Blackstone's Statutes on

Commercial & Consumer Law

D1328912

Blackstone's Statutes on

Commercial & Consumer Law

2012–2013

21st edition

edited by

F. D. Rose

PhD, LLD, DCL, of Gray's Inn, Barrister-at-Law
Professor of Commercial Law, University of Bristol

OXFORD
UNIVERSITY PRESS

OXFORD
UNIVERSITY PRESS

Great Clarendon Street, Oxford, OX2 6DP,
United Kingdom

Oxford University Press is a department of the University of Oxford.
It furthers the University's objective of excellence in research, scholarship,
and education by publishing worldwide. Oxford is a registered trade mark of
Oxford University Press in the UK and in certain other countries

This selection © F. D. Rose 2012

The moral rights of the author have been asserted

First published by Blackstone Press 1989
Eighteenth edition 2009
Nineteenth edition 2010
Twentieth edition 2011
Twenty-first edition 2012

Impression: 1

Public sector information reproduced under Open Government Licence v1.0
(http://www.nationalarchives.gov.uk/doc/open-government-licence/
open-government-licence.htm)

Crown Copyright material reproduced with the permission of the
Controller, HMSO (under the terms of the Click Use licence)

British Library Cataloguing in Publication Data
Data available

ISBN 978–0–19–965626–4

Printed in Great Britain by
MPG Books Group, Bodmin and King's Lynn

Links to third party websites are provided by Oxford in good faith and
for information only. Oxford disclaims any responsibility for the materials
contained in any third party website referenced in this work.

For Josephine

Contents

Alphabetical contents

Chronological contents

Editor's preface

The Queen's Diamond Jubilee coincides with the silver jubilee of the series of books on statutes and materials in which this was the second book—a series whose success, one could also say, has been of an Olympic nature—and so prompts some reflection. The series reflects the proverb that big oaks from little acorns grow, and has no doubt encouraged the rise and fall, and regeneration, of substantial forestation in order to support it. When I proposed the first book in the series, collections of statutory materials were not universally used. There had been statute books, but they were not commonly used and as necessary as modern developments have made them. There were also then fewer publishers, of a generally more conservative nature than nowadays. Fortunately, Alistair MacQueen was of a more unconventional mould; and, after a no-nonsense lunch in a Greek restaurant in Shepherd's Bush (which, as I note in passing it on most of my trips to London, also continues to flourish), the series began and has gone on from strength to strength and has inspired its imitators. Today's law students cannot successfully negotiate their courses without becoming familiar with at least some of the ever growing mountain of legislative overlays of our law; and I am gratified to note that this series remains at the forefront of assisting them to do so.

As in previous editions, this book sets out to present the principal legislative materials in the conventionally central areas of commercial and consumer law (including particularly relevant topics of general common law) but (in order to keep the collection manageable and its price reasonable) generally omitting more specialist subjects. This, of course, is more easily said than done. Commercial activity is infinitely varied and the pace of change continues to accelerate. For their part, our law makers (of which there are an increasing number) are engaged in responding to, facilitating and promoting such changes. Primarily their concern appears to be to create change (increasingly, it seems, for its own sake) and to devolve power to civil servants to effect changes. Legislation, both primary and secondary, is subject to constant expansion, revision and complication. And it is increasingly difficult to find in an easily accessible form for even electronic databases are dependent on fallible human masters, and even the best programmers have to grapple with an overabundance of unimplemented legislative amendments, some of which never have effect. These elements, coupled with the volume of new material each year, make revision of this book both challenging and exciting. They also require increased selectivity in combining the core features of our commercial law with a flavour of its diversity, particularly given the tension between its more obviously commercial and consumer protection aspects.

Commercial and Consumer Law and statute have in common that they are all in a permanent state of flux, making it essential continually to update this collection of materials. The book therefore has the usual range of necessary amendments to existing legislative provisions together with recent innovations.

Major innovations in this edition include the enactment of the Consumer Insurance (Disclosure and Representations) Act 2012. The continuing influence of European law on United Kingdom law is visible in the Proposal for a Regulation on a Common European Sales Law (CESL), which has obvious potential relevance to the core sector of Commercial Law and general significance for the potential development of the subject within the European Union and therefore the United Kingdom. As ever, Consumer Law remains incapable of standing still, and the Consumer Rights Directive 2011 will provoke further changes. Also, in the same week that this book was completed, revisions have been published to the Lending Code.

As in previous editions, whenever appropriate the material is reproduced in its complete, most recent form, amendments being enclosed in square brackets; occasional omissions are indicated by three dots. Supplementary notes and details of amending provisions, constantly changing and easily available in updated form elsewhere, are generally omitted for reasons of space.

I continue to be grateful to my wife, Lynda, for her contribution to revision of these materials. As always, I am happy to acknowledge the holders' rights in copyright materials. Also, I continue to be grateful for suggestions as to possible revisions of this collection of materials.

Francis Rose
5 May 2012

New to this edition

The twenty-first edition of *Blackstone's Statutes on Commercial & Consumer Law* has been fully revised and updated to include all relevant legislation and materials through to May 2012.

- Consumer Insurance (Disclosure and Representations) Act 2012
- Proposed Common European Sales Law Regulation ('CESL')
- Consumer Rights Directive 2011/83/EU
- Lending Code (revised 2012)

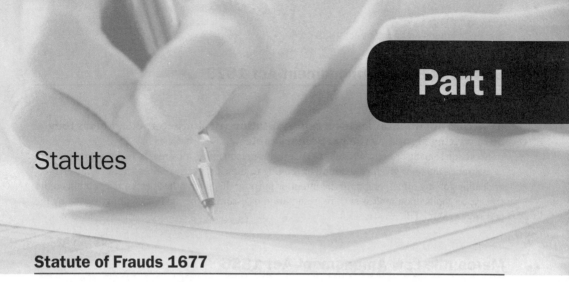

Part I

Statutes

Statute of Frauds 1677

(29 Chas. II, c. 3)

4   No action against executors, etc. upon a special promise, or upon any agreement, or contract for sale of lands, etc. unless agreement, etc. be in writing and signed

[…] noe action shall be brought […] whereby to charge the defendant upon any special promise to answere for the debt default or miscarriages of another person […] unlesse the agreement upon which such action shall be brought or some memorandum or note thereof shall be in writeing and signed by the partie to be charged therewith or some other person thereunto by him lawfully authorised.

Life Assurance Act 1774

(14 Geo. III, c. 48)

1   No insurance to be made on lives, etc., by persons having no interest, etc.

From and after the passing of this Act no insurance shall be made by any person or persons, bodies politick or corporate, on the life or lives of any person or persons, or on any other event or events whatsoever, wherein the person or persons for whose use, benefit, or on whose account such policy or policies shall be made, shall have no interest, or by way of gaming or wagering; and that every assurance made contrary to the true intent and meaning hereof shall be null and void to all intents and purposes whatsoever.

2   No policies on lives without inserting the names of persons interested, etc.

And […] it shall not be lawful to make any policy or policies on the life or lives of any person or persons, or other event or events, without inserting in such policy or policies the person or persons name or names interested therein, or for whose use, benefit, or on whose account such policy is so made or underwrote.

3   How much may be recovered where the insured hath interest in lives

And […] in all cases where the insured hath interest in such life or lives, event or events, no greater sum shall be recovered or received from the insurer or insurers than the amount of value of the interest of the insured in such life or lives, or other event or events.

4   Not to extend to insurances on ships, goods, etc.

Provided, always, that nothing herein contained shall extend or be construed to extend to insurances bona fide made by any person or persons on ships, goods, or merchandises, but every such insurance shall be as valid and effectual in the law as if this Act had not been made.

Statute of Frauds Amendment Act 1828

(9 Geo. IV, c. 14)

6   Action not maintainable on representations of character, etc., unless they be in writing signed by the party chargeable

... No action shall be brought whereby to charge any person upon or by reason of any representation or assurance made or given concerning or relating to the character, conduct, credit, ability, trade, or dealings of any other person, to the intent or purpose that such other person may obtain credit, money, or goods upon, unless such representation or assurance be made in writing, signed by the party to be charged therewith.

Mercantile Law Amendment Act 1856

(19 & 20 Vict., c. 97)

3   Consideration for guarantee need not appear in writing

No special promise to be made by any person [...] to answer for the debt, default, or miscarriage or another person, being in writing, and signed by the party to be charged therewith, or some other person by him thereunto lawfully authorised, shall be deemed invalid to support an action, suit, or other proceeding to charge the person by whom such promise shall have been made, by reason only that the consideration for such promise does not appear in writing, or by necessary inference from a written document.

5   A surety who discharges the liability to be entitled to assignment of all securities held by the creditor

Every person who, being surety for the debt or duty of another, or being liable with another for any debt or duty, shall pay such debt or perform such duty, shall be entitled to have assigned to him, or to a trustee for him, every judgment, specialty, or other security which shall be held by the creditor in respect of such debt or duty, whether such judgment, specialty, or other security shall or shall not be deemed at law to have been satisfied by the payment of the debt or performance of the duty, and such person shall be entitled to stand in the place of the creditor, and to use all the remedies, and, if need be, and upon a proper indemnity, to use the name of the creditor, in any action or other proceeding, at law or in equity, in order to obtain from the principal debtor, or any co-surety, co-contractor, or co-debtor, as the case may be, indemnification for the advances made and loss sustained by the person who shall have so paid such debt or performed such duty, and such payment or performance so made by such surety shall not be pleadable in bar of any such action or other proceeding by him: Provided always, that no co-surety, co-contractor, or co-debtor shall be entitled to recover from any other co-surety, co-contractor, or co-debtor, by the means aforesaid, more than the just proportion to which, as between those parties themselves, such last-mentioned person shall be justly liable.

Bills of Sale Act 1878

(41 & 42 Vict., c. 31)

An Act to consolidate and amend the Law for preventing Frauds upon Creditors by secret Bills of Sale of Personal Chattels.

3   Application

This Act shall apply to every bill of sale executed on or after the first day of January one thousand eight hundred and seventy-nine (whether the same be absolute, or subject or not subject to any trust) whereby the holder or grantee has power, either with or without notice, and either immediately or at any future time, to seize or take possession of any personal chattels comprised in or made subject to such bill of sale.

4   Interpretation of terms

In this Act the following words and expressions shall have the meanings in this section assigned to them respectively, unless there be something in the subject or context repugnant to such construction; (that is to say),

The expression 'bill of sale' shall include bills of sale, assignments, transfers, declarations of trust without transfer, inventories of goods with receipt thereto attached, or receipts for purchase moneys of goods, and other assurances of personal chattels, and also powers of attorney, authorities, or licenses to take possession of personal chattels as security for any debt, and also any agreement, whether intended or not to be followed by the execution of any other instrument, by which a right in equity to any personal chattels, or to any charge or security thereon, shall be conferred, but shall not include the following documents; that is to say, assignments for the benefit of the creditors of the person making or giving the same, marriage settlements, transfers or assignments of any ship or vessel or any share thereof, transfers of goods in the ordinary course of business of any trade or calling, bills of sale of goods in foreign parts or at sea, bills of lading, India warrants, warehouse-keepers' certificates, warrants or orders for the delivery of goods, or any other documents used in the ordinary course of business as proof of the possession or control of goods, or authorising or purporting to authorise, either by indorsement or by delivery, the possessor of such document to transfer or receive goods thereby represented:

The expression 'personal chattels' shall mean goods, furniture, and other articles capable of complete transfer by delivery, and (when separately assigned or charged) fixtures and growing crops, but shall not include chattel interests in real estate, nor fixtures (except trade machinery as hereinafter defined), when assigned together with a freehold or leasehold interest in any land or building to which they are affixed, nor growing crops when assigned together with any interest in the land on which they grow, nor shares or interests in the stock, funds, or securities of any government, or in the capital or property of incorporated or joint stock companies, nor choses in action, nor any stock or produce upon any farm or lands which by virtue of any covenant or agreement or of the custom of the country ought not to be removed from any farm where the same are at the time of making or giving of such bill of sale:

Personal chattels shall be deemed to be in the 'apparent possession' of the person making or giving a bill of sale, so long as they remain or are in or upon any house, mill, warehouse, building, works, yard, land, or other premises occupied by him, or are used and enjoyed by him in any place whatsoever, notwithstanding that formal possession thereof may have been taken by or given to any other person:

'Prescribed' means prescribed by rules made under the provisions of this Act.

5   Application of Act to trade machinery

From and after the commencement of this Act trade machinery shall, for the purposes of this Act, be deemed to be personal chattels, and any mode of disposition of trade machinery by the owner thereof which would be a bill of sale as to any other personal chattels shall be deemed to be a bill of sale within the meaning of this Act.

For the purposes of this Act—

'Trade machinery' means the machinery used in or attached to any factory or workshop;

1st.   Exclusive of the fixed motive-powers, such as the water-wheels and steam-engines, and the steam-boilers, donkey-engines, and other fixed appurtenances of the said motive-powers; and

2nd.   Exclusive of the fixed power machinery, such as the shafts, wheels, drums, and their fixed appurtenances, which transmit the action of the motive-powers to the other machinery, fixed and loose; and,

3rd.   Exclusive of the pipes for steam gas and water in the factory or workshop.

The machinery or effects excluded by this section from the definition of trade machinery shall not be deemed to be personal chattels within the meaning of this Act.

'Factory or workshop' means any premises on which any manual labour is exercised by way of trade, or for purposes of gain, in or incidental to the following purposes or any of them; that is to say,

      (a) In or incidental to the making of any article or part of an article; or

      (b) In or incidental to the altering repairing ornamenting finishing of any article; or

      (c) In or incidental to the adapting for sale of any article.

6   Certain instruments giving powers of distress to be subject to this Act

Every attornment instrument or agreement, not being a mining lease, whereby a power of distress is given or agreed to be given by any person to any other person by way of security for any present future or contingent debt or advance, and whereby any rent is reserved or made payable as a mode of providing for the payment of interest on such debt or advance, or otherwise for the purpose of such security only, shall be deemed to be a bill of sale, within the meaning of this Act, of any personal chattels which may be seized or taken under such power of distress.

Provided, that nothing in this section shall extend to any mortgage of any estate or interest in any land tenement or hereditament which the mortgagee, being in possession, shall have demised to the mortgagor as his tenant at a fair and reasonable rent.

7   Fixtures or growing crops not to be deemed separately assigned when the land passes by the same instrument

No fixtures or growing crops shall be deemed, under this Act, to be separately assigned or charged by reason only that they are assigned by separate words, or that power is given to sever them from the land or building to which they are affixed, or from the land on which they grow, without otherwise taking possession of or dealing with such land or building, or land, if by the same instrument any freehold or leasehold interest in the land or building to which such fixtures are affixed, or in the land on which such crops grow, is also conveyed or assigned to the same persons or person.

The same rule of construction shall be applied to all deeds or instruments, including fixtures or growing crops, executed before the commencement of this Act, and then subsisting and in force, in all questions arising under any bankruptcy liquidation assignment for the benefit of creditors, or execution of any process of any court, which shall take place or be issued after the commencement of this Act.

8   Avoidance of unregistered bills of sale in certain cases

Every bill of sale to which this Act applies shall be duly attested and shall be registered under this Act, within seven days after the making or giving thereof, and shall set forth the consideration for which such bill of sale was given, otherwise such bill of sale, as against all trustees or assignees of the estate of the person whose chattels, or any of them, are comprised in such bill of sale under the law relating to bankruptcy or liquidation, or under any assignment for the benefit of the creditors of such person, and also as against all sheriffs officers and other persons seizing any chattels comprised in such bill of sale, in the execution of any process of any court authorising the seizure of the chattels of the person by whom or of whose chattels such bill has been made, and also as against every person on whose behalf such process shall have been issued, shall be deemed fraudulent and void so far as regards the property in or right to the possession of any chattels comprised in such bill of sale which, at or after the time of filing the petition for bankruptcy or liquidation, or of the execution of such assignment, or of executing such process (as the case may be), and after the expiration of such seven days are in the possession or apparent possession of the person making such bill of sale (or of any person against whom the process has issued under or in the execution of which such bill has been made or given, as the case may be).

9   Avoidance of certain duplicate bills of sale

Where a subsequent bill of sale is executed within or on the expiration of seven days after the execution of a prior unregistered bill of sale, and comprises all or any part of the personal chattels comprised in such prior bill of sale, then, if such subsequent bill of sale is given as a security for the same debt as is secured by the prior bill of sale, or for any part of such debt, it shall, to the extent to which it is a security for the same debt or part thereof, and so far as respects the personal chattels or part thereof comprised in the prior bill, be absolutely void, unless it is proved to the satisfaction of the court having cognizance of the case that the subsequent bill of sale was bona fide given for the purpose of correcting some material error in the prior bill of sale, and not for the purpose of evading this Act.

10   Mode of registering bills of sale

A bill of sale shall be attested and registered under this Act in the following manner:

(1) The execution of every bill of sale shall be attested by a solicitor of the [Senior Courts], and the attestation shall state that before the execution of the bill of sale the effect thereof has been explained to the grantor by the attesting solicitor.

(2) Such bill, with every schedule or inventory thereto annexed or therein referred to, and also a true copy of such bill and of every such schedule or inventory, and of every attestation of the execution of such bill of sale, together with an affidavit of the time of such bill of sale being made or given, and of its due execution and attestation, and a description of the residence and occupation of the person making or giving the same (or in case the same is made or given by any person under or in the execution of any process, then a description of the residence and occupation of the person against whom such process issued), and of every attesting witness to such bill of sale, shall be presented to and the said copy and affidavit shall be filed with the registrar within seven clear days after the making or giving of such bill of sale, in like manner as a warrant of attorney in any personal action given by a trader is now by law required to be filed:

(3) If the bill of sale is made or given subject to any defeasance or condition, or declaration of trust not contained in the body thereof, such defeasance, condition, or declaration shall be deemed to be part of the bill, and shall be written on the same paper or parchment therewith before the registration, and shall be truly set forth in the copy filed under this Act therewith and as part thereof, otherwise the registration shall be void.

In case two or more bills of sale are given, comprising in whole or in part any of the same chattels, they shall have priority in the order of the date of their registration respectively as regards such chattels.

A transfer or assignment of a registered bill of sale need not be registered.

11   Renewal of registration

The registration of a bill of sale, whether executed before or after the commencement of this Act, must be renewed once at least every five years, and if a period of five years elapses from the registration or renewed registration of a bill of sale without a renewal or further renewal (as the case may be), the registration shall become void.

The renewal of a registration shall be effected by filing with the registrar an affidavit stating the date of the bill of sale and of the last registration thereof, and the names, residences, and occupations of the parties thereto as stated therein, and that the bill of sale is still a subsisting security.

Every such affidavit may be in the form set forth in the Schedule (A) to this Act annexed.

A renewal of registration shall not become necessary by reason only of a transfer or assignment of a bill of sale.

12   Form of register

The registrar shall keep a book (in this Act called 'the register') for the purposes of this Act, and shall, upon the filing of any bill of sale or copy under this Act, enter therein in the form set forth in the second schedule (B) to this Act annexed, or in any other prescribed form, the name residence and occupation of the person by whom the bill was made or given (or in case the same was made or given by any person under or in the execution of process, then the name residence and occupation of the person against whom such process was issued, and also the name of the person or persons to whom or in whose favour the bill was given), and the other particulars shown in the said schedule or to be prescribed under this Act, and shall number all such bills registered in each year consecutively, according to the respective dates of their registration.

Upon the registration of any affidavit of renewal the like entry shall be made, with the addition of the date and number of the last previous entry relating to the same bill, and the bill of sale or copy originally filed shall be thereupon marked with the number affixed to such affidavit of renewal.

The registrar shall also keep an index of the names of the grantors of registered bills of sale with reference to entries in the register of the bills of sale given by each such grantor.

Such index shall be arranged in divisions corresponding with the letters of the alphabet, so that all grantors whose surnames begin with the same letter (and no others) shall be comprised in one division, but the arrangement within each such division need not be strictly alphabetical.

13   The registrar

The masters of the [Senior Courts] attached to the Queen's Bench Division of the High Court of Justice, or such other officers as may for the time being be assigned for this purpose under the provisions of the Supreme Court of Judicature Acts 1873 and 1875, shall be the registrar for the purposes of this Act, and any one of the said masters may perform all or any of the duties of the registrar.

14   Rectification of register

Any judge of the High Court of Justice on being satisfied that the omission to register a bill of sale or an affidavit or renewal thereof within the time prescribed by this Act, or the omission or mis-statement of the name residence or occupation of any person, was accidental or due to inadvertence, may in his discretion order such omission or mis-statement to be rectified by the insertion in the register of the true name residence or occupation, or by extending the time for such registration on such terms and conditions (if any) as to security, notice by advertisement or otherwise, or as to any other matter, as he thinks fit to direct.

15   Entry of satisfaction

Subject to and in accordance with any rules to be made under and for the purposes of this Act, the registrar may order a memorandum of satisfaction to be written upon any registered copy of a bill of sale, upon the prescribed evidence being given that the debt (if any) for which such bill of sale was made or given has been satisfied or discharged.

16   Copies may be taken, etc.

Any person shall be entitled to have an office copy or extract of any registered bill of sale, and affidavit of execution filed therewith, or copy thereof, and of any affidavit filed therewith, if any, or registered affidavit of renewal, upon paying for the same at the like rate as for office copies of judgments of the High Court of Justice, and any copy of a registered bill of sale, and affidavit purporting to be an office copy thereof, shall in all courts and before all arbitrators or other persons, be admitted as prima facie evidence thereof, and of the fact and date of registration as shown thereon [...].

20   Order and disposition

Chattels comprised in a bill of sale which has been and continues to be duly registered under this Act shall not be deemed to be in the possession, order, or disposition of the grantor of the bill of sale within the meaning of the Bankruptcy Act 1869.

21   Rules

Rules for the purposes of this Act may be made and altered from time to time by the like persons and in the like manner in which rules and regulations may be made under and for the purposes of the Supreme Court of Judicature Acts 1873 and 1875.

22   Time for registration

When the time for registering a bill of sale expires on a Sunday, or other day on which the registrar's office is closed, the registration shall be valid if made on the next following day on which the office is open.

24   Extent of Act

This Act shall not extend to Scotland or to Ireland.

SCHEDULES

Section 11 ## SCHEDULE (A)

I [*A.B.*]   of   do swear that a bill of sale, bearing date the   day of   18 [*insert the date of the bill*], and made between [*insert the names and descriptions of the parties in the original bill of sale*] and which said bill of sale [*or, and a copy of which said bill of sale, as the case may be*] was registered on the   day of   18 [*insert date of registration*], is still a subsisting security.
 Sworn, &c.

SCHEDULE (B)

Statisfaction entered	No	By whom given (or against whom process issued)			To whom given	Nature of Instrument	Date	Date of Registration	Date of Registration of affidavit of renewal
		Name	Residence	Occupation					

Bills of Exchange Act 1882

(45 & 46 Vict., c. 61)

PART I PRELIMINARY

2 Interpretation of terms
In this Act, unless the context otherwise requires,—
 'Acceptance' means an acceptance completed by delivery or notification.
 'Action' includes counter claim and set off.
 'Banker' includes a body of persons whether incorporated or not who carry on the business of banking.
 'Bankrupt' includes any person whose estate is vested in a trustee or assignee under the law for the time being in force relating to bankruptcy.
 'Bearer' means the person in possession of a bill or note which is payable to bearer.
 'Bill' means bill of exchange, and 'note' means promissory note.
 'Delivery' means transfer of possession, actual or constructive, from one person to another.
 'Holder' means the payee or indorsee of a bill or note who is in possession of it, or the bearer thereof.
 'Indorsement' means an indorsement completed by delivery.
 'Issue' means the first delivery of a bill or note, complete in form to a person who takes it as a holder.
 'Person' includes a body of persons whether incorporated or not.
 ['postal operator' has the meaning given by section 125(1) of the Postal Services Act 2000.]
 'Value' means valuable consideration.
 'Written' includes printed, and 'writing' includes print.

PART II BILLS OF EXCHANGE

Form and interpretation

3 Bill of exchange defined

(1) A bill of exchange is an unconditional order in writing, addressed by one person to another, signed by the person giving it, requiring the person to whom it is addressed to pay on demand or at a fixed or determinable future time a sum certain in money to or to the order of a specified person, or to bearer.

(2) An instrument which does not comply with these conditions, or which orders any act to be done in addition to the payment of money, is not a bill of exchange.

(3) An order to pay out of a particular fund is not unconditional within the meaning of this section; but an unqualified order to pay, coupled with (a) an indication of a particular fund out of which the drawee is to re-imburse himself or a particular account to be debited with the amount, or (b) a statement of the transaction which gives rise to the bill, is unconditional.

(4) A bill is not invalid by reason—
   (a) That it is not dated;
   (b) That it does not specify the value given, or that any value has been given therefor;
   (c) That it does not specify the place where it is drawn or the place where it is payable.

4 Inland and foreign bills

(1) An inland bill is a bill which is or on the face of it purports to be (a) both drawn and payable within the British Islands, or (b) drawn within the British Islands upon some person resident therein. Any other bill is a foreign bill.

For the purposes of this Act 'British Islands' means any part of the United Kingdom of Great Britain and Ireland, the islands of Man, Guernsey, Jersey, Alderney, and Sark, and the islands adjacent to any of them being part of the dominions of Her Majesty.

(2) Unless the contrary appear on the face of the bill the holder may treat it as an inland bill.

5 Effect where different parties to bill are the same person

(1) A bill may be drawn payable to, or to the order of, the drawer; or it may be drawn payable to, or to the order of, the drawee.

(2) Where in a bill drawer and drawee are the same person, or where the drawee is a fictitious person or a person not having capacity to contract, the holder may treat the instrument, at his option, either as a bill of exchange or as a promissory note.

6 Address to drawee

(1) The drawee must be named or otherwise indicated in a bill with reasonable certainty.

(2) A bill may be addressed to two or more drawees whether they are partners or not, but an order addressed to two drawees in the alternative or to two or more drawees in succession is not a bill of exchange.

7 Certainty required as to payee

(1) Where a bill is not payable to bearer, the payee must be named or otherwise indicated therein with reasonable certainty.

(2) A bill may be made payable to two or more payees jointly, or it may be made payable in the alternative to one of two, or one or some of several payees. A bill may also be made payable to the holder of an office for the time being.

(3) Where the payee is a fictitious or non-existing person the bill may be treated as payable to bearer.

8 What bills are negotiable

(1) When a bill contains words prohibiting transfer, or indicating an intention that it should not be transferable, it is valid as between the parties thereto, but is not negotiable.

(2) A negotiable bill may be payable either to order or to bearer.

(3) A bill is payable to bearer which is expressed to be so payable, or on which the only or last indorsement is an indorsement in blank.

(4) A bill is payable to order which is expressed to be so payable, or which is expressed to be payable to a particular person, and does not contain words prohibiting transfer or indicating an intention that it should not be transferable.

(5) Where a bill, either originally or by indorsement, is expressed to be payable to the order of a specified person, and not to him or his order, it is nevertheless payable to him or his order at his option.

9   Sum payable

(1) The sum payable by a bill is a sum certain within the meaning of this Act, although it is required to be paid—

    (a) With interest.

    (b) By stated instalments.

    (c) By stated instalments, with a provision that upon default in payment of any instalment the whole shall become due.

    (d) According to an indicated rate of exchange or according to a rate of exchange to be ascertained as directed by the bill.

(2) Where the sum payable is expressed in words and also in figures, and there is a discrepancy between the two, the sum denoted by the words is the amount payable.

(3) Where a bill is expressed to be payable with interest, unless the instrument otherwise provides, interest runs from the date of the bill, and if the bill is undated from the issue thereof.

10   Bill payable on demand

(1) A bill is payable on demand—

    (a) Which is expressed to be payable on demand, or at sight, or on presentation; or

    (b) In which no time for payment is expressed.

(2) Where a bill is accepted or indorsed when it is overdue, it shall, as regards the acceptor who so accepts, or any indorser who so indorses it, be deemed a bill payable on demand.

11   Bill payable at a future time

A bill is payable at a determinable future time within the meaning of this Act which is expressed to be payable—

(1) At a fixed period after date or sight.

(2) On or at a fixed period after the occurrence of a specified event which is certain to happen, though the time of happening may be uncertain.

An instrument expressed to be payable on a contingency is not a bill, and the happening of the event does not cure the defect.

12   Omission of date in bill payable after date

Where a bill expressed to be payable at a fixed period after date is issued undated, or where the acceptance of a bill payable at a fixed period after sight is undated, any holder may insert therein the true date of issue or acceptance, and the bill shall be payable accordingly.

Provided that (1) where the holder in good faith and by mistake inserts a wrong date, and (2) in every case where a wrong date is inserted, if the bill subsequently comes into the hands of a holder in due course the bill shall not be avoided thereby, but shall operate and be payable as if the date so inserted had been the true date.

13   Ante-dating and post-dating

(1) Where a bill or an acceptance or any indorsement on a bill is dated, the date shall, unless the contrary be proved, be deemed to be the true date of the drawing, acceptance, or indorsement, as the case may be.

(2) A bill is not invalid by reason only that it is ante-dated or post-dated, or that it bears date on a Sunday.

14   Computation of time of payment

Where a bill is not payable on demand the day on which it falls due is determined as follows:

[(1) The bill is due and payable in all cases on the last day of the time of payment as fixed by the bill or, if that is a non-business day, on the succeeding business day.]

(2) Where a bill is payable at a fixed period after date, after sight, or after the happening of a specified event, the time of payment is determined by excluding the day from which the time is to begin to run and by including the day of payment.

(3) Where a bill is payable at a fixed period after sight, the time begins to run from the date of the acceptance if the bill be accepted, and from the date of noting or protest if the bill be noted or protested for non-acceptance, or for non-delivery.

15   Case of need

The drawer of a bill and any indorser may insert therein the name of a person to whom the holder may resort in case of need, that is to say, in case the bill is dishonoured by non-acceptance or non-payment. Such person is called the referee in case of need. It is in the option of the holder to resort to the referee in case of need or not as he may think fit.

16   Optional stipulations by drawer or indorser

The drawer of a bill, and any indorser may insert therein an express stipulation—

(1) Negativing or limiting his own liability to the holder:

(2) Waiving as regards himself some or all of the holder's duties.

17   Definition and requisites of acceptance

(1) The acceptance of a bill is the signification by the drawee of his assent to the order of the drawer.

(2) An acceptance is invalid unless it complies with the following conditions, namely:

(a) It must be written on the bill and be signed by the drawee. The mere signature of the drawee without additional words is sufficient.

(b) It must not express that the drawee will perform his promise by any other means than the payment of money.

18   Time for acceptance

A bill may be accepted—

(1) before it has been signed by the drawer, or while otherwise incomplete:

(2) When it is overdue, or after it has been dishonoured by a previous refusal to accept, or by non-payment:

(3) When a bill payable after sight is dishonoured by non-acceptance, and the drawee subsequently accepts it, the holder, in the absence of any different agreement, is entitled to have the bill accepted as of the date of first presentment to the drawee for acceptance.

19   General and qualified acceptance

(1) An acceptance is either (a) general or (b) qualified.

(2) A general acceptance assents without qualification to the order of the drawer. A qualified acceptance in express terms varies the effect of the bill as drawn.

In particular an acceptance is qualified which is—

(a) conditional, that is to say, which makes payment by the acceptor dependent on the fulfilment of a condition therein stated:

(b) partial, that is to say, an acceptance to pay part only of the amount for which the bill is drawn:

(c) local, that is to say, an acceptance to pay only at a particular specified place: An acceptance to pay at a particular place is a general acceptance, unless it expressly states that the bill is to be paid there only and not elsewhere:

(d) qualified as to time:

(e) the acceptance of some one or more of the drawees, but not of all.

20   Inchoate instruments

(1) Where a simple signature on a blank [...] paper is delivered by the signer in order that it may be converted into a bill, it operates as a prima facie authority to fill it up as a complete bill for any amount [...] using the signature for that of the drawer, or the acceptor, or an indorser; and, in like manner, when a bill is wanting in any material particular, the person in possession of it has a prima facie authority to fill up the omission in any way he thinks fit.

(2) In order that any such instrument when completed may be enforceable against any person who became a party thereto prior to its completion, it must be filled up within a reasonable time, and strictly in accordance with the authority given. Reasonable time for this purpose is a question of fact.

Provided that if any such instrument after completion is negotiated to a holder in due course it shall be valid and effectual for all purposes in his hands and he may enforce it as if it had been filled up within a reasonable time and strictly in accordance with the authority given.

21   Delivery

(1) Every contract on a bill, whether it be the drawer's, the acceptor's, or an indorser's is incomplete and revocable, until delivery of the instrument in order to give effect thereto.

Provided that where an acceptance is written on a bill, and the drawee gives notice to or according to the directions of the person entitled to the bill that he has accepted it, the acceptance then becomes complete and irrevocable.

(2) As between immediate parties, and as regards a remote party other than a holder in due course, the delivery—

> (a) in order to be effectual must be made either by or under the authority of the party drawing, accepting, or indorsing, as the case may be:
>
> (b) may be shown to have been conditional or for a special purpose only, and not for the purpose of transferring the property in the bill.

But if the bill be in the hands of a holder in due course a valid delivery of the bill by all parties prior to him so as to make them liable to him is conclusively presumed.

(3) Where a bill is no longer in the possession of a party who has signed it as drawer, acceptor, or indorser, a valid and unconditional delivery by him is presumed until the contrary is proved.

Capacity and authority of parties

22   Capacity of parties

(1) Capacity to incur liability as a party to a bill is coextensive with capacity to contract. Provided that nothing in this section shall enable a corporation to make itself liable as drawer, acceptor, or indorser of a bill unless it is competent to it so to do under the law for the time being in force relating to corporations.

(2) Where a bill is drawn or indorsed by an infant, minor, or corporation having no capacity or power to incur liability on a bill, the drawing or indorsement entitles the holder to receive payment of the bill, and to enforce it against any other party thereto.

23   Signature essential to liability

No person is liable as drawer, indorser, or acceptor of a bill who has not signed it as such: Provided that

(1) Where a person signs a bill in a trade or assumed name, he is liable thereon as if he had signed it in his own name:

(2) The signature of the name of a firm is equivalent to the signature by the person so signing of the names of all persons liable as partners in that firm.

24   Forged or unauthorised signature

Subject to the provisions of this Act, where a signature on a bill is forged or placed thereon without the authority of the person whose signature it purports to be, the forged or unauthorised signature is wholly inoperative, and no right to retain the bill or to give a discharge therefor or to enforce payment thereof against any party thereto can be acquired through or under that signature, unless the party against whom it is sought to retain or enforce payment of the bill is precluded from setting up the forgery or want of authority.

Provided that nothing in this section shall affect the ratification of an unauthorised signature not amounting to a forgery.

25   Procuration signatures

A signature by procuration operates as notice that the agent has but a limited authority to sign, and the principal is only bound by such signature if the agent in so signing was acting within the actual limits of his authority.

26   Person signing as agent or in representative capacity

(1) Where a person signs a bill as drawer, indorser, or acceptor, and adds words to his signature, indicating that he signs for or on behalf of a principal, or in a representative character, he is not personally liable thereon; but the mere addition to his signature of words describing him as an agent, or as filling a representative character, does not exempt him from personal liability.

(2) In determining whether a signature on a bill is that of the principal or that of the agent by whose hand it is written, the construction most favourable to the validity of the instrument shall be adopted.

The consideration for a bill

27   Value and holder for value

(1) Valuable consideration for a bill may be constituted by,—
   (a) Any consideration sufficient to support a simple contract;
   (b) An antecedent debt or liability. Such a debt or liability is deemed valuable consideration whether the bill is payable on demand or at a future time.

(2) Where value has at any time been given for a bill the holder is deemed to be a holder for value as regards the acceptor and all parties to the bill who became parties prior to such time.

(3) Where the holder of a bill has a lien on it, arising either from contract or by implication of law, he is deemed to be a holder for value to the extent of the sum for which he has a lien.

28   Accommodation bill or party

(1) An accommodation party to a bill is a person who has signed a bill as drawer, acceptor, or indorser, without receiving value therefor, and for the purpose of lending his name to some other person.

(2) An accommodation party is liable on the bill to a holder for value; and it is immaterial whether, when such holder took the bill, he knew such party to be an accommodation party or not.

29   Holder in due course

(1) A holder in due course is a holder who has taken a bill, complete and regular on the face of it, under the following conditions, namely,
   (a) That he became the holder of it before it was overdue, and without notice that it had been previously dishonoured, if such was the fact:
   (b) That he took the bill in good faith and for value, and that at the time the bill was negotiated to him he had no notice of any defect in the title of the person who negotiated it.

(2) In particular the title of a person who negotiates a bill is defective within the meaning of this Act when he obtained the bill, or the acceptance thereof, by fraud, duress or force and fear, or other unlawful means, or for an illegal consideration, or when he negotiates it in breach of faith, or under such circumstances as amount to a fraud.

(3) A holder (whether for value or not), who derives his title to a bill through a holder in due course, and who is not himself a party to any fraud or illegality affecting it, has all the rights of that holder in due course as regards the acceptor and all parties to the bill prior to that holder.

30   Presumption of value and good faith

(1) Every party whose signature appears on a bill is prima facie deemed to have become a party thereto for value.

(2) Every holder of a bill is prima facie deemed to be a holder in due course; but if in an action on a bill it is admitted or proved that the acceptance, issue, or subsequent negotiation of the bill is affected with fraud, duress, or force and fear, or illegality, the burden of proof is shifted, unless and until the holder proves that, subsequent to the alleged fraud or illegality, value has in good faith been given for the bill.

Negotiation of bills

31   Negotiation of bill

(1) A bill is negotiated when it is transferred from one person to another in such a manner as to constitute the transferee the holder of the bill.

(2) A bill payable to bearer is negotiated by delivery.

(3) A bill payable to order is negotiated by the indorsement of the holder completed by delivery.

(4) Where, the holder of a bill payable to his order transfers it for value without indorsing it, the transfer gives the transferee such title as the transferor had in the bill, and the transferee in addition acquires the right to have the indorsement of the transferor.

(5) Where any person is under obligation to indorse a bill in a representative capacity, he may indorse a bill in such terms as to negative personal liability.

32   Requisites of a valid indorsement

An indorsement in order to operate as a negotiation must comply with the following conditions, namely:—

(1) It must be written on the bill itself and signed by the indorser. The simple signature of the indorser on the bill, without additional words, is sufficient.

An indorsement written on an allonge or a 'copy' of a bill issued or negotiated in a country where 'copies' are recognised, is deemed to have been written on the bill itself.

(2) It must be an indorsement of the entire bill. A partial indorsement, that is to say, an indorsement which purports to transfer to the indorsee a part only of the amount payable, or which purports to transfer the bill to two or more indorsees severally, does not operate as a negotiation of the bill.

(3) Where a bill is payable to the order of two or more payees or indorsees who are not partners all must indorse, unless the one indorsing has authority to indorse for the others.

(4) Where, in a bill payable to order, the payee or indorsee is wrongly designated, or his name is mis-spelt, he may indorse the bill as therein described, adding, if he think fit, his proper signature.

(5) Where there are two or more indorsements on a bill, each indorsement is deemed to have been made in the order in which it appears on the bill, until the contrary is proved.

(6) An indorsement may be made in blank or special. It may also contain terms making it restrictive.

33   Conditional indorsement

Where a bill purports to be indorsed conditionally the condition may be disregarded by the payer, and payment to the indorsee is valid whether the condition has been fulfilled or not.

34   Indorsement in blank and special indorsement

(1) An indorsement in blank specifies no indorsee, and a bill so indorsed becomes payable to bearer.

(2) A special indorsement specifies the person to whom, or to whose order, the bill is to be payable.

(3) The provisions of this Act relating to a payee apply with the necessary modifications to an indorsee under a special indorsement.

(4) When a bill has been indorsed in blank, any holder may convert the blank indorsement into a special indorsement by writing above the indorser's signature a direction to pay the bill to or to the order of himself or some other person.

35   Restrictive indorsement

(1) An indorsement is restrictive which prohibits the further negotiation of the bill or which expresses that it is a mere authority to deal with the bill as thereby directed and not a transfer of ownership thereof, as, for example, if a bill be indorsed 'Pay D. only', or 'Pay D. for the account of X.,' or 'Pay D. or order for collection.'

(2) A restrictive indorsement gives the indorsee the right to receive payment of the bill and to sue any party thereto that his indorser could have sued, but gives him no power to transfer his rights as indorsee unless it expressly authorise him to do so.

(3) Where a restrictive indorsement authorises further transfer, all subsequent indorsees take the bill with the same rights and subject to the same liabilities as the first indorsee under the restrictive indorsement.

36   Negotiation of overdue or dishonoured bills

(1) Where a bill is negotiable in its origin it continues to be negotiable until it has been (a) restrictively indorsed or (b) discharged by payment or otherwise.

(2) Where an overdue bill is negotiated, it can only be negotiated subject to any defect of title affecting it at its maturity, and thenceforward no person who takes it can acquire or give a better title than that which the person from whom he took it had.

(3) A bill payable on demand is deemed to be overdue within the meaning and for the purposes of this section, when it appears on the face of it to have been in circulation for an unreasonable length of time. What is an unreasonable length of time for this purpose is a question of fact.

(4) Except where an indorsement bears date after the maturity of the bill, every negotiation is prima facie deemed to have been effected before the bill was overdue.

(5) Where a bill which is not overdue has been dishonoured any person who takes it with notice of the dishonour takes it subject to any defect of title attaching thereto at the time of dishonour, but nothing in this sub-section shall affect the rights of a holder in due course.

37   Negotiation of bill to party already liable thereon

Where a bill is negotiated back to the drawer, or to a prior indorser or to the acceptor, such party may, subject to the provisions of this Act, reissue and further negotiate the bill, but he is not entitled to enforce payment of the bill against any intervening party to whom he was previously liable.

38   Rights of the holder

The rights and powers of the holder of a bill are as follows:

(1) He may sue on the bill in his own name:

(2) Where he is a holder in due course, he holds the bill free from any defect of title of prior parties, as well as from mere personal defences available to prior parties among themselves, and may enforce payment against all parties liable on the bill:

(3) Where his title is defective (a) if he negotiates the bill to a holder in due course, that holder obtains a good and complete title to the bill, and (b) if he obtains payment of the bill the person who pays him in due course gets a valid discharge for the bill.

General duties of the holder

39   When presentment for acceptance is necessary

(1) Where a bill is payable after sight, presentment for acceptance is necessary in order to fix the maturity of the instrument.

(2) Where a bill expressly stipulates that it shall be presented for acceptance, or where a bill is drawn payable elsewhere than at the residence or place of business of the drawee, it must be presented for acceptance before it can be presented for payment.

(3) In no other case is presentment for acceptance necessary in order to render liable any party to the bill.

(4) Where the holder of a bill, drawn payable elsewhere than at the place of business or residence of the drawee, has not time, with the exercise of reasonable diligence, to present the bill for acceptance before presenting it for payment on the day that it falls due, the delay caused by presenting the bill for acceptance before presenting it for payment is excused, and does not discharge the drawer and the indorsers.

40 Time for presenting bill payable after sight

(1) Subject to the provisions of this Act, when a bill payable after sight is negotiated, the holder must either present it for acceptance or negotiate it within a reasonable time.

(2) If he do not do so, the drawer and all indorsers prior to that holder are discharged.

(3) In determining what is a reasonable time within the meaning of this section, regard shall be had to the nature of the bill, the usage of trade with respect to similar bills, and the facts of the particular case.

41 Rules as to presentment for acceptance and excuses for non-presentment

(1) A bill is duly presented for acceptance which is presented in accordance with the following rules:

    (a) The presentment must be made by or on behalf of the holder to the drawee or to some person authorised to accept or refuse acceptance on his behalf at a reasonable hour on a business day and before the bill is overdue:

    (b) Where a bill is addressed to two or more drawees, who are not partners, presentment must be made to them all, unless one has authority to accept for them all, then presentment must be made to him only:

    (c) Where the drawee is dead presentment may be made to his personal representative:

    (d) Where the drawee is bankrupt, presentment may be made to him or to his trustee:

    (e) Where authorised by agreement or usage, a presentment through [a postal operator] is sufficient.

(2) Presentment in accordance with these rules is excused, and a bill may be treated as dishonoured by non-acceptance—

    (a) Where the drawee is dead or bankrupt, or is a fictitious person or a person not having capacity to contract by bill:

    (b) Where, after the exercise of reasonable diligence, such presentment cannot be effected:

    (c) Where although the presentment has been irregular, acceptance has been refused on some other ground.

(3) The fact that the holder has reason to believe that the bill, on presentment, will be dishonoured does not excuse presentment.

42 Non-acceptance

(1) When a bill is duly presented for acceptance and is not accepted within the customary time, the person presenting it must treat it as dishonoured by non-acceptance. If he do not, the holder shall lose his right of recourse against the drawer and indorsers.

43 Dishonour by non-acceptance and its consequences

(1) A bill is dishonoured by non-acceptance—

    (a) when it is duly presented for acceptance, and such an acceptance as is prescribed by this Act is refused or cannot be obtained; or

    (b) when presentment for acceptance is excused and the bill is not accepted.

(2) Subject to the provisions of this Act when a bill is dishonoured by non-acceptance an immediate right of recourse against the drawer and indorsers accrues to the holder, and no presentment for payment is necessary.

44   Duties as to qualified acceptances

(1) The holder of a bill may refuse to take a qualified acceptance, and if he does not obtain an unqualified acceptance may treat the bill as dishonoured by non-acceptance.

(2) Where a qualified acceptance is taken, and the drawer or an indorser has not expressly or impliedly authorised the holder to take a qualified acceptance, or does not subsequently assent thereto, such drawer or indorser is discharged from his liability on the bill.

The provisions of this sub-section do not apply to a partial acceptance, whereof due notice has been given. Where a foreign bill has been accepted as to part, it must be protested as to the balance.

(3) When the drawer or indorser of a bill receives notice of a qualified acceptance, and does not within a reasonable time express his dissent to the holder he shall be deemed to have assented thereto.

45   Rules as to presentment for payment

Subject to the provisions of this Act a bill must be duly presented for payment. If it be not so presented the drawer and indorsers shall be discharged.

A bill is duly presented for payment which is presented in accordance with the following rules:—

(1) Where the bill is not payable on demand, presentment must be made on the day it falls due.

(2) Where the bill is payable on demand then, subject to the provisions of this Act, presentment must be made within a reasonable time after its issue in order to render the drawer liable, and within a reasonable time after the indorsement, in order to render the indorser liable.

In determining what is a reasonable time, regard shall be had to the nature of the bill, the usage of trade with regard to similar bills, and the facts of the particular case.

(3) Presentment must be made by the holder or by some person authorised to receive payment on his behalf at a reasonable hour on a business day, at the proper place as hereinafter defined, either to the person designated by the bill as payer, or to some person authorised to pay or refuse payment on his behalf if with the exercise of reasonable diligence such person can there be found.

(4) A bill is presented at the proper place:—

(a) Where a place of payment is specified in the bill and the bill is there presented.

(b) Where no place of payment is specified, but the address of the drawee or acceptor is given in the bill, and the bill is there presented.

(c) Where no place of payment is specified and no address given, and the bill is presented at the drawees or acceptor's place of business if known, and if not, at his ordinary residence if known.

(d) In any other case if presented to the drawer or acceptor wherever he can be found, or if presented at his last known place of business or residence.

(5) Where a bill is presented at the proper place, and after the exercise of reasonable diligence no person authorised to pay or refuse payment can be found there, no further presentment to the drawee or acceptor is required.

(6) Where a bill is drawn upon, or accepted by two or more persons who are not partners, and no place of payment is specified, presentment must be made to them all.

(7) Where the drawee or acceptor of a bill is dead, and no place of payment is specified, presentment must be made to a personal representative, if such there be, and with the exercise of reasonable diligence he can be found.

(8) Where authorised by agreement or usage a presentment through [a postal operator] is sufficient.

46   Excuses for delay or non-presentment for payment

(1) Delay in making presentment for payment is excused when the delay is caused by circumstances beyond the control of the holder, and not imputable to his default, misconduct, or negligence. When the cause of delay ceases to operate presentment must be made with reasonable diligence.

(2) Presentment for payment is dispensed with,—

(a) Where, after the exercise of reasonable diligence presentment, as required by this Act, cannot be effected.

    The fact that the holder has reason to believe that the bill will, on presentment, be dishonoured, does not dispense with the necessity for presentment.

(b) Where the drawee is a fictitious person.

(c) As regards the drawer where the drawee or acceptor is not bound, as between himself and the drawee, to accept or pay the bill, and the drawer has no reason to believe that the bill would be paid if presented.

(d) As regards an indorser, where the bill was accepted or made for the accommodation of the indorser, and he has no reason to expect that the bill would be paid if presented.

(e) By waiver of presentment, expressed or implied.

47 Dishonour by non-payment

(1) A bill is dishonoured by non-payment (a) when it is duly presented for payment and payment is refused or cannot be obtained, or (b) when presentment is excused and the bill is overdue and unpaid.

(2) Subject to the provisions of this Act, when a bill is dishonoured by non-payment, an immediate right of recourse against the drawer and indorsers accrues to the holder.

48 Notice of dishonour and effect of non-notice

Subject to the provisions of this Act, when a bill has been dishonoured by non-acceptance or by non-payment, notice of dishonour must be given to the drawer and each indorser, and any drawer or indorser to whom such notice is not given is discharged; Provided that—

(1) Where a bill is dishonoured by non-acceptance, and notice of dishonour is not given, the rights of the holder in due course subsequent to the omission, shall not be prejudiced by the omission.

(2) Where a bill is dishonoured by non-acceptance and due notice of dishonour is given, it shall not be necessary to give notice of a subsequent dishonour by non-payment unless the bill shall in the meantime have been accepted.

49 Rules as of notice of dishonour

Notice of dishonour in order to be valid and effectual must be given in accordance with the following rules:—

(1) The notice must be given by or on behalf of the holder, or by or on behalf of an indorser who, at the time of giving it, is himself liable on the bill.

(2) Notice of dishonour may be given by an agent either in his own name, or in the name of any party entitled to give notice whether that party be his principal or not.

(3) Where the notice is given by on on behalf of the holder, it enures for the benefit of all subsequent holders and all prior indorsers who have a right of recourse against the party to whom it is given.

(4) Where notice is given by or on behalf of an indorser entitled to give notice as herein-before provided, it enures for the benefit of the holder and all indorsers subsequent to the party to whom notice is given.

(5) The notice may be given in writing or by personal communication, and may be given in any terms which sufficiently identify the bill, and intimate that the bill has been dishonoured by non-acceptance or non-payment.

(6) The return of a dishonoured bill to the drawer or an indorser is, in point of form, deemed a sufficient notice of dishonour.

(7) A written notice need not be signed, and an insufficient written notice may be supplemented and validated by verbal communication. A misdescription of the bill shall not vitiate the notice unless the party to whom the notice is given is in fact misled thereby.

(8) Where notice of dishonour is required to be given to any person, it may be given either to the party himself, or to his agent in that behalf.

(9) Where the drawer or indorser is dead, and the party giving notice knows it, the notice must be given to a personal representative if such there be, and with the exercise of reasonable diligence he can be found.

(10) Where the drawer or indorser is bankrupt, notice may be given either to the party himself or to the trustee.

(11) Where there are two or more drawers or indorsers who are not partners, notice must be given to each of them, unless one of them has authority to receive such notice for the others.

(12) The notice may be given as soon as the bill is dishonoured and must be given within a reasonable time thereafter.

In the absence of special circumstances notice is not deemed to have been given within a reasonable time, unless—

>   (a) where the person giving and the person to receive notice reside in the same place, the notice is given or sent off in time to reach the latter on the day after the dishonour of the bill.

>   (b) where the person giving and the person to receive notice reside in different places, the notice is sent off on the day after the dishonour of the bill, if there be a post at a convenient hour on that day, and if there be no such post on that day then by the next post thereafter.

(13) Where a bill when dishonoured is in the hands of an agent, he may either himself give notice to the parties liable on the bill, or he may give notice to his principal. If he gives notice to his principal, he must do so within the same time as if he were the holder, and the principal upon receipt of such notice has himself the same time for giving notice as if the agent had been an independent holder.

(14) Where a party to a bill receives due notice of dishonour, he has after the receipt of such notice the same period of time for giving notice to antecedent parties that the holder has after the dishonour.

(15) Where a notice of dishonour is duly addressed and posted, the sender is deemed to have given due notice of dishonour, notwithstanding any miscarriage by the [postal operator concerned].

50   Excuses for non-notice and delay

(1) Delay in giving notice of dishonour is excused where the delay is caused by circumstances beyond the control of the party giving notice, and not imputable to his default, misconduct, or negligence. When the cause of delay ceases to operate the notice must be given with reasonable diligence.

(2) Notice of dishonour is dispensed with—

>   (a) When, after the exercise of reasonable diligence, notice as required by this Act cannot be given to or does not reach the drawer or indorser sought to be charged:

>   (b) By waiver express or implied. Notice of dishonour may be waived before the time of giving notice has arrived, or after the omission to give due notice:

>   (c) As regards the drawer in the following cases, namely, (1) where drawer and drawee are the same person, (2) where the drawee is a fictitious person or a person not having capacity to contract, (3) where the drawer is the person to whom the bill is presented for payment, (4) where the drawee or acceptor is as between himself and the drawer under no obligation to accept or pay the bill, (5) where the drawer has countermanded payment:

>   (d) As regards the indorser in the following cases, namely (1) where the drawee is a fictitious person or a person not having the capacity to contract and the indorser was aware of the fact at the time he indorsed the bill, (2) where the indorser is the person to whom the bill is presented for payment, (3) where the bill was accepted or made for his accommodation.

51   Noting or protest of bill

(1) Where an inland bill has been dishonoured it may, if the holder think fit, be noted for non-acceptance or non-payment, as the case may be; but it shall not be necessary to note or protest any such bill in order to preserve the recourse against the drawer or indorser.

(2) Where a foreign bill, appearing on the face of it to be such, has been dishonoured by non-acceptance it must be duly protested for non-acceptance and where such a bill, which has not been previously dishonoured by non-acceptance, is dishonoured by non-payment it must be duly protested for

non-payment. If it be not so protested the drawer and indorsers are discharged. Where a bill does not appear on the face of it to be a foreign bill, protest thereof in the case of dishonour is unnecessary.

(3) A bill which has been protested for non-acceptance may be subsequently protested for non-payment.

(4) Subject to the provisions of this Act, when a bill is noted or protested, [it may be noted on the day of its dishonour and must be noted not later than the next succeeding business day]. When a bill has been duly noted, the protest may be subsequently extended as of the date of the noting.

(5) Where the acceptor of the bill becomes bankrupt or insolvent or suspends payment before it matures, the holder may cause the bill to be protested for better security against the drawer and indorsers.

(6) A bill must be protested at the place where it is dishonoured: Provided that—

(a) When a bill is presented through [a postal operator], and returned by post dishonoured, it may be protested at the place to which it is returned and on the day of its return if received during business hours, and if not received during business hours, then not later than the next business day;

(b) When a bill drawn payable at the place of business or residence of some person other than the drawee, has been dishonoured by non-acceptance, it must be protested for non-payment at the place where it is expressed to be payable, and no further presentment for payment to, or demand on, the drawee is necessary.

(7) A protest must contain a copy of the bill, and must be signed by the notary making it, and must specify—

(a) The person at whose request the bill is protested:

(b) The place and date of protest, the cause or reason for protesting the bill, the demand made, and the answer given, if any, or the fact that the drawee or acceptor could not be found.

[(7A) In subsection (7) 'notary' includes a person who, for the purposes of the Legal Services Act 2007, is an authorised person in relation to any activity which constitutes a notarial activity (within the meaning of that Act).]

(8) Where a bill is lost or destroyed, or is wrongly detained from the person entitled to hold it, protest may be made on a copy or written particulars thereof.

(9) Protest is dispensed with by any circumstance which would dispense with notice of dishonour. Delay in noting or protesting is excused when the delay is caused by circumstances beyond the control of the holder, and not imputable to his default, misconduct, or negligence. When the cause of delay ceases to operate the bill must be noted or protested with reasonable diligence.

52   Duties of holder as regards drawee or acceptor

(1) When a bill is accepted generally presentment for payment is not necessary in order to render the acceptor liable.

(2) When by the terms of a qualified acceptance presentment for payment is required, the acceptor, in the absence of an express stipulation to that effect, is not discharged by the omission to present the bill for payment on the day that it matures.

(3) In order to render the acceptor of a bill liable it is not necessary to protest it, or that notice of dishonour should be given to him.

(4) Where the holder of a bill presents it for payment, he shall exhibit the bill to the person from whom he demands payment, and when a bill is paid the holder shall forthwith deliver it up to the party paying it.

Liabilities of parties

53   Funds in hands of drawee

(1) A bill, of itself, does not operate as an assignment of funds in the hands of the drawee available for the payment thereof, and the drawee of a bill who does not accept as required by this Act is not liable on the instrument. This sub-section shall not extend to Scotland.

54   Liability of acceptor
The acceptor of a bill, by accepting it—
    (1) Engages that he will pay it according to the tenor of his acceptance:
    (2) Is precluded from denying to a holder in due course:
        (a) The existence of the drawer, the genuineness of his signature, and his capacity and authority to draw the bill;
        (b) In the case of a bill payable to drawer's order, the then capacity of the drawer to indorse, but not the genuineness or validity of his indorsement;
        (c) In the case of a bill payable to the order of a third person, the existence of the payee and his then capacity to indorse, but not the genuineness or validity of his indorsement.

55   Liability of drawer or indorser
    (1) The drawer of a bill by drawing it—
        (a) Engages that on due presentment it shall be accepted and paid according to its tenor, and that if it be dishonoured he will compensate the holder or any indorser who is compelled to pay it, provided that the requisite proceedings on dishonour be duly taken;
        (b) Is precluded from denying to a holder in due course the existence of the payee and his then capacity to indorse.
    (2) The indorser of a bill by indorsing it—
        (a) Engages that on due presentment it shall be accepted and paid according to its tenor, and that if it be dishonoured he will compensate the holder or a subsequent indorser who is compelled to pay it, provided that the requisite proceedings on dishonour be duly taken;
        (b) Is precluded from denying to a holder in due course the genuineness and regularity in all respects of the drawer's signature and all previous indorsements;
        (c) Is precluded from denying to his immediate or a subsequent indorsee that the bill was at the time of his indorsement a valid and subsisting bill, and that he had then a good title thereto.

56   Stranger signing bill liable as indorser
Where a person signs a bill otherwise than as drawer or acceptor, he thereby incurs the liabilities of an indorser to a holder in due course.

57   Measure of damages against parties to dishonoured bill
Where a bill is dishonoured, the measure of damages, which shall be deemed to be liquidated damages, shall be as follows:
    (1) The holder may recover from any party liable on the bill, and the drawer who has been compelled to pay the bill may recover from the acceptor, and an indorser who has been compelled to pay the bill may recover from the acceptor or from the drawer, or from a prior indorser—
        (a) The amount of the bill:
        (b) Interest thereon from the time of presentment for payment if the bill is payable on demand, and from the maturity of the bill in any other case:
        (c) The expenses of noting, or, when protest is necessary, and the protest has been extended, the expenses of protest.
    [...]
    (3) Where by this Act interest may be recovered as damages, such interest may, if justice require it, be withheld wholly or in part, and where a bill is expressed to be payable with interest at a given rate, interest as damages may or may not be given at the same rate as interest proper.

58   Transferor by delivery and transferee
    (1) Where the holder of a bill payable to bearer negotiates it by delivery without indorsing it, he is called a 'transferor by delivery.'
    (2) A transferor by delivery is not liable on the instrument.

(3) A transferor by delivery who negotiates a bill thereby warrants to his immediate transferee being a holder for value that the bill is what it purports to be, that he has a right to transfer it, and that at the time of the transfer he is not aware of any fact which renders it valueless.

Discharge of bill

59   Payment in due course

(1) A bill is discharged by payment in due course by or on behalf of the drawee or acceptor. 'Payment in due course' means payment made at or after the maturity of the bill to the holder thereof in good faith and without notice that his title to the bill is defective.

(2) Subject to the provisions herein-after contained, when a bill is paid by the drawer or an indorser it is not discharged; but

    (a) Where a bill payable to, or to the order of, a third party is paid by the drawer, the drawer may enforce payment thereof against the acceptor, but may not re-issue the bill.

    (b) Where a bill is paid by an indorser, or where a bill payable to drawer's order is paid by the drawer, the party paying it is remitted to his former rights as regards the acceptor or antecedent parties, and he may, if he thinks fit, strike out his own and subsequent indorsements, and again negotiate the bill.

(3) Where an accommodation bill is paid in due course by the party accommodated the bill is discharged.

60   Banker paying demand draft whereon indorsement is forged

When a bill payable to order on demand is drawn on a banker, and the banker on whom it is drawn, pays the bill in good faith and in the ordinary course of business, it is not incumbent on the banker to show that the indorsement of the payee or any subsequent indorsement was made by or under the authority of the person whose indorsement it purports to be, and the banker is deemed to have paid the bill in due course, although such indorsement has been forged or made without authority.

61   Acceptor the holder at maturity

When the acceptor of a bill is or becomes the holder of it at or after its maturity, in his own right, the bill is discharged.

62   Express waiver

(1) When the holder of a bill at or after its maturity absolutely and unconditionally renounces his rights against the acceptor the bill is discharged.

The renunciation must be in writing, unless the bill is delivered up to the acceptor.

(2) The liabilities of any party to a bill may in like manner be renounced by the holder before, at, or after its maturity; but nothing in this section shall affect the rights of a holder in due course without notice of the renunciation.

63   Cancellation

(1) Where a bill is intentionally cancelled by the holder or his agent, and the cancellation is apparent thereon, the bill is discharged.

(2) In like manner any party liable on a bill may be discharged by the intentional cancellation of his signature by the holder or his agent. In such case any indorser who would have had a right of recourse against the party whose signature is cancelled, is also discharged.

(3) A cancellation made unintentionally, or under a mistake, or without the authority of the holder is inoperative; but where a bill or any signature thereon appears to have been cancelled the burden of proof lies on the party who alleges that the cancellation was made unintentionally, or under a mistake, or without authority.

64   Alteration of bill

(1) Where a bill or acceptance is materially altered without the assent of all parties liable on the bill, the bill is avoided except as against a party who has himself made, authorised, or assented to the alteration, and subsequent indorsers.

Provided that,

Where a bill has been materially altered, but the alteration is not apparent, and the bill is in the hands of a holder in due course, such holder may avail himself of the bill as if it had not been altered, and may enforce payment of it according to its original tenour.

(2) In particular the following alterations are material, namely, any alteration of the date, the sum payable, the time of payment, the place of payment, and where a bill has been accepted generally, the addition of a place of payment without the acceptor's assent.

Acceptance and payment for honour

65   Acceptance for honour supra protest

(1) Where a bill of exchange has been protested for dishonour by non-acceptance, or protested for better security, and is not overdue, any person, not being a party already liable thereon, may, with the consent of the holder, intervene and accept the bill *supra protest,* for the honour of any party liable thereon, or for the honour of the person for whose account the bill is drawn.

(2) A bill may be accepted for honour for part only of the sum for which it is drawn.

(3) An acceptance for honour supra protest in order to be valid must—

    (a) be written on the bill, and indicate that it is an acceptance for honour;

    (b) be signed by the acceptor for honour:

(4) Where an acceptance for honour does not expressly state for whose honour it is made, it is deemed to be an acceptance for the honour of the drawer.

(5) Where a bill payable after sight is accepted for honour, its maturity is calculated from the date of the noting for non-acceptance, and not from the date of the acceptance for honour.

66   Liability of acceptor for honour

(1) The acceptor for honour of a bill by accepting it engages that he will, on due presentment, pay the bill according to the tenor of his acceptance, if it is not paid by the drawee, provided it has been duly presented for payment, and protested for non-payment, and that he receives notice of these facts.

(2) The acceptor for honour is liable to the holder and to all parties to the bill subsequent to the party for whose honour he has accepted.

67   Presentment to acceptor for honour

(1) Where a dishonoured bill has been accepted for honour supra protest, or contains a reference in case of need, it must be protested for non-payment before it is presented for payment to the acceptor for honour, or referee in case of need.

(2) Where the address of the acceptor for honour is in the same place where the bill is protested for non-payment, the bill must be presented to him not later than the day following its maturity; and where the address of the acceptor for honour is in some place other than the place where it was protested for non-payment, the bill must be forwarded not later than the day following its maturity for presentment to him.

(3) Delay in presentment or non-presentment is excused by any circumstances which would excuse delay in presentment for payment or non-presentment for payment.

(4) When a bill of exchange is dishonoured by the acceptor for honour it must be protested for non-payment by him.

68   Payment for honour supra protest

(1) Where a bill has been protested for non-payment any person may intervene and pay it *supra protest* for the honour of any party liable thereon, or for the honour of the person for whose account the bill is drawn.

(2) Where two or more persons offer to pay a bill for the honour of different parties, the person whose payment will discharge most parties to the bill shall have the preference.

(3) Payment for honour *supra protest,* in order to operate as such and not as a mere voluntary payment, must be attested by a notarial act of honour which may be appended to the protest or form an extension of it.

(4) The notarial act of honour must be founded on a declaration made by the payer for honour, or his agent in that behalf, declaring his intention to pay the bill for honour, and for whose honour he pays.

(5) Where a bill has been paid for honour, all parties subsequent to the party for whose honour it is paid are discharged, but the payer for honour is subrogated for, and succeeds to both the rights and duties of, the holder as regards the party for whose honour he pays, and all parties liable to that party.

(6) The payer for honour on paying to the holder the amount of the bill and the notarial expenses incidental to its dishonour is entitled to receive both the bill itself and the protest. If the holder do not on demand deliver them up he shall be liable to the payer for honour in damages.

(7) Where the holder of a bill refuses to receive payment *supra protest* he shall lose his right of recourse against any party who would have been discharged by such payment.

Lost instruments

69 Holder's right to duplicate of lost bill

Where a bill has been lost before it is overdue, the person who was the holder of it may apply to the drawer to give him another bill of the same tenor, giving security to the drawer if required to indemnify him against all persons whatever in case the bill alleged to have been lost shall be found again.

If the drawer on request as aforesaid refuses to give such duplicate bill, he may be compelled to do so.

70 Action on lost bill

In any action or proceeding upon a bill, the court or a judge may order that the loss of the instrument shall not be set up, provided an indemnity be given to the satisfaction of the court or judge against the claims of any other person upon the instrument in question.

Bill in a set

71 Rules as to sets

(1) Where a bill is drawn in a set, each part of the set being numbered and containing a reference to the other parts, the whole of the parts constitute one bill.

(2) Where the holder of a set indorses two or more parts to different persons, he is liable to every such part, and every indorser subsequent to him is liable on the part he has himself indorsed as if the said parts were separate bills.

(3) Where two or more parts of a set are negotiated to different holders in due course, the holder whose title first accrues is as between such holders deemed the true owner of the bill; but nothing in this sub-section shall affect the rights of a person who in the course accepts or pays the part first presented to him.

(4) The acceptance may be written on any part, and it must be written on one part only.
If the drawee accepts more than one part, and such accepted parts get into the hands of different holders in due course, he is liable on every such part as if it were a separate bill.

(5) When the acceptor of a bill drawn in a set pays it without requiring the part bearing the acceptance to be delivered up to him, and that part at maturity is outstanding in the hands of a holder in due course, he is liable to the holder thereof.

(6) Subject to the preceding rules, where any one part of a bill drawn in a set is discharged by payment or otherwise, the whole bill is discharged.

Conflict of laws

72 Rules where laws conflict

Where a bill drawn in one country is negotiated, accepted, or payable in another, the rights, duties, and liabilities of the parties thereto are determined as follows:

(1) The validity of a bill as regards requisites in form is determined by the law of the place of issue, and the validity as regards requisites in form of the supervening contracts, such as acceptance, or indorsement, or acceptance supra protest, is determined by the law of the place where such contract was made.

Provided that—

    (a) Where a bill is issued out of the United Kingdom it is not invalid by reason only that it is not stamped in accordance with the law of the place of issue:

    (b) Where a bill, issued out of the United Kingdom, conforms, as regards requisites in form, to the law of the United Kingdom, it may, for the purpose of enforcing payment thereof, be treated as valid as between all persons who negotiate, hold, or become parties to it in the United Kingdom.

(2) Subject to the provisions of this Act, the interpretation of the drawing, indorsement, acceptance, or acceptance supra protest of a bill, is determined by the law of the place where such contract is made.

Provided that where an inland bill is indorsed in a foreign country the indorsement shall as regards the payer be interpreted according to the law of the United Kingdom.

(3) The duties of the holder with respect to presentment for acceptance or payment and the necessity for or sufficiency of a protest or notice of dishonour, or otherwise, are determined by the law of the place where the act is done or the bill is dishonoured.

[...]

(5) Where a bill is drawn in one country and is payable in another, the due date thereof is determined according to the law of the place where it is payable.

PART III CHEQUES ON A BANKER

73 Cheque defined

A cheque is a bill of exchange drawn on a banker payable on demand. Except as otherwise provided in this Part, the provisions of this Act applicable to a bill of exchange payable on demand apply to a cheque.

74 Presentment of cheque for payment

Subject to the provisions of this Act—

(1) Where a cheque is not presented for payment within a reasonable time of its issue, and the drawer or the person on whose account it is drawn had the right at the time of such presentment as between him and the banker to have the cheque paid and suffers actual damage through the delay, he is discharged to the extent of such damage, that is to say, to the extent to which such drawer or person is a creditor of such banker to a larger amount than he would have been had such cheque been paid.

(2) In determining what is a reasonable time regard shall be had to the nature of the instrument, the usage of trade and of bankers, and the facts of the particular case.

(3) The holder of such cheque as to which such drawer or person is discharged shall be a creditor, in lieu of such drawer or person, of such banker to the extent of such discharge, and entitled to recover the amount from him.

[74A Presentment of cheque for payment: alternative place of presentment

Where the banker on whom a cheque is drawn—

    (a) has by notice published in the London, Edinburgh and Belfast Gazettes specified an address at which cheques drawn on him may be presented, and

    (b) has not by notice so published cancelled the specification of that address, the cheque is also presented at the proper place if it is presented there.]

[74B   Presentment of cheque for payment: alternative means of presentment by banker

(1) A banker may present a cheque for payment to the banker on whom it is drawn by notifying him of its essential features by electronic means or otherwise, instead of by presenting the cheque itself.

(2) If a cheque is presented for payment under this section, presentment need not be made at the proper place or at a reasonable hour on a business day.

(3) If, before the close of business on the next business day following presentment of a cheque under this section, the banker on whom the cheque is drawn requests the banker by whom the cheque was presented to present the cheque itself—

(a) the presentment under this section shall be disregarded, and

(b) this section shall not apply in relation to the subsequent presentment of the cheque.

(4) A request under subsection (3) above for the presentment of a cheque shall not constitute dishonour of the cheque by non-payment.

(5) Where presentment of a cheque is made under this section, the banker who presented the cheque and the banker on whom it is drawn shall be subject to the same duties in relation to the collection and payment of the cheque as if the cheque itself had been presented for payment.

(6) For the purposes of this section, the essential features of a cheque are—

(a) the serial number of the cheque,

(b) the code which identifies the banker on whom the cheque is drawn,

(c) the account number of the drawer of the cheque, and

(d) the amount of the cheque is entered by the drawer of the cheque.]

[74C   Cheques presented for payment under section 74B: disapplication of section 52(4)

Section 52(4) above—

(a) so far as relating to presenting a bill for payment, shall not apply to presenting a cheque for payment under section 74B above, and

(b) so far as relating to a bill which is paid, shall not apply to a cheque which is paid following presentment under that section.]

75   Revocation of banker's authority

The duty and authority of a banker to pay a cheque drawn on him by his customer are determined by—

(1) Countermand of payment:

(2) Notice of the customer's death.

Crossed cheques

76   General and special crossings defined

(1) Where a cheque bears across its face an addition of—

(a) The words 'and company' or any abbreviation thereof between two parallel transverse lines either with or without the words 'not negotiable'; or

(b) Two parallel transverse lines simply, either with or without the words 'not negotiable'; that addition constitutes a crossing, and the cheque is crossed generally.

(2) Where a cheque bears across its face an addition of the name of a banker, either with or without the words 'not negotiable', that addition constitutes a crossing, and the cheque is crossed specially and to that banker.

77   Crossing by drawer or after issue

(1) A cheque may be crossed generally or specially by the drawer.

(2) Where a cheque is uncrossed, the holder may cross it generally or specially.

(3) Where a cheque is crossed generally the holder may cross it specially.

(4) Where a cheque is crossed generally or specially, the holder may add the words 'not negotiable.'

(5) Where a cheque is crossed specially, the banker to whom it is crossed may again cross it specially to another banker for collection.

(6) Where an uncrossed cheque, or a cheque crossed generally is sent to a banker for collection, he may cross it specially to himself.

78   Crossing a material part of cheque

A crossing authorised by this Act is a material part of the cheque; it shall not be lawful for any person to obliterate or except as authorised by this Act, to add to or alter the crossing.

79   Duties of banker as to crossed cheques

(1) Where a cheque is crossed specially to more than one banker except when crossed to an agent for collection being a banker, the banker on whom it is drawn shall refuse payment thereof.

(2) Where the banker on whom a cheque is drawn which is so crossed nevertheless pays the same, or pays a cheque crossed generally otherwise than to a banker, or if crossed specially otherwise than to the banker to whom it is crossed, or his agent for collection being a banker, he is liable to the true owner of the cheque for any loss he may sustain owing to the cheque having been so paid.

Provided that where a cheque is presented for payment which does not at the time of presentment appear to be crossed, or to have had a crossing which had been obliterated, or to have been added to or altered otherwise than as authorised by this Act, the banker paying the cheque in good faith and without negligence shall not be responsible or incur any liability, nor shall the payment be questioned by reason of the cheque having been crossed, or of the crossing having been obliterated on having been added to or altered otherwise than as authorised by this Act, and of payment having been made otherwise than to a banker or to the banker to whom the cheque is or was crossed, or to his agent for collection being a banker as the case may be.

80   Protection to banker and drawer where cheque is crossed

Where the banker, on whom a crossed cheque [(including a cheque which under section 81A below or otherwise is not transferable)] is drawn in good faith and without negligence pays it, if crossed generally to a banker, and if crossed specially, to the banker to whom it is crossed, or his agent for collection being a banker the banker paying the cheque, and, if the cheque has come into the hands of the payee, the drawer, shall respectively be entitled to the same rights and be placed in the same position as if payment of the cheque had been made to the true owner thereof.

81   Effect of crossing on holder

Where a person takes a crossed cheque which bears on it the words 'not negotiable,' he shall not have and shall not be capable of giving a better title to the cheque than that which the person from whom he took it had.

[81A   Non-transferable cheques

(1) Where a cheque is crossed and bears across its face the words 'account payee' or 'a/c payee', either with or without the words 'only', the cheque shall not be transferable, but shall only be valid as between the parties thereto.

(2) A banker is not to be treated for the purposes of section 80 above as having been negligent by reason only of his failure to concern himself with any purported indorsement of a cheque which under subsection (1) above or otherwise is not transferable.]

[...]

PART IV   PROMISSORY NOTES

83   Promissory note defined

(1) A promissory note is an unconditional promise in writing made by one person to another signed by the maker, engaging to pay, on demand or at a fixed or determinable future time, a sum certain in money, to, or to the order of, a specified person or to bearer.

(2) An instrument in the form of a note payable to maker's order is not a note within the meaning of this section unless and until it is indorsed by the maker.

(3) A note is not invalid by reason only that it contains also a pledge of collateral security with authority to sell or dispose thereof.

(4) A note which is, or on the face of it purports to be, both made and payable within the British Islands is an inland note. Any other note is a foreign note.

84 Delivery necessary

A promissory note is inchoate and incomplete until delivery thereof to the payee or bearer.

85 Joint and several notes

(1) A promissory note may be made by two or more makers, and they may be liable thereon jointly, or jointly and severally according to its tenor.

(2) Where a note runs 'I promise to pay' and is signed by two or more persons it is deemed to be their joint and several note.

86 Note payable on demand

(1) Where a note payable on demand has been indorsed, it must be presented for payment within a reasonable time of the indorsement. If it be not so presented the indorser is discharged.

(2) In determining what is a reasonable time, regard shall be had to the nature of the instrument, the usage of trade, and the facts of the particular case.

(3) Where a note payable on demand is negotiated, it is not deemed to be overdue for the purpose of affecting the holder with defects of title of which he had no notice, by reason that it appears that a reasonable time for presenting it for payment has elapsed since its issue.

87 Presentment of note for payment

(1) Where a promissory note is in the body of it made payable at a particular place, it must be presented for payment at that place in order to render the maker liable. In any other case, presentment for payment is not necessary to render the maker liable.

(2) Presentment for payment is necessary in order to render the indorser of a note liable.

(3) Where a note is in the body of it made payable at a particular place, presentment at that place is necessary in order to render an indorser liable; but when a place of payment is indicated by way of memorandum only, presentment at that place is sufficient to render the indorser liable, but a presentment to the maker elsewhere, if sufficient in other respects, shall also suffice.

88 Liability of maker

The maker of a promissory note by making it—

(1) Engages that he will pay it according to its tenour;

(2) Is precluded from denying to a holder in due course the existence of the payee and his then capacity to indorse.

89 Application of Part II to notes

(1) Subject to the provisions in this part and, except as by this section provided, the provisions of this Act relating to bills of exchange apply, with the necessary modifications, to promissory notes.

(2) In applying those provisions the maker of a note shall be deemed to correspond with the acceptor of a bill, and the first indorser of a note shall be deemed to correspond with the drawer of an accepted bill payable to drawer's order.

(3) The following provisions as to bills do not apply to notes; namely, provisions relating to—

  (a) Presentment for acceptance;

  (b) Acceptance;

  (c) Acceptance supra protest;

  (d) Bills in a set.

(4) Where a foreign note is dishonoured, protest thereof is unnecessary.

PART V   SUPPLEMENTARY

90   Good faith

A thing is deemed to be done in good faith, within the meaning of this Act, where it is in fact done honestly, whether it is done negligently or not.

91   Signature

(1) Where, by this Act, any instrument or writing is required to be signed by any person, it is not necessary that he should sign it with his own hand, but it is sufficient if his signature is written thereon by some other person by or under his authority.

(2) In the case of a corporation, where, by this Act, any instrument or writing is required to be signed, it is sufficient if the instrument or writing be sealed with the corporate seal.

But nothing in this section shall be construed as requiring the bill or note of a corporation to be under seal.

92   Computation of time

Where, by this Act, the time limited for doing any act or thing is less than three days, in reckoning time, non-business days are excluded.

'Non-business days' for the purposes of this Act mean—

    (a) [Saturday], Sunday, Good Friday, Christmas Day:

    (b) A bank holiday under [the Banking and Financial Dealings Act 1971.]

    (c) A day appointed by Royal proclamation as a public fast or thanksgiving day.

    [(d) a day declared by an order under section 2 of the Banking and Financial Dealings Act 1971 to be a non-business day.]

Any other day is a business day.

93   When noting equivalent to protest

For the purposes of this Act, where a bill or note is required to be protested within a specified time or before some further proceeding is taken, it is sufficient that the bill has been noted for protest before the expiration of the specified time or the taking of the proceeding; and the formal protest may be extended at any time thereafter as of the date of the noting.

94   Protest when notary not accessible

[(1)] Where a dishonoured bill or note is authorised or required to be protested, and the services of a notary cannot be obtained at the place where the bill is dishonoured, any householder, or substantial resident of the place may, in the presence of two witnesses, give a certificate, signed by them, attesting to the dishonour of the bill, and the certificate shall in all respects operate as if it were a formal protest of the bill.

The form given in Schedule I to this Act may be used with necessary modifications, and if used shall be sufficient.

[(2) In subsection (1), 'notary' includes a person who, for the purposes of the Legal Services Act 2007, is an authorised person in relation to any activity which constitutes a notarial activity (within the meaning of that Act).]

95   Dividend warrants may be crossed

The provisions of this Act as to crossed cheques shall apply to a warrant for payment of dividend. [...]

97   Savings

(1) The rules in bankruptcy relating to bills of exchange, promissory notes, and cheques, shall continue to apply thereto notwithstanding anything in this Act contained.

(2) The rules of common law including the law merchant, save in so far as they are inconsistent with the express provisions of this Act, shall continue to apply to bills of exchange, promissory notes, and cheques—

(3) Nothing in this Act or in any repeal effected thereby shall affect—

    (a) [...] any law or enactment for the time being in force relating to the revenue;

    (b) The provisions of the Companies Act, 1862, or Acts amending it, or any Act relating to joint stock banks or companies:

    (c) The provisions of any Act relating to or confirming the privileges of the Bank of England or the Bank of Ireland respectively:

    (d) The validity of any usage relating to dividend warrants, or the indorsements thereof.

99   Construction with other Acts, etc.

Where any Act or document refers to any enactment repealed by this Act, the Act or document shall be construed, and shall operate as if it referred to the corresponding provisions of this Act.

SCHEDULES

Section 94   **FIRST SCHEDULE**

Form of protest which may be used when the services of a notary cannot
be obtained.

Know all men that I, *A. B.* householder, of   in the county of
in the United Kingdom, at the request of *C. D.*, there being no notary
public available, did on the   day of   188   at————
demand payment [*or* acceptance] of the bill of exchange hereunder written, from *E. F*, to which demand he made answer [state answer, if any] wherefore I now, in the presence of *G. H.* and *J. K.* do protest the said bill of exchange.

      (Signed)   A. B. ⎫

                  G. H. ⎬ *Witnesses*

                  J. K. ⎭

N.B.—The bill itself should be annexed, or a copy of the bill and all that is written thereon should be underwritten.

Bills of Sale Act (1878) Amendment Act 1882

(45 & 46 Vict., c. 43)

1   Short title

This Act may be cited for all purposes as the Bills of Sale Act (1878) Amendment Act 1882; and this Act and the Bills of Sale Act 1878 may be cited together as the Bills of Sale Acts 1878 and 1882.

. . .

3   Construction of Act

The Bills of Sale Act 1878 is herein-after referred to as 'the principal Act', and this Act shall, so far as is consistent with the tenor thereof, be construed as one with the principal Act; but unless the context otherwise requires shall not apply to any bill of sale duly registered before the commencement of this Act so long as the registration thereof is not avoided by non-renewal or otherwise.

The expression 'bill of sale', and other expressions in this Act, have the same meaning as in the principal Act, except as to bills of sale or other documents mentioned in section four of the principal Act, which may be given otherwise than by way of security for the payment of money, to which last-mentioned bills of sale and other documents this Act shall not apply.

4   Bill of sale to have schedule of property attached thereto

Every bill of sale shall have annexed thereto or written thereon a schedule containing an inventory of the personal chattels comprised in the bill of sale; and such bill of sale, save as herein-after mentioned, shall have effect only in respect of the personal chattels specifically described in the said schedule; and shall be void, except as against the grantor, in respect of any personal chattels not so specifically described.

5   Bill of sale not to affect after acquired property

Save as herein-after mentioned, a bill of sale shall be void, except as against the grantor, in respect of any personal chattels specifically described in the schedule thereto of which the grantor was not the true owner at the time of the execution of the bill of sale.

6   Exception as to certain things

Nothing contained in the foregoing sections of this Act shall render a bill of sale void in respect of any of the following things; (that is to say,)

(1) Any growing crops separately assigned or charged where such crops were actually growing at the time when the bill of sale was executed.

(2) Any fixtures separately assigned or charged, and any plant, or trade machinery where such fixtures, plant, or trade machinery are used in, attached to, or brought upon any land, farm, factory, workshop, shop, house, warehouse, or other place in substitution for any of the like fixtures, plant, or trade machinery specifically described in the schedule to such bill of sale.

7   Bill of sale with power to seize except in certain events to be void

Personal chattels assigned under a bill of sale shall not be liable to be seized or taken possession of by the grantee for any other than the following causes:—

(1) If the grantor shall make default in payment of the sum or sums of money thereby secured at the time therein provided for payment, or in the performance of any covenant or agreement contained in the bill of sale and necessary for maintaining the security;

(2) If the grantor shall become a bankrupt, or suffer the said goods or any of them to be distrained [or taken control of using the power in Schedule 12 to the Tribunals, Courts and Enforcement Act 2007,] for rent, rates, or taxes;

(3) If the grantor shall fraudulently either remove or suffer the said goods, or any of them, to be removed from the premises;

(4) If the grantor shall not, without reasonable excuse, upon demand in writing by the grantee, produce to him his last receipts for rent, rates, and taxes;

(5) If execution shall have been levied against the goods of the grantor under any judgment at law:

Provided that the grantor may within five days from the seizure or taking possession of any chattels on account of any of the above-mentioned causes, apply to the High Court, or to a judge thereof in chambers, and such court or judge, if satisfied that by payment of money or otherwise the said cause of seizure no longer exists, may restrain the grantee from removing or selling the said chattels, or may make such other order as may seem just.

[7A   Defaults under consumer credit agreements

(1) Paragraph (1) of section 7 of this Act does not apply to a default relating to a bill of sale given by way of security for the payment of money under a regulated agreement to which section 87(1) of the Consumer Credit Act 1974 applies—

(a) unless the restriction imposed by section 88(2) of that Act has ceased to apply to the bill of sale; or

(b) if, by virtue of section 89 of that Act, the default is to be treated as not having occurred.

(2) Where paragraph (1) of section 7 of this Act does apply in relation to a bill of sale such as is mentioned in subsection (1) of this section, the proviso to that section shall have effect with the substitution of 'county court' for 'High Court'.]

8   Bill of sale to be void unless attested and registered

Every bill of sale shall be duly attested, and shall be registered under the principal Act within seven clear days after the execution thereof, or if it is executed in any place out of England then within seven clear days after the time at which it would in the ordinary course of post arrive in England if posted immediately after the execution thereof; and shall truly set forth the consideration for which it was given; otherwise such bill of sale shall be void in respect of the personal chattels comprised therein.

9   Form of bill of sale

A bill of sale made or given by way of security for the payment of money by the grantor thereof shall be void unless made in accordance with the form in the schedule to this Act annexed.

10   Attestation

The execution of every bill of sale by the grantor shall be attested by one or more credible witness or witnesses, not being a party or parties thereto. ...

11   Local registration of contents of bills of sale

Where the affidavit (which under section ten of the principal Act is required to accompany a bill of sale when presented for registration) describes the residence of the person making or giving the same or of the person against whom the process is issued to be in some place outside [the London insolvency district] or where the bill of sale describes the chattels enumerated therein as being in some place outside [the London insolvency district], the registrar under the principal Act shall forthwith and within three clear days after registration in the principal registry, and in accordance with the prescribed directions, transmit an abstract in the prescribed form of the contents of such bill of sale to the county court registrar in whose district such places are situate, and if such places are in the districts of different registrars to each such registrar.

Every abstract so transmitted shall be filed, kept, and indexed by the registrar of the county court in the prescribed manner, and any person may search, inspect, make extracts from, and obtain copies of the abstract so registered in the like manner and upon the like terms as to payment or otherwise as near as may be as in the case of bills of sale registered by the registrar under the principal Act.

12   Bill of sale under £30 to be void

Every bill of sale made or given in consideration of any sum under thirty pounds shall be void.

13   Chattels not to be removed or sold

All personal chattels seized or of which possession is taken [...] under or by virtue of any bill of sale (whether registered before or after the commencement of this Act), shall remain on the premises where they were so seized or so taken possession of, and shall not be removed or sold until after the expiration of five clear days from the day they were so seized or so taken possession of.

14   Bill of sale not to protect chattels against poor and parochial rates

A bill of sale to which this Act applies shall be no protection in respect of personal chattels included in such bill of sale which but for such bill of sale would have been liable to distress under a warrant[, or subject to a warrant of control,] for the recovery of taxes and poor and other parochial rates.

15   Repeal of part of Bills of Sale Act 1878

... All ... enactments contained in the principal Act which are inconsistent with this Act are repealed ...

16   Inspection of registered bills of sale

... Any person shall be entitled at all reasonable times to search the register, on payment of a fee of [5p], or such other fee as may be prescribed, and subject to such regulations as may be prescribed, and shall be entitled at all reasonable times to inspect, examine, and make extracts from any and every registered bill of sale without being required to make a written application, or to specify any particulars in reference thereto, upon payment of [5p] for each bill of sale inspected, and such payment shall be made by a judicature stamp. Provided that the said extracts shall be limited to the dates of execution, registration, renewal of registration, and satisfaction, to the names, addresses, and occupations of the parties, to the amount of the consideration, and to any further prescribed particulars.

17   Debentures to which Act not to apply

Nothing in this Act shall apply to any debentures issued by any mortgage, loan, or other incorporated company [or by any limited liability partnership], and secured upon the capital stock or goods, chattels, and effects of such company [or a limited liability partnership].

Section 9

SCHEDULE

FORM OF BILL OF SALE

This Indenture made the   day of   between *A.B.* of   of the one part, and *C.D.* of   of the other part, witnesseth that in consideration of the sum of £   now paid to *A.B.* by *C.D.*, the receipt of which the said *A.B.* hereby acknowledges [*or whatever else the consideration may be*], he the said *A.B.* doth hereby assign unto *C.D.*, his executors, administrators, and assigns, all and singular the several chattels and things specifically described in the schedule hereto annexed by way of security for the payment of the sum of £   and interest thereon at the rate of   per cent per annum [*or whatever else may be the rate*]. And the said *A.B.* doth further agree and declare that he will duly pay to the said *C.D.* the principal sum aforesaid, together with the interest then due, by equal payments of £   on the   day of   [*or whatever else may be the stipulated times or time of payment*]. And the said *A.B.* doth also agree with the said *C.D.* that he will [*here insert terms as to insurance, payment of rent, or otherwise, which the parties may agree to for the maintenance or defeasance of the security*].

Provided always, that the chattels hereby assigned shall not be liable to seizure or to be taken possession of by the said *C.D.* for any cause other than those specified in section seven of the Bills of Sale Act (1878) Amendment Act 1882.

In witness, &c.

Signed and sealed by the said *A.B.* in the presence of me *E.F.* [*add witness' name, address, and description*].

Factors Act 1889

(52 & 53 Vict., c. 45)

Preliminary

1   Definitions

For the purposes of this Act—

(1) The expression 'mercantile agent' shall mean a mercantile agent having in the customary course of his business as such agent authority either to sell goods or to consign goods for the purpose of sale, or to buy goods, or to raise money on the security of goods:

(2) A person shall be deemed to be in possession of goods or of the documents of title to goods, where the goods or documents are in the actual custody or are held by any other person subject to his control or for him or on his behalf:

(3) The expression 'goods' shall include wares and merchandise:

(4) The expression 'document of title' shall include any bill of lading, dock warrant, warehouse-keeper's certificate, and warrant or order for the delivery of goods, and any other document used in the ordinary course of business as proof of the possession or control of goods, or authorising or purporting to authorise, either by endorsement or by delivery, the possessor of the document to transfer or receive goods thereby represented:

(5) The expression 'pledge' shall include any contract pledging, or giving a lien or security on, goods, whether in consideration of an original advance or of any further or continuing advance or of any pecuniary liability:

(6) The expression 'person' shall include any body of persons corporate or unincorporate.

Dispositions by mercantile agents

2   Powers of mercantile agent with respect to disposition of goods

(1) Where a mercantile agent is, with the consent of the owner, in possession of goods or of the documents of title to goods, any sale, pledge, or other disposition of the goods, made by him when acting in the ordinary course of business of a mercantile agent, shall, subject to the provisions of this Act, be as valid as if he were expressly authorised by the owner of the goods to make the same; provided that the person taking under the disposition acts in good faith, and has not at the time of the disposition notice that the person making the disposition has not authority to make the same.

(2) Where a mercantile agent has, with the consent of the owner, been in possession of goods or of the documents of title to goods, any sale, pledge, or other disposition, which would have been valid if the consent had continued, shall be valid notwithstanding the determination of the consent; provided that the person taking under the disposition has not at the time thereof notice that the consent has been determined.

(3) Where a mercantile agent has obtained possession of any documents of title to goods by reason of his being or having been, with the consent of the owner, in possession of the goods represented thereby, or of any other documents of title to the goods, his possession of the first-mentioned documents shall, for the purposes of this Act, be deemed to be with the consent of the owner.

(4) For the purposes of this Act the consent of the owner shall be presumed in the absence of evidence to the contrary.

3   Effect of pledges of documents of title

A pledge of the documents of title to goods shall be deemed to be a pledge of the goods.

4   Pledge for antecedent debt

Where a mercantile agent pledges goods as security for a debt or liability due from the pledgor to the pledgee before the time of the pledge, the pledgee shall acquire no further right to the goods than could have been enforced by the pledgor at the time of the pledge.

5   Rights acquired by exchange of goods or documents

The consideration necessary for the validity of a sale, pledge, or other disposition of goods, in pursuance of this Act, may be either a payment in cash, or the delivery or transfer of other goods, or of a document of title to goods, or of a negotiable security, or any other valuable consideration; but where goods are pledged by a mercantile agent in consideration of the delivery or transfer of other goods, or of a document of title to goods, or of a negotiable security, the pledgee shall acquire no right or interest in the goods so pledged in excess of the value of the goods, documents, or security when so delivered or transferred in exchange.

6   Agreements through clerks, &c.

For the purposes of this Act an agreement made with a mercantile agent through a clerk or other person authorised in the ordinary course of business to make contracts of sale or pledge on his behalf shall be deemed to be an agreement with the agent.

7   Provisions as to consignors and consignees

(1) Where the owner of goods has given possession of the goods to another person for the purpose of consignment or sale, or has shipped the goods in the name of another person, and the consignee of the goods has not had notice that such person is not the owner of the goods, the consignee shall, in respect of advances made to or for the use of such person, have the same lien on the goods as if such person were the owner of the goods, and may transfer any such lien to another person.

(2) Nothing in this section shall limit or affect the validity of any sale, pledge, or disposition, by a mercantile agent.

Dispositions by sellers and buyers of goods

8   Disposition by seller remaining in possession

Where a person, having sold goods, continues, or is, in possession of the goods or of the documents of title to the goods, the delivery or transfer by that person, or by a mercantile agent acting for him, of the goods or documents of title under any sale, pledge, or other disposition thereof, or under any agreement for sale, pledge, or other disposition thereof, to any person receiving the same in good faith and without notice of the previous sale, shall have the same effect as if the person making the delivery or transfer were expressly authorised by the owner of the goods to make the same.

9   Disposition by buyer obtaining possession

Where a person, having bought or agreed to buy goods, obtains with the consent of the seller possession of the goods or the documents of title to the goods, the delivery or transfer, by that person or by a mercantile agent acting for him, of the goods or documents of title under any sale, pledge, or other disposition thereof, or under any agreement for sale, pledge, or other disposition thereof, to any person receiving the same in good faith and without notice of any lien or other right of the original seller in respect of the goods, shall have the same effect as if the person making the delivery or transfer were a mercantile agent in possession of the goods or documents of title with the consent of the owner.

[For the purposes of this section—

(i)   the buyer under a conditional sale agreement shall be deemed not to be a person who has bought or agreed to buy goods, and

(ii)   'conditional sale agreement' means an agreement for the sale of goods which is a consumer credit agreement within the meaning of the Consumer Credit Act 1974 under which the purchase price or part of it is payable in instalments, and the property in the goods is to remain in the seller (notwithstanding that the buyer is to be in possession of the goods) until such conditions as to the payment of instalments or otherwise as may be specified in the agreement are fulfilled.]

10   Effect of transfer of documents on vendor's lien or right of stoppage in transitu

Where a document of title to goods has been lawfully transferred to a person as a buyer or owner of the goods, and that person transfers the document to a person who takes the document in good faith and for valuable consideration, the last-mentioned transfer shall have the same effect for defeating any vendor's lien or right of stoppage in transitu as the transfer of a bill of lading has for defeating the right of stoppage in transitu.

Supplemental

11   Mode of transferring documents

For the purposes of this Act, the transfer of a document may be by endorsement, or, where the document is by custom or by its express terms transferable by delivery or makes the goods deliverable to the bearer, then by delivery.

12   Saving for rights of true owner

(1) Nothing in this Act shall authorise an agent to exceed or depart from his authority as between himself and his principal, or exempt him from any liability, civil or criminal, for so doing.

(2) Nothing in this Act shall prevent the owner of goods from recovering the goods from any agent or his trustee in bankruptcy at any time before the sale or pledge thereof, or shall prevent the owner of goods pledged by an agent from having the right to redeem the goods at any time before the sale thereof, on satisfying the claim for which the goods were pledged, and paying to the agent, if by him required, any money in respect of which the agent would by law be entitled to retain the goods or the documents of title thereto, or any of them, by way of lien as against the owner, or from recovering from any person with whom the goods have been pledged any balance of money remaining in his hands as the produce of the sale of the goods after deducting the amount of his lien.

(3) Nothing in this Act shall prevent the owner of goods sold by an agent from recovering from the buyer the price agreed to be paid for the same, or any part of that price, subject to any right of set off on the part of the buyer against the agent.

13 Saving for common law powers of agent

The provisions of this Act shall be construed in amplification and not in derogation of the powers exercisable by an agent independently of this Act.

Marine Insurance Act 1906

(6 Edw. 7, c. 41)

Marine insurance

1 Marine insurance defined

A contract of marine insurance is a contract whereby the insurer undertakes to indemnify the assured, in manner and to the extent thereby agreed, against marine losses, that is to say, the losses incident to marine adventure.

2 Mixed sea and land risks

(1) A contract of marine insurance may, by its express terms, or by usage of trade, be extended so as to protect the assured against losses on inland waters or on any land risk which may be incidental to any sea voyage.

(2) Where a ship in course of building, or the launch of a ship, or any adventure analogous to marine adventure, is covered by a policy in the form of a marine policy, the provisions of this Act, in so far as applicable, shall apply thereto; but, except as by this section provided, nothing in this Act shall alter or affect any rule of law applicable to any contract of insurance other than a contract of marine insurance as by this Act defined.

3 Marine adventure and maritime perils defined

(1) Subject to the provisions of this Act, every lawful marine adventure may be the subject of marine insurance.

(2) In particular there is a marine adventure where—

   (a) Any ship goods or other moveables are exposed to maritime perils. Such property is in this Act referred to as 'insurable property';

   (b) The earning or acquisition of any freight, passage money, commission, profit, or other pecuniary benefit, or the security for any advances, loan or disbursements, is endangered by the exposure of insurable property to maritime perils;

   (c) Any liability to a third party may be incurred by the owner of, or other person interested in or responsible for, insurable property, by reason of maritime perils.

'Maritime perils' means the perils consequent on, or incidental to, the navigation of the sea, that is to say, perils of the seas, fire, war perils, pirates, rovers, thieves, captures, seisures, restraints, and detainments of princes and peoples, jettisons, barratry, and any other perils, either of the like kind or which may be designated by the policy.

Insurable interest

4 Avoidance of wagering or gaming contracts

(1) Every contract of marine insurance by way of gaming or wagering is void.

(2) A contract of marine insurance is deemed to be a gaming or wagering contract—

   (a) Where the assured has not an insurable interest as defined by this Act, and the contract is entered into with no expectation of acquiring such an interest; or

(b) Where the policy is made 'interest or no interest,' or 'without further proof of interest than the policy itself,' or 'without benefit of salvage to the insurer,' or subject to any other like term:

Provided that, where there is no possibility of salvage, a policy may be effected without benefit of salvage to the insurer.

5   Insurable interest defined

(1) Subject to the provisions of this Act, every person has an insurable interest who is interested in a marine adventure.

(2) In particular a person is interested in a marine adventure where he stands in any legal or equitable relation to the adventure or to any insurable property at risk therein, in consequence of which he may benefit by the safety or due arrival of insurable property, or may be prejudiced by its loss, or damage thereto, or by the detention thereof, or may incur liability in respect thereof.

6   When interest must attach

(1) The assured must be interested in the subject-matter insured at the time of the loss though he need not be interested when the insurance is effected:

Provided that where the subject-matter is insured 'lost or not lost,' the assured may recover although he may not have acquired his interest until after the loss, unless at the time of effecting the contract of insurance the assured was aware of the loss, and the insurer was not.

(2) Where the assured has no interest at the time of the loss, he cannot acquire interest by any act or election after he is aware of the loss.

7   Defeasible or contingent interest

(1) A defeasible interest is insurable, as also is a contingent interest.

(2) In particular, where the buyer of goods has insured them, he has an insurable interest, notwithstanding that he might, at his election, have rejected the goods, or have treated them as at the seller's risk, by reason of the latter's delay in making delivery or otherwise.

8   Partial interest

A partial interest of any nature is insurable.

9   Re-insurance

(1) The insurer under a contract of marine insurance has an insurable interest in his risk, and may re-insure in respect of it.

(2) Unless the policy otherwise provides, the original assured has no right or interest in respect of such re-insurance.

10   Bottomry

The lender of money on bottomry or respondentia has an insurable interest in respect of the loan.

11   Master's and seamen's wages

The master or any member of the crew of a ship has an insurable interest in respect of his wages.

12   Advance freight

In the case of advance freight, the person advancing the freight has an insurable interest, in so far as such freight is not repayable in case of loss.

13   Charges of insurance

The assured has an insurable interest in the charges of any insurance which he may effect.

14   Quantum of interest

(1) Where the subject-matter insured is mortgaged, the mortgagor has an insurable interest in the full value thereof, and the mortgagee has an insurable interest in respect of any sum due or to become due under the mortgage.

(2) A mortgagee, consignee, or other person having an interest in the subject-matter insured may insure on his own behalf and for the benefit of other persons interested as well as for his own benefit.

(3) The owner of insurable property has an insurable interest in respect of the full value thereof, notwithstanding that some third person may have agreed, or be liable, to indemnify him in case of loss.

15   Assignment of interest

Where the assured assigns or otherwise parts with his interest in the subject-matter insured, he does not thereby transfer to the assignee his rights under the contract of insurance, unless there be an express or implied agreement with the assignee to that effect.

But the provisions of this section do not affect a transmission of interest by operation of law.

Insurable value

16   Measure of insurable value

Subject to any express provision or valuation in the policy, the insurable value of the subject-matter insured must be ascertained as follows:—

(1) In insurance on ship, the insurable value is the value, at the commencement of the risk, of the ship, including her outfit, provisions and stores for the officers and crew, money advanced for seamen's wages, and other disbursements (if any) incurred to make the ship fit for the voyage or adventure contemplated by the policy, plus the charges of insurance upon the whole:

The insurable value, in the case of a steamship, includes also the machinery, boilers, and coals and engine stores if owned by the assured, and, in the case of a ship engaged in a special trade, the ordinary fittings requisite for that trade:

(2) In insurance on freight, whether paid in advance or otherwise, the insurable value is the gross amount of freight at the risk of the assured, plus the charges of insurance:

(3) In insurance on goods or merchandise, the insurable value is the prime cost of the property insured, plus the expenses of and incidental to shipping and the charges of insurance upon the whole:

(4) In insurance on any other subject-matter, the insurable value is the amount at the risk of the assured when the policy attaches, plus the charges of insurance.

Disclosure and representations

17   Insurance is uberrimae fidei

A contract of marine insurance is a contract based upon the utmost good faith, and, if the utmost good faith is not observed by either party, the contract may be avoided by the other party.

18   Disclosure by assured

(1) Subject to the provisions of this section, the assured must disclose to the insurer, before the contract is concluded, every material circumstance which is known to the assured, and the assured is deemed to know every circumstance which, in the ordinary course of business, ought to be known by him. If the assured fails to make such disclosure, the insurer may avoid the contract.

(2) Every circumstance is material which would influence the judgment of a prudent insurer in fixing the premium, or determining whether he will take the risk.

(3) In the absence of inquiry the following circumstances need not be disclosed, namely:—

(a) Any circumstance which diminishes the risk;

(b) Any circumstance which is known or presumed to be known to the insurer. The insurer is presumed to know matters of common notoriety or knowledge, and matters which an insurer in the ordinary course of his business, as such, ought to know;

(c) Any circumstance as to which information is waived by the insurer.

(d) Any circumstance which it is superfluous to disclose by reason of any express or implied warranty.

(4) Whether any particular circumstance, which is not disclosed, be material or not is, in each case, a question of fact.

(5) The term 'circumstance' includes any communication made to, or information received by, the assured.

[(6) This section does not apply in relation to a contract of marine insurance if it is a consumer insurance contract within the meaning of the Consumer Insurance (Disclosure and Representations) Act 2012.]

19   Disclosure by agent effecting insurance

[(1)] Subjecttotheprovisionsoftheprecedingsectionastocircumstanceswhichneednotbedisclosed, where an insurance is effected for the assured by an agent, the agent must disclose to the insurer—

    (a) Every material circumstance which is known to himself, and an agent to insure is deemed to know every circumstance which, in the ordinary course of business, ought to be known by, or to have been communicated to, him; and

    (b) Every material circumstance which the assured is bound to disclose, unless it come to his knowledge too late to communicate it to the agent.

[(2) This section does not apply in relation to a contract of marine insurance if it is a consumer insurance contract within the meaning of the Consumer Insurance (Disclosure and Representations) Act 2012.]

20   Representations pending negotiation of contract

(1) Every material representation made by the assured or his agent to the insurer during the negotiations for contract, and before the contract is concluded, must be true. If it be untrue the insurer may avoid the contract.

(2) A representation is material which would influence the judgment of a prudent insurer in fixing the premium, or determining whether he will take the risk.

(3) A representation may be either a representation as to a matter of fact, or as to a matter of expectation or belief.

(4) A representation as to matter of fact is true, if it be substantially correct, that is to say, if the difference between what is represented and what is actually correct would not be considered material by a prudent insurer.

(5) A representation as to a matter of expectation or belief is true if it be made in good faith.

(6) A representation may be withdrawn or corrected before the contract is concluded.

(7) Whether a particular representation be material or not is, in each case, a question of fact.

[(8) This section does not apply in relation to a contract of marine insurance if it is a consumer insurance contract within the meaning of the Consumer Insurance (Disclosure and Representations) Act 2012.]

21   When contract is deemed to be concluded

A contract of marine insurance is deemed to be concluded when the proposal of the assured is accepted by the insurer, whether the policy be then issued or not; and, for the purpose of showing when the proposal was accepted, reference may be made to the slip or covering note or other customary memorandum of the contract, [...]

The policy

22   Contract must be embedded in policy

Subject to the provisions of any statute, a contract of marine insurance is inadmissible in evidence unless it is embodied in a marine policy in accordance with this Act. The policy may be executed and issued either at the time when the contract is concluded or afterwards.

23   What policy must specify

A marine policy must specify—

    (1) The name of the assured, or of some person who effects the insurance on his behalf:

[...]

24   Signature of insurer

(1) A marine policy must be signed by or on behalf of the insurer, provided that in the case of a corporation the corporate seal may be sufficient, but nothing in this section shall be construed as requiring the subscription of a corporation to be under seal.

(2) Where a policy is subscribed by or on behalf of two or more insurers, each subscription, unless the contrary be expressed, constitutes a distinct contract with the assured.

25   Voyage and time policies

(1) Where the contract is to insure the subject-matter 'at and from', or from one place to another or others, the policy is called a 'voyage policy', and where the contract is to insure the subject-matter for a definite period of time the policy is called a 'time policy'. A contract for both voyage and time may be included in the same policy.

[...]

26   Designation of subject-matter

(1) The subject-matter insured must be designated in a marine policy with reasonable certainty.

(2) The nature and extent of the interest of the assured in the subject-matter insured need not be specified in the policy.

(3) Where the policy designates the subject-matter insured in general terms, it shall be construed to apply to the interest intended by the assured to be covered.

(4) In the application of this section regard shall be had to any usage regulating the designation of the subject-matter insured.

27   Valued policy

(1) A policy may be either valued or unvalued.

(2) A valued policy is a policy which specifies the agreed value of the subject-matter insured.

(3) Subject to the provisions of this Act, and in the absence of fraud, the value fixed by the policy is, as between the insurer and the assured, conclusive of the insurable value of the subject intended to be insured, whether the loss be total or partial.

(4) Unless the policy otherwise provides, the value fixed by the policy is not conclusive for the purpose of determining whether there has been a constructive total loss.

28   Unvalued policy

An unvalued policy is a policy which does not specify the value of the subject-matter insured, but, subject to the limit of the sum insured, leaves the insurable value to be subsequently ascertained, in the manner herein-before specified.

29   Floating policy by ship or ships

(1) A floating policy is a policy which describes the insurance in general terms, and leaves the name of the ship or ships and other particulars to be defined by subsequent declaration.

(2) The subsequent declaration or declarations may be made by indorsement on the policy, or in other customary manner.

(3) Unless the policy otherwise provides, the declarations must be made in the order of dispatch or shipment. They must, in the case of goods, comprise all consignments within the terms of the policy, and the value of the goods or other property must be honestly stated, but an omission or erroneous declaration may be rectified even after loss or arrival, provided the omission or declaration was made in good faith.

(4) Unless the policy otherwise provides, where a declaration of value is not made until after notice of loss or arrival, the policy must be treated as an unvalued policy as regards the subject-matter of that declaration.

30   Construction of terms in policy

(1) A policy may be in the form in the First Schedule to this Act.

(2) Subject to the provisions of this Act, and unless the context of the policy otherwise requires, the terms and expressions mentioned in the First Schedule to this Act shall be construed as having the scope and meaning in that schedule assigned to them.

31   Premium to be arranged

(1) Where an insurance is effected at a premium to be arranged, and no arrangement is made, a reasonable premium is payable.

(2) Where an insurance is effected on the terms that an additional premium is to be arranged in a given event, and that event happens but no arrangement is made, then a reasonable additional premium is payable.

Double insurance

32   Double insurance

(1) Where two or more policies are effected by or on behalf of the assured on the same adventure and interest or any part thereof, and the sums insured exceed the indemnity allowed by this Act, the assured is said to be over-insured by double insurance.

(2) Where the assured is over-insured by double insurance—

    (a) The assured, unless the policy otherwise provides, may claim payment from the insurers in such order as he may think fit, provided that he is not entitled to receive any sum in excess of the indemnity allowed by this Act;

    (b) Where the policy under which the assured claims is a valued policy, the assured must give credit as against the valuation for any sum received by him under any other policy without regard to the actual value of the subject-matter insured;

    (c) Where the policy under which the assured claims is an unvalued policy he must give credit, as against the full insurable value, for any sum received by him under any other policy.

    (d) Where the assured receives any sum in excess of the indemnity allowed by this Act, he is deemed to hold such sum in trust for the insurers, according to their right of contribution among themselves.

Warranties, etc.

33   Nature of warranty

(1) A warranty, in the following sections relating to warranties, means a promissory warranty, that is to say, a warranty by which the assured undertakes that some particular thing shall or shall not be done, or that some condition shall be fulfilled, or whereby he affirms or negatives the existence of a particular state of facts.

(2) A warranty may be express or implied.

(3) A warranty, as above defined, is a condition which must be exactly complied with, whether it be material to the risk or not. If it be not so complied with, then, subject to any express provision in the policy, the insurer is discharged from liability as from the date of the breach of warranty, but without prejudice to any liability incurred by him before that date.

34   When breach of warranty excused

(1) Non-compliance with a warranty is excused when, by reason of a change of circumstances, the warranty ceases to be applicable to the circumstances of the contract, or when compliance with the warranty is rendered unlawful by any subsequent law.

(2) Where a warranty is broken, the assured cannot avail himself of the defence that the breach has been remedied, and the warranty complied with, before loss.

(3) A breach of warranty may be waived by the insurer.

35   Express warranties

(1) An express warranty may be in any form of words from which the intention to warrant is to be inferred.

(2) An express warranty must be included in, or written upon, the policy, or must be contained in some document incorporated by reference into the policy.

(3) An express warranty does not exclude an implied warranty, unless it be inconsistent therewith.

36　Warranty of neutrality

(1) Where insurable property, whether ship or goods, is expressly warranted neutral, there is an implied condition that the property shall have a neutral character at the commencement of the risk, and that, so far as the assured can control the matter, its neutral character shall be preserved during the risk.

(2) Where a ship is expressly warranted 'neutral' there is also an implied condition that, so far as the assured can control the matter, she shall be properly documented, that is to say, that she shall carry the necessary papers to establish her neutrality, and that she shall not falsify or suppress her papers, or use simulated papers. If any loss occurs through breach of this condition, the insurer may avoid the contract.

37　No implied warranty of nationality

There is no implied warranty as to the nationality of a ship, or that her nationality shall not be changed during the risk.

38　Warranty of good safety

Where the subject-matter insured is warranted 'well' or 'in good safety' on a particular day, it is sufficient if it be safe at any time during that day.

39　Warranty of seaworthiness of ship

(1) In a voyage policy there is an implied warranty that at the commencement of the voyage the ship shall be seaworthy for the purpose of the particular adventure insured.

(2) Where the policy attaches while the ship is in port, there is also an implied warranty that she shall, at the commencement of the risk, be reasonably fit to encounter the ordinary perils of the port.

(3) Where the policy relates to a voyage which is performed in different stages, during which the ship requires different kinds of or further preparation or equipment, there is an implied warranty that at the commencement of each stage the ship is seaworthy in respect of such preparation or equipment for the purposes of that stage.

(4) A ship is deemed to be seaworthy when she is reasonably fit in all respects to encounter the ordinary perils of the seas of the adventure insured.

(5) In a time policy there is no implied warranty that the ship shall be seaworthy at any stage of the adventure, but where, with the privity of the assured, the ship is sent to sea in an unseaworthy state, the insurer is not liable for any loss attributable to unseaworthiness.

40　No implied warranty that goods are seaworthy

(1) In a policy on goods or other moveables there is no implied warranty that the goods or moveables are seaworthy.

(2) In a voyage policy on goods or other moveables there is an implied warranty that at the commencement of the voyage the ship is not only seaworthy as a ship, but also that she is reasonably fit to carry the goods or other moveables to the destination contemplated by the policy.

41　Warranty of legality

There is an implied warranty that the adventure insured is a lawful one, and that, so far as the assured can control the matter, the adventure shall be carried out in a lawful manner.

The voyage

42　Implied condition as to commencement of risk

(1) Where the subject-matter is insured by a voyage policy 'at and from' or 'from' a particular place, it is not necessary that the ship should be at that place when the contract is concluded, but there is an implied condition that the adventure shall be commenced within a reasonable time, and that if the adventure be not so commenced the insurer may avoid the contract.

(2) The implied condition may be negatived by showing that the delay was caused by circumstances known to the insurer before the contract was concluded, or by showing that he waived the condition.

43   Alteration of port of departure

Where the place of departure is specified by the policy, and the ship instead of sailing from that place sails from any other place, the risk does not attach.

44   Sailing for different destination

Where the destination is specified in the policy, and the ship, instead of sailing for that destination, sails for any other destination, the risk does not attach.

45   Change of voyage

(1) Where, after the commencement of the risk, the destination of the ship is voluntarily changed from the destination contemplated by the policy, there is said to be a change of voyage.

(2) Unless the policy otherwise provides, where there is a change of voyage, the insurer is discharged from liability as from the time of the change, that it to say, as from the time when the determination to change it is manifested; and it is immaterial that the ship may not have left the course of voyage contemplated by the policy when the loss occurs.

46   Deviation

(1) Where a ship, without lawful excuse, deviates from the voyage contemplated by the policy, the insurer is discharged from liability as from the time of deviation, and it is immaterial that the ship may have regained her route before any loss occurs.

(2) There is a deviation from the voyage contemplated by the policy—
  (a) Where the course of the voyage is specifically designated by the policy, and that course is departed from; or
  (b) Where the course of the voyage is not specifically designated by the policy, but the usual and customary course is departed from.

(3) The intention to deviate is immaterial; there must be a deviation in fact to discharge the insurer from his liability under the contract.

47   Several ports of discharge

(1) Where several ports of discharge are specified by the policy, the ship may proceed to all or any of them, but, in the absence of any usage or sufficient cause to the contrary, she must proceed to them, or such of them as she goes to, in the order designated by the policy. If she does not there is a deviation.

(2) Where the policy is to 'ports of discharge', within a given area, which are not named, the ship must, in the absence of any usage or sufficient cause to the contrary, proceed to them, or such of them as she goes to, in their geographical order. If she does not there is a deviation.

48   Delay in voyage

In the case of a voyage policy, the adventure insured must be prosecuted throughout its course with reasonable dispatch, and, if without lawful excuse it is not so prosecuted, the insurer is discharged from liability as from the time when the delay becomes unreasonable.

49   Excuses for deviation or delay

(1) Deviation or delay in prosecuting the voyage contemplated by the policy is excused—
  (a) Where authorised by any special term in the policy; or
  (b) Where caused by circumstances beyond the control of the master and his employer; or
  (c) Where reasonably necessary in order to comply with an express or implied warranty; or
  (d) Where reasonably necessary for the safety of the ship or subject-matter insured; or
  (e) For the purpose of saving human life, or aiding a ship in distress where human life may be in danger; or
  (f) Where reasonably necessary for the purpose of obtaining medical or surgical aid for any person on board the ship; or

(g) Where caused by the barratrous conduct of the master or crew, if barratry be one of the perils insured against.

(2) When the cause excusing the deviation or delay ceases to operate, the ship must resume her course, and prosecute her voyage, with reasonable dispatch.

Assignment of policy

50   When and how policy is assignable

(1) A marine policy is assignable unless it contains terms expressly prohibiting assignment. It may be assigned either before or after loss.

(2) Where a marine policy has been assigned so as to pass the beneficial interest in such policy, the assignee of the policy is entitled to sue thereon in his own name; and the defendant is entitled to make any defence arising out of the contract which he would have been entitled to make if the action had been brought in the name of the person by or on behalf of whom the policy was effected.

(3) A marine policy may be assigned by indorsement thereon or in other customary manner.

51   Assured who has no interest cannot assign

Where the assured has parted with or lost his interest in the subject-matter insured, and has not, before or at the time of so doing, expressly or impliedly agreed to assign the policy, any subsequent assignment of the policy is inoperative:

  Provided that nothing in this section affects the assignment of a policy after loss.

The premium

52   When premium payable

Unless otherwise agreed, the duty of the assured or his agent to pay the premium, and the duty of the insurer to issue the policy to the assured or his agent, are concurrent conditions, and the insurer is not bound to issue the policy until payment or tender of the premium.

53   Policy effected through broker

(1) Unless otherwise agreed, where a marine policy is effected on behalf of the assured by a broker, the broker is directly responsible to the insurer for the premium, and the insurer is directly responsible to the assured for the amount which may be payable in respect of losses, or in respect of returnable premium.

(2) Unless otherwise agreed, the broker has, as against the assured, a lien upon the policy for the amount of the premium and his charges in respect of effecting the policy; and, where he has dealt with the person who employs him as a principal, he has also a lien on the policy in respect of any balance on any insurance account which may be due to him from such person, unless when the debt was incurred he had reason to believe that such person was only an agent.

54   Effect of receipt on policy

Where a marine policy effected on behalf of the assured by a broker acknowledges the receipt of the premium, such acknowledgement is, in the absence of fraud, conclusive as between the insurer and the assured, but not as between the insurer and broker.

Loss and abandonment

55   Included and excluded losses

(1) Subject to the provisions of this Act, and unless the policy otherwise provides, the insurer is liable for any loss proximately caused by a peril insured against, but, subject as aforesaid, he is not liable for any loss which is not proximately caused by a peril insured against.

(2) In particular,—

  (a) The insurer is not liable for any loss attributable to the wilful misconduct of the assured, but, unless the policy otherwise provides, he is liable for any loss proximately caused by a peril insured against, even though the loss would not have happened but for the misconduct or negligence of the master or crew;

(b) Unless the policy otherwise provides, the insurer on ship or goods is not liable for any loss proximately caused by delay, although the delay be caused by a peril insured against.

(c) Unless the policy otherwise provides, the insurer is not liable for ordinary wear and tear, ordinary leakage and breakage, inherent vice or nature of the subject-matter insured, or for any loss proximately caused by rats or vermin, or for any injury to machinery not proximately caused by maritime perils.

56   Partial and total loss

(1) A loss may be either total or partial. Any loss other than a total loss, as herein-after defined, is a partial loss.

(2) A total loss may be either an actual total loss, or a constructive total loss.

(3) Unless a different intention appears from the terms of the policy, an insurance against total loss includes a constructive, as well as an actual, total loss.

(4) Where the assured brings an action for a total loss and the evidence proves only a partial loss, he may, unless the policy otherwise provides, recover for a partial loss.

(5) Where goods reach their destination in specie, but by reason of obliteration of marks, or otherwise, they are incapable of identification, the loss, if any, is partial, and not total.

57   Actual total loss

(1) Where the subject-matter insured is destroyed, or so damaged as to cease to be a thing of the kind insured, or where the assured is irretrievably deprived thereof, there is an actual total loss.

(2) In the case of an actual total loss no notice of abandonment need be given.

58   Missing ship

Where the ship concerned in the adventure is missing, and after the lapse of a reasonable time no news of her has been received, an actual total loss may be presumed.

59   Effect of transhipment, etc.

Where, by a peril insured against, the voyage is interrupted at any intermediate port or place, under such circumstances as apart from any special stipulation in the contract of affreightment, to justify the master in landing and re-shipping the goods or other moveables, or in transhipping them, and sending them on to their destination, the liability of the insurer continues, notwithstanding the landing or transhipment.

60   Constructive total loss defined

(1) Subject to any express provision in the policy, there is a constructive total loss where the subject-matter insured is reasonably abandoned on account of its total loss appearing to be unavoidable, or because it could not be preserved from actual total loss without an expenditure which would exceed its value when the expenditure had been incurred.

(2) In particular, there is a constructive total loss—

   (i) Where the assured is deprived of the possession of his ship or goods by a peril insured against, and (a) it is unlikely that he can recover the ship or goods, as the case may be, or (b) the cost of recovering the ship or goods, as the case may be, would exceed their value when recovered; or

   (ii) In the case of damage to a ship, where she is so damaged by a peril insured against that the cost of repairing the damage would exceed the value of the ship when repaired.

   (iii) In estimating the cost of repairs, no deduction is to be made in respect of general average contributions to those repairs payable by other interests, but account is to be taken of the expense of future salvage operations and of any future general average contributions to which the ship would be liable if repaired; or

   (iv) In the case of damage to goods, where the cost of repairing the damage and forwarding the goods to their destination would exceed their value on arrival.

61   Effect of constructive total loss

Where there is a constructive total loss the assured may either treat the loss as a partial loss, or abandon the subject-matter insured to the insurer and treat the loss as if it were an actual total loss.

62   Notice of abandonment

(1) Subject to the provisions of this section, where the assured elects to abandon the subject-matter insured to the insurer, he must give notice of the abandonment. If he fails to do so the loss can only be treated as a partial loss.

(2) Notice of abandonment may be given in writing, or by word of mouth, or partly in writing and partly by word of mouth, and may be given in terms which indicate the intention of the assured to abandon his insured interest in the subject-matter insured unconditionally to the insurer.

(3) Notice of abandonment must be given with reasonable diligence after the receipt of reliable information of the loss, but where the information is of a doubtful character the assured is entitled to a reasonable time to make inquiry.

(4) Where notice of abandonment is properly given, the rights of the assured are not prejudiced by the fact that the insurer refuses to accept the abandonment.

(5) The acceptance of an abandonment may be either express or implied from the conduct of the insurer. The mere silence of the insurer after notice is not an acceptance.

(6) Where a notice of abandonment is accepted the abandonment is irrevocable. The acceptance of the notice conclusively admits liability for the loss and the sufficiency of the notice.

(7) Notice of abandonment is unnecessary where, at the time when the assured receives information of the loss, there would be no possibility of benefit to the insurer if notice were given to him.

(8) Notice of abandonment may be waived by the insurer.

(9) Where an insurer has re-insured his risk, no notice of abandonment need be given by him.

63   Effect of abandonment

(1) Where there is a valid abandonment the insurer is entitled to take over the interest of the assured in whatever may remain of the subject-matter insured, and all proprietary rights incidental thereto.

(2) Upon the abandonment of a ship, the insurer thereof is entitled to any freight in course of being earned, and which is earned by her subsequent to the casualty causing the loss, less the expenses of earning it incurred after the casualty; and, where a ship is carrying the owner's goods, the insurer is entitled to a reasonable remuneration for the carriage of them subsequent to the casualty causing the loss.

Partial losses (including salvage and general average and particular charges)

64   Particular average loss

(1) A particular average loss is a partial loss of the subject-matter insured, caused by a peril insured against, and which is not a general average loss.

(2) Expenses incurred by or on behalf of the assured for the safety or preservation of the subject-matter insured, other than general average and salvage charges, are called particular charges. Particular charges are not included in particular average.

65   Salvage charges

(1) Subject to any express provision in the policy, salvage charges incurred in preventing a loss by perils insured against may be recovered as a loss by those perils.

(2) 'Salvage charges' means the charges recoverable under maritime law by a salvor independently of contract. They do not include the expenses of services in the nature of salvage rendered by the assured or his agents, or any person employed for hire by them, for the purpose of averting a peril insured against. Such expenses, where properly incurred, may be recovered as particular charges or as a general average loss, according to the circumstances under which they were incurred.

66   General average loss

(1) A general average loss is a loss caused by or directly consequential on a general average act. It includes a general average expenditure as well as a general average sacrifice.

(2) There is a general average act where any extraordinary sacrifice or expenditure is voluntarily and reasonably made or incurred in the time of peril for the purpose of preserving the property imperilled in the common adventure.

(3) Where there is a general average loss, the party on whom it falls is entitled, subject to the conditions imposed by maritime law, to a rateable contribution from the other parties interested, and such contribution is called a general average contribution.

(4) Subject to any express provision in the policy, where the assured has incurred a general average expenditure, he may recover from the insurer in respect of the proportion of the loss which falls upon him; and, in the case of a general average sacrifice, he may recover from the insurer in respect of the whole loss without having enforced his right of contribution from the other parties liable to contribute.

(5) Subject to any express provision in the policy, where the assured has paid, or is liable to pay, a general average contribution in respect of the subject insured, he may recover therefor from the insurer.

(6) In the absence of express stipulation, the insurer is not liable for any general average loss or contribution where the loss was not incurred for the purpose of avoiding, or in connexion with the avoidance of, a peril insured against.

(7) Where ship, freight, and cargo, or any two of those interests, are owned by the same assured, the liability of the insurer in respect of general average losses or contributions is to be determined as if those subjects were owned by different persons.

Measure of indemnity

67   Extent of liability of insurer for loss

(1) The sum which the assured can recover in respect of a loss on a policy by which he is insured, in the case of an unvalued policy to the full extent of the insurable value, or in the case of a valued policy to the full extent of the value fixed by the policy, is called the measure of indemnity.

(2) Where there is a loss recoverable under the policy, the insurer, or each insurer if there be more than one, is liable for such proportion of the measure of indemnity as the amount of his subscription bears to the value fixed by the policy in the case of a valued policy, or to the insurable value in the case of an unvalued policy.

68   Total loss

Subject to the provisions of this Act and to any express provision in the policy, where there is a total loss of the subject-matter insured,—

(1) If the policy be a valued policy, the measure of indemnity is the sum fixed by the policy:

(2) If the policy be an unvalued policy, the measure of indemnity is the insurable value of the subject-matter insured.

69   Partial loss of ship

Where a ship is damaged, but not totally lost, the measure of indemnity, subject to any express provision in the policy, is as follows:—

(1) Where the ship has been repaired, the assured is entitled to the reasonable cost of the repairs, less the customary deductions, but not exceeding the sum insured in respect of any one casualty:

(2) Where the ship has been only partially repaired, the assured is entitled to the reasonable cost of such repairs, computed as above, and also to be indemnified for the reasonable depreciation, if any, arising from the unrepaired damage, provided that the aggregate amount shall not exceed the cost of repairing the whole damage, computed as above:

(3) Where the ship has not been repaired, and has not been sold in her damaged state during the risk, the assured is entitled to be indemnified for the reasonable depreciation arising from the unrepaired damage, but not exceeding the reasonable cost of repairing such damage, computed as above.

70   Partial loss of freight

Subject to any express provision in the policy, where there is a partial loss of freight, the measure of indemnity is such proportion of the sum fixed by the policy in the case of a valued policy, or of the insurable value in the case of an unvalued policy, as the proportion of freight lost by the assured bears to the whole freight at the risk of the assured under the policy.

71   Partial loss of goods, merchandise, etc.

Where there is a partial loss of goods, merchandise, or other moveables, the measure of indemnity, subject to any express provision in the policy, is as follows:—

(1) Where part of the goods, merchandise, or other moveables insured by a valued policy is totally lost, the measure of indemnity is such proportion of the sum fixed by the policy as the insurable value of the part lost bears to the insurable value of the whole, ascertained as in the case of an unvalued policy:

(2) Where part of the goods, merchandise, or other moveables insured by an unvalued policy is totally lost, the measure of indemnity is the insurable value of the part lost, ascertained as in the case of total loss:

(3) Where the whole or any part of the goods or merchandise insured has been delivered damaged at its destination, the measure of indemnity is such proportion of the sum fixed by the policy in the case of a valued policy, or of the insurable value in the case of an unvalued policy, as the difference between the gross sound and damaged values at the place of arrival bears to the gross sound value:

(4) 'Gross value' means the wholesale price or, if there be no such price, the estimated value, with, in either case, freight, landing charges, and duty paid before-hand; provided that, in the case of goods or merchandise customarily sold in bond, the bonded price is deemed to be the gross value. 'Gross proceeds' means the actual price obtained at a sale where all charges on sale are paid by the sellers.

72   Apportionment of valuation

(1) Where different species of property are insured under a single valuation, the valuation must be apportioned over the different species in proportion to their respective insurable values, as in the case of an unvalued policy. The insured value of any part of a species is such proportion of the total insured value of the same as the insurable value of the part bears to the insurable value of the whole, ascertained in both cases as provided by this Act.

(2) Where a valuation has to be apportioned, and particulars of the prime cost of each separate species, quality, or description of goods cannot be ascertained, the division of the valuation may be made over the net arrived sound values of the different species, qualities, or descriptions of goods.

73   General average contributions and salvage charges

(1) Subject to any express provision in the policy, where the assured has paid, or is liable for, any general average contribution, the measure of indemnity is the full amount of such contribution, if the subject-matter liable to contribution is insured for its full contributory value; but, if such subject-matter be not insured for its full contributory value, or if only part of it be insured, the indemnity payable by the insurer must be reduced in proportion to the under insurance, and where there has been a particular average loss which constitutes a deduction from the contributory value, and for which the insurer is liable, that amount must be deducted from the insured value in order to ascertain what the insurer is liable to contribute.

(2) Where the insurer is liable for salvage charges the extent of his liability must be determined on the like principle.

74   Liabilities to third parties

Where the assured has effected an insurance in express terms against any liability to a third party, the measure of indemnity, subject to any express provision in the policy, is the amount paid or payable by him to such third party in respect of such liability.

75   General provisions as to measure of indemnity

(1) Where there has been a loss in respect of any subject-matter not expressly provided for in the foregoing provisions of this Act, the measure of indemnity shall be ascertained, as nearly as may be, in accordance with those provisions, in so far as applicable to the particular case.

(2) Nothing in the provisions of this Act relating to the measure of indemnity shall affect the rules relating to double insurance, or prohibit the insurer from disproving interest wholly or in part, or from showing that at the time of the loss the whole or any part of the subject-matter insured was not at risk under the policy.

76 Particular average warranties

(1) Where the subject-matter insured is warranted free from particular average, the assured cannot recover for a loss of part, other than a loss incurred by a general average sacrificel unless the contract contained in the policy be apportionable; but, if the contract be apportionable, the assured may recover for a total loss of any apportionable part.

(2) Where the subject-matter insured is warranted free from particular average, either wholly or under a certain percentage, the insurer is nevertheless liable for salvage charges, and for particular charges and other expenses properly incurred pursuant to the provisions of the suing and labouring clause in order to avert a loss insured against.

(3) Unless the policy otherwise provides, where the subject-matter is warranted free from particular average under a specified percentage, a general average loss cannot be added to a particular average loss to make up the specified percentage.

(4) For the purpose of ascertaining whether the specified percentage has been reached, regard shall be had only to the actual loss suffered by the subject-matter insured. Particular charges and the expenses of and incidental to ascertaining and proving the loss must be excluded.

77 Successive losses

(1) Unless the policy otherwise provides, and subject to the provisions of this Act, the insurer is liable for successive losses, even though the total amount of such losses may exceed the sum insured.

(2) Where, under the same policy, a partial loss, which has not been repaired or otherwise made good, is followed by a total loss, the assured can only recover in respect of the total loss:

Provided that nothing in this section shall affect the liability of the insurer under the suing and labouring clause.

78 Suing and labouring clause

(1) Where the policy contains a suing and labouring clause, the engagement thereby entered into is deemed to be supplementary to the contract of insurance, and the assured may recover from the insurer any expenses properly incurred pursuant to the clause, notwithstanding that the insurer may have paid for a total loss, or that the subject-matter may have been warranted free from particular average, either wholly or under a certain percentage.

(2) General average losses and contributions and salvage charges, as defined by this Act, are not recoverable under the suing and labouring clause.

(3) Expenses incurred for the purpose of averting or diminishing any loss not covered by the policy are not recoverable under the suing and labouring clause.

(4) It is the duty of the assured and his agents, in all cases, to take such measures as may be reasonable for the purpose of averting or minimising a loss.

Rights of insurer on payment

79 Right of subrogation

(1) Where the insurer pays for a total loss, either of the whole, or in the case of goods of any apportionable part, of the subject-matter insured, he thereupon becomes entitled to take over the interest of the assured in whatever may remain of the subject-matter so paid for, and he is thereby subrogated to all the rights and remedies of the assured in and in respect of that subject-matter as from the time of the casualty causing the loss.

(2) Subject to the foregoing provisions, where the insurer pays for a partial loss, he acquires no title to the subject-matter insured, or such part of it as may remain, but he is thereupon subrogated to all rights and remedies of the assured in and in respect of the subject-matter insured as from the time of the casualty causing the loss, in so far as the assured has been indemnified, according to this Act, by such payment for the loss.

80   Right of contribution

(1) Where the assured is over-insured by double insurance, each insurer is bound, as between himself and the other insurers, to contribute rateably to the loss in proportion to the amount for which he is liable under his contract.

(2) If any insurer pays more than his proportion of the loss, he is entitled to maintain an action for contribution against the other insurers, and is entitled to the like remedies as a surety who has paid more than his proportion of the debt.

81   Effect of under insurance

Where the assured is insured for an amount less than the insurable value or, in the case of a valued policy, for an amount less than the policy valuation, he is deemed to be his own insurer in respect of the uninsured balance.

Return of premium

82   Enforcement of return

Where the premium or a proportionate part thereof is, by this Act, declared to be returnable,—

(a) If already paid, it may be recovered by the assured from the insurer; and

(b) If unpaid, it may be retained by the assured or his agent.

83   Return by agreement

Where the policy contains a stipulation for the return of the premium, or a proportionate part thereof, on the happening of a certain event, and that event happens, the premium, or, as the case may be, the proportionate part thereof, is thereupon returnable to the assured.

84   Return for failure of consideration

(1) Where the consideration for the payment of the premium totally fails, and there has been no fraud or illegality on the part of the assured or his agents, the premium is thereupon returnable to the assured.

(2) Where the consideration for the payment of the premium is apportionable and there is a total failure of any apportionable part of the consideration, a proportionate part of the premium is, under the like conditions, thereupon returnable to the assured.

(3) In particular—

(a) Where the policy is void, or is avoided by the insurer as from the commencement of the risk, the premium is returnable, provided that there has been no fraud or illegality on the part of the assured; but if the risk is not apportionable, and has once attached, the premium is not returnable;

(b) Where the subject-matter insured, or part thereof, has never been imperilled, the premium, or, as the case may be, a proportionate part thereof, is returnable: Provided that where the subject-matter has been insured 'lost or not lost' and has arrived in safety at the time when the contract is concluded, the premium is not returnable unless, at such time, the insurer knew of the safe arrival.

(c) Where the assured has no insurable interest throughout the currency of the risk, the premium is returnable, provided that this rule does not apply to a policy effected by way of gaming or wagering;

(d) Where the assured has a defeasible interest which is terminated during the currency of the risk, the premium is not returnable;

(e) Where the assured has over-insured under an unvalued policy, a proportionate part of the premium is returnable;

(f) Subject to the foregoing provisions, where the assured has over-insured by double insurance, a proportionate part of the several premiums is returnable:

Provided that, if the policies are effected at different times, and any earlier policy has at any time borne the entire risk, or if a claim has been paid on the policy in respect of the full sum insured thereby, no premium is returnable in respect of that policy, and when the double insurance is effected knowingly by the assured no premium is returnable.

Mutual insurance

85   Modification of Act in case of mutual insurance

(1) Where two or more persons mutually agree to insure each other against marine losses there is said to be a mutual insurance.

(2) The provisions of this Act relating to the premium do not apply to mutual insurance, but a guarantee, or such other arrangement as may be agreed upon, may be substituted for the premium.

(3) The provisions of this Act, in so far as they may be modified by the agreement of the parties, may in the case of mutual insurance be modified by the terms of the policies issued by the association, or by the rules and regulations of the association.

(4) Subject to the expectations mentioned in this section, the provisions of this Act apply to a mutual insurance.

Supplemental

86   Ratification by assured

Where a contract of marine insurance is in good faith effected by one person on behalf of another, the person on whose behalf it is effected may ratify the contract even after he is aware of a loss.

87   Implied obligations varied by agreement or usage

(1) Where any right, duty, or liability would arise under a contract of marine insurance by implication of law, it may be negatived or varied by express agreement or by usage, if the usage be such as to bind both parties to the contract.

(2) The provisions of this section extend to any right, duty, or liability declared by this Act which may be lawfully modified by agreement.

88   Reasonable time, etc, a question of fact

Where by this Act any reference is made to reasonable time, reasonable premium, or reasonable diligence, the question what is reasonable is a question of fact.

89   Slip as evidence

Where there is a duly stamped policy, reference may be made, as heretofore, to the slip or covering note, in any legal proceeding.

90   Interpretation of terms

In this Act, unless the context or subject-matter otherwise requires,—

'Action' includes counter-claim and set off:

'Freight' includes the profit derivable by a shipowner from the employment of his ship to carry his own goods or moveables, as well as freight payable by a third party, but does not include passage money:

'Moveables' means any moveable tangible property, other than the ship, and includes money, valuable securities, and other documents.

'Policy' means a marine policy.

91   Savings

(1) Nothing in this Act, or in any repeal effected thereby, shall affect—

    (a) The provisions of the Stamp Act 1891, or any enactment for the time being in force relating to the revenue;

    (b) The provisions of the Companies Act 1862, or any enactment amending or substituted for the same;

    (c) The provisions of any statute not expressly repealed by this Act.

(2) The rules of the common law including the law merchant, save in so far as they are inconsistent with the express provisions of this Act, shall continue to apply to contracts of marine insurance.

94   Short title

This Act may be cited as the Marine Insurance Act 1906.

Section 30

SCHEDULE 1

FORM OF POLICY

Lloyd's SG Policy

BE IT KNOWN THAT ... as well in ... own name as for and in the name and names of all and every other person or persons to whom the same doth, may, or shall appertain, in part or in all doth make assurance and cause ... and them, and every of them, to be insured lost or not lost, at and from ...

Upon any kind of goods and merchandise, and also upon the body, tackle, apparel, ordnance, munition, artillery, boat, and other furniture, of and in the good ship or vessel called the .....

whereof is master under God, for this present voyage, ... or whosoever else shall go for master in the said ship, or by whatsoever other name or names the said ship, or the master thereof, is or shall be named or called; beginning the adventure upon the said goods and merchandised from the loading thereof aboard the said ship, ...

upon the said ship, etc. ...

and so shall continue and endure, during her abode there, upon the said ship, etc. And further, until the said ship, with all her ordnance, tackle, apparel, etc., and goods and merchandises whatsoever shall be arrived at .....

upon the said ship, etc., until she hath moored at anchor for twenty-four hours in good safety; and upon the goods and merchandises, until the same be there discharged and safely landed. And it shall be lawful for the said ship, etc., in this voyage to proceed and sail to and touch and stay at any ports or places whatsoever ...

without prejudice to this insurance. The said ship, etc., goods and merchandises, etc., for so much as concerns the assured by agreement between the assured and assurers in this policy, are and shall be valued at ...

Touching the adventures and perils which we the assurers are contented to bear and do take upon us in this voyage: they are of the seas, men of war, fire, enemies, pirates, rovers, thieves, jettisons, letters of mart and countermart, surprisals, takings at sea, arrests, restraints, and detainments of all kings, princes, and people, of what nation, condition, or quality soever, barratry of the master and mariners, and of all other perils, losses, and misfortunes, that have or shall come to the hurt, detriment, or damage of the said goods and merchandises, and ship, etc., or any part thereof.

[*Sue and labour clause*] And in case of any loss or misfortune it shall be lawful to the assured, their factors, servants and assigns, to sue, labour, and travel for, in and about the defence, safeguards, and recovery of the said goods and merchandises, and ship, etc., or any part thereof, without prejudice to this insurance; to the charges whereof we, the assurers, will contribute each one according to the rate and quantity of his sum herein assured.

[*Waiver clause*] And it is especially declared and agreed that no acts of the insurer or insured in recovering, saving, or preserving the property insured shall be considered as a waiver, or acceptance of abandonment. And it is agreed by us, the insurers, that this writing or policy of assurance shall be of as much force and effect as the surest writing or policy of assurance heretofore made in Lombard Street, or in the Royal Exchange, or elsewhere in London. And so we, the assurers, are contented, and do hereby promise and bind ourselves, each one for his own part, our heirs, executors, and goods to the assured, their executors, administrators, and assigns, for the true performance of the premises, confessing ourselves paid the consideration due unto us for this assurance by the assured, at and after the rate of ...

IN WITNESS whereof we, the assurers, have subscribed our names and sums assured in London.

[*Memorandum*] N.B.—Corn, fish, salt, fruit, flour, and seed are warranted free from average, unless general, or the ship be stranded-sugar, tobacco, hemp, flax, hides and skins are warranted free from average, under five pounds per cent., and all other goods, also the ship and freight, are warranted free from average, under three pounds per cent. unless general, or the ship be stranded.

Rules for construction of policy

The following are the rules referred to by this Act for the construction of a policy in the above or other like form, where the context does not otherwise require:—

1. Where the subject-matter is insured 'lost or not lost,' and the loss has occurred before the contract is concluded, the risk attaches, unless at such time the assured was aware of the loss, and the insurer was not.

2. Where the subject-matter is insured 'from' a particular place, the risk does not attach until the ship starts on the voyage insured.

3. (a) Where a ship is insured 'at and from' a particular place, and she is at that place in good safety when the contract is concluded, the risk attaches immediately.

   (b) If she be not at that place when the contract is concluded, the risk attaches as soon as she arrives there in good safety, and, unless the policy otherwise provides, it is immaterial that she is covered by another policy for a specified time after arrival.

   (c) Where chartered freight is insured 'at and from' a particular place, and the ship is at that place in good safety when the contract is concluded the risk attaches immediately. If she be not there when the contract is concluded, the risk attaches as soon as she arrives there in good safety.

   (d) Where freight, other than chartered freight, is payable without special conditions and is insured 'at and from' a particular place, the risk attaches pro rata as the goods or merchandise are shipped; provided that if there be cargo in readiness which belongs to the shipowner, or which some other person has contracted with him to ship, the risk attaches as soon as the ship is ready to receive such cargo.

4. Where goods or other moveables are insured 'from the loading thereof,' the risk does not attach until such goods or moveables are actually on board, and the insurer is not liable for them while in transit from shore to ship.

5. Where the risk on goods or other moveables continues until they are 'safely landed,' they must be landed in the customary manner and within a reasonable time after arrival at the port of discharge, and if they are not so landed the risk ceases.

6. In the absence of any further licence or usage, the liberty to touch and stay 'at any port or place whatsoever' does not authorise the ship to depart from the course of her voyage from the port of departure to the port of destination.

7. The term 'perils of the seas' refers only to fortuitous accidents or casualties of the seas. It does not include the ordinary action of the winds and waves.

8. The term 'pirates' includes passengers who mutiny and rioters who attack the ship from the shore.

9. The term 'thieves' does not cover clandestine theft or a theft committed by anyone of the ship's company, whether crew or passengers.

10. The term 'arrests, etc., of kings, princes, and people' refers to political or executive acts, and does not include a loss caused by riot or by ordinary judicial process.

11. The term 'barratry' includes every wrongful act wilfully committed by the master or crew to the prejudice of the owner, or, as the case may be, the charterer.

12. The term 'all other perils' includes only perils similar in kind to the perils specifically mentioned in the policy.

13. The term 'average unless general' means a partial loss of the subject-matter insured other than a general average loss, and does not include 'particular charges.'

14. Where the ship has stranded, the insurer is liable for the excepted losses, although the loss is not attributable to the stranding, provided that when the stranding takes place the risk has attached and, if the policy be on goods, that the damaged goods are on board.

15. The term 'ship' includes the hull, materials and outfit, stores and provisions for the officers and crew, and, in the case of vessels engaged in a special trade, the ordinary fittings requisite for the trade, and also, in the case of a steamship, the machinery, boilers, and coals and engine stores, if owned by the assured.

16. The term 'freight' includes the profit derivable by a shipowner from the employment of his ship to carry his own goods or moveables, as well as freight payable by a third party, but does not include passage money.

17. The term 'goods' means goods in the nature of merchandise, and does not include personal effects or provisions and stores for use on board.

In the absence of any usage to the contrary, deck cargo and living animals must be insured specifically, and not under the general denomination of goods.

Marine Insurance (Gambling Policies) Act 1909

(9 Edw. 7, c. 12)

1 Prohibition of gambling on loss by maritime perils

(1) If—
  (a) any person effects a contract of marine insurance without having any bonâ fide interest, direct or indirect, either in the safe arrival of the ship in relation to which the contract is made or in the safety or preservation of the subject-matter insured, or a bonâ fide expectation of acquiring such an interest; or
  (b) any person in the employment of the owner of a ship, not being a part owner of the ship, effects a contract of marine insurance in relation to the ship, and the contract is made 'interest or no interest,' or 'without further proof of interest than the policy itself,' or 'without benefit of salvage to the insurer,' or subject to any other like term,

the contract shall be deemed to be a contract by way of gambling on loss by maritime perils, and the person effecting it shall be guilty of an offence, and shall be liable, on summary conviction, to imprisonment [...] for a term not exceeding six months or to a fine not exceeding [level 3 on the standard scale], and in either case to forfeit to the Crown any money he may receive under the contract.

(2) Any broker or other person through whom, and any insurer with whom, any such contract is effected shall be guilty of an offence and liable on summary conviction to the like penalties if he acted knowing that the contract was by way of gambling on loss by maritime perils within the meaning of this Act.

(3) Proceedings under this Act shall not be instituted without the consent in England of the Attorney-General, in Scotland of the Lord Advocate, and in Ireland of the [Attorney-General for Northern Ireland.]

(4) Proceedings shall not be instituted under this Act against a person (other than a person in the employment of the owner of the ship in relation to which the contract was made) alleged to have effected a contract by way of gambling on loss by maritime perils until an opportunity has been afforded him of showing that the contract was not such a contract as aforesaid, and any information given by that person for that purpose shall not be admissible in evidence against him in any prosecution under this Act.

(5) If proceedings under this Act are taken against any person (other than a person in the employment of the owner of the ship in relation to which the contract was made) for effecting such a contract, and the contract was made 'interest or no interest,' or 'without further proof of interest than the policy itself,' or 'without benefit of salvage to the insurer,' or subject to any other like term, the contract shall be deemed to be a contract by way of gambling on loss by maritime perils unless the contrary is proved.

(6) For the purpose of giving jurisdiction under this Act, every offence shall be deemed to have been committed either in the place in which the same actually was committed or in any place in which the offender may be.

(7) Any person aggrieved by an order or decision of a court of summary jurisdiction under this Act, may appeal to [the Crown Court].

(8) For the purposes of this Act the expression 'owner' includes charterer.

(9) Subsection (7) of this section shall not apply to Scotland.

2   Short title

This Act may be cited as the Marine Insurance (Gambling Policies) Act 1909, and the Marine Insurance Act 1906, and this Act may be cited together as the Marine Insurance Acts 1906 and 1909.

Law of Property Act 1925

(15 Geo. 5, c. 20)

136   Legal assignments of things in action

(1) Any absolute assignment by writing under the hand of the assignor (not purporting to be by way of charge only) of any debt or other legal thing in action, of which express notice in writing has been given to the debtor, trustee or other person from whom the assignor would have been entitled to claim such debt or thing in action, is effectual in law (subject to equities having priority over the right of the assignee) to pass and transfer from the date of such notice—

(a) the legal right to such debt or thing in action;

(b) all legal and other remedies for the same; and

(c) the power to give a good discharge for the same without the concurrence of the assignor:

Provided that, if the debtor, trustee or other person liable in respect of such debt or thing in action has notice—

(a) that the assignment is disputed by the assignor or any person claiming under him; or

(b) of any other opposing or conflicting claims to such debt or thing in action; he may, if he thinks fit, either call upon the persons making claim thereto to inter-plead concerning the same, or pay the debt or other thing in action into court under the provisions of the Trustee Act, 1925.

(2) This section does not affect the provisions of the Policies of Assurance Act, 1867.

Law Reform (Frustrated Contracts) Act 1943

(6 & 7 Geo. VI, c. 40)

1   Adjustment of rights and liabilities of parties to frustrated contracts

(1) Where a contract governed by English law has become impossible of performance or been otherwise frustrated, and the parties thereto have for that reason been discharged from the further performance of the contract, the following provisions of this section shall, subject to the provisions of section two of this Act, have effect in relation thereto.

(2) All sums paid or payable to any party in pursuance of the contract before the time when the parties were so discharged (in this Act referred to as 'the time of discharge') shall, in the case of sums so paid, be recoverable from him as money received by him for the use of the party by whom the sums were paid, and, in the case of sums so payable, cease to be so payable: Provided that, if the party to whom the sums were so paid or payable incurred expenses before the time of discharge in, or for the purpose of, the performance of the contract, the court may, if it considers it just to do so having regard to all the circumstances of the case, allow him to retain or, as the case may be, recover the whole or any part of the sums so paid or payable, not being an amount in excess of the expenses so incurred.

(3) Where any party to the contract has, by reason of anything done by any other party thereto in, or for the purpose of, the performance of the contract, obtained a valuable benefit (other than a payment of money to which the last foregoing subsection applies) before the time of discharge there shall be recoverable from him by the said other party such sum (if any), not exceeding the value of the said benefit to the party obtaining it, as the court considers just, having regard to all the circumstances of the case and, in particular,—

(a) the amount of any expenses incurred before the time of discharge by the benefited party in, or for the purpose of, the performance of the contract, including any sums paid or payable by him to any other party in pursuance of the contract and retained or recoverable by that party under the last foregoing subsection, and

(b) the effect, in relation to the said benefit, of the circumstances giving rise to the frustration of the contract.

(4) In estimating, for the purposes of the foregoing provisions of this section, the amount of any expenses incurred by any party to the contract, the court may, without prejudice to the generality of the said provisions, include any sum as appears to be reasonable in respect of overhead expenses and in respect of any work or services performed personally by the said party.

(5) In considering whether any sum ought to be recovered or retained under the foregoing provisions of this section by any party to the contract, the court shall not take into account any sums which have, by reason of the circumstances giving rise to the frustration of the contract, become payable to that party under any contract of insurance unless there was an obligation to insure imposed by an express term of the frustrated contract or by or under any enactment.

(6) Where any person has assumed obligations under the contract in consideration of the conferring of a benefit by any other party to the contract upon any other person, whether a party to the contract or not, the court may, if in all the circumstances of the case it considers it just to do so, treat for the purposes of subsection (3) of this section any benefit so conferred as a benefit obtained by the person who has assumed the obligations as aforesaid.

2 Provision as to application of this Act

(1) This Act shall apply to contracts, whether made before or after the commencement of this Act, as respects which the time of discharge is on or after the first day of July, nineteen hundred and forty-three, but not to contracts as respects which the time of discharge is before the said date.

(2) This Act shall apply to contracts to which the Crown is a party in like manner as to contracts between subjects.

(3) Where any contract to which this Act applies contains any provision which, upon the true construction of the contract, is intended to have effect in the event of circumstances arising which operate, or would but for the said provision operate, to frustrate the contract, or is intended to have effect whether such circumstances arise or not, the court shall give effect to the said provision and shall only give effect to the foregoing section of this Act to such extent, if any, as appears to the court to be consistent with the said provision.

(4) Where it appears to the court that a part of any contract to which this Act applies can be properly severed from the remainder of the contract, being a part wholly performed before the time of discharge, or so performed except for the payment in respect of that part of the contract of sums which are or can be ascertained under the contract, the court shall treat that part of the contract as if it were a separate contract and had not been frustrated and shall treat the foregoing section of this Act as only applicable to the remainder of that contract.

(5) This Act shall not apply—

(a) to any charterparty, except a time charterparty or a charterparty by way of demise, or to any contract (other than a charterparty) for the carriage of goods by sea; or

(b) to any contract of insurance, save as is provided by subsection (5) of the foregoing section; or

(c) to any contract to which [section 7 of the Sale of Goods Act 1979] (which avoids contracts for the sale of specific goods which perish before the risk has passed to the buyer) applies, or to any other contract for the sale, or for the sale and delivery, of specific goods, where the contract is frustrated by reason of the fact that the goods have perished.

3 Short title and interpretation

(2) In this Act the expression 'court' means, in relation to any matter, the court or arbitrator by or before whom the matter falls to be determined.

Cheques Act 1957

(5 & 6 Eliz. 2, c. 36)

1   Protection of bankers paying unindorsed or irregularly indorsed cheques, etc.

(1) Where a banker in good faith and in the ordinary course of business pays a cheque drawn on him which is not indorsed or is irregularly indorsed, he does not in doing so, incur any liability by reason only of the absence of, or irregularity in indorsement, and he is deemed to have paid it in due course.

(2) Where a banker in good faith and in the ordinary course of business pays any such instrument as the following namely—

(a) a document issued by a customer of his which, though not a bill of exchange, is intended to enable a person to obtain payment from him of the sum mentioned in the document;

(b) a draft payable on demand drawn by him upon himself, whether payable at the head office or some other office of his bank; he does not, in so doing, incur any liability by reason only of the absence of, or irregularity in, indorsement, and the payment discharges the instrument.

2   Rights of bankers collecting cheques not indorsed by holders

A banker who gives value for, or has a lien on, a cheque payable to order which the holder delivers to him for collection without indorsing it, has such (if any) rights as he would have had if, upon delivery, the holder had indorsed it in blank.

3   Unindorsed cheques as evidence of payment

[(1)] An unindorsed cheque which appears to have been paid by the banker on whom it is drawn is evidence of the receipt by the payee of the sum payable by the cheque.

[(2) For the purposes of subsection (1) above, a copy of a cheque to which that subsection applies is evidence of the cheque if—

(a) the copy is made by the banker in whose possession the cheque is after presentment and,

(b) it is certified by him to be a true copy of the original.]

4   Protection of bankers collecting payment of cheques, &c.

(1) Where a banker, in good faith and without negligence—

(a) receives payment for a customer of an instrument to which this section applies; or

(b) having credited a customer's account with the amount of such an instrument, receives payment thereof for himself;

and the customer has no title, or a defective title, to the instrument, the banker does not incur any liability to the true owner of the instrument by reason only of having received payment thereof.

(2) This section applies to the following instruments, namely:—

(a) cheques [(including cheques which under section 81A(1) of the Bills of Exchange Act 1882 or otherwise are not transferable)];

(b) any document issued by a customer of a banker which, though not a bill of exchange, is intended to enable a person to obtain payment from that banker of the sum mentioned in the document;

(c) any document issued by a public officer is intended to enable a person to obtain payment from the Paymaster General or the Queen's and Lord Treasurer's Remembrancer of the sum mentioned in the document but is not a bill of exchange;

(d) any draft payable on demand drawn by a banker upon himself whether payable at the head office or some other office of his bank.

(3) A banker is not to be treated for the purposes of this section as having been negligent by reason only of his failure to concern himself with absence of, or irregularity in, indorsement of an instrument.

5   Application of certain provisions of Bills of Exchange Act, 1882, to instruments not being bills of exchange

The provisions of the Bills of Exchange Act, 1882, relating to crossed cheques shall, so far as applicable, have effect in relation to instruments (other than cheques) to which the last foregoing section applies as they have effect in relation to cheques.

6   Construction, saving and repeal

(1) This Act shall be construed as one with the Bills of Exchange Act, 1882.

(2) The foregoing provisions of this Act do not make negotiable any instrument which, apart from them, is not negotiable.

Hire-Purchase Act 1964

(1964, c. 53)

[PART III TITLE TO MOTOR VEHICLES ON HIRE-PURCHASE OR CONDITIONAL SALE]

[27   Protection of purchasers of motor vehicles

(1) This section applies where a motor vehicle has been bailed or (in Scotland) hired under a hire-purchase agreement, or has been agreed to be sold under a conditional sale agreement, and, before the property in the vehicle has become vested in the debtor, he disposes of the vehicle to another person.

(2) Where the disposition referred to in subsection (1) above is to a private purchaser, and he is a purchaser of the motor vehicle in good faith without notice of the hire-purchase or conditional sale agreement (the 'relevant agreement') that disposition shall have effect as if the creditor's title to the vehicle has been vested in the debtor immediately before that disposition.

(3) Where the person to whom the disposition referred to in subsection (1) above is made (the 'original purchaser') is a trade or finance purchaser, then if the person who is the first private purchaser of the motor vehicle after that disposition (the 'first private purchaser') is a purchaser of the vehicle in good faith without notice of the relevant agreement, the disposition of the vehicle to the first private purchaser shall have effect as if the title of the creditor to the vehicle had been vested in the debtor immediately before he disposed of it to the original purchaser.

(4) Where, in a case within subsection (3) above—

(a) the disposition by which the first private purchaser becomes a purchaser of the motor vehicle in good faith without notice of the relevant agreement is itself a bailment or hiring under a hire-purchase agreement, and

(b) the person who is the creditor in relation to that agreement disposes of the vehicle to the first private purchaser, or a person claiming under him, by transferring to him the property in the vehicle in pursuance of a provision in the agreement in that behalf, the disposition referred to in paragraph (b) above (whether or not the person to whom it is made is a purchaser in good faith without notice of the relevant agreement) shall as well as the disposition referred to in paragraph (a) above, have effect as mentioned in subsection (3) above.

(5) The preceding provisions of this section apply—

(a) notwithstanding anything in [section 21 of the Sale of Goods Act 1979] (sale of goods by a person not the owner), but

(b) without prejudice to the provisions of the Factors Acts (as defined by [section 61(1) of the said Act of 1979)] or any other enactment enabling the apparent owner of goods to dispose of them as if he were the true owner.

(6) Nothing in this section shall exonerate the debtor from any liability (whether criminal or civil) to which he would be subject apart from this section; and, in a case where the debtor disposes of the motor vehicle to a trade or finance purchaser, nothing in this section shall exonerate—

(a) that trade or finance purchaser, or

(b) any other trade or finance purchaser who becomes a purchaser of the vehicle and is not a person claiming under the first private purchaser,

from any liability (whether criminal or civil) to which he would be subject apart from this section.]

[28 Presumptions relating to dealings with motor vehicles

(1) Where in any proceedings (whether criminal or civil) relating to a motor vehicle it is proved—

(a) that the vehicle was bailed or (in Scotland) hired under a hire-purchase agreement, or was agreed to be sold under a conditional sale agreement and

(b) that a person (whether a party to the proceedings or not) became a private purchaser of the vehicle in good faith without notice of the hire-purchase or conditional sale agreement (the 'relevant agreement'), this section shall have effect for the purposes of the operation of section 27 of this Act in relation to those proceedings.

(2) It shall be presumed for those purposes unless the contrary is proved, that the disposition of the vehicle to the person referred to in subsection (1)(b) above (the 'relevant purchaser') was made by the debtor.

(3) If it is proved that that disposition was not made by the debtor, then it shall be presumed for those purposes, unless the contrary is proved—

(a) that the debtor disposed of the vehicle to a private purchaser purchasing in good faith without notice of the relevant agreement, and

(b) that the relevant purchaser is or was a person claiming under the person to whom the debtor so disposed of the vehicle.

(4) If it is proved that the disposition of the vehicle to the relevant purchaser was not made by the debtor, and that the person to whom the debtor disposed of the vehicle (the 'original purchaser') was a trade or finance purchaser, then it shall be presumed for those purposes, unless the contrary is proved,

(a) that the person who, after the disposition of the vehicle to the original purchaser, first became a private purchaser of the vehicle was a purchaser in good faith without notice of the relevant agreement, and

(b) that the relevant purchaser is or was a person claiming under the original purchaser.

(5) Without prejudice to any other method of proof, where in any proceedings a party thereto admits a fact, that fact shall, for the purposes of this section, be taken as against him to be proved in relation to those proceedings.]

[29 Interpretation of Part III

(1) In this Part of this Act—

'conditional sale agreement' means an agreement for the sale of goods under which the purchase price or part of it is payable by instalments, and the property in the goods is to remain in the seller (notwithstanding that the buyer is to be in possession of the goods) until such conditions as to the payment of instalments or otherwise as may be specified in the agreement are fulfilled;

'creditor' means the person by whom goods are bailed or (in Scotland) hired under a hire-purchase agreement or as the case may be, the seller under a conditional sale agreement, or the person to whom his rights and duties have passed by assignment or operation of law;

'disposition' means any sale or contract of sale (including a conditional sale agreement), any bailment or (in Scotland) hiring under a hire-purchase agreement and any transfer of the property of goods in pursuance of a provision in that behalf contained in a hire-purchase agreement, and includes any transaction purporting to be a disposition (as so defined), and 'dispose of' shall be construed accordingly:

'hire-purchase agreement' means an agreement, other than a conditional sale agreement, under which—

(a) goods are bailed or (in Scotland) hired in return for periodical payments by the person to whom they are bailed or hired, and

(b) the property in the goods will pass to that person if the terms of the agreement are complied with and one or more of the following occurs—

(i) the exercise of an option to purchase by that person,

(ii) the doing of any other specified act by any party to the agreement,

(iii) the happening of any other specified events; and

'motor vehicle' means a mechanically propelled vehicle intended or adapted for use on roads to which the public has access.

(2) In this Part of this Act 'trade or finance purchaser' means a purchaser who, at the time of the disposition made to him, carries on a business which consists, wholly or partly—

(a) of purchasing motor vehicles for the purpose of offering or exposing them for sale, or

(b) of providing finance by purchasing motor vehicles for the purpose of bailing or (in Scotland) hiring them under hire-purchase agreements or agreeing to sell them under conditional sale agreements,

and 'private purchaser' means a purchaser who, at the time of the disposition made to him, does not carry on any such business.

(3) For the purposes of this Part of this Act a person becomes a purchaser of a motor vehicle if, and at the time when, a disposition of the vehicle is made to him; and a person shall be taken to be a purchaser of a motor vehicle without notice of a hire-purchase agreement or conditional sale agreement if, at the time of the disposition made to him, he has no actual notice that the vehicle is or was the subject of any such agreement.

(4) In this Part of this Act the 'debtor' in relation to a motor vehicle which has been bailed or hired under a hire-purchase agreement, or, as the case may be, agreed to be sold under a conditional sale agreement, means the person who at the material time (whether the agreement has before that time been terminated or not) either—

(a) is the person to whom the vehicle is bailed or hired under that agreement, or

(b) is, in relation to the agreement, the buyer, including a person who at that time is, by virtue of section 130(4) of the Consumer Credit Act 1974 treated as a bailee or (in Scotland) a custodier of the vehicle.

(5) In this Part of this Act any reference to the title of the creditor to a motor vehicle which has been bailed or (in Scotland) hired under a hire-purchase agreement or agreed to be sold under a conditional sale agreement, and is disposed of by the debtor, is a reference to such title (if any) to the vehicle as, immediately before that disposition, was vested in the person who then was the creditor in relation to the agreement.]

Misrepresentation Act 1967

(1967, c. 7)

1 Removal of certain bars to rescission for innocent misrepresentation

Where a person has entered into a contract after a misrepresentation has been made to him, and—

(a) the misrepresentation has become a term of the contract, or

(b) the contract has been performed;

or both, then, if otherwise he would be entitled to rescind the contract without alleging fraud, he shall be so entitled, subject to the provisions of this Act, notwithstanding the matters mentioned in paragraphs (a) and (b) of this section.

2 Damages for misrepresentation

(1) Where a person has entered into a contract after a misrepresentation has been made to him by another party thereto and as a result thereof he has suffered loss, then, if the person making the misrepresentation would be liable to damages in respect thereof had the misrepresentation been

made fraudulently, that person shall be so liable notwithstanding that the misrepresentation was not made fraudulently, unless he proves that he had reasonable ground to believe and did believe up to the time the contract was made that the facts represented were true.

(2) Where a person has entered into a contract after a misrepresentation has been made to him otherwise than fraudulently, and he would be entitled, by reason of the misrepresentation, to rescind the contract, then, if it is claimed, in any proceedings arising out of the contract, that the contract ought to be or has been rescinded, the court or arbitrator may declare the contract subsisting and award damages in lieu of rescission, if of opinion that it would be equitable to do so having regard to the nature of the misrepresentation and the loss that would be caused by it if the contract were upheld, as well as to the loss that rescission would cause to the other party.

(3) Damages may be awarded against a person under subsection (2) of this section whether or not he is liable to damages under subsection (1) thereof, but where he is so liable any award under the said subsection (2) shall be taken into account in assessing his liability under the said subsection (1).

3   Avoidance of provision excluding liability for misrepresentation

[If a contract contains a term which would exclude or restrict—

      (a) any liability to which a party to a contract may be subject by reason of any misrepresenta-tion made by him before the contract was made; or

      (b) any remedy available to another party to the contract by reason of such a misrepresentation,

that term shall be of no effect except in so far as it satisfies the requirement of reasonableness as stated in section 11(1) of the Unfair Contract Terms Act 1977; and it is for those claiming that the term sat-isfies that requirement to show that it does.]

Trade Descriptions Act 1968

(1968, c. 29)

Prohibition of false trade descriptions

1   Prohibition of false trade descriptions

[(2) Sections 2 to 4 shall have effect for the interpretation of expressions used in this Act.]

2   Trade description

(1) A trade description is an indication, direct or indirect, and by whatever means given, of any of the following matters with respect to any goods or parts of goods, that is to say—

      (a) quantity, size or gauge;

      (b) method of manufacture, production, processing or reconditioning;

      (c) composition;

      (d) fitness for purpose, strength, performance, behaviour or accuracy;

      (e) any physical characteristics not included in the preceding paragraphs;

      (f) testing by any person and results thereof;

      (g) approval by any person or conformity with a type approved by any person;

      (h) place or date of manufacture, production, processing or reconditioning;

      (i) person by whom manufactured, produced, processed or reconditioned;

      (j) other history, including previous ownership or use.

(2) The matters specified in subsection (1) of this section shall be taken—

      (a) in relation to any animal, to include sex, breed or cross, fertility and soundness;

      (b) in relation to any semen, to include the identity and characteristics of the animal from which it as taken and measure of dilution.

(3) In this section 'quantity' includes length, width, height, area, volume, capacity, weight and number.

(4) Notwithstanding anything in the preceding provisions of this section, the following shall be deemed not to be trade descriptions, that is to say, any description or mark applied in pursuance of—

(a)   [...]

(b)   section 2 of the Agricultural Produce (Grading and Marking) Act 1928 (as amended by the Agricultural Produce (Grading and Marking) Amendment Act 1931) or any corresponding enactment of the Parliament of Northern Ireland;

(c)   the Plant Varieties and Seeds Act 1964;

(d)   the Agriculture and Horticulture Act 1964 or any Community grading rules within the meaning of Part III of that Act;

(e)   the Seeds Act (Northern Ireland) 1965;

(f)   the Horticulture Act (Northern Ireland) 1966;

[(g)   the Consumer Protection Act 1987];

[(h)   the Plant Varieties Act 1997];

[any statement made in respect of, or mark applied to, any material in pursuance of Part IV of the Agriculture Act 1970, any name or expression to which a meaning has been assigned under section 70 of that Act when applied to any material in the circumstances specified in that section] [...] any mark prescribed by a system of classification compiled under section 5 of the Agriculture Act 1967 [and any designation, mark or description applied in pursuance of a scheme brought into force under section 6(1) or an order made under section 25(1) of the Agriculture Act 1970.]

(5) Notwithstanding anything in the preceding provisions of this section,

[(a)] where provision is made under [the Food Safety Act 1990] or the [Food Safety (Northern Ireland) Order 1991 or the Consumer Protection Act 1987] prohibiting the application of a description except to goods in the case of which the requirements specified in that provision are complied with, that description, when applied to such goods, shall be deemed not to be a trade description.

[(b)] where by virtue of any provision made under Part V of the Medicines Act 1968 (or made under any provisions of the said Part V as applied by an order made under section 104 or section 105 of that Act) anything which in accordance with this Act, constitutes the application of a trade description to goods is subject to any requirements or restrictions imposed by that provision, any particular description specified in that provision, when applied to goods in circumstances to which those requirements or restrictions are applicable, shall be deemed not to be a trade description.]

3   False trade description

(1) A false trade description is a trade description which is false to a material degree.

(2) A trade description which, though not false, is misleading, that is to say, likely to be taken for such an indication of any of the matters specified in section 2 of this Act as would be false to a material degree, shall be deemed to be a false trade description.

(3) Anything which, though not a trade description, is likely to be taken for an indication of any of those matters and, as such an indication, would be false to a material degree, shall be deemed to be a false trade description.

(4) A false indication, or anything likely to be taken as an indication which would be false, that any goods comply with a standard specified or recognised by any person or implied by the approval of any person shall be deemed to be a false trade description, if there is no such person or no standard so specified, recognised or implied.

4   Applying a trade description to goods

(1) A person applies a trade description to goods if he—

(a)   affixes or annexes it to or in any manner marks it on or incorporates it with—

(i)   the goods themselves, or

(ii)   anything in, on or with which the goods are supplied; or

(b)   places the goods in, on or with anything which the trade description has been affixed or annexed to, marked on or incorporated with, or places any such thing with the goods; or

(c) uses the trade description in any manner likely to be taken as referring to the goods.

(2) An oral statement may amount to the use of a trade description.

(3) Where goods are supplied in pursuance of a request in which a trade description is used and the circumstances are such as to make it reasonable to infer that the goods are supplied as goods corresponding to that trade description, the person supplying the goods shall be deemed to have applied the trade description to the goods.

Misstatements other than false trade descriptions

12 False representations as to royal approval or award, etc.

(1) If any person in the course of any trade or business, gives, by whatever means, any false indication, direct or indirect, that any goods or services supplied by him or any methods adopted by him are or are of a kind supplied to or approved by Her Majesty or any member of the Royal Family, he shall, subject to the provisions of this Act be guilty of an offence.

(2) If any person, in the course of any trade or business, uses, without the authority of Her Majesty, any device or emblem signifying the Queen's Award to Industry or anything so nearly resembling such a device or emblem as to be likely to deceive, he shall, subject to the provisions of this Act, be guilty of an offence.

[(3) A person shall not be guilty of an offence under subsection (1) or (2) by reason of doing anything that is a commercial practice unless the commercial practice is unfair.

In this subsection 'commercial practice' and 'unfair' have the same meaning as in the Consumer Protection from Unfair Trading Regulations 2008.]

Prohibition of importation of certain goods

16 Prohibition of importation of goods bearing false indication of origin

Where a false trade description is applied to any goods outside the United Kingdom and the false indication, or one of the false indications, given, or likely to be taken as given, thereby is an indication of the place of manufacture, production, processing or reconditioning of the goods or any part thereof, the goods shall not be imported into the United Kingdom.

Provisions as to offences

18 Penalty for offences

A person guilty of an offence under this Act for which no other penalty is specified shall be liable—

(a) on summary conviction, to a fine not exceeding [the prescribed sum]; and

(b) on conviction on indictment, to a fine or imprisonment for a term not exceeding two years or both.

19 Time limit for prosecutions

(1) No prosecution for an offence under this Act shall be commenced after the expiration of three years from the commission of the offence or one year from its discovery by the prosecutor, whichever is the earlier.

(2) Not withstanding anything in [section 127(1) of the Magistrates' Courts Act 1980], a magistrates' court may try an information for an offence under this Act if the information was laid at any time within twelve months from the commission of the offence.

(3) Notwithstanding anything in section 23 of the Summary jurisdiction (Scotland) Act 1954 (limitation of time for proceedings in statutory offences) summary proceedings in Scotland for an offence under this section may be commenced at any time within twelve months from the time when the offence was committed, and subsection (2) of the said section 23 shall apply for the purposes of this subsection as it applies for the purposes of that section.

(4) Subsections (2) and (3) of this section do not apply where—

(a) the offence was committed by the making of an oral statement; or [...]

20   Offences by corporations

(1) Where an offence under this Act which has been committed by a body corporate is proved to have been committed with the consent and connivance of, or to be attributable to any neglect on the part of, any director, manager, secretary or other similar officer of the body corporate, or any person who was purporting to act in any such capacity, he as well as the body corporate shall be liable to be proceeded against and punished accordingly.

(2) In this section 'director', in relation to any body corporate established by or under any enactment for the purpose of carrying on under national ownership any industry or part of an industry or undertaking, being a body corporate whose affairs are managed by the members thereof, means a member of that body corporate.

21   Accessories to offences committed abroad

(3) Any person who, in the United Kingdom, assists in or induces the commission outside the United Kingdom of an act which if committed in the United Kingdom, would be an offence under section 12 of this Act shall be guilty of an offence.

23   Offences due to fault of other person

Where the commission by any person of an offence under this Act is due to the act or default of some other person that other person shall be guilty of the offence, and a person may be charged with and convicted of the offence by virtue of this section whether or not proceedings are taken against the first-mentioned person.

Defences

24   Defence of mistake, accident, etc.

(1) In any proceedings for an offence under this Act it shall, subject to subsection (2) of this section, be a defence for the person charged to prove—

(a) that the commission of the offence was due to a mistake or to reliance on information supplied to him or to the act or default of another person, an accident or some other cause beyond his control; and

(b) that he took all reasonable precautions and exercised all due diligence to avoid the commission of such an offence by himself or any person under his control.

(2) If in any case the defence provided by the last foregoing subsection involves the allegation that the commission of the offence was due to the act or default of another person or to reliance on information supplied by another person, the person charged shall not, without leave of the court, be entitled to rely on that defence unless, within a period ending seven clear days before the hearing, he has served on the prosecutor a notice in writing giving such information identifying or assisting in the identification of that other person as was then in his possession.

25   Innocent publication of advertisement

In proceedings for an offence under this Act committed by the publication of an advertisement it shall be a defence for the person charged to prove that he is a person whose business it is to publish or arrange for the publication of advertisements and that he received the advertisement for publication in the ordinary course of business and did not know and had no reason to suspect that its publication would amount to an offence under this Act.

Enforcement

26   Enforcing authorities

(1) It shall be the duty of every local weights and measures authority [as defined in section 69(3) of the Weights and Measures Act 1985] to enforce within their area the provisions of this Act and of any order made under this Act [...]

(2) Every local weights and measures authority shall, whenever the Board of Trade so direct, make to the Board a report on the exercise of their functions under this Act in such form and containing such particulars as the Board may direct.

(5) Nothing in this section shall be taken as authorising a local weights and measures authority in Scotland to institute proceedings for an offence.

27   Power to make test purchases

A local weights and measures authority shall have power to make, or to authorise any of their officers to make on their behalf, such purchases of goods, and to authorise any of their officers to secure the provision of such services, accommodation or facilities, as may appear expedient for the purpose of determining whether or not the provisions of this Act and any order made thereunder are being complied with.

28   Power to enter premises and inspect and seize goods and documents

(1) A duly authorised officer of a local weights and measures authority or of a Government department may, at all reasonable hours and on production, if required, of his credentials, exercise the following powers, that is to say,—

    (a) he may, for the purpose of ascertaining whether any offence under this Act has been committed, inspect any goods and enter any premises other than premises used only as a dwelling;

    (b) if he has reasonable cause to suspect that an offence under this Act has been committed, he may, for the purpose of ascertaining whether it has been committed, require any person carrying on a trade or business or employed in connection with a trade or business to produce any books or documents relating to the trade or business and may take copies of, or of any entry in, any such book or document;

    (c) if he has reasonable cause to believe that an offence under this Act has been committed, he may seize and detain any goods for the purpose of ascertaining, by testing or otherwise, whether the offence has been committed;

    (d) he may seize and detain any goods or documents which he has reason to believe may be required as evidence in proceedings for an offence under this Act;

    (e) he may, for the purpose of exercising his powers under this subsection to seize goods, but only if and to the extent that it is reasonably necessary in order to secure that the provisions of this Act and of any order made thereunder are duly observed, require any person having authority to do so to break open any container or open any vending machine and, if that person does not comply with the requirement, he may do so himself.

(2) An officer seizing any goods or documents in the exercise of his powers under this section shall inform the person from whom they are seized and, in the case of goods seized from a vending machine, the person whose name and address are stated on the machine as being the proprietor's or, if no name and address are so stated, the occupier of the premises on which the machine stands or to which it is affixed.

(3) If a justice of the peace, on sworn information in writing—

    (a) is satisfied that there is reasonable ground to believe either—

        (i) that any goods, books or documents which a duly authorised officer has power under this section to inspect are on any premises and that their inspection is likely to disclose evidence of the commission of an offence under this Act; or

        (ii) that any offence under this Act has been, is being or is about to be committed on any premises; and

    (b) is also satisfied either—

        (i) that admission to the premises has been or is likely to be refused and that notice of intention to apply for a warrant under this subsection has been given to the occupier; or

        (ii) that an application for admission, or the giving of such a notice would defeat the object of the entry or that the premises are unoccupied or that the occupier is temporarily absent and it might defeat the object of the entry to await his return, the justice may by warrant under his hand, which shall continue in force for a period of one month, authorise an officer of a local weights and measures authority or of a Government department to enter the premises, if need be by force.

In the application of this subsection to Scotland, 'justice of the peace' shall be construed as including a sheriff and a magistrate.

(4) An officer entering any premises by virtue of this section may take with him such other persons and such equipment as may appear to him necessary; and on leaving any premises which he has entered by virtue of a warrant under the preceding subsection he shall, if the premises are unoccupied or the occupier is temporarily absent, leave them as effectively secured against trespassers as he found them.

(6) If any person who is not a duly authorised officer of a local weights and measures authority or of a Government department purports to act as such under this section he shall be guilty of an offence.

(7) Nothing in this section shall be taken to compel the production by a solicitor of a document containing a privileged communication made by or to him in that capacity or to authorise the taking of possession of any such document which is in his possession.

29 Obstruction of authorised officers

(1) Any person who—

    (a) wilfully obstructs an officer of a local weights and measures authority or of a Government department acting in pursuance of this Act; or

    (b) wilfully fails to comply with any requirement properly made to him by such an officer under section 28 of this Act; or

    (c) without reasonable cause fails to give such an officer so acting any other assistance or information which he may reasonably require of him for the purpose of the performance of his functions under this Act,

shall be guilty of an offence and liable, on summary conviction to a fine not exceeding [level 3 on the standard scale].

(2) If any person in giving any such information as is mentioned in the preceding subsection, makes any statement which he knows to be false, he shall be guilty of an offence.

(3) Nothing in this section shall be construed as requiring a person to answer any question or give any information if to do so might incriminate him.

30 Notice of test and intended prosecution

(1) Where any goods seized or purchased by an officer in pursuance of this Act are submitted to a test, then—

    (a) if the goods were seized the officer shall inform the person mentioned in section 28(2) of this Act of the result of the test;

    (b) if the goods were purchased and the test leads to the institution of proceedings for an offence under this Act, the officer shall inform the person from whom the goods were purchased, or, in the case of goods sold through a vending machine, the person mentioned in section 28(2) of this Act, of the result of the test; and shall, where as a result of the test proceedings for an offence under this Act are instituted against any person, allow him to have the goods tested on his behalf if it is reasonably practicable to do so.

31 Evidence by certificate

(1) The Board of Trade may by regulations provide that certificates issued by such persons as may be specified by the regulations in relation to such matters as may be so specified shall, subject to the provisions of this section be received in evidence of those matters in any proceedings under this Act.

(2) Such a certificate shall not be received in evidence—

    (a) unless the party against whom it is to be given in evidence has been served with a copy thereof not less than seven days before the hearing; or

    (b) if that party has, not less than three days before the hearing, served on the other party a notice requiring the attendance of the person issuing the certificate.

(3) In any proceedings under this Act in Scotland, a certificate received in evidence by virtue of this section or, where the attendance of a person issuing a certificate is required under subsection

(2)(b) of this section, the evidence of that person, shall be sufficient evidence of the matters stated in the certificate.

(4) For the purposes of this section any document purporting to be such a certificate as is mentioned in this section shall be deemed to be such a certificate unless the contrary is shown.

(5) Regulations under this section shall be made by statutory instrument which shall be subject to annulment in pursuance of a resolution of either House of Parliament.

Miscellaneous and supplemental

33   Compensation for loss, etc. of goods seized under s. 28

(1) Where, in the exercise of his powers under section 28 of this Act, an officer of a local weights and measures authority or of a Government department seizes and detains any goods and their owner suffers loss by reason thereof or by reason that the goods, during the detention, are lost or damaged or deteriorate, then, unless the owner is convicted of an offence under this Act committed in relation to the goods, the authority or department shall be liable to compensate him for the loss so suffered.

(2) Any disputed question as to the right to or the amount of any compensation payable under this section shall be determined by arbitration and, in Scotland, by a single arbiter appointed, failing agreement between the parties, by the sheriff.

34   Trade marks containing trade descriptions

The fact that a trade description is a trade mark, or part of a trade mark, [. . .] does not prevent it from being a false trade description when applied to any goods, except where the following conditions are satisfied, that is to say—

   (a) that it could have been lawfully applied to the goods if this Act had not been passed; and
   (b) that on the day this Act is passed the trade mark either is registered under the Trade Marks Act 1938 or is in use to indicate a connection in the course of trade between such goods and the proprietor of the trade mark; and
   (c) that the trade mark as applied is used to indicate such a connection between the goods and the proprietor of the trade mark or [, in the case of a registered trade mark, a person licensed to use it]; and
   (d) that the person who is the proprietor of the trade mark is the same person as, or a successor in title of, the proprietor on the day this Act is passed.

35   Saving for civil rights

A contract for the supply of any goods shall not be void or unenforceable by reason only of a contravention of any provision of this Act.

36   Country of origin

(1) For the purposes of this Act goods shall be deemed to have been manufactured or produced in the country in which they last underwent a treatment or process resulting in a substantial change.

(2) The Board of Trade may by order specify—

   (a) in relation to any description of goods, what treatment or process is to be regarded for the purposes of this section as resulting or not resulting in a substantial change;
   (b) in relation to any description of goods different parts of which were manufactured or produced in different countries, or of goods assembled in a country different from that in which their parts were manufactured or produced, in which of those countries the goods are to be regarded for the purposes of this Act as having been manufactured or produced.

38   Orders

(1) Any power to make an order under the preceding provisions of this Act shall be exercisable by statutory instrument, which shall be subject to annulment in pursuance of a resolution of either House of Parliament, and includes power to vary or revoke such an order by a subsequent order.

(2) Any order under the preceding provisions of this Act which relates to [. . .] fertilisers or any goods used as pesticides or for similar purposes shall be made by the Board of Trade acting jointly with the following Ministers, that is to say, if the order extends to England and Wales, the Minister

of Agriculture, Fisheries and Food, and if it extends to Scotland or Northern Ireland, the Secretary of State concerned.

(3) The following provisions shall apply to the making of an order under [section 36 of this Act], except in the case mentioned in section 10(2) thereof, that is to say—

(a) before making the order the Board of Trade shall consult with such organisations as appear to them to be representative of interests substantially affected by it and shall publish, in such manner as the Board think appropriate, notice of their intention to make the order and of the place where copies of the proposed order may be obtained; and

(b) the order shall not be made until the expiration of a period of twenty-eight days from the publication of the notice and may then be made with such modifications (if any) as the Board of Trade think appropriate having regard to any representations received by them.

39   Interpretation

(1) The following provisions shall have effect in addition to sections [2 to 4] of this Act, for the interpretation in this Act of expressions used therein, that is to say,—

'advertisement' includes a catalogue, a circular and a price list;

'goods' includes ships and aircraft, things attached to land and growing crops;

'premises' includes any place and any stall, vehicle, ship or aircraft; and

'ship' includes any boat and any other description of vessel used in navigation.

Carriage of Goods by Sea Act 1971

(1971, c. 19)

1   Application of Hague Rules as amended

(1) In this Act, 'the Rules' means the International Convention for the unification of certain rules of law relating to bills of lading signed at Brussels on 25th August 1924, as amended by the Protocol signed at Brussels on 23rd February 1968 [and by the protocol signed at Brussels on 21 December 1979].

(2) The provisions of the Rules, as set out in the Schedule to this Act, shall have the force of law.

(3) Without prejudice to subsection (2) above, the said provisions shall have effect (and have the force of law) in relation to and in connection with the carriage of goods by sea in ships where the port of shipment is a port in the United Kingdom, whether or not the carriage is between ports in two different States within the meaning of Article X of the Rules.

(4) Subject to subsection (6) below, nothing in this section shall be taken as applying anything in the Rules to any contract for the carriage of goods by sea, unless the contract expressly or by implication provides for the issue of a bill of lading or any similar document of title.

(5) [...]

(6) Without prejudice to Article X (c) of the Rules, the Rules shall have the force of law in relation to—

(a) any bill of lading if the contract contained in or evidenced by it expressly provides that the Rules shall govern the contract, and

(b) any receipt which is a non-negotiable document marked as such if the contract contained in or evidenced by it is a contract for the carriage of goods by sea which expressly provides that the Rules are to govern the contract as if the receipt were a bill of lading, but subject, where paragraph (b) applies, to any necessary modifications and in particular with the omission in Article III of the Rules of the second sentence of paragraph 4 and of paragraph 7.

(7) If and so far as the contract contained in or evidenced by a bill of lading or receipt within paragraph (a) or (b) of subsection (6) above applies to deck cargo or live animals, the Rules as given the force of law by that subsection shall have effect as if Article I(c) did not exclude deck cargo and live animals.

In this subsection 'deck cargo' means cargo which by the contract of carriage is stated as being carried on deck and is so carried.

[1A Conversion of special drawing rights into sterling

(1) For the purposes of Article IV of the Rules the value on a particular day of one special drawing right shall be treated as equal to such a sum in sterling as the International Monetary Fund have fixed as being the equivalent of one special drawing right—

    (a) for that day; or

    (b) if no sum has been so fixed for that day, for the last day before that day for which a sum has been so fixed.

(2) A certificate given by or on behalf of the Treasury stating—

    (a) that a particular sum in sterling has been fixed as aforesaid for a particular day; or

    (b) that no sum has been so fixed for a particular day and that a particular sum in sterling has been so fixed for a day which is the last day for which a sum has been so fixed before the particular day,

shall be conclusive evidence of those matters for the purposes of subsection (1) above; and a document purporting to be such a certificate shall in any proceedings be received in evidence and, unless the contrary is proved, be deemed to be such a certificate.

(3) The Treasury may charge a reasonable fee for any certificate given in pursuance of subsection (2) above, and any fee received by the Treasury by virtue of this subsection shall be paid into the Consolidated Fund.]

2 Contracting States, etc.

(1) If Her Majesty by Order in Council certifies to the following effect, that is to say, that for the purposes of the Rules—

    (a) a State specified in the Order is a contracting State, or is a contracting State in respect of any place or territory so specified; or

    (b) any place or territory specified in the Order forms part of a State so specified (whether a contracting State or not),

the Order shall, except so far as it has been superseded by a subsequent Order, be conclusive evidence of the matters so certified.

(2) An Order in Council under this section may be varied or revoked by a subsequent Order in Council.

3 Absolute warranty of seaworthiness not to be implied in contracts to which Rules apply

There shall not be implied in any contract for the carriage of goods by sea to which the Rules apply by virtue of this Act any absolute undertaking by the carrier of the goods to provide a seaworthy ship.

4 Application of Act to British possessions, etc.

(1) Her Majesty may by Order in Council direct that this Act shall extend, subject to such exceptions, adaptations and modifications as may be specified in the Order, to all or any of the following territories, that is—

    (a) any colony (not being a colony for whose external relations a country other than the United Kingdom is responsible),

    (b) any country outside Her Majesty's dominions in which Her Majesty has jurisdiction in right of Her Majesty's Government of the United Kingdom.

(2) An Order in Council under this section may contain such transitional and other consequential and incidental provisions as appear to Her Majesty to be expedient, including provisions amending or repealing any legislation about the carriage of goods by sea forming part of the law of any of the territories mentioned in paragraphs (a) and (b) above.

(3) An Order in Council under this section may be varied or revoked by a subsequent Order in Council.

5 Extension of application of Rules to carriage from ports in British possessions, etc.

(1) Her Majesty may by Order in Council provide that section 1(3) of this Act shall have effect as if the reference therein to the United Kingdom included a reference to all or any of the following territories, that is—

(a) the Isle of Man;

(b) any of the Channel Islands specified in the Order;

(c) any colony specified in the Order (not being a colony for whose external relations a country other than the United Kingdom is responsible);

[. . .]

(e) any country specified in the Order, being a country outside Her Majesty's dominions in which Her Majesty has jurisdiction in right of Her Majesty's Government of the United Kingdom.

(2) An Order in Council under this section may be varied or revoked by a subsequent Order in Council.

6 Supplemental

(1) This Act may be cited as the Carriage of Goods by Sea Act 1971.

(2) It is hereby declared that this Act extends to Northern Ireland.

(3) The following enactments shall be repealed, that is—

(a) the Carriage of Goods by Sea Act 1924,

(b) section 12(4)(a) of the Nuclear Installations Act 1965, and without prejudice to section [17(2)(a) of the Interpretation Act 1978], the reference to the said Act of 1924 in section 1(1)(i)(ii) of the Hovercraft Act 1968 shall include a reference to this Act.

[(4) It is hereby declared that for the purposes of Article VIII of the Rules [section 186 of the Merchant Shipping Act 1985 (which] entirely exempts shipowners and others in certain circumstances from liability for loss of, or damage to, goods) is a provision relating to limitation of liability.]

(5) This Act shall come into force on such day as Her Majesty may by Order in Council appoint, and, for the purposes of the transition from the law in force immediately before the day appointed under this subsection to the provisions of this Act, the Order appointing the day may provide that those provisions shall have effect subject to such transitional provisions as may be contained in the Order.

SCHEDULE

THE HAGUE RULES AS AMENDED BY THE BRUSSELS PROTOCOL 1968

Article I

In these Rules the following words are employed, with the meanings set out below:—

(a) 'Carrier' includes the owner or the charterer who enters into a contract of carriage with a shipper.

(b) 'Contract of carriage' applies only to contracts of carriage covered by a bill of lading or any similar document of title, in so far as such document relates to the carriage of goods by sea, including any bill of lading or any similar document as aforesaid issued under or pursuant to a charter party from the moment at which such bill of lading or similar document of title regulates the relations between a carrier and a holder of the same.

(c) 'Goods' includes goods, wares, merchandise, and articles of every kind whatsoever except live animals and cargo which by the contract of carriage is stated as being carried on deck and is so carried.

(d) 'Ship' means any vessel used for the carriage of goods by sea.

(e) 'Carriage of goods' covers the period from the time when the goods are loaded on to the time they are discharged from the ship.

Article II

Subject to the provisions of Article VI, under every contract of carriage of goods by sea the carrier, in relation to the loading, handling, stowage, carriage, custody, care and discharge of such goods, shall be subject to the responsibilities and liabilities, and entitled to the rights and immunities hereinafter set forth.

Article III

(1) The carrier shall be bound before and at the beginning of the voyage to exercise due diligence to—

    (a) Make the ship seaworthy.

    (b) Properly man, equip and supply the ship.

    (c) Make the holds, refrigerating and cool chambers, and all other parts of the ship in which goods are carried, fit and safe for their reception, carriage and preservation.

(2) Subject to the provisions of Article IV, the carrier shall properly and carefully load, handle, stow, carry, keep, care for, and discharge the goods carried.

(3) After receiving the goods into his charge the carrier or the master or agent of the carrier shall, on demand of the shipper, issue to the shipper a bill of lading showing among other things—

    (a) The leading marks necessary for identification of the goods as the same are furnished in writing by the shipper before the loading of such goods starts, provided such marks are stamped or otherwise shown clearly upon the goods if uncovered, or on the cases or coverings in which such goods are contained, in such a manner as should ordinarily remain legible until the end of the voyage.

    (b) Either the number of packages or pieces, or the quantity, or weight as the case may be, as furnished in writing by the shipper.

    (c) The apparent order and condition of the goods. Provided that no carrier, master or agent of the carrier shall be bound to state or show in the bill of lading any marks, number, quantity, or weight which he has reasonable ground for suspecting not accurately to represent the goods actually received, or which he has had no reasonable means of checking.

(4) Such a bill of lading shall be prima facie evidence of the receipt by the carrier of the goods as therein described in accordance with paragraph 3(a), (b) and (c). However, proof to the contrary shall not be admissible when the bill of lading has been transferred to a third party acting in good faith.

(5) The shipper shall be deemed to have guaranteed to the carrier the accuracy at the time of shipment of the marks, number, quantity and weight, as furnished by him, and the shipper shall indemnify the carrier against all loss, damages and expenses arising or resulting from inaccuracies in such particulars. The right of the carrier to such indemnity shall in no way limit his responsibility and liability under the contract of carriage to any person other than the shipper.

(6) Unless notice of loss or damage and the general nature of such loss or damage be given in writing to the carrier or his agent at the port of discharge before or at the time of the removal of the goods into the custody of the person entitled to delivery thereof under the contract of carriage, or, if the loss or damage be not apparent, within three days, such removal shall be prima facie evidence of the delivery by the carrier of the goods as described in the bill of lading.

The notice in writing need not be given if the state of the goods has, at the time of their receipt, been the subject of joint survey or inspection.

Subject to paragraph 6*bis* the carrier and the ship shall in any event be discharged from all liability whatsoever in respect of the goods, unless suit is brought within one year of their delivery or of the date when they should have been delivered. This period may, however, be extended if the parties so agree after the cause of action has arisen.

In the case of any actual or apprehended loss or damage the carrier and the receiver shall give all reasonable facilities to each other for inspecting and tallying the goods.

(6*bis*) An action for indemnity against a third person may be brought even after the expiration of the year provided for in the preceding paragraph if brought within the time allowed by the law of the

Court seized of the case. However, the time allowed shall be not less than three months, commencing from the day when the person bringing such action for indemnity has settled the claim or has been served with process in the action against himself.

(7) After the goods are loaded the bill of lading to be issued by the carrier, master, or agent of the carrier, to the shipper shall, if the shipper so demands, be a 'shipped' bill of lading, provided that if the shipper shall have previously taken up any document of title to such goods, he shall surrender the same as against the issue of the 'shipped' bill of lading, but at the option of the carrier such document of title may be noted at the port of shipment by the carrier, master, or agent with the name or names of the ship or ships upon which the goods have been shipped and the date or dates of shipment, and when so noted if it shows the particulars mentioned in paragraph 3 of Article III, shall for the purpose of this article be deemed to constitute a 'shipped' bill of lading.

(8) Any clause, covenant, or agreement in a contract of carriage relieving the carrier or the ship from liability for loss or damage to, or in connection with, goods arising from negligence, fault, or failure in the duties and obligations provided in this article or lessening such liability otherwise than as provided in these Rules, shall be null and void and of no effect. A benefit of insurance in favour of the carrier or similar clause shall be deemed to be a clause relieving the carrier from liability.

Article IV

(1) Neither the carrier nor the ship shall be liable for loss or damage arising or resulting from unseaworthiness unless caused by want of due diligence on the part of the carrier to make the ship seaworthy, and to secure that the ship is properly manned, equipped and supplied, and to make the holds, refrigerating and cool chambers and all other parts of the ship in which goods are carried fit and safe for their reception, carriage and preservation in accordance with the provisions of paragraph 1 of Article III. Whenever loss or damage has resulted from unseaworthiness the burden of proving the exercise of due diligence shall be on the carrier or other person claiming exemption under this article.

(2) Neither the carrier nor the ship shall be responsible for loss or damage arising or resulting from—

    (a) Act, neglect, or default of the master, mariner, pilot, or the servants of the carrier in the navigation or in the management of the ship.

    (b) Fire, unless caused by the actual fault or privity of the carrier.

    (c) Perils, dangers and accidents of the sea or other navigable waters.

    (d) Act of God.

    (e) Act of war.

    (f) Act of public enemies.

    (g) Arrest or restraint of princes, rulers or people, or seizure under legal process.

    (h) Quarantine restrictions.

    (i) Act or omission of the shipper or owner of the goods, his agent or representative.

    (j) Strikes or lockouts or stoppage or restraint of labour from whatever cause, whether partial or general.

    (k) Riots and civil commotions.

    (l) Saving or attempting to save life or property at sea.

    (m) Wastage in bulk or weight or any other loss or damage arising from inherent defect, quality or vice of the goods.

    (n) Insufficiency of packing.

    (o) Insufficiency or inadequacy of marks.

    (p) Latent defects not discoverable by due diligence.

    (q) Any other cause arising without the actual fault or privity of the carrier, or without the fault or neglect of the agents or servants of the carrier, but the burden of proof shall be on the person claiming the benefit of this exception to show that neither the actual fault or privity of the carrier nor the fault or neglect of the agents or servants of the carrier contributed to the loss or damage.

(3) The shipper shall not be responsible for the loss or damage sustained by the carrier or the ship arising or resulting from any cause without the act, fault or neglect of the shipper, his agents or his servants.

(4) Any deviation in saving or attempting to save life or property at sea or any reasonable deviation shall not be deemed to be an infringement or breach of these Rules or of the contract of carriage, and the carrier shall not be liable for any loss or damage resulting therefrom.

(5) (a) Unless the nature and value of such goods have been declared by the shipper before shipment and inserted in the bill of lading, neither the carrier nor the ship shall in any event be or become liable for any loss or damage to or in connection with the goods in an amount exceeding [666.67 units of account] per package or unit or [2 units of account per kilogramme] of gross weight of the goods lost or damaged, whichever is the higher.

(b) The total amount recoverable shall be calculated by reference to the value of such goods at the place and time at which the goods are discharged from the ship in accordance with the contract or should have been so discharged.

The value of the goods shall be fixed according to the commodity exchange price, or, if there be no such price, according to the current market price, or, if there be no commodity exchange price or current market price, by reference to the normal value of goods of the same kind and quality.

(c) Where a container, pallet or similar article of transport is used to consolidate goods, the number of packages or units enumerated in the bill of lading as packed in such article of transport shall be deemed the number of packages or units for the purpose of this paragraph as far as these packages or units are concerned. Except as aforesaid such article of transport shall be considered the package or unit.

[(d) The unit of account mentioned in this Article is the special drawing right as defined by the International Monetary Fund. The amounts mentioned in sub-paragraph (a) of this paragraph shall be converted into national currency on the basis of the value of that currency on a date to be determined by the law of the court seised of the case.]

(e) Neither the carrier nor the ship shall be entitled to the benefit of the limitation of liability provided for in this paragraph if it is proved that the damage resulted from an act or omission of the carrier done with intent to cause damage, or recklessly and with knowledge that damage would probably result.

(f) The declaration mentioned in sub-paragraph (a) of this paragraph, if embodied in the bill of lading, shall be prima facie evidence, but shall not be binding or conclusive on the carrier.

(g) By agreement between the carrier, master or agent of the carrier and the shipper other maximum amounts than those mentioned in sub-paragraph (a) of this paragraph may be fixed, provided that no maximum amount so fixed shall be less than the appropriate maximum mentioned in that sub-paragraph.

(h) Neither the carrier nor the ship shall be responsible in any event for loss or damage to, or in connection with, goods if the nature or value thereof has been knowingly mis-stated by the shipper in the bill of lading.

(6) Goods of an inflammable, explosive or dangerous nature to the shipment whereof the carrier, master or agent of the carrier has not consented with knowledge of their nature and character, may at any time before discharge be landed at any place, or destroyed or rendered innocuous by the carrier without compensation and the shipper of such goods shall be liable for all damages and expenses directly or indirectly arising out of or resulting from such shipment. If any such goods shipped with such knowledge and consent shall become a danger to the ship or cargo, they may in like manner be landed at any place, or destroyed or rendered innocuous by the carrier without liability on the part of the carrier except to general average, if any.

Article IV bis

(1) The defences and limits of liability provided for in these Rules shall apply in any action against the carrier in respect of loss or damage to goods covered by a contract of carriage whether the action be founded in contract or in tort.

(2) If such an action is brought against a servant or agent of the carrier (such servant or agent not being an independent contractor), such servant or agent shall be entitled to avail himself of the defences and limits of liability which the carrier is entitled to invoke under these Rules.

(3) The aggregate of the amounts recoverable from the carrier, and such servants and agents, shall in no case exceed the limit provided for in these Rules.

(4) Nevertheless, a servant or agent of the carrier shall not be entitled to avail himself of the provisions of this article, if it is proved that the damage resulted from an act or omission of the servant or agent done with intent to cause damage or recklessly and with knowledge that damage would probably result.

Article V

A carrier shall be at liberty to surrender in whole or in part all or any of his rights and immunities or to increase any of his responsibilities and obligations under these Rules, provided such surrender or increase shall be embodied in the bill of lading issued to the shipper. The provisions of the Rules shall not be applicable to charter parties, but if bills of lading are issued in the case of a ship under a charter party they shall comply with the terms of these Rules. Nothing in these Rules shall be held to prevent the insertion in a bill of lading of any lawful provisions regarding general average.

Article VI

Notwithstanding the provisions of the preceding articles, a carrier, master or agent of the carrier and a shipper shall in regard to any particular goods be at liberty to enter into any agreement in any terms as to the responsibility and liability of the carrier for such goods, and as to the rights and immunities of the carrier in respect of such goods, or his obligation as to seaworthiness, so far as this stipulation is not contrary to public policy, or the care or diligence of his servants or agents in regard to the loading, handling, stowage, carriage, custody, care and discharge of the goods carried by sea, provided that in this case no bill of lading has been or shall be issued and that the terms agreed shall be embodied in a receipt which shall be a non-negotiable document and shall be marked as such.

Any agreement so entered into shall have full legal effect.

Provided that this article shall not apply to ordinary commercial shipment made in the ordinary course of trade, but only to other shipments where the character or condition of the property to be carried or the circumstances, terms and conditions under which the carriage is to be performed are such as reasonably to justify a special agreement.

Article VII

Nothing herein contained shall prevent a carrier or a shipper from entering into any agreement, stipulation, condition, reservation or exemption as to the responsibility and liability of the carrier or the ship for the loss or damage to, or in connection with, the custody and care and handling of goods prior to the loading on, and subsequent to the discharge from, the ship on which the goods are carried by sea.

Article VIII

The provisions of these Rules shall not affect the rights and obligations of the carrier under any statute for the time being in force relating to the limitation of the liability of owners of sea-going vessels.

Article IX

These rules shall not affect the provisions of any international Convention or national law governing liability for nuclear damage.

Article X

The provisions of these Rules shall apply to every bill of lading relating to the carriage of goods between ports in two different States if:

(a) the bill of lading is issued in a contracting State, or

(b) the carriage is from a port in a contracting State, or

(c) the contract contained in or evidenced by the bill of lading provides that these Rules or legislation of any State giving effect to them are to govern the contract, whatever may be the nationality of the ship, the carrier, the shipper, the consignee, or any other interested person.

[*The last two paragraphs of this article are not reproduced. They require contracting States to apply the
Rules to bills of lading mentioned in the article and authorise them to apply the Rules to other bills of lading.*]

[*Articles 11 to 16 of the international Convention for the unification of certain rules of law relating to
bills of lading signed at Brussels on August 25 1974 are not reproduced. They deal with the coming into
force of the Convention, procedure for ratification, accession and denunciation and the right to call for a
fresh conference to consider amendments to the Rules contained in the Convention.*]

Unsolicited Goods and Services Act 1971

(1971, c. 30)

2   Demands and threats regarding payment

(1) A person who, not having reasonable cause to believe there is a right to payment, in the
course of any trade or business makes a demand for payment, or asserts a present or prospective right
to payment, for what he knows are unsolicited goods sent (after the commencement of this Act) to
another person with a view to his acquiring them [for the purposes of his trade or business], shall be
guilty of an offence and on summary conviction shall be liable to a fine not exceeding [level 4 on the
standard scale].

(2) A person who, not having reasonable cause to believe there is a right to payment in the course
of any trade or business and with a view to obtaining any payment for what he knows are unsolicited
goods sent as aforesaid—

(a) threatens to bring any legal proceedings; or

(b) places or causes to be placed the name of any person on a list of defaulters or debtors or
threatens to do so; or

(c) invokes or causes to be invoked any other collection procedure or threatens to do so,

shall be guilty of an offence and shall be liable on summary conviction to a fine not exceeding [level 5
on the standard scale].

3   Directory entries

[(1) A person ('the purchaser') shall not be liable to make any payment, and shall be entitled to
recover any payment made by him, by way of charge for including or arranging for the inclusion in a
directory of an entry relating to that person or his trade or business, unless—

(a) there has been signed by the purchaser or on his behalf an order complying with this
section,

(b) there has been signed by the purchaser or on his behalf a note complying with this section
of his agreement to the charge and before the note was signed, a copy of it was supplied,
for retention by him, to him or a person acting on his behalf, or

(c) there has been transmitted by the purchaser or a person acting on his behalf an electronic
communication which includes a statement that the purchaser agrees to the charge and
the relevant condition is satisfied in relation to that communication, or

(d) the charge arises under a contract in relation to which the conditions in section 3B(1)
(renewed and extended contracts) are met.]

(2) A person shall be guilty of an offence punishable on summary conviction with a fine not
exceeding £400 if, in a case where a payment in respect of a charge would [...] be recoverable from
him in accordance with the terms of subsection (1) above, he demands payment, or asserts a present
or prospective right to payment, of the charge or any part of it, without knowing or having reasonable
cause to believe [that—

(a) the entry to which the charge relates was ordered in accordance with this section,

(b) a proper note of the agreement has been duly signed, or

(c) the requirements set out in subsection (1)(c) or (d) above have been met.]

(3) For the purposes of [this section—

(a) an order for an entry in a directory must be made by means of an order form or other stationery belonging to the purchaser, which may be sent electronically but which must bear his name and address (or one or more of his addresses); and

(b) the note of a person's agreement to a charge must—

(i) specify the particulars set out in Part 1 of the Schedule to the Regulatory Reform (Unsolicited Goods and Services Act 1971) (Directory Entries and Demands for Payment) Order 2005, and

(ii) give reasonable particulars of the entry in respect of which the charge would be payable.]

[(3A) In relation to an electronic communication which includes a statement that the purchaser agrees to a charge for including or arranging the inclusion in a directory of any entry, the relevant condition is that—

(a) before the electronic communication was transmitted the information referred to in subsection (3B) below was communicated to the purchaser, and

(b) the electronic communication can readily be produced and retained in a visible and legible form.

(3B) that information is—

(a) the following particulars—

(i) the amount of the charge;

(ii) the name of the directory or proposed directory;

(iii) the name of the person producing the directory;

(iv) the geographic address at which that person is established;

(v) if the directory is or is to be available in printed form, the proposed date of publication of the directory or of the issue in which the entry is to be included;

(vi) if the directory or the issue in which the entry is to be included is to be put on sale, the price at which it is to be offered for sale and the minimum number of copies which are to be available for sale;

(vii) if the directory or the issue in which the entry is to be included is to be distributed free of charge (whether or not it is also to be put on sale), the minimum number of copies which are to be so distributed;

(viii) if the directory is or is to be available in a form other than in printed form, adequate details of how it may be accessed; and

(b) reasonable particulars of the entry in respect of which the charge would be payable.

(3C) In this section 'electronic communication' has the same meaning as in the Electronic Communications Act 2000.]

[3B   Renewed and extended contracts

(1) The conditions referred to in section 3(1)(d) above are met in relation to a contract ('the new contract') if—

(a) a person ('the purchaser') has entered into an earlier contract ('the earlier contract') for including or arranging for the inclusion in a particular issue or version of a directory ('the earlier directory') of an entry ('the earlier entry') relating to him or his trade or business;

(b) the purchaser was liable to make a payment by way of a charge arising under the earlier contract for including or arranging for the inclusion of the earlier entry in the earlier directory;

(c) the new contract is a contract for including or arranging for the inclusion in a later issue or version of a directory ('the later directory') of an entry ('the later entry') relating to the purchaser or his trade or business;

    (d) the form, content and distribution of the later directory is materially the same as the form, content and distribution of the earlier directory;

    (e) the form and content of the later entry is materially the same as the form and content of the earlier entry;

    (f) if the later directory is published other than in electronic form—

        (i) the earlier directory was the last, or the last but one, issue or version of the directory to be published before the later directory, and

        (ii) the date of publication of the later directory is not more than 13 months after the date of publication of the earlier directory;

    (g) if the later directory is published in electronic form, the first date on which the new contract requires the later entry to be published is not more than the relevant period after the last date on which the earlier contract required the earlier entry to be published;

    (h) if it was a term of the earlier contract that the purchaser renew or extend the contract—

        (i) before the start of the new contract the relevant publisher has given notice in writing to the purchaser containing the information set out in Part 3 of the Schedule to the Regulatory Reform (Unsolicited Goods and Services Act 1971) (Directory Entries and Demands for Payment) Order 2005; and

        (ii) the purchaser has not written to the relevant publisher withdrawing his agreement to the renewal or extension of the earlier contract within the period of 21 days starting when he receives the notice referred to in sub-paragraph (i); and

    (i) if the parties to the earlier contract and the new contract are different—

        (i) the parties to both contracts have entered into a novation agreement in respect of the earlier contract; or

        (ii) the relevant publisher has given the purchaser the information set out in Part 4 of the Schedule to the Regulatory Reform (Unsolicited Goods and Services Act 1971) (Directory Entries and Demands for Payment) Order 2005.

(2) For the purposes of subsection (1)(d) and (e), the form, content or distribution of the later directory, or the form or content of the later entry, shall be taken to be materially the same as that of the earlier directory or the earlier entry (as the case may be), if a reasonable person in the position of the purchaser would—

    (a) view the two as being materially the same; or

    (b) view that of the later directory or the later entry as being an improvement on that of the earlier directory or the earlier entry.

(3) For the purposes of subsection (1)(g) 'the relevant period' means the period of 13 months or (if shorter) the period of time between the first and last dates on which the earlier contract required the earlier entry to be published.

(4) For the purposes of subsection (1)(h) and (i) 'the relevant publisher' is the person with whom the purchaser has entered into the new contract.

(5) The information referred to in subsection (1)(i)(ii) must be given to the purchaser prior to the conclusion of the new contract.]

4 Unsolicited publications

(1) A person shall be guilty of an offence if he sends or causes to be sent to another person any book, magazine or leaflet (or advertising material for any such publication which he knows or ought reasonably to know is unsolicited and which describes or illustrates human sexual techniques.

(2) A person found guilty of an offence under this section shall be liable on summary conviction to a fine not exceeding [level 5 on the standard scale] for a first offence and to a fine not exceeding [level 5 on the standard scale] for any subsequent offence.

(3) A prosecution for an offence under this section shall not in England and Wales be instituted except by, or with the consent of, the Director of Public Prosecutions.

5 Offences by corporations

(1) Where an offence under this Act which has been committed by a body corporate is proved to have been committed with the consent or connivance of, or to be attributable to any neglect on the

part of, any director, manager, secretary, or other similar officer of the body corporate, or of any person who was purporting to act in any such capacity, he as well as the body corporate shall be guilty of that offence and shall be liable to be proceeded against and punished accordingly.

(2) Where the affairs of a body corporate are managed by its members, this section shall apply in relation to the acts or defaults of a member in connection with his functions of management as if he were a director of the body corporate.

6 Interpretation

(1) In this Act, unless the context or subject matter otherwise requires,—

'acquire' includes hire;

'send' includes deliver, and 'sender' shall be construed accordingly;

'unsolicited' means, in relation to goods sent to any person, that they are sent without any prior request made by him or on his behalf.

[(2) For the purposes of the Act, any invoice or similar document stating the amount of any payment shall be regarded as asserting a right to the payment unless it complies with the conditions set out in Part 2 of the Schedule to the Regulatory Reform (Unsolicited Goods and Services Act 1971) (Directory Entries and Demands for Payment) Order 2005.]

[(3) Nothing in sections 3 or 3B shall affect the rights of any consumer under the Consumer Protection (Distance Selling) Regulations 2000.]

Supply of Goods (Implied Terms) Act 1973

(1973, c. 13)

8 Implied terms as title

[(1) In every hire-purchase agreement, other than one to which subsection (2) below applies, there is—

(a) an implied term on the part of the creditor that he will have a right to sell the goods at the time when the property is to pass; and

(b) an implied term that—

(i) the goods are free, and will remain free until the time when the property is to pass, from any charge or encumbrance not disclosed or known to the person to whom the goods are bailed or (in Scotland) hired before the agreement is made, and

(ii) that person will enjoy quiet possession of the goods except so far as it may be disturbed by any person entitled to the benefit of any charge or encumbrance so disclosed or known.

(2) In a hire-purchase agreement, in the case of which there appears from the agreement or is to be inferred from the circumstances of the agreement an intention that the creditor should transfer only such title as he or a third person may have, there is—

(a) an implied term that all charges or encumbrances known to the creditor and not known to the person to whom the goods are bailed or hired have been disclosed to that person before the agreement is made; and

(b) an implied term that neither—

(i) the creditor; nor

(ii) in a case where the parties to the agreement intend that any title which may be transferred shall be only such title as a third person may have, that person; nor

(iii) anyone claiming through or under the creditor or that third person not otherwise than under a charge or encumbrance disclosed or known to the person to whom the goods are bailed or hired, before the agreement is made; will disturb the quiet possession of the person to whom the goods are bailed or hired.

(3) As regards England and Wales and Northern Ireland, the term implied by subsection (1)(a) above is a condition and the terms implied by subsections (1)(b), (2)(a) and (2)(b) above are warranties.]

9   Bailing or hiring by description

[(1) Where under a hire-purchase agreement goods are bailed or (in Scotland) hired by description, there is an implied term that the goods will correspond with the description, and if under the agreement the goods are bailed or hired by reference to a sample as well as a description, it is not sufficient that the bulk of the goods corresponds with the sample if the goods do not also correspond with the description.

(1A) As regards England and Wales and Northern Ireland, the term implied by subsection (1) above is a condition.

(2) Goods shall not be prevented from being bailed or hired by description by reason only that, being exposed for sale, bailment or hire, they are selected by the person to whom they are bailed or hired.]

10   Implied undertakings as to quality or fitness

[(1) Except as provided by this section and section 11 below and subject to the provisions of any other enactment, including any enactment of the Parliament of Northern Ireland or the Northern Ireland Assembly, there is no implied term as to the quality or fitness for any particular purpose of goods bailed or (in Scotland) hired under a hire-purchase agreement.

(2) Where the creditor bails or hires goods under a hire purchase agreement in the course of a business, there is an implied term that the goods supplied under the agreement are of satisfactory quality.

(2A) For the purposes of this Act, goods are of satisfactory quality if they meet the standard that a reasonable person would regard as satisfactory, taking account of any description of the goods, the price (if relevant) and all the other relevant circumstances.

(2B) For the purposes of this Act, the quality of goods includes their state and condition and the following (among others) are in appropriate cases aspects of the quality of goods—

  (a) fitness for all the purposes for which goods of the kind in question are commonly supplied,
  (b) appearance and finish.
  (c) freedom from minor defects,
  (d) safety, and
  (e) durability.

(2C) The term implied by subsection (2) above does not extend to any matter making the quality of goods unsatisfactory—

  (a) which is specifically drawn to the attention of the person to whom the goods are bailed or hired before the agreement is made,
  (b) where that person examines the goods before the agreement is made, which that examination ought to reveal, or
  (c) where the goods are bailed or hired by reference to a sample, which would have been apparent on a reasonable examination of the sample.

[(2D) If the person to whom the goods are bailed or hired deals as consumer or, in Scotland, if the goods are hired to a person under a consumer contract, the relevant circumstances mentioned in subsection (2A) above include any public statements on the specific characteristics of the goods made about them by the creditor, the producer or his representative, particularly in advertising or on labelling.

(2E) A public statement is not by virtue of subsection (2D) above a relevant circumstance for the purposes of subsection (2A) above in the case of a contract of hire-purchase, if the creditor shows that—

  (a) at the time the contract was made, he was not, and could not reasonably have been, aware of the statement,
  (b) before the contract was made, the statement had been withdrawn in public or, to the extent that it contained anything which was incorrect or misleading, it had been corrected in public, or
  (c) the decision to acquire the goods could not have been influenced by the statement.

(2F) Subsections (2D) and (2E) above do not prevent any public statement from being a relevant circumstance for the purposes of subsection (2A) above (whether or not the person to whom the goods are bailed or hired deals as consumer or, in Scotland, whether or not the goods are hired to a person under a consumer contract) if the statement would have been such a circumstance apart from those subsections.]

(3) Where the creditor bails or hires goods under a hire-purchase agreement in the course of a business and the person to whom the goods are bailed or hired, expressly or by implication, makes known—

(a) to the creditor in the course of negotiations conducted by the creditor in relation to the making of the hire-purchase agreement, or

(b) to a credit-broker in the course of negotiations conducted by that broker in relation to goods sold by him to the creditor before forming the subject matter of the hire-purchase agreement,

any particular purpose for which the goods are being bailed or hired, there is an implied term that the goods supplied under the agreement are reasonably fit for that purpose, whether or not that is a purpose for which such goods are commonly supplied, except where the circumstances show that the person to whom the goods are bailed or hired does not rely, or that it is unreasonable for him to rely, on the skill or judgment of the creditor or credit-broker.

(4) An implied term as to quality or fitness for a particular purpose may be annexed to a hire-purchase agreement by usage.

(5) The preceding provisions of this section apply to a hire-purchase agreement made by a person who in the course of a business is acting as agent for the creditor as they apply to an agreement made by the creditor in the course of a business, except where the creditor is not bailing or hiring in the course of a business and either the person to whom the goods are bailed or hired knows that fact or reasonable steps are taken to bring it to the notice of that person before the agreement is made.

(6) In subsection (3) above and this subsection—

(a) 'credit-broker' means a person acting in the course of a business of credit brokerage;

(b) 'credit brokerage' means the effecting of introductions of individuals desiring to obtain credit—

(i)   to persons carrying on any business so far as it relates to the provision of credit, or

(ii)   to other persons engaged in credit brokerage.

(7) As regards England and Wales and Northern Ireland, the terms implied by subsections (2) and (3) above are conditions.]

11 Samples

[(1) Where under a hire-purchase agreement goods are bailed or (in Scotland) hired by reference to a sample, there is an implied term—

(a) that the bulk will correspond with the sample in quality; and

(b) that the person to whom the goods are bailed or hired will have a reasonable opportunity of comparing the bulk with the sample; and

(c) that the goods will be free from any defect, making their quality unsatisfactory, which would not be apparent on reasonable examination of the sample.

(2) As regards England and Wales and Northern Ireland, the term implied by subsection (1) above is a condition.]

[11A Modification of remedies for breach of statutory condition in non-consumer cases

(1) Where in the case of a hire purchase agreement—

(a) the person to whom goods are bailed would, apart from this subsection, have the right to reject them by reason of a breach on the part of the creditor of a term implied by section 9, 10 or 11(1)(a) or (c) above, but

(b) the breach is so slight that it would be unreasonable for him to reject them, then, if the person to whom the goods are bailed does not deal as consumer, the breach is not to be treated as a breach of condition but may be treated as a breach of warranty.

(2) This section applies unless a contrary intention appears in, or is to be implied from, the agreement.

(3) It is for the creditor to show—

(a) that a breach fell within subsection (1)(b) above, and

(b) that the person to whom the goods were bailed did not deal as consumer.

(4) The references in this section to dealing as consumer are to be construed in accordance with Part I of the Unfair Contract Terms Act 1977.]

[12   Exclusion of implied terms

An express term does not negative a term implied by this Act unless inconsistent with it.]

14   Special provisions as to conditional sale agreements

[(1) Section 11(4) of the Sale of Goods Act 1979 (whereby in certain circumstances a breach of a condition in a contract of sale is treated only as a breach of warranty) shall not apply to a conditional sale agreement where the buyer deals as consumer within Part I of the Unfair Contract Terms Act 1977...

(2) In England and Wales and Northern Ireland a breach of a condition (whether express or implied) to be fulfilled by the seller under any such agreement shall be treated as a breach of warranty, and not as grounds for rejecting the goods and treating the agreement as repudiated, if (but only if) it would have fallen to be so treated had the condition been contained or implied in a corresponding hire-purchase agreement as a condition to be fulfilled by the creditor.]

15   Supplementary

[(1) In sections 8 to 14 above and this section—

'business' includes a profession and the activities of any government department (including a Northern Ireland department), [or local or public authority];

'buyer' and 'seller' includes a person to whom rights and duties under a conditional sale agreement have passed by assignment or operation of law;

'conditional sale agreement' means an agreement for the sale of goods under which the purchase price or part of it is payable by instalments, and the property in the goods is to remain in the seller (notwithstanding that the buyer is to be in possession of the goods) until such conditions as to the payment of instalments or otherwise as may be specified in the agreement are fulfilled;

['consumer sale' has the same meaning as in section 55 of the Sale of Goods Act 1979 (as set out in paragraph 11 of Schedule 1 to that Act)];

'creditor' means the person by whom the goods are bailed or (in Scotland) hired under a hire-purchase agreement or the person to whom his rights and duties under the agreement have passed by assignment or operation of law; and

'hire-purchase agreement' means an agreement, other than conditional sale agreement, under which—

(a) goods are bailed or (in Scotland) hired in return for periodical payments by the person to whom they are bailed or hired, and

(b) the property in the goods will pass to that person if the terms of the agreement are complied with and one or more of the following occurs—

(i)   the exercise of an option to purchase by that person,

(ii) the doing of any other specified act by any party to the agreement,

(iii) the happening of any other specified event.

['producer' means the manufacturer of goods, the importer of goods into the European Economic Area or any person purporting to be a producer by placing his name, trade mark or other distinctive sign on the goods;]

(3) In section 14(2) above 'corresponding hire-purchase agreement' means, in relation to a conditional sale agreement, a hire-purchase agreement relating to the same goods as the conditional sale

agreement and made between the same parties and at the same time and in the same circumstances and, as nearly as may be, in the same terms as the conditional sale agreement.

(4) Nothing in sections 8 to 13 above shall prejudice the operation of any other enactment including any enactment of the Parliament of Northern Ireland or the Northern Ireland Assembly or any rule of law whereby any term, other than one relating to quality or fitness, is to be implied in any hire-purchase agreement.]

Consumer Credit Act 1974

(1974, c. 39)

PART I [OFFICE OF FAIR TRADING]

1 General functions of [OFT]

(1) It is the duty of [the Office of Fair Trading ('the OFT'])—

  (a) to administer the licensing system set up by this Act,

  (b) to exercise the adjudicating functions conferred on [it] by this Act in relation to the issue, renewal, variation, suspension and revocation of licences, and other matters,

  [(ba) to monitor, as it sees fit, businesses being carried on under licences;]

  (c) generally to superintend the working and enforcement of this Act, and regulations made under it, and

  (d) where necessary or expedient, [itself] to take steps to enforce this Act, and regulations so made.

(2) It is the duty of the [OFT], so far as appears to [it] to be practicable and having regard both to the national interest and the interests of persons carrying on businesses to which this Act applies and their customers, to keep under review and from time to time advise the Secretary of State about—

  (a) social and commercial developments in the United Kingdom and elsewhere relating to the provision of credit or bailment or (in Scotland) hiring of goods to individuals, and related activities; and

  (b) the working and enforcement of this Act and orders and regulations made under it.

2 Powers of Secretary of State

(1) The Secretary of State may by order—

  (a) confer on the [OFT] additional functions concerning the provision of credit or bailment or (in Scotland) hiring of goods to individuals, and related activities, and

  (b) regulate the carrying out by the [OFT] of [its] functions under this Act.

(2) The Secretary of State may give general directions indicating considerations to which the [OFT] should have particular regard in carrying out [its] functions under this Act, and may give specific directions on any matter connected with the carrying out by the [OFT] of those functions.

(3) The Secretary of State, on giving any directions under subsection (2), shall arrange for them to be published in such manner as he thinks most suitable for drawing them to the attention of interested persons.

(4) With the approval of the Secretary of State and the Treasury, the [OFT] may charge, for any service or facility provided by [it] under this Act, a fee of an amount specified by general notice (the 'specified fee').

(5) Provision may be made under subsection (4) for reduced fees, or no fees at all, to be paid for certain services or facilities by persons of a specified description, and references in this Act to the specified fee shall, in such cases, be construed accordingly.

(6) An order under subsection (1)(a) shall be made by statutory instrument and shall be of no effect unless a draft of the order has been laid before and approved by each House of Parliament.

(7) References in subsection (2) to the functions of the [OFT] under this Act do not include the making of a determination to which section 41 [...] (appeals from [OFT] to [the First-tier Tribunal]) applies.

4   Dissemination of information and advice

The [OFT] shall arrange for the dissemination, in such form and manner as [it] considers appropriate, of such information and advice as it may appear to [it] expedient to give to the public in the United Kingdom about the operation of this Act, [the consumer credit juridiction under Part 16 of the Financial Services and Markets Act 2000,] the credit facilities available to them, and other matters within the scope of [its] functions under this Act.

6   Form etc. of applications

(1) An application to the [OFT] under this Act is of no effect unless the requirements of this section are satisfied.

(2) The application must be in writing, and in such form, and accompanied by such [information and documents], as the [OFT] may specify [or describe in a] general notice, [...].

[(2A) The application must also be accompanied—

  (a) in the case of an application for a licence or for the renewal of a licence, by the charge payable by virtue of section 6A;

  (b) in any other case, by the specified fee.]

[(3) Where the OFT receives an application, it may by notice to the applicant at any time before the determination of the application require him to provide such information or documents relevant to the application as may be specified or described in the notice.]

(4) The [OFT] may by notice require the applicant to publish details of his applicant at a time or times and in a manner specified in the notice

[(5) Subsection (6) applies where a general notice under subsection (2) comes into effect—

  (a) after an application has been made; but

  (b) before its determination.

(6) The applicant shall, within such period as may be specified in the general notice, provide the OFT with any information or document—

  (a) which he has not previously provided in relation to the application by virtue of this section;

  (b) which he would have been required to provide with his application had it been made after the general notice came into effect; and

  (c) which the general notice requires to be provided for the purposes of this subsection.

(7) An applicant shall notify the OFT, giving details, if before his application is determined—

  (a) any information or document provided by him in relation to the application by virtue of this section is, to any extent, superseded or otherwise affected by a change in circumstances; or

  (b) he becomes aware of an error in or omission from any such information or document.

(8) A notification for the purposes of subsection (7) shall be given within the period of 28 days beginning with the day on which (as the case may be)—

  (a) the information or document is superseded;

  (b) the change in circumstances occurs; or

  (c) the applicant becomes aware of the error or omission.

(9) Subsection (7) does not require an applicant to notify the OFT about—

  (a) anything of which he is required to notify it under section 36; or

  (b) an error in or omission from any information or document which is a clerical error or omission not affecting the substance of the information or document.]

[6A   Charge on applicants for licences etc.

(1) An applicant for a licence, or for the renewal of a licence, shall pay the OFT a charge towards the costs of carrying out its functions under this Act.

(2) The amount of the charge payable by an applicant shall be determined in accordance with provision made by the OFT by general notice.

(3) The provision that may be made by the OFT under subsection (2) includes—

  (a) different provision in relation to persons of different descriptions;

  (b) provision for no charge at all to be payable by persons of specified descriptions.

(4) The approval of the Secretary of State and the Treasury is required for a general notice under subsection (2).]

[7   Penalty for false information

A person commits an offence if, for the purposes of, or in connection with, any requirement imposed or other provision made by or under this Act, he knowingly or recklessly gives information to the OFT, or to an officer of the OFT, which, in a material particular, is false or misleading.]

PART II   CREDIT AGREEMENTS, HIRE AGREEMENTS AND LINKED TRANSACTIONS

8   Consumer credit agreements

(1) A [consumer] credit agreement is an agreement between an individual ('the debtor') and any other person ('the creditor') by which the creditor provides the debtor with credit of any amount.

[...]

(3) A consumer credit agreement is a regulated agreement within the meaning of this Act if it is not an agreement (an 'exempt agreement') specified in or under section 16 [, 16A , 16B or 16C].

9   Meaning of credit

(1) In this Act 'credit' includes a cash loan, and any other form of financial accommodation.

(2) Where credit is provided otherwise than in sterling it shall be treated for the purposes of this Act as provided in sterling of an equivalent amount.

(3) Without prejudice to the generality of subsection (1), the person by whom goods are bailed or (in Scotland) hired to an individual under a hire-purchase agreement shall be taken to provide him with fixed-sum credit to finance the transaction of an amount equal to the total price of the goods less the aggregate of the deposit (if any) and the total charge for credit.

(4) For the purposes of this Act, an item entering into the total charge for credit shall not be treated as credit even though time is allowed for its payment.

10   Running-account credit and fixed-sum credit

(1) For the purposes of this Act—

(a) running-account credit is a facility under a [consumer] credit agreement whereby the debtor is enabled to receive from time to time (whether in his own person, or by another person) from the creditor or a third party cash, goods and services (or any of them) to an amount or value such that, taking into account payments made by or to the credit of the debtor, the credit limit (if any) is not at any time exceeded; and

(b) fixed-sum credit is any other facility under a [consumer] credit agreement whereby the debtor is enabled to receive credit (whether in one amount or by instalments).

(2) In relation to running-account credit, 'credit limit' means, as respects any period, the maximum debit balance which, under the credit agreement, is allowed to stand on the account during that period, disregarding any term of the agreement allowing that maximum to be exceeded merely temporarily.

(3) For the purposes of [any provision of this Act that specifies an amount of credit (except section 17(1)(a))], running-account credit shall be taken not to exceed the amount specified in [that provision] ('the specified amount') if—

(a) the credit limit does not exceed the specified amount; or

(b) whether or not there is a credit limit, and if there is, notwithstanding that it exceeds the specified amount,—

(i) the debtor is not enabled to draw at any one time an amount which, so far as (having regard to section 9(4)) it represents credit, exceeds the specified amount, or

(ii) the agreement provides that, if the debit balance rises above a given amount (not exceeding the specified amount), the rate of the total charge for credit increases or any other condition favouring the creditor or his associate comes into operation, or

(iii) at the time the agreement is made it is probable, having regard to the terms of the agreement and any other relevant considerations, that the debit balance will not at any time rise above the specified amount.

11   Restricted-use credit and unrestricted-use credit

(1) A restricted-use credit agreement is a regulated consumer credit agreement—

(a) to finance a transaction between the debtor and the creditor, whether forming part of that agreement or not, or

(b) to finance a transaction between the debtor and a person (the 'supplier') other than the creditor, or

(c) to refinance any existing indebtedness of the debtor's, whether to the creditor or another person, and 'restricted-use credit' shall be construed accordingly.

(2) An unrestricted-use credit agreement is a regulated consumer credit agreement not falling within subsection (1), and 'unrestricted-use credit' shall be construed accordingly.

(3) An agreement does not fall within subsection (1) if the credit is in fact provided in such a way as to leave the debtor free to use it as he chooses, even though certain uses would contravene that or any other agreement.

(4) An agreement may fall within subsection (1)(b) although the identity of the supplier is unknown at the time the agreement is made.

12   Debtor-creditor supplier agreements

A debtor-creditor-supplier agreement is a regulated consumer credit agreement being—

(a) a restricted-use credit agreement which falls within section 11(1)(a), or

(b) a restricted-use credit agreement which falls within section 11(1)(b) and is made by the creditor under pre-existing arrangements, or in contemplation of future arrangements, between himself and the supplier, or

(c) an unrestricted-use credit agreement which is made by the creditor under pre-existing arrangements between himself and a person (the 'supplier') other than the debtor in the knowledge that the credit is to be used to finance a transaction between the debtor and the supplier.

13   Debtor-creditor agreements

A debtor-creditor agreement is a regulated consumer credit agreement being—

(a) a restricted-use credit agreement which falls within section 11(1)(b) but is not made by the creditor under pre-existing arrangements, or in contemplation of future arrangements, between himself and the supplier, or

(b) a restricted-use credit agreement which falls within section 11(1)(c), or

(c) an unrestricted-use credit agreement which is not made by the creditor under pre-existing arrangements between himself and a person (the 'supplier') other than the debtor in the knowledge that the credit is to be used to finance a transaction between the debtor and the supplier.

14   Credit-token agreements

(1) A credit-token is a card, check, voucher, coupon, stamp, form, booklet or other document or thing given to an individual by a person carrying on a consumer credit business, who undertakes—

(a) that on the production of it (whether or not some other action is also required) he will supply cash, goods and services (or any of them) on credit, or

(b) that where, on the production of it to a third party (whether or not any other action is also required), the third party supplies cash, goods and services (or any of them), he will pay the third party for them (whether or not deducting any discount or commission), in return for payment to him by the individual.

(2) A credit-token agreement is a regulated agreement for the provision of credit in connection with the use of a credit-token.

(3) Without prejudice to the generality of section 9(1), the person who gives to an individual an undertaking falling within subsection (1)(b) shall be taken to provide him with credit drawn on whenever a third party supplies him with cash, goods or services.

(4) For the purposes of subsection (1), use of an object to operate a machine provided by the person giving the object or a third party shall be treated as the production of the object to him.

15   Consumer hire agreements

(1) A consumer hire agreement is an agreement made by a person with an individual (the 'hirer') for the bailment or (in Scotland) the hiring of goods to the hirer, being an agreement which—

    (a) is not a hire-purchase agreement, and

    (b) is capable of subsisting for more than three months, [...].

(2) A consumer hire agreement is a regulated agreement if it is not an exempt agreement.

16   Exempt agreements

(1) This Act does not regulate a consumer credit agreement where the creditor is a local authority [...], or a body specified, or of a description specified, in an order made by the Secretary of State, being—

    [(a) an insurer;]

    (b) a friendly society,

    (c) an organisation of employers or organisation of workers,

    (d) a charity,

    (e) a land improvement company, or

    (f) a body corporate named or specifically referred to in any public general Act.

    [(ff) a body corporate named or specifically referred to in an order made under—

        section 156(4) or 447(2)(a) of the Housing Act 1985,

        section 156(4) of that Act as it has effect by virtue of section 17 of the Housing Act 1996 (the right to acquire),

        section 223 or 229 of the Housing (Scotland) Act 1987, or

        Article 154(1)(a) or 156AA of the Housing (Northern Ireland) Order 1981 or Article 10(6A) of the Housing (Northern Ireland) Order 1983; or]

    (g) a building society, or

    [(h) a deposit taker.]

(2) Subsection (1ww) applies only where the agreement is—

    (a) a debtor-creditor-supplier agreement financing—

        (i)   the purchase of land, or

        (ii) the provision of dwellings on any land, and secured by a land mortgage on that land; or

    (b) a debtor-creditor agreement secured by any land mortgage; or

    (c) a debtor-creditor-supplier agreement financing a transaction which is a linked transaction in relation to—

        (i)   an agreement falling within paragraph (a), or

        (ii) an agreement failing within paragraph (b) financing—

            (aa) the purchase of any land, or

            (bb) the provision of dwellings on any land, and secured by a land mortgage on the land referred to in paragraph (a) or, as the case may be, the land referred to in sub-paragraph (ii).

[(3) Before he makes, varies or revokes an order under subsection (1), the Secretary of State must undertake the necessary consultation.

(3A) The necessary consultation means consultation with the bodies mentioned in the following table in relation to the provision under which the order is to be made, varied or revoked:

Table

Provision of subsection (1)	Consultee
Paragraph (a) or (b)	The Financial Services Authority
Paragraph (d)	The Charity Commissioners
Paragraph (e), (f) or (ff)	Any Minister of the Crown with responsibilities in relation to the body in question
Paragraph (g) or (h)	The Treasury and the Financial Services Authority

(4) An order under subsection (1) relating to a body may be limited so as to apply only to agreements by that body of a description specified in the order.

(5) The Secretary of State may by order provide that this Act shall not regulate other consumer credit agreements where—

    (a) the number of payments to be made by the debtor does not exceed the number specified for that purpose in the order, or

    (b) the rate of the total charge for credit does not exceed the rate so specified, or

    (c) an agreement has a connection with a country outside the United Kingdom.

(6) The Secretary of State may by order provide that this Act shall not regulate consumer hire agreements of a description specified in the order where—

    (a) the owner is a body corporate authorised by or under any enactment to supply electricity, gas or water, and

    (b) the subject of the agreement is a meter or metering equipment or where the owner is a provider of a public electronic communications service who is specified in the order].

[(6A) This Act does not regulate a consumer credit agreement where the creditor is a housing authority and the agreement is secured by a land mortgage of a dwelling.

(6B) In subsection (6A) 'housing authority' means—

    (a) as regards England and Wales, [the Homes and Communities Agency, the Welsh new towns residuary body,] the Housing Corporation, … and an authority or body within section 80(1) of the Housing Act 1985 (the landlord condition for secure tenancies), other than a housing association or a housing trust which is a charity;

    (b) as regards Scotland, a development corporation established under an order made, or having effect as if made under the New Towns (Scotland) Act 1968, the Scottish Special Housing Association or the Housing Corporation;

    (c) as regards Northern Ireland, the Northern Ireland Housing Executive.

(6BA) In subsection (6B)(a) "the Welsh new towns residuary body" means the Welsh Ministers so far as exercising functions in relation to anything transferred (or to be transferred) to them as mentioned in section 36(1)(a)(i) to (iii) of the New Towns Act 1981.

(6C) This Act does not regulate a consumer credit agreement if—

    (a) it is secured by a land mortgage and entering into that agreement as lender is a regulated activity for the purposes of the Financial Services and Markets Act 2000; or

    (b) it is or forms part of a regulated home purchase plan and entering into the agreement as home purchase provider is a regulated activity for the purposes of that Act.

(6D) But section 126, and any other provision so far as it relates to section 126, applies to an agreement which would (but for subsection (6C)(a)) be a regulated agreement.

(6E) Subsection (6C) must be read with—

    (a) section 22 of the Financial Services and Markets Act 2000 (regulated activities: power to specify classes of activity and categories of investment);

(b) any order for the time being in force under that section; and

(c) Schedule 2 to that Act.

(7A) Nothing in this section affects the application of sections 140A to 140C.

(8) In the application of this section to Scotland, subsection (3A) shall have effect as if the reference to the Charity Commissioners were a reference to the Lord Advocate.]

(9) In the application of this section to Northern Ireland [subsection (3A)] shall have effect as if any reference to a Minister of the Crown were a reference to a Northern Ireland department, [...] and any reference to the Charity Commissioners were a reference to the Department of Finance for Northern Ireland.

[(10) In this section—

(a) 'deposit-taker' means—

(i) a person who has permission under Part 4 of the Financial Services and Markets Act 2000 to accept deposits,

(ii) an EEA firm of the kind mentioned in paragraph 5(b) of Schedule 3 to that Act which has permission under paragraph 15 of that Schedule (as a result of qualifying for authorisation under paragraph 12 of that Schedule) to accept deposits,

(iii) any wholly owned subsidiary (within the meaning of [the Companies Acts (see section 1159 of the Companies Act 2006)]) of a person mentioned in sub-paragraph (i), or

(iv) any undertaking which, in relation to a person mentioned in sub-paragraph (ii), is a subsidiary undertaking within the meaning of any rule of law in force in the EEA State in question for purposes connected with the implementation of the European Council Seventh Company Law Directive of 13 June 1983 on consolidated accounts (No. 83/349/EEC), and which has no members other than that person;

(b) 'insurer' means—

(i) a person who has permission under Part 4 of the Financial Services and Markets Act 2000 to effect or carry out contracts of insurance, or

(ii) an EEA firm of the kind mentioned in paragraph 5(d) of Schedule 3 to that Act, which has permission under paragraph 15 of that Schedule (as a result of qualifying for authorisation under paragraph 12 of that Schedule) to effect or carry out contracts of insurance,

but does not include a friendly society or an organisation of workers or of employers.

(11) Subsection (10) must be read with—

(a) section 22 of the Financial Services and Markets Act 2000;

(b) any relevant order under that section; and

(c) Schedule 2 to that Act.]

[16A Exemption relating to high net worth debtors and hirers

(1) The Secretary of State may by order provide that this Act shall not regulate a consumer credit agreement or a consumer hire agreement where—

(a) the debtor or hirer is a natural person;

(b) the agreement includes a declaration made by him to the effect that he agrees to forgo the protection and remedies that would be available to him under this Act if the agreement were a regulated agreement;

(c) a statement of high net worth has been made in relation to him; and

(d) that statement is current in relation to the agreement and a copy of it was provided to the creditor or owner before the agreement was made.

(2) For the purposes of this section a statement of high net worth is a statement to the effect that, in the opinion of the person making it, the natural person in relation to whom it is made—

(a) received during the previous financial year income of a specified description totalling an amount of not less than the specified amount; or

(b) had throughout that year net assets of a specified description with a total value of not less than the specified value.

(3) Such a statement—
  (a) may not be made by the person in relation to whom it is made;
  (b) must be made by a person of a specified description; and
  (c) is current in relation to an agreement if it was made during the period of one year ending with the day on which the agreement is made.

(4) An order under this section may make provision about—
  (a) how amounts of income and values of net assets are to be determined for the purposes of subsection (2)(a) and (b);
  (b) the form, content and signing of—
    (i) statements of high net worth;
    (ii) declarations for the purposes of subsection (1)(b).

(5) Where an agreement has two or more debtors or hirers, for the purposes of paragraph (c) of subsection (1) a separate statement of high net worth must have been made in relation to each of them; and paragraph (d) of that subsection shall have effect accordingly.

(6) In this section—
  'previous financial year' means, in relation to a statement of high net worth, the financial year immediately preceding the financial year during which the statement is made;
  'specified' means specified in an order under this section.

(7) In subsection (6) 'financial year' means a period of one year ending with 31st March.

(8) Nothing in this section affects the application of sections 140A to 140C.]

[16B   Exemption relating to businesses

(1) This Act does not regulate—
  (a) a consumer credit agreement by which the creditor provides the debtor with credit exceeding £25,000, or
  (b) a consumer hire agreement that requires the hirer to make payments exceeding £25,000,
if the agreement is entered into by the debtor or hirer wholly or predominantly for the purposes of a business carried on, or intended to be carried on, by him.

[(1A) This Act does not regulate a consumer credit agreement if—
  (a) the credit provided by the creditor to the debtor by the agreement does not exceed £25,000,
  (b) the agreement is entered into by the debtor wholly for the purposes of a business carried on, or intended to be carried on, by the debtor, and
  (c) the agreement is a green deal plan (within the meaning of section 1 of the Energy Act 2011).]

(2) If an agreement [falling within subsection (1)] includes a declaration made by the debtor or hirer to the effect that the agreement is entered into by him wholly or predominantly for the purposes of a business carried on, or intended to be carried on, by him, the agreement shall be presumed to have been entered into by him wholly or predominantly for such purposes.

(3) But that presumption does not apply if, when the agreement is entered into—
  (a) the creditor or owner, or
  (b) any person who has acted on his behalf in connection with the entering into of the agreement,
knows, or has reasonable cause to suspect, that the agreement is not entered into by the debtor or hirer wholly or predominantly for the purposes of a business carried on, or intended to be carried on, by him.

[(3A) Subsections (2) and (3) also apply in relation to an agreement falling within subsection (1A) but with the omission of the words "or predominantly".]

(4) The Secretary of State may by order make provision about the form, content and signing of declarations for the purposes of subsection (2).

(5) Where an agreement has two or more creditors or owners, in subsection (3) references to the creditor or owner are references to any one or more of them.

(6) Nothing in this section affects the application of sections 140A to 140C.]

[16C Exemption relating to investment properties

(1) This Act does not regulate a consumer credit agreement if, at the time the agreement is entered into, any sums due under it are secured by a land mortgage on land where the condition in subsection (2) is satisfied.

(2) The condition is that less than 40% of the land is used, or is intended to be used, as or in connection with a dwelling—

(a) by the debtor or a person connected with the debtor, or

(b) in the case of credit provided to trustees, by an individual who is the beneficiary of the trust or a person connected with such an individual.

(3) For the purposes of subsection (2) the area of any land which comprises a building or other structure containing two or more storeys is to be taken to be the aggregate of the floor areas of each of those storeys.

(4) For the purposes of subsection (2) a person is "connected with" the debtor or an individual who is the beneficiary of a trust if he is—

(a) that person's spouse or civil partner;

(b) a person (whether or not of the opposite sex) whose relationship with that person has the characteristics of the relationship between husband and wife; or

(c) that person's parent, brother, sister, child, grandparent or grandchild.

(5) Section 126 (enforcement of land mortgages) applies to an agreement which would but for this section be a regulated agreement.

(6) Nothing in this section affects the application of sections 140A to 140C.]

17 Small agreements

(1) A small agreement is—

(a) a regulated consumer credit agreement for credit not exceeding [£50], other than a hire-purchase or conditional sale agreement; or

(b) a regulated consumer hire agreement which does not require the hirer to make payments exceeding [£50],

being an agreement which is either unsecured or secured by a guarantee or indemnity only (whether or not the guarantee or indemnity is itself secured).

[(2) For the purposes of paragraph (a) of subsection (1), running-account credit shall be taken not to exceed the amount specified in that paragraph if the credit limit does not exceed that amount.]

(3) Where—

(a) two or more small agreements are made at or about the same time between the same parties, and

(b) it appears probable that they would instead have been made as a single agreement but for the desire to avoid the operation of provisions of this Act which would have applied to that single agreement but, apart from this subsection, are not applicable to the small agreements,

this Act applies to the small agreements as if they were regulated agreements other than small agreements.

(4) If, apart from this subsection, subsection (3) does not apply to any agreements but would apply if, for any party or parties to any of the agreements, there were substituted an associate of that party, or associates of each of those parties, as the case may be, then subsection (3) shall apply to the agreements.

18 Multiple agreements

(1) This section applies to an agreement (a 'multiple agreement') if its terms are such as—

(a) to place a part of it within one category of agreement mentioned in this Act, and another part of it within a different category of agreement so mentioned, or within a category of agreement not so mentioned, or

(b) to place it, or a part of it, within two or more categories of agreement so mentioned.

(2) Where a part of an agreement falls within subsection (1), that part shall be treated for the purposes of this Act as a separate agreement.

(3) Where an agreement falls within subsection (1)(b), it shall be treated as an agreement in each of the categories in question, and this Act shall apply to it accordingly.

(4) Where under subsection (2) a part of a multiple agreement is to be treated as a separate agreement, the multiple agreement shall (with any necessary modifications) be construed accordingly; and any sum payable under the multiple agreement, if not apportioned by the parties, shall for the purposes of proceedings in any court relating to the multiple agreement be apportioned by the court as may be requisite.

(5) In the case of an agreement for running-account credit, a term of the agreement allowing the credit limit to be exceeded merely temporarily shall not be treated as a separate agreement or as providing fixed-sum credit in respect of the excess.

(6) This Act does not apply to a multiple agreement so far as the agreement relates to goods if under the agreement payments are to be made in respect of the goods in the form of rent (other than a rentcharge) issuing out of land.

19   Linked transactions

(1) A transaction entered into by the debtor or hirer, or a relative of his, with any other person ('the other party'), except one for the provision of security, is a linked transaction in relation to an actual or prospective regulated agreement (the 'principal agreement') of which it does not form part if—

  (a) the transaction is entered into in compliance with a term of the principal agreement; or
  (b) the principal agreement is a debtor-creditor-supplier agreement and the transaction is financed, or to be financed, by the principal agreement; or
  (c) the other party is a person mentioned in subsection (2), and a person so mentioned initiated the transaction by suggesting it to the debtor or hirer, or his relative, who enters into it—
    (i)   to induce the creditor or owner to enter into the principal agreement, or
    (ii) for another purpose related to the principal agreement, or
    (iii) where the principal agreement is a restricted-use credit agreement, for a purpose related to a transaction financed, or to be financed, by the principal agreement.

(2) The persons referred to in subsection (1)(c) are—

  (a) the creditor or owner, or his associate;
  (b) a person who, in the negotiation of the transaction, is represented by a credit-broker who is also a negotiator in antecedent negotiations for the principal agreement;
  (c) a person who, at the time the transaction is initiated, knows that the principal agreement has been made or contemplates that it might be made.

(3) A linked transaction entered into before the making of the principal agreement has no effect until such time (if any) as that agreement is made.

(4) Regulations may exclude linked transactions of the prescribed description from the operation of subsection (3).

20   Total charge for credit

(1) The Secretary of State shall make regulations containing such provisions as appear to him appropriate for determining the true cost to the debtor of the credit provided or to be provided under an actual or prospective consumer credit agreement (the 'total charge for credit'), and regulations so made shall prescribe—

  (a) what items are to be treated as entering into the total charge for credit, and how their amount is to be ascertained;
  (b) the method of calculating the rate of the total charge for credit.

(2) Regulations under subsection (1) may provide for the whole or part of the amount payable by the debtor or his relative under any linked transaction to be included in the total charge for credit, whether or not the creditor is a party to the transaction or derives benefit from it.

PART III   LICENSING OF CREDIT AND HIRE BUSINESSES

Licensing principles

21   Businesses needing a licence

(1) Subject to this section, a licence is required to carry on a consumer credit business or [a consumer hire business or an ancillary credit business].

(2) A local authority does not need a licence to carry on a business.

(3) A body corporate empowered by a public general Act naming it to carry on a business does not need a licence to do so.

[(4) A relevant energy supplier acting in that capacity does not need a licence to carry on an ancillary credit business so far as it comprises or relates to debt-adjusting, debt-counselling, debt-collecting or debt administration in relation to debts due under a green deal plan associated with the supplier.

(5) A green deal plan is associated with a relevant energy supplier if the payments under the plan are to be made to the supplier.

(6) In this section—
   (a) "green deal plan" has the meaning given by section 1 of the Energy Act 2011; and
   (b) "relevant energy supplier" has the meaning given in regulations made for the purposes of section 2(9) of that Act.]

22   Standard and group licences

(1) A licence may be—
   (a) a standard licence, that is a licence, issued by the [OFT] to a person named in the licence on an application made by him, which, [whilst the licence is in effect], covers such activities as are described in the licence, or
   (b) a group licence, that is a licence, issued by the [OFT] (whether on the application of any person or of [its] own motion), which, [whilst the licence is in effect], covers such persons and activities as are described in the licence.

[(1A) The terms of a licence shall specify—
   (a) whether it has effect indefinitely or only for a limited period; and
   (b) if it has effect for a limited period, that period.

(1B) For the purposes of subsection (1A)(b) the period specified shall be such period not exceeding the prescribed period as the OFT thinks fit (subject to subsection (1E)).

(1C) A standard licence shall have effect indefinitely unless—
   (a) the application for its issue requests that it have effect for a limited period only; or
   (b) the OFT otherwise thinks there is good reason why it should have effect for such a period only.

(1D) A group licence shall have effect for a limited period only unless the OFT thinks there is good reason why it should have effect indefinitely.

(1E) Where a licence which has effect indefinitely is to be varied under section 30 or 31 for the purpose of limiting the licence's duration, the variation shall provide for the licence to expire—
   (a) in the case of a variation under section 30, at the end of such period from the time of the variation as is set out in the application for the variation; or
   (b) in the case of a variation under section 31, at the end of such period from the time of the variation as the OFT thinks fit;
but a period mentioned in paragraph (a) or (b) shall not exceed the prescribed period.]

(2) A licence is not assignable or, subject to section 37, transmissible on death or in any other way.

(3) Except in the case of a partnership or an unincorporated body of persons, a standard licence shall not be issued to more than one person.

(4) A standard licence issued to a partnership or an unincorporated body of persons shall be issued in the name of the partnership or body.

(5) The [OFT] may issue a group licence only if it appears to [it] that the public interest is better served by doing so than by obliging the persons concerned to apply separately for standard licences.

[(5A) A group licence to carry on a business may limit the activities it covers in any way the OFT thinks fit.]

(6) The persons covered by a group licence may be described by general words, whether or not coupled with the exclusion of named persons, or in any other way the [OFT] thinks fit.

(7) The fact that a person is covered by a group licence in respect of certain activities does not prevent a standard licence being issued to him in respect of those activities or any of them.

(8) A group licence issued on the application of any person shall be issued to that person, and general notice shall be given of the issue of any group licence (whether on application or not).

23   Authorisation of specific activities

(1) Subject to [the terms of the licence], a licence to carry on a business covers all lawful activities done in the course of that business, whether by the licensee or other persons on his behalf.

(3) A licence covers the canvassing off trade premises of debtor-creditor-supplier agreements or regulated consumer hire agreements only if, and to the extent that, the licence specifically so provides; and such provision shall not be included in a group licence.

(4) [The OFT may by general notice specify] other activities which, if engaged in by or on behalf of the person carrying on a business, require to be covered by an express term in his licence.

24   Control of name of business

A standard licence authorises the licensee to carry on a business under the name or names specified in the licence, but not under any other name.

[24A   Applications for standard licences

(1) An application for a standard licence shall, in relation to each type of business which is covered by the application, state whether the applicant is applying—

  (a) for the licence to cover the carrying on of that type of business with no limitation; or
  (b) for the licence to cover the carrying on of that type of business only so far as it falls within one or more descriptions of business.

(2) An application within subsection (1)(b) in relation to a type of business shall set out the description or descriptions of business in question.

(3) References in this Part to a type of business are references to a type of business within subsection (4).

(4) The types of business within this subsection are—

  (a) a consumer credit business;
  (b) a consumer hire business;
  (c) a business so far as it comprises or relates to credit brokerage;
  (d) a business so far as it comprises or relates to debt-adjusting;
  (e) a business so far as it comprises or relates to debt-counselling;
  (f) a business so far as it comprises or relates to debt-collecting;
  (g) a business so far as it comprises or relates to debt administration;
  (h) a business so far as it comprises or relates to the provision of credit information services;
  (i) a business so far as it comprises or relates to the operation of a credit reference agency.

(5) The OFT—

  (a) shall by general notice specify the descriptions of business which can be set out in an application for the purposes of subsection (2) in relation to a type of business;
  (b) may by general notice provide that applications within subsection (1)(b) cannot be made in relation to one or more of the types of business within subsection (4)(c) to (i).

(6) The power of the OFT under subsection (5) includes power to make different provision for different cases or classes of case.]

25   Licensee to be a fit person

[(1) If an applicant for a standard licence—

(a) makes an application within section 24A(1)(a) in relation to a type of business, and

(b) satisfies the OFT that he is a fit person to carry on that type of business with no limitation,

he shall be entitled to be issued with a standard licence covering the carrying on of that type of business with no limitation.

(1AA) If such an applicant—

(a) makes an application within subsection (1)(b) of section 24A in relation to a type of business, and

(b) satisfies the OFT that he is a fit person to carry on that type of business so far as it falls within the description or descriptions of business set out in his application in accordance with subsection (2) of that section,

he shall be entitled to be issued with a standard licence covering the carrying on of that type of business so far as it falls within the description or descriptions in question.

(1AB) If such an applicant makes an application within section 24A(1)(a) or (b) in relation to a type of business but fails to satisfy the OFT as mentioned in subsection (1) or (1AA) (as the case may be), he shall nevertheless be entitled to be issued with a standard licence covering the carrying on of that type of business so far as it falls within one or more descriptions of business if—

(a) he satisfies the OFT that he is a fit person to carry on that type of business so far as it falls within the description or descriptions in question;

(b) he could have applied for the licence to be limited in that way; and

(c) the licence would not cover any activity which was not covered by his application.

(1AC) In this section 'description of business' means, in relation to a type of business, a description of business specified in a general notice under section 24A(5)(a).

(1AD) An applicant shall not, by virtue of this section, be issued with a licence unless he satisfies the OFT that the name or names under which he would be licensed is or are not misleading or otherwise undesirable.]

(1B) If an application for the grant of a standard licence—

(a) is made by a person with permission under Part 4 of the Financial Services and Markets Act 2000 to accept deposits, and

(b) relates to a listed activity,

the Financial Services Authority may, if it considers that the [OFT] ought to refuse the application, notify him of that fact.

(1C) In subsection (1B) 'listed activity' means an activity listed in Annex 1 to Directive 2006/48/EC of the European Parliament and of the Council of 14 June 2006 relating to the taking up and pursuit of the business of credit institutions (as that Annex was last amended by Directive 2009/111/EC) or in Annex I to the markets in financial instruments directive (2004/39/EEC) and references to deposits and to their acceptance must be read with—

(a) section 22 of the Financial Services and Markets Act 2000;

(b) any relevant order under that section; and

(c) Schedule 2 to that Act.]

[(2) In determining whether an applicant for a licence is a fit person for the purposes of this section the OFT shall have regard to any matters appearing to it to be relevant including (amongst other things)—

(a) the applicant's skills, knowledge and experience in relation to consumer credit businesses, consumer hire businesses or ancillary credit businesses;

(b) such skills, knowledge and experience of other persons who the applicant proposes will participate in any business that would be carried on by him under the licence;

(c) practices and procedures that the applicant proposes to implement in connection with any such business;

(d) evidence of the kind mentioned in subsection (2A).

(2A) That evidence is evidence tending to show that the applicant, or any of the applicant's employees, agents or associates (whether past or present) or, where the applicant is a body corporate, any person appearing to the OFT to be a controller of the body corporate or an associate of any such person, has—

    (a) committed any offence involving fraud or other dishonesty or violence;

    (b) contravened any provision made by or under—

        (i)   this Act;

        [(ia) paragraph 13 of Schedule 1A to the Financial Services and Markets Act 2000;]

        (ii) Part 16 of the Financial Services and Markets Act 2000 so far as it relates to the consumer credit jurisdiction under that Part;

        (iii) any other enactment regulating the provision of credit to individuals or other transactions with individuals;

    (c) contravened any provision in force in an EEA State which corresponds to a provision of the kind mentioned in paragraph (b);

    (d) practised discrimination on grounds of sex, colour, race or ethnic or national origins in, or in connection with, the carrying on of any business; or

    (e) engaged in business practices appearing to the OFT to be deceitful or oppressive or otherwise unfair or improper (whether unlawful or not).

(2B) For the purposes of subsection (2A)(e), the business practices which the OFT may consider to be deceitful or oppressive or otherwise unfair or improper include practices in the carrying on of a consumer credit business that appear to the OFT to involve irresponsible lending.]

(3) In subsection [(2A)], 'associate', in addition to the persons specified in section 184, includes a business associate.

[25A   Guidance on fitness test

(1) The OFT shall prepare and publish guidance in relation to how it determines, or how it proposes to determine, whether persons are fit persons as mentioned in section 25.

(2) If the OFT revises the guidance at any time after it has been published, the OFT shall publish it as revised.

(3) The guidance shall be published in such manner as the OFT thinks fit for the purpose of bringing it to the attention of those likely to be affected by it.

(4) In preparing or revising the guidance the OFT shall consult such persons as it thinks fit.

(5) In carrying out its functions under this Part the OFT shall have regard to the guidance as most recently published.]

[26   Conduct of business

(1) Regulations may be made as to—

    (a) the conduct by a licensee of his business; and

    (b) the conduct by a consumer credit EEA firm of its business in the United Kingdom.

(2) The regulations may in particular specify—

    (a) the books or other records to be kept by any person to whom the regulations apply;

    (b) the information to be furnished by such a person to those persons with whom—

        (i)   that person does business, or

        (ii) that person seeks to do business, and the way in which that information is to be furnished.]

Issue of licences

27   Determination of applications

(1) Unless the [OFT] determines to issue a licence in accordance with an application [it] shall, before determining the application, by notice—

    (a) inform the applicant, giving [its] reasons, that, as the case may be, [it] is minded to refuse the application, or to grant it in terms different from those applied for, describing them, and

    (b) invite the applicant to submit to the [OFT] representations in support of his application in accordance with section 34.

(2) If the [OFT] grants the application in terms different from those applied for then, whether or not the applicant appeals, the [OFT] shall issue the licence in the terms approved by [it] unless the applicant by notice informs [it] that he does not desire a licence in those terms.

[27A   Consumer credit EEA firms

(1) Where—
   (a) a consumer credit EEA firm makes an application for a standard licence, and
   (b) the activities covered by the application are all permitted activities,
the OFT shall refuse the application.

(2) Subsection (3) applies where—
   (a) a consumer credit EEA firm makes an application for a standard licence; and
   (b) some (but not all) of the activities covered by the application are permitted activities.

(3) In order to be entitled to be issued with a standard licence in accordance with section 25(1) to (1AB) in relation to a type of business, the firm need not satisfy the OFT that it is a fit person to carry on that type of business so far as it would involve any of the permitted activities covered by the application.

(4) A standard licence held by a consumer credit EEA firm does not at any time authorise the carrying on of an activity which is a permitted activity at that time.

(5) In this section 'permitted activity' means, in relation to a consumer credit EEA firm, an activity for which the firm has, or could obtain, permission under paragraph 15 of Schedule 3 to the Financial Services and Markets Act 2000.]

28   Exclusion from group licence

Where the [OFT] is minded to issue a group licence (whether on the application of any person or not), and in doing so to exclude any person from the group by name, [it] shall, before determining the matter,—
   (a) give notice of that fact to the person proposed to be excluded, giving [its] reasons, and
   (b) invite that person to submit to the [OFT] representations against his exclusion in accordance with section 34.

Charges for indefinite licences

[28A   Charges to be paid by licensees etc. before end of payment periods

(1) The licensee under a standard licence which has effect indefinitely shall, before the end of each payment period of his, pay the OFT a charge towards the costs of carrying out its functions under this Act.

(2) The original applicant for a group licence which has effect indefinitely shall, before the end of each payment period of his, pay the OFT such a charge.

(3) The amount of the charge payable by a person under subsection (1) or (2) before the end of a payment period shall be determined in accordance with provision which—
   (a) is made by the OFT by general notice; and
   (b) is current on such day as may be determined in accordance with provision made by regulations.

(4) The provision that may be made by the OFT under subsection (3)(a) includes—
   (a) different provision in relation to persons of different descriptions (including persons whose payment periods end at different times);
   (b) provision for no charge at all to be payable by persons of specified descriptions.

(5) The approval of the Secretary of State and the Treasury is required for a general notice under subsection (3)(a).

(6) For the purposes of this section a person's payment periods are to be determined in accordance with provision made by regulations.]

[28B   Extension of period to pay charge under s. 28A

(1) A person who is required under section 28A to pay a charge before the end of a period may apply once to the OFT for that period to be extended.

(2) The application shall be made before such day as may be determined in accordance with provision made by the OFT by general notice.

(3) If the OFT is satisfied that there is a good reason—

(a) why the applicant has not paid that charge prior to his making of the application, and

(b) why he cannot pay that charge before the end of that period,

it may, if it thinks fit, by notice to him extend that period by such time as it thinks fit having regard to that reason.

(4) The power of the OFT under this section to extend a period in relation to a charge—

(a) includes the power to extend the period in relation to a part of the charge only;

(b) may be exercised even though the period has ended.]

[28C   Failure to pay charge under s. 28A

(1) This section applies if a person (the 'defaulter') fails to pay a charge—

(a) before the end of a period (the 'payment period') as required under section 28A; or

(b) where the payment period is extended under section 28B, before the end of the payment period as extended (subject to subsection (2)).

(2) Where the payment period is extended under section 28B in relation to a part of the charge only, this section applies if the defaulter fails—

(a) to pay so much of the charge as is not covered by the extension before the end of the payment period disregarding the extension; or

(b) to pay so much of the charge as is covered by the extension before the end of the payment period as extended.

(3) Subject to subsection (4), if the charge is a charge under section 28A(1), the defaulter's licence terminates.

(4) If the defaulter has applied to the OFT under section 28B for the payment period to be extended and that application has not been determined—

(a) his licence shall not terminate before the application has been determined and the OFT has notified him of the determination; and

(b) if the OFT extends the payment period on that application, this section shall have effect accordingly.

(5) If the charge is a charge under section 28A(2), the charge shall be recoverable by the OFT.]

Renewal, variation, suspension and revocation of licences

29   Renewal

(1) If the licensee under a standard licence [of limited duration], or the original applicant for, or any licensee under, a group licence of limited duration, wishes the [OFT] to renew the licence, whether on the same terms (except as to expiry) or on varied terms, he must, during the period specified by the [OFT] by general notice or such longer period as the [OFT] may allow, make an application to the Director for its renewal.

(2) The [OFT] may of [its] own motion renew any group licence.

(3) The preceding provisions of this Part apply to the renewal of a licence as they apply to the issue of a licence, except that section 28 does not apply to a person who was already excluded in the licence up for renewal.

[(3A) In its application to the renewal of standard licences by virtue of subsection (3) of this section, section 27(1) shall have effect as if for paragraph (b) there were substituted—

'(b) invite the applicant to submit to the OFT in accordance with section 34 representations—

(i)   in support of his application; and

(ii) about the provision (if any) that should be included under section 34A as part of the determination were the OFT to refuse the application or grant it in terms different from those applied for.']

(4) Until the determination of an application under subsection (1) and, where an appeal lies from the determination, until the end of the appeal period, the licence shall continue [to have effect], notwithstanding that apart from this subsection it would expire earlier.

(6) General notice shall be given of the renewal of a group licence.

30 Variation by request

[(1) If it thinks fit, the OFT may by notice to the licensee under a standard licence—

    (a) in the case of a licence which covers the carrying on of a type of business only so far as it falls within one or more descriptions of business, vary the licence by—

        (i)   removing that limitation;

        (ii) adding a description of business to that limitation; or

        (iii) removing a description of business from that limitation;

    (c) in the case of a licence which covers the carrying on of a type of business with no limitation, vary the licence so that it covers the carrying on of that type of business only so far as it falls within one or more descriptions of business;

    (d) vary the licence so that it no longer covers the carrying on of a type of business at all;

    (e) vary the licence so that a type of business the carrying on of which is not covered at all by the licence is covered either—

        (i)   with no limitation; or

        (ii) only so far as it falls within one or more descriptions of business; or

    (j) vary the licence in any other way except for the purpose of varying the descriptions of activities covered by the licence.

(1A) The OFT may vary a licence under subsection (1) only in accordance with an application made by the licensee.

(1B) References in this section to a description of business in relation to a type of business—

    (a) are references to a description of business specified in a general notice under section 24A(5)(a); and

    (b) in subsection (1)(a) (apart from sub-paragraph (ii)) include references to a description of business that was, but is no longer, so specified.]

(2) In the case of a group licence issued on the application of any person, the [OFT], on an application made by that person, may if [it] thinks fit by notice to that person vary the terms of the licence in accordance with the application; but the [OFT] shall not vary a group licence under this subsection by excluding a named person, other than the person making the request, unless that named person consents in writing to his exclusion.

(3) In the case of a group licence from which (whether by name or description) a person is excluded, the [OFT], on an application made by that person, may if [it] thinks fit, by notice to that person, vary the terms of the licence so as to remove the exclusion.

(4) Unless the [OFT] determines to vary a licence in accordance with an application [it] shall, before determining the application, by notice—

    (a) inform the applicant, giving [its] reasons, that [it] is minded to refuse the application, and

    (b) invite the applicant to submit to the [OFT] representations in suppprt of his application in accordance with section 34.

(5) General notice shall be given that a variation of a group licence has been made under this section.

31 Compulsory variation

(1) Where at a time during the currency of a licence the [OFT] is of the opinion that, if the licence had expired at that time [(assuming, in the case of a licence which has effect indefinitely, that it were a licence of limited duration)], [it] would on an application for its renewal or futher renewal on the same terms (except as to expiry), have been minded to grant the application but on different terms, and that therefore [it should take steps mentioned in subsection (1A)], [it] shall proceed as follows.

[(1A) Those steps are—

    (a) in the case of a standard licence, steps mentioned in section 30(1)(a)(ii) and (iii), (b), (c) and (e);

(b) in the case of a group licence, the varying of terms of the licence.]

[(1B) The OFT shall also proceed as follows if, having regard to section 22 (1B) to (1E), it is of the opinion—

(a) that a licence which has effect indefinitely should have its duration limited; or

(b) in the case of a licence of limited duration, that the period during which it has effect should be shortened.]

(2) In the case of a standard licence the [OFT] shall, by notice—

(a) inform the licensee of the variations the [OFT] is minded to make in the terms of the licence, stating [its] reasons, and

[(b) invite him to submit to the OFT in accordance with section 34 representations—

(i)   as to the proposed variations; and

(ii) about the provision (if any) that should be included under section 34A as part of the determination were the OFT to vary the licence.]

(3) In the case of a group licence the [OFT] shall—

(a) give general notice of the variations [it] is minded to make in the terms of the licence, stating [its] reasons, and

(b) in the notice invite any licensee to submit to [it] representations as to the proposed variations in accordance with section 34.

(4) In the case of a group licence issued on application the [OFT] shall also—

(a) inform the original applicant of the variations the [OFT] is minded to make in the terms of the licence, stating [its] reasons, and

(b) invite him to submit to the [OFT] representations as to the proposed variations in accordance with section 34.

(5) If the [OFT] is minded to vary a group licence by excluding any person (other than the original applicant) from the group by name the [OFT] shall, in addition, take the like steps under section 28 as are required in the case mentioned in that section.

(6) General notice shall be given that a variation of any group licence has been made under this section.

(7) A variation under this section shall not take effect before the end of the appeal period.

[(8) Subsection (1) shall have effect in relation to a standard licence as if an application could be made for the renewal or further renewal of the licence on the same terms (except as to expiry) even if such an application could not be made because of provision made in a general notice under section 24A(5).

(9) Accordingly, in applying subsection (1AA) of section 25 in relation to the licence for the purposes of this section, the OFT shall treat references in that subsection to the description or descriptions of business in relation to a type of business as references to the description or descriptions of business included in the licence in relation to that type of business, notwithstanding that provision under section 24A(5).]

32   Suspension and revocation

(1) Where at a time during the currency of a licence the [OFT] is of the opinion that if the licence had expired at that time [(assuming, in the case of a licence which has effect indefinitely, that it were a licence of limited duration)] [it] would have been minded not to renew it, and that therefore it should be revoked or suspended, [it] shall proceed as follows.

(2) In the case of a standard licence the [OFT] shall, by notice—

(a) inform the licensee that, as the case may be, the [OFT] is minded to revoke the licence, or suspend it until a specified date or indefinitely, stating [its] reasons, and

[(b) invite him to submit to the OFT in accordance with section 34 representations—

(i)   as to the proposed revocation or suspension; and

(ii) about the provision (if any) that should be included under section 34A as part of the determination were the OFT to revoke or suspend the licence.]

(3) In the case of a group licence the [OFT] shall—

(a) give general notice that, as the case may be, [it] is minded to revoke the licence, or suspend it until a specified date or indefinitely, stating [its] reasons, and

(b) in the notice invite any licensee to submit to [it] representations as to the proposed revocation or suspension in accordance with section 34.

(4) In the case of a group licence issued on application the [OFT] shall also—

(a) inform the original applicant that, as the case may be, the [OFT] is minded to revoke the licence, or suspend it until a specified date or indefinitely, stating its reasons, and

(b) invite him to submit representations as to the proposed revocation or suspension in accordance with section 34.

(6) General notice shall be given of the revocation or suspension of a group licence.

(7) A revocation or suspension under this section shall not take effect before the end of the appeal period.

(8) Except for the purposes of section 29, a licensee under a suspended licence shall be treated, in respect of the period of suspension, as if the licence had not been issued; and where the suspension is not expressed to end on a specified date it may, if the [OFT] thinks fit, be ended by notice given by [it] to the licensee or, in the case of a group licence, by general notice.

[(9) The OFT has no power to revoke or to suspend a standard licence simply because, by virtue of provision made in a general notice under sections 24A(5), a person cannot apply for the renewal of such a licence on terms which are the same as the terms of the licence in question.]

33 Application to end suspension

(1) On an application made by a licensee the [OFT] may, if [it] thinks fit, by notice to the licensee end the suspension of a licence, whether the suspension was for a fixed or indefinite period.

(2) Unless the [OFT] determines to end the suspension in accordance with the application [it] shall, before determining the application, by notice—

(a) inform the applicant, giving [its] reasons, that [it] is minded to refuse the application, and

(b) invite the applicant to submit to the [OFT] representations in support of his application in accordance with section 34.

(3) General notice shall be given that a suspension of a group licence has been ended under this section.

(4) In the case of a group licence issued on application—

(a) the references in subsection (1) to a licensee include the original applicant;

(b) the [OFT] shall inform the original applicant that a suspension of a group licence has been ended under this section.

[Further powers of OFT to regulate conduct of licensees etc.]

[33A Power of OFT to impose requirements on licensees

(1) This section applies where the OFT is dissatisfied with any matter in connection with—

(a) a business being carried on, or which has been carried on, by a licensee or by an associate or a former associate of a licensee;

(b) a proposal to carry on a business which has been made by a licensee or by an associate or a former associate of a licensee; or

(c) any conduct not covered by paragraph (a) or (b) of a licensee or of an associate or a former associate of a licensee.

(2) The OFT may by notice to the licensee require him to do or not to do (or to cease doing) anything specified in the notice for purposes connected with—

(a) addressing the matter with which the OFT is dissatisfied; or

(b) securing that matters of the same or a similar kind do not arise.

(3) A requirement imposed under this section on a licensee shall only relate to a business which the licensee is carrying on, or is proposing to carry on, under the licence under which he is a licensee.

(4) Such a requirement may be framed by reference to a named person other than the licensee.

(5) For the purposes of subsection (1) it is immaterial whether the matter with which the OFT is dissatisfied arose before or after the licensee became a licensee.

(6) If—

    (a) a person makes an application for a standard licence, and

    (b) while dealing with that application the OFT forms the opinion that, if such a licence were to be issued to that person, it would be minded to impose on him a requirement under this section,

the OFT may, before issuing such a licence to that person, do (in whole or in part) anything that it must do under section 33D or 34(1) or (2) in relation to the imposing of the requirement.

(7) In this section 'associate', in addition to the persons specified in section 184, includes a business associate.]

[33B   Power of OFT to impose requirements on supervisory bodies

(1) This section applies where the OFT is dissatisfied with the way in which a responsible person in relation to a group licence—

    (a) is regulating or otherwise supervising, or has regulated or otherwise supervised, persons who are licensees under that licence; or

    (b) is proposing to regulate or otherwise to supervise such persons.

(2) The OFT may by notice to the responsible person require him to do or not to do (or to cease doing) anything specified in the notice for purposes connected with—

    (a) addressing the matters giving rise to the OFT's dissatisfaction; or

    (b) securing that matters of the same or a similar kind do not arise.

(3) A requirement imposed under this section on a responsible person in relation to a group licence shall only relate to practices and procedures for regulating or otherwise supervising licensees under the licence in connection with their carrying on of businesses under the licence.

(4) For the purposes of subsection (1) it is immaterial whether the matters giving rise to the OFT's dissatisfaction arose before or after the issue of the group licence in question.

(5) If—

    (a) a person makes an application for a group licence, and

    (b) while dealing with that application the OFT forms the opinion that, if such a licence were to be issued to that person, it would be minded to impose on him a requirement under this section,

the OFT may, before issuing such a licence to that person, do (in whole or in part) anything that it must do under section 33D or 34(1) or (2) in relation to the imposing of the requirement.

(6) For the purposes of this Part a person is a responsible person in relation to a group licence if—

    (a) he is the original applicant for it; and

    (b) he has a responsibility (whether by virtue of an enactment, an agreement or otherwise) for regulating or otherwise supervising persons who are licensees under the licence.]

[33C   Supplementary provision relating to requirements

(1) A notice imposing a requirement under section 33A or 33B may include provision about the time at or by which, or the period during which, the requirement is to be complied with.

(2) A requirement imposed under section 33A or 33B shall not have effect after the licence by reference to which it is imposed has itself ceased to have effect.

(3) A person shall not be required under section 33A or 33B to compensate, or otherwise to make amends to, another person.

(4) The OFT may by notice to the person on whom a requirement has been imposed under section 33A or 33B vary or revoke the requirement (including any provision made under subsection (1) of this section in relation to it) with effect from such date as may be specified in the notice.

(5) The OFT may exercise its power under subsection (4) in relation to a requirement either on its own motion or on the application of a person falling within subsection (6) or (7) in relation to the requirement.

(6) A person falls within this subsection in relation to a requirement if he is the person on whom the requirement is imposed.

(7) A person falls within this subsection in relation to a requirement if—

(a) the requirement is imposed under section 33A;

(b) he is not the person on whom the requirement is imposed;

(c) the requirement is framed by reference to him by name; and

(d) the effect of the requirement is—

    (i) to prevent him being an employee of the person on whom the requirement is imposed;

    (ii) to restrict the activities that he may engage in as an employee of that person; or

    (iii) otherwise to prevent him from doing something, or to restrict his doing something, in connection with a business being carried on by that person.]

[33D Procedure in relation to requirements

(1) Before making a determination—

(a) to impose a requirement on a person under section 33A or 33B,

(b) to refuse an application under section 33C(5) in relation to a requirement imposed under either of those sections, or

(c) to vary or to revoke a requirement so imposed,

the OFT shall proceed as follows.

(2) The OFT shall give a notice to every person to whom subsection (3) applies in relation to the determination—

(a) informing him, with reasons, that it is minded to make the determination; and

(b) inviting him to submit to it representations as to the determination under section 34.

(3) This subsection applies to a person in relation to the determination if he falls within, or as a consequence of the determination would fall within, section 33C(6) or (7) in relation to the requirement in question.

(4) This section does not require the OFT to give a notice to a person if the determination in question is in the same terms as a proposal made to the OFT by that person (whether as part of an application under this Part or otherwise).]

[33E Guidance on requirements

(1) The OFT shall prepare and publish guidance in relation to how it exercises, or how it proposes to exercise, its powers under sections 33A to 33C.

(2) If the OFT revises the guidance at any time after it has been published, the OFT shall publish it as revised.

(3) The guidance shall be published in such manner as the OFT thinks fit for the purpose of bringing it to the attention of those likely to be affected by it.

(4) In preparing or revising the guidance the OFT shall consult such persons as it thinks fit.

(5) In exercising its powers under sections 33A to 33C the OFT shall have regard to the guidance as most recently published.]

Miscellaneous

34 Representations to [OFT]

(1) Where this section applies to an invitation by the [OFT] to any person to submit representations, the [OFT] shall invite that person, within 21 days after the notice containing the invitation is given to him or published, or such longer period as the [OFT] may allow—

(a) to submit his representations in writing to the [OFT], and

(b) to give notice to the [OFT], if he thinks fit, that he wishes to make representations orally,

and where notice is given under paragraph (b) the [OFT] shall arrange for the oral representations to be heard.

(2) In reaching [its] determination the [OFT] shall take into account any representations submitted or made under this section.

(3) The [OFT] shall give notice of [its] determination to the persons who were required to be invited to submit representations about it or, where the invitation to submit representations was required to be given by general notice, shall give general notice of the determination.

[34A   Winding-up of standard licensee's business

(1) If it thinks fit, the OFT may, for the purpose of enabling the licensee's business, or any part of his business, to be transferred or wound up, include as part of a determination to which subsection (2) applies provision authorising the licensee to carry on for a specified period—

    (a) specified activities, or

    (b) activities of specified descriptions,

which, because of that determination, the licensee will no longer be licensed to carry on.

(2) This subsection applies to the following determinations—

    (a) a determination to refuse to renew a standard licence in accordance with the terms of the application for its renewal;

    (b) a determination to vary such a licence under section 31;

    (c) a determination to suspend or revoke such a licence.

(3) Such provision—

    (a) may specify different periods for different activities or activities of different description;

    (b) may provide for persons other than the licensee to carry on activities under the authorisation;

    (c) may specify requirements which must be complied with by a person carrying on activities under the authorisation in relation to those activities;

and, if a requirement specified under paragraph (c) is not complied with, the OFT may by notice to a person carrying on activities under the authorisation terminate the authorisation (in whole or in part) from a specified date.

(4) Without prejudice to the generality of paragraph (c) of subsection (3), a requirement specified under that paragraph may have the effect of—

    (a) preventing a named person from being an employee of a person carrying on activities under the authorisation, or restricting the activities he may engage in as an employee of such a person;

    (b) preventing a named person from doing something, or restricting his doing something, in connection with activities being carried on by a person under the authorisation;

    (c) securing that access to premises is given to officers of the OFT for the purpose of enabling them to inspect documents or to observe the carrying on of activities.

(5) Activities carried on under an authorisation shall be treated for the purposes of sections 39(1), 40, 148 and 149 as if carried on under a standard licence.]

35   The register

(1) The [OFT] shall establish and maintain a register, in which [it] shall cause to be kept particulars of—

    (a) applications not yet determined for the issue, variation or renewal of licences, or for ending the suspension of a licence;

    (b) licences which are in [effect], or have at any time been suspended or revoked [or terminated by section 28C], with details of any variation of the terms of a licence;

    [(ba) requirements imposed under section 33A or 33B which are in effect or which have been in effect, with details of any variation of such a requirement;]

    (c) decisions given by [it] under this Act, and any appeal from those decisions; and

    (d) such other matters (if any) as [it] thinks fit.

[(1A) The [OFT] shall also cause to be kept in the register any copy of any notice or other document relating to a consumer credit EEA firm which is given to the [OFT] by the Financial Services Authority for inclusion in the register.]

(2) The [OFT] shall give general notice of the various matters required to be entered in the register, and of any change in them made under subsection (1)(d).

(3) Any person shall be entitled on payment of the specified fee—

(a) to inspect the register during ordinary office hours and take copies of any entry, or

(b) to obtain from the [OFT] a copy, certified by the [OFT] to be correct, of any entry in the register.

(4) The [OFT] may, if [it] thinks fit, determine that the right conferred by subsection (3)(a) shall be exercisable in relation to a copy of the register instead of, or in addition to, the original.

(5) The [OFT] shall give general notice of the place or places where, and times when, the register or a copy of it may be inspected.

36 Duty to notify changes

(1) Within 21 working days after change takes place in any particulars entered in the register in respect of a standard licence or the licensee under section 35(1)(d) (not being a change resulting from action taken by the [OFT]), the licensee shall give the [OFT] notice of the change; and the [OFT] shall cause any necessary amendment to be made in the register.

(2) Within 21 working days after—

(a) any change takes place in the officers of—

(i) a body corporate, or an unincorporated body of persons, which is the licensee under a standard licence, or

(ii) a body corporate which is a controller of a body corporate which is such a licensee, or

(b) a body corporate which is such a licensee becomes aware that a person has become or ceased to be a controller of the body corporate, or

(c) any change takes place in the members of a partnership which is such a licensee (including a change on the amalgamation of the partnership with another firm, or a change whereby the number of partners is reduced to one), the licensee shall give the [OFT] notice of the change.

(3) Within 14 working days after any change takes place in the officers of a body corporate which is a controller of another body corporate which is a licensee under a standard licence, the controller shall give the licensee notice of the change.

(4) Within 14 working days after a person becomes or ceases to be a controller of a body corporate which is a licensee under a standard licence, that person shall give the licensee notice of the fact.

(5) Where a change in a partnership has the result that the business ceases to be carried on under the name, or any of the names, specified in a standard licence the licence shall cease to have effect.

[36A Further duties to notify changes etc.

(1) Subsections (2) to (4) apply where a general notice under section 6(2) comes into effect.

(2) A person who is the licensee under a standard licence or who is the original applicant for a group licence shall, in relation to each relevant application which he has made and which was determined before the general notice came into effect, provide the OFT with any information or document—

(a) which he would have been required to provide with the application had the application been made after the general notice came into effect; and

(b) which the general notice requires to be provided for the purposes of this subsection.

(3) Any such information or document shall be provided within such period as may be specified in the general notice.

(4) Subsection (2) does not require a person to provide any information or document—

(a) which he provided in relation to the application by virtue of section 6;

(b) which he has previously provided in relation to the application by virtue of this section; or

(c) which he would have been required to provide in relation to the application by virtue of subsection (5) but for subsection (6).

(5) A person who is the licensee under a standard licence or who is the original applicant for a group licence shall, in relation to each relevant application which he has made, notify the OFT giving details if, after the application is determined, any information or document which he—

(a) provided in relation to the application by virtue of section 6, or

(b) has so provided by virtue of this section,

is, to any extent, superseded or otherwise affected by a change in circumstances.

(6) Subsection (5) does not require a person to notify the OFT about a matter unless it falls within a description of matters specified by the OFT in a general notice.

(7) A description may be specified for the purposes of subsection (6) only if the OFT is satisfied that the matters which would fall within that description are matters which would be relevant to the question of—

(a) whether, having regard to section 25(2), a person is a fit person to carry on a business under a standard licence; or

(b) whether the public interest is better served by a group licence remaining in effect than by obliging the licensees under it to apply separately for standard licences.

(8) A person who is the licensee under a standard licence or who is the original applicant for a group licence shall, in relation to each relevant application which he has made, notify the OFT about every error or omission—

(a) in or from any information or document which he provided by virtue of section 6, or which he has provided by virtue of this section, in relation to the application; and

(b) of which he becomes aware after the determination of the application.

(9) A notification for the purposes of subsection (5) or (8) shall be given within the period of 28 days beginning with the day on which (as the case may be)—

(a) the information or document is superseded;

(b) the change in circumstances occurs; or

(c) the licensee or the original applicant becomes aware of the error or omission.

(10) This section does not require a person to notify the OFT about—

(a) anything of which he is required to notify it under section 36; or

(b) an error in or omission from any information or document which is a clerical error or omission not affecting the substance of the information or document.

(11) In this section 'relevant application' means, in relation to a person who is the licensee under a standard licence or who is the original applicant for a group licence—

(a) the original application for the licence; or

(b) an application for its renewal or for its variation.]

[36B Power of OFT to require information generally

(1) The OFT may by notice to a person require him—

(a) to provide such information as may be specified or described in the notice; or

(b) to produce such documents as may be so specified or described.

(2) The notice shall set out the reasons why the OFT requires the information or documents to be provided or produced.

(3) The information or documents shall be provided or produced—

(a) before the end of such reasonable period as may be specified in the notice; and

(b) at such place as may be so specified.

(4) A requirement may be imposed under subsection (1) on a person who is—

(a) the licensee under a standard licence, or

(b) the original applicant for a group licence,

only if the provision or production of the information or documents in question is reasonably required for purposes connected with the OFT's functions under this Act.

(5) A requirement may be imposed under subsection (1) on any other person only if—

(a) an act or omission mentioned in subsection (6) has occurred or the OFT has reason to suspect that such an act or omission has occurred; and

(b) the provision or production of the information or documents in question is reasonably required for purposes connected with—

(i)   the taking by the OFT of steps under this Part as a consequence; or

(ii) its consideration of whether to take such steps as a consequence.

(6) Those acts or omissions are acts or omissions which—

    (a) cast doubt on whether, having regard to section 25(2), a person is a fit person to carry on a business under a standard licence;

    (b) cast doubt on whether the public interest is better served by a group licence remaining in effect, or being issued, than by obliging the persons who are licensees under it, or who would be licensees under it, to apply separately for standard licences;

    (c) give rise, or are likely to give rise, to dissatisfaction for the purposes of section 33A(1) or 33B(1); or

    (d) constitute or give rise to a failure of the kind mentioned in section 39A(1).]

[36C   Power of OFT to require access to premises

(1) The OFT may by notice to a licensee under a licence require him to secure that access to the premises specified or described in the notice is given to an officer of an enforcement authority in order for the officer—

    (a) to observe the carrying on of a business under the licence by the licensee; or

    (b) to inspect such documents of the licensee relating to such a business as are—

        (i)   specified or described in the notice; and

        (ii) situated on the premises.

(2) The notice shall set out the reasons why the access is required.

(3) The premises which may be specified or described in the notice—

    (a) include premises which are not premises of the licensee if they are premises from which he carries on activities in connection with the business in question; but

    (b) do not include premises which are used only as a dwelling.

(4) The licensee shall secure that the required access is given at such times as the OFT reasonably requires.

(5) The OFT shall give reasonable notice of those times.

(6) Where an officer is given access to any premises by virtue of this section, the licensee shall also secure that persons on the premises give the officer such assistance or information as he may reasonably require in connection with his observation or inspection of documents (as the case may be).

(7) The assistance that may be required under subsection (6) includes (amongst other things) the giving to the officer of an explanation of a document which he is inspecting.

(8) A requirement may be imposed under subsection (1) on a person who is—

    (a) the licensee under a standard licence, or

    (b) the original applicant for a group licence,

only if the observation or inspection in question is reasonably required for purposes connected with the OFT's functions under this Act.

(9) A requirement may be imposed under subsection (1) on any other person only if—

    (a) an act or omission mentioned in section 36B(6) has occurred or the OFT has reason to suspect that such an act or omission has occurred; and

    (b) the observation or inspection in question is reasonably required for purposes connected with—

        (i)   the taking by the OFT of steps under this Part as a consequence; or

        (ii) its consideration of whether to take such steps as a consequence.

(10) In this section—

    (a) references to a licensee under a licence include, in relation to a group licence issued on application, references to the original applicant; and

    (b) references to a business being carried on under a licence by a licensee include, in relation to the original applicant for a group licence, activities being carried on by him for the purpose of regulating or otherwise supervising (whether by virtue of an enactment, an agreement or otherwise) licensees under that licence in connection with their carrying on of businesses under that licence.]

[36D   Entry to premises under warrant

(1) A justice of the peace may issue a warrant under this section if satisfied on information on oath given on behalf of the OFT that there are reasonable grounds for believing that the following conditions are satisfied.

(2) Those conditions are—

    (a) that there is on the premises specified in the warrant information or documents in relation to which a requirement could be imposed under section 36B; and

    (b) that if such a requirement were to be imposed in relation to the information or documents—

        (i)   it would not be complied with; or

        (ii)   the information or documents would be tampered with.

(3) A warrant under this section shall authorise an officer of an enforcement authority—

    (a) to enter the premises specified in the warrant;

    (b) to search the premises and to seize and detain any information or documents appearing to be information or documents specified in the warrant or information or documents of a description so specified;

    (c) to take any other steps which may appear to be reasonably necessary for preserving such information or documents or preventing interference with them; and

    (d) to use such force as may be reasonably necessary.

(4) An officer entering premises by virtue of this section may take such persons and equipment with him as he thinks necessary.

(5) In the application of this section to Scotland—

    (a) the reference to a justice of the peace includes a reference to a sheriff;

    (b) for 'information on oath' there is substituted 'evidence on oath'.

(6) In the application of this section to Northern Ireland the reference to a justice of the peace shall be construed as a reference to a lay magistrate.]

[36E   Failure to comply with information requirement

(1) If on an application made by the OFT it appears to the court that a person (the 'information defaulter') has failed to do something that he was required to do by virtue of section 36B or 36C, the court may make an order under this section.

(2) An order under this section may require the information defaulter—

    (a) to do the thing that it appears he failed to do within such period as may be specified in the order;

    (b) otherwise to take such steps to remedy the consequences of the failure as may be so specified.

(3) If the information defaulter is a body corporate, a partnership or an unincorporated body of persons which is not a partnership, the order may require any officer who is (wholly or partly) responsible for the failure to meet such costs of the application as are specified in the order.

(4) In this section—

'court' means—

    (a) in England and Wales and Northern Ireland, the High Court or the county court;

    (b) in Scotland, the Court of Session or the sheriff;

'officer' means—

    (a) in relation to a body corporate, a person holding a position of director, manager or secretary of the body or any similar position;

    (b) in relation to a partnership or to an unincorporated body of persons, a member of the partnership or body.

(5) In subsection (4) 'director' means, in relation to a body corporate whose affairs are managed by its members, a member of the body.]

[36F   Officers of enforcement authorities other than OFT

(1) A relevant officer may only exercise powers by virtue of section 36C or 36D in pursuance of arrangements made with the OFT by or on behalf of the enforcement authority of which he is an officer.

(2) Anything done or omitted to be done by, or in relation to, a relevant officer in the exercise or purported exercise of a power by virtue of section 36C or 36D shall be treated for all purposes as having been done or omitted to be done by, or in relation to, an officer of the OFT.

(3) Subsection (2) does not apply for the purposes of any criminal proceedings brought against the officer, the enforcement authority of which he is an officer or the OFT in respect of anything done or omitted to be done by the officer.

(4) A relevant officer shall not disclose to a person other than the OFT information obtained by his exercise of a power by virtue of section 36C or 36D unless—

    (a) he has the approval of the OFT to do so; or

    (b) he is under a duty to make the disclosure.

(5) In this section 'relevant officer' means an officer of an enforcement authority other than the OFT.]

37 Death, bankruptcy etc. of licensee

(1) A licence held by one individual terminates if he—

    (a) dies, or

    (b) is adjudged bankrupt, or

    [(c) becomes a person who lacks capacity (within the meaning of the Mental Capacity Act 2005) to carry on the activities covered by the licence.]

[(1A) A licence terminates if the licensee gives the OFT a notice under subsection (1B).

(1B) A notice under this subsection shall—

    (a) be in such form as the OFT may by general notice specify;

    (b) contain such information as may be so specified;

    (c) be accompanied by the licence or give reasons as to why it is not accompanied by the licence; and

    (d) be signed by or on behalf of the licensee.]

(2) In relation to a licence held by one individual, or a partnership or other unincorporated body of persons, or a body corporate, regulations may specify other events relating to the licensee on the occurrence of which the licence is to terminate.

(3) Regulations may—

    (a) provide for the termination of a licence by subsection (1) [or (1A)], or under subsection (2), to be deferred for a period not exceeding 12 months, and

    (b) authorise the business of the licensee to be carried on under the licence by some other person during the period of deferment, subject to such conditions as may be prescribed.

(4) This section does not apply to group licences.

38 Application of s. 37 to Scotland and Northern Ireland

[(2) In the application of section 37 to Northern Ireland the following shall be substituted for subsection (1)—

'(1) A licence held by one individual terminates if—

    (a) he dies, or

    (b) he is adjudged bankrupt or his estate and effects vest in the official assignee under section 349 of the Irish Bankrupt and Insolvent Act 1857, or

    (c) a declaration is made under section 15 of the Lunacy Regulation (Ireland) Act 1871 that he is of unsound mind and incapable of managing his person or property, or an order is made under section 68 of that Act in consequence of its being found that he is of unsound mind and incapable of managing his affairs.']

39 Offences against Part III

(1) A person who engages in any activities for which a licence is required when he is not a licensee under a licence covering those activities commits an offence.

(2) A licensee under a standard licence who carries on business under a name not specified in the licence commits an offence.

(3) A person who fails to give the [OFT] or a licensee notice under section 36 within the period required commits an offence.

[39A   Power of OFT to impose civil penalties

(1) Where the OFT is satisfied that a person (the 'defaulter') has failed or is failing to comply with a requirement imposed on him by virtue of section 33A, 33B or 36A, it may by notice to him (a 'penalty notice') impose on him a penalty of such amount as it thinks fit.

The penalty notice shall—

> (a) specify the amount of the penalty that is being imposed;
> (b) set out the OFT's reasons for imposing a penalty and for specifying that amount;
> (c) specify how the payment of the penalty may be made to the OFT; and
> (d) specify the period within which the penalty is required to be paid.

(3) The amount of the penalty shall not exceed £50,000.

(4) The period specified in the penalty notice for the purposes of subsection (2)(d) shall not end earlier than the end of the period during which an appeal may be brought against the imposition of the penalty under section 41.

(5) If the defaulter does not pay the penalty to the OFT within the period so specified—

> (a) the unpaid balance from time to time shall carry interest at the rate for the time being specified in section 17 of the Judgments Act 1838; and
> (b) the penalty and any interest payable on it shall be recoverable by the OFT.]

[39B   Further provision relating to civil penalties

(1) Before determining to impose a penalty on a person under section 39A the OFT shall give a notice to that person—

> (a) informing him that it is minded to impose a penalty on him;
> (b) stating the proposed amount of the penalty;
> (c) setting out its reasons for being minded to impose a penalty on him and for proposing that amount;
> (d) setting out the proposed period for the payment of the penalty; and
> (e) inviting him to submit representations to it about the matters mentioned in the preceding paragraphs in accordance with section 34.

(2) In determining whether and how to exercise its powers under section 39A in relation to a person's failure, the OFT shall have regard to (amongst other things)—

> (a) any penalty or fine that has been imposed on that person by another body in relation to the conduct giving rise to the failure;
> (b) other steps that the OFT has taken or might take under this Part in relation to that conduct.

(3) General notice shall be given of the imposition of a penalty under section 39A on a person who is a responsible person in relation to a group licence.

(4) That notice shall include the matters set out in the notice imposing the penalty in accordance with section 39A(2)(a) and (b).]

[39C   Statement of policy in relation to civil penalties

(1) The OFT shall prepare and publish a statement of policy in relation to how it exercises, or how it proposes to exercise, its powers under section 39A.

(2) If the OFT revises the statement of policy at any time after it has been published, the OFT shall publish it as revised.

(3) No statement of policy shall be published without the approval of the Secretary of State.

(4) The statement of policy shall be published in such manner as the OFT thinks fit for the purpose of bringing it to the attention of those likely to be affected by it.

(5) In preparing or revising the statement of policy the OFT shall consult such persons as it thinks fit.

(6) In determining whether and how to exercise its powers under section 39A in relation to a person's failure, the OFT shall have regard to the statement of policy as most recently published at the time the failure occurred.

(7) The OFT shall not impose a penalty on a person under section 39A in relation to a failure occurring before it has published a statement of policy.]

40   Enforcement of agreements made by unlicensed trader

[(1) A regulated agreement is not enforceable against the debtor or hirer by a person acting in the course of a consumer credit business or a consumer hire business (as the case may be) if that person is not licensed to carry on a consumer credit business or a consumer hire business (as the case may be) of a description which covers the enforcement of the agreement.

(1A) Unless the OFT has made an order under subsection (2) which applies to the agreement, a regulated agreement is not enforceable against the debtor or hirer if—

    (a) it was made by the creditor or owner in the course of a consumer credit business or a consumer hire business (as the case may be); and

    (b) at the time the agreement was made he was not licensed to carry on a consumer credit business or a consumer hire business (as the case may be) of a description which covered the making of the agreement.

(2) Where—

    (a) during any period a person (the 'trader' has) made regulated agreements in the course of a consumer credit business or a consumer hire business (as the case may be), and

    (b) during that period he was not licensed to carry on a consumer credit business or a consumer hire business (as the case may be) of a description which covered the making of those agreements,

he or his successor in title may apply to the OFT for an order that the agreements are to be treated for the purposes of subsection (1A) as if he had been licensed as required.]

(3) Unless the [OFT] determines to make an order under subsection (2) in accordance with the application, [it] shall, before determining the application, by notice—

    (a) inform the applicant, giving [its] reasons, that, as the case may be, [it] is minded to refuse the application, or to grant it in terms different from those applied for, describing them, and

    (b) invite the applicant to submit to the [OFT] representations in support of his application in accordance with section 34.

(4) In determining whether or not to make an order under subsection (2) in respect of any period the [OFT] shall consider, in addition to any other relevant factors—

    (a) how far, if at all, debtors or hirers under [the regulated agreements in question] were prejudiced by the trader's conduct,

    (b) whether or not the [OFT] would have been likely to grant a licence covering [the making of those agreements during] that period on an application by the trader, and

    (c) the degree of culpability for the failure [to be licensed as required].

(5) If the [OFT] thinks fit, [it] may in an order under subsection (2)—

    (a) limit the order to specified agreements, or agreements of a specified description or made at a specified time;

    (b) make the order conditional on the doing of specified acts by the applicant.

[(6) This section (apart from subsection (1)) does not apply to a regulated agreement [...] made by a consumer credit EEA firm unless at the time it was made that firm was precluded from entering into it as a result of—

    (a) a consumer credit prohibition imposed under section 203 of the Financial Services and Markets Act 2000; or

    (b) a restriction imposed on the firm under section 204 of that Act.]

[(7) Subsection (1) does not apply to the enforcement of a regulated agreement by a consumer credit EEA firm unless that firm is precluded from enforcing it as a result of a prohibition or restriction mentioned in subsection (6)(a) or (b).

(8) This section (apart from subsection (1)) does not apply to a regulated agreement made by a person if by virtue of section 21(2) or (3) he was not required to be licensed to make the agreement.

(9) Subsection (1) does not apply to the enforcement of a regulated agreement by a person if by virtue of section 21(2) or (3) he is not required to be licensed to enforce the agreement.]

[Appeals]

41   Appeals to [First-tier Tribunal] under Part III

(1) If, in the case of a determination by the [OFT] such as is mentioned in column 1 of the table set out at the end of this section, a person mentioned in relation to that determination in column 2 of the table is aggrieved by the determination he may, within the [specified period, appeal to the First-tier Tribunal].

Determination	Appellant
Refusal to issue, renew or vary licence in accordance with terms of application.	The applicant.
Exclusion of person from group licence.	The person excluded.
[...]	
Compulsory variation, or suspension or revocation, of standard licence.	The licensee.
Compulsory variation, or suspension or revocation, of group licence.	The original applicant or any licensee.
Refusal to end suspension of licence in accordance with terms of application.	The applicant.
[Determination— (a) to impose a requirement under section 33A or 33B; (b) to refuse an application under section 33C(5) in relation to a requirement imposed under either of those sections; or (c) to vary or revoke a requirement so imposed.	A person who falls within section 33C(6) or (7) in relation to the requirement unless the OFT was not required to give a notice to him in relation to the determination by virtue of section 33D(4).]
[Imposition of penalty under section 39A	The person on whom the penalty is imposed.]
Refusal to make order under section 40(2)[, 148(2) or 149(2)] in accordance with terms of application.	The applicant.
[Imposition of, or refusal to withdraw, consumer credit prohibition under section 203 of the Financial Services and Markers Act 2000.	The consumer credit EEA firm concerned.]
[Imposition of, or refusal to withdraw, a restriction under section 204 of the Financial Services and Markets Act 2000.	The consumer credit EEA firm concerned.]

[41ZA   Tribunal Procedure Rules: suspension of OFT determinations

In the case of appeals to the First-tier Tribunal under section 41, Tribunal Procedure Rules may make provision for the suspension of determinations of the OFT.]

[41ZB   Disposal of appeals

(1) The First-tier Tribunal shall decide an appeal under section 41 by way of a rehearing of the determination appealed against.

(2) In disposing of an appeal under section 41 the First-tier Tribunal may do one or more of the following—

    (a) confirm the determination appealed against;

    (b) quash that determination;

    (c) vary that determination;

    (d) remit the matter to the OFT for reconsideration and determination in accordance with the directions (if any) given to it by the tribunal;

    (e) give the OFT directions for the purpose of giving effect to its decision.

(3) In the case of an appeal under section 41 against a determination to impose a penalty, the First-tier Tribunal—

    (a) has no power by virtue of subsection (2)(c) to increase the penalty;

    (b) may extend the period within which the penalty is to be paid (including in cases where that period has already ended).

(4) Subsection (3) does not affect—

    (a) the tribunal's power to give directions to the OFT under subsection (2)(d); or

    (b) what the OFT can do where a matter is remitted to it under subsection (2)(d).

(5) Where the First-tier Tribunal remits a matter to the OFT, it may direct that the requirements of section 34 of this Act are not to apply, or are only to apply to a specified extent, in relation to the OFT's reconsideration of the matter.

(6) Subject to subsections (7) and (8), where the First-tier Tribunal remits an application to the OFT, section 6(1) and (3) to (9) of this Act shall apply as if the application had not been previously determined by the OFT.

(7) In the case of a general notice which came into effect after the determination appealed against was made but before the application was remitted, the applicant shall provide any information or document which he is required to provide under section 6(6) within—

    (a) the period of 28 days beginning with the day on which the application was remitted; or

    (b) such longer period as the OFT may allow.

(8) In the case of—

    (a) any information or document which was superseded,

    (b) any change in circumstances which occurred, or

    (c) any error or omission of which the applicant became aware,

after the determination appealed against was made but before the application was remitted, any notification that is required to be given by the applicant under section 6(7) shall be given within the period of 28 days beginning with the day on which the application was remitted.]

PART IV SEEKING BUSINESS

Advertising

43   Advertisements to which Part IV applies

(1) This Part applies to any advertisement, published for the purposes of a business carried on by the advertiser, indicating that he is willing—

    (a) to provide credit, or

    (b) to enter into an agreement for the bailment or (in Scotland) the hiring of goods by him.

(2) An advertisement does not fall within subsection (1) if the advertiser does not carry on—

    (a) a consumer credit business or consumer hire business, or

    (b) a business in the course of which he provides credit to individuals secured on land, or

    (c) a business which comprises or relates to unregulated agreements where—

        (i) the law applicable to the agreement is the law of a country outside the United Kingdom, and

        (ii) if the law applicable to the agreement were the law of a part of the United Kingdom it would be a regulated agreement.

(3) An advertisement does not fall within subsection (1)(a) if it indicates—

(b) that the credit is available only to a body corporate.

[(3A) An advertisement does not fall within subsection (1)(a) in so far as it is a communication of an invitation or inducement to engage in investment activity within the meaning of section 21 of the Financial Services and Markets Act 2000, other than an exempt generic communication.

(3B) An 'exempt generic communication' is a communication to which subsection (1) of section 21 of the Financial Services and Markets Act 2000 does not apply, as a result of an order under subsection (5) of that section, because it does not identify a person as providing an investment or as carrying on an activity to which the communication relates.]

(4) An advertisement does not fall within subsection (1)(b) if it indicates that the advertiser is not willing to enter into a consumer hire agreement.

(5) The Secretary of State may by order provide that this Part shall not apply to other advertisements of a description specified in the order.

44   Form and content of advertisements

(1) The Secretary of State shall make regulations as to the form and content of advertisements to which this Part applies, and the regulations shall contain such provisions as appear to him appropriate with a view to ensuring that, having regard to its subject-matter and the amount of detail included in it, an advertisement conveys a fair and reasonably comprehensive indication of the nature of the credit or hire facilities offered by the advertiser and of their true cost to persons using them.

(2) Regulations under subsection (1) may in particular—

(a) require specified information to be included in the prescribed manner in advertisements, and other specified material to be excluded;

(b) contain requirements to ensure that specified information is clearly brought to the attention of persons to whom advertisements are directed, and that one part of an advertisement is not given insufficient or excessive prominence compared with another.

45   Prohibition of advertisement where goods etc. not sold for cash

If an advertisement to which this Part applies indicates that the advertiser is willing to provide credit under a restricted-use credit agreement relating to goods or services to be supplied by any person, but at the time when the advertisement is published that person is not holding himself out as prepared to sell the goods or provide the services (as the case may be) for cash, the advertiser commits an offence.

47   Advertising infringements

(1) Where an advertiser commits an offence against regulations made under section 44 or against section 45 [. . .] or would be taken to commit such an offence but for the defence provided by section 168, a like offence is committed by—

(a) the publisher of the advertisement, and

(b) any person who, in the course of a business carried on by him, devised the advertisement, or a part of it relevant to the first-mentioned offence, and

(c) where the advertiser did not procure the publication of the advertisement, the person who did procure it.

(2) In proceedings for an offence under subsection (1)(a) it is a defence for the person charged to prove that—

(a) the advertisement was published in the course of a business carried on by him, and

(b) he received the advertisement in the course of that business, and did not know and had no reason to suspect that its publication would be an offence under this Part.

Canvassing, etc.

48   Definition of canvassing off trade premises (regulated agreements)

(1) An individual (the 'canvasser') canvasses a regulated agreement off trade premises if he solicits the entry (as debtor or hirer) of another individual (the 'consumer') into the agreement by making

oral representations to the consumer, or any other individual, during a visit by the canvasser to any place (not excluded by subsection (2)) where the consumer, or that other individual, as the case may be, is, being a visit—

    (a) carried out for the purpose of making such oral representations to individuals who are at that place, but

    (b) not carried out in response to a request made on a previous occasion.

  (2) A place is excluded from subsection (1) if it is a place where a business is carried on (whether on a permanent or temporary basis) by—

    (a) the creditor or owner, or

    (b) a supplier, or

    (c) the canvasser, or the person whose employee or agent the canvasser is, or

    (d) the consumer.

49 Prohibition of canvassing debtor-creditor agreements off trade premises

  (1) It is an offence to canvass debtor-creditor agreements off trade premises.

  (2) It is also an offence to solicit the entry of an individual (as debtor) into a debtor-creditor agreement during a visit carried out in response to a request made on a previous occasion, where—

    (a) the request was not in writing signed by or on behalf of the person making it, and

    (b) if no request for the visit had been made, the soliciting would have constituted the canvassing of a debtor-creditor agreement off trade premises.

  (3) Subsections (1) and (2) do not apply to any soliciting for an agreement enabling the debtor to overdraw on a current account of any description kept with the creditor, where—

    (a) the [OFT] has determined that current accounts of that description kept with the creditor are excluded from subsections (1) and (2), and

    (b) the debtor already keeps an account with the creditor (whether a current account or not).

  (4) A determination under subsection (3)(a)—

    (a) may be made subject to such conditions as the [OFT] thinks fit, and

    (b) shall be made only where the [OFT] is of opinion that it is not against the interests of debtors.

  (5) If soliciting is done in breach of a condition imposed under subsection (4)(a), the determination under subsection (3)(a) does not apply to it.

50 Circulars to minors

  (1) A person commits an offence who, with a view to financial gain, sends to a minor any document inviting him to—

    (a) borrow money, or

    (b) obtain goods on credit or hire, or

    (c) obtain services on credit, or

    (d) apply for information or advice on borrowing money or otherwise obtaining credit, or hiring goods.

  (2) In proceedings under subsection (1) in respect of the sending of a document to a minor, it is a defence for the person charged to prove that he did not know, and had no reasonable cause to suspect, that he was a minor.

  (3) Where a document is received by a minor at any school or other educational establishment for minors, a person sending it to him at that establishment knowing or suspecting it to be such an establishment shall be taken to have reasonable cause to suspect that he is a minor.

51 Prohibition of unsolicited credit-tokens

  (1) It is an offence to give a person a credit-token if he has not asked for it.

  (2) To comply with subsection (1) a request must be contained in a document signed by the person making the request, unless the credit-token agreement is a small debtor-creditor-supplier agreement.

  (3) Subsection (1) does not apply to the giving of a credit-token to a person—

    (a) for use under a credit-token agreement already made, or

(b) in renewal or replacement of a credit-token previously accepted by him under a credit-token agreement which continues in force, whether or not varied.

[51A   Restrictions on provision of credit card cheques

(1) A person who provides credit card cheques otherwise than in accordance with this section commits an offence.

(2) Credit card cheques may be provided only to a person who has asked for them.

(3) They may be provided only on a single occasion in respect of each request that is made.

(4) The number of cheques provided in respect of a request must not exceed three (or, if less, the number requested).

(5) Where a single request is made for the provision of credit card cheques in connection with more than one credit-token agreement, subsections (3) and (4) apply as if a separate request had been made in relation to each agreement.

(6) Where more than one request for the provision of cheques is made in the same document or at the same time—

(a) they may be provided in respect of only one of the requests, but

(b) if the requests relate to more than one credit-token agreement, in relation to each agreement they may be provided only in respect of one of the requests made in relation to that agreement.

(7) "Credit card cheque" means a cheque (whether or not drawn on a banker) which, whenever used, will result in the provision of credit under a credit-token agreement.

(8) Accordingly, "credit card cheque" does not include a cheque to be used only in connection with a current account.]

[51B   Section 51A: exemption for business

(1) Section 51A does not apply to credit card cheques provided in connection with a credit-token agreement that is entered into by the debtor wholly or predominantly for the purposes of a business carried on, or intended to be carried on, by the debtor.

(2) If a credit-token agreement includes a declaration made by the debtor to the effect that the agreement is entered into as mentioned in subsection (1), the agreement is treated for the purposes of that subsection as having been so entered into.

(3) Subsection (2) does not apply if, when the agreement is entered into—

(a) the creditor, or

(b) any person who has acted on behalf of the creditor in connection with the entering into of the agreement,

knows, or has reasonable cause to suspect, that the agreement is not entered into as mentioned in subsection (1).

(4) The Secretary of State may by order make provision about the form, content and signing of declarations for the purposes of subsection (2).

(5) Where an agreement has two or more creditors, references in subsection (3) to the creditor are to any one or more of them.]

Miscellaneous

52   Quotations

(1) Regulations may be made—

(a) as to the form and content of any document (a 'quotation') by which a person who carries on a consumer credit business or consumer hire business, or a business in the course of which he provides credit to individuals secured on land, gives prospective customers information about the terms on which he is prepared to do business;

(b) requiring a person carrying on such a business to provide quotations to such persons and in such circumstances as are prescribed.

(2) Regulations under subsection (1)(a) may in particular contain provisions relating to quotations such as are set out in relation to advertisements in section 44.

[(3) In this section, 'quotation' does not include—

    (a) any document which is a communication of an invitation or inducement to engage in investment activity within the meaning of section 21 of the Financial Services and Markets Act 2000; or

    (b) any document (other than one falling within paragraph (a)) provided by an authorised person (within the meaning of that Act) in connection with an agreement which would or might be an exempt agreement as a result of section 16(6C).]

53 Duty to display information

Regulations may require a person who carries on a consumer credit business or consumer hire business, or a business in the course of which he provides credit to individuals secured on land [(other than credit provided under an agreement which is an exempt agreement as a result of section 16(6C)(a)], to display in the prescribed manner, at any premises where the business is carried on to which the public have access, prescribed information about the business.

54 Conduct of business regulations

Without prejudice to the generality of section 26, regulations under that section may include provisions further regulating the seeking of business by [a person to whom the regulations apply] who carries on a consumer credit business or a consumer hire business.

PART V ENTRY INTO CREDIT OR HIRE AGREEMENTS

Preliminary matters

55 Disclosure of information

(1) Regulations may require specified information to be disclosed in the prescribed manner to the debtor or hirer before a regulated agreement is made.

[(2) If regulations under subsection (1) are not complied with, the agreement is enforceable against the debtor or hirer on an order of the court only (and for these purposes a retaking of goods or land to which the agreement relates is an enforcement of the agreement).]

[55A Pre-contractual explanations etc

(1) Before a regulated consumer credit agreement, other than an excluded agreement, is made, the creditor must—

    (a) provide the debtor with an adequate explanation of the matters referred to in subsection (2) in order to place him in a position enabling him to assess whether the agreement is adapted to his needs and his financial situation,

    (b) advise the debtor—

        (i) to consider the information which is required to be disclosed under section 55(1), and

        (ii) where this information is disclosed in person to the debtor, that the debtor is able to take it away,

    (c) provide the debtor with an opportunity to ask questions about the agreement, and

    (d) advise the debtor how to ask the creditor for further information and explanation.

(2) The matters referred to in subsection (1)(a) are—

    (a) the features of the agreement which may make the credit to be provided under the agreement unsuitable for particular types of use,

    (b) how much the debtor will have to pay periodically and, where the amount can be determined, in total under the agreement,

    (c) the features of the agreement which may operate in a manner which would have a significant adverse effect on the debtor in a way which the debtor is unlikely to foresee,

    (d) the principal consequences for the debtor arising from a failure to make payments under the agreement at the times required by the agreement including legal proceedings and, where this is a possibility, repossession of the debtor's home, and

(e) the effect of the exercise of any right to withdraw from the agreement and how and when this right may be exercised.

(3) The advice and explanation may be given orally or in writing except as provided in subsection (4).

(4) Where the explanation of the matters specified in paragraphs (a), (b) or (e) of subsection (2) is given orally or in person to a debtor, the explanation of the other matters specified in that paragraph, and the advice required to be given by subsection (1)(b), must be given orally to him.

(5) Subsections (1) to (4) do not apply to a creditor if a credit intermediary (see section 160A) has complied with those subsections in respect of the agreement.

(6) For the purposes of this section an agreement is an excluded agreement if it is—

(a) an agreement under which the creditor provides the debtor with credit which exceeds £60, 260, or

(b) an agreement secured on land.

(7) Where the regulated consumer credit agreement is an agreement under which a person takes an article in pawn—

(a) the obligation in subsection (1)(a) only relates to the matters listed in paragraphs (d) and (e) of subsection (2), and

(b) the obligations in subsection (1)(b) and (d) do not apply.]

[55B   Assessment of creditworthiness

(1) Before making a regulated consumer credit agreement, other than an excluded agreement, the creditor must undertake an assessment of the creditworthiness of the debtor.

(2) Before significantly increasing—

(a) the amount of credit to be provided under a regulated consumer credit agreement, other than an excluded agreement, or

(b) a credit limit for running-account credit under a regulated consumer credit agreement, other than an excluded agreement,

the creditor must undertake an assessment of the debtor's creditworthiness.

(3) A creditworthiness assessment must be based on sufficient information obtained from—

(a) the debtor, where appropriate, and

(b) a credit reference agency, where necessary.

(4) For the purposes of this section an agreement is an excluded agreement if it is—

(a) an agreement secured on land, or

(b) an agreement under which a person takes an article in pawn.]

[55C   Copy of draft consumer credit agreement

(1) Before a regulated consumer credit agreement, other than an excluded agreement, is made, the creditor must, if requested, give to the debtor without delay a copy of the prospective agreement (or such of its terms as have at that time been reduced to writing).

(2) Subsection (1) does not apply if at the time the request is made, the creditor is unwilling to proceed with the agreement.

(3) A breach of the duty imposed by subsection (1) is actionable as a breach of statutory duty.

(4) For the purposes of this section an agreement is an excluded agreement if it is—

(a) an agreement secured on land,

(b) an agreement under which a person takes an article in pawn,

(c) an agreement under which the creditor provides the debtor with credit which exceeds £60, 260, or

(d) an agreement entered into by the debtor wholly or predominantly for the purposes of a business carried on, or intended to be carried on, by him.

(5) Subsections (2) to (5) of section 16B (declaration by the debtor as to the purposes of the agreement) apply for the purposes of subsection (4)(d).]

56 Antecedent negotiations

(1) In this Act 'antecedent negotiations' means any negotiations with the debtor or hirer—

    (a) conducted by the creditor or owner in relation to the making of any regulated agreement, or

    (b) conducted by a credit-broker in relation to goods sold or proposed to be sold by the credit-broker to the creditor before forming the subject-matter of a debtor-creditor-supplier agreement within section 12(a), or

    (c) conducted by the supplier in relation to a transaction financed or proposed to be financed by a debtor-creditor-supplier agreement within section 12(b) or (c), and 'negotiator' means the person by whom negotiations are so conducted with the debtor or hirer.

(2) Negotiations with the debtor in a case falling within subsection (1)(b) or (c) shall be deemed to be conducted by the negotiator in the capacity of agent of the creditor as well as in his actual capacity.

(3) An agreement is void if, and to the extent that, it purports in relation to an actual or prospective regulated agreement—

    (a) to provide that a person acting as, or on behalf of, a negotiator is to be treated as the agent of the debtor or hirer, or

    (b) to relieve a person from liability for acts or omissions of any person acting as, or on behalf of, a negotiator.

(4) For the purposes of this Act, antecedent negotiations shall be taken to begin when the negotiator and the debtor or hirer first enter into communication (including communication by advertisement), and to include any representations made by the negotiator to the debtor or hirer and any other dealings between them.

57 Withdrawal from prospective agreement

(1) The withdrawal of a party from a prospective regulated agreement shall operate to apply this Part to the agreement, any linked transaction and any other thing done in anticipation of the making of the agreement as it would apply if the agreement were made and then cancelled under section 69.

(2) The giving to a party of a written or oral notice which, however expressed, indicates the intention of the other party to withdraw from a prospective regulated agreement operates as a withdrawal from it.

(3) Each of the following shall be deemed to be the agent of the creditor or owner for the purpose of receiving a notice under subsection (2)—

    (a) a credit-broker or supplier who is the negotiator in antecedent negotiations,

    (b) any person who, in the course of a business carried on by him, acts on behalf of the debtor or hirer in any negotiations for the agreement.

(4) Where the agreement, if made, would not be a cancellable agreement, subsection (1) shall nevertheless apply as if the contrary were the case.

58 Opportunity for withdrawal from prospective land mortgage

(1) Before sending to the debtor or hirer, for his signature, an unexecuted agreement in a case where the prospective regulated agreement is to be secured on land (the 'mortgaged land'), the creditor or owner shall give the debtor or hirer a copy of the unexecuted agreement which contains a notice in the prescribed form indicating the right of the debtor or hirer to withdraw from the prospective agreement, and how and when the right is exercisable, together with a copy of any other document referred to in the unexecuted agreement.

(2) Subsection (1) does not apply to—

    (a) a restricted-use credit agreement to finance the purchase of the mortgaged land, or

    (b) an agreement for a bridging loan in connection with the purchase of the mortgaged land or other land.

59 Agreement to enter future agreement void

(1) An agreement is void if, and to the extent that, it purports to bind a person to enter as debtor or hirer into a prospective regulated agreement.

(2) Regulations may exclude from the operation of subsection (1) agreements such as are described in the regulations.

Making the agreement

60　Form and content of agreements

(1) The Secretary of State shall make regulations as to the form and content of documents embodying regulated agreements, and the regulations shall contain such provisions as appear to him appropriate with a view to ensuring that the debtor or hirer is made aware of—

    (a) the rights and duties conferred or imposed on him by the agreement,

    (b) the amount and rate of the total charge for credit (in the case of a consumer credit agreement),

    (c) the protection and remedies available to him under this Act, and

    (d) any other matters which, in the opinion of the Secretary of State, it is desirable for him to know about in connection with the agreement.

(2) Regulations under subsection (1) may in particular—

    (a) require specified information to be included in the prescribed manner in documents, and other specified material to be excluded;

    (b) contain requirements to ensure that specified information is clearly brought to the attention of the debtor or hirer, and that one part of a document is not given insufficient or excessive prominence compared with another.

(3) If, on an application made to the [OFT] by a person carrying on a consumer credit business or a consumer hire business, it appears to the [OFT] impracticable for the applicant to comply with any requirement of regulations under subsection (1) in a particular case, [it] may, by notice to the applicant direct that the requirement be waived or varied in relation to such agreements, and subject to such conditions (if any), as [it] may specify, and this Act and the regulations shall have effect accordingly.

(4) The [OFT] shall give a notice under subsection (3) only if [it] is satisfied that to do so would not prejudice the interests of debtors or hirers'.

[(5) An application may be made under subsection (3) only if it relates to—

    (a) a consumer credit agreement secured on land,

    (b) a consumer credit agreement under which a person takes an article in pawn,

    (c) a consumer credit agreement under which the creditor provides the debtor with credit which exceeds £60,260,

    (d) a consumer credit agreement entered into by the debtor wholly or predominantly for the purposes of a business carried on, or intended to be carried on, by him, or

    (e) a consumer hire agreement.

(6) Subsections (2) to (5) of section 16B (declaration by the debtor as to the purposes of the agreement) apply for the purposes of subsection (5)(d).]

61　Signing of agreement

(1) A regulated agreement is not properly executed unless—

    (a) a document in the prescribed form itself containing all the prescribed terms and conforming to regulations under section 60(1) is signed in the prescribed manner both by the debtor or hirer and by or on behalf of the creditor or owner, and

    (b) the document embodies all the terms of the agreement, other than implied terms, and

    (c) the document is, when presented or sent to the debtor or hirer for signature, in such a state that all its terms are readily legible.

(2) In addition, where the agreement is one to which section 58(1) applies, it is not properly executed unless—

    (a) the requirements of section 58(1) were complied with, and

    (b) the unexecuted agreement was sent, for his signature, to the debtor or hirer by an appropriate method not less than seven days after a copy of it was given to him under section 58(1), and

(c) during the consideration period, the creditor or owner refrained from approaching the debtor or hirer (whether in person, by telephone or letter, or in any other way) except in response to a specific request made by the debtor or hirer after the beginning of the consideration period, and

(d) no notice of withdrawal by the debtor or hirer was received by the creditor or owner before the sending of the unexecuted agreement.

(3) In subsection (2)(c), 'the consideration period' means the period beginning with the giving of the copy under section 58(1) and ending—

(a) at the expiry of seven days after the day on which the unexecuted agreement is sent, for his signature, to the debtor or hirer, or

(b) on its return by the debtor or hirer after signature by him, whichever first occurs.

(4) Where the debtor or hirer is a partnership or an unincorporated body of persons, subsection (1)(a) shall apply with the substitution for 'by the debtor or hirer' of 'by or on behalf of the debtor or hirer's'.

[61A   Duty to supply copy of executed consumer credit agreement

(1) Where a regulated consumer credit agreement, other than an excluded agreement, has been made, the creditor must give a copy of the executed agreement, and any other document referred to in it, to the debtor.

(2) Subsection (1) does not apply if—

(a) a copy of the unexecuted agreement (and of any other document referred to in it) has already been given to the debtor, and

(b) the unexecuted agreement is in identical terms to the executed agreement.

(3) In a case referred to in subsection (2), the creditor must inform the debtor in writing—

(a) that the agreement has been executed,

(b) that the executed agreement is in identical terms to the unexecuted agreement a copy of which has already been given to the debtor, and

(c) that the debtor has the right to receive a copy of the executed agreement if the debtor makes a request for it at any time before the end of the period referred to in section 66A(2).

(4) Where a request is made under subsection (3)(c) the creditor must give a copy of the executed agreement to the debtor without delay.

(5) If the requirements of this section are not observed, the agreement is not properly executed.

(6) For the purposes of this section, an agreement is an excluded agreement if it is—

(a) a cancellable agreement, or

(b) an agreement—

(i)   secured on land,

(ii) under which the creditor provides the debtor with credit which exceeds £60,260, or

(iii) entered into by the debtor wholly or predominantly for the purposes of a business carried on, or intended to be carried on, by him,

unless the creditor or a credit intermediary has complied with or purported to comply with regulation 3(2) of the Consumer Credit (Disclosure of Information) Regulations 2010.

(7) Subsections (2) to (5) of section 16B (declaration by the debtor as to the purposes of the agreement) apply for the purposes of subsection (6)(b)(iii).]

[61B   Duty to supply copy of overdraft agreement

(1) Where an authorised business overdraft agreement or an authorised non-business overdraft agreement has been made, a document containing the terms of the agreement must be given to the debtor.

(2) The creditor must provide the document referred to in subsection (1) to the debtor before or at the time the agreement is made unless—

(a) the creditor has provided the debtor with the information referred to in regulation 10(3) of the Consumer Credit (Disclosure of Information) Regulations 2010, in which case it must be provided after the agreement is made,

(b) the creditor has provided the debtor with the information referred to in regulation 10(3)(c), (e), (f), (h) and (k) of those Regulations, in which case it must be provided immediately after the agreement is made, or

(c) the agreement is an agreement of a description referred to in regulation 10(4)(b) of those Regulations, in which case it must be provided immediately after the agreement is made.

(3) If the requirements of this section are not observed, the agreement is enforceable against the debtor on an order of the court only (and for these purposes a retaking of goods or land to which the agreement relates is an enforcement of the agreement).]

62   Duty to supply copy of unexecuted agreement[: excluded agreements]

(1) If [in the case of a regulated agreement which is an excluded agreement] the unexecuted agreement is presented personally to the debtor or hirer for his signature, but on the occasion when he signs it the document does not become an executed agreement, a copy of it, and of any other document referred to in it, must be there and then delivered to him.

(2) If the unexecuted agreement is sent to the debtor or hirer for his signature, a copy of it, and of any other document referred to in it, must be sent to him at the same time.

(3) A regulated agreement [which is an excluded agreement] is not properly executed if the requirements of this section are not observed.

[(4) In this section, "excluded agreement" has the same meaning as in section 61A.]

63   Duty to supply copy of executed agreement[: excluded agreements]

(1) If [in the case of a regulated agreement which is an excluded agreement] the unexecuted agreement is presented personally to the debtor or hirer for his signature, and on the occasion when he signs it the document becomes an executed agreement, a copy of the executed agreement, and of any other document referred to in it, must be there and then delivered to him.

(2) A copy of the executed agreement, and of any other document referred to in it, must be given to the debtor or hirer within the seven days following the making of the agreement unless—

(a) subsection (1) applies, or

(b) the unexecuted agreement was sent to the debtor or hirer for his signature and, on the occasion of his signing it, the document became an executed agreement.

(3) In the case of a cancellable agreement, a copy under subsection (2) must be sent by an appropriate method.

(4) In the case of a credit-token agreement, a copy under subsection (2) need not be given within the seven days following the making of the agreement if it is given before or at the time when the credit-token is given to the debtor.

(5) A regulated agreement [which is an excluded agreement] is not properly executed if the requirements of this section are not observed.

[(6) In this section, "excluded agreement" has the same meaning as in section 61A.]

64   Duty to give notice of cancellation rights

(1) In the case of a cancellable agreement, a notice in the prescribed form indicating the right of the debtor or hirer to cancel the agreement, how and when that right is exercisable, and the name and address of a person to whom notice of cancellation may be given,—

(a) must be included in every copy given to the debtor or hirer under section 62 or 63, and

(b) except where section 63(2) applied, must also be sent [by an appropriate method] to the debtor or hirer within the seven days following the making of the agreement.

(2) In the case of a credit-token agreement, a notice under subsection (1)(b) need not be sent [by an appropriate method] within the seven days following the making of the agreement if either—

(a) it is sent [by an appropriate method] to the debtor or hirer before the credit-token is given
to him, or

(b) it is sent [by an appropriate method] to him together with the credit-token.

(3) Regulations may provide that except where section 63(2) applied a notice sent under subsection (1)(b) shall be accompanied by a further copy of the executed agreement, and of any other
document referred to in it.

(4) Regulations may provide that subsection (1)(b) is not to apply in the case of agreements such
as are described in the regulations, being agreements made by a particular person, if—

(a) on an application by that person to the [OFT], the [OFT] has determined that, having
regard to—

(i)   the manner in which antecedent negotiations for agreements with the applicant of
that description are conducted, and

(ii)   the information provided to debtors or hirers before such agreements are made, the
requirement imposed by subsection (1)(b) can be dispensed with without prejudicing the interests of debtors or hirers, and

(b) any conditions imposed by the [OFT] in making the determination are complied with.

(5) A cancellable agreement is not properly executed if the requirements of this section are not
observed.

65   Consequences of improper execution

(1) An improperly-executed regulated agreement is enforceable against the debtor or hirer on
an order of the court only.

(2) A retaking of goods or land to which a regulated agreement relates is an enforcement of the
agreement.

66   Acceptance of credit-tokens

(1) The debtor shall not be liable under a credit-token agreement for use made of the credit-
token by any person unless the debtor had previously accepted the credit-token, or the use constituted
an acceptance of it by him.

(2) The debtor accepts a credit-token when—

(a) it is signed, or

(b) a receipt for it is signed, or

(c) it is first used, either by the debtor himself or by a person who, pursuant to the agreement,
is authorised by him to use it.

[Withdrawal from certain agreements]

[66A   Withdrawal from consumer credit agreement

(1) The debtor under a regulated consumer credit agreement, other than an excluded agreement, may withdraw from the agreement, without giving any reason, in accordance with this
section.

(2) To withdraw from an agreement under this section the debtor must give oral or written
notice of the withdrawal to the creditor before the end of the period of 14 days beginning with the
relevant day.

(3) For the purposes of subsection (2) the relevant day is whichever is the latest of the
following—

(a) the day on which the agreement is made;

(b) where the creditor is required to inform the debtor of the credit limit under the agreement, the day on which the creditor first does so;

(c) in the case of an agreement to which section 61A (duty to supply copy of executed consumer credit agreement) applies, the day on which the debtor receives a copy of the agreement under that section or on which the debtor is informed as specified in subsection (3)
of that section;

(d) in the case of an agreement to which section 63 (duty to supply copy of executed agreement: excluded agreements) applies, the day on which the debtor receives a copy of the agreement under that section.

(4) Where oral notice under this section is given to the creditor it must be given in a manner specified in the agreement.

(5) Where written notice under this section is given by facsimile transmission or electronically—

(a) it must be sent to the number or electronic address specified for the purpose in the agreement, and

(b) where it is so sent, it is to be regarded as having been received by the creditor at the time it is sent (and section 176A does not apply).

(6) Where written notice under this section is given in any other form—

(a) it must be sent by post to, or left at, the postal address specified for the purpose in the agreement, and

(b) where it is sent by post to that address, it is to be regarded as having been received by the creditor at the time of posting (and section 176 does not apply).

(7) Subject as follows, where the debtor withdraws from a regulated consumer credit agreement under this section—

(a) the agreement shall be treated as if it had never been entered into, and

(b) where an ancillary service relating to the agreement is or is to be provided by the creditor, or by a third party on the basis of an agreement between the third party and the creditor, the ancillary service contract shall be treated as if it had never been entered into.

(8) In the case referred to in subsection (7)(b) the creditor must without delay notify any third party of the fact that the debtor has withdrawn from the agreement.

(9) Where the debtor withdraws from an agreement under this section—

(a) the debtor must repay to the creditor any credit provided and the interest accrued on it (at the rate provided for under the agreement), but

(b) the debtor is not liable to pay to the creditor any compensation, fees or charges except any non-returnable charges paid by the creditor to a public administrative body.

(10) An amount payable under subsection (9) must be paid without undue delay and no later than the end of the period of 30 days beginning with the day after the day on which the notice of withdrawal was given (and if not paid by the end of that period may be recovered by the creditor as a debt).

(11) Where a regulated consumer credit agreement is a conditional sale, hire-purchase or credit-sale agreement and—

(a) the debtor withdraws from the agreement under this section after the credit has been provided, and

(b) the sum payable under subsection (9)(a) is paid in full by the debtor,

title to the goods purchased or supplied under the agreement is to pass to the debtor on the same terms as would have applied had the debtor not withdrawn from the agreement.

(12) In subsections (2), (4), (5), (6) and (9)(a) references to the creditor include a person specified by the creditor in the agreement.

(13) In subsection (7)(b) the reference to an ancillary service means a service that relates to the provision of credit under the agreement and includes in particular an insurance or payment protection policy.

(14) For the purposes of this section, an agreement is an excluded agreement if it is—

(a) an agreement for credit exceeding £60, 260,

(b) an agreement secured on land,

(c) a restricted-use credit agreement to finance the purchase of land, or

(d) an agreement for a bridging loan in connection with the purchase of land.]

Cancellation of certain agreements within cooling-off period

67 Cancellable agreements

[(1) Subject to subsection (2)] A regulated agreement may be cancelled by the debtor or hirer in accordance with this Part if the antecedent negotiations included oral representations made when in the presence of the debtor or hirer by an individual acting as, or on behalf of, the negotiator, unless—

(a) the agreement is secured on land, or is a restricted-use credit agreement to finance the purchase of land or is an agreement for a bridging loan in connection with the purchase of land, or

(b) the unexecuted agreement is signed by the debtor or hirer at premises at which any of the following is carrying on any business (whether on a permanent or temporary basis)—

(i)   the creditor or owner;

(ii) any party to a linked transaction (other than the debtor or hirer or a relative of his);

(iii) the negotiator in any antecedent negotiations.

[(2) This section does not apply where section 66A applies.]

68 Cooling-off period

The debtor or hirer may serve notice of cancellation of a cancellable agreement between his signing of the unexecuted agreement and—

(a) the end of the fifth day following the day on which he received a copy under section 63(2) or a notice under section 64(1)(b), or

(b) if (by virtue of regulations made under section 64(4) section 64(1)(b) does not apply, the end of the fourteenth day following the day on which he signed the unexecuted agreement.

69 Notice of cancellation

(1) If within the period specified in section 68 the debtor or hirer under a cancellable agreement serves on—

(a) the creditor or owner, or

(b) the person specified in the notice under section 64(1), or

(c) a person who (whether by virtue of subsection (6) or otherwise) is the agent of the creditor or owner, a notice (a 'notice of cancellation') which, however expressed and whether or not conforming to the notice given under section 64(1), indicates the intention of the debtor or hirer to withdraw from the agreement, the notice shall operate—

(i)   to cancel the agreement, and any linked transaction, and

(ii) to withdraw any offer by the debtor or hirer, or his relative, to enter into a linked transaction.

(2) In the case of a debtor-creditor-supplier agreement for restricted-use credit financing—

(a) the doing of work or supply of goods to meet an emergency, or

(b) the supply of goods which, before service of the notice of cancellation, had by the act of the debtor or his relative become incorporated in any land or thing not comprised in the agreement or any linked transaction,

subsection (1) shall apply with the substitution of the following for paragraph (i)—

'(i) to cancel only such provisions of the agreement and any linked transaction as—

(aa) relate to the provision of credit, or

(bb) require the debtor to pay an item in the total charge for credit, or

(cc) subject the debtor to any obligation other than to pay for the doing of the said work, or the supply of the said goods'.

(3) Except so far as is otherwise provided, references in this Act to the cancellation of an agreement or transaction do not include a case within subsection (2).

(4) Except as otherwise provided by or under this Act, an agreement or transaction cancelled under subsection (1) shall be treated as if it had never been entered into.

(5) Regulations may exclude linked transactions of the prescribed description from subsection (1)(i) or (ii).

(6) Each of the following shall be deemed to be the agent of the creditor or owner for the purpose of receiving a notice of cancellation—

    (a) a credit-broker or supplier who is the negotiator in antecedent negotiations,

    (b) any person who, in the course of a business carried on by him, acts on behalf of the debtor or hirer in any negotiations for the agreement.

[(7) Whether or not it is actually received by him, a notice of cancellation sent to a person shall be deemed to be served on him—

    (a) in the case of a notice sent by post, at the time of posting, and

    (b) in the case of a notice transmitted in the form of an electronic communication in accordance with section 176A(1), at the time of the transmission.]

70   Cancellation: recovery of money paid by debtor or hirer

(1) On the cancellation of a regulated agreement, and of any linked transaction,—

    (a) any sum paid by the debtor or hirer, or his relative, under or in contemplation of the agreement or transaction, including any item in the total charge for credit, shall become repayable, and

    (b) any sum, including any item in the total charge for credit, which but for the cancellation is, or would or might become, payable by the debtor or hirer, or his relative, under the agreement or transaction shall cease to be, or shall not become, so payable, and

    (c) in the case of a debtor-creditor-supplier agreement falling within section 12(b), any sum paid on the debtor's behalf by the creditor to the supplier shall become repayable to the creditor.

(2) If, under the terms of a cancelled agreement or transaction, the debtor or hirer, or his relative, is in possession of any goods, he shall have a lien on them for any sum repayable to him under subsection (1) in respect of that agreement or transaction, or any other linked transaction.

(3) A sum repayable under subsection (1) is repayable by the person to whom it was originally paid, but in the case of a debtor-creditor-supplier agreement falling within section 12(b) the creditor and the supplier shall be under a joint and several liability to repay sums paid by the debtor, or his relative, under the agreement or under a linked transaction falling within section 19(1)(b) and accordingly, in such a case, the creditor shall be entitled, in accordance with rules of court, to have the supplier made a party to any proceedings brought against the creditor to recover any such sums.

(4) Subject to any agreement between them, the creditor shall be entitled to be indemnified by the supplier for loss suffered by the creditor in satisfying his liability under subsection (3), including costs reasonably incurred by him in defending proceedings instituted by the debtor.

(5) Subsection (1) does not apply to any sum which, if not paid by a debtor, would be payable by virtue of section 71, and applies to a sum paid or payable by a debtor for the issue of a credit-token only where the credit-token has been returned to the creditor or surrendered to a supplier.

(6) If the total charge for credit includes an item in respect of a fee or commission charged by a credit-broker, the amount repayable under subsection (1) in respect of that item shall be the excess over [£5] of the fee or commission.

(7) If the total charge for credit includes any sum payable or paid by the debtor to a credit-broker otherwise than in respect of a fee or commission charged by him, that sum shall for the purposes of subsection (6) be treated as if it were such a fee or commission.

(8) So far only as is necessary to give effect to section 69(2), this section applies to an agreement or transaction within that subsection as it applies to a cancelled agreement or transaction.

71   Cancellation: repayment of credit

(1) Notwithstanding the cancellation of a regulated consumer credit agreement, other than a debtor-creditor-supplier agreement for restricted-use credit, the agreement shall continue in force so far as it relates to repayment of credit and payment of interest.

(2) If, following the cancellation of a regulated consumer credit agreement, the debtor repays the whole or a portion of the credit—

    (a) before the expiry of one month following service of the notice of cancellation, or

    (b) in the case of a credit repayable by instalments, before the date on which the first instalment is due,

no interest shall be payable on the amount repaid.

(3) If the whole of a credit repayable by instalments is not repaid on or before the date specified in subsection (2)(b), the debtor shall not be liable to repay any of the credit except on receipt of a request in writing in the prescribed form, signed by or on behalf of the creditor, stating the amounts of the remaining instalments (recalculated by the creditor as nearly as may be in accordance with the agreement and without extending the repayment period), but excluding any sum other than principal and interest.

(4) Repayment of a credit, or payment of interest, under a cancelled agreement shall be treated as duly made if it is made to any person on whom, under section 69, a notice of cancellation could have been served, other than a person referred to in section 69(6)(b).

72 Cancellation: return of goods

(1) This section applies where any agreement or transaction relating to goods, being—

    (a) a restricted-use debtor-creditor-supplier agreement, a consumer hire agreement, or a linked transaction to which the debtor or hirer under any regulated agreement is a party, or

    (b) a linked transaction to which a relative of the debtor or hirer under any regulated agreement is a party,

is cancelled after the debtor or hirer (in a case within paragraph (a)) or the relative (in a case within paragraph (b)) has acquired possession of the goods by virtue of the agreement or transaction.

(2) In this section—

    (a) 'the possessor' means the person who has acquired possession of the goods as mentioned in subsection (1),

    (b) 'the other party' means the person from whom the possessor acquired possession, and

    (c) 'the pre-cancellation period' means the period beginning when the possessor acquired possession and ending with the cancellation.

(3) The possessor shall be treated as having been under a duty throughout the pre-cancellation period—

    (a) to retain possession of the goods, and

    (b) to take reasonable care of them.

(4) On the cancellation, the possessor shall be under a duty, subject to any lien, to restore the goods to the other party in accordance with this section, and meanwhile to retain possession of the goods and take reasonable care of them.

(5) The possessor shall not be under any duty to deliver the goods except at his own premises and in pursuance of a request in writing signed by or on behalf of the other party and served on the possessor either before, or at the time when, the goods are collected from those premises.

(6) If the possessor—

    (a) delivers the goods (whether at his own premises or elsewhere) to any person on whom, under section 69, a notice of cancellation could have been served (other than a person referred to in section 69(6)(b), or

    (b) sends the goods at his own expense to such a person, he shall be discharged from any duty to retain the goods or deliver them to any person.

(7) Where the possessor delivers the goods as mentioned in subsection (6)(a), his obligation to take care of the goods shall cease: and if he sends the goods as mentioned in subsection (6)(b), he shall be under a duty to take reasonable care to see that they are received by the other party and not damaged in transit, but in other respects his duty to take care of the goods shall cease.

(8) Where, at any time during the period of 21 days following the cancellation, the possessor receives such a request as is mentioned in subsection (5), and unreasonably refuses or unreasonably fails to comply with it, his duty to take reasonable care of the goods shall continue until he delivers or

sends the goods as mentioned in subsection (6), but if within that period he does not receive such a request his duty to take reasonable care of the goods shall cease at the end of that period.

(9) The preceding provisions of this section do not apply to—

    (a) perishable goods, or

    (b) goods which by their nature are consumed by use and which, before the cancellation, were so consumed, or

    (c) goods supplied to meet an emergency, or

    (d) goods which, before the cancellation, had become incorporated in any land or thing not comprised in the cancelled agreement or a linked transaction.

(10) Where the address of the possessor is specified in the executed agreement, references in this section to his own premises are to that address and no other.

(11) Breach of a duty imposed by this section is actionable as a breach of statutory duty.

73 Cancellation: goods given in part-exchange

(1) This section applies on the cancellation of a regulated agreement where, in antecedent negotiations, the negotiator agreed to take goods in part-exchange (the 'part-exchange goods') and those goods have been delivered to him.

(2) Unless, before the end of the period of ten days beginning with the date of cancellation, the part-exchange goods are returned to the debtor or hirer in a condition substantially as good as when they were delivered to the negotiator, the debtor or hirer shall be entitled to recover from the negotiator a sum equal to the part-exchange allowance (as defined in subsection (7)(b)).

(3) In the case of a debtor-creditor-supplier agreement within section 12(b), the negotiator and the creditor shall be under a joint and several liability to pay to the debtor a sum recoverable under subsection (2).

(4) Subject to any agreement between them, the creditor shall be entitled to be indemnified by the negotiator for loss suffered by the creditor in satisfying his liability under subsection (3), including costs reasonably incurred by him in defending proceedings instituted by the debtor.

(5) During the period of ten days beginning with the date of cancellation, the debtor or hirer, if he is in possession of goods to which the cancelled agreement relates, shall have a lien on them for—

    (a) delivery of the part-exchange goods, in a condition substantially as good as when they were delivered to the negotiator, or

    (b) a sum equal to the part-exchange allowance; and if the lien continues to the end of that period it shall thereafter subsist only as a lien for a sum equal to the part-exchange allowance.

(6) Where the debtor or hirer recovers from the negotiator or creditor, or both of them jointly, a sum equal to the part-exchange allowance, then, if the title of the debtor or hirer to the part-exchange goods has not vested in the negotiator, it shall so vest on the recovery of that sum.

(7) For the purposes of this section—

    (a) the negotiator shall be treated as having agreed to take goods in part-exchange if, in pursuance of the antecedent negotiations, he either purchased or agreed to purchase those goods or accepted or agreed to accept them as part of the consideration for the cancelled agreement, and

    (b) the part-exchange allowance shall be the sum agreed as such in the antecedent negotiations or, if no such agreement was arrived at, such sum as it would have been reasonable to allow in respect of the part-exchange goods if no notice of cancellation had been served.

(8) In an action brought against the creditor for a sum recoverable under subsection (2), he shall be entitled, in accordance with rules of court, to have the negotiator made a party to the proceedings.

Exclusion of certain agreements from Part V

74 Exclusion of certain agreements from Part V

[(1) Except as provided in subsections (1A) to (2), this Part does not apply to—

(a) a non-commercial agreement,

(b) a debtor-creditor agreement enabling the debtor to overdraw on a current account,

(c) a debtor-creditor agreement to finance the making of such payments arising on, or connected with, the death of a person as may be prescribed, or

(d) a small debtor-creditor-supplier agreement for restricted-use credit.

(1A) Section 56 (antecedent negotiations) applies to a non-commercial agreement.

(1B) Where an agreement that falls within subsection (1)(b) is an authorised business overdraft agreement the following provisions apply—

(a) section 55B (assessment of creditworthiness);

(b) section 56 (antecedent negotiations);

(c) section 60 (regulations on form and content of agreements);

(d) section 61B (duty to supply copy of overdraft agreement).

(1C) Where an agreement that falls within subsection (1)(b) is an authorised non-business overdraft agreement the following provisions apply—

(a) section 55 (regulations on disclosure of information);

(b) section 55B (assessment of creditworthiness);

(c) section 55C (copy of draft consumer credit agreement);

(d) section 56 (antecedent negotiations);

(e) section 60 (regulations on form and content of agreements);

(f) section 61B (duty to supply copy of overdraft agreement).

(1D) Where an agreement that falls within subsection (1)(b) would be an authorised non-business overdraft agreement but for the fact that the credit is not repayable on demand or within three months the following provisions apply—

(a) section 55 (regulations on disclosure of information);

(b) section 55A (adequate explanations);

(c) section 55B (credit assessment);

(d) section 55C (copy of draft consumer credit agreement);

(e) section 56 (antecedent negotiations);

(f) section 60 (regulations on form and content of agreements);

(g) section 61 (signing of agreement);

(h) section 61A (duty to supply copy of executed agreement);

(i) section 66A (withdrawal from consumer credit agreement).

(1E) In the case of an agreement that falls within subsection (1)(b) but does not fall within subsection (1B), (1C) or (1D), section 56 (antecedent negotiations) applies.

(1F) The following provisions apply to a debtor-creditor agreement to finance the making of such payments arising on, or connected with, the death of a person as may be prescribed—

(a) section 55 (regulations on disclosure of information);

(b) section 55A (adequate explanations);

(c) section 55B (assessment of creditworthiness);

(d) section 55C (copy of draft consumer credit agreement);

(e) section 56 (antecedent negotiations);

(f) section 60 (regulations on form and content of agreements);

(g) section 61 (signing of agreement);

(h) section 61A (duty to supply copy of executed agreement);

(i) section 66A (withdrawal from consumer credit agreement).

(2) The following provisions apply to a small debtor-creditor-supplier agreement for restricted-use credit—

(a) section 55 (regulations on disclosure of information);

(b) section 56 (antecedent negotiations);

(c) section 66A (withdrawal from consumer credit agreement).]

[(2A) In the case of an agreement to which the Cancellation of Contracts made in a Consumer's Home or Place of Work etc. Regulations 2008 apply the reference in subsection (2) to a small agreement shall be construed as if in section 17(1)(a) and (b) '£35' were substituted for '£50'.]

(3) [Subsection (1)(c) applies] only where the [OFT] so determines, and such a determination—

(a) may be made subject to such conditions as the [OFT] thinks fit, and

(b) shall be made only if the [OFT] is of opinion that it is not against the interests of debtors.

(4) If any term of an agreement falling within subsection [1(d)] is expressed in writing, regulations under section 60(1) shall apply to that term (subject to section 60(3)) as if the agreement were a regulated agreement not falling within subsection [1(d)].

[PART VA   CURRENT ACCOUNT OVERDRAFTS]

[74A   Information to be provided on a current account agreement

(1) This section applies to a current account agreement where there is the possibility that the account-holder may be allowed to overdraw on the current account without a pre-arranged overdraft or exceed a pre-arranged overdraft limit.

(2) The current account agreement must include the following information at the time it is made—

(a) the rate of interest charged on the amount by which an account-holder overdraws on the current account or exceeds the pre-arranged overdraft limit,

(b) any conditions applicable to that rate,

(c) any reference rate on which that rate is based,

(d) information on any changes to the rate of interest (including the periods that the rate applies and any conditions or procedure applicable to changing that rate), and

(e) any other charges payable by the debtor under the agreement (and the conditions under which those charges may be varied).

(3) The account-holder must be informed at least annually of the information in subsection (2).

(4) For the purposes of subsections (2) and (3) where different rates of interest are charged in different circumstances, the creditor must provide the information in subsection (2)(a) to (d) in respect of each rate.

(5) Subsection (3) does not apply where the overdraft or excess would be secured on land.]

[74B   Information to be provided on significant overdrawing without prior arrangement

(1) Where—

(a) the holder of a current account overdraws on the account without a pre-arranged overdraft, or exceeds a pre-arranged overdraft limit, for a period exceeding one month,

(b) the amount of that overdraft or excess is significant throughout that period, and

(c) the account-holder has not been informed in writing of the matters mentioned in subsection (2) within that period,

the account-holder must be informed in writing of those matters without delay.

(2) The matters referred to in subsection (1) are—

(a) the fact that the current account is overdrawn or the overdraft limit has been exceeded,

(b) the amount of that overdraft or excess,

(c) the rate of interest charged on it, and

(d) any other charges payable by the debtor in relation to it (including any penalties and any interest on those charges).

(3) For the purposes of subsection (1)(b) the amount of the overdraft or excess is to be treated as significant if—

(a) the account-holder is liable to pay a charge for which he would not otherwise be liable,

(b) the overdraft or excess is likely to have an adverse effect on the debtor's ability to receive further credit (including any effect on the information about the debtor held by a credit reference agency), or

(c) it otherwise appears significant, having regard to all the circumstances.

(4) Where the overdraft or excess is secured on land, subsection (1)(a) is to be read as if the reference to one month were a reference to three months.]

PART VI MATTERS ARISING DURING CURRENCY OF CREDIT OR HIRE AGREEMENTS

75 Liability of creditor for breaches by supplier

(1) If the debtor under a debtor-creditor-supplier agreement falling within section 12(b) or (c) has, in relation to a transaction financed by the agreement, any claim against the supplier in respect of a misrepresentation or breach of contract, he shall have a like claim against the creditor, who, with the supplier, shall accordingly be jointly and severally liable to the debtor.

(2) Subject to any agreement between them, the creditor shall be entitled to be indemnified by the supplier for loss suffered by the creditor in satisfying his liability under subsection (1), including costs reasonably incurred by him in defending proceedings instituted by the debtor.

(3) Subsection (1) does not apply to a claim—

(a) under a non-commercial agreement, [. . .]

(b) so far as the claim relates to any single item to which the supplier has attached a cash price not exceeding [£100] or more than [£30,000][, or.

(c) under a debtor-creditor-supplier agreement for running-account credit—

(i) which provides for the making of payments by the debtor in relation to specified periods which, in the case of an agreement which is not secured on land, do not exceed three months, and

(ii) which requires that the number of payments to be made by the debtor in repayments of the whole amount of the credit provided in each such period shall not exceed one.].

(4) This section applies notwithstanding that the debtor, in entering into the transaction, exceeded the credit limit or otherwise contravened any term of the agreement.

(5) In an action brought against the creditor under subsection (1) he shall be entitled, in accordance with rules of court, to have the supplier made a party to the proceedings.

[75A Further provision for liability of creditor for breaches by supplier

(1) If the debtor under a linked credit agreement has a claim against the supplier in respect of a breach of contract the debtor may pursue that claim against the creditor where any of the conditions in subsection (2) are met.

(2) The conditions in subsection (1) are—

(a) that the supplier cannot be traced,

(b) that the debtor has contacted the supplier but the supplier has not responded,

(c) that the supplier is insolvent, or

(d) that the debtor has taken reasonable steps to pursue his claim against the supplier but has not obtained satisfaction for his claim.

(3) The steps referred to in subsection (2)(d) need not include litigation.

(4) For the purposes of subsection (2)(d) a debtor is to be deemed to have obtained satisfaction where he has accepted a replacement product or service or other compensation from the supplier in settlement of his claim.

(5) In this section "linked credit agreement" means a regulated consumer credit agreement which serves exclusively to finance an agreement for the supply of specific goods or the provision of a specific service and where—

(a) the creditor uses the services of the supplier in connection with the preparation or making of the credit agreement, or

(b) the specific goods or provision of a specific service are explicitly specified in the credit agreement.

(6) This section does not apply where—

(a) the cash value of the goods or service is £30, 000 or less,

(b) the linked credit agreement is for credit which exceeds £60, 260, or

(c) the linked credit agreement is entered into by the debtor wholly or predominantly for the purposes of a business carried on, or intended to be carried on, by him.

(7) Subsections (2) to (5) of section 16B (declaration by the debtor as to the purposes of the agreement) apply for the purposes of subsection (6)(c).]

76   Duty to give notice before taking certain action

(1) The creditor or owner is not entitled to enforce a term of a regulated agreement by—

(a) demanding earlier payment of any sum, or

(b) recovering possession of any goods or land, or

(c) treating any right conferred on the debtor or hirer by the agreement as terminated, restricted or deferred,

except by or after giving the debtor or hirer not less than seven days' notice of his intention to do so.

(2) Subsection (1) applies only where—

(a) a period for the duration of the agreement is specified in the agreement, and

(b) that period has not ended when the creditor or owner does an act mentioned in subsection (1),

but so applies notwithstanding that, under the agreement, any party is entitled to terminate it before the end of the period so specified.

(3) A notice under subsection (1) is ineffective if not in the prescribed form.

(4) Subsection (1) does not prevent a creditor from treating the right to draw on any credit as restricted or deferred and taking such steps as may be necessary to make the restriction or deferment effective.

(5) Regulations may provide that subsection (1) is not to apply to agreements described by the regulations.

(6) Subsection (1) does not apply to a right of enforcement arising by reason of any breach by the debtor or hirer of the regulated agreement.

77   Duty to give information to debtor under fixed-sum credit agreement

(1) The creditor under a regulated agreement for fixed-sum credit, within the prescribed period after receiving a request in writing to that effect from the debtor and payment of a fee of [£1], shall give the debtor a copy of the executed agreement (if any) and of any other document referred to in it, together with a statement signed by or on behalf of the creditor showing, according to the information to which it is practicable for him to refer,—

(a) the total sum paid under the agreement by the debtor;

(b) the total sum which has become payable under the agreement by the debtor but remains unpaid, and the various amounts comprised in that total sum, with the date when each became due; and

(c) the total sum which is to become payable under the agreement by the debtor, and the various amounts comprised in that total sum, with the date, or mode of determining the date, when each becomes due.

(2) If the creditor possesses insufficient information to enable him to ascertain the amounts and dates mentioned in subsection (1)(c), he shall be taken to comply with that paragraph if his statement under subsection (1) gives the basis on which, under the regulated agreement, they would fall to be ascertained.

[(2A) Subsection (2B) applies if the regulated agreement is a green deal plan (within the meaning of section 1 of the Energy Act 2011).

(2B) The duty imposed on the creditor by subsection (1) may be discharged by another person acting on the creditor's behalf.]

(3) Subsection (1) does not apply to—

(a) an agreement under which no sum is, or will or may become, payable by the debtor, or

(b) a request made less than one month after a previous request under that subsection relating to the same agreement was complied with.

(4) If the creditor under an agreement fails to comply with subsection (1)—

(a) he is not entitled, while the default continues, to enforce the agreement; [...].

(5) This section does not apply to a non-commercial agreement.

[77A Statements to be provided in relation to fixed-sum credit agreements

(1) The creditor under a regulated agreement for fixed-sum credit must give the debtor statements under this section.

(1A) The statements must relate to consecutive periods.

(1B) The first such period must begin with either—

(a) the day on which the agreement is made, or

(b) the day the first movement occurs on the debtor's account with the creditor relating to the agreement.

(1C) No such period may exceed a year.

(1D) For the purposes of subsection (1C), a period of a year which expires on a non-working day may be regarded as expiring on the next working day.

(1E) Each statement under this section must be given to the debtor before the end of the period of thirty days beginning with the day after the end of the period to which the statement relates.

(2) Regulations may make provision about the form and content of statements under this section.

[(2A) Subsection (2B) applies if the regulated agreement is a green deal plan (within the meaning of section 1 of the Energy Act 2011).

(2B) Any duty imposed on the creditor by this section may be discharged by another person acting on the creditor's behalf.]

(3) The debtor shall have no liability to pay any sum in connection with the preparation or the giving to him of a statement under this section.

(4) The creditor is not required to give the debtor any statement under this section once the following conditions are satisfied—

(a) that there is no sum payable under the agreement by the debtor; and

(b) that there is no sum which will or may become so payable.

(5) Subsection (6) applies if at a time before the conditions mentioned in subsection (4) are satisfied the creditor fails to give the debtor—

(a) a statement under this section within the period mentioned in subsection (1E);

(6) Where this subsection applies in relation to a failure to give a statement under this section to the debtor—

(a) the creditor shall not be entitled to enforce the agreement during the period of non-compliance;

(b) the debtor shall have no liability to pay any sum of interest to the extent calculated by reference to the period of non-compliance or to any part of it; and

(c) the debtor shall have no liability to pay any default sum which (apart from this paragraph)—

(i) would have become payable during the period of non-compliance; or

(ii) would have become payable after the end of that period in connection with a breach of the agreement which occurs during that period (whether or not the breach continues after the end of that period).

(7) In this section 'the period of non-compliance' means, in relation to a failure to give a statement under this section to the debtor, the period which—

    (a) begins immediately after the end of the period mentioned in subsection (5); and

    (b) ends at the end of the day on which the statement is given to the debtor or on which the conditions mentioned in subsection (4) are satisfied, whichever is earlier.

(8) This section does not apply in relation to a non-commercial agreement or to a small agreement.]

[(9) This section does not apply where the holder of a current account overdraws on the account without a pre-arranged overdraft or exceeds a pre-arranged overdraft limit.]

[77B   Fixed-sum credit agreement: statement of account to be provided on request

(1) This section applies to a regulated consumer credit agreement—

    (a) which is for fixed-sum credit,

    (b) which is of fixed duration,

    (c) where the credit is repayable in instalments by the debtor, and

    (d) which is not an excluded agreement.

(2) Upon a request from the debtor, the creditor must as soon as reasonably practicable give to the debtor a statement in writing which complies with subsections (3) to (5).

(3) The statement must include a table showing the details of each instalment owing under the agreement as at the date of the request.

(4) Details to be provided under subsection (3) must include—

    (a) the date on which the instalment is due,

    (b) the amount of the instalment,

    (c) any conditions relating to payment of the instalment, and

    (d) a breakdown of the instalment showing how much of it is made up of capital repayment, interest payment and other charges.

(5) Where the rate of interest is variable or the charges under the agreement may be varied, the statement must also indicate clearly and concisely that the information in the table is valid only until the rate of interest or charges are varied.

(6) The debtor may make a request under subsection (2) at any time that the agreement is in force unless a previous request has been made less than a month before and has been complied with.

(7) The debtor shall have no liability to pay any sum in connection with the preparation or the giving of a statement under this section.

[(7A) Subsection (7B) applies if the regulated agreement is a green deal plan (within the meaning of section 1 of the Energy Act 2011).

(7B) The duty imposed on the creditor by this section may be discharged by another person acting on the creditor's behalf.]

(8) A breach of the duty imposed by this section is actionable as a breach of statutory duty.

(9) For the purposes of this section, an agreement is an excluded agreement if it is—

    (a) an agreement secured on land,

    (b) an agreement under which a person takes an article in pawn,

    (c) an agreement under which the creditor provides the debtor with credit which exceeds £60, 260, or

    (d) an agreement entered into by the debtor wholly or predominantly for the purpose of a business carried on, or intended to be carried on, by him.

(10) Subsections (2) to (5) of section 16B (declaration by the debtor as to the purposes of the agreement) apply for the purposes of subsection (9)(d).]

78   Duty to give information to debtor under running-account credit agreement

(1) The creditor under a regulated agreement for running-account credit, within the prescribed period after receiving a request in writing to that effect from the debtor and payment of a fee of [£1],

shall give the debtor a copy of the executed agreement (if any) and of any other document referred to in it, together with a statement signed by or on behalf of the creditor showing, according to the information to which it is practicable for him to refer,—

    (a) the state of the account, and

    (b) the amount, if any, currently payable under the agreement by the debtor to the creditor, and

    (c) the amounts and due dates of any payments which, if the debtor does not draw further on the account, will later become payable under the agreement by the debtor to the creditor.

(2) If the creditor possesses insufficient information to enable him to ascertain the amounts and dates mentioned in subsection (1)(c), he shall be taken to comply with that paragraph if his statement under subsection (1) gives the basis on which, under the regulated agreement, they would fall to be ascertained.

(3) Subsection (1) does not apply to—

    (a) an agreement under which no sum is, or will or may become, payable by the debtor, or

    (b) a request made less than one month after a previous request under that subsection relating to the same agreement was complied with.

(4) Where running-account credit is provided under a regulated agreement, the creditor shall give the debtor statements in the prescribed form, and with the prescribed contents—

    (a) showing according to the information to which it is practicable for him to refer, the state of the account at regular intervals of not more than twelve months, and

    (b) where the agreement provides, in relation to specified periods, for the making of payments by the debtor, or the charging against him of interest or any other sum, showing according to the information to which it is practicable for him to refer the state of the account at the end of each of those periods during which there is any movement in the account.

[(4A) Regulations may require a statement under subsection (4) to contain also information in the prescribed terms about the consequences of the debtor—

    (a) failing to make payments as required by the agreement; or

    (b) only making payments of a prescribed description in prescribed circumstances.]

(5) A statement under subsection (4) shall be given within the prescribed period after the end of the period to which the statement relates.

(6) If the creditor under an agreement fails to comply with subsection (1)—

    (a) he is not entitled, while the default continues, to enforce the agreement; [...].

(7) This section does not apply to a non-commercial agreement, and subsections [(4) to (5)] do not apply to a small agreement.

[78A Duty to give information to debtor on change of rate of interest

(1) Where the rate of interest charged under a regulated consumer credit agreement, other than an excluded agreement, is to be varied, the creditor must inform the debtor in writing of the matters mentioned in subsection (3) before the variation can take effect.

(2) But subsection (1) does not apply where—

    (a) the agreement provides that the creditor is to inform the debtor in writing periodically of the matters mentioned in subsection (3) in relation to any variation, at such times as may be provided for in the agreement,

    (b) the agreement provides that the rate of interest is to vary according to a reference rate,

    (c) the reference rate is publicly available,

    (d) information about the reference rate is available on the premises of the creditor, and

    (e) the variation of the rate of interest results from a change to the reference rate.

(3) The matters referred to in subsections (1) and (2)(a) are—

    (a) the variation in the rate of interest,

(b) the amount of any payments that are to be made after the variation has effect, if different, expressed as a sum of money where practicable, and

(c) if the number or frequency of payments changes as a result of the variation, the new number or frequency.

(4) In the case of an agreement mentioned in subsection (5) this section applies as follows—

(a) the obligation in subsection (1) only applies if the rate of interest increases, and

(b) subsection (3) is to be read as if paragraphs (b) and (c) were omitted.

(5) The agreements referred to in subsection (4) are—

(a) an authorised business overdraft agreement,

(b) an authorised non-business overdraft agreement, or

(c) an agreement which would be an authorised non-business overdraft agreement but for the fact that the credit is not repayable on demand or within three months.

(6) For the purposes of this section an agreement is an excluded agreement if it is—

(a) a debtor-creditor agreement arising where the holder of a current account overdraws on the account without a pre-arranged overdraft or exceeds a pre-arranged overdraft limit, or

(b) an agreement secured on land.]

79 Duty to give hirer information

(1) The owner under a regulated consumer hire agreement, within the prescribed period after receiving a request in writing to that effect from the hirer and payment of a fee of [£1], shall give to the hirer a copy of the executed agreement and of any other document referred to in it, together with a statement signed by or on behalf of the owner showing, according to the information to which it is practicable for him to refer, the total sum which has become payable under the agreement by the hirer but remains unpaid and the various amounts comprised in that total sum, with the date when each became due.

(2) Subsection (1) does not apply to—

(a) an agreement under which no sum is, or will or may become, payable by the hirer, or

(b) a request made less than one month after a previous request under that subsection relating to the same agreement was complied with.

(3) If the owner under an agreement fails to comply with subsection (1)—

(a) he is not entitled, while the default continues, to enforce the agreement; [...].

(4) This section does not apply to a non-commercial agreement.

80 Debtor or hirer to give information about goods

(1) Where a regulated agreement, other than a non-commercial agreement, requires the debtor or hirer to keep goods to which the agreement relates in his possession or control, he shall, within seven working days after he has received a request in writing to that effect from the creditor or owner, tell the creditor or owner where the goods are.

(2) If the debtor or hirer fails to comply with subsection (1), and the default continues for 14 days, he commits an offence.

81 Appropriation of payments

(1) Where a debtor or hirer is liable to make to the same person payments in respect of two or more regulated agreements, he shall be entitled, on making any payment in respect of the agreements which is not sufficient to discharge the total amount then due under all the agreements, to appropriate the sum so paid by him—

(a) in or towards the satisfaction of the sum due under any one of the agreements, or

(b) in or towards the satisfaction of the sums due under any two or more of the agreements in such proportions as he thinks fit.

(2) If the debtor or hirer fails to make any such appropriation where one or more of the agreements is—

(a) a hire-purchase agreement or conditional sale agreement, or

(b) a consumer hire agreement, or

(c) an agreement in relation to which any security is provided, the payment shall be appropriated towards the satisfaction of the sums due under the several agreements respectively in the proportions which those sums bear to one another.

82   Variation of agreements

(1) Where, under a power contained in a regulated agreement, the creditor or owner varies the agreement, the variation shall not take effect before notice of it is given to the debtor or hirer in the prescribed manner.

[(1A) Subsection (1) does not apply to a variation in the rate of interest charged under an agreement not secured on land (see section 78A).

(1B) Subsection (1) does not apply to a variation in the rate of interest charged under an agreement secured on land if—

(a) the agreement falls within subsection (1D), and

(b) the variation is a reduction in the rate.

(1C) Subsection (1) does not apply to a variation in any other charge under an agreement if—

(a) the agreement falls within subsection (1D), and

(b) the variation is a reduction in the charge.

(1D) The agreements referred to in subsections (1B) and (1C) are—

(a) an authorised business overdraft agreement,

(b) an authorised non-business overdraft agreement, or

(c) an agreement which would be an authorised non-business overdraft agreement but for the fact that the credit is not repayable on demand or within three months.

(1E) Subsection (1) does not apply to a debtor-creditor agreement arising where the holder of a current account overdraws on the account without a pre-arranged overdraft or exceeds a pre-arranged overdraft limit.]

(2) Where an agreement (a 'modifying agreement') varies or supplements an earlier agreement, the modifying agreement shall for the purposes of this Act be treated as—

(a) revoking the earlier agreement, and

(b) containing provisions reproducing the combined effect of the two agreements, and obligations outstanding in relation to the earlier agreement shall accordingly be treated as outstanding instead in relation to the modifying agreement.

[(2A) Subsection (2) does not apply if the earlier agreement or the modifying agreement is an exempt agreement as a result of section 16(6C) or 16C.]

[(2B) Subsection (2) does not apply if the modifying agreement varies—

(a) the amount of the repayment to be made under the earlier agreement, or

(b) the duration of the agreement,

as a result of the discharge of part of the debtor's indebtedness under the earlier agreement by virtue of section 94(3).]

(3) If the earlier agreement is a regulated agreement but (apart from this subsection) the modifying agreement is not then, [unless the modifying agreement is—

(a) for running account credit; or

(b) is an exempt agreement as a result of section 16(6C) or 16C,

it shall be treated as a regulated agreement.]

(4) If the earlier agreement is a regulated agreement for running-account credit, and by the modifying agreement the creditor allows the credit limit to be exceeded but intends the excess to be merely temporary, Part V (except section 56) shall not apply to the modifying agreement.

(5) If—

(a) the earlier agreement is a cancellable agreement, and

(b) the modifying agreement is made within the period applicable under section 68 to the earlier agreement,

then, whether or not the modifying agreement would, apart from this subsection, be a cancellable agreement, it shall be treated as a cancellable agreement in respect of which a notice may be served under section 68 not later than the end of the period applicable under that section to the earlier agreement.

[(5A) Subsection 5 does not apply where the modifying agreement is an exempt agreement as a result of section 16(6C) or 16C.]

(6) Except under subsection (5), a modifying agreement shall not be treated as a cancellable agreement.

[(6A) If—

    (a) the earlier agreement is an agreement to which section 66A (right of withdrawal) applies, and

    (b) the modifying agreement is made within the period during which the debtor may give notice of withdrawal from the earlier agreement (see section 66A(2)),

then, whether or not the modifying agreement would, apart from this subsection, be an agreement to which section 66A applies, it shall be treated as such an agreement in respect of which notice may be given under subsection (2) of that section within the period referred to in paragraph (b) above.

(6B) Except as provided for under subsection (6A) section 66A does not apply to a modifying agreement.]

(7) This section does not apply to a non-commercial agreement.

[82A   Assignment of rights

(1) Where rights of a creditor under a regulated consumer credit agreement are assigned to a third party, the assignee must arrange for notice of the assignment to be given to the debtor—

    (a) as soon as reasonably possible, or

    (b) if, after the assignment, the arrangements for servicing the credit under the agreement do not change as far as the debtor is concerned, on or before the first occasion that they do.

(2) This section does not apply to an agreement secured on land.]

83   Liability for misuse of credit facilities

(1) The debtor under a regulated consumer credit agreement shall not be liable to the creditor for any loss arising from use of the credit facility by another person not acting, or to be treated as acting, as the debtor's agent.

(2) This section does not apply to a non-commercial agreement, or to any loss in so far as it arises from misuse of an instrument to which section 4 of the Cheques Act 1957 applies.

84   Misuse of credit-tokens

(1) Section 83 does not prevent the debtor under a credit-token agreement from being made liable to the extent of [£50] (or the credit limit if lower) for loss to the creditor arising from use of the credit-token by other persons during a period beginning when the credit-token ceases to be in the possession of any authorized person and ending when the credit-token is once more in the possession of an authorised person.

(2) Section 83 does not prevent the debtor under a credit-token agreement from being made liable to any extent for loss to the creditor from use of the credit-token by a person who acquired possession of it with the debtor's consent.

(3) Subsection (1) and (2) shall not apply to any use of the credit-token after the creditor has been given oral or written notice that it is lost or stolen, or is for any other reason liable to misuse.

[(3A) Subsections (1) and (2) shall not apply to any use, in connection with a distance contract (other than an excepted contract), of a card which is a credit-token.

(3B) In subsection (3A), 'distance contract' and 'excepted contract' have the meanings given in the Consumer Protection (Distance Selling) Regulations 2000.]

[(3C) Subsections (1) and (2) shall not apply to any use, in connection with a distance contract within the meaning of the Financial Services (Distance Marketing) Regulations 2004, of a card which is a credit-token.]

(4) Subsections (1) and (2) shall not apply unless there are contained in the credit-token agreement in the prescribed manner particulars of the name, address and telephone number of a person stated to be the person to whom notice is to be given under subsection (3).

(5) Notice under subsection (3) takes effect when received, but where it is given orally, and the agreement so requires, it shall be treated as not taking effect if not confirmed in writing within seven days.

(6) Any sum paid by the debtor for the issue of the credit-token to the extent (if any) that it has not been previously offset by use made of the credit-token, shall be treated as paid towards satisfaction of any liability under subsection (1) or (2).

(7) The debtor, the creditor, and any person authorised by the debtor to use the credit-token, shall be authorised persons for the purposes of subsection (1).

(8) Where two or more credit-tokens are given under one credit-token agreement, the preceding provisions of this section apply to each credit-token separately.

85   Duty on issue of new credit-tokens

(1) Whenever, in connection with a credit-token agreement, a credit-token (other than the first) is given by the creditor to the debtor, the creditor shall give the debtor a copy of the executed agreement (if any) and of any other document referred to in it.

(2) If the creditor fails to comply with this section—

(a) he is not entitled, while the default continues, to enforce the agreement, [...].

(3) This section does not apply to a small agreement.

86   Death of debtor or hirer

(1) The creditor or owner under a regulated agreement is not entitled, by reason of the death of the debtor or hirer, to do an act specified in paragraphs (a) to (e) of section 87(1) if at the death the agreement is fully secured.

(2) If at the death of the debtor or hirer a regulated agreement is only partly secured or is unsecured, the creditor or owner is entitled, by reason of the death of the debtor or hirer, to do an act specified in paragraphs (a) to (e) of section 87(1) on an order of the court only.

(3) This section applies in relation to the termination of an agreement only where—

(a) a period for its duration is specified in the agreement, and

(b) that period has not ended when the creditor or owner purports to terminate the agreement,

but so applies notwithstanding that, under the agreement, any party is entitled to terminate it before the end of the period so specified.

(4) This section does not prevent the creditor from treating the right to draw on any credit as restricted or deferred, and taking such steps as may be necessary to make the restriction or deferment effective.

(5) This section does not affect the operation of any agreement providing for payment of sums—

(a) due under the regulated agreement, or

(b) becoming due under it on the death of the debtor or hirer, out of the proceeds of a policy of assurance on his life.

(6) For the purposes of this section an act is done by reason of the death of the debtor or hirer if it is done under a power conferred by the agreement which is—

(a) exercisable on his death, or

(b) exercisable at will and exercised at any time after his death.

PART VII   DEFAULT AND TERMINATION

[Information sheets]

[86A   OFT to prepare information sheets on arrears and default

(1) The OFT shall prepare, and give general notice of, an arrears information sheet and a default information sheet.

(2) The arrears information sheet shall include information to help debtors and hirers who receive notices under section 86B or 86C.

(3) The default information sheet shall include information to help debtors and hirers who receive default notices.

(4) Regulations may make provision about the information to be included in an information sheet.

(5) An information sheet takes effect for the purposes of this Part at the end of the period of three months beginning with the day on which general notice of it is given.

(6) If the OFT revises an information sheet after general notice of it has been given, it shall give general notice of the information sheet as revised.

(7) A revised information sheet takes effect for the purposes of this Part at the end of the period of three months beginning with the day on which general notice of it is given.]

[Sums in arrears and default sums]

[86B   Notice of sums in arrears under fixed-sum credit agreements etc.

(1) This section applies where at any time the following conditions are satisfied—

(a) that the debtor or hirer under an applicable agreement is required to have made at least two payments under the agreement before that time;

(b) that the total sum paid under the agreement by him is less than the total sum which he is required to have paid before that time;

(c) that the amount of the shortfall is no less than the sum of the last two payments which he is required to have made before that time;

(d) that the creditor or owner is not already under a duty to give him notices under this section in relation to the agreement; and

(e) if a judgment has been given in relation to the agreement before that time, that there is no sum still to be paid under the judgment by the debtor or hirer.

(2) The creditor or owner—

(a) shall, within the period of 14 days beginning with the day on which the conditions mentioned in subsection (1) are satisfied, give the debtor or hirer a notice under this section; and

(b) after the giving of that notice, shall give him further notices under this section at intervals of not more than six months.

(3) The duty of the creditor or owner to give the debtor or hirer notices under this section shall cease when either of the conditions mentioned in subsection (4) is satisfied; but if either of those conditions is satisfied before the notice required by subsection (2)(a) is given, the duty shall not cease until that notice is given.

(4) The conditions referred to in subsection (3) are—

(a) that the debtor or hirer ceases to be in arrears;

(b) that a judgment is given in relation to the agreement under which a sum is required to be paid by the debtor or hirer.

(5) For the purposes of subsection (4)(a) the debtor or hirer ceases to be in arrears when—

(a) no payments, which he has ever failed to make under the agreement when required, are still owing;

(b) no default sum, which has ever become payable under the agreement in connection with his failure to pay any sum under the agreement when required, is still owing;

(c) no sum of interest, which has ever become payable under the agreement in connection with such a default sum, is still owing; and

(d) no other sum of interest, which has ever become payable under the agreement in connection with his failure to pay any sum under the agreement when required, is still owing.

(6) A notice under this section shall include a copy of the current arrears information sheet under section 86A.

(7) The debtor or hirer shall have no liability to pay any sum in connection with the preparation or the giving to him of a notice under this section.

(8) Regulations may make provision about the form and content of notices under this section.

(9) In the case of an applicable agreement under which the debtor or hirer must make all payments he is required to make at intervals of one week or less, this section shall have effect as if in subsection (1)(a) and (c) for 'two' there were substituted 'four'.

(10) If an agreement mentioned in subsection (9) was made before the beginning of the relevant period, only amounts resulting from failures by the debtor or hirer to make payments he is required to have made during that period shall be taken into account in determining any shortfall for the purposes of subsection (1)(c).

(11) In subsection (10) 'relevant period' means the period of 20 weeks ending with the day on which the debtor or hirer is required to have made the most recent payment under the agreement.]

[(12) In this section "applicable agreement" means an agreement which falls within subsection (12A) or (12B).

(12A) An agreement falls within this subsection if—

    (a) it is a regulated agreement for fixed-sum credit; and

    (b) it is not—

        (i) a non-commercial agreement;

        (ii) a small agreement; or

        (iii) a green deal plan (within the meaning of section 1 of the Energy Act 2011).

(12B) An agreement falls within this subsection if—

    (a) it is a regulated consumer hire agreement; and

    (b) it is neither a non-commercial agreement nor a small agreement.]

[(13) In this section—

    (a) "payments" in relation to an applicable agreement which is a regulated agreement for fixed-sum credit means payments to be made at predetermined intervals provided for under the terms of the agreement; and

    (b) "payments" in relation to an applicable agreement which is a regulated consumer hire agreement means any payments to be made by the hirer in relation to any period in consideration of the bailment or hiring to him of goods under the agreement.]

[86C Notice of sums in arrears under running-account credit agreements

(1) This section applies where at any time the following conditions are satisfied—

    (a) that the debtor under an applicable agreement is required to have made at least two payments under the agreement before that time;

    (b) that the last two payments which he is required to have made before that time have not been made;

    (c) that the creditor has not already been required to give a notice under this section in relation to either of those payments; and

    (d) if a judgment has been given in relation to the agreement before that time, that there is no sum still to be paid under the judgment by the debtor.

(2) The creditor shall, no later than the end of the period within which he is next required to give a statement under section 78(4) in relation to the agreement, give the debtor a notice under this section.

(3) The notice shall include a copy of the current arrears information sheet under section 86A.

(4) The notice may be incorporated in a statement or other notice which the creditor gives the debtor in relation to the agreement by virtue of another provision of this Act.

(5) The debtor shall have no liability to pay any sum in connection with the preparation or the giving to him of the notice.

(6) Regulations may make provision about the form and content of notices under this section.

(7) In this section 'applicable agreement' means an agreement which—

    (a) is a regulated agreement for running-account credit; and

    (b) is neither a non-commercial agreement nor a small agreement.

(8) In this section "payments" means payments to be made at predetermined intervals provided for under the terms of the agreement.]

[86D   Failure to give notice of sums in arrears

(1) This section applies where the creditor or owner under an agreement is under a duty to give the debtor or hirer notices under section 86B but fails to give him such a notice—

    (a) within the period mentioned in subsection (2)(a) of that section; or

    (b) within the period of six months beginning with the day after the day on which such a notice was last given to him.

(2) This section also applies where the creditor under an agreement is under a duty to give the debtor a notice under section 86C but fails to do so before the end of the period mentioned in subsection (2) of that section.

(3) The creditor or owner shall not be entitled to enforce the agreement during the period of non-compliance.

(4) The debtor or hirer shall have no liability to pay—

    (a) any sum of interest to the extent calculated by reference to the period of non-compliance or to any part of it; or

    (b) any default sum which (apart from this paragraph)—

        (i) would have become payable during the period of non-compliance; or

        (ii) would have become payable after the end of that period in connection with a breach of the agreement which occurs during that period (whether or not the breach continues after the end of that period).

(5) In this section 'the period of non-compliance' means, in relation to a failure to give a notice under section 86B or 86C to the debtor or hirer, the period which—

    (a) begins immediately after the end of the period mentioned in (as the case may be) subsection (1)(a) or (b) or (2); and

    (b) ends at the end of the day mentioned in subsection (6).

(6) That day is—

    (a) in the case of a failure to give a notice under section 86B as mentioned in subsection (1)(a) of this section, the day on which the notice is given to the debtor or hirer;

    (b) in the case of a failure to give a notice under that section as mentioned in subsection (1)(b) of this section, the earlier of the following—

        (i) the day on which the notice is given to the debtor or hirer;

        (ii) the day on which the condition mentioned in subsection (4)(a) of that section is satisfied;

    (c) in the case of a failure to give a notice under section 86C, the day on which the notice is given to the debtor.]

[86E   Notice of default sums

(1) This section applies where a default sum becomes payable under a regulated agreement by the debtor or hirer.

(2) The creditor or owner shall, within the prescribed period after the default sum becomes payable, give the debtor or hirer a notice under this section.

(3) The notice under this section may be incorporated in a statement or other notice which the creditor or owner gives the debtor or hirer in relation to the agreement by virtue of another provision of this Act.

(4) The debtor or hirer shall have no liability to pay interest in connection with the default sum to the extent that the interest is calculated by reference to a period occurring before the 29th day after the day on which the debtor or hirer is given the notice under this section.

(5) If the creditor or owner fails to give the debtor or hirer the notice under this section within the period mentioned in subsection (2), he shall not be entitled to enforce the agreement until the notice is given to the debtor or hirer.

(6) The debtor or hirer shall have no liability to pay any sum in connection with the preparation or the giving to him of the notice under this section.

(7) Regulations may—

    (a) provide that this section does not apply in relation to a default sum which is less than a prescribed amount;

    (b) make provision about the form and content of notices under this section.

(8) This section does not apply in relation to a non-commercial agreement or to a small agreement.]

[86F   Interest on default sums

(1) This section applies where a default sum becomes payable under a regulated agreement by the debtor or hirer.

(2) The debtor or hirer shall only be liable to pay interest in connection with the default sum if the interest is simple interest.]

Default notices

87   Need for default notice

(1) Service of a notice on the debtor or hirer in accordance with section 88 (a 'default notice') is necessary before the creditor or owner can become entitled, by reason of any breach by the debtor or hirer of a regulated agreement,—

    (a) to terminate the agreement, or

    (b) to demand earlier payment of any sum, or

    (c) to recover possession of any goods or land, or

    (d) to treat any right conferred on the debtor or hirer by the agreement as terminated, restricted or deferred, or

    (e) to enforce any security.

(2) Subsection (1) does not prevent the creditor from treating the right to draw upon any credit as restricted or deferred, and taking such steps as may be necessary to make the restriction or deferment effective.

(3) The doing of an act by which a floating charge becomes fixed is not enforcement of a security.

(4) Regulations may provide that section (1) is not to apply to agreements described by the regulations.

[(5) Subsection (1)(d) does not apply in a case referred to in section 98A(4) (termination or suspension of debtor's right to draw on credit under open-end agreement).]

88   Contents and effect of default notice

(1) The default notice must be in the prescribed form and specify—

    (a) the nature of the alleged breach;

    (b) if the breach is capable of remedy, what action is required to remedy it and the date before which that action is to be taken;

    (c) if the breach is not capable of remedy, the sum (if any) required to be paid as compensation for the breach, and the date before which it is to be paid.

(2) A date specified under subsection (1) must not be less than [14] days after the date of service of the default notice, and the creditor or owner shall not take action such as is mentioned in section 87(1) before the date so specified or (if no requirement is made under subsection (1)) before those [14] days have elapsed.

(3) The default notice must not treat as a breach failure to comply with a provision of the agreement which becomes operative only on breach of some other provision, but if the breach of that other provision is not duly remedied or compensation demanded under subsection (1) is not duly paid, or (where no requirement is made under subsection (1)) if the seven days mentioned in subsection (2) have elapsed, the creditor or owner may treat the failure as a breach and section 87(1) shall not apply to it.

(4) The default notice must contain information in the prescribed terms about the consequences of failure to comply with it and any other prescribed matters relating to the agreement.

[(4A) The default notice must also include a copy of the current default information sheet under section 86A.]

(5) A default notice making a requirement under subsection (1) may include a provision for the taking of action such as is mentioned in section 87(1) at any time after the restriction imposed by subsection (2) will cease, together with a statement that the provision will be ineffective if the breach is duly remedied or the compensation duly paid.

89 Compliance with default notice

If before the date specified for that purpose in the default notice the debtor or hirer takes the action specified under section 88(1)(b) or (c) the breach shall be treated as not having occurred.

Further restriction of remedies for default

90 Retaking of protected hire-purchase etc. goods

(1) At any time when—
> (a) the debtor is in breach of a regulated hire-purchase or a regulated conditional sale agreement relating to goods, and
> (b) the debtor has paid to the creditor one-third or more of the total price of the goods and
> (c) the property in the goods remains in the creditor, the creditor is not entitled to recover possession of the goods from the debtor except on an order of the court.

(2) Where under a hire-purchase or conditional sale agreement the creditor is required to carry out any installation and the agreement specifies, as part of the total price, the amount to be paid in respect of the installation (the 'installation charge') the reference in subsection (1)(b) to one-third of the total price shall be construed as a reference to the aggregate of the installation charge and one-third of the remainder of the total price.

(3) In a case where—
> (a) subsection (1)(a) is satisfied, but not subsection (1)(b), and
> (b) subsection (1)(b) was satisfied on a previous occasion in relation to an earlier agreement, being a regulated hire-purchase or regulated conditional sale agreement, between the same parties, and relating to any of the goods comprised in the later agreement (whether or not other goods were also included),

subsection (1) shall apply to the later agreement with the omission of paragraph (b).

(4) If the later agreement is a modifying agreement, subsection (3) shall apply with the substitution, for the second reference to the later agreement, of a reference to the modifying agreement.

(5) Subsection (1) shall not apply, or shall cease to apply, to an agreement if the debtor has terminated, or terminates, the agreement.

(6) Where subsection (1) applies to an agreement at the death of the debtor, it shall continue to apply (in relation to the possessor of the goods) until the grant of probate or administration, or (in Scotland) confirmation (on which the personal representative would fall to be treated as the debtor).

(7) Goods falling within this section are in this Act referred to as 'protected goods'.

91 Consequences of breach of s. 90

If goods are recovered by the creditor in contravention of section 90—
> (a) the regulated agreement, if not previously terminated, shall terminate, and
> (b) the debtor shall be released from all liability under the agreement, and shall be entitled to recover from the creditor all sums paid by the debtor under the agreement.

92 Recovery of possession of goods or land

(1) Except under an order of the court, the creditor or owner shall not be entitled to enter any premises to take possession of goods subject to a regulated hire-purchase agreement, regulated conditional sale agreement or regulated consumer hire agreement.

(2) At any time when the debtor is in breach of a regulated conditional sale agreement relating to land, the creditor is entitled to recover possession of the land from the debtor, or any person claiming under him, on an order of the court only.

(3) An entry in contravention of section (1) or (2) is actionable as a breach of statutory duty.

93   Interest not to be increased on default

The debtor under a regulated consumer credit agreement shall not be obliged to pay interest on sums which, in breach of the agreement, are unpaid by him at a rate—

    (a) where the total charge for credit includes an item in respect of interest, exceeding the rate of that interest, or

    (b) in any other case, exceeding what would be the rate of the total charge for credit if any items included in the total charge for credit by virtue of section 20(2) were disregarded.

Early payment by debtor

94   Right to complete payments ahead of time

(1) The debtor under a regulated consumer credit agreement is entitled at any time, by notice to the creditor and the payment to the creditor of all amounts payable by the debtor to him under the agreement [and any amount which the creditor claims under section 95A(2) or section 95B(2)] (less any rebate allowable under section 95), to discharge the debtor's indebtedness under the agreement.

(2) A notice under subsection (1) may embody the exercise by the debtor of any option to purchase goods conferred on him by the agreement, and deal with any other matter arising on, or in relation to, the termination of the agreement.

[(3) The debtor under a regulated consumer credit agreement, other than an agreement secured on land, is entitled at any time to discharge part of his indebtedness by taking the steps in subsection (4).

(4) The steps referred to in subsection (3) are as follows—

    (a) he provides notice to the creditor,

    (b) he pays to the creditor some of the amount payable by him to the creditor under the agreement before the time fixed by the agreement, and

    (c) he makes the payment—

        (i) before the end of the period of 28 days beginning with the day following that on which notice under paragraph (a) was received by the creditor, or

        (ii) on or before any later date specified in the notice.

(5) Where a debtor takes the steps in subsection (4) his indebtedness shall be discharged by an amount equal to the sum of the amount paid and any rebate allowable under section 95 less any amount which the creditor claims under section 95A(2) or section 95B(2).

(6) A notice—

    (a) under subsection (1), other than a notice relating to a regulated consumer credit agreement secured on land, or

    (b) under subsection (4)(a),

need not be in writing.]

95   Rebate on early settlement

(1) Regulations may provide for the allowance of a rebate of charges for credit to the debtor under a regulated consumer credit agreement where, under section 94, on refinancing, on breach of the agreement, or for any other reason, his indebtedness is discharged [or is discharged in part] or becomes payable before the time fixed by the agreement, or any sum becomes payable by him before the time so fixed.

(2) Regulations under subsection (1) may provide for calculation of the rebate by reference to any sums paid or payable by the debtor or his relative under or in connection with the agreement (whether to the creditor or some other person), including sums under linked transactions and other items in the total charge for credit.

[95A   Compensatory amount

(1) This section applies where—

  (a) a regulated consumer credit agreement, other than an agreement secured on land, provides for the rate of interest on the credit to be fixed for a period of time, and

  (b) under section 94 the debtor discharges all or part of his indebtedness during that period.

(2) The creditor may claim an amount equal to the cost which the creditor has incurred as a result only of the debtor's indebtedness being discharged during that period if—

  (a) the amount of the payment under section 94 exceeds £8,000 or, where more than one such payment is made in any 12 month period, the total of those payments exceeds £8,000,

  (b) the agreement is not a debtor-creditor agreement enabling the debtor to overdraw on a current account, and

  (c) the amount of the payment under section 94 is not paid from the proceeds of a contract of payment protection insurance.

(3) The amount in subsection (2)—

  (a) must be fair,

  (b) must be objectively justified, and

  (c) must not exceed whichever is the higher of—

    (i) the relevant percentage of the amount of the payment under section 94, and

    (ii) the total amount of interest that would have been paid by the debtor under the agreement in the period from the date on which the debtor makes the payment under section 94 to the date fixed by the agreement for the discharge of the indebtedness of the debtor.

(4) In subsection (3)(c)(i) "relevant percentage" means—

  (a) 1%, where the period from the date on which the debtor makes the payment under section 94 to the date fixed by the agreement for the discharge of the indebtedness of the debtor is more than one year, or

  (b) 0.5%, where that period is equal to or less than one year.]

[95B   Compensatory amount: green deal finance

(1) This section applies where—

  (a) a regulated consumer credit agreement provides for the rate of interest on the credit to be fixed for a period of time ("the fixed rate period"),

  (b) the agreement is a green deal plan (within the meaning of section 1 of the Energy Act 2011) which is of a duration specified for the purposes of this section in regulations, and

  (c) under section 94 the debtor discharges all or part of his indebtedness during the fixed rate period.

(2) The creditor may claim an amount equal to the cost which the creditor has incurred as a result only of the debtor's indebtedness being discharged during the fixed rate period if—

  (a) the amount of the payment under section 94 is not paid from the proceeds of a contract of payment protection insurance, and

  (b) such other conditions as may be specified for the purposes of this section in regulations are satisfied.

(3) The amount in subsection (2)—

  (a) must be fair,

  (b) must be objectively justified,

  (c) must be calculated by the creditor in accordance with provision made for the purposes of this section in regulations, and

  (d) must not exceed the total amount of interest that would have been paid by the debtor under the agreement in the period from the date on which the debtor makes the payment under section 94 to the date fixed by the agreement for the discharge of the indebtedness of the debtor.

(4) If a creditor could claim under either section 95A or this section, the creditor may choose under which section to claim.]

96   Effect on linked transactions

(1) Where for any reason the indebtedness of the debtor under a regulated consumer credit agreement is discharged before the time fixed by the agreement, he, and any relative of his, shall at the same time be discharged from any liability under a linked transaction, other than a debt which has already become payable.

(2) Subsection (1) does not apply to a linked transaction which is itself an agreement providing the debtor or his relative with credit.

(3) Regulations may exclude linked transactions of the prescribed description from the operation of subsection (1).

97   Duty to give information

(1) The creditor under a regulated consumer credit agreement, within the prescribed period after he has received a request [...] to that effect from the debtor, shall give the debtor a statement in the prescribed form indicating, according to the information to which it is practicable for him to refer, the amount of the payment required to discharge the debtor's indebtedness under the agreement, together with the prescribed particulars showing how the amount is arrived at.

(2) Subsection (1) does not apply to a request made less than one month after a previous request under that subsection relating to the same agreement was complied with.

[(2A) A request under subsection (1) need not be in writing unless the agreement is secured on land.]

(3) If the creditor fails to comply with subsection (1)—
   (a) he is not entitled, while the default continues, to enforce the agreement; [...].

[97A   Duty to give information on partial repayment

(1) Where a debtor under a regulated consumer credit agreement—
   (a) makes a payment by virtue of which part of his indebtedness is discharged under section 94, and
   (b) at the same time or subsequently requests the creditor to give him a statement concerning the effect of the payment on the debtor's indebtedness,
the creditor must give the statement to the debtor before the end of the period of seven working days beginning with the day following that on which the creditor receives the request.

(2) The statement shall be in writing and shall contain the following particulars—
   (a) a description of the agreement sufficient to identify it,
   (b) the name, postal address and, where appropriate, any other address of the creditor and the debtor,
   (c) where the creditor is claiming an amount under section 95A(2) or section 95B(2), that amount and the method used to determine it,
   (d) the amount of any rebate to which the debtor is entitled—
      (i) under the agreement, or
      (ii) by virtue of section 95 where that is higher,
   (e) where the amount of the rebate mentioned in paragraph (d)(ii) is given, a statement indicating that this amount has been calculated having regard to the Consumer Credit (Early Settlement) Regulations 2004,
   (f) where the debtor is not entitled to any rebate, a statement to this effect,
   (g) any change to—
      (i) the number, timing or amount of repayments to be made under the agreement, or
      (ii) the duration of the agreement,
      which results from the partial discharge of the indebtedness of the debtor, and
   (h) the amount of the debtor's indebtedness remaining under the agreement at the date the creditor gives the statement.]

Termination of agreements

98   Duty to give notice of termination (non-default cases)

(1) The creditor or owner is not entitled to terminate a regulated agreement except by or after giving the debtor or hirer not less than seven days' notice of the termination.

(2) Subsection (1) applies only where—

(a) a period for the duration of the agreement is specified in the agreement, and

(b) that period has not ended when the creditor or owner does an act mentioned in subsection (1),

but so applies notwithstanding that, under the agreement, any party is entitled to terminate it before the end of the period so specified.

(3) A notice under subsection (1) is ineffective if not in the prescribed form.

(4) Subsection (1) does not prevent a creditor from treating the right to draw on any credit as restricted or deferred and taking such steps as may be necessary to make the restriction or deferment effective.

(5) Regulations may provide that subsection (1) is not to apply to agreements described by the regulations.

(6) Subsection (1) does not apply to the termination of a regulated agreement by reason of any breach by the debtor or hirer of the agreement.

[98A   Termination etc of open-end consumer credit agreements

(1) The debtor under a regulated open-end consumer credit agreement, other than an excluded agreement, may by notice terminate the agreement, free of charge, at any time, subject to any period of notice not exceeding one month provided for by the agreement.

(2) Notice under subsection (1) need not be in writing unless the creditor so requires.

(3) Where a regulated open-end consumer credit agreement, other than an excluded agreement, provides for termination of the agreement by the creditor—

(a) the termination must be by notice served on the debtor, and

(b) the termination may not take effect until after the end of the period of two months, or such longer period as the agreement may provide, beginning with the day after the day on which notice is served.

(4) Where a regulated open-end consumer credit agreement, other than an excluded agreement, provides for termination or suspension by the creditor of the debtor's right to draw on credit—

(a) to terminate or suspend the right to draw on credit the creditor must serve a notice on the debtor before the termination or suspension or, if that is not practicable, immediately afterwards,

(b) the notice must give reasons for the termination or suspension, and

(c) the reasons must be objectively justified.

(5) Subsection (4)(a) and (b) does not apply where giving the notice—

(a) is prohibited by an EU obligation, or

(b) would, or would be likely to, prejudice—

(i)   the prevention or detection of crime,

(ii)   the apprehension or prosecution of offenders, or

(iii) the administration of justice.

(6) An objectively justified reason under subsection (4)(c) may, for example, relate to—

(a) the unauthorised or fraudulent use of credit, or

(b) a significantly increased risk of the debtor being unable to fulfil his obligation to repay the credit.

(7) Subsections (1) and (3) do not affect any right to terminate an agreement for breach of contract.

(8) For the purposes of this section an agreement is an excluded agreement if it is—

(a) an authorised non-business overdraft agreement,

(b) an authorised business overdraft agreement,

(c) a debtor-creditor agreement arising where the holder of a current account overdraws on the account without a pre-arranged overdraft or exceeds a pre-arranged overdraft limit, or

(d) an agreement secured on land.]

99   Right to terminate hire-purchase etc. agreements

(1) At any time before the final payment by the debtor under a regulated hire-purchase or regulated conditional sale agreement falls due, the debtor shall be entitled to terminate the agreement by giving notice to any person entitled or authorised to receive the sums payable under the agreement.

(2) Termination of an agreement under subsection (1) does not affect any liability under the agreement which has accrued before the termination.

(3) Subsection (1) does not apply to a conditional sale agreement relating to land after the title to the land has passed to the debtor.

(4) In the case of a conditional sale agreement relating to goods, where the property in the goods, having become vested in the debtor, is transferred to a person who does not become the debtor under the agreement, the debtor shall not thereafter be entitled to terminate the agreement under subsection (1).

(5) Subject to subsection (4), where a debtor under a conditional sale agreement relating to goods terminates the agreement under this section after the property in the goods has become vested in him, the property in the goods shall thereupon vest in the person (the 'previous owner') in whom it was vested immediately before it became vested in the debtor:

Provided that if the previous owner has died, or any other event has occurred whereby that property, if vested in him immediately before that event, would thereupon have vested in some other person, the property shall be treated as having devolved as if it had been vested in the previous owner immediately before his death or immediately before that event, as the case may be.

100   Liability of debtor on termination of hire-purchase etc. agreement

(1) Where a regulated hire-purchase or regulated conditional sale agreement is terminated under section 99 the debtor shall be liable, unless the agreement provides for a smaller payment, or does not provide for any payment, to pay to the creditor the amount (if any) by which one-half of the total price exceeds the aggregate of the sums paid and the sums due in respect of the total price immediately before the termination.

(2) Where under a hire-purchase or conditional sale agreement the creditor is required to carry out any installation and the agreement specifies, as part of the total price, the amount to be paid in respect of the installation (the 'installation charge') the reference in subsection (1) to one-half of the total price shall be construed as a reference to the aggregate of the installation charge and one-half of the remainder of the total price.

(3) If in any action the court is satisfied that a sum less than the amount specified in subsection (1) would be equal to the loss sustained by the creditor in consequence of the termination of the agreement by the debtor, the court may make an order for the payment of that sum in lieu of the amount specified in subsection (1).

(4) If the debtor has contravened an obligation to take reasonable care of the goods or land, the amount arrived at under subsection (1) shall be increased by the sum required to recompense the creditor for that contravention, and subsection (2) shall have effect accordingly.

(5) Where the debtor, on the termination of the agreement, wrongfully retains possession of goods to which the agreement relates, then, in any action brought by the creditor to recover possession of the goods from the debtor, the court, unless it is satisfied that having regard to the circumstances it would not be just to do so, shall order the goods to be delivered to the creditor without giving the debtor an option to pay the value of the goods.

101   Right to terminate hire agreement

(1) The hirer under a regulated consumer hire agreement is entitled to terminate the agreement by giving notice to any person entitled or authorised to receive the sums payable under the agreement.

(2) Termination of an agreement under subsection (1) does not affect any liability under the agreement which has accrued before the termination.

(3) A notice under subsection (1) shall not expire earlier than eighteen months after the making of the agreement, but apart from that the minimum period of notice to be given under subsection (1), unless the agreement provides for a shorter period, is as follows.

(4) If the agreement provides for the making of payments by the hirer to the owner at equal intervals, the minimum period of notice is the length of one interval or three months, whichever is less.

(5) If the agreement provides for the making of such payments at differing intervals, the minimum period of notice is the length of the shortest interval or three months, whichever is less.

(6) In any other case, the minimum period of notice is three months.

(7) This section does not apply to—

    (a) any agreement which provides for the making by the hirer of payments which in total (and without breach of the agreement) exceed [£1,500] in any year, or

    (b) any agreement where—

        (i) goods are bailed or (in Scotland) hired to the hirer for the purposes of a business carried on by him, or the hirer holds himself out as requiring the goods for those purposes, and

        (ii) the goods are selected by the hirer, and acquired by the owner for the purposes of the agreement at the request of the hirer from any person other than the owner's associate, or

    (c) any agreement where the hirer requires, or holds himself out as requiring, the goods for the purpose of bailing or hiring them to other persons in the course of a business carried on by him.

(8) If, on an application made to the [OFT] by a person carrying on a consumer hire business, it appears to the [OFT] that it would be in the interest of hirers to do so, [it] may by notice to the applicant direct that [, subject to such conditions (if any) as it may specify, this section shall not apply to consumer hire agreements made by the applicant; and this Act shall have effect accordingly].

[(8A) If it appears to the OFT that it would be in the interests of hirers to do so, it may by general notice direct that, subject to such conditions (if any) as it may specify, this section shall not apply to a consumer hire agreement if the agreement falls within a specified description; and this Act shall have effect accordingly.]

(9) In the case of a modifying agreement, subsection (3) shall apply with the substitution for 'the making of the agreement' of 'the making of the original agreement'.

102 Agency for receiving notice of rescission

(1) Where the debtor or hirer under a regulated agreement claims to have a right to rescind the agreement, each of the following shall be deemed to be the agent of the creditor or owner for the purpose of receiving any notice rescinding the agreement which is served by the debtor or hirer—

    (a) a credit-broker or supplier who was the negotiator in antecedent negotiations, and

    (b) any person who, in the course of a business carried on by him, acted on behalf of the debtor or hirer in any negotiations for the agreement.

(2) In subsection (1) 'rescind' does not include—

    (a) service of a notice of cancellation, or

    (b) termination of an agreement under section 99 or 101 or by the exercise of a right or power in that behalf expressly conferred by the agreement.

103 Termination statements

(1) If an individual (the 'customer') serves on any person (the 'trader') a notice—

    (a) stating that—

        (i) the customer was the debtor or hirer under a regulated agreement described in the notice, and the trader was the creditor or owner under the agreement, and

        (ii) the customer has discharged his indebtedness to the trader under the agreement, and

        (iii) the agreement has ceased to have any operation; and

(b) requiring the trader to give the customer a notice, signed by or on behalf of the trader, confirming that those statements are correct,

the trader shall, within the prescribed period after receiving the notice, either comply with it or serve on the customer a counter-notice stating that, as the case may be, he disputes the correctness of the notice or asserts that the customer is not indebted to him under the agreement.

(2) Where the trader disputes the correctness of the notice he shall give particulars of the way in which he alleges it to be wrong.

(3) Subsection (1) does not apply in relation to any agreement if the trader has previously complied with that subsection on the service of a notice under it with respect to that agreement.

(4) Subsection (1) does not apply to a non-commercial agreement.

[(6) A breach of the duty imposed by subsection (1) is actionable as a breach of statutory duty.]

104   Goods not to be treated as subject to landlord's hypothec in Scotland

Goods comprised in a hire-purchase agreement or goods comprised in a conditional sale agreement which have not become vested in the debtor shall not be treated in Scotland as subject to the landlord's hypothec—

(a) during the period between the service of a default notice in respect of the goods and the date on which the notice expires or is earlier complied with; or

(b) if the agreement is enforceable on an order of the court only, during the period between the commencement and termination of an action by the creditor to enforce the agreement.

PART VIII SECURITY

General

105   Form and content of securities

(1) Any security provided in relation to a regulated agreement shall be expressed in writing.

(2) Regulations may prescribe the form and content of documents ('security instruments') to be made in compliance with subsection (1).

(3) Regulations under subsection (2) may in particular—

(a) require specified information to be included in the prescribed manner in documents, and other specified material to be excluded;

(b) contain requirements to ensure that specified information is clearly brought to the attention of the surety, and that one part of a document is not given insufficient or excessive prominence compared with another.

(4) A security instrument is not properly executed unless—

(a) a document in the prescribed form, itself containing all the prescribed terms and conforming to regulations under subsection (2), is signed in the prescribed manner by or on behalf of the surety, and

(b) the document embodies all the terms of the security, other than implied terms, and

(c) the document, when presented or sent for the purpose of being signed by or on behalf of the surety, is in such state that its terms are readily legible, and

(d) when the document is presented or sent for the purpose of being signed by or on behalf of the surety there is also presented or sent a copy of the document.

(5) A security instrument is not properly executed unless—

(a) where the security is provided after, or at the time when, the regulated agreement is made, a copy of the executed agreement, together with a copy of any other document referred to in it, is given to the surety at the time the security is provided, or

(b) where the security is provided before the regulated agreement is made, a copy of the executed agreement, together with a copy of any other document referred to in it, is given to the surety within seven days after the regulated agreement is made.

(6) Subsection (1) does not apply to a security provided by the debtor or hirer.

(7) If—

    (a) in contravention of subsection (1) a security is not expressed in writing, or

    (b) a security instrument is improperly executed, the security, so far as provided in relation to a regulated agreement, is enforceable against the surety on an order of the court only.

(8) If an application for an order under subsection (7) is dismissed (except on technical grounds only) section 106 (ineffective securities) shall apply to the security.

(9) Regulations under section 60(1) shall include provision requiring documents embodying regulated agreements also to embody any security provided in relation to a regulated agreement by the debtor or hirer.

106 Ineffective securities

Where, under any provision of this Act, this section is applied to any security provided in relation to a regulated agreement, then, subject to section 177 (saving for registered charges)—

    (a) the security, so far as it is so provided, shall be treated as never having effect;

    (b) any property lodged with the creditor or owner solely for the purposes of the security as so provided shall be returned by him forthwith;

    (c) the creditor or owner shall take any necessary action to remove or cancel an entry in any register, so far as the entry relates to the security as so provided; and

    (d) any amount received by the creditor or owner on realisation of the security shall, so far as it is referable to the agreement, be repaid to the surety.

107 Duty to give information to surety under fixed-sum credit agreement

(1) The creditor under a regulated agreement for fixed-sum credit in relation to which security is provided, within the prescribed period after receiving a request in writing to that effect from the surety and payment of a fee of [£1], shall give to the surety (if a different person from the debtor)—

    (a) a copy of the executed agreement (if any) and of any other document referred to in it;

    (b) a copy of the security instrument (if any); and

    (c) a statement signed by or on behalf of the creditor showing, according to the information to which it is practicable for him to refer,—

        (i) the total sum paid under the agreement by the debtor,

        (ii) the total sum which has become payable under the agreement by the debtor but remains unpaid, and the various amounts comprised in that total sum, with the date when each became due, and

        (iii) the total sum which is to become payable under the agreement by the debtor, and the various amounts comprised in that total sum, with the date, or mode of determining the date, when each becomes due.

(2) If the creditor possesses insufficient information to enable him to ascertain the amounts and dates mentioned in subsection (1)(c)(iii), he shall be taken to comply with that sub-paragraph if his statement under subsection (1)(c) gives the basis on which, under the regulated agreement, they would fall to be ascertained.

(3) Subsection (1) does not apply to—

    (a) an agreement under which no sum is, or will or may become, payable by the debtor, or

    (b) a request made less than one month after a previous request under that subsection relating to the same agreement was complied with.

(4) If the creditor under an agreement fails to comply with subsection (1)—

    (a) he is not entitled, while the default continues, to enforce the security, so far as provided in relation to the agreement; [...].

(5) This section does not apply to a non-commercial agreement.

108   Duty to give information to surety under running-account credit agreement

(1) The creditor under a regulated agreement for running-account credit in relation to which security is provided, within the prescribed period after receiving a request in writing to that effect from the surety and payment of a fee of [£1], shall give to the surety (if a different person from the debtor)—

    (a) a copy of the executed agreement (if any) and of any other document referred to in it;

    (b) a copy of the security instrument (if any); and

    (c) a statement signed by or on behalf of the creditor showing, according to the information to which it is practicable for him to refer,—

        (i)   the state of the account, and

        (ii) the amount, if any, currently payable under the agreement by the debtor to the creditor, and

        (iii) the amounts and due dates of any payments which, if the debtor does not draw further on the account, will later become payable under the agreement by the debtor to the creditor.

(2) If the creditor possesses insufficient information to enable him to ascertain the amounts and dates mentioned in subsection (1)(c)(iii), he shall be taken to comply with that sub-paragraph if his statement under subsection (1)(c) gives the basis on which, under the regulated agreement, they would fall to be ascertained.

(3) Subsection (1) does not apply to—

    (a) an agreement under which no sum is, or will or may become, payable by the debtor, or

    (b) a request made less than one month after a previous request under that subsection relating to the same agreement was complied with.

(4) If the creditor under an agreement fails to comply with subsection (1)—

    (a) he is not entitled, while the default continues, to enforce the security, so far as provided in relation to the agreement; [...].

(5) This section does not apply to a non-commercial agreement.

109   Duty to give information to surety under consumer hire agreement

(1) The owner under a regulated consumer hire agreement in relation to which security is provided, within the prescribed period after receiving a request in writing to that effect from the surety and payment of a fee of [£1], shall give to the surety (if a different person from the hirer)—

    (a) a copy of the executed agreement and of any other document referred to in it;

    (b) a copy of the security instrument (if any); and

    (c) a statement signed by or on behalf of the owner showing, according to the information to which it is practicable for him to refer, the total sum which has become payable under the agreement by the hirer but remains unpaid and the various amounts comprised in that total sum, with the date when each became due.

(2) Subsection (1) does not apply to—

    (a) an agreement under which no sum is, or will or may become, payable by the hirer, or

    (b) a request made less than one month after a previous request under that subsection relating to the same agreement was complied with.

(3) If the owner under an agreement fails to comply with subsection (1)—

    (a) he is not entitled, while the default continues, to enforce the security, so far as provided in relation to the agreement; [...].

(4) This section does not apply to a non-commercial agreement.

110   Duty to give information to debtor or hirer

(1) The creditor or owner under a regulated agreement, within the prescribed period after receiving a request in writing to that effect from the debtor or hirer and payment of a fee of [£1], shall give the debtor or hirer a copy of any security instrument executed in relation to the agreement after the making of the agreement.

(2) Subsection (1) does not apply to—

(a) a non-commercial agreement, or

(b) an agreement under which no sum is, or will or may become, payable by the debtor or hirer, or

(c) a request made less than one month after a previous request under subsection (1) relating to the same agreement was complied with.

(3) If the creditor or owner under an agreement fails to comply with subsection (1)—

(a) he is not entitled, while the default continues, to enforce the security (so far as provided in relation to the agreement); [...].

111 Duty to give surety copy of default etc. notice

(1) When a default notice or a notice under section 76(1) or 98(1) is served on a debtor or hirer, a copy of the notice shall be served by the creditor or owner on any surety (if a different person from the debtor or hirer).

(2) If the creditor or owner fails to comply with subsection (1) in the case of any surety, the security is enforceable against the surety (in respect of the breach or other matter to which the notice relates) on an order of the court only.

112 Realisation of securities

Subject to section 121, regulations may provide for any matters relating to the sale or other realisation, by the creditor or owner, of property over which any right has been provided by way of security in relation to an actual or prospective regulated agreement, other than a non-commercial agreement.

113 Act not to be evaded by use of security

(1) Where a security is provided in relation to an actual or prospective regulated agreement, the security shall not be enforced so as to benefit the creditor or owner, directly or indirectly, to an extent greater (whether as respects the amount of any payment or the time or manner of its being made) than would be the case if the security were not provided and any obligations of the debtor or hirer, or his relative, under or in relation to the agreement were carried out to the extent (if any) to which they would be enforced under this Act.

(2) In accordance with subsection (1), where a regulated agreement is enforceable on an order of the court or the [OFT] only, any security provided in relation to the agreement is enforceable (so far as provided in relation to the agreement) where such an order has been made in relation to the agreement, but not otherwise.

(3) Where—

(a) a regulated agreement is cancelled under section 69(1) or becomes subject to section 69(2), or

(b) a regulated agreement is terminated under section 91, or

(c) in relation to any agreement an application for an order under section 40(2), 65(1), 124(1) or 149(2) is dismissed (except on technical grounds only), or

(d) a declaration is made by the court under section 142(1) (refusal of enforcement order) as respects any regulated agreement,

section 106 shall apply to any security provided in relation to the agreement.

(4) Where subsection (3)(d) applies and the declaration relates to a part only of the regulated agreement, section 106 shall apply to the security only so far as it concerns that part.

(5) In the case of a cancelled agreement, the duty imposed on the debtor or hirer by section 71 or 72 shall not be enforceable before the creditor or owner has discharged any duty imposed on him by section 106 (as applied by subsection (3)(a)).

(6) If the security is provided in relation to a prospective agreement or transaction, the security shall be enforceable in relation to the agreement or transaction only after the time (if any) when the agreement is made; and until that time the person providing the security shall be entitled, by notice to the creditor or owner, to require that section 106 shall thereupon apply to the security.

(7) Where an indemnity [or guarantee] is given in a case where the debtor or hirer is a minor, or [an indemnity is given in a case where he is] otherwise not of full capacity, the reference in subsection

(1) to the extent to which his obligations would be enforced shall be read in relation to the indemnity [or guarantee] as a reference to the extent to which [those obligations] would be enforced if he were of full capacity.

(8) Subsections (1) and (3) also apply where a security is provided in relation to an actual or prospective linked transaction, and in that case—

   (a) references to the agreement shall be read as references to the linked transaction, and

   (b) references to the creditor or owner shall be read as references to any person (other than the debtor or hirer, or his relative) who is a party, or prospective party, to the linked transaction.

Pledges

114   Pawn-receipts

(1)   At the time he receives the article, a person who takes any article in pawn under a regulated agreement shall give to the person from whom he receives it a receipt in the prescribed form (a 'pawn-receipt').

(2)   A person who takes any article in pawn from an individual whom he knows to be, or who appears to be and is, a minor commits an offence.

(3)   This section and sections 115 to 122 do not apply to—

   (a)   a pledge of documents of title [or of bearer bonds], or

   (b)   a non-commercial agreement.

115   Penalty for failure to supply copies of pledge agreement, etc.

If the creditor under a regulated agreement to take any article in pawn fails to observe the requirements of section 62 to 64 or 114(1) in relation to the agreement he commits an offence.

116   Redemption period

(1)   A pawn is redeemable at any time within six months after it was taken.

(2)   Subject to subsection (1), the period within which a pawn is redeemable shall be the same as the period fixed by the parties for the duration of the credit secured by the pledge, or such longer period as they may agree.

(3)   If the pawn is not redeemed by the end of the period laid down by subsections (1) and (2) (the 'redemption period'), it nevertheless remains redeemable until it is realised by the pawnee under section 121 except where under section 120(1)(a) the property in it passes to the pawnee.

(4)   No special charge shall be made for redemption of a pawn after the end of the redemption period, and charges in respect of the safe keeping of the pawn shall not be at a higher rate after the end of the redemption period than before.

117   Redemption procedure

(1)   On surrender of the pawn-receipt, and payment of the amount owing, at any time when the pawn is redeemable, the pawnee shall deliver the pawn to the bearer of the pawn-receipt.

(2)   Subsection (1) does not apply if the pawnee knows or has reasonable cause to suspect that the bearer of the pawn-receipt is neither the owner of the pawn nor authorised by the owner to redeem it.

(3)   The pawnee is not liable to any person in tort or delict for delivering the pawn where subsection (1) applies, or refusing to deliver it where the person demanding delivery does not comply with subsection (1) or, by reason of subsection (2), subsection (1) does not apply.

118   Loss etc. of pawn-receipt

(1)   A person (the 'claimant') who is not in possession of the pawn-receipt but claims to be the owner of the pawn, or to be otherwise entitled or authorised to redeem it, may do so at any time when it is redeemable by tendering to the pawnee in place of the pawn-receipt—

   (a)   a statutory declaration made by the claimant in the prescribed form, and with the prescribed contents, or

(b) where the pawn is security for fixed-sum credit not exceeding [£75] or running-account credit on which the credit limit does not exceed [£75], and the pawnee agrees, a statement in writing in the prescribed form, and with the prescribed contents, signed by the claimant.

(2) On compliance by the claimant with subsection (1), section 117 shall apply as if the declaration or statement were the pawn-receipt, and the pawn-receipt itself shall become inoperative for the purposes of section 117.

119   Unreasonable refusal to deliver pawn

(1) If a person who has taken a pawn under a regulated agreement refuses without reasonable cause to allow the pawn to be redeemed, he commits an offence.

(2) On the conviction in England and Wales of a pawnee under subsection (1) where the offence does not amount to theft, [section 148 of the Powers of Criminal Courts (Sentencing) Act 2000 (restitution orders)] shall apply as if the pawnee had been convicted of stealing the pawn.

(3) On the conviction in Northern Ireland of a pawnee under subsection (1) where the offence does not amount to theft, section 27 (orders for restitution) of the Theft Act (Northern Ireland) 1969, and any provision of the Theft Act (Northern Ireland) 1969 relating to that section, shall apply as if the pawnee had been convicted of stealing the pawn.

120   Consequence of failure to redeem

(1) If at the end of the redemption period the pawn has not been redeemed—

(a) notwithstanding anything in section 113, the property in the pawn passes to the pawnee where

[(i) the redemption period is six months,

(ii) the pawn is security for fixed-sum credit not exceeding £75 or running-account credit on which the credit limit does not exceed £75, and

(iii) the pawn was not immediately before the making of the regulated consumer credit agreement a pawn under another regulated consumer credit agreement in respect of which the debtor has discharged his indebtedness in part under section 94(3); or]

(b) in any other case the pawn becomes realisable by the pawnee.

(2) Where the debtor or hirer is entitled to apply to the court for a time order under section 129, subsection (1) shall apply with the substitution, for 'at the end of the redemption period' of 'after the expiry of five days following the end of the redemption period'.

121   Realisation of pawn

(1) When a pawn has become realisable by him, the pawnee may sell it, after giving to the pawnor (except in such cases as may be prescribed) not less than the prescribed period of notice of the intention to sell, indicating in the notice the asking price and such other particulars as may be prescribed.

(2) Within the prescribed period after the sale takes place, the pawnee shall give the pawnor the prescribed information in writing as to the sale, its proceeds and expenses.

(3) Where the net proceeds of sale are not less than the sum which, if the pawn had been redeemed on the date of the sale, would have been payable for its redemption, the debt secured by the pawn is discharged and any surplus shall be paid by the pawnee to the pawnor.

(4) Where subsection (3) does not apply, the debt shall be treated as from the date of sale as equal to the amount by which the net proceeds of sale fall short of the sum which would have been payable for the redemption of the pawn on that date.

(5) In this section the 'net proceeds of sale' is the amount realised (the 'gross amount') less the expenses (if any) of the sale.

(6) If the pawnor alleges that the gross amount is less than the true market value of the pawn on the date of sale, it is for the pawnee to prove that he and any agents employed by him in the sale used reasonable care to ensure that the true market value was obtained, and if he fails to do so subsections (3) and (4) shall have effect as if the reference in subsection (5) to the gross amount were a reference to the true market value.

(7) If the pawnor alleges that the expenses of the sale were unreasonably high, it is for the pawnee to prove that they were reasonable, and if he fails to do so subsections (3) and (4) shall have effect as if the reference in subsection (5) to expenses were a reference to reasonable expenses.

Negotiable instruments

123   Restrictions on taking and negotiating instruments

(1) A creditor or owner shall not take a negotiable instrument, other than a bank note or cheque, in discharge of any sum payable—

    (a) by the debtor or hirer under a regulated agreement, or

    (b) by any person as surety in relation to the agreement.

(2) The creditor or owner shall not negotiate a cheque taken by him in discharge of a sum payable as mentioned in subsection (1) except to a banker (within the meaning of the Bills of Exchange Act 1882).

(3) The creditor or owner shall not take a negotiable instrument as security for the discharge of any sum payable as mentioned in subsection (1).

(4) A person takes a negotiable instrument as security for the discharge of a sum if the sum is intended to be paid in some other way, and the negotiable instrument is to be presented for payment only if the sum is not paid in that way.

(5) This section does not apply where the regulated agreement is a non-commercial agreement.

(6) The Secretary of State may by order provide that this section shall not apply where the regulated agreement has a connection with a country outside the United Kingdom.

124   Consequences of breach of s. 123

(1) After any contravention of section 123 has occurred in relation to a sum payable as mentioned in section 123(1)(a), the agreement under which the sum is payable is enforceable against the debtor or hirer on an order of the court only.

(2) After any contravention of section 123 has occurred in relation to a sum payable by any surety, the security is enforceable on an order of the court only.

(3) Where an application for an order under subsection (2) is dismissed (except on technical grounds only) section 106 shall apply to the security.

125   Holders in due course

(1) A person who takes a negotiable instrument in contravention of section 123(1) or (3) is not a holder in due course, and is not entitled to enforce the instrument.

(2) Where a person negotiates a cheque in contravention of section 123(2), his doing so constitutes a defect in his title within the meaning of the Bills of Exchange Act 1882.

(3) If a person mentioned in section 123(1)(a) and (b) ('the protected person') becomes liable to a holder in due course of an instrument taken from the protected person in contravention of section 123(1) or (3), or taken from the protected person and negotiated in contravention of section 123(2), the creditor or owner shall indemnify the protected person in respect of that liability.

(4) Nothing in this Act affects the rights of the holder in due course of any negotiable instrument.

Land mortgages

126   Enforcement of land mortgages

A land mortgage securing a regulated agreement is enforceable (so far as provided in relation to the agreement) on an order of the court only.

PART IX JUDICIAL CONTROL

Enforcement of certain regulated agreements and securities

127   Enforcement orders in cases of infringement

(1) In the case of an application for an enforcement order under—

    [(za) section 55(2) (disclosure of information), or]

    [(zb) section 61B(3) (duty to supply copy of overdraft agreement), or]

(a)   section 65(1) (improperly executed agreements), or

(b)   section 105(7)(a) or (b) (improperly executed security instruments), or

(c)   section 111(2) (failure to serve copy of notice on surety), or

(d)   section 124(1) or (2) (taking of negotiable instrument in contravention of section 123),

the court shall dismiss the application if, but […] only if, it considers it just to do so having regard to—

(i)   prejudice caused to any person by the contravention in question, and the degree of culpability for it; and

(ii)   the powers conferred on the court by subsection (2) and sections 135 and 136.

(2) If it appears to the court just to do so, it may in an enforcement order reduce or discharge any sum payable by the debtor or hirer, or any surety, so as to compensate him for prejudice suffered as a result of the contravention in question.

128   Enforcement orders on death of debtor or hirer

The court shall make an order under section 86(2) if, but only if, the creditor or owner proves that he has been unable to satisfy himself that the present and future obligations of the debtor or hirer under the agreement are likely to be discharged.

Extension of time

129   Time orders

(1) [Subject to subsection (3) below,] If it appears to the court just to do so—

(a) on an application for an enforcement order; or

(b) on an application made by a debtor or hirer under this paragraph after service on him of—

(i)   a default notice, or

(ii)   a notice under section 76(1) or 98(1);

[(ba) on an application made by a debtor or hirer under this paragraph after he has been given a notice under section 86B or 86c; or]

(c) in an action brought by a creditor or owner to enforce a regulated agreement or any security, or recover possession of any goods or land to which a regulated agreement relates,

the court may make an order under this section (a 'time order').

(2) A time order shall provide for one or both of the following, as the court considers just—

(a) the payment by the debtor or hirer or any surety of any sum owed under a regulated agreement or a security by such instalments, payable at such times, as the court having regard to the means of the debtor or hirer and any surety, considers reasonable;

(b) the remedying by the debtor or hirer of any breach of a regulated agreement (other than non-payment of money) within such period as the court may specify.

[(3) Where in Scotland a time to pay direction or a time order has been made in relation to a debt, it shall not thereafter be competent to make a time order in relation to the same debt.]

[129A   Debtor or hirer to give notice of intent etc. to creditor or owner

(1) A debtor or hirer may make an application under section 129(1)(ba) in relation to a regulated agreement only if—

(a) following his being given the notice under section 86B or 86C, he gave a notice within subsection (2) to the creditor or owner; and

(b) a period of at least 14 days has elapsed after the day on which he gave that notice to the creditor or owner.

(2) A notice is within this subsection if it—

(a) indicates that the debtor or hirer intends to make the application;

(b) indicates that he wants to make a proposal to the creditor or owner in relation to his making of payments under the agreement; and

(c) gives details of that proposal.]

130 Supplemental provisions about time orders

(1) Where in accordance with rules of court an offer to pay any sum by instalments is made by the debtor or hirer and accepted by the creditor or owner, the court may in accordance with rules of court make a time order under section 129(2)(a) giving effect to the offer without hearing evidence of means.

(2) In the case of a hire-purchase or conditional sale agreement only, a time order under section 129(2)(a) may deal with sums which, although not payable by the debtor at the time the order is made, would if the agreement continued in force become payable under it subsequently.

(3) A time order under section 129(2)(a) shall not be made where the regulated agreement is secured by a pledge if, by virtue of regulations made under section 76(5), 87(4) or 98(5), service of a notice is not necessary for enforcement of the pledge.

(4) Where, following the making of a time order in relation to a regulated hire-purchase or conditional sale agreement or a regulated consumer hire agreement, the debtor or hirer is in possession of the goods, he shall be treated (except in the case of a debtor to whom the creditor's title has passed) as a bailee or (in Scotland) a custodier of the goods under the terms of the agreement, notwithstanding that the agreement has been terminated.

(5) Without prejudice to anything done by the creditor or owner before the commencement of the period specified in a time order made under section 129(2)(b) ('the relevant period'),—

    (a) he shall not while the relevant period subsists take in relation to the agreement any action such as is mentioned in section 87(1);

    (b) where—

        (i)   a provision of the agreement ('the secondary provision') becomes operative only on breach of another provision of the agreement ('the primary provision'), and

        (ii) the time order provides for the remedying of such a breach of the primary provision within the relevant period,

    he shall not treat the secondary provision as operative before the end of that period;

    (c) if while the relevant period subsists the breach to which the order relates is remedied it shall be treated as not having occurred.

(6) On the application of any person affected by a time order, the court may vary or revoke the order.

[Interest]

[130A   Interest payable on judgment debts etc.

(1) If the creditor or owner under a regulated agreement wants to be able to recover from the debtor or hirer post-judgment interest in connection with a sum that is required to be paid under a judgment given in relation to the agreement (the 'judgment sum'), he—

    (a) after the giving of that judgment, shall give the debtor or hirer a notice under this section (the 'first required notice'); and

    (b) after the giving of the first required notice, shall give the debtor or hirer further notices under this section at intervals of not more than six months.

(2) The debtor or hirer shall have no liability to pay post-judgment interest in connection with the judgment sum to the extent that the interest is calculated by reference to a period occurring before the day on which he is given the first required notice.

(3) If the creditor or owner fails to give the debtor or hirer a notice under this section within the period of six months beginning with the day after the day on which such a notice was last given to the debtor or hirer, the debtor or hirer shall have no liability to pay post-judgment interest in connection with the judgment sum to the extent that the interest is calculated by reference to the whole or to a part of the period which—

    (a) begins immediately after the end of that period of six months; and

    (b) ends at the end of the day on which the notice is given to the debtor or hirer.

(4) The debtor or hirer shall have no liability to pay any sum in connection with the preparation or the giving to him of a notice under this section.

(5) A notice under this section may be incorporated in a statement or other notice which the creditor or owner gives the debtor or hirer in relation to the agreement by virtue of another provision of this Act.

(6) Regulations may make provision about the form and content of notices under this section.

(7) This section does not apply in relation to post-judgment interest which is required to be paid by virtue of any of the following—

(a) section 4 of the Administration of Justice (Scotland) Act 1972;

(b) Article 127 of the Judgments Enforcement (Northern Ireland) Order 1981;

(c) section 74 of the County Courts Act 1984.

(8) This section does not apply in relation to a non-commercial agreement or to a small agreement.

(9) In this section 'post-judgment interest' means interest to the extent calculated by reference to a period occurring after the giving of the judgment under which the judgment sum is required to be paid.]

Protection of property pending proceedings

131   Protection orders

The court, on application of the creditor or owner under a regulated agreement, may make such orders as it thinks just for protecting any property of the creditor or owner, or property subject to any security, from damage or depreciation pending the determination of any proceedings under this Act, including orders restricting or prohibiting use of the property or giving directions as to its custody.

Hire and hire-purchase etc. agreements

132   Financial relief for hirer

(1) Where the owner under a regulated consumer hire agreement recovers possession of goods to which the agreement relates otherwise than by action, the hirer may apply to the court for an order that—

(a) the whole or part of any sum paid by the hirer to the owner in respect of the goods shall be repaid, and

(b) the obligation to pay the whole or part of any sum owed by the hirer to the owner in respect of the goods shall cease,

and if it appears to the court just to do so, having regard to the extent of the enjoyment of the goods by the hirer, the court shall grant the application in full or in part.

(2) Where in proceedings relating to a regulated consumer hire agreement the court makes an order for the delivery to the owner of goods to which the agreement relates the court may include in the order the like provision as may be made in an order under subsection (1).

133   Hire-purchase etc. agreements: special powers of court

(1) If, in relation to a regulated hire-purchase or conditional sale agreement, it appears to the court just to do so—

(a) on an application for an enforcement order or time order; or

(b) in an action brought by the creditor to recover possession of goods to which the agreement relates,

the court may—

(i)   make an order (a 'return order') for the return to the creditor of goods to which the agreement relates;

(ii) make an order (a 'transfer order') for the transfer to the debtor of the creditor's title to certain goods to which the agreement relates ('the transferred goods'), and the return to the creditor of the remainder of the goods.

(2) In determining for the purposes of this section how much of the total price has been paid ('the paid-up sum'), the court may—

    (a) treat any sum paid by the debtor, or owed by the creditor, in relation to the goods as part of the paid-up sum;

    (b) deduct any sum owed by the debtor in relation to the goods (otherwise than as part of the total price) from the paid-up sum,

and make corresponding reductions in amounts so owed.

    (3) Where a transfer order is made, the transferred goods shall be such of the goods to which the agreement relates as the court thinks just; but a transfer order shall be made only where the paid-up sum exceeds the part of the total price referable to the transferred goods by an amount equal to at least one-third of the unpaid balance of the total price.

    (4) Notwithstanding the making of a return order or transfer order, the debtor may at any time before the goods enter the possession of the creditor, on payment of the balance of the total price and the fulfilment of any other necessary conditions, claim the goods ordered to be returned to the creditor.

    (5) When, in pursuance of a time order or under this section, the total price of goods under a regulated hire-purchase agreement or regulated conditional sale agreement is paid and any other necessary conditions are fulfilled, the creditor's title to the goods vests in the debtor.

    (6) If, in contravention of a return order or transfer order, any goods to which the order relates are not returned to the creditor, the court, on the application of the creditor, may—

    (a) revoke so much of the order as relates to those goods, and

    (b) order the debtor to pay the creditor the unpaid portion of so much of the total price as is referable to those goods.

    (7) For the purposes of this section, the part of the total price referable to any goods is the part assigned to those goods by the agreement or (if no such assignment is made) the part determined by the court to be reasonable.

134 Evidence of adverse detention in hire-purchase etc. cases

    (1) Where goods are comprised in a regulated hire-purchase agreement, regulated conditional sale agreement or regulated consumer hire agreement, and the creditor or owner—

    (a) brings an action or makes an application to enforce a right to recover possession of the goods from the debtor or hirer and

    (b) proves that a demand for the delivery of the goods was included in the default notice under section 88(5), or that, after the right to recover possession of the goods accrued but before the action was begun or the application was made, he made a request in writing to the debtor or hirer to surrender the goods,

then, for the purposes of the claim of the creditor or owner to recover possession of the goods, the possession of them by the debtor or hirer shall be deemed to be adverse to the creditor or owner.

    (2) In subsection (1) 'the debtor or hirer' includes a person in possession of the goods at any time between the debtor's or hirer's death and the grant of probate or administration, or (in Scotland) confirmation.

    (3) Nothing in this section affects a claim for damages for conversion or (in Scotland) for delict.

Supplemental provisions as to orders

135 Power to impose conditions, or suspend operation of order

    (1) If it considers it just to do so, the court may in an order made by it in relation to a regulated agreement include provisions—

    (a) making the operation of any term of the order conditional on the doing of specified acts by any party to the proceedings;

    (b) suspending the operation of any term of the order either—

      (i)   until such time as the court subsequently directs, or

      (ii) until the occurrence of a specified act or omission.

    (2) The court shall not suspend the operation of a term requiring the delivery up of goods by any person unless satisfied that the goods are in his possession or control.

(3) In the case of a consumer hire agreement, the court shall not so use its powers under subsection (1)(b) as to extend the period for which, under the terms of the agreement, the hirer is entitled to possession of the goods to which the agreement relates.

(4) On the application of any person affected by a provision included under subsection (1), the court may vary the provision.

136   Power to vary agreements and securities

(1) The court may in an order made by it under this Act include such provision as it considers just for amending any agreement or security in consequence of a term of the order.

[Unfair relationships]

[140A   Unfair relationships between creditors and debtors

(1) The court may make an order under section 140B in connection with a credit agreement if it determines that the relationship between the creditor and the debtor arising out of the agreement (or the agreement taken with any related agreement) is unfair to the debtor because of one or more of the following—

    (a) any of the terms of the agreement or of any related agreement;

    (b) the way in which the creditor has exercised or enforced any of his rights under the agreement or any related agreement;

    (c) any other thing done (or not done) by, or on behalf of, the creditor (either before or after the making of the agreement or any related agreement).

(2) In deciding whether to make a determination under this section the court shall have regard to all matters it thinks relevant (including matters relating to the creditor and matters relating to the debtor).

(3) For the purposes of this section the court shall (except to the extent that it is not appropriate to do so) treat anything done (or not done) by, or on behalf of, or in relation to, an associate or a former associate of the creditor as if done (or not done) by, or on behalf of, or in relation to, the creditor.

(4) A determination may be made under this section in relation to a relationship notwithstanding that the relationship may have ended.

(5) An order under section 140B shall not be made in connection with a credit agreement which is an exempt agreement by virtue of section 16(6C).]

[140B   Powers of court in relation to unfair relationships

(1) An order under this section in connection with a credit agreement may do one or more of the following—

    (a) require the creditor, or any associate or former associate of his, to repay (in whole or in part) any sum paid by the debtor or by a surety by virtue of the agreement or any related agreement (whether paid to the creditor, the associate or the former associate or to any other person);

    (b) require the creditor, or any associate or former associate of his, to do or not to do (or to cease doing) anything specified in the order in connection with the agreement or any related agreement;

    (c) reduce or discharge any sum payable by the debtor or by a surety by virtue of the agreement or any related agreement;

    (d) direct the return to a surety of any property provided by him for the purposes of a security;

    (e) otherwise set aside (in whole or in part) any duty imposed on the debtor or on a surety by virtue of the agreement or any related agreement;

    (f) alter the terms of the agreement or of any related agreement;

    (g) direct accounts to be taken, or (in Scotland) an accounting to be made, between any persons.

(2) An order under this section may be made in connection with a credit agreement only—

    (a) on an application made by the debtor or by a surety;

(b) at the instance of the debtor or a surety in any proceedings in any court to which the debtor and the creditor are parties, being proceedings to enforce the agreement or any related agreement; or

(c) at the instance of the debtor or a surety in any other proceedings in any court where the amount paid or payable under the agreement or any related agreement is relevant.

(3) An order under this section may be made notwithstanding that its effect is to place on the creditor, or any associate or former associate of his, a burden in respect of an advantage enjoyed by another person.

(4) An application under subsection (2)(a) may only be made—

(a) in England and Wales, to the county court;

(b) in Scotland, to the sheriff court;

(c) in Northern Ireland, to the High Court (subject to subsection (6)).

(5) In Scotland such an application may be made in the sheriff court for the district in which the debtor or surety resides or carries on business.

(6) In Northern Ireland such an application may be made to the county court if the credit agreement is an agreement under which the creditor provides the debtor with—

(a) fixed-sum credit not exceeding £15,000; or

(b) running-account credit on which the credit limit does not exceed £15,000.

(7) Without prejudice to any provision which may be made by rules of court made in relation to county courts in Northern Ireland, such rules may provide that an application made by virtue of subsection (6) may be made in the county court for the division in which the debtor or surety resides or carries on business.

(8) A party to any proceedings mentioned in subsection (2) shall be entitled, in accordance with rules of court, to have any person who might be the subject of an order under this section made a party to the proceedings.

(9) If, in any such proceedings, the debtor or a surety alleges that the relationship between the creditor and the debtor is unfair to the debtor, it is for the creditor to prove to the contrary.]

[140C   Interpretation of ss. 140A and 140B

(1) In this section and in sections 140A and 140B 'credit agreement' means any agreement between an individual (the 'debtor') and any other person (the 'creditor') by which the creditor provides the debtor with credit of any amount.

(2) References in this section and in sections 140A and 140B to the creditor or to the debtor under a credit agreement include—

(a) references to the person to whom his rights and duties under the agreement have passed by assignment or operation of law;

(b) where two or more persons are the creditor or the debtor, references to any one or more of those persons.

(3) The definition of 'court' in section 189(1) does not apply for the purposes of sections 140A and 140B.

(4) References in sections 140A and 140B to an agreement related to a credit agreement (the 'main agreement') are references to—

(a) a credit agreement consolidated by the main agreement;

(b) a linked transaction in relation to the main agreement or to a credit agreement within paragraph (a);

(c) a security provided in relation to the main agreement, to a credit agreement within paragraph (a) or to a linked transaction within paragraph (b).

(5) In the case of a credit agreement which is not a regulated consumer credit agreement, for the purposes of subsection (4) a transaction shall be treated as being a linked transaction in relation to that agreement if it would have been such a transaction had that agreement been a regulated consumer credit agreement.

(6) For the purposes of this section and section 140B the definitions of 'security' and 'surety' in section 189(1) apply (with any appropriate changes) in relation to—

(a) a credit agreement which is not a consumer credit agreement as if it were a consumer credit agreement; and

(b) a transaction which is a linked transaction by virtue of subsection (5).

(7) For the purposes of this section a credit agreement (the 'earlier agreement') is consolidated by another credit agreement (the 'later agreement') if—

(a) the later agreement is entered into by the debtor (in whole or in part) for purposes connected with debts owed by virtue of the earlier agreement; and

(b) at any time prior to the later agreement being entered into the parties to the earlier agreement included—

(i)   the debtor under the later agreement; and

(ii) the creditor under the later agreement or an associate or a former associate of his.

(8) Further, if the later agreement is itself consolidated by another credit agreement (whether by virtue of this subsection or subsection (7)), then the earlier agreement is consolidated by that other agreement as well.]

[140D Advice and information

The advice and information published by the OFT under section 229 of the Enterprise Act 2002 shall indicate how the OFT expects sections 140A to 140C of this Act to interact with Part 8 of that Act.]

Miscellaneous

141 Jurisdiction and parties

(1) In England and Wales the county court shall have jurisdiction to hear and determine—

(a) any action by the creditor or owner to enforce a regulated agreement or any security relating to it;

(b) any action to enforce any linked transaction against the debtor or hirer or his relative, and such an action shall not be brought in any other court.

(2) Where an action or application is brought in the High Court which, by virtue of this Act, ought to have been brought in the county court it shall not be treated as improperly brought, but shall be transferred to the county court.

[(3) In Scotland the sheriff court shall have jurisdiction to hear and determine any action falling within subsection (1) and such an action shall not be brought in any other court.]

[(3A) Subject to subsection (3B) an action which is brought in the sheriff court by virtue of subsection (3) shall be brought only in one of the following courts, namely—

(a) the court for the place where the debtor or hirer is domiciled (within the meaning of section 41 or 42 of the Civil Jurisdiction and Judgments Act 1982);

(b) the court for the place where the debtor or hirer carries on business; and

(c) where the purpose of the action is to assert, declare or determine proprietary or possessory rights, or rights of security, in or over movable property, or to obtain authority to dispose of movable property, the court for the place where the property is situated.

(3B) Subsection (3A) shall not apply—

(a) where Rule 3 of Schedule 8 to the said Act of 1982 applies; or

(b) where the jurisdiction of another court has been prorogated by an agreement entered into after the dispute has arisen.]

(4) In Northern Ireland the county court shall have jurisdiction to hear and determine any action or application falling within subsection (1).

(5) Except as may be provided by rules of court, all the parties to a regulated agreement, and any surety, shall be made parties to any proceedings relating to the agreement.

142 Power to declare rights of parties

(1) Where under any provision of this Act a thing can be done by a creditor or owner on an enforcement order only, and either—

(a) the court dismisses (except on technical grounds only) an application for an enforcement order, or

(b) where no such application has been made or such an application has been dismissed on technical grounds only an interested party applies to the court for a declaration under this subsection,

the court may if it thinks just make a declaration that the creditor or owner is not entitled to do that thing, and thereafter no application for an enforcement order in respect of it shall be entertained.

(2) Where—

(a) a regulated agreement or linked transaction is cancelled under section 69(1), or becomes subject to section 69(2), or

(b) a regulated agreement is terminated under section 91, and an interested party applies to the court for a declaration under this subsection, the court may make a declaration to that effect.

PART X ANCILLARY CREDIT BUSINESSES

Definitions

145 Types of ancillary credit business

(1) An ancillary credit business is any business so far as it comprises or relates to—

(a)   credit brokerage,

(b)   debt-adjusting,

(c)   debt-counselling,

(d)   debt-collecting,

[(da) debt administration,]

[(db) the provision of credit information services, or]

(e)   the operation of a credit reference agency.

(2) Subject to section 146(5) [and (5A)], credit brokerage is the effecting of introductions—

(a) of individuals desiring to obtain credit—

(i)   to persons carrying on businesses to which this sub-paragraph applies, or

(ii) in the case of an individual desiring to obtain credit to finance the acquisition or provision of a dwelling occupied by himself or his relative, to any person carrying on a business in the course of which he provides credit secured on land, or

(b) of individuals desiring to obtain goods on hire to persons carrying on businesses to which this paragraph applies, or

(c) of individuals desiring to obtain credit, or to obtain goods on hire, to other credit-brokers.

(3) Subsection (2)(a)(i) applies to—

(a) a consumer credit business;

(b) a business which comprises or relates to consumer credit agreements being, otherwise than by virtue of section 16(5)(a), exempt agreements;

(c) a business which comprises or relates to unregulated agreements where—

(i)   the [law applicable to] the agreement is the law of a country outside the United Kingdom, and

(ii) if the [law applicable to] the agreement were the law of a part of the United Kingdom it would be a regulated consumer credit agreement.

(4) Subsection (2)(b) applies to—

(a) a consumer hire business;

[(aa) a business which comprises or relates to consumer hire agreements being, otherwise than by virtue of section 16(6), exempt agreements;]

(b) a business which comprises or relates to unregulated agreements where—

(i)   the [law applicable to] the agreement is the law of a country outside the United Kingdom, and

       (ii) if the [law applicable to] the agreement were the law of a part of the United Kingdom it would be a regulated consumer hire agreement.

(5) Subject to [section 146(5B) and (6)], debt-adjusting is, in relation to debts due under consumer credit agreements or consumer hire agreements,—

    (a) negotiating with the creditor or owner, on behalf of the debtor or hirer, terms for the discharge of a debt, or

    (b) taking over, in return for payments by the debtor or hirer, his obligation to discharge a debt, or

    (c) any similar activity concerned with the liquidation of a debt.

(6) Subject to [section 146 (5C) and (6)], debt-counselling is the giving of advice to debtors or hirers about the liquidation of debts due under consumer credit agreements or consumer hire agreements.

(7) Subject to section 146(6), debt-collecting is the taking of steps to procure payment of debts due under consumer credit agreements or consumer hire agreements.

[(7A) Subject to section 146(7), debt administration is the taking of steps—

    (a) to perform duties under a consumer credit agreement or a consumer hire agreement on behalf of the creditor or owner, or

    (b) to exercise or to enforce rights under such an agreement on behalf of the creditor or owner,

so far as the taking of such steps is not debt-collecting.]

[(7B) A person provides credit information services if—

    (a) he takes any steps mentioned in subsection (7C) on behalf of an individual; or

    (b) he gives advice to an individual in relation to the taking of any such steps.

(7C) Those steps are steps taken with a view—

    (a) to ascertaining whether a credit information agency (other than that person himself if he is one) holds information relevant to the financial standing of an individual;

    (b) to ascertaining the contents of such information held by such an agency;

    (c) to securing the correction of, the omission of anything from, or the making of any other kind of modification of, such information so held; or

    (d) to securing that such an agency which holds such information—

        (i) stops holding it; or

        (ii) does not provide it to another person.

(7D) In subsection (7C) 'credit information agency' means—

    (a) a person carrying on a consumer credit business or a consumer hire business;

    (b) a person carrying on a business so far as it comprises or relates to credit brokerage, debt-adjusting, debt-counselling, debt-collecting, debt administration or the operation of a credit reference agency;

    (c) a person carrying on a business which would be a consumer credit business except that it comprises or relates to consumer credit agreements being, otherwise than by virtue of section 16(5)(a), exempt agreements; or

    (d) a person carrying on a business which would be a consumer hire business except that it comprises or relates to consumer hire agreements being, otherwise than by virtue of section 16(6), exempt agreements.]

(8) A credit reference agency is a person carrying on a business comprising the furnishing of persons with information relevant to the financial standing of individuals, being information collected by the agency for that purpose.

146 Exceptions from section 145

(1) A barrister or advocate acting in that capacity is not to be treated as doing so in the course of any ancillary credit business.

(2) A solicitor engaging in contentious business (as defined in [section 87(1) of the Solicitors Act 1974]) is not to be treated as doing so in the course of any ancillary credit business.

[(2A) An authorised person (other than a barrister or solicitor) engaging in contentious business is not to be treated as doing so in the course of any ancillary credit business.

(2B) In subsection (2A)—

'authorised person' means a person who, for the purposes of the Legal Services Act 2007, is an authorised person in relation to an activity which constitutes the exercise of a right of audience or the conduct of litigation (within the meaning of that Act);

'contentious business' means business done in or for the purposes of proceedings begun before a court or before an arbitrator, not being non-contentious or common form probate business (within the meaning of section 128 of the Supreme Court Act 1981).]

(3) A solicitor within the meaning of the Solicitors (Scotland) Act 1933 engaging in business done in or for the purposes of proceedings before a court or before an arbiter is not to be treated as doing so in the course of any ancillary credit business.

(4) A solicitor in Northern Ireland engaging in [contentious business (as defined in Article 3(2) of the Solicitors (Northern Ireland) Order 1976], is not to be treated as doing so in the course of any ancillary credit business.

(5) For the purposes of section 145(2), introductions effected by an individual by canvassing off trade premises either debtor-creditor-supplier agreements falling within section 12(a) or regulated consumer hire agreements shall be disregarded if—

(a) the introductions are not effected by him in the capacity of an employee, and

(b) he does not by any other method effect introductions falling within section 145(2).

[(5A) It is not credit brokerage for a person to effect the introduction of an individual desiring to obtain credit if the introduction is made—

(a) to an authorised person, within the meaning of the 2000 Act, who has permission under that Act to enter into a relevant agreement as lender or home purchase provider (as the case may be); or

(b) to a qualifying broker,

with a view to that individual obtaining credit under the relevant agreement.

(5B) It is not debt-adjusting for a person to carry on an activity mentioned in paragraph (a), (b) or (c) of section 145(5) if—

(a) the debt in question is due under a relevant agreement; and

(b) that activity is a regulated activity for the purposes of the 2000 Act.

(5C) It is not debt-counselling for a person to give advice to debtors about the liquidation of debts if—

(a) the debt in question is due under a relevant agreement; and

(b) giving that advice is a regulated activity for the purposes of the 2000 Act.

(5D) In this section—

'the 2000 Act' means the Financial Services and Markets Act 2000;

'relevant agreement' means an agreement which—

(a) is secured by a land mortgage, or

(b) is or forms part of a regulated home purchase plan,

but only if entering into the agreement as lender or home purchase provider (as the case may be) is a regulated activity for the purposes of the 2000 Act.;]

'qualifying broker' means a person who may effect introductions of the kind mentioned in sub-section (5A) without contravening the general prohibition, within the meaning of section 19 of the 2000 Act, and references to 'regulated activities', 'regulated home purchase plan' and 'home purchase provider' and the definition of 'qualifying broker' must be read with—

(a) section 22 of the 2000 Act (regulated activities: power to specify classes of activity and categories of investment);

(b) any order for the time being in force under that section; and

(c) Schedule 2 to that Act.]

(6) It is not debt-adjusting, debt-counselling or debt-collecting for a person to do anything in relation to a debt arising under an agreement if [any of the following conditions is satisfied]—

[(aa) that he is the creditor or owner under the agreement, or]

(c) [that] he is the supplier in relation to the agreement, or

> (d)   [that] he is a credit-broker who has acquired the business of the person who was the supplier in relation to the agreement, or
>
> (e)   [that] he is a person prevented by subsection (5) from being treated as a credit-broker, and the agreement was made in consequence of an introduction (whether made by him or another person) which, under subsection (5), is to be disregarded.

[(7) It is not debt administration for a person to take steps to perform duties, or to exercise or enforce rights, under an agreement on behalf of the creditor or owner if any of the conditions mentioned in subsection (6)(aa) to (e) is satisfied in relation to that person.]

Licensing

147   Application of Part III

(2) Without prejudice to the generality of section 26, regulations under that section […] may include provisions regulating the collection and dissemination of information by credit reference agencies.

148   Agreement for services of unlicensed trader

(1) An agreement for the services of a person carrying on ancillary credit business (the 'trader'), if made when the trader was unlicensed, is enforceable against the other party (the 'customer') only where the [OFT] has made an order under subsection (2) which applies to the agreement.

(2) The trader or his successor in title may apply to the [OFT] for an order that agreements within subsection (1) are to be treated as if made when the trader was licensed.

(3) Unless the [OFT] determines to make an order under subsection (2) in accordance with the application, [it] shall, before determining the application, by notice—

> (a) inform the trader, giving [its] reasons, that, as the case may be, [it] is minded to refuse the application, or to grant it in terms different from those applied for, describing them, and
>
> (b) invite the trader to submit to the [OFT] representations in support of his application in accordance with section 34.

(4) In determining whether or not to make an order under subsection (2) in respect of any period the [OFT] shall consider, in addition to any other relevant factors,—

> (a) how far, if at all, customers under agreements made by the trader during that period were prejudiced by the trader's conduct,
>
> (b) whether or not the [OFT] would have been likely to grant a licence covering that period on an application by the trader, and
>
> (c) the degree of culpability for the failure to obtain a licence.

(5) If the [OFT] thinks fit, [it] may in an order under subsection (2)—

> (a) limit the order to specified agreements, or agreements of a specified description or made at a specified time;
>
> (b) make the order conditional on the doing of specified acts by the trader.

[(6) This section does not apply to an agreement made by a consumer credit EEA firm unless at the time it was made that firm was precluded from entering into it as a result of—

> (a) a consumer credit prohibition imposed under section 203 of the Financial Services and Markets Act 2000; or
>
> (b) a restriction imposed on the firm under section 204 of that Act.]

149   Regulated agreements made on introductions by unlicensed credit-broker

(1) A regulated agreement made by a debtor or hirer who, for the purpose of making that agreement, was introduced to the creditor or owner by an unlicensed credit-broker is enforceable against the debtor or hirer only where—

> (a) on the application of the credit-broker, the [OFT] has made an order under section 148(2) in respect of a period including the time when the introduction was made, and the order does not (whether in general terms or specifically) exclude the application of this paragraph to the regulated agreement, or
>
> (b) the [OFT] has made an order under subsection (2) which applies to the agreement.

(2) Where during any period individuals were introduced to a person carrying on a consumer credit business or consumer hire business by an unlicensed credit-broker for the purpose of making regulated agreements with the person carrying on that business, that person or his successor in title may apply to the Director for an order that regulated agreements so made are to be treated as if the credit-broker had been licensed at the time of the introduction.

(3) Unless the [OFT] determines to make an order under subsection (2) in accordance with the application, [it] shall, before determining the application, by notice—

    (a) inform the applicant, giving [its] reasons, that, as the case may be, [it] is minded to refuse the application, or to grant it in terms different from those applied for, describing them, and

    (b) invite the applicant to submit to the [OFT] representations in support of his application in accordance with section 34.

(4) In determining whether or not to make an order under subsection (2) the [OFT] shall consider, in addition to any other relevant factors—

    (a) how far, if at all, debtors or hirers under regulated agreements to which the application relates were prejudiced by the credit-broker's conduct, and

    (b) the degree of culpability of the applicant in facilitating the carrying on by the credit-broker of his business when unlicensed.

(5) If the [OFT] thinks fit, [it] may in an order under subsection (2)—

    (a) limit the order to specified agreements, or agreements of a specified description or made at a specified time;

    (b) make the order conditional on the doing of specified acts by the applicant.

[(6) For the purposes of this section, 'unlicensed credit-broker' does not include a consumer credit EEA firm unless at the time the introduction was made that firm was precluded from making it as a result of—

    (a) a consumer credit prohibition imposed under section 203 of the Financial Services and Markets Act 2000; or

    (b) a restriction imposed on the firm under section 204 of that Act.]

Seeking business

151 Advertisements

(1) Sections 44 to 47 apply to an advertisement published for the purposes of a business of credit brokerage carried on by any person, whether it advertises the services of that person or the services of persons to whom he effects introductions, as they apply to an advertisement to which Part IV applies.

(2) Sections 44 [. . .] and 47 apply to an advertisement, published for the purposes of a business carried on by the advertiser, indicating that he is willing to advise on debts, [to] engage in transactions concerned with the liquidation of debts [or to provide credit information services], as they apply to an advertisement to which Part IV applies.

[(2A) An advertisement does not fall within subsection (1) or (2) in so far as it is a communication of an invitation or inducement to engage in investment activity within the meaning of section 21 of the Financial Services and Markets Act 2000, other than an exempt generic communication (as defined in section 43(3B)).]

(3) The Secretary of State may by order provide that an advertisement published for the purposes of a business of credit brokerage, debt adjusting [, debt-counselling or the provision of credit information services] shall not fall within subsection (1) or (2) if it is of a description specified in the order.

(4) An advertisement [(other than one for credit information services)] does not fall within subsection (2) if it indicates that the advertiser is not willing to act in relation to consumer credit agreements and consumer hire agreements.

(5) In subsections (1) and (3) 'credit brokerage' includes the effecting of introductions of individuals desiring to obtain credit to any person carrying on a business in the course of which he provides credit secured on land.

152 Application of sections 52 to 54 to credit brokerage etc.

(1) Sections 52 to 54 apply to a business of credit brokerage, debt-adjusting [, debt-counselling or the provision of credit information services] as they apply to a consumer credit business.

(2) In their application to a business of credit brokerage, sections 52 and 53 shall apply to the giving of quotations and information about the business of any person to whom the credit-broker effects introductions as well as to the giving of quotations and information about his own business.

153 Definition of canvassing off trade premises (agreements for ancillary credit services)

(1) An individual (the 'canvasser') canvasses off trade premises the services of a person carrying on an ancillary credit business if he solicits the entry of another individual (the 'consumer') into an agreement for the provision to the consumer of those services by making oral representations to the consumer, or any other individual, during a visit by the canvasser to any place (not excluded by subsection (2)) where the consumer, or that other individual as the case may be, is, being a visit—

  (a) carried out for the purpose of making such oral representations to individuals who are at that place, but

  (b) not carried out in response to a request made on a previous occasion.

(2) A place is excluded from subsection (1) if it is a place where (whether on a permanent or temporary basis)—

  (a) the ancillary credit business is carried on, or

  (b) any business is carried on by the canvasser or the person whose employee or agent the canvasser is, or by the consumer.

154 Prohibition of canvassing certain ancillary credit services off trade premises

It is an offence to canvass off trade premises the services of a person carrying on a business of credit-brokerage, debt-adjusting [, debt-counselling or the provision of credit information services].

155 Right to recover brokerage fees

(1) [Subject to subsection (2A),] The excess over [£5] of a fee or commission for his services charged by a credit-broker to an individual to whom this subsection applies shall cease to be payable or, as the case may be, shall be recoverable by the individual if the introduction does not result in his entering into a relevant agreement within the six months following the introduction (disregarding any agreement which is cancelled under section 69(1) or becomes subject to section 69(2)).

(2) Subsection (1) applies to an individual who sought an introduction for a purpose which would have been fulfilled by his entry into—

  (a) a regulated agreement, or

  (b) in the case of an individual such as is referred to in section 145(2)(a)(ii), an agreement for credit secured on land, or

  (c) an agreement such as is referred to in section 145(3)(b) or (c) or (4)(b).

[(2A) But subsection (1) does not apply where—

  (a) the fee or commission relates to the effecting of an introduction of a kind mentioned in section 146(5A); and

  (b) the person charging that fee or commission is an authorised person or an appointed representative, within the meaning of the Financial Services and Markets Act 2000.]

(3) An agreement is a relevant agreement for the purposes of subsection (1) in relation to an individual if it is an agreement such as is referred to in subsection (2) in relation to that individual.

(4) In the case of an individual desiring to obtain credit under a consumer credit agreement, any sum payable or paid by him to a credit-broker otherwise than as a fee or commission for the credit-broker's services shall for the purposes of subsection (1) be treated as such a fee or commission if it enters, or would enter, into the total charge for credit.

Entry into agreements

156 Entry into agreements
Regulations may make provision, in relation to agreements entered into in the course of a business of credit brokerage, debt-adjusting, debt-counselling or the provision of credit information services, corresponding, with such modifications as the Secretary of State thinks fit, to the provision which is or may be made by or under sections 55, 60, 61, 62, 63, 65, 127, 179 or 180 in relation to agreements to which those sections apply.

Credit reference agencies

157 Duty to disclose name etc. of agency
[(A1) Where a creditor under a prospective regulated agreement, other than an excluded agreement, decides not to proceed with it on the basis of information obtained by the creditor from a credit reference agency, the creditor must, when informing the debtor of the decision—
  (a) inform the debtor that this decision has been reached on the basis of information from a credit reference agency, and
  (b) provide the debtor with the particulars of the agency including its name, address and telephone number.]
  (1) [In any other case,] A creditor, owner or negotiator, within the prescribed period after receiving a request in writing to that effect from the debtor or hirer, shall give him notice of the name and address of any credit reference agency from which the creditor, owner or negotiator has, during the antecedent negotiations, applied for information about his financial standing.
  (2) Subsection (1) does not apply to a request received more than 28 days after the termination of the antecedent negotiations, whether on the making of the regulated agreement or otherwise.
  [(2A) A creditor is not required to disclose information under this section if such disclosure—
  (a) contravenes the Data Protection Act 1998,
  (b) is prohibited by any EU obligation,
  (c) would create or be likely to create a serious risk that any person would be subject to violence or intimidation, or
  (d) would, or would be likely to, prejudice—
    (i)   the prevention or detection of crime,
    (ii) the apprehension or prosecution of offenders, or
    (iii) the administration of justice.]
  (3) If the creditor, owner or negotiator fails to comply with subsection [(A1) or] (1) he commits an offence.
  [(4) For the purposes of subsection (A1) an agreement is an excluded agreement if it is—
  (a) a consumer hire agreement, or
  (b) an agreement secured on land.]

158 Duty of agency to disclose filed information
  (1) A credit reference agency, within the prescribed period after receiving,—
  [(a) a request in writing to that effect from a consumer,] and
  (b) such particulars as the agency may reasonably require to enable them to identify the file, and
  (c) a fee of [£2],
shall give the consumer a copy of the file relating to [it] kept by the agency.
  (2) When giving a copy of the file under subsection (1), the agency shall also give the consumer a statement in the prescribed form of [the consumer's] rights under section 159.
  (3) If the agency does not keep a file relating to the consumer it shall give [the consumer] notice of that fact, but need not return any money paid.
  (4) If the agency contravenes any provision of this section it commits an offence.
  [(4A) In this section 'consumer' means—
  (a) a partnership consisting of two or three persons not all of whom are bodies corporate; or

(b) an unincorporated body of persons which does not consist entirely of bodies corporate and is not a partnership.]

(5) In this Act 'file', in relation to an individual, means all the information about him kept by a credit reference agency, regardless of how the information is stored, and 'copy of the file', as respects information not in plain English, means a transcript reduced into plain English.

159   Correction of wrong information

[(1) Any individual (the 'objector') given—

(a) information under section 7 of the Data Protection Act 1998 by a credit reference agency, or

(b) information under section 158, who considers that an entry in his file is incorrect, and that if it is not corrected he is likely to be prejudiced, may give notice to the agency requiring it either to remove the entry from the file or amend it.]

(2) Within 28 days after receiving a notice under subsection (1), the agency shall by notice inform the [objector] that it has—

(a) removed the entry from the file, or

(b) amended the entry, or

(c) taken no action, and if the notice states that the agency has amended the entry it shall include a copy of the file so far as it comprises the amended entry.

(3) Within 28 days after receiving a notice under subsection (2), or where no such notice was given, within 28 days after the expiry of the period mentioned in subsection (2), the [objector] may, unless he has been informed by the agency that it has removed the entry from his file, serve a further notice on the agency requiring it to add to the file an accompanying notice of correction (not exceeding 200 words) drawn up by the [objector], and include a copy of it when furnishing information included in or based on that entry.

(4) Within 28 days after receiving a notice under subsection (3), the agency, unless it intends to apply to the [the relevant authority] under subsection (5), shall by notice inform the [objector] that it has received the notice under subsection (3) and intends to comply with it.

(5) If—

(a) the [objector] has not received a notice under subsection (4) within the time required, or

(b) it appears to the agency that it would be improper for it to publish a notice of correction because it is incorrect, or unjustly defames any person, or is frivolous or scandalous, or is for any other reason unsuitable,

the [objector] or, as the case may be, the agency may, in the prescribed manner and on payment of the specified fee, apply to [the relevant authority], who may make such order on the application as he thinks fit.

(6) If a person to whom an order under this section is directed fails to comply with it within the period specified in the order he commits an offence.

[(7) The Information Commissioner may vary or revoke any order made by him under this section.

(8) In this section 'the relevant authority' means

(a) where the objector is a partnership or other unincorporated body of persons, the OFT, and

(b) in any other case, the Information Commissioner.]

160   Alternative procedure for business consumers

(1) The [OFT], on an application made by a credit reference agency, may direct that this section shall apply to the agency if [it] is satisfied—

(a) that compliance with section 158 in the case of consumers who carry on a business would adversely affect the service provided to its customers by the agency, and

(b) that, having regard to the methods employed by the agency and to any other relevant facts, it is probable that consumers carrying on a business would not be prejudiced by the making of the direction.

(2) Where an agency to which this section applies receives a request, particulars and a fee under section 158(1) from a consumer who carries on a business and section 158(3) does not apply, the agency, instead of complying with section 158, may elect to deal with the matter under the following subsections.

(3) Instead of giving the consumer a copy of the file, the agency shall within the prescribed period give notice to the consumer that it is proceeding under this section, and by notice give the consumer such information included in or based on entries in the file as the [OFT] may direct, together with a statement in the prescribed form of the consumer's rights under subsections (4) and (5).

(4) If within 28 days after receiving the information given to [the consumer] under subsection (3), or such longer period as the [OFT] may allow, the consumer—

> (a) gives notice to the [OFT] that [the consumer] is dissatisfied with the information, and
> (b) satisfies the [OFT] that the [consumer] has taken such steps in relation to the agency as may be reasonable with a view to removing the cause of [the consumer's] dissatisfaction, and
> (c) pays the [OFT] the specified fee, the [OFT] may direct the agency to give the [OFT] a copy of the file, and the [OFT] may disclose to the consumer such of the information on the file as the [OFT] thinks fit.

(5) Section 159 applies with any necessary modifications to information given to the consumer under this section as it applies to information given under section 158.

(6) If an agency making an election under subsection (2) fails to comply with subsection (3) or (4) it commits an offence.

[(7) In this section 'consumer' has the same meaning as in section 158.]

[160A Credit intermediaries

(1) In this section "credit intermediary" means a person who in the course of business—

> (a) carries out any of the activities specified in subsection (2) for a consideration that is or includes a financial consideration, and
> (b) does not do so as a creditor.

(2) The activities are—

> (a) recommending or making available prospective regulated consumer credit agreements, other than agreements secured on land, to individuals,
> (b) assisting individuals by undertaking other preparatory work in relation to such agreements, or
> (c) entering into regulated consumer credit agreements, other than agreements secured on land, with individuals on behalf of creditors.

(3) A credit intermediary must in—

> (a) advertising of his relating to an activity in subsection (2) which is intended for individuals not acting the course of a business, or
> (b) documentation of his relating to an activity in subsection (2) which is intended for individuals,

indicate the extent to which the intermediary is acting independently and in particular whether he works exclusively with a creditor.

(4) Where a credit intermediary carries on an activity specified in subsection (2) for a debtor, the intermediary must secure that any financial consideration payable to him by the debtor for the activity is disclosed to the debtor and then agreed in writing before the regulated consumer credit agreement is concluded.

(5) Where a credit intermediary carries on an activity specified in subsection (2) for a debtor, the intermediary must disclose to the creditor the financial consideration for the activity payable by the debtor if the annual percentage rate of the total charge for credit prescribed under section 20 is to be ascertained by the creditor.

(6) A credit intermediary who fails to comply with a requirement of this section commits an offence.

(7) An offence under this section is to be treated for the purposes of the definition of "relevant offence" in section 38(1) and (2) of the Regulatory Enforcement and Sanctions Act 2008 as an offence contained in this Act immediately before the day on which that Act was passed.]

PART XI ENFORCEMENT OF ACT

161 Enforcement authorities

(1) The following authorities ('enforcement authorities') have a duty to enforce this Act and regulations made under it—

    (a) the [OFT],

    (b) in Great Britain, the local weights and measures authority,

    (c) In Northern Ireland, the Department of Commerce for Northern Ireland.

(3) Every local weights and measures authority shall, whenever the [OFT] requires, report to [it] in such form and with such particulars as [it] requires on the exercise of their functions under this Act.

162 Powers of entry and inspection

(1) A duly authorised officer of an enforcement authority, at all reasonable hours and on production, if required, of his credentials, may—

    (a) in order to ascertain whether a breach of any provision of or under this Act has been committed, inspect any goods and enter any premises (other than premises used only as a dwelling);

    (b) if he has reasonable cause to suspect that a breach of any provision of or under this Act has been committed, in order to ascertain whether it has been committed, require any person—

        (i)   carrying on, or employed in connection with, a business to produce any [...] documents relating to it; or

        (ii) having control of any information relating to a business [to provide him with that information],

    (c) if he has reasonable cause to believe that a breach of any provision of or under this Act has been committed, seize and detain any goods in order to ascertain (by testing or otherwise) whether such a breach has been committed;

    (d) seize and detain any goods, [...] or documents which he has reason to believe may be required as evidence in proceedings for an offence under this Act;

    (e) for the purpose of exercising his powers under this subsection to seize goods, [...] or documents, but only if and to the extent that it is reasonably necessary for securing that the provision of this Act and of any regulations made under it are duly observed, require any person having authority to do so to break open any container and, if that person does not comply, break it open himself.

(2) An officer seizing goods, [...] or documents in exercise of his powers under this section shall not do so without informing the person he seizes them from.

(3) If a justice of the peace, on sworn information in writing, or, in Scotland, a sheriff or a magistrate or justice of the peace, on evidence on oath,—

    (a) is satisfied that there is reasonable ground to believe either—

        (i)   that any goods, [...] or documents which a duly authorised officer has power to inspect under this section are on any premises and their inspection is likely to disclose evidence of a breach of any provision of or under this Act; or

        (ii) that a breach of any provision of or under this Act has been, is being or is about to be committed on any premises; and

    (b) is also satisfied either—

        (i)   that admission to the premises has been or is likely to be refused and that notice of intention to apply for a warrant under this subsection has been given to the occupier; or

(ii) that an application for admission, or the giving of such a notice, would defeat the object of the entry or that the premises are unoccupied or that the occupier is temporarily absent and it might defeat the object of the entry to wait for his return,

the justice or, as the case may be, the sheriff or magistrate may by warrant under his hand, which shall continue in force for a period of one month, authorise an officer of an enforcement authority to enter the premises (by force if need be).

(4) An officer entering premises by virtue of this section may take such other persons and equipment with him as he thinks necessary; and on leaving premises entered by virtue of a warrant under subsection (3) shall, if they are unoccupied or the occupier is temporarily absent, leave them as effectively secured against trespassers as he found them.

(5) Regulations may provide that, in cases described by the regulations, an officer of a local weights and measures authority is not to be taken to be duly authorised for the purposes of this section unless he is authorised by the [OFT].

(6) A person who is not a duly authorised officer of an enforcement authority, but purports to act as such under this section, commits an offence.

[(8) References in this section to a breach of any provision of or under this Act do not include references to—

(a) a failure to comply with a requirement imposed under section 33A or 33B;

(b) a failure to comply with section 36A; or

(c) a failure in relation to which the OFT can apply for an order under section 36E.]

163 Compensation for loss

(1) Where, in exercising his powers under section 162, an officer of an enforcement authority seizes and detains goods and their owner suffers loss by reason of—

(a) that seizure, or

(b) the loss, damage or deterioration of the goods during detention,

then, unless the owner is convicted of an offence under this Act committed in relation to the goods, the authority shall compensate him for the loss so suffered.

(2) Any dispute as to the right to or amount of any compensation under subsection (1) shall be determined by arbitration.

164 Power to make test purchases etc.

(1) An enforcement authority may—

(a) make, or authorise any of their officers to make on their behalf, such purchases of goods; and

(b) authorise any of their officers to procure the provision of such services or facilities or to enter into such agreements or other transactions, as may appear to them expedient for determining whether any provisions made by or under this Act are being complied with.

(2) Any act done by an officer authorised to do it under subsection (1) shall be treated for the purposes of this Act as done by him as an individual on his own behalf.

(3) Any goods seized by an officer under this Act may be tested, and in the event of such a test he shall inform the person mentioned in section 162(2) of the test results.

(4) Where any test leads to proceedings under this Act, the enforcement authority shall—

(a) if the goods were purchased, inform the person they were purchased from of the test results, and

(b) allow any person against whom the proceedings are taken to have the goods tested on his behalf if it is reasonably practicable to do so.

165 Obstruction of authorised officers

(1) Any person who—

(a) wilfully obstructs an officer of an enforcement authority acting in pursuance of this Act; or

  (b) wilfully fails to comply with any requirement properly made to him by such an officer under section 162; or

  (c) without reasonable cause fails to give such an officer (so acting) other assistance or information he may reasonably require in performing his functions under this Act, commits an offence.

[(1A) A failure to give assistance or information shall not constitute an offence under subsection (1)(c) if it is also—

  (a) a failure to comply with a requirement imposed under section 33A or 33B;

  (b) a failure to comply with section 36A; or

  (c) a failure in relation to which the OFT can apply for an order under section 36E.]

(2) If any person, in giving such information as is mentioned in subsection (1)(c), makes any statement which he knows to be false, he commits an offence.

(3) Nothing in this section requires a person to answer any question or give any information if to do so might incriminate that person or (where that person [is married or a civil partner) the spouse or civil partner.]

166   Notification of convictions and judgments to [OFT]

Where a person is convicted of an offence or has a judgment given against him by or before any court in the United Kingdom and it appears to the court—

  (a) having regard to the functions of the [OFT] under this Act, that the conviction or judgment should be brought to the [OFT's] attention, and

  (b) that it may not be brought to [its] attention unless arrangements for that purpose are made by the court,

the court may make such arrangements notwithstanding that the proceedings have been finally disposed of.

167   Penalties

(1) An offence under a provision of this Act specified in column 1 of Schedule 1 is triable in the mode or modes indicated in column 3, and on conviction is punishable as indicated in column 4 (where a period of time indicates the maximum term of imprisonment, and a monetary amount indicates the maximum fine, for the offence in question).

(2) A person who contravenes any regulations made under section 44, 52, 53, or 112, or made under section 26 by virtue of section 54, commits an offence.

168   Defences

(1) In any proceedings for an offence under this Act it is a defence for the person charged to prove—

  (a) that his act or omission was due to a mistake, or to reliance on information supplied to him, or to an act or omission by another person, or to an accident or some other cause beyond his control, and

  (b) that he took all reasonable precautions and exercised all due diligence to avoid such an act or omission by himself or any person under his control.

(2) If in any case the defence provided by subsection (1) involves the allegation that the act or omission was due to an act or omission by another person or to reliance on information supplied by another person, the person charged shall not, without leave of the court, be entitled to rely on that defence unless, within a period ending seven clear days before the hearing, he has served on the prosecutor a notice giving such information identifying or assisting in the identification of that other person as was then in his possession.

169   Offences by bodies corporate

Where at any time a body corporate commits an offence under this Act with the consent or connivance of, or because of neglect by, any individual, the individual commits the like offence if at that time—

  (a) he is a director, manager, secretary or similar officer of the body corporate, or

(b) he is purporting to act as such an officer, or

(c) the body corporate is managed by its members of whom he is one.

170   No further sanctions for breach of Act

(1) A breach of any requirement made (otherwise than by any court) by or under this Act shall incur no civil or criminal sanction as being such a breach, except to the extent (if any) expressly provided by or under this Act.

(2) In exercising its functions under this Act the [OFT] may take account of any matter appearing to [it] to constitute a breach of a requirement made by or under this Act, whether or not any sanction for that breach is provided by or under this Act and, if it is so provided, whether or not proceedings have been brought in respect of the breach.

(3) Subsection (1) does not prevent the grant of an injunction, or the making of an order of certiorari, mandamus or prohibition or as respects Scotland the grant of an interdict or of an order under section 91 of the Court of Session Act 1868 (order for specific performance of statutory duty).

171   Onus of proof in various proceedings

(1) If an agreement contains a term signifying that in the opinion of the parties section 10(3)(b)(iii) does not apply to the agreement, it shall be taken not to apply unless the contrary is proved.

(2) It shall be assumed in any proceedings, unless the contrary is proved, that when a person initiated a transaction as mentioned in section 19(1)(c) he knew the principal agreement had been made, or contemplated that it might be made.

(3) Regulations under section 44 or 52 may make provision as to the onus of proof in any proceedings to enforce the regulations.

(4) In proceedings brought by the creditor under a credit-token agreement—

    (a) it is for the creditor to prove that the credit-token was lawfully supplied to the debtor, and was accepted by him, and

    (b) if the debtor alleges that any use made of the credit-token was not authorised by him, it is for the creditor to prove either—

        (i)   that the use was so authorised, or

        (ii) that the use occurred before the creditor had been given notice under section 84(3).

(5) In proceedings under section 50(1) in respect of a document received by a minor at any school or other educational establishment for minors, it is for the person sending it to him at that establishment to prove that he did not know or suspect it to be such an establishment.

(6) In proceedings under section 119(1) it is for the pawnee to prove that he had reasonable cause to refuse to allow the pawn to be redeemed.

172   Statements by creditor or owner to be binding

(1) A statement by a creditor or owner is binding on him if given under—

section 77(1),

section 78(1),

section 79(1),

section 97(1),

section 107(1)(c),

section 108(1)(c), or

section 109(1)(c).

(2) Where a trader—

    (a) gives a customer a notice in compliance with section 103(1)(b), or

    (b) gives a customer a notice under section 103(1) asserting that the customer is not indebted to him under an agreement,

the notice is binding on the trader.

(3) Where in proceedings before any court—

    (a) it is sought to reply on a statement or notice given as mentioned in subsection (1) or (2), and

(b) the statement or notice is shown to be incorrect,

the court may direct such relief (if any) to be given to the creditor or owner from the operation of sub-section (1) or (2) as appears to the court to be just.

173   Contracting-out forbidden

(1) A term contained in a regulated agreement or linked transaction, or in any other agreement relating to an actual or prospective regulated agreement or linked transaction, is void if, and to the extent that, it is inconsistent with a provision for the protection of the debtor or hirer or his relative or any surety contained in this Act or in any regulation made under this Act.

(2) Where a provision specifies the duty or liability of the debtor or hirer or his relative or any surety in certain circumstances, a term is inconsistent with that provision if it purports to impose, directly or indirectly, an additional duty or liability on him in those circumstances.

(3) Notwithstanding subsection (1), a provision of this Act under which a thing may be done in relation to any person on an order of the court or the [OFT] only shall not be taken to prevent its being done at any time with that person's consent given at that time, but the refusal of such consent shall not give rise to any liability.

PART XII   SUPPLEMENTAL

[174A   Powers to require provision of information or documents etc.

(1) Every power conferred on a relevant authority by or under this Act (however expressed) to require the provision or production of information or documents includes the power—

    (a) to require information to be provided or produced in such form as the authority may specify, including, in relation to information recorded otherwise than in a legible form, in a legible form;

    (b) to take copies of, or extracts from, any documents provided or produced by virtue of the exercise of the power;

    (c) to require the person who is required to provide or produce any information or document by virtue of the exercise of the power—

        (i)   to state, to the best of his knowledge and belief, where the information or document is

        (ii)   to give an explanation of the information or document;

        (iii) to secure that any information provided or produced, whether in a document or otherwise, is verified in such manner as may be specified by the authority;

        (iv) to secure that any document provided or produced is authenticated in such manner as may be so specified;

    (d) to specify a time at or by which a requirement imposed by virtue of paragraph (c) must be complied with.

(2) Every power conferred on a relevant authority by or under this Act (however expressed) to inspect or to seize documents at any premises includes the power to take copies of, or extracts from, any documents inspected or seized by virtue of the exercise of the power.

(3) But a relevant authority has no power under this Act—

    (a) to require another person to provide or to produce,

    (b) to seize from another person, or

    (c) to require another person to give access to premises for the purposes of the inspection of,

any information or document which the other person would be entitled to refuse to provide or produce in proceedings in the High Court on the grounds of legal professional privilege or (in Scotland) in proceedings in the Court of Session on the grounds of confidentiality of communications.

(4) In subsection (3) 'communications' means—

    (a) communications between a professional legal adviser and his client;

    (b) communications made in connection with or in contemplation of legal proceedings and for the purposes of those proceedings.

(5) In this section 'relevant authority' means—

    (a) the OFT or an enforcement authority (other than the OFT);

    (b) an officer of the OFT or of an enforcement authority (other than the OFT).]

175   Duty of persons deemed to be agents

Where under this Act a person is deemed to receive a notice or payment as agent of the creditor or owner under regulated agreement, he shall be deemed to be under a contractual duty to the creditor or owner to transmit the notice, or remit the payment, to him forthwith.

176   Service of documents

(1) A document to be served under this Act by one person ('the server') on another person ('the subject') is to be treated as properly served on the subject if dealt with as mentioned in the following subsections.

(2) The document may be delivered or sent [by an appropriate method] to the subject, or addressed to him by name and left at his proper address.

(3) For the purposes of this Act, a document sent [by an appropriate method] to, or left at, the address last known to the server as the address of a person shall be treated as sent by post to, or left at, his proper address.

(4) Where the document is to be served on the subject as being the person having any interest in land, and it is not practicable after reasonable inquiry to ascertain the subject's name or address, the document may be served by—

   (a) addressing it to the subject by the description of the person having that interest in the land (naming it), and

   (b) delivering the document to some responsible person on the land or affixing it, or a copy of it, in a conspicuous position on the land.

(5) Where a document to be served on the subject as being a debtor, hirer or surety, or as having any other capacity relevant for the purposes of this Act, is served at any time on another person who—

   (a) is the person last known to the server as having that capacity, but

   (b) before that time had ceased to have it, the document shall be treated as having been served at that time on the subject.

(6) Anything done to a document in relation to a person who (whether to the knowledge of the server or not) has died shall be treated for the purposes of subsection (5) as service of the document on that person if it would have been so treated had he not died.

[(7) The following enactments shall not be construed as authorising service on the Public Trustee (in England and Wales) or the Probate Judge (in Northern Ireland) of any document which is to be served under this Act—

   section 9 of the Administration of Estates Act 1925;

   section 3 of the Administration of Estates Act (Northern Ireland) 1955.]

(8) References in the preceding subsections to the serving of a document on a person include the giving of the document to that person.

[176A   Electronic transmission of documents

(1) A document is transmitted in accordance with this subsection if—

   (a) the person to whom it is transmitted agrees that it may be delivered to him by being transmitted to a particular electronic address in a particular electronic form,

   (b) it is transmitted to that address in that form, and

   (c) the form in which the document is transmitted is such that any information in the document which is addressed to the person to whom the document is transmitted is capable of being stored for future reference for an appropriate period in a way which allows the information to be reproduced without change.

(2) A document transmitted in accordance with subsection (1) shall, unless the contrary is proved, be treated for the purposes of this Act, except section 69, as having been delivered on the working day immediately following the day on which it is transmitted.

(3) In this section, 'electronic address' includes any number or address used for the purposes of receiving electronic communications.]

177   Saving for registered charges

(1) Nothing in this Act affects the rights of a proprietor of a registered charge (within the meaning of the [Land Registration Act 2002]), who—

    (a) became the proprietor under a transfer for valuable consideration without notice of any defect in the title arising (apart from this section) by virtue of this Act, or

    (b) derives title from such a proprietor.

(2) Nothing in this Act affects the operation of section 104 of the Law of Property Act 1925 (protection of purchaser where mortgagee exercises power of sale).

(3) Subsection (1) does not apply to a proprietor carrying on a business of debt-collecting.

(4) Where, by virtue of subsection (1), a land mortgage is enforced which apart from this section would be treated as never having effect, the original creditor or owner shall be liable to indemnify the debtor or hirer against any loss thereby suffered by him.

(5) In the application of this section to Scotland for subsections (1) to (3) there shall be substituted the following subsections—

'(1) Nothing in this Act affects the rights of a creditor in a heritable security who—

    (a) became the creditor under a transfer for value without notice of any defect in the title arising (apart from this section) by virtue of this Act; or

    (b) derives title from such a creditor.

(2) Nothing in this Act affects the operation of section 41 of the Conveyancing (Scotland) Act 1924 (protection of purchasers), or of that section as applied to standard securities by section 32 of the Conveyancing and Feudal Reform (Scotland) Act 1970.

(3) Subsection (1) does not apply to a creditor carrying on [a consumer credit business, a consumer hire business or a business of debt-collecting or debt administration].'

(6) In the application of this section to Northern Ireland—

    (a) any reference to the proprietor of a registered charge (within the meaning of the [Land Registration Act 2002]) shall be construed as a reference to the registered owner of a charge under the Local Registration of Title (Ireland) Act 1891 or Part IV of the Land Registration Act (Northern Ireland) 1970, and

    (b) for the reference to section 104 of the Law Property Act 1925 there shall be substituted a reference to section 21 of the Conveyancing and Law Property Act 1881 and section 5 of the Conveyancing Act 1911.

178   Local Acts

The Secretary of State or the Department of Commerce for Northern Ireland may by order make such amendments or repeals of any provision of any local Act as appears to the Secretary of State or, as the case may be, the Department, necessary or expedient in consequence of the replacement by this Act of the enactments relating to pawnbrokers and moneylenders.

Regulations, orders, etc.

179   Power to prescribe form etc. of secondary documents

(1) Regulations may be made as to the form and content of credit-cards, trading-checks, receipts, vouchers and other documents or things issued by creditors, owners or suppliers under or in connection with regulated agreements or by other persons in connection with linked transactions, and may in particular—

    (a) require specified information to be included in the prescribed manner in documents, and other specified material to be excluded;

    (b) contain requirements to ensure that specified information is clearly brought to the attention of the debtor or hirer, or his relative, and that one part of a document is not given insufficient or excessive prominence compared with another.

(2) If a person issues any document or thing in contravention of regulations under subsection (1) then, as from the time of the contravention but without prejudice to anything done before it, this Act

shall apply as if the regulated agreement had been improperly executed by reason of a contravention of regulations under section 60(1).

180 Power to prescribe form etc. of copies

(1) Regulations may be made as to the form and content of documents to be issued as copies of any executed agreement, security instrument or other document referred to in this Act, and may in particular—

(a) require specified information to be included in the prescribed manner in any copy, and contain requirements to ensure that such information is clearly brought to the attention of a reader of the copy;

(b) authorise the omission from a copy of certain material contained in the original, or the inclusion of such material in condensed form.

(2) A duty imposed by any provision of this Act (except section 35) to supply a copy of any document—

(a) is not satisfied unless the copy supplied is in the prescribed form and conforms to the prescribed requirements;

(b) is not infringed by the omission of any material, or its inclusion in condensed form, if that is authorised by regulations;

and references in this Act to copies shall be construed accordingly.

(3) Regulations may provide that a duty imposed by this Act to supply a copy of a document referred to in an unexecuted agreement or an executed agreement shall not apply to documents of a kind specified in the regulations.

181 Power to alter monetary limits etc.

(1) The Secretary of State may by order made by statutory instrument amend, or further amend, any of the following provisions of this Act so as to reduce or increase a sum mentioned in that provision, namely, sections [16B(1)], 17(1), [39A(3)], 70(6), 75(3)(b), 77(1), 78(1), 79(1), 84(1), 101(7)(a), 107(1), 108(1), 109(1), 110(1), 118(1)(b), 120(1)(a), [140B(6),] 155(1) and 158(1).

(2) An order under subsection (1) amending section [16B(1)] 17(1), [39A(3),] 75(3)(b) [or 140B(6)] shall be of no effect unless a draft of the order has been laid before and approved by each House of Parliament.

182 Regulations and orders

(1) Any power of the Secretary of State to make regulations or orders under this Act, except the power conferred by sections 2(1)(a), 181 and 192 shall be exercisable by statutory instrument subject to annulment in pursuance of a resolution of either House of Parliament.

(2) Where a power to make regulations or orders [...] is exercisable by the Secretary of State [...] by virtue of this Act, regulations or orders [...] made in the exercise of that power may—

(a) make different provision in relation to different cases or classes of case, and

(b) exclude certain cases or classes of case, and

(c) contain such transitional provision as the [Secretary of State] thinks fit.

(3) Regulations may provide that specified expressions, when used as described by the regulations, are to be given the prescribed meaning, notwithstanding that another meaning is intended by the person using them.

(4) Any power conferred on the Secretary of State by this Act to make orders includes power to vary or revoke an order so made.

[183 Determinations etc. by OFT

(1) The OFT may vary or revoke any determination made, or direction given, by it under this Act.

(2) Subsection (1) does not apply to—

(a) a determination to issue, renew or vary a licence;

(b) a determination to extend a period under section 28B or to refuse to extend a period under that section;

(c) a determination to end a suspension under section 33;

(d) a determination to make an order under section 40(2), 148(2) or 149(2);

(e) a determination mentioned in column 1 of the Table in section 41.]

Interpretation

184 Associates

[(1) A person is an associate of an individual if that person is—

(a) the individual's husband or wife or civil partner,

(b) a relative of—

(i)   the individual, or

(ii) the individual's husband or wife or civil partner, or

(c) the husband or wife or civil partner of a relative of—

(i)   the individual, or

(ii) the individual's husband or wife or civil partner.]

(2) A person is an associate of any person with whom he is in partnership, and of the husband or wife [or civil partner] or a relative of any individual with whom he is in partnership.

(3) A body corporate is an associate of another body corporate—

(a) if the same person is a controller of both, or a person is a controller of one and persons who are his associates, or he and persons who are his associates, are controllers of the other; or

(b) if a group of two or more persons is controller of each company, and the groups either consist of the same persons or could be regarded as consisting of the same persons by treating (in one or more cases) a member of either group as replaced by a person of whom he is an associate.

(4) A body corporate is an associate of another person if that person is a controller of it or if that person and persons who are his associates together are controllers of it.

(5) In this section 'relative' means brother, sister, uncle, aunt, nephew, niece, lineal ancestor or lineal descendant, [...] references to a husband or wife include a former husband or wife and a reputed husband [or wife, and references to a civil partner include a former civil partner and a reputed civil partner;] and for the purposes of this subsection a relationship shall be established as if any illegitimate child, step-child or adopted child of a person [were the legitimate child of the relationship in question].

185 Agreement with more than one debtor or hirer

(1) Where an actual or prospective regulated agreement has two or more debtors or hirers (not being a partnership or an unincorporated body of persons)—

(a) anything required by or under this Act to be done to or in relation to the debtor or hirer shall be done to or in relation to each of them; and

(b) anything done under this Act by or on behalf of one of them shall have effect as if done by or on behalf of all of them.

[(1A) Notwithstanding subsection (1) above, subsection (4) of section 55A (pre-contractual explanations etc) does not require an oral explanation to be given to any debtor to whom an explanation of the matters referred to in subsection (2)(a), (b) and (e) of that section has not been given orally or in person.]

[(2) Notwithstanding subsection (1)(a), where credit is provided under an agreement to two or more debtors jointly, in performing his duties—

(a) in the case of fixed-sum credit, under section 77A, or

(b) in the case of running-account credit, under section 78(4),

the creditor need not give statements to any debtor who has signed and given to him a notice (a 'dispensing notice') authorising him not to comply in the debtor's case with section 77A or (as the case may be) 78(4).

(2A) A dispensing notice given by a debtor is operative from when it is given to the creditor until it is revoked by a further notice given to the creditor by the debtor.

(2B) But subsection (2) does not apply if (apart from this subsection) dispensing notices would be operative in relation to all of the debtors to whom the credit is provided.

(2C) Any dispensing notices operative in relation to an agreement shall cease to have effect if any of the debtors dies.

(2D) A dispensing notice which is operative in relation to an agreement shall be operative also in relation to any subsequent agreement which, in relation to the earlier agreement, is a modifying agreement.]

(3) Subsection (1)(b) does not apply for the purposes of section 61(1)(a) [...].

(4) Where a regulated agreement has two or more debtors or hirers (not being a partnership or an unincorporated body of persons), section 86 applies to the death of any of them.

(5) An agreement for the provision of credit, or the bailment or (in Scotland) the hiring of goods, to two or more persons jointly where—

    (a) one or more of those persons is an individual, and

    (b) one or more of them is [not an individual],

is a consumer credit agreement or consumer hire agreement if it would have been one had they all been individuals; and [each person within paragraph (b)] shall accordingly be included among the debtors or hirers under the agreement.

(6) Where subsection (5) applies, references in this Act to the signing of any document by the debtor or hirer shall be construed in relation to a body corporate [within paragraph (b) of that subsection] as referring to a signing on behalf of the body corporate.

186 Agreement with more than one creditor or owner

Where an actual or prospective regulated agreement has two or more creditors or owners, anything required by or under this Act to be done to, or in relation to, or by, the creditor or owner shall be effective if done to, or in relation to, or by, any one of them.

187 Arrangements between creditor and supplier

(1) A consumer credit agreement shall be treated as entered into under pre-existing arrangements between a creditor and a supplier if it is entered into in accordance with, or in furtherance of, arrangements previously made between persons mentioned in subsection (4)(a), (b) or (c).

(2) A consumer credit agreement shall be treated as entered into in contemplation of future arrangements between a creditor and a supplier if it is entered into in the expectation that arrangements will subsequently be made between persons mentioned in subsection (4)(a), (b) or (c) for the supply of cash, goods and services (or any of them) to be financed by the consumer credit agreement.

(3) Arrangements shall be disregarded for the purposes of subsection (1) or (2) if—

    (a) they are arrangements for the making, in specified circumstances, of payments to the supplier by the creditor, and

    (b) the creditor holds himself out as willing to make, in such circumstances, payments of the kind to suppliers generally.

[(3A) Arrangements shall also be disregarded for the purposes of subsections (1) and (2) if they are arrangements for the electronic transfer of funds from a current account at a bank within the meaning of the Bankers' Book Evidence Act 1879.]

(4) The persons referred to in subsections (1) and (2) are—

    (a) the creditor and the supplier;

    (b) one of them and an associate of the other's;

    (c) an associate of one and an associate of the other's.

(5) Where the creditor is an associate of the supplier's. the consumer credit agreement shall be treated, unless the contrary is proved, as entered into under pre-existing arrangements between the creditor and the supplier.

[187A Definition of 'default sum'

(1) In this Act 'default sum' means, in relation to the debtor or hirer under a regulated agreement, a sum (other than a sum of interest) which is payable by him under the agreement in connection with a breach of the agreement by him.

(2) But a sum is not a default sum in relation to the debtor or hirer simply because, as a consequence of his breach of the agreement, he is required to pay it earlier than he would otherwise have had to.]

188 Examples of use of new terminology

(1) Schedule 2 shall have effect for illustrating the use of terminology employed in this Act.

(2) The examples given in Schedule 2 are not exhaustive.

(3) In the case of conflict between Schedule 2 and any other provision of this Act, that other provision shall prevail.

(4) The Secretary of State may by order amend Schedule 2 by adding further examples or in any other way.

189 Definitions

(1) In this Act, unless the context otherwise requires—

'advertisement' includes every form of advertising, whether in a publication, by television or radio, by display of notices, signs, labels, showcards or goods, by distribution of samples, circulars, catalogues, price lists or other material, by exhibition of pictures, models or films, or in any other way, and references to the publishing of advertisements shall be construed accordingly;

'advertiser' in relation to an advertisement, means any person indicated by the advertisement as willing to enter into transactions to which the advertisement relates;

'ancillary credit business' has the meaning given by section 145(1), 'antecedent negotiations' has the meaning given by section 56;

'appeal period' means the period beginning on the first day on which an appeal to the [First-tier Tribunal] may be brought and ending on the last day on which it may be brought or, if it is brought, ending on its final determination, or abandonment;

['appropriate method' means—

(a) post, or

(b) transmission in the form of an electronic communication in accordance with section 176A(1);]

'assignment', in relation to Scotland, means assignation;

'associate' shall be construed in accordance with section 184;

["authorised business overdraft agreement" means a debtor-creditor agreement which provides authorisation in advance for the debtor to overdraw on a current account, where the agreement is entered into by the debtor wholly or predominantly for the purposes of the debtor's business (see subsection (2A));

["authorised non-business overdraft agreement" means a debtor-creditor agreement which provides authorisation in advance for the debtor to overdraw on a current account where—

(a) the credit must be repaid on demand or within three months, and

(b) the agreement is not entered into by the debtor wholly or predominantly for the purposes of the debtor's business (see subsection (2A));]

['authorised institution' means an institution authorised under the Banking Act 1987;]

'bill of sale' has the meaning given by section 4 of the Bills of Sale Act 1878 or, for Northern Ireland, by section 4 of the Bills of Sale (Ireland) Act 1879;

['building society' means a building society within the meaning of the Building Societies Act 1986;]

'business' includes profession or trade, and references to a business apply subject to subsection (2);

'cancellable agreement' means a regulated agreement which, by virtue of section 67, may be cancelled by the debtor or hirer;

'canvass' shall be construed in accordance with sections 48 and 153;

'cash' includes money in any form;

'charity' means as respects England and Wales a charity registered under [the Charities Act 2011] or an exempt charity (within the meaning of that Act), [as respects] Northern Ireland an institution or other organization established for charitable purposes only ('organisation' including any persons administering a trust and 'charitable' being construed in the same way as if it were contained in the Income Tax Acts) [and as respects Scotland a body entered in the Scottish Charity Register];

'conditional sale agreement' means an agreement for the sale of goods or land under which the purchase price or part of it is payable by instalments, and the property in the goods or land is to remain in the seller (notwithstanding that the buyer is to be in possession of the goods or land) until such conditions as to the payment of instalments or otherwise as may be specified in the agreement are fulfilled;

'consumer credit agreement' has the meaning given by section 8, and includes a consumer credit agreement which is cancelled under section 69(1), or becomes subject to section 69(2), so far as the agreement remains in force;

['consumer credit business' means any business being carried on by a person so far as it comprises or relates to—

(a) the provision of credit by him, or

(b) otherwise his being a creditor,

under regulated consumer credit agreements;]

'consumer hire agreement' has the meaning given by section 15;

['consumer hire business' means any business being carried on by a person so far as it comprises or relates to—

(a) the bailment or (in Scotland) the hiring of goods by him, or

(b) otherwise his being an owner,

under regulated consumer hire agreements;]

'controller', in relation to a body corporate, means a person—

(a) in accordance with whose directions or instructions the directors of the body corporate or of another body corporate which is its controller (or any of them) are accustomed to act, or

(b) who, either alone or with any associate or associates, is entitled to exercise, or control the exercise of, one third or more of the voting power at any general meeting of the body corporate or of another body corporate which is its controller;

'copy' shall be construed in accordance with section 180;

'court' means in relation to England and Wales the county court, in relation to Scotland the sheriff court and in relation to Northern Ireland the High Court or the county court;

'credit' shall be construed in accordance with section 9;

'credit-broker' means a person carrying on a business of credit-brokerage;

'credit-brokerage' has the meaning given by section 145(2);

['credit information services' has the meaning given by section 145(7B);]

["credit intermediary" has the meaning given by section 160A;]

'credit limit' has the meaning given by section 10(2);

'creditor' means the person providing credit under a consumer credit agreement or the person to whom his rights and duties under the agreement have passed by assignment or operation of law, and in relation to a prospective consumer agreement, includes the prospective creditor;

'credit reference agency' has the meaning given by section 145(8);

'credit-sale agreement' means an agreement for the sale of goods, under which the purchase price or part of it is payable by instalments, but which is not a conditional sale agreement;

'credit-token' has the meaning given by section 14(1);

'credit-token agreement' means a regulated agreement for the provision of credit in connection with the use of a credit-token;

'debt-adjusting' has the meaning given by section 145(5);

['debt administration' has the meaning given by section 145(7A);]

'debt-collecting' has the meaning given by section 145(7);

'debt-counselling' has the meaning given by section 145(6);

'debtor' means the individual receiving credit under a consumer credit agreement or the person to whom his rights and duties under the agreement have passed by assignment or operation of law, and in relation to a prospective consumer credit agreement includes the prospective debtor;

'debtor-creditor agreement' has the meaning given by section 13;

'debtor-creditor-supplier agreement' has the meaning given by section 12;

'default notice' has the meaning given by section 87(1);

['default sum' has the meaning given by section 187A;]

'deposit' means [(except in section 16(10) and 25(1B)] any sum payable by a debtor or hirer by way of deposit or downpayment, or credited or to be credited to him on account of any deposit or downpayment, whether the sum is to be or has been paid to the creditor or owner or any other person, or is to be or has been discharged by a payment of money or a transfer or delivery of goods or by any other means;

['documents' includes information recorded in any form;]

'electric line' has the meaning given by [the Electricity Act 1989] or, for Northern Ireland the Electricity Supply (Northern Ireland) Order 1972;

['electronic communication' means an electronic communication within the meaning of the Electronic Communications Act 2000 (c.7);]

'embodies' and related words shall be construed in accordance with subsection (4);

'enforcement authority' has the meaning given by section 161(1);

'enforcement order' means an order under section 65(1), 105(7)(a) or (b), 111(2) or 124(1) or (2);

'executed agreement' means a document, signed by or on behalf of the parties, embodying the terms of a regulated agreement, or such of them as have been reduced to writing;

'exempt agreement' means an agreement specified in or under section 16[, 16A, 16B or 16C];

'finance' means to finance wholly or partly, and 'financed' and 'refinanced' shall be construed accordingly;

'file' and 'copy of the file' have the meanings given by section 158(5);

'fixed-sum credit' has the meaning given by section 10(1)(b);

'friendly society' means a society registered [or treated as registered under the Friendly Societies Act 1974 or the Friendly Societies Act 1992];

'future arrangements' shall be construed in accordance with section 187;

'general notice' means a notice published by the [OFT] at a time and in a manner appearing to [it] suitable for securing that the notice is seen within a reasonable time by persons likely to be affected by it;

'give' means deliver or send [by an appropriate method] to;

'goods' has the meaning given by [section 61(1) of the Sale of Goods Act 1979];

'group licence' has the meaning given by section 22(1)(b);

'High Court' means Her Majesty's High Court of Justice, or the Court of Session in Scotland or the High Court of Justice in Northern Ireland;

'hire-purchase agreement' means an agreement, other than a conditional sale agreement, under which—

(a) goods are bailed or (in Scotland) hired in return for periodical payments by the person to whom they are bailed or hired, and

(b) the property in the goods will pass to that person if the terms of the agreement are complied with and one or more of the following occurs—

(i) the exercise of an option to purchase by that person,

(ii) the doing of any other specified act by any party to the agreement,

(iii) the happening of any other specified event;

'hirer' means the individual to whom goods are bailed or (in Scotland) hired under a consumer hire agreement, or the person to whom his rights and duties under the agreement have passed by assignment or operation of law, and in relation to a prospective consumer hire agreement includes the prospective hirer;

['individual' includes—

    (a) a partnership consisting of two or three persons not all of whom are bodies corporate; and

    (b) an unincorporated body of persons which does not consist entirely of bodies corporate and is not a partnership;]

'installation' means—

    (a) the installing of any electric line or any gas or water pipe,

    (b) the fixing of goods to the premises where they are to be used, and the alteration of premises to enable goods to be used on them,

    (c) where it is reasonably necessary that goods should be constructed or erected on the premises where they are to be used, any work carried out for the purpose of constructing or erecting them on those premises;

'judgment' includes an order or decree made by any court;

'land' includes an interest in land, and in relation to Scotland includes heritable subjects of whatever description;

'land improvement company' means an improvement company as defined by section 7 of the improvement of Land Act 1899;

'land mortgage' includes any security charged on land;

'licence' means a licence under Part III [...];

'licensed', in relation to any act, means authorised by a licence to do the act or cause or permit another person to do it;

'licensee', in the case of a group licence, includes any person covered by the licence;

'linked transaction' has the meaning given by section 19(1);

'local authority', in relation to England and Wales, means the Greater London Council, a county council, a London borough council, a district council, the Common Council of the City of London, or the Council of the Isles of Scilly, [in relation to Wales means a county council or a county borough council,] and in relation to Scotland, means a [council constituted under section 2 of the Local Government etc. (Scotland) Act 1994], and, in relation to Northern Ireland, means a district council;

'modifying agreement' has the meaning given by section 82(2);

'mortgage', in relation to Scotland, includes any heritable security;

'multiple agreement' has the meaning given by section 18(1);

'negotiator' has the meaning given by section 56(1);

'non-commercial agreement' means a consumer credit agreement or a consumer hire agreement not made by the creditor or owner in the course of a business carried on by him;

'notice' means notice in writing;

'notice of cancellation' has the meaning given by section 69(1);

['OFT' means the Office of Fair Trading;]

["open-end" in relation to a consumer credit agreement, means of no fixed duration;]

'owner' means a person who bails or (in Scotland) hires out goods under a consumer hire agreement or the person to whom his rights and duties under the agreement have passed by assignment or operation of law, and in relation to a prospective consumer hire agreement, includes the prospective bailor or person from whom the goods are to be hired;

'pawn' means any article subject to a pledge;

'pawn-receipt' has the meaning given by section 114;

'pawnee' and 'pawnor' include any person to whom the rights and duties of the original pawnee or the original pawnor, as the case may be, have passed by assignment or operation of law;

'payment' includes tender;

'pledge' means the pawnee's rights over an article taken in pawn;

'prescribed' means prescribed by regulations made by the Secretary of State;

'pre-existing arrangements' shall be construed in accordance with section 187;

'principal agreement' has the meaning given by section 19(1);

'protected goods' has the meaning given by section 90(7);

'quotation' has the meaning given by section 52(1)(a);

'redemption period' has the meaning given by section 116(3);

'register' means the register kept by the [OFT] under section 35;

'regulated agreement' means a consumer credit agreement, or consumer hire agreement, other than an exempt agreement, and 'regulated' and 'unregulated' shall be construed accordingly;

'regulations' means regulations made by the Secretary of State;

'relative', except in section 184, means a person who is an associate by virtue of section 184(1);

'representation' includes any condition or warranty, and any other statement or undertaking, whether oral or in writing;

'restricted-use credit agreement' and 'restricted-use credit' have the meanings given by section 11(1);

'rules of court', in relation to Northern Ireland means, in relation to the High Court, rules made under section 7 of the Northern Ireland Act 1962, and, in relation to any other court, rules made by the authority having for the time being power to make rules regulating the practice and procedure in that court;

'running-account credit' shall be construed in accordance with section 10;

'security', in relation to an actual or prospective consumer credit agreement or consumer hire agreement, or any linked transaction, means a mortgage, charge, pledge, bond, debenture, indemnity, guarantee, bill, note or other right provided by the debtor or hirer, or at his request (express or implied), to secure the carrying out of the obligations of the debtor or hirer under the agreement;

'security instrument' has the meaning given by section 105(2);

'serve on' means deliver or send [by an appropriate method] to;

'signed' shall be construed in accordance with subsection (3);

'small agreement' has the meaning given by section 17(1), and 'small' in relation to an agreement within any category shall be construed accordingly;

'specified fee' shall be construed in accordance with section 2(4) and (5);

'standard licence' has the meaning given by section 22(1)(a);

'supplier' has the meaning given by section 11(1)(b) or 12(c) or 13(c) or, in relation to an agreement failing within section 11(1)(a), means the creditor, and includes a person to whom the rights and duties of a supplier (as so defined) have passed by assignment or operation of law, or (in relation to a prospective agreement) the prospective supplier;

'surety' means the person by whom any security is provided, or the person to whom his rights and duties in relation to the security have passed by assignment or operation of law;

'technical grounds' shall be construed in accordance with subsection (5);

'time order' has the meaning given by section 129(1);

'total charge for credit' means a sum calculated in accordance with regulations under section 20(1);

'total price' means the total sum payable by the debtor under a hire-purchase agreement or a conditional sale agreement, including any sum payable on the exercise of an option to purchase, but excluding any sum payable as a penalty or as compensation or damages for a breach of the agreement;

'unexecuted agreement' means a document embodying the terms of a prospective regulated agreement, or such of them as it is intended to reduce to writing;

'unlicensed' means without a licence, but applies only in relation to acts for which a licence is required;

'unrestricted-use credit agreement' and 'unrestricted-use credit' have the meanings given by section 11(2);

'working day' means any day other than—
>   (a) Saturday or Sunday,
>   (b) Christmas Day or Good Friday,
>   (c) a bank holiday within the meaning given by section 1 of the Banking and Financial Dealings Act 1971.

[(1A) In sections 36E(3), 70(4), 73(4) and 75(2) and … 'costs', in relation to proceedings in Scotland, means expenses.]

(2) A person is not to be treated as carrying on a particular type of business merely because occasionally he enters into transactions belonging to a business of that type.

[(2A) For the purpose of the definitions of "authorised business overdraft agreement" and "authorised non-business overdraft agreement" subsections (2) to (5) of section 16B (declaration by the debtor as to the purposes of the agreement) apply.]

(3) Any provision of this Act requiring a document to be signed is complied with by a body corporate if the document is sealed by that body.

This subsection does not apply to Scotland.

(4) A document embodies a provision if the provision is set out either in the document itself or in another document referred to in it.

(5) An application dismissed by the court or the Director shall, if the court or the Director (as the case may be) so certifies, be taken to be dismissed on technical grounds only.

(6) Except in so far as the context otherwise requires, any reference in this Act to an enactment shall be construed as a reference to that enactment as amended by or under any other enactment, including this Act.

(7) In this Act, except where otherwise indicated—
>   (a) a reference to a numbered Part, section or Schedule is a reference to the Part or section of, or the Schedule to, this Act so numbered, and
>   (b) a reference in a section to a numbered subsection is a reference to the subsection of that section so numbered, and
>   (c) a reference in a section, subsection or Schedule to a numbered paragraph is a reference to the paragraph of that section, subsection or Schedule so numbered.

[189A   Meaning of 'consumer credit EEA firm'
In this Act 'consumer credit EEA firm' means an EEA firm falling within sub-paragraph (a), (b) or (c) of paragraph 5 of Schedule 3 to the Financial Services and Markets Act 2000 carrying on, or seeking to carry on, consumer credit business, consumer hire business or ancillary credit business for which a licence would be required under this Act but for paragraph 15(3) of Schedule 3 to the Financial Services and Markets Act 2000.]

190   Financial provisions
(1) There shall be defrayed out of money provided by Parliament—
>   (a) all expenses incurred by the Secretary of State in consequence of the provisions of this Act;
>   (b) any expenses incurred in consequence of those provisions by any other Minister of the Crown or Government department;
>   (c) any increase attributable to this Act in the sums payable out of money so provided under the Superannuation Act 1972 or the Fair Trading Act 1973.

(2) Any fees[, charges, penalties or others sums] received by the [OFT] under this Act shall be paid into the Consolidated Fund.

SCHEDULE 1

PROSECUTION AND PUNISHMENT OF OFFENCES

Section 167

1 Section	2 Offence	3 Mode of prosecution	4 Imprisonment or fine
7 …	Knowingly or recklessly giving false information to [OFT].	(a) Summarily. (b) On indictment.	[The prescribed sum.] 2 years or a fine or both.
39(1) …	Engaging in activities requiring a licence when not a licensee.	(a) Summarily. (b) On indictment.	[The prescribed sum.] 2 years or a fine or both.
39(2) …	Carrying on a business under a name not specified in licence.	(a) Summarily. (b) On indictment.	[The prescribed sum.] 2 years or a fine or both.
39(3) …	Failure to notify changes in registered particulars.	(a) Summarily. (b) On indictment.	[The prescribed sum.] 2 years or a fine or both.
45 …	Advertising credit where goods etc. not available for cash.	(a) Summarily. (b) On indictment.	[The prescribed sum.] 2 years or a fine or both.
47(1) …	Advertising infringements.	(a) Summarily. (b) On indictment.	[The prescribed sum.] 2 years or a fine or both.
49(1) …	Canvassing debtor-creditor agreements off trade premises.	(a) Summarily. (b) On indictment.	[The prescribed sum.] 2 years or a fine or both.
49(2) …	Soliciting debtor-creditor agreements during visits made in response to previous oral requests.	(a) Summarily. (b) On indictment.	[The prescribed sum.] 2 years or a fine or both.
50(1) …	Sending circulars to minors.	(a) Summarily. (b) On indictment.	[The prescribed sum.] 2 years or a fine or both.
51(1) …	Supplying unsolicited credit-tokens.	(a) Summarily. (b) On indictment.	[The prescribed sum.] 2 years or a fine or both.
[51A(1)	Breach of restrictions on provision of credit card cheques.	(a) Summarily. (b) On indictment.	The statutory maximum. [A fine.]
	Failure to tell creditor or owner whereabouts of goods.	(a) Summarily.	[Level 3 on the standard scale.]

1 Section	2 Offence	3 Mode of prosecution	4 Imprisonment or fine
114(2) …	Taking pledges from minors.	(a) Summarily. (b) On indictment.	[The prescribed sum.] 1 year or a fine or both.
115 …	Failure to supply copies of a pledge agreement or pawn-receipt.	(a) Summarily.	[Level 4 on the standard scale.]
119(1) …	Unreasonable refusal to allow pawn to be redeemed.	(a) Summarily.	[Level 4 on the standard scale.]
154 …	Canvassing ancillary credit services off trade premises.	(a) Summarily. (b) On indictment.	[The prescribed sum.] 1 year or a fine or both.
157(3) …	Refusal to give name etc. of credit reference agency.	(a) Summarily.	[Level 4 on the standard scale.]
158(4) …	Failure of credit reference agency to disclose filed information.	(a) Summarily.	[Level 4 on the standard scale.]
159(6) …	Failure of credit reference agency to correct information.	(a) Summarily.	[Level 4 on the standard scale.]
160(6) …	Failure of credit reference agency to comply with section 160(3) or (4).	(a) Summarily. (b) On indictment.	[Level 4 on the standard scale.] [1 year or a fine or both.]
[160A]	[Failure of credit intermediary to comply with section 160A(3), (4) or (5).]	[Summarily.]	[Level 4 on the standard scale.]
162(6) …	Impersonation of enforcement authority officers.	(a) Summarily. (b) On indictment.	[The prescribed sum.] [1 year or a fine or both.]
165(1) …	Impersonation of enforcement authority officers.	(a) Summarily. (b) On indictment.	[Level 4 on the standard scale.] [1 year or a fine or both.]
165(1) …	Objection of enforcement authority officers.	(a) Summarily.	[Level 4 on the standard scale.]
165(2) …	Giving false information to enforcement authority officers.	(a) Summarily. (b) On indictment.	[The prescribed sum.] [2 years or a fine or both.]
167(2) …	Contravention of regulations under section 44, 52, 53, 54, or 112.	(a) Summarily. (b) On indictment.	[Level 4 on the standard scale.] [2 years or a fine or both.]
174(5) …	Wrongful disclosure of information.	(a) Summarily. (b) On indictment.	[Level 4 on the standard scale.] [2 years or a fine or both.]

Section 188(1)   **SCHEDULE 2**

EXAMPLES OF USE OF NEW TERMINOLOGY

PART I LIST OF TERMS

Term	Defined in section	Illustrated by example(s)
Advertisement	189(1)	2
Advertiser	189(1)	2
Antecedent negotiations	56	1, 2, 3, 4
Cancellable agreement	67	4
Consumer credit agreement ...	8	5, 6, 7, 15, 19, 21
Consumer hire agreement ...	15	20, 24
Credit	9	16, 19, 21
Credit-broker	189(1)	2
Credit limit	10(2)	6, 7, 19, 22, 23
Creditor	189(1)	1, 2, 3, 4
Credit-sale agreement	189(1)	5
Credit-token	14	3, 14, 16
Credit-token agreement ...	14	3, 14, 16, 21
Debtor-creditor agreement ...	13	8, 16, 17, 18
Debtor-creditor-supplier agreement ...	12	8, 16
Fixed-sum credit	10	9, 10, 17, 23
Hire-purchase agreement ...	189(1)	10
Individual	189(1)	19, 24
Linked transaction	19	11
Modifying agreement	82(2)	24
Multiple agreement	18	16, 18
Negotiator	56(1)	1, 2, 3, 4
[...]		
Pre-existing arrangements... ...	187	8, 21
Restricted-use credit	11	10, 12, 13, 14, 16
Running-account credit ...	10	15, 16, 18, 23
Small agreement	17	16, 17, 22
Supplier	189(1)	3, 14
Total charge for credit	20	5, 10
Total price	189(1)	10
Unrestricted-use credit	11	8, 12, 16, 17, 18

PART II EXAMPLES

Example 1

Facts Correspondence passes between an employee of a money-lending company (writing on behalf of the company) and an individual about the terms on which the company would grant him a loan under a regulated agreement.

Analysis The correspondence constitutes antecedent negotiations falling within section 56(1)(a), the money-lending company being both creditor and negotiator.

Example 2

Facts Representations are made about goods in a poster displayed by a shopkeeper near the goods, the goods being selected by a customer who has read the poster and then sold by the shopkeeper to a finance company introduced by him (with whom he has a business relationship). The goods are disposed of by the finance company to the customer under a regulated hire-purchase agreement.

Analysis The representations in the poster constitute antecedent negotiations falling within section 56(1)(b), the shopkeeper being the credit-broker and negotiator and the finance company being the creditor. The poster is an advertisement and the shopkeeper is the advertiser.

Example 3

Facts Discussions take place between a shopkeeper and a customer about goods the customer wishes to buy using a credit-card issued by the D Bank under a regulated agreement.

Analysis The discussions constitute antecedent negotiations falling within section 56(1)(c), the shopkeeper being the supplier and negotiator and the D Bank the creditor. The credit-card is a credit-token as defined in section 14(1), and the regulated agreement under which it was issued is a credit-token agreement as defined in section 14(2).

Example 4

Facts Discussions take place and correspondence passes between a secondhand car dealer and a customer about a car, which is then sold by the dealer to the customer under a regulated conditional sale agreement. Subsequently, on a revocation of that agreement by consent, the car is resold by the dealer to a finance company introduced by him (with whom he has a business relationship), who in turn dispose of it to the same customer under a regulated hire-purchase agreement.

Analysis The discussions and correspondence constitute antecedent negotiations in relation both to the conditional sale agreement and the hire-purchase agreement. They fall under section 56(1)(a) in relation to the conditional sale agreement, the dealer being the creditor and the negotiator. In relation to the hire-purchase agreement they fall within section 56(1)(b), the dealer continuing to be treated as the negotiator but the finance company now being the creditor. Both agreements are cancellable if the discussions took place when the individual conducting the negotiations (whether the 'negotiator' or his employee or agent) was in the presence of the debtor, unless the unexecuted agreement was signed by the debtor at trade premises (as defined in section 67(b)). If the discussions all took place by telephone however, or the unexecuted agreement was signed by the debtor on trade premises (as so defined) the agreements are not cancellable.

Example 5

Facts E agrees to sell to F (an individual) an item of furniture in return for 24 monthly instalments of £10 payable in arrear. The property in the goods passes to F immediately.

Analysis This is a credit-sale agreement (see definition of 'credit-sale agreement' in section 189(1)). The credit provided amounts to £240 less the amount which, according to regulations made under section 20(1), constitutes the total charge for credit. (This amount is required to be deducted by section 9(4).) Accordingly the agreement falls within section 8(2) and is a consumer credit agreement.

Example 6

Facts The G Bank grants H (an individual) an unlimited overdraft, with an increased rate of interest on so much of any debit balance as exceeds £2,000.

Analysis Although the overdraft purports to be unlimited, the stipulation for increased interest above £2,000 brings the agreement within section 10(3)(b)(ii) and it is a consumer credit agreement.

Example 7

Facts J is an individual who owns a small shop which usually carries a stock worth about £1,000. K makes a stocking agreement under which he undertakes to provide on short-term credit the stock needed from time to time by J without any specified limit.

Analysis Although the agreement appears to provide unlimited credit, it is probable, having regard to the stock usually carried by J, that his indebtedness to K will not at any time rise above £5,000. Accordingly the agreement falls within section 10(3)(b)(iii) and is a consumer credit agreement.

Example 8

Facts U, a moneylender, lends £500 to V (an individual) knowing he intends to use it to buy office equipment from W. W introduced V to U, it being his practice to introduce customers needing finance to him. Sometimes U gives W a commission for this and sometimes not. U pays the £500 direct to V.

Analysis Although this appears to fall under section 11(1)(b), it is excluded by section 11(3) and is therefore (by section 11(2)) an unrestricted-use credit agreement. Whether it is a debtor-creditor agreement (by section 13(c)) or a debtor-creditor-supplier agreement (by section 12(c)) depends on whether the previous dealings between U and W amount to 'pre-existing arrangements', that is whether the agreement can be taken to have been entered into 'in accordance with, or in furtherance of' arrangements previously made between U and W, as laid down in section 187(1).

Example 9

Facts A agrees to lend B (an individual) £4,500 in nine monthly instalments of £500.

Analysis This is a cash loan and is a form of credit (see section 9 and definition of 'cash' in section 189(1)). Accordingly it falls within section 10(1)(b) and is fixed-sum credit amounting to £4,500.

Example 10

Facts C (in England) agrees to bail goods to D (an individual) in return for periodical payments. The agreement provides for the property in the goods to pass to D on payment of a total of £7,500 and the exercise by D of an option to purchase. The sum of £7,500 includes a down-payment of £1,000. It also includes an amount which, according to regulations made under section 20(1), constitutes a total charge for credit of £1,500.

Analysis This is a hire-purchase agreement with a deposit of £1,000 and a total price of £7,500 (see definitions of 'hire-purchase agreement', 'deposit' and 'total price' in section 189(1)). By section 9(3), it is taken to provide credit amounting to £7,500 − (£1,500 + £1,000), which equals £5,000. Under section 8(2), the agreement is therefore a consumer credit agreement, and under sections 9(3) and 11(l) it is a restricted-use credit agreement for fixed-sum credit. A similar result would follow if the agreement by C had been a hiring agreement in Scotland.

Example 11

Facts X (an individual) borrows £500 from Y (Finance). As a condition of the granting of the loan X is required—

    (a) to execute a second mortgage on his house in favour of Y (Finance), and

    (b) to take out a policy of insurance on his life with Y (Insurances).

In accordance with the loan agreement, the policy is charged to Y (Finance) as collateral security for the loan. The two companies are associates within the meaning of section 184(3).

Analysis The second mortgage is a transaction for the provision of security and accordingly does not fall within section 19(1), but the taking out of the insurance policy is a linked transaction falling within section 19(1)(a). The charging of the policy is a separate transaction (made between different parties) for the provision of security and again is excluded from section 19(1). The only linked transaction is therefore the taking out of the insurance policy. If X had not been required by the loan agreement to take out the policy, but it had been done at the suggestion of Y (Finance) to induce them to enter into the loan agreement, it would have been a linked transaction under section 19(1)(c)(i) by virtue of section 19(2)(a).

Example 12

Facts The N Bank agrees to lend O (an individual) £2,000 to buy a car from P. To make sure the loan is used as intended, the N Bank stipulates that the money must be paid by it direct to P.

Analysis The agreement is a consumer credit agreement by virtue of section 8(2). Since it falls within section 11(1)(b), it is a restricted-use credit agreement, P being the supplier. If the N Bank had not stipulated for direct payment to the supplier, section 11(3) would have operated and made the agreement into one for unrestricted-use credit.

Example 13

Facts Q, a debt-adjuster, agrees to pay off debts owed by R (an individual) to various money-lenders. For this purpose the agreement provides for the making of a loan by Q to R in return for R's agreeing to repay the loan by instalments with interest. The loan money is not paid over to R but retained by Q and used to pay off the money lenders.

Analysis This is an agreement to refinance existing indebtedness of the debtor's, and if the loan by Q does not exceed £5,000 is a restricted-use credit agreement falling within section 11(1)(c).

Example 14

Facts On payment of £1, S issues to T (an individual) a trading check under which T can spend up to £20 at any shop which has agreed, or in future agrees, to accept S's trading checks.

Analysis The trading check is a credit-token falling within section 14(1)(b). The credit-token agreement is a restricted-use credit agreement within section 11(1)(b), any shop in which the credit-token is used being the 'supplier'. The fact that further shops may be added after the issue of the credit-token is irrelevant in view of section 11(4).

Example 15

Facts A retailer L agrees with M (an individual) to open an account in M's name and, in return for M's promise to pay a specified minimum sum into the account each month and to pay a monthly charge for credit, agrees to allow to be debited to the account, in respect of purchases made by M from L, such sums as will not increase the debit balance at any time beyond the credit limit, defined in the agreement as a given multiple of the specified minimum sum.

Analysis This agreement provides credit falling within the definition of running-account credit in section 10(1)(a). Provided the credit limit is not over £5,000, the agreement falls within section 8(2) and is a consumer credit agreement for running-account credit.

Example 16

Facts Under an unsecured agreement, A (Credit), an associate of the A Bank, issues to B (an individual) a credit-card for use in obtaining cash on credit from A (Credit), to be paid by branches of the A Bank (acting as agent of A (Credit)), or goods or cash from suppliers or banks who have agreed to honour credit-cards issued by A (Credit). The credit limit is £30.

Analysis This is a credit-token agreement falling within section 14(1)(a) and (b). It is a regulated consumer credit agreement for running-account credit. Since the credit limit does not exceed £30, the agreement is a small agreement. So far as the agreement relates to goods it is a debtor-creditor-supplier agreement within section 12(b), since it provides restricted-use credit under section 11(1)(b). So far as it relates to cash it is a debtor-creditor agreement within section 13(c) and the credit it provides is unrestricted-use credit. This is therefore a multiple agreement. In that the whole agreement falls within several of the categories of agreement mentioned in this Act, it is, by section 18(3), to be treated as an agreement in each of those categories. So far as it is a debtor-creditor-supplier agreement providing restricted-use credit it is, by section 18(2), to be treated as a separate agreement; and similarly so far as it is a debtor-creditor agreement providing unrestricted-use credit. (See also Example 22.)

Example 17

Facts The manager of the C Bank agrees orally with D (an individual) to open a current account in D's name. Nothing is said about overdraft facilities. After maintaining the account in credit for some weeks, D draws a cheque in favour of E for an amount exceeding D's credit balance by £20. E presents the cheque and the Bank pay it.

Analysis In drawing the cheque D, by implication, requests the Bank to grant him an overdraft of £20 on its usual terms as to interest and other charges. In deciding to honour the cheque, the Bank by implication accept the offer. This constitutes a regulated small consumer credit agreement for unrestricted-use, fixed sum credit. It is a debtor-creditor agreement, and falls within section 74(1)(b) if covered by a determination under section 74(3). (Compare Example 18.)

Example 18

Facts F (an individual) has had a current account with the G Bank for many years. Although usually in credit, the account has been allowed by the Bank to become overdrawn from time to time. The maximum such overdraft has been is about £1,000. No explicit agreement has ever been made about overdraft facilities. Now, with a credit balance of £500, F draws a cheque for £1,300.

Analysis It might well be held that the agreement with F (express or implied) under which the Bank operate his account includes an implied term giving him the right to overdraft facilities up to say £1,000. If so, the agreement is a regulated consumer credit agreement for unrestricted-use, running-account credit. It is a debtor-creditor agreement, and falls within section 74(1)(b) if covered by a direction under section 74(3). It is also a multiple agreement, part of which (i.e. the part not dealing with the overdraft), as referred to in section 18(1)(a), falls within a category of agreement not mentioned in this Act. (Compare Example 17.)

Example 19

Facts H (a finance house) agrees with J (a partnership of individuals) to open an unsecured loan account in J's name on which the debit balance is not to exceed £7,500 (having regard to payments into the account made from time to time by J). Interest is to be payable in advance on this sum, with provision for yearly adjustments. H is entitled to debit the account with interest, a 'setting-up' charge, and other charges. Before J has an opportunity to draw on the account it is initially debited with £2,250 for advance interest and other charges.

Analysis This is a personal running-account credit agreement (see sections 8(1) and 10(1)(a), and definition of 'individual' in section 189(1)). By section 10(2) the credit limit is £7,000. By section 9(4) however the initial debit of £2,250, and any other charges later debited to the account by H, are not to be treated as credit even though time is allowed for their payment. Effect is given to this by section 10(3). Although the credit limit of £7,000 exceeds the amount (£5,000) specified in section 8(2) as the maximum for a consumer credit agreement, so that the agreement is not within section 10(3)(a), it is caught by section 10(3)(b)(i). At the beginning J can effectively draw (as credit) no more than £4,750, so the agreement is a consumer credit agreement.

Example 20

Facts K (in England) agrees with L (an individual) to bail goods to L for a period of three years certain at £2,200 a year, payable quarterly. The agreement contains no provision for the passing of the property in the goods to L.

Analysis This is not a hire-purchase agreement (see paragraph (b) of the definition of that term in section 189(1)), and is capable of subsisting for more than three months. Paragraphs(a) and (b) of section 15(1) are therefore satisfied, but paragraph (c) is not. The payments by L must exceed £5,000 if he conforms to the agreement. It is true that under section 101 L has a right to terminate the agreement on giving K three month's notice expiring not earlier than eighteen months after the making of the agreement, but that section applies only where the agreement is a regulated consumer hire agreement apart from the section (see subsection (1)). So the agreement is not a consumer hire agreement, though it would be if the hire charge were say £1,500 a year, or there were a 'break' clause in it operable by either party before the hire charges exceeded £5,000. A similar result would follow if the agreement by K had been a hiring agreement in Scotland.

Example 21

Facts The P Bank decides to issue cheque cards to its customers under a scheme whereby the bank undertakes to honour cheques of up to £30 in every case where the payee has taken the cheque in reliance on the cheque card, whether the customer has funds in his account or not. The P Bank writes to the major retailers advising them of this scheme and also publicises it by advertising. The Bank issues a cheque card to Q (an individual), who uses it to pay by cheque for goods costing £20 bought by Q from R, a major retailer. At the time, Q has £500 in his account at the P Bank.

Analysis The agreement under which the cheque card is issued to Q is a consumer credit agreement even though at all relevant times Q has more than £30 in his account. This is because Q is free to draw out his whole balance and then use the cheque card, in which case the Bank has bound itself to honour the cheque. In other words the cheque card agreement provides Q with credit, whether he avails himself of it or not. Since the amount of the credit is not subject to any express limit, the cheque card can be used any number of times. It may be presumed however that section 10(3)(b)(iii) will apply. The agreement is an unrestricted-use debtor-creditor agreement (by section 13(c)). Although the P Bank wrote to R informing R of the P Bank's willingness to honour any cheque taken by R in reliance on a cheque card, this does not constitute pre-existing arrangements as mentioned in section 13(c) because section 187(3) operates to prevent it. The agreement is not a credit-token agreement within section 14(1)(b) because payment by the P Bank to R, would be a payment of the cheque and not a payment for the goods.

Example 22

Facts The facts are as in Example 16. On one occasion B uses the credit-card in a way which increases his debit balance with A (Credit) to £40. A (Credit) writes to B agreeing to allow the excess on that occasion only, but stating that it must be paid off within one month.

Analysis In exceeding his credit limit B, by implication, requests A (Credit) to allow him a temporary excess (compare Example 17). A (Credit) is thus faced by B's action with the choice of treating it as a breach of contract or granting his implied request. He does the latter. If he had done the former, B would be treated as taking credit to which he was not entitled (see section 14(3)) and, subject to the terms of his contract with A (Credit), would be liable to damages for breach of contract. As it is, the agreement to allow the excess varies the original credit-token agreement by adding a new term. Under section 10(2), the new term is to be disregarded in arriving at the credit limit, so that the credit-token agreement at no time ceases to be a small agreement. By section 82(2) the later agreement is deemed to revoke the original agreement and contain provisions reproducing the combined effect of the two agreements. By section 82(4), this later agreement is exempted from Part V (except section 56).

Example 23

Facts Under an oral agreement made on 10th January, X (an individual) has an overdraft on his current account at the Y bank with a credit limit of £100. On 15th February, when his overdraft stands at £90, X draws a cheque for £25. It is the first time that X has exceeded his credit limit, and on 16th February the bank honours the cheque.

Analysis The agreement of 10th January is a consumer credit agreement for running-account credit. The agreement of 15th–16th February varies the earlier agreement by adding a term allowing the credit limit to be exceeded merely temporarily. By section 82(2) the later agreement is deemed to revoke the earlier agreement and reproduce the combined effect of the two agreements. By section 82(4), Part V of this Act (except section 56) does not apply to the later agreement. By section 18(5), a term allowing a merely temporary excess over the credit limit is not to be treated as a separate agreement, or as providing fixed-sum credit. The whole of the £115 owed to the bank by X on 16th February is therefore running-account credit.

Example 24

Facts On 1st March 1975 Z (in England) enters into an agreement with A (an unincorporated body of persons) to bail to A equipment consisting of two components (component P and component Q). The agreement is not a hire-purchase agreement and is for a fixed term of 3 years, so paragraphs (a) and (b) of section 15(1) are both satisfied. The rental is payable monthly at a rate of £2,400 a year, but the agreement provides that this is to be reduced to £1,200 a year for the remainder of the agreement if at any time during its currency A returns component Q to the owner Z. On 5th May 1976 A is incorporated as A Ltd., taking over A's assets and liabilities. On 1st March 1977, A Ltd. returns component Q. On 1st January 1978, Z and A Ltd. agree to extend the earlier agreement by one year, increasing the rental for the final year by £250 to £1,450.

Analysis When entered into on 1st March 1975, the agreement is a consumer hire agreement. A falls within the definition of 'individual' in section 189(1) and if A returns component Q before 1st May 1976 the total rental will not exceed £5,000 (see section 15(1)(c)). When this date is passed without component Q having been returned it is obvious that the total rental must now exceed £5,000. Does this mean that the agreement then ceases to be a consumer hire agreement? The answer is no, because there has been no change in the terms of the agreement, and without such a change the agreement cannot move from one category to the other. Similarly, the fact that A's rights and duties under the agreement pass to a body corporate on 5th May 1976 does not cause the agreement to cease to be a consumer hire agreement (see definition of 'hirer' in section 189(1)).

The effect of the modifying agreement of 1st January 1978 is governed by section 82(2), which requires it to be treated as containing provisions reproducing the combined effect of the two actual agreements, that is to say as providing that—

    (a) obligations outstanding on 1st January 1978 are to be treated as outstanding under the modifying agreement;

    (b) the modifying agreement applies at the old rate of hire for the months of January and February 1978, and

    (c) for the year beginning 1st March 1978 A Ltd. will be the bailee of component P at a rental of £1,450.

The total rental under the modifying agreement is £1,850. Accordingly the modifying agreement is a regulated agreement. Even if the total rental under the modifying agreement exceeded £5,000 it would still be regulated because of the provisions of section 82(3).

Torts (Interference with Goods) Act 1977

(1977, c. 32)

1 Definition of 'wrongful interference with goods'

In this Act 'wrongful interference', or 'wrongful interference with goods', means—

    (a) conversion of goods (also called trover),

    (b) trespass to goods,

    (c) negligence so far as it results in damage to goods or to an interest in goods,

    (d) subject to section 2, any other tort so far as it results in damage to goods or to an interest in goods

[and references in this Act (however worded) to proceedings for wrongful interference or to a claim or right to claim for wrongful interference shall include references to proceedings by virtue of Part I of the Consumer Protection Act 1987 (product liability) in respect of any damage to goods and to the interest in goods or, as the case may be, to a claim or right to claim by virtue of that Part in respect of any such damage].

2 Abolition of detinue

    (1) Detinue is abolished.

(2) An action lies in conversion for loss or destruction of goods which a bailee has allowed to happen in breach of his duty to his bailor (that is to say it lies in a case which is not otherwise conversion, but would have been detinue before detinue was abolished).

3   Forms of judgment where goods are detained

(1) In proceedings for wrongful interference against a person who is in possession or in control of the goods relief may be given in accordance with this section, so far as appropriate.

(2) The relief is—

(a) an order for delivery of goods, and for payment of any consequential damages, or

(b) an order for delivery of the goods, but giving the defendant the alternative of paying damages by reference to the value of the goods, together in either alternative with payment of any consequential damages, or

(c) damages.

(3) Subject to rules of court—

(a) relief shall be given under only one of paragraphs (a), (b) and (c) of subsection (2),

(b) relief under paragraph (a) of subsection (2) is at the discretion of the court, and the claimant may choose between the others.

(4) If it is shown to the satisfaction of the court that an order under subsection (2)(a) had not been complied with, the court may—

(a) revoke the order, or the relevant part of it, and

(b) make an order for payment of damages by reference to the value of the goods.

(5) Where an order is made under subsection (2)(b) the defendant may satisfy the order by returning the goods at any time before execution of judgment, but without prejudice to liability to pay any consequential damages.

(6) An order for delivery of the goods under subsection (2)(a) or (b) may impose such conditions as may be determined by the court, or pursuant to rules of court, and in particular, where damages by reference to the value of the goods would not be the whole of the value of the goods, may require an allowance to be made by the claimant to reflect the difference.

For example, a bailor's action against the bailee may be one in which the measure of damages is not the full value of the goods, and then the court may order delivery of the goods, but require the bailor to pay the bailee a sum reflecting the difference.

(7) Where under subsection (1) or subsection (2) of section 6 an allowance is to be made in respect of an improvement of the goods, and an order is made under subsection (2)(a) or (b), the court may assess the allowance to be made in respect of the improvement, and by the order require, as a condition for delivery of the goods, that allowance to be made by the claimant.

(8) This section is without prejudice—

(a) to the remedies afforded by section 133 of the Consumer Credit Act, or

...

(c) to any jurisdiction to afford ancillary or incidental relief.

4   Interlocutory relief where goods are detained

(1) In this section 'proceedings' means proceedings for wrongful interference.

(2) On the application of any person in accordance with rules of court, the High Court shall, in such circumstances as may be specified in the rules, have power to make an order providing for the delivery up of any goods which are or may become subject matter of subsequent proceedings in the court, or as to which any question may arise in proceedings.

(3) Delivery shall be, as the order may provide, to the claimant or to a person appointed by the court for the purpose, and shall be on such terms and conditions as may be specified in the order.

5   Extinction of title on satisfaction of claim for damages

(1) Where damages for wrongful interference are, or would fall to be, assessed on the footing that the claimant is being compensated—

(a) for the whole of his interest in the goods, or

(b) for the whole of his interest in the goods subject to a reduction for contributory negligence, payment of the assessed damages (under all heads), or as the case may be settlement of a claim for damages for the wrong (under all heads), extinguishes the claimant's title to that interest.

(2) In subsection (1) the reference to the settlement of the claim includes—

(a) where the claim is made in court proceedings, and the defendant has paid a sum into court to meet the whole claim, the taking of that sum by the claimant, and

(b) where the claim is made in court proceedings, and the proceedings are settled or compromised, the payment of what is due in accordance with the settlement or compromise, and

(c) where the claim is made out of court and is settled or compromised, the payment of what is due in accordance with the settlement or compromise.

(3) It is hereby declared that subsection (1) does not apply where damages are assessed on the footing that the claimant is being compensated for the whole of his interest in the goods, but the damages paid are limited to some lesser amount by virtue of any enactment or rule of law.

(4) Where under section 7(3) the claimant accounts over to another person (the 'third party') so as to compensate (under all heads) the third party for the whole of his interest in the goods, the third party's title to that interest is extinguished.

(5) This section has effect subject to any agreement varying the respective rights of the parties to the agreement, and where the claim is made in court proceedings has effect subject to any court.

6 Allowance for improvement of the goods

(1) If in proceedings for wrongful interference against a person (the 'improver') who has improved the goods, it is shown that the improver acted in the mistaken but honest belief that he had a good title to them, an allowance shall be made for the extent to which, at the time as at which the goods fall to be valued in assessing damages, the value of the goods is attributable to the improvement.

(2) If, in proceedings for wrongful interference against a person ('the purchaser') who has purported to purchase the goods—

(a) from the improver, or

(b) where after such a purported sale the goods passed by a further purported sale on one or more occasions, on any such occasion,

it is shown that the purchaser acted in good faith, an allowance shall be made on the principle set out in subsection (1).

For example, where a person in good faith buys a stolen car from the improver and is sued in conversion by the true owner the damages may be reduced to reflect the improvement, but if the person who bought the stolen car from the improver sues the improver for failure of consideration, and the improver acted in good faith, subsection (3) below will ordinarily make a comparable reduction in the damages he recovers from the improver.

(3) If in a case within subsection (2) the person purporting to sell the goods acted in good faith, then in proceedings by the purchaser for recovery of the purchase price because of failure of consideration, or in any other proceedings founded on that failure of consideration, an allowance shall, where appropriate, be made on the principle set out in subsection (1).

(4) This section applies, with the necessary modifications, to a purported bailment or other disposition of goods as it applies to a purported sale of goods.

7 Double liability

(1) In this section 'double liability' means the double liability of the wrongdoer which can arise—

(a) where one of two or more rights of action for wrongful interference is founded on a possessory title, or

(b) where the measure of damages in an action for wrongful interference founded on a proprietary title is or includes the entire value of the goods, although the interest is one of two or more interests in the goods.

(2) In proceedings to which any two or more claimants are parties, the relief shall be such as to avoid double liability of the wrongdoer as between those claimants.

(3) On satisfaction, in whole or in part, of any claim for an amount exceeding that recoverable if subsection (2) applied, the claimant is liable to account over to the other person having a right to claim to such extent as will avoid double liability.

(4) Where, as the result of enforcement of a double liability, any claimant is unjustly enriched to an extent, he shall be liable to reimburse the wrongdoer to that extent.

For example, if a converter of goods pays damages first to a finder of the goods, and then to the true owner, the finder is unjustly enriched unless he accounts over to the true owner under subsection (3); and then the true owner is unjustly enriched and becomes liable to reimburse the converter of the goods.

8 Competing rights to the goods

(1) The defendant in an action for wrongful interference shall be entitled to show, in accordance with rules of court, that a third party has a better right than the plaintiff as respects all or any part of the interest claimed by the plaintiff, or in right of which he sues, and any rule of law (sometimes called jus tertii) to the contrary is abolished.

(2) Rules of court relating to proceedings for wrongful interference may—

(a) require the plaintiff to give particulars of his title,

(b) require the plaintiff to identify any person who, to his knowledge, has or claims any interest in the goods,

(c) authorise the defendant to apply for directions as to whether any person should be joined with a view to establishing whether he has a better right than the plaintiff, or has a claim of a result of which the defendant might be doubly liable,

(d) where a party fails to appear on an application within paragraph (c), or to comply with any direction given by the court on such an application, authorise the court to deprive him of any right of action against the defendant for the wrong either unconditionally, or subject to such terms or conditions as may be specified.

(3) Subsection (2) is without prejudice to any power of making rules of court.

9 Concurrent actions

...

10 Co-owners

(1) Co-ownership is no defence to an action founded on conversion or trespass to goods where the defendant without the authority of the other co-owner—

(a) destroys the goods, or disposes of the goods in a way giving a good title to the entire property in the goods, or otherwise does anything equivalent to the destruction of the other's interest in the goods, or

(b) purports to dispose of the goods in a way which would give a good title to the entire property in the goods if he was acting with the authority of all co-owners of the goods.

(2) Subsection (1) shall not affect the law concerning execution or enforcement of judgments, or concerning any form of distress.

(3) Subsection (1)(a) is by the way of restatement of existing law so far as it relates to conversion.

11 Minor amendments

(1) Contributory negligence is no defence in proceedings founded on conversion, or on intentional trespass to goods.

(2) Receipt of goods by way of pledge is conversion if the delivery of the goods is conversion.

(3) Denial of title is not of itself conversion.

12 Bailee's power of sale

(1) This section applies to goods in the possession or under the control of a bailee where—

(a) the bailor is in breach of an obligation to take delivery of the goods or, if the terms of the bailment so provide, to give directions as to their delivery, or

(b) the bailee could impose such an obligation by giving notice to the bailor, but is unable to trace or communicate with the bailor, or

(c) the bailee can reasonably expect to be relieved of any duty to safeguard the goods on giving notice to the bailor, but is unable to trace or communicate with the bailor.

(2) In the cases of Part I of Schedule 1 to this Act a bailee may, for the purposes of subsection (1), impose an obligation on the bailor to take delivery of the goods, or as the case may be to give directions as to their delivery, and in those cases the said Part I sets out the method of notification.

(3) If the bailee—

(a) has in accordance with Part II of Schedule 1 to this Act given notice to the bailor of his intention to sell the goods under this subsection, or

(b) has failed to trace or communicate with the bailor with a view to giving him such a notice, after having taken reasonable steps for the purpose, and is reasonably satisfied that the bailor owns the goods, he shall be entitled, as against the bailor, to sell the goods.

(4) Where subsection (3) applies but the bailor did not in fact own the goods, a sale under this section, or under section 13, shall not give a good title as against the owner, or as against a person claiming under the owner.

(5) A bailee exercising his powers under subsection (3) shall be liable to account to the bailor for the proceeds of sale, less any cost of sale, and—

(a) the account shall be taken on the footing that the bailee should have adopted the best method of sale reasonably available in the circumstances, and

(b) where subsection (3)(a) applies, any sum payable in respect of the goods by the bailor to the bailee which accrued due before the bailee gave notice of intention to sell the goods shall be deductible from the proceeds of sale.

(6) A sale duly made under this section gives a good title to the purchaser as against the bailor.

(7) In this section, section 13, and Schedule 1 to the Act,

(a) 'bailor' and 'bailee' include their respective successors in title, and

(b) references to what is payable, paid or due to the bailee in respect of the goods include references to what would be payable by the bailor to the bailee as a condition of delivery of the goods at the relevant time.

(8) This section, and Schedule 1 to this Act, have effect subject to the terms of the bailment.

(9) this section shall not apply where the goods were bailed before the commencement of this Act.

13   Sale authorised by the court

(1) If a bailee of the goods to which section 12 applies satisfies the court that he is entitled to see the goods under section 12, or that he would be so entitled if he had given any notice required in accordance with Schedule 1 to this Act, the court—

(a) may authorise the sale of the goods subject to such terms and conditions, if any, as may be specified in the order and,

(b) may authorise the bailee to deduct from the proceeds of sale any costs of sale and any amount due from the bailor to the bailee in respect of the goods, and

(c) may direct the payment into court of the net proceeds of sale, less any amount deducted under paragraph (b), to be held to the credit of the bailor.

(2) A decision of the court authorising a sale under this section shall, subject to any right of appeal, be conclusive, as against the bailor, of the bailee's entitlement to sell the goods, and gives a good title to the purchaser as against the bailor.

(3) In this section 'the court' means the High Court or a county court, and a county court shall have jurisdiction in the proceedings if the value of the goods does not exceed the county court limit.

14   Interpretation

(1) In this Act, unless the context otherwise requires—

...

'goods' includes all chattels personal other than things in action and money.

...

16   Extent and application to the Crown

(3) This Act shall bind the Crown, but as regards the Crown's liability in tort shall not bind the Crown further than the Crown is made liable in tort by the Crown Proceedings Act 1947.

Section 12

SCHEDULE 1

UNCOLLECTED GOODS

PART I POWER TO IMPOSE OBLIGATION TO COLLECT GOODS

1. (1) For the purposes of section 12(1) a bailee may, in the circumstances specified in this Part of this Schedule, by notice given to the bailor impose on him an obligation to take delivery of the goods.

(2) The notice shall be in writing, and may be given either—

(a) by delivering it to the bailor, or

(b) by leaving it at his proper address, or

(c) by post.

(3) The notice shall—

(a) specify the name and address of the bailee, and give sufficient particulars of the goods and the address or place where they are held, and

(b) state that the goods are ready for delivery to the bailor, or where combined with a notice terminating the contract of bailment, will be ready for delivery when the contract is terminated, and

(c) specify the amount, if any, which is payable by the bailor to the bailee in respect of the goods and which became due before the giving of the notice.

(4) Where the notice is sent by post it may be combined with a notice under Part II of this Schedule if the notice is sent by post in a way complying with paragraph 6(4).

(5) References in this Part of this Schedule to taking delivery of the goods include, where the terms of the bailment admit, references to giving directions as to their delivery.

(6) This Part of this Schedule is without prejudice to the provisions of any contract requiring the bailor to take delivery of the goods.

Goods accepted for repair or other treatment

2. If a bailee has accepted goods for repair or other treatment on the terms (expressed or implied) that they will be re-delivered to the bailor when the repair or other treatment has been carried out, the notice may be given at any time after the repair or other treatment has been carried out.

Goods accepted for valuation or appraisal

3. If a bailee has accepted goods in order to value or appraise them, the notice may be given at any time after the bailee has carried out the valuation or appraisal.

Storage, warehousing, etc.

4. (1) If a bailee is in possession of goods which he has held as custodian, and his obligation as custodian has come to an end, the notice may be given at any time after the ending of the obligation, or may be combined with any notice terminating his obligation as custodian.

(2) This paragraph shall not apply to goods held by a person as mercantile agent, that is to say by a person having in the customary course of his business as a mercantile agent authority either to sell goods or to consign goods for the purpose of sale, or to buy goods, or to raise money on the security of goods.

Supplemental

5. Paragraphs 2, 3 and 4 apply whether or not the bailor has paid any amount due to the bailee in respect of the goods, and whether or not the bailment is for reward, or in the course of business, or gratuitous.

PART II NOTICE OF INTENTION TO SELL GOODS

6. (1) A notice under section 12(3) shall—
  (a) specify the name and address of the bailee, and give sufficient particulars of the goods and the address or place where they are held, and
  (b) specify the date on or after which the bailee proposes to sell the goods, and
  (c) specify the amount, if any, which is payable by the bailor to the bailee in respect of the goods, and which became due before giving of the notice.

(2) The period between giving of the notice and the date specified in the notice as that on or after which the bailee proposes to exercise the power of sale shall be such as will afford the bailor a reasonable opportunity of taking delivery of the goods.

(3) If any amount is payable in respect of the goods by the bailor to the bailee, and become due before giving of the notice, the said period shall be not less than three months.

(4) The notice shall be in writing and shall be sent by post in a registered letter, or by the recorded delivery service.

7. (1) The bailee shall not give a notice under section 12(3), or exercise his right to send the goods pursuant to such a notice, at a time when he has notice that, because of a dispute concerning the goods, the bailor is questioning or refusing to pay all or any part of what the bailee claims to be due to him in respect of the goods.

(2) This paragraph shall be left out of account in determining under section 13(1) whether a bailee of goods is entitled to see the goods under section 12, or would be so entitled if he had given any notice required in accordance with this Schedule.

Unfair Contract Terms Act 1977

(1977, c. 50)

PART I

AMENDMENT OF LAW FOR ENGLAND AND WALES AND NORTHERN IRELAND

1 Scope of Part I
  (1) For the purposes of this Part of this Act, 'negligence' means the breach—
    (a) of any obligation, arising from the express or implied terms of a contract, to take reasonable care or exercise reasonable skill in the performance of the contract;
    (b) of any common law duty to take reasonable care or exercise reasonable skill (but not any stricter duty);
    (c) of the common duty of care imposed by the Occupiers' Liability Act 1957 or the Occupier's Liability Act (Northern Ireland) 1957.

(2) This Part of the Act is subject to Part III; and in relation to contracts, the operation of sections 2 to 4 and 7 is subject to the exceptions made by Schedule I.

(3) In the case of both contract and tort, sections 2 to 7 apply (except where the contrary is stated in section 6(4)) only to business liability, that is liability to breach of obligations or duties arising—

    (a) from things done or to be done by a person in the course of a business (whether his own business or another's); or

    (b) from the occupation of premises used for business purposes of the occupier; and references to liability are to be read accordingly [but liability of an occupier of premises for breach of an obligation or duty towards a person obtaining access to the premises for recreational or educational purposes, being liability for loss or damage suffered by reason of the dangerous state of the premises, is not a business liability of the occupier unless granting that person such access for the purposes concerned falls within the business purposes of the occupier.]

(4) In relation to any breach of duty or obligation, it is immaterial for any purpose of this Part of this Act whether the breach was inadvertent or intentional, or whether liability for it arises directly or vicariously.

2   Negligence liability

(1) A person cannot by reference to any contract term or to a notice given to persons generally or to particular persons exclude or restrict his liability for death or personal injury resulting from negligence.

(2) In the case of other loss or damage, a person cannot so exclude or restrict his liability for negligence except in so far as the term or notice satisfies the requirement of reasonableness.

(3) Where a contract term or notice purports to exclude or restrict liability for negligence a person's agreement to or awareness of it is not of itself to be taken as indicating his voluntary acceptance of any risk.

3   Liability arising in contract

(1) This section applies as between contracting parties where one of them deals as consumer or on the other's written standard terms of business.

(2) As against that party, the other cannot by reference to any contract term—

    (a) when himself in breach of contract, exclude or restrict any liability of his in respect of the breach; or

    (b) claim to be entitled—

        (i)   to render a contractual performance substantially different from that which was reasonably expected of him, or

        (ii) in respect of the whole of any part of his contractual obligation, to render no performance at all,

except in so far as (in any of the cases mentioned above in this subsection) the contract term satisfies the requirement of reasonableness.

4   Unreasonable indemnity clauses

(1) A person dealing as consumer cannot by reference to any contract term be made to indemnify another person (whether a party to the contract or not) in respect of liability that may be incurred by the other for negligence or breach of contract, except in so far as the contract term satisfies the requirement of reasonableness.

(2) This section applies whether the liability in question—

    (a) is directly that of the person to be indemnified or is incurred by him vicariously;

    (b) is to the person dealing as consumer or to someone else.

5   'Guarantee' of consumer goods

(1) In the case of goods of a type ordinarily supplied for private use of consumption, where loss or damage—

    (a) arises from the goods proving defective while in consumer use; and

    (b) results from the negligence of a person concerned in the manufacture or distribution of the goods, liability for the loss or damage cannot be excluded or restricted by reference to any contract term or notice contained in or operating by reference to a guarantee of the goods.

(2) For these purposes—

(a) goods are to be regarded as 'in consumer use' when a person is using them, or has them in his possession for use, otherwise than exclusively for the purposes of a business; and

(b) anything in writing is a guarantee if it contains or purports to contain some promise or assurance (however worded or presented) that defects will be made good by complete or partial replacement, or by repair, monetary compensation or otherwise.

(3) This section does not apply as between the parties to a contract under or in pursuance of which possession or ownership of the goods passed.

6 Sale and hire-purchase

(1) Liability for breach of the obligations arising from—

(a) [section 12 of the Sale of Goods Act 1979] (seller's implied undertakings as to title, etc.);

(b) section 8 of the Supply of Goods (Implied Terms) Act 1973 (the corresponding thing in relation to hire-purchase),

cannot be excluded or restricted by reference to any contract term.

(2) As against a person dealing as consumer, liability for breach of the obligations arising from—

(a) [section 13, 14 or 15 of the [1979] Act] (seller's implied undertakings as to conformity of goods with description or sample, or as to their quality of fitness for a particular purpose);

(b) section 9, 10 or 11 of the 1973 Act (the corresponding things in relation to hire-purchase),

cannot be excluded or restricted by reference to any contract term.

(3) As against a person dealing otherwise than as consumer, the liability specified in subsection (2) above can be excluded or restricted by reference to a contract term, but only in so far as the term satisfies the requirement of reasonableness.

(4) The liabilities referred to in this section are not only the business liabilities defined by section 1(3), but include those arising under any contract of sale of goods or hire-purchase agreement.

7 Miscellaneous contracts under which goods pass

(1) Where the possession or ownership of goods passes under or in pursuance of a contract not governed by the law of sale of goods or hire-purchase, subsections (2) to (4) below apply as regards the effect (if any) to be given to contract terms excluding or restricting liability for breach of obligation arising by implication of law from the nature of the contract.

(2) As against a person dealing as consumer, liability in respect of the goods' correspondence with description or sample, or their quality or fitness for any particular purpose, cannot be excluded or restricted by reference to any such term.

(3) As against a person dealing otherwise than as consumer, that liability can be excluded or restricted by reference to such a term, but only in so far as the term satisfies the requirement of reasonableness.

[(3A) Liability for breach of the obligations arising under section 2 of the Supply of Goods and Services Act 1982 (implied terms about title etc. in certain contracts for the transfer of the property in goods) cannot be excluded or restricted by reference to any such term.]

(4) Liability in respect of—

(a) the right to transfer ownership of the goods, or give possession; or

(b) the assurance of quiet possession to a person taking goods in pursuance of the contract,

cannot [(in a case to which subsection (3A) above does not apply)] be excluded or restricted by reference to any such term except in so far as the term satisfies the requirement of reasonableness.

9 Effect of breach

(1) Where for reliance upon it a contract term has to satisfy the requirement of reasonableness, it may be found to do so-and be given effect accordingly notwithstanding that the contract has been terminated either by breach or by a party electing to treat it as repudiated.

(2) Where on a breach the contract is nevertheless affirmed by a party entitled to treat it as repudiated, this does not of itself exclude the requirement of reasonableness in relation to any contract term.

10 Evasion by means of secondary contract

A person is not bound by any contract term prejudicing or taking away rights of his which arise under, or in connection with the performance of, another contract, so far as those rights extend to the enforcement of another's liability which this Part of this Act prevents that other from excluding or restricting.

11 The 'reasonableness' test

(1) In relation to a contract term, the requirement of reasonableness for the purposes of this Part of this Act, section 3 of the Misrepresentation Act 1967 and section 3 of the Misrepresentation Act (Northern Ireland) 1967 is that the term shall have been a fair and reasonable one to be included having regard to the circumstances which were, or ought reasonably to have been, known to or in the contemplation of the parties when the contract was made.

(2) In determining for the purposes of section 6 or 7 above whether a contract term satisfies the requirement of reasonableness, regard shall be had in particular to the matters specified in Schedule 2 to this Act; but this subsection does not prevent the court or arbitrator from holding, in accordance with any rule of law, that a term which purports to exclude or restrict any relevant liability is not a term of the contract.

(3) In relation to a notice (not being a notice having contractual effect), the requirement of reasonableness under this Act is that it should be fair and reasonable to allow reliance on it, having regard to all the circumstances obtaining when the liability arose or (but for the notice) would have arisen.

(4) Where by reference to a contract term or notice a person seeks to restrict liability to a specified sum of money, and the question arises (under this or any other Act) whether the term or notice satisfies the requirement of reasonableness, regard shall be had in particular (but without prejudice to subsection (2) above in the case of contract terms) to—

(a) the resources which he could expect to be available to him for the purpose of meeting the liability should it arise; and

(b) how far it was open to him to cover himself by insurance.

(5) It is for those claiming that a contract term or notice satisfies the requirement of reasonableness to show that it does.

12 'Dealing as consumer'

(1) A party to contract 'deals as consumer' in relation to another party if—

(a) he neither makes the contract in the course of a business nor holds himself out as doing so; and

(b) the other party does make the contract in the course of a business; and

(c) in the case of a contract governed by the law of sale of goods or hire-purchase, or by section 7 of this Act, the goods passing under or in pursuance of the contract are of a type ordinarily supplied for private use or consumption.

[(1A) But if the first party mentioned in subsection (1) is an individual paragraph (c) of that subsection must be ignored.]

[(2) But the buyer is not in any circumstances to be regarded as dealing as consumer—

(a) if he is an individual and the goods are second hand goods sold at public auction at which individuals have the opportunity of attending the sale in person;

(b) if he is not an individual and the goods are sold by auction or by competitive tender.]

(3) Subject to this, it is for those claiming that a party does not deal as consumer to show that he does not.

13   Varieties of exemption clause

(1) To the extent that this Part of this Act prevents the exclusion or restriction of any liability it also prevents—

(a) making the liability or its enforcement subject to restrictive or onerous conditions;

(b) excluding or restricting any right or remedy in respect of the liability, or subjecting a person to any prejudice in consequence of his pursuing any such right or remedy;

(c) excluding or restricting rules of evidence or procedure; and (to that extent) sections 2 and 5 to 7 also prevent excluding or restricting liability by reference to terms and notices which exclude or restrict the relevant obligation or duty.

(2) But an agreement in writing to submit present or future differences to arbitration is not to be treated under this Part of this Act as excluding or restricting any liability.

14   Interpretation of Part I

In this Part of the Act—

'business' includes a profession and the activities of any government department or local or public authority;

'goods' has the same meaning as in [the Sales of Goods Act 1979];

'hire-purchase agreement' has the same meaning as in the Consumer Credit Act 1974;

'negligence' has the meaning given by section 1(1);

'notice' includes an announcement, whether or not in writing, and any other communication or pretended communication; and

'personal injury' includes any disease and any impairment of physical or mental condition.

PART III

PROVISIONS APPLYING TO WHOLE OF UNITED KINGDOM

26   International supply contracts

(1) The limits imposed by this Act on the extent to which a person may exclude or restrict liability by reference to a contract term do not apply to liability arising under such a contract as is described in subsection (3) below.

(2) The terms of such a contract are not subject to any requirement of reasonableness under section 3 or 4: and nothing in Part II of this Act should require the incorporation of the terms of such a contract to be fair and reasonable for them to have effect.

(3) Subject to subsection (4), that description of contract is one whose characteristics are the following—

(a) either it is a contract of sale of goods or it is one under or in pursuance of which the possession of ownership of goods passes, and

(b) it is made by parties whose places of business (or, if they have none, habitual residences) are in the territories of different States (the Channel Islands and the Isle of Man being treated for this purpose as different States from the United Kingdom).

(4) A contract falls within subsection (3) above only if either—

(a) the goods in question are, at the time of the conclusion of the contract, in the course of carriage, or will be carried, from the territory of one State to the territory of another; or

(b) the acts constituting the offer and acceptance have been done in the territories of different States; or

(c) the contract provides for the goods to be delivered to the territory of a state other than that within whose territory those acts were done.

27   Choice of law clauses

(1) Where the [law applicable to] a contract is the law of any part of the United Kingdom only by choice of the parties (and apart from that choice would be the law of some country outside the United Kingdom) sections 2 to 7 and 16 to 21 of this Act do not operate as part [of the law applicable to the contract.]

(2) This Act has effect notwithstanding any contract term which applies or purports to apply the law of some country outside the United Kingdom, where (either or both)—

  (a) the term appears to the court, or arbitrator or arbiter to have been imposed wholly or mainly for the purpose of enabling the party imposing it to evade the operation of this Act; or

  (b) in the making of the contract one of the parties dealt as consumer, and he was then habitually resident in the United Kingdom, and the essential steps necessary for the making of the contract were taken there, whether by him or by others on his behalf.

(3) In the application of subsection (2) above to Scotland, for paragraph (b) there shall be substituted—

  '(b) the contract is a consumer contract as defined in Part 11 of this Act, and the consumer at the date when the contract was made was habitually resident in the United Kingdom, and the essential steps necessary for the making of the contract were taken there, whether by him or by others on his behalf.'

28   Temporary provision for sea carriage of passengers

(1) This section applies to a contract for carriage by sea of a passenger or of a passenger and his luggage where the provisions of the Athens Convention (with or without modification) do not have, in relation to the contract, the force of law in the United Kingdom.

(2) In a case where—

  (a) the contract is not made in the United Kingdom, and

  (b) neither the place of departure nor the place of destination under it is in the United Kingdom, a person is not precluded by this Act from excluding or restricting liability for loss or damage, being loss or damage for which the provisions of the Convention would, if they had the force of law in relation to the contract, impose liability on him.

(3) In any other case, a person is not precluded by this Act from excluding or restricting liability for that loss or damage—

  (a) in so far as the exclusion or restriction would have been effective in that case had the provisions of the Convention had the force of law in relation to the contract; or

  (b) in such circumstances and to such extent as may be prescribed, by reference to a prescribed term of the contract.

(4) For the purposes of subsection (3)(a), the values which shall be taken to be the official values in the United Kingdom of the amounts (expressed in gold francs) by reference to which liability under the provisions of the Convention is limited shall be such amounts in sterling as the Secretary of State may from time to time by order made by statutory instrument specify.

(5) In this section,—

  (a) the references to excluding or restricting liability include doing any of those things in relation to the liability which are mentioned in section 13 or section 25(3) and (5); and

  (b) 'the Athens Convention' means the Athens Convention relating to the Carriage of Passengers and their Luggage by Sea, 1974; and

  (c) 'prescribed' means prescribed by the Secretary of State by regulations made by statutory instrument;

and a statutory instrument containing the regulations shall be subject to annulment in pursuance of a resolution of either House of Parliament.

29   Saving for other relevant legislation

(1) Nothing in this Act removes or restricts the effect of, or prevents reliance upon, any contractual provision which—

(a) is authorised or required by the express terms or necessary implication of an enactment; or

(b) being made with a view to compliance with an international agreement to which the United Kingdom is a party, does not operate more restrictively than is contemplated by the agreement.

(2) A contract term is to be taken—

(a) for the purposes of Part I of this Act, as satisfying the requirement of reasonableness; and

(b) for those of Part II, to have been fair and reasonable to incorporate,

if it is incorporated or approved by, or incorporated pursuant to a decision or ruling of, a competent authority acting in the exercise of any statutory jurisdiction or function and is not a term in a contract to which the competent authority is itself a party.

(3) In this section—

'competent authority' means any court, arbitrator or arbiter, government department or public authority;

'enactment' means any legislation (including subordinate legislation) of the United Kingdom or Northern Ireland and any instrument having effect by virtue of such legislation; and

'statutory' means conferred by an enactment.

Section 1(2)   # SCHEDULE 1

SCOPE OF SECTIONS 2 TO 4 AND 7

1. Sections 2 to 4 of this Act do not extend to—

   (a) any contract of insurance (including a contract to pay an annuity on human life);

   (b) any contract so far as it relates to the creation or transfer of an interest in land, or to the termination of such an interest, whether by extinction, merger, surrender, forfeiture or otherwise;

   (c) any contract so far as it relates to the creation or transfer of a right or interest in any patent, trade mark, copyright [or design right];

   (d) any contract so far as it relates—

      (i) to the formation or dissolution of a company (which means any body corporate or unincorporated association and includes a partnership), or

      (ii) to its constitution or the rights or obligations of its corporators or members;

   (e) any contract so far as it relates to the creation or transfer of securities or of any right or interest in securities.

2. Section 2(1) extends to—

   (a) any contract of marine salvage or towage;

   (b) any charterparty of a ship or hovercraft; and

   (c) any contract for the carriage of goods by ship or hovercraft;

but subject to this sections 2 to 4 and 7 do not extend to any such contract except in favour of a person dealing as a consumer.

3. Where goods are carried by ship or hovercraft in pursuance of a contract which either—

   (a) specifies that as the means of carriage over part of the journey to be covered, or

   (b) makes no provision as to the means of carriage and does not exclude that means,

then sections 2(2), 3 and 4 do not, except in favour of a person dealing as consumer, extend to the contract as it operates for and in relation to the carriage of the goods by that means.

4. Section 2(1) and (2) do not extend to a contract of employment, except in favour of the employee.

5. Section 2(1) does not affect the validity of any discharge and indemnity given by a person, on or in connection with an award to him of compensation for pneumoconiosis attributable to employment in the coal industry, in respect of any further claim arising from his contracting the disease.

Sections 11(2) and 24(2)   SCHEDULE 2

'GUIDELINES' FOR APPLICATION OF
REASONABLENESS TEST

The matters to which regard is to be had in particular for the purposes of sections 6(3), 7(3) and (4), 20 and 21 are any of the following which appear to be relevant—

(a) the strength of the bargaining positions of the parties relative to each other, taking into account (among other things) alternative means by which the customer's requirements could have been met;

(b) whether the customer received an inducement to agree to the term, or in accepting it had an opportunity of entering into a similar contract with other persons, but without having to accept a similar term;

(c) whether the customer knew or ought reasonably to have known of the existence and extent of the term (having regard, among other things, to any custom of the trade and any previous course of dealing between the parties);

(d) where the term excludes or restricts any relevant liability if some condition is not complied with, whether it was reasonable at the time of the contract to expect that compliance with that condition would be practicable;

(e) whether the goods were manufactured, processed or adapted to the special order of the customer.

Sale of Goods Act 1979

(1979, c. 54)

PART I CONTRACTS TO WHICH ACT APPLIES

1   Contracts to which Act applies

(1) This Act applies to contracts of sale of goods made on or after (but not to those made before) 1 January 1894.

(2) In relation to contracts made on certain dates, this Act applies subject to the modification of certain of its sections as mentioned in Schedule 1 below.

(3) Any such modification is indicated in the section concerned by a reference to Schedule 1 below.

(4) Accordingly, where a section does not contain such a reference, this Act applies in relation to the contract concerned without such modification of the section.

PART II FORMATION OF THE CONTRACT

Contract of sale

2   Contract of sale

(1) A contract of sale of goods is a contract by which the seller transfers or agrees to transfer the property in goods to the buyer for a money consideration, called the price.

(2) There may a contract of sale between one part owner and another.

(3) A contract of sale may be absolute or conditional.

(4) Where under a contract of sale the property in the goods is transferred from the seller to the buyer the contact is called a sale.

(5) Where under a contract of sale the transfer of the property in the goods is to take place at a future time or subject to some condition later to be fulfilled the contract is called an agreement to sell.

(6) An agreement to sell becomes a sale when the time elapses or the conditions are fulfilled subject to which the property in the goods is to be transferred.

3 Capacity to buy and sell

(1) Capacity to buy and sell is regulated by the general law concerning capacity to contract and to transfer and acquire property.

(2) Where necessaries are sold and delivered to a minor or to a person who by reason of [...] drunkenness is incompetent to contract, he must pay a reasonable price for them.

(3) In subsection (2) above 'necessaries' means goods suitable to the condition in life of the minor or other person concerned and to his actual requirements at the time of the sale and delivery.

Formalities of contract

4 How contract of sale is made

(1) Subject to this and any other Act, a contract of sale may be made in writing (either with or without seal), or by word of mouth, or partly in writing and partly by word of mouth, or may be implied from the conduct of the parties.

(2) Nothing in this section affects the law relating to corporations.

Subject matter of contract

5 Existing or future goods

(1) The goods which form the subject of a contract of sale may be either existing goods, owned or possessed by the seller, or goods to be manufactured or acquired by him after the making of the contract of sale, in this Act called future goods.

(2) There may be a contract for the sale of goods the acquisition of which by the seller depends on a contingency which may or may not happen.

(3) Where by a contract of sale the seller purports to effect a present sale of future goods, the contract operates as an agreement to sell the goods.

6 Goods which have perished

Where there is a contract for the sale of specific goods, and the goods without the knowledge of the seller have perished at the time when a contract is made, the contract is void.

7 Goods perishing before sale but after agreement to sell

Where there is an agreement to sell specific goods and subsequently the goods, without any fault on the part of the seller or buyer, perish before the risk passes to the buyer, the agreement is avoided.

The price

8 Ascertainment of price

(1) The price in a contract of sale may be fixed by the contract, or may be left to be fixed in a manner agreed by the contract, or may be determined by the course of dealing between the parties.

(2) Where the price is not determined as mentioned in subsection (1) above the buyer must pay a reasonable price.

(3) What is a reasonable price is a question of fact dependent on the circumstances of each particular case.

9 Agreement to sell at valuation

(1) Where there is an agreement to sell goods on the terms that the price is to be fixed by the valuation of a third party, and he cannot or does not make the valuation, the agreement is avoided; but if the goods or any part of them have been delivered to and appropriated by the buyer he must pay a reasonable price for them.

(2) Where the third party is prevented from making the valuation by the fault of the seller or buyer, the party not at fault may maintain an action for damages against the party at fault.

[Implied terms etc.]

10   Stipulations about time

(1) Unless a different intention appears from the terms of the contract, stipulations as to time of payment are not of the essence of a contract of sale.

(2) Whether any other stipulation as to time is or is not of the essence of the contract depends on the terms of the contract.

(3) In a contract of sale 'month' prima facie means calendar month.

11   When condition to be treated as warranty

(2) Where a contract of sale is subject to a condition to be fulfilled by the seller, the buyer may waive the condition, or may elect to treat the breach of the condition as a breach of warranty and not as a ground for treating the contract as repudiated.

(3) Whether a stipulation in a contract of sale is a condition, the breach of which may give rise to a right to treat the contract as repudiated, or a warranty, the breach of which may give rise to a claim for damages but not to a right to reject the goods and treat the contract as repudiated, depends in each case on the construction of the contract; and a stipulation may be a condition, though called a warranty in the contract.

(4) [Subject to section 35A below] Where a contract of sale is not severable and the buyer has accepted the goods or part of them, the breach of a condition to be fulfilled by the seller can only be treated as a breach of warranty, and not as a ground for rejecting the goods and treating the contract as repudiated, unless there is an express or implied term of the contract to that effect.

(6) Nothing in this section affects a condition or warranty whose fulfilment is excused by law by reason of impossibility or otherwise.

12   Implied terms about title, etc.

(1) In a contract of sale, other than one to which subsection (3) below applies, there is an implied [term] on the part of the seller that in the case of a sale he has a right to sell the goods, and in the case of an agreement to sell he will have such a right at the time when the property is to pass.

(2) In a contract of sale, other than one to which subsection (3) below applies, there is also an implied [term] that—

    (a) the goods are free, and will remain free until the time when the property is to pass, from any charge or encumbrance not disclosed or known to the buyer before the contract is made, and

    (b) the buyer will enjoy quiet possession of the goods except so far as it may be disturbed by the owner or other person entitled to the benefit of any charge or encumbrance so disclosed or known.

(3) This subsection applies to a contract of sale in the case of which there appears from the contract or is to be inferred from its circumstances an intention that the seller should transfer only such title as he or a third person may have.

(4) In a contract to which subsection (3) above applies there is an implied [term] that all charges or encumbrances known to the seller and not known to the buyer have been disclosed to the buyer before the contract is made.

(5) In a contract to which subsection (3) above applies there is also an implied [term] that none of the following will disturb the buyer's quiet possession of the goods, namely—

    (a) the seller;

    (b) in a case where the parties to the contract intend that the seller should transfer only such title as a third person may have, that person;

    (c) anyone claiming through or under the seller or that third person otherwise than under a charge or encumbrance disclosed or known to the buyer before the contract is made.

[(5A) As regards England and Wales and Northern Ireland, the term implied by subsection (1) above is a condition and the terms implied by subsections (2), (4) and (5) above are warranties.]

(6) Paragraph 3 of Schedule 1 below applies in relation to a contract made before 18 May 1973.

13 Sale by description

(1) Where there is a contract for the sale of goods by description, there is an implied [term] that the goods will correspond with the description.

[(1A) As regards England and Wales and Northern Ireland, the term implied by subsection (1) above is a condition.]

(2) If the sale is by sample as well as by description it is not sufficient that the bulk of the goods corresponds with the sample if the goods do not also correspond with the description.

(3) A sale of goods is not prevented from being a sale by description by reason only that, being exposed for sale or hire, they are selected by the buyer.

(4) Paragraph 4 of Schedule 1 below applies in relation to a contract made before 18 May 1973.

14 Implied terms about quality or fitness

(1) Except as provided by this section and section 15 below and subject to any other enactment, there is no implied [term] about the quality or fitness for any particular purpose of goods supplied under a contract of sale.

[(2) Where the seller sells goods in the course of a business, there is an implied term that the goods supplied under the contract are of satisfactory quality.

(2A) For the purposes of this Act, goods are of satisfactory quality if they meet the standard that a reasonable person would regard as satisfactory, taking account of any description of the goods, the price (if relevant) and all the other relevant circumstances.

(2B) For the purposes of this Act, the quality of goods includes their state and condition and the following (among others) are in appropriate cases aspects of the quality of goods—

(a) fitness for all the purposes for which goods of the kind in question are commonly supplied,

(b) appearance and finish,

(c) freedom from minor defects,

(d) safety, and

(e) durability.

(2C) The term implied by subsection (2) above does not extend to any matter making the quality of goods unsatisfactory—

(a) which is specifically drawn to the buyer's attention before the contract is made,

(b) where the buyer examines the goods before the contract is made, which that examination ought to reveal, or

(c) in the case of a contract for sale by sample, which would have been apparent on a reasonable examination of the sample.]

[(2D) If the buyer deals as consumer or, in Scotland, if a contract of sale is a consumer contract, the relevant circumstances mentioned in subsection (2A) above include any public statements on the specific characteristics of the goods made about them by the seller, the producer or his representative, particularly in advertising or on labelling.

(2E) A public statement is not by virtue of subsection (2D) above a relevant circumstance for the purposes of subsection (2A) above in the case of a contract of sale, if the seller shows that—

(a) at the time the contract was made, he was not, and could not reasonably have been aware of the statement,

(b) before the contract was made, the statement had been withdrawn in public or, to the extent that it contained anything which was incorrect or misleading, it had been corrected in public, or

(c) the decision to buy the goods could not have been influenced by the statement.

(2F) Subsections (2D) and (2E) above do not prevent any public statement from being a relevant circumstance for the purposes of subsection (2A) above (whether or not the buyer deals as consumer or, in Scotland, whether or not the contract of sale is a consumer contract) if the statement would have been such a circumstance apart from those subsections.]

(3) Where the seller sells goods in the course of a business and the buyer, expressly or by implication, makes known—

(a) to the seller, or

(b) where the purchase price of part of it is payable by instalments and the goods were previously sold by a credit-broker to the seller, to that credit-broker,

any particular purpose for which the goods are being bought, there is an implied [term] that the goods supplied under the contract are reasonably fit for that purpose, whether or not that is a purpose for which such goods are commonly supplied, except where the circumstances show that the buyer does not rely, or that it is unreasonable for him to rely, on the skill or judgment of the seller or credit-broker.

(4) An implied [term] about quality or fitness for a particular purpose may be annexed to a contract of sale by usage.

(5) The preceding provisions of this section apply to a sale by a person who in the course of a business is acting as agent for another as they apply to a sale by a principal in the course of a business, except where that other is not selling in the course of a business and either the buyer knows that fact or reasonable steps are taken to bring it to the notice of the buyer before the contract is made.

[(6) As regards England and Wales and Northern Ireland, the terms implied by subsections (2) and (3) above are conditions.]

(7) Paragraph 5 of Schedule 1 below applies in relation to a contract made on or after 18 May 1973 and before the appointed day, and paragraph 6 in relation to one made before 18 May 1973.

(8) In subsection (7) above and paragraph 5 of Schedule 1 below references to the appointed day are to the day appointed for the purposes of those provisions by an order of the Secretary of State made by statutory instrument.

Sale by sample

15   Sale by sample

(1) A contract of sale is a contract for sale by sample where there is an express or implied term to that effect in the contract.

(2) In the case of a contract for sale by sample there is an implied [term]—

(a) that the bulk will correspond with the sample in quality;

[...]

(c) that the goods will be free from any defect, [making their quality unsatisfactory], which would not be apparent on reasonable examination of the sample.

[(3) As regards England and Wales and Northern Ireland, the term implied by subsection (2) above is a condition.]

(4) Paragraph 7 of Schedule 1 below applies in relation to a contract made before 18 May 1973.

Miscellaneous

[15A   Modification of remedies for breach of condition in non-consumer cases

(1) Where in the case of a contract of sale—

(a) the buyer would, apart from this subsection, have the right to reject goods by reason of a breach on the part of the seller of a term implied by section 13, 14 or 15 above, but

(b) the breach is so slight that it would be unreasonable for him to reject them, then, if the buyer does not deal as consumer, the breach is not to be treated as a breach of condition but may be treated as a breach of warranty.

(2) This section applies unless a contrary intention appears in, or is to be implied from, the contract.

(3) It is for the seller to show that a breach fell within subsection (1)(b) above.

(4) This section does not apply to Scotland.]

PART III   EFFECTS OF THE CONTRACT

Transfer of property as between seller and buyer

16   Goods must be ascertained

[Subject to section 20A below] Where there is a contract for the sale of unascertained goods no property in the goods is transferred to the buyer unless and until the goods are ascertained.

17   Property passes when intended to pass

(1) Where there is a contract for the sale of specific or ascertained goods the property in them is transferred to the buyer at such time as the parties to the contract intend it to be transferred.

(2) For the purpose of ascertaining the intention of the parties regard shall be had to the terms of the contract, the conduct of the parties and the circumstances of the case.

18   Rules for ascertaining intention

Unless a different intention appears, the following are rules for ascertaining the intention of the parties as to the time at which the property in the goods is to pass to the buyer.

Rule 1.—Where there is an unconditional contract for the sale of specific goods in a deliverable state the property in the goods passes to the buyer when the contract is made, and it is immaterial whether the time of payment or the time of delivery, or both, be postponed.

Rule 2.—Where there is a contract for the sale of specific goods and the seller is bound to do something to the goods for the purpose of putting them into a deliverable state, the property does not pass until the thing is done and the buyer has notice that it has been done.

Rule 3.—Where there is a contract for the sale of specific goods in a deliverable state but the seller is bound to weigh, measure, test, or do some other act or thing with reference to the goods for the purpose of ascertaining the price, the property does not pass until the act or thing is done and the buyer has notice that it has been done.

Rule 4.—When goods are delivered to the buyer on approval or on sale or return or other similar terms the property in the goods passes to the buyer:—

    (a) when he signifies his approval or acceptance to the seller or does any other act adopting the transaction;

    (b) if he does not signify his approval or acceptance to the seller but retains the goods without giving notice of rejection, then, if a time has been fixed for the return of the goods, on the expiration of that time, and, if no time has been fixed, on the expiration of a reasonable time.

Rule 5.—(1) Where there is a contract for the sale of unascertained or future goods by description, and goods of that description and in a deliverable state are unconditionally appropriated to the contract, either by the seller with the assent of the buyer or by the buyer with the assent of the seller, the property in the goods then passes to the buyer; and the assent may be express or implied, and may be given either before of after the appropriation is made.

(2) Where, in pursuance of the contract, the seller delivers the goods to the buyer or to a carrier or other bailee or custodier (whether named by the buyer or not) for the purpose of transmission to the buyer, and does not reserve the right of disposal, he is to be taken to have unconditionally appropriated the goods to the contract.

[(3) Where there is a contract for the sale of a specified quantity of unascertained goods in a deliverable state forming part of a bulk which is identified either in the contract or by subsequent agreement between the parties and the bulk is reduced to (or to less than) that quantity, then, if the buyer under that contract is the only buyer to whom goods are then due out of the bulk—

    (a) the remaining goods are to be taken as appropriated to that contract at the time when the bulk is so reduced; and

    (b) the property in those goods then passes to that buyer.

(4) Paragraph (3) above applies also (with the necessary modifications) where a bulk is reduced to (or to less than) the aggregate of the quantities due to a single buyer under separate contracts relating to that bulk and he is the only buyer to whom goods are then due out of that bulk.]

19 Reservation of right of disposal

(1) Where there is a contract for the sale of specific goods or where goods are subsequently appropriated to the contract, the seller may, by the terms of the contract or appropriation, reserve the right of disposal of the goods until certain conditions are fulfilled; and in such a case, notwithstanding the delivery of the goods to the buyer, or to a carrier or other bailee or custodier for the purpose of transmission to the buyer, the property in the goods does not pass to the buyer until the conditions imposed by the seller are fulfilled.

(2) Where goods are shipped, and by the bill of lading the goods are deliverable to the order of the seller or his agent, the seller is prima facie to be taken to reserve the right of disposal.

(3) Where the seller of goods draws on the buyer for the price, and transmits the bill of exchange and bill of lading to the buyer together to secure acceptance or payment of the bill of exchange, the buyer is bound to return the bill of lading if he does not honour the bill of exchange, and if he wrongfully retains the bill of lading the property in the goods does not pass to him.

20 [Passing of risk]

(1) Unless otherwise agreed, the goods remain at the seller's risk until the property in them is transferred to the buyer, but when the property in them is transferred to the buyer the goods are at the buyer's risk whether delivery has been made or not.

(2) But where delivery has been delayed through the fault of either buyer or seller the goods are at the risk of the party at fault as regards any loss which might not have occurred but for such fault.

(3) Nothing in this section affects the duties or liabilities of either seller or buyer as a bailee or custodier of the goods of the other party.

[(4) In a case where the buyer deals as consumer or, in Scotland, where there is a consumer contract in which the buyer is a consumer, subsections (1) to (3) above must be ignored and the goods remain at the seller's risk until they are delivered to the consumer.]

[20A Undivided shares in goods forming part of a bulk

(1) This section applies to a contract for the sale of a specified quantity of unascertained goods if the following conditions are met—

    (a) the goods or some of them form part of a bulk which is identified either in the contract or by subsequent agreement between the parties; and

    (b) the buyer has paid the price for some or all of the goods which are the subject of the contract and which form part of the bulk.

(2) Where this section applies, then (unless the parties agree otherwise), as soon as the conditions specified in paragraphs (a) and (b) of subsection (1) above are met or at such later time as the parties may agree—

    (a) property in an undivided share in the bulk is transferred to the buyer; and

    (b) the buyer becomes an owner in common of the bulk.

(3) Subject to subsection (4) below, for the purposes of this section, the undivided share of a buyer in a bulk at any time shall be such share as the quantity of goods paid for and due to the buyer out of the bulk bears to the quantity of goods in the bulk at that time.

(4) Where the aggregate of the undivided shares of buyers in a bulk determined under subsection (3) above would at any time exceed the whole of the bulk at that time, the undivided share in the bulk of each buyer shall be reduced proportionately so that the aggregate of the undivided shares is equal to the whole bulk.

(5) Where a buyer has paid the price for only some of the goods due to him out of a bulk, any delivery to the buyer out of the bulk shall, for the purposes of this section, be ascribed in the first place to the goods in respect of which payment has been made.]

(6) For the purpose of this section payment of part of the price for any goods shall be treated as payment for a corresponding part of the goods.]

[20B   Deemed consent by co-owner to dealings in bulk goods

(1) A person who has become an owner in common of a bulk by virtue of section 20A above shall be deemed to have consented to—

    (a) any delivery of goods out of the bulk to any other owner in common of the bulk, being goods which are due to him under his contract;

    (b) any removal, dealing with, delivery or disposal of goods in the bulk by any other person who is an owner in common of the bulk in so far as the goods fall within that co-owner's undivided share in the bulk at the time of the removal, dealing, delivery or disposal.

(2) No cause of action shall accrue to anyone against a person by reason of that person having acted in accordance with paragraph (a) or (b) of subsection (1) above in reliance on any consent deemed to have been given under that subsection.

(3) Nothing in this section or section 20A above shall—

    (a) impose an obligation on a buyer of goods out of a bulk to compensate any other buyer of goods out of that bulk for any shortfall in the goods received by that other buyer;

    (b) affects any contractual arrangement between buyers of goods out of a bulk for adjustments between themselves; or

    (c) affect the rights of any buyer under his contract.]

Transfer of title

21   Sale by person not the owner

(1) Subject to this Act, where goods are sold by a person who is not their owner, and who does not sell them under the authority or with the consent of the owner, the buyer acquires no better title to the goods than the seller had, unless the owner of the goods is by his conduct precluded from denying the seller's authority to sell.

(2) Nothing in this Act affects—

    (a) the provisions of the Factors Acts or any enactment enabling the apparent owner of goods to dispose of them as if he were their true owner;

    (b) the validity of any contract of sale under any special common law or statutory power of sale or under the order of a court of competent jurisdiction.

22   Market overt

[...]

23   Sale under voidable title

When the seller of goods has a voidable title to them, but his title has not been avoided at the time of the sale, the buyer acquires a good title to the goods, provided he buys them in good faith and without notice of the seller's defect of title.

24   Seller in possession after sale

Where a person having sold goods continues or is in possession of the goods, or of the documents of title to the goods, the delivery or transfer by that person, or by a mercantile agent acting for him, of the goods or documents of title under any sale, pledge, or other disposition thereof, to any person receiving the same in good faith and without notice of the previous sale, has the same effect as if the person making the delivery or transfer were expressly authorised by the owner of the goods to make the same.

25   Buyer in possession after sale

(1) Where a person having bought or agreed to buy goods obtains, with the consent of the seller, possession of the goods or the documents of title to the goods, the delivery or transfer by that person, or by a mercantile agent acting for him, of the goods or documents of title, under any sale, pledge, or

other disposition thereof, to any person receiving the same in good faith and without notice of any lien or other right of the original seller in respect of the goods, has the same effect as if the person making the delivery or transfer were a mercantile agent in possession of the goods or documents of title with the consent of the owner.

(2) For the purposes of subsection (1) above—

(a) the buyer under a conditional sale agreement is to be taken not to be a person who has bought or agreed to buy goods, and

(b) 'conditional sale agreement' means an agreement for the sale of goods which is a consumer credit agreement within the meaning of the Consumer Credit Act 1974 under which the purchase price or part of it is payable by instalments, and the property in the goods is to remain in the seller (notwithstanding that the buyer is to be in possession of the goods) until such conditions as to the payment of instalments or otherwise as may be specified in the agreement are fulfilled.

(3) Paragraph 9 of Schedule 1 below applies in relation to a contract under which a person buys or agrees to buy goods and which is made before the appointed day.

(4) In subsection (3) above and paragraph 9 of Schedule 1 below references to the appointed day are to the day appointed for the purposes of those provisions by an order of the Secretary of State made by statutory instrument.

26   Supplementary to sections 24 and 25

In sections 24 and 25 above 'mercantile agent' means a mercantile agent having in the customary course of his business as such agent authority either—

(a) to sell goods, or

(b) to consign goods for the purpose of sale, or

(c) to buy goods, or

(d) to raise money on the security of goods.

PART IV PERFORMANCE OF THE CONTRACT

27   Duties of seller and buyer

It is the duty of the seller to deliver the goods, and of the buyer to accept and pay for them, in accordance with the terms of the contract of sale.

28   Payment and delivery are concurrent conditions

Unless otherwise agreed, delivery of the goods and payment of the price are concurrent conditions, that is to say, the seller must be ready and willing to give possession of the goods to the buyer in exchange for the price and the buyer must be ready and willing to pay the price in exchange for possession of the goods.

29   Rules about delivery

(1) Whether it is for the buyer to take possession of the goods or for the seller to send them to the buyer is a question depending in each case on the contract, express or implied, between the parties.

(2) Apart from any such contract, express or implied, the place of delivery is the seller's place of business if he has one, and if not, his residence; except that, if the contract is for the sale of specific goods, which to the knowledge of the parties when the contract is made are in some other place, then that place is the place of delivery.

(3) Where under the contract of sale the seller is bound to send the goods to the buyer, but no time for sending them is fixed, the seller is bound to send them within a reasonable time.

(4) Where the goods at the time of sale are in the possession of a third person, there is no delivery by seller to buyer unless and until the third person acknowledges to the buyer that he holds the goods on his behalf; but nothing in this section affects the operation of the issue or transfer of any document of title to goods.

(5) Demand or tender of delivery may be treated as ineffectual unless made at a reasonable hour; and what is a reasonable hour is a question of fact.

(6) Unless otherwise agreed, the expenses of and incidental to putting the goods into a deliverable state must be borne by the seller.

30   Delivery of wrong quantity

(1) Where the seller delivers to the buyer a quantity of goods less than he contracted to sell, the buyer may reject them, but if the buyer accepts the goods so delivered he must pay for them at the contract rate.

(2) Where the seller delivers to the buyer a quantity of goods larger than he contracted to sell, the buyer may accept the goods included in the contract and reject the rest, or he may reject the whole.

    [(2A) A buyer who does not deal as consumer may not—

      (a) where the seller delivers a quantity of goods less than he contracted to sell, reject the goods under subsection (1) above, or

      (b) where the seller delivers a quantity of goods larger than he contracted to sell, reject the whole under subsection (2) above,

if the shortfall or, as the case may be, excess is so slight that it would be unreasonable for him to do so.

    (2B) It is for the seller to show that a shortfall or excess fell within subsection (2A) above.

    (2C) Subsections (2A) and (2B) above do not apply to Scotland.]

    [(2D) Where the seller delivers a quantity of goods—

      (a) less than he contracted to sell, the buyer shall not be entitled to reject the goods under subsection (1) above,

      (b) larger than he contracted to sell, the buyer shall not be entitled to reject the whole under subsection (2) above,

unless the shortfall or excess is material.

    (2E) Subsection (2D) above applies to Scotland only.]

(3) Where the seller delivers to the buyer a quantity of goods larger than he contracted to sell and the buyer accepts the whole of the goods so delivered he must pay for them at the contract rate.

(5) This section is subject to any usage of trade, special agreement, or course of dealing between the parties.

31   Instalment deliveries

(1) Unless otherwise agreed, the buyer of goods is not bound to accept delivery of them by instalments.

(2) Where there is a contract for the sale of goods to be delivered by stated instalments, which are to be separately paid for, and the seller makes defective deliveries in respect of one or more instalments, or the buyer neglects or refuses to take delivery of or pay for one or more instalments, it is a question in each case depending on the terms of the contract and the circumstances of the case whether the breach of contract is a repudiation of the whole contract or whether it is a severable breach giving rise to a claim for compensation but not to a right to treat the whole contract as repudiated.

32   Delivery to carrier

(1) Where, in pursuance of a contract of sale, the seller is authorised or required to send the goods to the buyer, delivery of the goods to a carrier (whether named by the buyer or not) for the purpose of transmission to the buyer is prima facie deemed to be delivery of the goods to the buyer.

(2) Unless otherwise authorised by the buyer, the seller must make such contact with the carrier on behalf of the buyer as may be reasonable having regard to the nature of the goods and the other circumstances of the case; and if the seller omits to do so, and the goods are lost or damaged in course

of transit, the buyer may decline to treat the delivery to the carrier as a delivery to himself or may hold the seller responsible in damages.

(3) Unless otherwise agreed, where goods are sent by the seller to the buyer by a route involving sea transit, under circumstances in which it is usual to insure, the seller must give such notice to the buyer as may enable him to insure them during their sea transit, and if the seller fails to do so, the goods are at his risk during such sea transit.

[(4) In a case where the buyer deals as consumer or, in Scotland where there is a consumer contract in which the buyer is a consumer, subsections (1) to (3) above must be ignored, but if in pursuance of a contract of sale the seller is authorised or required to send the goods to the buyer, delivery of the goods to the carrier is not delivery of the goods to the buyer.]

33   Risk where goods are delivered at distant place

Where the seller of goods agrees to deliver them at his own risk at a place other than that where they are when sold, the buyer must nevertheless (unless otherwise agreed) take any risk of deterioration in the goods necessarily incident to the course of transit.

34   Buyer's right of examining the goods

[Unless otherwise agreed, when the seller tenders delivery of goods to the buyer, he is bound on request to afford the buyer a reasonable opportunity of examining the goods for the purpose of ascertaining whether they are in conformity with the contract and, in the case of a contract for sale by sample, of comparing the bulk with the sample.]

35   Acceptance

(1) The buyer is deemed to have accepted the goods [subject to subsection (2) below—
   (a) when he intimates to the seller that he has accepted them, or
   (b) when the goods have been delivered to him and he does any act in relation to them which is inconsistent with the ownership of the seller.

(2) Where goods are delivered to the buyer, and he has not previously examined them, he is not deemed to have accepted them under subsection (1) above until he has had a reasonable opportunity of examining them for the purpose—
   (a) of ascertaining whether they are in conformity with the contract, and
   (b) in the case of a contract for sale by sample, of comparing the bulk with the sample.

(3) Where the buyer deals as consumer or (in Scotland) the contract of sale is a consumer contract, the buyer cannot lose his right to rely on subsection (2) above by agreement, waiver or otherwise.

(4) The buyer is also deemed to have accepted the goods when after the lapse of a reasonable time he retains the goods without intimating to the seller that he has rejected them.

(5) The questions that are material in determining for the purposes of subsection (4) above whether a reasonable time has elapsed include whether the buyer has had a reasonable opportunity of examining the goods for the purpose mentioned in subsection (2) above.

(6) The buyer is not by virtue of this section deemed to have accepted the goods merely because—
   (a) he asks for, or agrees to, their repair by or under an arrangement with the seller, or
   (b) the goods are delivered to another under a sub-sale or other disposition.

(7) Where the contract is for the sale of goods making one or more commercial units, a buyer accepting any goods included in a unit is deemed to have accepted all the goods making the unit; and in this subsection 'commercial unit' means a unit division of which would materially impair the value of the goods or the character of the unit.

[35A   Right of partial rejection

(1) If the buyer—
   (a) has the right to reject the goods by reason of a breach on the part of the seller that affects some or all of them, but

(b) accepts some of the goods, including, where there are any goods unaffected by the breach, all such goods,

he does not by accepting them lose his right to reject the rest.

(2) In the case of a buyer having the right to reject an instalment of goods, subsection (1) above applies as if references to the goods were references to the goods comprised in the instalment.

(3) For the purposes of subsection (1) above, goods are affected by a breach if by reason of the breach they are not in conformity with the contract.

(4) This section applies unless a contrary intention appears in, or is to be implied from, the contract.]

36   Buyer not bound to return rejected goods

Unless otherwise agreed, where goods are delivered to the buyer, and he refuses to accept them, having the right to do so, he is not bound to return them to the seller, but it is sufficient if he intimates to the seller that he refuses to accept them.

37   Buyer's liability for not taking delivery of goods

(1) When the seller is ready and willing to deliver the goods, and requests the buyer to take delivery, and the buyer does not within a reasonable time after such request take delivery of the goods, he is liable to the seller for any loss occasioned by his neglect or refusal to take delivery, and also for a reasonable charge for the care and custody of the goods.

(2) Nothing in this section affects the rights of the seller where the neglect or refusal of the buyer to take delivery amounts to a repudiation of the contract.

PART V   RIGHTS OF UNPAID SELLER AGAINST THE GOODS

Preliminary

38   Unpaid seller defined

(1) The seller of goods is an unpaid seller within the meaning of this Act—

    (a) when the whole of the price has not been paid or tendered;

    (b) when a bill of exchange or other negotiable instrument has been received as conditional payment, and the condition on which it was received has not been fulfilled by reason of the dishonour of the instrument or otherwise.

(2) In this Part of this Act 'seller' includes any person who is in the position of a seller, as, for instance, an agent of the seller to whom the bill of lading has been indorsed, or a consignor or agent who has himself paid (or is directly responsible for) the price.

39   Unpaid seller's rights

(1) Subject to this and any other Act, notwithstanding that the property in the goods may have passed to the buyer, the unpaid seller of goods, as such, has by implication of law—

    (a) a lien on the goods or right to retain them for the price while he is in possession of them;

    (b) in the case of the insolvency of the buyer, a right of stopping the goods in transit after he has parted with the possession of them;

    (c) a right of re-sale as limited by this Act.

(2) Where the property in goods has not passed to the buyer, the unpaid seller has (in addition to his other remedies) a right of withholding delivery similar to and coextensive with his rights of lien or retention and stoppage in transit where the property has passed to the buyer.

Unpaid seller's lien

41   Seller's lien

(1) Subject to this Act, the unpaid seller of goods who is in possession of them is entitled to retain possession of them until payment or tender of the price in the following cases:—

(a) where the goods have been sold without any stipulation as to credit;

(b) where the goods have been sold on credit but the term of credit has expired;

(c) where the buyer becomes insolvent.

(2) The seller may exercise his lien or right of retention notwithstanding that he is in possession of the goods as agent or bailee or custodier for the buyer.

42 Part delivery

Where an unpaid seller has made part delivery of the goods, he may exercise his lien or right of retention on the remainder, unless such part delivery has been made under such circumstances as to show an agreement to waive the lien or right of retention.

43 Termination of lien

(1) The unpaid seller of goods loses his lien or right of retention in respect of them—

(a) when he delivers the goods to a carrier or other bailee or custodier for the purpose of transmission to the buyer without reserving the right of disposal of the goods;

(b) when the buyer or his agent lawfully obtains possession of the goods;

(c) by waiver of the lien or right of retention.

(2) An unpaid seller of goods who has a lien or right of retention in respect of them does not lose his lien or right of retention by reason only that he has obtained judgment or decree for the price of the goods.

Stoppage in transit

44 Right of stoppage in transit

Subject to this Act, when the buyer of goods becomes insolvent the unpaid seller who has parted with the possession of the goods has the right of stopping them in transit, that is to say, he may resume possession of the goods as long as they are in course of transit, and may retain them until payment or tender of the price.

45 Duration of transit

(1) Goods are deemed to be in course of transit from the time when they are delivered to a carrier or other bailee or custodier for the purpose of transmission to the buyer, until the buyer or his agent in that behalf takes delivery of them from the carrier or other bailee or custodier.

(2) If the buyer or his agent in that behalf obtains delivery of the goods before their arrival at the appointed destination, the transit is at an end.

(3) If, after the arrival of the goods at the appointed destination, the carrier or other bailee or custodier acknowledges to the buyer or his agent that he holds the goods on his behalf and continues in possession of them as bailee or custodier for the buyer or his agent, the transit is at an end, and it is immaterial that a further destination for the goods may have been indicated by the buyer.

(4) If the goods are rejected by the buyer, and the carrier or other bailee or custodier continues in possession of them, the transit is not deemed to be at an end, even if the seller has refused to receive them back.

(5) When goods are delivered to a ship chartered by the buyer it is a question depending on the circumstances of the particular case whether they are in the possession of the master as a carrier or as agent to the buyer.

(6) Where the carrier or other bailee or custodier wrongfully refuses to deliver the goods to the buyer or his agent in that behalf, the transit is deemed to be at an end.

(7) Where part delivery of the goods has been made to the buyer or his agent in that behalf, the remainder of the goods may be stopped in transit, unless such part delivery has been made under such circumstances as to show an agreement to give up possession of the whole of the goods.

46   How stoppage in transit is effected

(1) The unpaid seller may exercise his right of stoppage in transit either by taking actual possession of the goods or by giving notice of his claim to the carrier or other bailee or custodier in whose possession the goods are.

(2) The notice may be given either to the person in actual possession of the goods or to his principal.

(3) If given to the principal, the notice is ineffective unless given at such time and under such circumstances that the principal, by the exercise of reasonable diligence, may communicate it to his servant or agent in time to prevent a delivery to the buyer.

(4) When notice of stoppage in transit is given by the seller to the carrier or other bailee or custodier in possession of the goods, he must re-deliver the goods to, or according to the directions of, the seller; and the expenses of the re-delivery must be borne by the seller.

Re-sale etc. by buyer

47   Effect of sub-sale etc. by buyer

(1) Subject to this Act, the unpaid seller's right of lien or retention or stoppage in transit is not affected by any sale or other disposition of the goods which the buyer may have made, unless the seller has assented to it.

(2) Where a document of title to goods has been lawfully transferred to any person as buyer or owner of the goods, and that person transfers the document to a person who takes it in good faith and for valuable consideration, then—

  (a) if the last-mentioned transfer was by way of sale the unpaid seller's right of lien or retention or stoppage in transit is defeated; and

  (b) if the last-mentioned transfer was made by way of pledge or other disposition for value, the unpaid seller's right of lien or retention of stoppage in transit can only be exercised subject to the rights of the transferee.

Rescission: and re-sale by seller

48   Rescission: and re-sale by seller

(1) Subject to this section, a contract of sale is not rescinded by the mere exercise by an unpaid seller of his right of lien or retention or stoppage in transit.

(2) Where an unpaid seller who has exercised his right of lien or retention or stoppage in transit re-sells the goods, the buyer acquires a good title to them as against the original buyer.

(3) Where the goods are of a perishable nature, or where the unpaid seller gives notice to the buyer of his intention to re-sell, and the buyer does not within a reasonable time pay or tender the price, the unpaid seller may re-sell the goods and recover from the original buyer damages for any loss occasioned by his breach of contract.

(4) Where the seller expressly reserves the right of re-sale in case the buyer should make default, and on the buyer making default re-sells the goods, the original contract of sale is rescinded but without prejudice to any claim the seller may have for damages.

[PART 5A ADDITIONAL RIGHTS OF BUYER IN CONSUMER CASES]

[48A   Introductory

(1) This section applies if—

  (a) the buyer deals as consumer or, in Scotland, there is a consumer contract in which the buyer is a consumer, and

  (b) the goods do not conform to the contract of sale at the time of delivery.

(2) If this section applies, the buyer has the right—

(a) under and in accordance with section 48B below, to require the seller to repair or replace the goods, or

(b) under and in accordance with section 48C below—

    (i)   to require the seller to reduce the purchase price of the goods to the buyer by an appropriate amount, or

    (ii) to rescind the contract with regard to the goods in question.

(3) For the purposes of subsection (1)(b) above goods which do not conform to the contract of sale at any time within the period of six months starting with the date on which the goods were delivered to the buyer must be taken not to have so conformed at that date.

(4) Subsection (3) above does not apply if—

(a) it is established that the goods did so conform at that date;

(b) its application is incompatible with the nature of the goods or the nature of the lack of conformity.]

[48B   Repair or replacement of the goods

(1) If section 48A above applies, the buyer may require the seller—

(a) to repair the goods, or

(b) to replace the goods.

(2) If the buyer requires the seller to repair or replace the goods, the seller must—

(a) repair or, as the case may be, replace the goods within a reasonable time but without causing significant inconvenience to the buyer;

(b) bear any necessary costs incurred in doing so (including in particular the cost of any labour, materials or postage).

(3) The buyer must not require the seller to repair or, as the case may be, replace the goods if that remedy is—

(a) impossible, or

(b) disproportionate in comparison to the other of those remedies, or

(c) disproportionate in comparison to an appropriate reduction in the purchase price under paragraph (a), or rescission under paragraph (b), of section 48C(1) below.

(4) One remedy is disproportionate in comparison to the other if the one imposes costs on the seller which, in comparison to those imposed on him by the other, are unreasonable, taking into account—

(a) the value which the goods would have if they conformed to the contract of sale,

(b) the significance of the lack of conformity, and

(c) whether the other remedy could be effected without significant inconvenience to the buyer.

(5) Any question as to what is a reasonable time or significant inconvenience is to be determined by reference to—

(a) the nature of the goods, and

(b) the purpose for which the goods were acquired.]

[48C   Reduction of purchase price or rescission of contract

(1) If section 48A above applies, the buyer may—

(a) require the seller to reduce the purchase price of the goods in question to the buyer by an appropriate amount, or

(b) rescind the contract with regard to those goods,

if the condition in subsection (2) below is satisfied.

(2) The condition is that—

(a) by virtue of section 48B(3) above the buyer may require neither repair nor replacement of the goods; or

(b) the buyer has required the seller to repair or replace the goods, but the seller is in breach of the requirement of section 48B(2)(a) above to do so within a reasonable time and without significant inconvenience to the buyer.

(3) For the purposes of this Part, if the buyer rescinds the contract, any reimbursement to the buyer may be reduced to take account of the use he has had of the goods since they were delivered to him.]

[48D Relation to other remedies etc.

(1) If the buyer requires the seller to repair or replace the goods the buyer must not act under subsection (2) until he has given the seller a reasonable time in which to repair or replace (as the case may be) the goods.

(2) The buyer acts under this subsection if—

(a) in England and Wales or Northern Ireland he rejects the goods and terminates the contract for breach of condition;

(b) in Scotland he rejects any goods delivered under the contract and treats it as repudiated;

(c) he requires the goods to be replaced or repaired (as the case may be).]

[48E Powers of the court

(1) In any proceedings in which a remedy is sought by virtue of this Part the court, in addition to any other power it has, may act under this section.

(2) On the application of the buyer the court may make an order requiring specific performance or, in Scotland, specific implement by the seller of any obligation imposed on him by virtue of section 48B above.

(3) Subsection (4) applies if—

(a) the buyer requires the seller to give effect to a remedy under section 48B or 48C above or has claims to rescind under section 48C, but

(b) the court decides that another remedy under section 48B or 48C is appropriate.

(4) The court may proceed—

(a) as if the buyer had required the seller to give effect to the other remedy, or if the other remedy is rescission under section 48C

(b) as if the buyer had claimed to rescind the contract under that section.

(5) If the buyer has claimed to rescind the contract the court may order that any reimbursement to the buyer is reduced to take account of the use he has had of the goods since they were delivered to him.

(6) The court may make an order under this section unconditionally or on such terms and conditions as to damages, payment of the price and otherwise as it thinks just.]

[48F Conformity with the contract

For the purposes of this Part, goods do not conform to a contract of sale if there is, in relation to the goods, a breach of an express term of the contract or a term implied by section 13, 14 or 15 above.]

PART VI ACTIONS FOR BREACH OF THE CONTRACT

Seller's remedies

49 Action for price

(1) Where, under a contract of sale, the property in the goods has passed to the buyer and he wrongfully neglects or refuses to pay for the goods according to the terms of the contract, the seller may maintain an action against him for the price of the goods.

(2) Where, under a contract of sale, the price is payable on a day certain irrespective of delivery and the buyer wrongfully neglects or refuses to pay such price, the seller may maintain an action for the price, although the property in goods has not passed and the goods have not been appropriated to the contract.

(3) Nothing in this section prejudices the right of the seller in Scotland to recover interest on the price from the date of tender of the goods, or from the date on which the price was payable, as the case may be.

50   Damages for non-acceptance

(1) Where the buyer wrongfully neglects or refuses to accept and pay for the goods, the seller may maintain an action against him for damages for non-acceptance.

(2) The measure of damages is the estimated loss directly and naturally resulting in the ordinary course of events, from the buyer's breach of contract.

(3) Where there is an available market for the goods in question the measure of damages is prima facie to be ascertained by the difference between the contract price and the market or current price at the time or times when the goods ought to have been accepted or (if no time was fixed for acceptance) at the time of the refusal to accept.

Buyer's remedies

51   Damages for non-delivery

(1) Where the seller wrongfully neglects or refuses to deliver the goods to the buyer, the buyer may maintain an action against the seller for damages for non-delivery.

(2) The measure of damages is the estimated loss directly and naturally resulting, in the ordinary course of events, from the seller's breach of contract.

(3) Where there is an available market for the goods in question the measure of damages is prima facie to be ascertained by the difference between the contract price and the market or current price of the goods at the time or times when they ought to have been delivered or (if no time was fixed) at the time of the refusal to deliver.

52   Specific performance

(1) If any action for breach of contract to deliver specific or ascertained goods the court may, if it thinks fit, on the plaintiff s application, by its judgment or decree direct that the contract shall be performed specifically, without giving the defendant the option of retaining the goods on payment of damages.

(2) The plaintiff s application may be made at any time before judgment or decree.

(3) The judgment or decree may be unconditional, or on such terms and conditions as to damages, payment of the price and otherwise as seem just to the court.

(4) The provisions of this section shall be deemed to be supplementary to, and not in derogation of, the right of specific implement in Scotland.

53   Remedy for breach of warranty

(1) Where there is a breach of warranty by the seller, or where the buyer elects (or is compelled) to treat any breach of a condition on the part of the seller as a breach of warranty, the buyer is not by reason only of such breach of warranty entitled to reject the goods; but he may—

   (a) set up against the seller the breach of warranty in diminution of extinction of the price, or

   (b) maintain an action against the seller for damages for the breach of warranty.

(2) The measure of damages for breach of warranty is the estimated loss directly and naturally resulting, in the ordinary course of events, from the breach of warranty.

(3) In the case of breach of warranty of quality such loss is prima facie the difference between the value of the goods at the time of delivery to the buyer and the value they would have had if they had fulfilled the warranty.

(4) The fact that the buyer has set up the breach of warranty in diminution or extinction of the price does not prevent him from maintaining an action for the same breach of warranty if he has suffered further damage.

Interest, etc.

54 Interest, etc.

Nothing in this Act affects the right of the buyer or the seller to recover interest or special damages in any case where by law interest or special damages may be recoverable, or to recover money paid where the consideration for the payment of it has failed.

PART VII SUPPLEMENTARY

55 Exclusion of implied terms

(1) Where a right duty or liability would arise under a contract of sale of goods by implication of law, it may (subject to the Unfair Contract Terms Act 1977) be negatived or varied by express agreement, or by the course of dealing between the parties, or by such usage as binds both parties to the contract.

(2) An express [term] does not negative a [term] implied by this Act unless inconsistent with it.

57 Auction sales

(1) Where goods are put up for sale by auction in lots, each lot is prima facie deemed to be the subject of a separate contract of sale.

(2) A sale by auction is complete when the auctioneer announces its completion by the fall of the hammer, or in other customary manner; and until the announcement is made any bidder may retract his bid.

(3) A sale by auction may be notified to be subject to a reserve or upset price, and a right to bid may also be reserved expressly by or on behalf of the seller.

(4) Where a sale by auction is not notified to be subject to a right to bid by or on behalf of the seller, it is not lawful for the seller to bid himself or to employ any person to bid at the sale, or for the auctioneer knowingly to take any bid from the seller or any such person.

(5) A sale contravening subsection (4) above may be treated as fraudulent by the buyer.

(6) Where, in respect of a sale by auction, a right to bid is expressly reserved (but not otherwise) the seller or any one person on his behalf may bid at the auction.

59 Reasonable time a question of fact

Where a reference is made in this Act to a reasonable time the question what is a reasonable time is a question of fact.

60 Rights, etc. enforceable by action

Where a right, duty or liability is declared by this Act, it may (unless otherwise provided by this Act) be enforced by action.

61 Interpretation

(1) In this Act, unless the context or subject matter otherwise requires,— 'action' includes counterclaim and set-off, and in Scotland condescendence and claim and compensation;

['bulk' means a mass or collection of goods of the same kind which—

(a) is contained in a defined space or area; and

(b) is such that any goods in the bulk are interchangeable with any other goods therein of the same number or quantity;]

'business' includes a profession and the activities of any government department (including a Northern Ireland department) or local or public authority;

'buyer' means a person who buys or agrees to buy goods;

['consumer contract' has the same meaning as in section 25(1) of the Unfair Contract Terms Act 1977; and for the purposes of this Act the onus of proving that a contract is not to be regarded as a consumer contract shall lie on the seller] 'contract of sale' includes an agreement to sell as well as a sale,

'credit-broker' means a person acting in the course of a business of credit brokerage carried on by him, that is a business of effecting introductions of individuals desiring to obtain credit—

(a) to persons carrying on any business so far as it relates to the provision of credit, or

(b) to other persons engaged in credit brokerage;

'defendant' includes in Scotland defender, respondent, and claimant in a multiple-poinding;

'delivery' means voluntary transfer of possession from one person to another; [except that in relation to sections 20A and 20B above it includes such appropriation of goods to the contract as results in property in the goods being transferred to the buyer;]

'document of title to goods' has the same meaning as it has in the Factors Acts;

'Factors Acts' means the Factors Act 1889, the Factors (Scotland) Act 1890, and any enactment amending or substituted for the same;

'fault' means wrongful act or default;

'future goods' means goods to be manufactured or acquired by the seller after the making of the contract of sale;

'goods' includes all personal chattels other than things in action and money, and in Scotland all corporeal moveables except money; and in particular 'goods' includes emblements, industrial growing crops, and things attached to or forming part of the land which are agreed to be severed before sale or under the contract of sale; [and includes an undivided share in goods;]

'plaintiff' includes pursuer, complainer, claimant in a multiplepoinding and defendant or defender counter-claiming;

['producer' means the manufacturer of goods, the importer of goods into the European Economic Area or any person purporting to be a producer by placing his name, trade mark or other distinctive sign on the goods;]

'property' means the general property in goods, and not merely a special property;

['repair' means, in cases where there is a lack of conformity in goods for purposes of section 48F of this Act, to bring the goods into conformity with the contract;]

'sale' includes a bargain and sale as well as a sale and delivery;

'seller' means a person who sells or agrees to sell goods;

'specific goods' means goods identified and agreed on at the time a contract of sale is made; [and includes an undivided share, specified as a fraction or percentage, of goods identified and agreed on as aforesaid;]

'warranty' (as regards England and Wales and Northern Ireland) means an agreement with reference to goods which are the subject of a contract of sale, but collateral to the main purpose of such contract, the breach of which gives rise to a claim for damages, but not to a right to reject the goods and treat the contract as repudiated.

(3) A thing is deemed to be done in good faith within the meaning of this Act when it is in fact done honestly, whether it is done negligently or not.

(4) A person is deemed to be insolvent within the meaning of this Act if he has either ceased to pay his debts in the ordinary course of business or he cannot pay his debts as they become due, [...]

(5) Goods are in a deliverable state within the meaning of this Act when they are in such a state that the buyer would under the contract be bound to take delivery of them.

[(5A) References in this Act to dealing as consumer are to be construed in accordance with Part I of the Unfair Contract Terms Act 1977; and, for the purposes of this Act, it is for a seller claiming that the buyer does not deal as consumer to show that he does not.]

(6) As regards the definition of 'business' in subsection (1) above, paragraph 14 of Schedule 1 below applies in relation to a contract made on or after 18 May 1973 and before 1 February 1978, and paragraph 15 in relation to one made before 18 May 1973.

62   Savings: rules of law, etc.

(1) The rules in bankruptcy relating to contracts of sale apply to those contracts, notwithstanding anything in this Act.

(2) The rules of the common law, including the law merchant, except in so far as they are inconsistent with the provisions of this Act, and in particular the rules relating to the law of principal and agent and the effect of fraud, misrepresentation, duress or coercion, mistake, or other invalidating cause, apply to contracts for the sale of goods.

(3) Nothing in this Act or the Sale of Goods Act 1893 affects the enactments relating to bills of sale, or any enactment relating to the sale of goods which is not expressly repealed or amended by this Act or that.

(4) The provisions of this Act about contracts of sale do not apply to a transaction in the form of a contract of sale which is intended to operate by way of mortgage, pledge, charge, or other security.

Supply of Goods and Services Act 1982

(1982, c. 29)

PART I SUPPLY OF GOODS

Contracts for the transfer of property in goods

1 The contracts concerned

(1) In this Act [in its application to England and Wales and Northern Ireland] a 'contract for the transfer of goods' means a contract under which one person transfers or agrees to transfer to another the property in goods, other than an excepted contract.

(2) For the purposes of this section an excepted contract means any of the following:—

    (a) a contract of sale of goods;

    (b) a hire-purchase agreement;

    [...]

    (d) a transfer or agreement to transfer which is made by deed and for which there is no consideration other than the presumed consideration imported by the deed;

    (e) a contract intended to operate by way of mortgage, pledge, charge or other security.

(3) For the purposes of this Act [in its application to England and Wales and Northern Ireland] a contract is a contract for the transfer of goods whether or not services are also provided or to be provided under the contract, and (subject to subsection (2) above) whatever is the nature of the consideration for the transfer or agreement to transfer.

2 Implied terms about title, etc.

(1) In a contract for the transfer of goods, other than one to which subsection (3) below applies, there is an implied condition on the part of the transferor that in the case of a transfer of the property in the goods he has a right to transfer the property and in the case of an agreement to transfer the property in the goods he will have such a right at the time when the property is to be transferred.

(2) In a contract for the transfer of goods, other than one to which subsection (3) below applies, there is also an implied warranty that—

    (a) the goods are free, and will remain free until the time when the property is to be transferred, from any charge or encumbrance not disclosed or known to the transferee before the contract is made, and

    (b) the transferee will enjoy quiet possession of the goods except so far as it may be disturbed by the owner or other person entitled to the benefit of any charge or encumbrance so disclosed or known.

(3) This subsection applies to a contract for the transfer of goods in the case of which there appears from the contract or is to be inferred from its circumstances an intention that the transferor should transfer only such title as he or a third person may have.

(4) In a contract to which subsection (3) above applies there is an implied warranty that all charges or encumbrances known to the transferor and not known to the transferee have been disclosed to the transferee before the contract is made.

(5) In a contract to which subsection (3) above applies, there is also an implied warranty that none of the following will disturb the transferee's quiet possession of the goods, namely—

    (a) the transferor;

    (b) in a case where the parties to the contract intend that the transferor should transfer only such title as a third person may have, that person;

    (c) anyone claiming through or under the transferor or that third person otherwise than under a charge or encumbrance disclosed or known to the transferee before the contract is made.

3 Implied terms where transfer is by description

(1) This section applies where, under a contract for the transfer of goods, the transferor transfers or agrees to transfer the property in the goods by description.

(2) In such case there is an implied condition that the goods will correspond with the description.

(3) If the transferor transfers or agrees to transfer the property in the goods by sample as well as by description it is not sufficient that the bulk of the goods corresponds with the sample if the goods do not also correspond with the description.

(4) A contract is not prevented from falling within subsection (1) above by reason only that, being exposed for supply, the goods are selected by the transferee.

4 Implied terms about quality or fitness

(1) Except as provided by this section and section 5 below and subject to the provision of any other enactment, there is no implied condition or warranty about the quality or fitness for any particular purpose of goods supplied under a contract for the transfer of goods.

[(2) Where, under such a contract, the transferor transfers the property in goods in the course of a business, there is an implied condition that the goods supplied under the contract are of satisfactory quality.

(2A) For the purposes of this section and section 5 below, goods are of satisfactory quality if they meet the standard that a reasonable person would regard as satisfactory, taking account of any description of the goods, the price (if relevant) and all the other relevant circumstances.]

[(2B) If the transferee deals as consumer, the relevant circumstances mentioned in subsection (2A) above include any public statements on the specific characteristics of the goods made about them by the transferor, the producer or his representative, particularly in advertising or on labelling.

(2C) A public statement is not by virtue of subsection (2B) above a relevant circumstance for the purposes of subsection (2A) above in the case of a contract for the transfer of goods, if the transferor shows that—

    (a) at the time the contract was made, he was not, and could not reasonably have been, aware of the statement,

    (b) before the contract was made, the statement had been withdrawn in public or, to the extent that it contained anything which was incorrect or misleading, it had been corrected in public, or

    (c) the decision to acquire the goods could not have been influenced by the statement.

(2D) Subsections (2B) and (2C) above do not prevent any public statement from being a relevant circumstance for the purposes of subsection (2A) above (whether or not the transferee deals as consumer) if the statement would have been such a circumstance apart from those subsections.]

[(3) The condition implied by subsection (2) above does not extend to any matter making the quality of goods unsatisfactory—

    (a) which is specifically drawn to the transferee's attention before the contract is made,

    (b) where the transferee examines the goods before the contract is made, which that examination ought to reveal, or

    (c) where the property in the goods is transferred by reference to a sample, which would have been apparent on a reasonable examination of the sample.]

(4) Subsection (5) below applies where, under a contract for the transfer of goods, the transferor transfers the property in goods in the course of a business and the transferee, expressly or by implication, makes known—

(a) to the transferor, or

(b) where the consideration or part of the consideration for the transfer is a sum payable by instalments and the goods were previously sold by a credit-broker to the transferor, to that credit-broker,

any particular purpose for which the goods are being acquired.

(5) In that case there is (subject to subsection (6) below) an implied condition that the goods supplied under the contract are reasonably fit for that purpose, whether or not that is a purpose for which such goods are commonly supplied.

(6) Subsection (5) above does not apply where the circumstances show that the transferee does not rely, or that it is unreasonable for him to rely, on the skill or judgment of the transferor or credit-broker.

(7) An implied condition or warranty about quality or fitness for a particular purpose may be annexed by usage to a contract for the transfer of goods.

(8) The preceding provisions of this section apply to a transfer by a person who in the course of a business is acting as agent for another as they apply to a transfer by a principal in the course of a business, except where that other is not transferring in the course of a business and either the transferee knows that fact or reasonable steps are taken to bring it to the transferee's notice before the contract concerned is made.

5   Implied terms where transfer is by sample

(1) This section applies where, under a contract for the transfer of goods, the transferor transfers or agrees to transfer the property in the goods by reference to a sample.

(2) In such a case there is an implied condition—

(a) that the bulk will correspond with the sample in quality; and

(b) that the transferee will have a reasonable opportunity of comparing the bulk with the sample; and

(c) that the goods will be free from any defect, [making their quality unsatisfactory], which would not be apparent on reasonable examination of the sample.

(4) For the purposes of this section a transferor transfers or agrees to transfer the property in goods by reference to a sample where there is an express or implied term to that effect in the contract concerned.

[5A   Modification of remedies for breach of statutory condition in non-consumer cases

(1) Where in the case of a contract for the transfer of goods—

(a) the transferee would, apart from this subsection, have the right to treat the contract as repudiated by reason of a breach on the part of the transferor of a term implied by section 3, 4 or 5(2)(a) or (c) above, but

(b) the breach is so slight that it would be unreasonable for him to do so,

then, if the transferee does not deal as consumer, the breach is not to be treated as a breach of condition but may be treated as a breach of warranty.

(2) This section applies unless a contrary intention appears in, or is to be implied from, the contract.

(3) It is for the transferor to show that a breach fell within subsection (1)(b) above.]

Contracts for the hire of goods

6   The contracts concerned

(1) In this Act [in its application to England and Wales and Northern Ireland] a 'contract for the hire of goods' means a contract under which one person bails or agrees to bail goods to another by way of hire, other than [a hire-purchase agreement].

[...]

(3) For the purposes of this Act [in its application to England and Wales and Northern Ireland] a contract is a contract for the hire of goods whether or not services are also provided or to be provided under the contract, and [...] whatever is the nature of the consideration for the bailment or agreement to bail by way of hire.

7 Implied terms about right to transfer possession, etc.

(1) In a contract for the hire of goods there is an implied condition on the part of the bailor that in the case of a bailment he has a right to transfer possession of the goods by way of hire for the period of the bailment and in the case of an agreement to bail he will have such a right at the time of the bailment.

(2) In a contract for the hire of goods there is also an implied warranty that the bailee will enjoy quiet possession of the goods for the period of the bailment except so far as the possession may be disturbed by the owner or other person entitled to the benefit of any charge or encumbrance disclosed or known to the bailee before the contract is made.

(3) The preceding provisions of this section do not affect the right of the bailor to repossess the goods under an express or implied term of contract.

8 Implied terms where hire is by description

(1) This section applies where, under a contract for the hire of goods, the bailor bails or agrees to bail the goods by description.

(2) In such a case there is an implied condition that the goods will correspond with the description.

(3) If under the contract the bailor bails or agrees to bail the goods by reference to a sample as well as a description it is not sufficient that the bulk of the goods corresponds with the sample if the goods do not also correspond with the description.

(4) A contract is not prevented from falling within subsection (1) above by reason only that, being exposed for supply, the goods are selected by the bailee.

9 Implied terms about quality or fitness

(1) Except as provided by this section and section 10 below and subject to the provisions of any other enactment, there is no implied condition or warranty about the quality or fitness for any particular purpose of goods bailed under a contract for the hire of goods.

[(2) Where, under such a contract, the bailor bails goods in the course of a business, there is an implied condition that the goods supplied under the contract are of satisfactory quality.

(2A) For the purposes of this section and section 10 below, goods are of satisfactory quality if they meet the standard that a reasonable person would regard as satisfactory, taking account of any description of the goods, the consideration for the bailment (if relevant) and all the other relevant circumstances.]

[(2B) If the bailee deals as consumer, the relevant circumstances mentioned in subsection (2A) above include any public statements on the specific characteristics of the goods made about them by the bailor, the producer or his representative, particularly in advertising or on labelling.

(2C) A public statement is not by virtue of subsection (2B) above a relevant circumstance for the purposes of subsection (2A) above in the case of a contract for the hire of goods, if the bailor shows that—

    (a) at the time the contract was made, he was not, and could not reasonably have been, aware of the statement,

    (b) before the contract was made, the statement had been withdrawn in public or, to the extent that it contained anything which was incorrect or misleading, it had been corrected in public, or

    (c) the decision to acquire the goods could not have been influenced by the statement.

(2D) Subsections (2B) and (2C) above do not prevent any public statement from being a relevant circumstance for the purposes of subsection (2A) above (whether or not the bailee deals as consumer) if the statement would have been such a circumstance apart from those subsections.]

[(3) The condition implied by subsection (2) above does not extend to any matter making the quality of goods unsatisfactory—

(a) which is specifically drawn to the bailee's attention before the contract is made,

(b) where the bailee examines the goods before the contract is made, which that examination ought to reveal, or

(c) where the goods are bailed by reference to a sample, which would have been apparent on a reasonable examination of the sample.]

(4) Subsection (5) below applies where, under a contract for the hire of goods, the bailor bails goods in the course of a business and the bailee, expressly or by implication, makes known—

(a) to the bailor in the course of negotiations conducted by him in relation to the making of the contract, or

(b) to a credit-broker in the course of negotiations conducted by that broker in relation to goods sold by him to the bailor before forming the subject matter of the contract,

any particular purpose for which the goods are being bailed.

(5) In that case there is (subject to subsection (6) below) an implied condition that the goods supplied under the contract are reasonably fit for that purpose, whether or not that is a purpose for which such goods are commonly supplied.

(6) Subsection (5) above does not apply where the circumstances show that the bailee does not rely, or that it is unreasonable for him to rely, on the skill or judgment of the bailor or credit-broker.

(7) An implied condition or warranty about quality or fitness for a particular purpose may be annexed by usage to a contract for the hire of goods.

(8) The preceding provisions of this section apply to a bailment by a person who in the course of a business is acting as agent for another as they apply to a bailment by a principal in the course of a business, except where that other is not bailing in the course of a business and either the bailee knows that fact or reasonable steps are taken to bring it to the bailee's notice before the contract concerned is made.

10   Implied terms where hire is by sample

(1) This section applies where, under a contract for the hire of goods, the bailor bails or agrees to bail the goods by reference to a sample.

(2) In such a case there is an implied condition—

(a) that the bulk will correspond with the sample in quality; and

(b) that the bailee will have a reasonable opportunity of comparing the bulk with the sample; and

(c) that the goods will be free from any defect, [making their quality unsatisfactory], which would not be apparent on reasonable examination of the sample.

(4) For the purposes of this section a bailor bails or agrees to bail goods by reference to a sample where there is an express or implied term to that effect in the contract concerned.

[10A   Modification of remedies for breach of statutory condition in non-consumer cases

(1) Where in the case of a contract for the hire of goods—

(a) the bailee would, apart from this subsection, have the right to treat the contract as repudiated by reason of a breach on the part of the bailor of a term implied by section 8, 9 or 10(2)(a) or (c) above, but

(b) the breach is so slight that it would be unreasonable for him to do so, then, if the bailee does not deal as consumer, the breach is not to be treated as a breach of condition but may be treated as a breach of warranty.

(2) This section applies unless a contrary intention appears in, or is to be implied from, the contract.

(3) It is for the bailor to show that a breach fell within subsection (1)(b) above.]

Exclusion of implied terms, etc.

11 Exclusion of implied terms, etc.

(1) Where a right, duty or liability would arise under a contract for the transfer of goods or a contract for the hire of goods by implication of law, it may (subject to subsection (2) below and the 1977 Act) be negatived or varied by express agreement, or by the course of dealing between the parties, or by such usage as binds both parties to the contract.

(2) An express condition or warranty does not negative a condition or warranty implied by the preceding provisions of this Act unless inconsistent with it.

(3) Nothing in the preceding provisions of this Act prejudices the operation of any other enact-ment or any rule of law whereby any condition or warranty (other than one relating to quality or fitness) is to be implied in a contract for the transfer of goods or a contract for hire of goods.

[PART IB ADDITIONAL RIGHTS OF TRANSFEREE IN CONSUMER CASES]

[11M Introductory

(1) This section applies if—
-   (a) the transferee deals as consumer or, in Scotland, there is a consumer contract in which the transferee is a consumer, and
-   (b) the goods do not conform to the contract for the transfer of goods at the time of delivery.

(2) If this section applies, the transferee has the right—
-   (a) under and in accordance with section 11N below, to require the transferor to repair or replace the goods, or
-   (b) under and in accordance with section 11P below—
    -   (i) to require the transferor to reduce the amount to be paid for the transfer by the trans-feree by an appropriate amount, or
    -   (ii) to rescind the contract with regard to the goods in question.

(3) For the purposes of subsection (1)(b) above, goods which do not conform to the contract for the transfer of goods at any time within the period of six months starting with the date on which the goods were delivered to the transferee must be taken not to have so conformed at that date.

(4) Subsection (3) above does not apply if—
-   (a) it is established that the goods did so conform at that date;
-   (b) its application is incompatible with the nature of the goods or the nature of the lack of conformity.

(5) For the purposes of this section, 'consumer contract' has the same meaning as in section 11F(3) above.]

[11N Repair or replacement of the goods

(1) If section 11M above applies, the transferee may require the transferor—
-   (a) to repair the goods, or
-   (b) to replace the goods.

(2) If the transferee requires the transferor to repair or replace the goods, the transferor must—
-   (a) repair or, as the case may be, replace the goods within a reasonable time but without causing significant inconvenience to the transferee;

    (b) bear any necessary costs incurred in doing so (including in particular the cost of any labour, materials or postage).

    (3) The transferee must not require the transferor to repair or, as the case may be, replace the goods if that remedy is—

        (a) impossible,

        (b) disproportionate in comparison to the other of those remedies, or

        (c) disproportionate in comparison to an appropriate reduction in the purchase price under paragraph (a), or rescission under paragraph (b), of section 11P(1) below.

    (4) One remedy is disproportionate in comparison to the other if the one imposes costs on the transferor which, in comparison to those imposed on him by the other, are unreasonable, taking into account—

        (a) the value which the goods would have if they conformed to the contract for the transfer of goods,

        (b) the significance of the lack of conformity to the contract for the transfer of goods, and

        (c) whether the other remedy could be effected without significant inconvenience to the transferee.

    (5) Any question as to what is a reasonable time or significant inconvenience is to be determined by reference to—

        (a) the nature of the goods, and

        (b) the purpose for which the goods were acquired.]

[11P   Reduction of purchase price or rescission of contract

    (1) If section 11M above applies, the transferee may—

        (a) require the transferor to reduce the purchase price of the goods in question to the transferee by an appropriate amount, or

        (b) rescind the contract with regard to those goods,

if the condition in subsection (2) below is satisfied.

    (2) The condition is that—

        (a) by virtue of section 11N(3) above the transferee may require neither repair nor replacement of the goods, or

        (b) the transferee has required the transferor to repair or replace the goods, but the transferor is in breach of the requirement of section 11N(2)(a) above to do so within a reasonable time and without significant inconvenience to the transferee.

    (3) If the transferee rescinds the contract, any reimbursement to the transferee may be reduced to take account of the use he has had of the goods since they were delivered to him.]

[11Q   Relation to other remedies, etc.

    (1) If the transferee requires the transferor to repair or replace the goods the transferee must not act under subsection (2) until he has given the transferor a reasonable time in which to repair or replace (as the case may be) the goods.

    (2) The transferee acts under this subsection if—

        (a) in England and Wales or Northern Ireland he rejects the goods and terminates the contract for breach of condition;

        (b) in Scotland he rejects any goods delivered under the contract and treats it as repudiated; or

        (c) he requires the goods to be replaced or repaired (as the case may be).]

[11R   Powers of the court

    (1) In any proceedings in which a remedy is sought by virtue of this Part the court, in addition to any other power it has, may act under this section.

    (2) On the application of the transferee the court may make an order requiring specific performance or, in Scotland, specific implement by the transferor of any obligation imposed on him by virtue of section 11N above.

    (3) Subsection (4) applies if—

(a) the transferee requires the transferor to give effect to a remedy under section 11N or 11P above or has claims to rescind under section 11P, but

(b) the court decides that another remedy under section 11N or 11P is appropriate.

(4) The court may proceed—

(a) as if the transferee had required the transferor to give effect to the other remedy, or if the other remedy is rescission under section 11P,

(b) as if the transferee had claimed to rescind the contract under that section.

(5) If the transferee has claimed to rescind the contract the court may order that any reimbursement to the transferee is reduced to take account of the use he has had of the goods since they were delivered to him.

(6) The court may make an order under this section unconditionally or on such terms and conditions as to damages, payment of the price and otherwise as it thinks just.]

[11S   Conformity with the contract

(1) Goods do not conform to a contract for the supply or transfer of goods if—

(a) there is, in relation to the goods, a breach of an express term of the contract or a term implied by section 3, 4 or 5 above or, in Scotland, by section 11C, 11D or 11E above, or

(b) installation of the goods forms part of the contract for the transfer of goods, and the goods were installed by the transferor, or under his responsibility, in breach of the term implied by section 13 below or (in Scotland) in breach of any term implied by any rule of law as to the manner in which the installation is carried out.]

PART II SUPPLY OF SERVICES

12   The contracts concerned

(1) In this Act a 'contract for the supply of a service' means, subject to subsection (2) below a contract under which a person ('the supplier') agrees to carry out a service.

(2) For the purposes of this Act, a contract of service or apprenticeship is not a contract for the supply of a service.

(3) Subject to subsection (2) above, a contract is a contract for the supply of a service for the purposes of this Act whether or not goods are also—

(a) transferred or to be transferred, or

(b) bailed or to be bailed by way of hire, under the contract, and whatever is the nature of the consideration for which the service is to be carried out.

(4) The Secretary of State may by order provide that one or more of sections 13 to 15 below shall not apply to services of a description specified in the order, and such an order may make different provision for different circumstances.

(5) The power to make an order under subsection (4) above shall be exercisable by statutory instrument subject to annulment in pursuance of a resolution of either House of Parliament.

13   Implied term about care and skill

In a contract for the supply of a service where the supplier is acting in the course of a business, there is an implied term that the supplier will carry out the service with reasonable care and skill.

14   Implied term about time of performance

(1) Where, under a contract for the supply of a service by a supplier acting in the course of a business, the time for the service to be carried out is not fixed by the contract, left to be fixed in a manner agreed by the contract or determined by the course of dealing between the parties, there is an implied term that the supplier will carry out the service within a reasonable time.

(2) What is a reasonable time is a question of fact.

15   Implied term about consideration

(1) Where, under a contract for the supply of a service, the consideration for the service is not determined by the contract, left to be determined in a manner agreed by the contract or determined by the course of dealing between the parties, there is an implied term that the party contracting with the supplier will pay a reasonable charge.

(2) What is a reasonable charge is a question of fact.

16   Exclusion of implied terms, etc.

(1) Where a right, duty or liability would arise under contract for the supply of a service by virtue of this Part of this Act, it may (subject to subsection (2) below and the 1977 Act) be negatived or varied by express agreement, or by the course of dealing between the parties, or by such usage as binds both parties to the contract.

(2) An express term does not negative a term implied by this Part of this Act unless inconsistent with it.

(3) Nothing in this Part of this Act prejudices—

(a) any rule of law which imposes on the supplier a duty stricter than that imposed by section 13 or 14 above; or

(b) subject to paragraph (a) above, any rule of law whereby any term not inconsistent with this Part of this Act is to be implied in a contract for the supply of a service.

(4) This Part of this Act has effect to any other enactment which defines or restricts the rights, duties or liabilities arising in connection with a service of any description.

PART III SUPPLEMENTARY

18   Interpretation: general

(1) In the preceding provisions of this Act and this section—

'bailee', in relation to a contract for the hire of goods means (depending on the context) a person to whom the goods are bailed under a contract, or a person to whom they are to be so bailed, or a person to whom the rights under the contract of either of those persons have passed;

'bailor', in relation to a contract for the hire of goods, means (depending on the context) a person who bails the goods under the contract, or a person who agrees to do so, or a person to whom the duties under the contract of either of those persons have passed;

'business' includes a profession and the activities of any government department or local or public authority;

'credit-broker' means a person acting in the course of a business of credit brokerage carried on by him;

'credit brokerage' means the effecting of introductions—

(a) of individuals desiring to obtain credit to persons carrying on any business so far as it relates to the provision of credit; or

(b) of individuals desiring to obtain goods on hire to persons carrying on a business which comprises or relates to the bailment [or as regards Scotland the hire] of goods under a contract for the hire of goods; or

(c) of individuals desiring to obtain credit, or to obtain goods on hire, to other credit-brokers;

'enactment' means any legislation (including subordinate legislation) of the United Kingdom or Northern Ireland;

'goods' [includes all personal chattels, other than things in action and money, and as regards Scotland all corporeal moveables; and in particular 'goods' includes] emblements, industrial growing crops, and things attached to or forming part of the land which are agreed to be severed before the transfer [bailment or hire] concerned or under the contract concerned [...];

'hire-purchase agreement' has the same meaning as in the 1974 Act;

['producer' means the manufacturer of goods, the importer of goods into the European Economic Area or any person purporting to be a producer by placing his name, trade mark or other distinctive sign on the goods;]

'property', in relation to goods, means the general property in them and not merely a special property;

['repair' means, in cases where there is a lack of conformity in goods for the purposes of this Act, to bring the goods into conformity with the contract.]

'transferee', in relation to a contract for the transfer of goods, means (depending on the context) a person to whom the property in the goods is transferred under the contract, or a person to whom the property is to be so transferred, or a person to whom the rights under the contract of either of those persons have passed;

'transferor', in relation to a contract for the transfer of goods, means (depending on the context) a person who transfers the property in the goods under the contract, or a person who agrees to do so, or a person to whom the duties under the contract of either of those persons have passed.

(2) In subsection (1) above, in the definitions of bailee, bailor, transferee and transferor, a reference to rights or duties passing is to their passing by assignment, [assignation] operation of law or otherwise.

[(3) For the purposes of this Act, the quality of goods includes their state and condition and the following (among others) are in appropriate cases aspects of the quality of goods—

(a) fitness for all the purposes for which goods of the kind in question are commonly supplied,
(b) appearance and finish,
(c) freedom from minor defects,
(d) safety, and
(e) durability.

(4) References in this Act to dealing as consumer are to be construed in accordance with Part I of the Unfair Contract Terms Act 1977; and, for the purposes of this Act, it is for the transferor or bailor claiming that the transferee or bailee does not deal as consumer to show that he does not.]

19   Interpretation: references to Acts

In this Act—

'the 1973 Act' means the Supply of Goods (Implied Terms) Act 1973;
'the 1974 Act' means the Consumer Credit Act 1974;
'the 1977 Act' means the Unfair Contract Terms Act 1977;
and 'the 1979 Act' means the Sale of Goods Act 1979.

Insolvency Act 1986

(1986, c. 45)

[8   Administration

Schedule B1 to this Act (which makes provision about the administration of companies) shall have effect.]

40   Payment of debts out of assets subject to floating charge

(1) The following applies, in the case of a company, where a receiver is appointed on behalf of the holders of any debentures of the company secured by a charge which, as created, was a floating charge.

(2) If the company is not at the time in course of being wound up, its preferential debts (within the meaning given to that expression by section 386 in Part XII) shall be paid out of the assets coming to the hands of the receiver in priority to any claims for principal or interest in respect of the debentures.

(3) Payments made under this section shall be recouped, as far as may be, out of the assets of the company available for payment of general creditors.

[72A   Floating charge holder not to appoint administrative receiver

(1) The holder of a qualifying floating charge in respect of a company's property may not appoint an administrative receiver of the company.

(6) This section is subject to the exceptions specified in sections 72B to 72G.]

127   Avoidance of property dispositions, etc.

[(1)] In a winding up by the court, any disposition of the company's property, and any transfer of shares, or alteration in the status of the company's members, made after the commencement of the winding up is, unless the court otherwise orders, void.

[(2) This section has no effect in respect of anything done by an administrator of a company while a winding-up petition is suspended under paragraph 40 of Schedule B1.]

175   Preferential debts (general provision)

(1) In a winding up the company's preferential debts (within the meaning given by section 386 in Part XII) shall be paid in priority to all other debts.

(2) Preferential debts—

  (a) rank equally among themselves after the expenses of the winding up and shall be paid in full, unless the assets are insufficient to meet them, in which case they abate in equal proportions; and

  (b) so far as the assets of the company available for payment of general creditors are insufficient to meet them, have priority over the claims of holders of debentures secured by, or holders of, any floating charge created by the company, and shall be paid accordingly out of any property comprised in or subject to that charge.

[176ZA   Payment of expenses of winding up (England and Wales)

(1) The expenses of winding up in England and Wales, so far as the assets of the company available for payment of general creditors are insufficient to meet them, have priority over any claims to property comprised in or subject to any floating charge created by the company and shall be paid out of any such property accordingly.

(2) In subsection (1)—

  (a) the reference to assets of the company available for payment of general creditors does not include any amount made available under section 176A(2)(a);

  (b) the reference to claims to property comprised in or subject to a floating charge is to the claims of—

    (i) the holders of debentures secured by, or holders of, the floating charge, and

    (ii) any preferential creditors entitled to be paid out of that property in priority to them.

(3) Provision may be made by rules restricting the application of subsection (1), in such circumstances as may be prescribed, to expenses authorised or approved—

  (a) by the holders of debentures secured by, or holders of, the floating charge and by any preferential creditors entitled to be paid in priority to them, or

  (b) by the court.

(4) References in this section to the expenses of the winding up are to all expenses properly incurred in the winding up, including the remuneration of the liquidator.]

[176A   Share of assets for unsecured creditors

(1) This section applies where a floating charge relates to property of a company—

  (a) which has gone into liquidation,

  (b) which is in administration,

  (c) of which there is a provisional liquidator, or

  (d) of which there is a receiver.

(2) The liquidator, administrator or receiver—

(a) shall make a prescribed part of the company's net property available for the satisfaction of unsecured debts, and

(b) shall not distribute that part to the proprietor of a floating charge except in so far as it exceeds the amount required for the satisfaction of unsecured debts.

(3) Subsection (2) shall not apply to a company if—

(a) the company's net property is less than the prescribed minimum, and

(b) the liquidator, administrator or receiver thinks that the cost of making a distribution to unsecured creditors would be disproportionate to the benefits.

(4) Subsection (2) shall also not apply to a company if or in so far as it is disapplied by—

(a) a voluntary arrangement in respect of the company, or

(b) a compromise or arrangement agreed under section 425 of the Companies Act (compromise with creditors and members).

(5) Subsection (2) shall also not apply to a company if—

(a) the liquidator, administrator or receiver applies to the court for an order under this subsection on the ground that the cost of making a distribution to unsecured creditors would be disproportionate to the benefits, and

(b) the court orders that subsection (2) shall not apply.

(6) In subsections (2) and (3) a company's net property is the amount of its property which would, but for this section, be available for satisfaction of claims of holders of debentures secured by, or holders of, any floating charge created by the company.

(7) An order under subsection (2) prescribing part of a company's net property may, in particular, provide for its calculation—

(a) as a percentage of the company's net property, or

(b) as an aggregate of different percentages of different parts of the company's net property.

(8) An order under this section—

(a) must be made by statutory instrument, and

(b) shall be subject to annulment pursuant to a resolution of either House of Parliament.

(9) In this section—

'floating charge' means a charge which is a floating charge on its creation and which is created after the first order under subsection (2)(a) comes into force, and

'prescribed' means prescribed by order by the Secretary of State.

(10) An order under this section may include transitional or incidental provision.]

213 Fraudulent trading

(1) If in the course of the winding up of a company it appears that any business of the company has been carried on with intent to defraud creditors of the company or creditors of any other person, or for any fraudulent purpose, the following has effect.

(2) The court, on the application of the liquidator may declare that any persons who were knowingly parties to the carrying on of the business in the manner above-mentioned are to be liable to make such contributions (if any) to the company's assets as the court thinks proper.

238 Transactions at an undervalue (England and Wales)

(1) This section applies in the case of a company where—

[(a) the company enters administration,]

(b) the company goes into liquidation;

and 'the office-holder' means the administrator or the liquidator, as the case may be.

(2) Where the company has at a relevant time (defined in section 240) entered into a transaction with any person at an undervalue, the office-holder may apply to the court for an order under this section.

(3) Subject as follows, the court shall, on such an application, make such order as it thinks fit for restoring the position to what it would have been if the company had not entered into that transaction.

(4) For the purposes of this section and section 241, a company enters into a transaction with a person at an undervalue if—

    (a) the company makes a gift to that person or otherwise enters into a transaction with that person on terms that provide for the company to receive no consideration, or

    (b) the company enters into a transaction with that person for a consideration the value of which, in money or money's worth, is significantly less than the value, in money or money's worth, of the consideration provided by the company.

(5) The court shall not make an order under this section in respect of a transaction at an undervalue if it is satisfied—

    (a) that the company which entered into the transaction did so in good faith and for the purpose of carrying on its business, and

    (b) that at the time it did so there were reasonable grounds for believing that the transaction would benefit the company.

239   Preferences (England and Wales)

(1) This section applies as does section 238.

(2) Where the company has at a relevant time (defined in the next section) given a preference to any person, the office-holder may apply to the court for an order under this section.

(3) Subject as follows, the court shall, on such an application, make such order as it thinks fit for restoring the position to what it would have been if the company had not given that preference.

(4) For the purposes of this section and section 241, a company gives a preference to a person if—

    (a) that person is one of the company's creditors or a surety or guarantor for any of the company's debts or other liabilities, and

    (b) the company does anything or suffers anything to be done which (in either case) has the effect of putting that person into a position which, in the event of the company going into insolvent liquidation, will be better than the position he would have been in if that thing had not been done.

(5) The court shall not make an order under this section in respect of a preference given to any person unless the company which gave the preference was influenced in deciding to give it by a desire to produce in relation to that person the effect mentioned in subsection (4)(b).

(6) A company which has given a preference to a person connected with the company (otherwise than by reason only of being its employee) at the time the preference was given is presumed, unless the contrary is shown, to have been influenced in deciding to give it by such a desire as is mentioned in subsection (5).

(7) The fact that something has been done in pursuance of the order of a court does not, without more, prevent the doing or suffering of that thing from constituting the giving of a preference.

240   'Relevant time' under ss. 238, 239

. . .

241   Orders under ss. 238, 239

(1) Without prejudice to the generality of sections 238(3) and 239(3), an order under either of those sections with respect to a transaction or preference entered into or given by a company may (subject to the next subsection)—

    (a) require any property transferred as part of the transaction, or in connection with the giving of the preference, to be vested in the company,

    (b) require any property to be so vested if it represents in any person's hands the application either of the proceeds of sale of property so transferred or of money so transferred,

    (c) release or discharge (in whole or in part) any security given by the company,

    (d) require any person to pay, in respect of benefits received by him from the company, such sums to the office-holder as the court may direct,

(e) provide for any surety or guarantor whose obligations to any person were released or discharged (in whole or in part) under the transaction, or by the giving of the preference, to be under such new or revived obligations to that person as the court thinks appropriate,

(f) provide for security to be provided for the discharge of any obligation imposed by or arising under the order, for such an obligation to be charged on any property and for the security or charge to have the same priority as a security or charge released or discharged (in whole or in part) under the transaction or by the giving of the preference, and

(g) provide for the extent to which any person whose property is vested by the order in the company, or on whom obligations are imposed by the order, is to be able to prove in the winding up of the company for debts or other liabilities which arose from, or were released or discharged (in whole or in part) under or by, the transaction or the giving of the preference.

(2) An order under section 238 or 239 may affect the property of, or impose any obligation on, any person whether or not he is the person with whom the company in question entered into the transaction or (as the case may be) the person to whom the preference was given; but such an order—

(a) shall not prejudice any interest in property which was acquired from a person other than the company and was acquired [in good faith and for value], or prejudice any interest deriving from such an interest, and

(b) shall not require a person who received a benefit from the transaction or preference [in good faith and for value] to pay a sum to the office-holder, except where that person was a party to the transaction or the payment is to be in respect of a preference given to that person at a time when he was a creditor of the company.

[(2A) Where a person has acquired an interest in property from a person other than the company in question, or has received a benefit from the transaction or preference, and at the time of that acquisition or receipt—

(a) he had notice of the relevant surrounding circumstances and of the relevant proceedings, or

(b) he was connected with, or was an associate of, either the company in question or the person with whom that company entered into the transaction or to whom that company gave the preference,

then, unless the contrary is shown, it shall be presumed for the purposes of paragraph (a) or (as the case may be) paragraph (b) of subsection (2) that the interest was acquired or the benefit was received otherwise than in good faith.]

[(3) For the purposes of subsection (2A)(a), the relevant surrounding circumstances are (as the case may require)—

(a) the fact that the company in question entered into the transaction at an under-value; or

(b) the circumstances which amounted to the giving of the preference by the company in question;

and subsections (3A) to (3C) have effect to determine whether, for those purposes, a person has notice of the relevant proceedings.]

[(3A) Where section 238 or 239 applies by reason of a company's entering administration, a person has notice of the relevant proceedings if he has notice that—

(a) an administration application has been made,

(b) an administration order has been made,

(c) a copy of a notice of intention to appoint an administrator under paragraph 14 or 22 of Schedule B1 has been filed, or

(d) notice of the appointment of an administrator has been filed under paragraph 18 or 29 of that Schedule.

(3B) Where section 238 or 239 applies by reason of a company's going into liquidation at the time when the appointment of an administrator of the company ceases to have effect, a person has notice of the relevant proceedings if he has notice that—

>   (a) an administration application has been made,
>   (b) an administration order has been made,
>   (c) a copy of a notice of intention to appoint an administrator under paragraph 14 or 22 of Schedule B1 has been filed,
>   (d) notice of the appointment of an administrator has been filed under paragraph 18 or 29 of that Schedule, or
>   (e) the company has gone into liquidation.]

[(3C) In a case where section 238 or 239 applies by reason of the company in question going into liquidation at any other time, a person has notice of the relevant proceedings if he has notice—

>   (a) where the company goes into liquidation on the making of a winding-up order, of the fact that the petition on which the winding-up order is made has been presented or of the fact that the company has gone into liquidation;
>   (b) in any other case, of the fact that the company has gone into liquidation.]

(4) The provisions of sections 238 to 241 apply without prejudice to the availability of any other remedy, even in relation to a transaction or preference which the company had no power to enter into or give.

244   Extortionate credit transactions

(1) This section applies as does section 238, and where the company is, or has been, a party to a transaction for, or involving, the provision of credit to the company.

(2) The court may, on the application of the office-holder, make an order with respect to the transaction if the transaction is or was extortionate and was entered into in the period of 3 years ending with [the day on which the company entered administration or went into liquidation.]

(3) For the purposes of this section a transaction is extortionate if, having regard to the risk accepted by the person providing the credit—

>   (a) the terms of it are or were such as to require grossly exorbitant payments to be made (whether unconditionally or in certain contingencies) in respect of the provision of the credit, or
>   (b) it otherwise grossly contravened ordinary principles of fair dealing;

and it shall be presumed, unless the contrary is proved, that a transaction with respect to which an application is made under this section is or, as the case may be, was extortionate.

(4) An order under this section with respect to any transaction may contain such one or more of the following as the court thinks fit, that is to say—

>   (a) provision setting aside the whole or part of any obligation created by the transaction,
>   (b) provision otherwise varying the terms of the transaction or varying the terms on which any security for the purposes of the transaction is held,
>   (c) provision requiring any person who is or was a party to the transaction to pay to the office-holder any sums paid to that person, by virtue of the transaction, by the company,
>   (d) provision requiring any person to surrender to the office-holder any property held by him as security for the purposes of the transaction,
>   (e) provision directing accounts to be taken between any persons.

(5) The powers conferred by this section are exercisable in relation to any transaction concurrently with any powers exercisable in relation to that transaction as a transaction at an undervalue or under section 242 (gratuitous alienations in Scotland).

245   Avoidance of certain floating charges

(1) This section applies as does section 238, but applies to Scotland as well as to England and Wales.

(2) Subject as follows, a floating charge on the company's undertaking or property created at a relevant time is invalid except to the extent of the aggregate of—

(a) the value of so much of the consideration for the creation of the charge as consists of money paid, or goods or services supplied, to the company at the same time as, or after, the creation of the charge,

(b) the value of so much of that consideration as consists of the discharge or reduction, at the same time as, or after, the creation of the charge, of any debt of the company, and

(c) the amount of such interest (if any) as is payable on the amount falling within paragraph (a) or (b) in pursuance of any agreement under which the money was so paid, the goods or services were so supplied or the debt was so discharged or reduced.

(3) Subject to the next subsection, the time at which a floating charge is created by a company is a relevant time for the purposes of this section if the charge is created—

(a) in the case of a charge which is created in favour of a person who is connected with the company, at a time in the period of 2 years ending with the onset of insolvency,

(b) in the case of a charge which is created in favour of any other person, at a time in the period of 12 months ending with the onset of insolvency,

(c) in either case, at a time between the making of an administration application in respect of the company and the making of an administration order on that application, or

(d) in either case, at a time between the filing with the court of a copy of notice of intention to appoint an administrator under paragraph 14 or 22 of Schedule B1 and the making of an appointment under that paragraph.

(4) Where a company creates a floating charge at a time mentioned in subsection (3)(b) and the person in favour of whom the charge is created is not connected with the company, that time is not a relevant time for the purposes of this section unless the company—

(a) is at that time unable to pay its debts within the meaning of section 123 in Chapter VI of Part IV, or

(b) becomes unable to pay its debts within the meaning of that section in consequence of the transaction under which the charge is created.

(5) For the purposes of subsection (3), the onset of insolvency is—

[(a) in a case where this section applies by reason of an administrator of a company being appointed by administration order, the date on which the administration application is made,

(b) in a case where this section applies by reason of an administrator of a company being appointed under paragraph 14 or 22 of Schedule B1 following filing with the court of a copy of notice of intention to appoint under that paragraph, the date on which the copy of the notice is filed,

(c) in a case where this section applies by reason of an administrator of a company being appointed otherwise than as mentioned in paragraph (a) or (b), the date on which the appointment takes effect, and

(d) in a case where this section applies by reason of a company going into liquidation, the date of the commencement of the winding up.]

(6) For the purposes of subsection (2)(a) the value of any goods or services supplied by way of consideration for a floating charge is the amount in money which at the time they were supplied could reasonably have been expected to be obtained for supplying the goods or services in the ordinary course of business and on the same terms (apart from the consideration) as those on which they were supplied to the company.

251 Expressions used generally

In this Group of Parts, except in so far as the context otherwise requires— ...

'administrative receiver' means—

(a) an administrative receiver as defined by section 29(2) in Chapter I of Part III, or

(b) a receiver appointed under section 51 in Chapter II of that Part in a case where the whole (or substantially the whole) of the company's property is attached by the floating charge;

["agent" does not include a person's counsel acting as such;]

["books and papers" and "books or papers" includes accounts, deeds, writing and documents;]

'business day' means any day other than a Saturday, a Sunday, Christmas Day, Good Friday or a day which is a bank holiday in any part of Great Britain;

'chattel leasing agreement' means an agreement for the bailment or, in Scotland, the hiring of goods which is capable of subsisting for more than 3 months;

'contributory' has the meaning given by section 79;

["the court", in relation to a company, means a court having jurisdiction to wind up the company;]

'director' includes any person occupying the position of director, by whatever named called;

["document" includes summons, notice, order and other legal process, and registers;]

'floating charge' means a charge which, as created, was a floating charge and includes a floating charge within section 462 of the Companies Act (Scottish floating charges);

["the Gazette" means—

      (a) as respects companies registered in England and Wales, the London Gazette;

      (b) as respects companies registered in Scotland, the Edinburgh Gazette;]

'office copy', in relation to Scotland, means a copy certified by the clerk of court;

["officer", in relation to a body corporate, includes a director, manager or secretary;]

'the official rate', in relation to interest, means the rate payable under section 189(4);

'prescribed' means prescribed by the rules;

'receiver', in the expression 'receiver or manager', does not include a receiver appointed under section 51 in Chapter II of Part III;

'retention of title agreement' means an agreement for the sale of goods to a company, being an agreement—

      (a) which does not constitute a charge on the goods, but

      (b) under which, if the seller is not paid and the company is wound up, the seller will have priority over all other creditors of the company as respects the goods or any property representing the goods;

'the rules' means rules under section 411 in Part XV; and

'shadow director', in relation to a company, means a person in accordance with whose directions or instructions the directors of the company are accustomed to act (but so that a person is not deemed a shadow director by reason only that the directors act on advice given by him in a professional capacity); and any expression for whose interpretation provision is made by Part XXVI of the Companies Act, other than an expression defined above in this section, is to be constructed in accordance with that provision.

344   Avoidance of general assignment of book debts

(1) The following applies where a person engaged in any business makes a general assignment to another person of his existing or future book debts, or any class of them, and is subsequently adjudged bankrupt.

(2) The assignment is void against the trustee of the bankrupt's estate as regards book debts which were not paid before the presentation of the bankruptcy petition, unless the assignment has been registered under the Bills of Sale Act 1878.

(3) For the purpose of subsections (1) and (2)—

      (a) 'assignment' includes an assignment by way of security or charge on book debts, and

      (b) 'general assignment' does not include—

          (i)   an assignment of book debts due at the date of the assignment from specified debtors or of debts becoming due under specified contracts, or

          (ii) an assignment of book debts included either in a transfer of a business made in good faith and for value or in an assignment of assets for the benefit of creditors generally.

(4) For the purposes of registration under the Act of 1878 an assignment of book debts is to be treated as if it were a bill of sale given otherwise than by way of security for the payment of a sum of

money; and the provisions of that Act with respect to the registration of bills of sale apply accordingly with such necessary modifications as may be made by rules under that Act.

423   Transactions defrauding creditors

(1) This section relates to transactions entered into at an undervalue; and a person enters into such a transaction with another person if—

    (a) he makes a gift to the other person or he otherwise enters into a transaction with the other on terms that provide for him to receive no consideration;

    (b) he enters into a transaction with the other in consideration of marriage [or the formation of a civil partnership]; or

    (c) he enters into a transaction with the other for a consideration the value of which, in money or money's worth, is significantly less than the value, in money or money's worth, of the consideration provided by himself.

(2) Where a person has entered into such a transaction, the court may, if satisfied under the next subsection, make such order as it thinks fit for—

    (a) restoring the position to what it would have been if the transaction had not been entered into, and

    (b) protecting the interests of persons who are victims of the transaction.

(3) In the case of a person entering into such a transaction, an order shall only be made if the court is satisfied that it was entered into by him for the purpose—

    (a) of putting assets beyond the reach of a person who is making, or may at some time make, a claim against him, or

    (b) of otherwise prejudicing the interests of such a person in relation to the claim which he is making or may make.

(5) In relation to a transaction at an undervalue, references here and below to a victim of the transaction are to a person who is, or is capable of being, prejudiced by it; and in the following two sections the person entering into the transaction is referred to as 'the debtor'.

425   Provision which may be made by order under s. 423

(1) Without prejudice to the generality of section 423, an order made under that section with respect to a transaction may (subject as follows)—

    (a) require any property transferred as part of the transaction to be vested in any person, either absolutely or for the benefit of all the persons on whose behalf the application for the order is treated as made;

    (b) require any property to be so vested if it represents, in any person's hands, the application either of the proceeds of sale of property so transferred or of money so transferred;

    (c) release or discharge (in whole or in part) any security given by the debtor;

    (d) require any person to pay to any other person in respect of benefits received from the debtor such sums as the court may direct;

    (e) provide for any surety or guarantor whose obligations to any person were released or discharged (in whole or in part) under the transaction to be under such new or revived obligations as the court thinks appropriate;

    (f) provide for security to be provided for the discharge of any obligation imposed by or arising under the order, for such an obligation to be charged on any property and for such security or charge to have the same priority as a security or charge released or discharged (in whole or in part) under the transaction.

(2) An order under section 423 may affect the property of, or impose any obligation on, any person whether or not he is the person with whom the debtor entered into the transaction; but such an order—

    (a) shall not prejudice any interest in property which was acquired from a person other than the debtor and was acquired in good faith, for value and without notice of the relevant circumstances, or prejudice any interest deriving from such an interest, and

(b) shall not require a person who received a benefit from the transaction in good faith, for value and without notice of the relevant circumstances to pay any sum unless he was a party to the transaction.

(3) For the purposes of this section the relevant circumstances in relation to a transaction are the circumstances by virtue of which an order under section 423 may be made in respect of the transaction.

(4) In this section 'security' means any mortgage, charge, lien or other security.

[SCHEDULE B1
ADMINISTRATION

NATURE OF ADMINISTRATION

Administration

1.—(1) For the purposes of this Act "administrator" of a company means a person appointed under this Schedule to manage the company's affairs, business and property.

(2) For the purposes of this Act—

(a) a company is "in administration" while the appointment of an administrator of the company has effect,

(b) a company "enters administration" when the appointment of an administrator takes effect,

(c) a company ceases to be in administration when the appointment of an administrator of the company ceases to have effect in accordance with this Schedule, and

(d) a company does not cease to be in administration merely because an administrator vacates office (by reason of resignation, death or otherwise) or is removed from office.

2. A person may be appointed as administrator of a company—

(a) by administration order of the court under paragraph 10,

(b) by the holder of a floating charge under paragraph 14, or

(c) by the company or its directors under paragraph 22.

Purpose of administration

3.—(1) The administrator of a company must perform his functions with the objective of—

(a) rescuing the company as a going concern, or

(b) achieving a better result for the company's creditors as a whole than would be likely if the company were wound up (without first being in administration), or

(c) realising property in order to make a distribution to one or more secured or preferential creditors.

(2) Subject to sub-paragraph (4), the administrator of a company must perform his functions in the interests of the company's creditors as a whole.

(3) The administrator must perform his functions with the objective specified in sub-paragraph (1)(a) unless he thinks either—

(a) that it is not reasonably practicable to achieve that objective, or

(b) that the objective specified in sub-paragraph (1)(b) would achieve a better result for the company's creditors as a whole.

(4) The administrator may perform his functions with the objective specified in sub-paragraph (1)(c) only if—

(a) he thinks that it is not reasonably practicable to achieve either of the objectives specified in sub-paragraph (1)(a) and (b), and

(b) he does not unnecessarily harm the interests of the creditors of the company as a whole.

4. The administrator of a company must perform his functions as quickly and efficiently as is reasonably practicable.

Status of administrator

5. An administrator is an officer of the court (whether or not he is appointed by the court).

APPOINTMENT OF ADMINISTRATOR BY COURT

Administration order

10. An administration order is an order appointing a person as the administrator of a company.

Conditions for making order

11. The court may make an administration order in relation to a company only if satisfied—

(a) that the company is or is likely to become unable to pay its debts, and

(b) that the administration order is reasonably likely to achieve the purpose of administration.

Administration application

12.—(1) An application to the court for an administration order in respect of a company (an "administration application") may be made only by—

(a) the company,

(b) the directors of the company,

(c) one or more creditors of the company,

(d) the [designated officer] for a magistrates' court in the exercise of the power conferred by section 87A of the Magistrates' Courts Act 1980 (c. 43)(fine imposed on company), or

(e) a combination of persons listed in paragraphs (a) to (d).

APPOINTMENT OF ADMINISTRATOR BY HOLDER
OF FLOATING CHARGE

Power to appoint

14.—(1) The holder of a qualifying floating charge in respect of a company's property may appoint an administrator of the company.

(2) For the purposes of sub-paragraph (1) a floating charge qualifies if created by an instrument which—

(a) states that this paragraph applies to the floating charge,

(b) purports to empower the holder of the floating charge to appoint an administrator of the company,

(c) purports to empower the holder of the floating charge to make an appointment which would be the appointment of an administrative receiver within the meaning given by section 29(2), or

(d) purports to empower the holder of a floating charge in Scotland to appoint a receiver who on appointment would be an administrative receiver.

(3) For the purposes of sub-paragraph (1) a person is the holder of a qualifying floating charge in respect of a company's property if he holds one or more debentures of the company secured—

(a) by a qualifying floating charge which relates to the whole or substantially the whole of the company's property,

(b) by a number of qualifying floating charges which together relate to the whole or substantially the whole of the company's property, or

(c) by charges and other forms of security which together relate to the whole or substantially the whole of the company's property and at least one of which is a qualifying floating charge.

Restrictions on power to appoint

16. An administrator may not be appointed under paragraph 14 while a floating charge on which the appointment relies is not enforceable.

17. An administrator of a company may not be appointed under paragraph 14 if—

(a) a provisional liquidator of the company has been appointed under section 135, or

(b) an administrative receiver of the company is in office.

EFFECT OF ADMINISTRATION

Dismissal of pending winding-up petition

40.—(1) A petition for the winding up of a company—

(a) shall be dismissed on the making of an administration order in respect of the company, and

(b) shall be suspended while the company is in administration following an appointment under paragraph 14.

(2) Sub-paragraph (1)(b) does not apply to a petition presented under—

(a) section 124A (public interest), or

[(aa) section 124B (SEs),]

(b) section 367 of the Financial Services and Markets Act 2000 (c. 8)(petition by Financial Services Authority).

(3) Where an administrator becomes aware that a petition was presented under a provision referred to in sub-paragraph (2) before his appointment, he shall apply to the court for directions under paragraph 63.

Dismissal of administrative or other receiver

41.—(1) When an administration order takes effect in respect of a company any administrative receiver of the company shall vacate office.

(2) Where a company is in administration, any receiver of part of the company's property shall vacate office if the administrator requires him to.

Moratorium on insolvency proceedings

42.—(1) This paragraph applies to a company in administration.

(2) No resolution may be passed for the winding up of the company.

(3) No order may be made for the winding up of the company.

(4) Sub-paragraph (3) does not apply to an order made on a petition presented under—

(a) section 124A (public interest), or

[(aa) section 124B (SEs),]

(b) section 367 of the Financial Services and Markets Act 2000 (c. 8)(petition by Financial Services Authority).

(5) If a petition presented under a provision referred to in sub-paragraph (4) comes to the attention of the administrator, he shall apply to the court for directions under paragraph 63.

Moratorium on other legal process

43.—(1) This paragraph applies to a company in administration.

(2) No step may be taken to enforce security over the company's property except—

(a) with the consent of the administrator, or

(b) with the permission of the court.

. . .

Publicity

45.—[(1) While a company is in administration, every business document issued by or on behalf of the company or the administrator, and all the company's websites, must state—

(a) the name of the administrator, and

(b) that the affairs, business and property of the company are being managed by the administrator.]

PROCESS OF ADMINISTRATION

Administrator's proposals

49.—(1) The administrator of a company shall make a statement setting out proposals for achieving the purpose of administration.

FUNCTIONS OF ADMINISTRATOR

General powers

59.—(1) The administrator of a company may do anything necessary or expedient for the management of the affairs, business and property of the company.

(3) A person who deals with the administrator of a company in good faith and for value need not inquire whether the administrator is acting within his powers.

60. The administrator of a company has the powers specified in Schedule 1 to this Act.

Administrator as agent of company

69. In exercising his functions under this Schedule the administrator of a company acts as its agent.

Charged property: floating charge

70.—(1) The administrator of a company may dispose of or take action relating to property which is subject to a floating charge as if it were not subject to the charge.

(2) Where property is disposed of in reliance on sub-paragraph (1) the holder of the floating charge shall have the same priority in respect of acquired property as he had in respect of the property disposed of.

(3) In sub-paragraph (2) "acquired property" means property of the company which directly or indirectly represents the property disposed of.

Charged property: non-floating charge

71.—(1) The court may by order enable the administrator of a company to dispose of property which is subject to a security (other than a floating charge) as if it were not subject to the security.

(2) An order under sub-paragraph (1) may be made only—
    (a) on the application of the administrator, and
    (b) where the court thinks that disposal of the property would be likely to promote the purpose of administration in respect of the company.

(3) An order under this paragraph is subject to the condition that there be applied towards discharging the sums secured by the security—
    (a) the net proceeds of disposal of the property, and
    (b) any additional money required to be added to the net proceeds so as to produce the amount determined by the court as the net amount which would be realised on a sale of the property at market value.

(4) If an order under this paragraph relates to more than one security, application of money under sub-paragraph (3) shall be in the order of the priorities of the securities.

(5) An administrator who makes a successful application for an order under this paragraph shall send a copy of the order to the registrar of companies before the end of the period of 14 days starting with the date of the order.

(6) An administrator commits an offence if he fails to comply with sub-paragraph (5) without reasonable excuse.

Hire-purchase property

72.—(1) The court may by order enable the administrator of a company to dispose of goods which are in the possession of the company under a hire-purchase agreement as if all the rights of the owner under the agreement were vested in the company.

Protection for secured or preferential creditor

73.—(1) An administrator's statement of proposals under paragraph 49 may not include any action which—

      (a) affects the right of a secured creditor of the company to enforce his security,

      (b) would result in a preferential debt of the company being paid otherwise than in priority to its non-preferential debts, or

      (c) would result in one preferential creditor of the company being paid a smaller proportion of his debt than another.

    (2) Sub-paragraph (1) does not apply to—

      (a) action to which the relevant creditor consents,

      (b) a proposal for a voluntary arrangement under Part I of this Act (although this sub-paragraph is without prejudice to section 4(3)), or

      (c) a proposal for a compromise or arrangement to be sanctioned under [Part 26 of the Companies Act 2006 (arrangements and reconstructions) or

      (d) a proposal for a cross-border merger within the meaning of regulation 2 of the Companies (Cross-Border Mergers) Regulations 2007.]

Consumer Protection Act 1987

(1987, c. 43)

PART I   PRODUCT LIABILITY

1   Purpose and construction of Part I

(1) This Part shall have effect for the purpose of making such provision as is necessary in order to comply with the product liability Directive and shall be construed accordingly.

(2) In this Part, except in so far as the context otherwise requires—

['agricultural produce' means any produce of the soil, of stock-farming or of fisheries;]

'dependant' and 'relative' have the same meaning as they have in, respectively, the Fatal Accidents Act 1976 and the [Damages (Scotland) Act 2011];

'producer', in relation to a product, means—

      (a) the person who manufactured it;

      (b) in the case of a substance which has not been manufactured but has been won or abstracted, the person who won or abstracted it;

      (c) in the case of a product which has not been manufactured, won or abstracted but essential characteristics of which are attributable to an industrial or other process having been carried out (for example, in relation to agricultural produce), the person who carried out that process;

'product', means any goods or electricity and (subject to subsection (3) below) includes a product which is comprised in another product, whether by virtue of being a component part or raw material or otherwise; and

'the product liability Directive' means the Directive of the Council of the European Communities, dated 25th July 1985, (No. 85/374/EEC) on the approximation of the laws, regulations and administrative provisions of the member States concerning liability for defective products.

(3) For the purposes of this Part a person who supplies any product in which products are comprised, whether by virtue of being component parts or raw materials or otherwise, shall not be treated by reason only of his supply of that product as supplying any of the products so comprised.

2 Liability for defective products

(1) Subject to the following provisions of this Part, where any damage is caused wholly or partly by a defect in a product, every person to whom subsection (2) below applies shall be liable for the damage.

(2) This subsection applies to—

(a) the producer of the product;

(b) any person who, by putting his name on the product or using a trade mark or other distinguishing mark in relation to the product, has held himself out to be the producer of the product;

(c) any person who has imported the product into a member State from a place outside the member States in order, in the course of any business of his, to supply it to another.

(3) Subject as aforesaid, where any damage is caused wholly or partly by a defect in a product, any person who supplied the product (whether to the person who suffered the damage, to the producer of any product in which the product in question is comprised or to any other person) shall be liable for the damage if—

(a) the person who suffered the damage requests the supplier to identify one or more of the persons (whether still in existence or not) to whom subsection (2) above applies in relation to the product;

(b) that request is made within a reasonable period after the damage occurs and at a time when it is not reasonably practicable for the person making the request to identify all those persons; and

(c) the supplier fails, within a reasonable period after receiving the request, either to comply with the request or to identify the person who supplied the product to him.

(5) Where two or more persons are liable by virtue of this Part for the same damage, their liability shall be joint and several.

(6) This section shall be without prejudice to any liability arising otherwise than by virtue of this Part.

3 Meaning of 'defect'

(1) Subject to the following provisions of the section, there is a defect in a product for the purposes of this Part if the safety of the product is not such as persons generally are entitled to expect; and for those purposes 'safety', in relation to a product, shall include safety with respect to products comprised in that product and safety in the context of risks of damage to property, as well as in the context of risks of death or personal injury.

(2) In determining for the purposes of subsection (1) above what persons generally are entitled to expect in relation to a product all the circumstances shall be taken into account, including—

(a) the manner in which, and purposes for which, the product has been marketed, its get-up, the use of any mark in relation to the product and any instructions for, or warnings with respect to, doing or refraining from doing anything with or in relation to the product;

(b) what might reasonably be expected to be done with or in relation to the product; and

(c) the time when the product was supplied by its producer to another;

and nothing in this section shall require a defect to be inferred from the fact alone that the safety of a product which is supplied after that time is greater than the safety of the product in question.

4 Defences

(1) In any civil proceedings by virtue of this Part against any person ('the person proceeded against') in respect of a defect in a product it shall be a defence for him to show—

(a) that the defect is attributable to compliance with any requirement imposed by or under any enactment or with any Community obligation; or

(b) that the person proceeded against did not at any time supply the product to another; or

(c) that the following conditions are satisfied, that is to say—

    (i)   that the only supply of the product to another by the person proceeded against was otherwise than in the course of a business of that person's; and

    (ii)   that section 2(2) above does not apply to that person or applies to him by virtue only of things done otherwise than with a view to profit; or

(d) that the defect did not exist in the product at the relevant time; or

(e) that the state of scientific and technical knowledge at the relevant time was not such that a producer of products of the same description as the product in question might be expected to have discovered the defect if it had existed in his products while they were under his control; or

(f) that the defect—

    (i)   constituted a defect in a product ('the subsequent product') in which the product in question had been comprised; and

    (ii)   was wholly attributable to the design of the subsequent product or to compliance by the producer of the product in question with instructions given by the producer of the subsequent product.

(2) In this section 'the relevant time', in relation to electricity, means the time at which it was generated, being a time before it was transmitted or distributed, and in relation to any other product, means—

(a) if the person proceeded against is a person to whom subsection (2) of section 2 above applies in relation to the product, the time when he supplied the product to another;

(b) if that subsection does not apply to that person in relation to the product, the time when the product was last supplied by a person to whom that subsection does apply in relation to the product.

5   Damage giving rise to liability

(1) Subject to the following provisions of this section, in this Part 'damages' means death or personal injury or any loss of or damage to any property (including land).

(2) A person shall not be liable under section 2 above in respect of any defect in a product for the loss of or any damage to the product itself or for the loss of or any damage to the whole or any part of any product which has been supplied with the product in question comprised in it.

(3) A person shall not be liable under section 2 above for any loss of or damage to any property which, at the time it is lost or damaged, is not—

(a) of a description of property ordinarily intended for private use, occupation or consumption; and

(b) intended by the person suffering the loss or damage mainly for his own private use, occupation or consumption.

(4) No damages shall be awarded to any person by virtue of this Part in respect of any loss of or damage to any property if the amount which would fall to be so awarded to that person, apart from this subsection and any liability for interest, does not exceed £275.

(5) In determining for the purposes of this Part who has suffered any loss of or damage to property and when any such loss or damage occurred, the loss or damage shall be regarded as having occurred at the earliest time at which a person with an interest in the property had knowledge of the material facts about the loss or damage.

(6) For the purposes of subsection (5) above the material facts about any loss of or damage to any property are such facts about the loss or damage as would lead a reasonable person with an interest in the property to consider the loss or damage sufficiently serious to justify his instituting proceedings for damages against a defendant who did not dispute liability and was able to satisfy a judgment.

(7) For the purposes of subsection (5) above a person's knowledge includes knowledge which he might reasonably have been expected to acquire—

(a) from facts observable or ascertainable by him; or

(b) from facts ascertainable by him with help of appropriate expert advice which it is reasonable for him to seek;

but a person shall not be taken by virtue of this subsection to have knowledge of a fact ascertainable by him only with the help of expert advice unless he has failed to take all reasonable steps to obtain (and, where appropriate, to act on) that advice.

(8) Subsections (5) to (7) above shall not extend to Scotland.

6   Application of certain enactments etc.

(1) Any damage for which a person is liable under section 2 above shall be deemed to have been caused—

(a) for the purposes of the Fatal Accidents Act 1976, by that person's wrongful act, neglect or default;

(b) for the purposes of section 3 of the Law Reform (Miscellaneous Provisions) (Scotland) Act 1940 (contribution among joint wrongdoers), by that person's wrongful act or negligent act or omission; . . .

(2) Where—

(a) a person's death is caused wholly or partly by a defect in a product, or a person dies after suffering damage which has been so caused;

(b) a request such as mentioned in paragraph (a) of subsection (3) of section 2 above is made to a supplier of the product by that person's personal representatives or, in the case of a person whose death is caused wholly or partly by the defect, by any dependant or relative of that person; and

(c) the conditions specified in paragraphs (b) and (c) of that subsection are satisfied in relation to that request,

this Part shall have effect for the purposes of the Law Reform (Miscellaneous Provisions) Act 1934, the Fatal Accidents Acts 1976 and the [Damages (Scotland) Act 2011] as if liability of the supplier to that person under that subsection did not depend on that person having requested the supplier to identify certain persons or on the said conditions having been satisfied in relation to a request made by that person.

(3) Section 1 of the Congenital Disabilities (Civil Liability) Act 1976 shall have effect for the purposes of this Part as if—

(a) a person were answerable to a child in respect of an occurrence caused wholly or partly by a defect in a product if he is or has been liable under section 2 above in respect of any effect of the occurrence on a parent of the child, or would be so liable if the occurrence caused a parent of the child to suffer damage;

(b) the provisions of this Part relating to liability under section 2 above applied in relation to liability by virtue of paragraph (a) above under the said section 1; and

(c) subsection (6) of the said section 1 (exclusion of liability) were omitted.

(4) Where any damage is caused partly by a defect in a product and partly by the fault of the person suffering the damage, the Law Reform (Contributory Negligence) Act 1945 and section 5 of the Fatal Accidents Act 1976 (contributory negligence) shall have effect as if the defect were the fault of every person liable by virtue of this Part for the damage caused by the defect.

(5) In subsection (4) above 'fault' has the same meaning as in the said Act of 1945.

(6) Schedule 1 to this Act shall have effect for the purpose of amending the Limitation Act 1980 and the Prescription and Limitation (Scotland) Act 1973 in their application in relation to the bringing of actions by virtue of this Part.

(7) It is hereby declared that liability by virtue of this Part is to be treated as liability in tort for the purposes of any enactment conferring jurisdiction on any court with respect to any matter.

(8) Nothing in this Part shall prejudice the operation of section 12 of the Nuclear Installations Act 1965 (rights to compensation for certain breaches of duties confined to rights under that Act).

7   Prohibition on exclusions from liability

The liability of a person by virtue of this Part to person who has suffered damage caused wholly or partly by a defect in a product, or to a dependant or relative of such a person, shall not be limited or excluded by any contract term, by any notice or by any other provision.

8   Power to modify Part I

(1) Her Majesty may by Order in Council make such modifications of this Part and of any other enactment (including an enactment contained in the following Parts of this Act, or in an Act passed after this Act) as appear to Her Majesty in Council to be necessary or expedient in consequence of any modification of the product liability Directive which is made at any time after the passing of this Act.

(2) An Order in Council under subsection (1) above shall not be submitted to Her Majesty in Council unless a draft of the Order has been laid before, and approved by a resolution of, each House of Parliament.

9   Application of Part I to Crown

(1) Subject to subsection (2) below, this Part shall bind the Crown.

(2) The Crown shall not, as regards the Crown's liability by virtue of this Part, be bound by this Part further than the Crown is made liable in tort or in reparation under the Crown Proceedings Act 1947, as that Act has effect from time to time.

PART II CONSUMER SAFETY

11   Safety regulations

(1) The Secretary of State may by regulations under this section ('safety regulations') make such provision as he considers appropriate [. . .] for the purpose of securing—

(a) that goods to which this section applies are safe;

(b) that goods to which this section applies which are unsafe, or would be unsafe in the hands of persons of a particular description, are not made available to persons generally or, as the case may be, to persons of that description, and

(c) that appropriate information is, and inappropriate information is not, provided in relation to goods to which this section applies.

(2) Without prejudice to the generality of subsection (1) above, safety regulations may contain provision—

(a) with respect to the composition or contents, design, construction, finish or packing of goods to which this section applies, with respect to standards for such goods and with respect to other matters relating to such goods;

(b) with respect to the giving, refusal, alteration or cancellation of approvals of such goods, of descriptions of such goods or of standards for such goods;

(c) with respect to the conditions that may be attached to any approval given under the regulations;

(d) for requiring such fees as may be determined by or under the regulations to be paid on the giving or alteration of any approval under the regulations and on the making of an application for such an approval or alteration;

(e) with respect to appeals against refusals, alterations and cancellations of approvals given under the regulations and against the conditions contained in such approvals;

(f) for requiring goods to which this section applies to be approved under the regulations or to conform to the requirements of the regulations or to descriptions or standards specified in or approved by or under the regulations;

(g) with respect to the testing or inspection of goods to which this section applies (including provision for determining the standards to be applied in carrying out any test or inspection);

(h) with respect to the way of dealing with goods of which some or all do not satisfy a test required by or under the regulations or a standard connected with a procedure so required;

(i) for requiring a mark, warning or instruction or any other information relating to goods to be put on or to accompany the goods or to be used or provided in some other manner in relation to the goods, and for securing that inappropriate information is not given in relation to goods either by means of misleading marks or otherwise;

(j) for prohibiting persons from supplying, or from offering to supply, agreeing to supply, exposing for supply or possessing for supply, goods to which this section applies and component parts and raw materials for such goods;

(k) for requiring information to be given to any such person as may be determined by or under the regulations for the purpose of enabling that person to exercise any function conferred on him by the regulations.

(3) Without prejudice as aforesaid, safety regulations may contain provision—

(a) for requiring persons on whom functions are conferred by or under section 27 below to have regard, in exercising their functions so far as relating to any provision of safety regulations, to matters specified in a direction issued by the Secretary of State with respect to that provision;

(b) for securing that a person shall not be guilty of an offence under section 12 below unless it is shown that the goods in question do not conform to a particular standard;

(c) for securing that proceedings for such an offence are not brought in England and Wales except by or with the consent of the Secretary of State or the Director of Public Prosecutions;

(d) for securing that proceedings for such an offence are not brought in Northern Ireland except by or with consent of the Secretary of State or the Director of Public Prosecutions for Northern Ireland;

(e) for enabling a magistrate's court in England and Wales or Northern Ireland to try an information or, in Northern Ireland, a complaint in respect of such an offence if the information was laid or the complaint made within twelve months from the time when the offence was committed;

(f) for enabling summary proceedings for such an offence to be brought in Scotland at any time within twelve months from the time when the offence was committed; and

(g) for determining the persons by whom, and the manner in which, anything required to be done by or under the regulations is to be done.

(4) Safety regulations shall not provide for any contravention of the regulations to be an offence.

(5) Where the Secretary of State proposes to make safety regulations it shall be his duty before he makes them—

(a) to consult such organisations as appear to him to be representative of interests substantially affected by the proposal;

(b) to consult such other persons as he considers appropriate; and

(c) in the case of proposed regulations relating to goods suitable for use at work to consult [the Health and Safety Executive] in relation to the application of the proposed regulations to Great Britain;

but the preceding provisions of this subsection shall not apply in the case of regulations which provide for the regulations to cease to have effect at the end of a period of not more than twelve months beginning with the day on which they come into force and which contain a statement that it appears to the Secretary of State that the need to protect the public requires that the regulations should be made without delay.

(6) The power to make safety regulations shall be exercisable by statutory instrument subject to annulment in pursuance of a resolution of either House of Parliament and shall include power—

(a) to make different provision for different cases; and

(b) to make such supplemental, consequential and transitional provision as the Secretary of State considers appropriate.

(7) This section applies to any goods other than—

    (a) growing crops and things comprised in land by virtue of being attached to it;
    (b) water, food, feeding stuff and fertiliser;
    (c) gas which is, is to be or has been supplied by a person authorised to supply it by or under [section 7A of the Gas Act 1986 (licensing of gas suppliers and gas shippers) or paragraph 5 of Schedule 2A to that Act (supply to very large customers an exception to prohibition on unlicensed activities or under Article 8(1)(c) of the Gas (Northern Ireland) Order 1996];
    (d) controlled drugs and licensed medicinal products.

12   Offences against the safety regulations

(1) Where safety regulations prohibit a person from supplying or offering or agreeing to supply any goods or from exposing or possessing any goods for supply that person shall be guilty of an offence if he contravenes the prohibition.

(2) Where safety regulations require a person who makes or processes any goods in the course of carrying on a business—

    (a) to carry out a particular test or use a particular procedure in connection with the making or processing of the goods with a view to ascertaining whether the goods satisfy any requirements of such regulations; or
    (b) to deal or not to deal in a particular way with a quantity of the goods of which the whole or part does not satisfy such a test or does not satisfy standards connected with such a procedure,

that person shall be guilty of an offence if he does not comply with the requirement.

(3) If a person contravenes a provision of safety regulations which prohibits or requires the provision, by means of a mark or otherwise, of information of a particular kind in relation to goods, he shall be guilty of an offence.

(4) Where safety regulations require any person to give information to another for the purpose of enabling that other to exercise any function, that person shall be guilty of an offence if—

    (a) he fails without reasonable cause to comply with the requirement; or
    (b) in giving the information which is required of him—
        (i)   he makes any statement which he knows is false in a material particular; or
        (ii) he recklessly makes any statement which is false in a material particular.

(5) A person guilty of an offence under this section shall be liable on summary conviction to imprisonment for a term not exceeding six months or to a fine not exceeding level 5 on the standard scale or to both.

13   Prohibition notices and notices to warn

(1) The Secretary of State may—

    (a) serve on any person a notice ('a prohibition notice') prohibiting that person, except with the consent of the Secretary of State, from supplying, or from offering to supply, agreeing to supply or possessing for supply, any relevant goods which the Secretary of State considers are unsafe and which are described in the notice;
    (b) serve on any person a notice ('a notice to warn') requiring that person at his own expense to publish, in a form and manner and on occasions specified in the notice, a warning about any relevant goods which the Secretary of State considers are unsafe, which that person supplies or has supplied and which are described in the notice.

(2) Schedule 2 to this Act shall have effect with respect to prohibition notices and notices to warn, and the Secretary of State may by regulations make provision specifying the manner in which information is to be given to any person under that Schedule.

(3) A consent given by the Secretary of State for the purposes of a prohibition notice may impose such conditions on the doing of anything for which the consent is required as the Secretary of State considers appropriate.

(4) A person who contravenes a prohibition notice or a notice to warn shall be guilty of an offence and liable on summary conviction to imprisonment for a term not exceeding [three months] or to a fine not exceeding level 5 on the standard scale or to both.

(5) The power to make regulations under subsection (2) above shall be exercisable by statutory instrument subject to annulment in pursuance of a resolution of either House of Parliament and shall include power—

(a) to make different provision for different cases; and

(b) to make such supplemental, consequential and transitional provision as the Secretary of State considers appropriate.

(6) In this section 'relevant goods' means—

(a) in relation to a prohibition notice, any goods to which section 11 above applies; and

(b) in relation to a notice to warn, any goods to which that section applies or any growing crops or things comprised in land by virtue of being attached to it.

[(7) A notice may not be given under this section in respect of any aspect of the safety of goods, or any risk or category of risk associated with goods, concerning which provision is contained in the General Product Safety Regulations 2005.]

14 Suspension notices

(1) Where an enforcement authority has reasonable grounds for suspecting that any safety provision has been contravened in relation to any goods, the authority may serve a notice ('suspension notice') prohibiting the person on whom it is served, for such period ending not more than six months after the date of the notice as is specified therein, from doing any of the following things without the consent of the authority, that is to say, supplying the goods, offering to supply them, agreeing to supply them or exposing them for supply.

(2) A suspension notice served by an enforcement authority in respect of any goods shall—

(a) describe the goods in a manner sufficient to identify them;

(b) set out the grounds on which the authority suspects that a safety provision has been contravened in relation to the goods, and

(c) state that, and the manner in which, the person on whom the notice is served may appeal against the notice under section 15 below.

(3) A suspension notice served by an enforcement authority for the purpose of prohibiting a person for any period from doing the things mentioned in subsection (1) above in relation to any goods may also require that person to keep the authority informed of the whereabouts throughout that period of any of those goods in which he has an interest.

(4) Where a suspension notice has been served on any person in respect of any goods, no further such notice shall be served on that person in respect of the same goods unless—

(a) proceedings against that person for an offence in respect of a contravention in relation to the goods of a safety provision (not being an offence under this section); or

(b) proceedings for the forfeiture of the goods under section 16 or 17 below, are pending at the end of the period specified in the first-mentioned notice.

(5) A consent given by an enforcement authority for the purposes of subsection (1) above may impose such conditions on the doing of anything for which the consent is required as the authority considers appropriate.

(6) Any person who contravenes a suspension notice shall be guilty of an offence and liable on summary conviction to imprisonment for a term not exceeding [three months] or to a fine not exceeding level 5 on the standard scale or to both.

(7) Where an enforcement authority serves a suspension notice in respect of any goods, the authority shall be liable to pay compensation to any person having an interest in the goods in respect of any loss or damage caused by reason of the service of the notice if—

(a) there has been no contravention in relation to the goods of any safety provision; and

(b) the exercise of the power is not attributable to any neglect or default by that person.

(8) Any disputed question as to the right to or the amount of any compensation payable under this section shall be determined by arbitration or, in Scotland, by a single arbiter appointed, failing agreement between the parties, by the sheriff.

15   Appeals against suspension notices

(1) Any person having an interest in any goods in respect of which a suspension notice is for the time being in force may apply for an order setting aside the notice.

(2) An application under this section may be made—

    (a) to any magistrates' court in which proceedings have been brought in England and Wales or Northern Ireland—

        (i)   for an offence in respect of a contravention in relation to the goods of any safety provision; or

        (ii)   for the forfeiture of the goods under section 16 below;

    (b) where no such proceedings have been so brought, by way of complaint to a magistrates' court; or

    (c) in Scotland, by summary application to the sheriff.

(3) On an application under this section to a magistrates' court in England and Wales or Northern Ireland the court shall make an order setting aside the suspension notice only if the court is satisfied that there has been no contravention in relation to the goods of any safety provision.

(4) On an application under this section to the sheriff he shall make an order setting aside the suspension notice only if he is satisfied that at the date of making the order—

    (a) proceedings for an offence in respect of a contravention in relation to the goods of any safety provision; or

    (b) proceedings for the forfeiture of the goods under section 17 below, have not been brought or, having been brought, have been concluded.

(5) Any person aggrieved by an order made under this section by a magistrates' court in England and Wales or Northern Ireland, or by a decision of such a court not to make such an order, may appeal against that order or decision—

    (a) in England and Wales, to the Crown Court;

    (b) in Northern Ireland, to the county court;

and an order so made may contain such provision as appears to the court to be appropriate for delaying the coming into force of the order pending the making and determination of any appeal (including any application under section Ill of the Magistrates' Courts Act 1980 or Article 146 of the Magistrates' Courts (Northern Ireland) Order 1981 (statement of case)).

16   Forfeiture: England and Wales and Northern Ireland

(1) An enforcement authority in England and Wales or Northern Ireland may apply under this section for an order for the forfeiture of any goods on the grounds that there has been a contravention in relation to the goods of a safety provision.

(2) An application under this section may be made—

    (a) where proceedings have been brought in a magistrates' court for an offence in respect of a contravention in relation to some or all of the goods of any safety provision, to that court;

    (b) where an application with respect to some or all of the goods has been made to a magistrates' court under section 15 above or section 33 below, to that court; and

    (c) where no application for the forfeiture of the goods has been made under paragraph (a) or (b) above, by way of complaint to a magistrates' court.

(3) On an application under this section the court shall make an order for the forfeiture of any goods only if it is satisfied that there has been a contravention in relation to the goods of a safety provision.

(4) For the avoidance of doubt it is declared that a court may infer for the purposes of this section that there has been a contravention in relation to any goods of a safety provision if it is satisfied that any such provision has been contravened in relation to goods which are representative of those goods (whether by reason of being of the same design or part of the same consignment or batch or otherwise).

(5) Any person aggrieved by an order made under this section by a magistrates' court, or by a decision of such a court not to make such an order, may appeal against that order or decision—

(a) in England and Wales, to the Crown Court;

(b) in Northern Ireland, to the county court;

and an order so made may contain such provision as appears to the court to be appropriate for delaying the coming into force of the order pending the making and determination of any appeal (including any application under section III of the Magistrates' Courts Act 1980 or Article 146 of the Magistrates' Courts (Northern Ireland) Order 1981 (statement of case)).

(6) Subject to subsection (7) below, where any goods are forfeited under this section they shall be destroyed in accordance with such directions as the court may give.

(7) On making an order under this section a magistrates' court may, if it considers it appropriate to do so, direct that the goods to which the order relates shall (instead of being destroyed) be released, to such person as the court may specify, on condition that that person—

(a) does not supply those goods to any person otherwise than as mentioned in section 46(7)(a) or (b) below, and

(b) complies with any order to pay costs or expenses (including any order under section 35 below) which has been made against that person in the proceedings for the order for forfeiture.

18   Power to obtain information

(1) If the Secretary of State considers that, for the purpose of deciding whether—

(a) to make, vary or revoke any safety regulations; or

(b) to serve, vary or revoke a prohibition notice; or

(c) to serve or revoke a notice to warn,

he requires information which another person is likely to be able to furnish, the Secretary of State may serve on the other person a notice under this section.

(2) A notice served on any person under this section may require that person—

(a) to furnish to the Secretary of State, within a period specified in the notice, such information as is so specified;

(b) to produce such records as are specified in the notice at a time and place so specified and to permit a person appointed by the Secretary of State for the purpose to take copies of the records at that time and place.

(3) A person shall be guilty of an offence if he—

(a) fails, without reasonable cause, to comply with a notice served on him under this section; or

(b) in purporting to comply with a requirement which by virtue of paragraph (a) of subsection (2) above is contained in such a notice—

(i)   furnishes information which he knows is false in a material particular;

(ii) recklessly furnishes information which is false in a material particular.

(4) A person guilty of an offence under subsection (3) above shall—

(a) in the case of an offence under paragraph (a) of that subsection, be liable on summary conviction to a fine not exceeding level 5 on the standard scale; and

(b) in the case of an offence under paragraph (b) of that subsection be liable—

(i)   on conviction on indictment, to a fine,

(ii) on summary conviction, to a fine not exceeding the statutory maximum.

19   Interpretation of Part II

(1) In this Part—

'controlled drug' means a controlled drug within the meaning of the Misuse of Drugs Act 1971;

'feeding stuff' and 'fertiliser' have the same meaning as in Part IV of the Agriculture Act 1970;

'food' does not include anything containing tobacco but, subject to that, has the same meaning as in the [Food Safety Act 1990] or, in relation to Northern Ireland, the same meaning as in the [Food Safety (Northern Ireland) Order 1991];

'licensed medicinal product' means—

(a) any medicinal product within the meaning of the Medicines Act 1968 in respect of which a product licence within the meaning of that Act is for the time being in force; or

(b) any other article or substance in respect of which any such licence is for the time being in force in pursuance of an order under section 104 or 105 of that Act (application of Act to other articles and substances); [or

(c) a veterinary medicinal product that has a marketing authorisation under the Veterinary Medicines Regulations 2006.]

'safe', in relation to any goods, means such that there is no risk, or no risk apart from one reduced to a minimum, that any of the following will (whether immediately or after a definite or indefinite period) cause the death of, or any personal injury to, any person whatsoever, that is to say—

(a) the goods;

(b) the keeping, use or consumption of the goods;

(c) the assembly of any of the goods which are, or are to be supplied unassembled;

(d) any emission or leakage from the goods or, as a result of the keeping, use or consumption of the goods, from anything else; or

(e) reliance on the accuracy of any measurement, calculation or other reading made by or by means of the goods,

and [...] 'unsafe' shall be construed accordingly;

'tobacco' includes any tobacco product within the meaning of the Tobacco Products Duty Act 1979 and any article or substance containing tobacco and intended for oral or nasal use.

(2) In the definition of 'safe' in subsection (1) above, references to the keeping, use or consumption of any goods are references to—

(a) the keeping, use or consumption of the goods by the persons by whom, and in all or any of the ways or circumstances in which, they might reasonably be expected to be kept, used or consumed; and

(b) the keeping, use or consumption of the goods either alone or in conjunction with other goods in conjunction with which they might reasonably be expected to be kept, used or consumed.

PART IV ENFORCEMENT OF PARTS II AND III

27 Enforcement

(1) Subject to the following provisions of this section—

(a) it shall be the duty of every weights and measures authority in Great Britain to enforce within their area the safety provisions [...]; and

(b) it shall be the duty of every district council in Northern Ireland to enforce within their area the safety provisions.

(2) The Secretary of State may by regulations—

(a) wholly or partly transfer any duty imposed by subsection (1) above on a weights and measures authority or a district council in Northern Ireland to such other person who has agreed to the transfer as is specified in the regulations;

(b) relieve such an authority or council of any such duty so far as it is exercisable in relation to such goods as may be described in the regulations.

(3) The power to make regulations under subsection (2) above shall be exercisable by statutory instrument subject to annulment in pursuance of a resolution of either House of Parliament and shall include power—

(a) to make different provision for different cases; and

(b) to make such supplemental, consequential and transitional provision as the Secretary of State considers appropriate.

(4) Nothing in this section shall authorise any weights and measures authority, or any person whom functions are conferred by regulations under subsection (2) above, to bring proceedings in Scotland for an offence.

28 Test purchases

(1) An enforcement authority shall have power, for the purpose of ascertaining whether any safety provision [...] has been contravened in relation to any goods, services, accommodation or facilities—

(a) to make, or to authorise an officer of the authority to make, any purchase of any goods; or

(b) to secure, or to authorise an officer of the authority to secure, the provision of any services, accommodation or facilities.

(2) Where—

(a) any goods purchased under this section by or on behalf of an enforcement authority are submitted to a test; and

(b) the test leads to—

(i) the bringing of proceedings for an offence in respect of a contravention in relation to the goods of any safety provision [...] or for the forfeiture of the goods under section 16 or 17 above; or

(ii) the serving of a suspension notice in respect of any goods; and

(c) the authority is requested to do so and it is practicable for the authority to comply with the request,

the authority shall allow the person from whom the goods were purchased or any person who is a party to the proceedings or has an interest in any goods to which the notice relates to have the goods tested.

(3) The Secretary of State may by regulations provide that any test of goods under this section by or on behalf of an enforcement authority shall—

(a) be carried out at the expense of the authority in a manner and by a person prescribed by or determined under the regulations; or

(b) be carried out either as mentioned in paragraph (a) above or by the authority in a manner prescribed by the regulations.

(4) The power to make regulations under subsection (3) above shall be exercisable by statutory instrument subject to annulment in pursuance of a resolution of either House of Parliament and shall include power—

(a) to make different provision for different cases; and

(b) to make such supplemental, consequential and transitional provision as the Secretary of State considers appropriate.

(5) Nothing in this section shall authorise the acquisition by or on behalf of an enforcement authority of any interest in land.

29 Powers of search etc.

(1) Subject to the following provisions of this Part, a duly authorised officer of an enforcement authority may at any reasonable hour and on production, if required, of his credentials exercise any of the powers conferred by the following provisions of this section.

(2) The officer may, for the purpose of ascertaining whether there has been any contravention of any safety provision [...], inspect any goods and enter any premises other than premises occupied only as a person's residence.

(3) The officer may, for the purpose of ascertaining whether there has been any contravention of any safety provision, examine any procedure (including any arrangements for carrying out a test) connected with the production of any goods.

(4) If the officer has reasonable grounds for suspecting that any goods are manufactured or imported goods which have not been supplied in the United Kingdom since they were manufactured or imported he may—

    (a) for the purpose of ascertaining whether there has been any contravention of any safety provision in relation to the goods, require any person carrying on a business, or employed in connection with a business, to produce any records relating to the business;

    (b) for the purpose of ascertaining (by testing or otherwise) whether there has been any such contravention, seize and detain the goods;

    (c) take copies of, or of any entry in, any records produced by virtue of paragraph (a) above.

(5) If the officer has reasonable grounds for suspecting that there has been a contravention in relation to any goods of any safety provision [. . .], he may—

    (a) for the purpose of ascertaining whether there has been any such contravention, require any person carrying on a business, or employed in connection with a business, to produce any records relating to the business;

    (b) for the purpose of ascertaining (by testing or otherwise) whether there has been any such contravention, seize and detain the goods;

    (c) take copies of, or of any entry in, any records produced by virtue of paragraph (a) above.

(6) The officer may seize and detain—

    (a) any goods or records which he has reasonable grounds for believing may be required as evidence in proceedings for an offence in respect of a contravention of any safety provision [. . .];

    (b) any goods which he has reasonable grounds for suspecting may be liable to be forfeited under section 16 or 17 above.

(7) If and to the extent that it is reasonably necessary to do so to prevent a contravention of any safety provision [. . .], the officer may, for the purpose of exercising his power under subsection (4), (5) or (6) above to seize any goods or records—

    (a) require any person having authority to do so to open any container or to open any vending machine; and

    (b) himself open or break open any such container or machine where a requirement made under paragraph (a) above in relation to the container or machine has not been complied with.

30   Provisions supplemental to s. 29

(1) An officer seizing any goods or records under section 29 above shall inform the following persons that the goods or records have been so seized, that is to say—

    (a) the person from whom they are seized; and

    (b) in the case of imported goods seized on any premises under the control of the Commissioners of Customs and Excise, the importer of those goods (within the meaning of the Customs and Excise Management Act 1979).

(2) If a justice of the peace—

    (a) is satisfied by any written information on oath that there are reasonable grounds for believing either—

        (i) that any goods or records which any officer has power to inspect under section 29 above are on any premises and that their inspection is likely to disclose evidence that there has been a contravention of any safety provision or of any provision [. . .]; or

        (ii) that such a contravention has taken place, is taking place or is about to take place on any premises; and

    (b) is also satisfied by any such information either—

        (i) that admission to the premises has been or is likely to be refused and that notice of intention to apply for a warrant under this section has been given to the occupier; or

(ii) that an application for admission, or the giving of such a notice, would defeat the object of entry or that the premises are unoccupied or that the occupier is temporarily absent and it might defeat the object of the entry to await his return,

the justice may by warrant under his hand, which shall continue in force for a period of one month, authorise any officer of an enforcement authority to enter the premises, if need be by force.

(3) An officer entering any premises by virtue of section 29 above or a warrant under subsection (2) above may take with him such other persons and such equipment as may appear to him necessary.

(4) On leaving any premises which a person is authorised to enter by a warrant under subsection (2) above, that person shall, if the premises are unoccupied or the occupier is temporarily absent, leave the premises as effectively secured against trespassers as he found them.

(5) If any person who is not an officer of an enforcement authority purports to act as such under section 29 above of this section he shall be guilty of an offence and liable on summary conviction to a fine not exceeding level 5 on the standard scale.

(6) Where any goods seized by an officer under section 29 above are submitted to a test, the officer shall inform the persons mentioned in subsection (1) above of the result of the test and, if—

(a) proceedings are brought for an offence in respect of a contravention in relation to the goods of any safety provision [...] or for the forfeiture of the goods under section 16 or 17 above, or a suspension notice is served in respect of any goods; and

(b) the officer is requested to do so and it is practicable to comply with the request,

the officer shall allow any person who is a party to the proceedings or, as the case may be, has an interest in the goods to which the notice relates to have the goods tested.

(7) The Secretary of State may by regulations provide that any test of goods seized under section 29 above by an officer of an enforcement authority shall—

(a) be carried out at the expense of the authority in a manner and by a person prescribed by or determined under the regulations; or

(b) be carried out either as mentioned in paragraph (a) above or by the authority in a manner prescribed by the regulations.

(8) The power to make regulations under subsection (7) above shall be exercisable by statutory instrument subject to annulment in pursuance of a resolution of either House of Parliament and shall include power—

(a) to make different provision for different cases; and

(b) to make such supplemental, consequential and transitional provisions as the Secretary of State considers appropriate.

(9) In the application of this section to Scotland, the reference in subsection (2) above to a justice of the peace shall include a reference to a sheriff and the references to written information on oath shall be construed as references to evidence on oath.

(10) In the application of this section to Northern Ireland, the references in subsection (2) above to any information on oath shall be construed as references to any complaint on oath.

31 Power of customs officer to detain goods

(1) A customs officer may, for the purpose of facilitating the exercise by an enforcement authority or officer of such an authority of any functions conferred on the authority or officer by or under Part II of this Act, or by or under this Part in its application for the purposes of the safety provisions, seize any imported goods and detain them for not more than two working days.

(2) Anything seized and detained under this section shall be dealt with during the period of its detention in such manner as the Commissioners of Customs and Excise may direct.

(3) In subsection (1) above the reference to two working days is a reference to a period of forty-eight hours calculated from the time when the goods in question are seized but disregarding so much of any period as falls on a Saturday or Sunday or on Christmas Day, Good Friday or a day which is a bank holiday under the Banking and Financial Dealings Act 1971 in the part of the United Kingdom where the goods are seized.

(4) In this section and section 32 below 'customs officer' means any officer within the meaning of the Customs and Excise Management Act 1979.

32   Obstruction of authorised officer

(1) Any person who—

    (a) intentionally obstructs any officer of an enforcement authority who is acting in pursuance of any provision of this Part or any customs officer who is so acting; or

    (b) intentionally fails to comply with any requirements made of him by any officer of an enforcement authority under any provision of this Part, or

    (c) without reasonable cause fails to give any officer of an enforcement authority who is so acting any other assistance or information which the officer may reasonably require of him for the purposes of the exercise of the officer's functions under any provision of this Part,

shall be guilty of an offence and liable on summary conviction to a fine not exceeding level 5 on the standard scale.

(2) A person shall be guilty of an offence if, in giving any information which is required of him by virtue of subsection (1)(c) above—

    (a) he makes any statement which he knows is false in a material particular, or

    (b) he recklessly makes a statement which is false in a material particular.

(3) A person guilty of an offence under subsection (2) above shall be liable—

    (a) on conviction on indictment to a fine;

    (b) on summary conviction, to a fine not exceeding the statutory maximum.

33   Appeals against detention of goods

(1) Any person having an interest in any goods which are for the time being detained under any provision of this Part by an enforcement authority or by an officer of such an authority may apply for an order requiring the goods to be released to him or to another person.

(2) An application under this section may be made—

    (a) to any magistrates' court in which proceedings have been brought in England and Wales or Northern Ireland—

        (i) for an offence in respect of a contravention in relation to the goods of any safety provision [...]; or

        (ii) for the forfeiture of the goods under section 16 above;

    (b) where no such proceedings have been so brought, by way of complaint to a magistrates' court; or

    (c) makes an order under section 16 or 17 above for the forfeiture of any goods.

34   Compensation for seizure and detention

(1) Where an officer of an enforcement authority exercises any power under section 29 above to seize and detain goods, the enforcement authority shall be liable to pay compensation to any person having an interest in the goods in respect of any loss or damage caused by reason of the exercise of the power if—

    (a) there has been no contravention in relation to the goods of any safety provision [...]; and

    (b) the exercise of the power is not attributable to any neglect or default by that person.

(2) Any disputed question as to the right to or the amount of any compensation payable under this section shall be determined by arbitration ...

35   Recovery of expenses of enforcement

(2) The court may (in addition to any other order it may make as to costs or expenses) order the person convicted or, as the case may be, any person having an interest in the goods to reimburse an enforcement authority for any expenditure which has been or may be incurred by that authority—

    (a) in connection with any seizure or detention of the goods by or on behalf of the authority; or

(b) in connection with any compliance by the authority with directions given by the court for the purposes of any order for the forfeiture of the goods.

PART V MISCELLANEOUS AND SUPPLEMENTAL

37 [Power of Commissioners for Revenue and Customs to disclose information]

(1) If they think it appropriate to do so for the purpose of facilitating the exercise by any person to whom subsection (2) below applies of any function conferred on that person by or under Part II of this Act, or by or under Part IV of this Act in its application for the purposes of the safety provisions, [the Commissioners for Her Majesty's Revenue and Customs] may authorise the disclosure to that person of any information obtained [or held] for the purposes of the exercise [by Her Majesty's Revenue and Customs] of their functions in relation to imported goods.

(2) This subsection applies to an enforcement authority and to any officer of an enforcement authority.

(3) A disclosure of information made to any person under subsection (1) above shall be made in such manner as may be directed by [the Commissioners for Her Majesty's Revenue and Customs] and may be through such persons acting on behalf of that person as may be so directed.

(4) Information may be disclosed to a person under subsection (1) above whether or not the disclosure of the information has been requested by or on behalf of that person.

39 Defence of due diligence

(1) Subject to the following provisions of this section, in proceedings against any person for an offence to which this section applies it shall be a defence for that person to show that he took all reasonable steps and exercised all due diligence to avoid committing the offence.

(2) Where in any proceedings against any person for such an offence the defence provided by subsection (1) above involves an allegation that the commission of the offence was due—

(a) to the act or default of another; or

(b) to reliance on information given by another,

that person shall not, without the leave of the court, be entitled to rely on the defence unless, not less than seven clear days before the hearing of the proceedings, he has served a notice under subsection (3) below on the person bringing the proceedings.

(3) A notice under this subsection shall give such information identifying or assisting in the identification of the person who committed the act or default or gave the information as is in the possession of the person serving the notice at the time he serves it.

(4) It is hereby declared that a person shall not be entitled to rely on the defence provided by subsection (1) above by reason of his reliance on information supplied by another, unless he shows that it was reasonable in all the circumstances for him to have relied on the information, having regard in particular—

(a) to the steps which he took, and those which might reasonably have been taken, for the purpose of verifying the information, and

(b) to whether he had any reason to disbelieve the information.

(5) This section shall apply to an offence under section [...] 12(1), (2) or (3), 13(4) [or 14(6)] above.

40 Liability of persons other than principal offender

(1) Where the commission by any person of an offence to which section 39 above applies is due to an act or default committed by some other person in the course of any business of his, the other person shall be guilty of the offence and may be proceeded against and punished by virtue of this subsection whether or not proceedings are taken against the first-mentioned person.

(2) Where a body corporate is guilty of an offence under this Act (including where it is so guilty by virtue of subsection (1) above) in respect of any act or default which is shown to have been committed with the consent or connivance of, or to be attributable to any neglect on the part of, any director, manager, secretary or other similar officer of the body corporate or any person who was purporting to act in any such capacity he, as well as the body corporate, shall be guilty of that offence and shall be liable to be proceeded against and punished accordingly.

(3) Where the affairs of a body corporate are managed by its members, subsection (2) above shall apply in relation to the acts and defaults of a member in connection with his functions of management as if he were a director of the body corporate.

41   Civil proceedings

(1) An obligation imposed by safety regulations shall be a duty owed to any person who may be affected by a contravention of the obligation and, subject to any provisions to the contrary in the regulations and to the defences and other incidents applying to actions for breach of statutory duty, a contravention of any such obligation shall be actionable accordingly.

(2) This Act shall not be construed as conferring any other right of action in civil proceedings, apart from the right conferred by virtue of Part I of this Act, in respect of any loss or damage suffered in consequence of a contravention of a safety provision [...].

(3) Subject to any provision to the contrary in the agreement itself, an agreement shall not be void or unenforceable by reason only of a contravention of a safety provision [...].

(4) Liability by virtue of subsection (1) above shall not be limited or excluded by any contract term, by any notice or (subject to the power contained in subsection (1) above to limit or exclude it in safety regulations) by any other provision.

(5) Nothing in subsection (1) above shall prejudice the operation of section 12 of the Nuclear Installations Act 1965 (rights to compensation for certain breaches of duties confined to rights under that Act).

(6) In this section 'damage' includes personal injury and death.

42   Reports etc.

(1) It shall be the duty of the Secretary of State at least once in every five years to lay before each House of Parliament a report on the exercise during the period to which the report relates of the functions which under Part II of this Act, or under Part IV of this Act in its application for the purposes of the safety provisions, are exercisable by the Secretary of State, weights and measures authorities, district councils in Northern Ireland and persons on whom functions are conferred by regulations made under section 27(2) above.

(2) The Secretary of State may from time to time prepare and lay before each House of Parliament such other reports on the exercise of those functions as he considers appropriate.

(3) Every weights and measures authority, every district council in Northern Ireland and every person on whom functions are conferred by regulations under subsection (2) of section 27 above shall, whenever the Secretary of State so directs, make a report to the Secretary of State on the exercise of the functions exercisable by that authority or council under that section or by that person by virtue of any such regulations.

(4) A report under subsection (3) above shall be in such form and shall contain such particulars as are specified in the direction of the Secretary of State.

(5) The first report under subsection (1) above shall be laid before each House of Parliament not more than five years after the laying of the last report under section 8(2) of the Consumer Safety Act 1978.

43   Financial provisions

(1) There shall be paid out of money provided by Parliament—

(a) any expenses incurred or compensation payable by a Minister of the Crown or Government department in consequence of any provision of this Act; and

(b) any increase attributable to this Act in the sums payable out of money so provided under any other Act.

(2) Any sums received by a Minister of the Crown or Government department by virtue of this Act shall be paid into the Consolidated Fund.

44 Service of documents etc.

(1) Any documents required or authorised by virtue of this Act to be served on a person may be so served—

(a) by delivering it to him or by leaving it at his proper address or by sending it by post to him at that address; or

(b) if the person is a body corporate, by serving it in accordance with paragraph (a) above on the secretary or clerk of that body; or

(c) if the person is a partnership, by serving it in accordance with that paragraph on a partner or on a person having control or management of the partnership business.

(2) For the purposes of subsection (1) above, and for the purposes of section 7 of the Interpretation Act 1978 (which relates to the service of documents by post) in its application to that subsection, the proper address of any person on whom a document is to be served by virtue of this Act shall be his last known address except that—

(a) in the case of service on a body corporate or its secretary or clerk, it shall be the address of the registered or principal office of the body corporate;

(b) in the case of service on a partnership or a partner or a person having the control or management of a partnership business, it shall be the principal office of the partnership; and for the purposes of this subsection the principal office of a company registered outside the United Kingdom or of a partnership carrying on business outside the United Kingdom is its principal office within the United Kingdom.

(3) The Secretary of State may by regulations make provision for the manner in which any information is to be given to any person under any provision of Part IV of this Act.

(4) Without prejudice to the generality of subsection (3) above regulations made by the Secretary of State may prescribe the person, or manner of determining the person, who is to be treated for the purposes of section 28(2) or 30 above as the person from whom goods were purchased or seized where the goods were purchased or seized from a vending machine.

(5) The power to make regulations under subsection (3) or (4) above shall be exercisable by statutory instrument subject to annulment in pursuance of a resolution of either House of Parliament and shall include power—

(a) to make different provision for different cases; and

(b) to make such supplemental, consequential and transitional provision as the Secretary of State considers appropriate.

45 Interpretation

(1) In this Act, expect in so far as the context otherwise requires—

'aircraft' includes gliders, balloons and hovercraft;

'business' includes a trade or profession and the activities of a professional or trade association or of a local authority or other public authority;

'conditional sale agreement', 'credit-sale agreement' and 'hire-purchase agreement' have the same meanings as in the Consumer Credit Act 1974 but as if in the definitions in that Act 'goods' had the same meaning as in this Act;

'contravention' includes a failure to comply and cognate expressions shall be construed accordingly;

'enforcement authority' means the Secretary of State, any other Minister of the Crown in charge of a Government department, any such department and any authority, council or other person on whom functions under this Act are conferred by or under section 27 above;

'gas' has the same meaning as in Part I of the Gas Act 1986;

'goods' includes substances, growing crops and things comprised in land by virtue of being attached to it and any ship, aircraft or vehicle;

'information' includes accounts, estimates and returns;

'magistrates' court', in relation to Northern Ireland, means a court of summary jurisdiction;

'modifications' includes additions, alterations and omissions, and cognate expressions shall be construed accordingly;

'motor vehicle' has the same meaning as in [the Road Traffic Act 1988];

'notice' means a notice in writing;

'notice to warn' means a notice under section 13(1)(b) above;

'officer', in relation to an enforcement authority, means a person authorised in writing to assist the authority in carrying out its functions under or for the purposes of the enforcement of any of the safety provisions or of any of the provisions made by or under Part III of this Act;

'personal injury' includes any disease and any other impairment of a person's physical or mental condition;

'premises' includes any place and any ship, aircraft or vehicle;

'prohibition notice' means a notice under section 13(1)(a) above;

'records' includes any books or documents and any records in non-documentary form;

'safety provision' means [...] any provision of safety regulations, a prohibition notice or a suspension notice;

'safety regulations' means regulations under section 11 above;

'ship' includes any boat and any other description of vessel used in navigation;

'subordinate legislation' has the same meaning as in the Interpretation Act 1978;

'substance' means any natural or artificial substance, whether in solid, liquid or gaseous form or in the form of a vapour, and includes substances that are comprised in or mixed with other goods;

'supply' and cognate expressions shall be construed in accordance with section 46 below;

'suspension notice' means a notice under section 14 above.

(2) Except in so far as the context otherwise requires, references in this Act to a contravention of a safety provision shall, in relation to any goods, include references to anything which would constitute such a contravention if the goods were supplied to any person.

(3) References in this Act to any goods in relation to which any safety provision has been or may have been contravened shall include references to any goods which it is not reasonably practicable to separate from any such goods.

(5) In Scotland, any reference in this Act to things comprised in land by virtue of being attached to it is a reference to moveables which have become heritable by accession to heritable property.

46 Meaning of 'supply'

(1) Subject to the following provisions of this section, references in this Act to supplying goods shall be construed as references to doing any of the following, whether as principal or agent, that is to say—

(a) selling, hiring out or lending the goods;

(b) entering into a hire-purchase agreement to furnish the goods;

(c) the performance of any contract for work and materials to furnish the goods;

(d) providing the goods in exchange for any consideration [...] other than money;

(e) providing the goods in or in connection with the performance of any statutory function; or

(f) giving the goods as a prize or otherwise making a gift of the goods;

and, in relation to gas or water, those references shall be construed as including references to providing the service by which the gas or water is made available for use.

(2) For the purposes of any reference in this Act to supplying goods, where a person ('the ostensible supplier') supplies goods to another person ('the customer') under a hire-purchase

agreement, conditional sale agreement or credit-sale agreement or under an agreement for the hiring of goods (other than a hire-purchase agreement) and the ostensible supplier—

    (a) carries on the business of financing the provision of goods for others by means of such agreements; and

    (b) in the course of that business acquired his interest in the goods supplied to the customer as a means of financing the provision of them for the customer by a further person ('the effective supplier'),

the effective supplier and not the ostensible supplier shall be treated as supplying the goods to the customer.

(3) Subject to subsection (4) below, the performance of any contract by the erection of any building or structure on any land or by the carrying out of any other building works shall be treated for the purposes of this Act as a supply of goods in so far as, but only in so far as, it involves the provision of any goods to any person by means of their incorporation into the building, structure or works.

(4) Except for the purposes of, and in relation to, notices to warn [...], references in this Act to supplying goods shall not include references to supplying goods comprised in land where the supply is effected by the creation or disposal of an interest in the land.

(5) Except in Part I of this Act references in this Act to a person's supplying goods shall be confined to references to that person's supplying goods in the course of a business of his, but for the purposes of this subsection it shall be immaterial whether the business is a business of dealing in the goods.

(6) For the purposes of subsection (5) above goods shall not be treated as supplied in the course of a business if they are supplied, in pursuance of an obligation arising under or in connection with the insurance of the goods, to the person with whom they were insured.

(7) Except for the purposes of, and in relation to, prohibition notices or suspension notices, references in [Part 2 or Part 4] of this Act to supplying goods shall not include—

    (a) references to supplying goods where the person supplied carries on a business of buying goods of the same description as those goods and repairing or reconditioning them,

    (b) references to supplying goods by a sale of articles as scrap (that is to say, for the value of materials included in the articles rather that for the value of the articles themselves).

(8) Where any goods have at any time been supplied by being hired out or lent to any person, neither a continuation or renewal of the hire or loan (whether on the same or different terms) nor any transaction for the transfer after that time of any interest in the goods to the person to whom they were hired or lent shall be treated for the purposes of this Act as a further supply of the goods to that person.

(9) A ship, aircraft or motor vehicle shall not be treated for the purposes of this Act as supplied to any person by reason only that services consisting in the carriage of goods or passengers in that ship, aircraft or vehicle, or in its use for any other purpose, are provided to that person in pursuance of an agreement relating to the use of the ship, aircraft or vehicle for a particular period or for particular voyages, flights or journeys.

47   Savings for certain privileges

(1) Nothing in this Act shall be taken as requiring any person to produce any records if he would be entitled to refuse to produce those records in any proceedings in any court on the ground that they are the subject of legal professional privilege or, in Scotland, that they contain a confidential communication made by or to an advocate or solicitor in that capacity, or as authorising any person to take possession of any records which are in the possession of a person who would be so entitled.

(2) Nothing in this Act shall be construed as requiring a person to answer any question or give any information if to do so would incriminate that person or that person's spouse [or civil partner].

Section 13

SCHEDULE 2

PROHIBITION NOTICES AND NOTICES TO WARN

PART I PROHIBITION NOTICES

1. A prohibition notice in respect of any goods shall—
   (a) state that the Secretary of State considers that the goods are unsafe;
   (b) set out the reasons why the Secretary of State considers that the goods are unsafe;
   (c) specify the day on which the notice is to come into force; and
   (d) state that the trader may at any time make representations in writing to the Secretary of State for the purpose of establishing that the goods are safe.

2.—(1) If representations in writing about a prohibition notice are made by the trader to the Secretary of State, it shall be the duty of the Secretary of State to consider whether to revoke the notice and—
   (a) if he decides to revoke it, to do so;
   (b) in any other case, to appoint a person to consider those representations, any further representations made (whether in writing or orally) by the trader about the notice and the statements of any witnesses examined under this Part of this Schedule.

(2) Where the Secretary of State has appointed a person to consider representations about a prohibition notice, he shall serve a notification on the trader which—
   (a) states that the trader may make oral representations to the appointed person for the purpose of establishing that the goods to which the notice relates are safe; and
   (b) specifies the place and time at which the oral representations may be made.

(3) The time specified in a notification served under sub-paragraph (2) above shall not be before the end of the period of twenty-one days beginning with the day on which the notification is served, unless the trader otherwise agrees.

(4) A person on whom a notification has been served under sub-paragraph (2) above or his representative may, at the place and time specified in the notification—
   (a) make oral representations to the appointed person for the purpose of establishing that the goods in question are safe; and
   (b) call and examine witnesses in connection with representations.

3.—(1) Where representations in writing about a prohibition notice are made by the trader to the Secretary of State at any time after a person has been appointed to consider representations about that notice, then, whether or not the appointed person has made a report to the Secretary of State, the following provisions of this paragraph shall apply instead of paragraph 2 above.

(2) The Secretary of State shall, before the end of the period of one month beginning with the day on which he receives the representations, serve a notification on the trader which states—
   (a) that the Secretary of State has decided to revoke the notice, has decided to vary it or, as the case may be, has decided neither to revoke nor to vary it; or
   (b) that, a person having been appointed to consider representations about the notice, the trader may, at a place and time specified in the notification, make oral representations to the appointed person for the purpose of establishing that the goods to which the notice relates are safe.

(3) The time specified in a notification served for the purposes of sub-paragraph (2)(b) above shall not be before the end of the period of twenty-one days beginning with the day on which the notification is served, unless the trader otherwise agrees or the time is the time already specified for the purposes of paragraph 2(2)(b) above.

(4) A person on whom a notification has been served for the purposes of sub-paragraph (2)(b) above or his representative may, at the place and time specified in the notification—

(a) make oral representations to the appointed person for the purpose of establishing that the goods in question are safe; and

(b) call and examine witnesses in connection with the representations.

4.—(1) Where a person is appointed to consider representations about a prohibition notice, it shall be his duty to consider—

(a) any written representations made by the trader about the notice, other than those in respect of which a notification is served under paragraph 3(2)(a) above;

(b) any oral representations made under paragraph 2(4) or 3(4) above; and

(c) any statements made by witnesses in connection with the oral representations,

and, after considering any matters under this paragraph, to make a report (including recommendations) to the Secretary of State about the matters considered by him and the notice.

(2) It shall be the duty of the Secretary of State to consider any report made to him under subparagraph (1) above and, after considering the report, to inform the trader of his decision with respect to the prohibition notice to which the report relates.

5.—(1) The Secretary of State may revoke or vary a prohibition notice by serving on the trader a notification stating that the notice is revoked or, as the case may be, is varied as specified in the notification.

(2) The Secretary of State shall not vary a prohibition notice so as to make the effect of the notice more restrictive for the trader.

(3) Without prejudice to the power conferred by section 13(2) of this Act, the service of a notification under sub-paragraph (1) above shall be sufficient to satisfy the requirement of paragraph 4(2) above that the trader shall be informed of the Secretary of State's decision.

PART II NOTICES TO WARN

6.—(1) If the Secretary of State proposes to serve a notice to warn on any person in respect of any goods, the Secretary of State, before he serves the notice shall serve on that person a notification which—

(a) contains a draft of the proposed notice;

(b) states that the Secretary of State proposes to serve a notice in the form of the draft on that person;

(c) states that the Secretary of State considers that the goods described in the draft are unsafe;

(d) sets out the reasons why the Secretary of State considers that those goods are unsafe; and

(e) states that that person may make representations to the Secretary of State for the purpose of establishing that the goods are safe if, before the end of the period of fourteen days beginning with the day on which the notification is served, he informs the Secretary of State—

(i) of his intention to make representations; and

(ii) whether the representations will be made only in writing or both in writing and orally.

(2) Where the Secretary of State has served a notification containing a draft of a proposed notice to warn on any person, he shall not serve a notice to warn on that person in respect of the goods to which the proposed notice relates unless—

(a) the period of fourteen days beginning with the day on which the notification was served expires without the Secretary of State being informed as mentioned in sub-paragraph (1)(e) above;

(b) the period of twenty-eight days beginning with that day expires without any written representations being made by that person to the Secretary of State about the proposed notice; or

(c) the Secretary of State has considered a report about the proposed notice by a person appointed under paragraph 7(1) below.

7.—(1) Where a person on whom a notification containing a draft of a proposed notice to warn has been served—

    (a) informs the Secretary of State as mentioned in paragraph 6(1)(e) above before the end of the period of fourteen days beginning with the day on which the notification was served; and

    (b) makes written representations to the Secretary of State about the proposed notice before the end of the period of twenty-eight days beginning with that day,

the Secretary of State shall appoint a person to consider those representations, any further representations made by that person about the draft notice and the statements of any witnesses examined under this Part of this Schedule.

(2) Where—

    (a) the Secretary of State has appointed a person to consider representations about a proposed notice to warn; and

    (b) the person whose representations are to be considered has informed the Secretary of State for the purposes of paragraph 6(1)(e) above that the representations he intends to make will include oral representations,

the Secretary of State shall inform the person intending to make the representations of the place and time at which oral representations may be made to the appointed person.

(3) Where a person on whom a notification containing a draft of a proposed notice to warn has been served is informed of a time for the purposes of sub-paragraph (2) above, that time shall not be—

    (a) before the end of the period of twenty-eight days beginning with the day on which the notification was served; or

    (b) before the end of the period of seven days beginning with the day on which that person is informed of the time.

(4) A person who has been informed of a place and time for the purposes of sub-paragraph (2) above or his representative may, at that place and time—

    (a) make oral representations to the appointed person for the purpose of establishing that the goods to which the proposed notice relates are safe; and

    (b) call and examine witnesses in connection with the representations.

8.—(1) Where a person is appointed to consider representations about a proposed notice to warn, it shall be his duty to consider—

    (a) any written representations made by the person on whom it is proposed to serve the notice; and

    (b) in a case where a place and time has been appointed under paragraph 7(2) above for oral representations to be made by that person or his representative, any representations so made and any statements made by witnesses in connection with those representations,

and, after considering those matters to make a report (including recommendations) to the Secretary of State about the matters considered by him and the proposal to serve the notice.

(2) It shall be the duty of the Secretary of State to consider any report made to him under sub-paragraph (1) above, and after considering the report, to inform the person on whom it was proposed that a notice to warn should be served of his decision with respect to the proposal.

(3) If at any time after serving a notification on a person under paragraph 6 above the Secretary of State decides not to serve on that person either the proposed notice to warn or that notice with modifications, the Secretary of State shall inform that person of the decision, and nothing done for the purposes of any of the preceding provisions of this Part
of this Schedule before that person was so informed shall—

    (a) entitle the Secretary of State subsequently to serve the proposed notice or the notice with modifications; or

    (b) require the Secretary of State, or any person appointed to consider representations about the proposed notice, subsequently to do anything in respect of, or in consequence of, any such representations.

(4) Where a notification containing a draft of a proposed notice to warn is served on a person in respect of any goods, a notice to warn served on him in consequence of a decision made under sub-paragraph (2) above shall either be in the form of the draft or shall be less onerous than the draft.

9. The Secretary of State may revoke a notice to warn by serving on the person on whom the notice was served a notification stating that the notice is revoked.

PART III GENERAL

10.—(1) Where in a notification served on any person under this Schedule the Secretary of State has appointed a time for the making of oral representations or the examination of witnesses, he may, by giving that person such notification as the Secretary of State considers appropriate, change that time to a later time or appoint further times at which further representations may be made or the examination of witnesses may be continued; and paragraphs 2(4), 3(4) and 7(4) above shall have effect accordingly.

(2) For the purposes of this Schedule the Secretary of State may appoint a person (instead of the appointed person) to consider any representations or statements, if the person originally appointed, or last appointed under this sub-paragraph, to consider those representations or statements has died or appears to the Secretary of State to be otherwise unable to act.

11. In this Schedule—

'the appointed person' in relation to a prohibition notice or a proposal to serve a notice to warn, means the person for the time being appointed under this Schedule to consider representations about the notice or, as the case may be, about the proposed notice;

'notification' means a notification in writing;

'trader', in relation to a prohibition notice, means the person on whom the notice is or was served.

Carriage of Goods by Sea Act 1992

(1992, c. 50)

1 Shipping documents etc. to which Act applies

(1) This Act applies to the following documents, that is to say—

    (a) any bill of lading;

    (b) any sea waybill; and

    (c) any ship's delivery order.

(2) References in this Act to a bill of lading—

    (a) do not include references to a document which is incapable of transfer either by indorsement or, as a bearer bill, by delivery without indorsement; but

    (b) subject to that, do include references to a received for shipment bill of lading.

(3) References in this Act to a sea waybill are references to any document which is not a bill of lading but—

    (a) is such a receipt for goods as contains or evidences a contract for the carriage of goods by sea; and

    (b) identifies the person to whom delivery of the goods is to be made by the carrier in accordance with that contract.

(4) References in this Act to a ship's delivery order are references to any document which is neither a bill of lading nor a sea waybill but contains an undertaking which—

    (a) is given under or for the purposes of a contract for the carriage by sea of the goods to which the document relates, or of goods which include those goods; and

(b) is an undertaking by the carrier to a person identified in the document to deliver the goods to which the document relates to that person.

(5) The Secretary of State may by regulations make provision for the application of this Act to cases where [an electronic communications network] or any other information technology is used for effecting transactions corresponding to—

(a) the issue of a document to which this Act applies;

(b) the indorsement, delivery or other transfer of such a document; or

(c) the doing of anything else in relation to such a document.

(6) Regulations under subsection (5) above may—

(a) make such modifications of the following provisions of this Act as the Secretary of State considers appropriate in connection with the application of this Act to any case mentioned in that subsection; and

(b) contain supplemental, incidental, consequential and transitional provision;

and the power to make regulations under that subsection shall be exercisable by statutory instrument subject to annulment in pursuance of a resolution of either House of Parliament.

2 Rights under shipping documents

(1) Subject to the following provisions of this section, a person who becomes—

(a) the lawful holder of a bill of lading;

(b) the person who (without being an original party to the contract of carriage) is the person to whom delivery of the goods to which a sea waybill relates is to be made by the carrier in accordance with that contract; or

(c) the person to whom delivery of the goods to which a ship's delivery order relates is to be made in accordance with the undertaking contained in the order,

shall (by virtue of becoming the holder of the bill or, as the case may be, the person to whom delivery is to be made) have transferred to and vested in him all rights of suit under the contract of carriage as if he had been a party to that contract.

(2) Where, when a person becomes the lawful holder of a bill of lading, possession of the bill no longer gives a right (as against the carrier) to possession of the goods to which the bill relates, that person shall not have any rights transferred to him by virtue of subsection (1) above unless he becomes the holder of the bill—

(a) by virtue of a transaction effected in pursuance of any contractual or other arrangements made before the time when such a right to possession ceased to attach to possession of the bill; or

(b) as a result of the rejection to that person by another person of goods or documents delivered to the other person in pursuance of any such arrangements.

(3) The rights vested in any person by virtue of the operation of subsection (1) above in relation to a ship's delivery order—

(a) shall be so vested subject to the terms of the order; and

(b) where the goods to which the order relates form a part only of the goods to which the contract of carriage relates, shall be confined to rights in respect of the goods to which the order relates.

(4) Where, in the case of any document to which this Act applies—

(a) a person with any interest or right in or in relation to goods to which the document relates sustains loss or damage in consequence of a breach of the contract of carriage; but

(b) subsection (1) above operates in relation to that document so that rights of suit in respect of that breach are vested in another person,

the other person shall be entitled to exercise those rights for the benefit of the person who sustained the loss or damage to the same extent as they could have been exercised if they had been vested in the person for whose benefit they are exercised.

(5) Where rights are transferred by virtue of the operation of subsection (1) above in relation to any document, the transfer for which that subsection provides shall extinguish any entitlement to those rights which derives—

(a) where that document is a bill of lading, from a person's having been an original party to the contract of carriage; or

(b) in the case of any document to which this Act applies, from the previous operation of that subsection in relation to that document;

but the operation of that subsection shall be without prejudice to any rights which derive from a person's having been an original party to the contract contained in, or evidenced by, a sea waybill and, in relation to a ship's delivery order, shall be without prejudice to any rights deriving otherwise than from the previous operation of that subsection in relation to that order.

3   Liabilities under shipping documents

(1) Where subsection (1) of section 2 of this Act operates in relation to any document to which this Act applies and the person in whom rights are vested by virtue of that subsection—

(a) takes or demands delivery from the carrier of any of the goods to which the document relates;

(b) makes a claim under the contract of carriage against the carrier in respect of any of those goods; or

(c) is a person who, at a time before those rights were vested in him, took or demanded delivery from the carrier of any of those goods,

that person shall (by virtue of taking or demanding delivery or making the claim or, in a case falling within paragraph (c) above, of having the rights vested in him) become subject to the same liabilities under that contract as if he had been a party to that contract.

(2) Where the goods to which a ship's delivery order relates form a part only of the goods to which the contract of carriage relates, the liabilities to which any person is subject by virtue of the operation of this section in relation to that order shall exclude liabilities in respect of any goods to which the order does not relate.

(3) This section, so far as it imposes liabilities under any contract on any person, shall be without prejudice to the liabilities under the contract of any person as an original party to the contract.

4   Representations in bills of lading

A bill of lading which—

(a) represents goods to have been shipped on board a vessel or to have been received for shipment on board a vessel; and

(b) has been signed by the master of the vessel or by a person who was not the master but had the express, implied or apparent authority of the carrier to sign bills of lading,

shall, in favour of a person who has become the lawful holder of the bill, be conclusive evidence against the carrier of the shipment of the goods or, as the case may be, of their receipt for shipment.

5   Interpretation etc.

(1) In this Act—

'bill of lading', 'sea waybill' and 'ship's delivery order' shall be construed in accordance with section 1 above;

'the contract of carriage'—

(a) in relation to a bill of lading or sea waybill, means the contract contained in or evidenced by that bill or waybill; and

(b) in relation to a ship's delivery order, means the contract under or for the purposes of which the undertaking contained in the order is given;

'holder', in relation to a bill of lading, shall be construed in accordance with subsection (2) below;

'information technology' includes any computer or other technology by means of which information or other matter may be recorded or communicated without being reduced to documentary form;

[...].

(2) References in this Act to the holder of a bill of lading are references to any of the following persons, that is to say—

(a) a person with possession of the bill who, by virtue of being the person identified in the bill, is the consignee of the goods to which the bill relates;

(b) a person with possession of the bill as a result of the completion, by delivery of the bill, of any indorsement of the bill or, in the case of a bearer bill, of any other transfer of the bill;

(c) a person with possession of the bill as a result of any transaction by virtue of which he would have become a holder falling within paragraph (a) or (b) above had not the transaction been effected at a time when possession of the bill no longer gave a right (as against the carrier) to possession of the goods to which the bill relates;

and a person shall be regarded for the purposes of this Act as having become the lawful holder of a bill of lading wherever he has become the holder of the bill in good faith.

(3) References in this Act to a person's being identified in a document include references to his being identified by a description which allows for the identity of the person in question to be varied, in accordance with the terms of the document, after its issue; and the reference in section 1(3)(b) of this Act to a document's identifying a person shall be construed accordingly.

(4) Without prejudice to sections 2(2) and 4 above, nothing in this Act shall preclude its operation in relation to a case where the goods to which a document relates—

(a) cease to exist after the issue of the document; or

(b) cannot be identified (whether because they are mixed with other goods or for any other reason);

and references in this Act to the goods to which a document relates shall be construed accordingly.

(5) The preceding provisions of this Act shall have effect without prejudice to the application, in relation to any case, of the rules (the Hague-Visby Rules) which for the time being have the force of law by virtue of section 1 of the Carriage of Goods by Sea Act 1971.

6   Short title, repeal, commencement and extent

(4) This Act extends to Northern Ireland.

Arbitration Act 1996

(1996, c. 23)

PART I   ARBITRATION PURSUANT TO AN ARBITRATION AGREEMENT

Introductory

1   General principles

The provisions of this Part are founded on the following principles, and shall be construed accordingly—

(a) the object of arbitration is to obtain the fair resolution of disputes by an impartial tribunal without unnecessary delay or expense;

(b) the parties should be free to agree how their disputes are resolved, subject only to such safeguards as are necessary in the public interest;

(c) in matters governed by this Part the court should not intervene except as provided by this Part.

2   Scope of application of provisions

(1) The provisions of this Part apply where the seat of the arbitration is in England and Wales or Northern Ireland.

(2) The following sections apply even if the seat of the arbitration is outside England and Wales or Northern Ireland or no seat has been designated or determined—

(a) sections 9 to 11 (stay of legal proceedings, &c.), and

(b) section 66 (enforcement of arbitral awards).

(3) The powers conferred by the following sections apply even if the seat of the arbitration is outside England and Wales or Northern Ireland or no seat has been designated or determined—

(a) section 43 (securing the attendance of witnesses), and

(b) section 44 (court powers exercisable in support of arbitral proceedings);

but the court may refuse to exercise any such power if, in the opinion of the court, the fact that the seat of the arbitration is outside England and Wales or Northern Ireland, or that when designated or determined the seat is likely to be outside England and Wales or Northern Ireland, makes it inappropriate to do so.

(4) The court may exercise a power conferred by any provision of this Part not mentioned in subsection (2) or (3) for the purpose of supporting the arbitral process where—

(a) no seat of the arbitration has been designated or determined, and

(b) by reason of a connection with England and Wales or Northern Ireland the court is satisfied that it is appropriate to do so.

(5) Section 7 (separability of arbitration agreement) and section 8 (death of a party) apply where the law applicable to the arbitration agreement is the law of England and Wales or Northern Ireland even if the seat of the arbitration is outside England and Wales or Northern Ireland or has not been designated or determined.

3   The seat of the arbitration

In this Part 'the seat of the arbitration' means the juridical seat of the arbitration designated—

(a) by the parties to the arbitration agreement, or

(b) by any arbitral or other institution or person vested by the parties with powers in that regard, or

(c) by the arbitral tribunal if so authorised by the parties,

or determined, in the absence of any such designation, having regard to the parties' agreement and all the relevant circumstances.

4   Mandatory and non-mandatory provisions

(1) The mandatory provisions of this Part are listed in Schedule 1 and have effect notwithstanding any agreement to the contrary.

(2) The other provisions of this Part (the 'non-mandatory provisions') allow the parties to make their own arrangements by agreement but provide rules which apply in the absence of such agreement.

(3) The parties may make such arrangements by agreeing to the application of institutional rules or providing any other means by which a matter may be decided.

(4) It is immaterial whether or not the law applicable to the parties' agreement is the law of England and Wales or, as the case may be, Northern Ireland.

(5) The choice of a law other than the law of England and Wales or Northern Ireland as the applicable law in respect of a matter provided for by a non-mandatory provision of this Part is equivalent to an agreement making provision about that matter.

For this purpose an applicable law determined in accordance with the parties' agreement, or which is objectively determined in the absence of any express or implied choice, shall be treated as chosen by the parties.

5   Agreements to be in writing

(1) The provisions of this Part apply only where the arbitration agreement is in writing, and any other agreement between the parties as to any matter is effective for the purposes of this Part only if in writing.

The expressions 'agreement', 'agree' and 'agreed' shall be construed accordingly.

(2) There is an agreement in writing—

(a) if the agreement is made in writing (whether or not it is signed by the parties),

(b) if the agreement is made by exchange of communications in writing, or

(c) if the agreement is evidenced in writing.

(3) Where parties agree otherwise than in writing by reference to terms which are in writing, they make an agreement in writing.

(4) An agreement is evidenced in writing if an agreement made otherwise than in writing is recorded by one of the parties, or by a third party, with the authority of the parties to the agreement.

(5) An exchange of written submissions in arbitral or legal proceedings in which the existence of an agreement otherwise than in writing is alleged by one party against another party and not denied by the other party in his response constitutes as between those parties an agreement in writing to the effect alleged.

(6) References in this Part to anything being written or in writing include its being recorded by any means.

6 Definition of arbitration agreement

(1) In this Part an 'arbitration agreement' means an agreement to submit to arbitration present or future disputes (whether they are contractual or not).

(2) The reference in an agreement to a written form of arbitration clause or to a document containing an arbitration clause constitutes an arbitration agreement if the reference is such as to make that clause part of the agreement.

7 Separability of arbitration agreement

Unless otherwise agreed by the parties, an arbitration agreement which forms or was intended to form part of another agreement (whether or not in writing) shall not be regarded as invalid, non-existent or ineffective because that other agreement is invalid, or did not come into existence or has become ineffective, and it shall for that purpose be treated as a distinct agreement.

8 Whether agreement discharged by death of a party

(1) Unless otherwise agreed by the parties, an arbitration agreement is not discharged by the death of a party and may be enforced by or against the personal representatives of that party.

(2) Subsection (1) does not affect the operation of any enactment or rule of law by virtue of which a substantive right or obligation is extinguished by death.

Stay of legal proceedings

9 Stay of legal proceedings

(1) A party to an arbitration agreement against whom legal proceedings are brought (whether by way of claim or counterclaim) in respect of a matter which under the agreement is to be referred to arbitration may (upon notice to the other parties to the proceedings) apply to the court in which the proceedings have been brought to stay the proceedings so far as they concern that matter.

(2) An application may be made notwithstanding that the matter is to be referred to arbitration only after the exhaustion of other dispute resolution procedures.

(3) An application may not be made by a person before taking the appropriate procedural step (if any) to acknowledge the legal proceedings against him or after he has taken any step in those proceedings to answer the substantive claim.

(4) On an application under this section the court shall grant a stay unless satisfied that the arbitration agreement is null and void, inoperative, or incapable of being performed.

(5) If the court refuses to stay the legal proceedings, any provision that an award is a condition precedent to the bringing of legal proceedings in respect of any matter is of no effect in relation to those proceedings.

10 Reference of interpleader issue to arbitration

(1) Where in legal proceedings relief by way of interpleader is granted and any issue between the claimants is one in respect of which there is an arbitration agreement between them, the court granting the relief shall direct that the issue be determined in accordance with the agreement unless the circumstances are such that proceedings brought by a claimant in respect of the matter would not be stayed.

(2) Where subsection (1) applies but the court does not direct that the issue be determined in accordance with the arbitration agreement, any provision that an award is a condition precedent to the bringing of legal proceedings in respect of any matter shall not affect the determination of that issue by the court.

11 Retention of security where Admiralty proceedings stayed

(1) Where Admiralty proceedings are stayed on the ground that the dispute in question should be submitted to arbitration, the court granting the stay may, if in those proceedings property has been arrested or bail or other security has been given to prevent or obtain release from arrest—

    (a) order that the property arrested be retained as security for the satisfaction of any award given in the arbitration in respect of that dispute, or

    (b) order that the stay of those proceedings be conditional on the provision of equivalent security for the satisfaction of any such award.

(2) Subject to any provision made by rules of court and to any necessary modifications, the same law and practice shall apply in relation to property retained in pursuance of an order as would apply if it were held for the purposes of proceedings in the court making the order.

Commencement of arbitral proceedings

12 Power of court to extend time for beginning arbitral proceedings, &c.

(1) Where an arbitration agreement to refer future disputes to arbitration provides that a claim shall be barred, or the claimant's right extinguished, unless the claimant takes within a time fixed by the agreement some step—

    (a) to begin arbitral proceedings, or

    (b) to begin other dispute resolution procedures which must be exhausted before arbitral proceedings can be begun,

the court may by order extend the time for taking that step.

(2) Any party to the arbitration agreement may apply for such an order (upon notice to the other parties), but only after a claim has arisen and after exhausting any available arbitral process for obtaining an extension of time.

(3) The court shall make an order only if satisfied—

    (a) that the circumstances are such as were outside the reasonable contemplation of the parties when they agreed the provision in question, and that it would be just to extend the time, or

    (b) that the conduct of one party makes it unjust to hold the other party to the strict terms of the provision in question.

(4) The court may extend the time for such period and on such terms as it thinks fit, and may do so whether or not the time previously fixed (by agreement or by a previous order) has expired.

(5) An order under this section does not affect the operation of the Limitation Acts (see section 13).

(6) The leave of the court is required for any appeal from a decision of the court under this section.

13 Application of limitation acts

(1) The Limitation Acts apply to arbitral proceedings as they apply to legal proceedings.

(2) The court may order that in computing the time prescribed by the Limitation Acts for the commencement of proceedings (including arbitral proceedings) in respect of a dispute which was the subject matter—

    (a) of an award which the court orders to be set aside or declares to be of no effect, or

(b) of the affected part of an award which the court orders to be set aside in part, or declares to be in part of no effect,

the period between the commencement of the arbitration and the date of the order referred to in paragraph (a) or (b) shall be excluded.

(3) In determining for the purposes of the Limitation Acts when a cause of action accrued, any provision that an award is a condition precedent to the bringing of legal proceedings in respect of a matter to which an arbitration agreement applies shall be disregarded.

(4) In this Part 'the Limitation Acts' means—

(a) in England and Wales, the Limitation Act 1980, the Foreign Limitation Periods Act 1984 and any other enactment (whenever passed) relating to the limitation of actions;

(b) in Northern Ireland, the Limitation (Northern Ireland) Order 1989, the Foreign Limitation Periods (Northern Ireland) Order 1985 and any other enactment (whenever passed) relating to the limitation of actions.

14   Commencement of arbitral proceedings

(1) The parties are free to agree when arbitral proceedings are to be regarded as commenced for the purposes of this Part and for the purposes of the Limitation Acts.

(2) If there is no such agreement the following provisions apply.

(3) Where the arbitrator is named or designated in the arbitration agreement, arbitral proceedings are commenced in respect of a matter when one party serves on the other party or parties a notice in writing requiring him or them to submit that matter to the person so named or designated.

(4) Where the arbitrator or arbitrators are to be appointed by the parties, arbitral proceedings are commenced in respect of a matter when one party serves on the other party or parties notice in writing requiring him or them to appoint an arbitrator or to agree to the appointment of an arbitrator in respect of that matter.

(5) Where the arbitrator or arbitrators are to be appointed by a person other than a party to the proceedings, arbitral proceedings are commenced in respect of a matter when one party gives notice in writing to that person requesting him to make the appointment in respect of that matter.

The arbitral tribunal

15   The arbitral tribunal

(1) The parties are free to agree on the number of arbitrators to form the tribunal and whether there is to be a chairman or umpire.

(2) Unless otherwise agreed by the parties, an agreement that the number of arbitrators shall be two or any other even number shall be understood as requiring the appointment of an additional arbitrator as chairman of the tribunal.

(3) If there is no agreement as to the number of arbitrators, the tribunal shall consist of a sole arbitrator.

16   Procedure for appointment of arbitrators

(1) The parties are free to agree on the procedure for appointing the arbitrator or arbitrators, including the procedure for appointing any chairman or umpire.

(2) If or to the extent that there is no such agreement, the following provisions apply.

(3) If the tribunal is to consist of a sole arbitrator, the parties shall jointly appoint the arbitrator not later than 28 days after service of a request in writing by either party to do so.

(4) If the tribunal is to consist of two arbitrators, each party shall appoint one arbitrator not later than 14 days after service of a request in writing by either party to do so.

(5) If the tribunal is to consist of three arbitrators—

(a) each party shall appoint one arbitrator not later than 14 days after service of a request in writing by either party to do so, and

(b) the two so appointed shall forthwith appoint a third arbitrator as the chairman of the tribunal.

(6) If the tribunal is to consist of two arbitrators and an umpire—

    (a) each party shall appoint one arbitrator not later than 14 days after service of a request in writing by either party to do so, and

    (b) the two so appointed may appoint an umpire at any time after they themselves are appointed and shall do so before any substantive hearing or forthwith if they cannot agree on a matter relating to the arbitration.

(7) In any other case (in particular, if there are more than two parties) section 18 applies as in the case of a failure of the agreed appointment procedure.

17   Power in case of default to appoint sole arbitrator

(1) Unless the parties otherwise agree, where each of two parties to an arbitration agreement is to appoint an arbitrator and one party ('the party in default') refuses to do so, or fails to do so within the time specified, the other party, having duly appointed his arbitrator, may give notice in writing to the party in default that he proposes to appoint his arbitrator to act as sole arbitrator.

(2) If the party in default does not within 7 clear days of that notice being given—

    (a) make the required appointment, and

    (b) notify the other party that he has done so,

the other party may appoint his arbitrator as sole arbitrator whose award shall be binding on both parties as if he had been so appointed by agreement.

(3) Where a sole arbitrator has been appointed under subsection (2), the party in default may (upon notice to the appointing party) apply to the court which may set aside the appointment.

(4) The leave of the court is required for any appeal from a decision of the court under this section.

18   Failure of appointment procedure

(1) The parties are free to agree what is to happen in the event of a failure of the procedure for the appointment of the arbitral tribunal.

There is no failure if an appointment is duly made under section 17 (power in case of default to appoint sole arbitrator), unless that appointment is set aside.

(2) If or to the extent that there is no such agreement any party to the arbitration agreement may (upon notice to the other parties) apply to the court to exercise its powers under this section.

(3) Those powers are—

    (a) to give directions as to the making of any necessary appointments;

    (b) to direct that the tribunal shall be constituted by such appointments (or any one or more of them) as have been made;

    (c) to revoke any appointments already made;

    (d) to make any necessary appointments itself.

(4) An appointment made by the court under this section has effect as if made with the agreement of the parties.

(5) The leave of the court is required for any appeal from a decision of the court under this section.

19   Court to have regard to agreed qualifications

In deciding whether to exercise, and in considering how to exercise, any of its powers under section 16 (procedure for appointment of arbitrators) or section 18 (failure of appointment procedure), the court shall have due regard to any agreement of the parties as to the qualifications required of the arbitrators.

20   Chairman

(1) Where the parties have agreed that there is to be a chairman, they are free to agree what the functions of the chairman are to be in relation to the making of decisions, orders and awards.

(2) If or to the extent that there is no such agreement, the following provisions apply.

(3) Decisions, orders and awards shall be made by all or a majority of the arbitrators (including the chairman).

(4) The view of the chairman shall prevail in relation to a decision, order or award in respect of which there is neither unanimity nor a majority under subsection (3).

21　Umpire

(1) Where the parties have agreed that there is to be an umpire, they are free to agree what the functions of the umpire are to be, and in particular—

(a) whether he is to attend the proceedings, and

(b) when he is to replace the other arbitrators as the tribunal with power to make decisions, orders and awards.

(2) If or to the extent that there is no such agreement, the following provisions apply.

(3) The umpire shall attend the proceedings and be supplied with the same documents and other materials as are supplied to the other arbitrators.

(4) Decisions, orders and awards shall be made by the other arbitrators unless and until they cannot agree on a matter relating to the arbitration.

In that event they shall forthwith give notice in writing to the parties and the umpire, whereupon the umpire shall replace them as the tribunal with power to make decisions, orders and awards as if he were sole arbitrator.

(5) If the arbitrators cannot agree but fail to give notice of that fact, or if any of them fails to join in the giving of notice, any party to the arbitral proceedings may (upon notice to the other parties and to the tribunal) apply to the court which may order that the umpire shall replace the other arbitrators as the tribunal with power to make decisions, orders and awards as if he were sole arbitrator.

(6) The leave of the court is required for any appeal from a decision of the court under this section.

22　Decision-making where no chairman or umpire

(1) Where the parties agree that there shall be two or more arbitrators with no chairman or umpire, the parties are free to agree how the tribunal is to make decisions, orders and awards.

(2) If there is no such agreement, decisions, orders and awards shall be made by all or a majority of the arbitrators.

23　Revocation of arbitrator's authority

(1) The parties are free to agree in what circumstances the authority of an arbitrator may be revoked.

(2) If or to the extent that there is no such agreement the following provisions apply.

(3) The authority of an arbitrator may not be revoked except—

(a) by the parties acting jointly, or

(b) by an arbitral or other institution or person vested by the parties with powers in that regard.

(4) Revocation of the authority of an arbitrator by the parties acting jointly must be agreed in writing unless the parties also agree (whether or not in writing) to terminate the arbitration agreement.

(5) Nothing in this section affects the power of the court—

(a) to revoke an appointment under section 18 (powers exercisable in case of failure of appointment procedure), or

(b) to remove an arbitrator on the grounds specified in section 24.

24　Power of court to remove arbitrator

(1) A party to arbitral proceedings may (upon notice to the other parties, to the arbitrator concerned and to any other arbitrator) apply to the court to remove an arbitrator on any of the following grounds—

(a) that circumstances exist that give rise to justifiable doubts as to his impartiality;

(b) that he does not possess the qualifications required by the arbitration agreement;

(c) that he is physically or mentally incapable of conducting the proceedings or there are justifiable doubts as to his capacity to do so;

    (d) that he has refused or failed—

        (i)   properly to conduct the proceedings, or

        (ii) to use all reasonable despatch in conducting the proceedings or making an award,

and that substantial injustice has been or will be caused to the applicant.

    (2) If there is an arbitral or other institution or person vested by the parties with power to remove an arbitrator, the court shall not exercise its power of removal unless satisfied that the applicant has first exhausted any available recourse to that institution or person.

    (3) The arbitral tribunal may continue the arbitral proceedings and make an award while an application to the court under this section is pending.

    (4) Where the court removes an arbitrator, it may make such order as it thinks fit with respect to his entitlement (if any) to fees or expenses, or the repayment of any fees or expenses already paid.

    (5) The arbitrator concerned is entitled to appear and be heard by the court before it makes any order under this section.

    (6) The leave of the court is required for any appeal from a decision of the court under this section.

25   Resignation of arbitrator

    (1) The parties are free to agree with an arbitrator as to the consequences of his resignation as regards—

        (a) his entitlement (if any) to fees or expenses, and

        (b) any liability thereby incurred by him.

    (2) If or to the extent that there is no such agreement the following provisions apply.

    (3) An arbitrator who resigns his appointment may (upon notice to the parties) apply to the court—

        (a) to grant him relief from any liability thereby incurred by him, and

        (b) to make such order as it thinks fit with respect to his entitlement (if any) to fees or expenses or the repayment of any fees or expenses already paid.

    (4) If the court is satisfied that in all the circumstances it was reasonable for the arbitrator to resign, it may grant such relief as is mentioned in subsection (3)(a) on such terms as it thinks fit.

    (5) The leave of the court is required for any appeal from a decision of the court under this section.

26   Death of arbitrator or person appointing him

    (1) The authority of an arbitrator is personal and ceases on his death.

    (2) Unless otherwise agreed by the parties, the death of the person by whom an arbitrator was appointed does not revoke the arbitrator's authority.

27   Filling of vacancy, &c.

    (1) Where an arbitrator ceases to hold office, the parties are free to agree—

        (a) whether and if so how the vacancy is to be filled,

        (b) whether and if so to what extent the previous proceedings should stand, and

        (c) what effect (if any) his ceasing to hold office has on any appointment made by him (alone or jointly).

    (2) If or to the extent that there is no such agreement, the following provisions apply.

    (3) The provisions of sections 16 (procedure for appointment of arbitrators) and 18 (failure of appointment procedure) apply in relation to the filling of the vacancy as in relation to an original appointment.

    (4) The tribunal (when reconstituted) shall determine whether and if so to what extent the previous proceedings should stand.

This does not affect any right of a party to challenge those proceedings on any ground which had arisen before the arbitrator ceased to hold office.

    (5) His ceasing to hold office does not affect any appointment by him (alone or jointly) of another arbitrator, in particular any appointment of a chairman or umpire.

28   Joint and several liability of parties to arbitrators for fees and expenses

(1) The parties are jointly and severally liable to pay to the arbitrators such reasonable fees and expenses (if any) as are appropriate in the circumstances.

(2) Any party may apply to the court (upon notice to the other parties and to the arbitrators) which may order that the amount of the arbitrators' fees and expenses shall be considered and adjusted by such means and upon such terms as it may direct.

(3) If the application is made after any amount has been paid to the arbitrators by way of fees or expenses, the court may order the repayment of such amount (if any) as is shown to be excessive, but shall not do so unless it is shown that it is reasonable in the circumstances to order repayment.

(4) The above provisions have effect subject to any order of the court under section 24(4) or 25(3)(b) (order as to entitlement to fees or expenses in case of removal or resignation of arbitrator).

(5) Nothing in this section affects any liability of a party to any other party to pay all or any of the costs of the arbitration (see sections 59 to 65) or any contractual right of an arbitrator to payment of his fees and expenses.

(6) In this section references to arbitrators include an arbitrator who has ceased to act and an umpire who has not replaced the other arbitrators.

29   Immunity of arbitrator

(1) An arbitrator is not liable for anything done or omitted in the discharge or purported discharge of his functions as arbitrator unless the act or omission is shown to have been in bad faith.

(2) Subsection (1) applies to an employee or agent of an arbitrator as it applies to the arbitrator himself.

(3) This section does not affect any liability incurred by an arbitrator by reason of his resigning (but see section 25).

Jurisdiction of the arbitral tribunal

30   Competence of tribunal to rule on its own jurisdiction

(1) Unless otherwise agreed by the parties, the arbitral tribunal may rule on its own substantive jurisdiction, that is, as to—

> (a) whether there is a valid arbitration agreement,
> (b) whether the tribunal is properly constituted, and
> (c) what matters have been submitted to arbitration in accordance with the arbitration agreement.

(2) Any such ruling may be challenged by any available arbitral process of appeal or review or in accordance with the provisions of this Part.

31   Objection to substantive jurisdiction of tribunal

(1) An objection that the arbitral tribunal lacks substantive jurisdiction at the outset of the proceedings must be raised by a party not later than the time he takes the first step in the proceedings to contest the merits of any matter in relation to which he challenges the tribunal's jurisdiction.

A party is not precluded from raising such an objection by the fact that he has appointed or participated in the appointment of an arbitrator.

(2) Any objection during the course of the arbitral proceedings that the arbitral tribunal is exceeding its substantive jurisdiction must be made as soon as possible after the matter alleged to be beyond its jurisdiction is raised.

(3) The arbitral tribunal may admit an objection later than the time specified in subsection (1) or (2) if it considers the delay justified.

(4) Where an objection is duly taken to the tribunal's substantive jurisdiction and the tribunal has power to rule on its own jurisdiction, it may—

> (a) rule on the matter in an award as to jurisdiction, or
> (b) deal with the objection in its award on the merits.

If the parties agree which of these courses the tribunal should take, the tribunal shall proceed accordingly.

(5) The tribunal may in any case, and shall if the parties so agree, stay proceedings whilst an application is made to the court under section 32 (determination of preliminary point of jurisdiction).

32 Determination of preliminary point of jurisdiction

(1) The court may, on the application of a party to arbitral proceedings (upon notice to the other parties), determine any question as to the substantive jurisdiction of the tribunal.

A party may lose the right to object (see section 73).

(2) An application under this section shall not be considered unless—
  (a) it is made with the agreement in writing of all the other parties to the proceedings, or
  (b) it is made with the permission of the tribunal and the court is satisfied—
      (i)   that the determination of the question is likely to produce substantial savings in costs,
      (ii) that the application was made without delay, and
      (iii) that there is good reason why the matter should be decided by the court.

(3) An application under this section, unless made with the agreement of all the other parties to the proceedings, shall state the grounds on which it is said that the matter should be decided by the court.

(4) Unless otherwise agreed by the parties, the arbitral tribunal may continue the arbitral proceedings and make an award while an application to the court under this section is pending.

(5) Unless the court gives leave, no appeal lies from a decision of the court whether the conditions specified in subsection (2) are met.

(6) The decision of the court on the question of jurisdiction shall be treated as a judgment of the court for the purposes of an appeal.

But no appeal lies without the leave of the court which shall not be given unless the court considers that the question involves a point of law which is one of general importance or is one which for some other special reason should be considered by the Court of Appeal.

The arbitral proceedings

33 General duty of the tribunal

(1) The tribunal shall—
  (a) act fairly and impartially as between the parties, giving each party a reasonable opportunity of putting his case and dealing with that of his opponent, and
  (b) adopt procedures suitable to the circumstances of the particular case, avoiding unnecessary delay or expense, so as to provide a fair means for the resolution of the matters falling to be determined.

(2) The tribunal shall comply with that general duty in conducting the arbitral proceedings, in its decisions on matters of procedure and evidence and in the exercise of all other powers conferred on it.

34 Procedural and evidential matters

(1) It shall be for the tribunal to decide all procedural and evidential matters, subject to the right of the parties to agree any matter.

(2) Procedural and evidential matters include—
  (a) when and where any part of the proceedings is to be held;
  (b) the language or languages to be used in the proceedings and whether translations of any relevant documents are to be supplied;
  (c) whether any and if so what form of written statements of claim and defence are to be used, when these should be supplied and the extent to which such statements can be later amended;
  (d) whether any and if so which documents or classes of documents should be disclosed between and produced by the parties and at what stage;

    (e) whether any and if so what questions should be put to and answered by the respective parties and when and in what form this should be done;

    (f) whether to apply strict rules of evidence (or any other rules) as to the admissibility, relevance or weight of any material (oral, written or other) sought to be tendered on any matters of fact or opinion, and the time, manner and form in which such material should be exchanged and presented;

    (g) whether and to what extent the tribunal should itself take the initiative in ascertaining the facts and the law;

    (h) whether and to what extent there should be oral or written evidence or submissions.

    (3) The tribunal may fix the time within which any directions given by it are to be complied with, and may if it thinks fit extend the time so fixed (whether or not it has expired).

35   Consolidation of proceedings and concurrent hearings

    (1) The parties are free to agree—

    (a) that the arbitral proceedings shall be consolidated with other arbitral proceedings, or

    (b) that concurrent hearings shall be held,

on such terms as may be agreed.

    (2) Unless the parties agree to confer such power on the tribunal, the tribunal has no power to order consolidation of proceedings or concurrent hearings.

36   Legal or other representation

Unless otherwise agreed by the parties, a party to arbitral proceedings may be represented in the proceedings by a lawyer or other person chosen by him.

37   Power to appoint experts, legal advisers or assessors

    (1) Unless otherwise agreed by the parties—

    (a) the tribunal may—

        (i)   appoint experts or legal advisers to report to it and the parties, or

        (ii) appoint assessors to assist it on technical matters,

        and may allow any such expert, legal adviser or assessor to attend the proceedings; and

    (b) the parties shall be given a reasonable opportunity to comment on any information, opinion or advice offered by any such person.

    (2) The fees and expenses of an expert, legal adviser or assessor appointed by the tribunal for which the arbitrators are liable are expenses of the arbitrators for the purposes of this Part.

38   General powers exercisable by the tribunal

    (1) The parties are free to agree on the powers exercisable by the arbitral tribunal for the purposes of and in relation to the proceedings.

    (2) Unless otherwise agreed by the parties the tribunal has the following powers.

    (3) The tribunal may order a claimant to provide security for the costs of the arbitration. This power shall not be exercised on the ground that the claimant is—

    (a) an individual ordinarily resident outside the United Kingdom, or

    (b) a corporation or association incorporated or formed under the law of a country outside the United Kingdom, or whose central management and control is exercised outside the United Kingdom.

    (4) The tribunal may give directions in relation to any property which is the subject of the proceedings or as to which any question arises in the proceedings, and which is owned by or is in the possession of a party to the proceedings—

    (a) for the inspection, photographing, preservation, custody or detention of the property by the tribunal, an expert or a party, or

    (b) ordering that samples be taken from, or any observation be made of or experiment conducted upon, the property.

(5) The tribunal may direct that a party or witness shall be examined on oath or affirmation, and may for that purpose administer any necessary oath or take any necessary affirmation.

(6) The tribunal may give directions to a party for the preservation for the purposes of the proceedings of any evidence in his custody or control.

39   Power to make provisional awards

(1) The parties are free to agree that the tribunal shall have power to order on a provisional basis any relief which it would have power to grant in a final award.

(2) This includes, for instance, making—

(a) a provisional order for the payment of money or the disposition of property as between the parties, or

(b) an order to make an interim payment on account of the costs of the arbitration.

(3) Any such order shall be subject to the tribunal's final adjudication; and the tribunal's final award, on the merits or as to costs, shall take account of any such order.

(4) Unless the parties agree to confer such power on the tribunal, the tribunal has no such power.

This does not affect its powers under section 47 (awards on different issues, &c.).

40   General duty of parties

(1) The parties shall do all things necessary for the proper and expeditious conduct of the arbitral proceedings.

(2) This includes—

(a) complying without delay with any determination of the tribunal as to procedural or evidential matters, or with any order or directions of the tribunal, and

(b) where appropriate, taking without delay any necessary steps to obtain a decision of the court on a preliminary question of jurisdiction or law (see sections 32 and 45).

41   Powers of tribunal in case of party's default

(1) The parties are free to agree on the powers of the tribunal in case of a party's failure to do something necessary for the proper and expeditious conduct of the arbitration.

(2) Unless otherwise agreed by the parties, the following provisions apply.

(3) If the tribunal is satisfied that there has been inordinate and inexcusable delay on the part of the claimant in pursuing his claim and that the delay—

(a) gives rise, or is likely to give rise, to a substantial risk that it is not possible to have a fair resolution of the issues in that claim, or

(b) has caused, or is likely to cause, serious prejudice to the respondent, the tribunal may make an award dismissing the claim.

(4) If without showing sufficient cause a party—

(a) fails to attend or be represented at an oral hearing of which due notice was given, or

(b) where matters are to be dealt with in writing, fails after due notice to submit written evidence or make written submissions,

the tribunal may continue the proceedings in the absence of that party or, as the case may be, without any written evidence or submissions on his behalf, and may make an award on the basis of the evidence before it.

(5) If without showing sufficient cause a party fails to comply with any order or directions of the tribunal, the tribunal may make a peremptory order to the same effect, prescribing such time for compliance with it as the tribunal considers appropriate.

(6) If a claimant fails to comply with a peremptory order of the tribunal to provide security for costs, the tribunal may make an award dismissing his claim.

(7) If a party fails to comply with any other kind of peremptory order, then, without prejudice to section 42 (enforcement by court of tribunal's peremptory orders), the tribunal may do any of the following—

(a) direct that the party in default shall not be entitled to rely upon any allegation or material which was the subject matter of the order;

(b) draw such adverse inferences from the act of non-compliance as the circumstances justify;

(c) proceed to an award on the basis of such materials as have been properly provided to it;

(d) make such order as it thinks fit as to the payment of costs of the arbitration incurred in consequence of the non-compliance.

Powers of court in relation to arbitral proceedings

42   Enforcement of peremptory orders of tribunal

(1) Unless otherwise agreed by the parties, the court may make an order requiring a party to comply with a peremptory order made by the tribunal.

(2) An application for an order under this section may be made—

(a) by the tribunal (upon notice to the parties),

(b) by a party to the arbitral proceedings with the permission of the tribunal (and upon notice to the other parties), or

(c) where the parties have agreed that the powers of the court under this section shall be available.

(3) The court shall not act unless it is satisfied that the applicant has exhausted any available arbitral process in respect of failure to comply with the tribunal's order.

(4) No order shall be made under this section unless the court is satisfied that the person to whom the tribunal's order was directed has failed to comply with it within the time prescribed in the order or, if no time was prescribed, within a reasonable time.

(5) The leave of the court is required for any appeal from a decision of the court under this section.

43   Securing the attendance of witnesses

(1) A party to arbitral proceedings may use the same court procedures as are available in relation to legal proceedings to secure the attendance before the tribunal of a witness in order to give oral testimony or to produce documents or other material evidence.

(2) This may only be done with the permission of the tribunal or the agreement of the other parties.

(3) The court procedures may only be used if—

(a) the witness is in the United Kingdom, and

(b) the arbitral proceedings are being conducted in England and Wales or, as the case may be, Northern Ireland.

(4) A person shall not be compelled by virtue of this section to produce any document or other material evidence which he could not be compelled to produce in legal proceedings.

44   Court powers exercisable in support of arbitral proceedings

(1) Unless otherwise agreed by the parties, the court has for the purposes of and in relation to arbitral proceedings the same power of making orders about the matters listed below as it has for the purposes of and in relation to legal proceedings.

(2) Those matters are—

(a) the taking of the evidence of witnesses;

(b) the preservation of evidence;

(c) making orders relating to property which is the subject of the proceedings or as to which any question arises in the proceedings—

(i)   for the inspection, photographing, preservation, custody or detention of the property, or

(ii) ordering that samples be taken from, or any observation be made of or experiment conducted upon, the property; and for that purpose authorising any person to enter any premises in the possession or control of a party to the arbitration;

(d) the sale of any goods the subject of the proceedings;

(e) the granting of an interim injunction or the appointment of a receiver.

(3) If the case is one of urgency, the court may, on the application of a party or proposed party to the arbitral proceedings, make such orders as it thinks necessary for the purpose of preserving evidence or assets.

(4) If the case is not one of urgency, the court shall act only on the application of a party to the arbitral proceedings (upon notice to the other parties and to the tribunal) made with the permission of the tribunal or the agreement in writing of the other parties.

(5) In any case the court shall act only if or to the extent that the arbitral tribunal, and any arbitral or other institution or person vested by the parties with power in that regard, has no power or is unable for the time being to act effectively.

(6) If the court so orders, an order made by it under this section shall cease to have effect in whole or in part on the order of the tribunal or of any such arbitral or other institution or person having power to act in relation to the subject-matter of the order.

(7) The leave of the court is required for any appeal from a decision of the court under this section.

45 Determination of preliminary point of law

(1) Unless otherwise agreed by the parties, the court may on the application of a party to arbitral proceedings (upon notice to the other parties) determine any question of law arising in the course of the proceedings which the court is satisfied substantially affects the rights of one or more of the parties.

An agreement to dispense with reasons for the tribunal's award shall be considered an agreement to exclude the court's jurisdiction under this section.

(2) An application under this section shall not be considered unless—

    (a) it is made with the agreement of all the other parties to the proceedings, or

    (b) it is made with the permission of the tribunal and the court is satisfied—

        (i) that the determination of the question is likely to produce substantial savings in costs, and

        (ii) that the application was made without delay.

(3) The application shall identify the question of law to be determined and, unless made with the agreement of all the other parties to the proceedings, shall state the grounds on which it is said that the question should be decided by the court.

(4) Unless otherwise agreed by the parties, the arbitral tribunal may continue the arbitral proceedings and make an award while an application to the court under this section is pending.

(5) Unless the court gives leave, no appeal lies from a decision of the court whether the conditions specified in subsection (2) are met.

(6) The decision of the court on the question of law shall be treated as a judgment of the court for the purposes of an appeal.

But no appeal lies without the leave of the court which shall not be given unless the court considers that the question is one of general importance, or is one which for some other special reason should be considered by the Court of Appeal.

The award

46 Rules applicable to substance of dispute

(1) The arbitral tribunal shall decide the dispute—

    (a) in accordance with the law chosen by the parties as applicable to the substance of the dispute, or

    (b) if the parties so agree, in accordance with such other considerations as are agreed by them or determined by the tribunal.

(2) For this purpose the choice of the laws of a country shall be understood to refer to the substantive laws of that country and not its conflict of laws rules.

(3) If or to the extent that there is no such choice or agreement, the tribunal shall apply the law determined by the conflict of laws rules which it considers applicable.

47   Awards on different issues, &c.

(1) Unless otherwise agreed by the parties, the tribunal may make more than one award at different times on different aspects of the matters to be determined.

(2) The tribunal may, in particular, make an award relating—

(a) to an issue affecting the whole claim, or

(b) to a part only of the claims or cross-claims submitted to it for decision.

(3) If the tribunal does so, it shall specify in its award the issue, or the claim or part of a claim, which is the subject matter of the award.

48   Remedies

(1) The parties are free to agree on the powers exercisable by the arbitral tribunal as regards remedies.

(2) Unless otherwise agreed by the parties, the tribunal has the following powers.

(3) The tribunal may make a declaration as to any matter to be determined in the proceedings.

(4) The tribunal may order the payment of a sum of money, in any currency.

(5) The tribunal has the same powers as the court—

(a) to order a party to do or refrain from doing anything;

(b) to order specific performance of a contract (other than a contract relating to land);

(c) to order the rectification, setting aside or cancellation of a deed or other document.

49   Interest

(1) The parties are free to agree on the powers of the tribunal as regards the award of interest.

(2) Unless otherwise agreed by the parties the following provisions apply.

(3) The tribunal may award simple or compound interest from such dates, at such rates and with such rests as it considers meets the justice of the case—

(a) on the whole or part of any amount awarded by the tribunal, in respect of any period up to the date of the award;

(b) on the whole or part of any amount claimed in the arbitration and outstanding at the commencement of the arbitral proceedings but paid before the award was made, in respect of any period up to the date of payment.

(4) The tribunal may award simple or compound interest from the date of the award (or any later date) until payment, at such rates and with such rests as it considers meets the justice of the case, on the outstanding amount of any award (including any award of interest under subsection (3) and any award as to costs).

(5) References in this section to an amount awarded by the tribunal include an amount payable in consequence of a declaratory award by the tribunal.

(6) The above provisions do not affect any other power of the tribunal to award interest.

50   Extension of time for making award

(1) Where the time for making an award is limited by or in pursuance of the arbitration agreement, then, unless otherwise agreed by the parties, the court may in accordance with the following provisions by order extend that time.

(2) An application for an order under this section may be made—

(a) by the tribunal (upon notice to the parties), or

(b) by any party to the proceedings (upon notice to the tribunal and the other parties), but only after exhausting any available arbitral process for obtaining an extension of time.

(3) The court shall only make an order if satisfied that a substantial injustice would otherwise be done.

(4) The court may extend the time for such period and on such terms as it thinks fit, and may do so whether or not the time previously fixed (by or under the agreement or by a previous order) has expired.

(5) The leave of the court is required for any appeal from a decision of the court under this section.

51   Settlement

(1) If during arbitral proceedings the parties settle the dispute, the following provisions apply unless otherwise agreed by the parties.

(2) The tribunal shall terminate the substantive proceedings and, if so requested by the parties and not objected to by the tribunal, shall record the settlement in the form of an agreed award.

(3) An agreed award shall state that it is an award of the tribunal and shall have the same status and effect as any other award on the merits of the case.

(4) The following provisions of this Part relating to awards (sections 52 to 58) apply to an agreed award.

(5) Unless the parties have also settled the matter of the payment of the costs of the arbitration, the provisions of this Part relating to costs (sections 59 to 65) continue to apply.

52   Form of award

(1) The parties are free to agree on the form of an award.

(2) If or to the extent that there is no such agreement, the following provisions apply.

(3) The award shall be in writing signed by all the arbitrators or all those assenting to the award.

(4) The award shall contain the reasons for the award unless it is an agreed award or the parties have agreed to dispense with reasons.

(5) The award shall state the seat of the arbitration and the date when the award is made.

53   Place where award treated as made

Unless otherwise agreed by the parties, where the seat of the arbitration is in England and Wales or Northern Ireland, any award in the proceedings shall be treated as made there, regardless of where it was signed, despatched or delivered to any of the parties.

54   Date of award

(1) Unless otherwise agreed by the parties, the tribunal may decide what is to be taken to be the date on which the award was made.

(2) In the absence of any such decision, the date of the award shall be taken to be the date on which it is signed by the arbitrator or, where more than one arbitrator signs the award, by the last of them.

55   Notification of award

(1) The parties are free to agree on the requirements as to notification of the award to the parties.

(2) If there is no such agreement, the award shall be notified to the parties by service on them of copies of the award, which shall be done without delay after the award is made.

(3) Nothing in this section affects section 56 (power to withhold award in case of non-payment).

56   Power to withhold award in case of non-payment

(1) The tribunal may refuse to deliver an award to the parties except upon full payment of the fees and expenses of the arbitrators.

(2) If the tribunal refuses on that ground to deliver an award, a party to the arbitral proceedings may (upon notice to the other parties and the tribunal) apply to the court, which may order that—

    (a) the tribunal shall deliver the award on the payment into court by the applicant of the fees and expenses demanded, or such lesser amount as the court may specify,

(b) the amount of the fees and expenses properly payable shall be determined by such means and upon such terms as the court may direct, and

(c) that out of the money paid into court there shall be paid out such fees and expenses as may be found to be properly payable and the balance of the money (if any) shall be paid out to the applicant.

(3) For this purpose the amount of fees and expenses properly payable is the amount the applicant is liable to pay under section 28 or any agreement relating to the payment of the arbitrators.

(4) No application to the court may be made where there is any available arbitral process for appeal or review of the amount of the fees or expenses demanded.

(5) References in this section to arbitrators include an arbitrator who has ceased to act and an umpire who has not replaced the other arbitrators.

(6) The above provisions of this section also apply in relation to any arbitral or other institution or person vested by the parties with powers in relation to the delivery of the tribunal's award.

As they so apply, the references to the fees and expenses of the arbitrators shall be construed as including the fees and expenses of that institution or person.

(7) The leave of the court is required for any appeal from a decision of the court under this section.

(8) Nothing in this section shall be construed as excluding an application under section 28 where payment has been made to the arbitrators in order to obtain the award.

57   Correction of award or additional award

(1) The parties are free to agree on the powers of the tribunal to correct an award or make an additional award.

(2) If or to the extent there is no such agreement, the following provisions apply.

(3) The tribunal may on its own initiative or on the application of a party—

(a) correct an award so as to remove any clerical mistake or error arising from an accidental slip or omission or clarify or remove any ambiguity in the award, or

(b) make an additional award in respect of any claim (including a claim for interest or costs) which was presented to the tribunal but was not dealt with in the award.

These powers shall not be exercised without first affording the other parties a reasonable opportunity to make representations to the tribunal.

(4) Any application for the exercise of those powers must be made within 28 days of the date of the award or such longer period as the parties may agree.

(5) Any correction of an award shall be made within 28 days of the date the application was received by the tribunal or, where the correction is made by the tribunal on its own initiative, within 28 days of the date of the award or, in either case, such longer period as the parties may agree.

(6) Any additional award shall be made within 56 days of the date of the original award or such longer period as the parties may agree.

(7) Any correction of an award shall form part of the award.

58   Effect of award

(1) Unless otherwise agreed by the parties, an award made by the tribunal pursuant to an arbitration agreement is final and binding both on the parties and on any persons claiming through or under them.

(2) This does not affect the right of a person to challenge the award by any available arbitral process of appeal or review or in accordance with the provisions of this Part.

Costs of the arbitration

59   Costs of the arbitration

(1) References in this Part to the costs of the arbitration are to—

(a) the arbitrators' fees and expenses,

(b) the fees and expenses of any arbitral institution concerned, and

(c) the legal or other costs of the parties.

(2) Any such reference includes the costs of or incidental to any proceedings to determine the amount of the recoverable costs of the arbitration (see section 63).

60 Agreement to pay costs in any event

An agreement which has the effect that a party is to pay the whole or part of the costs of the arbitration in any event is only valid if made after the dispute in question has arisen.

61 Award of costs

(1) The tribunal may make an award allocating the costs of the arbitration as between the parties, subject to any agreement of the parties.

(2) Unless the parties otherwise agree, the tribunal shall award costs on the general principle that costs should follow the event except where it appears to the tribunal that in the circumstances this is not appropriate in relation to the whole or part of the costs.

62 Effect of agreement or award about costs

Unless the parties otherwise agree, any obligation under an agreement between them as to how the costs of the arbitration are to be borne, or under an award allocating the costs of the arbitration, extends only to such costs as are recoverable.

63 The recoverable costs of the arbitration

(1) The parties are free to agree what costs of the arbitration are recoverable.

(2) If or to the extent there is no such agreement, the following provisions apply.

(3) The tribunal may determine by award the recoverable costs of the arbitration on such basis as it thinks fit.

If it does so, it shall specify—

    (a) the basis on which it has acted, and

    (b) the items of recoverable costs and the amount referable to each.

(4) If the tribunal does not determine the recoverable costs of the arbitration, any party to the arbitral proceedings may apply to the court (upon notice to the other parties) which may—

    (a) determine the recoverable costs of the arbitration on such basis as it thinks fit, or

    (b) order that they shall be determined by such means and upon such terms as it may specify.

(5) Unless the tribunal or the court determines otherwise—

    (a) the recoverable costs of the arbitration shall be determined on the basis that there shall be allowed a reasonable amount in respect of all costs reasonably incurred, and

    (b) any doubt as to whether costs were reasonably incurred or were reasonable in amount shall be resolved in favour of the paying party.

(6) The above provisions have effect subject to section 64 (recoverable fees and expenses of arbitrators).

(7) Nothing in this section affects any right of the arbitrators, any expert, legal adviser or assessor appointed by the tribunal, or any arbitral institution, to payment of their fees and expenses.

64 Recoverable fees and expenses of arbitrators

(1) Unless otherwise agreed by the parties, the recoverable costs of the arbitration shall include in respect of the fees and expenses of the arbitrators only such reasonable fees and expenses as are appropriate in the circumstances.

(2) If there is any question as to what reasonable fees and expenses are appropriate in the circumstances, and the matter is not already before the court on an application under section 63(4), the court may on the application of any party (upon notice to the other parties)—

    (a) determine the matter, or

    (b) order that it be determined by such means and upon such terms as the court may specify.

(3) Subsection (1) has effect subject to any order of the court under section 24(4) or 25(3)(b) (order as to entitlement to fees or expenses in case of removal or resignation of arbitrator).

(4) Nothing in this section affects any right of the arbitrator to payment of his fees and expenses.

65 Power to limit recoverable costs

(1) Unless otherwise agreed by the parties, the tribunal may direct that the recoverable costs of the arbitration, or of any part of the arbitral proceedings, shall be limited to a specified amount.

(2) Any direction may be made or varied at any stage, but this must be done sufficiently in advance of the incurring of costs to which it relates, or the taking of any steps in the proceedings which may be affected by it, for the limit to be taken into account.

Powers of the court in relation to award

66 Enforcement of the award

(1) An award made by the tribunal pursuant to an arbitration agreement may, by leave of the court, be enforced in the same manner as a judgment or order of the court to the same effect.

(2) Where leave is so given, judgment may be entered in terms of the award.

(3) Leave to enforce an award shall not be given where, or to the extent that, the person against whom it is sought to be enforced shows that the tribunal lacked substantive jurisdiction to make the award.

The right to raise such an objection may have been lost (see section 73).

(4) Nothing in this section affects the recognition or enforcement of an award under any other enactment or rule of law, in particular under Part II of the Arbitration Act 1950 (enforcement of awards under Geneva Convention) or the provisions of Part III of this Act relating to the recognition and enforcement of awards under the New York Convention or by an action on the award.

67 Challenging the award: substantive jurisdiction

(1) A party to arbitral proceedings may (upon notice to the other parties and to the tribunal) apply to the court—

(a) challenging any award of the arbitral tribunal as to its substantive jurisdiction; or

(b) for an order declaring an award made by the tribunal on the merits to be of no effect, in whole or in part, because the tribunal did not have substantive jurisdiction.

A party may lose the right to object (see section 73) and the right to apply is subject to the restrictions in section 70(2) and (3).

(2) The arbitral tribunal may continue the arbitral proceedings and make a further award while an application to the court under this section is pending in relation to an award as to jurisdiction.

(3) On an application under this section challenging an award of the arbitral tribunal as to its substantive jurisdiction, the court may by order—

(a) confirm the award,

(b) vary the award, or

(c) set aside the award in whole or in part.

(4) The leave of the court is required for any appeal from a decision of the court under this section.

68 Challenging the award: serious irregularity

(1) A party to arbitral proceedings may (upon notice to the other parties and to the tribunal) apply to the court challenging an award in the proceedings on the ground of serious irregularity affecting the tribunal, the proceedings or the award.

A party may lose the right to object (see section 73) and the right to apply is subject to the restrictions in section 70(2) and (3).

(2) Serious irregularity means an irregularity of one or more of the following kinds which the court considers has caused or will cause substantial injustice to the applicant—

(a) failure by the tribunal to comply with section 33 (general duty of tribunal);

(b) the tribunal exceeding its powers (otherwise than by exceeding its substantive jurisdiction: see section 67);

(c) failure by the tribunal to conduct the proceedings in accordance with the procedure agreed by the parties;

(d) failure by the tribunal to deal with all the issues that were put to it;

(e) any arbitral or other institution or person vested by the parties with powers in relation to the proceedings or the award exceeding its powers;

(f) uncertainty or ambiguity as to the effect of the award;

(g) the award being obtained by fraud or the award or the way in which it was procured being contrary to public policy;

(h) failure to comply with the requirements as to the form of the award; or

(i) any irregularity in the conduct of the proceedings or in the award which is admitted by the tribunal or by any arbitral or other institution or person vested by the parties with powers in relation to the proceedings or the award.

(3) If there is shown to be serious irregularity affecting the tribunal, the proceedings or the award, the court may—

(a) remit the award to the tribunal, in whole or in part, for reconsideration,

(b) set the award aside in whole or in part, or

(c) declare the award to be of no effect, in whole or in part.

The court shall not exercise its power to set aside or to declare an award to be of no effect, in whole or in part, unless it is satisfied that it would be inappropriate to remit the matters in question to the tribunal for reconsideration.

(4) The leave of the court is required for any appeal from a decision of the court under this section.

69 Appeal on point of law

(1) Unless otherwise agreed by the parties, a party to arbitral proceedings may (upon notice to the other parties and to the tribunal) appeal to the court on a question of law arising out of an award made in the proceedings.

An agreement to dispense with reasons for the tribunal's award shall be considered an agreement to exclude the court's jurisdiction under this section.

(2) An appeal shall not be brought under this section except—

(a) with the agreement of all the other parties to the proceedings, or

(b) with the leave of the court.

The right to appeal is also subject to the restrictions in section 70(2) and (3).

(3) Leave to appeal shall be given only if the court is satisfied—

(a) that the determination of the question will substantially affect the rights of one or more of the parties,

(b) that the question is one which the tribunal was asked to determine,

(c) that, on the basis of the findings of fact in the award—

(i)   the decision of the tribunal on the question is obviously wrong, or

(ii) the question is one of general public importance and the decision of the tribunal is at least open to serious doubt, and

(d) that, despite the agreement of the parties to resolve the matter by arbitration, it is just and proper in all the circumstances for the court to determine the question.

(4) An application for leave to appeal under this section shall identify the question of law to be determined and state the grounds on which it is alleged that leave to appeal should be granted.

(5) The court shall determine an application for leave to appeal under this section without a hearing unless it appears to the court that a hearing is required.

(6) The leave of the court is required for any appeal from a decision of the court under this section to grant or refuse leave to appeal.

(7) On an appeal under this section the court may by order—

(a) confirm the award,

(b) vary the award,

(c) remit the award to the tribunal, in whole or in part, for reconsideration in the light of the court's determination, or

(d) set aside the award in whole or in part.

The court shall not exercise its power to set aside an award, in whole or in part, unless it is satisfied that it would be inappropriate to remit the matters in question to the tribunal for reconsideration.

(8) The decision of the court on an appeal under this section shall be treated as a judgment of the court for the purposes of a further appeal.

But no such appeal lies without the leave of the court which shall not be given unless the court considers that the question is one of general importance or is one which for some other special reason should be considered by the Court of Appeal.

70   Challenge or appeal: supplementary provisions

(1) The following provisions apply to an application or appeal under section 67, 68 or 69.

(2) An application or appeal may not be brought if the applicant or appellant has not first exhausted—

(a) any available arbitral process of appeal or review, and

(b) any available recourse under section 57 (correction of award or additional award).

(3) Any application or appeal must be brought within 28 days of the date of the award or, if there has been any arbitral process of appeal or review, of the date when the applicant or appellant was notified of the result of that process.

(4) If on an application or appeal it appears to the court that the award—

(a) does not contain the tribunal's reasons, or

(b) does not set out the tribunal's reasons in sufficient detail to enable the court properly to consider the application or appeal,

the court may order the tribunal to state the reasons for its award in sufficient detail for that purpose.

(5) Where the court makes an order under subsection (4), it may make such further order as it thinks fit with respect to any additional costs of the arbitration resulting from its order.

(6) The court may order the applicant or appellant to provide security for the costs of the application or appeal, and may direct that the application or appeal be dismissed if the order is not complied with.

The power to order security for costs shall not be exercised on the ground that the applicant or appellant is—

(a) an individual ordinarily resident outside the United Kingdom, or

(b) a corporation or association incorporated or formed under the law of a country outside the United Kingdom, or whose central management and control is exercised outside the United Kingdom.

(7) The court may order that any money payable under the award shall be brought into court or otherwise secured pending the determination of the application or appeal, and may direct that the application or appeal be dismissed if the order is not complied with.

(8) The court may grant leave to appeal subject to conditions to the same or similar effect as an order under subsection (6) or (7).

This does not affect the general discretion of the court to grant leave subject to conditions.

71   Challenge or appeal: effect of order of court

(1) The following provisions have effect where the court makes an order under section 67, 68 or 69 with respect to an award.

(2) Where the award is varied, the variation has effect as part of the tribunal's award.

(3) Where the award is remitted to the tribunal, in whole or in part, for reconsideration, the tribunal shall make a fresh award in respect of the matters remitted within three months of the date of the order for remission or such longer or shorter period as the court may direct.

(4) Where the award is set aside or declared to be of no effect, in whole or in part, the court may also order that any provision that an award is a condition precedent to the bringing of legal proceedings in respect of a matter to which the arbitration agreement applies, is of no effect as regards the subject matter of the award or, as the case may be, the relevant part of the award.

Miscellaneous

72 Saving for rights of person who takes no part in proceedings

(1) A person alleged to be a party to arbitral proceedings but who takes no part in the proceedings may question—

(a) whether there is a valid arbitration agreement,

(b) whether the tribunal is properly constituted, or

(c) what matters have been submitted to arbitration in accordance with the arbitration agreement,

by proceedings in the court for a declaration or injunction or other appropriate relief.

(2) He also has the same right as a party to the arbitral proceedings to challenge an award—

(a) by an application under section 67 on the ground of lack of substantive jurisdiction in relation to him, or

(b) by an application under section 68 on the ground of serious irregularity (within the meaning of that section) affecting him;

and section 70(2) (duty to exhaust arbitral procedures) does not apply in his case.

73 Loss of right to object

(1) If a party to arbitral proceedings takes part, or continues to take part, in the proceedings without making, either forthwith or within such time as is allowed by the arbitration agreement or the tribunal or by any provision of this Part, any objection—

(a) that the tribunal lacks substantive jurisdiction,

(b) that the proceedings have been improperly conducted,

(c) that there has been a failure to comply with the arbitration agreement or with any provision of this Part, or

(d) that there has been any other irregularity affecting the tribunal or the proceedings,

he may not raise that objection later, before the tribunal or the court, unless he shows that, at the time he took part or continued to take part in the proceedings, he did not know and could not with reasonable diligence have discovered the grounds for the objection.

(2) Where the arbitral tribunal rules that it has substantive jurisdiction and a party to arbitral proceedings who could have questioned that ruling—

(a) by any available arbitral process of appeal or review, or

(b) by challenging the award,

does not do so, or does not do so within the time allowed by the arbitration agreement or any provision of this Part, he may not object later to the tribunal's substantive jurisdiction on any ground which was the subject of that ruling.

74 Immunity of arbitral institutions, &c.

(1) An arbitral or other institution or person designated or requested by the parties to appoint or nominate an arbitrator is not liable for anything done or omitted in the discharge or purported discharge of that function unless the act or omission is shown to have been in bad faith.

(2) An arbitral or other institution or person by whom an arbitrator is appointed or nominated is not liable, by reason of having appointed or nominated him, for anything done or omitted by the arbitrator (or his employees or agents) in the discharge or purported discharge of his functions as arbitrator.

(3) The above provisions apply to an employee or agent of an arbitral or other institution or person as they apply to the institution or the person himself.

75 Charge to secure payment of solicitors' costs

The powers of the court to make declarations and orders under section 73 of the Solicitors Act 1974 or Article 71H of the Solicitors (Northern Ireland) Order 1976 (power to charge property recovered in the proceedings with the payment of solicitors' costs) may be exercised in relation to arbitral proceedings as if those proceedings were proceedings in the court.

Supplementary

76 Service of notices, &c.

(1) The parties are free to agree on the manner of service of any notice or other document required or authorised to be given or served in pursuance of the arbitration agreement or for the purposes of the arbitral proceedings.

(2) If or to the extent that there is no such agreement the following provisions apply.

(3) A notice or other document may be served on a person by any effective means.

(4) If a notice or other document is addressed, pre-paid and delivered by post—

    (a) to the addressee's last known principal residence or, if he is or has been carrying on a trade, profession or business, his last known principal business address, or

    (b) where the addressee is a body corporate, to the body's registered or principal office,

it shall be treated as effectively served.

(5) This section does not apply to the service of documents for the purposes of legal proceedings, for which provision is made by rules of court.

(6) References in this Part to a notice or other document include any form of communication in writing and references to giving or serving a notice or other document shall be construed accordingly.

77 Powers of court in relation to service of documents

(1) This section applies where service of a document on a person in the manner agreed by the parties, or in accordance with provisions of section 76 having effect in default of agreement, is not reasonably practicable.

(2) Unless otherwise agreed by the parties, the court may make such order as it thinks fit—

    (a) for service in such manner as the court may direct, or

    (b) dispensing with service of the document.

(3) Any party to the arbitration agreement may apply for an order, but only after exhausting any available arbitral process for resolving the matter.

(4) The leave of the court is required for any appeal from a decision of the court under this section.

78 Reckoning periods of time

(1) The parties are free to agree on the method of reckoning periods of time for the purposes of any provision agreed by them or any provision of this Part having effect in default of such agreement.

(2) If or to the extent there is no such agreement, periods of time shall be reckoned in accordance with the following provisions.

(3) Where the act is required to be done within a specified period after or from a specified date, the period begins immediately after that date.

(4) Where the act is required to be done a specified number of clear days after a specified date, at least that number of days must intervene between the day on which the act is done and that date.

(5) Where the period is a period of seven days or less which would include a Saturday, Sunday or a public holiday in the place where anything which has to be done within the period falls to be done, that day shall be excluded.

In relation to England and Wales or Northern Ireland, a 'public holiday' means Christmas Day, Good Friday or a day which under the Banking and Financial Dealings Act 1971 is a bank holiday.

79 Power of court to extend time limits relating to arbitral proceedings

(1) Unless the parties otherwise agree, the court may by order extend any time limit agreed by them in relation to any matter relating to the arbitral proceedings or specified in any provision of this Part having effect in default of such agreement.

This section does not apply to a time limit to which section 12 applies (power of court to extend time for beginning arbitral proceedings, &c.).

(2) An application for an order may be made—

> (a) by any party to the arbitral proceedings (upon notice to the other parties and to the tribunal), or
>
> (b) by the arbitral tribunal (upon notice to the parties).

(3) The court shall not exercise its power to extend a time limit unless it is satisfied—

> (a) that any available recourse to the tribunal, or to any arbitral or other institution or person vested by the parties with power in that regard, has first been exhausted, and
>
> (b) that a substantial injustice would otherwise be done.

(4) The court's power under this section may be exercised whether or not the time has already expired.

(5) An order under this section may be made on such terms as the court thinks fit.

(6) The leave of the court is required for any appeal from a decision of the court under this section.

80 Notice and other requirements in connection with legal proceedings

(1) References in this Part to an application, appeal or other step in relation to legal proceedings being taken 'upon notice' to the other parties to the arbitral proceedings, or to the tribunal, are to such notice of the originating process as is required by rules of court and do not impose any separate requirement.

(2) Rules of court shall be made—

> (a) requiring such notice to be given as indicated by any provision of this Part, and
>
> (b) as to the manner, form and content of any such notice.

(3) Subject to any provision made by rules of court, a requirement to give notice to the tribunal of legal proceedings shall be construed—

> (a) if there is more than one arbitrator, as a requirement to give notice to each of them; and
>
> (b) if the tribunal is not fully constituted, as a requirement to give notice to any arbitrator who has been appointed.

(4) References in this Part to making an application or appeal to the court within a specified period are to the issue within that period of the appropriate originating process in accordance with rules of court.

(5) Where any provision of this Part requires an application or appeal to be made to the court within a specified time, the rules of court relating to the reckoning of periods, the extending or abridging of periods, and the consequences of not taking a step within the period prescribed by the rules, apply in relation to that requirement.

(6) Provision may be made by rules of court amending the provisions of this Part—

> (a) with respect to the time within which any application or appeal to the court must be made,
>
> (b) so as to keep any provision made by this Part in relation to arbitral proceedings in step with the corresponding provision of rules of court applying in relation to proceedings in the court, or
>
> (c) so as to keep any provision made by this Part in relation to legal proceedings in step with the corresponding provision of rules of court applying generally in relation to proceedings in the court.

(7) Nothing in this section affects the generality of the power to make rules of court.

81 Saving for certain matters governed by common law

(1) Nothing in this Part shall be construed as excluding the operation of any rule of law consistent with the provisions of this Part, in particular, any rule of law as to—

> (a) matters which are not capable of settlement by arbitration;
>
> (b) the effect of an oral arbitration agreement; or
>
> (c) the refusal of recognition or enforcement of an arbitral award on grounds of public policy.

(2) Nothing in this Act shall be construed as reviving any jurisdiction of the court to set aside or remit an award on the ground of errors of fact or law on the face of the award.

82   Minor definitions

(1) In this Part—

'arbitrator', unless the context otherwise requires, includes an umpire;

'available arbitral process', in relation to any matter, includes any process of appeal to or review by an arbitral or other institution or person vested by the parties with powers in relation to that matter;

'claimant', unless the context otherwise requires, includes a counterclaimant, and related expressions shall be construed accordingly;

'dispute' includes any difference;

'enactment' includes an enactment contained in Northern Ireland legislation;

'legal proceedings' means civil proceedings in the High Court or a county court;

'peremptory order' means an order made under section 41(5) or made in exercise of any corresponding power conferred by the parties;

'premises' includes land, buildings, moveable structures, vehicles, vessels, aircraft and hovercraft;

'question of law' means—

(a) for a court in England and Wales, a question of the law of England and Wales, and

(b) for a court in Northern Ireland, a question of the law of Northern Ireland;

'substantive jurisdiction', in relation to an arbitral tribunal, refers to the matters specified in section 30(1)(a) to (c), and references to the tribunal exceeding its substantive jurisdiction shall be construed accordingly.

(2) References in this Part to a party to an arbitration agreement include any person claiming under or through a party to the agreement.

83   Index of defined expressions: Part I

In this Part the expressions listed below are defined or otherwise explained by the provisions indicated—

agreement, agree and agreed	section 5(1)
agreement in writing	section 5(2) to (5)
arbitration agreement	sections 6 and 5(1)
arbitrator	section 82(1)
available arbitral process	section 82(1)
claimant	section 82(1)
commencement (in relation to arbitral proceedings)	section 14
costs of the arbitration	section 59
the court	section 105
dispute	section 82(1)
enactment	section 82(1)
legal proceedings	section 82(1)
Limitation Acts	section 13(4)
notice (or other document)	section 76(6)
party—	
—in relation to an arbitration agreement	section 82(2)
—where section 106(4) or (3) applies	section 106(4)
question of law	section 82(1)
peremptory order	section 82(1) (and see section 41(5))
premises	section 82(1)
question of law	section 82(1)
recoverable costs	sections 63 and 64
seat of the arbitration	section 3
serve and service (of notice or other document)	section 76(6)
substantive jurisdiction (in relation to an arbitral tribunal)	section 82(1) (and see section 30(1)(a) to (c))

| upon notice (to the parties or the tribunal) | section 80 |
| written and in writing | section 5(6) |

84 Transitional provisions

(1) The provisions of this Part do not apply to arbitral proceedings commenced before the date on which this Part comes into force.

(2) They apply to arbitral proceedings commenced on or after that date under an arbitration agreement whenever made.

(3) The above provisions have effect subject to any transitional provision made by an order under section 109(2) (power to include transitional provisions in commencement order).

PART II OTHER PROVISIONS RELATING TO ARBITRATION

Domestic arbitration agreements

85 Modification of Part I in relation to domestic arbitration agreement

(1) In the case of a domestic arbitration agreement the provisions of Part I are modified in accordance with the following sections.

(2) For this purpose a 'domestic arbitration agreement' means an arbitration agreement to which none of the parties is—

   (a) an individual who is a national of, or habitually resident in, a state other than the United Kingdom, or

   (b) a body corporate which is incorporated in, or whose central control and management is exercised in, a state other than the United Kingdom,

and under which the seat of the arbitration (if the seat has been designated or determined) is in the United Kingdom.

(3) In subsection (2) 'arbitration agreement' and 'seat of the arbitration' have the same meaning as in Part I (see sections 3, 5(1) and 6).

86 Staying of legal proceedings

(1) In section 9 (stay of legal proceedings), subsection (4) (stay unless the arbitration agreement is null and void, inoperative, or incapable of being performed) does not apply to a domestic arbitration agreement.

(2) On an application under that section in relation to a domestic arbitration agreement the court shall grant a stay unless satisfied—

   (a) that the arbitration agreement is null and void, inoperative, or incapable of being performed, or

   (b) that there are other sufficient grounds for not requiring the parties to abide by the arbitration agreement.

(3) The court may treat as a sufficient ground under subsection (2)(b) the fact that the applicant is or was at any material time not ready and willing to do all things necessary for the proper conduct of the arbitration or of any other dispute resolution procedures required to be exhausted before resorting to arbitration.

(4) For the purposes of this section the question whether an arbitration agreement is a domestic arbitration agreement shall be determined by reference to the facts at the time the legal proceedings are commenced.

87 Effectiveness of agreement to exclude court's jurisdiction

(1) In the case of a domestic arbitration agreement any agreement to exclude the jurisdiction of the court under—

(a) section 45 (determination of preliminary point of law), or

(b) section 69 (challenging the award: appeal on point of law),

is not effective unless entered into after the commencement of the arbitral proceedings in which the question arises or the award is made.

(2) For this purpose the commencement of the arbitral proceedings has the same meaning as in Part I (see section 14).

(3) For the purposes of this section the question whether an arbitration agreement is a domestic arbitration agreement shall be determined by reference to the facts at the time the agreement is entered into.

88 Power to repeal or amend sections 85 to 87

(1) The Secretary of State may by order repeal or amend the provisions of sections 85 to 87.

(2) An order under this section may contain such supplementary, incidental and transitional provisions as appear to the Secretary of State to be appropriate.

(3) An order under this section shall be made by statutory instrument and no such order shall be made unless a draft of it has been laid before and approved by a resolution of each House of Parliament.

Consumer arbitration agreements

89 Application of unfair terms regulations to consumer arbitration agreements

(1) The following sections extend the application of the Unfair Terms in Consumer Contracts Regulations 1994 in relation to a term which constitutes an arbitration agreement.

For this purpose 'arbitration agreement' means an agreement to submit to arbitration present or future disputes or differences (whether or not contractual).

(2) In those sections 'the Regulations' means those regulations and includes any regulations amending or replacing those regulations.

(3) Those sections apply whatever the law applicable to the arbitration agreement.

90 Regulations apply where consumer is a legal person

The Regulations apply where the consumer is a legal person as they apply where the consumer is a natural person.

91 Arbitration agreement unfair where modest amount sought

(1) A term which constitutes an arbitration agreement is unfair for the purposes of the Regulations so far as it relates to a claim for a pecuniary remedy which does not exceed the amount specified by order for the purposes of this section.

(2) Orders under this section may make different provision for different cases and for different purposes.

(3) The power to make orders under this section is exercisable—

(a) for England and Wales, by the Secretary of State with the concurrence of the Lord Chancellor,

(b) for Scotland, by the Secretary of State [...] , and

(c) for Northern Ireland, by the Department of Economic Development for Northern Ireland with the concurrence of the Lord Chancellor.

(4) Any such order for England and Wales or Scotland shall be made by statutory instrument which shall be subject to annulment in pursuance of a resolution of either House of Parliament.

(5) Any such order for Northern Ireland shall be a statutory rule for the purposes of the Statutory Rules (Northern Ireland) Order 1979 and shall be subject to negative resolution, within the meaning of section 41(6) of the Interpretation Act (Northern Ireland) 1954.

Small claims arbitration in the county court

92 Exclusion of Part I in relation to small claims arbitration in the county court

Nothing in Part I of this Act applies to arbitration under section 64 of the County Courts Act 1984.

Appointment of judges as arbitrators

93 Appointment of judges as arbitrators

(1) A judge of the Commercial Court or an official referee may, if in all the circumstances he thinks fit, accept appointment as a sole arbitrator or as umpire by or by virtue of an arbitration agreement.

(2) A judge of the Commercial Court shall not do so unless the Lord Chief Justice has informed him that, having regard to the state of business in the High Court and the Crown Court, he can be made available.

(3) An official referee shall not do so unless the Lord Chief Justice has informed him that, having regard to the state of official referees' business, he can be made available.

(4) The fees payable for the services of a judge of the Commercial Court or official referee as arbitrator or umpire shall be taken in the High Court.

(5) In this section—

'arbitration agreement' has the same meaning as in Part I; and

'official referee' means a person nominated under section 68(1)(a) of [the Senior Courts Act 1981] to deal with official referees' business.

(6) The provisions of Part I of this Act apply to arbitration before a person appointed under this section with the modifications specified in Schedule 2.

Statutory arbitrations

94 Application of Part I to statutory arbitrations

(1) The provisions of Part I apply to every arbitration under an enactment (a 'statutory arbitration'), whether the enactment was passed or made before or after the commencement of this Act, subject to the adaptations and exclusions specified in sections 95 to 98.

(2) The provisions of Part I do not apply to a statutory arbitration if or to the extent that their application—

    (a) is inconsistent with the provisions of the enactment concerned, with any rules or procedure authorised or recognised by it, or

    (b) is excluded by any other enactment.

(3) In this section and the following provisions of this Part 'enactment'—

    (a) in England and Wales, includes an enactment contained in subordinate legislation within the meaning of the Interpretation Act 1978;

    (b) in Northern Ireland, means a statutory provision within the meaning of section 1(f) of the Interpretation Act (Northern Ireland) 1954.

95 General adaptation of provisions in relation to statutory arbitrations

(1) The provisions of Part I apply to a statutory arbitration—

    (a) as if the arbitration were pursuant to an arbitration agreement and as if the enactment were that agreement, and

    (b) as if the persons by and against whom a claim subject to arbitration in pursuance of the enactment may be or has been made were parties to that agreement.

(2) Every statutory arbitration shall be taken to have its seat in England and Wales, or, as the case may be, in Northern Ireland.

96 Specific adaptations of provisions in relation to statutory arbitrations

(1) The following provisions of Part I apply to a statutory arbitration with the following adaptations.

(2) In section 30(1) (competence of tribunal to rule on its own jurisdiction), the reference in paragraph (a) to whether there is a valid arbitration agreement shall be construed as a reference to whether the enactment applies to the dispute or difference in question.

(3) Section 35 (consolidation of proceedings and concurrent hearings) applies only so as to authorise the consolidation of proceedings, or concurrent hearings in proceedings, under the same enactment.

(4) Section 46 (rules applicable to substance of dispute) applies with the omission of subsection (1)(b) (determination in accordance with considerations agreed by parties).

97 Provisions excluded from applying to statutory arbitrations
The following provisions of Part I do not apply in relation to a statutory arbitration—
  (a) section 8 (whether agreement discharged by death of a party);
  (b) section 12 (power of court to extend agreed time limits);
  (c) sections 9(5), 10(2) and 71(4) (restrictions on effect of provision that award condition precedent to right to bring legal proceedings).

98 Power to make further provision by regulations
(1) The Secretary of State may make provision by regulations for adapting or excluding any provision of Part I in relation to statutory arbitrations in general or statutory arbitrations of any particular description.

(2) The power is exercisable whether the enactment concerned is passed or made before or after the commencement of this Act.

(3) Regulations under this section shall be made by statutory instrument which shall be subject to annulment in pursuance of a resolution of either House of Parliament.

PART III RECOGNITION AND ENFORCEMENT OF CERTAIN FOREIGN AWARDS

Enforcement of Geneva Convention awards

99 Continuation of Part II of the Arbitration Act 1950
Part II of the Arbitration Act 1950 (enforcement of certain foreign awards) continues to apply in relation to foreign awards within the meaning of that Part which are not also New York Convention awards.

Recognition and enforcement of New York Convention awards

100 New York Convention awards
(1) In this Part a 'New York Convention award' means an award made, in pursuance of an arbitration agreement, in the territory of a state (other than the United Kingdom) which is a party to the New York Convention.

(2) For the purposes of subsection (1) and of the provisions of this Part relating to such awards—
  (a) 'arbitration agreement' means an arbitration agreement in writing, and
  (b) an award shall be treated as made at the seat of the arbitration, regardless of where it was signed, despatched or delivered to any of the parties.
In this subsection 'agreement in writing' and 'seat of the arbitration' have the same meaning as in Part I.

(3) If Her Majesty by Order in Council declares that a state specified in the Order is a party to the New York Convention, or is a party in respect of any territory so specified, the Order shall, while in force, be conclusive evidence of that fact.

(4) In this section 'the New York Convention' means the Convention on the Recognition and Enforcement of Foreign Arbitral Awards adopted by the United Nations Conference on International Commercial Arbitration on 10th June 1958.

101 Recognition and enforcement of awards

(1) A New York Convention award shall be recognised as binding on the persons as between whom it was made, and may accordingly be relied on by those persons by way of defence, set-off or otherwise in any legal proceedings in England and Wales or Northern Ireland.

(2) A New York Convention award may, by leave of the court, be enforced in the same manner as a judgment or order of the court to the same effect.

As to the meaning of 'the court' see section 105.

(3) Where leave is so given, judgment may be entered in terms of the award.

102 Evidence to be produced by party seeking recognition or enforcement

(1) A party seeking the recognition or enforcement of a New York Convention award must produce—

    (a) the duly authenticated original award or a duly certified copy of it, and

    (b) the original arbitration agreement or a duly certified copy of it.

(2) If the award or agreement is in a foreign language, the party must also produce a translation of it certified by an official or sworn translator or by a diplomatic or consular agent.

103 Refusal of recognition or enforcement

(1) Recognition or enforcement of a New York Convention award shall not be refused except in the following cases.

(2) Recognition or enforcement of the award may be refused if the person against whom it is revoked proves—

    (a) that a party to the arbitration agreement was (under the law applicable to him) under some incapacity;

    (b) that the arbitration agreement was not valid under the law to which the parties subjected it or, failing any indication thereon, under the law of the country where the award was made;

    (c) that he was not given proper notice of the appointment of the arbitrator or of the arbitration proceedings or was otherwise unable to present his case;

    (d) that the award deals with a difference not contemplated by or not falling within the terms of the submission to arbitration or contains decisions on matters beyond the scope of the submission to arbitration (but see subsection (4))

    (e) that the composition of the arbitral tribunal or the arbitral procedure was not in accordance with the agreement of the parties or, failing such arrangement, withe the law of the country in which the arbitration took place;

    (f) that the award has not yet become binding on the parties, or has been set aside or suspended by a competent authority of the country in which, or under the law of which, it was made.

(3) Recognition or enforcement of the award may also be refused if the award is in respect of a matter which is not capable of settlement by arbitration, or if it would be contrary to public policy to recognise or enforce the award.

(4) An award which contains decisions on matters not submitted to arbitration may be recognised or enforced to the extent that it contains decisions on matters submitted to arbitration which can be separated from those on matters not so submitted.

(5) Where an application for the setting aside or suspension of the award has been made to such a competent authority as is mentioned in subsection (2)(f), the court before which the award

is sought to be relied upon may, if it considers it proper, adjourn the decision on the recognition or enforcement of the award.

It may also on the application of the party claiming recognition or enforcement of the award order the other party to give suitable security.

104   Saving for other bases of recognition or enforcement
Nothing in the preceding provisions of this Part affects any right to rely upon or enforce a New York Convention award at common law or under section 66.

PART IV GENERAL PROVISIONS

105   Meaning of 'the court': jurisdiction of High Court and county court
(1) In this Act 'the court' means the High Court or a county court, subject to the following provisions.

(2) The Lord Chancellor may by order make provision—

(a) allocating proceedings under this Act to the High Court or to county courts; or

(b) specifying proceedings under this Act which may be commenced or taken only in the High Court or in a county court.

(3) The Lord Chancellor may by order make provision requiring proceedings of any specified description under this Act in relation to which a county court has jurisdiction to be commenced or taken in one or more specified county courts.

Any jurisdiction so exercisable by a specified county court is exercisable throughout England and Wales or, as the case may be, Northern Ireland.

[(3A) The Lord Chancellor must consult the Lord Chief Justice of England and Wales or the Lord Chief Justice of Northern Ireland (as the case may be) before making an order under this section.

(3B) The Lord Chief Justice of England and Wales may nominate a judicial office holder (as defined in section 109(4) of the Constitutional Reform Act 2005) to exercise his functions under this section.

(3C) The Lord Chief Justice of Northern Ireland may nominate any of the following to exercise his functions under this section—

(a) the holder of one of the offices listed in Schedule 1 to the Justice (Northern Ireland) Act 2002;

(b) a Lord Justice of Appeal (as defined in section 88 of that Act).]

(4) An order under this section—

(a) may differentiate between categories of proceedings by reference to such criteria as the Lord Chancellor sees fit to specify, and

(b) may make such incidental or transitional provision as the Lord Chancellor considers necessary or expedient.

(5) An order under this section for England and Wales shall be made by statutory instrument which shall be subject to annulment in pursuance of a resolution of either House of Parliament.

(6) An order under this section for Northern Ireland shall be a statutory rule for the purposes of the Statutory Rules (Northern Ireland) Order 1979 which shall be subject to annulment in pursuance of a resolution of either House of Parliament in like manner as a statutory instrument and section 5 of the Statutory Instruments Act 1946 shall apply accordingly.

106   Crown application
(1) Part I of this Act applies to any arbitration agreement to which Her Majesty, either in right of the Crown or of the Duchy of Lancaster or otherwise, or the Duke of Cornwall, is a party.

(2) Where Her Majesty is party to an arbitration agreement otherwise than in right of the Crown, Her Majesty shall be represented for the purposes of any arbitral proceedings—

(a) where the agreement was entered into by Her Majesty in right of the Duchy of Lancaster, by the Chancellor of the Duchy or such person as he may appoint, and

(b) in any other case, by such person as Her Majesty may appoint in writing under the Royal Sign Manual.

(3) Where the Duke of Cornwall is party to an arbitration agreement, he shall be represented for the purposes of any arbitral proceedings by such person as he may appoint.

(4) References in Part I to a party or the parties to the arbitration agreement or to arbitral proceedings shall be construed, where subsection (2) or (3) applies, as references to the person representing Her Majesty or the Duke of Cornwall.

Section 4(1)   **SCHEDULE 1**

MANDATORY PROVISIONS OF PART I

sections 9 to 11 (stay of legal proceedings);
section 12 (power of court to extend agreed time limits);
section 13 (application of Limitation Acts);
section 24 (power of court to remove arbitrator);
section 26(1) (effect of death of arbitrator);
section 28 (liability of parties for fees and expenses of arbitrators);
section 29 (immunity of arbitrator);
section 31 (objection to substantive jurisdiction of tribunal);
section 32 (determination of preliminary point of jurisdiction);
section 33 (general duty of tribunal);
section 37(2) (items to be treated as expenses of arbitrators);
section 40 (general duty of parties);
section 43 (securing the attendance of witnesses);
section 56 (power to withhold award in case of non-payment);
section 60 (effectiveness of agreement for payment of costs in any event);
section 66 (enforcement of award);
sections 67 and 68 (challenging the award: substantive jurisdiction and serious irregularity), and sections 70 and 71 (supplementary provisions; effect of order of court) so far as relating to those sections;
section 72 (saving for rights of person who takes no part in proceedings);
section 73 (loss of right to object);
section 74 (immunity of arbitral institutions, &c.);
section 75 (charge to secure payment of solicitors' costs).

Section 93(6)   **SCHEDULE 2**

MODIFICATIONS OF PART I IN RELATION TO JUDGE-ARBITRATORS

Introductory

1. In this Schedule 'judge-arbitrator' means a judge of the Commercial Court or official referee appointed as arbitrator or umpire under section 93.

General

2.—(1) Subject to the following provisions of this Schedule, references in Part I to the court shall be construed in relation to a judge-arbitrator, or in relation to the appointment of a judge-arbitrator, as references to the Court of Appeal.

(2) The references in sections 32(6), 45(6) and 69(8) to the Court of Appeal shall in such a case be construed as references to the [Supreme Court].

Arbitrator's fees

3.—(1) The power of the court in section 28(2) to order consideration and adjustment of the liability of a party for the fees of an arbitrator may be exercised by a judge-arbitrator.

(2) Any such exercise of the power is subject to the powers of the Court of Appeal under sections 24(4) and 25(3)(b) (directions as to entitlement to fees or expenses in case of removal or resignation).

Exercise of court powers in support of arbitration

4.—(1) Where the arbitral tribunal consists of or includes a judge-arbitrator the powers of the court under sections 42 to 44 (enforcement of peremptory orders, summoning witnesses, and other court powers) are exercisable by the High Court and also by the judge-arbitrator himself.

(2) Anything done by a judge-arbitrator in the exercise of those powers shall be regarded as done by him in his capacity as judge of the High Court and have effect as if done by that court.

Nothing in this sub-paragraph prejudices any power vested in him as arbitrator or umpire.

Extension of time for making award

5.—(1) The power conferred by section 50 (extension of time for making award) is exercisable by the judge-arbitrator himself.

(2) Any appeal from a decision of a judge-arbitrator under that section lies to the Court of Appeal with the leave of that court.

Withholding award in case of non-payment

6.—(1) The provisions of paragraph 7 apply in place of the provisions of section 56 (power to withhold award in the case of non-payment) in relation to the withholding of an award for non-payment of the fees and expenses of a judge-arbitrator.

(2) This does not affect the application of section 56 in relation to the delivery of such an award by an arbitral or other institution or person vested by the parties with powers in relation to the delivery of the award

7.—(1) A judge-arbitrator may refuse to deliver an award except upon payment of the fees and expenses mentioned in section 56(1).

(2) The judge-arbitrator may, on an application by a party to the arbitral proceedings, order that if he pays into the High Court the fees and expenses demanded, or such lesser amount as the judge-arbitrator may specify—

    (a) the award shall be delivered,

    (b) the amount of the fees and expenses properly payable shall be determined by such means and upon such terms as he may direct, and

    (c) out of the money paid into court there shall be paid out such fees and expenses as may be found to be properly payable and the balance of the money (if any) shall be paid out to the applicant.

(3) For this purpose the amount of fees and expenses properly payable is the amount the applicant is liable to pay under section 28 or any agreement relating to the payment of the arbitrator.

(4) No application to the judge-arbitrator under this paragraph may be made where there is any available arbitral process for appeal or review of the amount of the fees or expenses demanded.

(5) Any appeal from a decision of a judge-arbitrator under this paragraph lies to the Court of Appeal with the leave of that court.

(6) Where a party to arbitral proceedings appeals under sub-paragraph (5), an arbitrator is entitled to appear and be heard.

Correction of award or additional award

8. Subsections (4) to (6) of section 57 (correction of award or additional award: time limit for application or exercise of power) do not apply to a judge-arbitrator.

Costs

9. Where the arbitral tribunal consists of or includes a judge-arbitrator the powers of the court under section 63(4) (determination of recoverable costs) shall be exercised by the High Court.

10.—(1) The power of the court under section 64 to determine an arbitrator's reasonable fees and expenses may be exercised by a judge-arbitrator.

(2) Any such exercise of the power is subject to the powers of the Court of Appeal under sections 24(4) and 25(3)(b) (directions as to entitlement to fees or expenses in case of removal or resignation).

Enforcement of award

11. The leave of the court required by section 66 (enforcement of award) may in the case of an award of a judge-arbitrator be given by the judge-arbitrator himself.

Solicitors' costs

12. The powers of the court to make declarations and orders under the provisions applied by section 75 (power to charge property recovered in arbitral proceedings with the payment of solicitors' costs) may be exercised by the judge-arbitrator.

Powers of court in relation to service of documents

13.—(1) The power of the court under section 77(2) (powers of court in relation to service of documents) is exercisable by the judge-arbitrator.

(2) Any appeal from a decision of a judge-arbitrator under that section lies to the Court of Appeal with the leave of that court.

Powers of court to extend time limits relating to arbitral proceedings

14.—(1) The power conferred by section 79 (power of court to extend time limits relating to arbitral proceedings) is exercisable by the judge-arbitrator himself.

(2) Any appeal from a decision of a judge-arbitrator under that section lies to the Court of Appeal with the leave of that court.

Late Payment of Commercial Debts (Interest) Act 1998

(1998, c. 20)

PART I STATUTORY INTEREST ON QUALIFYING DEBTS

1 Statutory interest

(1) It is an implied term in a contract to which this Act applies that any qualifying debt created by the contract carries simple interest subject to and in accordance with this Part.

(2) Interest carried under that implied term (in this Act referred to as 'statutory interest') shall be treated, for the purposes of any rule of law or enactment (other than this Act) relating to interest on debts, in the same way as interest carried under an express contract term.

(3) This Part has effect subject to Part II (which in certain circumstances permits contract terms to oust or vary the right to statutory interest that would otherwise be conferred by virtue of the term implied by subsection (1)).

2   Contracts to which Act applies

(1) This Act applies to a contract for the supply of goods or services where the purchaser and the supplier are each acting in the course of a business, other than an excepted contract.

(2) In this Act 'contract for the supply of goods or services' means—

(a) a contract of sale of goods; or

(b) a contract (other than a contract of sale of goods) by which a person does any, or any combination, of the things mentioned in subsection (3) for a consideration that is (or includes) a money consideration.

(3) Those things are—

(a) transferring or agreeing to transfer to another the property in goods;

(b) bailing or agreeing to bail goods to another by way of hire or, in Scotland, hiring or agreeing to hire goods to another; and

(c) agreeing to carry out a service

(4) For the avoidance of doubt a contract of service or apprenticeship is nor a contract for the supply of goods or services.

(5) The following are excepted contracts—

(a) a consumer credit agreement;

(b) a contract intended to operate by way of mortgage, pledge, charge or other security; and

(7) In this section—

'business' includes a profession and the activities of any government department or local or public authority;

'consumer credit agreement' has the same meaning as in the Consumer Credit Act 1974;

'contract of sale of goods' and 'goods' have the same meaning as in the Sale of Goods Act 1979;

['government department' includes any part of the Scottish Administration;]

'property in goods' means the general property in them and not merely a special property.

3   Qualifying debts

(1) A debt created by virtue of an obligation under a contract to which this Act applies to pay the whole or any part of the contract price is a 'qualifying debt' for the purposes of this Act, unless (when created) the whole of the debt is prevented from carrying statutory interest by this section.

(2) A debt does not carry statutory interest if or to the extent that it consists of a sum to which a right to interest or to charge interest applies by virtue of any enactment (other than section 1 of this Act).

This subsection does not prevent a sum from carrying statutory interest by reason of the fact that a court, arbitrator or arbiter would, apart from this Act, have power to award interest on it.

(3) A debt does not carry (and shall be treated as never having carried) statutory interest if or to the extent that a right to demand interest on it, which exists by virtue of any rule of law, is exercised.

4   Period for which statutory interest runs

(1) Statutory interest runs in relation to a qualifying debt in accordance with this section (unless section 5 applies).

(2) Statutory interest starts to run on the day after the relevant day for the debt, at the rate prevailing under section 6 at the end of the relevant day.

(3) Where the supplier and the purchaser agree a date for payment of the debt (that is, the day on which the debt is to be created by the contract), that is the relevant day unless the debt relates to an obligation to make an advance payment.

A date so agreed may be a fixed one or may depend on the happening of an event or the failure of an event to happen.

(4) Where the debt relates to an obligation to make an advance payment, the relevant day is the day on which the debt is treated by section 11 as having been created.

(5) In any other case, the relevant day is the last day of the period of 30 days beginning with—

    (a) the day on which the obligation of the supplier to which the debt relates is performed; or

    (b) the day on which the purchaser has notice of the amount of the debt or (where that amount is unascertained) the sum which the supplier claims is the amount of the debt,

whichever is the later.

    (6) Where the debt is created by virtue of an obligation to pay a sum due in respect of a period of hire of goods, subsection (5)(a) has effect as if it referred to the last day of that period.

    (7) Statutory interest ceases to run when the interest would cease to run if it were carried under an express contract term.

    (8) In this section 'advance payment' has the same meaning as in section 11.

5 Remission of statutory interest

    (1) This section applies where, by reason of any conduct of the supplier, the interests of justice require that statutory interest should be remitted in whole or part in respect of a period for which it would otherwise run in relation to a qualifying debt.

    (2) If the interests of justice require that the supplier should receive no statutory interest for a period, statutory interest shall not run for that period.

    (3) If the interests of justice require that the supplier should receive statutory interest at a reduced rate for a period, statutory interest shall run at such rate as meets the justice of the case for that period.

    (4) Remission of statutory interest under this section may be required—

    (a) by reason of conduct at any time (whether before or after the time at which the debt is created); and

    (b) for the whole period for which statutory interest would otherwise run or for one or more parts of that period.

    (5) In this section 'conduct' includes any act or omission.

[5A Compensation arising out of late payment

    (1) Once statutory interest begins to run in relation to a qualifying debt, the supplier shall be entitled to a fixed sum (in addition to the statutory interest on the debt).

    (2) That sum shall be—

    (a) for a debt less than £1,000, the sum of £40;

    (b) for a debt of £1,000 or more, but less than £10,000, the sum of £70;

    (c) for a debt of £10,000 or more, the sum of £100.

    (3) The obligation to pay an additional fixed sum under this section in respect of a qualifying debt shall be treated as part of the term implied by section 1(1) in the contract creating the debt.]

6 Rate of statutory interest

    (1) The Secretary of State shall by order made with the consent of the Treasury set the rate of statutory interest by prescribing—

    (a) a formula for calculating the rate of statutory interest; or

    (b) the rate of statutory interest.

    (2) Before making such an order the Secretary of State shall, among other things, consider the extent to which it may be desirable to set the rate so as to—

    (a) protect suppliers whose financial position makes them particularly vulnerable if their qualifying debts are paid late; and

    (b) deter generally the late payment of qualifying debts.

PART II CONTRACT TERMS RELATING TO LATE PAYMENT OF QUALIFYING DEBTS

7   Purpose of Part II

(1) This Part deals with the extent to which the parties to a contract to which this Act applies may by reference to contract terms oust or vary the right to statutory interest that would otherwise apply when a qualifying debt created by the contract (in this Part referred to as 'the debt') is not paid.

(2) This Part applies to contract terms agreed before the debt is created; after that time the parties are free to agree terms dealing with the debt.

(3) This Part has effect without prejudice to any other ground which may affect the validity of a contract term.

8   Circumstances where statutory interest may be ousted or varied

(1) Any contract terms are void to the extent that they purport to exclude the right to statutory interest in relation to the debt, unless there is a substantial contractual remedy for late payment of the debt.

(2) Where the parties agree a contractual remedy for late payment of the debt that is a substantial remedy, statutory interest is not carried by the debt (unless they agree otherwise).

(3) The parties may not agree to vary the right to statutory interest in relation to the debt unless either the right to statutory interest as varied or the overall remedy for late payment of the debt is a substantial remedy.

(4) Any contract terms are void to the extent that they purport to—

   (a) confer a contractual right to interest that is not a substantial remedy for late payment of the debt, or

   (b) vary the right to statutory interest so as to provide for a right to statutory interest that is not a substantial remedy for late payment of the debt,

unless the overall remedy for late payment of the debt is a substantial remedy.

(5) Subject to this section, the parties are free to agree contract terms which deal with the consequences of late payment of the debt.

9   Meaning of 'substantial remedy'

(1) A remedy for the late payment of the debt shall be regarded as a substantial remedy unless—

   (a) the remedy is insufficient either for the purpose of compensating the supplier for late payment or for deterring late payment; and

   (b) it would not be fair or reasonable to allow the remedy to be relied on to oust or (as the case may be) to vary the right to statutory interest that would otherwise apply in relation to the debt.

(2) In determining whether a remedy is not a substantial remedy, regard shall be had to all the relevant circumstances at the time the terms in question are agreed.

(3) In determining whether subsection (1)(b) applies, regard shall be had (without prejudice to the generality of subsection (2)) to the following matters—

   (a) the benefits of commercial certainty;

   (b) the strength of the bargaining positions of the parties relative to each other;

   (c) whether the term was imposed by one party to the detriment of the other (whether by the use of standard terms or otherwise); and

   (d) whether the supplier received an inducement to agree to the term.

10   Interpretation of Part II

(1) In this Part—

'contract term' means a term of the contract creating the debt or any other contract term binding the parties (or either of them);

'contractual remedy' means a contractual right to interest or any contractual remedy other than interest;

'contractual right to interest' includes a reference to a contractual right to charge interest;

'overall remedy', in relation to the late payment of the debt, means any combination of a contractual right to interest, a varied right to statutory interest or a contractual remedy other than interest;

'substantial remedy' shall be construed in accordance with section 9.

(2) In this Part a reference (however worded) to contract terms which vary the right to statutory interest is a reference to terms altering in any way the effect of Part I in relation to the debt (for example by postponing the time at which interest starts to run or by imposing conditions on the right to interest).

(3) In this Part a reference to late payment of the debt is a reference to late payment of the sum due when the debt is created (excluding any part of that sum which is prevented from carrying statutory interest by section 3).

PART III GENERAL AND SUPPLEMENTARY

11 Treatment of advance payments of the contract price

(1) A qualifying debt created by virtue of an obligation to make an advance payment shall be treated for the purposes of this Act as if it was created on the day mentioned in subsection (3), (4) or (5) (as the case may be).

(2) In this section 'advance payment' means a payment falling due before the obligation of the supplier to which the whole contract price relates ('the supplier's obligation') is performed, other than a payment of a part of the contract price that is due in respect of any part performance of that obligation and payable on or after the day on which that part performance is completed.

(3) Where the advance payment is the whole contract price, the debt shall be treated as created on the day on which the supplier's obligation is performed.

(4) Where the advance payment is a part of the contract price, but the sum is not due in respect of any part performance of the supplier's obligation, the debt shall be treated as created on the day on which the supplier's obligation is performed.

(5) Where the advance payment is a part of the contract price due in respect of any part performance of the supplier's obligation, but is payable before that part performance is completed, the debt shall be treated as created on the day on which the relevant part performance is completed.

(6) Where the debt is created by virtue of an obligation to pay a sum due in respect of a period of hire of goods, this section has effect as if—

(a) references to the day on which the supplier's obligation is performed were references to the last day of that period; and

(b) references to part performance of that obligation were references to part of that period.

(7) For the purposes of this section an obligation to pay the whole outstanding balance of the contract price shall be regarded as an obligation to pay the whole contract price and not as an obligation to pay a part of the contract price.

12 Conflict of laws

(1) This Act does not have effect in relation to a contract governed by the law of a part of the United Kingdom by choice of the parties if—

(a) there is no significant connection between the contract and that part of the United Kingdom; and

(b) but for that choice, the applicable law would be a foreign law.

(2) This Act has effect in relation to a contract governed by a foreign law by choice of the parties if—

(a) but for that choice, the applicable law would be the law of a part of the United Kingdom; and

(b) there is no significant connection between the contract and any country other than that part of the United Kingdom.

(3) In this section—

'contract' means a contract falling within section 2(1);and

'foreign law' means the law of a country outside the United Kingdom.

13   Assignments, etc.

(1) The operation of this Act in relation to a qualifying debt is not affected by—

(a) any change in the identity of the parties to the contract creating the debt; or

(b) the passing of the right to be paid the debt, or the duty to pay it (in whole or in part) to a person other than the person who is the original creditor or the original debtor when the debt is created.

(2) Any reference in this Act to the supplier or the purchaser is a reference to the person who is for the time being the supplier or the purchaser or, in relation to a time after the debt in question has been created, the person who is for the time being the creditor or the debtor, as the case may be.

(3) Where the right to be paid part of a debt passes to a person other than the person who is the original creditor when the debt is created, any reference in this Act to a debt shall be construed as (or, if the context so requires, as including) a reference to part of a debt.

(4) A reference in this section to the identity of the parties to a contract changing, or to a right or duty passing, is a reference to it changing or passing by assignment or assignation, by operation of law or otherwise.

14   Contract terms relating to the date for payment of the contract price

(1) This section applies to any contract term which purports to have the effect of postponing the time at which a qualifying debt would otherwise be created by a contract to which this Act applies.

(2) Sections 3(2)(b) and 17(1)(b) of the Unfair Contract Terms Act 1977 (no reliance to be placed on certain contract terms) shall apply in cases where such a contract term is not contained in written standard terms of the purchaser as well as in cases where the term is contained in such standard terms.

(3) In this section 'contract term' has the same meaning as in section 10(1).

15   Orders and regulations

(1) Any power to make an order or regulations under this Act is exercisable by statutory instrument.

(2) Any statutory instrument containing an order or regulations under this Act, other than an order under section 17(2), shall be subject to annulment in pursuance of a resolution of either House of Parliament.

16   Interpretation

(1) In this Act—

'contract for the supply of goods or services' has the meaning given in section 2(2);

'contract price' means the price in a contract of sale of goods or the money consideration referred to in section 2(2)(b) in any other contract for the supply of goods or services;

'purchaser' means (subject to section 13(2)) the seller in a contract of sale or the person who contracts with the supplier in any other contract for the supply of goods or services;

'qualifiying debt' means a debt falling within section 3(1);

'statutory interest' means interest carried by virtue of the term implied by section 1(1); and

'supplier' means (subject to section 13(2)) the seller in a contract of sale of goods or the person who does one or more of the things mentioned in section 2(3) in any other contract for the supply of goods or services

(2) In this Act any reference (however worded) to an agreement or to contract terms includes a reference to both express and implied terms (including terms established by a course of dealing or by such usage as binds the parties).

Contracts (Rights of Third Parties) Act 1999

(1999, c. 31)

1 Right of third party to enforce contractual term

(1) Subject to the provisions of this Act, a person who is not a party to a contract (a 'third party') may in his own right enforce a term of the contract if—

  (a) the contract expressly provides that he may, or

  (b) subject to subsection (2), the term purports to confer a benefit on him.

(2) Subsection (1)(b) does not apply if on a proper construction of the contract it appears that the parties did not intend the term to be enforceable by the third party.

(3) The third party must be expressly identified in the contract by name, as a member of a class or as answering a particular description but need not be in existence when the contract is entered into.

(4) This section does not confer a right on a third party to enforce a term of a contract otherwise than subject to and in accordance with any other relevant terms of the contract.

(5) For the purpose of exercising his right to enforce a term of the contract, there shall be available to the third party any remedy that would have been available to him in an action for breach of contract if he had been a party to the contract (and the rules relating to damages, injunctions, specific performance and other relief shall apply accordingly).

(6) Where a term of a contract excludes or limits liability in relation to any matter references in this Act to the third party enforcing the term shall be construed as references to his availing himself of the exclusion or limitation.

(7) In this Act, in relation to a term of a contract which is enforceable by a third party—

'the promisor' means the party to the contract against whom the term is enforceable by the third party, and

'the promisee' means the party to the contract by whom the term is enforceable against the promisor.

2 Variation and rescission of contract

(1) Subject to the provisions of this section, where a third party has a right under section 1 to enforce a term of the contract, the parties to the contract may not, by agreement, rescind the contract, or vary it in such a way as to extinguish or alter his entitlement under that right, without his consent if—

  (a) the third party has communicated his assent to the term to the promisor,

  (b) the promisor is aware that the third party has relied on the term, or

  (c) the promisor can reasonably be expected to have foreseen that the third party would rely on the term and the third party has in fact relied on it.

(2) The assent referred to in subsection (1)(a)—

  (a) may be by words or conduct, and

  (b) if sent to the promisor by post or other means, shall not be regarded as communicated to the promisor until received by him.

(3) Subsection (1) is subject to any express term of the contract under which—

  (a) the parties to the contract may by agreement rescind or vary the contract without the consent of the third party, or

  (b) the consent of the third party is required in circumstances specified in the contract instead of those set out in subsection (1)(a) to (c).

(4) Where the consent of a third party is required under subsection (1) or (3), the court or arbitral tribunal may, on the application of the parties to the contract, dispense with his consent if satisfied—

  (a) that his consent cannot be obtained because his whereabouts cannot reasonably be ascertained, or

  (b) that he is mentally incapable of giving his consent.

(5) The court or arbital tribunal may, on the application of the parties to a contract, dispense with any consent that may be required under subsection (1)(c) if satisfied that it cannot reasonably be ascertained whether or not the third party has in fact relied on the term.

(6) If the court or arbitral tribunal dispenses with a third party's consent, it may impose such conditions as it thinks fit, including a condition requiring the payment of compensation to the third party.

(7) The jurisdiction conferred on the court by subsections (4) to (6) is exercisable by both the High Court and a county court.

3   Defences etc. available to promisor

(1) Subsections (2) to (5) apply where, in reliance on section 1, proceedings for the enforcement of a term of a contract are brought by a third party.

(2) The promisor shall have available to him by way of defence or set-off any matter that—

(a) arises from or in connection with the contract and is relevant to the term, and

(b) would have been available to him by way of defence or set-off if the proceedings had been brought by the promisee.

(3) The promisor shall also have available to him by way of defence or set-off any matter if—

(a) an express term of the contract provides for it to be available to him in proceedings brought by the third party, and

(b) it would have been available to him by way of defence or set-off if the proceedings had been brought by the promisee.

(4) The promisor shall also have available to him—

(a) by way of defence or set-off any matter, and

(b) by way of counterclaim any matter not arising from the contract,

that would have been available to him by way of defence or set-off or, as the case may be, by way of counterclaim against the third party if the third party had been a party to the contract.

(5) Subsections (2) and (4) are subject to any express term of the contract as to the matters that are not available to the promisor by way of defence, set-off or counterclaim.

(6) Where in any proceedings brought against him a third party seeks in reliance on section 1 to enforce a term of a contract (including, in particular, a term purporting to exclude or limit liability), he may not do so if he could not have done so (whether by reason of any particular circumstances relating to him or otherwise) had he been a party to the contract.

4   Enforcement of contract by promisee

Section 1 does not affect any right of the promisee to enforce any term of contract.

5   Protection of promisor from double liability

Where under section 1 a term of a contract is enforceable by a third party, and the promisee has recovered from the promisor a sum in respect of—

(a) the third party's loss in respect of the term, or

(b) the expense to the promisee of making good to the third party the default of the promisor,

then, in any proceedings brought in reliance on that section by the third party, the court or arbital tribunal shall reduce any award to the third party to such extent as it thinks appropriate to take account of the sum recovered by the promisee.

6   Exceptions

(1) Section 1 confers no rights on a third party in the case of a contract on a bill of exchange, promissory note or other negotiable instrument.

(2) Section 1 confers no rights on a third party in the case of any contract binding on a company and its members under [section 33 of the Companies Act 2006 (effect of company's constitution)].

[(2A) Section 1 confers no rights on a third party in the case of any incorporation document of a limited liability partnership or any agreement (express or implied) between the members of a limited liability partnership, or between a limited liability partnership and its members, that determines the mutual rights and duties of the members and their rights and duties in relation to the limited liability partnership.]

(3) Section 1 confers no right on a third party to enforce—

(a) any term of a contract of employment against an employee,

(b) any term of a worker's contract against a worker (including a home worker), or

(c) any term of a relevant contract against an agency worker.

(4) In subsection (3)—

(a) 'contract of employment', 'employee', 'worker's contract', and 'worker' have the meaning given by section 54 of the National Minimum Wage Act 1998,

(b) 'home worker' has the meaning given by section 35(2) of that Act

(c) 'agency worker' has the same meaning as in section 34(1) of that Act, and

(d) 'relevant contract' means a contract entered into, in a case where section 34 of that Act applies, by the agency worker as respects work falling within subsection (1)(a) of that section.

(5) Section 1 confers no rights on a third party in the case of—

(a) a contract for the carriage of goods by sea, or

(b) a contract for the carriage of goods by rail or road, or for the carriage of cargo by air, which is subject to the rules of the appropriate international transport convention,

except that a third party may in reliance on that section avail himself of an exclusion or limitation of liability in such a contract.

(6) In subsection (5) 'contract for the carriage of goods by sea' means a contract of carriage—

(a) contained in or evidenced by a bill of lading, sea waybill or a corresponding electronic transaction, or

(b) under or for the purposes of which there is given an undertaking which is contained in a ship's delivery order or a corresponding electronic transaction.

(7) For the purposes of subsection (6)—

(a) 'bill of lading', 'sea waybill' and 'ship's delivery order' have the same meaning as in the Carriage of Goods by Sea Act 1992, and

(b) a corresponding electronic transaction is a transaction within section 1(5) of that Act which corresponds to the issue, indorsement, delivery or transfer of a bill of lading, sea waybill or ship's delivery order.

(8) In subsection (5) 'the appropriate international transport convention' means—

(a) in relation to a contract for the carriage of goods by rail, the Convention which has the force of law in the United Kingdom under [regulation 3 of the Railways (Convention on International Carriage by Rail) Regulations 2005,]

(b) in relation to a contract for the carriage of goods by road, the Convention which has the force of law in the United Kingdom under section 1 of the Carriage of Goods by Road Act 1965, and

(c) in relation to a contract for the carriage of cargo by air—

(i)   the Convention which has the force of law in the United Kingdom under section 1 of the Carriage by Air act 1961, or

(ii) the Convention which has the force of law under section 1 of the Carriage by Air (Supplementary Provisions) Act 1962, or

(iii) either of the amended Conventions set out in Part B of Schedule 2 or 3 to the Carriage by Air Acts (Application of Provisions) Order 1967.

7   Supplementary provisions relating to third party

(1) Section 1 does not affect any right or remedy of a third party that exists or is available from this Act.

(2) Section 2(2) of the Unfair Contract Terms Act 1977 (restriction on exclusion etc. of liability for negligence) shall not apply where the negligence consists of the breach of an obligation arising from a term of a contract and the person seeking to enforce it is a third party acting in reliance on section 1.

(3) In sections 5 and 8 of the Limitation Act 1980 the references to an action founded on a simple contract and an action upon a specialty shall respectively include references to an action brought in reliance on section 1 relating to a simple contract and an action brought in reliance on that section relating to a specialty.

(4) A third party shall not, by virtue of section 1(5) or 3(4) or (6), be treated as a party to the contract for the purposes of any other Act (or any instrument made under any other Act).

8   Arbitration provisions

(1) Where—

    (a) a right under section 1 to enforce a term ('the substantive term') is subject to a term providing for the submission of disputes to arbitration ('the arbitration agreement'), and

    (b) the arbitration agreement is an agreement in writing for the purposes of Part I of the Arbitration Act 1996,

the third party shall be treated for the purposes of that Act as a party to the arbitration agreement as regards disputes between himself and the promisor relating to the enforcement of the substantive term by the third party.

(2) Where—

    (a) a third party has a right under section 1 to enforce a term providing for one or more descriptions of dispute between the third party and the promisor to be submitted to arbitration ('the arbitration agreement'),

    (b) the arbitration agreement is an agreement in writing for the purposes of Part I of the Arbitration Act 1996, and

    (c) the third party does not fall to be treated under subsection (1) as a party to the arbitration agreement,

the third party shall, if he exercises the right, be treated for the purposes of that Act as a party to the arbitration agreement in relation to the matter with respect to which the right is exercised, and be treated as having been so immediately before the exercise of the right.

Financial Services and Markets Act 2000

(2000, c. 8)

1   The Financial Services Authority

(1) The body corporate known as the Financial Services Authority ('the Authority') is to have the functions conferred on it by or under this Act.

2   The Authority's general duties

(1) In discharging its general functions the Authority must, so far as is reasonably possible, act in a way—

    (a) which is compatible with the regulatory objectives; and

    (b) which the Authority considers most appropriate for the purpose of meeting these objectives.

(2) The regulatory objectives are—

    (a)   market confidence;

    [(ab) financial stability;]

    (b)   public awareness;

    (c)   the protection of consumers; and

    (d)   the reduction of financial crime.

(3) In discharging its general functions the Authority must have regard to—

    (a) the need to use its resources in the most efficient and economic way;

    (b) the responsibilities of those who manage the affairs of authorised persons;

   (c) the principle that a burden or restriction which is imposed on a person, or on the carrying on of an activity, should be proportionate to the benefits, considered in general terms, which are expected to result from the imposition of that burden or restriction;

   (d) the desirability of facilitating innovation in connection with regulated activities;

   (e) the international character of financial services and markets and the desirability of maintaining the competitive position of the United Kingdom;

   (f) the need to minimise the adverse effects on competition that may arise from anything done in the discharge of those functions;

   (g) the desirability of facilitating competition between those who are subject to any form of regulation by the Authority.

   [(h) the desirability of enhancing the understanding and knowledge of members of the public of financial matters (including the UK financial system).]

(4) The Authority's general functions are—

   (a) its function of making rules under this Act (considered as a whole);

   (b) its function of preparing and issuing codes under this Act (considered as a whole);

   (c) its functions in relation to the giving of general guidance (considered as a whole); and

   (d) its function of determining the general policy and principles by reference to which it performs particular functions.

(5) 'General Guidance' has the meaning given in section 158(5).

3   Market confidence

(1) The market confidence objective is: maintaining confidence in [the UK financial system].

(2) ['The UK financial system'] means the financial system operating in the United Kingdom and includes—

   (a) financial markets and exchanges;

   (b) regulated activities; and

   (c) other activities connected with financial markets and exchanges.

[3A   Financial stability

(1) The financial stability objective is: contributing to the protection and enhancement of the stability of the UK financial system.

(2) In considering that objective the Authority must have regard to—

   (a) the economic and fiscal consequences for the United Kingdom of instability of the UK financial system;

   (b) the effects (if any) on the growth of the economy of the United Kingdom of anything done for the purpose of meeting that objective; and

   (c) the impact (if any) on the stability of the UK financial system of events or circumstances outside the United Kingdom (as well as in the United Kingdom).

(3) The Authority must, consulting the Treasury, determine and review its strategy in relation to the financial stability objective.]

5   The protection of consumers

(1) The protection of consumers objective is: securing the appropriate degree of protection for consumers.

(2) In considering what degree of protection may be appropriate, the Authority must have regard to—

   (a)   the differing degrees of risk involved in different kinds of investment or other transaction;

   (b)   the differing degrees of experience and expertise that different consumers may have in relation to different kinds of regulated activity;

   [(ba) any information which the consumer financial education body has provided to the Authority in the exercise of the consumer financial education function;]

   (c)   the needs that consumers may have for advice and accurate information; and

(d)   the general principle that consumers should take responsibility for their decisions.

(3) 'Consumers' means persons—

(a) who are consumers for the purposes of section 138; or

(b) who, in relation to regulated activities carried on otherwise than by authorised persons, would be consumers for those purposes if the activities were carried on by authorised persons.

6   The reduction of financial crime

(1) The reduction of financial crime objective is: reducing the extent to which it is possible for a business carried on—

(a) by a regulated person, or

(b) in contravention of the general prohibition,

to be used for a purpose connected with financial crime.

(2) In considering that objective the Authority must, in particular, have regard to the desirability of—

(a) regulated persons being aware of the risk of their businesses being used in connection with the commission of financial crime;

(b) regulated persons taking appropriate measures (in relation to their administration and employment practices, the conduct of transactions by them and otherwise) to prevent financial crime, facilitate its detection and monitor its incidence;

(c) regulated persons devoting adequate resources to the matters mentioned in paragraph (b).

(3) 'Financial crime' includes any offence involving—

(a) fraud or dishonesty

(b) misconduct in, or misuse of information relating to, a financial market; or

(c) handling the proceeds of crime

(4) 'Offence' includes an act or omission which would be an offence if it had taken place in the United Kingdom.

(5) 'Regulated person' means an authorised person, a recognised investment exchange or a recognised clearing house.

[6A   Enhancing public understanding of financial matters etc

(1) The Authority must establish a body corporate ("the consumer financial education body") whose function ("the consumer financial education function") is to enhance—

(a) the understanding and knowledge of members of the public of financial matters (including the UK financial system); and

(b) the ability of members of the public to manage their own financial affairs.

(2) The consumer financial education function includes, in particular—

(a) promoting awareness of the benefits of financial planning;

(b) promoting awareness of the financial advantages and disadvantages in relation to the supply of particular kinds of goods or services;

(c) promoting awareness of the benefits and risks associated with different kinds of financial dealing (which includes informing the Authority and other bodies of those benefits and risks);

(d) the publication of educational materials or the carrying out of other educational activities; and

(e) the provision of information and advice to members of the public.

(3) Schedule 1A makes further provision about the consumer financial education body.]

7   Duty of Authority to follow principles of good governance

In managing its affairs, the Authority must have regard to such generally accepted principles of good corporate governance as it is reasonable to regard as applicable to it.

8   The Authority's general duty to consult

The Authority must make and maintain effective arrangements for consulting practitioners and consumers on the extent to which its general policies and practices are consistent with its general duties under section 2.

9   The Practitioner Panel

(1) Arrangements under section 8 must include the establishment and maintenance of a panel of persons (to be known as 'the Practitioner Panel') to represent the interests of practitioners.

10   The Consumer Panel

(1) Arrangements under section 8 must include the establishment and maintenance of a panel of persons (to be known as 'the Consumer Panel') to represent the interests of consumers.

(2) The Authority must appoint one of the members of the Consumer Panel to be its chairman.

(3) The Treasury's approval is required for the appointment or dismissal of the chairman.

(4) The Authority must have regard to any representations made to it by the Consumer Panel.

(5) The Authority must appoint to the Consumer Panel such consumers, or persons representing the interests of consumers, as it considers appropriate.

[(5A) The Secretary of State may direct the Authority to appoint as a member of the Consumer Panel a person specified by the Secretary of State who—

(a) is a non-executive member of the National Consumer Council, and

(b) is nominated for the purposes of this subsection by the National Consumer Council after consultation with the Authority.

(5B) Only one person may, at any time, be a member of the Consumer Panel appointed in accordance with a direction under subsection (5A); but that does not prevent the Authority appointing as a member of the Consumer Panel any person who is also a member of the National Consumer Council.

(5C) A person appointed in accordance with a direction under subsection (5A) ceases to be a member of the Panel on ceasing to be a non-executive member of the National Consumer Council.]

(6) The Authority must secure that the membership of the Consumer Panel is such as to give a fair degree of representation to those who are using, or are or may be contemplating using, services otherwise than in connection with businesses carried on by them.

(7) 'Consumers' means persons, other than authorised persons—

(a) who are consumers for the purposes of section 138; or

(b) who, in relation to regulated activities carried on otherwise than by authorised persons, would be consumers for those purposes if the activities were carried on by authorised persons.

[(7) Sections 425A and 425B (meaning of "consumers") apply for the purposes of this section, but the references to consumers in this section do not include consumers who are authorised persons.]

11   Duty to consider representations by the Panels

(1) This section applies to a representation made, in accordance with arrangements under section 8, by the Practitioner Panel or by the Consumer Panel.

(2) The Authority must consider the representation.

(3) If the Authority disagrees with a view expressed, or proposal made, in the representation, it must give the Panel a statement in writing of its reasons for disagreeing.

19   The general prohibition

(1) No person may carry on a regulated activity in the United Kingdom, or purport to do so, unless he is—

(a) an authorised person; or

(b) an exempt person.

(2) The prohibition is referred to in this Act as the general prohibition.

21   Restrictions on financial promotion

(1) A person ('A') must not, in the course of business, communicate an invitation or inducement to engage in investment activity.

(2) But subsection (1) does not apply if—

(a) A is an authorised person; or

(b) the content of the communication is approved for the purposes of this section by an authorised person.

(3) In the case of a communication originating outside the United Kingdom, subsection (1) applies only if the communication is capable of having an effect in the United Kingdom.

(4) The Treasury may by order specify circumstances in which a person is to be regarded for the purposes of subsection (1) as—

(a) acting in the course of business;

(b) not acting in the course of business.

(5) The Treasury may by order specify circumstances (which may include compliance with financial promotion rules) in which subsection (1) does not apply.

(6) An order under subsection (5) may, in particular, provide that subsection (1) does not apply in relation to communications—

(a) of a specified description;

(b) originating in a specified country or territory outside the United Kingdom;

(c) originating in a country or territory which falls within a specified description of country or territory outside the United Kingdom; or

(d) originating outside the United Kingdom.

(7) The Treasury may by order repeal subsection (3).

(8) 'Engaging in investment activity' means—

(a) entering or offering to enter into an agreement the making or performance of which by either party constitutes a controlled activity; or

(b) exercising any rights conferred by a controlled investment to acquire, dispose of, underwrite or convert a controlled investment.

(9) An activity is a controlled activity if—

(a) it is an activity of a specified kind or one which falls within a specified class of activity; and

(b) it relates to an investment of a specified kind, or to one which falls within a specified class of investment.

(10) An investment is a controlled investment if it is an investment of a specified kind or one which falls within a specified class of investment.

22   The classes of activity and categories of investment

(1) An activity is a regulated activity for the purposes of this Act if it is an activity of a specified kind which is carried on by way of business and—

(a) relates to an investment of a specified kind; or

(b) in the case of an activity of a kind which is also specified for the purposes of this paragraph, is carried on in relation to property of any kind.

26   Agreements made by unauthorised persons

(1) An agreement made by a person in the course of carrying on a regulated activity in contravention of the general prohibition is unenforceable against the other party.

(2) The other party is entitled to recover—

(a) any money or other property paid or transferred by him under the agreement; and

(b) compensation for any loss sustained by him as a result of having parted with it.

(3) 'Agreement' means an agreement—

(a) made after this section comes into force; and

(b) the making or performance of which constitutes, or is part of, the regulated activity in question.

42 Giving permission

(1) 'The applicant' means an applicant for permission under section 40.

(2) The Authority may give permission for the applicant to carry on the regulated activity or activities to which his application relates or such of them as may be specified in the permission.

56 Prohibition orders

(1) Subsection (2) applies if it appears to the Authority that an individual is not a fit and proper person to perform functions in relation to a regulated activity carried on by an authorised person.

(2) The Authority may make an order ('a prohibition order') prohibiting the individual from performing a specified function, any function falling within a specified description or any function.

(4) An individual who performs or agrees to perform a function in breach of a prohibition order is guilty of an offence and liable on summary conviction to a fine not exceeding level 5 on the standard scale.

(5) In proceedings for an offence under subsection (4) it is a defence for the accused to show that he took all reasonable precautions and exercised all due diligence to avoid committing the offence.

(6) An authorised person must take reasonable care to ensure that no function of his, in relation to the carrying on of a regulated activity, is performed by a person who is prohibited from performing that function by a prohibition order.

64 Conduct: statements and codes

(1) The Authority may issue statements of principle with respect to the conduct expected of approved persons.

(2) If the Authority issues a statement of principle under subsection (1), it must also issue a code of practice for the purpose of helping to determine whether or not a person's conduct complies with the statement of principle.

(3) A code issued under subsection (2) may specify—
  (a) descriptions of conduct which, in the opinion of the Authority, comply with a statement of principle;
  (b) descriptions of conduct which, in the opinion of the Authority, do not comply with a statement of principle;
  (c) factors which, in the opinion of the Authority, are to be taken into account in determining whether or not a person's conduct complies with a statement of principle.

(4) The Authority may at any time alter or replace a statement or code issued under this section.

(5) If a statement or code is altered or replaced, the altered or replacement statement or code must be issued by the Authority.

(6) A statement or code issued under this section must be published by the Authority in the way appearing to the Authority to be best calculated to bring it to the attention of the public.

(7) A code published under this section and in force at the time when any particular conduct takes place may be relied on so far as it tends to establish whether or not that conduct complies with a statement of principle.

(8) Failure to comply with a statement of principle under this section does not of itself give rise to any right of action by persons affected or affect the validity of any transaction.

(9) A person is not to be taken to have failed to comply with a statement of principle if he shows that, at the time of the alleged failure, it or its associated code of practice had not been published.

(10) The Authority must, without delay, give the Treasury a copy of any statement or code which it publishes under this section.

90 [Compensation for statements in listing particulars or prospectus]

(1) Any person responsible for listing particulars is liable to pay compensation to a person who has—

(a) acquired securities to which the particulars apply; and

(b) suffered loss in respect of them as a result of—

    (i) any untrue or misleading statement in the particulars; or

    (ii) the omission from the particulars of any matter required to be included by section 80 or 81.

[118 Market abuse

(1) For the purposes of this Act, market abuse is behaviour (whether by one person alone or by two or more persons jointly or in concert) which—

    (a) occurs in relation to—

        (i) qualifying investments admitted to trading on a prescribed market,

        (ii) qualifying investments in respect of which a request for admission to trading on such a market has been made, or

        (iii) in the case of subsection (2) or (3) behaviour, investments which are related investments in relation to such qualifying investments, and

    (b) falls within any one or more of the types of behaviour set out in subsections (2) to (8).

(2) The first type of behaviour is where an insider deals, or attempts to deal, in a qualifying investment or related investment on the basis of inside information relating to the investment in question.

(3) The second is where an insider discloses inside information to another person otherwise than in the proper course of the exercise of his employment, profession or duties.

(4) The third is where the behaviour (not falling within subsection (2) or (3))—

    (a) is based on information which is not generally available to those using the market but which, if available to a regular user of the market, would be, or would be likely to be, regarded by him as relevant when deciding the terms on which transactions in qualifying investments should be effected, and

    (b) is likely to be regarded by a regular user of the market as a failure on the part of the person concerned to observe the standard of behaviour reasonably expected of a person in his position in relation to the market.

(5) The fourth is where the behaviour consists of effecting transactions or orders to trade (otherwise than for legitimate reasons and in conformity with accepted market practices on the relevant market) which—

    (a) give, or are likely to give, a false or misleading impression as to the supply of, or demand for, or as to the price of, one or more qualifying investments, or

    (b) secure the price of one or more such investments at an abnormal or artificial level.

(6) The fifth is where the behaviour consists of effecting transactions or orders to trade which employ fictitious devices or any other form of deception or contrivance.

(7) The sixth is where the behaviour consists of the dissemination of information by any means which gives, or is likely to give, a false or misleading impression as to a qualifying investment by a person who knew or could reasonably be expected to have known that the information was false or misleading.

(8) The seventh is where the behaviour (not falling within subsection (5), (6) or (7))—

    (a) is likely to give a regular user of the market a false or misleading impression as to the supply of, demand for or price or value of, qualifying investments, or

    (b) would be, or would be likely to be, regarded by a regular user of the market as behaviour that would distort, or would be likely to distort, the market in such an investment,

and the behaviour is likely to be regarded by a regular user of the market as a failure on the part of the person concerned to observe the standard of behaviour reasonably expected of a person in his position in relation to the market.

(9) Subsections (4) and (8) and the definition of 'regular user' in section 130A(3) cease to have effect on [31 December 2011] and subsection (1)(b) is then to be read as no longer referring to those subsections.]

[See also ss 118A (Supplementary provision about certain behaviour), 118B (Insiders) and 118C (Inside information).]

119   The code

(1) The Authority must prepare and issue a code containing such provisions as the Authority considers will give appropriate guidance to those determining whether or not behaviour amounts to market abuse.

(2) The code may among other things specify—

(a) descriptions of behaviour that, in the opinion of the Authority, amount to market abuse;

(b) descriptions of behaviour that, in the opinion of the Authority, do not amount to market abuse;

(c) factors that, in the opinion of the Authority, are to be taken into account in determining whether or not behaviour amounts to market abuse.

[(d) descriptions of behaviour that are accepted market practices in relation to one or more specified markets;

(e) descriptions of behaviour that are not accepted market practices in relation to one or more specified markets.].

[(2A) In determining, for the purposes of subsections (2)(d) and (2)(e) or otherwise, what are and what are not accepted market practices, the Authority must have regard to the factors and procedures laid down in Articles 2 and 3 respectively of Commission Directive 2004/72/EC of 29 April 2004 implementing Directive 2003/6/EC of the European Parliament and of the Council.]

122   Effect of the code

(1) If a person behaves in a way which is described (in the code in force under section 119 at the time of the behaviour) as behaviour that, in the Authority's opinion, does not amount to market abuse that behaviour of his is to be taken, for the purposes of this Act, as not amounting to market abuse.

(2) Otherwise, the code in force under section 119 at the time when particular behaviour occurs may be relied on so far as it indicates whether or not that behaviour should be taken to amount to market abuse.

138   General rule-making power

(1) The Authority may make such rules applying to authorised persons—

(a) with respect to the carrying on by them of regulated activities, or

(b) with respect to the carrying on by them of activities which are not regulated activities,

as appear to it to be necessary or expedient for the purpose of [meeting any of its regulatory objectives or for the purpose of, to facilitate or in consequence of a transfer under section 3 of the Banking (Special Provisions) Act 2008].

[139A   General rules about remuneration

(1) The Authority must exercise its power to make general rules so as to make rules requiring each authorised person (or each authorised person of a specified description) to have, and act in accordance with, a remuneration policy.

(2) A "remuneration policy" is a policy about the remuneration by the authorised person of—

(a) officers,

(b) employees, and

(c) other persons,

of a specified description.

(3) The rules must secure that any remuneration policy that an authorised person is required by the rules to have is consistent with—

(a) the effective management of risks; and

(b) the Implementation Standards.

(4) When making rules about remuneration policies, the Authority must have regard to any other international standards about the remuneration of individuals working in the financial sector (or certain such individuals).

(5) The Treasury may direct the Authority to consider whether the remuneration policies of authorised persons specified in the direction (or of authorised persons of a description so specified) comply with requirements imposed by the rules as to the contents of the policies.

(6) Before giving a direction under subsection (5), the Treasury must consult the Authority.

(7) If the Authority considers that a remuneration policy fails to make provision which complies with the requirements mentioned in subsection (5), the Authority must take such steps as it considers appropriate to deal with the failure.

(8) The steps that the Authority may take include requiring the remuneration policy to be revised.

(9) General rules may—

(a) prohibit persons (or persons of a specified description) from being remunerated in a specified way;

(b) provide that any provision of an agreement that contravenes such a prohibition is void;
and

(c) provide for the recovery of any payment made, or other property transferred, in pursuance of a provision that is void by virtue of paragraph (b).

(10) A prohibition may be imposed under subsection (9)(a) only for the purpose of ensuring that the provision of remuneration is consistent with—

(a) the effective management of risks; or

(b) the Implementation Standards.

(11) A provision that, at the time the rules are made, is contained in an agreement made before that time may not be rendered void under subsection (9)(b) unless it is subsequently amended so as to contravene a prohibition under subsection (9)(a).

(12) In this section—

"the Implementation Standards" means the Implementation Standards for Principles for Sound Compensation Practices, issued by the Financial Stability Board on 25 September 2009; and

"specified" (except in subsection (5)) means specified by the rules.

(13) References to the Implementation Standards or to international standards of a kind mentioned in subsection (4) are to standards that are for the time being in force.]

[139B   Rules about recovery plans

(1) The Authority must exercise its power to make general rules so as to make rules requiring each authorised person (or each authorised person of a specified description) to prepare, and keep up-to-date, a recovery plan.

(2) A "recovery plan" is a document containing information within subsection (3) or (4) of a specified description.

(3) Information is within this subsection if it relates to action to be taken to secure that, in the event of specified circumstances affecting the carrying on of the business (or any part of the business) of the authorised person—

(a) the business of the authorised person, or

(b) a specified part of the business of the authorised person,

is capable of being carried on (whether or not by the authorised person and whether or not in the same way as previously).

(4) Information is within this subsection if it would facilitate the carrying on of the business (or any part of the business) of the authorised person by any other person.

(5) The Authority must consider whether each recovery plan makes satisfactory provision in relation to the matters required by the rules to be covered by the plan.

(6) If the Authority considers that a recovery plan fails to make satisfactory provision in relation to any such matter, the Authority must take such steps as it considers appropriate to deal with the failure.

(7) The steps that the Authority may take include requiring the recovery plan to be revised.

(8) The authorised persons subject to general rules about recovery plans must include authorised persons in relation to whom any power under Part 1 of the Banking Act 2009 (special resolution regime) is exercisable.

(9) Before preparing a draft of general rules about recovery plans having effect in relation to those persons, the Authority must consult—

    (a) the Treasury; and

    (b) the Bank of England.]

[139C   Rules about resolution plans

(1) The Authority must exercise its power to make general rules so as to make rules requiring each authorised person (or each authorised person of a specified description) to prepare, and keep up-to-date, a resolution plan.

(2) A "resolution plan" is a document containing information within subsection (3) or (4) of a specified description.

(3) Information is within this subsection if it relates to action to be taken in the event of—

    (a) circumstances arising in which it is likely that the business (or any part of the business) of the authorised person will fail; or

    (b) the failure of the business (or any part of the business) of the authorised person.

(4) Information is within this subsection if it would facilitate anything falling to be done by any person in consequence of that failure.

(5) An example of information within subsection (4) is information that, in the event of that failure, would facilitate—

    (a) planning by the Treasury in relation to the possible exercise of any of their powers under Part 1 of the Banking Act 2009; or

    (b) planning by the Bank of England in relation to the possible exercise of any of its powers under Part 1, 2 or 3 of that Act.

(6) The Authority must consider whether each resolution plan makes satisfactory provision in relation to the matters required by the rules to be covered by the plan.

(7) If the Authority considers that a resolution plan fails to make satisfactory provision in relation to any such matter, the Authority must take such steps as it considers appropriate to deal with the failure.

(8) The steps that the Authority may take include requiring the resolution plan to be revised.

(9) The authorised persons subject to general rules about resolution plans must include authorised persons in relation to whom any power under Part 1 of the Banking Act 2009 is exercisable.

(10) Before preparing a draft of general rules about resolution plans having effect in relation to those persons, the Authority must consult—

    (a) the Treasury; and

    (b) the Bank of England.]

203   Power to prohibit the carrying on of Consumer Credit Act business

(1) If it appears to [the Office of Fair Trading ('the OFT')] that subsection (4) has been, or is likely to be, contravened as respects a consumer credit EEA firm, [it] may by written notice given to the firm impose on the firm a consumer credit prohibition.

(2) If it appears to the [OFT] that a restriction imposed under section 204 on an EEA consumer credit firm has not been complied with, [it] may by written notice given to the firm impose a consumer credit prohibition.

(3) 'Consumer credit prohibition' means a prohibition on carrying on, or purporting to carry on, in the United Kingdom any Consumer Credit Act business which consists of or includes carrying on one or more listed activities.

(4) This subsection is contravened as respects a firm if—

    (a) the firm or any of its employees, agents or associates (whether past or present), or

    (b) if the firm is a body corporate, any controller of the firm or an associate of any such controller,

does any of the things specified in paragraphs [(a) to (e) of section 25(2A)] of the Consumer Credit Act 1974.

(5) A consumer credit prohibition may be absolute or may be imposed—

    (a) for such period,

    (b) until the occurrence of such event, or

    (c) until such conditions are complied with,

as may be specified in the notice given under subsection (1) or (2).

(6) Any period, event or condition so specified may be varied by the [OFT] on the application of the firm concerned.

(7) A consumer credit prohibition may be withdrawn by written notice served by the [OFT] on the firm concerned, and any such notice takes effect on such date as is specified in the notice.

(8) Schedule 16 has effect as respects consumer credit prohibitions and restrictions under section 204.

(9) A firm contravening a prohibition under this section is guilty of an offence and liable—

    (a) on summary conviction, to a fine not exceeding the statutory maximum;

    (b) on conviction on indictment, to a fine.

(10) In this section and section 204—

'a consumer credit EEA firm' means an EEA firm falling within any of paragraphs (a) to (c) of paragraph 5 of Schedule 3 whose EEA authorisation covers any Consumer Credit Act business;

'Consumer Credit Act business' means consumer credit business, consumer hire business or ancillary credit business;

'consumer credit business', 'consumer hire business' and 'ancillary credit business' have the same meaning as in the Consumer Credit Act 1974;

'listed activity' means an activity listed in [Annex 1 to the banking consolidation directive] or the Annex to the investment services directive;

'associate' has the same meaning as in section [25(2A)] of the Consumer Credit Act 1974;

'controller' has the meaning given by section 189(1) of that Act.

204 Power to restrict the carrying on of Consumer Credit Act business

(1) In this section 'restriction' means a direction that a consumer credit EEA firm may not carry on in the United Kingdom, otherwise than in accordance with such condition or conditions as may be specified in the direction, any Consumer Credit Act business which—

    (a) consists of or includes carrying on any listed activity; and

    (b) is specified in the direction.

(2) If it appears to the [OFT] that the situation as respects a consumer credit EEA firm is such that the powers conferred by section 203(1) are exercisable, the [OFT] may, instead of imposing a prohibition, impose such restriction as appears to [it] desirable.

(3) A restriction—

    (a) may be withdrawn, or

    (b) may be varied with the agreement of the firm concerned, by written notice served by the [OFT] on the firm, and any such notice takes effect on such date as is specified in the notice.

(4) A firm contravening a restriction is guilty of an offence and liable—

    (a) on summary conviction, to a fine not exceeding the statutory maximum;

    (b) on conviction on indictment, to a fine.

[226A Consumer credit jurisdiction

(1) A complaint which relates to an act or omission of a person ('the respondent') is to be dealt with under the ombudsman scheme if the conditions mentioned in subsection (2) are satisfied.

(2) The conditions are that—
  (a) the complainant is eligible and wishes to have the complaint dealt with under the scheme;
  (b) the complaint falls within a description specified in consumer credit rules;
  (c) at the time of the act or omission the respondent was the licensee under a standard licence or was authorised to carry on an activity by virtue of section 34A of the Consumer Credit Act 1974;
  (d) the act or omission occurred in the course of a business being carried on by the respondent which was of a type mentioned in subsection (3);
  (e) at the time of the act or omission that type of business was specified in an order made by the Secretary of State; and
  (f) the complaint cannot be dealt with under the compulsory jurisdiction.
(3) The types of business referred to in subsection (2)(d) are—
  (a) a consumer credit business;
  (b) a consumer hire business;
  (c) a business so far as it comprises or relates to credit brokerage;
  (d) a business so far as it comprises or relates to debt-adjusting;
  (e) a business so far as it comprises or relates to debt-counselling;
  (f) a business so far as it comprises or relates to debt-collecting;
  (g) a business so far as it comprises or relates to debt administration;
  (h) a business so far as it comprises or relates to the provision of credit information services;
  (i) a business so far as it comprises or relates to the operation of a credit reference agency.
(4) A complainant is eligible if—
  (a) he is—
    (i) an individual; or
    (ii) a surety in relation to a security provided to the respondent in connection with the business mentioned in subsection (2)(d); and
  (b) he falls within a class of person specified in consumer credit rules.
(5) The approval of the Treasury is required for an order under subsection (2)(e).
(6) The jurisdiction of the scheme which results from this section is referred to in this Act as the 'consumer credit jurisdiction'.
(7) In this Act 'consumer credit rules' means rules made by the scheme operator with the approval of the Authority for the purposes of the consumer credit jurisdiction.
(8) Consumer credit rules under this section may make different provision for different cases.
(9) Expressions used in the Consumer Credit Act 1974 have the same meaning in this section as they have in that Act.]

[234A Funding by consumer credit licensees etc.

(1) For the purpose of funding—
  (a) the establishment of the ombudsman scheme so far as it relates to the consumer credit jurisdiction (whenever any relevant expense is incurred), and
  (b) its operation in relation to the consumer credit jurisdiction,
the scheme operator may from time to time with the approval of the Authority determine a sum which is to be raised by way of contributions under this section.
(2) A sum determined under subsection (1) may include a component to cover the costs of the collection of contributions to that sum ('collection costs') under this section.
(3) The scheme operator must notify the OFT of every determination under subsection (1).
(4) The OFT must give general notice of every determination so notified
(5) The OFT may by general notice impose requirements on—
  (a) licensees to whom this section applies, or
  (b) persons who make applications to which this section applies,
to pay contributions to the OFT for the purpose of raising sums determined under subsection (1).
(6) The amount of the contribution payable by a person under such a requirement—

(a) shall be the amount specified in or determined under the general notice; and

(b) shall be paid before the end of the period or at the time so specified or determined.

(7) A general notice under subsection (5) may—

(a) impose requirements only on descriptions of licensees or applicants specified in the notice;

(b) provide for exceptions from any requirement imposed on a description of licensees or applicants;

(c) impose different requirements on different descriptions of licensees or applicants;

(d) make provision for refunds in specified circumstances.

(8) Contributions received by the OFT must be paid to the scheme operator.

(9) As soon as practicable after the end of—

(a) each financial year of the scheme operator, or

(b) if the OFT and the scheme operator agree that this paragraph is to apply instead of paragraph (a) for the time being, each period agreed by them,

the scheme operator must pay to the OFT an amount representing the extent to which collection costs are covered in accordance with subsection (2) by the total amount of the contributions paid by the OFT to it during the year or (as the case may be) the agreed period.

(10) Amounts received by the OFT from the scheme operator are to be retained by it for the purpose of meeting its costs.

(11) The Secretary of State may by order provide that the functions of the OFT under this section are for the time being to be carried out by the scheme operator.

(12) An order under subsection (11) may provide that while the order is in force this section shall have effect subject to such modifications as may be set out in the order.

(13) The licensees to whom this section applies are licensees under standard licences which cover to any extent the carrying on of a type of business specified in an order under section 226A(2)(e).

(14) The applications to which this section applies are applications for—

(a) standard licences covering to any extent the carrying on of a business of such a type;

(b) the renewal of standard licences on terms covering to any extent the carrying on of a business of such a type.

(15) Expressions used in the Consumer Credit Act 1974 have the same meaning in this section as they have in that Act.]

380 Injunctions

(1) If, on the application of the Authority or the Secretary of State, the court is satisfied—

(a) that there is a reasonable likelihood that any person will contravene a relevant requirement, or

(b) that any person has contravened a relevant requirement and that there is a reasonable likelihood that the contravention will continue or be repeated,

the court may make an order restraining (or in Scotland an interdict prohibiting) the contravention.

(2) If on the application of the Authority or the Secretary of State the court is satisfied—

(a) that any person has contravened a relevant requirement, and

(b) that there are steps which could be taken for remedying the contravention,

the court may make an order requiring that person, and any other person who appears to have been knowingly concerned in the contravention, to take such steps as the court may direct to remedy it.

381 Injunctions in cases of market abuse

(1) If, on the application of the Authority, the court is satisfied—

(a) that there is a reasonable likelihood that any person will engage in market abuse, or

(b) that any person is or has engaged in market abuse and that there is a reasonable likelihood that the market abuse will continue or be repeated,

the court may make an order restraining (or in Scotland an interdict prohibiting) the market abuse.

(2) If on the application of the Authority the court is satisfied—

(a) that any person is or has engaged in market abuse, and

(b) that there are steps which could be taken for remedying the market abuse,

the court may make an order requiring him to take such steps as the court may direct to remedy it.

382 Restitution orders

(1) The court may, on the application of the Authority or the Secretary of State, make an order under subsection (2) if it is satisfied that a person has contravened a relevant requirement, or been knowingly concerned in the contravention of such a requirement, and—

(a) that profits have accrued to him as a result of the contravention; or

(b) that one or more persons have suffered loss or been otherwise adversely affected as a result of the contravention.

(2) The court may order the person concerned to pay to the Authority such sum as appears to the court to be just having regard—

(a) in a case within paragraph (a) of subsection (1), to the profits appearing to the court to have accrued;

(b) in a case within paragraph (b) of that subsection, to the extent of the loss or other adverse effect;

(c) in a case within both of those paragraphs, to the profits appearing to the court to have accrued and to the extent of the loss or other adverse effect.

(3) Any amount paid to the Authority in pursuance of an order under subsection (2) must be paid by it to such qualifying person or distributed by it among such qualifying persons as the court may direct.

(8) 'Qualifying person' means a person appearing to the court to be someone—

(a) to whom the profits mentioned in subsection (1)(a) are attributable; or

(b) who has suffered the loss or adverse effect mentioned in subsection (1)(b).

[404 Consumer redress schemes

(1) This section applies if—

(a) it appears to the Authority that there may have been a widespread or regular failure by relevant firms to comply with requirements applicable to the carrying on by them of any activity;

(b) it appears to it that, as a result, consumers have suffered (or may suffer) loss or damage in respect of which, if they brought legal proceedings, a remedy or relief would be available in the proceedings; and

(c) it considers that it is desirable to make rules for the purpose of securing that redress is made to the consumers in respect of the failure (having regard to other ways in which consumers may obtain redress).

(2) "Relevant firms" means—

(a) authorised persons; [...]

(b) payment service providers [or

(c) electronic money issuers].

(3) The Authority may make rules requiring each relevant firm (or each relevant firm of a specified description) which has carried on the activity on or after the specified date to establish and operate a consumer redress scheme.

(4) A "consumer redress scheme" is a scheme under which the firm is required to take one or more of the following steps in relation to the activity.

(5) The firm must first investigate whether, on or after the specified date, it has failed to comply with the requirements mentioned in subsection (1)(a) that are applicable to the carrying on by it of the activity.

(6) The next step is for the firm to determine whether the failure has caused (or may cause) loss or damage to consumers.

(7) If the firm determines that the failure has caused (or may cause) loss or damage to consumers, it must then—

(a) determine what the redress should be in respect of the failure; and

(b) make the redress to the consumers.

(8) A relevant firm is required to take the above steps in relation to any particular consumer even if, after the rules are made, a defence of limitation becomes available to the firm in respect of the loss or damage in question.

(9) Before making rules under this section, the Authority must consult the scheme operator of the ombudsman scheme.

(10) For the meaning of consumers, see section 404E.]

[404A   Rules under s. 404: supplementary

(1) Rules under section 404 may make provision—

(a) specifying the activities and requirements in relation to which relevant firms are to carry out investigations under consumer redress schemes;

(b) setting out, in relation to any specified description of case, examples of things done, or omitted to be done, that are to be regarded as constituting a failure to comply with a requirement;

(c) setting out, in relation to any specified description of case, matters to be taken into account, or steps to be taken, by relevant firms for the purpose of—

   (i) assessing evidence as to a failure to comply with a requirement; or

   (ii) determining whether such a failure has caused (or may cause) loss or damage to consumers;

(d) as to the kinds of redress that are, or are not, to be made to consumers in specified descriptions of case and the way in which redress is to be determined in specified descriptions of case;

(e) as to the things that relevant firms are, or are not, to do in establishing and operating consumer redress schemes;

(f) securing that relevant firms are not required to investigate anything occurring after a specified date;

(g) specifying the times by which anything required to be done under any consumer redress scheme is to be done;

(h) requiring relevant firms to provide information to the Authority;

(i) authorising one or more competent persons to do anything for the purposes of, or in connection with, the establishment or operation of any consumer redress scheme;

(j) for the nomination or approval by the Authority of persons authorised under paragraph (i);

(k) as to the circumstances in which, instead of a relevant firm, the Authority (or one or more competent persons acting on the Authority's behalf) may carry out the investigation and take the other relevant steps under any consumer redress scheme;

(l) as to the powers to be available to those carrying out an investigation by virtue of paragraph (k);

(m) as to the enforcement of any redress (for example, in the case of a money award, as a debt owed by a relevant firm).

(2) The only examples that may be set out in the rules as a result of subsection (1)(b) are examples of things done, or omitted to be done, that have been, or would be, held by a court or tribunal to constitute a failure to comply with a requirement.

(3) Matters may not be set out in the rules as a result of subsection (1)(c) if they have not been, or would not be, taken into account by a court or tribunal for the purpose mentioned there.

(4) The Authority must exercise the power conferred as a result of subsection (1)(d) so as to secure that, in relation to any description of case, the only kinds of redress to be made are those which it considers to be just in relation to that description of case.

(5) In acting under subsection (4), the Authority must have regard (among other things) to the nature and extent of the losses or damage in question.

(7) The reference in subsection (1)(k) to the other relevant steps under any consumer redress scheme is a reference to the Authority making the determinations mentioned in section 404(6) and (7) (with the firm still required to make the redress).

(8) If the rules include provision under subsection (1)(k), they must also include provision for—

    (a) giving warning and decision notices, and

    (b) conferring rights on relevant firms to refer matters to the Tribunal,

in relation to any determination mentioned in section 404(6) and (7) made by the Authority.

(9) Nothing in this section is to be taken as limiting the power conferred by section 404.]

[404B Complaints to the ombudsman scheme

(1) If—

    (a) a consumer makes a complaint under the ombudsman scheme in respect of an act or omission of a relevant firm, and

    (b) at the time the complaint is made, the subject-matter of the complaint falls to be dealt with (or has been dealt with) under a consumer redress scheme,

the way in which the complaint is to be determined by the ombudsman is to be as mentioned in subsection (4).

(2) If a consumer—

    (a) is not satisfied with a determination made by a relevant firm under a consumer redress scheme, or

    (b) considers that a relevant firm has failed to make a determination in accordance with a consumer redress scheme,

the consumer may, in respect of that determination or failure, make a complaint under the ombudsman scheme.

(3) A complaint mentioned in subsection (1) or (2) is referred to in the following provisions of this section as a "relevant complaint".

(4) A relevant complaint is to be determined by reference to what, in the opinion of the ombudsman, the determination under the consumer redress scheme should be or should have been (subject to subsection (5)).

(5) If, in determining a relevant complaint, the ombudsman determines that the firm should make (or should have made) a payment of an amount to the consumer, the amount awarded by the ombudsman (a "money award") must not exceed the monetary limit (within the meaning of section 229).

(6) But the ombudsman may recommend that the firm pay a larger amount.

(7) A money award—

    (a) may specify the date by which the amount awarded is to be paid;

    (b) may provide for interest to be payable, at a rate specified in the award, on any amount which is not paid by that date; and

    (c) is enforceable by the consumer in accordance with Part 3 or 3A of Schedule 17 (as the case may be).

(8) If, in determining a relevant complaint, the ombudsman determines that the firm should take (or should have taken) particular action in relation to the consumer, the ombudsman may direct the firm to take that action.

(9) Compliance with a direction under subsection (8) is enforceable, on the application of the consumer, by an injunction . . .

(11) The compulsory jurisdiction of the ombudsman scheme is to include the jurisdiction resulting from this section.]

[404E Meaning of "consumers"

(1) For the purposes of sections 404 to 404B "consumers" means persons who—

    (a) have used, or may have contemplated using, any of the services within subsection (2); or

    (b) have relevant rights or interests in relation to any of the services within that subsection.

(2) The services within this subsection are services provided by—

    (a) authorised persons in carrying on regulated activities;

    (b) authorised persons in carrying on a consumer credit business in connection with the accepting of deposits;

    (c) authorised persons in communicating, or approving the communication by others of, invitations or inducements to engage in investment activity;

    (d) authorised persons who are investment firms, or credit institutions, in providing relevant ancillary services;

    (e) persons acting as appointed representatives; [...]

    (f) payment service providers in providing payment services [or

    (g) electronic money issuers].

(3) A person ("P") has a "relevant right or interest" in relation to any services within subsection (2) if P has a right or interest—

    (a) which is derived from, or is otherwise attributable to, the use of the services by others; or

    (b) which may be adversely affected by the use of the services by persons acting on P's behalf or in a fiduciary capacity in relation to P.

(4) If a person is providing a service within subsection (2) as a trustee, the persons who have been, or may have been, beneficiaries of the trust are to be treated as persons who have used, or may have contemplated using, the service.

(5) A person who deals with another person ("B") in the course of B providing a service within subsection (2) is to be treated as using the service.

(6) In this section—

"accepting", in relation to deposits, includes agreeing to accept;

"consumer credit business" has the same meaning as in the Consumer Credit Act 1974 (see section 189(1));

"credit institution" has the meaning given by section 138(1B);

"engage in investment activity" has the meaning given by section 21;

["electronic money" has the same meaning as in the Electronic Money Regulations 2011 and any reference to issuing electronic money must be read accordingly;]

"payment services" has the same meaning as in the Payment Services Regulations 2009;

"payment service provider" means a person who is a payment service provider for the purposes of those regulations as a result of falling within any of paragraphs (a) to (e) of the definition in regulation 2(1);

"relevant ancillary services" has the meaning given by section 138(1C).]

[404F   Other definitions etc

(1) For the purposes of sections 404 to 404B—

"redress" includes—

    (a) interest; and

    (b) a remedy or relief which could not be awarded in legal proceedings;

"specified" means specified in rules made under section 404.

(2) In determining for the purposes of those sections whether an authorised person has failed to comply with a requirement, anything which an appointed representative has done or omitted as respects business for which the authorised person has accepted responsibility is to be treated as having been done or omitted by the authorised person.

(3) References in those sections to the failure by a relevant firm to comply with a requirement applicable to the carrying on by it of any activity include anything done, or omitted to be done, by it in carrying on the activity—

    (a) which is in breach of a duty or other obligation, prohibition or restriction; or

    (b) which otherwise gives rise to the availability of a remedy or relief in legal proceedings.]

[404G Power to widen the scope of consumer redress schemes

(1) The Treasury may by order amend the definition of "relevant firms" in section 404 or the definition of "consumers" in section 404E (or both).

(2) An order under this section may make consequential amendments of any provision of sections 404 to 404F.]

[415A Powers of the Authority

Any power which the Authority has under any provision of this Act is not limited in any way by any other power which it has under any other provision of this Act.]

[425A Consumers: regulated activities etc carried on by authorised persons

(1) This section has effect for the purposes of the provisions of this Act which apply this section.

(2) "Consumers" means persons who—

    (a) use, have used or may use any of the services within subsection (3); or

    (b) have relevant rights or interests in relation to any of those services.

(3) The services within this subsection are services provided by—

    (a) authorised persons in carrying on regulated activities;

    (b) authorised persons who are investment firms, or credit institutions, in providing relevant ancillary services; or

    (c) persons acting as appointed representatives.

(4) A person ("P") has a "relevant right or interest" in relation to any services within subsection (3) if P has a right or interest—

    (a) which is derived from, or is otherwise attributable to, the use of the services by others; or

    (b) which may be adversely affected by the use of the services by persons acting on P's behalf or in a fiduciary capacity in relation to P.

(5) If a person is providing a service within subsection (3) as a trustee, the persons who are, have been or may be beneficiaries of the trust are to be treated as persons who use, have used or may use the service.

(6) A person who deals with another person ("A") in the course of A providing a service within subsection (3) is to be treated as using the service.

(7) In this section—

"credit institution" means—

    (a) a credit institution authorised under the banking consolidation directive; or

    (b) an institution which would satisfy the requirements for authorisation as a credit institution under that directive if it had its registered office (or if does not have one, its head office) in an EEA State;

"relevant ancillary service" means any service of a kind mentioned in Section B of Annex I to the markets in financial instruments directive the provision of which does not involve the carrying on of a regulated activity.]

[425B Consumers: regulated activities carried on by others

(1) This section has effect for the purposes of the provisions of this Act which apply this section.

(2) "Consumers" means persons who, in relation to regulated activities carried on otherwise than by authorised persons, would be consumers as defined by section 425A if the activities were carried on by authorised persons.]

[Section 6A   **SCHEDULE 1A**

FURTHER PROVISION ABOUT THE CONSUMER FINANCIAL EDUCATION BODY

1　Ensuring exercise of consumer financial education function etc

(1) The Authority must take such steps as are necessary to ensure that the consumer financial education body is, at all times, capable of exercising the consumer financial education function.

2　Constitution

(1) The constitution of the consumer financial education body must provide for it to have—

(a) a chair;

(b) a chief executive; and

(c) a board (which must include the chair and chief executive) whose members are the body's directors.

(2) The members of the board must be persons appointed, and liable to removal from office, by the Authority (acting, in the case of the chair or chief executive, with the approval of the Treasury).

(3) But the terms of appointment of members of the board (and in particular those governing removal from office) must be such as to secure their independence from the Authority in the exercise of the consumer financial education function.

(4) The Authority may appoint a person to be a member of the board only if it is satisfied that the person has knowledge or experience which is likely to be relevant to the exercise by the body of the consumer financial education function.

3　Status

(1) The consumer financial education body is not to be regarded as exercising functions on behalf of the Crown.

4　Discharge of function by others

(1) The consumer financial education body may discharge the consumer financial education function by—

(a) supporting the doing by other persons of anything that it considers would enhance the understanding, knowledge or ability mentioned in section 6A(1); or

(b) arranging for other persons to do anything that it considers would enhance that understanding, knowledge or ability.

6　Market confidence and financial stability

In discharging the consumer financial education function, the consumer financial education body must have regard to the importance of—

(a) maintaining confidence in the UK financial system; and

(b) maintaining the stability of the UK financial system.

13　Funding of the relevant costs by consumer credit licensees etc

(1) For the purpose of meeting a proportion of the relevant costs the OFT may, with the approval of the Secretary of State and the Treasury, from time to time require—

(a) qualifying consumer credit licensees or applicants, or

(b) any specified class of qualifying consumer credit licensee or applicant,

to pay to the OFT specified amounts or amounts calculated in a specified way.

(2) The requirements are to be imposed by general notice.

(3) "Qualifying consumer credit licensee or applicant" means—

(a) a licensee under a licence which covers to any extent the carrying on of a type of business specified in an order under section 226A(2)(e); or

(b) an applicant for a licence, or for the renewal of a licence, which (if granted or renewed) will fall within paragraph (a) above.

(4) Before giving a general notice the OFT must have regard to other anticipated sources of funding of the relevant costs.

(5) Before giving a general notice, the OFT must consult—

(a) the Authority;

(b) the consumer financial education body; and

(c) such other persons (if any) as the OFT considers appropriate.]

Section 203(8) **SCHEDULE 16**

PROHIBITIONS AND RESTRICTIONS IMPOSED BY [OFFICE OF FAIR TRADING]

Preliminary

1. In this Schedule—

'appeal period' has the same meaning as in the Consumer Credit Act 1974;

'prohibition' means a consumer credit prohibition under section 203;

'restriction' means a restriction under section 204.

Notice of prohibition or restriction

2.—(1) This paragraph applies if the [OFT] proposes, in relation to a firm—

(a) to impose a prohibition;

(b) to impose a restriction; or

(c) to vary a restriction otherwise than with the agreement of the firm.

(2) The [OFT] must by notice—

(a) inform the firm of [its] proposal, stating [its] reasons; and

(b) invite the firm to submit representations in accordance with paragraph 4.

(3) If the [OFT] imposes the prohibition or restriction or varies the restriction, the [OFT] may give directions authorising the firm to carry into effect agreements made before the coming into force of the prohibition, restriction or variation.

(4) A prohibition, restriction or variation is not to come into force before the end of the appeal period.

(5) If the [OFT] imposes a prohibition or restriction or varies a restriction, [it] must serve a copy of the prohibition, restriction or variation—

(a) on the Authority; and

(b) on the firm's home state regulator.

Application to revoke prohibition or restriction

3.—(1) This paragraph applies if the [OFT] proposes to refuse an application made by a firm for the revocation of a prohibition or restriction.

(2) The [OFT] must by notice—

(a) inform the firm of the proposed refusal, stating [its] reasons; and

(b) invite the firm to submit representations in accordance with paragraph 4.

Representations to [OFT]

4.—(1) If this paragraph applies to an invitation to submit representations, the [OFT] must invite the firm, within 21 days after the notice containing the invitation is given to it or such longer period as [the OFT] may allow—

(a) to submit its representations in writing to [it] and

(b) to give notice to [it], if the firm thinks fit, that it wishes to make representations orally.

(2) If notice is given under sub-paragraph (1)(b), the [OFT] must arrange for the oral representations to be heard.

(3) The [OFT] must give the firm notice of its determination.

Appeals

5. Section 41 of the Consumer Credit Act 1974 (appeals to the Secretary of State) has effect as if—

    (a) the following determinations were mentioned in column 1 of the table set out at the end of that section—

        (i)   imposition of a prohibition or restriction or the variation of a restriction; and

        (ii)   refusal of an application for the revocation of a prohibition or restriction;

    (b) the firm concerned were mentioned in column 2 of that table in relation to those determinations.

Section 225(4)

SCHEDULE 17

THE OMBUDSMAN SCHEME

[PART 3A THE CONSUMER CREDIT JURISDICTION

16A   Introduction

This Part of this Schedule applies only in relation to the consumer credit jurisdiction.

16B   Procedure for complaints etc.

(1) Consumer credit rules—

    (a) must provide that a complaint is not to be entertained unless the complainant has referred it under the ombudsman scheme before the applicable time limit (determined in accordance with the rules) has expired;

    (b) may provide that an ombudsman may extend that time limit in specified circumstances;

    (c) may provide that a complaint is not to be entertained (except in specified circumstances) if the complainant has not previously communicated its substance to the respondent and given him a reasonable opportunity to deal with it;

    (d) may make provision about the procedure for the reference of complaints and for their investigation, consideration and determination by an ombudsman.

(2) Sub-paragraphs (2) and (3) of paragraph 14 apply in relation to consumer credit rules under sub-paragraph (1) of this paragraph as they apply in relation to scheme rules under that paragraph.

(3) Consumer credit rules may require persons falling within sub-paragraph (6) to establish such procedures as the scheme operator considers appropriate for the resolution of complaints which may be referred to the scheme.

(4) Consumer credit rules under sub-paragraph (3) may make different provision in relation to persons of different descriptions or to complaints of different descriptions.

(5) Consumer credit rules under sub-paragraph (3) may authorise the scheme operator to dispense with or modify the application of such rules in particular cases where the scheme operator—

    (a) considers it appropriate to do so; and

    (b) is satisfied that the specified conditions (if any) are met.

(6) A person falls within this sub-paragraph if he is licensed by a standard licence (within the meaning of the Consumer Credit Act 1974) to carry on to any extent a business of a type specified in an order under section 226A(2)(e) of this Act.

16C Fees

(1) Consumer credit rules may require a respondent to pay to the scheme operator such fees as may be specified in the rules.

(2) Sub-paragraph (2) of paragraph 15 applies in relation to consumer credit rules under this paragraph as it applies in relation to scheme rules under that paragraph.

16D Enforcement of money awards

A money award, including interest, which has been registered in accordance with consumer credit rules may—

> (a) if a county court so orders in England and Wales, be recovered by execution issued from the county court (or otherwise) as if it were payable under an order of that court;
>
> (b) be enforced in Northern Ireland as a money judgment under the Judgments Enforcement (Northern Ireland) Order 1981;
>
> (c) be enforced in Scotland as if it were a decree of the sheriff and whether or not the sheriff could himself have granted such a decree.

16E Procedure for consumer credit rules

(1) If the scheme operator makes any consumer credit rules, it must give a copy of them to the Authority without delay.

(2) If the scheme operator revokes any such rules, it must give written notice to the Authority without delay.

(3) The power to make such rules is exercisable in writing.

(4) Immediately after the making of such rules, the scheme operator must arrange for them to be printed and made available to the public.

(5) The scheme operator may charge a reasonable fee for providing a person with a copy of any such rules.

16F Verification of consumer credit rules

(1) The production of a printed copy of consumer credit rules purporting to be made by the scheme operator—

> (a) on which there is endorsed a certificate signed by a member of the scheme operator's staff authorised by the scheme operator for that purpose, and
>
> (b) which contains the required statements,

is evidence (or in Scotland sufficient evidence) of the facts stated in the certificate.

(2) The required statements are—

> (a) that the rules were made by the scheme operator;
>
> (b) that the copy is a true copy of the rules; and
>
> (c) that on a specified date the rules were made available to the public in accordance with paragraph 16E(4).

(3) A certificate purporting to be signed as mentioned in sub-paragraph (1) is to be taken to have been duly signed unless the contrary is shown.

16G Consultation

(1) If the scheme operator proposes to make consumer credit rules, it must publish a draft of the proposed rules in the way appearing to it to be best calculated to bring the draft to the attention of the public.

(2) The draft must be accompanied by—

> (a) an explanation of the proposed rules; and
>
> (b) a statement that representations about the proposals may be made to the scheme operator within a specified time.

(3) Before making any consumer credit rules, the scheme operator must have regard to any representations made to it in accordance with sub-paragraph (2)(b).

(4) If consumer credit rules made by the scheme operator differ from the draft published under sub-paragraph (1) in a way which the scheme operator considers significant, the scheme operator must publish a statement of the difference.]

Enterprise Act 2002

(2002, c. 40)

PART 1 THE OFFICE OF FAIR TRADING

Establishment of OFT

1 The Office of Fair Trading

(1) There shall be a body corporate to be known as the Office of Fair Trading (in this Act referred to as 'the OFT').

(2) The functions of the OFT are carried out on behalf of the Crown.

(3) Schedule 1 (which makes further provision about the OFT) has effect.

(4) In managing its affairs the OFT shall have regard, in addition to any relevant general guidance as to the governance of public bodies, to such generally accepted principles of good corporate governance as it is reasonable to regard as applicable to the OFT.

2 The Director General of Fair Trading

(1) The functions of the Director General of Fair Trading (in this Act referred to as 'the Director'), and his property, rights and liabilities, are transferred to the OFT.

(2) The office of the Director is abolished.

(3) Any enactment, instrument or other document passed or made before the commencement of subsection (1) which refers to the Director shall have effect, so far as necessary for the purposes of or in consequence of anything being transferred, as if any reference to the Director were a reference to the OFT.

3 Annual plan

(1) The OFT shall, before each financial year, publish a document (the 'annual plan') containing a statement of its main objectives and priorities for the year.

(2) The OFT shall for the purposes of public consultation publish a document containing proposals for its annual plan at least two months before publishing the annual plan for any year.

(3) The OFT shall lay before Parliament a copy of each document published under subsection (2) and each annual plan.

4 Annual and other reports

(1) The OFT shall, as soon as practicable after the end of each financial year, make to the Secretary of State a report (the 'annual report') on its activities and performance during that year.

(2) The annual report for each year shall include—

(a) a general survey of developments in respect of matters relating to the OFT's functions;

(b) an assessment of the extent to which the OFT's main objectives and priorities for the year (as set out in the annual plan) have been met;

(c) a summary of the significant decisions, investigations or other activities made or carried out by the OFT during the year;

(d) a summary of the allocation of the OFT's financial resources to its various activities during the year; and

(e) an assessment of the OFT's performance and practices in relation to its enforcement functions.

(3) The OFT shall lay a copy of each annual report before Parliament and arrange for the report to be published.

(4) The OFT may—

    (a) prepare other reports in respect of matters relating to any of its functions; and

    (b) arrange for any such report to be published.

General functions of OFT

5   Acquisition of information etc

(1) The OFT has the function of obtaining, compiling and keeping under review information about matters relating to the carrying out of its functions.

(2) That function is to be carried out with a view to (among other things) ensuring that the OFT has sufficient information to take informed decisions and to carry out its other functions effectively.

(3) In carrying out that function the OFT may carry out, commission or support (financially or otherwise) research.

6   Provision of information etc. to the public

(1) The OFT has the function of—

    (a) making the public aware of the ways in which competition may benefit consumers in, and the economy of, the United Kingdom; and

    (b) giving information or advice in respect of matters relating to any of its functions to the public.

(2) In carrying out those functions the OFT may—

    (a) publish educational materials or carry out other educational activities; or

    (b) support (financially or otherwise) the carrying out by others of such activities or the provision by others of information or advice.

7   Provision of information and advice to Ministers etc.

(1) The OFT has the function of—

    (a) making proposals, or

    (b) giving other information or advice,

on matters relating to any of its functions to any Minister of the Crown or other public authority (including proposals, information or advice as to any aspect of the law or a proposed change in the law).

(2) A Minister of the Crown may request the OFT to make proposals or give other information or advice on any matter relating to any of its functions; and the OFT shall, so far as is reasonably practicable and consistent with its other functions, comply with the request.

8   Promoting good consumer practice

(1) The OFT has the function of promoting good practice in the carrying out of activities which may affect the economic interests of consumers in the United Kingdom.

(2) In carrying out that function the OFT may (without prejudice to the generality of subsection (1)) make arrangements for approving consumer codes and may, in accordance with the arrangements, give its approval to or withdraw its approval from any consumer code.

(3) Any such arrangements must specify the criteria to be applied by the OFT in determining whether to give approval to or withdraw approval from a consumer code.

(4) Any such arrangements may in particular—

    (a) specify descriptions of consumer code which may be the subject of an application to the OFT for approval (and any such description may be framed by reference to any feature of a consumer code, including the persons who are, or are to be, subject to the code, the manner in which it is, or is to be, operated and the persons responsible for its operation); and

(b) provide for the use in accordance with the arrangements of an official symbol intended to signify that a consumer code is approved by the OFT.

(5) The OFT shall publish any arrangements under subsection (2) in such manner it considers appropriate.

(6) In this section 'consumer code' means a code of practice or other document (however described) intended, with a view to safeguarding or promoting the interests of consumers, to regulate by any means the conduct of persons engaged in the supply of goods or services to consumers (or the conduct of their employees or representatives).

Miscellaneous

11   Super-complaints to OFT

(1) This section applies where a designated consumer body makes a complaint to the OFT that any feature, or combination of features, of a market in the United Kingdom for goods or services is or appears to be significantly harming the interests of consumers.

(2) The OFT must, within 90 days after the day on which it receives the complaint, publish a response stating how it proposes to deal with the complaint, and in particular—

(a) whether it has decided to take any action, or to take no action, in response to the complaint, and

(b) if it has decided to take action, what action it proposes to take.

(3) The response must state the OFT's reasons for its proposals.

(4) The Secretary of State may by order amend subsection (2) by substituting any period for the period for the time being specified there.

(5) 'Designated consumer body' means a body designated by the Secretary of State by order.

(6) The Secretary of State—

(a) may designate a body only if it appears to him to represent the interests of consumers of any description, and

(b) must publish (and may from time to time vary) other criteria to be applied by him in determining whether to make or revoke a designation.

(7) The OFT—

(a) must issue guidance as to the presentation by the complainant of a reasoned case for the complaint, and

(b) may issue such other guidance as appears to it to be appropriate for the purposes of this section.

(8) An order under this section—

(a) shall be made by statutory instrument, and

(b) shall be subject to annulment in pursuance of a resolution of either House of Parliament.

(9) In this section—

(a) references to a feature of a market in the United Kingdom for goods or services have the same meaning as if contained in Part 4, and

(b) 'consumer' means an individual who is a consumer within the meaning of that Part.

PART 8 ENFORCEMENT OF CERTAIN CONSUMER LEGISLATION

Introduction

210   Consumers

(1) In this Part references to consumers must be construed in accordance with this section.

(2) In relation to a domestic infringement a consumer is an individual in respect of whom the first and second conditions are satisfied.

(3) The first condition is that—

    (a) goods are or are sought to be supplied to the individual (whether by way of sale or other-wise) in the course of a business carried on by the person supplying or seeking to supply them, or

    (b) services are or are sought to be supplied to the individual in the course of a business carried on by the person supplying or seeking to supply them.

(4) The second condition is that—

    (a) the individual receives or seeks to receive the goods or services otherwise than in the course of a business carried on by him, or

    (b) the individual receives or seeks to receive the goods or services with a view to carrying on a business but not in the course of a business carried on by him.

(5) For the purposes of a domestic infringement it is immaterial whether a person supplying goods or services has a place of business in the United Kingdom.

(6) In relation to a Community infringement a consumer is a person who is a consumer for the purposes of—

    (a) the Injunctions Directive, and

    (b) the listed Directive [or the listed Regulation] concerned.

(7) A Directive is a listed Directive—

    (a) if it is a Directive of the Council of the European Communities or of the European Parliament and of the Council, and

    (b) if it is specified in Schedule 13 or to the extent that any of its provisions is so specified.

[(7A) A Regulation is a listed Regulation—

    (a) if it is a Regulation of the Council of the European Communities or of the European Parliament and of the Council, and

    (b) if it is specified in Schedule 13 or to the extent that any of its provisions is so specified.]

(8) A business includes—

    (a) a professional practice;

    (b) any other undertaking carried on for gain or reward;

    (c) any undertaking in the course of which goods or services are supplied otherwise than free of charge.

(9) The Secretary of State may by order modify Schedule 13.

(10) An order under this section must be made by statutory instrument subject to annulment in pursuance of a resolution of either House of Parliament.

211 Domestic infringements

(1) In this Part a domestic infringement is an act or omission which—

    (a) is done or made by a person in the course of a business,

    (b) falls within subsection (2), and

    (c) harms the collective interests of consumers in the United Kingdom.

(2) An act or omission falls within this subsection if it is of a description specified by the Secretary of State by order and consists of any of the following—

    (a) a contravention of an enactment which imposes a duty, prohibition or restriction enforce-able by criminal proceedings;

    (b) an act done or omission made in breach of contract;

    (c) an act done or omission made in breach of a non-contractual duty owed to a person by virtue of an enactment or rule of law and enforceable by civil proceedings;

    (d) an act or omission in respect of which an enactment provides for a remedy or sanction enforceable by civil proceedings;

    (e) an act done or omission made by a person supplying or seeking to supply goods or services as a result of which an agreement or security relating to the supply is void or unenforce-able to any extent;

    (f) an act or omission by which a person supplying or seeking to supply goods or services purports or attempts to exercise a right or remedy relating to the supply in circumstances where the exercise of the right or remedy is restricted or excluded under or by virtue of an enactment;

(g) an act or omission by which a person supplying or seeking to supply goods or services purports or attempts to avoid (to any extent) liability relating to the supply in circumstances where such avoidance is restricted or prevented under an enactment.

(3) But an order under this section may provide that any description of act or omission falling within subsection (2) is not a domestic infringement.

(4) For the purposes of subsection (2) it is immaterial—

(a) whether or not any duty, prohibition or restriction exists in relation to consumers as such;

(b) whether or not any remedy or sanction is provided for the benefit of consumers as such;

(c) whether or not any proceedings have been brought in relation to the act or omission;

(d) whether or not any person has been convicted of an offence in respect of the contravention mentioned in subsection (2)(a);

(e) whether or not there is a waiver in respect of the breach of contract mentioned in subsection (2)(b).

(5) References to an enactment include references to subordinate legislation (within the meaning of the Interpretation Act 1978 (c. 30)).

(6) The power to make an order under this section must be exercised by statutory instrument.

(7) But no such order may be made unless a draft of it has been laid before Parliament and approved by a resolution of each House.

212　Community infringements

(1) In this Part a Community infringement is an act or omission which harms the collective interests of consumers and which—

(a) contravenes a listed Directive as given effect by the laws, regulations or administrative provisions of an EEA State, [...]

(b) contravenes such laws, regulations or administrative provisions which provide additional permitted protections.

[(c) contravenes a listed Regulation, or

(d) contravenes any laws, regulations or administrative provisions of an EEA State which give effect to a listed Regulation.]

(2) The laws, regulations or administrative provisions of an EEA State which give effect to a listed Directive provide additional permitted protections if—

(a) they provide protection for consumers which is in addition to the minimum protection required by the Directive concerned, and

(b) such additional protection is permitted by that Directive.

(3) The Secretary of State may by order specify for the purposes of this section the law in the United Kingdom which—

(a) gives effect to the listed Directives;

(b) provides additional permitted protections [; or

(c) gives effect to a listed regulation].

(4) References to a listed Directive [or to a listed Regulation] must be construed in accordance with section 210.

(5) An EEA State is a State which is a contracting party to the Agreement on the European Economic Area signed at Oporto on 2nd May 1992 as adjusted by the Protocol signed at Brussels on 17th March 1993.

(6) An order under this section must be made by statutory instrument subject to annulment in pursuance of a resolution of either House of Parliament.

213　Enforcers

(1) Each of the following is a general enforcer—

(a) the OFT;

(b) every local weights and measures authority in Great Britain;

(c) the Department of Enterprise, Trade and Investment in Northern Ireland.

(2) A designated enforcer is any person or body (whether or not incorporated) which the Secretary of State—

(a) thinks has as one of its purposes the protection of the collective interests of consumers, and

(b) designates by order.

(3) The Secretary of State may designate a public body only if he is satisfied that it is independent.

(4) The Secretary of State may designate a person or body which is not a public body only if the person or body (as the case may be) satisfies such criteria as the Secretary of State specifies by order.

(5) A Community enforcer is a qualified entity for the purposes of the Injunctions Directive—

(a) which is for the time being specified in the list published in the Official Journal of the European Communities in pursuance of Article 4.3 of that Directive, but

[(b) which is not a general enforcer, a designated enforcer or a CPC enforcer].

[(5A) Each of the following (being bodies or persons designated by the Secretary of State under Article 4(1) or 4(2) of the CPC Regulation) is a CPC enforcer—

(a) the OFT;

(b) the Civil Aviation Authority;

(c) the Financial Services Authority;

(d) the Secretary of State for Health;

(e) the Department of Health, Social Services and Public Safety in Northern Ireland;

(f) the Office of Communications;

(g) the Department of Enterprise, Trade and Investment in Northern Ireland;

(h) every local weights and measures authority in Great Britain;

(i) the Independent Committee for the Supervision of Standards of the Telephone Information Services.]

(6) An order under this section may designate an enforcer in respect of—

(a) all infringements;

(b) infringements of such descriptions as are specified in the order.

(7) An order under this section may make different provision for different purposes.

(8) The designation of a body by virtue of subsection (3) is conclusive evidence for the purposes of any question arising under this Part that the body is a public body.

(9) An order under this section must be made by statutory instrument subject to annulment in pursuance of a resolution of either House of Parliament.

(10) If requested to do so by a designated enforcer which is designated in respect of one or more Community infringements the Secretary of State must notify the Commission of the European Communities—

(a) of its name and purpose;

(b) of the Community infringements in respect of which it is designated.

(11) The Secretary of State must also notify the Commission—

(a) of the fact that a person or body in respect of which he has given notice under subsection (10) ceases to be a designated enforcer;

(b) of any change in the name or purpose of a designated enforcer in respect of which he has given such notice;

(c) of any change to the Community infringements in respect of which a designated enforcer is designated.

Enforcement procedure

214   Consultation

(1) An enforcer must not make an application for an enforcement order unless he has engaged in appropriate consultation with—

 (a) the person against whom the enforcement order would be made, and

 (b) the OFT (if it is not the enforcer).

(2) Appropriate consultation is consultation for the purpose of—

 (a) achieving the cessation of the infringement in a case where an infringement is occurring;

 (b) ensuring that there will be no repetition of the infringement in a case where the infringement has occurred;

 (c) ensuring that there will be no repetition of the infringement in a case where the cessation of the infringement is achieved under paragraph (a);

 (d) ensuring that the infringement does not take place in the case of a Community infringement which the enforcer believes is likely to take place.

(3) Subsection (1) does not apply if the OFT thinks that an application for an enforcement order should be made without delay.

(4) Subsection (1) ceases to apply—

 (a) for the purposes of an application for an enforcement order at the end of the period of 14 days beginning with the day after the person against whom the enforcement order would be made receives a request for consultation from the enforcer;

 (b) for the purposes of an application for an interim enforcement order at the end of the period of seven days beginning with the day after the person against whom the interim enforcement order would be made receives a request for consultation from the enforcer.

(5) The Secretary of State may by order make rules in relation to consultation under this section.

(6) Such an order must be made by statutory instrument subject to annulment in pursuance of a resolution of either House of Parliament.

(7) In this section (except subsection (4)) and in sections 215 and 216 references to an enforcement order include references to an interim enforcement order.

215   Applications

(1) An application for an enforcement order must name the person the enforcer thinks—

 (a) has engaged or is engaging in conduct which constitutes a domestic or a Community infringement, or

 (b) is likely to engage in conduct which constitutes a Community infringement.

(2) A general enforcer may make an application for an enforcement order in respect of any infringement.

(3) A designated enforcer may make an application for an enforcement order in respect of any infringement to which his designation relates.

(4) A Community enforcer may make an application for an enforcement order in respect of a Community infringement.

[(4A) A CPC enforcer may make an application for an enforcement order in respect of a Community infringement.]

(5) The following courts have jurisdiction to make an enforcement order—

 (a) the High Court or a county court if the person against whom the order is sought carries on business or has a place of business in England and Wales or Northern Ireland;

 (b) the Court of Session or the sheriff if the person against whom the order is sought carries on business or has a place of business in Scotland.

(6) If an application for an enforcement order is made by a Community enforcer the court may examine whether the purpose of the enforcer justifies its making the application.

(7) If the court thinks that the purpose of the Community enforcer does not justify its making the application the court may refuse the application on that ground alone.

(8) The purpose of a Community enforcer must be construed by reference to the Injunctions Directive.

(9) An enforcer which is not the OFT must notify the OFT of the result of an application under this section.

216 Applications: directions by OFT

(1) This section applies if the OFT believes that an enforcer other than the OFT intends to apply for an enforcement order.

(2) In such a case the OFT may direct that if an application in respect of a particular infringement is to be made it must be made—

(a) only by the OFT, or

(b) only by such other enforcer as the OFT directs.

(3) If the OFT directs that only it may make an application that does not prevent—

(a) the OFT or any enforcer from accepting an undertaking under section 219, or

(b) the OFT from taking such other steps it thinks appropriate (apart from making an application) for the purpose of securing that the infringement is not committed, continued or repeated.

(4) The OFT may vary or withdraw a direction given under this section.

(5) The OFT must take such steps as it thinks appropriate to bring a direction (or a variation or withdrawal of a direction) to the attention of enforcers it thinks may be affected by it.

(6) But this section does not prevent an application for an enforcement order being made by a Community enforcer.

217 Enforcement orders

(1) This section applies if an application for an enforcement order is made under section 215 and the court finds that the person named in the application has engaged in conduct which constitutes the infringement.

(2) This section also applies if such an application is made in relation to a Community infringement and the court finds that the person named in the application is likely to engage in conduct which constitutes the infringement.

(3) If this section applies the court may make an enforcement order against the person.

(4) In considering whether to make an enforcement order the court must have regard to whether the person named in the application—

(a) has given an undertaking under section 219 in respect of conduct such as is mentioned in subsection (3) of that section;

(b) has failed to comply with the undertaking.

(5) An enforcement order must—

(a) indicate the nature of the conduct to which the finding under subsection (1) or (2) relates, and

(b) direct the person to comply with subsection (6).

(6) A person complies with this subsection if he—

(a) does not continue or repeat the conduct;

(b) does not engage in such conduct in the course of his business or another business;

(c) does not consent to or connive in the carrying out of such conduct by a body corporate with which he has a special relationship (within the meaning of section 222(3)).

(7) But subsection (6)(a) does not apply in the case of a finding under subsection (2).

(8) An enforcement order may require a person against whom the order is made to publish in such form and manner and to such extent as the court thinks appropriate for the purpose of eliminating any continuing effects of the infringement—

(a) the order;

(b) a corrective statement.

(9) If the court makes a finding under subsection (1) or (2) it may accept an undertaking by the person—

(a) to comply with subsection (6), or

(b) to take steps which the court believes will secure that he complies with subsection (6).

(10) An undertaking under subsection (9) may include a further undertaking by the person to publish in such form and manner and to such extent as the court thinks appropriate for the purpose of eliminating any continuing effects of the infringement—

    (a) the terms of the undertaking;

    (b) a corrective statement.

(11) If the court—

    (a) makes a finding under subsection (1) or (2), and

    (b) accepts an undertaking under subsection (9),

it must not make an enforcement order in respect of the infringement to which the undertaking relates.

(12) An enforcement order made by a court in one part of the United Kingdom has effect in any other part of the United Kingdom as if made by a court in that part.

218   Interim enforcement order

(1) The court may make an interim enforcement order against a person named in the application for the order if it appears to the court—

    (a) that it is alleged that the person is engaged in conduct which constitutes a domestic or Community infringement or is likely to engage in conduct which constitutes a Community infringement,

    (b) that if the application had been an application for an enforcement order it would be likely to be granted,

    (c) that it is expedient that the conduct is prohibited or prevented (as the case may be) immediately, and

    (d) if no notice of the application has been given to the person named in the application that it is appropriate to make an interim enforcement order without notice.

(2) An interim enforcement order must—

    (a) indicate the nature of the alleged conduct, and

    (b) direct the person to comply with subsection (3).

(3) A person complies with this subsection if he—

    (a) does not continue or repeat the conduct;

    (b) does not engage in such conduct in the course of his business or another business;

    (c) does not consent to or connive in the carrying out of such conduct by a body corporate with which he has a special relationship (within the meaning of section 222(3)).

(4) But subsection (3)(a) does not apply in so far as the application is made in respect of an allegation that the person is likely to engage in conduct which constitutes a Community infringement.

(5) An application for an interim enforcement order against a person may be made at any time before an application for an enforcement order against the person in respect of the same conduct is determined.

(6) An application for an interim enforcement order must refer to all matters—

    (a) which are known to the applicant, and

    (b) which are material to the question whether or not the application is granted.

(7) If an application for an interim enforcement order is made without notice the application must state why no notice has been given.

(8) The court may vary or discharge an interim enforcement order on the application of—

    (a) the enforcer who applied for the order;

    (b) the person against whom it is made.

(9) An interim enforcement order against a person is discharged on the determination of an application for an enforcement order made against the person in respect of the same conduct.

(10) If it appears to the court as mentioned in subsection (1)(a) to (c) the court may instead of making an interim enforcement order accept an undertaking from the person named in the application—

(a) to comply with subsection (3), or

(b) to take steps which the court believes will secure that he complies with subsection (3).

(11) An interim enforcement order made by a court in one part of the United Kingdom has effect in any other part of the United Kingdom as if made by a court in that part.

[218A   Unfair commercial practices: substantiation of claims

(1) This section applies where an application for an enforcement order or for an interim enforcement order is made in respect of a Community infringement involving a contravention of Directive 2005/29/EC of the European Parliament and of the Council of 11 May 2005 concerning unfair business-to-consumer commercial practices in the internal market.

(2) For the purposes of considering the application the court may require the person named in the application to provide evidence as to the accuracy of any factual claim made as part of a commercial practice of that person if, taking into account the legitimate interests of that person and any other party to the proceedings, it appears appropriate in the circumstances.

(3) If, having been required under subsection (2) to provide evidence as to the accuracy of a factual claim, a person—

(a) fails to provide such evidence, or

(b) provides evidence as to the accuracy of the factual claim that the court considers inadequate,

the court may consider that the factual claim is inaccurate.

(4) In this section 'commercial practice' has the meaning given by regulation 2 of the Consumer Protection from Unfair Trading Regulations 2008.]

219   Undertakings

(1) This section applies if an enforcer has power to make an application under section 215.

(2) In such a case the enforcer may accept from a person to whom subsection (3) applies an undertaking that the person will comply with subsection (4).

(3) This subsection applies to a person who the enforcer believes—

(a) has engaged in conduct which constitutes an infringement;

(b) is engaging in such conduct;

(c) is likely to engage in conduct which constitutes a Community infringement.

(4) A person complies with this subsection if he—

(a) does not continue or repeat the conduct;

(b) does not engage in such conduct in the course of his business or another business;

(c) does not consent to or connive in the carrying out of such conduct by a body corporate with which he has a special relationship (within the meaning of section 222(3)).

(5) But subsection (4)(a) does not apply in the case of an undertaking given by a person in so far as subsection (3) applies to him by virtue of paragraph (c).

[(5A) A CPC enforcer who has accepted an undertaking under this section may—

(a) accept a further undertaking from the person concerned to publish the terms of the undertaking; or

(b) take steps itself to publish the undertaking.

(5B) In each case the undertaking shall be published in such form and manner and to such extent as the CPC enforcer thinks appropriate for the purpose of eliminating any continuing effects of the Community infringement.]

(6) If an enforcer accepts an undertaking under this section it must notify the OFT—

(a) of the terms of the undertaking;

(b) of the identity of the person who gave it.

220   Further proceedings

(1) This section applies if the court—

(a) makes an enforcement order under section 217,

(b) makes an interim enforcement order under section 218, or

(c) accepts an undertaking under either of those sections.

(2) In such a case the OFT has the same right to apply to the court in respect of a failure to comply with the order or undertaking as the enforcer who made the application for the order.

(3) An application to the court in respect of a failure to comply with an undertaking may include an application for an enforcement order or for an interim enforcement order.

(4) If the court finds that an undertaking is not being complied with it may make an enforcement order or an interim enforcement order (instead of making any other order it has power to make).

(5) In the case of an application for an enforcement order or for an interim enforcement order as mentioned in subsection (3) sections 214 and 216 must be ignored and sections 215 and 217 or 218 (as the case may be) apply subject to the following modifications—

(a) section 215(1)(b) must be ignored;

(b) section 215(5) must be ignored and the application must be made to the court which accepted the undertaking;

(c) section 217(9) to (11) must be ignored;

(d) section 218(10) must be ignored.

(6) If an enforcer which is not the OFT makes an application in respect of the failure of a person to comply with an enforcement order, an interim enforcement order or an undertaking given under section 217 or 218 the enforcer must notify the OFT—

(a) of the application;

(b) of any order made by the court on the application.

221 Community infringements: proceedings

(1) Subsection (2) applies to—

(a) every general enforcer;

(b) every designated enforcer which is a public body.

(2) An enforcer to which this subsection applies has power to take proceedings in EEA States other than the United Kingdom for the cessation or prohibition of a Community infringement.

(3) Subsection (4) applies to—

(a) every general enforcer;

(b) every designated enforcer

[(c) every CPC enforcer.].

(4) An enforcer to which this subsection applies may co-operate with a Community enforcer—

(a) for the purpose of bringing proceedings mentioned in subsection (2);

(b) in connection with the exercise by the Community enforcer of its functions under this Part.

(5) An EEA State is a State which is a contracting party to the Agreement on the European Economic Area signed at Oporto on 2nd May 1992 as adjusted by the Protocol signed at Brussels on 17th March 1993.

222 Bodies corporate: accessories

(1) This section applies if the person whose conduct constitutes a domestic infringement or a Community infringement is a body corporate.

(2) If the conduct takes place with the consent or connivance of a person (an accessory) who has a special relationship with the body corporate, the consent or connivance is also conduct which constitutes the infringement.

(3) A person has a special relationship with a body corporate if he is—

(a) a controller of the body corporate, or

(b) a director, manager, secretary or other similar officer of the body corporate or a person purporting to act in such a capacity.

(4) A person is a controller of a body corporate if—

(a) the directors of the body corporate or of another body corporate which is its controller are accustomed to act in accordance with the person's directions or instructions, or

(b) either alone or with an associate or associates he is entitled to exercise or control the exercise of one third or more of the voting power at any general meeting of the body corporate or of another body corporate which is its controller.

(5) An enforcement order or an interim enforcement order may be made against an accessory in respect of an infringement whether or not such an order is made against the body corporate.

(6) The court may accept an undertaking under section 217(9) or 218(10) from an accessory in respect of an infringement whether or not it accepts such an undertaking from the body corporate.

(7) An enforcer may accept an undertaking under section 219 from an accessory in respect of an infringement whether or not it accepts such an undertaking from the body corporate.

(8) Subsection (9) applies if—

    (a) an order is made as mentioned in subsection (5), or

    (b) an undertaking is accepted as mentioned in subsection (6) or (7).

(9) In such a case for subsection (6) of section 217, subsection (3) of section 218 or subsection (4) of section 219 (as the case may be) there is substituted the following subsection—

    '( ) A person complies with this subsection if he—

        (a) does not continue or repeat the conduct;

        (b) does not in the course of any business carried on by him engage in conduct such as that which constitutes the infringement committed by the body corporate mentioned in section 222(1);

        (c) does not consent to or connive in the carrying out of such conduct by another body corporate with which he has a special relationship (within the meaning of section 222(3)).'

(10) A person is an associate of an individual if—

    (a) he is the spouse [or civil partner] of the individual;

    (b) he is a relative of the individual;

    (c) he is a relative of the individual's spouse [or civil partner];

    (d) he is the spouse [or civil partner] of a relative of the individual;

    (e) he is the spouse [or civil partner] of a relative of the individual's spouse;

    (f) he lives in the same household as the individual otherwise than merely because he or the individual is the other's employer, tenant, lodger or boarder;

    (g) he is a relative of a person who is an associate of the individual by virtue of paragraph (f);

    (h) he has at some time in the past fallen within any of paragraphs (a) to (g).

(11) A person is also an associate of—

    (a) an individual with whom he is in partnership;

    (b) an individual who is an associate of the individual mentioned in paragraph (a);

    (c) a body corporate if he is a controller of it or he is an associate of a person who is a controller of the body corporate.

(12) A body corporate is an associate of another body corporate if—

    (a) the same person is a controller of both;

    (b) a person is a controller of one and persons who are his associates are controllers of the other;

    (c) a person is a controller of one and he and persons who are his associates are controllers of the other;

    (d) a group of two or more persons is a controller of each company and the groups consist of the same persons;

    (e) a group of two or more persons is a controller of each company and the groups may be regarded as consisting of the same persons by treating (in one or more cases) a member of either group as replaced by a person of whom he is an associate.

(13) A relative is a brother, sister, uncle, aunt, nephew, niece, lineal ancestor or lineal descendant.

223 Bodies corporate: orders

(1) This section applies if a court makes an enforcement order or an interim enforcement order against a body corporate and—

(a) at the time the order is made the body corporate is a member of a group of interconnected bodies corporate,

(b) at any time when the order is in force the body corporate becomes a member of a group of interconnected bodies corporate, or

(c) at any time when the order is in force a group of interconnected bodies corporate of which the body corporate is a member is increased by the addition of one or more further members.

(2) The court may direct that the order is binding upon all of the members of the group as if each of them were the body corporate against which the order is made.

(3) A group of interconnected bodies corporate is a group consisting of two or more bodies corporate all of whom are interconnected with each other.

(4) Any two bodies corporate are interconnected—

(a) if one of them is a subsidiary of the other, or

(b) if both of them are subsidiaries of the same body corporate.

[(5) In this section "subsidiary" has the meaning given by section 1159 of the Companies Act 2006.]

Information

224   OFT

(1) The OFT may for any of the purposes mentioned in subsection (2) give notice to any person requiring the person to provide it with the information specified in the notice.

(2) The purposes are—

(a) to enable the OFT to exercise or to consider whether to exercise any function it has under this Part;

(b) to enable a designated enforcer to which section 225 does not apply to consider whether to exercise any function it has under this Part;

(c) to enable a Community enforcer to consider whether to exercise any function it has under this Part;

(d) to ascertain whether a person has complied with or is complying with an enforcement order, an interim enforcement order or an undertaking given under section 217(9), 218(10) or 219.

225   Other enforcers

(1) This section applies to—

(a)   every general enforcer (other than the OFT);

(b)   every designated enforcer which is a public body

[(c)   every CPC enforcer (other than the OFT).].

(2) An enforcer to which this section applies may for any of the purposes mentioned in subsection (3) give notice to any person requiring the person to provide the enforcer with the information specified in the notice.

(3) The purposes are—

(a) to enable the enforcer to exercise or to consider whether to exercise any function it has under this Part;

(b) to ascertain whether a person has complied with or is complying with an enforcement order or an interim enforcement order made on the application of the enforcer or an undertaking given under section 217(9) or 218(10) (as the case may be) following such an application or an undertaking given to the enforcer under section 219.

226   Notices: procedure

(1) This section applies to a notice given under section 224 or 225.

(2) The notice must—

(a) be in writing;

(b) specify the purpose for which the information is required.

(3) If the purpose is as mentioned in section 224(2)(a), (b) or (c) or 225(3)(a) the notice must specify the function concerned.

(4) A notice may specify the time within which and manner in which it is to be complied with.

(5) A notice may require the production of documents or any description of documents.

(6) An enforcer may take copies of any documents produced in compliance with such a requirement.

[(6A) A notice may specify the form in which information is to be provided.]

(7) A notice may be varied or revoked by a subsequent notice.

(8) But a notice must not require a person to provide any information or produce any document which he would be entitled to refuse to provide or produce—

    (a) in proceedings in the High Court on the grounds of legal professional privilege;

    (b) in proceedings in the Court of Session on the grounds of confidentiality of communications.

227 Notices: enforcement

(1) If a person fails to comply with a notice given under section 224 or 225 the enforcer who gave the notice may make an application under this section.

(2) If it appears to the court that the person to whom the notice was given has failed to comply with the notice the court may make an order under this section.

(3) An order under this section may require the person to whom the notice was given to do anything the court thinks it is reasonable for him to do for any of the purposes mentioned in section 224 or 225 (as the case may be) to ensure that the notice is complied with.

(4) An order under this section may require the person to meet all the costs or expenses of the application.

(5) If the person is a company or association the court in proceeding under subsection (4) may require any officer of the company or association who is responsible for the failure to meet the costs or expenses.

(6) The court is a court which may make an enforcement order.

(7) In subsection (5) an officer of a company is a person who is a director, manager, secretary or other similar officer of the company.

[227A Power to enter premises without warrant

(1) An officer of a CPC enforcer who reasonably suspects that there has been, or is likely to be, a Community infringement may for any purpose relating to the functions of the CPC enforcer under this Part enter any premises to investigate whether there has been, or is likely to be, such an infringement.

(2) An officer of a CPC enforcer who reasonably suspects that there is, or has been, a failure to comply with a relevant enforcement measure may for any purpose relating to the functions of the CPC enforcer under this Part enter any premises to investigate whether a person is complying with, or has complied with, the relevant enforcement measure.

(3) An appropriate notice must be given to the occupier of the premises before an officer of a CPC enforcer enters them under subsection (1) and (2).]

[227B Powers exercisable on the premises

(1) An officer of a CPC enforcer may, in the exercise of his powers under section 227A—

    (a) observe the carrying on of a business on the premises;

    (b) inspect goods or documents on the premises;

    (c) require any person on the premises to produce goods or documents within such period as the officer considers to be reasonable;

    (d) seize goods or documents to carry out tests on them on the premises or seize, remove and retain them to carry out tests on them elsewhere; or

    (e) seize, remove and retain goods or documents which he reasonably suspects may be required as evidence of a Community infringement or a breach of a relevant enforcement measure.]

Miscellaneous

228 Evidence

(1) Proceedings under this Part are civil proceedings for the purposes of—

>   (a) section 11 of the Civil Evidence Act 1968 (c. 64) (convictions admissible as evidence in civil proceedings);
>
>   (b) section 10 of the Law Reform (Miscellaneous Provisions) (Scotland) Act 1968 (c. 70) (corresponding provision in Scotland);
>
>   (c) section 7 of the Civil Evidence Act (Northern Ireland) 1971 (c. 36 (N.I.)) (corresponding provision in Northern Ireland).

(2) In proceedings under this Part any finding by a court in civil proceedings that an act or omission mentioned in section 211(2)(b), (c) or (d) or 212(1) has occurred—

>   (a) is admissible as evidence that the act or omission occurred;
>
>   (b) unless the contrary is proved, is sufficient evidence that the act or omission occurred.

(3) But subsection (2) does not apply to any finding—

>   (a) which has been reversed on appeal;
>
>   (b) which has been varied on appeal so as to negative it.

[(4) This section does not apply to proceedings for an offence under section 227E.]

229 Advice and information

(1) As soon as is reasonably practicable after the passing of this Act the OFT must prepare and publish advice and information with a view to—

>   (a) explaining the provisions of this Part to persons who are likely to be affected by them, and
>
>   (b) indicating how the OFT expects such provisions to operate.

(2) The OFT may at any time publish revised or new advice or information.

(3) Advice or information published in pursuance of subsection (1)(b) may include advice or information about the factors which the OFT may take into account in considering how to exercise the functions conferred on it by this Part.

(4) Advice or information published by the OFT under this section is to be published in such form and in such manner as it considers appropriate.

(5) In preparing advice or information under this section the OFT must consult such persons as it thinks are representative of persons affected by this Part.

(6) If any proposed advice or information relates to a matter in respect of which another general [or CPC] enforcer or a designated enforcer may act the persons to be consulted must include that enforcer.

230 Notice to OFT of intended prosecution

(1) This section applies if a local weights and measures authority in England and Wales intends to start proceedings for an offence under an enactment or subordinate legislation specified by the Secretary of State by order for the purposes of this section.

(2) The authority must give the OFT—

>   (a) notice of its intention to start the proceedings;
>
>   (b) a summary of the evidence it intends to lead in respect of the charges.

(3) The authority must not start the proceedings until whichever is the earlier of the following—

>   (a) the end of the period of 14 days starting with the day on which the authority gives the notice;
>
>   (b) the day on which it is notified by the OFT that the OFT has received the notice and summary given under subsection (2).

(4) The authority must also notify the OFT of the outcome of the proceedings after they are finally determined.

(5) But such proceedings are not invalid by reason only of the failure of the authority to comply with this section.

(6) Subordinate legislation has the same meaning as in section 21(1) of the Interpretation Act 1978 (c. 30).

(7) An order under this section must be made by statutory instrument subject to annulment in pursuance of a resolution of either House of Parliament.

231 Notice of convictions and judgments to OFT

(1) This section applies if—

    (a) a person is convicted of an offence by or before a court in the United Kingdom, or

    (b) a judgment is given against a person by a court in civil proceedings in the United Kingdom.

(2) The court may make arrangements to bring the conviction or judgment to the attention of the OFT if it appears to the court—

    (a) having regard to the functions of the OFT under this Part or under the Estate Agents Act 1979 (c. 38) that it is expedient for the conviction or judgment to be brought to the attention of the OFT, and

    (b) without such arrangements the conviction or judgment may not be brought to the attention of the OFT.

(3) For the purposes of subsection (2) it is immaterial that the proceedings have been finally disposed of by the court.

(4) Judgment includes an order or decree and references to the giving of the judgment must be construed accordingly.

Interpretation

232 Goods and services

(1) References in this Part to goods and services must be construed in accordance with this section.

(2) Goods include—

    (a) buildings and other structures;

    (b) ships, aircraft and hovercraft.

(3) The supply of goods includes—

    (a) supply by way of sale, lease, hire or hire purchase;

    (b) in relation to buildings and other structures, construction of them by one person for another.

(4) Goods or services which are supplied wholly or partly outside the United Kingdom must be taken to be supplied to or for a person in the United Kingdom if they are supplied in accordance with arrangements falling within subsection (5).

(5) Arrangements fall within this subsection if they are made by any means and—

    (a) at the time the arrangements are made the person seeking the supply is in the United Kingdom, or

    (b) at the time the goods or services are supplied (or ought to be supplied in accordance with the arrangements) the person responsible under the arrangements for effecting the supply is in or has a place of business in the United Kingdom.

233 Person supplying goods

(1) This section has effect for the purpose of references in this Part to a person supplying or seeking to supply goods under—

    (a) a hire-purchase agreement;

    (b) a credit-sale agreement;

    (c) a conditional sale agreement.

(2) The references include references to a person who conducts any antecedent negotiations relating to the agreement.

(3) The following expressions must be construed in accordance with section 189 of the Consumer Credit Act 1974 (c. 39)—

    (a) hire-purchase agreement;

    (b) credit-sale agreement;

    (c) conditional sale agreement;

    (d) antecedent negotiations.

234 Supply of services

(1) References in this Part to the supply of services must be construed in accordance with this section.

(2) The supply of services does not include the provision of services under a contract of service or of apprenticeship whether it is express or implied and (if it is express) whether it is oral or in writing.

(3) The supply of services includes—

    (a) performing for gain or reward any activity other than the supply of goods;

    (b) rendering services to order;

    (c) the provision of services by making them available to potential users.

(4) The supply of services includes making arrangements for the use of computer software or for granting access to data stored in any form which is not readily accessible.

(5) The supply of services includes making arrangements by means of a relevant agreement (within the meaning of [paragraph 29 of Schedule 2 to the Telecommunications Act 1984]) for sharing the use of telecommunications apparatus.

(6) The supply of services includes permitting or making arrangements to permit the use of land in such circumstances as the Secretary of State specifies by order.

(7) The power to make an order under subsection (6) must be exercised by statutory instrument.

(8) But no such order may be made unless a draft of it has been laid before Parliament and approved by a resolution of each House.

235 Injunctions Directive

In this Part the Injunctions Directive is Directive 98/27/EC of the European Parliament and of the Council on injunctions for the protection of consumers' interests.

[235A CPC Regulation

In this Part—

    (a) the CPC Regulation is Regulation (EC) No. 2006/2004 of the European Parliament and of the Council of 27 October 2004 on cooperation between national authorities responsible for the enforcement of consumer protection laws as amended by the Unfair Commercial Practices Directive;

    (b) the Unfair Commercial Practices Directive is Directive 2005/29/EC of the European Parliament and of the Council of 11 May 2005 concerning unfair business-to-consumer commercial practices in the internal market.]

Crown

[236 Crown

(1) This Part binds the Crown.

(2) But the powers conferred by sections 227A to 227D are not exercisable in relation to premises occupied by the Crown.]

Companies Act 2006

(2006, c. 46)

17   A company's constitution

Unless the context otherwise requires, references in the Companies Acts to a company's constitution include—

(a) the company's articles, and

(b) any resolutions and agreements to which Chapter 3 applies (**see** section 29).

31   Statement of company's objects

(1) Unless a company's articles specifically restrict the objects of the company, its objects are unrestricted.

33   Effect of company's constitution

(1) The provisions of a company's constitution bind the company and its members to the same extent as if there were covenants on the part of the company and of each member to observe those provisions.

39   A company's capacity

(1) The validity of an act done by a company shall not be called into question on the ground of lack of capacity by reason of anything in the company's constitution.

40   Power of directors to bind the company

(1) In favour of a person dealing with a company in good faith, the power of the directors to bind the company, or authorise others to do so, is deemed to be free of any limitation under the company's constitution.

(2) For this purpose—

(a) a person 'deals with' a company if he is a party to any transaction or other act to which the company is a party,

(b) a person dealing with a company—

(i)   is not bound to enquire as to any limitation on the powers of the directors to bind the company or authorise others to do so,

(ii) is presumed to have acted in good faith unless the contrary is proved, and

(iii) is not to be regarded as acting in bad faith by reason only of his knowing that an act is beyond the powers of the directors under the company's constitution.

41   Constitutional limitations: transactions involving directors or their associates

(1) This section applies to a transaction if or to the extent that its validity depends on section 40 (power of directors deemed to be free of limitations under company's constitution in favour of person dealing with company in good faith).

Nothing in this section shall be read as excluding the operation of any other enactment or rule of law by virtue of which the transaction may be called in question or any liability to the company may arise.

(2) Where—

(a) a company enters into such a transaction, and

(b) the parties to the transaction include—

(i)   a director of the company or of its holding company, or

(ii) a person connected with any such director,

the transaction is voidable at the instance of the company.

(3) Whether or not it is avoided, any such party to the transaction as is mentioned in subsection (2)(b)(i) or (ii), and any director of the company who authorised the transaction, is liable—

(a) to account to the company for any gain he has made directly or indirectly by the transaction, and

(b) to indemnify the company for any loss or damage resulting from the transaction.

(4) The transaction ceases to be voidable if—

(a) restitution of any money or other asset which was the subject matter of the transaction is no longer possible, or

(b) the company is indemnified for any loss or damage resulting from the transaction, or

(c) rights acquired bona fide for value and without actual notice of the directors' exceeding their powers by a person who is not party to the transaction would be affected by the avoidance, or

(d) the transaction is affirmed by the company.

(5) A person other than a director of the company is not liable under subsection (3) if he shows that at the time the transaction was entered into he did not know that the directors were exceeding their powers.

(6) Nothing in the preceding provisions of this section affects the rights of any party to the transaction not within subsection (2)(b)(i) or (ii).

But the court may, on the application of the company or any such party, make an order affirming, severing or setting aside the transaction on such terms as appear to the court to be just.

(7) In this section—

(a) 'transaction' includes any act; and

(b) the reference to a person connected with a director has the same meaning as in Part 10 (company directors).

43   Company contracts

(1) Under the law of England and Wales or Northern Ireland a contract may be made—

(a) by a company, by writing under its common seal, or

(b) on behalf of a company, by a person acting under its authority, express or implied.

(2) Any formalities required by law in the case of a contract made by an individual also apply, unless a contrary intention appears, to a contract made by or on behalf of a company.

51   Pre-incorporation contracts, deeds and obligations

(1) A contract that purports to be made by or on behalf of a company at a time when the company has not been formed has effect, subject to any agreement to the contrary, as one made with the person purporting to act for the company or as agent for it, and he is personally liable on the contract accordingly.

(2) Subsection (1) applies—

(a) to the making of a deed under the law of England and Wales or Northern Ireland, and

(b) to the undertaking of an obligation under the law of Scotland, as it applies to the making of a contract.

82   Requirement to disclose company name etc.

(1) The Secretary of State may by regulations make provision requiring companies—

(a) to display specified information in specified locations,

(b) to state specified information in specified descriptions of document or communication, and

(c) to provide specified information on request to those they deal with in the course of their business.

83   Civil consequences of failure to make required disclosure

(1) This section applies to any legal proceedings brought by a company to which section 82 applies (requirement to disclose company name etc) to enforce a right arising out of a contract made in the course of a business in respect of which the company was, at the time the contract was made, in breach of regulations under that section.

(2) The proceedings shall be dismissed if the defendant (in Scotland, the defender) to the proceedings shows—

(a) that he has a claim against the claimant (pursuer) arising out of the contract that he has been unable to pursue by reason of the latter's breach of the regulations, or

(b) that he has suffered some financial loss in connection with the contract by reason of the claimant's (pursuer's) breach of the regulations,

unless the court before which the proceedings are brought is satisfied that it is just and equitable to permit the proceedings to continue.

(3) This section does not affect the right of any person to enforce such rights as he may have against another person in any proceedings brought by that person.

161 Validity of acts of directors

(1) The acts of a person acting as a director are valid notwithstanding that it is afterwards discovered—

(a) that there was a defect in his appointment;

(b) that he was disqualified from holding office;

(c) that he had ceased to hold office;

(d) that he was not entitled to vote on the matter in question.

170 Scope and nature of general duties

(1) The general duties specified in sections 171 to 177 are owed by a director of a company to the company.

(2) A person who ceases to be a director continues to be subject—

(a) to the duty in section 175 (duty to avoid conflicts of interest) as regards the exploitation of any property, information or opportunity of which he became aware at a time when he was a director, and

(b) to the duty in section 176 (duty not to accept benefits from third parties) as regards things done or omitted by him before he ceased to be a director.

To that extent those duties apply to a former director as to a director, subject to any necessary adaptations.

(3) The general duties are based on certain common law rules and equitable principles as they apply in relation to directors and have effect in place of those rules and principles as regards the duties owed to a company by a director.

(4) The general duties shall be interpreted and applied in the same way as common law rules or equitable principles, and regard shall be had to the corresponding common law rules and equitable principles in interpreting and applying the general duties.

171 Duty to act within powers

A director of a company must—

(a) act in accordance with the company's constitution, and

(b) only exercise powers for the purposes for which they are conferred.

174 Duty to exercise reasonable care, skill and diligence

(1) A director of a company must exercise reasonable care, skill and diligence.

(2) This means the care, skill and diligence that would be exercised by a reasonably diligent person with—

(a) the general knowledge, skill and experience that may reasonably be expected of a person carrying out the functions carried out by the director in relation to the company, and

(b) the general knowledge, skill and experience that the director has.

175   Duty to avoid conflicts of interest

(1) A director of a company must avoid a situation in which he has, or can have, a direct or indirect interest that conflicts, or possibly may conflict, with the interests of the company.

(4) This duty is not infringed—

(a) if the situation cannot reasonably be regarded as likely to give rise to a conflict of interest; or

(b) if the matter has been authorised by the directors.

(7) Any reference in this section to a conflict of interest includes a conflict of interest and duty and a conflict of duties.

176   Duty not to accept benefits from third parties

(1) A director of a company must not accept a benefit from a third party conferred by reason of—

(a) his being a director, or

(b) his doing (or not doing) anything as director.

(5) Any reference in this section to a conflict of interest includes a conflict of interest and duty and a conflict of duties.

177   Duty to declare interest in proposed transaction or arrangement

. . .

178   Civil consequences of breach of general duties

(1) The consequences of breach (or threatened breach) of sections 171 to 177 are the same as would apply if the corresponding common law rule or equitable principle applied.

(3) The duties in those sections (with the exception of section 174 (duty to exercise reasonable care, skill and diligence)) are, accordingly, enforceable in the same way as any other fiduciary duty owed to a company by its directors.

180   Consent, approval or authorisation by members

(1) In a case where—

(a) section 175 (duty to avoid conflicts of interest) is complied with by authorisation by the directors, or

(b) section 177 (duty to declare interest in proposed transaction or arrangement) is complied with,

the transaction or arrangement is not liable to be set aside by virtue of any common law rule or equitable principle requiring the consent or approval of the members of the company.

754   Priorities where debentures secured by floating charge

(1) This section applies where debentures of a company registered in England and Wales or Northern Ireland are secured by a charge that, as created, was a floating charge.

(2) If possession is taken, by or on behalf of the holders of the debentures, of any property comprised in or subject to the charge, and the company is not at that time in the course of being wound up, the company's preferential debts shall be paid out of assets coming to the hands of the persons taking possession in priority to any claims for principal or interest in respect of the debentures.

(3) 'Preferential debts' means the categories of debts listed in Schedule 6 to the Insolvency Act 1986 (c. 45) or Schedule 4 to the Insolvency (Northern Ireland) Order 1989 (S.I. 1989/2405 (N.I. 19)).

For the purposes of those Schedules 'the relevant date' is the date of possession being taken as mentioned in subsection (2).

(4) Payments under this section shall be recouped, as far as may be, out of the assets of the company available for payment of general creditors.

860   Charges created by a company

(1) A company that creates a charge to which this section applies must deliver the prescribed particulars of the charge, together with the instrument (if any) by which the charge is created or evidenced, to the registrar for registration before the end of the period allowed for registration.

(2) Registration of a charge to which this section applies may instead be effected on the application of a person interested in it.

(3) Where registration is effected on the application of some person other than the company, that person is entitled to recover from the company the amount of any fees properly paid by him to the registrar on registration.

(4) If a company fails to comply with subsection (1), an offence is committed by—

    (a) the company, and

    (b) every officer of it who is in default.

(5) A person guilty of an offence under this section is liable—

    (a) on conviction on indictment, to a fine;

    (b) on summary conviction, to a fine not exceeding the statutory maximum.

(6) Subsection (4) does not apply if registration of the charge has been effected on the application of some other person.

(7) This section applies to the following charges—

    (a) a charge on land or any interest in land, other than a charge for any rent or other periodical sum issuing out of land,

    (b) a charge created or evidenced by an instrument which, if executed by an individual, would require registration as a bill of sale,

    (c) a charge for the purposes of securing any issue of debentures,

    (d) a charge on uncalled share capital of the company,

    (e) a charge on calls made but not paid,

    (f) a charge on book debts of the company,

    (g) a floating charge on the company's property or undertaking,

    (h) a charge on a ship or aircraft, or any share in a ship,

    (i) a charge on goodwill or on any intellectual property.

861   Charges which have to be registered: supplementary

(1) The holding of debentures entitling the holder to a charge on land is not, for the purposes of section 860(7)(a), an interest in the land.

(2) It is immaterial for the purposes of this Chapter where land subject to a charge is situated.

(3) The deposit by way of security of a negotiable instrument given to secure the payment of book debts is not, for the purposes of section 860(7)(f), a charge on those book debts.

(4) For the purposes of section 860(7)(i), 'intellectual property' means—

    (a) any patent, trade mark, registered design, copyright or design right;

    (b) any licence under or in respect of any such right.

(5) In this Chapter—

'charge' includes mortgage, and

'company' means a company registered in England and Wales or in Northern Ireland.

874   Consequence of failure to register charges created by a company

(1) If a company creates a charge to which section 860 applies, the charge is void (so far as any security on the company's property or undertaking is conferred by it) against—

    (a) a liquidator of the company,

    (b) an administrator of the company, and

    (c) a creditor of the company,

unless that section is complied with.

(2) Subsection (1) is subject to the provisions of this Chapter.

(3) Subsection (1) is without prejudice to any contract or obligation for repayment of the money secured by the charge; and when a charge becomes void under this section, the money secured by it immediately becomes payable.

Banking Act 2009

(2009, c. 1)

PART 1 SPECIAL RESOLUTION REGIME

Introduction

1 Overview

(1) The purpose of the special resolution regime for banks is to address the situation where all or part of the business of a bank has encountered, or is likely to encounter, financial difficulties.

(2) The special resolution regime consists of—

    (a) the three stabilisation options,

    (b) the bank insolvency procedure (provided by Part 2), and

    (c) the bank administration procedure (provided by Part 3).

(3) The three "stabilisation options" are—

    (a) transfer to a private sector purchaser (section 11),

    (b) transfer to a bridge bank (section 12), and

    (c) transfer to temporary public ownership (section 13).

(4) Each of the three stabilisation options is achieved through the exercise of one or more of the "stabilisation powers", which are—

    (a) the share transfer powers (sections 15, 16, 26 to 31 and 85), and

    (b) the property transfer powers (sections 33 and 42 to 46).

(5) Each of the following has a role in the operation of the special resolution regime—

    (a) the Bank of England,

    (b) the Treasury, and

    (c) the Financial Services Authority.

(6) The Table describes the provisions of this Part.

Sections	Topic
Sections 1 to 3	Introduction
Sections 4 to 6	Objectives and code
Sections 7 to 10	Exercise of powers: general
Sections 11 to 13	The stabilisation options
Sections 14 to 32	Transfer of securities
Sections 33 to [48A]	Transfer of property
Sections 49 to 62	Compensation
Sections 63 to 75	Incidental functions
Sections 76 to 81	Treasury
Sections 82 and 83	Holding companies
Sections 84 to 89	Building societies, &c.

Objectives and code

4   Special resolution objectives

(1) This section sets out the special resolution objectives.

(2) The relevant authorities shall have regard to the special resolution objectives in using, or considering the use of—

(a) the stabilisation powers,

(b) the bank insolvency procedure, or

(c) the bank administration procedure.

(3) For the purpose of this section the relevant authorities are—

(a) the Treasury,

(b) the FSA, and

(c) the Bank of England.

(4) Objective 1 is to protect and enhance the stability of the financial systems of the United Kingdom.

(5) Objective 2 is to protect and enhance public confidence in the stability of the banking systems of the United Kingdom.

(6) Objective 3 is to protect depositors.

(7) Objective 4 is to protect public funds.

(8) Objective 5 is to avoid interfering with property rights in contravention of a Convention right (within the meaning of the Human Rights Act 1998).

(9) In subsection (4), the reference to the stability of the financial systems of the United Kingdom includes, in particular, a reference to the continuity of banking services.

(10) The order in which the objectives are listed in this section is not significant; they are to be balanced as appropriate in each case.

5   Code of practice

(1) The Treasury shall issue a code of practice about the use of—

(a) the stabilisation powers,

(b) the bank insolvency procedure, and

(c) the bank administration procedure.

(2) The code may, in particular, provide guidance on—

(a) how the special resolution objectives are to be understood and achieved,

(b) the choice between different options,

(c) the information to be provided in the course of a consultation under this Part,

(d) the giving of advice by one relevant authority to another about whether, when and how the stabilisation powers are to be used,

(e) how to determine whether Condition 2 in section 7 is met,

(f) how to determine whether the test for the use of stabilisation powers in section 8 is satisfied,

(g) sections 63 and 66, and

(h) compensation.

(3) Sections 12 and 13 require the inclusion in the code of certain matters about bridge banks and temporary public ownership.

(4) The relevant authorities shall have regard to the code.

(5) For the purpose of this section the relevant authorities are—

(a) the Treasury,

(b) the FSA, and

(c) the Bank of England.

Exercise of powers: general

7 General conditions

(1) A stabilisation power may be exercised in respect of a bank only if the FSA is satisfied that the following conditions are met.

(2) Condition 1 is that the bank is failing, or is likely to fail, to satisfy the threshold conditions (within the meaning of section 41(1) of the Financial Services and Markets Act 2000 (permission to carry on regulated activities)).

(3) Condition 2 is that having regard to timing and other relevant circumstances it is not reasonably likely that (ignoring the stabilisation powers) action will be taken by or in respect of the bank that will enable the bank to satisfy the threshold conditions.

(4) The FSA shall treat Conditions 1 and 2 as met if satisfied that they would be met but for financial assistance provided by—

    (a) the Treasury, or

    (b) the Bank of England (disregarding ordinary market assistance offered by the Bank on its usual terms).

(5) Before determining whether or not Condition 2 is met the FSA must consult—

    (a) the Bank of England, and

    (b) the Treasury.

(6) The special resolution objectives are not relevant to Conditions 1 and 2.

(7) The conditions for applying for and making a bank insolvency order are set out in sections 96 and 97.

(8) The conditions for applying for and making a bank administration order are set out in sections 143 and 144.

8 Specific conditions: private sector purchaser and bridge bank

(1) The Bank of England may exercise a stabilisation power in respect of a bank in accordance with section 11(2) or 12(2) only if satisfied that Condition A is met.

(2) Condition A is that the exercise of the power is necessary, having regard to the public interest in—

    (a) the stability of the financial systems of the United Kingdom,

    (b) the maintenance of public confidence in the stability of the banking systems of the United Kingdom, or

    (c) the protection of depositors.

(3) Before determining whether Condition A is met, and if so how to react, the Bank of England must consult—

    (a) the FSA, and

    (b) the Treasury.

(4) Where the Treasury notify the Bank of England that they have provided financial assistance in respect of a bank for the purpose of resolving or reducing a serious threat to the stability of the financial systems of the United Kingdom, the Bank may exercise a stabilisation power in respect of the bank in accordance with section 11(2) or 12(2) only if satisfied that Condition B is met (instead of Condition A).

(5) Condition B is that—

    (a) the Treasury have recommended the Bank of England to exercise the stabilisation power on the grounds that it is necessary to protect the public interest, and

    (b) in the Bank's opinion, exercise of the stabilisation power is an appropriate way to provide that protection.

(6) The conditions in this section are in addition to the conditions in section 7.

9 Specific conditions: temporary public ownership

(1) The Treasury may exercise a stabilisation power in respect of a bank in accordance with section 13(2) only if satisfied that one of the following conditions is met.

(2) Condition A is that the exercise of the power is necessary to resolve or reduce a serious threat to the stability of the financial systems of the United Kingdom.

(3) Condition B is that exercise of the power is necessary to protect the public interest, where the Treasury have provided financial assistance in respect of the bank for the purpose of resolving or reducing a serious threat to the stability of the financial systems of the United Kingdom.

(4) Before determining whether a condition is met the Treasury must consult—

(a) the FSA, and

(b) the Bank of England.

(5) The conditions in this section are in addition to the conditions in section 7.

10   Banking Liaison Panel

(1) The Treasury shall make arrangements for a panel to advise the Treasury about the effect of the special resolution regime on—

(a) banks,

(b) persons with whom banks do business, and

(c) the financial markets.

(2) In particular, the panel may advise the Treasury about—

(a) the exercise of powers to make statutory instruments under or by virtue of this Part, Part 2 or Part 3 (excluding the stabilisation powers, compensation scheme orders, resolution fund orders, third party compensation orders and orders under section 75(2)(b) and (c)),

(b) the code of practice under section 5, and

(c) anything else referred to the panel by the Treasury.

(3) The Treasury shall ensure that the panel includes—

(a) a member appointed by the Treasury,

(b) a member appointed by the Bank of England,

(c) a member appointed by the FSA,

(d) a member appointed by the scheme manager of the Financial Services Compensation Scheme,

(e) one or more persons who in the Treasury's opinion represent the interests of banks,

(f) one or more persons who in the Treasury's opinion have expertise in law relating to the financial systems of the United Kingdom, and

(g) one or more persons who in the Treasury's opinion have expertise in insolvency law and practice.

12   Bridge bank

(1) The second stabilisation option is to transfer all or part of the business of the bank to a company which is wholly owned by the Bank of England (a "bridge bank").

(2) For that purpose the Bank of England may make one or more property transfer instruments.

(3) The code of practice under section 5 must include provision about the management and control of bridge banks including, in particular, provision about—

(a) setting objectives,

(b) the content of the articles of association,

(c) the content of reports under section 80(1),

(d) different arrangements for management and control at different stages, and

(e) eventual disposal.

(4) Where property, rights or liabilities are first transferred by property transfer instrument to a bridge bank and later transferred (whether or not by the exercise of a power under this Part) to another company which is wholly owned by the Bank of England, that other company is an "onward bridge bank".

(5) An onward bridge bank—

(a) is a bridge bank for the purposes of—

(i)   subsection (3),

        (ii)   section 77,

        (iii) section 79, and

        (iv) section 80(5), but

   (b) is not a bridge bank for the purposes of—

        (i)   section 30(1),

        (ii)   section 43(1), or

        (iii) section 80(1).

13   Temporary public ownership

(1) The third stabilisation option is to take the bank into temporary public ownership.

(2) For that purpose the Treasury may make one or more share transfer orders in which the transferee is—

   (a) a nominee of the Treasury, or

   (b) a company wholly owned by the Treasury.

(3) The code of practice under section 5 must include provision about the management of banks taken into temporary public ownership under this section.

PART 2 BANK INSOLVENCY

Bank insolvency order

94   The order

(1) A bank insolvency order is an order appointing a person as the bank liquidator of a bank.

(2) A person is eligible for appointment as a bank liquidator if qualified to act as an insolvency practitioner.

(3) An appointment may be made only if the person has consented to act.

(4) A bank insolvency order takes effect in accordance with section 98; and—

   (a) the process of a bank insolvency order having effect may be described as "bank insolvency" in relation to the bank, and

   (b) while the order has effect the bank may be described as being "in bank insolvency".

95   Application

(1) An application for a bank insolvency order may be made to the court by—

   (a) the Bank of England,

   (b) the FSA, or

   (c) the Secretary of State.

(2) An application must nominate a person to be appointed as the bank liquidator.

(3) The bank must be given notice of an application, in accordance with rules under section 411 of the Insolvency Act 1986 (as applied by section 125 below).

96   Grounds for applying

(1) In this section—

   (a) Ground A is that a bank is unable, or likely to become unable, to pay its debts,

   (b) Ground B is that the winding up of a bank would be in the public interest, and

   (c) Ground C is that the winding up of a bank would be fair.

(2) The Bank of England may apply for a bank insolvency order only if—

   (a) the FSA has informed the Bank of England that the FSA is satisfied that Conditions 1 and 2 in section 7 are met, and

   (b) the Bank of England is satisfied—

        (i)   that the bank has eligible depositors, and

        (ii) that Ground A or C applies.

(3) The FSA may apply for a bank insolvency order only if—

   (a) the Bank of England consents, and

    (b) the FSA is satisfied—
        (i)   that Conditions 1 and 2 in section 7 are met,
        (ii) that the bank has eligible depositors, and
        (iii) that Ground A or C applies.

(4) The Secretary of State may apply for a bank insolvency order only if satisfied—
    (a) that the bank has eligible depositors, and
    (b) that Ground B applies.

(5) The sources of information on the basis of which the Secretary of State may be satisfied of the matters specified in subsection (4) include those listed in section 124A(1) of the Insolvency Act 1986 (petition for winding up on grounds of public interest).

97   Grounds for making

(1) The court may make a bank insolvency order on the application of the Bank of England or the FSA if satisfied—
    (a) that the bank has eligible depositors, and
    (b) that Ground A or C of section 96 applies.

(2) The court may make a bank insolvency order on the application of the Secretary of State if satisfied—
    (a) that the bank has eligible depositors, and
    (b) that Grounds B and C of section 96 apply.

(3) On an application for a bank insolvency order the court may—
    (a) grant the application in accordance with subsection (1) or (2),
    (b) adjourn the application (generally or to a specified date), or
    (c) dismiss the application.

98   Commencement

(1) A bank insolvency order shall be treated as having taken effect in accordance with this section.

(2) In the case where—
    (a) notice has been given to the FSA under section 120 of an application for an administration order or a petition for a winding up order, and
    (b) the FSA or the Bank of England applies for a bank insolvency order in the period of 2 weeks specified in Condition 3 in that section,
the bank insolvency order is treated as having taken effect when the application or petition was made or presented.

(3) In any other case, the bank insolvency order is treated as having taken effect when the application for the order was made.

(4) Unless the court directs otherwise on proof of fraud or mistake, proceedings taken in the bank insolvency, during the period for which it is treated as having had effect, are treated as having been taken validly.

Process of bank liquidation

99   Objectives

(1) A bank liquidator has two objectives.

(2) Objective 1 is to work with the FSCS so as to ensure that as soon as is reasonably practicable each eligible depositor—
    (a) has the relevant account transferred to another financial institution, or
    (b) receives payment from (or on behalf of) the FSCS.

(3) Objective 2 is to wind up the affairs of the bank so as to achieve the best result for the bank's creditors as a whole.

(4) Objective 1 takes precedence over Objective 2 (but the bank liquidator is obliged to begin working towards both objectives immediately upon appointment).

100   Liquidation committee

(1) Following a bank insolvency order a liquidation committee must be established, for the purpose of ensuring that the bank liquidator properly exercises the functions under this Part.

(2) The liquidation committee shall consist initially of 3 individuals, one nominated by each of—

    (a) the Bank of England,

    (b) the FSA, and

    (c) the FSCS.

(3) The bank liquidator must report to the liquidation committee about any matter—

    (a) on request, or

    (b) which the bank liquidator thinks is likely to be of interest to the liquidation committee.

(4) In particular, the bank liquidator—

    (a) must keep the liquidation committee informed of progress towards Objective 1 in section 99, and

    (b) must notify the liquidation committee when in the bank liquidator's opinion Objective 1 in section 99 has been achieved entirely or so far as is reasonably practicable.

(5) As soon as is reasonably practicable after receiving notice under subsection (4)(b) the liquidation committee must either—

    (a) resolve that Objective 1 in section 99 has been achieved entirely or so far as is reasonably practicable (a "full payment resolution"), or

    (b) apply to the court under section 168(5) of the Insolvency Act 1986 (as applied by section 103 below).

103   General powers, duties and effect

(1) A bank liquidator may do anything necessary or expedient for the pursuit of the Objectives in section 99.

(2) The following provisions of this section provide for—

    (a) general powers and duties of bank liquidators (by application of provisions about liquidators), and

    (b) the general process and effects of bank insolvency (by application of provisions about winding up).

Termination of process, &c.

113   Company voluntary arrangement

(1) A bank liquidator may make a proposal in accordance with section 1 of the Insolvency Act 1986 (company voluntary arrangement).

114   Administration

(1) A bank liquidator who thinks that administration would achieve a better result for the bank's creditors as a whole than bank insolvency may apply to the court for an administration order (under paragraph 38 of Schedule B1 to the Insolvency Act 1986).

(2) An application may be made only if the following conditions are satisfied.

(3) Condition 1 is that the liquidation committee has passed a full payment resolution.

(4) Condition 2 is that the liquidation committee has resolved that moving to administration might enable the rescue of the bank as a going concern.

(5) Condition 3 is that the bank liquidator is satisfied, as a result of arrangements made with the FSCS, that any depositors still eligible for compensation under the scheme will receive their payments or have their accounts transferred during administration.

Other processes

117 Bank insolvency as alternative order

(1) On a petition for a winding up order or an application for an administration order in respect of a bank the court may, instead, make a bank insolvency order.

(2) A bank insolvency order may be made under subsection (1) only—

(a) on the application of the FSA made with the consent of the Bank of England, or

(b) on the application of the Bank of England.

118 Voluntary winding-up

A resolution for voluntary winding up of a bank under section 84 of the Insolvency Act 1986 shall have no effect without the prior approval of the court.

120 Notice to FSA of preliminary steps

(1) An application for an administration order in respect of a bank may not be determined unless the conditions below are satisfied.

(2) A petition for a winding up order in respect of a bank may not be determined unless the conditions below are satisfied.

(3) A resolution for voluntary winding up of a bank may not be made unless the conditions below are satisfied.

(4) An administrator of a bank may not be appointed unless the conditions below are satisfied.

(5) Condition 1 is that the FSA has been notified—

(a) by the applicant for an administration order, that the application has been made,

(b) by the petitioner for a winding up order, that the petition has been presented,

(c) by the bank, that a resolution for voluntary winding up may be made, or

(d) by the person proposing to appoint an administrator, of the proposed appointment.

(6) Condition 2 is that a copy of the notice complying with Condition 1 has been filed with the court (and made available for public inspection by the court).

(7) Condition 3 is that—

(a) the period of 2 weeks, beginning with the day on which the notice is received, has ended, or

(b) both—

(i)   the FSA has informed the person who gave the notice that it does not intend to apply for a bank insolvency order, and

(ii) the Bank of England has informed the person who gave the notice that it does not intend to apply for a bank insolvency order or to exercise a stabilisation power under Part 1.

(8) Condition 4 is that no application for a bank insolvency order is pending.

(9) Arranging for the giving of notice in order to satisfy Condition 1 can be a step with a view to minimising the potential loss to a bank's creditors for the purpose of section 214 of the Insolvency Act 1986 (wrongful trading).

(10) Where the FSA receives notice under Condition 1—

(a) the FSA shall inform the Bank of England,

(b) the FSA shall inform the person who gave the notice, within the period in Condition 3(a), whether it intends to apply for a bank insolvency order, and

(c) if the Bank of England decides to apply for a bank insolvency order or to exercise a stabilisation power under Part 1, the Bank shall inform the person who gave the notice, within the period in Condition 3(a).

Miscellaneous

123 Role of FSCS

(1) For the purpose of co-operating in the pursuit of Objective 1 in section 99 the FSCS—

(a) may make or arrange for payments to or in respect of eligible depositors of the bank, and

(b) may make money available to facilitate the transfer of accounts of eligible depositors of the bank.

PART 3 BANK ADMINISTRATION

Introduction

136 Overview

(1) This Part provides for a procedure to be known as bank administration.

(2) The main features of bank administration are that—

(a) it is used where part of the business of a bank is sold to a commercial purchaser in accordance with section 11 or transferred to a bridge bank in accordance with section 12 (and it can also be used in certain cases of multiple transfers under Part 1),

(b) the court appoints a bank administrator on the application of the Bank of England,

(c) the bank administrator is able and required to ensure that the non-sold or non-transferred part of the bank ("the residual bank") provides services or facilities required to enable the commercial purchaser ("the private sector purchaser") or the transferee ("the bridge bank") to operate effectively, and

(d) in other respects the process is the same as for normal administration under the Insolvency Act 1986, subject to specified modifications.

137 Objectives

(1) A bank administrator has two objectives—

(a) Objective 1: support for commercial purchaser or bridge bank (see section 138), and

(b) Objective 2: "normal" administration (see section 140).

(2) Objective 1 takes priority over Objective 2 (but a bank administrator is obliged to begin working towards both objectives immediately upon appointment).

138 Objective 1: supporting private sector purchaser or bridge bank

(1) Objective 1 is to ensure the supply to the private sector purchaser or bridge bank of such services and facilities as are required to enable it, in the opinion of the Bank of England, to operate effectively.

140 Objective 2: "normal" administration

(1) Objective 2 is to—

(a) rescue the residual bank as a going concern ("Objective 2(a)"), or

(b) achieve a better result for the residual bank's creditors as a whole than would be likely if the residual bank were wound up without first being in bank administration ("Objective 2(b)").

(2) In pursuing Objective 2 a bank administrator must aim to achieve Objective 2(a) unless of the opinion either—

(a) that it is not reasonably practicable to achieve it, or

(b) that Objective 2(b) would achieve a better result for the residual bank's creditors as a whole.

147 Administrator's proposals

(1) This section applies before the giving of an Objective 1 Achievement Notice (at which point paragraph 49 of Schedule B1 to the Insolvency Act 1986 applies in accordance with section 145).

(2) The bank administrator must as soon as is reasonably practicable after appointment make a statement setting out proposals for achieving the Objectives in section 137.

(3) The statement must say whether the bank administrator proposes to pursue Objective 2(a) or 2(b) in section 140.

(4) The statement must have been agreed with the Bank of England.

(5) But a bank administrator who is unable to agree a statement with the Bank of England may apply to the court for directions under paragraph 63 of Schedule B1 to the Insolvency Act 1986 (as applied by section 145); and the court may make any order, including dispensing with the need for the Bank of England's agreement.

(6) The bank administrator must send the statement to the FSA.

PART 5 INTER-BANK PAYMENT SYSTEMS

Introduction

181 Overview

This Part enables the Bank of England to oversee certain systems for payments between financial institutions.

182 Interpretation: "inter-bank payment system"

(1) In this Part "inter-bank payment system" means arrangements designed to facilitate or control the transfer of money between financial institutions who participate in the arrangements.

(2) The fact that persons other than financial institutions can participate does not prevent arrangements from being an inter-bank payment system.

(3) In subsection (1) "financial institutions" means—

    (a) banks, and

    (b) building societies.

(4) In subsection (1) "money" includes credit.

(5) A system is an inter-bank payment system for the purposes of this Part whether or not it operates wholly or partly in relation to persons or places outside the United Kingdom.

Regulation

188 Principles

(1) The Bank of England may publish principles to which operators of recognised inter-bank payment systems are to have regard in operating the systems.

(2) Before publishing principles the Bank must obtain the approval of the Treasury.

189 Codes of practice

The Bank of England may publish codes of practice about the operation of recognised inter-bank payment systems.

190 System rules

(1) The Bank of England may require the operator of a recognised inter-bank payment system—

    (a) to establish rules for the operation of the system;

    (b) to change the rules in a specified way or so as to achieve a specified purpose;

    (c) to notify the Bank of any proposed change to the rules;

    (d) not to change the rules without the approval of the Bank.

(2) A requirement under subsection (1)(c) or (d) may be general or specific.

191 Directions

(1) The Bank of England may give directions to the operator of a recognised inter-bank payment system.

(2) A direction may—

    (a) require or prohibit the taking of specified action in the operation of the system;

    (b) set standards to be met in the operation of the system.

(3) Before giving a direction the Bank must notify the Treasury.

(4) The Treasury may by order confer immunity from liability in damages in respect of action or inaction in accordance with a direction.

(5) An immunity does not extend to action or inaction—

    (a) in bad faith, or

    (b) in contravention of section 6(1) of the Human Rights Act 1998.

(6) An order—

    (a) shall be made by statutory instrument, and

    (b) shall be subject to annulment in pursuance of a resolution of either House of Parliament.

192   Role of FSA

(1) In exercising powers under this Part the Bank of England shall have regard to any action that the FSA has taken or could take.

(2) Before taking action under this Part in respect of a recognised inter-bank payment system the operator of which satisfies section 186(2), the Bank of England must consult the FSA.

(3) If the FSA gives the Bank of England notice that the FSA is considering taking action in respect of the operator of a recognised inter-bank payment system who satisfies section 186(2), the Bank may not take action under this Part in respect of the operator unless—

    (a) the FSA consents, or

    (b) the notice is withdrawn.

199   Closure

(1) This section applies if the Bank of England thinks that a compliance failure—

    (a) threatens the stability of, or confidence in, the UK financial system, or

    (b) has serious consequences for business or other interests throughout the United Kingdom.

(2) The Bank may give the operator of the inter-bank payment system concerned an order to stop operating the system (a "closure order")—

    (a) for a specified period,

    (b) until further notice, or

    (c) permanently.

200   Management disqualification

(1) The Bank of England may by order prohibit a specified person from being an operator of a recognised inter-bank payment system—

    (a) for a specified period,

    (b) until further notice, or

    (c) permanently.

(2) The Bank may by order prohibit a specified person from holding an office or position involving responsibility for taking decisions about the management of a recognised inter-bank payment system—

    (a) for a specified period,

    (b) until further notice, or

    (c) permanently.

Third Parties (Rights against Insurers) Act 2010

(2010, c. 10)

Transfer of rights to third parties

1   Rights against insurer of insolvent person etc

(1) This section applies if—

    (a) a relevant person incurs a liability against which that person is insured under a contract of insurance, or

    (b) a person who is subject to such a liability becomes a relevant person.

(2) The rights of the relevant person under the contract against the insurer in respect of the liability are transferred to and vest in the person to whom the liability is or was incurred (the "third party").

(3) The third party may bring proceedings to enforce the rights against the insurer without having established the relevant person's liability; but the third party may not enforce those rights without having established that liability.

(4) For the purposes of this Act, a liability is established only if its existence and amount are established; and, for that purpose, "establish" means establish—

(a) by virtue of a declaration under section 2 or a declarator under section 3,

(b) by a judgment or decree,

(c) by an award in arbitral proceedings or by an arbitration, or

(d) by an enforceable agreement.

(5) In this Act—

(a) references to an "insured" are to a person who incurs or who is subject to a liability to a third party against which that person is insured under a contract of insurance;

(b) references to a "relevant person" are to a person within sections 4 to 7;

(c) references to a "third party" are to be construed in accordance with subsection (2);

(d) references to "transferred rights" are to rights under a contract of insurance which are transferred under this section.

2 Establishing liability in England and Wales and Northern Ireland

(1) This section applies where a person (P)—

(a) claims to have rights under a contract of insurance by virtue of a transfer under section 1, but

(b) has not yet established the insured's liability which is insured under that contract.

(2) P may bring proceedings against the insurer for either or both of the following—

(a) a declaration as to the insured's liability to P;

(b) a declaration as to the insurer's potential liability to P.

(3) In such proceedings P is entitled, subject to any defence on which the insurer may rely, to a declaration under subsection (2)(a) or (b) on proof of the insured's liability to P or (as the case may be) the insurer's potential liability to P.

(4) Where proceedings are brought under subsection (2)(a) the insurer may rely on any defence on which the insured could rely if those proceedings were proceedings brought against the insured in respect of the insured's liability to P.

(5) Subsection (4) is subject to section 12(1).

(6) Where the court makes a declaration under this section, the effect of which is that the insurer is liable to P, the court may give the appropriate judgment against the insurer.

(7) Where a person applying for a declaration under subsection (2)(b) is entitled or required, by virtue of the contract of insurance, to do so in arbitral proceedings, that person may also apply in the same proceedings for a declaration under subsection (2)(a).

(8) In the application of this section to arbitral proceedings, subsection (6) is to be read as if "tribunal" were substituted for "court" and "make the appropriate award" for "give the appropriate judgment".

(9) When bringing proceedings under subsection (2)(a), P may also make the insured a defendant to those proceedings.

(10) If (but only if) the insured is a defendant to proceedings under this section (whether by virtue of subsection (9) or otherwise), a declaration under subsection (2) binds the insured as well as the insurer.

(11) In this section, references to the insurer's potential liability to P are references to the insurer's liability in respect of the insured's liability to P, if established.

Relevant persons

4 Individuals

(1) An individual is a relevant person if any of the following is in force in respect of that individual in England and Wales—

> (a) a deed of arrangement registered in accordance with the Deeds of Arrangement Act 1914,
>
> (b) an administration order made under Part 6 of the County Courts Act 1984,
>
> (c) an enforcement restriction order made under Part 6A of that Act,
>
> (d) subject to subsection (4), a debt relief order made under Part 7A of the Insolvency Act 1986,
>
> (e) a voluntary arrangement approved in accordance with Part 8 of that Act, or
>
> (f) a bankruptcy order made under Part 9 of that Act.

(4) If an individual is a relevant person by virtue of subsection (1)(d), that person is a relevant person for the purposes of section 1(1)(b) only.

5 Individuals who die insolvent

(1) An individual who dies insolvent is a relevant person for the purposes of section 1(1)(b) only.

(2) For the purposes of this section an individual (D) is to be regarded as having died insolvent if, following D's death—

> (a) D's estate falls to be administered in accordance with an order under section 421 of the Insolvency Act 1986 . . .

(3) Where a transfer of rights under section 1 takes place as a result of an insured person being a relevant person by virtue of this section, references in this Act to an insured are, where the context so requires, to be read as references to the insured's estate.

6 Corporate bodies etc

(1) A body corporate or an unincorporated body is a relevant person if—

> (a) a compromise or arrangement between the body and its creditors (or a class of them) is in force, having been sanctioned in accordance with section 899 of the Companies Act 2006, or
>
> (b) the body has been dissolved under section 1000, 1001 or 1003 of that Act, and the body has not been—
>
>> (i)   restored to the register by virtue of section 1025 of that Act, or
>>
>> (ii) ordered to be restored to the register by virtue of section 1031 of that Act.

(2) A body corporate or an unincorporated body is a relevant person if, in England and Wales or Scotland—

> (a) a voluntary arrangement approved in accordance with Part 1 of the Insolvency Act 1986 is in force in respect of it,
>
> (b) an administration order made under Part 2 of that Act is in force in respect of it,
>
> (c) there is a person appointed in accordance with Part 3 of that Act who is acting as receiver or manager of the body's property (or there would be such a person so acting but for a temporary vacancy),
>
> (d) the body is, or is being, wound up voluntarily in accordance with Chapter 2 of Part 4 of that Act,
>
> (e) there is a person appointed under section 135 of that Act who is acting as provisional liquidator in respect of the body (or there would be such a person so acting but for a temporary vacancy), or
>
> (f) the body is, or is being, wound up by the court following the making of a winding-up order under Chapter 6 of Part 4 of that Act or Part 5 of that Act.

(5) A body within subsection (1)(a) is not a relevant person in relation to a liability that is transferred to another body by the order sanctioning the compromise or arrangement.

(6) Where a body is a relevant person by virtue of subsection (1)(a), section 1 has effect to transfer rights only to a person on whom the compromise or arrangement is binding.

(9) In this section—

(a) a reference to a person appointed in accordance with Part 3 of the Insolvency Act 1986 includes a reference to a person appointed under section 101 of the Law of Property Act 1925;

(b) a reference to a receiver or manager of a body's property includes a reference to a receiver or manager of part only of the property and to a receiver only of the income arising from the property or from part of it; ...

Transferred rights: supplemental

8   Limit on rights transferred

Where the liability of an insured to a third party is less than the liability of the insurer to the insured (ignoring the effect of section 1), no rights are transferred under that section in respect of the difference.

9   Conditions affecting transferred rights

(1) This section applies where transferred rights are subject to a condition (whether under the contract of insurance from which the transferred rights are derived or otherwise) that the insured has to fulfil.

(2) Anything done by the third party which, if done by the insured, would have amounted to or contributed to fulfilment of the condition is to be treated as if done by the insured.

(3) The transferred rights are not subject to a condition requiring the insured to provide information or assistance to the insurer if that condition cannot be fulfilled because the insured is—

(a) an individual who has died, or

(b) a body corporate that has been dissolved.

(4) A condition requiring the insured to provide information or assistance to the insurer does not include a condition requiring the insured to notify the insurer of the existence of a claim under the contract of insurance.

(5) The transferred rights are not subject to a condition requiring the prior discharge by the insured of the insured's liability to the third party.

(6) In the case of a contract of marine insurance, subsection (5) applies only to the extent that the liability of the insured is a liability in respect of death or personal injury.

(7) In this section—

"contract of marine insurance" has the meaning given by section 1 of the Marine Insurance Act 1906;

"dissolved" means dissolved under—

(a) Chapter 9 of Part 4 of the Insolvency Act 1986,

(b) section 1000, 1001 or 1003 of the Companies Act 2006, ...

"personal injury" includes any disease and any impairment of a person's physical or mental condition.

10   Insurer's right of set off

(1) This section applies if—

(a) rights of an insured under a contract of insurance have been transferred to a third party under section 1,

(b) the insured is under a liability to the insurer under the contract ("the insured's liability"), and

(c) if there had been no transfer, the insurer would have been entitled to set off the amount of the insured's liability against the amount of the insurer's own liability to the insured.

(2) The insurer is entitled to set off the amount of the insured's liability against the amount of the insurer's own liability to the third party in relation to the transferred rights.

Provision of information etc

11 Information and disclosure for third parties

Schedule 1 (information and disclosure for third parties) has effect.

Enforcement of transferred rights

12 Limitation and prescription

(1) Subsection (2) applies where a person brings proceedings for a declaration under section 2(2)(a), ... and the proceedings are started ...—

(a) after the expiry of a period of limitation applicable to an action against the insured to enforce the insured's liability, or of a period of prescription applicable to that liability, but

(b) while such an action is in progress.

(2) The insurer may not rely on the expiry of that period as a defence unless the insured is able to rely on it in the action against the insured.

(3) For the purposes of subsection (1), an action is to be treated as no longer in progress if it has been concluded by a judgment or decree, or by an award, even if there is an appeal or a right of appeal.

(4) Where a person who has already established an insured's liability to that person brings proceedings under this Act against the insurer, nothing in this Act is to be read as meaning—

(a) that, for the purposes of the law of limitation in England and Wales, that person's cause of action against the insurer arose otherwise than at the time when that person established the liability of the insured, ...

13 Jurisdiction within the United Kingdom

(1) Where a person (P) domiciled in a part of the United Kingdom is entitled to bring proceedings under this Act against an insurer domiciled in another part, P may do so in the part where P is domiciled or in the part where the insurer is domiciled (whatever the contract of insurance may stipulate as to where proceedings are to be brought).

Enforcement of insured's liability

14 Effect of transfer on insured's liability

(1) Where rights in respect of an insured's liability to a third party are transferred under section 1, the third party may enforce that liability against the insured only to the extent (if any) that it exceeds the amount recoverable from the insurer by virtue of the transfer.

(2) Subsection (3) applies if a transfer of rights under section 1 occurs because the insured person is a relevant person by virtue of—

(a) section 4(1)(a) or (e), (2)(b) or (3)(b) or (c),

(b) section 6(1)(a), (2)(a), (3)(c) or (4)(a), or

(c) section 7(1)(b).

(3) If the liability is subject to the arrangement, trust deed or compromise by virtue of which the insured is a relevant person, the liability is to be treated as subject to that arrangement, trust deed or compromise only to the extent that the liability exceeds the amount recoverable from the insurer by virtue of the transfer.

(6) For the purposes of this section the amount recoverable from the insurer does not include any amount that the third party is unable to recover as a result of—

(a) a shortage of assets on the insurer's part, in a case where the insurer is a relevant person, or

  (b) a limit set by the contract of insurance on the fund available to meet claims in respect of a particular description of liability of the insured.

 (7) Where a third party is eligible to make a claim in respect of the insurer's liability under or by virtue of rules made under Part 15 of the Financial Services and Markets Act 2000 (the Financial Services Compensation Scheme)—

  (a) subsection (6)(a) applies only if the third party has made such a claim, and

  (b) the third party is to be treated as being able to recover from the insurer any amount paid to, or due to, the third party as a result of the claim.

Application of Act

15 Reinsurance

This Act does not apply to a case where the liability referred to in section 1(1) is itself a liability incurred by an insurer under a contract of insurance.

16 Voluntarily-incurred liabilities

It is irrelevant for the purposes of section 1 whether or not the liability of the insured is or was incurred voluntarily.

17 Avoidance

 (1) A contract of insurance to which this section applies is of no effect in so far as it purports, whether directly or indirectly, to avoid or terminate the contract or alter the rights of the parties under it in the event of the insured—

  (a) becoming a relevant person, or

  (b) dying insolvent (within the meaning given by section 5(2)).

 (2) A contract of insurance is one to which this section applies if the insured's rights under it are capable of being transferred under section 1.

18 Cases with a foreign element

Except as expressly provided, the application of this Act does not depend on whether there is a connection with a part of the United Kingdom; and in particular it does not depend on—

  (a) whether or not the liability (or the alleged liability) of the insured to the third party was incurred in, or under the law of, England and Wales, Scotland or Northern Ireland;

  (b) the place of residence or domicile of any of the parties;

  (c) whether or not the contract of insurance (or a part of it) is governed by the law of England and Wales, Scotland or Northern Ireland;

  (d) the place where sums due under the contract of insurance are payable.

Section 11   # SCHEDULES

SCHEDULE 1
INFORMATION AND DISCLOSURE FOR THIRD PARTIES

1 Notices requesting information

 (1) If a person (A) reasonably believes that—

  (a) another person (B) has incurred a liability to A, and

  (b) B is a relevant person,

A may, by notice in writing, request from B such information falling within sub-paragraph (3) as the notice specifies.

 (2) If a person (A) reasonably believes that—

  (a) a liability has been incurred to A,

  (b) the person who incurred the liability is insured against it under a contract of insurance,

  (c) rights of that person under the contract have been transferred to A under section 1, and

  (d) there is a person (C) who is able to provide information falling within sub-paragraph (3),

A may, by notice in writing, request from C such information falling within that sub-paragraph as the notice specifies.

    (3) The following is the information that falls within this sub-paragraph—

        (a) whether there is a contract of insurance that covers the supposed liability or might reasonably be regarded as covering it;

        (b) if there is such a contract—

            (i)   who the insurer is;

            (ii) what the terms of the contract are;

            (iii) whether the insured has been informed that the insurer has claimed not to be liable under the contract in respect of the supposed liability;

            (iv) whether there are or have been any proceedings between the insurer and the insured in respect of the supposed liability and, if so, relevant details of those proceedings;

            (v) in a case where the contract sets a limit on the fund available to meet claims in respect of the supposed liability and other liabilities, how much of it (if any) has been paid out in respect of other liabilities;

            (vi) whether there is a fixed charge to which any sums paid out under the contract in respect of the supposed liability would be subject.

    (4) For the purpose of sub-paragraph (3)(b)(iv), relevant details of proceedings are—

        (a) in the case of court proceedings—

            (i)   the name of the court;

            (ii) the case number;

            (iii) the contents of all documents served in the proceedings in accordance with rules of court or orders made in the proceedings, and the contents of any such orders;

        (b) in the case of arbitral proceedings or, in Scotland, an arbitration—

            (i)   the name of the arbitrator;

            (ii) information corresponding with that mentioned in paragraph (a)(iii).

    (6) A notice given by a person under this paragraph must include particulars of the facts on which that person relies as entitlement to give the notice.

2   Provision of information where notice given under paragraph 1

    (1) A person (R) who receives a notice under paragraph 1 must, within the period of 28 days beginning with the day of receipt of the notice—

        (a) provide to the person who gave the notice any information specified in it that R is able to provide;

        (b) in relation to any such information that R is not able to provide, notify that person why R is not able to provide it.

    (2) Where—

        (a) a person (R) receives a notice under paragraph 1,

        (b) there is information specified in the notice that R is not able to provide because it is contained in a document that is not in R's control,

        (c) the document was at one time in R's control, and

        (d) R knows or believes that it is now in another person's control,

R must, within the period of 28 days beginning with the day of receipt of the notice, provide the person who gave the notice with whatever particulars R can as to the nature of the information and the identity of that other person.

    (3) If R fails to comply with a duty imposed on R by this paragraph, the person who gave R the notice may apply to court for an order requiring R to comply with the duty.

    (4) No duty arises by virtue of this paragraph in respect of information as to which a claim to legal professional privilege . . . could be maintained in legal proceedings.

3   Notices requiring disclosure: defunct bodies

    (1) If—

        (a) a person (P) has started proceedings under this Act against an insurer in respect of a liability that P claims has been incurred to P by a body corporate, and

        (b) the body is defunct,

P may by notice in writing require a person to whom sub-paragraph (2) applies to disclose to P any documents that are relevant to that liability.

(2) This sub-paragraph applies to a person if—

(a) immediately before the time of the alleged transfer under section 1, that person was an officer or employee of the body, or

(b) immediately before the body became defunct, that person was—

(i) acting as an insolvency practitioner in relation to the body (within the meaning given by section 388(1) of the Insolvency Act 1986 . . ., or

(ii) acting as the official receiver in relation to the winding up of the body.

(3) A notice under this paragraph must be accompanied by—

(a) a copy of the particulars of claim required to be served in connection with the proceedings mentioned in sub-paragraph (1), or

(b) where those proceedings are arbitral proceedings, the particulars of claim that would be required to be so served if they were court proceedings.

(4) For the purposes of this paragraph a body corporate is defunct if, subject to sub-paragraph (5), it has been dissolved under—

(a) Chapter 9 of Part 4 of the Insolvency Act 1986,

. . . or

(c) section 1000, 1001 or 1003 of the Companies Act 2006.

(5) But a body corporate is not defunct for the purposes of this paragraph if the body has been—

(a) restored to the register by virtue of section 1025 of the Companies Act 2006, or

(b) ordered to be restored to the register by virtue of section 1031 of that Act.

4 Disclosure and inspection where notice given under paragraph 3

(1) Subject to the provisions of this paragraph and to any necessary modifications—

(a) the duties of disclosure of a person who receives a notice under paragraph 3, and

(b) the rights of inspection of the person giving the notice,

are the same as the corresponding duties and rights under Civil Procedure Rules of parties to court proceedings in which an order for standard disclosure has been made.

(3) A person who by virtue of sub-paragraph (1) or (2) has to serve a list of documents must do so within the period of 28 days beginning with the day of receipt of the notice.

(4) A person who has received a notice under paragraph 3 and has served a list of documents in response to it is not under a duty of disclosure by reason of that notice in relation to documents that the person did not have when the list was served.

5 Avoidance

A contract of insurance is of no effect in so far as it purports, whether directly or indirectly—

(a) to avoid or terminate the contract or alter the rights of the parties under it in the event of a person providing information, or giving disclosure, that the person is required to provide or give by virtue of a notice under paragraph 1 or 3, or

(b) otherwise to prohibit, prevent or restrict a person from providing such information or giving such disclosure.

6 Other rights to information etc

Rights to information, or to inspection of documents, that a person has by virtue of paragraph 1 or 3 are in addition to any such rights as the person has apart from that paragraph.

7 Interpretation

For the purposes of this Schedule—

(a) a person is able to provide information only if—

(i) that person can obtain it without undue difficulty from a document that is in that person's control, or

(ii) where that person is an individual, the information is within that person's knowledge;

(b) a document is in a person's control if it is in that person's possession or if that person has a right to possession of it or to inspect or take copies of it.

Consumer Insurance (Disclosure and Representations) Act 2012

(2012, c. 6)

Main definitions

1   Main definitions

In this Act—

"consumer insurance contract" means a contract of insurance between—

(a) an individual who enters into the contract wholly or mainly for purposes unrelated to the individual's trade, business or profession, and

(b) a person who carries on the business of insurance and who becomes a party to the contract by way of that business (whether or not in accordance with permission for the purposes of the Financial Services and Markets Act 2000);

"consumer" means the individual who enters into a consumer insurance contract, or proposes to do so;

"insurer" means the person who is, or would become, the other party to a consumer insurance contract.

Pre-contract and pre-variation information

2   Disclosure and representations before contract or variation

(1) This section makes provision about disclosure and representations by a consumer to an insurer before a consumer insurance contract is entered into or varied.

(2) It is the duty of the consumer to take reasonable care not to make a misrepresentation to the insurer.

(3) A failure by the consumer to comply with the insurer's request to confirm or amend particulars previously given is capable of being a misrepresentation for the purposes of this Act (whether or not it could be apart from this subsection).

(4) The duty set out in subsection (2) replaces any duty relating to disclosure or representations by a consumer to an insurer which existed in the same circumstances before this Act applied.

(5) Accordingly—

(a) any rule of law to the effect that a consumer insurance contract is one of the utmost good faith is modified to the extent required by the provisions of this Act, and

(b) the application of section 17 of the Marine Insurance Act 1906 (contracts of marine insurance are of utmost good faith), in relation to a contract of marine insurance which is a consumer insurance contract, is subject to the provisions of this Act.

3   Reasonable care

(1) Whether or not a consumer has taken reasonable care not to make a misrepresentation is to be determined in the light of all the relevant circumstances.

(2) The following are examples of things which may need to be taken into account in making a determination under subsection (1)—

(a) the type of consumer insurance contract in question, and its target market,

(b) any relevant explanatory material or publicity produced or authorised by the insurer,

(c) how clear, and how specific, the insurer's questions were,

(d) in the case of a failure to respond to the insurer's questions in connection with the renewal or variation of a consumer insurance contract, how clearly the insurer communicated the importance of answering those questions (or the possible consequences of failing to do so),

(e) whether or not an agent was acting for the consumer.

(3) The standard of care required is that of a reasonable consumer: but this is subject to subsections (4) and (5).

(4) If the insurer was, or ought to have been, aware of any particular characteristics or circumstances of the actual consumer, those are to be taken into account.

(5) A misrepresentation made dishonestly is always to be taken as showing lack of reasonable care.

Qualifying misrepresentations

4   Qualifying misrepresentations: definition and remedies

(1) An insurer has a remedy against a consumer for a misrepresentation made by the consumer before a consumer insurance contract was entered into or varied only if—

(a) the consumer made the misrepresentation in breach of the duty set out in section 2(2), and

(b) the insurer shows that without the misrepresentation, that insurer would not have entered into the contract (or agreed to the variation) at all, or would have done so only on different terms.

(2) A misrepresentation for which the insurer has a remedy against the consumer is referred to in this Act as a "qualifying misrepresentation".

(3) The only such remedies available are set out in Schedule 1.

5   Qualifying misrepresentations: classification and presumptions

(1) For the purposes of this Act, a qualifying misrepresentation (see section 4(2)) is either—

(a) deliberate or reckless, or

(b) careless.

(2) A qualifying misrepresentation is deliberate or reckless if the consumer—

(a) knew that it was untrue or misleading, or did not care whether or not it was untrue or misleading, and

(b) knew that the matter to which the misrepresentation related was relevant to the insurer, or did not care whether or not it was relevant to the insurer.

(3) A qualifying misrepresentation is careless if it is not deliberate or reckless.

(4) It is for the insurer to show that a qualifying misrepresentation was deliberate or reckless.

(5) But it is to be presumed, unless the contrary is shown—

(a) that the consumer had the knowledge of a reasonable consumer, and

(b) that the consumer knew that a matter about which the insurer asked a clear and specific question was relevant to the insurer.

Specific issues

6   Warranties and representations

(1) This section applies to representations made by a consumer—

(a) in connection with a proposed consumer insurance contract, or

(b) in connection with a proposed variation to a consumer insurance contract.

(2) Such a representation is not capable of being converted into a warranty by means of any provision of the consumer insurance contract (or of the terms of the variation), or of any other contract (and whether by declaring the representation to form the basis of the contract or otherwise).

7   Group insurance

(1) This section applies where—

(a) a contract of insurance is entered into by a person ("A") in order to provide cover for another person ("C"), or is varied or extended so as to do so,

(b) C is not a party to the contract,

(c) so far as the cover for C is concerned, the contract would have been a consumer insurance contract if entered into by C rather than by A, and

(d) C provided information directly or indirectly to the insurer before the contract was entered into, or before it was varied or extended to provide cover for C.

(2) So far as the cover for C is concerned—

(a) sections 2 and 3 apply in relation to disclosure and representations by C to the insurer as if C were proposing to enter into a consumer insurance contract for the relevant cover with the insurer, and

(b) subject to subsections (3) to (5) and the modifications in relation to the insurer's remedies set out in Part 3 of Schedule 1, the remainder of this Act applies in relation to the cover for C as if C had entered into a consumer insurance contract for that cover with the insurer.

(3) Section 4(1)(b) applies as if it read as follows—

"(b) the insurer shows that without the misrepresentation, that insurer would not have agreed to provide cover for C at all, or would have done so only on different terms."

(4) If there is more than one C, a breach on the part of one of them of the duty imposed (by virtue of subsection (2)(a)) by section 2(2) does not affect the contract so far as it relates to the others.

(5) Nothing in this section affects any duty owed by A to the insurer, or any remedy which the insurer may have against A for breach of such a duty.

8   Insurance on life of another

(1) This section applies in relation to a consumer insurance contract for life insurance on the life of an individual ("L") who is not a party to the contract.

(2) If this section applies—

(a) information provided to the insurer by L is to be treated for the purposes of this Act as if it were provided by the person who is the party to the contract, but

(b) in relation to such information, if anything turns on the state of mind, knowledge, circumstances or characteristics of the individual providing the information, it is to be determined by reference to L and not the party to the contract.

9   Agents

Schedule 2 applies for determining, for the purposes of this Act only, whether an agent through whom a consumer insurance contract is effected is the agent of the consumer or of the insurer.

10   Contracting out

(1) A term of a consumer insurance contract, or of any other contract, which would put the consumer in a worse position as respects the matters mentioned in subsection (2) than the consumer would be in by virtue of the provisions of this Act is to that extent of no effect.

(2) The matters are—

(a) disclosure and representations by the consumer to the insurer before the contract is entered into or varied, and

(b) any remedies for qualifying misrepresentations (see section 4(2)).

(3) This section does not apply in relation to a contract for the settlement of a claim arising under a consumer insurance contract.

Final provision

11   Consequential provision

(1) Any rule of law to the same effect as the following is abolished in relation to consumer insurance contracts—

      (a) section 18 of the Marine Insurance Act 1906 (disclosure by assured),

      (b) section 19 of that Act (disclosure by agent effecting insurance),

      (c) section 20 of that Act (representations pending negotiation of contract).

12   Short title, commencement, application and extent

(4) This Act applies only in relation to consumer insurance contracts entered into, and variations to consumer insurance contracts agreed, after the Act comes into force.

In the case of group insurance (see section 7), that includes the provision of cover for C by means of an insurance contract entered into by A after the Act comes into force, or varied or extended so as to do so after the Act comes into force.

(5) Nothing in this Act affects the circumstances in which a person is bound by the acts or omissions of that person's agent.

SCHEDULES

Section 4(3)   ## SCHEDULE 1

INSURERS' REMEDIES FOR QUALIFYING MISREPRESENTATIONS

PART 1   CONTRACTS

1. General

This Part of this Schedule applies in relation to qualifying misrepresentations made in connection with consumer insurance contracts (for variations to them, see Part 2).

2. Deliberate or reckless misrepresentations

If a qualifying misrepresentation was deliberate or reckless, the insurer—

      (a) may avoid the contract and refuse all claims, and

      (b) need not return any of the premiums paid, except to the extent (if any) that it would be unfair to the consumer to retain them.

Careless misrepresentations—claims

3. If the qualifying misrepresentation was careless, paragraphs 4 to 8 apply in relation to any claim.

    4. The insurer's remedies are based on what it would have done if the consumer had complied with the duty set out in section 2(2), and paragraphs 5 to 8 are to be read accordingly.

    5. If the insurer would not have entered into the consumer insurance contract on any terms, the insurer may avoid the contract and refuse all claims, but must return the premiums paid.

    6. If the insurer would have entered into the consumer insurance contract, but on different terms (excluding terms relating to the premium), the contract is to be treated as if it had been entered into on those different terms if the insurer so requires.

    7. In addition, if the insurer would have entered into the consumer insurance contract (whether the terms relating to matters other than the premium would have been the same or different), but would have charged a higher premium, the insurer may reduce proportionately the amount to be paid on a claim.

8. "Reduce proportionately" means that the insurer need pay on the claim only X% of what it would otherwise have been under an obligation to pay under the terms of the contract (or, if applicable, under the different terms provided for by virtue of paragraph 6), where—

$$X = \frac{\text{Premium actually charged}}{\text{Higher premium}} \times 100$$

9. Careless misrepresentations—treatment of contract for the future

(1) This paragraph—

    (a) applies if the qualifying misrepresentation was careless, but

    (b) does not relate to any outstanding claim.

(2) Paragraphs 5 and 6 (as read with paragraph 4) apply as they apply where a claim has been made.

(3) Paragraph 7 (as read with paragraph 4) applies in relation to a claim yet to be made as it applies in relation to a claim which has been made.

(4) If by virtue of sub-paragraph (2) or (3), the insurer would have either (or both) of the rights conferred by paragraph 6 or 7, the insurer may—

    (a) give notice to that effect to the consumer, or

    (b) terminate the contract by giving reasonable notice to the consumer.

(5) But the insurer may not terminate a contract under sub-paragraph (4)(b) if it is wholly or mainly one of life insurance.

(6) If the insurer gives notice to the consumer under sub-paragraph (4)(a), the consumer may terminate the contract by giving reasonable notice to the insurer.

(7) If either party terminates the contract under this paragraph, the insurer must refund any premiums paid for the terminated cover in respect of the balance of the contract term.

(8) Termination of the contract under this paragraph does not affect the treatment of any claim arising under the contract in the period before termination.

(9) Nothing in this paragraph affects any contractual right to terminate the contract.

PART 2 VARIATIONS

10. This Part of this Schedule applies in relation to qualifying misrepresentations made in connection with variations to consumer insurance contracts.

11. If the subject-matter of a variation can reasonably be treated separately from the subject-matter of the rest of the contract, Part 1 of this Schedule applies (with any necessary modifications) in relation to the variation as it applies in relation to a contract.

12. Otherwise, Part 1 applies (with any necessary modifications) as if the qualifying misrepresentation had been made in relation to the whole contract (for this purpose treated as including the variation) rather than merely in relation to the variation.

PART 3 MODIFICATIONS FOR GROUP INSURANCE

13. Part 1 is to be read subject to the following modifications in relation to cover provided for C under a group insurance contract as mentioned in section 7 (and in this Part "A" and "C" mean the same as in that section).

14. References to the consumer insurance contract (however described) are to that part of the contract which provides for cover for C.

15. References to claims and premiums are to claims and premiums in relation to that cover.

16. The reference to the consumer is to be read—

    (a) in paragraph 2(b), as a reference to whoever paid the premiums, or the part of them that related to the cover for C,

    (b) in paragraph 9(4) and (6), as a reference to A.

PART 4 SUPPLEMENTARY

17. Section 84 of the Marine Insurance Act 1906 (return of premium for failure of consideration) is to be read subject to the provisions of this Schedule in relation to contracts of marine insurance which are consumer insurance contracts.

Section 9

SCHEDULE 2

RULES FOR DETERMINING STATUS OF AGENTS

1. This Schedule sets out rules for determining, for the purposes of this Act only, whether an agent through whom a consumer insurance contract is effected is acting as the agent of the consumer or of the insurer.

    2. The agent is to be taken as the insurer's agent in each of the following cases—

        (a) when the agent does something in the agent's capacity as the appointed representative of the insurer for the purposes of the Financial Services and Markets Act 2000 (see section 39 of that Act),

        (b) when the agent collects information from the consumer, if the insurer had given the agent express authority to do so as the insurer's agent,

        (c) when the agent enters into the contract as the insurer's agent, if the insurer had given the agent express authority to do so.

    3.—(1) In any other case, it is to be presumed that the agent is acting as the consumer's agent unless, in the light of all the relevant circumstances, it appears that the agent is acting as the insurer's agent.

    (2) Some factors which may be relevant are set out below.

    (3) Examples of factors which may tend to confirm that the agent is acting for the consumer are—

        (a) the agent undertakes to give impartial advice to the consumer,

        (b) the agent undertakes to conduct a fair analysis of the market,

        (c) the consumer pays the agent a fee.

    (4) Examples of factors which may tend to show that the agent is acting for the insurer are—

        (a) the agent places insurance of the type in question with only one of the insurers who provide insurance of that type,

        (b) the agent is under a contractual obligation which has the effect of restricting the number of insurers with whom the agent places insurance of the type in question,

        (c) the insurer provides insurance of the type in question through only a small proportion of the agents who deal in that type of insurance,

        (d) the insurer permits the agent to use the insurer's name in providing the agent's services,

        (e) the insurance in question is marketed under the name of the agent,

        (f) the insurer asks the agent to solicit the consumer's custom.

    4. (1) If it appears to the Treasury that the list of factors in sub-paragraph (3) or (4) of paragraph 3 has become outdated, the Treasury may by order made by statutory instrument bring the list up to date by amending the subparagraph so as to add, omit or alter any factor.

    (2) A statutory instrument containing an order under sub-paragraph (1) may not be made unless a draft of the instrument has been laid before and approved by a resolution of each House of Parliament.

Part II

Statutory Instruments

Commercial Agents (Council Directive) Regulations 1993

(SI 1993, No. 3053)

PART I GENERAL

1 Citation, commencement and applicable law

(1) These Regulations may be cited as the Commercial Agents (Council Directive) Regulations 1993 and shall come into force on 1st January 1994.

(2) These Regulations govern the relations between commercial agents and their principals and, subject to paragraph (3), apply in relation to the activities of commercial agents in Great Britain.

[(3) A court or tribunal shall:

    (a) apply the law of the other member State concerned in place of regulations 3 to 22 where the parties have agreed that the agency contract is to be governed by the law of that member State;

    (b) (whether or not it would otherwise be required to do so) apply these Regulations where the law of another member State corresponding to these Regulations enables the parties to agree that the agency contract is to be governed by the law of a different member State and the parties have agreed that it is to be governed by the law of England and Wales or Scotland.]

2 Interpretation, application and extent

(1) In these Regulations—

'commercial agent' means a self-employed intermediary who has continuing authority to negotiate the sale or purchase of goods on behalf of another person (the 'principal'), or to negotiate and conclude the sale or purchase of goods on behalf of and in the name of that principal; but shall be understood as not including in particular:

    (i) a person who, in his capacity as an officer of a company or association, is empowered to enter into commitments binding on that company or association;

    (ii) a partner who is lawfully authorised to enter into commitments binding on his partners;

    (iii) a person who acts as an insolvency practitioner (as that expression is defined in section 388 of the Insolvency Act 1986) or the equivalent in any other jurisdiction;

'commission' means any part of the remuneration of a commercial agent which varies with the number or value of business transactions;

['EEA Agreement' means the Agreement on the European Economic Area signed at Oporto on 2nd May 1992 as adjusted by the Protocol signed at Brussels on 17th March 1993;

'member State' includes a State which is a contracting party to the EEA Agreement;]

'restraint of trade clause' means an agreement restricting the business activities of a commercial agent following termination of the agency contract.

(2) These Regulations do not apply to—

(a) commercial agents whose activities are unpaid;

(b) commercial agents when they operate on commodity exchanges or in the commodity market;

(c) the Crown Agents for Overseas Governments and Administrations, as set up under the Crown Agents Act 1979, or its subsidiaries.

(3) The provisions of the Schedule to these Regulations have effect for the purpose of determining the persons whose activities as commercial agents are to be considered secondary.

(4) These Regulations shall not apply to the persons referred to in paragraph (3) above.

(5) These Regulations do not extend to Northern Ireland.

PART II   RIGHTS AND OBLIGATIONS

3   Duties of a commercial agent to his principal

(1) In performing his activities a commercial agent must look after the interests of his principal and act dutifully and in good faith.

(2) In particular, a commercial agent must—

(a) make proper efforts to negotiate and, where appropriate, conclude the transactions he is instructed to take care of;

(b) communicate to his principal all the necessary information available to him;

(c) comply with reasonable instructions given by his principal.

4   Duties of a principal to his commercial agent

(1) In his relations with his commercial agent a principal must act dutifully and in good faith.

(2) In particular, a principal must—

(a) provide his commercial agent with the necessary documentation relating to the goods concerned;

(b) obtain for his commercial agent the information necessary for the performance of the agency contract, and in particular notify his commercial agent within a reasonable period once he anticipates that the volume of commercial transactions will be significantly lower than that which the commercial agent could normally have expected.

(3) A principal shall, in addition, inform his commercial agent within a reasonable period of his acceptance or refusal of, and of any non-execution by him of, a commercial transaction which the commercial agent has procured for him.

5   Prohibition on derogation from regulations 3   and 4   and consequence of breach

(1) The parties may not derogate from regulations 3 and 4 above.

(2) The law applicable to the contract shall govern the consequence of breach of the rights and obligations under regulations 3 and 4 above.

PART III   REMUNERATION

6   Form and amount of remuneration in absence of agreement

(1) In the absence of any agreement as to remuneration between the parties, a commercial agent shall be entitled to the remuneration that commercial agents appointed for the goods forming the subject of his agency contract are customarily allowed in the place where he carries on his activities and, if there is no such customary practice, a commercial agent shall be entitled to reasonable remuneration taking into account all the aspects of the transaction.

(2) This regulation is without prejudice to the application of any enactment or rule of law concerning the level of remuneration.

(3) Where a commercial agent is not remunerated (wholly or in part) by commission, regulations 7 to 12 below shall not apply.

7 Entitlement to commission on transactions concluded during agency contract

(1) A commercial agent shall be entitled to commission on commercial transactions concluded during the period covered by the agency contract—

> (a) where the transaction has been concluded as a result of his action; or
>
> (b) where the transaction is concluded with a third party whom he has previously acquired as a customer for transactions of the same kind.

(2) A commercial agent shall also be entitled to commission on transactions concluded during the period covered by the agency contract where he has an exclusive right to a specific geographical area or to a specific group of customers and where the transaction has been entered into with a customer belonging to that area or group.

8 Entitlement to commission on transactions concluded after agency contract has terminated

Subject to regulation 9 below, a commercial agent shall be entitled to commission on commercial transactions concluded after the agency contract has terminated if—

> (a) the transaction is mainly attributable to his efforts during the period covered by the agency contract and if the transaction was entered into within a reasonable period after that contract terminated; or
>
> (b) in accordance with the conditions mentioned in regulation 7 above, the order of the third party reached the principal or the commercial agent before the agency contract terminated.

9 Apportionment of commission between new and previous commercial agents

(1) A commercial agent shall not be entitled to the commission referred to in regulation 7 above if that commission is payable, by virtue of regulation 8 above, to the previous commercial agent, unless it is equitable because of the circumstances for the commission to be shared between the commercial agents.

(2) The principal shall be liable for any sum due under paragraph (1) above to the person entitled to it in accordance with that paragraph, and any sum which the other commercial agent receives to which he is not entitled shall be refunded to the principal.

10 When commission due and date for payment

(1) Commission shall become due as soon as, and to the extent that, one of the following circumstances occurs:

> (a) the principal has executed the transaction; or
>
> (b) the principal should, according to his agreement with the third party, have executed the transaction; or
>
> (c) the third party has executed the transaction.

(2) Commission shall become due at the latest when the third party has executed his part of the transaction or should have done so if the principal had executed his part of the transaction, as he should have.

(3) The commission shall be paid not later than on the last day of the month following the quarter in which it became due, and, for the purposes of these Regulations, unless otherwise agreed between the parties, the first quarter period shall run from the date the agency contract takes effect, and subsequent periods shall run from that date in the third month thereafter or the beginning of the fourth month, whichever is the sooner.

(4) Any agreement to derogate from paragraphs (2) and (3) above to the detriment of the commercial agent shall be void.

11 Extinction of right to commission

(1) The right to commission can be extinguished only if and to the extent that—

(a) it is established that the contract between the third party and the principal will not be executed; and

(b) that fact is due to a reason for which the principal is not to blame.

(2) Any commission which the commercial agent has already received shall be refunded if the right to it is extinguished.

(3) any agreement to derogate from paragraph (1) above to the detriment of the commercial agent shall be void.

12   Periodic supply of information as to commission due and right of inspection of principal's books

(1) The principal shall supply his commercial agent with a statement of the commission due, not later than the last day of the month following the quarter in which the commission has become due, and such statement shall set out the main components used in calculating the amount of the commission.

(2) A commercial agent shall be entitled to demand that he be provided with all the information (and in particular an extract from the books) which is available to his principal and which he needs in order to check the amount of the commission due to him.

(3) Any agreement to derogate from paragraphs (1) and (2) above shall be void.

(4) Nothing in this regulation shall remove or restrict the effect of, or prevent reliance upon, any enactment or rule of law which recognises the right of an agent to inspect the books of a principal.

PART IV CONCLUSION AND TERMINATION OF THE AGENCY CONTRACT

13   Right to signed written statement of terms of agency contract

(1) The commercial agent and principal shall each be entitled to receive from the other, on request, a signed written document setting out the terms of the agency contract including any terms subsequently agreed.

(2) Any purported waiver of the right referred to in paragraph (1) above shall be void.

14   Conversion of agency contract after expiry of fixed period

An agency contract for a fixed period which continues to be performed by both parties after that period has expired shall be deemed to be converted into an agency contract for an indefinite period.

15   Minimum periods of notice for termination of agency contract

(1) Where an agency contract is concluded for an indefinite period either party may terminate it by notice.

(2) The period of notice shall be—

(a) 1 month for the first year of the contract;

(b) 2 months for the second year commenced;

(c) 3 months for the third year commenced and for the subsequent years;

and the parties may not agree on any shorter periods of notice.

(3) If the parties agree on longer periods than those laid down in paragraph (2) above, the period of notice to be observed by the principal must not be shorter than that to be observed by the commercial agent.

(4) Unless otherwise agreed by the parties, the end of the period of notice must coincide with the end of a calendar month.

(5) The provisions of this regulation shall also apply to an agency contract for a fixed period where it is converted under regulation 14 above into an agency contract for an indefinite period subject to the proviso that the earlier fixed period must be taken into account in the calculation of the period of notice.

16   Savings with regard to immediate termination

These Regulations shall not affect the application of any enactment or rule of law which provides for the immediate termination of the agency contract—

(a) because of the failure of one party to carry out all or part of his obligations under that contract; or

(b) where exceptional circumstances arise.

17   Entitlement of commercial agent to indemnity or compensation on termination of agency contract

(1) This regulation has effect for the purpose of ensuring that the commercial agent is, after termination of the agency contract, indemnified in accordance with paragraphs (3) to (5) below or compensated for damage in accordance with paragraphs (6) and (7) below.

(2) Except where the agency [contract] otherwise provides, the commercial agent shall be entitled to be compensated rather than indemnified.

(3) Subject to paragraph (9) and to regulation 18 below, the commercial agent shall be entitled to an indemnity if and to the extent that—

(a) he has brought the principal new customers or has significantly increased the volume of business with existing customers and the principal continues to derive substantial benefits from the business with such customers; and

(b) the payment of this indemnity is equitable having regard to all the circumstances and, in particular, the commission lost by the commercial agent on the business transacted with such customers.

(4) The amount of the indemnity shall not exceed a figure equivalent to an indemnity for one year calculated from the commercial agent's average annual remuneration over the preceding five years and if the contract goes back less than five years the indemnity shall be calculated on the average for the period in question.

(5) The grant of an indemnity as mentioned above shall not prevent the commercial agent from seeking damages.

(6) Subject to paragraph (9) and to regulation 18 below, the commercial agent shall be entitled to compensation for the damage he suffers as a result of the termination of his relations with his principal.

(7) For the purpose of these Regulations such damage shall be deemed to occur particularly when the termination takes place in either or both of the following circumstances, namely circumstances which—

(a) deprive the commercial agent of the commission which proper performance of the agency contract would have procured for him whilst providing his principal with substantial benefits linked to the activities of the commercial agent; or

(b) have not enabled the commercial agent to amortize the costs and expenses that he had incurred in the performance of the agency contract on the advice of his principal.

(8) Entitlement to the indemnity or compensation for damage as provided for under paragraphs (2) to (7) above shall also arise where the agency contract is terminated as a result of the death of the commercial agent.

(9) The commercial agent shall lose his entitlement to the indemnity or compensation for damage in the instances provided for in paragraphs (2) to (8) above if within one year following termination of his agency contract he has not notified his principal that he intends pursuing his entitlement.

18   Grounds for excluding payment of indemnity or compensation under regulation 17

The [indemnity or] compensation referred to in regulation 17 above shall not be payable to the commercial agent where—

(a) the principal has terminated the agency contract because of default attributable to the commercial agent which would justify immediate termination of the agency contract pursuant to regulation 16 above; or

(b) the commercial agent has himself terminated the agency contract, unless such termination is justified—
   (i) by circumstances attributable to the principal, or
   (ii) on grounds of the age, infirmity or illness of the commercial agent in consequence of which he cannot reasonably be required to continue his activities; or

(c) the commercial agent, with the agreement of his principal, assigns his rights and duties under the agency contract to another person.

19 Prohibition on derogation from regulations 17 and 18

The parties may not derogate from regulations 17 and 18 to the detriment of the commercial agent before the agency contract expires.

20 Restraint of trade clauses

(1) A restraint of trade clause shall be valid only if and to the extent that—
   (a) it is concluded in writing; and
   (b) it relates to the geographical area or the group of customers and the geographical area entrusted to the commercial agent and to the kind of goods covered by his agency under the contract.

(2) A restraint of trade clause shall be valid for not more than two years after termination of the agency contract.

(3) Nothing in this regulation shall affect any enactment or rule of law which imposes other restrictions on the validity or enforceability of restraint of trade clauses or which enables a court to reduce the obligations on the parties resulting from such clauses.

PART V MISCELLANEOUS AND SUPPLEMENTAL

21 Disclosure of information

Nothing in these Regulations shall require information to be given where such disclosure would be contrary to public policy.

22 Service of notice etc

(1) Any notice, statement or other document to be given or supplied to a commercial agent or to be given or supplied to the principal under these Regulations may be so given or supplied:
   (a) by delivering it to him;
   (b) by leaving it at his proper address addressed to him by name;
   (c) by sending it by post to him addressed either to his registered address or to the address of his registered or principal office;
or by any other means provided for in the agency contract.

(2) Any such notice, statement or document may—
   (a) in the case of a body corporate, be given or served on the secretary or clerk of that body;
   (b) in the case of a partnership, be given to or served on any partner or on any person having the control or management of the partnership business.

23 Transitional provisions

(1) Notwithstanding any provision in an agency contract made before 1st January 1994, these Regulations shall apply to that contract after that date and, accordingly any provision which is inconsistent with these Regulations shall have effect subject to them.

(2) Nothing in these Regulations shall affect the rights and liabilities of a commercial agent or a principal which have accrued before 1st January 1994.

Regulation 2(3)   **THE SCHEDULE**

1. The activities of a person as a commercial agent are to be considered secondary where it may reasonably be taken that the primary purpose of the arrangement with his principal is other than as set out in paragraph 2 below.

2. An arrangement falls within this paragraph if—

(a) the business of the principal is the sale, or as the case may be purchase, of goods of a particular kind; and

(b) the goods concerned are such that—

(i) transactions are normally individually negotiated and concluded on a commercial basis, and

(ii) procuring a transaction on one occasion is likely to lead to further transactions in those goods with that customer on future occasions, or to transactions in those goods with other customers in the same geographical area or among the same group of customers, and

that accordingly it is in the commercial interests of the principal in developing the market in those goods to appoint a representative to such customers with a view to the representative devoting effort, skill and expenditure from his own resources to that end.

3. The following are indications that an arrangement falls within paragraph 2 above, and the absence of any of them is an indication to the contrary—

(a) the principal is the manufacturer, importer or distributor of the goods;

(b) the goods are specifically identified with the principal in the market in question rather than, or to a greater extent than, with any other person;

(c) the agent devotes substantially the whole of his time to representative activities (whether for one principal or for a number of principals whose interests are not conflicting);

(d) the goods are not normally available in the market in question other than by means of the agent;

(e) the arrangement is described as one of commercial agency.

4. The following are indications that an arrangement does not fall within paragraph 2 above—

(a) promotional material is supplied direct to potential customers;

(b) persons are granted agencies without reference to existing agents in a particular area or in relation to a particular group;

(c) customers normally select the goods for themselves and merely place their orders through the agent.

5. The activities of the following categories of persons are presumed, unless the contrary is established, not to fall within paragraph 2 above—

Mail order catalogue agents for consumer goods.

Consumer credit agents.

Unfair Terms in Consumer Contracts Regulations 1999

(SI 1999, No. 2083)

3 Interpretation

(1) In these Regulations—

'the Community' means the European Community;

'consumer' means any natural person who, in contracts covered by these Regulations, is acting for purposes which are outside his trade, business or profession;

'court' in relation to England and Wales and Northern Ireland means a county court or the High Court, and in relation to Scotland, the Sheriff or the Court of Session;

'Director' means the Director General of Fair Trading;

'EEA Agreement' means the Agreement on the European Economic Area signed at Oporto on 2nd May 1992 as adjusted by the protocol signed at Brussels on 17th March 1993;

'Member State' means a State which is a contracting party to the EEA Agreement;

'notified' means notified in writing;

'qualifying body' means a person specified in Schedule 1;

'seller or supplier' means any natural or legal person who, in contracts covered by these Regulations, is acting for purposes relating to his trade, business or profession, whether publicly owned or privately owned;

'unfair terms' means the contractual terms referred to in regulation 5.

[(1A) The references—

    (a) in regulation 4(1) to a seller or a supplier, and

    (b) in regulation 8(1) to a seller or supplier,

include references to a distance supplier and to an intermediary.

(1B) In paragraph (1A) and regulation 5(6)—

'distance supplier' means—

    (a) a supplier under a distance contract within the meaning of the Financial Services (Distance Marketing) Regulations 2004, or

    (b) a supplier of unsolicited financial services within regulation 15 of those Regulations; and

'intermediary' has the same meaning as in those Regulations.]

(2) In the application of these Regulations to Scotland for references to an 'injunction' or an 'interim injunction' there shall be substituted references to an 'interdict' or 'interim interdict' respectively.

4   Terms to which these Regulations apply

(1) These Regulations apply in relation to unfair terms in contracts concluded between a seller or a supplier and a consumer.

(2) These Regulations do not apply to contractual terms which reflect—

    (a) mandatory statutory or regulatory provisions (including such provisions under the law of any Member State or in Community legislation having effect in the United Kingdom without further enactment);

    (b) the provisions or principles of international conventions to which the Member States or the Community are party.

5   Unfair terms

(1) A contractual term which has not been individually negotiated shall be regarded as unfair if, contrary to the requirement of good faith, it causes a significant imbalance in the parties' rights and obligations arising under the contract, to the detriment of the consumer.

(2) A term shall always be regarded as not having been individually negotiated where it has been drafted in advance and the consumer has therefore not been able to influence the substance of the term.

(3) Notwithstanding that a specific term or certain aspects of it in a contract has been individually negotiated, these Regulations shall apply to the rest of a contract if an overall assessment of it indicates that it is a pre-formulated standard contract.

(4) It shall be for any seller or supplier who claims that a term was individually negotiated to show that it was.

(5) Schedule 2 to these Regulations contains an indicative and non-exhaustive list of the terms which may be regarded as unfair.

[(6) Any contractual term providing that a consumer bears the burden of proof in respect of showing whether a distance supplier or an intermediary complied with any or all of the obligations placed upon him resulting from the Directive and any rule or enactment implementing it shall always be regarded as unfair.

(7) In paragraph (6)—

'the Directive' means Directive 2002/65/EC of the European Parliament and of the Council of 23 September 2002 concerning the distance marketing of consumer financial services and amending Council Directive 90/619/EEC and Directives 97/7/EC and 98/27/EC; and

'rule' means a rule made by the Financial Services Authority under the Financial Services and Markets Act 2000 or by a designated professional body within the meaning of section 326(2) of that Act.]

6 Assessment of unfair terms

(1) Without prejudice to regulation 12, the unfairness of a contractual term shall be assessed, taking into account the nature of the goods or services for which the contract was concluded and by referring, at the time of conclusion of the contract, to all the circumstances attending the conclusion of the contract and to all the other terms of the contract or of another contract on which it is dependent.

(2) In so far as it is in plain intelligible language, the assessment of fairness of a term shall not relate—

    (a) to the definition of the main subject matter of the contract, or

    (b) to the adequacy of the price or remuneration, as against the goods or services supplied in exchange.

7 Written contracts

(1) A seller or supplier shall ensure that any written term of a contract is expressed in plain, intelligible language.

(2) If there is doubt about the meaning of a written term, the interpretation which is most favourable to the consumer shall prevail but this rule shall not apply in proceedings brought under regulation 12.

8 Effect of unfair term

(1) An unfair term in a contract concluded with a consumer by a seller or supplier shall not be binding on the consumer.

(2) The contract shall continue to bind the parties if it is capable of continuing in existence without the unfair term.

9 Choice of law clauses

These Regulations shall apply notwithstanding any contract term which applies or purports to apply the law of a non-Member State, if the contract has a close connection with the territory of the Member States.

10 Complaints—consideration by [OFT]

(1) It shall be the duty of the [OFT] to consider any complaint made to [it] that any contract term drawn up for general use is unfair, unless—

    (a) the complaint appears to the [OFT] to be frivolous or vexatious; or

    (b) a qualifying body has notified the [OFT] that it agrees to consider the complaint.

(2) The [OFT] shall give reasons for [its] decision to apply or not to apply, as the case may be, for an injunction under regulation 12 in relation to any complaint which these Regulations require him to consider.

(3) In deciding whether or not to apply for an injunction in respect of a term which the [OFT] considers to be unfair, [it] may, if [it] considers it appropriate to do so, have regard to any undertakings given to [it] by or on behalf of any person as to the continued use of such a term in contracts concluded with consumers.

11 Complaints—consideration by qualifying bodies

(1) If a qualifying body specified in Part One of Schedule 1 notifies the [OFT] that it agrees to consider a complaint that any contract term drawn up for general use is unfair, it shall be under a duty to consider that complaint.

(2) Regulation 10(2) and (3) shall apply to a qualifying body which is under a duty to consider a complaint as they apply to the Director.

12   Injunctions to prevent continued use of unfair terms

(1) The [OFT] or, subject to paragraph (2), any qualifying body may apply for an injunction (including an interim injunction) against any person appearing to the [OFT] or that body to be using, or recommending use of, an unfair term drawn up for general use in contracts concluded with consumers.

(2) A qualifying body may apply for an injunction only where—

(a) it has notified the [OFT] of its intention to apply at least fourteen days before the date on which the application is made, beginning with the date on which the notification was given; or

(b) the [OFT] consents to the application being made within a shorter period.

(3) The court on an application under this regulation may grant an injunction on such terms as it thinks fit.

(4) An injunction may relate not only to use of a particular contract term drawn up for general use but to any similar term, or a term having like effect, used or recommended for use by any person.

13   Powers of the [OFT] and qualifying bodies to obtain documents and information

(1) The [OFT] may exercise the power conferred by this regulation for the purpose of—

(a) facilitating his consideration of a complaint that a contract term drawn up for general use is unfair; or

(b) ascertaining whether a person has complied with an undertaking or court order as to the continued use, or recommendation for use, of a term in contracts concluded with consumers.

(2) A qualifying body specified in Part One of Schedule 1 may exercise the power conferred by this regulation for the purpose of—

(a) facilitating its consideration of a complaint that a contract term drawn up for general use is unfair; or

(b) ascertaining whether a person has complied with—

(i)   an undertaking given to it or to the court following an application by that body, or

(ii) a court order made on an application by that body,

as to the continued use, or recommendation for use, of a term in contracts concluded with consumers.

(3) The [OFT] may require any person to supply to [it], and a qualifying body specified in Part One of Schedule 1 may require any person to supply to it—

(a) a copy of any document which that person has used or recommended for use, at the time the notice referred to in paragraph (4) below is given, as a pre-formulated standard contract in dealings with consumers;

(b) information about the use, or recommendation for use, by that person of that document or any other such document in dealings with consumers.

(4) The power conferred by this regulation is to be exercised by a notice in writing which may—

(a) specify the way in which and the time within which it is to be complied with; and

(b) be varied or revoked by a subsequent notice.

(5) Nothing in this regulation compels a person to supply any document or information which he would be entitled to refuse to produce or give in civil proceedings before the court.

(6) If a person makes default in complying with a notice under this regulation, the court may, on the application of the [OFT] or of the qualifying body, make such order as the court thinks fit for requiring the default to be made good, and any such order may provide that all the costs or expenses of and incidental to the application shall be borne by the person in default or by any officers of a company or other association who are responsible for its default.

14   Notification of undertakings and orders to [OFT]

A qualifying body shall notify the [OFT]—

    (a) of any undertaking given to it by or on behalf of any person as to the continued use of a term which that body considers to be unfair in contracts concluded with consumers;

    (b) of the outcome of any application made by it under regulation 12, and of the terms of any undertaking given to, or order made by, the court;

    (c) of the outcome of any application made by it to enforce a previous order of the court.

15   Publication, information and advice

    (1) The [OFT] shall arrange for the publication in such form and manner as [it] considers appropriate, of—

    (a) details of any undertaking or order notified to [it] under regulation 14;

    (b) details of any undertaking given to [it] by or on behalf of any person as to the continued use of a term which the [OFT] considers to be unfair in contracts concluded with consumers;

    (c) details of any application made by [it] under regulation 12, and of the terms of any undertaking given to, or order made by, the court;

    (d) details of any application made by the [OFT] to enforce a previous order of the court.

    (2) The [OFT] shall inform any person on request whether a particular term to which these Regulations apply has been—

    (a) the subject of an undertaking given to the [OFT] or notified to [it] by a qualifying body; or

    (b) the subject of an order of the court made upon application by [it] or notified to [it] by a qualifying body;

and shall give that person details of the undertaking or a copy of the order, as the case may be, together with a copy of any amendments which the person giving the undertaking has agreed to make to the term in question.

    (3) The [OFT] may arrange for the dissemination in such form and manner as [it] considers appropriate of such information and advice concerning the operation of these Regulations as may appear to him to be expedient to give to the public and to all persons likely to be affected by these Regulations.

[16   The functions of the Financial Services Authority

The functions of the Financial Services Authority under these Regulations shall be treated as functions of the Financial Services Authority under the Financial Services and Markets Act 2000.]

Regulation 3

SCHEDULE 1

QUALIFYING BODIES

PART ONE

    [1.   The Information Commissioner.
    2.   The Gas and Electricity Markets Authority.
    3.   The Director General of Electricity Supply for Northern Ireland.
    4.   The Director General of Gas for Northern Ireland.
    5.   [The Office of Communications.]
    6.   [The Water Services Regulation Authority.]
    7.   The Rail Regulator.
    8.   Every weights and measures authority in Great Britain.
    9.   The Department of Enterprise, Trade and Investment in Northern Ireland.

10. The Financial Services Authority.]

PART TWO

11. Consumers' Association.

Regulation 5(5)   # SCHEDULE 2

INDICATIVE AND NON-EXHAUSTIVE LIST OF TERMS WHICH MAY BE REGARDED AS UNFAIR

1. Terms which have the object or effect of—
    (a) excluding or limiting the legal liability of a seller or supplier in the event of the death of a consumer or personal injury to the latter resulting from an act or omission of that seller or supplier;
    (b) inappropriately excluding or limiting the legal rights of the consumer vis-à-vis the seller or supplier or another party in the event of total or partial non-performance or inadequate performance by the seller or supplier of any of the contractual obligations, including the option of offsetting a debt owed to the seller or supplier against any claim which the consumer may have against him;
    (c) making an agreement binding on the consumer whereas provision of services by the seller or supplier is subject to a condition whose realisation depends on his own will alone;
    (d) permitting the seller or supplier to retain sums paid by the consumer where the latter decides not to conclude or perform the contract, without providing for the consumer to receive compensation of an equivalent amount from the seller or supplier where the latter is the party cancelling the contract;
    (e) requiring any consumer who fails to fulfil his obligation to pay a disproportionately high sum in compensation;
    (f) authorising the seller or supplier to dissolve the contract on a discretionary basis where the same facility is not granted to the consumer, or permitting the seller or supplier to retain the sums paid for services not yet supplied by him where it is the seller or supplier himself who dissolves the contract;
    (g) enabling the seller or supplier to terminate a contract of indeterminate duration without reasonable notice except where there are serious grounds for doing so;
    (h) automatically extending a contract of fixed duration where the consumer does not indicate otherwise, when the deadline fixed for the consumer to express his desire not to extend the contract is unreasonably early;
    (i) irrevocably binding the consumer to terms with which he had no real opportunity of becoming acquainted before the conclusion of the contract;
    (j) enabling the seller or supplier to alter the terms of the contract unilaterally without a valid reason which is specified in the contract;
    (k) enabling the seller or supplier to alter unilaterally without a valid reason any characteristics of the product or service to be provided;
    (l) providing for the price of goods to be determined at the time of delivery or allowing a seller of goods or supplier of services to increase their price without in both cases giving the consumer the corresponding right to cancel the contract if the final price is too high in relation to the price agreed when the contract was concluded;
    (m) giving the seller or supplier the right to determine whether the goods or services supplied are in conformity with the contract, or giving him the exclusive right to interpret any term of the contract;

(n) limiting the seller's or supplier's obligation to respect commitments undertaken by his agents or making his commitments subject to compliance with a particular formality;

(o) obliging the consumer to fulfil all his obligations where the seller or supplier does not perform his;

(p) giving the seller or supplier the possibility of transferring his rights and obligations under the contract, where this may serve to reduce the guarantees for the consumer, without the latter's agreement;

(q) excluding or hindering the consumer's right to take legal action or exercise any other legal remedy, particularly by requiring the consumer to take disputes exclusively to arbitration not covered by legal provisions, unduly restricting the evidence available to him or imposing on him a burden of proof which, according to the applicable law, should lie with another party to the contract.

2. Scope of paragraphs 1(g), (j) and (l)—

(a) Paragraph 1(g) is without hindrance to terms by which a supplier of financial services reserves the right to terminate unilaterally a contract of indeterminate duration without notice where there is a valid reason provided that the supplier is required to inform the other contracting party or parties thereof immediately.

(b) Paragraph 1(j) is without hindrance to terms under which a supplier of financial services reserves the right to alter the rate of interest payable by the consumer or due to the latter, or the amount of other charges for financial services without notice where there is a valid reason, provided that the supplier is required to inform the other contracting party or parties thereof at the earliest opportunity and that the latter are free to dissolve the contract immediately.

Paragraph 1(j) is also without hindrance to terms under which a seller or supplier reserves the right to alter unilaterally the conditions of a contract of indeterminate duration, provided that he is required to inform the consumer with reasonable notice and that the consumer is free to dissolve the contract.

(c) Paragraphs 1(g), (j) and (l) do not apply to:

– transactions in transferable securities, financial instruments and other products or services where the price is linked to fluctuations in a stock exchange quotation or index or a financial market rate that the seller or supplier does not control;

– contracts for the purchase or sale of foreign currency, traveller's cheques or international money orders denominated in foreign currency;

(d) Paragraph 1(1) is without hindrance to price indexation clauses, where lawful, provided that the method by which prices vary is explicitly described.

Consumer Protection (Distance Selling) Regulations 2000

(SI 2000, No. 2334)

3   Interpretation

(1) In these Regulations—

['the 2000 Act' means the Financial Services and Markets Act 2000;

'appointed representative' has the same meaning as in section 39(2) of the 2000 Act;

'authorised person' has the same meaning as in section 31(2) of the 2000 Act;]

'breach' means contravention by a supplier of a prohibition in, or failure to comply with a requirement of, these Regulations;

'business' includes a trade or profession;

'consumer' means any natural person who, in contracts to which these Regulations apply, is acting for purposes which are outside his business;

'court' in relation to England and Wales and Northern Ireland means a county court or the High Court, and in relation to Scotland means the Sheriff Court or the Court of Session;

'credit' includes a cash loan and any other form of financial accommodation, and for this purpose 'cash' includes money in any form;

'[OFT] means the [Office of Fair Trading];

'distance contract' means any contract concerning goods or services concluded between a supplier and a consumer under an organised distance sales or service provision scheme run by the supplier who, for the purpose of the contract, makes exclusive use of one or more means of distance communication up to and including the moment at which the contract is concluded;

'EEA Agreement' means the Agreement on the European Economic Area signed at Oporto on 2 May 1992 as adjusted by the Protocol signed at Brussels on 17 March 1993;

'enactment' includes an enactment comprised in, or in an instrument made under, an Act of the Scottish Parliament;

'enforcement authority' means the [OFT], every weights and measures authority in Great Britain, and the Department of Enterprise, Trade and Investment in Northern Ireland;

'excepted contract' means a contract such as is mentioned in regulation 5(1);

['financial service' means any service of a banking, credit, insurance, personal pension, investment or payment nature;]

'means of distance communication' means any means which, without the simultaneous physical presence of the supplier and the consumer, may be used for the conclusion of a contract between those parties; and an indicative list of such means is contained in Schedule 1;

'Member State' means a State which is a contracting party to the EEA Agreement;

'operator of a means of communication' means any public or private person whose business involves making one or more means of distance communication available to suppliers;

'period for performance' has the meaning given by regulation 19(2);

'personal credit agreement' has the meaning given by regulation 14(8);

['regulated activity' has the same meaning as in section 22 of the 2000 Act;]

'related credit agreement' has the meaning given by regulation 15(5);

'supplier' means any person who, in contracts to which these Regulations apply, is acting in his commercial or professional capacity; and

'working days' means all days other than Saturdays, Sundays and public holidays.

(2) In the application of these Regulations to Scotland, for references to an 'injunction' or an 'interim injunction' there shall be substituted references to an 'interdict' or an 'interim interdict' respectively.

4   Contracts to which these Regulations apply

These Regulations apply, subject to regulation 6, to distance contracts other than excepted contracts.

5   Excepted contracts

(1) The following are excepted contracts, namely any contract—
- (a) for the sale or other disposition of an interest in land except for a rental agreement;
- (b) for the construction of a building where the contract also provides for a sale or other disposition of an interest in land on which the building is constructed, except for a rental agreement;
- (c) relating to financial services [. . .];
- (d) concluded by means of an automated vending machine or automated commercial premises;

(e) concluded with a telecommunications operator through the use of a public pay-phone;

(f) concluded at an auction.

(2) References in paragraph (1) to a rental agreement—

(a) if the land is situated in England and Wales, are references to any agreement which does not have to be made in writing (whether or not in fact made in writing) because of section 2(5)(a) of the Law of Property (Miscellaneous Provisions) Act 1989;

(b) if the land is situated in Scotland, are references to any agreement for the creation, transfer, variation or extinction of an interest in land, which does not have to be made in writing (whether or not in fact made in writing) as provided for in section 1(2) and (7) of the Requirements of Writing (Scotland) Act 1995; and

(c) if the land is situated in Northern Ireland, are references to any agreement which is not one to which section II of the Statute of Frauds, (Ireland) 1695 applies.

(3) Paragraph (2) shall not be taken to mean that a rental agreement in respect of land situated outside the United Kingdom is not capable of being a distance contract to which these Regulations apply.

6   Contracts to which only part of these Regulations apply

[(1) Regulations 7 to 20 shall not apply to a contract which is a regulated contract within the meaning of the Timeshare, Holiday Products, Resale and Exchange Contracts Regulations 2010.]

(2) Regulations 7 to 19(1) shall not apply to—

(a) contracts for the supply of food, beverages or other goods intended for everyday consumption supplied to the consumer's residence or to his workplace by regular roundsmen; or

(b) contracts for the provision of accommodation, transport, catering or leisure services, where the supplier undertakes, when the contract is concluded, to provide these services on a specific date or within a specific period.

(3) Regulations 19(2) to (8) and 20 do not apply to a contract for a 'package' within the meaning of the Package Travel, Package Holidays and Package Tours Regulations 1992 which is sold or offered for sale in the territory of the Member States.

[(4) Regulations 7 to 14, 17 to 20 and 25 do not apply to any contract which is made, and regulation 24 does not apply to any unsolicited services which are supplied, by an authorised person where the making or performance of that contract or the supply of those services, as the case may be, constitutes or is part of a regulated activity carried on by him.

(5) Regulations 7 to 9, 17 to 20 and 25 do not apply to any contract which is made, and regulation 24 does not apply to any unsolicited services which are supplied, by an appointed representative where the making or performance of that contract or the supply of those services, as the case may be, constitutes or is part of a regulated activity carried on by him.]

7   Information required prior to the conclusion of the contract

(1) Subject to paragraph (4), in good time prior to the conclusion of the contract the supplier shall—

(a) provide to the consumer the following information—

(i)   the identity of the supplier and, where the contract requires payment in advance, the supplier's address;

(ii) a description of the main characteristics of the goods or services;

(iii) the price of the goods or services including all taxes;

(iv) delivery costs where appropriate;

(v)   the arrangements for payment, delivery or performance;

(vi) the existence of a right of cancellation except in the cases referred to in regulation 13;

(vii) the cost of using the means of distance communication where it is calculated other than at the basic rate;

(viii) the period for which the offer or the price remains valid; and

(ix) where appropriate, the minimum duration of the contract, in the case of contracts for the supply of goods or services to be performed permanently or recurrently;

(b) inform the consumer if he proposes, in the event of the goods or services ordered by the consumer being unavailable, to provide substitute goods or services (as the case may be) of equivalent quality and price; and

(c) inform the consumer that the cost of returning any such substitute goods to the supplier in the event of cancellation by the consumer would be met by the supplier.

(2) The supplier shall ensure that the information required by paragraph (1) is provided in a clear and comprehensible manner appropriate to the means of distance communication used, with due regard in particular to the principles of good faith in commercial transactions and the principles governing the protection of those who are unable to give their consent such as minors.

(3) Subject to paragraph (4), the supplier shall ensure that his commercial purpose is made clear when providing the information required by paragraph (1).

(4) In the case of a telephone communication, the identity of the supplier and the commercial purpose of the call shall be made clear at the beginning of the conversation with the consumer.

8 Written and additional information

(1) Subject to regulation 9, the supplier shall provide to the consumer in writing, or in another durable medium which is available and accessible to the consumer, the information referred to in paragraph (2), either—

(a) prior to the conclusion of the contract, or

(b) thereafter, in good time and in any event—

(i) during the performance of the contract, in the case of services; and

(ii) at the latest at the time of delivery where goods not for delivery to third parties are concerned.

(2) The information required to be provided by paragraph (1) is—

(a) the information set out in paragraphs (i) to (vi) of Regulation 7(1)(a);

(b) information about the conditions and procedures for exercising the right to cancel under regulation 10, including—

(i) where a term of the contract requires (or the supplier intends that it will require) that the consumer shall return the goods to the supplier in the event of cancellation, notification of that requirement; [. . .]

(ii) information as to whether the consumer or the supplier would be responsible under these Regulations for the cost of returning any goods to the supplier, or the cost of his recovering them, if the consumer cancels the contract under regulation 10;

[(iii) in the case of a contract for the supply of services, information as to how the right to cancel may be affected by the consumer agreeing to performance of the services beginning before the end of the seven working day period referred to in regulation 12;]

(c) the geographical address of the place of business of the supplier to which the consumer may address any complaints;

(d) information about any after-sales services and guarantees; and

(e) the conditions for exercising any contractual right to cancel the contract, where the contract is of an unspecified duration or a duration exceeding one year.

9 Services performed through the use of a means of distance communication

(1) Regulation 8 shall not apply to a contract for the supply of services which are performed through the use of a means of distance communication, where those services are supplied on only one occasion and are invoiced by the operator of the means of distance communication.

(2) But the supplier shall take all necessary steps to ensure that a consumer who is a party to a contract to which paragraph (1) applies is able to obtain the supplier's geographical address and the place of business to which the consumer may address any complaints.

10   Right to cancel

(1) Subject to regulation 13, if within the cancellation period set out in regulations 11 and 12, the consumer gives a notice of cancellation to the supplier, or any other person previously notified by the supplier to the consumer as a person to whom notice of cancellation may be given, the notice of cancellation shall operate to cancel the contract.

(2) Except as otherwise provided by these Regulations, the effect of a notice of cancellation is that the contract shall be treated as if it had not been made.

(3) For the purposes of these Regulations, a notice of cancellation is a notice in writing or in another durable medium available and accessible to the supplier (or to the other person to whom it is given) which, however expressed, indicates the intention of the consumer to cancel the contract.

(4) A notice of cancellation given under this regulation by a consumer to a supplier or other person is to be treated as having been properly given if the consumer—

    (a) leaves it at the address last known to the consumer and addressed to the supplier or other person by name (in which case it is to be taken to have been given on the day on which it was left);

    (b) sends it by post to the address last known to the consumer and addressed to the supplier or other person by name (in which case, it is to be taken to have been given on the day on which it was posted);

    (c) sends it by facsimile to the business facsimile number last known to the consumer (in which case it is to be taken to have been given on the day on which it is sent); or

    (d) sends it by electronic mail, to the business electronic mail address last known to the consumer (in which case it is to be taken to have been given on the day on which it is sent).

(5) Where a consumer gives a notice in accordance with paragraph (4)(a) or (b) to a supplier who is a body corporate or a partnership, the notice is to be treated as having been properly given if—

    (a) in the case of a body corporate, it is left at the address of, or sent to, the secretary or clerk of that body; or

    (b) in the case of a partnership, it is left with or sent to a partner or a person having control or management of the partnership business.

11   Cancellation period in the case of contracts for the supply of goods

(1) For the purposes of regulation 10, the cancellation period in the case of contracts for the supply of goods begins with the day on which the contract is concluded and ends as provided in paragraphs (2) to (5).

(2) Where the supplier complies with regulation 8, the cancellation period ends on the expiry of the period of seven working days beginning with the day after the day on which the consumer receives the goods.

(3) Where a supplier who has not complied with regulation 8 provides to the consumer the information referred to in regulation 8(2), and does so in writing or in another durable medium available and accessible to the consumer, within the period of three months beginning with the day after the day on which the consumer receives the goods, the cancellation period ends on the expiry of the period of seven working days beginning with the day after the day on which the consumer receives the information.

(4) Where neither paragraph (2) nor (3) applies, the cancellation period ends on the expiry of the period of three months and seven working days beginning with the day after the day on which the consumer receives the goods.

(5) In the case of contracts for goods for delivery to third parties, paragraphs (2) to (4) shall apply as if the consumer had received the goods on the day on which they were received by the third party.

12   Cancellation period in the case of contracts for the supply of services

(1) For the purposes of regulation 10, the cancellation period in the case of contracts for the supply of services begins with the day on which the contract is concluded and ends as provided in paragraphs (2) to (4).

(2) Where the supplier complies with regulation 8 on or before the day on which the contract is concluded, the cancellation period ends on the expiry of the period of seven working days beginning with the day after the day on which the contract is concluded.

(3) [Subject to paragraph (3A)] Where a supplier who has not complied with regulation 8 on or before the day on which the contract is concluded provides to the consumer the information referred to in regulation 8(2) [. . .], and does so in writing or in another durable medium available and accessible to the consumer, within the period of three months beginning with the day after the day on which the contract is concluded, the cancellation period ends on the expiry of the period of seven working days beginning with the day after the day on which the consumer receives the information.

[(3A) Where the performance of the contract has begun with the consumer's agreement before the expiry of the period of seven working days beginning with the day after the day on which the contract was concluded and the supplier has not complied with regulation 8 on or before the day on which performance began, but provides to the consumer the information referred to in regulation 8(2) in good time during the performance of the contract, the cancellation period ends—

    (a) on the expiry of the period of seven working days beginning with the day after the day on which the consumer receives the information; or

    (b) if the performance of the contract is completed before the expiry of the period referred to in sub-paragraph (a), on the day when the performance of the contract is completed.]

(4) Where [none of paragraphs (2) to (3A) applies], the cancellation period ends on the expiry of the period of three months and seven working days beginning with the day after the day on which the contract is concluded.

13   Exceptions to the right to cancel

(1) Unless the parties have agreed otherwise, the consumer will not have the right to cancel the contract by giving notice of cancellation pursuant to regulation 10 in respect of contracts—

    [(a) for the supply of services if the performance of the contract has begun with the consumer's agreement—

        (i) before the end of the cancellation period applicable under regulation 12(2); and

        (ii) after the supplier has provided the information referred to in regulation 8(2)];

    (b) for the supply of goods or services the price of which is dependent on fluctuations in the financial market which cannot be controlled by the supplier;

    (c) for the supply of goods made to the consumer's specifications or clearly personalised or which by reason of their nature cannot be returned or are liable to deteriorate or expire rapidly;

    (d) for the supply of audio or video recordings or computer software if they are unsealed by the consumer;

    (e) for the supply of newspapers, periodicals or magazines; or

    (f) for gaming, betting or lottery services.

14   Recovery of sums paid by or on behalf of the consumer on cancellation, and return of security

(1) On the cancellation of a contract under regulation 10, the supplier shall reimburse any sum paid by or on behalf of the consumer under or in relation to the contract to the person by whom it was made free of any charge, less any charge made in accordance with paragraph (5).

(2) The reference in paragraph (1) to any sum paid on behalf of the consumer includes any sum paid by a creditor who is not the same person as the supplier under a personal credit agreement with the consumer.

(3) The supplier shall make the reimbursement referred to in paragraph (1) as soon as possible and in any case within a period not exceeding 30 days beginning with the day on which the notice of cancellation was given.

(4) Where any security has been provided in relation to the contract, the security (so far as it is so provided) shall, on cancellation under regulation 10, be treated as never having had effect and any property lodged with the supplier solely for the purposes of the security as so provided shall be returned by him forthwith.

(5) Subject to paragraphs (6) and (7), the supplier may make a charge, not exceeding the direct costs of recovering any goods supplied under the contract, where a term of the contract provides that the consumer must return any goods supplied if he cancels the contract under regulation 10 but the consumer does not comply with this provision or returns the goods at the expense of the supplier.

(6) Paragraph (5) shall not apply where—
    (a) the consumer cancels in circumstances where he has the right to reject the goods under a term of the contract, including a term implied by virtue of any enactment, or
    (b) the term requiring the consumer to return any goods supplied if he cancels the contract is an 'unfair term' within the meaning of the Unfair Terms in Consumer Contracts Regulations 1999.

(7) Paragraph (5) shall not apply to the cost of recovering any goods which were supplied as substitutes for the goods ordered by the consumer.

(8) For the purposes of these Regulations, a personal credit agreement is an agreement between the consumer and any other person ('the creditor') by which the creditor provides the consumer with credit of any amount.

15 Automatic cancellation of a related credit agreement

(1) Where a notice of cancellation is given under regulation 10 which has the effect of cancelling the contract, the giving of the notice shall also have the effect of cancelling any related credit agreement.

(2) Where a related credit agreement is cancelled by virtue of paragraph (1), the supplier shall, if he is not the same person as the creditor under that agreement, forthwith on receipt of the notice of cancellation inform the creditor that the notice has been given.

(3) Where a related credit agreement is cancelled by virtue of paragraph (1)—
    (a) any sum paid by or on behalf of the consumer under, or in relation to, the credit agreement which the supplier is not obliged to reimburse under regulation 14(1) shall be reimbursed, except for any sum which, if it had not already been paid, would have to be paid under subparagraph (b);
    (b) the agreement shall continue in force so far as it relates to repayment of the credit and payment of interest, subject to regulation 16; and
    (c) subject to subparagraph (b), the agreement shall cease to be enforceable.

(4) Where any security has been provided under a related credit agreement, the security, so far as it is so provided, shall be treated as never having had effect and any property lodged with the creditor solely for the purposes of the security as so provided shall be returned by him forthwith.

(5) For the purposes of this regulation and regulation 16, a 'related credit agreement' means an agreement under which fixed sum credit which fully or partly covers the price under a contract cancelled under regulation 10 is granted—
    (a) by the supplier, or
    (b) by another person, under an arrangement between that person and the supplier.

(6) For the purposes of this regulation and regulation 16—
    (a) 'creditor' is a person who grants credit under a related credit agreement;
    (b) 'fixed sum credit' has the same meaning as in section 10 of the Consumer Credit Act 1974;
    (c) 'repayment' in relation to credit means repayment of money received by the consumer, and cognate expressions shall be construed accordingly; and
    (d) 'interest' means interest on money so received.

16   Repayment of credit and interest after cancellation of a related credit agreement

(1) This regulation applies following the cancellation of a related credit agreement by virtue of regulation 15(1).

(2) If the consumer repays the whole or a portion of the credit—

(a) before the expiry of one month following the cancellation of the credit agreement, or

(b) in the case of a credit repayable by instalments, before the date on which the first instalment is due,

no interest shall be payable on the amount repaid.

(3) If the whole of a credit repayable by instalments is not repaid on or before the date referred to in paragraph (2)(b), the consumer shall not be liable to repay any of the credit except on receipt of a request in writing, signed by the creditor, stating the amounts of the remaining instalments (recalculated by the creditor as nearly as may be in accordance with the agreement and without extending the repayment period), but excluding any sum other than principal and interest.

(4) Where any security has been provided under a related credit agreement the duty imposed on the consumer to repay credit and to pay interest shall not be enforceable before the creditor has discharged any duty imposed on him by regulation 15(4) to return any property lodged with him as security on cancellation.

17   Restoration of goods by consumer after cancellation

(1) This regulation applies where a contract is cancelled under regulation 10 after the consumer has acquired possession of any goods under the contract other than any goods mentioned in regulation 13(1)(b) to (e).

(2) The consumer shall be treated as having been under a duty throughout the period prior to cancellation—

(a) to retain possession of the goods, and

(b) to take reasonable care of them.

(3) On cancellation, the consumer shall be under a duty to restore the goods to the supplier in accordance with this regulation, and in the meanwhile to retain possession of the goods and take reasonable care of them.

(4) The consumer shall not be under any duty to deliver the goods except at his own premises and in pursuance of a request in writing, or in another durable medium available and accessible to the consumer, from the supplier and given to the consumer either before, or at the time when, the goods are collected from those premises.

(5) If the consumer—

(a) delivers the goods (whether at his own premises or elsewhere) to any person to whom, under regulation 10(1), a notice of cancellation could have been given; or

(b) sends the goods at his own expense to such a person, he shall be discharged from any duty to retain possession of the goods or restore them to the supplier.

(6) Where the consumer delivers the goods in accordance with paragraph (5)(a), his obligation to take care of the goods shall cease; and if he sends the goods in accordance with paragraph (5)(b), he shall be under a duty to take reasonable care to see that they are received by the supplier and not damaged in transit, but in other respects his duty to take care of the goods shall cease when he sends them.

(7) Where, at any time during the period of 21 days beginning with the day notice of cancellation was given, the consumer receives such a request as is mentioned in paragraph (4), and unreasonably refuses or unreasonably fails to comply with it, his duty to retain possession and take reasonable care of the goods shall continue until he delivers or sends the goods as mentioned in paragraph (5), but if within that period he does not receive such a request his duty to take reasonable care of the goods shall cease at the end of that period.

(8) Where—

(a) a term of the contract provides that if the consumer cancels the contract, he must return the goods to the supplier, and

(b) the consumer is not otherwise entitled to reject the goods under the terms of the contract or by virtue of any enactment,

paragraph (7) shall apply as if for the period of 21 days there were substituted the period of 6 months.

(9) Where any security has been provided in relation to the cancelled contract, the duty to restore goods imposed on the consumer by this regulation shall not be enforceable before the supplier has discharged any duty imposed on him by regulation 14(4) to return any property lodged with him as security on cancellation.

(10) Breach of a duty imposed by this regulation on a consumer is actionable as a breach of statutory duty.

18   Goods given in part-exchange

(1) This regulation applies on the cancellation of a contract under regulation 10 where the supplier agreed to take goods in part-exchange (the 'part-exchange goods') and those goods have been delivered to him.

(2) Unless, before the end of the period of 10 days beginning with the date of cancellation, the part-exchange goods are returned to the consumer in a condition substantially as good as when they were delivered to the supplier, the consumer shall be entitled to recover from the supplier a sum equal to the part-exchange allowance.

(3) In this regulation the part-exchange allowance means the sum agreed as such in the cancelled contract, or if no such sum was agreed, such sum as it would have been reasonable to allow in respect of the part-exchange goods if no notice of cancellation had been served.

(4) Where the consumer recovers from the supplier a sum equal to the part-exchange allowance, the title of the consumer to the part-exchange goods shall vest in the supplier (if it has not already done so) on recovery of that sum.

19   Performance

(1) Unless the parties agree otherwise, the supplier shall perform the contract within a maximum of 30 days beginning with the day after the day the consumer sent his order to the supplier.

(2) Subject to paragraphs (7) and (8), where the supplier is unable to perform the contract because the goods or services ordered are not available, within the period for performance referred to in paragraph (1) or such other period as the parties agree ('the period for performance'), he shall—

(a) inform the consumer; and

(b) reimburse any sum paid by or on behalf of the consumer under or in relation to the contract to the person by whom it was made.

(3) The reference in paragraph (2)(b) to any sum paid on behalf of the consumer includes any sum paid by a creditor who is not the same person as the supplier under a personal credit agreement with the consumer.

(4) The supplier shall make the reimbursement referred to in paragraph (2)(b) as soon as possible and in any event within a period of 30 days beginning with the day after the day on which the period for performance expired.

(5) A contract which has not been performed within the period for performance shall be treated as if it had not been made, save for any rights or remedies which the consumer has under it as a result of the non-performance.

(6) Where any security has been provided in relation to the contract, the security (so far as it is so provided) shall, where the supplier is unable to perform the contract within the period for performance, be treated as never having had any effect and any property lodged with the supplier solely for the purposes of the security as so provided shall be returned by him forthwith.

(7) Where the supplier is unable to supply the goods or services ordered by the consumer, the supplier may perform the contract for the purposes of these Regulations by providing substitute goods or services (as the case may be) of equivalent quality and price provided that—

(a) this possibility was provided for in the contract;

(b) prior to the conclusion of the contract the supplier gave the consumer the information required by regulation 7(1)(b) and (c) in the manner required by regulation 7(2).

(8) In the case of outdoor leisure events which by their nature cannot be rescheduled, paragraph 2(b) shall not apply where the consumer and the supplier so agree.

20   Effect of non-performance on related credit agreement

Where a supplier is unable to perform the contract within the period for performance—

(a) regulations 15 and 16 shall apply to any related credit agreement as if the consumer had given a valid notice of cancellation under regulation 10 on the expiry of the period for performance; and

(b) the reference in regulation 15(3)(a) to regulation 14(1) shall be read, for the purposes of this regulation, as a reference to regulation 19(2).

24   Inertia selling

(1) Paragraphs (2) and (3) apply if—

(a) unsolicited goods are sent to a person ('the recipient') with a view to his acquiring them;

(b) the recipient has no reasonable cause to believe that they were sent with a view to their being acquired for the purposes of a business; and

(c) the recipient has neither agreed to acquire nor agreed to return them.

(2) The recipient may, as between himself and the sender, use, deal with or dispose of the goods as if they were an unconditional gift to him.

(3) The rights of the sender to the goods are extinguished.

(6) In this regulation—

'acquire' includes hire;

'send' includes deliver;

'sender', in relation to any goods, includes—

(a) any person on whose behalf or with whose consent the goods are sent;

(b) any other person claiming through or under the sender or any person mentioned in paragraph (a); and

(c) any person who delivers the goods; and

'unsolicited' means, in relation to goods sent or services supplied to any person, that they are sent or supplied without any prior request made by or on behalf of the recipient.

(10) This regulation applies only to goods sent and services supplied after the date on which it comes into force.

25   No contracting-out

(1) A term contained in any contract to which these Regulations apply is void if, and to the extent that, it is inconsistent with a provision for the protection of the consumer contained in these Regulations.

(2) Where a provision of these Regulations specifies a duty or liability of the consumer in certain circumstances, a term contained in a contract to which these Regulations apply, other than a term to which paragraph (3) applies, is inconsistent with that provision if it purports to impose, directly or indirectly, an additional duty or liability on him in those circumstances.

(3) This paragraph applies to a term which requires the consumer to return any goods supplied to him under the contract if he cancels it under regulation 10.

(4) A term to which paragraph (3) applies shall, in the event of cancellation by the consumer under regulation 10, have effect only for the purposes of regulation 14(5) and 17(8).

(5) These Regulations shall apply notwithstanding any contract term which applies or purports to apply the law of a non-Member State if the contract has a close connection with the territory of a Member State.

26   Consideration of complaints

(1) It shall be the duty of an enforcement authority to consider any complaint made to it about a breach unless—

(a) the complaint appears to the authority to be frivolous or vexatious; or

(b) another enforcement authority has notified the [OFT] that it agrees to consider the complaint.

(2) If an enforcement authority notifies the [OFT] that it agrees to consider a complaint made to another enforcement authority, the first mentioned authority shall be under a duty to consider the complaint.

(3) An enforcement authority which is under a duty to consider a complaint shall give reasons for its decision to apply or not to apply, as the case may be, for an injunction under regulation 27.

(4) In deciding whether or not to apply for an injunction in respect of a breach an enforcement authority may, if it considers it appropriate to do so, have regard to any undertaking given to it or another enforcement authority by or on behalf of any person as to compliance with these Regulations.

27   Injunctions to secure compliance with these Regulations

(1) The [OFT] or, subject to paragraph (2), any other enforcement authority may apply for an injunction (including an interim injunction) against any person who appears to the [OFT] or that authority to be responsible for a breach.

(2) An enforcement authority other than the [OFT] may apply for an injunction only where—

(a) it has notified the [OFT] of its intention to apply at least fourteen days before the date on which the application is to be made, beginning with the date on which the notification was given; or

(b) the [OFT] consents to the application being made within a shorter period.

(3) The court on an application under this regulation may grant an injunction on such terms as it thinks fit to secure compliance with these Regulations.

28   Notification of undertakings and orders to the [OFT]

An enforcement authority other than the [OFT] shall notify the [OFT]—

(a) of any undertaking given to it by or on behalf of any person who appears to it to be responsible for a breach;

(b) of the outcome of any application made by it under regulation 27 and of the terms of any undertaking given to or order made by the court;

(c) of the outcome of any application made by it to enforce a previous order of the court.

29   Publication, information and advice

(1) The [OFT] shall arrange for the publication in such form and manner as [it] considers appropriate of—

(a) details of any undertaking or order notified to [it] under regulation 28;

(b) details of any undertaking given to [it] by or on behalf of any person as to compliance with these Regulations;

(c) details of any application made by [it] under regulation 27, and of the terms of any undertaking given to, or order made by, the court;

(d) details of any application made by the [OFT] to enforce a previous order of the court.

(2) The [OFT] may arrange for the dissemination in such form and manner as [it] considers appropriate of such information and advice concerning the operation of these Regulations as it may appear to [it] to be expedient to give to the public and to all persons likely to be affected by these Regulations.

Regulation 3   **SCHEDULE 1**

INDICATIVE LIST OF MEANS OF DISTANCE COMMUNICATION

1.   Unaddressed printed matter.
2.   Addressed printed matter.

3. Letter.
4. Press advertising with order form.
5. Catalogue.
6. Telephone with human intervention.
7. Telephone without human intervention (automatic calling machine, audiotext).
8. Radio.
9. Videophone (telephone with screen).
10. Videotext (microcomputer and television screen) with keyboard or touch screen.
11. Electronic mail.
12. Facsimile machine (fax).
13. Television (teleshopping).

Electronic Commerce Directive (Financial Services and Markets) Regulations 2002

(SI 2002, No. 1775)

PART 1 GENERAL

2   Interpretation

(1) In these Regulations—

'the 2000 Act' means the Financial Services and Markets Act 2000;

'authorised incoming provider' means an incoming provider who is an authorised person within the meaning of the 2000 Act;

'the Authority' means the Financial Services Authority;

'commercial communication' means a communication, in any form, designed to promote, directly or indirectly, the goods, services or image of any person pursuing a commercial activity or exercising a regulated profession, other than a communication—

    (a) consisting only of information allowing direct access to the activity of that person, including a geographic address, domain name or electronic mail address; or

    (b) relating to the goods, services or image of that person provided that the communication has been prepared independently of the person making it (and for this purpose, a communication prepared without financial consideration is to be taken to have been prepared independently unless the contrary is shown);

'the Commission' means the Commission of the European Communities;

'consumer' means any individual who is acting for purposes other than those of his trade, business or profession;

'country of origin' in relation to an incoming electronic commerce activity means the EEA State in which is situated the establishment from which the information society service in question is provided;

'criminal conduct' means conduct which constitutes an offence in any part of the United Kingdom, or would constitute an offence in any part of the United Kingdom if it occurred there;

'direction' means a direction made, or proposed to be made, by the Authority under regulation 6;

'EEA regulator' means an authority in an EEA State other than the United Kingdom which exercises any function of a kind mentioned in section 195(4) of the 2000 Act;

['EEA State' has the meaning given by Schedule 1 to the Interpretation Act 1978;]

'electronic commerce directive' means Directive 2000/31/EC of the European Parliament and of the Council of 8 June 2000 on certain legal aspects of information society services, in particular electronic commerce, in the Internal Market (Directive on electronic commerce);

'financial instrument' includes an investment of a kind specified by any of articles 76 to 85 of the Regulated Activities Order;

'incoming electronic commerce activity' means an activity—

    (a) which consists of the provision of an information society service from an establishment in an EEA State other than the United Kingdom to a person or persons in the United Kingdom, and

    (b) which would, but for article 72A of the Regulated Activities Order (and irrespective of the effect of article 72 of that Order), be a regulated activity within the meaning of the 2000 Act;

'incoming provider' means a person carrying on an incoming electronic commerce activity;

'information society service' means an information society service within the meaning of Article 2(a) of the electronic commerce directive;

'investment' means an investment of a kind specified by any provision of Part III of the Regulated Activities Order;

'Regulated Activities Order' means the Financial Services and Markets Act 2000 (Regulated Activities) Order 2001;

'regulated profession' means any profession within the meaning of—

    (a) Article 1(d) of Directive 89/48/EEC of the Council of the European Communities of 21 December 1988 on a general system for the recognition of higher-education diplomas awarded on completion of professional education and training of at least three years' duration, or

    (b) Article 1(f) of Directive 92/51/EEC of the Council of the European Communities of 18 June 1992 on a second general system for the recognition of professional education and training to supplement Directive 89/48/EEC;

'relevant EEA regulator', in relation to a direction, means the EEA regulator in the country of origin of the incoming electronic commerce activity to which the direction does, or would if made, relate, and which is responsible in that country for the regulation of that activity;

'rule' means a rule made by the Authority under the 2000 Act;

'UCITS Directive' means [Directive 2009/65/EC of the European Parliament and of the Council of 13 July 2009] on the co-ordination of laws, regulations and administrative provisions relating to undertakings for collective investment in transferable securities;

'UCITS Directive scheme' means an undertaking for collective investment in transferable securities which is subject to the UCITS Directive, and has been authorised in accordance with [Article 5] of that Directive;

'unauthorised incoming provider' means an incoming provider who is not an authorised person within the meaning of the 2000 Act.

(2) A reference in these Regulations to a requirement imposed by the Authority under these Regulations is a reference to—

    (a) a requirement (including a requirement that a person no longer carry on an incoming electronic commerce activity) imposed by a direction; or

    (b) a requirement imposed by a rule applicable to incoming providers in accordance with regulation 3(4).

(3) For the purposes of these Regulations—

    (a) an establishment, in connection with an information society service, is the place at which the provider of the service (being a national of an EEA State or a company or firm as mentioned in Article 48 of the treaty establishing the European Community) effectively pursues an economic activity for an indefinite period;

(b) the presence or use in a particular place of equipment or other technical means of providing an information society service does not, of itself, constitute that place as an establishment of the kind mentioned in sub-paragraph (a);

(c) where it cannot be determined from which of a number of establishments a given information society service is provided, that service is to be regarded as provided from the establishment where the provider has the centre of his activities relating to the service;

(d) a communication by electronic mail is to be regarded as unsolicited, unless it is made in response to an express request from the recipient of the communication.

PART 2 MODIFICATION OF FUNCTIONS OF THE FINANCIAL SERVICES AUTHORITY

3   Consumer contract requirements: modification of rule-making power

(1) The power to make rules conferred by section 138 of the 2000 Act is to be taken to include a power to make rules applying to unauthorised incoming providers.

(2) In consequence of paragraph (1)—

(a) any reference in sections 138(4), (5) and (7) to (9), 148, 150 and 156 of the 2000 Act to an authorised person includes a reference to an unauthorised incoming provider;

(b) any reference in those sections to a regulated activity includes a reference to an incoming electronic commerce activity.

(3) For the purpose of the exercise by the Authority of the power conferred by section 138 of the 2000 Act to make rules applying to incoming providers with respect to the carrying on by them of incoming electronic commerce activities, subsections (7) and (9) of that section have effect as if the reference to 'person' where first occurring were a reference to an individual acting for purposes other than those of his trade, business or profession.

(4) Rules made by the Authority under section 138 of the 2000 Act do not apply to incoming providers with respect to the carrying on by them of incoming electronic commerce activities unless they—

(a) impose consumer contract requirements;

(b) apply with respect to communications that constitute an advertisement by the operator of a UCITS Directive scheme of units in that scheme; or

(c) relate to the permissibility of unsolicited commercial communications by electronic mail.

[(4A) Notwithstanding paragraph (4)(a), rules made by the Authority under section 138 of the 2000 Act which impose consumer contract requirements do not apply to an incoming provider with respect to the carrying on by him of an incoming electronic commerce activity which consists of the provision of an information society service from an establishment in an EEA State other than the United Kingdom, if the provisions by which that State has transposed the Financial Services Distance Marketing Directive, or the obligations in the domestic law of that State corresponding to those provided for in that Directive, as the case may be, apply to that activity.]

(5) A consumer contract rule may provide that conduct engaged in by a person to whom the rule applies, and which is in conformity with a provision corresponding to the rule made by a body or authority in an EEA State other than the United Kingdom, is to be treated as conduct in conformity with the rule.

(6) 'Consumer contract requirement' means a requirement—

(a) that information of a kind referred to in regulation 4 be provided to a consumer before he enters into a contract for the provision of one or more information society services, or

(b) as to the manner in which such information is to be provided.

[(6A) 'The Financial Services Distance Marketing Directive' means Directive 2002/65/EC of the European Parliament and the Council of 23 September 2002 concerning the distance marketing of consumer financial services and amending Council Directive 90/619/EEC and Directives 97/7/EC and 98/27/EC.]

(7) 'Consumer contract rule' means a rule made by the Authority under section 138 of the 2000 Act which imposes a consumer contract requirement on incoming providers.

4   Consumer contract requirements: information

The information which may be the subject of a consumer contract requirement is—

    (a) the identity and description of the main business of the other party to the proposed contract ('the supplier'), the geographic address at which the supplier is established, and any other geographic address relevant to the consumer's relations with the supplier;

    (b) if the supplier has a representative established in the consumer's country of residence with whom the consumer is to have dealings, the identity and geographic address of the representative, and any other geographic address relevant to the consumer's relations with the representative;

    (c) if the consumer is to have dealings with any professional person in connection with the contract, the identity of that person, a statement of the capacity in which he is to act, and the geographic address relevant to the consumer's relations with him;

    (d) if the supplier is registered on any public register in connection with the carrying on of his business (or such of his business as is relevant to the contract), the name of that register, and any registration number or other means of identifying the relevant entry on the register;

    (e) if the carrying on of the supplier's business (or such of it as is relevant to the contract) is subject to a requirement that he be authorised by a person or body in order to carry it on, the name and geographic address of that person or body;

    (f) a description of the main features of the service or services to which the contract relates;

    (g) either—

        (aa) the total price to be paid by the consumer under the contract, including all related fees, charges and expenses, and all taxes paid by or through the supplier (in so far as these are reflected in the total price); or

        (bb) if the total price cannot be given, the basis for the calculation of the total price, in a form enabling the consumer to verify the total price when calculated by the supplier;

    (h) where the service to be provided under the contract relates to one or more financial instruments—

        (aa) if the instruments are subject to special risks relating to their specific features or operations to be executed in relation to them, notice of the existence of those risks,

        (bb) if the price of the instruments is subject to fluctuation depending on market conditions outside the supplier's control, notice of that fact, and

        (cc) notice that movements in the price of the instruments in the past are not necessarily an indicator of future performance;

    (i) notice of the possibility that taxes or other costs may exist which are not imposed or paid by or through the supplier;

    (j) the arrangements for payment under, and the performance of, the contract;

    (k) any specific additional cost imposed by the supplier on the consumer in relation to the consumer's use of the means for concluding the contract or communicating with the supplier;

    (l) the existence or absence of any legal right of the consumer to withdraw from the contract after it has been entered into, the conditions attached to the exercise of any such right, and the consequences for the consumer of not exercising it;

    (m) where the contract relates to services to be performed on an indefinite or recurrent basis, the minimum duration of the contract;

    (n) any rights of the consumer or the supplier to terminate the contract in accordance with one of its express terms, any contractual penalties which may apply in that event, and the procedure to be followed by the consumer in that event (including the address to which any notification of withdrawal from the contract should be sent);

(o) the state or states whose laws are taken by the supplier as a basis for the establishment of relations with the consumer before the contract is concluded;

(p) any express term in the contract relating to the law governing it, or to the jurisdiction of courts;

(q) the language or languages in which the supplier— (aa) proposes to offer the terms of, and information concerning, the contract, and (bb) undertakes (with the agreement of the consumer) to communicate with the consumer during the existence of the contract;

(r) whether any mechanism other than redress through a court (including guarantee funds and compensation schemes and arrangements) is available to the consumer in relation to matters arising in connection with the contract, and if so, the procedure to be followed by the consumer in order to gain access to it;

(s) any limitations, of which the supplier could reasonably be taken to be aware, of the period for which any information referred to in paragraphs (a) to (r) will be valid.

5   Application of certain rules

Rules made by the Authority under section 140 or 141 of the 2000 Act do not apply to incoming providers to the extent that they specify an activity which is an incoming electronic commerce activity.

Electronic Commerce (EC Directive) Regulations 2002

(SI 2002, No. 2013)

2   Interpretation

(1) In these Regulations and in the Schedule—

'commercial communication' means a communication, in any form, designed to promote, directly or indirectly, the goods, services or image of any person pursuing a commercial, industrial or craft activity or exercising a regulated profession, other than a communication—

(a) consisting only of information allowing direct access to the activity of that person including a geographic address, a domain name or an electronic mail address; or

(b) relating to the goods, services or image of that person provided that the communication has been prepared independently of the person making it (and for this purpose, a communication prepared without financial consideration is to be taken to have been prepared independently unless the contrary is shown);

'the Commission' means the Commission of the European Communities;

'consumer' means any natural person who is acting for purposes other than those of his trade, business or profession;

'coordinated field' means requirements applicable to information society service providers or information society services, regardless of whether they are of a general nature or specifically designed for them, and covers requirements with which the service provider has to comply in respect of—

(a) the taking up of the activity of an information society service, such as requirements concerning qualifications, authorisation or notification, and

(b) the pursuit of the activity of an information society service, such as requirements concerning the behaviour of the service provider, requirements regarding the quality or content of the service including those applicable to advertising and contracts, or requirements concerning the liability of the service provider,

but does not cover requirements such as those applicable to goods as such, to the delivery of goods or to services not provided by electronic means;

'the Directive' means Directive 2000/31/EC of the European Parliament and of the Council of 8 June 2000 on certain legal aspects of information society services, in particular electronic commerce, in the Internal Market (Directive on electronic commerce);

'EEA Agreement' means the Agreement on the European Economic Area signed at Oporto on 2 May 1992 as adjusted by the Protocol signed at Brussels on 17 March 1993;

'enactment' includes an enactment comprised in Northern Ireland legislation and comprised in, or an instrument made under, an Act of the Scottish Parliament;

'enforcement action' means any form of enforcement action including, in particular—

> (a) in relation to any legal requirement imposed by or under any enactment, any action taken with a view to or in connection with imposing any sanction (whether criminal or otherwise) for failure to observe or comply with it; and
>
> (b) in relation to a permission or authorisation, anything done with a view to removing or restricting that permission or authorisation;

'enforcement authority' does not include courts but, subject to that, means any person who is authorised, whether by or under an enactment or otherwise, to take enforcement action;

'established service provider' means a service provider who is a national of a member State or a company or firm as mentioned in Article 48 of the Treaty and who effectively pursues an economic activity by virtue of which he is a service provider using a fixed establishment in a member State for an indefinite period, but the presence and use of the technical means and technologies required to provide the information society service do not, in themselves, constitute an establishment of the provider; in cases where it cannot be determined from which of a number of places of establishment a given service is provided, that service is to be regarded as provided from the place of establishment where the provider has the centre of his activities relating to that service; references to a service provider being established or to the establishment of a service provider shall be construed accordingly;

'information society services' (which is summarised in recital 17 of the Directive as covering 'any service normally provided for remuneration, at a distance, by means of electronic equipment for the processing (including digital compression) and storage of data, and at the individual request of a recipient of a service') has the meaning set out in Article 2(a) of the Directive, (which refers to Article 1(2) of Directive 98/34/EC of the European Parliament and of the Council of 22 June 1998 laying down a procedure for the provision of information in the field of technical standards and regulations, as amended by Directive 98/48/EC of 20 July 1998);

'member State' includes a State which is a contracting party to the EEA Agreement;

'recipient of the service' means any person who, for professional ends or otherwise, uses an information society service, in particular for the purposes of seeking information or making it accessible;

'regulated profession' means any profession within the meaning of either Article 1(d) of Council Directive 89/48/EEC of 21 December 1988 on a general system for the recognition of higher-education diplomas awarded on completion of professional education and training of at least three years' duration or of Article 1(f) of Council Directive 92/51/EEC of 18 June 1992 on a second general system for the recognition of professional education and training to supplement Directive 89/48/EEC;

'service provider' means any person providing an information society service;

'the Treaty' means the treaty establishing the European Community.

(2) In regulation 4 and 5, 'requirement' means any legal requirement under the law of the United Kingdom, or any part of it, imposed by or under any enactment or otherwise.

(3) Terms used in the Directive other than those in paragraph (1) above shall have the same meaning as in the Directive.

3   Exclusions

. . .

4   Internal market

(1) Subject to paragraph (4) below, any requirement which falls within the coordinated field shall apply to the provision of an information society service by a service provider established in the United Kingdom irrespective of whether that information society service is provided in the United Kingdom or another member State.

(2) Subject to paragraph (4) below, an enforcement authority with responsibility in relation to any requirement in paragraph (1) shall ensure that the provision of an information society service by a service provider established in the United Kingdom complies with that requirement irrespective of whether that service is provided in the United Kingdom or another member State and any power, remedy or procedure for taking enforcement action shall be available to secure compliance.

(3) Subject to paragraphs (4), (5) and (6) below, any requirement shall not be applied to the provision of an information society service by a service provider established in a member State other than the United Kingdom for reasons which fall within the coordinated field where its application would restrict the freedom to provide information society services to a person in the United Kingdom from that member State.

(4) Paragraphs (1), (2) and (3) shall not apply to those fields in the annex to the Directive set out in the Schedule.

(5) The reference to any requirements the application of which would restrict the freedom to provide information society services from another member State in paragraph (3) above does not include any requirement maintaining the level of protection for public health and consumer interests established by Community acts.

(6) To the extent that anything in these Regulations creates any new criminal offence, it shall not be punishable with imprisonment for more than two years or punishable on summary conviction with imprisonment for more than three months or with a fine of more than level 5 on the standard scale (if not calculated on a daily basis) or with a fine of more than £100 a day.

5 Derogations from regulation 4

(1) Notwithstanding regulation 4(3), an enforcement authority may take measures, including applying any requirement which would otherwise not apply by virtue of regulation 4(3) in respect of a given information society service, where those measures are necessary for reasons of—

   (a) public policy, in particular the prevention, investigation, detection and prosecution of criminal offences, including the protection of minors and the fight against any incitement to hatred on grounds of race, sex, religion or nationality, and violations of human dignity concerning individual persons;

   (b) the protection of public health;

   (c) public security, including the safeguarding of national security and defence, or

   (d) the protection of consumers, including investors,

and proportionate to those objectives.

(2) Notwithstanding regulation 4(3), in any case where an enforcement authority with responsibility in relation to the requirement in question is not party to the proceedings, a court may, on the application of any person or of its own motion, apply any requirement which would otherwise not apply by virtue of regulation 4(3) in respect of a given information society service, if the application of that enactment or requirement is necessary for and proportionate to any of the objectives set out in paragraph (1) above.

(3) Paragraphs (1) and (2) shall only apply where the information society service prejudices or presents a serious and grave risk of prejudice to an objective in paragraph (1)(a) to (d).

(4) Subject to paragraphs (5) and (6), an enforcement authority shall not take the measures in paragraph (1) above, unless it—

   (a) asks the member State in which the service provider is established to take measures and the member State does not take such measures or they are inadequate; and

   (b) notifies the Commission and the member State in which the service provider is established of its intention to take such measures.

(5) Paragraph (4) shall not apply to court proceedings, including preliminary proceedings and acts carried out in the course of a criminal investigation.

(6) If it appears to the enforcement authority that the matter is one of urgency, it may take the measures under paragraph (1) without first asking the member State in which the service provider is established to take measures and notifying the Commission and the member State in derogation from paragraph (4).

(7) In a case where a measure is taken pursuant to paragraph (6) above, the enforcement authority shall notify the measures taken to the Commission and to the member State concerned in the shortest possible time thereafter and indicate the reasons for urgency.

(8) In paragraph (2), 'court' means any court or tribunal.

6   General information to be provided by a person providing an information society service

(1) A person providing an information society service shall make available to the recipient of the service and any relevant enforcement authority, in a form and manner which is easily, directly and permanently accessible, the following information—

    (a) the name of the service provider;

    (b) the geographic address at which the service provider is established;

    (c) the details of the service provider, including his electronic mail address, which make it possible to contact him rapidly and communicate with him in a direct and effective manner;

    (d) where the service provider is registered in a trade or similar register available to the public, details of the register in which the service provider is entered and his registration number, or equivalent means of identification in that register;

    (e) where the provision of the service is subject to an authorisation scheme, the particulars of the relevant supervisory authority;

    (f) where the service provider exercises a regulated profession—

        (i)   the details of any professional body or similar institution with which the service provider is registered;

        (ii)   his professional title and the member State where that title has been granted;

        (iii) a reference to the professional rules applicable to the service provider in the member State of establishment and the means to access them; and

    (g) where the service provider undertakes an activity that is subject to value added tax, the identification number referred to in Article 22(1) of the sixth Council Directive 77/388/EEC of 17 May 1977 on the harmonisation of the laws of the member States relating to turnover taxes—Common system of value added tax: uniform basis of assessment.

(2) Where a person providing an information society service refers to prices, these shall be indicated clearly and unambiguously and, in particular, shall indicate whether they are inclusive of tax and delivery costs.

7   Commercial communications

A service provider shall ensure that any commercial communication provided by him and which constitutes or forms part of an information society service shall—

    (a) be clearly identifiable as a commercial communication;

    (b) clearly identify the person on whose behalf the commercial communication is made;

    (c) clearly identify as such any promotional offer (including any discount, premium or gift) and ensure that any conditions which must be met to qualify for it are easily accessible, and presented clearly and unambiguously; and

    (d) clearly identify as such any promotional competition or game and ensure that any conditions for participation are easily accessible and presented clearly and unambiguously.

8   Unsolicited commercial communications

A service provider shall ensure that any unsolicited commercial communication sent by him by electronic mail is clearly and unambiguously identifiable as such as soon as it is received.

9   Information to be provided where contracts are concluded by electronic means

(1) Unless parties who are not consumers have agreed otherwise, where a contract is to be concluded by electronic means a service provider shall, prior to an order being placed by the recipient of a service, provide to that recipient in a clear, comprehensible and unambiguous manner the information set out in (a) to (d) below—

    (a) the different technical steps to follow to conclude the contract;

    (b) whether or not the concluded contract will be filed by the service provider and whether it will be accessible;

    (c) the technical means for identifying and correcting input errors prior to the placing of the order; and

    (d) the languages offered for the conclusion of the contract.

(2) Unless parties who are not consumers have agreed otherwise, a service provider shall indicate which relevant codes of conduct he subscribes to and give information on how those codes can be consulted electronically.

(3) Where the service provider provides terms and conditions applicable to the contract to the recipient, the service provider shall make them available to him in a way that allows him to store and reproduce them.

(4) The requirements of paragraphs (1) and (2) above shall not apply to contracts concluded exclusively by exchange of electronic mail or by equivalent individual communications.

10   Other information requirements

Regulations 6, 7, 8 and 9(1) have effect in addition to any other information requirements in legislation giving effect to Community law.

11   Placing of the order

(1) Unless parties who are not consumers have agreed otherwise, where the recipient of the service places his order through technological means, a service provider shall—

    (a) acknowledge receipt of the order to the recipient of the service without undue delay and by electronic means; and

    (b) make available to the recipient of the service appropriate, effective and accessible technical means allowing him to identify and correct input errors prior to the placing of the order.

(2) For the purposes of paragraph (1)(a) above—

    (a) the order and the acknowledgement of receipt will be deemed to be received when the parties to whom they are addressed are able to access them; and

    (b) the acknowledgement of receipt may take the form of the provision of the service paid for where that service is an information society service.

(3) The requirements of paragraph (1) above shall not apply to contracts concluded exclusively by exchange of electronic mail or by equivalent individual communications.

12   Meaning of the term 'order'

Except in relation to regulation 9(1)(c) and regulation 11(1)(b) where 'order' shall be the contractual offer, 'order' may be but need not be the contractual offer for the purposes of regulations 9 and 11.

13   Liability of the service provider

The duties imposed by regulations 6, 7, 8, 9(1) and 11(1)(a) shall be enforceable, at the suit of any recipient of a service, by an action against the service provider for damages for breach of statutory duty.

14   Compliance with Regulation 9(3)

Where on request a service provider has failed to comply with the requirement in regulation 9(3), the recipient may seek an order from any court having jurisdiction in relation to the contract requiring that service provider to comply with that requirement.

15   Right to rescind contract

Where a person—

    (a) has entered into a contract to which these Regulations apply, and

    (b) the service provider has not made available means of allowing him to identify and correct input errors in compliance with regulation 11(1)(b),

he shall be entitled to rescind the contract unless any court having jurisdiction in relation to the contract in question orders otherwise on the application of the service provider.

17 Mere conduit

(1) Where an information society service is provided which consists of the transmission in a communication network of information provided by a recipient of the service or the provision of access to a communication network, the service provider (if he otherwise would) shall not be liable for damages or for any other pecuniary remedy or for any criminal sanction as a result of that transmission where the service provider—

(a) did not initiate the transmission;

(b) did not select the receiver of the transmission; and

(c) did not select or modify the information contained in the transmission.

(2) The acts of transmission and of provision of access referred to in paragraph (1) include the automatic, intermediate and transient storage of the information transmitted where:

(a) this takes place for the sole purpose of carrying out the transmission in the communication network, and

(b) the information is not stored for any period longer than is reasonably necessary for the transmission.

18 Caching

Where an information society service is provided which consists of the transmission in a communication network of information provided by a recipient of the service, the service provider (if he otherwise would) shall not be liable for damages or for any other pecuniary remedy or for any criminal sanction as a result of that transmission where—

(a) the information is the subject of automatic, intermediate and temporary storage where that storage is for the sole purpose of making more efficient onward transmission of the information to other recipients of the service upon their request, and

(b) the service provider—

(i) does not modify the information;

(ii) complies with conditions on access to the information;

(iii) complies with any rules regarding the updating of the information, specified in a manner widely recognised and used by industry;

(iv) does not interfere with the lawful use of technology, widely recognised and used by industry, to obtain data on the use of the information; and

(v) acts expeditiously to remove or to disable access to the information he has stored upon obtaining actual knowledge of the fact that the information at the initial source of the transmission has been removed from the network, or access to it has been disabled, or that a court or an administrative authority has ordered such removal or disablement.

19 Hosting

Where an information society service is provided which consists of the storage of information provided by a recipient of the service, the service provider (if he otherwise would) shall not be liable for damages or for any other pecuniary remedy or for any criminal sanction as a result of that storage where—

(a) the service provider—

(i) does not have actual knowledge of unlawful activity or information and, where a claim for damages is made, is not aware of facts or circumstances from which it would have been apparent to the service provider that the activity or information was unlawful; or

(ii) upon obtaining such knowledge or awareness, acts expeditiously to remove or to disable access to the information, and

(b) the recipient of the service was not acting under the authority or the control of the service provider.

20   Protection of rights

(1) Nothing in regulations 17, 18 and 19 shall—

(a) prevent a person agreeing different contractual terms; or

(b) affect the rights of any party to apply to a court for relief to prevent or stop infringement of any rights.

(2) Any power of an administrative authority to prevent or stop infringement of any rights shall continue to apply notwithstanding regulations 17, 18 and 19.

21   Defence in criminal proceedings: burden of proof

(1) This regulation applies where a service provider charged with an offence in criminal proceedings arising out of any transmission, provision of access or storage falling within regulation 17, 18 or 19 relies on a defence under any of regulations 17, 18 and 19.

(2) Where evidence is adduced which is sufficient to raise an issue with respect to that defence, the court or jury shall assume that the defence is satisfied unless the prosecution proves beyond reasonable doubt that it is not.

22   Notice for the purposes of actual knowledge

In determining whether a service provider has actual knowledge for the purposes of regulations 18(b)(v) and 19(a)(i), a court shall take into account all matters which appear to it in the particular circumstances to be relevant and, among other things, shall have regard to—

(a) whether a service provider has received a notice through a means of contact made available in accordance with regulation 6(1)(c), and

(b) the extent to which any notice includes—

(i)   the full name and address of the sender of the notice;

(ii) details of the location of the information in question; and

(iii) details of the unlawful nature of the activity or information in question.

Regulation 4   **SCHEDULE**

1. Copyright, neighbouring rights, rights referred to in Directive 87/54/EEC and Directive 96/9/EC and industrial property rights.

2. The freedom of the parties to a contract to choose the applicable law.

3. Contractual obligations concerning consumer contracts.

4. Formal validity of contracts creating or transferring rights in real estate where such contracts are subject to mandatory formal requirements of the law of the member State where the real estate is situated.

5. The permissibility of unsolicited commercial communications by electronic mail.

Sale and Supply of Goods to Consumers Regulations 2002

(S1 2002, No. 3045)

2   Interpretation

In these Regulations—

'consumer' means any natural person who, in the contracts covered by these Regulations, is acting for purposes which are outside his trade, business or profession;

'consumer guarantee' means any undertaking to a consumer by a person acting in the course of his business, given without extra charge, to reimburse the price paid or to replace, repair or handle consumer goods in any way if they do not meet the specifications set out in the guarantee statement or in the relevant advertising;

'court' in relation to England and Wales and Northern Ireland means a county court or the High Court, and in relation to Scotland, the sheriff or the Court of Session;

'enforcement authority' means the [Office of Fair Trading], every local weights and measures authority in Great Britain and the Department of Enterprise, Trade and Investment for Northern Ireland;

'goods' has the same meaning as in section 61 of the Sale of Goods Act 1979;

'guarantor' means a person who offers a consumer guarantee to a consumer; and

'supply' includes supply by way of sale, lease, hire or hire-purchase.

15   Consumer guarantees

(1) Where goods are sold or otherwise supplied to a consumer which are offered with a consumer guarantee, the consumer guarantee takes effect at the time the goods are delivered as a contractual obligation owed by the guarantor under the conditions set out in the guarantee statement and the associated advertising.

(2) The guarantor shall ensure that the guarantee sets out in plain intelligible language the contents of the guarantee and the essential particulars necessary for making claims under the guarantee, notably the duration and territorial scope of the guarantee as well as the name and address of the guarantor.

[(2A) The guarantor shall also ensure that the guarantee contains a statement that the consumer has statutory rights in relation to the goods which are sold or supplied and that those rights are not affected by the guarantee.]

(3) On request by the consumer to a person to whom paragraph (4) applies, the guarantee shall within a reasonable time be made available in writing or in another durable medium available and accessible to him.

(4) This paragraph applies to the guarantor and any other person who offers to consumers the goods which are the subject of the guarantee for sale or supply.

(5) Where consumer goods are offered with a consumer guarantee, and where those goods are offered within the territory of the United Kingdom, then the guarantor shall ensure that the consumer guarantee is written in English.

(6) If the guarantor fails to comply with the provisions of paragraphs (2) or (5) above, or a person to whom paragraph (4) applies fails to comply with paragraph (3) then the enforcement authority may apply for an injunction or (in Scotland) an order of specific implement against that person requiring him to comply.

(7) The court on application under this Regulation may grant an injunction or (in Scotland) an order of specific implement on such terms as it thinks fit.

Insolvency Act 1986 (Prescribed Part) Order 2003

(SI 2003, No. 2097)

1   Citation, Commencement and Interpretation

(2) In this order 'the 1986 Act' means the Insolvency Act 1986.

2   Minimum value of the company's net property

For the purposes of section 176A(3)(a) of the 1986 Act the minimum value of the company's net property is £10,000.

3   Calculation of prescribed part

(1) The prescribed part of the company's net property to be made available for the satisfaction of unsecured debts of the company pursuant to section 176A of the 1986 Act shall be calculated as follows—

    (a) where the company's net property does not exceed £10,000 in value, 50% of that property;

(b) subject to paragraph (2), where the company's net property exceeds £10,000 in value the sum of—

    (i)   50% of the first £10,000 in value; and

    (ii) 20% of that part of the company's net property which exceeds £10,000 in value.

(2) The value of the prescribed part of the company's net property to be made available for the satisfaction of unsecured debts of the company pursuant to section 176A shall not exceed £600,000.

Consumer Credit (Disclosure of Information) Regulations 2004

(SI 2004, No. 1481)

1   Citation, commencement and interpretation

(2) In these Regulations—

["the Act" means the Consumer Credit Act 1974;]

'the Agreements Regulations' mean the Consumer Credit (Agreements) Regulations 1983;

'distance contract' means any regulated agreement made under an organised distance sales or service-provision scheme run by the creditor or owner or by an intermediary of the creditor or owner who, in any such case, for the purpose of that agreement makes exclusive use of one or more means of distance communication up to and including the time at which the agreement is made and for this purpose any means of communication is a means of distance communication if, without the simultaneous physical presence of the creditor or owner or any intermediary of the creditor or owner and of the debtor or hirer, it may be used for the distance marketing of a regulated agreement between the parties to that agreement;

'durable medium' means any instrument which enables the debtor or hirer to store information addressed personally to him in a way accessible for future reference for a period of time adequate for the purposes of the information and which allows the unchanged reproduction of the information stored.

2   Agreements to which these Regulations apply

[(1) Subject to paragraph (3) these Regulations apply in respect of the following regulated agreements—

    (a) consumer credit agreements secured on land except those to which section 58 of the Act (opportunity for withdrawal from prospective land mortgage) applies,

    (b) consumer hire agreements,

    (c) consumer credit agreements under which the creditor provides the debtor with credit which exceeds £60,260,

    (d) consumer credit agreements entered into by the debtor wholly or predominantly for the purposes of a business carried on, or intended to be carried on, by him, and

    (e) small debtor-creditor-supplier agreements for restricted-use credit,

except to the extent the Consumer Credit (Disclosure of Information) Regulations 2010 apply to such agreements.

(2) Subsections (2) to (5) of section 16B of the Act (declaration by the debtor as to the purposes of the agreement) apply for the purposes of paragraph (1)(d).

(3) These Regulations do not apply to distance contracts.]

3   Information to be disclosed to a debtor or hirer before a regulated agreement is made

(1) Before a regulated agreement ('the relevant agreement') is made, the creditor or owner must disclose to the debtor or hirer in the manner set out in regulation 4 the information and statements of protection and remedies that are required to be given—

    (a) in the case of a regulated consumer credit agreement, under regulation 2 of the Agreements Regulations;

    (b) in the case of a regulated consumer hire agreement, under regulation 3 of the Agreements Regulations;

    (c) in the case of a modifying agreement which is, or is treated as, a regulated consumer credit agreement, under regulations 2(3) and 7(2) of the Agreements Regulations;

    (d) in the case of a modifying agreement which is or is treated as a regulated consumer hirer agreement, under regulations 3(3) and 7(9) of the Agreements Regulations.

[(1A) In the case of an agreement falling within regulation 2(1)(c), (d) or (e), the creditor shall provide, in addition to the information specified in paragraph (1), a statement in accordance with section 157(A1) of the Act that if the creditor decides not to proceed with a prospective regulated consumer credit agreement he must, when informing the debtor of this decision, inform the debtor that this decision has been reached on the basis of information from a credit reference agency and of the particulars of that agency.]

(2) The information and statements of protection required to be disclosed under paragraph (1) shall be the information and statements that will be included in the document embodying the relevant agreement save that, where any of the information is not known at the time of disclosure, the creditor or owner shall disclose estimated information based on such assumptions as he may reasonably make in all the circumstances of the case.

4 Manner of disclosure

The information and statements of protection and remedies required to be disclosed under regulation 3 must be—

    (a) easily legible and, where applicable, of a colour which is readily distinguishable from the background medium upon which they are displayed;

    (b) not interspersed with any other information or wording apart from subtotals of total amounts and cross references to the terms of the agreement;

    (c) of equal prominence except that headings may be afforded more prominence whether by capital letters, underlining, larger or bold print or otherwise; and

    (d) contained in a document which:

        (i) is separate from the document embodying the relevant agreement (within the meaning of regulation 3) and any other document referred to in the document embodying that agreement;

        (ii) is headed with the words 'Pre-contract Information';

        (iii) does not contain any other information or wording apart from the heading referred to in sub-paragraph (ii);

        (iv) is on paper or on another durable medium which is available and accessible to the debtor or hirer; and

        (v) is of a nature that enables the debtor or hirer to remove it from the place where it is disclosed to him.

General Product Safety Regulations 2005

(SI 2005, No. 1803)

PART 1 GENERAL

2. Interpretation

In these Regulations:—

'the 1987 Act' means the Consumer Protection Act 1987;

'[EU] law' includes a law in any part of the United Kingdom which implements [an EU] obligation [and does not include Regulation (EC) No 765/2008 of the European Parliament and the Council setting out the requirements for accreditation and market surveillance relating to the marketing of products and repealing Regulation (EEC) No 339/93];

'contravention' includes a failure to comply and cognate expressions shall be construed accordingly;

'dangerous product' means a product other than a safe product;

'distributor' means a professional in the supply chain whose activity does not affect the safety properties of a product;

'enforcement authority' means the Secretary of State, any other Minister of the Crown in charge of a government department, any such department and any authority or council mentioned in regulation 10;

'general safety requirement' means the requirement that only safe products should be placed on the market;

'the GPS Directive' means Directive 2001/95/EC of the European Parliament and of the Council of 3 December 2001 on general product safety;

'magistrates' court' in relation to Northern Ireland, means a court of summary jurisdiction;

'Member State' means a member State, Norway, Iceland or Liechtenstein;

'notice' means a notice in writing;

'officer', in relation to an enforcement authority, means a person authorised in writing to assist the authority in carrying out its functions under or for the purposes of the enforcement of these Regulations and safety notices, except in relation to an enforcement authority which is a government department where it means an officer of that department;

'producer' means—

(a) the manufacturer of a product, when he is established in a Member State and any other person presenting himself as the manufacturer by affixing to the product his name, trade mark or other distinctive mark, or the person who reconditions the product;

(b) when the manufacturer is not established in a Member State—

   (i) if he has a representative established in a Member State, the representative,

   (ii) in any other case, the importer of the product from a state that is not a Member State into a Member State;

(c) other professionals in the supply chain, insofar as their activities may affect the safety properties of a product;

'product' means a product which is intended for consumers or likely, under reasonably foreseeable conditions, to be used by consumers even if not intended for them and which is supplied or made available, whether for consideration or not, in the course of a commercial activity and whether it is new, used or reconditioned and includes a product that is supplied or made available to consumers for their own use in the context of providing a service. 'product' does not include equipment used by service providers themselves to supply a service to consumers, in particular equipment on which consumers ride or travel which is operated by a service provider;

'recall' means any measure aimed at achieving the return of a dangerous product that has already been supplied or made available to consumers;

'recall notice' means a notice under regulation 15;

'record' includes any book or document and any record in any form;

'requirement to mark' means a notice under regulation 12;

'requirement to warn' means a notice under regulation 13;

'safe product' means a product which, under normal or reasonably foreseeable conditions of use including duration and, where applicable, putting into service, installation and maintenance requirements, does not present any risk or only the minimum risks compatible with the product's use, considered to be acceptable and consistent with a high level of protection for the safety and health of persons. In determining the foregoing, the following shall be taken into account in particular—

    (a) the characteristics of the product, including its composition, packaging, instructions for assembly and, where applicable, instructions for installation and maintenance,

    (b) the effect of the product on other products, where it is reasonably foreseeable that it will be used with other products,

    (c) the presentation of the product, the labelling, any warnings and instructions for its use and disposal and any other indication or information regarding the product, and

    (d) the categories of consumers at risk when using the product, in particular children and the elderly.

The feasibility of obtaining higher levels of safety or the availability of other products presenting a lesser degree of risk shall not constitute grounds for considering a product to be a dangerous product;

'safety notice' means a suspension notice, a requirement to mark, a requirement to warn, a withdrawal notice or a recall notice;

'serious risk' means a serious risk, including one the effects of which are not immediate, requiring rapid intervention;

'supply' in relation to a product includes making it available, in the context of providing a service, for use by consumers;

'suspension notice' means a notice under regulation 11;

'withdrawal' means any measure aimed at preventing the distribution, display or offer of a dangerous product to a consumer;

'withdrawal notice' means a notice under regulation 14.

3. Application

(1) Each provision of these Regulations applies to a product in so far as there are no specific provisions with the same objective in rules of [EU] law governing the safety of the product other than the GPS Directive.

(2) Where a product is subject to specific safety requirements imposed by rules of [EU] law other than the GPS Directive, these Regulations shall apply only to the aspects and risks or category of risks not covered by those requirements. This means that:

    (a) the definition of 'safe product' and 'dangerous product' in regulation 2 and regulations 5 and 6 shall not apply to such a product in so far as concerns the risks or category of risks covered by the specific rules, and

    (b) the remainder of these Regulations shall apply except where there are specific provisions governing the aspects covered by those regulations with the same objective.

4. These Regulations do not apply to a second-hand product supplied as a product to be repaired or reconditioned prior to being used, provided the supplier clearly informs the person to whom he supplies the product to that effect.

PART 2 OBLIGATIONS OF PRODUCERS AND DISTRIBUTORS

5. General safety requirement

(1) No producer shall place a product on the market unless the product is a safe product.

(2) No producer shall offer or agree to place a product on the market or expose or possess a product for placing on the market unless the product is a safe product.

(3) No producer shall offer or agree to supply a product or expose or possess a product for supply unless the product is a safe product.

(4) No producer shall supply a product unless the product is a safe product.

6. Presumption of conformity

(1) Where, in the absence of specific provisions in rules of [EU] law governing the safety of a product, the product conforms to the specific rules of the law of part of the United Kingdom laying

down the health and safety requirements which the product must satisfy in order to be marketed in the United Kingdom, the product shall be deemed safe so far as concerns the aspects covered by such rules.

(2) Where a product conforms to a voluntary national standard of the United Kingdom giving effect to a European standard the reference of which has been published in the Official Journal of the European Union in accordance with Article 4 of the GPS Directive, the product shall be presumed to be a safe product so far as concerns the risks and categories of risk covered by that national standard. The Secretary of State shall publish the reference number of such national standards in such manner as he considers appropriate.

(3) In circumstances other than those referred to in paragraphs (1) and (2), the conformity of a product to the general safety requirement shall be assessed taking into account—

    (a) any voluntary national standard of the United Kingdom giving effect to a European stand-ard, other than one referred to in paragraph (2),

    (b) other national standards drawn up in the United Kingdom,

    (c) recommendations of the European Commission setting guidelines on product safety assessment,

    (d) product safety codes of good practice in the sector concerned,

    (e) the state of the art and technology, and

    (f) reasonable consumer expectations concerning safety.

(4) Conformity of a product with the criteria designed to ensure the general safety requirement is complied with, in particular the provisions mentioned in paragraphs (1) to (3), shall not bar an enforcement authority from exercising its powers under these Regulations in relation to that product where there is evidence that, despite such conformity, it is dangerous.

7. Other obligations of producers

(1) Within the limits of his activities, a producer shall provide consumers with the relevant infor-mation to enable them—

    (a) to assess the risks inherent in a product throughout the normal or reasonably foreseeable period of its use, where such risks are not immediately obvious without adequate warn-ings, and

    (b) to take precautions against those risks.

(2) The presence of warnings does not exempt any person from compliance with the other requirements of these Regulations.

(3) Within the limits of his activities, a producer shall adopt measures commensurate with the characteristics of the products which he supplies to enable him to—

    (a) be informed of the risks which the products might pose, and

    (b) take appropriate action including, where necessary to avoid such risks, withdrawal, adequately and effectively warning consumers as to the risks or, as a last resort, recall.

(4) The measures referred to in paragraph (3) include—

    (a) except where it is not reasonable to do so, an indication by means of the product or its packaging of—

        (i) the name and address of the producer, and

        (ii) the product reference or where applicable the batch of products to which it belongs; and

    (b) where and to the extent that it is reasonable to do so—

        (i) sample testing of marketed products,

        (ii) investigating and if necessary keeping a register of complaints concerning the safety of the product, and

        (iii) keeping distributors informed of the results of such monitoring where a product presents a risk or may present a risk.

8. Obligations of distributors

(1) A distributor shall act with due care in order to help ensure compliance with the applicable safety requirements and in particular he—

    (a) shall not expose or possess for supply or offer or agree to supply, or supply, a product to any person which he knows or should have presumed, on the basis of the information in his possession and as a professional, is a dangerous product; and

    (b) shall, within the limits of his activities, participate in monitoring the safety of a product placed on the market, in particular by—

        (i)   passing on information on the risks posed by the product,

        (ii) keeping the documentation necessary for tracing the origin of the product,

        (iii) producing the documentation necessary for tracing the origin of the product, and cooperating in action taken by a producer or an enforcement authority to avoid the risks.

(2) Within the limits of his activities, a distributor shall take measures enabling him to cooperate efficiently in the action referred to in paragraph (1)(b)(iii).

9. Obligations of producers and distributors

(1) Subject to paragraph (2), where a producer or a distributor knows that a product he has placed on the market or supplied poses risks to the consumer that are incompatible with the general safety requirement, he shall forthwith notify an enforcement authority in writing of that information and—

    (a) the action taken to prevent risk to the consumer; and

    (b) where the product is being or has been marketed or otherwise supplied to consumers outside the United Kingdom, of the identity of each Member State in which, to the best of his knowledge, it is being or has been so marketed or supplied.

(2) Paragraph (1) shall not apply—

    (a) in the case of a second-hand product supplied as an antique or as a product to be repaired or reconditioned prior to being used, provided the supplier clearly informed the person to whom he supplied the product to that effect,

    (b) in conditions concerning isolated circumstances or products.

(3) In the event of a serious risk the notification under paragraph (1) shall include the following—

    (a) information enabling a precise identification of the product or batch of products in question,

    (b) a full description of the risks that the product presents,

    (c) all available information relevant for tracing the product, and

    (d) a description of the action undertaken to prevent risks to the consumer.

(4) Within the limits of his activities, a person who is a producer or a distributor shall co-operate with an enforcement authority (at the enforcement authority's request) in action taken to avoid the risks posed by a product which he supplies or has supplied. Every enforcement authority shall maintain procedures for such co-operation, including procedures for dialogue with the producers and distributors concerned on issues related to product safety.

PART 3 ENFORCEMENT

10. Enforcement

(1) It shall be the duty of every authority to which paragraph (4) applies to enforce within its area these Regulations and safety notices.

(2) An authority in England or Wales to which paragraph (4) applies shall have the power to investigate and prosecute for an alleged contravention of any provision imposed by or under these Regulations which was committed outside its area in any part of England and Wales.

(3) A district council in Northern Ireland shall have the power to investigate and prosecute for an alleged contravention of any provision imposed by or under these Regulations which was committed outside its area in any part of Northern Ireland.

(4) The authorities to which this paragraph applies are:

(a) in England, a county council, district council, London Borough Council, the Common Council of the City of London in its capacity as a local authority and the Council of the Isles of Scilly,

(b) in Wales, a county council or a county borough council,

(c) in Scotland, a council constituted under section 2 of the Local Government etc. (Scotland) Act 1994,

(d) in Northern Ireland any district council.

(5) An enforcement authority shall in enforcing these Regulations act in a manner proportionate to the seriousness of the risk and shall take due account of the precautionary principle. In this context, it shall encourage and promote voluntary action by producers and distributors. Notwithstanding the foregoing, an enforcement authority may take any action under these Regulations urgently and without first encouraging and promoting voluntary action if a product poses a serious risk.

11. Suspension notices

(1) Where an enforcement authority has reasonable grounds for suspecting that a requirement of these Regulations has been contravened in relation to a product, the authority may, for the period needed to organise appropriate safety evaluations, checks and controls, serve a notice ('a suspension notice') prohibiting the person on whom it is served from doing any of the following things without the consent of the authority, that is to say—

(a) placing the product on the market, offering to place it on the market, agreeing to place it on the market or exposing it for placing on the market, or

(b) supplying the product, offering to supply it, agreeing to supply it or exposing it for supply.

(2) A suspension notice served by an enforcement authority in relation to a product may require the person on whom it is served to keep the authority informed of the whereabouts of any such product in which he has an interest.

(3) A consent given by the enforcement authority for the purposes of paragraph (1) may impose such conditions on the doing of anything for which the consent is required as the authority considers appropriate.

12. Requirements to mark

(1) Where an enforcement authority has reasonable grounds for believing that a product is a dangerous product in that it could pose risks in certain conditions, the authority may serve a notice ('a requirement to mark') requiring the person on whom the notice is served at his own expense to undertake either or both of the following, as specified in the notice—

(a) to ensure that the product is marked in accordance with requirements specified in the notice with warnings as to the risks it may present,

(b) to make the marketing of the product subject to prior conditions as specified in the notice so as to ensure the product is a safe product.

(2) The requirements referred to in paragraph (1)(a) shall be such as to ensure that the product is marked with a warning which is suitable, clearly worded and easily comprehensible.

13. Requirements to warn

Where an enforcement authority has reasonable grounds for believing that a product is a dangerous product in that it could pose risks for certain persons, the authority may serve a notice ('a requirement to warn') requiring the person on whom the notice is served at his own expense to undertake one or more of the following, as specified in the notice—

(a) where and to the extent it is practicable to do so, to ensure that any person who could be subject to such risks and who has been supplied with the product be given warning of the risks in good time and in a form specified in the notice,

(b) to publish a warning of the risks in such form and manner as is likely to bring those risks to the attention of any such person,

(c) to ensure that the product carries a warning of the risks in a form specified in the notice.

14. Withdrawal notices

(1) Where an enforcement authority has reasonable grounds for believing that a product is a dangerous product, the authority may serve a notice ('a withdrawal notice') prohibiting the person on whom it is served from doing any of the following things without the consent of the authority, that is to say—

(a) placing the product on the market, offering to place it on the market, agreeing to place it on the market or exposing it for placing on the market, or

(b) supplying the product, offering to supply it, agreeing to supply it or exposing it for supply.

(2) A withdrawal notice may require the person on whom it is served to take action to alert consumers to the risks that the product presents.

(3) In relation to a product that is already on the market, a withdrawal notice may only be served by an enforcement authority where the action being undertaken by the producer or the distributor concerned in fulfilment of his obligations under these Regulations is unsatisfactory or insufficient to prevent the risks concerned to the health and safety of persons.

(4) Paragraph (3) shall not apply in the case of a product posing a serious risk requiring, in the view of the enforcement authority, urgent action.

(5) A withdrawal notice served by an enforcement authority in relation to a product may require the person on whom it is served to keep the authority informed of the whereabouts of any such product in which he has an interest.

(6) A consent given by the enforcement authority for the purposes of paragraph (1) may impose such conditions on the doing of anything for which the consent is required as the authority considers appropriate.

15. Recall notices

(1) Subject to paragraph (4), where an enforcement authority has reasonable grounds for believing that a product is a dangerous product and that it has already been supplied or made available to consumers, the authority may serve a notice ('a recall notice') requiring the person on whom it is served to use his reasonable endeavours to organise the return of the product from consumers to that person or to such other person as is specified in the notice.

(2) A recall notice may require—

(a) the recall to be effected in accordance with a code of practice applicable to the product concerned, or

(b) the recipient of the recall notice to—

(i)   contact consumers who have purchased the product in order to inform them of the recall, where and to the extent it is practicable to do so,

(ii) publish a notice in such form and such manner as is likely to bring to the attention of purchasers of the product the risk the product poses and the fact of the recall, or

(iii) make arrangements for the collection or return of the product from consumers who have purchased it or for its disposal,

and may impose such additional requirements on the recipient of the notice as are reasonable and practicable with a view to achieving the return of the product from consumers to the person specified in the notice or its disposal.

(3) In determining what requirements to include in a recall notice, the enforcement authority shall take into consideration the need to encourage distributors, users and consumers to contribute to its implementation.

(4) A recall notice may only be issued by an enforcement authority where—

(a) other action which it may require under these Regulations would not suffice to prevent the risks concerned to the health and safety of persons,

    (b) the action being undertaken by the producer or the distributor concerned in fulfilment of his obligations under these Regulations is unsatisfactory or insufficient to prevent the risks concerned to the health and safety of persons, and

    (c) the authority has given not less than seven days notice to the person on whom the recall notice is to be served of its intention to serve such a notice and where that person has before the expiry of that period by notice required the authority to seek the advice of such person as the Institute determines on the questions of—

        (i) whether the product is a dangerous product,

        (ii) whether the issue of a recall notice is proportionate to the seriousness of the risk, and

    the authority has taken account of such advice.

    (5) Paragraphs (4)(b) and (c) shall not apply in the case of a product posing a serious risk requiring, in the view of the enforcement authority, urgent action.

    (6) Where a person requires an enforcement authority to seek advice as referred to in paragraph (4)(c), that person shall be responsible for the fees, costs and expenses of the Institute and of the person appointed by the Institute to advise the authority.

    (7) In paragraphs 4(c) and (6) 'the Institute' means the charitable organisation with registered number 803725 and known as the Chartered Institute of Arbitrators.

    (8) A recall notice served by an enforcement authority in relation to a product may require the person on whom it is served to keep the authority informed of the whereabouts of any such product to which the recall notice relates, so far as he is able to do so.

    (9) Where the conditions in paragraph (1) for serving a recall notice are satisfied and either the enforcement authority has been unable to identify any person on whom to serve a recall notice, or the person on whom such a notice has been served has failed to comply with it, then the authority may itself take such action as could have been required by a recall notice.

    (10) Where—

    (a) an authority has complied with the requirements of paragraph (4); and

    (b) the authority has exercised its powers under paragraph (9) to take action following the failure of the person on whom the recall notice has been served to comply with that notice,

then the authority may recover from the person on whom the notice was served summarily as a civil debt, any costs or expenses reasonably incurred by it in undertaking the action referred to in sub-paragraph (b).

    (11) A civil debt recoverable under the preceding paragraph may be recovered—

    (a) in England and Wales by way of complaint (as mentioned in section 58 of the Magistrates' Courts Act 1980,

    (b) in Northern Ireland in proceedings under Article 62 of the Magistrate's Court (Northern Ireland) Order 1981.

16. Supplementary provisions relating to safety notices

    (1) Whenever feasible, prior to serving a safety notice the authority shall give an opportunity to the person on whom the notice is to be served to submit his views to the authority. Where, due to the urgency of the situation, this is not feasible the person shall be given an opportunity to submit his views to the authority after service of the notice.

    (2) A safety notice served by an enforcement authority in respect of a product shall—

    (a) describe the product in a manner sufficient to identify it;

    (b) state the reasons on which the notice is based;

    (c) indicate the rights available to the recipient of the notice under these Regulations and (where applicable) the time limits applying to their exercise; and

    (d) in the case of a suspension notice, state the period of time for which it applies.

    (3) A safety notice shall have effect throughout the United Kingdom.

(4) Where an enforcement authority serves a suspension notice in respect of a product, the authority shall be liable to pay compensation to a person having an interest in the product in respect of any loss or damage suffered by reason of the notice if—

(a) there has been no contravention of any requirement of these Regulations in relation to the product; and

(b) the exercise by the authority of the power to serve the suspension notice was not attributable to any neglect or default by that person.

(5) Where an enforcement authority serves a withdrawal notice in respect of a product, the authority shall be liable to pay compensation to a person having an interest in the product in respect of any loss or damage suffered by reason of the notice if—

(a) the product was not a dangerous product; and

(b) the exercise by the authority of the power to serve the withdrawal notice was not attributable to any neglect or default by that person.

(6) Where an enforcement authority serves a recall notice in respect of a product, the authority shall be liable to pay compensation to the person on whom the notice was served in respect of any loss or damage suffered by reason of the notice if—

(a) the product was not a dangerous product; and

(b) the exercise by the authority of the power to serve the recall notice was not attributable to any neglect or default by that person.

(7) An enforcement authority may vary or revoke a safety notice which it has served provided that the notice is not made more restrictive for the person on whom it is served or more onerous for that person to comply with.

(8) Wherever feasible prior to varying a safety notice the authority shall give an opportunity to the person on whom the original notice was served to submit his views to the authority.

17. Appeals against safety notices

(1) A person on whom a safety notice has been served and a person having an interest in a product in respect of which a safety notice (other than a recall notice) has been served may, before the end of the period of 21 days beginning with the day on which the notice was served, apply for an order to vary or set aside the terms of the notice.

(2) On an application under paragraph (1) the court or the sheriff, as the case may be, shall make an order setting aside the notice only if satisfied that—

(a) in the case of a suspension notice, there has been no contravention in relation to the product of any requirement of these Regulations,

(b) in the case of a requirement to mark or a requirement to warn, the product is not a dangerous product,

(c) in the case of a withdrawal notice—

(i) the product is not a dangerous product, or

(ii) where applicable, regulation 14(3) has not been complied with by the enforcement authority concerned,

(d) in the case of a recall notice—

(i) the product is not a dangerous product, or

(ii) regulation 15(4) has not been complied with,

(e) in any case, the serving of the safety notice concerned was not proportionate to the seriousness of the risk.

(3) On an application concerning the period of time specified in a suspension notice as the period for which it applies, the court or the sheriff, as the case may be, may reduce the period to such period as it considers sufficient for organising appropriate safety evaluations, checks and controls.

(4) On an application to vary the terms of a notice, the court or the sheriff, as the case may be, may vary the requirements specified in the notice as it considers appropriate.

(5) A person on whom a recall notice has been served and who proposes to make an application under paragraph (1) in relation to the notice may, before the end of the period of seven days beginning with the day on which the notice was served, apply to the court or the sheriff for an order suspending the effect of the notice and the court or the sheriff may, in any case where it considers it appropriate to do so, make an order suspending the effect of the notice.

(6) If the court or the sheriff makes an order suspending the effect of a recall notice under paragraph (5) in the absence of the enforcement authority, the enforcement authority may apply for the revocation of such order.

(7) An order under paragraph (5) shall take effect from the time it is made until—

(a) it is revoked under paragraph (6),

(b) where no application is made under paragraph (1) in respect of the recall notice within the time specified in that paragraph, the expiration of that time,

(c) where such an application is made but is withdrawn or dismissed for want of prosecution, the date of dismissal or withdrawal of the application, or

(d) where such an application is made and is not withdrawn or dismissed for want of prosecution, the determination of the application.

(8) Subject to paragraph (6), in Scotland the sheriff's decision under paragraph (5) shall be final.

(9) An application under this regulation may be made—

(a) by way of complaint to any magistrates' court in which proceedings have been brought in England and Wales or Northern Ireland—

(i) in respect of a contravention in relation to the product of a requirement imposed by or under these Regulations; or

(ii) for the forfeiture of the product under regulation 18;

(b) where no such proceedings have been brought, by way of complaint to any magistrates' court; or

(c) in Scotland, by summary application to the sheriff.

(10) A person aggrieved by an order made pursuant to an application under paragraph (1) by a magistrates' court in England, Wales or Northern Ireland, or by a decision of such a court not to make such an order, may appeal against that order or decision—

(a) in England and Wales, to the Crown Court;

(b) in Northern Ireland, to the county court.

18. Forfeiture: England and Wales and Northern Ireland

(1) An enforcement authority in England and Wales or Northern Ireland may apply for an order for the forfeiture of a product on the grounds that the product is a dangerous product.

(2) An application under paragraph (1) may be made—

(a) where proceedings have been brought in a magistrates' court for an offence in respect of a contravention in relation to the product of a requirement imposed by or under these Regulations, to that court,

(b) where an application with respect to the product has been made to a magistrates' court under regulation 17 (appeals against safety notices) or 25 (appeals against detention of products and records) to that court, and

(c) otherwise, by way of complaint to a magistrates' court.

(3) An enforcement authority making an application under paragraph (1) shall serve a copy of the application on any person appearing to it to be the owner of, or otherwise to have an interest in, the product to which the application relates, together with a notice giving him the opportunity to appear at the hearing of the application to show cause why the product should not be forfeited.

(4) A person on whom notice is served under paragraph (3) and any other person claiming to be the owner of, or otherwise to have an interest in, the product to which the application relates shall be entitled to appear at the hearing of the application and show cause why the product should not be forfeited.

(5) The court shall not make an order for the forfeiture of a product—

(a) if any person on whom notice is served under paragraph (3) does not appear, unless service of the notice on that person is proved, or

(b) if no notice under paragraph (3) has been served, unless the court is satisfied that in the circumstances it was reasonable not to serve notice on any person.

(6) The court may make an order for the forfeiture of a product only if it is satisfied that the product is a dangerous product.

(7) Any person aggrieved by an order made by a magistrates' court for the forfeiture of a product, or by a decision of such a court not to make such an order, may appeal against that order or decision—

(a) in England and Wales, to the Crown Court;

(b) in Northern Ireland, to the county court.

(8) An order for the forfeiture of a product shall not take effect until the later of—

(i)   the end of the period within which an appeal under paragraph (7) may be brought or within which an application under section 111 of the Magistrates' Courts Act 1980 or article 146 of the Magistrates' Courts (Northern Ireland) Order 1981 (statement of case) may be made, or

(ii) if an appeal or an application is so made, when the appeal or application is determined or abandoned.

(9) Subject to the following paragraph, where a product is forfeited it shall be destroyed in accordance with such directions as the court may give.

(10) On making an order for forfeiture of a product a magistrates' court may, if it considers it appropriate to do so, direct that the product shall (instead of being destroyed) be delivered up to such person as the court may specify, on condition that the person—

(a) does not supply the product to any person otherwise than as mentioned in paragraph (11), and

(b) on condition, if the court considers it appropriate, that he complies with any order to pay costs or expenses (including any order under regulation 28) which has been made against him in the proceedings for the order for forfeiture.

(11) The supplies which may be permitted under the preceding paragraph are—

(a) a supply to a person who carries on a business of buying products of the same description as the product concerned and repairing or reconditioning them,

(b) a supply to a person as scrap (that is to say, for the value of materials included in the product rather than for the value of the product itself),

(c) a supply to any person, provided that being so supplied the product is repaired by or on behalf of the person to whom the product was delivered up by direction of the court and that following such repair it is not a dangerous product.

20. Offences

(1) A person who contravenes regulations 5 or 8(1)(a) shall be guilty of an offence and liable on conviction on indictment to imprisonment for a term not exceeding 12 months or to a fine not exceeding £20,000 or to both, or on summary conviction to imprisonment for a term not exceeding three months or to a fine not exceeding the statutory maximum or to both.

(2) A person who contravenes regulation 7(1), 7(3) (by failing to take any of the measures specified in regulation 7(4)), 8(1)(b)(i), (ii) or (iii) or 9(1) shall be guilty of an offence and liable on summary conviction to imprisonment for a term not exceeding three months or to a fine not exceeding level 5 on the standard scale or to both.

(3) A producer or distributor who does not give notice to an enforcement authority under regulation 9(1) in respect of a product he has placed on the market or supplied commits an offence where it is proved that he ought to have known that the product poses risks to consumers that are incompatible with the general safety requirement and he shall be liable on summary conviction to imprisonment for a term not exceeding three months or to a fine not exceeding level 5 on the standard scale or to both.

(4) A person who contravenes a safety notice shall be guilty of an offence and liable on conviction on indictment to imprisonment for a term not exceeding 12 months or to a fine not exceeding £20,000 or to both, or on summary conviction to imprisonment for a term not exceeding three months or to a fine not exceeding the statutory maximum or to both.

21. Test purchases

(1) An enforcement authority shall have power to organise appropriate checks on the safety properties of a product, on an adequate scale, up to the final stage of use or consumption and for that purpose may make a purchase of a product or authorise an officer of the authority to make a purchase of a product.

(2) Where a product purchased under paragraph (1) is submitted to a test and the test leads to—

(a) the bringing of proceedings for an offence in respect of a contravention in relation to the product of any requirement imposed by or under these Regulations or for the forfeiture of the product under regulation 18 or 19, or

(b) the serving of a safety notice in respect of the product, and

(c) the authority is requested to do so and it is practicable for the authority to comply with the request,

then the authority shall allow the person from whom the product was purchased, a person who is a party to the proceedings, on whom the notice was served or who has an interest in the product to which the notice relates, to have the product tested.

22. Powers of entry and search etc.

(1) An officer of an enforcement authority may at any reasonable hour and on production, if required, of his credentials exercise any of the powers conferred by the following provisions of this regulation.

(2) The officer may, for the purposes of ascertaining whether there has been a contravention of a requirement imposed by or under these Regulations, enter any premises other than premises occupied only as a person's residence and inspect any record or product.

(3) The officer may, for the purpose of ascertaining whether there has been a contravention of a requirement imposed by or under these Regulations, examine any procedure (including any arrangements for carrying out a test) connected with the production of a product.

(4) If the officer has reasonable grounds for suspecting that the product has not been placed on the market or supplied in the United Kingdom since it was manufactured or imported he may for the purpose of ascertaining whether there has been a contravention in relation to the product of a requirement imposed by or under these Regulations—

(a) require a person carrying on a commercial activity, or employed in connection with a commercial activity, to supply all necessary information relating to the activity, including by the production of records,

(b) require any record which is stored in an electronic form and is accessible from the premises to be produced in a form —

(i) in which it can be taken away, and

(ii) in which it is visible and legible.

(c) for the purpose of ascertaining (by testing or otherwise) whether there has been any such contravention, seize and detain samples of the product,

(d) take copies of, or of an entry in, any records produced by virtue of sub-paragraph (a).

(5) If the officer has reasonable grounds for suspecting that there has been a contravention in relation to a product of a requirement imposed by or under these Regulations, he may—

    (a) for the purpose of ascertaining whether there has been any such contravention, require a person carrying on a commercial activity, or employed in connection with a commercial activity, to supply all necessary information relating to the activity, including by the production of records,

    (b) for the purpose of ascertaining whether there has been any such contravention, require any record which is stored in an electronic form and is accessible from the premises to be produced in a form—

        (i) in which it can be taken away, and

        (ii) in which it is visible and legible,

    (c) for the purpose of ascertaining (by testing or otherwise) whether there has been any such contravention, seize and detain samples of the product,

    (d) take copies of, or of an entry in, any records produced by virtue of sub-paragraph (a).

  (6) The officer may seize and detain any products or records which he has reasonable grounds for believing may be required as evidence in proceedings for an offence in respect of a contravention of any requirement imposed by or under these Regulations.

  (7) If and to the extent that it is reasonably necessary to do so to prevent a contravention of any requirement imposed by or under these Regulations, the officer may, for the purpose of exercising his power under paragraphs (4) to (6) to seize products or records—

    (a) require any person having authority to do so to open any container or to open any vending machine; and

    (b) himself open or break open any such container or machine where a requirement made under sub-paragraph (a) in relation to the container or machine has not been complied with.

23. Provisions supplemental to regulation 22—and search warrants etc.

  (1) An officer seizing any products or records shall, before he leaves the premises, provide to the person from whom they were seized a written notice—

    (a) specifying the products (including the quantity thereof) and records seized,

    (b) stating the reasons for their seizure, and

    (c) explaining the right of appeal under regulation 25.

  (2) References in paragraph (1) and regulation 25 to the person from whom something has been seized, in relation to a case in which the power of seizure was exercisable by reason of the product having been found on any premises, are references to the occupier of the premises at the time of the seizure.

  (3) If a justice of the peace—

    (a) is satisfied by written information on oath that there are reasonable grounds for believing either—

        (i) that any products or records which an officer has power to inspect under regulation 22 are on any premises and that their inspection is likely to disclose evidence that there has been a contravention of any requirement imposed by or under these Regulations, or

        (ii) that such a contravention has taken place, is taking place or is about to take place on any premises, and

    (b) is also satisfied by such information either—

        (i) that admission to the premises has been or is likely to be refused and that notice of the intention to apply for a warrant under this paragraph has been given to the occupier, or

        (ii) that an application for admission, or the giving of such a notice, would defeat the object of the entry or that the premises are unoccupied or that the occupier is temporarily absent and it might defeat the object of the entry to await his return.

    the justice may by warrant under his hand, which shall continue in force for a period of one month, authorise any officer of an enforcement authority to enter the premises, if need be by force.

(4) An officer entering premises by virtue of regulation 22 or a warrant under paragraph (3) may take him such other persons and equipment as may appear to him necessary.

(5) On leaving any premises which a person is authorised to enter by a warrant under paragraph (3), that person shall, if the premises are unoccupied or the occupier is temporarily absent—

  (a) leave the premises as effectively secured against trespassers as he found them,
  (b) attach a notice such as is mentioned in paragraph (1) in a prominent place at the premises.

(6) Where a product seized by an officer of an enforcement authority under regulation 22 or 23 is submitted to a test, the authority shall inform the person mentioned in paragraph (1) of the result of the test and, if—

  (a) proceedings are brought for an offence in respect of a contravention in relation to the product of any requirement imposed by or under these Regulations or for the forfeiture of the product under regulation 18 or 19; or
  (b) a safety notice is served in respect of the product; and
  (c) the authority is requested to do so and it is practicable for him to comply with the request,

then the authority shall allow a person who is a party to the proceedings or, on whom the notice was served or who has an interest in the product to which the notice relates to have the product tested.

(7) If a person who is not an officer of an enforcement authority purports to act as such under regulation 22 or under this regulation he shall be guilty of an offence and liable on summary conviction to a fine not exceeding level 5 on the standard scale.

24. Obstruction of officers

(1) A person who—

  (a) intentionally obstructs an officer of an enforcement authority who is acting in pursuance of any provision of regulations 22 or 23; or
  (b) intentionally fails to comply with a requirement made of him by an officer of an enforcement authority under any provision of those regulations; or
  (c) without reasonable cause fails to give an officer of an enforcement authority who is so acting any other assistance or information which the officer may reasonably require of him for the purposes of the exercise of the officer's functions under any provision of those regulations,

shall be guilty of an offence and liable on summary conviction to a fine not exceeding level 5 on the standard scale.

(2) A person shall be guilty of an offence if, in giving any information which is required by him by virtue of paragraph (1)(c)—

  (a) he makes a statement which he knows is false in a material particular; or
  (b) he recklessly makes a statement which is false in a material particular.

(3) A person guilty of an offence under paragraph (2) shall be liable—

  (a) on conviction on indictment, to a fine;
  (b) on summary conviction, to a fine not exceeding the statutory maximum.

25. Appeals against detention of products and records

(1) A person referred to in regulation 23(1) may apply for an order requiring any product or record which is for the time being detained under regulation 22 or 23 by an enforcement authority or by an officer of such an authority to be released to him or to another person.

(2) An application under the preceding paragraph may be made—

  (a) to any magistrates' court in which proceedings have been brought in England and Wales or Northern Ireland—
    (i) for an offence in respect of a contravention in relation to the product of a requirement imposed by or under these Regulation, or
    (ii) for the forfeiture of the product under regulation 18,
  (b) where no such proceedings have been brought, by way of complaint to a magistrates' court;
  (c) in Scotland, by summary application to the sheriff.

(3) On an application under paragraph (1) to a magistrates' court or to the sheriff, the court or the sheriff may make an order requiring a product or record to be released only if the court or sheriff is satisfied—

    (a) that proceedings

        (i) for an offence in respect of any contravention in relation to the product or, in the case of a record, the product to which the record relates, of any requirement imposed by or under these Regulations; or

        (ii) for the forfeiture of the product or, in the case of a record, the product to which the record relate, under regulation 18 or 19,

        have not been brought or, having been brought, have been concluded without the product being forfeited; and

    (b) where no such proceedings have been brought, that more than six months have elapsed since the product or records was seized.

(4) In determining whether to make an order under this regulation requiring the release of a product or record the court or sheriff shall take all the circumstances into account including the results of any tests on the product which have been carried out by or on behalf of the enforcement authority and any statement made by the enforcement authority to the court or sheriff as to its intention to bring proceedings for an offence in respect of a contravention in relation to the product of any requirement imposed by or under these Regulations.

(5) Where—

    (a) more than 12 months have elapsed since a product or records were seized and the enforcement authority has not commenced proceedings for an offence in respect of a contravention in relation to the product (or, in the case of records, the product to which the records relate) of any requirement imposed by or under these Regulations or for the forfeiture of the product under regulation 18 or 19, or

    (b) an enforcement authority has brought proceedings for an offence as mentioned in sub-paragraph (a) and the proceedings were dismissed and all rights of appeal have been exercised or the time for appealing has expired,

the authority shall be under a duty to return the product or records detained under regulation 22 or 23 to the person from whom they were seized.

(6) Where the authority is satisfied that some other person has a better right to a product or record than the person from whom they were seized, the authority shall, instead of the duty in paragraph (5), be under a duty to return it to that other person or, as the case may be, to the person appearing to the authority to have the best right to the product or record in question.

(7) Where different persons claim to be entitled to the return of a product or record that is required to be returned under paragraph (5), then it may be retained for as long as it reasonably necessary for the determination in accordance with paragraph (6) of the person to whom it must be returned.

(8) A person aggrieved by an order made under this regulation by a magistrates' court in England and Wales or Northern Ireland, or by a decision of such a court not to make such an order, may appeal against that order or decision—

    (a) in England and Wales, to the Crown Court;

    (b) in Northern Ireland, to the county court;

and an order so made may contain such provision as appears to the court to be appropriate for delaying the coming into force of the order pending the making and determination of any appeal (including any application under section 111 of the Magistrates' Courts Act 1980 or article 146 of the Magistrates' Courts (Northern Ireland) Order 1981 (statement of case)).

26. Compensation for seizure and detention

Where an officer of an enforcement authority exercises any power under regulation 22 or 23 to seize and detain a product, the enforcement authority shall be liable to pay compensation to any person having an interest in the product in respect of any loss or damage caused by reason of the exercise of the power if—

    (a) there has been no contravention in relation to the product of any requirement imposed by or under these Regulations, and

    (b) the exercise of the power is not attributable to any neglect or default by that person.

27. Recovery of expenses of enforcement

    (1) This regulation shall apply where a court—

        (a) convicts a person of an offence in respect of a contravention in relation to a product of any requirement imposed by or under these Regulations, or

        (b) makes an order under regulation 18 or 19 for the forfeiture of a product.

    (2) The court may (in addition to any other order it may make as to costs or expenses) order the person convicted or, as the case may be, any person having an interest in the product to reimburse an enforcement authority for any expenditure which has been or may be incurred by that authority—

        (a) in connection with any seizure or detention of the product by or on behalf of the authority, or

        (b) in connection with any compliance by the authority with directions given by the court for the purposes of any order for the forfeiture of the product.

28. Power of Secretary of State to obtain information

    (1) If the Secretary of State considers that, for the purposes of deciding whether to serve a safety notice, or to vary or revoke a safety notice which he has already served, he requires information or a sample of a product he may serve on a person a notice requiring him:

        (a) to furnish to the Secretary of State, within a period specified in the notice, such information as is specified;

        (b) to produce such records as are specified in the notice at a time and place so specified (and to produce any such records which are stored in any electronic form in a form in which they are visible and legible) and to permit a person appointed by the Secretary of State for that purpose to take copies of the records at that time and place;

        (c) to produce such samples of a product as are specified in the notice at a time and place so specified.

    (2) A person shall be guilty of an offence if he—

        (a) fails, without reasonable cause, to comply with a notice served on him under paragraph (1); or

        (b) in purporting to comply with a requirement which by virtue of paragraph (1)(a) or (b) is contained in such a notice—

            (i) furnishes information or records which he knows are false in a material particular, or

            (ii) recklessly furnishes information or records which are false in a material particular.

    (3) A person guilty of an offence under paragraph (2) shall—

        (a) in the case of an offence under sub-paragraph (a) of that paragraph, be liable on summary conviction to a fine not exceeding level 5 on the standard scale; and

        (b) in the case of an offence under sub-paragraph (b) of that paragraph, be liable—

            (i) on conviction on indictment, to a fine;

            (ii) on summary conviction, to a fine not exceeding the statutory maximum.

29. Defence of due diligence

    (1) Subject to the following provisions of this regulation, in proceedings against a person for an offence under these Regulations it shall be a defence for that person to show that he took all reasonable steps and exercised all due diligence to avoid committing the offence.

    (2) Where in any proceedings against any person for such an offence the defence provided by paragraph (1) involves an allegation that the commission of the offence was due—

(a) to the act or default of another, or

(b) to reliance on information given by another,

that person shall not, without the leave of the court, be entitled to rely on the defence unless, not less than seven clear days before, in England, Wales and Northern Ireland, the hearing of the proceedings or, in Scotland, the trial diet, he has served a notice under paragraph (3) on the person bringing the proceedings.

(3) A notice under this paragraph shall give such information identifying or assisting in the identification of the person who—

(a) committed the act or default, or

(b) gave the information,

as is in the possession of the person serving the notice at the time he serves it.

(4) A person may not rely on the defence provided by paragraph (1) by reason of his reliance on information supplied by another, unless he shows that it was reasonable in all the circumstances to have relied on the information, having regard in particular—

(a) to the steps which he took, and those which might reasonably have been taken, for the purpose of verifying the information; and

(b) to whether he had any reason to disbelieve the information.

30. Defence in relation to antiques

(1) This regulation shall apply in proceedings against any person for an offence under regulation 20(1) in respect of the supply, offer or agreement to supply or exposure or possession for supply of second hand products supplied as antiques.

(2) It shall be a defence for that person to show that the terms on which he supplied the product or agreed or offered to supply the product or, in the case of a product which he exposed or possessed for supply, the terms on which he intended to supply the product, contemplated the acquisition of an interest in the product by the person supplied or to be supplied.

(3) Paragraph (2) applies only if the producer or distributor clearly informed the person to whom he supplied the product, or offered or agreed to supply the product or, in the case of a product which he exposed or possessed for supply, he intended to so inform that person, that the product is an antique.

31. Liability of person other than principal offender

(1) Where the commission by a person of an offence under these Regulations is due to an act or default committed by some other person in the course of a commercial activity of his, the other person shall be guilty of the offence and may be proceeded against and punished by virtue of this paragraph whether or not proceedings are taken against the first-mentioned person.

(2) Where a body corporate is guilty of an offence under these Regulations (including where it is so guilty by virtue of paragraph (1)) in respect of any act or default which is shown to have been committed with the consent or connivance of, or to be attributable to any neglect on the part of, any director, manager, secretary or other similar officer of the body corporate or any person who was purporting to act in any such capacity he, as well as the body corporate, shall be guilty of that offence and shall be liable to be proceeded against and punished accordingly.

(3) Where the affairs of a body corporate are managed by its members, paragraph (2) shall apply in relation to the acts and defaults of a member in connection with his functions of management as if he were a director of the body corporate.

(4) Where a Scottish partnership is guilty of an offence under these Regulations (including where it is so guilty by virtue of paragraph (1)) in respect of any act or default which is shown to have been committed with the consent or connivance of, or to be attributable to any neglect on the part of, a partner in the partnership, he, as well as the partnership, shall be guilty of that offence and shall be liable to be proceeded against and punished accordingly.

PART 4 MISCELLANEOUS

32. Reports

(1) It shall be the duty of the Secretary of State to lay before each House of Parliament a report on the exercise during the period to which the report relates of the functions which are exercisable by enforcement authorities under these Regulations.

(2) The first such report shall relate to the period beginning on the day on which these Regulations come into force and ending on 31 March 2008 and subsequent reports shall relate to a period of not more than five years beginning on the day after the day on which the period to which the previous report relates ends.

(3) The Secretary of State may from time to time prepare and lay before each House of Parliament such other reports on the exercise of those functions as he considers appropriate.

(4) The Secretary of State may direct an enforcement authority to report at such intervals as he may specify in the direction on the discharge by that authority of the functions exercisable by it under these Regulations.

(5) A report under paragraph (4) shall be in such form and shall contain such particulars as are specified in the direction of the Secretary of State.

33. Duty to notify Secretary of State and Commission

(1) An enforcement authority which has received a notification under regulation 9(1) shall immediately pass the same on to the Secretary of State, who shall immediately pass it on to the competent authorities appointed for the purpose in the Member States where the product in question is or has been marketed or otherwise supplied to consumers.

(2) Where an enforcement authority takes a measure which restricts the placing on the market of a product, or requires its withdrawal or recall, it shall immediately notify the Secretary of State, specifying its reasons for taking the action. It shall also immediately notify the Secretary of State of any modification or lifting of such a measure.

(3) On receiving a notification under paragraph (2), or if he takes a measure which restricts the placing on the market of a product, or requires its withdrawal or recall, the Secretary of State shall (to the extent that such notification is not required under article 12 of the GPS Directive or any other [EU] legislation) immediately notify the European Commission of the measure taken, specifying the reasons for taking it. The Secretary of State shall also immediately notify the European Commission of any modification or lifting of such a measure. If the Secretary of State considers that the effects of the risk do not or cannot go beyond the territory of the United Kingdom, he shall notify the European Commission of the measure concerned insofar as it involves information likely to be of interest to Member States from the product safety standpoint, and in particular if it is in response to a new risk which has not yet been reported in other notifications.

(4) Where an enforcement authority adopts or decides to adopt, recommend or agree with producers and distributors, whether on a compulsory or voluntary basis, a measure or action to prevent, restrict or impose specific conditions on the possible marketing or use of a product (other than a pharmaceutical product) by reason of a serious risk, it shall immediately notify the Secretary of State. It shall also immediately notify the Secretary of State of any modification or withdrawal of any such measure or action.

(5) On receiving a notification under paragraph (4), or if he adopts or decides to adopt, recommend or agree with producers and distributors, whether on a compulsory or voluntary basis, a measure or action to prevent, restrict or impose specific conditions on the possible marketing or use of a product (other than a pharmaceutical product) by reason of a serious risk, the Secretary of State shall immediately notify the European Commission of it through the Community Rapid Information System, known as RAPEX. The Secretary of State shall also inform the European Commission without delay of any modification or withdrawal of any such measure or action.

(6) If the Secretary of State considers that the effects of the risk do not or cannot go beyond the territory of the United Kingdom, he shall notify the European Commission of the measures or

action concerned insofar as they involve information likely to be of interest to Member States of the European Union from the product safety standpoint, and in particular if they are in response to a new risk which has not been reported in other notifications.

(7) Before deciding to adopt such a measure or take such an action as is referred to in paragraph (5), the Secretary of State may pass on to the European Commission any information in his possession regarding the existence of a serious risk. Where he does so, he must inform the European Commission, within 45 days of the day of passing the information to it, whether he confirms or modifies that information.

(8) Upon receipt of a notification from the European Commission under article 12(2) of the GPS Directive, the Secretary of State shall notify the Commission of the following—

(a) whether the product the subject of the notification has been marketed in the United Kingdom;

(b) what measure concerning the product the enforcement authorities in the United Kingdom may be adopting, stating the reasons, including any differing assessment of risk or any other special circumstance justifying the decision as to the measure, in particular lack of action or follow-up; and

(c) any relevant supplementary information he has obtained on the risk involved, including the results of any test or analysis carried out.

(9) The Secretary of State shall notify the European Commission without delay of any modification or withdrawal of any measures notified to it under paragraph (8)(b).

(10) In this regulation—

(a) references to a product excludes a second hand product supplied as an antique or as a product to be repaired or reconditioned prior to being used, provided the supplier clearly informs the person to whom he supplies the product to that effect;

(b) 'pharmaceutical product' means a product falling within Council Directive 2001/83/EC of the European Parliament and of the Council on the Community code relating to medicinal products for human use [as amended by Directive 2002/98/EC of the European Parliament and of the Council setting standards of quality and safety for the collection, testing, processing, storage and distribution of human blood and blood components, Commission Directive 2003/63/EC amending Directive 2001/83/EC on the Community code relating to medicinal products for human use, Directive 2004/24/EC of the European Parliament and of the Council amending, as regards traditional herbal medicinal products, Directive 2001/83/EC on the Community code relating to medicinal products for human use and Directive 2004/27/EC of the European Parliament and of the Council amending Directive 2001/83/EC on the Community code relating to medicinal products for human use].

34. Provisions supplemental to regulation 33

(1) A notification under regulation 33(2) to (6), (8) or (9) to the Secretary of State or the Commission shall be in writing and shall provide all available details and at least the following information—

(a) information enabling the product to be identified,

(b) a description of the risk involved, including a summary of the results of any test or analysis and of their conclusions which are relevant to assessing the level of risk,

(c) the nature and the duration of the measures or action taken or decided on, if applicable,

(d) information on supply chains and distribution of the product, in particular on destination countries.

(2) Where a measure notified to the Commission under regulation 33 seeks to limit the marketing or use of a chemical substance or preparation, the Secretary of State shall provide to the Commission as soon as possible either a summary or the references of the relevant data relating to the substance or preparation considered and to known and available substitutes, where such information is available. The Secretary of State shall also notify the Commission of the anticipated effects of the measure on consumer health and safety together with the assessment of the risk carried out in accordance with the general principles for the risk evaluation of chemical substances as referred

to in article 10(4) of Council Regulation (EEC) No. 793/93 of 23 March 1993 on the evaluation and control of the risks of existing substances, in the case of an existing substance, or in article 3(2) of Council Directive 67/548/EEC on the approximation of laws, regulations and administrative provisions relating to the classification, packaging and labelling of dangerous substances in the case of a new substance.

(3) Where the Commission carries out an investigation under paragraph 5 of Annex II to the GPS Directive, the Secretary of State shall supply the Commission with such information as it requests, to the best of his ability.

35. Implementation of Commission decisions

(1) This regulation applies where the Commission adopts a decision pursuant to article 13 of the GPS Directive.

(2) The Secretary of State shall—

    (a) take such action under these Regulations, or

    (b) direct another enforcement authority to take such action under these Regulations as is necessary to comply with the decision.

(3) Where an enforcement authority serves a safety notice pursuant to paragraph (2), the following provisions of these Regulations shall not apply in relation to that notice, namely regulations 14(3), 15(4) to (6) and 16(1), 16(2)(c) and (d), 16(5) to (7) and 17.

(4) Unless the Commission's decision provides otherwise, export from the Community of a dangerous product which is the subject of such a decision is prohibited with effect from the date the decision comes into force.

(5) The enforcement of the prohibition in paragraph (4) shall be treated as an assigned matter within the meaning of section 1(1) of the Customs and Excise Management Act 1979.

(6) The measures necessary to implement the decision shall be taken within 20 days, unless the decision specifies a different period.

(7) The Secretary of State or, where the Secretary of State has directed another enforcement authority to take action under paragraph (2)(b), that enforcement authority shall, within one month, give the parties concerned an opportunity to submit their views and shall inform the Commission accordingly.

36. Market surveillance

In order to ensure a high level of consumer health and safety protection, enforcement authorities shall within the limits of their responsibility and to the extent of their ability undertake market surveillance of products employing appropriate means and procedures and co-operating with other enforcement authorities and competent authorities of other Member States which may include:

    (a) establishment, periodical updating and implementation of sectoral surveillance programmes by categories of products or risks and the monitoring of surveillance activities, findings and results,

    (b) follow-up and updating of scientific and technical knowledge concerning the safety of products,

    (c) the periodical review and assessment of the functioning of the control activities and their effectiveness and, if necessary revision of the surveillance approach and organisation put in place.

37. Complaints procedures

An enforcement authority shall maintain and publish a procedure by which complaints may be submitted by any person on product safety and on surveillance and control activities, which complaints shall be followed up as appropriate.

38. Co-operation between enforcement authorities

(1) It shall be the duty of an enforcement authority to co-operate with other enforcement authorities in carrying out the functions conferred on them by these Regulations. In particular—

(a) enforcement authorities shall share their expertise and best practices with each other;

(b) enforcement authorities shall undertake collaborative working where they have a shared interest.

(2) The Secretary of State shall inform the European Commission as to the arrangements for the enforcement of these Regulations, including which bodies are enforcement authorities.

39. Information

(1) An enforcement authority shall in general make available to the public such information as is available to it on the following matters relating to the risks to consumer health and safety posed by a product—

(a) the nature of the risk,

(b) the product identification,

and the measures taken in respect of the risk, without prejudice to the need not to disclose information for effective monitoring and investigation activities.

(2) Paragraph (1) shall not apply to any information obtained by an enforcement authority for the purposes of these Regulations which, by its nature, is covered by professional secrecy, unless the circumstances require such information to be made public in order to protect the health and safety of consumers.

40. Service of documents

(1) A document required or authorised by virtue of these Regulations to be served on a person may be so served—

(a) on an individual by delivering it to him or by leaving it at his proper address or by sending it by post to him at that address;

(b) on a body corporate other than a limited liability partnership, by serving it in accordance with sub-paragraph (a) on the secretary of the body;

(c) on a limited liability partnership, by serving it in accordance with sub-paragraph (a) on a member of the partnership; or

(d) on a partnership, by serving it in accordance with sub-paragraph (a) on a partner or a person having the control or management of the partnership business;

(e) on any other person by leaving it at his proper address or by sending it by post to him at that address.

(2) For the purposes of paragraph (1), and for the purposes of section 7 of the Interpretation Act 1978 (which relates to the service of documents by post) in its application to that paragraph, the proper address of a person on whom a document is to be served by virtue of these Regulations shall be his last known address except that—

(a) in the case of a body corporate (other than a limited liability partnership) or its secretary, it shall be the address of the registered or principal office of the body;

(b) in the case of a limited liability partnership or a member of the partnership, it shall be the address of the registered or principal office of the partnership;

(c) in the case of a partnership or a partner or a person having the control or management of a partnership business, it shall be the address of the principal office of the partnership,

and for the purposes of this paragraph the principal officer of a company constituted under the law of a country or territory outside the United Kingdom or of a partnership carrying on business outside the United Kingdom is its principal office within the United Kingdom.

(3) A document required or authorised by virtue of these Regulations to be served on a person may also be served by transmitting the request by any means of electronic communication to an electronic address (which includes a fax number and an e-mail address) being an address which the person has held out as an address at which he or it can be contacted for the purposes of receiving such documents.

(4) A document transmitted by any means of electronic communication in accordance with the preceding paragraph is, unless the contrary is proved, deemed to be received on the business day after the notice was transmitted over a public electronic communications network.

41. Extension of time for bringing summary proceedings

(1) Notwithstanding section 127 of the Magistrates' Courts Act 1980 or article 19 of the Magistrates' Courts (Northern Ireland) Order 1981, in England, Wales and Northern Ireland a magistrates' court may try an information (in the case of England and Wales) or a complaint (in the case of Northern Ireland) in respect of an offence under these Regulations if (in the case of England and Wales) the information is laid or (in the case of Northern Ireland) the complaint is made within three years from the date of the offence or within one year from the discovery of the offence by the prosecutor whichever is the earlier.

(2) Notwithstanding section 136 of the Criminal Procedure (Scotland) Act 1995, in Scotland summary proceedings for an offence under these Regulations may be commenced within three years from the date of the offence or within one year from the discovery of the offence by the prosecutor whichever is the earlier.

(3) For the purposes of paragraph (2), section 136(3) of the Criminal Procedure (Scotland) Act 1995 shall apply as it applies for the purposes of that section.

42. Civil proceedings

These Regulations shall not be construed as conferring any right of action in civil proceedings in respect of any loss or damage suffered in consequence of a contravention of these Regulations.

43. Privileged information

(1) Nothing in these Regulations shall be taken as requiring a person to produce any records if he would be entitled to refuse to produce those records in any proceedings in any court on the grounds that they are the subject of legal professional privilege or, in Scotland, that they contain a confidential communication made by or to an advocate or solicitor in that capacity, or as authorising a person to take possession of any records which are in the possession of a person who would be so entitled.

(2) Nothing in these Regulations shall be construed as requiring a person to answer any question or give any information if to do so would incriminate that person or that person's spouse or civil partner.

44. Evidence in proceedings for offence relating to regulation 9(1)

(1) This regulation applies where a person has given a notification to an enforcement authority pursuant to regulation 9(1).

(2) No evidence relating to that statement may be adduced and no question relating to it may be asked by the prosecution in any criminal proceedings (other than proceedings in which that person is charged with an offence under regulation 20 for a contravention of regulation 9(1)), unless evidence relating to it is adduced, or a question relating to it is asked, in the proceedings by or on behalf of that person.

Business Protection from Misleading Marketing Regulations 2008

(SI 2008, No. 1276)

[Implementing Directive 2006/114/EC of the European Parliament and of the Council concerning misleading and comparative advertising [2006] OJ L376/21.]

2. Interpretation

(1) In these Regulations—

'advertising' means any form of representation which is made in connection with a trade, business, craft or profession in order to promote the supply or transfer of a product and 'advertiser' shall be construed accordingly;

'code owner' means a trader or a body responsible for—

(a) the formulation and revision of a code of conduct; or

(b) monitoring compliance with the code by those who have undertaken to be bound by it;

'comparative advertising' means advertising which in any way, either explicitly or by implication, identifies a competitor or a product offered by a competitor;

'court', in relation to England and Wales and Northern Ireland, means a county court or the High Court, and, in relation to Scotland, the sheriff or the Court of Session;

'enforcement authority' means the OFT, every local weights and measures authority in Great Britain (within the meaning of section 69 of the Weights and Measure Act 1985) and the Department of Enterprise, Trade and Investment in Northern Ireland;

'goods' includes ships, aircraft, animals, things attached to land and growing crops;

'OFT' means the Office of Fair Trading;

'premises' includes any place and any stall, vehicle, ship or aircraft;

'product' means any goods or services and includes immovable property, rights and obligations;

'ship' includes any boat and any other description of vessel used in navigation; and

'trader' means any person who is acting for purposes relating to his trade, craft, business or profession and anyone acting in the name of or on behalf of a trader.

(2) In the application of these Regulations to Scotland for references to an 'injunction' or an 'interim injunction' there shall be substituted references to an 'interdict' or an 'interim interdict' respectively.

3.   Prohibition of advertising which misleads traders

(1) Advertising which is misleading is prohibited.

(2) Advertising is misleading which—

(a) in any way, including its presentation, deceives or is likely to deceive the traders to whom it is addressed or whom it reaches; and by reason of its deceptive nature, is likely to affect their economic behaviour; or

(b) for those reasons, injures or is likely to injure a competitor.

(3) In determining whether advertising is misleading, account shall be taken of all its features, and in particular of any information it contains concerning—

(a) the characteristics of the product (as defined in paragraph (4));

(b) the price or manner in which the price is calculated;

(c) the conditions on which the product is supplied or provided; and

(d) the nature, attributes and rights of the advertiser (as defined in paragraph (5)).

(4) In paragraph (3)(a) the 'characteristics of the product' include—

(a) availability of the product;

(b) nature of the product;

(c) execution of the product;

(d) composition of the product;

(e) method and date of manufacture of the product;

(f) method and date of provision of the product;

(g) fitness for purpose of the product;

(h) uses of the product;

(i) quantity of the product;

(j) specification of the product;

(k) geographical or commercial origin of the product;

(l) results to be expected from use of the product; or

(m) results and material features of tests or checks carried out on the product.

(5) In paragraph (3)(d) the 'nature, attributes and rights' of the advertiser include the advertiser's—

(a) identity;

    (b) assets;

    (c) qualifications;

    (d) ownership of industrial, commercial or intellectual property rights; or

    (e) awards and distinctions.

4. Comparative advertising

Comparative advertising shall, as far as the comparison is concerned, be permitted only when the following conditions are met—

    (a) it is not misleading under regulation 3;

    (b) it is not a misleading action under regulation 5 of the Consumer Protection from Unfair Trading Regulations 2008 or a misleading omission under regulation 6 of those Regulations;

    (c) it compares products meeting the same needs or intended for the same purpose;

    (d) it objectively compares one or more material, relevant, verifiable and representative features of those products, which may include price;

    (e) it does not create confusion among traders—

        (i) between the advertiser and a competitor, or

        (ii) between the trade marks, trade names, other distinguishing marks or products of the advertiser and those of a competitor;

    (f) it does not discredit or denigrate the trade marks, trade names, other distinguishing marks, products, activities, or circumstances of a competitor;

    (g) for products with designation of origin, it relates in each case to products with the same designation;

    (h) it does not take unfair advantage of the reputation of a trade mark, trade name or other distinguishing marks of a competitor or of the designation of origin of competing products;

    (i) it does not present products as imitations or replicas of products bearing a protected trade mark or trade name.

5. Promotion of misleading advertising and comparative advertising which is not permitted

A code owner shall not promote in a code of conduct—

    (a) advertising which is misleading under regulation 3; or

    (b) comparative advertising which is not permitted under regulation 4.

6. Misleading advertising

A trader is guilty of an offence if he engages in advertising which is misleading under regulation 3.

7. Penalty for offence under regulation 6

A person guilty of an offence under regulation 6 shall be liable—

    (a) on summary conviction, to a fine not exceeding the statutory maximum; or

    (b) on conviction on indictment, to a fine or imprisonment for a term not exceeding two years or both.

8. Offences committed by bodies of persons

    (1) Where an offence under these Regulations committed by a body corporate is proved—

        (a) to have been committed with the consent or connivance of an officer of the body, or

        (b) to be attributable to any neglect on his part,

the officer as well as the body corporate is guilty of the offence and liable to be proceeded against and punished accordingly.

    (2) In paragraph (1) a reference to an officer of a body corporate includes a reference to—

        (a) a director, manager, secretary or other similar officer; and

        (b) a person purporting to act as a director, manager, secretary or other similar officer.

    (3) Where an offence under these Regulations committed by a Scottish partnership is proved—

(a) to have been committed with the consent or connivance of a partner, or

(b) to be attributable to any neglect on his part,

the partner as well as the partnership is guilty of the offence and liable to be proceeded against and punished accordingly.

(4) In paragraph (3) a reference to a partner includes a person purporting to act as a partner.

9. Offence due to the default of another person

(1) This regulation applies where a person 'X'—

(a) commits an offence under regulation 6, or

(b) would have committed an offence under regulation 6 but for a defence under regulation 11 or 12,

and the commission of the offence, or of what would have been an offence but for X being able to rely on a defence under regulations 11 or 12, is due to the act or default of some other person 'Y'.

(2) Where this regulation applies Y shall be guilty of the offence subject to regulations 11 and 12 whether or not Y is a trader and whether or not Y's act or default is advertising.

(3) Y may be charged with and convicted of the offence by virtue of paragraph (2) whether or not proceedings are taken against X.

10. Time limit for prosecution

(1) No proceedings for an offence under these Regulations shall be commenced after—

(a) the end of the period of three years beginning with the date of the commission of the offence; or

(b) the end of the period of one year beginning with the date of discovery of the offence by the prosecutor,

whichever is earlier.

11. Due diligence defence

(1) In any proceedings against a person for an offence under regulation 6 it is a defence for that person to prove—

(a) that the commission of the offence was due to—

(i) a mistake;

(ii) reliance on information supplied to him by another person;

(iii) the act or default of another person;

(iv) an accident; or

(v) another cause beyond his control; and

(b) that he took all reasonable precautions and exercised all due diligence to avoid the commission of such an offence by himself or any person under his control.

(2) A person shall not be entitled to rely on the defence provided by paragraph (1) by reason of the matters referred to in paragraph (ii) or (iii) of paragraph (1)(a) without the leave of the court unless—

(a) he has served on the prosecutor a notice in writing giving such information identifying or assisting in the identification of that other person as was in his possession; and

(b) the notice is served on the prosecutor at least seven clear days before the date of the hearing.

12. Innocent publication defence

In any proceedings against a person for an offence under regulation 6 committed by the publication of advertising it is a defence for that person to prove that—

(a) he is a person whose business it is to publish or to arrange for the publication of advertising;

(b) he received the advertising for publication in the ordinary course of business; and

(c) he did not know and had no reason to suspect that its publication would amount to an offence under regulation 6.

PART 3

ENFORCEMENT

13.   Duty to enforce

(4) In determining how to comply with its duty of enforcement every enforcement authority shall have regard to the desirability of encouraging control of advertising which is misleading under regulation 3 and comparative advertising which is not permitted under regulation 4 by such established means as it considers appropriate having regard to all the circumstances of the particular case.

14.   Notice to OFT of intended prosecution

(1) Where an enforcement authority is a local weights and measures authority in England and Wales it may bring proceedings for an offence under regulation 6 only if—

    (a) it has notified the OFT of its intention to bring proceedings at least fourteen days before the date on which proceedings are brought; or

    (b) the OFT consents to proceedings being brought in a shorter period.

(2) The enforcement authority must also notify the OFT of the outcome of the proceedings after they are finally determined.

(3) Such proceedings are not invalid by reason only of the failure to comply with this regulation.

15.   Injunctions to secure compliance with the Regulations

(1) This regulation applies where an enforcement authority considers that there has been or is likely to be a breach of regulation 3, 4 or 5.

(2) Where this regulation applies an enforcement authority may, subject to paragraph (3), if it thinks it appropriate to do so, bring proceedings for an injunction (in which proceedings it may also apply for an interim injunction) against any person appearing to it to be concerned or likely to be concerned with the breach.

(3) Where the enforcement authority is a local weights and measures authority in Great Britain it may apply for an injunction only if—

    (a) it has notified the OFT of its intention to apply for an injunction at least fourteen days before the date on which the application is made; or

    (b) the OFT consents to the application for an injunction being made within a shorter period.

(4) Proceedings referred to in paragraph (2) are not invalid by reason only of the failure to comply with paragraph (3).

16.   Undertakings

Where an enforcement authority considers that there has been or is likely to be a breach of regulation 3, 4 or 5 it may accept from the person concerned or likely to be concerned with the breach an undertaking that he will comply with those regulations.

17.   Co-ordination

(1) If more than one local weights and measures authority in Great Britain is contemplating bringing proceedings under regulation 15 in any particular case, the OFT may direct which enforcement authority is to bring the proceedings or decide that only it may do so.

(2) Where the OFT directs that only it may bring such proceedings it may take into account whether compliance with regulation 3, 4 or 5 could be achieved by other means in deciding whether to bring proceedings.

18.   Powers of the court

(1) The court on an application by an enforcement authority may grant an injunction on such terms as it may think fit to secure compliance with regulation 3, 4 or 5.

(2) Before granting an injunction the court shall have regard to all the interests involved and in particular the public interest.

(3) An injunction may relate not only to particular advertising but to any advertising in similar terms or likely to convey a similar impression.

(4) The court may also require any person against whom an injunction (other than an interim injunction) is granted to publish in such form and manner and to such extent as the court thinks appropriate for the purpose of eliminating any continuing effects of the advertising—

    (a) the injunction; and

    (b) a corrective statement.

(5) In considering an application for an injunction the court may require the person named in the application to provide evidence as to the accuracy of any factual claim made as part of the advertising of that person if, taking into account the legitimate interests of that person and any other party to the proceedings, it appears appropriate in the circumstances.

(6) If, having been required under paragraph (5) to provide evidence as to the accuracy of a factual claim, a person—

    (a) fails to provide such evidence, or

    (b) provides evidence as to the accuracy of the factual claim that the court considers inadequate,

the court may consider that the factual claim is inaccurate.

(7) The court may grant an injunction even where there is no evidence of proof of actual loss or damage or of intention or negligence on the part of the advertiser.

19.   Notifications of undertakings and orders to the OFT

An enforcement authority, other than the OFT, shall notify the OFT—

    (a) of any undertaking given to it under regulation 16;

    (b) of the outcome of any application made by it under regulation 15 and the terms of any order made by the court; and

    (c) of the outcome of any application made by it to enforce a previous order of the court.

20.   Publication, information and advice

(1) The OFT must arrange for the publication, in such form and manner as it considers appropriate, of—

    (a) details of any undertaking or order notified to it under regulation 19;

    (b) details of any undertaking given to it under regulation 16;

    (c) details of any application made by it under regulation 15 and of the terms of any undertaking given to, or order made by, the court;

    (d) details of any application made by it to enforce a previous order of the court.

(2) The OFT may arrange for the dissemination, in such form and manner as it considers appropriate, of such information and advice concerning the operation of these Regulations as appear to it to be expedient to give to the public and to all persons likely to be affected by these Regulations.

PART 4

INVESTIGATION POWERS

[21 (powers of enforcement authorities to obtain information); 22 (power to make test purchases); 23 (power of entry and investigation, etc.); 24 (power to enter premises with a warrant); 25 (obstruction of authorised officers); 26 (notice of test and intended proceedings); 27 (compensation).]

28.   Crown

(1) The powers conferred by regulations 23 and 24 are not exercisable in relation to premises occupied by the Crown.

(2) The Crown is not criminally liable as a result of any provision of these Regulations.

(3) Paragraph (2) does not affect the application of any provision of these Regulations in relation to a person in the public service of the Crown.

29. Validity of agreements
An agreement shall not be void or unenforceable by reason only of a breach of these Regulations.

Cancellation of Contracts made in a Consumer's Home or Place of Work etc. Regulations 2008

(SI 2008, No. 1816)

2. Interpretation
(1) In these Regulations:

"the 1974 Act" means the Consumer Credit Act 1974;

"cancellable agreement" has the same meaning as in section 189(1) of the 1974 Act;

"cancellation notice" means a notice in writing given by the consumer which indicates that he wishes to cancel the contract;

"cancellation period" means the period of 7 days starting with the date of receipt by the consumer of a notice of the right to cancel;

"consumer" means a natural person who in making a contract to which these Regulations apply is acting for purposes which can be regarded as outside his trade or profession;

"consumer credit agreement" means an agreement between the consumer and any other person by which the other person provides the consumer with credit of any amount;

"credit" includes a cash loan and any other form of financial accommodation, and for this purpose "cash" includes money in any form;

"enforcement authority" means any person mentioned in regulation 21;

"fixed sum credit" has the same meaning as in section 10(1) of the 1974 Act;

"notice of the right to cancel" means a notice given in accordance with regulation 7;

"related credit agreement" means a consumer credit agreement under which fixed sum credit which fully or partly covers the price under a contract which may be cancelled under regulation 7 is granted—

(i) by the trader; or

(ii) by another person, under an arrangement made between that person and the trader;

"solicited visit" has the meaning given in regulation 6(3);

"specified contract" has the meaning given in regulation 9; and

"trader" means a person who, in making a contract to which these Regulations apply, is acting in his commercial or professional capacity and anyone acting in the name or on behalf of a trader.

(2) Paragraph 8(2) of Schedule 3 has effect for the purposes of paragraphs 7 and 8(1).

Scope of application
5. These Regulations apply to a contract, including a consumer credit agreement, between a consumer and a trader which is for the supply of goods or services to the consumer by a trader and which is made—

(a) during a visit by the trader to the consumer's home or place of work, or to the home of another individual;

(b) during an excursion organised by the trader away from his business premises; or

(c) after an offer made by the consumer during such a visit or excursion.

6.—(1) These Regulations do not apply to—

(a) any contracts listed in Schedule 3 (Excepted Contracts);

(b) a cancellable agreement;

    (c) a consumer credit agreement which may be cancelled by the consumer in accordance with the terms of the agreement conferring upon him similar rights as if the agreement were a cancellable agreement; or

    [(ca) a consumer credit agreement regulated under the 1974 Act to which the right of withdrawal applies under section 66A of that Act]

    (d) a contract made during a solicited visit or a contract made after an offer made by a consumer during a solicited visit where the contract is—

        (i) a regulated mortgage, home purchase plan or home reversion plan if the making or performance of such a contract constitutes a regulated activity for the purposes of the Financial Services and Markets Act 2000;

        (ii) a consumer credit agreement secured on land which is—

            (aa) regulated under the 1974 Act; or

            (bb) to the extent that it is not regulated under the 1974 Act, exempt under that Act; or

        (iii) any other consumer credit agreement regulated under the 1974 Act.

(2) Where any agreement referred to in paragraph (1)(b), [(c), (ca) or (d)(iii)] is a related credit agreement the provisions of regulations 11 and 12 shall apply to the cancellation of that agreement.

(3) A solicited visit means a visit by a trader, whether or not he is the trader who supplies the goods or services, to a consumer's home or place of work or to the home of another individual, which is made at the express request of the consumer but does not include—

    (a) a visit by a trader which is made after he, or a person acting in his name or on his behalf—

        (i) telephones the consumer (otherwise than at the consumer's express request) and indicates during the course of the telephone call (either expressly or by implication) that he, or the trader in whose name or on whose behalf he is acting, is willing to visit the consumer; or

        (ii) visits the consumer (otherwise than at the consumer's express request) and indicates during the course of that visit (either expressly or by implication) that he, or the trader in whose name or on whose behalf he is acting, is willing to make a subsequent visit to the consumer; or

    (b) a visit during which the contract which is made relates to goods and services other than those concerning which the consumer requested the visit of the trader, provided that when the visit was requested the consumer did not know, or could not reasonably have known, that the supply of such goods or services formed part of the trader's commercial or professional activities.

7. Right to cancel a contract to which these Regulations apply

(1) A consumer has the right to cancel a contract to which these Regulations apply within the cancellation period.

(2) The trader must give the consumer a written notice of his right to cancel the contract and such notice must be given at the time the contract is made except in the case of a contract to which regulation 5(c) applies in which case the notice must be given at the time the offer is made by the consumer.

(3) The notice must—

    (a) be dated;

    (b) indicate the right of the consumer to cancel the contract within the cancellation period;

    (c) be easily legible;

    (d) contain—

        (i) the information set out in Part I of Schedule 4; and

        (ii) a cancellation form in the form set out in Part II of that Schedule provided as a detachable slip and completed by or on behalf of the trader in accordance with the notes; and

  (e) indicate if applicable—

    (i) that the consumer may be required to pay for the goods or services supplied if the performance of the contract has begun with his written agreement before the end of the cancellation period;

    (ii) that a related credit agreement will be automatically cancelled if the contract for goods or services is cancelled.

 (4) Where the contract is wholly or partly in writing the notice must be incorporated in the same document.

 (5) If incorporated in the contract or another document the notice of the right to cancel must—

  (a) be set out in a separate box with the heading "Notice of the Right to Cancel"; and

  (b) have as much prominence as any other information in the contract or document apart from the heading and the names of the parties to the contract and any information inserted in handwriting.

 (6) A contract to which these Regulations apply shall not be enforceable against the consumer unless the trader has given the consumer a notice of the right to cancel and the information required in accordance with this regulation.

8. Exercise of the right to cancel a contract

 (1) If the consumer serves a cancellation notice within the cancellation period then the contract is cancelled.

 (2) A contract which is cancelled shall be treated as if it had never been entered into by the consumer except where these Regulations provide otherwise.

 (3) The cancellation notice must indicate the intention of the consumer to cancel the contract and does not need to follow the form of cancellation notice set out in Part II of Schedule 4.

 (4) The cancellation notice must be served on the trader or another person specified in the notice of the right to cancel as a person to whom the cancellation notice may be given.

 (5) A cancellation notice sent by post is taken to have been served at the time of posting, whether or not it is actually received.

 (6) Where a cancellation notice is sent by electronic mail it is taken to have been served on the day on which it is sent.

9. Cancellation of specified contracts commenced before expiry of the right to cancel

 (1) Where the consumer enters into a specified contract and he wishes the performance of the contract to begin before the end of the cancellation period, he must request this in writing.

 (2) Where the consumer cancels a specified contract in accordance with regulation 8 he shall be under a duty to pay in accordance with the reasonable requirements of the cancelled contract for goods or services that were supplied before the cancellation.

 (3) If the consumer fails to provide the request in writing referred to in paragraph (1) then—

  (a) the trader is not obliged to begin performance of the specified contract before the end of the cancellation period; and

  (b) the consumer is not bound by the duty referred to in paragraph (2) if he cancels the contract in accordance with regulation 8.

 (4) For the purposes of this regulation and regulation 13, a "specified contact" means a contract for any of the following—

  (a) the supply of newspapers, periodicals or magazines;

  (b) advertising in any medium;

  (c) the supply of goods the price of which is dependent on fluctuations in the financial markets which cannot be controlled by the trader;

  (d) the supply of goods to meet an emergency;

  (e) the supply of goods made to a customer's specifications or clearly personalised and any services in connection with the provision of such goods;

  (f) the supply of perishable goods;

(g) the supply of goods which by their nature are consumed by use and which, before the cancellation, were so consumed;

(h) the supply of goods which, before the cancellation, had become incorporated in any land or thing not comprised in the cancelled contract;

(i) the supply of goods or services relating to a funeral; or

(j) the supply of services of any other kind.

10. Recovery of money paid by consumer

(1) On the cancellation of a contract under regulation 8 any sum paid by or on behalf of the consumer in respect of the contract shall become repayable except where these Regulations provide otherwise.

(2) If the consumer or any person on his behalf is in possession of any goods under the terms of the cancelled contract then he shall have a lien on them for any sum repayable to him under paragraph (1).

(3) Where any security has been provided in relation to the cancelled contract, the security shall be treated as never having had effect for that purpose and the trader must immediately return any property lodged with him solely as security for the purposes of the cancelled contract.

11. Automatic cancellation of related credit agreement

(1) A cancellation notice which cancels a contract for goods or services shall have the effect of cancelling any related credit agreement.

(2) Subject to paragraphs (3) and (4), where a related credit agreement has been cancelled under paragraph (1)—

(a) the trader must, if he is not the same person as the creditor under that agreement, immediately on receipt of the cancellation notice inform the creditor that the notice has been given;

(b) any sum paid by or on behalf of the consumer in relation to the credit agreement must be reimbursed, except for any sum which would have to be paid under sub-paragraph (c);

(c) the agreement shall continue in force so far as it relates to repayment of the credit and payment of interest in accordance with regulation 12, but shall otherwise cease to be enforceable; and

(d) any security provided under the related credit agreement shall be treated as never having had effect for that purpose and the creditor must immediately return any property lodged with him solely as security for the purposes of the related credit agreement.

(3) Where a related credit agreement is a cancellable agreement—

(a) its cancellation under paragraph (1) shall take effect as if a notice of cancellation within the meaning of the 1974 Act had been served;

(b) that Act shall apply in respect of the consequences of such cancellation;

(c) paragraph (2)(b) to (d) and regulation 12 shall not apply in respect of its cancellation; and

(d) regulations 13 and 14 shall not apply in respect of the cancellation of the related contract for goods or services.

(4) Where a related credit agreement of a kind referred to in regulation 6(1)(c) is cancelled under paragraph (1)—

(a) paragraph (2)(b) to (d) and regulation 12 shall not apply in respect of its cancellation; and

(b) regulations 13 and 14 shall not apply in respect of the cancellation of the related contract for goods or services.

(5) Where a related credit agreement of a kind referred to in [regulation 6(1)(ca) or 6(1)(d)(iii)] is cancelled under paragraph (1)—

(a) the provisions of this regulation and regulation 12 shall apply in respect of its cancellation; and

(b) the provisions of regulations 13 and 14 shall apply in respect of the cancellation of the related contract for goods or services.

(6) For the purposes of this regulation and regulation 12 "creditor" is the person who grants credit under a related credit agreement.

12. Repayment of credit and interest

(1) Where—

    (a) a contract under which credit is provided to the consumer is cancelled under regulation 8; or

    (b) a related credit agreement (other than a cancellable agreement or an agreement of a kind referred to in regulation 6(1)(c)) is cancelled as a result of the cancellation of a contract for goods or services,

the contract or agreement shall continue in force so far as it relates to repayment of the credit and payment of interest.

(2) If, following the cancellation of a contract or related credit agreement to which paragraph (1) applies, the consumer repays the whole or a portion of the credit—

    (a) before the expiry of one month following service of the cancellation notice; or

    (b) in the case of a credit repayable by instalments, before the date on which the first instalment is due,

no interest shall be payable on the amount repaid.

(3) If the whole of a credit repayable by instalments is not repaid on or before the date specified in paragraph (2)(b), the consumer shall not be liable to repay any of the credit except on receipt of a request in writing signed by the trader stating the amounts of the remaining instalments (recalculated by the trader as nearly as may be in accordance with the contract and without extending the repayment period), but excluding any sum other than principal and interest.

(4) Repayment of a credit, or payment of interest, under a cancelled contract or related credit agreement shall be treated as duly made if it is made to any person on whom, under regulation 8(4), a cancellation notice could have been served.

(5) Where any security has been provided in relation to the contract or consumer credit agreement, the duty imposed on the consumer by this regulation shall not be enforceable before the trader or creditor has discharged any duty imposed on him by regulation 10(3) or 11(2)(d) respectively.

13. Return of goods by consumer after cancellation

(1) A consumer who has acquired possession of any goods by virtue of the contract shall on the cancellation of that contract be under a duty, subject to any lien, to restore the goods to the trader and meanwhile to retain possession of the goods and take reasonable care of them.

(2) The consumer shall not be under a duty to restore goods supplied under a specified contract in circumstances where—

    (a) he is required to pay, in accordance with the reasonable requirements of the cancelled contract, for the supply of such goods before cancellation; or

    (b) the trader has begun performance of the contract before the end of the cancellation period without a prior request in writing by the consumer.

(3) The consumer shall not be under any duty to deliver the goods except at his own premises and following a request in writing signed by the trader and served on the consumer either before, or at the time when, the goods are collected from those premises.

(4) If the consumer—

    (a) delivers the goods (whether at his own premises or elsewhere) to any person on whom, under regulation 8(4), a cancellation notice could have been served; or

    (b) sends the goods at his own expense to such a person,

he shall be discharged from any duty to retain possession of the goods or restore them to the trader.

(5) Where the consumer delivers the goods as mentioned in paragraph (4)(a), his obligation to take care of the goods shall cease; and if he sends the goods as mentioned in paragraph (4)(b), he shall

be under a duty to take reasonable care to see that they are received by the trader and not damaged in transit, but in other respects his duty to take care of the goods shall cease.

(6) Where, at any time during the period of 21 days following the cancellation, the consumer receives such a request as is mentioned in paragraph (3) and unreasonably refuses or unreasonably fails to comply with it, his duty to retain possession and take reasonable care of the goods shall continue until he delivers or sends the goods as mentioned in paragraph (4); but if within that period he does not receive such a request his duty to take reasonable care of the goods shall cease at the end of that period.

(7) Where any security has been provided in relation to the cancelled contract, the duty imposed on the consumer to restore goods shall not be enforceable before the trader has discharged any duty imposed on him by regulation 10(3).

(8) Breach of a duty imposed on a consumer by this regulation is actionable as a breach of statutory duty.

14. Goods given in part-exchange

(1) This regulation applies on the cancellation of a contract where the trader agreed to take goods in part-exchange (the "part-exchange goods") and those goods have been delivered to him.

(2) Unless, before the end of the period of ten days beginning with the date of cancellation, the part-exchange goods are returned to the consumer in a condition substantially as good as when they were delivered to the trader, the consumer shall be entitled to recover from the trader a sum equal to the part-exchange allowance.

(3) During the period of ten days beginning with the date of cancellation, the consumer, if he is in possession of goods to which the cancelled contract relates, shall have a lien on them for—

    (a) delivery of the part-exchange goods in a condition substantially as good as when they were delivered to the trader; or

    (b) a sum equal to the part-exchange allowance,

and if the lien continues to the end of that period it shall thereafter subsist only as a lien for a sum equal to the part-exchange allowance.

(4) In this regulation the part-exchange allowance means the sum agreed as such in the cancelled contract, or if no such sum was agreed, such sum as it would have been reasonable to allow in respect of the part-exchange goods if no notice of cancellation had been served.

15. No contracting-out of contracts to which these Regulations apply

(1) A term contained in a contract is void if, and to the extent that, it is inconsistent with a provision for the protection of the consumer contained in these Regulations.

(2) Where a provision of these Regulations specifies the duty or liability of the consumer in certain circumstances, a term contained in a contract is inconsistent with that provision if it purports to impose, directly or indirectly, an additional or different duty or liability on the consumer in those circumstances.

16. Service of documents

(1) A document to be served under these Regulations on a person may be so served—

    (a) by delivering it to him, or by leaving it at his proper address or by sending it to him at that address;

    (b) if the person is a body corporate, by serving it in accordance with sub-paragraph (a) on the secretary or clerk of that body;

    (c) if the person is a partnership, by serving it in accordance with sub-paragraph (a) on a partner or on a person having the control or management of the partnership business; and

    (d) if the person is an unincorporated body, by serving it in accordance with sub-paragraph (a) on a person having control or management of that body.

(2) For the purposes of paragraph (1), the proper address of any person on whom a document is to be served under these Regulations is his last known address except that—

    (a) in the case of service on a body corporate or its secretary or clerk, it is the address of the registered or principal office of the body corporate in the United Kingdom; and

    (b) in the case of service on a partnership or partner or person having the control or management of a partnership business, it is the partnership's principal place of business in the United Kingdom.

    (3) A person's electronic mail address may also be his proper address for the purposes of paragraph (1).

Enforcement

17. Offence relating to the failure to give notice of the right to cancel

    (1) A trader is guilty of an offence if he enters into a contract to which these Regulations apply but fails to give the consumer a notice of the right to cancel in accordance with regulation 7.

    (2) A person who is guilty of an offence under paragraph (1) shall be liable on summary conviction to a fine not exceeding level 5 on the standard scale.

18. Defence of due diligence

    (1) In any proceedings against a person for an offence under regulation 17 it is a defence for that person to prove—

       (a) that the commission of the offence was due to—

          (i)   the act or default of another, or

          (ii) reliance on information given by another, and

       (b) that he took all reasonable precautions and exercised all due diligence to avoid the commission of such an offence by himself or any person under his control.

    (2) A person shall not be entitled to rely on the defence provided by paragraph (1) without leave of the court unless—

       (a) he has served on the prosecutor a notice in writing giving such information identifying or assisting in the identification of that other person as was in his possession; and

       (b) the notice is served on the prosecutor not less than seven clear days before the hearing of the proceedings or, in Scotland, the diet of trial.

19. Liability of persons other than the principal offender

Where the commission by a person of an offence under regulation 17 is due to the act or default of another person, that other person is guilty of the offence and may be proceeded against and punished whether or not proceedings are taken against the first person.

20. Offences committed by bodies of persons

    (1) Where an offence under regulation 17 committed by a body corporate is proved—

       (a) to have been committed with the consent or connivance of an officer of the body corporate or

       (b) to be attributable to any neglect on his part,

the officer, as well as the body corporate shall be guilty of the offence and liable to be proceeded against and punished accordingly.

    (2) In paragraph (1) a reference to an officer of a body corporate includes a reference to—

       (a) a director, manager, secretary or other similar officer; and

       (b) a person purporting to act as a director, manager, secretary or other similar officer.

    (3) Where an offence under regulation 17 committed in Scotland by a Scottish partnership is proved—

       (a) to have been committed with the consent or connivance of a partner; or

       (b) to be attributable to any neglect on his part,

that partner, as well as the partnership shall be guilty of the offence and liable to be proceeded against and punished accordingly.

    (4) In paragraph (3) a reference to a partner includes a person purporting to act as a partner.

21. Duty to enforce

    (1) Subject to paragraphs (2) and (3)—

(a) it shall be the duty of every weights and measures authority in Great Britain to enforce regulation 17 within its area; and

(b) it shall be the duty of the Department of Enterprise Trade and Investment in Northern Ireland to enforce regulation 17 within Northern Ireland.

(2) No proceedings for an offence under these Regulations may be instituted in England and Wales except by or on behalf of an enforcement authority.

(3) Nothing in paragraph (1) shall authorise any weights and measures authority to bring proceedings in Scotland for an offence.

22.   Powers of investigation

(1) If a duly authorised officer of an enforcement authority has reasonable grounds for suspecting that an offence has been committed under regulation 17, he may require a person carrying on or employed in a business to produce any document relating to the business, and take copies of it or any entry in it for the purposes of ascertaining whether such an offence has been committed.

(2) If the officer has reasonable grounds for believing that any documents may be required as evidence in proceedings for such an offence, he may seize and detain them and shall, if he does so, inform the person from whom they are seized.

(3) In this regulation "document" includes information recorded in any form.

(4) The reference in paragraph (1) to production of documents is, in the case of a document which contains information recorded otherwise than in a legible form, a reference to the production of a copy of the information in a legible form.

(5) An officer seeking to exercise a power under this regulation must do so only at a reasonable hour and on production (if required) of his identification and authority.

(6) Nothing in this regulation requires a person to produce, or authorises the taking from a person of, a document which the other person would be entitled to refuse to produce in proceedings in the High Court on the grounds of legal professional privilege or (in Scotland) in the Court of Session on the grounds of confidentiality of communications.

(7) In paragraph (6) "communications" means—

(a) communications between a professional legal adviser and his client; or

(b) communications made in connection with, or in contemplation of legal proceedings and for the purpose of those proceedings.

Obstruction of authorised officers

23.—(1) A person is guilty of an offence if he—

(a) intentionally obstructs an officer of an enforcement authority acting in pursuance of his functions under these Regulations;

(b) without reasonable cause fails to comply with any requirement properly made of him by such an officer under regulation 22; or

(c) without reasonable cause fails to give such an officer any other assistance or information which he may reasonably require of him for the purpose of the performance of his functions under these Regulations.

(2) A person is guilty of an offence if, in giving any information which is required of him under paragraph (1)(c), he makes any statement which he knows to be false in a material particular.

(3) A person guilty of an offence under paragraph (1) or (2) shall be liable on summary conviction to a fine not exceeding level 3 on the standard scale.

24. Nothing in regulation 22 or 23 shall be construed as requiring a person to answer any question or give any information if to do so might incriminate him.

Regulations 2(2) and 6(1)(a) SCHEDULE 3

EXCEPTED CONTRACTS

1. A contract for the construction, sale or rental of immovable property or a contract concerning other rights relating to immovable property other than—

    (a) a contract for the construction of extensions, patios, conservatories or driveways;

    (b) a contract for the supply of goods and their incorporation in immovable property; and

    (c) a contract for the repair, refurbishment or improvement of immovable property.

2. A contract for the supply of foodstuffs or beverages or other goods intended for current consumption in the household and supplied by a regular roundsman.

3. A contract for the supply of goods or services provided that each of the following conditions is met:

    (a) the contract is concluded on the basis of a trader's catalogue which the consumer has a proper opportunity of reading in the absence of the trader's representative;

    (b) there is intended to be continuity of contact between the trader's representative and the consumer in relation to that or any subsequent transaction; and

    (c) both the catalogue and the contract contain a prominent notice informing the consumer of his rights to return goods to the supplier within a period of not less than seven days of receipt or otherwise to cancel the contract within that period without obligation of any kind other than to take reasonable care of the goods.

4. A contract of insurance.

5. Any contract under which credit within the meaning of the 1974 Act is provided not exceeding £35 other than a hire purchase or conditional sale agreement.

6. Any contract not falling within paragraph 5 under which the total payments to be made by the consumer do not exceed £35.

7. Any agreement the making or performance of which by either party constitutes a relevant regulated activity.

8.—(1) For the purposes of paragraph 7—

    (a) "a relevant regulated activity" means an activity of the following kind—

        (i)   dealing in investments, as principal or as agent;

        (ii) arranging deals in investments;

        (iii) operating a multilateral trading facility;

        (iv) managing investments;

        (v) safeguarding and administering investments;

        (vi) establishing, operating or winding up a collective investment scheme; and

    (b) for these purposes "investment" means—

        (i)   shares;

        (ii) instruments creating or acknowledging indebtedness;

        (iii) instruments giving entitlement to investments

        (iv) certificates representing securities;

        (v) units in a collective investment scheme;

        (vi) options;

        (vii) futures;

        (viii) contracts for differences; and

        (ix) rights to or interests in investments.

  (2) Paragraph 7 and this paragraph must be read with—

    (a) section 22 of the Financial Services and Markets Act 2000;

    (b) any relevant order under that section; and

    (c) Schedule 2 to that Act,

but any restriction on or exclusion from the meaning of a regulated activity for the purposes of paragraph 7 which arises from the identity of the person carrying on such activity is to be disregarded.

Regulations 2(2) and 6(1)(a) **SCHEDULE 4**

NOTICE OF THE RIGHT TO CANCEL

PART I INFORMATION TO BE CONTAINED IN NOTICE OF THE RIGHT TO CANCEL

1. The identity of the trader including trading name if any.

2. The trader's reference number, code or other details to enable the contract or offer to be identified.

3. A statement that the consumer has a right to cancel the contract if he wishes and that this right can be exercised by delivering, or sending (including by electronic mail) a cancellation notice to the person mentioned in the next paragraph at any time within the period of 7 days starting with the day of receipt of a notice in writing of the right to cancel the contract.

4. The name and address, (including any electronic mail address as well as the postal address), of a person to whom a cancellation notice may be given.

5. A statement that notice of cancellation is deemed to be served as soon as it is posted or sent to a trader or in the case of an electronic communication from the day it is sent to the trader.

6. A statement that the consumer can use the cancellation form provided if he wishes.

PART II CANCELLATION NOTICE TO BE INCLUDED IN NOTICE OF THE RIGHT TO CANCEL

If you wish to cancel the contract you MUST DO SO IN WRITING and deliver personally or send (which may be by electronic mail) this to the person named below. You may use this form if you want to but you do not have to.

(Complete, detach and return this form ONLY IF YOU WISH TO CANCEL THE CONTRACT.)

To:.........................[trader to insert name and address of person to whom notice may be given.]

I/We (delete as appropriate) hereby give notice that I/we (delete as appropriate) wish to cancel my/our (delete as appropriate) contract..................... [trader to insert reference number, code or other details to enable the contract or offer to be identified. He may also insert the name and address of the consumer.]

Signed

Name and Address

Date

Consumer Protection from Unfair Trading Regulations 2008

(SI 2008, No. 1277)

PART 1 GENERAL

2. Interpretation

(1) In these Regulations—

'average consumer' shall be construed in accordance with paragraphs (2) to (6);

'business' includes a trade, craft or profession;

'code of conduct' means an agreement or set of rules (which is not imposed by legal or administrative requirements), which defines the behaviour of traders who undertake to be bound by it in relation to one or more commercial practices or business sectors;

'code owner' means a trader or a body responsible for—

    (a) the formulation and revision of a code of conduct; or

    (b) monitoring compliance with the code by those who have undertaken to be bound by it;

'commercial practice' means any act, omission, course of conduct, representation or commercial communication (including advertising and marketing) by a trader, which is directly connected with the promotion, sale or supply of a product to or from consumers, whether occurring before, during or after a commercial transaction (if any) in relation to a product;

'consumer' means any individual who in relation to a commercial practice is acting for purposes which are outside his business;

'enforcement authority' means the OFT, every local weights and measures authority in Great Britain (within the meaning of section 69 of the Weights and Measures Act 1985) and the Department of Enterprise, Trade and Investment in Northern Ireland;

'goods' includes ships, aircraft, animals, things attached to land and growing crops;

'invitation to purchase' means a commercial communication which indicates characteristics of the product and the price in a way appropriate to the means of that commercial communication and thereby enables the consumer to make a purchase;

'materially distort the economic behaviour' means in relation to an average consumer, appreciably to impair the average consumer's ability to make an informed decision thereby causing him to take a transactional decision that he would not have taken otherwise;

'OFT' means the Office of Fair Trading;

'premises' includes any place and any stall, vehicle, ship or aircraft;

'product' means any goods or service and includes immovable property, rights and obligations;

'professional diligence' means the standard of special skill and care which a trader may reasonably be expected to exercise towards consumers which is commensurate with either—

    (a) honest market practice in the trader's field of activity, or

    (b) the general principle of good faith in the trader's field of activity;

'ship' includes any boat and any other description of vessel used in navigation;

'trader' means any person who in relation to a commercial practice is acting for purposes relating to his business, and anyone acting in the name of or on behalf of a trader;

'transactional decision' means any decision taken by a consumer, whether it is to act or to refrain from acting, concerning—

    (a) whether, how and on what terms to purchase, make payment in whole or in part for, retain or dispose of a product; or

    (b) whether, how and on what terms to exercise a contractual right in relation to a product.

(2) In determining the effect of a commercial practice on the average consumer where the practice reaches or is addressed to a consumer or consumers account shall be taken of the material characteristics of such an average consumer including his being reasonably well informed, reasonably observant and circumspect.

(3) Paragraphs (4) and (5) set out the circumstances in which a reference to the average consumer shall be read as in addition referring to the average member of a particular group of consumers.

(4) In determining the effect of a commercial practice on the average consumer where the practice is directed to a particular group of consumers, a reference to the average consumer shall be read as referring to the average member of that group.

(5) In determining the effect of a commercial practice on the average consumer—

(a) where a clearly identifiable group of consumers is particularly vulnerable to the practice or the underlying product because of their mental or physical infirmity, age or credulity in a way which the trader could reasonably be expected to foresee, and

(b) where the practice is likely to materially distort the economic behaviour only of that group,

a reference to the average consumer shall be read as referring to the average member of that group.

(6) Paragraph (5) is without prejudice to the common and legitimate advertising practice of making exaggerated statements which are not meant to be taken literally.

PART 2 PROHIBITIONS

3. Prohibition of unfair commercial practices

(1) Unfair commercial practices are prohibited.

(2) Paragraphs (3) and (4) set out the circumstances when a commercial practice is unfair.

(3) A commercial practice is unfair if—

(a) it contravenes the requirements of professional diligence; and

(b) it materially distorts or is likely to materially distort the economic behaviour of the average consumer with regard to the product.

(4) A commercial practice is unfair if—

(a) it is a misleading action under the provisions of regulation 5;

(b) it is a misleading omission under the provisions of regulation 6;

(c) it is aggressive under the provisions of regulation 7; or

(d) it is listed in Schedule 1.

4. Prohibition of the promotion of unfair commercial practices

The promotion of any unfair commercial practice by a code owner in a code of conduct is prohibited.

5. Misleading actions

(1) A commercial practice is a misleading action if it satisfies the conditions in either paragraph (2) or paragraph (3).

(2) A commercial practice satisfies the conditions of this paragraph—

(a) if it contains false information and is therefore untruthful in relation to any of the matters in paragraph (4) or if it or its overall presentation in any way deceives or is likely to deceive the average consumer in relation to any of the matters in that paragraph, even if the information is factually correct; and

(b) it causes or is likely to cause the average consumer to take a transactional decision he would not have taken otherwise.

(3) A commercial practice satisfies the conditions of this paragraph if—

(a) it concerns any marketing of a product (including comparative advertising) which creates confusion with any products, trade marks, trade names or other distinguishing marks of a competitor; or

(b) it concerns any failure by a trader to comply with a commitment contained in a code of conduct which the trader has undertaken to comply with, if—

(i)   the trader indicates in a commercial practice that he is bound by that code of conduct, and

(ii) the commitment is firm and capable of being verified and is not aspirational,

and it causes or is likely to cause the average consumer to take a transactional decision he would not have taken otherwise, taking account of its factual context and of all its features and circumstances.

(4) The matters referred to in paragraph (2)(a) are—

    (a) the existence or nature of the product;

    (b) the main characteristics of the product (as defined in paragraph 5);

    (c) the extent of the trader's commitments;

    (d) the motives for the commercial practice;

    (e) the nature of the sales process;

    (f) any statement or symbol relating to direct or indirect sponsorship or approval of the trader or the product;

    (g) the price or the manner in which the price is calculated;

    (h) the existence of a specific price advantage;

    (i) the need for a service, part, replacement or repair;

    (j) the nature, attributes and rights of the trader (as defined in paragraph 6);

    (k) the consumer's rights or the risks he may face.

(5) In paragraph (4)(b), the 'main characteristics of the product' include—

    (a) availability of the product;

    (b) benefits of the product;

    (c) risks of the product;

    (d) execution of the product;

    (e) composition of the product;

    (f) accessories of the product;

    (g) after-sale customer assistance concerning the product;

    (h) the handling of complaints about the product;

    (i) the method and date of manufacture of the product;

    (j) the method and date of provision of the product;

    (k) delivery of the product;

    (l) fitness for purpose of the product;

    (m) usage of the product;

    (n) quantity of the product;

    (o) specification of the product;

    (p) geographical or commercial origin of the product;

    (q) results to be expected from use of the product; and

    (r) results and material features of tests or checks carried out on the product.

(6) In paragraph (4)(j), the 'nature, attributes and rights' as far as concern the trader include the trader's—

    (a) identity;

    (b) assets;

    (c) qualifications;

    (d) status;

    (e) approval;

    (f) affiliations or connections;

    (g) ownership of industrial, commercial or intellectual property rights; and

    (h) awards and distinctions.

(7) In paragraph (4)(k) 'consumer's rights' include rights the consumer may have under Part 5A of the Sale of Goods Act 1979 or Part 1B of the Supply of Goods and Services Act 1982.

6. Misleading omissions

(1) A commercial practice is a misleading omission if, in its factual context, taking account of the matters in paragraph (2)—

    (a) the commercial practice omits material information,

    (b) the commercial practice hides material information,

    (c) the commercial practice provides material information in a manner which is unclear, unintelligible, ambiguous or untimely, or

    (d) the commercial practice fails to identify its commercial intent, unless this is already apparent from the context, and as a result it causes or is likely to cause the average consumer to take a transactional decision he would not have taken otherwise.

(2) The matters referred to in paragraph (1) are—

(a) all the features and circumstances of the commercial practice;

(b) the limitations of the medium used to communicate the commercial practice (including limitations of space or time); and

(c) where the medium used to communicate the commercial practice imposes limitations of space or time, any measures taken by the trader to make the information available to consumers by other means.

(3) In paragraph (1) 'material information' means—

(a) the information which the average consumer needs, according to the context, to take an informed transactional decision; and

(b) any information requirement which applies in relation to a commercial communication as a result of a Community obligation.

(4) Where a commercial practice is an invitation to purchase, the following information will be material if not already apparent from the context in addition to any other information which is material information under paragraph (3)—

(a) the main characteristics of the product, to the extent appropriate to the medium by which the invitation to purchase is communicated and the product;

(b) the identity of the trader, such as his trading name, and the identity of any other trader on whose behalf the trader is acting;

(c) the geographical address of the trader and the geographical address of any other trader on whose behalf the trader is acting;

(d) either—

(i) the price, including any taxes; or

(ii) where the nature of the product is such that the price cannot reasonably be calculated in advance, the manner in which the price is calculated;

(e) where appropriate, either—

(i) all additional freight, delivery or postal charges; or

(ii) where such charges cannot reasonably be calculated in advance, the fact that such charges may be payable;

(f) the following matters where they depart from the requirements of professional diligence—

(i) arrangements for payment,

(ii) arrangements for delivery,

(iii) arrangements for performance,

(iv) complaint handling policy;

(g) for products and transactions involving a right of withdrawal or cancellation, the existence of such a right.

7. Aggressive commercial practices

(1) A commercial practice is aggressive if, in its factual context, taking account of all of its features and circumstances—

(a) it significantly impairs or is likely significantly to impair the average consumer's freedom of choice or conduct in relation to the product concerned through the use of harassment, coercion or undue influence; and

(b) it thereby causes or is likely to cause him to take a transactional decision he would not have taken otherwise.

(2) In determining whether a commercial practice uses harassment, coercion or undue influence account shall be taken of—

(a) its timing, location, nature or persistence;

(b) the use of threatening or abusive language or behaviour;

(c) the exploitation by the trader of any specific misfortune or circumstance of such gravity as to impair the consumer's judgment, of which the trader is aware, to influence the consumer's decision with regard to the product;

(d) any onerous or disproportionate non-contractual barrier imposed by the trader where a consumer wishes to exercise rights under the contract, including rights to terminate a contract or to switch to another product or another trader; and

(e) any threat to take any action which cannot legally be taken.

(3) In this regulation—

(a) 'coercion' includes the use of physical force; and

(b) 'undue influence' means exploiting a position of power in relation to the consumer so as to apply pressure, even without using or threatening to use physical force, in a way which significantly limits the consumer's ability to make an informed decision.

PART 3 OFFENCES

Offences relating to unfair commercial practices

8.—(1) A trader is guilty of an offence if—

(a) he knowingly or recklessly engages in a commercial practice which contravenes the requirements of professional diligence under regulation 3(3)(a); and

(b) the practice materially distorts or is likely to materially distort the economic behaviour of the average consumer with regard to the product under regulation 3(3)(b).

(2) For the purposes of paragraph (1)(a) a trader who engages in a commercial practice without regard to whether the practice contravenes the requirements of professional diligence shall be deemed recklessly to engage in the practice, whether or not the trader has reason for believing that the practice might contravene those requirements.

9. A trader is guilty of an offence if he engages in a commercial practice which is a misleading action under regulation 5 otherwise than by reason of the commercial practice satisfying the condition in regulation 5(3)(b).

10. A trader is guilty of an offence if he engages in a commercial practice which is a misleading omission under regulation 6.

11. A trader is guilty of an offence if he engages in a commercial practice which is aggressive under regulation 7.

12. A trader is guilty of an offence if he engages in a commercial practice set out in any of paragraphs 1 to 10, 12 to 27 and 29 to 31 of Schedule 1.

13. Penalty for offences

A person guilty of an offence under regulation 8, 9, 10, 11 or 12 shall be liable—

(a) on summary conviction, to a fine not exceeding the statutory maximum; or

(b) on conviction on indictment, to a fine or imprisonment for a term not exceeding two years or both.

14. Time limit for prosecution

(1) No proceedings for an offence under these Regulations shall be commenced after—

(a) the end of the period of three years beginning with the date of the commission of the offence, or

(b) the end of the period of one year beginning with the date of discovery of the offence by the prosecutor,

whichever is earlier.

(2) For the purposes of paragraph (1)(b) a certificate signed by or on behalf of the prosecutor and stating the date on which the offence was discovered by him shall be conclusive evidence of that fact and a certificate stating that matter and purporting to be so signed shall be treated as so signed unless the contrary is proved.

(3) Notwithstanding anything in section 127(1) of the Magistrates' Courts Act 1980, an information relating to an offence under these Regulations which is triable by a magistrates' court in England and Wales may be so tried if it is laid at any time before the end of the period of twelve months beginning with the date of the commission of the offence.

(4) Notwithstanding anything in section 136 of the Criminal Procedure (Scotland) Act 1995 summary proceedings in Scotland for an offence under these Regulations may be commenced at any time before the end of the period of twelve months beginning with the date of the commission of the offence.

(5) For the purposes of paragraph (4), section 136(3) of the Criminal Procedure (Scotland) Act 1995 shall apply as it applies for the purposes of that subsection.

(6) Notwithstanding anything in Article 19(1) of the Magistrates' Courts (Northern Ireland) Order 1981 a complaint charging an offence under these Regulations which is triable by a magistrates' court in Northern Ireland may be so tried if it is made at any time before the end of the period of twelve months beginning with the date of the commission of the offence.

15. Offences committed by bodies of persons

(1) Where an offence under these Regulations committed by a body corporate is proved—

(a) to have been committed with the consent or connivance of an officer of the body, or

(b) to be attributable to any neglect on his part,

the officer as well as the body corporate is guilty of the offence and liable to be proceeded against and punished accordingly.

(2) In paragraph (1) a reference to an officer of a body corporate includes a reference to—

(a) a director, manager, secretary or other similar officer; and

(b) a person purporting to act as a director, manager, secretary or other similar officer.

(3) Where an offence under these Regulations committed by a Scottish partnership is proved—

(a) to have been committed with the consent or connivance of a partner, or

(b) to be attributable to any neglect on his part,

the partner as well as the partnership is guilty of the offence and liable to be proceeded against and punished accordingly.

(4) In paragraph (3) a reference to a partner includes a person purporting to act as a partner.

16. Offence due to the default of another person

(1) This regulation applies where a person 'X'—

(a) commits an offence under regulation 9, 10, 11 or 12, or

(b) would have committed an offence under those regulations but for a defence under regulation 17 or 18,

and the commission of the offence, or of what would have been an offence but for X being able to rely on a defence under regulation 17 or 18, is due to the act or default of some other person 'Y'.

(2) Where this regulation applies Y is guilty of the offence, subject to regulations 17 and 18, whether or not Y is a trader and whether or not Y's act or default is a commercial practice.

(3) Y may be charged with and convicted of the offence by virtue of paragraph (2) whether or not proceedings are taken against X.

17. Due diligence defence

(1) In any proceedings against a person for an offence under regulation 9, 10, 11 or 12 it is a defence for that person to prove—

(a) that the commission of the offence was due to—

(i)   a mistake;

(ii) reliance on information supplied to him by another person;

(iii) the act or default of another person;

(iv) an accident; or

(v)   another cause beyond his control; and

(b) that he took all reasonable precautions and exercised all due diligence to avoid the commission of such an offence by himself or any person under his control.

(2) A person shall not be entitled to rely on the defence provided by paragraph (1) by reason of the matters referred to in paragraph (ii) or (iii) of paragraph (1)(a) without leave of the court unless—

(a) he has served on the prosecutor a notice in writing giving such information identifying or assisting in the identification of that other person as was in his possession; and

(b) the notice is served on the prosecutor at least seven clear days before the date of the hearing.

18. Innocent publication of advertisement defence

(1) In any proceedings against a person for an offence under regulation 9, 10, 11 or 12 committed by the publication of an advertisement it shall be a defence for a person to prove that—

(a) he is a person whose business it is to publish or to arrange for the publication of advertisements;

(b) he received the advertisement for publication in the ordinary course of business; and

(c) he did not know and had no reason to suspect that its publication would amount to an offence under the regulation to which the proceedings relate.

(2) In paragraph (1) 'advertisement' includes a catalogue, a circular and a price list.

PART 4 ENFORCEMENT

19. Duty to enforce

(1) It shall be the duty of every enforcement authority to enforce these Regulations.

(2) Where the enforcement authority is a local weights and measures authority the duty referred to in paragraph (1) shall apply to the enforcement of these Regulations within the authority's area.

(3) Where the enforcement authority is the Department of Enterprise, Trade and Investment in Northern Ireland the duty referred to in paragraph (1) shall apply to the enforcement of these Regulations within Northern Ireland.

(4) In determining how to comply with its duty of enforcement every enforcement authority shall have regard to the desirability of encouraging control of unfair commercial practices by such established means as it considers appropriate having regard to all the circumstances of the particular case.

(5) Nothing in this regulation shall authorise any enforcement authority to bring proceedings in Scotland for an offence.

20. Power to make test purchases

An enforcement authority may or may authorise any of its officers on its behalf to—

(a) make a purchase of a product, or

(b) enter into an agreement to secure the provision of a product,

for the purposes of determining whether these Regulations are being complied with.

21. Power of entry and investigation, etc.

(1) A duly authorised officer of an enforcement authority may at all reasonable hours exercise the following powers—

(a) he may, for the purposes of ascertaining whether a breach of these Regulations has been committed, inspect any goods and enter any premises other than premises used only as a dwelling;

(b) if he has reasonable cause to suspect that a breach of these Regulations has been committed, he may, for the purpose of ascertaining whether it has been committed, require any trader to produce any documents relating to his business and may take copies of, or of any entry in, any such document;

(c) if he has reasonable cause to believe that a breach of these Regulations has been committed, he may seize and detain any goods for the purpose of ascertaining, by testing or otherwise, whether the breach has been committed; and

(d) he may seize and detain goods or documents which he has reason to believe may be required as evidence in proceedings for a breach of these Regulations.

(2) If and to the extent that it is reasonably necessary to secure that the provisions of these Regulations are observed, the officer may for the purpose of exercising his powers under paragraphs (1)(c) and (d) to seize goods or documents—
- (a) require any person having authority to do so to break open any container or open any vending machine; and
- (b) himself open or break open any such container or open any vending machine where a requirement made under sub-paragraph (a) in relation to the container or vending machine has not been complied with.

(3) An officer seizing any goods or documents in exercise of his powers under this regulation shall—
- (a) inform the person from whom they are seized, and,
- (b) where goods are seized from a vending machine, inform—
  - (i) the person whose name and address are stated on the machine as being the proprietor's; or
  - (ii) if there is no such name or address stated on the machine the occupier of the premises on which the machine stands or to which it is affixed,

that the goods or documents have been so seized.

(4) In this regulation 'document' includes information recorded in any form.

(5) The reference in paragraph (1)(b) to the production of documents is, in the case of a document which contains information recorded otherwise than in legible form, a reference to the production of a copy of the information in legible form.

(6) An officer seeking to exercise a power under this regulation must produce evidence of his identity and authority to a person (if there is one) who appears to the officer to be the occupier of the premises.

(7) Where an officer seizes goods or documents in exercise of a power under this regulation they may not be detained—
- (a) for a period of more than 3 months; or
- (b) where the goods or documents are reasonably required by the enforcement authority in connection with the enforcement of these Regulations, for longer than they are so required.

(8) An officer entering any premises under this regulation may take with him such other persons and such equipment as may appear to him to be necessary.

(9) Nothing in this regulation or in regulation 22 gives any power to an officer of an enforcement authority—
- (a) to require any person to produce, or
- (b) to seize from another person,

any document which the other person would be entitled to refuse to produce in proceedings in the High Court on the grounds of legal professional privilege or (in Scotland) in proceedings in the Court of Session on the grounds of confidentiality of communications.

(10) In paragraph (9) 'communications' means—
- (a) communications between a professional legal adviser and his client; or
- (b) communications made in connection with or in contemplation of legal proceedings and for the purposes of those proceedings.

(11) If any person who is not an officer of an enforcement authority purports to act as such under this regulation or under regulation 22 he shall be guilty of an offence and liable on summary conviction to a fine not exceeding level 5 on the standard scale.

22. Power to enter premises with a warrant
(1) If a justice of the peace by any written information on oath is satisfied—
- (a) that there are reasonable grounds for believing that Condition A or B is met, and
- (b) that Condition C, D or E is met,

the justice may by warrant under his hand authorise an officer of an enforcement authority to enter the premises at all reasonable times, if necessary by force.

(2) Condition A is that there are on any premises goods or documents which a duly authorised officer of the enforcement authority has power under regulation 21(1) to inspect and that their inspection is likely to disclose evidence of a breach of these Regulations.

(3) Condition B is that a breach of these Regulations has been, is being or is about to be committed on any premises.

(4) Condition C is that the admission to the premises has been or is likely to be refused and that notice of intention to apply for a warrant under this regulation has been given to the occupier.

(5) Condition D is that an application for admission, or the giving of a notice of intention to apply for a warrant, would defeat the object of the entry.

(6) Condition E is that the premises are unoccupied or that the occupier is absent and it might defeat the object of the entry to await his return.

(7) A warrant under paragraph (1)—
  (a) ceases to have effect at the end of the period of one month beginning with the day it is issued;
  (b) must be produced for inspection to the person (if there is one) who appears to the officer to be the occupier of the premises.

(8) An officer entering any premises under this regulation may take with him such other persons and such equipment as may appear to him to be necessary.

(9) On leaving any premises which an officer is authorised to enter by warrant under this regulation the officer shall, if the premises are unoccupied or the occupier is temporarily absent, leave the premises as effectively secured against trespassers as he found them.

(10) In its application to Scotland, this regulation has effect as if—
  (a) the references in paragraph (1) to a justice of the peace included references to a sheriff; and
  (b) the reference in paragraph (1) to information on oath were a reference to evidence on oath.

(11) In its application to Northern Ireland, this regulation has effect as if the references in paragraph (1) to a justice of the peace were references to a lay magistrate.

23. Obstruction of authorised officers

(1) Any person who—
  (a) intentionally obstructs an officer of an enforcement authority acting in pursuance of these Regulations,
  (b) intentionally fails to comply with any requirement properly made of him by such an officer under regulation 21, or
  (c) without reasonable cause fails to give such an officer any other assistance or information which he may reasonably require of him for the purpose of the performance of his functions under these Regulations,

is guilty of an offence and liable, on summary conviction, to a fine not exceeding level 5 on the standard scale.

(2) Any person who, in giving any information which is required of him under paragraph (1)(c), makes any statement which he knows to be false in a material particular is guilty of an offence and liable—
  (a) on summary conviction, to a fine not exceeding the statutory maximum; or
  (b) on conviction on indictment, to a fine or imprisonment for a term not exceeding two years or both.

(3) Nothing in this regulation shall be construed as requiring a person to answer any question or give any information if to do so might incriminate him.

24   Notice of test and intended proceedings

(1) Where goods purchased by an officer pursuant to regulation 20 are submitted to a test and the test leads to the institution of any proceedings for a breach of these Regulations the officer shall inform—

    (a) the person from whom the goods were purchased, or

    (b) where the goods were sold through a vending machine, the person mentioned in regulation 21(3)(b),

of the result of the test.

(2) Where goods seized by an officer pursuant to regulation 21 are submitted to a test then the officer shall inform the person mentioned in regulation 21(3) of the result of the test.

(3) Where, as a result of the test, any proceedings in respect of a breach of these Regulations are taken against any person, the officer shall allow him to have the goods tested on his behalf if it is reasonably practicable to do so.

25.   Compensation

(1) Where an officer of an enforcement authority seizes and detains goods in exercise of the powers under regulation 21 the enforcement authority shall be liable to pay compensation to any person having an interest in the goods in respect of any loss or damage caused by reason of the exercise of the power if—

    (a) there has been no breach of these Regulations in relation to the goods, and

    (b) the exercise of that power is not attributable to any neglect or default by that person.

(2) Any disputed question as to the right to or the amount of any compensation payable under this provision shall be determined by arbitration or, in Scotland, by a single arbiter appointed, failing agreement between the parties, by the sheriff.

PART 5 SUPPLEMENTARY

28.   Crown

(1) The powers conferred by regulations 21 and 22 are not exercisable in relation to premises occupied by the Crown.

(2) The Crown is not criminally liable as a result of any provision of these Regulations.

(3) Paragraph (2) does not affect the application of any provision of these Regulations in relation to a person in the public service of the Crown.

29.   Validity of agreements

An agreement shall not be void or unenforceable by reason only of a breach of these Regulations.

Regulation 3(4)(d)   # SCHEDULE 1

COMMERCIAL PRACTICES WHICH ARE IN ALL CIRCUMSTANCES CONSIDERED UNFAIR

1. Claiming to be a signatory to a code of conduct when the trader is not.

2. Displaying a trust mark, quality mark or equivalent without having obtained the necessary authorisation.

3. Claiming that a code of conduct has an endorsement from a public or other body which it does not have.

4. Claiming that a trader (including his commercial practices) or a product has been approved, endorsed or authorised by a public or private body when the trader, the commercial practices or the product have not or making such a claim without complying with the terms of the approval, endorsement or authorisation.

5. Making an invitation to purchase products at a specified price without disclosing the existence of any reasonable grounds the trader may have for believing that he will not be able to offer for supply, or to procure another trader to supply, those products or equivalent products at that price for a period that is, and in quantities that are, reasonable having regard to the product, the scale of advertising of the product and the price offered (bait advertising).

6. Making an invitation to purchase products at a specified price and then—

(a) refusing to show the advertised item to consumers,

(b) refusing to take orders for it or deliver it within a reasonable time, or

(c) demonstrating a defective sample of it,

with the intention of promoting a different product (bait and switch).

7. Falsely stating that a product will only be available for a very limited time, or that it will only be available on particular terms for a very limited time, in order to elicit an immediate decision and deprive consumers of sufficient opportunity or time to make an informed choice.

8. Undertaking to provide after-sales service to consumers with whom the trader has communicated prior to a transaction in a language which is not an official language of the EEA State where the trader is located and then making such service available only in another language without clearly disclosing this to the consumer before the consumer is committed to the transaction.

9. Stating or otherwise creating the impression that a product can legally be sold when it cannot.

10. Presenting rights given to consumers in law as a distinctive feature of the trader's offer.

11. Using editorial content in the media to promote a product where a trader has paid for the promotion without making that clear in the content or by images or sounds clearly identifiable by the consumer (advertorial).

12. Making a materially inaccurate claim concerning the nature and extent of the risk to the personal security of the consumer or his family if the consumer does not purchase the product.

13. Promoting a product similar to a product made by a particular manufacturer in such a manner as deliberately to mislead the consumer into believing that the product is made by that same manufacturer when it is not.

14. Establishing, operating or promoting a pyramid promotional scheme where a consumer gives consideration for the opportunity to receive compensation that is derived primarily from the introduction of other consumers into the scheme rather than from the sale or consumption of products.

15. Claiming that the trader is about to cease trading or move premises when he is not.

16. Claiming that products are able to facilitate winning in games of chance.

17. Falsely claiming that a product is able to cure illnesses, dysfunction or malformations.

18. Passing on materially inaccurate information on market conditions or on the possibility of finding the product with the intention of inducing the consumer to acquire the product at conditions less favourable than normal market conditions.

19. Claiming in a commercial practice to offer a competition or prize promotion without awarding the prizes described or a reasonable equivalent.

20. Describing a product as 'gratis', 'free', 'without charge' or similar if the consumer has to pay anything other than the unavoidable cost of responding to the commercial practice and collecting or paying for delivery of the item.

21. Including in marketing material an invoice or similar document seeking payment which gives the consumer the impression that he has already ordered the marketed product when he has not.

22. Falsely claiming or creating the impression that the trader is not acting for purposes relating to his trade, business, craft or profession, or falsely representing oneself as a consumer.

23. Creating the false impression that after-sales service in relation to a product is available in an EEA State other than the one in which the product is sold.

24. Creating the impression that the consumer cannot leave the premises until a contract is formed.

25. Conducting personal visits to the consumer's home ignoring the consumer's request to leave or not to return, except in circumstances and to the extent justified to enforce a contractual obligation.

26. Making persistent and unwanted solicitations by telephone, fax, e-mail or other remote media except in circumstances and to the extent justified to enforce a contractual obligation.

27. Requiring a consumer who wishes to claim on an insurance policy to produce documents which could not reasonably be considered relevant as to whether the claim was valid, or failing systematically to respond to pertinent correspondence, in order to dissuade a consumer from exercising his contractual rights.

28. Including in an advertisement a direct exhortation to children to buy advertised products or persuade their parents or other adults to buy advertised products for them.

29. Demanding immediate or deferred payment for or the return or safekeeping of products supplied by the trader, but not solicited by the consumer, except where the product is a substitute supplied in accordance with regulation 19(7) of the Consumer Protection (Distance Selling) Regulations 2000 (inertia selling).

30. Explicitly informing a consumer that if he does not buy the product or service, the trader's job or livelihood will be in jeopardy.

31. Creating the false impression that the consumer has already won, will win, or will on doing a particular act win, a prize or other equivalent benefit, when in fact either—

    (a) there is no prize or other equivalent benefit, or

    (b) taking any action in relation to claiming the prize or other equivalent benefit is subject to the consumer paying money or incurring a cost.

Payment Services Regulations 2009

(SI 2009, No. 209)

PART 1 INTRODUCTORY PROVISIONS

2 Interpretation

(1) In these Regulations —

"the 2000 Act" means the Financial Services and Markets Act 2000(3);

"agent" means a person who acts on behalf of an authorised payment institution or a small payment institution in the provision of payment services;

"authorised payment institution" means—

    (a) a person included by the Authority in the register as an authorised payment institution pursuant to regulation 4(1)(a); or

    (b) a person deemed to have been granted authorisation by the Authority by virtue of regulation 121;

"the Authority" means the Financial Services Authority;

"the banking consolidation directive" means Directive 2006/48/EC of the European Parliament and of the Council of 14th June 2006 relating to the taking up and pursuit of the business of credit institutions [as last amended by Directive 2009/111/EC];

"branch" means a place of business of an authorised payment institution, a small payment institution, or an EEA authorised payment institution, other than its head office, which forms a legally dependent part of the institution and which carries out directly all or some of the transactions inherent in its business; and, for the purposes of these Regulations, all places of business set up in the same EEA State other than the United Kingdom by an authorised payment institution are to be regarded as a single branch;

"business day" means any day on which the relevant payment service provider is open for business as required for the execution of a payment transaction;

"charity" means a body whose annual income is less than £1 million and is—

    (c) in England and Wales, a charity as defined by section 1(1) of the Charities Act 2006(5);

(d) in Scotland, a charity as defined by section 106 of the Charities and Trustee Investment (Scotland) Act 2005(6);

(e) in Northern Ireland, a charity as defined by section 1(1) of the Charities Act (Northern Ireland) 2008(7) or, until that section comes into force, a body which is recognised as a charity for tax purposes by Her Majesty's Revenue and Customs;

"the Commissioners" means the Commissioners for Her Majesty's Revenue and Customs;

"consumer" means an individual who, in contracts for payment services to which these Regulations apply, is acting for purposes other than a trade, business or profession;

"credit institution" has the meaning given in [Article 4(1)] of the banking consolidation directive;

"direct debit" means a payment service for debiting the payer's payment account where a payment transaction is initiated by the payee on the basis of consent given by the payer to the payee, to the payee's payment service provider or to the payer's own payment service provider;

"durable medium" means any instrument which enables the payment service user to store information addressed personally to them in a way accessible for future reference for a period of time adequate for the purposes of the information and which allows the unchanged reproduction of the information stored;

"the EEA" means the European Economic Area;

"EEA agent" means an agent through which an authorised payment institution, in the exercise of its passport rights, provides payment services in an EEA State other than the United Kingdom;

"EEA authorised payment institution" means a person authorised in an EEA State other than the United Kingdom to provide payment services in accordance with the payment services directive;

"EEA branch" means a branch established by an authorised payment institution, in the exercise of its passport rights, to carry out payment services in an EEA State other than the United Kingdom;

["the electronic money directive" means Directive 2009/110/EC of the European Parliament and of the Council of 16th September 2009 on the taking up, pursuit and prudential supervision of the business of electronic money institutions;]

"electronic money institution" has the meaning given in [Article 2(1)] of the electronic money directive;

"framework contract" means a contract for payment services which governs the future execution of individual and successive payment transactions and which may contain the obligation and conditions for setting up a payment account;

"funds" means banknotes and coins, scriptural money, and electronic money as defined in [Article 2(2)] of the electronic money directive;

"group" means a group of undertakings which consists of a parent undertaking, its subsidiary undertakings and the entities in which the parent undertaking or its subsidiary undertakings have a holding, as well as undertakings linked to each other by a relationship referred to in Article 12(1) of the Seventh Council Directive 83/349/EEC of 13th June 1983 based on Article 54(3)(g) of the Treaty on consolidated accounts;

"home state competent authority" means the competent authority designated in accordance with Article 20 of the payment services directive as being responsible for the authorisation and prudential supervision of an EEA authorised payment institution which is exercising (or intends to exercise) its passport rights in the United Kingdom;

"host state competent authority" means the competent authority designated in accordance with Article 20 of the payment services directive in an EEA State in which an authorised payment institution exercises (or intends to exercise) its passport rights;

"means of distance communication" means any means which, without the simultaneous physical presence of the payment service provider and the payment service user, may be used for the conclusion of a contract for payment services between those parties;

"micro-enterprise" means an enterprise which, at the time at which the contract for payment services is entered into, is an enterprise as defined in Article 1 and Article 2(1) and (3) of the Annex to Recommendation 2003/361/EC;

"the money laundering directive" means Directive 2005/60/EC of the European Parliament and of the Council of 26th October 2005 on the prevention of the use of the financial system for the purpose of money laundering and terrorist financing;

"money remittance" means a service for the transmission of money (or any representation of monetary value), without any payment accounts being created in the name of the payer or the payee, where—

(a) funds are received from a payer for the sole purpose of transferring a corresponding amount to a payee or to another payment service provider acting on behalf of the payee; or

(b) funds are received on behalf of, and made available to, the payee;

"notice" means a notice in writing;

"the OFT" means the Office of Fair Trading;

"parent undertaking" has the same meaning as in the Companies Acts (see section 1162 of, and Schedule 7 to, the Companies Act 2006);

"passport right" (except for the purposes of regulation 26(1)) means the entitlement of a person to establish a branch or provide services in an EEA State other than that in which they are authorised to provide payment services—

(a) in accordance with the Treaty establishing the European Community as applied in the EEA; and

(b) subject to the conditions of the payment services directive;

"payee" means a person who is the intended recipient of funds which have been the subject of a payment transaction;

"payer" means—

(a) a person who holds a payment account and initiates, or consents to the initiation of, a payment order from that payment account; or

(b) where there is no payment account, a person who gives a payment order;

"payment account" means an account held in the name of one or more payment service users which is used for the execution of payment transactions;

"payment instrument" means any—

(a) personalised device; or

(b) personalised set of procedures agreed between the payment service user and the payment service provider,

used by the payment service user in order to initiate a payment order;

"payment order" means any instruction by—

(a) a payer; or

(b) a payee,

to their respective payment service provider requesting the execution of a payment transaction;

"payment services" means any of the activities specified in Part 1 of Schedule 1 when carried out as a regular occupation or business activity, other than any of the activities specified in Part 2 of that Schedule;

"payment services directive" means Directive 2007/64/EC of the European Parliament and of the Council of 13th November 2007 on payment services in the internal market;

"payment service provider" means any of the following persons when they carry out payment services—

(a) authorised payment institutions;

(b) small payment institutions;

(c) EEA authorised payment institutions;

(d) credit institutions;

(e) electronic money institutions;

(f) the Post Office Limited;

(g) the Bank of England, the European Central Bank and the national central banks of EEA States other than the United Kingdom, other than when acting in their capacity as a monetary authority or carrying out other functions of a public nature; and

(h) government departments and local authorities, other than when carrying out functions of a public nature;

"payment service user" means a person when making use of a payment service in the capacity of either payer or payee, or both;

"payment system" means a funds transfer system with formal and standardised arrangements and common rules for the processing, clearing and settlement of payment transactions;

"payment transaction" means an act, initiated by the payer or payee, of placing, transferring or withdrawing funds, irrespective of any underlying obligations between the payer and payee;

"qualifying holding" has the meaning given in article 4(11) of the banking consolidation directive;

"reference exchange rate" means the exchange rate which is used as the basis to calculate any currency exchange and which is made available by the payment service provider or comes from a publicly available source;

"reference interest rate" means the interest rate which is used as the basis for calculating any interest to be applied and which comes from a publicly available source which can be verified by both parties to a contract for payment services;

"the register" means the register maintained by the Authority under regulation 4;

"regulated agreement" has the meaning given by section 189(1) of the Consumer Credit Act 1974 (definitions);

"single payment service contract" means a contract for a single payment transaction not covered by a framework contract;

"small payment institution" means a person included by the Authority in the register pursuant to regulation 4(1)(b);

"subsidiary undertaking" has the same meaning as in the Companies Acts (see section 1162 of, and Schedule 7 to, the Companies Act 2006);

[...]

"unique identifier" means a combination of letters, numbers or symbols specified to the payment service user by the payment service provider and to be provided by the payment service user in relation to a payment transaction in order to identify unambiguously one or both of—

(a) the other payment service user who is a party to the payment transaction;

(b) the other payment service user's payment account;

"value date" means a reference time used by a payment service provider for the calculation of interest on the funds debited from or credited to a payment account.

(2) In these Regulations references to amounts in euro include references to equivalent amounts in another currency.

(3) Unless otherwise defined, expressions used in these Regulations which are also used in the payment services directive have the same meaning as in that directive.

(4) Expressions used in these Regulations and in a modification to a provision in primary or secondary legislation applied by these Regulations have the same meaning as in these Regulations.

3   Exemption for certain bodies

(1) Subject to paragraph (2) and regulation 4(1)(d), these Regulations do not apply to the following persons—

(a) credit unions;

(b) municipal banks; and

(c) the National Savings Bank.

(2) Where municipal banks provide or propose to provide payment services they must give notice to the Authority.

(3) In this regulation—

"credit union" means a credit union within the meaning of—

    (a) the Credit Unions Act 1979;

    (b) the Credit Unions (Northern Ireland) Order 1985;

"municipal bank" means a company which, immediately before 1st December 2001, fell within the definition in section 103 of the Banking Act 1987.

PART 2 REGISTRATION

The register

4 The register of certain payment service providers

(1) The Authority must maintain a register of—

    (a) authorised payment institutions and their EEA branches;

    (b) small payment institutions;

    (c) agents of authorised payment institutions and small payment institutions required to be registered under regulation 29; and

    (d) the persons specified in regulation 3(1) where they provide payment services.

(2) The Authority may include on the register any of the persons mentioned in paragraphs (c) to (h) of the definition of a payment service provider in regulation 2(1) where such persons provide payment services.

(3) Where a person mentioned in paragraph (f), (g) or (h) of the definition of a payment service provider in regulation 2(1)—

    (a) is not included on the register; and

    (b) provides, or proposes to provide, payment services,

the person must give notice to the Authority.

(4) The Authority may—

    (a) keep the register in any form it thinks fit;

    (b) include on it such information as the Authority considers appropriate, provided that the register identifies the payment services for which an institution is authorised or registered under this Part; and

    (c) exploit commercially the information contained in the register, or any part of that information.

(5) The Authority must—

    (a) publish the register online and make it available for public inspection;

    (b) update the register on a regular basis; and

    (c) provide a certified copy of the register, or any part of it, to any person who asks for it—

        (i) on payment of the fee (if any) fixed by the Authority; and

        (ii) in a form (either written or electronic) in which it is legible to the person asking for it.

Authorisation as a payment institution

5 Application for authorisation as a payment institution or variation of an existing authorisation

(1) An application for authorisation as a payment institution must contain or be accompanied by the information specified in Schedule 2.

(2) An application for the variation of an authorisation as a payment institution must—

    (a) contain a statement of the proposed variation;

    (b) contain a statement of the payment services which the applicant proposes to carry on if the authorisation is varied; and

    (c) contain, or be accompanied by, such other information as the Authority may reasonably require.

(3) An application under paragraph (1) or (2) must be made in such manner as the Authority may direct.

(4) At any time after receiving an application and before determining it, the Authority may require the applicant to provide it with such further information as it reasonably considers necessary to enable it to determine the application.

(5) Different directions may be given, and different requirements imposed, in relation to different applications or categories of application.

6   Conditions for authorisation as a payment institution

(1) The Authority may refuse to grant all or part of an application for authorisation as a payment institution only if any of the conditions set out in paragraphs (2) to (8) is not met.

(2) The application must comply with the requirements of, and any requirements imposed under, regulation 5.

(3) The applicant must immediately before the time of authorisation hold the amount of initial capital required in accordance with Part 1 of Schedule 3.

(4) The applicant must be a body corporate constituted under the law of a part of the United Kingdom having—

    (a) its head office, and

    (b) if it has a registered office, that office,

in the United Kingdom.

(5) The applicant must satisfy the Authority that, taking into account the need to ensure the sound and prudent conduct of the affairs of the institution, it has—

    (a) robust governance arrangements for its payment service business, including a clear organisational structure with well-defined, transparent and consistent lines of responsibility;

    (b) effective procedures to identify, manage, monitor and report any risks to which it might be exposed;

    (c) adequate internal control mechanisms, including sound administrative, risk management and accounting procedures,

which are comprehensive and proportionate to the nature, scale and complexity of the payment services to be provided by the institution.

(6) The applicant must satisfy the Authority that—

    (a) any persons having a qualifying holding in it are fit and proper persons having regard to the need to ensure the sound and prudent conduct of the affairs of an authorised payment institution;

    (b) the directors and persons responsible for the management of the institution and, where relevant, the persons responsible for the management of payment services, are of good repute and possess appropriate knowledge and experience to provide payment services;

    (c) it has a business plan (including, for the first three years, a forecast budget calculation) under which appropriate and proportionate systems, resources and procedures will be employed by the institution to operate soundly; and

    (d) it has taken adequate measures for the purpose of safeguarding payment service users' funds in accordance with regulation 19.

(7) The applicant must comply with a requirement of the Money Laundering Regulations 2007 to be included in a register maintained under those Regulations where such a requirement applies to the applicant.

(8) If the applicant has close links with another person ("CL") the applicant must satisfy the Authority—

    (a) that those links are not likely to prevent the Authority's effective supervision of the applicant; and

    (b) if it appears to the Authority that CL is subject to the laws, regulations or administrative provisions of a territory which is not an EEA State ("the foreign provisions"), that neither the foreign provisions, nor any deficiency in their enforcement, would prevent the Authority's effective supervision of the applicant.

(9) For the purposes of paragraph (8), an applicant has close links with CL if—

(a) CL is a parent undertaking of the applicant;

(b) CL is a subsidiary undertaking of the applicant;

(c) CL is a parent undertaking of a subsidiary undertaking of the applicant;

(d) CL is a subsidiary undertaking of a parent undertaking of the applicant;

(e) CL owns or controls 20% or more of the voting rights or capital of the applicant; or

(f) the applicant owns or controls 20% or more of the voting rights or capital of CL.

7   Imposition of requirements

(1) The Authority may include in an authorisation such requirements as it considers appropriate.

(2) A requirement may, in particular, be imposed so as to require the person concerned to—

(a) take a specified action;

(b) refrain from taking a specified action.

(3) A requirement may be imposed by reference to the person's relationship with its group or other members of its group.

(4) Where—

(a) an applicant for authorisation as a payment institution intends to carry on business activities other than the provision of payment services; and

(b) the Authority considers that the carrying on of such other business activities will impair, or is likely to impair—

(i) the financial soundness of the applicant, or

(ii) the Authority's effective supervision of the applicant,

the Authority may require the applicant to establish a separate body corporate to carry on the payment service business.

(5) A requirement expires at the end of such period as the Authority may specify in the authorisation.

(6) Paragraph (5) does not affect the Authority's powers under regulation 8 or 11.

8   Variation etc at request of authorised payment institution

The Authority may, on the application of an authorised payment institution, vary that person's authorisation by—

(a) adding a payment service to those for which it has granted authorisation;

(b) removing a payment service from those for which it has granted authorisation;

(c) imposing a requirement such as may, under regulation 7, be included in an authorisation;

(d) cancelling a requirement included in the authorisation or previously imposed under paragraph (c); or

(e) varying such a requirement,

provided that the conditions set out in regulation 6(4) to (8) and, if applicable, the requirement in regulation 18(1) to maintain own funds, will continue to be met.

9   Determination of application for authorisation or variation of authorisation

(1) The Authority must determine an application for authorisation or the variation of an authorisation before the end of the period of three months beginning with the date on which it received the completed application.

(2) The Authority may determine an incomplete application if it considers it appropriate to do so, and it must in any event determine any such application within 12 months beginning with the date on which it received the application.

(3) The applicant may withdraw its application, by giving the Authority notice, at any time before the Authority determines it.

(4) The Authority may grant authorisation to carry out the payment services to which the application relates or such of them as may be specified in the grant of the authorisation.

(5) If the Authority decides to grant an application for authorisation, or for the variation of an authorisation, it must give the applicant notice of its decision specifying—

    (a) the payment services for which authorisation has been granted; or

    (b) the variation granted,

described in such manner as the Authority considers appropriate.

(6) The notice must state the date on which the authorisation or variation takes effect.

(7) If the Authority proposes to refuse an application or to impose a requirement it must give the applicant a warning notice.

(8) The Authority must, having considered any representations made in response to the warning notice—

    (a) if it decides to refuse the application or to impose a requirement, give the applicant a decision notice; or

    (b) if it grants the application without imposing a requirement, give the applicant notice of its decision, stating the date on which the authorisation or variation takes effect.

(9) If the Authority decides to refuse the application or to impose a requirement the applicant may refer the matter to the [Upper Tribunal].

(10) If the Authority decides to authorise the applicant, or vary its authorisation, it must update the register as soon as practicable.

10 Cancellation of authorisation

(1) The Authority may cancel a person's authorisation and remove the person from the register where—

    (a) the person does not provide payment services within 12 months beginning with the date on which the authorisation took effect;

    (b) the person requests, or consents to, the cancellation of the authorisation;

    (c) the person ceases to engage in business activity for more than six months;

    (d) the person has obtained authorisation through false statements or any other irregular means;

    (e) the person no longer meets, or is unlikely to continue to meet, any of the conditions set out in regulation 6(4) to (8) or, if applicable, the requirement in regulation 18(1) to maintain own funds;

    (f) the person has provided payment services other than in accordance with the authorisation granted to it;

    (g) the person would constitute a threat to the stability of a payment system by continuing its payment services business;

    (h) the cancellation is desirable in order to protect the interests of consumers; or

    (i) the person's provision of payment services is otherwise unlawful.

(2) Where the Authority proposes to cancel a person's authorisation, other than at the person's request, it must give the person a warning notice.

(3) The Authority must, having considered any representations made in response to the warning notice—

    (a) if it decides to cancel the authorisation, give the person a decision notice; or

    (b) if it decides not to cancel the authorisation, give the person notice of its decision.

(4) If the Authority decides to cancel the authorisation, other than at the person's request, the person may refer the matter to the [Upper Tribunal].

(5) Where the period for a reference to the [Upper Tribunal] has expired without a reference being made, the Authority must as soon as practicable update the register accordingly.

[10A Request for cancellation of authorisation

(1) A request for cancellation of a person's authorisation under regulation 10(1)(b) must be made in such manner as the Authority may direct.

(2) At any time after receiving a request and before determining it, the Authority may require the person making the request to provide it with such further information as it reasonably considers necessary to enable it to determine the request.

(3) Different directions may be given and different requirements imposed, in relation to different requests or cate-gories of request.]

11 Variation of authorisation on Authority's own initiative

(1) The Authority may vary a person's authorisation in any of the ways mentioned in regulation 8 if it appears to the Authority that—

    (a) the person no longer meets, or is unlikely to continue to meet, any of the conditions set out in regulation 6(4) to (8) or, if applicable, the requirement in regulation 18(1) to maintain own funds;

    (b) the person has provided a particular payment service or payment services other than in accordance with the authorisation granted to it;

    (c) the person would constitute a threat to the stability of a payment system by continuing to provide a particular payment service or payment services;

    (d) the variation is desirable in order to protect the interests of consumers; or

    (e) the person's provision of a particular payment service or payment services is otherwise unlawful.

(2) A variation under this regulation takes effect—

    (a) immediately, if the notice given under paragraph (6) states that that is the case;

    (b) on such date as may be specified in the notice; or

    (c) if no date is specified in the notice, when the matter to which the notice relates is no longer open to review.

(3) A variation may be expressed to take effect immediately or on a specified date only if the Authority, having regard to the ground on which it is exercising the power under paragraph (1), reasonably considers that it is necessary for the variation to take effect immediately or, as the case may be, on that date.

(4) The Authority must as soon as practicable after the variation takes effect update the register accordingly.

(5) A person who is aggrieved by the variation of their authorisation under this regulation may refer the matter to the [Upper Tribunal].

(6) Where the Authority proposes to vary a person's authorisation under this regulation, it must give the person notice.

(7) The notice must—

    (a) give details of the variation;

    (b) state the Authority's reasons for the variation and for its determination as to when the variation takes effect;

    (c) inform the person that they may make representations to the Authority within such period as may be specified in the notice (whether or not the person has referred the matter to the [Upper Tribunal]);

    (d) inform the person of the date on which the variation takes effect; and

    (e) inform the person of their right to refer the matter to the [Upper Tribunal] and the procedure for such a reference.

(8) The Authority may extend the period allowed under the notice for making representations.

(9) If, having considered any representations made by the person, the Authority decides—

    (a) to vary the authorisation in the way proposed, or

    (b) if the authorisation has been varied, not to rescind the variation,

it must give the person notice.

(10) If, having considered any representations made by the person, the Authority decides—

    (a) not to vary the authorisation in the way proposed,

    (b) to vary the authorisation in a different way, or

    (c) to rescind a variation which has taken effect,

it must give the person notice.

(11) A notice given under paragraph (9) must inform the person of their right to refer the matter to the [Upper Tribunal] and the procedure for such a reference.

(12) A notice under paragraph (10)(b) must comply with paragraph (7).

(13) For the purposes of paragraph (2)(c), paragraphs (a) to (d) of section 391(8) of the 2000 Act (publication) apply to determine whether a matter is open to review.

Registration as a small payment institution

12 Application for registration as a small payment institution or variation of an existing registration

(1) An application for registration as a small payment institution must contain, or be accompanied by, such information as the Authority may reasonably require.

(2) An application for the variation of a registration as a small payment institution must—
  (a) contain a statement of the proposed variation;
  (b) contain a statement of the payment services which the applicant proposes to carry on if the registration is varied; and
  (c) contain, or be accompanied by, such other information as the Authority may reasonably require.

(3) An application under paragraph (1) or (2) must be made in such manner as the Authority may direct.

(4) At any time after receiving an application and before determining it, the Authority may require the applicant to provide it with such further information as it reasonably considers necessary to enable it to determine the application.

(5) Different directions may be given, and different requirements imposed, in relation to different applications or categories of application.

13 Conditions for registration as a small payment institution

(1) The Authority may refuse to register an applicant as a small payment institution only if any of the conditions set out in paragraphs (2) to (6) is not met.

(2) The application must comply with the requirements of, and any requirements imposed under, regulation 12.

(3) The monthly average over the period of 12 months preceding the application of the total amount of payment transactions executed by the applicant, including any of its agents in the United Kingdom, must not exceed 3 million euros.

(4) None of the individuals responsible for the management or operation of the business has been convicted of—
  (a) an offence under Part 7 of the Proceeds of Crime Act 2002(money laundering) or under the Money Laundering Regulations 2007;
  (b) an offence under section 15 (fund-raising), 16 (use and possession), 17 (funding arrangements), 18 (money laundering) or 63 (terrorist finance: jurisdiction) of the Terrorism Act 2000;
  (c) an offence under the 2000 Act;
  [(d) an offence under regulation 3, 4 or 6 of the Al-Qaida and Taliban (Asset-Freezing) Regulations 2010, or regulation 10 of the Al-Qaida (Asset-Freezing) Regulations 2011;]
  [(da) an offence under section 11, 12, 13, 14, 15 or 18 of the Terrorist Asset-Freezing etc Act 2010 (offences relating to the freezing of funds etc of designated persons);]
  (e) an offence under these Regulations [or the Electronic Money Regulations 2011]; or
  (f) any other financial crimes.

(5) The applicant's head office, registered office or place of residence, as the case may be, must be in the United Kingdom.

(6) The applicant must comply with a requirement of the Money Laundering Regulations 2007 to be included in a register maintained under those Regulations where such a requirement applies to the applicant.

(7) For the purposes of paragraph (3), where the applicant has yet to commence the provision of payment services, or has been providing payment services for less than 12 months, the monthly average may be based on the projected total amount of payment transactions over a 12 month period.

(8) In paragraph (4) "financial crime" includes any offence involving fraud or dishonesty and, for this purpose, "offence" includes any act or omission which would be an offence if it had taken place in the United Kingdom.

14   Supplementary provisions

Regulations 7 to 11 apply to registration as a small payment institution as they apply to authorisation as a payment institution with the following modifications—

(a) references to authorisation are to be treated as references to registration;

(b) omit regulation 7(4);

(c) in regulation 8 for "an authorised payment institution" substitute "small payment institution" and for "provided that" to the end substitute—

"provided that the conditions set out in regulation 13(4) to (6) will continue to be met and that the monthly average over any period of 12 months of the total amount of payment transactions executed by the institution, including any of its agents in the United Kingdom, continues not to exceed 3 million euro ("the financial limit").";

(d) in regulation 10 for paragraph (1)(e) substitute—

"(e) the person no longer meets, or is unlikely to continue to meet, any of the conditions set out in regulation 13(4) to (6) or the financial limit referred to in regulation 8;"; and

(e) in regulation 11 for paragraph (1)(a) substitute—

"(a) the person no longer meets, or is unlikely to continue to meet, any of the conditions set out in regulation 13(4) to (6) or the financial limit referred to in regulation 8;".

15   Application for authorisation as a payment institution where the financial limit is exceeded

Where the financial limit referred to in regulation 8 (as applied by regulation 14(c)) is exceeded, the institution concerned must, within 30 days of becoming aware of the change in circumstances, apply for authorisation as a payment institution under regulation 5 if it intends to continue providing payment services in the United Kingdom.

Common provisions

16   Duty to notify changes

(1) If at any time after an applicant has provided the Authority with any information under regulation 5(1), (2), or (4), or 12(1), (2) or (4) and before the Authority has determined the application—

(a) there is, or is likely to be, a material change affecting any matter contained in that information; or

(b) it becomes apparent to the applicant that the information is incomplete or contains a material inaccuracy,

the applicant must provide the Authority with details of the change, the complete information or a correction of the inaccuracy (as the case may be) without undue delay, or, in the case of a material change which has not yet taken place, the applicant must provide details of the likely change as soon as the applicant is aware of such change.

(2) The obligation in paragraph (1) also applies to material changes or significant inaccuracies affecting any matter contained in any supplementary information provided pursuant to that paragraph.

(3) Any information to be provided to the Authority under this regulation must be in such form or verified in such manner as it may direct.

17   Authorised payment institutions and small payment institutions acting without permission

If an authorised payment institution or a small payment institution carries on a payment service in the United Kingdom, or purports to do so, other than in accordance with an authorisation or registration granted, or deemed to be granted under regulation 121, to it by the Authority under these Regulations, it is to be taken to have contravened a requirement imposed on it under these Regulations.

PART 3   AUTHORISED PAYMENT INSTITUTIONS

18   Capital requirements

(1) Subject to paragraph (2), an authorised payment institution must maintain at all times own funds as defined for the purposes of Part 2 of Schedule 3 equal to or in excess of—

    (a) the amount of initial capital specified in Part 1 of Schedule 3, or

    (b) the amount of the own funds requirement calculated in accordance with paragraph 11 of Schedule 3 subject to any adjustment directed by the Authority under paragraph 12 of that Schedule,

whichever is greater.

(2) Paragraph (1) does not apply to an authorised payment institution—

    (a) which is included in the consolidated supervision of a parent credit institution pursuant to the banking consolidation directive; and

    (b) in respect of which all of the conditions specified in Article 69(1) of the banking consolidation directive are met.

19   Safeguarding requirements

(1) For the purposes of this regulation "relevant funds" comprise the following—

    (a) sums received from, or for the benefit of, a payment service user for the execution of a payment transaction; and

    (b) sums received from a payment service provider for the execution of a payment transaction on behalf of a payment service user.

(2) Where—

    (a) only a portion of the sums referred to in paragraph (1)(a) or (b) is to be used for the execution of a payment transaction (with the remainder being used for non-payment services); and

    (b) the precise portion attributable to the execution of the payment transaction is variable or unknown in advance,

the relevant funds are such amount as may be reasonably estimated, on the basis of historical data and to the satisfaction of the Authority, to be representative of the portion attributable to the execution of the payment transaction.

(3) Where the relevant funds in respect of a payment transaction exceed £50, an authorised payment institution must safeguard such funds in accordance with either—

    (a) paragraphs (4) to (8); or

    (b) paragraphs (9) and (10).

(4) An authorised payment institution must keep relevant funds segregated from any other funds that it holds.

(5) Where the authorised payment institution continues to hold the relevant funds at the end of the business day following the day on which they were received it must—

    (a) place them in a separate account that it holds with an authorised credit institution; or

    (b) invest the relevant funds in such secure, liquid assets as the Authority may approve ("relevant assets") and place those assets in a separate account with an authorised custodian.

(6) An account in which relevant funds or relevant assets are placed under paragraph (5) must—

    (a) be designated in such a way as to show that it is an account which is held for the purpose of safeguarding relevant funds or relevant assets in accordance with this regulation; and

    (b) be used only for holding those funds or assets.

(7) No person other than the authorised payment institution may have any interest in or right over the relevant funds or relevant assets placed in an account in accordance with paragraph (5)(a) or (b) except as provided by this regulation.

(8) The authorised payment institution must keep a record of—

    (a) any relevant funds segregated in accordance with paragraph (4);

    (b) any relevant funds placed in an account in accordance with paragraph (5)(a); and

    (c) any relevant assets placed in an account in accordance with paragraph (5)(b).

(9) The authorised payment institution must ensure that—

    (a) any relevant funds are covered by—

        (i)   an insurance policy with an authorised insurer;

        (ii) a guarantee from an authorised insurer; or

        (iii) a guarantee from an authorised credit institution; and

    (b) the proceeds of any such insurance policy or guarantee are payable upon an insolvency event into a separate account held by the authorised payment institution which must—

        (i) be designated in such a way as to show that it is an account which is held for the purpose of safeguarding relevant funds in accordance with this regulation; and

        (ii) be used only for holding such proceeds.

(10) No person other than the authorised payment institution may have any interest in or right over the proceeds placed in an account in accordance with paragraph (9)(b) except as provided by this regulation.

(11) Subject to paragraph (12), where there is an insolvency event—

    (a) the claims of payment service users are to be paid from the asset pool in priority to all other creditors; and

    (b) until all the claims of payment service users have been paid, no right of set-off or security right may be exercised in respect of the asset pool except to the extent that the right of set-off relates to fees and expenses in relation to operating an account held in accordance with paragraph (5)(a) or (b) or (9)(b).

(12) The claims referred to in paragraph (11)(a) shall not be subject to the priority of expenses of an insolvency proceeding except in respect of the costs of distributing the asset pool.

(13) Paragraphs (11) and (12) shall apply to any relevant funds which a small payment institution (or an authorised payment institution in relation to relevant funds of £50 or less) voluntarily safeguards in accordance with either paragraphs (4) to (8) or paragraphs (9) and (10).

(14) An authorised payment institution (and any small payment institution which voluntarily safeguards relevant funds) must maintain organisational arrangements sufficient to minimise the risk of the loss or diminution of relevant funds or relevant assets through fraud, misuse, negligence or poor administration.

(15) In this regulation—

"asset pool" means—

    (a) any relevant funds segregated in accordance with paragraph (4);

    (b) any relevant funds held in an account in accordance with paragraph (5)(a);

    (c) any relevant assets held in an account in accordance with paragraph (5)(b); and

    (d) any proceeds of an insurance policy or guarantee held in an account in accordance with paragraph (9)(b);

"authorised insurer" means a person authorised for the purposes of the 2000 Act to effect and carry out a contract of general insurance as principal or otherwise authorised in accordance with Article 6 of the First Council Directive 73/239/EEC of 24th July 1973 on the business of direct insurance other than life insurance, other than a person in the same group as the authorised payment institution;

"authorised credit institution" means a person authorised for the purposes of the 2000 Act to accept deposits or otherwise authorised as a credit institution in accordance with Article 6 of the banking consolidation directive other than a person in the same group as the authorised payment institution;

"authorised custodian" means a person authorised for the purposes of the 2000 Act to safeguard and administer investments or authorised as an investment firm under Article 5 of Directive 2004/39/EC of 12th April 2004 on markets in financial instruments which holds those investments under regulatory standards at least equivalent to those set out under Article 13 of that directive;

"insolvency event" means any of the following procedures in relation to an authorised payment institution or small payment institution—

    (e) the making of a winding-up order;

    (f) the passing of a resolution for voluntary winding-up;

    (g) the entry of the institution into administration;

    (h) the appointment of a receiver or manager of the institution's property;

    (i) the approval of a proposed voluntary arrangement (being a composition in satisfaction of debts or a scheme of arrangement);

    (j) the making of a bankruptcy order;

    (k) in Scotland, the award of sequestration;

    (l) the making of any deed of arrangement for the benefit of creditors or, in Scotland, the execution of a trust deed for creditors;

    (m) the conclusion of any composition contract with creditors; or

    (n) the making of an insolvency administration order or, in Scotland, sequestration, in respect of the estate of a deceased person;

"insolvency proceeding" means—

    (o) winding-up, administration, receivership, bankruptcy or, in Scotland, sequestration;

    (p) a voluntary arrangement, deed of arrangement or trust deed for the benefit of creditors; or

    (q) the administration of the insolvent estate of a deceased person;

"security right" means—

    (r) security for a debt owed by an authorised payment institution or a small payment institution and includes any charge, lien, mortgage or other security over the asset pool or any part of the asset pool; and

    (s) any charge arising in respect of the expenses of a voluntary arrangement.

20 Accounting and statutory audit

(1) Where an authorised payment institution carries on activities other than the provision of payment services, it must provide to the Authority separate accounting information in respect of its provision of payment services.

(2) Such accounting information must be subject, where relevant, to an auditor's report prepared by the institution's statutory auditors or an audit firm (within the meaning of Directive 2006/43/EC of the European Parliament and of the Council of 17th May 2006 on statutory audits of annual accounts and consolidated accounts).

(3) A statutory auditor or audit firm ("the auditor") must, in any of the circumstances referred to in paragraph (4), communicate to the Authority information on, or its opinion on, matters—

    (a) of which it has become aware in its capacity as auditor of an authorised payment institution or of a person with close links to an authorised payment institution; and

    (b) which relate to payment services provided by that institution.

(4) The circumstances are that—

    (a) the auditor reasonably believes that—

      (i)   there is or has been, or may be or may have been, a contravention of any requirement imposed on the authorised payment institution by or under these Regulations; and

      (ii) the contravention may be of material significance to the Authority in determining whether to exercise, in relation to that institution, any functions conferred on the Authority by these Regulations;

  (b) the auditor reasonably believes that the information on, or his opinion on, those matters may be of material significance to the Authority in determining whether the institution meets or will continue to meet the conditions set out in regulation 6(4) to (8) and, if applicable, the requirement in regulation 18(1) to maintain own funds;

  (c) the auditor reasonably believes that the institution is not, may not be or may cease to be, a going concern;

  (d) the auditor is precluded from stating in his report that the annual accounts have been properly prepared in accordance with the Companies Act 2006;

  (e) the auditor is precluded from stating in his report, where applicable, that the annual accounts give a true and fair view of the matters referred to in section 495 of the Companies Act 2006 (auditor's report on company's annual accounts) including as it is applied and modified by regulation 39 of the Limited Liability Partnerships (Accounts and Audit) (Application of Companies Act 2006) Regulations 2008 ("the LLP Regulations"); or

  (f) the auditor is required to state in his report in relation to the person concerned any of the facts referred to in subsection (2), (3) or (5) of section 498 of the Companies Act 2006 (duties of auditor) or, in the case of limited liability partnerships, subsection (2), (3) or (4) of section 498 as applied and modified by regulation 40 of the LLP Regulations.

(5) In this regulation a person has close links with an authorised payment institution ("A") if that person is—

  (a) a parent undertaking of A;

  (b) a subsidiary undertaking of A;

  (c) a parent undertaking of a subsidiary undertaking of A; or

  (d) a subsidiary undertaking of a parent undertaking of A.

21 Outsourcing

(1) An authorised payment institution must notify the Authority of its intention to enter into a contract with another person under which that other person will carry out any operational function relating to its provision of payment services ("outsourcing").

(2) Where an authorised payment institution intends to outsource any important operational function, all of the following conditions must be met—

  (a) the outsourcing is not undertaken in such a way as to impair—

      (i)   the quality of the authorised payment institution's internal control; or

      (ii) the ability of the Authority to monitor the authorised payment institution's compliance with these Regulations;

  (b) the outsourcing does not result in any delegation by the senior management of the authorised payment institution of responsibility for complying with the requirements imposed by or under these Regulations;

  (c) the relationship and obligations of the authorised payment institution towards its payment service users under these Regulations is not substantially altered;

  (d) compliance with the conditions which the authorised payment institution must observe in order to be authorised and remain so is not adversely affected; and

  (e) none of the conditions of the payment institution's authorisation requires removal or variation.

(3) For the purposes of paragraph (2), an operational function is important if a defect or failure in its performance would materially impair—

  (a) compliance by the authorised payment institution with these Regulations and any requirements of its authorisation;

(b) the financial performance of the authorised payment institution; or

(c) the soundness or continuity of the authorised payment institution's payment services.

22 Record keeping

(1) An authorised payment institution must maintain relevant records and keep them for at least five years from the date on which the record was created.

(2) For the purposes of paragraph (1), records are relevant where they relate to the authorised payment institution's compliance with this Part and, in particular, would enable the Authority to supervise effectively such compliance.

Exercise of passport rights

23 Notice of intention

(1) Where an authorised payment institution intends to exercise its passport rights for the first time in a particular EEA State it must give the Authority, in such manner as the Authority may direct, notice of its intention to do so ("a notice of intention") which—

(a) identifies the payment services which it seeks to carry on in exercise of those rights in that State;

(b) gives the names of those responsible for the management of a proposed EEA branch, if any; and

(c) provides details of the organisational structure of a proposed EEA branch, if any.

(2) The Authority must, within one month beginning with the date on which it receives the notice of intention, inform the host state competent authority of—

(a) the name and address of the authorised payment institution; and

(b) the information contained in the notice of intention.

(3) Where an authorised payment institution intends to exercise its passport rights through an EEA agent, the provisions of regulation 29 apply.

24 Registration of EEA branch

(1) If the Authority, taking into account any information received from the host state competent authority, has reasonable grounds to suspect that, in connection with the establishment of an EEA branch by an authorised payment institution—

(a) money laundering or terrorist financing within the meaning of the money laundering directive is taking place, has taken place, or has been attempted; or

(b) the risk of such activities taking place would be increased,

the Authority may refuse to register the EEA branch or cancel any such registration already made and remove the branch from the register.

(2) If the Authority proposes to refuse to register, or cancel the registration of, an EEA branch, it must give the relevant authorised payment institution a warning notice.

(3) The Authority must, having considered any representations made in response to the warning notice—

(a) if it decides not to register the branch, or to cancel its registration, give the authorised payment institution a decision notice; or

(b) if it decides to register the branch, or not to cancel the registration, give the authorised payment institution notice of its decision.

(4) If the Authority decides not to register the branch, or to cancel its registration, the authorised payment institution may refer the matter to the [Upper Tribunal].

(5) If the Authority decides to register an EEA branch, it must update the register as soon as practicable.

(6) If the Authority decides to cancel the registration, the Authority must, where the period for a reference to the [Upper Tribunal] has expired without a reference being made, as soon as practicable update the register accordingly.

25   Supervision of firms exercising passport rights

(1) Without prejudice to the generality of regulation 119, the Authority must co-operate with the relevant host state competent authority or home state competent authority, as the case may be, in relation to the exercise of passport rights by any authorised payment institution or EEA authorised payment institution.

(2) The Authority must, in particular—

(a) notify the host state competent authority whenever it intends to carry out an on-site inspection in the host state competent authority's territory; and

(b) provide the host state competent authority or home state competent authority, as the case may be—

(i) on request, with all relevant information; and

(ii) on its own initiative, with all essential information,

relating to the exercise of passport rights by an authorised payment institution or EEA authorised payment institution, including where there is an infringement or suspected infringement of these Regulations or of the provisions of the payment services directive by an agent, branch or entity carrying out activities on behalf of such an institution.

(3) Where the Authority and the home state competent authority agree, the Authority may carry out on-site inspections on behalf of the home state competent authority in respect of payment services provided by an EEA authorised payment institution exercising its passport rights.

(4) If the Authority has reasonable grounds to suspect that, in connection with the proposed establishment of a branch or the proposed provision of services by an EEA authorised payment institution—

(a) money laundering or terrorist financing within the meaning of the Money Laundering Regulations 2007 is taking place, has taken place, or has been attempted; or

(b) the risk of such activities taking place would be increased,

it must inform the relevant home state competent authority of its grounds for suspicion.

26   Carrying on of Consumer Credit Act business by EEA authorised payment institutions

(1) Sections 203 (power to prohibit the carrying on of Consumer Credit Act business) and 204 (power to restrict the carrying on of Consumer Credit Act business) of, and Schedule 16 (prohibitions and restrictions imposed by OFT) to, the 2000 Act apply in relation to EEA authorised payment institutions exercising passport rights in the United Kingdom under these Regulations as they apply in relation to EEA firms exercising passport rights under Part 2 of Schedule 3 to the 2000 Act (EEA passport rights) with the following modifications—

(a) in section 203(10)—

(i) for the definition of "a consumer credit EEA firm" substitute—

""a consumer credit EEA firm" means an EEA authorised payment institution (as defined by regulation 2(1) of the Payment Services Regulations 2009) which is exercising passport rights in the United Kingdom and is carrying on any Consumer Credit Act business;" and

(ii) for the definition of "listed activity" substitute—

""listed activity" means an activity listed in the Annex to the payment services directive and any activity carried on in accordance with Article 16 of that directive;";

(b) in paragraph 2(5)(b) of Schedule 16, for "the firm's home state regulator" substitute "the home state competent authority (as defined by regulation 2(1) of the Payment Services Regulations 2009)".

(2) Sections 21 (businesses needing a licence) and 39(1) (offences against Part 3) of the Consumer Credit Act 1974 do not apply in relation to the carrying on by an EEA authorised payment institution of a payment service which is Consumer Credit Act business, unless the OFT has exercised the power conferred on it by section 203 of the 2000 Act, as applied with modifications by paragraph (1), in relation to that institution.

(3) In this regulation "Consumer Credit Act business" has the same meaning as in section 203 of the 2000 Act.

PART 4 PROVISIONS APPLICABLE TO AUTHORISED PAYMENT INSTITUTIONS AND SMALL PAYMENT INSTITUTIONS

27 Additional activities

(1) Authorised payment institutions and small payment institutions may, in addition to providing payment services, engage in the following activities—

    (a) the provision of operational and closely related ancillary services, including—

        (i)   ensuring the execution of payment transactions;

        (ii) foreign exchange services;

        (iii) safe-keeping activities; and

        (iv) the storage and processing of data;

    (b) the operation of payment systems; and

    (c) business activities other than the provision of payment services, subject to any relevant Community or national law.

(2) Authorised payment institutions and small payment institutions may grant credit in relation to the provision of the payment services specified in paragraph 1(d), (e) and (g) of Schedule 1 only if—

    (a) such credit is ancillary and granted exclusively in connection with the execution of a payment transaction;

    (b) such credit is not granted from the funds received or held for the purposes of executing payment transactions;

    (c) in cases where such credit is granted by an authorised payment institution exercising its passport rights, there is an obligation upon the payment service user to repay the credit within a period not exceeding 12 months; and

    (d) in relation to an authorised payment institution, in the opinion of the Authority the institution's own funds (comprising the items specified in paragraph 3(a) to (j) of Schedule 3) are, and continue to be, adequate in the light of the overall amount of credit granted.

28 Payment accounts and sums received for the execution of payment transactions

Any payment account held by an authorised payment institution or a small payment institution must be used only in relation to payment transactions.

29 Use of agents

(1) Authorised payment institutions and small payment institutions may not provide payment services in the United Kingdom through an agent unless the agent is included on the register.

(2) Authorised payment institutions may not provide payment services in the exercise of their passport rights through an EEA agent unless the agent is included on the register.

(3) An application for an agent to be included on the register must—

    (a) contain, or be accompanied by, the following information—

        (i)   the name and address of the agent;

        (ii) where relevant, a description of the internal control mechanisms that will be used by the agent—

            (aa) in the case of an agent in the United Kingdom, to comply with the Money Laundering Regulations 2007; and

            (bb) in the case of an EEA agent, to comply with provisions of the money laundering directive; and

      (iii) in the case of an agent of an authorised payment institution, the identity of the direc-
tors and persons responsible for the management of the agent and evidence that they
are fit and proper persons; and

      (iv) such other information as the Authority may reasonably require; and

  (b) be made in such manner as the Authority may direct.

(4) Different directions may be given, and different requirements imposed, in relation to different applications or categories of application.

(5) At any time after receiving an application and before determining it, the Authority may
require the applicant to provide it with such further information as it reasonably considers necessary
to enable it to determine the application.

(6) The Authority may refuse to include the agent on the register only if—

  (a) it has not received the information referred to in paragraph (3)(a), or is not satisfied that
such information is correct;

  (b) it is not satisfied that the directors and persons responsible for the management of the
agent are fit and proper persons;

  (c) it has reasonable grounds to suspect that, in connection with the provision of services
through the agent—

      (i) money laundering or terrorist financing within the meaning of the money laundering
directive (or, in the United Kingdom, the Money Laundering Regulations 2007) is
taking place, has taken place, or has been attempted; or

      (ii) the risk of such activities taking place would be increased.

(7) Where—

  (a) an authorised payment institution intends to provide payment services through an EEA
agent; and

  (b) the Authority proposes to include the EEA agent on the register,

the Authority must inform the host state competent authority and take account of its opinion (if provided within such reasonable period as the Authority specifies) on any of the matters referred to in
paragraph (6)(b) or (c).

(8) The Authority must decide whether to include the agent on the register within a reasonable
period of it having received a completed application.

(9) If the Authority proposes to refuse to include the agent on the register, it must give the authorised payment institution or the small payment institution, as the case may be, a warning notice.

(10) The Authority must, having considered any representations made in response to the warning
notice—

  (a) if it decides not to include the agent on the register, give the applicant a decision notice;
or

  (b) if it decides to include the agent on the register, give the applicant notice of its decision,
stating the date on which the registration takes effect.

(11) If the Authority decides not to include the agent on the register the applicant may refer the
matter to the [Upper Tribunal].

(12) If the Authority decides to include the agent on the register, it must update the register as
soon as practicable.

(13) An application under paragraph (3) may be combined with an application under regulation
5 or 12, in which case the application must be determined in the manner set out in regulation 9 (if
relevant, as applied by regulation 14).

(14) An authorised payment institution or a small payment institution must ensure that agents
acting on its behalf inform payment service users of the agency arrangement.

30 Removal of agent from register

(1) The Authority may remove an agent of an authorised payment institution or small payment
institution from the register where—

  (a) the authorised payment institution or small payment institution requests, or consents to,
the agent's removal from the register;

(b) the authorised payment institution or small payment institution has obtained registration through false statements or any other irregular means;

(c) regulation 29(6)(b) or (c) applies;

(d) the removal is desirable in order to protect the interests of consumers; or

(e) the agent's provision of payment services is otherwise unlawful.

(2) Where the Authority proposes to remove an agent from the register, other than at the request of the authorised payment institution or small payment institution, it must give the authorised payment institution or small payment institution a warning notice.

(3) The Authority must, having considered any representations made in response to the warning notice—

(a) if it decides to remove the agent, give the authorised payment institution or small payment institution a decision notice; or

(b) if it decides not to remove the agent, give the authorised payment institution or small payment institution notice of its decision.

(4) If the Authority decides to remove the agent, other than at the request of the authorised payment institution or small payment institution, the institution concerned may refer the matter to the [Upper Tribunal].

(5) Where the period for a reference to the [Upper Tribunal] has expired without a reference being made, the Authority must as soon as practicable update the register accordingly.

31   Reliance

(1) Where an authorised payment institution or a small payment institution relies on a third party for the performance of operational functions it must take all reasonable steps to ensure that these Regulations are complied with.

(2) Without prejudice to paragraph (1), an authorised payment institution or a small payment institution is responsible, to the same extent as if it had expressly permitted it, for anything done or omitted by any of its employees, any agent or branch providing payment services on its behalf, or any entity to which activities are outsourced.

32   Duty to notify change in circumstance

(1) Where it becomes apparent to an authorised payment institution or a small payment institution that there is, or is likely to be, a significant change in circumstances which is relevant to—

(a) in the case of an authorised payment institution—

(i) its fulfilment of any of the conditions set out in regulation 6(4) to (8) and, if applicable, the requirement in regulation 18(1) to maintain own funds;

(ii) the payment services which it seeks to carry on in exercise of its passport rights;

(b) in the case of a small payment institution, its fulfilment of any of the conditions set out in regulation 13(4) to (6) and compliance with the financial limit referred to in regulation 8 (as applied by regulation 14(c)); and

(c) in the case of the use of an agent to provide payment services, the matters referred to in regulation 29(6)(b) and (c),

it must provide the Authority with details of the change without undue delay, or, in the case of a substantial change in circumstances which has not yet taken place, details of the likely change a reasonable period before it takes place.

(2) Any information to be provided to the Authority under this regulation must be in such form or verified in such manner as it may direct.

PART 5 INFORMATION REQUIREMENTS
FOR APPLICATION

33   Application of Part 5

(1)   This Part applies to a contract for payment services where—

(a)   the services are provided from an establishment maintained by a payment service provider or its agent in the United Kingdom;

(b)   the payment service providers of both the payer and the payee are located within the EEA; and

(c)   the payment services are carried out either in euro or in the currency of an EEA State that has not adopted the euro as its currency.

(2)   Regulations 36 to 39 apply to payment services provided under a single payment service contract.

(3)   Regulations 40 to 46 apply to payment services provided under a framework contract.

(4)   Except where the payment service user is—

(a)   a consumer,

(b)   a micro-enterprise, or

(c)   a charity,

the parties may agree that any or all of the provisions of this Part do not apply to a contract for payment services.

34   Disapplication of certain regulations in the case of consumer credit agreements

Where the contract under which a payment service is provided is, or would be, when entered into, a regulated agreement—

(a)   regulations 41, 42 and 43 do not apply;

(b)   the payment service provider is only required under regulation 40(1) to provide the information specified in paragraph 3(b) of Schedule 4; and

(c)   the payment service provider is only required under regulation 45(1) to provide the information specified in paragraph (2)(d) of regulation 45.

35   Disapplication of certain regulations in the case of low-value payment instruments

(1)   This regulation applies in respect of payment instruments which, under the framework contract governing their use—

(a)   can be used only to execute individual payment transactions of 30 euro or less, or in relation to payment transactions executed wholly within the United Kingdom, 60 euro or less;

(b)   have a spending limit of 150 euro, or where payment transactions must be executed wholly within the United Kingdom, 300 euro; or

(c)   store funds that do not exceed 500 euro at any time.

(2)   Where this regulation applies—

(a)   regulations 40 and 44 do not apply and the payment service provider is only required to provide the payer with information about the main characteristics of the payment service, including—

(i)   the way in which the payment instrument can be used;

(ii)   the liability of the payer, as set out in regulation 62;

(iii) charges levied;

(iv)   any other material information the payer might need to take an informed decision; and

(v)   an indication of where the information specified in Schedule 4 is made available in an easily accessible manner;

(b)   the parties may agree that regulations 45 and 46 do not apply and instead—

(i)   the payment service provider must provide or make available a reference enabling the payment service user to identify—

(aa) the payment transaction;

(bb) the amount of the payment transaction;

(cc)   any charges payable in respect of the payment transaction;

(ii) in the case of several payment transactions of the same kind made to the same payee, the payment service provider must provide or make available to the payment service user information about the total amount of the payment transactions and any charges for those payment transactions; or

(iii) where the payment instrument is used anonymously or the payment service provider is not otherwise technically able to provide or make available the information specified in paragraph (i) or (ii), the payment service provider must enable the payer to verify the amount of funds stored; and

(c) the parties may agree that regulation 47(1) does not apply to information provided or made available in accordance with regulation 42.

Single payment service contracts

36   Information required prior to the conclusion of a single payment service contract

(1) A payment service provider must provide or make available to the payment service user the information specified in paragraph (2), whether by supplying a copy of the draft single payment service contract or supplying a copy of the draft payment order or otherwise, either—

(a) before the payment service user is bound by the single payment service contract; or

(b) immediately after the execution of the payment transaction, where the contract is concluded at the payment service user's request using a means of distance communication which does not enable provision of such information in accordance with sub-paragraph (a).

(2) The information referred to in paragraph (1) is—

(a) the information or unique identifier that has to be provided by the payment service user in order for a payment order to be properly executed;

(b) the maximum time in which the payment service will be executed;

(c) the charges payable by the payment service user to the user's payment service provider and, where applicable, a breakdown of the amounts of such charges;

(d) where applicable, the actual or reference exchange rate to be applied to the payment transaction; and

(e) such of the information specified in Schedule 4 as is relevant to the single payment service contract in question.

37   Information required after receipt of the payment order

(1) The payer's payment service provider must, immediately after receipt of the payment order, provide or make available to the payer the information specified in paragraph (2).

(2) The information referred to in paragraph (1) is—

(a) a reference enabling the payer to identify the payment transaction and, where appropriate, information relating to the payee;

(b) the amount of the payment transaction in the currency used in the payment order;

(c) the amount of any charges for the payment transaction payable by the payer and, where applicable, a breakdown of the amounts of such charges;

(d) where an exchange rate is used in the payment transaction and the actual rate used in the payment transaction differs from the rate provided in accordance with regulation 36(2) (d), the actual rate used or a reference to it, and the amount of the payment transaction after that currency conversion; and

(e) the date on which the payment service provider received the payment order.

38 Information for the payee after execution

(1) The payee's payment service provider must, immediately after the execution of the payment transaction, provide or make available to the payee the information specified in paragraph (2).

(2) The information referred to in paragraph (1) is—

(a) a reference enabling the payee to identify the payment transaction and, where appropriate, the payer and any information transferred with the payment transaction;

(b) the amount of the payment transaction in the currency in which the funds are at the payee's disposal;

(c) the amount of any charges for the payment transaction payable by the payee and, where applicable, a breakdown of the amount of such charges;

(d) where applicable, the exchange rate used in the payment transaction by the payee's payment service provider, and the amount of the payment transaction before that currency conversion; and

(e) the credit value date.

39 Avoidance of duplication of information

Where a payment order for a single payment transaction is transmitted by way of a payment instrument issued under a framework contract, the payment service provider in respect of that single payment transaction need not provide or make available under regulations 36 to 38 information which has been provided or made available, or will be provided or made available, under regulations 40 to 45 by another payment service provider in respect of the framework contract.

Framework contracts

40 Prior general information for framework contracts

(1) A payment service provider must provide to the payment service user the information specified in Schedule 4, either—

(a) in good time before the payment service user is bound by the framework contract; or

(b) where the contract is concluded at the payment service user's request using a means of distance communication which does not enable provision of such information in accordance with sub-paragraph (a), immediately after the conclusion of the contract.

(2) The payment service provider may discharge the duty under paragraph (1) by supplying a copy of the draft framework contract provided that such contract includes the information specified in Schedule 4.

41 Information during period of contract

If the payment service user so requests at any time during the contractual relationship, the payment service provider must provide the information specified in Schedule 4 and the terms of the framework contract.

42 Changes in contractual information

(1) Subject to paragraph (4), any proposed changes to—

(a) the existing terms of the framework contract; or

(b) the information specified in Schedule 4,

must be [provided] by the payment service provider to the payment service user no later than two months before the date on which they are to take effect.

(2) The framework contract may provide for any such proposed changes to be made unilaterally by the payment service provider where the payment service user does not, before the proposed date of entry into force of the changes, notify the payment service provider to the contrary.

(3) Where paragraph (2) applies, the payment service provider must inform the payment service user that—

(a) the payment service user will be deemed to have accepted the changes in the circumstances referred to in that paragraph; and

(b) the payment service user has the right to terminate the framework contract immediately and without charge before the proposed date of their entry into force.

(4) Changes in the interest or exchange rates may be applied immediately and without notice where—

    (a) such a right is agreed under the framework contract and the changes are based on the reference interest or exchange rates information on which has been provided to the payment service user in accordance with this Part; or

    (b) the changes are more favourable to the payment service user.

(5) The payment service provider must inform the payment service user of any change to the interest rate as soon as possible unless the parties have agreed on a specific frequency or manner in which the information is to be provided or made available.

(6) Any change in the interest or exchange rate used in payment transactions must be implemented and calculated in a neutral manner that does not discriminate against payment service users.

43 Termination of framework contract

(1) The payment service user may terminate the framework contract at any time unless the parties have agreed on a period of notice not exceeding one month.

(2) Subject to paragraph (3), any charges for the termination of the contract must reasonably correspond to the actual costs to the payment service provider of termination.

(3) The payment service provider may not charge the payment service user for the termination, after the expiry of 12 months, of a framework contract concluded for a fixed period of more than 12 months or for an indefinite period.

(4) The payment service provider may terminate a framework contract concluded for an indefinite period by giving at least two months' notice, if the contract so provides.

(5) Notice of termination given in accordance with paragraph (4) must be provided in the same way as information is required by regulation 47(1) to be provided or made available.

(6) Where charges for the payment service are levied on a regular basis, such charges must be apportioned up until the time of the termination of the contract and any charges paid in advance must be reimbursed proportionally.

(7) This regulation does not affect any right of a party to the framework contract to treat it [, in accordance with the general law of contract, as unenforceable, void or discharged].

44 Information prior to execution of individual payment transaction

Where an individual payment transaction under a framework contract is initiated by the payer, at the payer's request the payer's payment service provider must inform the payer of—

    (a) the maximum execution time;

    (b) the charges payable by the payer in respect of the payment transaction; and

    (c) where applicable, a breakdown of the amounts of such charges.

45 Information for the payer on individual payment transactions

(1) The payer's payment service provider under a framework contract must provide to the payer the information specified in paragraph (2) as soon as reasonably practicable either—

    (a) after the amount of an individual payment transaction is debited from the payer's payment account; or

    (b) where the payer does not use a payment account, after receipt of the payment order.

(2) The information referred to in paragraph (1) is—

    (a) a reference enabling the payer to identify each payment transaction and, where appropriate, information relating to the payee;

    (b) the amount of the payment transaction in the currency in which the payer's payment account is debited or in the currency used for the payment order;

    (c) the amount of any charges for the payment transaction and, where applicable, a breakdown of the amounts of such charges, or the interest payable by the payer;

   (d) where applicable, the exchange rate used in the payment transaction by the payer's pay-
       ment service provider and the amount of the payment transaction after that currency con-
       version; and
   (e) the debit value date or the date of receipt of the payment order.

   (3) A framework contract may include a condition that the information specified in paragraph
(2) be provided or made available periodically at least once a month and in an agreed manner which
enables the payer to store and reproduce the information unchanged.

46 Information for the payee on individual payment transactions

   (1) As soon as reasonably practicable after the execution of an individual payment transaction
under a framework contract, the payee's payment service provider must provide to the payee the
information specified in paragraph (2).

   (2) The information referred to in paragraph (1) is—
   (a) a reference enabling the payee to identify the payment transaction and, where appropri-
       ate, the payer, and any information transferred with the payment transaction;
   (b) the amount of the payment transaction in the currency in which the payee's payment
       account is credited;
   (c) the amount of any charges for the payment transaction and, where applicable, a break-
       down of the amounts of such charges, or the interest payable by the payee;
   (d) where applicable, the exchange rate used in the payment transaction by the payee's pay-
       ment service provider, and the amount of the payment transaction before that currency
       conversion; and
   (e) the credit value date.

   (3) A framework contract may include a condition that the information specified in paragraph
(2) is to be provided or made available periodically at least once a month and in an agreed manner
which enables the payee to store and reproduce the information unchanged.

Common provisions

47 Communication of information

   (1) Subject to regulation 35(2)(c), any information provided or made available in accordance
with this Part must be provided or made available—
   (a) [in the case of single payment service contracts,] in an easily accessible manner;
   (b) [subject to paragraph (2)], on paper or on another durable medium;
   (c) in easily understandable language and in a clear and comprehensible form; and
   (d) in English or in the language agreed by the parties.
   [(2) Paragraph (1)(b)—
   (a) in the case of single payment service contracts, only applies where the payment service
       user so requests; and
   (b) in the case of framework contracts, is subject to any agreement in accordance with regulation
       45(3) or 46(3) as to the manner in which information is to be provided or made available.]

48 Charges for information

   (1) A payment service provider may not charge for providing or making available information
which is required to be provided or made available by this Part.

   (2) The payment service provider and the payment service user may agree on charges for any
information which is provided at the request of the payment service user where such information is—
   (a) additional to the information required to be provided or made available by this Part;
   (b) provided more frequently than is specified in this Part; or
   (c) transmitted by means of communication other than those specified in the framework
       contract.

   (3) Any charges imposed under paragraph (2) must reasonably correspond to the payment service provider's actual costs.

49   Currency and currency conversion

(1) Payment transactions must be executed in the currency agreed between the parties.

(2) Where a currency conversion service is offered before the initiation of the payment transaction—

(a) at the point of sale; or

(b) by the payee,

the party offering the currency conversion service to the payer must disclose to the payer all charges as well as the exchange rate to be used for converting the payment transaction.

50   Information on additional charges or reductions

(1) The payee must inform the payer of any charge requested or reduction offered by the payee for the use of a particular payment instrument before the initiation of the payment transaction.

(2) The payment service provider, or any relevant third party, must inform the payment service user of any charge requested by the payment service provider or third party, as the case may be, for the use of a particular payment instrument before the initiation of the payment transaction.

PART 6 RIGHTS AND OBLIGATIONS IN RELATION TO THE PROVISION OF APPLICATION

51   Application of Part 6

(1) This Part applies to a contract for payment services where—

(a) the services are provided from an establishment maintained by a payment service provider or its agent in the United Kingdom;

(b) subject to paragraph (2), the payment service providers of both the payer and the payee are located within the EEA; and

(c) where the payment services are carried out in euro or in the currency of an EEA State that has not adopted the euro as its currency.

(2) Regulation 73 applies whether or not the payment service providers of both the payer and the payee are located within the EEA.

(3) Except where the payment service user is a consumer, a micro-enterprise or a charity, the parties may agree that—

(a) any or all of regulations 54(1), [55(3) or (4)], 60, 62, 63, 64, 67, 75, 76 and 77 do not apply;

(b) a different time period applies for the purposes of regulation 59(1).

52   Disapplication of certain regulations in the case of consumer credit agreements

The following provisions of the Consumer Credit Act 1974 shall apply in relation to contracts for the provision of payment services which are regulated agreements for the purposes of that Act in place of the following provisions of these Regulations—

(a) section 51 (prohibition of unsolicited credit tokens) in place of regulation 58(1)(b);

(b) sections 66 (acceptance of credit tokens) and 84 (misuse of credit tokens) in place of regulations 59, 61 and 62;

(c) section 83 (liability for misuse of credit facilities) in place of regulations 59, 61 and 62;

(d) sections 76 (duty to give notice before taking certain action) and 87 (need for default notice) in relation to the grounds mentioned in regulation 56(2) in place of regulation 56(3) to (6) [; and]

[(e) section 98A(4) to (6) (termination of open-end consumer credit agreement) in place of regulation 56(2) to (6).]

53 Disapplication of certain regulations in the case of low value payment instruments

(1) This regulation applies in respect of payment instruments which, under the framework contract governing their use—

    (a) can be used only to execute individual payment transactions of 30 euro or less, or in relation to payment transactions executed wholly within the United Kingdom, 60 euro or less;

    (b) have a spending limit of 150 euro, or where payment transactions must be executed wholly within the United Kingdom, 300 euro; or

    (c) store funds that do not exceed 500 euro at any time.

(2) Where this regulation applies the parties may agree that—

    (a) regulations 57(1)(b), 58(1)(c), (d) and (e) and 62(3) do not apply where the payment instrument does not allow for the stopping or prevention of its use;

    (b) regulations 60, 61 and 62(1) and (2) do not apply where the payment instrument is used anonymously or the payment service provider is not in a position, for other reasons concerning the payment instrument, to prove that a payment transaction was authorised;

    (c) the payment service provider is not required under regulation 66(1) to notify the payment service user of the refusal of a payment order if the non-execution is apparent from the context;

    (d) the payer may not revoke the payment order under regulation 67 after transmitting the payment order or giving their consent to execute the payment transaction to the payee;

    (e) execution periods other than those provided by regulations 70 and 71 apply.

(3) Subject to paragraph (2)(b), regulations 61 and 62(1) and (2) apply to electronic money as defined in [Article 2(2)] of the electronic money directive unless the payer's payment service provider does not have the ability under the contract to—

    (a) freeze the payment account; or

    (b) stop the use of the payment instrument.

Charges

54 Charges

(1) The payment service provider may only charge the payment service user for the fulfilment of any of its obligations under this Part—

    (a) in accordance with regulation 66(3), 67(6) or 74(2)(b);

    (b) where agreed between the parties; and

    (c) where such charges reasonably correspond to the payment service provider's actual costs.

(2) Where a payment transaction does not involve any currency conversion, the respective payment service providers must ensure that—

    (a) the payee pays any charges levied by the payee's payment service provider; and

    (b) the payer pays any charges levied by the payer's payment service provider.

(3) The payee's payment service provider may not prevent the payee from—

    (a) requiring payment of a charge by; or

    (b) offering a reduction to,

the payer for the use of a particular payment instrument.

Authorisation of payment transactions

55 Consent and withdrawal of consent

(1) A payment transaction is to be regarded as having been authorised by the payer for the purposes of this Part only if the payer has given its consent to—

(a) the execution of the payment transaction; or

(b) the execution of a series of payment transactions of which that payment transaction forms part.

(2) Such consent—

(a) may be given before or, if agreed between the payer and its payment service provider, after the execution of the payment transaction; and

(b) must be given in the form, and in accordance with the procedure, agreed between the payer and its payment service provider.

(3) The payer may withdraw its consent to a payment transaction at any time before the point at which the payment order can no longer be revoked under regulation 67.

(4) Subject to regulation 67(3) to (5), the payer may withdraw its consent to the execution of a series of payment transactions at any time with the effect that any future payment transactions are not regarded as authorised for the purposes of this Part.

56   Limits on the use of payment instruments

(1) Where a specific payment instrument is used for the purpose of giving consent to the execution of a payment transaction, the payer and its payment service provider may agree on spending limits for any payment transactions executed through that payment instrument.

(2) A framework contract may provide for the payment service provider to have the right to stop the use of a payment instrument on reasonable grounds relating to—

(a) the security of the payment instrument;

(b) the suspected unauthorised or fraudulent use of the payment instrument; or

(c) in the case of a payment instrument with a credit line, a significantly increased risk that the payer may be unable to fulfil its liability to pay.

(3) The payment service provider must, in the manner agreed between the payment service provider and the payer and before carrying out any measures to stop the use of the payment instrument—

(a) inform the payer that it intends to stop the use of the payment instrument; and

(b) give its reasons for doing so.

(4) Where the payment service provider is unable to inform the payer in accordance with paragraph (3) before carrying out any measures to stop the use of the payment instrument, it must do so immediately after.

(5) Paragraphs (3) and (4) do not apply where provision of the information in accordance with paragraph (3) would compromise reasonable security measures or is otherwise unlawful.

(6) The payment service provider must allow the use of the payment instrument or replace it with a new payment instrument as soon as practicable after the reasons for stopping its use cease to exist.

57   Obligations of the payment service user in relation to payment instruments

(1) A payment service user to whom a payment instrument has been issued must—

(a) use the payment instrument in accordance with the terms and conditions governing its issue and use; and

(b) notify the payment service provider in the agreed manner and without undue delay on becoming aware of the loss, theft, misappropriation or unauthorised use of the payment instrument.

(2) The payment service user must on receiving a payment instrument take all reasonable steps to keep its personalised security features safe.

58   Obligations of the payment service provider in relation to payment instruments

(1) A payment service provider issuing a payment instrument must—

(a) subject to regulation 57, ensure that the personalised security features of the payment instrument are not accessible to persons other than the payment service user to whom the payment instrument has been issued;

(b) not send an unsolicited payment instrument, except where a payment instrument already issued to a payment service user is to be replaced;

(c) ensure that appropriate means are available at all times to enable the payment service user to notify the payment service provider in accordance with regulation 57(1)(b) or to request that the use of the payment instrument is no longer stopped in accordance with regulation 56(6);

(d) on request, provide the payment service user at any time during a period of 18 months after the alleged date of notification under regulation 57(1)(b) with the means to prove that such notification to the payment service provider was made;

(e) prevent any use of the payment instrument once notification has been made under regulation 57(1)(b).

(2) The payment service provider bears the risk of sending a payment instrument or any of its personalised security features to the payment service user.

59 Notification of unauthorised or incorrectly executed payment transactions

(1) A payment service user is entitled to redress under regulation 61, 75, 76 or 77 only if it notifies the payment service provider without undue delay, and in any event no later than 13 months after the debit date, on becoming aware of any unauthorised or incorrectly executed payment transaction.

(2) Where the payment service provider has failed to provide or make available information concerning the payment transaction in accordance with Part 5 of these Regulations, the payment service user is entitled to redress under the regulations referred to in paragraph (1) notwithstanding that the payment service user has failed to notify the payment service provider as mentioned in that paragraph.

60 Evidence on authentication and execution of payment transactions

(1) Where a payment service user—

(a) denies having authorised an executed payment transaction; or

(b) claims that a payment transaction has not been correctly executed,

it is for the payment service provider to prove that the payment transaction was authenticated, accurately recorded, entered in the payment service provider's accounts and not affected by a technical breakdown or some other deficiency.

(2) In paragraph (1) "authenticated" means the use of any procedure by which a payment service provider is able to verify the use of a specific payment instrument, including its personalised security features.

(3) Where a payment service user denies having authorised an executed payment transaction, the use of a payment instrument recorded by the payment service provider is not in itself necessarily sufficient to prove either that—

(a) the payment transaction was authorised by the payer; or

(b) the payer acted fraudulently or failed with intent or gross negligence to comply with regulation 57.

61 Payment service provider's liability for unauthorised payment transactions

Subject to regulations 59 and 60, where an executed payment transaction was not authorised in accordance with regulation 55, the payment service provider must immediately—

(a) refund the amount of the unauthorised payment transaction to the payer; and

(b) where applicable, restore the debited payment account to the state it would have been in had the unauthorised payment transaction not taken place.

62 Payer's liability for unauthorised payment transaction

(1) Subject to paragraphs (2) and (3), the payer is liable up to a maximum of £50 for any losses incurred in respect of unauthorised payment transactions arising—

(a) from the use of a lost or stolen payment instrument; or

(b) where the payer has failed to keep the personalised security features of the payment instrument safe, from the misappropriation of the payment instrument.

(2) The payer is liable for all losses incurred in respect of an unauthorised payment transaction where the payer—

(a) has acted fraudulently; or

(b) has with intent or gross negligence failed to comply with regulation 57.

(3) Except where the payer has acted fraudulently, the payer is not liable for any losses incurred in respect of an unauthorised payment transaction—

(a) arising after notification under regulation 57(1)(b);

(b) where the payment service provider has failed at any time to provide, in accordance with regulation 58(1)(c), appropriate means for notification; or

(c) where the payment instrument has been used in connection with a distance contract (other than an excepted contract).

(4) In paragraph (3)(c) "distance contract" and "excepted contract" have the meanings given in the Consumer Protection (Distance Selling) Regulations 2000.

63 Refunds for payment transactions initiated by or through a payee

(1) Where the conditions in paragraph (2) and the requirement in regulation 64(1) are satisfied, the payer is entitled to a refund from its payment service provider of the full amount of any authorised payment transaction initiated by or through the payee.

(2) The conditions are that—

(a) the authorisation did not specify the exact amount of the payment transaction when the authorisation was given in accordance with regulation 55; and

(b) the amount of the payment transaction exceeded the amount that the payer could reasonably have expected taking into account the payer's previous spending pattern, the conditions of the framework contract and the circumstances of the case.

(3) The payer and payment service provider may agree in the framework contract, in respect of direct debits, that the conditions in paragraph (2) need not be satisfied in order for the payer to be entitled to a refund.

(4) For the purposes of paragraph (2)(b), the payer cannot rely on currency exchange fluctuations where the reference exchange rate provided under regulation 36(2)(d) or paragraph 3(b) of Schedule 4 was applied.

(5) The payer and payment service provider may agree in the framework contract that the right to a refund does not apply where—

(a) the payer has given consent directly to the payment service provider for the payment transaction to be executed; and

(b) if applicable, information on the payment transaction was provided or made available in an agreed manner to the payer for at least four weeks before the due date by the payment service provider or by the payee.

64 Requests for refunds for payment transactions initiated by or through a payee

(1) The payer must request a refund under regulation 63 from its payment service provider within 8 weeks from the date on which the funds were debited.

(2) The payment service provider may require the payer to provide such information as is reasonably necessary to ascertain whether the conditions in regulation 63(2) are satisfied.

(3) Subject to paragraph (4), the payment service provider must either—

(a) refund the full amount of the payment transaction; or

(b) provide justification for refusing to refund the payment transaction, indicating the bodies to which the payer may refer the matter if the payer does not accept the justification provided.

(4) Where an agreement in accordance with regulation 63(3) applies, the payment service provider must, notwithstanding that a condition in regulation 63(2) is not satisfied, refund the full amount of the payment transaction.

(5) Any refund or justification for refusing a refund must be provided within 10 business days of receiving a request for a refund or, where applicable, within 10 business days of receiving any further information requested under paragraph (2).

Execution of payment transactions

65   Receipt of payment orders

(1) Subject to paragraphs (2) to (5), for the purposes of these Regulations the time of receipt of a payment order is the time at which the payment order, given directly by the payer or indirectly by or through a payee, is received by the payer's payment service provider.

(2) If the time of receipt of a payment order does not fall on a business day for the payer's payment service provider, the payment order is deemed to have been received on the first business day thereafter.

(3) The payment service provider may set a time towards the end of a business day after which any payment order received will be deemed to have been received on the following business day.

(4) Where the payment service user initiating a payment order agrees with its payment service provider that execution of the payment order is to take place—

(a) on a specific day;

(b) on the last day of a certain period; or

(c) on the day on which the payer has put funds at the disposal of its payment service provider,

the time of receipt is deemed to be the day so agreed.

(5) If the day agreed under paragraph (4) is not a business day for the payer's payment service provider, the payment order is deemed to have been received on the first business day thereafter.

66   Refusal of payment orders

(1) Subject to paragraph (4), where a payment service provider refuses to execute a payment order, it must notify the payment service user of—

(a) the refusal;

(b) if possible, the reasons for such refusal; and

(c) [where it is possible to provide reasons for the refusal and those reasons relate to factual matters,] the procedure for rectifying any factual errors that led to the refusal.

(2) Any notification under paragraph (1) must be given or made available in an agreed manner and at the earliest opportunity, and in any event within the periods specified in regulation 70.

(3) The framework contract may provide for the payment service provider to charge the payment service user for such notification where the refusal is reasonably justified.

(4) The payment service provider is not required to notify the payment service user under paragraph (1) where such notification would be otherwise unlawful.

(5) Where all the conditions set out in the payer's framework contract have been satisfied, the payment service provider may not refuse to execute an authorised payment order irrespective of whether the payment order is initiated by the payer or by or through a payee, unless such execution is otherwise unlawful.

(6) For the purposes of regulations 70, 75 and 76 a payment order of which execution has been refused is deemed not to have been received.

67   Revocation of a payment order

(1) Subject to paragraphs (2) to (5), a payment service user may not revoke a payment order after it has been received by the payer's payment service provider.

(2) In the case of a payment transaction initiated by or through the payee, the payer may not revoke the payment order after transmitting the payment order or giving consent to execute the payment transaction to the payee.

(3) In the case of a direct debit, the payer may not revoke the payment order after the end of the business day preceding the day agreed for debiting the funds.

(4) Where a day is agreed under regulation 65(4), the payment service user may not revoke a payment order after the end of the business day preceding the agreed day.

(5) At any time after the time limits for revocation set out in paragraphs (1) to (4), the payment order may only be revoked if the revocation is—

  (a) agreed between the payment service user and its payment service provider; and

  (b) in the case of a payment transaction initiated by or through the payee, including in the case of a direct debit, also agreed with the payee.

(6) A framework contract may provide for the payment service provider to charge for revocation under this regulation.

68   Amounts transferred and amounts received

(1) Subject to paragraph (2), the payment service providers of the payer and payee must ensure that the full amount of the payment transaction is transferred and that no charges are deducted from the amount transferred.

(2) The payee and its payment service provider may agree for the payment service provider to deduct its charges from the amount transferred before crediting it to the payee provided that the full amount of the payment transaction and the amount of the charges are clearly stated in the information provided to the payee.

(3) If charges other than those provided for by paragraph (2) are deducted from the amount transferred—

  (a) in the case of a payment transaction initiated by the payer, the payer's payment service provider must ensure that the payee receives the full amount of the payment transaction;

  (b) in the case of a payment transaction initiated by the payee, the payee's payment service provider must ensure that the payee receives the full amount of the payment transaction.

Execution time and value date

69   Application of regulations 70 to 72

(1) Regulations 70 to 72 apply to any [payment] transaction—

  (a) in euro;

  [(b) executed wholly within the United Kingdom in sterling; or]

  (c) involving only one currency conversion between the euro and sterling, provided that—

    (i) the currency conversion is carried out in the United Kingdom; and

    (ii) in the case of cross-border payment transactions, the cross-border transfer takes place in euro.

(2) In respect of any other [payment] transaction, the payment service user may agree with the payment service provider that regulations 70 (other than regulation 70(4)) to 72 do not apply.

70   Payment transactions to a payment account

(1) Subject to paragraphs (2), (3) and (4), the payer's payment service provider must ensure that the amount of the payment transaction is credited to the payee's payment service provider's account by the end of the business day following the time of receipt of the payment order.

(2) Until 1st January 2012, the payer and their payment service provider may agree that the amount of the payment transaction is to be credited to the payee's payment service provider's account by the end of the third business day following the time of receipt of the payment order.

(3) Where a payment transaction is initiated by way of a paper payment order—

(a) the reference in paragraph (1) to the end of the business day following the time of receipt of the payment order is to be treated as a reference to the end of the second business day following the time of receipt of the payment order; and

(b) the reference in paragraph (2) to the end of the third business day following the time of receipt of the payment order is to be treated as a reference to the end of the fourth business day following the time of receipt of the payment order.

(4) Where a payment transaction—

(a) does not fall within paragraphs (a) to (c) of regulation 69(1); but

(b) is to be executed wholly within the EEA,

the payer's payment service provider must ensure that the amount of the payment transaction is credited to the payee's payment service provider's account by the end of the fourth business day following the time of receipt of the payment order.

(5) The payee's payment service provider must value date and credit the amount of the payment transaction to the payee's payment account following its receipt of the funds.

(6) The payee's payment service provider must transmit a payment order initiated by or through the payee to the payer's payment service provider within the time limits agreed between the payee and its payment service provider, enabling settlement in respect of a direct debit to occur on the agreed due date.

71 Absence of payee's payment account with the payment service provider

(1) Paragraph (2) applies where a payment service provider accepts funds on behalf of a payee who does not have a payment account with that payment service provider.

(2) The payment service provider must make the funds available to the payee immediately after the funds have been credited to that payment service provider's account.

72 Cash placed on a payment account

Where a payment service user places cash on its payment account with a payment service provider in the same currency as that payment account, the payment service provider must—

(a) if the user is a consumer, micro-enterprise or charity, ensure that the amount is made available and value dated immediately after the receipt of the funds;

(b) in any other case, ensure that the amount is made available and value dated no later than the end of the [next] business day after the receipt of the funds.

73 Value date and availability of funds

(1) The credit value date for the payee's payment account must be no later than the business day on which the amount of the payment transaction is credited to the account of the payee's payment service provider.

(2) The payee's payment service provider must ensure that the amount of the payment transaction is at the payee's disposal immediately after that amount has been credited to that payment service provider's account.

(3) The debit value date for the payer's payment account must be no earlier than the time at which the amount of the payment transaction is debited to that payment account.

Liability

74 Incorrect unique identifiers

(1) Where a payment order is executed in accordance with the unique identifier, the payment order is deemed to have been correctly executed by each payment service provider involved in executing the payment order with respect to the payee specified by the unique identifier.

(2) Where the unique identifier provided by the payment service user is incorrect, the payment service provider is not liable under regulation 75 or 76 for non-execution or defective execution of the payment transaction, but the payment service provider—

(a) must make reasonable efforts to recover the funds involved in the payment transaction; and

(b) may, if agreed in the framework contract, charge the payment service user for any such recovery.

(3) Where the payment service user provides information additional to that specified in regulation 36(2)(a) or paragraph 2(b) of Schedule 4, the payment service provider is liable only for the execution of payment transactions in accordance with the unique identifier provided by the payment service user.

75 Non-execution or defective execution of payment transactions initiated by the payer

(1) This regulation applies where a payment order is initiated by the payer.

(2) The payer's payment service provider is liable to the payer for the correct execution of the payment transaction unless it can prove to the payer and, where relevant, to the payee's payment service provider, that the payee's payment service provider received the amount of the payment transaction in accordance with regulation 70.

(3) The payer's payment service provider must, on request, make immediate efforts to trace the payment transaction and notify the payer of the outcome.

(4) Where the payer's payment service provider is liable under paragraph (2), it must without undue delay refund to the payer the amount of the non-executed or defective payment transaction and, where applicable, restore the debited payment account to the state in which it would have been had the defective payment transaction not taken place.

(5) Where the payer's payment service provider can prove (as set out in paragraph (2)) that the payee's payment service provider received the amount of the payment transaction in accordance with regulation 70, the payee's payment service provider is liable to the payee for the correct execution of the payment transaction and must—

(a) immediately make available the amount of the payment transaction to the payee; and

(b) where applicable, credit the corresponding amount to the payee's payment account.

76 Non-execution or defective execution of payment transactions initiated by the payee

(1) This regulation applies where a payment order is initiated by the payee.

(2) The payee's payment service provider is liable to the payee for the correct transmission of the payment order to the payer's payment service provider in accordance with regulation 70(6).

(3) Where the payee's payment service provider is liable under paragraph (2), it must immediately re-transmit the payment order in question to the payer's payment service provider.

(4) The payee's payment service provider must, on request, make immediate efforts to trace the payment transaction and notify the payee of the outcome.

(5) Where the payee's payment service provider can prove to the payee and, where relevant, to the payer's payment service provider, that it is not liable under paragraph (2) in respect of a non-executed or defectively executed payment transaction, the payer's payment service provider is liable to the payer and must, as appropriate and without undue delay—

(a) refund to the payer the amount of the payment transaction; and

(b) restore the debited payment account to the state in which it would have been had the defective payment transaction not taken place.

77 Liability of payment service provider for charges and interest

A payment service provider is liable to its payment service user for—

(a) any charges for which the payment service user is responsible; and

(b) any interest which the payment service user must pay,

as a consequence of the non-execution or defective execution of the payment transaction.

78   Right of recourse

Where the liability of a payment service provider ("the first provider") under regulation 75 or 76 is attributable to another payment service provider or an intermediary, the other payment service provider or intermediary must compensate the first provider for any losses incurred or sums paid pursuant to those regulations.

79   Force majeure

(1) A person is not liable for any contravention of a requirement imposed on it by or under this Part where the contravention is due to abnormal and unforeseeable circumstances beyond the person's control, the consequences of which would have been unavoidable despite all efforts to the contrary.

(2) A payment service provider is not liable for any contravention of a requirement imposed on it by or under this Part where the contravention is due to the obligations of the payment service provider under other provisions of Community or national law.

PART 7 THE AUTHORITY

The functions of the Authority

80   Functions of the Authority

(1) The Authority is to have the functions conferred on it by these Regulations.

(2) In discharging its function of determining the general policy and principles by reference to which it performs particular functions under these Regulations, the Authority must have regard to—

    (a) the need to use its resources in the most efficient and economic way;

    (b) the responsibilities of those who manage the affairs of payment service providers;

    (c) the principle that a burden or restriction which is imposed on a person, or on the carrying on of an activity, should be proportionate to the benefits, considered in general terms, which are expected to result from the imposition of that burden or restriction;

    (d) the desirability of facilitating innovation in connection with payment services;

    (e) the international character of financial services and markets and the desirability of maintaining the competitive position of the United Kingdom;

    (f) the need to minimise the adverse effects on competition that may arise from anything done in the discharge of those functions; and

    (g) the desirability of facilitating competition in relation to payment services.

Supervision and enforcement

81   Monitoring and enforcement

(1) The Authority must maintain arrangements designed to enable it to determine whether—

    (a) persons on whom requirements are imposed by or under Part 2, 3 or 4 of these Regulations are complying with them;

    (b) there has been any contravention of regulation 110(1), 111(1) or 114(1)(a) or (2).

(2) The Authority may maintain arrangements designed to enable it to determine whether persons on whom requirements are imposed by or under Part 5 or 6 of these Regulations are complying with them.

(3) The arrangements referred to in paragraphs (1) and (2) may provide for functions to be performed on behalf of the Authority by any body or person who is, in its opinion, competent to perform them.

(4) The Authority must also maintain arrangements for enforcing the provisions of these Regulations.

(5) Paragraph (3) does not affect the Authority's duty under paragraph (1).

82 Reporting requirements

(1) A payment service provider must give the Authority such information in respect of its provision of payment services and its compliance with requirements imposed by or under Parts 2 to 6 of these Regulations as the Authority may direct.

(2) Information required under this regulation must be given at such times and in such form, and verified in such manner, as the Authority may direct.

84 Public censure

If the Authority considers that a payment service provider has contravened a requirement imposed on them by or under these Regulations the Authority may publish a statement to that effect.

85 Financial penalties

(1) The Authority may impose a penalty of such amount as it considers appropriate on—

    (a) a payment service provider who has contravened a requirement imposed on them by or under these Regulations; or

    (b) a person who has contravened regulation 110(1),111(1) or 114(1)(a) or (2).

(2) The Authority may not in respect of any contravention both require a person to pay a penalty under this regulation and cancel their authorisation as a payment institution or their registration as a small payment institution (as the case may be).

(3) A penalty under this regulation is a debt due from that person to the Authority, and is recoverable accordingly.

86 Proposal to take disciplinary measures

(1) Where the Authority proposes to publish a statement under regulation 84 or to impose a penalty under regulation 85, it must give the person concerned a warning notice.

(2) The warning notice must set out the terms of the proposed statement or state the amount of the proposed penalty.

(3) If, having considered any representations made in response to the warning notice, the Authority decides to publish a statement under regulation 84 or to impose a penalty under regulation 85, it must without delay give the person concerned a decision notice.

(4) The decision notice must set out the terms of the statement or state the amount of the penalty.

(5) If the Authority decides to publish a statement under regulation 84 or impose a penalty on a person under regulation 85, the person concerned may refer the matter to the [Upper Tribunal].

(6) Sections 210 (statements of policy) and 211 (statements of policy: procedure) of the 2000 Act apply in respect of the imposition of penalties under regulation 85 and the amount of such penalties as they apply in respect of the imposition of penalties under Part 14 of the 2000 Act (disciplinary measures) and the amount of penalties under that Part of that Act.

(7) After a statement under regulation 84 is published, the Authority must send a copy of it to the person concerned and to any person to whom a copy of the decision notice was given under section 393(4) of the 2000 Act (third party rights) (as applied by paragraph 7 of Schedule 5 to these Regulations).

87 Injunctions

(1) If, on the application of the Authority, the court is satisfied—

    (a) that there is a reasonable likelihood that any person will contravene a requirement imposed by or under these Regulations; or

    (b) that any person has contravened such a requirement and that there is a reasonable likelihood that the contravention will continue or be repeated,

the court may make an order restraining (or in Scotland an interdict prohibiting) the contravention.

(2) If, on the application of the Authority, the court is satisfied—

(a) that any person has contravened a requirement imposed by or under these Regulations, and

(b) that there are steps which could be taken for remedying the contravention,

the court may make an order requiring that person, and any other person who appears to have been knowingly concerned in the contravention, to take such steps as the court may direct to remedy it.

(3) If, on the application of the Authority, the court is satisfied that any person may have—

(a) contravened a requirement imposed by or under these Regulations, or

(b) been knowingly concerned in the contravention of such a requirement,

it may make an order restraining (or in Scotland an interdict prohibiting) them from disposing of, or otherwise dealing with, any assets of theirs which it is satisfied they are reasonably likely to dispose of or otherwise deal with.

(4) The jurisdiction conferred by this regulation is exercisable by the High Court and the Court of Session.

(5) In paragraph (2), references to remedying a contravention include references to mitigating its effect.

88   Power of Authority to require restitution

(1) The Authority may exercise the power in paragraph (2) if it is satisfied that a payment service provider (referred to in this regulation and regulation 89 as "the person concerned") has contravened a requirement imposed by or under these Regulations, or been knowingly concerned in the contravention of such a requirement, and that—

(a) profits have accrued to the person concerned as a result of the contravention; or

(b) one or more persons have suffered loss or been otherwise adversely affected as a result of the contravention.

(2) The power referred to in paragraph (1) is a power to require the person concerned, in accordance with such arrangements as the Authority considers appropriate, to pay to the appropriate person or distribute among the appropriate persons such amount as appears to the Authority to be just having regard—

(a) in a case within sub-paragraph (a) of paragraph (1), to the profits appearing to the Authority to have accrued;

(b) in a case within sub-paragraph (b) of that paragraph, to the extent of the loss or other adverse effect;

(c) in a case within both of those paragraphs, to the profits appearing to the Authority to have accrued and to the extent of the loss or other adverse effect.

(3) In paragraph (2) "appropriate person" means a person appearing to the Authority to be someone—

(a) to whom the profits mentioned in paragraph (1)(a) are attributable; or

(b) who has suffered the loss or adverse effect mentioned in paragraph (1)(b).

89   Proposal to require restitution

(1) If the Authority proposes to exercise the power under regulation 88(2), it must give the person concerned a warning notice.

(2) The warning notice must state the amount which the Authority propose to require the person concerned to pay or distribute as mentioned in regulation 88(2).

(3) If, having considered any representations made in response to the warning notice, the Authority decides to exercise the power under regulation 88(2), it must without delay give the person concerned a decision notice.

(4) The decision notice must—

(a) state the amount that the person concerned is to pay or distribute;

(b) identify the person or persons to whom that amount is to be paid or among whom that amount is to be distributed; and

(c) state the arrangements in accordance with which the payment or distribution is to be made.

(5) If the Authority decides to exercise the power under regulation 88(2), the person concerned may refer the matter to the [Upper Tribunal].

90   Restitution orders

(1) The court may, on the application of the Authority, make an order under paragraph (2) if it is satisfied that a payment service provider has contravened a requirement imposed by or under these Regulations, or been knowingly concerned in the contravention of such a requirement, and that—

(a) profits have accrued to them as a result of the contravention; or

(b) one or more persons have suffered loss or been otherwise adversely affected as a result of the contravention.

(2) The court may order the person concerned to pay to the Authority such sum as appears to the court to be just having regard—

(a) in a case within sub-paragraph (a) of paragraph (1), to the profits appearing to the court to have accrued;

(b) in a case within sub-paragraph (b) of that paragraph, to the extent of the loss or other adverse effect;

(c) in a case within both of those sub-paragraphs, to the profits appearing to the court to have accrued and to the extent of the loss or other adverse effect.

(3) Any amount paid to the Authority in pursuance of an order under paragraph (2) must be paid by it to such qualifying person or distributed by it among such qualifying persons as the court may direct.

(4) In paragraph (3), "qualifying person" means a person appearing to the court to be someone—

(a) to whom the profits mentioned in paragraph (1)(a) are attributable; or

(b) who has suffered the loss or adverse effect mentioned in paragraph (1)(b).

(5) On an application under paragraph (1) the court may require the person concerned to supply it with such accounts or other information as it may require for any one or more of the following purposes—

(a) establishing whether any and, if so, what profits have accrued to them as mentioned in sub-paragraph (a) of that paragraph;

(b) establishing whether any person or persons have suffered any loss or adverse effect as mentioned in sub-paragraph (b) of that paragraph; and

(c) determining how any amounts are to be paid or distributed under paragraph (3).

(6) The court may require any accounts or other information supplied under paragraph (5) to be verified in such manner as it may direct.

(7) The jurisdiction conferred by this regulation is exercisable by the High Court and the Court of Session.

(8) Nothing in this regulation affects the right of any person other than the Authority to bring proceedings in respect of the matters to which this regulation applies.

91   Complaints

(1) The Authority must maintain arrangements designed to enable payment service users and other interested parties to submit complaints to it that a requirement imposed by or under Parts 2 to 6 of these Regulations has been breached by a payment service provider.

(2) Where it considers it appropriate, the Authority must include in any reply to a complaint under paragraph (1) details of the ombudsman scheme established under Part 16 of the 2000 Act (the ombudsman scheme).

Miscellaneous

92   Costs of supervision

(1) The functions of the Authority under these Regulations are to be treated for the purposes of paragraph 17 (fees) of Part 3 of Schedule 1 to the 2000 Act as functions conferred on the Authority under that Act with the following modifications—

(a) section 2(3) of the 2000 Act (the Authority's general duties) does not apply to the making of rules under paragraph 17 by virtue of this regulation;

(b) rules made under paragraph 17 by virtue of this regulation are not to be treated as regulating provisions for the purposes of section 159(1) of the 2000 Act (competition scrutiny);

(c) paragraph 17(2) and (3) are omitted.

(2) The Authority must apply amounts paid to it by way of penalties imposed under regulation 85 towards expenses incurred in carrying out its functions under these Regulations or for any incidental purpose.

93   Guidance

(1) The Authority may give guidance consisting of such information and advice as it considers appropriate with respect to—

(a) the operation of these Regulations;

(b) any matters relating to the functions of the Authority under these Regulations;

(c) any other matters about which it appears to the Authority to be desirable to give information or advice in connection with these Regulations.

(2) The Authority may—

(a) publish its guidance;

(b) offer copies of its published guidance for sale at a reasonable price;

(c) if it gives guidance in response to a request made by any person, make a reasonable charge for that guidance.

94   Authority's exemption from liability in damages

The functions of the Authority under these Regulations are to be treated for the purposes of paragraph 19 (exemption from liability in damages) of Part 4 of Schedule 1 to the 2000 Act as functions conferred on the Authority under that Act.

95   Application and modification of primary and secondary legislation

The provisions of primary and secondary legislation set out in Schedule 5 apply in respect of the Authority's functions under these Regulations with the modifications set out in that Schedule.

PART 8   ACCESS TO PAYMENT SYSTEMS

General

96   Application of Part 8

(1) This Part does not apply to the following kinds of payment systems—

(a) a designated system;

(b) a payment system consisting solely of payment service providers belonging to the same group where one of the payment service providers enjoys effective control over the others;

(c) a payment system where the sole payment service provider (whether as a single entity or a group)—

(i) acts or is able to act as the payment service provider for both the payer and the payee and is solely responsible for the management of the system; and

(ii) licenses other payment service providers to participate in the system subject to their having no right to negotiate fees in respect of the system between or amongst themselves (although they may establish their own pricing in relation to payers and payees).

(2) In paragraph (1)(a), "designated system" means a system which is declared by a designation order for the time being in force under regulation 4 of the Financial Markets and Insolvency (Settlement Finality) Regulations 1999 to be a designated system for the purposes of those Regulations.

97 Prohibition on restrictive rules on access to payment systems

(1) Rules or conditions governing access to, or participation in, a payment system by authorised payment institutions, EEA authorised payment institutions and small payment institutions must—

    (a) be objective, proportionate and non-discriminatory; and

    (b) not prevent, restrict or inhibit access or participation more than is necessary to—

        (i) safeguard against specific risks such as settlement risk, operational risk or business risk; or

        (ii) protect the financial and operational stability of the payment system.

(2) Paragraph (1) applies only to such small payment institutions as are legal persons.

(3) Rules or conditions governing access to, or participation in, a payment system which, in respect of payment service providers, payment service users or other payment systems—

    (a) restrict effective participation in other payment systems;

    (b) discriminate (whether directly or indirectly) between—

        (i) different authorised payment institutions, or

        (ii) different small payment institutions,

    in relation to the rights, obligations or entitlements of participants in the payment system; or

    (c) impose any restrictions on the basis that a person is not of a particular institutional status,

are prohibited.

Supervision and enforcement

98 Power of OFT to investigate

(1) The OFT may conduct an investigation where there are reasonable grounds for suspecting that any rule or condition governing access to, or participation in, a payment system contravenes regulation 97(1) or (3).

(2) Where the investigation relates to a possible breach of regulation 97(1)(b)(ii), the OFT must consult the Bank of England and the Authority.

99 OFT power to require information

(1) For the purposes of an investigation under regulation 98 the OFT may require any person—

    (a) to produce to it or to a person appointed by it, at a specified time and place, any specified document, or

    (b) to provide to it or to a person appointed by it, at a specified time and place, any specified information,

which the OFT considers relates to any matter relevant to the investigation.

(2) The power conferred by paragraph (1) is to be exercised by a notice indicating the subject matter and purpose of the investigation.

(3) Information required to be provided under paragraph (1) must be provided in the specified manner and form, or, if that is not possible, in the nearest equivalent manner and form.

(4) The power conferred by paragraph (1) to require a person to produce a document includes power—

    (a) to require them to provide an explanation of the document, or

(b) if the document is not produced, to require them to state, to the best of their knowledge and belief, where it is.

(5) In this regulation—

"document" includes information recorded in any form;

"information" includes estimates and forecasts;

"specified" means—

(a) specified, or described, in the notice referred to in paragraph (2), or

(b) falling within a category which is specified, or described, in such notice.

100   Failure to comply with information requirement

(1) If, on an application made by the OFT, it appears to the court that a person (the "information defaulter") has failed to do something that they were required to do under regulation 99, the court may make an order under this regulation.

(2) An order under this regulation may require the information defaulter—

(a) to do the thing that they failed to do within such period as may be specified in the order;

(b) otherwise to take such steps to remedy the consequence of the failure as may be so specified.

(3) In this regulation, "the court" means—

(a) in England and Wales and Northern Ireland, the High Court or the county court;

(b) in Scotland, the Court of Session or the sheriff court.

101   Privileged communications

(1) A person is not required under regulation 99 to produce or disclose a privileged communication.

(2) In paragraph (1) "privileged communication" means a communication—

(a) between a professional legal adviser and their client, or

(b) made in connection with, or in contemplation of, legal proceedings and for the purposes of those proceedings,

which in proceedings in the High Court would be protected from disclosure on grounds of legal professional privilege.

(3) In the application of this regulation to Scotland the reference in paragraph (2) to—

(a) proceedings in the High Court is to be read as a reference to legal proceedings generally; and

(b) an entitlement on grounds of legal professional privilege is to be read as a reference to an entitlement on the grounds of confidentiality of communications.

102   Notice of OFT decision

Before the OFT, as the result of an investigation under regulation 98, makes a decision that any rules or conditions governing access to, or participation in, a payment system contravene regulation 97(1) or (3), the OFT must—

(a) give notice to the person (or persons) who the OFT considers are responsible for the contravention, and

(b) give that person (or those persons) an opportunity to make representations.

103   Publication of OFT decision

Where the OFT makes a decision after an investigation under regulation 98, the OFT must publish its decision, together with its reasons for making it.

104   Enforcement of decisions

(1) If the OFT makes a decision that any rules or conditions governing access to, or participation in, a payment system contravene regulation 97(1) or (3), the OFT may give such directions as the OFT considers appropriate to such person or persons as it considers appropriate.

(2) A direction under paragraph (1) may (in particular)—

(a) require the person concerned to change any rule or condition so that it no longer contravenes regulation 97(1) or (3); and

(b) relate to the conduct of the person in implementing any rule or condition.

(3) A direction under paragraph (1) must be given in writing.

(4) If a person fails, without reasonable excuse, to comply with a direction under paragraph (1), the OFT may apply to the High Court (or, in Scotland, the Court of Session) for an order requiring that person to comply with the direction within a time specified in the order.

(5) An order under paragraph (4) may provide for all of the costs of, or incidental to, the application for the order to be borne by the person in default.

105   Power of OFT to impose financial penalties

(1) Where the OFT is satisfied that any rules or conditions governing access to, or participation in, a payment system contravene regulation 97(1) or (3), the OFT may impose a penalty of such amount as it considers appropriate on such persons as it considers appropriate.

(2) The OFT may impose a penalty on a person under paragraph (1) only if the OFT is satisfied that the infringement has been committed intentionally or negligently by that person.

(3) Notice of a penalty under this regulation must—

(a) be in writing; and

(b) specify the date before which the penalty is required to be paid.

(4) The date specified must not be earlier than the end of the period within which an appeal against the notice may be brought under regulation 106.

(5) Any sums received by the OFT under this regulation are to be paid into the Consolidated Fund.

Miscellaneous

106   Appeal to the Competition Appeal Tribunal

(1) A person may appeal to the Competition Appeal Tribunal from a decision by the OFT to give a direction under regulation 104(1) to that person or to impose a penalty under regulation 105 on that person.

(2) In determining an appeal under paragraph (1) the Competition Appeal Tribunal shall apply the same principles as would be applied by a court on an application for judicial review.

(3) Sections 14 (constitution of tribunal) and 15 (tribunal rules) of the Enterprise Act 2002 apply in respect of appeals to the Competition Appeal Tribunal under paragraph (1) as they apply in respect of appeals to the Competition Appeal Tribunal under that Act.

107   Disclosure of information by OFT

Subject to regulation 119(2) and (3), Part 9 of the Enterprise Act 2002 (information) applies in respect of information which comes to the OFT by virtue of these Regulations as it applies in respect of information which is specified information for the purposes of Part 9.

108   Defamation

For the purposes of the law relating to defamation, absolute privilege attaches to any decision made or notice given by the OFT in the exercise of any of its functions under this Part.

109   Guidance

(1) The OFT may give guidance consisting of such information and advice as it considers appropriate with respect to the exercise of its functions under this Part.

(2) The OFT may—

(a) publish its guidance;

(b) if it gives guidance in response to a request made by any person, make a reasonable charge for that guidance.

PART 9 GENERAL

Criminal Offences

110   Prohibition on provision of payment services by persons other than payment service providers

(1) A person may not provide a payment service in the United Kingdom, or purport to do so, unless the person is—

    (a) an authorised payment institution;

    (b) a small payment institution;

    (c) an EEA authorised payment institution exercising its passport rights;

    [(d) a credit institution authorised in the UK or exercising an EEA right in accordance with Part 2 of Schedule 3 to the 2000 Act (exercise of passport rights by EEA firms);

    (e) an electronic money institution authorised in the UK or exercising an EEA right in accordance with Part 2 of Schedule 3 to the 2000 Act;

    (f) the Post Office Limited;

    (g) the Bank of England, the European Central Bank or a national central bank of an EEA State other than the United Kingdom,

    (h) a government department or a local authority; or

    (i) exempt under regulation 3].

(2) A person who contravenes paragraph (1) is guilty of an offence and is liable—

    (a) on summary conviction, to imprisonment for a term not exceeding three months or to a fine not exceeding the statutory maximum, or both;

    (b) on conviction on indictment, to imprisonment for a term not exceeding two years or to a fine, or both.

111   False claims to be a payment service provider or exempt

(1) A person who does not fall within any of sub-paragraphs (a) to (e) of regulation 110(1) may not—

    (a) describe themselves (in whatever terms) as a person falling within any of those sub-paragraphs; or

    (b) behave, or otherwise hold themselves out, in a manner which indicates (or which is reasonably likely to be understood as indicating) that they are such a person.

(2) A person who contravenes paragraph (1) is guilty of an offence and is liable on summary conviction to imprisonment for a term not exceeding three months or to a fine not exceeding level 5 on the standard scale, or both.

112   Defences

In proceedings for an offence under regulation 110 or 111 it is a defence for the accused to show that they took all reasonable precautions and exercised all due diligence to avoid committing the offence.

113   Contravention of regulations 49 and 50

(1) A person (not being a payment service provider) who contravenes regulation 49(2) or 50(2) is guilty of an offence and liable on summary conviction to a fine not exceeding level 5 on the standard scale.

(2) No offence is committed if the person took all reasonable steps and exercised all due diligence to ensure that the requirement imposed on the person by regulation 49(2) or 50(2), as the case may be, would be complied with.

114   Misleading the Authority or the OFT

(1) A person may not, in purported compliance with any requirement imposed by or under these Regulations, knowingly or recklessly give—

    (a) the Authority; or

    (b) the OFT,

information which is false or misleading in a material particular.

(2) A person may not—

    (a) provide any information to another person, knowing the information to be false or misleading in a material particular, or

    (b) recklessly provide to another person any information which is false or misleading in a material particular,

knowing that the information is to be used for the purpose of providing information to the Authority in connection with its functions under these Regulations.

(3) A person may not—

    (a) provide any information to another person, knowing the information to be false or misleading in a material particular, or

    (b) recklessly provide to another person any information which is false or misleading in a material particular,

knowing that the information is to be used for the purpose of providing information to the OFT in connection with their functions under these Regulations.

(4) A person who knows or suspects that an investigation by the OFT under regulation 98 is being or is likely to be conducted may not—

    (a) intentionally or recklessly destroy or otherwise dispose of, falsify or conceal a document (as defined by regulation 99(5)) which may be relevant to such an investigation; or

    (b) cause or permit its destruction, disposal, falsification or concealment.

(5) A person who contravenes paragraph (1), (2), (3) or (4) is guilty of an offence and is liable—

    (a) on summary conviction, to a fine not exceeding the statutory maximum;

    (b) on conviction on indictment, to a fine.

115 Restriction on penalties

A person who is convicted of an offence under these Regulations is not liable to a penalty under regulation 85 or 105 in respect of the same contravention of a requirement imposed by or under these Regulations.

116 Liability of officers of bodies corporate etc

(1) If an offence under these Regulations committed by a body corporate is shown—

    (a) to have been committed with the consent or connivance of an officer, or

    (b) to be attributable to any neglect on their part,

the officer as well as the body corporate is guilty of the offence and liable to be proceeded against and punished accordingly.

(2) If the affairs of a body corporate are managed by its members, paragraph (1) applies in relation to the acts and defaults of a member in connection with such member's functions of management as if the member were a director of the body.

(3) If an offence under these Regulations committed by a partnership is shown—

    (a) to have been committed with the consent or connivance of a partner, or

    (b) to be attributable to any neglect on their part,

the partner as well as the partnership is guilty of the offence and liable to be proceeded against and punished accordingly.

(4) If an offence under these Regulations committed by an unincorporated association (other than a partnership) is shown—

    (a) to have been committed with the consent or connivance of an officer, or

    (b) to be attributable to any neglect of such officer,

the officer as well as the association is guilty of the offence and liable to be proceeded against and punished accordingly.

(5) In this regulation—

"officer"—

    (a) in relation to a body corporate, means a director, manager, secretary, chief executive, member of the committee of management, or a person purporting to act in such a capacity; and

(b) in relation to an unincorporated association, means any officer of the association or any member of its governing body, or a person purporting to act in such capacity; and

"partner" includes a person purporting to act as a partner.

117 Prosecution of offences

(1) Proceedings for an offence under these Regulations may be instituted only—

    (a) in respect of an offence under regulation 110, 111, 113, or 114(1)(a) or (2), by the Authority;

    (b) in respect of an offence under regulation 114(1)(b), (3) or (4), by the OFT; or

    (c) by or with the consent of the Director of Public Prosecutions.

(2) Paragraph (1) does not apply to proceedings in Scotland.

118 Proceedings against unincorporated bodies

(1) Proceedings for an offence alleged to have been committed by a partnership or an unincorporated association must be brought in the name of the partnership or association (and not in that of its members).

(2) A fine imposed on the partnership or association on its conviction of an offence is to be paid out of the funds of the partnership or association.

(3) Rules of court relating to the service of documents are to have effect as if the partnership or association were a body corporate.

(4) In proceedings for an offence brought against the partnership or association—

    (a) section 33 of the Criminal Justice Act 1925 (procedure on charge of offence against corporation) and section 46 of and Schedule 3 to the Magistrates' Courts Act 1980 (corporations) apply as they do in relation to a body corporate;

    (b) section 70 of the Criminal Procedure (Scotland) Act 1995 (proceedings against bodies corporate) applies as it does in relation to a body corporate;

    (c) section 18 of the Criminal Justice (Northern Ireland) Act 1945 (procedure on charge) and Schedule 4 to the Magistrates' Courts (Northern Ireland) Order 1981 (corporations) apply as they do in relation to a body corporate.

(5) Summary proceedings for an offence under these Regulations may be taken—

    (a) against a body corporate or unincorporated association at any place at which it has a place of business;

    (b) against an individual at any place where they are for the time being.

(6) Paragraph (5) does not affect any jurisdiction exercisable apart from this regulation.

Duties of the Authority, the Commissioners and the OFT to cooperate

119 Duty to co-operate and exchange of information

(1) The Authority, the Commissioners and the OFT must take such steps as they consider appropriate to co-operate with each other and—

    (a) the competent authorities designated under Article 20(1), or referred to in Article 82(1), of the payment services directive, of EEA States other than the United Kingdom;

    (b) the European Central Bank, the Bank of England and the national central banks of EEA States other than the United Kingdom; and

    (c) any other relevant competent authorities designated under Community law or the law of the United Kingdom or any other EEA State which is applicable to payment service providers,

for the purposes of the exercise by those bodies of their functions under the payment services directive and other relevant Community or national legislation.

(2) Subject to the requirements of the Data Protection Act 1998, sections 348 and 349 of the 2000 Act (as applied with modifications by paragraph 5 of Schedule 5 to these Regulations), regulation 49A of the Money Laundering Regulations 2007 (as inserted by paragraph 6(g) of Schedule

6 to these Regulations) and any other applicable restrictions on the disclosure of information, the Authority, the Commissioners and the OFT may provide information to each other and—

    (a) the bodies mentioned in paragraph (1)(a) and (c);

    (b) the European Central Bank, the Bank of England and the national central banks of EEA States other than the United Kingdom when acting in their capacity as monetary and oversight authorities;

    (c) where relevant, other public authorities responsible for the oversight of payment and settlement systems;

for the purposes of the exercise by those bodies of their functions under the payment services directive and other relevant Community or national legislation.

    (3) Part 9 of the Enterprise Act 2002 does not prohibit disclosure by the OFT under paragraph (2) but the OFT must have regard to the considerations mentioned in section 244 of that Act (specified information: considerations relevant to disclosure) before making any such disclosure.

Actions for breach of requirements

120   Right to bring actions

    (1) A contravention—

    (a) which is to be taken to have occurred by virtue of regulation 17;

    (b) of a requirement imposed by regulation 19; or

    (c) of a requirement imposed by or under Part 5 or 6,

is actionable at the suit of a private person who suffers loss as a result of the contravention, subject to the defences and other incidents applying to actions for breach of statutory duty.

    (2) A person acting in a fiduciary or representative capacity may bring an action under paragraph (1) on behalf of a private person if any remedy—

    (a) will be exclusively for the benefit of the private person; and

    (b) cannot be obtained by way of an action brought otherwise than at the suit of the fiduciary or representative.

    (3) In this regulation "private person" means—

    (a) any individual, except where the individual suffers the loss in question in the course of providing payment services; and

    (b) any person who is not an individual, except where that person suffers the loss in question in the course of carrying on business of any kind;

but does not include a government, a local authority (in the United Kingdom or elsewhere) or an international organisation.

Regulation 2(1)   # SCHEDULE 1

PAYMENT SERVICES

PART 1 PAYMENT SERVICES

1. Subject to Part 2, the following activities, when carried out as a regular occupation or business activity, are payment services—

    (a) services enabling cash to be placed on a payment account and all of the operations required for operating a payment account;

    (b) services enabling cash withdrawals from a payment account and all of the operations required for operating a payment account;

    (c) the execution of the following types of payment transaction—

        (i)   direct debits, including one-off direct debits;

        (ii) payment transactions executed through a payment card or a similar device;

        (iii) credit transfers, including standing orders;

    (d) the execution of the following types of payment transaction where the funds are covered by a credit line for the payment service user—

        (i)   direct debits, including one-off direct debits;

        (ii) payment transactions executed through a payment card or a similar device;

        (iii) credit transfers, including standing orders;

    (e) issuing payment instruments or acquiring payment transactions;

    (f) money remittance;

    (g) the execution of payment transactions where the consent of the payer to execute the payment transaction is given by means of any telecommunication, digital or IT device and the payment is made to the telecommunication, IT system or network operator acting only as an intermediary between the payment service user and the supplier of the goods or services.

PART 2   ACTIVITIES WHICH DO NOT CONSTITUTE PAYMENT SERVICES

2. The following activities do not constitute payment services—

    (a) payment transactions executed wholly in cash and directly between the payer and the payee, without any intermediary intervention;

    (b) payment transactions between the payer and the payee through a commercial agent authorised to negotiate or conclude the sale or purchase of goods or services on behalf of the payer or the payee;

    (c) the professional physical transport of banknotes and coins, including their collection, processing and delivery;

    (d) payment transactions consisting of non-professional cash collection and delivery as part of a not-for-profit or charitable activity;

    (e) services where cash is provided by the payee to the payer as part of a payment transaction for the purchase of goods or services following an explicit request by the payer immediately before the execution of the payment transaction;

    (f) money exchange business consisting of cash-to-cash operations where the funds are not held on a payment account;

    (g) payment transactions based on any of the following documents drawn on the payment service provider with a view to placing funds at the disposal of the payee—

        (i)   paper cheques of any kind, including traveller's cheques;

        (ii) bankers' drafts;

        (iii) paper-based vouchers;

        (iv) paper postal orders;

    (h) payment transactions carried out within a payment or securities settlement system between payment service providers and settlement agents, central counterparties, clearing houses, central banks or other participants in the system;

    (i) payment transactions related to securities asset servicing, including dividends, income or other distributions, or redemption or sale, carried out by persons referred to in sub-paragraph (h) or by investment firms, credit institutions, collective investment undertakings or asset management companies providing investment services or by any other entities allowed to have the custody of financial instruments;

    (j) services provided by technical service providers, which support the provision of payment services, without the provider entering at any time into possession of the funds to be transferred, including—

        (i)   the processing and storage of data;

        (ii) trust and privacy protection services;

        (iii) data and entity authentication;

        (iv) information technology;

        (v) communication network provision; and

(vi) the provision and maintenance of terminals and devices used for payment services;

(k) services based on instruments that can be used to acquire goods or services only—

(i) in or on the issuer's premises; or

(ii) under a commercial agreement with the issuer, either within a limited network of service providers or for a limited range of goods or services,

and for these purposes the "issuer" is the person who issues the instrument in question;

(l) payment transactions executed by means of any telecommunication, digital or IT device, where the goods or services purchased are delivered to and are to be used through a telecommunication, digital or IT device, provided that the telecommunication, digital or IT operator does not act only as an intermediary between the payment service user and the supplier of the goods and services;

(m) payment transactions carried out between payment service providers, or their agents or branches, for their own account;

(n) payment transactions between a parent undertaking and its subsidiary or between subsidiaries of the same parent undertaking, without any intermediary intervention by a payment service provider other than an undertaking belonging to the same group;

(o) services by providers to withdraw cash by means of automated teller machines acting on behalf of one or more card issuers, which are not party to the framework contract with the customer withdrawing money from a payment account, where no other payment service is conducted by the provider.

Regulation 5(1)

SCHEDULE 2

INFORMATION TO BE INCLUDED IN OR WITH AN APPLICATION FOR AUTHORISATION

1. A programme of operations setting out, in particular, the type of payment services envisaged.

2. A business plan including a forecast budget calculation for the first three financial years which demonstrates that the applicant is able to employ appropriate and proportionate systems, resources and procedures to operate soundly.

3. Evidence that the applicant holds initial capital for the purposes of regulation 6(3).

4. Where regulation 19 applies, a description of the measures taken for safeguarding payment service users' funds in accordance with that regulation.

5. A description of the applicant's governance arrangements and internal control mechanisms, including administrative risk management and accounting procedures, which demonstrates that such arrangements, mechanisms and procedures are proportionate, appropriate, sound and adequate.

6. A description of the internal control mechanisms which the applicant has established in order to comply with the Money Laundering Regulations 2007 and Regulation (EC) No 1781/2006 of the European Parliament and of the Council of 15 November 2006 on information on the payer accompanying transfers of funds.

7. A description of the applicant's structural organisation, including, where applicable, a description of the intended use of agents and branches and a description of outsourcing arrangements, and of its participation in a national or international payment system.

8.—(1) In relation to each person holding, directly or indirectly, a qualifying holding in the applicant—

(a) the size and nature of their qualifying holding; and

(b) evidence of their suitability taking into account the need to ensure the sound and prudent management of a payment institution.

9.—(1) The identity of directors and persons who are or will be responsible for the management of the applicant and, where relevant, persons who are or will be responsible for the management of the payment services activities of the applicant.

(2) Evidence that the persons described in sub-paragraph (1) are of good repute and that they possess appropriate knowledge and experience to perform payment services.

10. The identity of the auditors of the applicant, if any.

11.—(1) The legal status of the applicant and, where the applicant is a limited company, its articles.

(2) In this paragraph "articles" has the meaning given in section 7 of the Companies Act 1985 (articles prescribing regulations for companies) until the coming into force of section 18 of the Companies Act 2006 (articles of association) when it will have the meaning given by that section.

12. The address of the head office of the applicant.

13. For the purposes of paragraphs 4, 5 and 7, a description of the audit arrangements of the applicant and of the organisational arrangements the applicant has set up with a view to taking all reasonable steps to protect the interests of its payment service users and to ensure continuity and reliability in the performance of payment services.

Regulations 6(3), 18

SCHEDULE 3

CAPITAL REQUIREMENTS

PART 1 INITIAL CAPITAL

1. For the purposes of this Part, "initial capital" comprises the items specified in paragraph 3(a), (b) and (c) of this Schedule.

2.—(1) An applicant for authorisation as a payment institution must hold the amount of initial capital specified in the second column of the table, corresponding to the payment services provided or to be provided (as specified in the first column).

(2) Where more than one initial capital requirement applies, the applicant must hold initial capital of whichever is the greater amount.

Payment services	Initial capital requirement (euro)
Payment services specified in paragraph 127(f) of Schedule 1	20,000
Payment services specified in paragraph 127(g) of Schedule 1	50,000
Any of the payment services specified in paragraph 127(a) to (e) of Schedule 1	125,000

PART 2 OWN FUNDS

Qualifying items

3. For the purposes of this Part, "own funds" means the following items, subject to the deductions specified in paragraph 147 and to the limits specified in paragraph 149—

(a) paid up capital, including share premium accounts but excluding amounts arising in respect of cumulative preference shares;

(b) reserves other than—

(i) revaluation reserves;

(ii) fair value reserves related to gains or losses on cash flow hedges of financial instruments measured at amortised cost; and

(iii) that part of profit and loss reserves that arises from any gains on liabilities valued at fair value that are due to changes in the authorised payment institution's credit standing;

(c) profit or loss brought forward as a result of the application of the final profit or loss, provided that—

    (i) interim profits may only be included if they are—

        (aa) verified by persons responsible for the auditing of the authorised payment institution's accounts;

        (bb) shown to the satisfaction of the Authority that the amount has been evaluated in accordance with the principles set out in directive 86/635/EEC of the Council of the 8th December 1986 on the annual accounts and consolidated accounts of banks and other financial institutions; and

        (cc) net of any foreseeable charge or dividend;

    (ii) in the case of an authorised payment institution which is the originator of a securitisation, net gains arising from the capitalisation of future income from the securitised assets and providing credit enhancement to positions in the securitisation are excluded;

(d) revaluation reserves;

(e) general or collective provisions if—

    (i) they are freely available to the authorised payment institution to cover normal payment services risks where revenue or capital losses have not yet been identified;

    (ii) their existence is disclosed in internal accounting records; and

    (iii) their amount is determined by the management of the authorised payment institution, verified by a statutory auditor or audit firm (as defined by regulation 20(2)) and notified to the Authority;

(f) securities of indeterminate duration and other instruments that fulfil the following conditions—

    (i) they may not be reimbursed on the bearer's initiative or without the prior agreement of the Authority;

    (ii) the debt agreement provides for the authorised payment institution to have the option of deferring the payment of interest on the debt;

    (iii) the lender's claim on the authorised payment institution is wholly subordinated to those of all non-subordinated creditors;

    (iv) the documents governing the issue of the securities provide for debt and unpaid interest to be such as to absorb losses, whilst leaving the authorised payment institution in a position to continue trading;

    provided that only fully paid-up amounts are to be taken into account;

(g) cumulative preferential shares, other than fixed-term cumulative preference shares referred to in paragraph (j);

(h) the commitments of the members of an authorised payment institution set up as a cooperative, comprising—

    (i) that institution's uncalled capital; and

    (ii) the legal commitments of the members of that institution to make additional non-refundable payments should the institution incur a loss provided that such payments can be demanded without delay;

(i) the joint and several commitments of the borrower in the case of an authorised payment institution organised as a fund, comprising—

    (i) that institution's uncalled capital; and

    (ii) the legal commitments of the borrowers of that institution to make additional non-refundable payments should the institution incur a loss provided that such payments can be demanded without delay;

(j) fixed-term cumulative preferential shares and subordinated loan capital if—

      (i)   binding agreements exist under which, in the event of the winding-up of the author-ised payment institution, they rank after the claims of all other creditors and are not to be repaid until all other debts outstanding at the time have been settled; and

      (ii) in the case of subordinated loan capital—

         (aa) only fully paid-up funds are taken into account;

         (bb) the loans involved have an original maturity of at least five years, after which they may be repaid;

         (cc) the extent to which they may rank as own funds is gradually reduced during at least the last five years before the repayment date; and

         (dd) the loan agreement does not include any clause providing that in specified cir-cumstances, other than the winding-up of the authorised payment institution, the debt will become repayable before the agreed repayment date.

4. The items specified in paragraph 144(a) to (d) must be—

    (a) available to the authorised payment institution for unrestricted and immediate use to cover risks or losses as soon as these occur; and

    (b) net of any foreseeable tax charge at the moment of their calculation or be suitably adjusted in so far as such tax charges reduce the amount up to which these items may be applied to cover risks or losses.

5. Own funds are not to include guarantees provided by the Crown or a local authority to a payment institution which is a public sector entity for the purposes of the banking consolidation directive.

Deductions from own funds

6. The deductions from own funds are—

    (a) own shares at book value held by the authorised payment institution;

    (b) intangible assets;

    (c) material losses of the current financial year;

    (d) holdings of shares in credit institutions and financial institutions exceeding 10% of their capital;

    (e) if sub-paragraph (d) applies, the items specified in paragraph 144(f), (g) and (j) held in the relevant credit institution or financial institution;

    (f) holdings of shares or of the items specified in paragraph 3(f), (g) and (j) held in other credit institutions or financial institutions where—

      (i)   the holding has not been deducted in accordance with sub-paragraph (d) or (e) of this paragraph; and

      (ii) the total amount of such holdings exceeds 10% of the authorised payment institu-tion's own funds calculated before deduction of the items specified in this sub-para-graph and sub-paragraphs (d), (e), (g) and (h);

    (g) participations which the authorised payment institution holds in an insurance undertak-ing, reinsurance undertaking or insurance holding company; and

    (h) the following instruments held in an insurance undertaking, reinsurance undertak-ing or insurance holding company in which the authorised payment institution holds a participation—

      (i)   instruments referred to in article 16(3) of directive 73/239/EEC of the Council on the coordination of laws, regulations and administrative provisions relating to the taking-up and pursuit of the business of direct insurance other than life assurance;

      (ii) instruments referred to in article 27(3) of directive 2002/83/EC of the European Parliament and of the Council of 5th November 2002 concerning life assurance.

7. Where shares in another credit institution, financial institution, insurance undertaking, reinsur-ance undertaking or insurance holding company are held temporarily for the purposes of a financial assistance operation designed to reorganise and save that entity, the Authority may direct that any or all of the items specified in paragraph 147(d) to (h) are not to be deducted from own funds.

Limits on qualifying items

8.—(1) The limits referred to in paragraph 144 are—

    (a) that A must not exceed B; and

    (b) that C must not exceed 50% of B.

(2) After applying such limits—

    (a) 50% of the total of the items specified in paragraph 6(d) to (h) must be deducted from A and the remaining 50% must be deducted from B; and

    (b) the amount, if any, by which the amount to be deducted from A exceeds A must be deducted from B.

(3) In this paragraph—

    (a) "A" means the total of the items specified in paragraph 144(d) to (j);

    (b) "B" means the total of the items specified in paragraph 144(a) to (c) less the total of the items specified in paragraph 147(a) to (c); and

    (c) "C" means the total of the items specified in paragraph 144(h) to (j).

9. The Authority may in temporary and exceptional circumstances direct that an authorised payment institution may exceed one or more of the limits described in paragraph 8(1).

10. An authorised payment institution must not include in its own funds calculation any item—

    (a) used in an equivalent calculation by an authorised payment institution, credit institution, investment firm, asset management company or insurance undertaking in the same group; or

    (b) in the case of an authorised payment institution which carries out activities other than providing payment services, is used in carrying out those activities.

Own funds requirement

11. An authorised payment institution must hold own funds calculated in accordance with such of Method A, Method B or Method C as the Authority may direct.

Adjustment by the Authority

12. The Authority may direct that an authorised payment institution must hold own funds up to 20% higher, or up to 20% lower, than the amount which would result from paragraph 152.

13. A direction made under paragraph 153 must be on the basis of an evaluation of the relevant authorised payment institution including, if available and where the Authority considers it appropriate, any risk-management processes, risk loss database or internal control mechanisms of the authorised payment institution.

14. The Authority may make a reasonable charge for making an evaluation required under paragraph 154.

Provision for start-up payment institutions

15. If an authorised payment institution has not completed a full financial year's business, references to a figure for the preceding financial year are to be read as the equivalent figure projected in the business plan provided in the payment institution's application for authorisation, subject to any adjustment to that plan required by the Authority.

Method A

16.—(1) "Method A" means the calculation method set out in this paragraph.

(2) The own funds requirement is 10% of the authorised payment institution's fixed overheads for the preceding financial year.

(3) If a material change has occurred in an authorised payment institution's business since the preceding financial year, the Authority may direct that the own funds requirement is to be a higher or lower amount than that calculated in accordance with sub-paragraph (2).

Method B

17.—(1) "Method B" means the calculation method set out in this paragraph.

(2) The own funds requirement is the sum of the following elements multiplied by the scaling factor—

    (a) 4% of the first 5,000,000 euro of payment volume;

    (b) 2.5% of the next 5,000,000 euro of payment volume;

    (c) 1% of the next 90,000,000 euro of payment volume;

    (d) 0.5% of the next 150,000,000 euro of payment volume; and

    (e) 0.25% of any remaining payment volume.

(3) "Payment volume" means the total amount of payment transactions executed by the authorised payment institution in the preceding financial year divided by the number of months in that year.

(4) The "scaling factor" is—

    (a) 0.5 for a payment institution that is authorised to provide the payment service specified in paragraph 127(f) of Schedule 1;

    (b) 0.8 for a payment institution that is authorised to provide the payment service specified in paragraph 127(g) of Schedule 1; and

    (c) 1 for a payment institution that is authorised to provide any other payment service.

Method C

18.—(1) "Method C" means the calculation method set out in this paragraph.

(2) The own funds requirement is the relevant indicator multiplied by—

    (a) the multiplication factor; and

    (b) the scaling factor;

subject to the proviso in sub-paragraph (7).

(3) The "relevant indicator" is the sum of the following elements—

    (a) interest income;

    (b) interest expenses;

    (c) gross commissions and fees received; and

    (d) gross other operating income.

(4) For the purpose of calculating the relevant indicator—

    (a) each element must be included in the sum with its positive or negative sign;

    (b) income from extraordinary or irregular items may not be used;

    (c) expenditure on the outsourcing of services rendered by third parties may reduce the relevant indicator if the expenditure is incurred from a payment service provider;

    (d) the relevant indicator is calculated on the basis of the twelve-monthly observation at the end of the previous financial year;

    (e) the relevant indicator must be calculated over the previous financial year; and

    (f) audited figures must be used unless they are not available in which case business estimates may be used.

(5) The "multiplication factor" is the sum of—

    (a) 10% of the first 2,500,000 euro of the relevant indicator;

    (b) 8% of the next 2,500,000 euro of the relevant indicator;

    (c) 6% of the next 20,000,000 euro of the relevant indicator;

    (d) 3% of the next 25,000,000 euro of the relevant indicator; and

    (e) 1.5% of any remaining amount of the relevant indicator.

(6) "Scaling factor" has the meaning given in paragraph 158(4).

(7) The proviso is that the own funds requirement must not be less than 80 % of the average of the previous three financial years for the relevant indicator.

Application of accounting standards

19. Except where this Schedule provides for a different method of recognition, measurement or valuation, whenever a provision in this Schedule refers to an asset, liability, equity or income statement item, an authorised payment institution must, for the purpose of that provision, recognise the asset, liability, equity or income statement item and measure its value in accordance with whichever of the following are applicable for the purpose of the institution's external financial reporting—

(a) Financial Reporting Standards and Statements of Standard Accounting Practice issued or adopted by the Accounting Standards Board;

(b) Statements of Recommended Practice, issued by industry or sectoral bodies recognised for this purpose by the Accounting Standards Board;

(c) International Financial Reporting Standards and International Accounting Standards issued or adopted by the International Accounting Standards Board;

(d) International Standards on Auditing (United Kingdom and Ireland) issued by the Auditing Practices Board; and

(e) the Companies Act 2006.

Regulations 36(2), 40(1)   **SCHEDULE 4**

PRIOR GENERAL INFORMATION FOR FRAMEWORK CONTRACTS

1. The following information about the payment service provider—

(a) the name of the payment service provider;

(b) the address and contact details of the payment service provider's head office;

(c) if different from the information under sub-paragraph (b), the address and contact details of the branch or agent from which the payment service is being provided;

(d) details of the payment service provider's regulators, including any reference or registration number of the payment service provider.

2. The following information about the payment service—

(a) a description of the main characteristics of the payment service to be provided;

(b) the information or unique identifier that must be provided by the payment service user in order for a payment order to be properly executed;

(c) the form and procedure for giving consent to the execution of a payment transaction and for the withdrawal of consent in accordance with regulation 55;

(d) a reference to the time of receipt of a payment order, as defined in regulation 65, and the cut-off time, if any, established by the payment service provider;

(e) the maximum execution time for the payment services to be provided;

(f) whether spending limits for the use of a payment instrument may be agreed in accordance with regulation 56(1).

3. The following information about charges, interest and exchange rates—

(a) details of all charges payable by the payment service user to the payment service provider and, where applicable, a breakdown of the amounts of any charges;

(b) where relevant, details of the interest and exchange rates to be applied or, if reference interest and exchange rates are to be used, the method of calculating the actual interest and the relevant date and index or base for determining such reference interest or exchange rates;

(c) if agreed, the immediate application of changes in reference interest or exchange rates and information requirements relating to the changes in accordance with regulation 42(4).

4. The following information about communication—

    (a) the means of communication agreed between the parties for the transmission of information or notifications under these Regulations including, where relevant, any technical requirements for the payment service user's equipment for receipt of the information or notifications;

    (b) the manner in which and frequency with which information under these Regulations is to be provided or made available;

    (c) the language or languages in which the framework contract will be concluded and in which any information or notifications under these Regulations will be communicated;

    (d) the payment service user's right to receive the terms of the framework contract and information in accordance with regulation 41.

5. The following information about safeguards and corrective measures—

    (a) where relevant, a description of the steps that the payment service user is to take in order to keep safe a payment instrument and how to notify the payment service provider for the purposes of regulation 57(1)(b);

    (b) where relevant, the conditions under which the payment service provider proposes to reserve the right to stop or prevent the use of a payment instrument in accordance with regulation 56;

    (c) the payer's liability under regulation 62, including details of any limits on such liability;

    (d) how and within what period of time the payment service user is to notify the payment service provider of any unauthorised or incorrectly executed payment transaction under regulation 59, and the payment service provider's liability for unauthorised payment transactions under regulation 61;

    (e) the payment service provider's liability for the execution of payment transactions under regulation 75 or 76;

    (f) the conditions for the payment of any refund under regulation 63.

6. The following information about changes to and termination of the framework contract—

    (a) where relevant, the proposed terms under which the payment service user will be deemed to have accepted changes to the framework contract in accordance with regulation 42(2), unless they notify the payment service provider that they do not accept such changes before the proposed date of their entry into force;

    (b) the duration of the framework contract;

    (c) the right of the payment service user to terminate the framework contract and any agreements relating to termination in accordance with regulation 43.

7. The following information about redress—

    (a) any contractual clause on—

        (i) the law applicable to the framework contract;

        (ii) the competent courts;

    (b) the availability of out-of-court complaint and redress procedures for the payment service user and the methods for having access to them.

Consumer Credit (Disclosure of Information) Regulations 2010

(SI 2010, No. 1013)

1 Citation, commencement and interpretation

    (2) In these Regulations—

"the Act" means the Consumer Credit Act 1974;

"advance payment" includes any deposit and in relation to a regulated consumer credit agreement includes also any part-exchange allowance in respect of any goods agreed in antecedent negotiations

[...] to be taken by the creditor in part exchange but does not include a repayment of credit or any insurance premium or any amount entering into the total charge for credit;

"ancillary service" means a service that relates to the provision of credit under the agreement and includes in particular an insurance or payment protection policy;

"the APR" means the annual percentage rate of charge for credit determined in accordance with Schedule 2 to these Regulations and the Total Charge for Credit Regulations;

"cash price" in relation to any goods, services, land or other things means the price or charge at which the goods, services, land or other things may be purchased by, or supplied to, the debtor for cash account being taken of any discount generally available from the dealer or supplier in question;

"credit intermediary" has the same meaning as in section 160A of the Act;

"distance contract" means any regulated agreement made under an organised distance sales or service-provision scheme run by or on behalf of the creditor who, in any such case, for the purpose of that agreement makes exclusive use of one or more means of distance communication up to and including the time at which the agreement is made. For this purpose, "means of distance communication" means any means which, without the simultaneous physical presence of the creditor or a person acting on behalf of the creditor and of the debtor, may be used for the making of a regulated agreement between the parties to that agreement;

"excluded pawn agreement" means a pawn agreement—

(a) where the debtor is not a new customer of the creditor ([paragraph (6)]), and

(b) where, before the agreement is made, the creditor has not received a request from the debtor for the pre-contract credit information (see regulation 9);

"linked credit agreement" means a regulated consumer credit agreement which—

(a) serves exclusively to finance an agreement for the supply of specific goods or the provision of a specific service or land, and

(b) (i) where the supplier or service provider himself finances the credit for the debtor, or if it is financed by a third party, where the creditor uses the services of the supplier or service provider in connection with the preparation or making of the credit agreement, or

(ii) where the specific goods or land or the provision of a specific service are explicitly specified in the credit agreement;

"pawn agreement" means a consumer credit agreement under which the creditor takes an article in pawn;

"pre-contract credit information" means the information specified in regulation 3(4);

"total amount of credit" means the credit limit or the total sums made available under a consumer credit agreement;

"total amount payable" means the sum of the total charge for credit and the total amount of credit payable under the agreement as well as any advance payment;

"total charge for credit" means the total charge for credit determined in accordance with the Total Charge for Credit Regulations and the Schedule to these Regulations;

"the Total Charge for Credit Regulations" means the Consumer Credit (Total Charge for Credit) Regulations 2010.

(3) In these Regulations, a reference to a repayment is a reference to—

(a) a repayment of the whole or any part of the credit,

(b) a payment of the whole or any part of the total charge for credit, or

(c) a combination of such repayments and payments.

(4) In these Regulations, a reference to rate of interest is a reference to the interest rate expressed as a fixed or variable percentage applied on an annual basis to the amount of credit drawn down.

(5) In these Regulations, a reference to an agreement includes a reference to a prospective agreement.

(6) For the purposes of the definition of "excluded pawn agreement" and regulation 8 the debtor is a new customer if the debtor has not entered into a pawn agreement with the creditor in the three years preceding the start of the negotiations antecedent to the agreement.

(7) In relation to a regulated consumer credit agreement secured on land and to which these Regulations do not apply, the definition of Total Charge for Credit Regulations shall apply as if for the words "Consumer Credit (Total Charge for Credit) Regulations 2010" there were substituted "Consumer Credit (Total Charge for Credit) Regulations 1980".

2   Agreements to which these Regulations apply

(1) These Regulations apply in respect of a regulated consumer credit agreement, except as provided for in paragraphs (2) to (4).

(2) These regulations do not apply to an agreement to which section 58 of the Act (opportunity for withdrawal from prospective land mortgage) applies.

(3) These Regulations do not apply to an authorised non-business overdraft agreement which is—

    (a) for credit which exceeds £60,260, or

    (b) secured on land.

(4) Except as provided for in paragraph (5) these Regulations do not apply to an agreement—

    (a) under which the creditor provides the debtor with credit exceeding £60,260,

    (b) secured on land,

    (c) entered into by the debtor wholly or predominantly for the purposes of a business also carried on, or intended to be carried on, by him, or

    (d) made before 1st February 2011.

(5) These Regulations apply to an agreement mentioned in paragraph (4) (which is not also an agreement mentioned in paragraph (2) or (3)) where a creditor or, where applicable a credit intermediary, discloses or purports to disclose the pre-contract credit information in accordance with these Regulations rather than in accordance with the Consumer Credit (Disclosure of Information) Regulations 2004 or the Financial Services (Distance Marketing) Regulations 2004 (as the case may be).

(6) Subsections (2) to (5) of section 16B of the Act (declaration by the debtor as to the purposes of the agreement) apply for the purposes of [paragraph (4)(c)].

3   Information to be disclosed: agreements other than telephone contracts, non-telephone distance contracts, excluded pawn agreements and overdraft agreements

(1) This regulation applies to an agreement other than—

    [(a) an agreement made by voice telephone communication where it is a distance contract and the debtor consents to the disclosure of the information referred to in regulation 4(2);

   (aa) an agreement made by voice telephone communication where it is not a distance contract (see regulation 4(3));]

    (b) an agreement made using a means of distance communication other than a voice telephone communication, which does not enable the provision of the pre-contract credit information before the agreement is made (see regulation 5);

    (c) an excluded pawn agreement;

    (d) an authorised non-business overdraft agreement (see regulations 10 and 11).

(2) In good time before the agreement is made, the creditor must disclose to the debtor, in the manner set out in regulation 8, the pre-contract credit information.

(3) Paragraph (2) does not require a creditor to disclose the pre-contract credit information where it has already been disclosed to the debtor by a credit intermediary in a manner which complies with paragraph (2).

(4) For the purposes of these Regulations, the pre-contract credit information comprises—

    (a) the type of credit,

    (b) the identity and geographical address of the creditor and, where applicable, of the credit intermediary,

(c) the total amount of credit to be provided under the agreement and the conditions governing the draw down of credit. In the case of an agreement for running-account credit, the total amount of credit may be expressed as a statement indicating the manner in which the credit limit will be determined where it is not practicable to express the limit as a sum of money,

(d) the duration or minimum duration of the agreement or a statement that the agreement has no fixed or minimum duration,

(e) in the case of—
    (i) credit in the form of deferred payment for specific goods, services or land, or
    (ii) a linked credit agreement,
    a description of the goods, services or land and the cash price of each and the total cash price,

(f) the rate of interest charged, any conditions applicable to that rate, where available, any reference rate on which that rate is based and any information on any changes to the rate of interest (including the periods that the rate applies, and any conditions or procedure applicable to changing the rate),

(g) where different rates of interest are charged in different circumstances the creditor must provide the information in paragraph (f) in respect of each rate,

(h) the APR and the total amount payable under the agreement illustrated (if not known) by way of a representative example mentioning all the assumptions used in order to calculate that rate and amount,

(i) the amount (expressed as a sum of money), number (if applicable) and frequency of repayments to be made by the debtor and, where appropriate, the order in which repayments will be allocated to different outstanding balances charged at different rates of interest,

(j) in the case of an agreement for running-account credit, the amount of each repayment is to be expressed as (a) a sum of money; (b) a specified proportion of a specified amount; (c) a combination of (a) or (b); or (d) in a case where the amount of any repayment cannot be expressed in accordance with (a), (b) or (c), a statement indicating the manner in which the amount will be determined,

(k) if applicable, any charges for maintaining an account recording both payment transactions and draw downs, unless the opening of an account is optional, and any charge payable for using a method of payment in respect of payment transactions or draw downs,

(l) any other charges payable deriving from the credit agreement and the conditions under which those charges may be changed,

(m) if applicable, a statement that fees will be payable by the debtor to a notary on conclusion of the credit agreement,

(n) the obligation, if any, to enter into a contract for ancillary services relating to the consumer credit agreement, in particular insurance services, where the conclusion of such a contract is compulsory in order to obtain the credit or to obtain it on the terms and conditions marketed,

(o) the rate of interest applicable in the case of late payments and the arrangements for its adjustment, and, where applicable, any charges payable for default,

(p) a warning regarding the consequences of missing payments (for example, the possibility of legal proceedings and the possibility that the debtor's home may be repossessed),

(q) where applicable, any security to be provided by the debtor or on behalf of the debtor,

(r) the existence or absence of a right of withdrawal,

(s) the debtor's right of early repayment under section 94 of the Act, and where applicable, information concerning the creditor's right to compensation and the way in which that compensation will be determined,

(t) the requirement for a creditor to inform a debtor in accordance with section 157(A1) of the Act that a decision not to proceed with a prospective regulated consumer credit agreement has been reached on the basis of information from a credit reference agency and of the particulars of that agency,

(u) the debtor's right to be supplied under section 55C of the Act on request and free of charge, with a copy of the draft agreement except where—

    (i) the creditor is at the time of the request unwilling to proceed to the making of the agreement, or

    (ii) the agreement is an agreement referred to in regulation 2(4)(a) to (c) or a pawn agreement, and

(v) if applicable, the period of time during which the creditor is bound by the pre-contract credit information.

(5) For the purpose of the representative example referred to in paragraph (4)(h)—

    (a)(i) where the debtor has informed the creditor or credit intermediary of one or more components of his preferred credit, such as the duration of the consumer credit agreement or the total amount of credit, and

    (ii) where the creditor would in principle agree to offer credit on such terms,

    the creditor or credit intermediary must take those components into account when calculating the representative APR and the total amount payable;

    (b) where the creditor uses the assumption set out in regulation 6(g) of the Consumer Credit (Total Charge for Credit) Regulations 2010 the creditor must indicate that other draw down mechanisms for this type of consumer credit agreement may result in a higher APR;

    (c) subject to paragraph (a), in the case of an agreement for running-account credit, where the credit limit is not known at the date on which the pre-contract credit information is disclosed, the total amount of credit is to be assumed to be £1,200 or in a case where credit is to be provided subject to a maximum credit limit of less than £1,200, an amount equal to that maximum limit.

(6) In the case of a consumer credit agreement under which repayments do not give rise to an immediate reduction in the total amount of credit advanced but are used to constitute capital as provided for under the agreement or under an ancillary agreement, the creditor or credit intermediary must provide a clear and concise statement that such agreements do not provide for a guarantee of repayment of the total amount of credit drawn down under the credit agreement unless such a guarantee is given.

4   Information to be disclosed: telephone contracts

(1) This regulation applies to an agreement (other than an authorised non-business overdraft agreement) made by way of a voice telephone communication (whether or not it is a distance contract).

(2) Where the agreement is a distance contract and where the debtor explicitly consents, the creditor must disclose the following information before the agreement is made—

    (a) the identity of the person in contact with the debtor and that person's link with the creditor,

    (b) a description of the main characteristics of the credit agreement which includes the information set out in regulation 3(4)(c), (d), (e), (f), (g), (h), (i) and (j),

    (c) the total price to be paid by the debtor to the creditor for the credit including all taxes paid via the creditor or, if an exact price cannot be indicated, the basis for the calculation of the price enabling the debtor to verify it,

    (d) notice of the possibility that other taxes or costs may exist that are not paid via the creditor or imposed by the creditor,

    (e) whether or not there is—

        (i) a right to withdraw under section 66A of the Act, or

        (ii) a right to cancel under regulation 9 of the Financial Services (Distance Marketing) Regulations 2004 and, where there is such a right, its duration and the conditions for exercising it, including information on the amount which the consumer may be required to pay in accordance with regulation 13 of those Regulations, as well as the consequences of not exercising that right,

 (f) that other information is available on request and the nature of that information.

 (3) Where the agreement is not a distance contract the creditor must disclose the information in paragraph (2)(b) before the agreement is made.

 (4) The creditor must disclose the pre-contract credit information in the manner set out in regulation 8 immediately after the agreement is made.

5 Information to be disclosed: non-telephone distance contracts

 (1) This regulation applies to an agreement (other than an authorised non-business overdraft agreement) made—

  (a) at the debtor's request, and

  (b) using a means of distance communication other than a voice telephone communication which does not enable the provision before the agreement is made of the pre-contract credit information.

 (2) The creditor must disclose the pre-contract credit information in the manner set out in regulation 8 immediately after the agreement is made.

6 Information to be disclosed: distance contracts for the purpose of a business

 (1) This regulation applies to an agreement that is a distance contract entered into by the debtor wholly or predominantly for the purposes of a business carried on, or intended to be carried on by him.

 (2) Where the agreement is an agreement to which [regulations 3, 4 or 5] would otherwise apply the creditor may comply with those regulations by disclosing the pre-contract credit information immediately after the agreement is entered into.

 (3) Subsections (2) to (5) of section 16B of the Act (declaration by the debtor as to the purposes of the agreement) apply for the purposes of paragraph (1).

7 Information about contractual terms and conditions: [regulations 3, 4 and 5]

 (1) This regulation applies to an agreement which is—

  (a) a distance contract to which [regulation 3, 4 or 5] applies, and

  (b) which is not entered into by the debtor wholly or predominantly for the purposes of a business carried on, or intended to be carried on, by him.

 (2) The creditor must ensure that—

  (a) the information provided to the debtor pursuant to [regulation 3, 4 or 5] includes the contractual terms and conditions, and

  (b) the information provided to the debtor in relation to the contractual obligations which would arise if the distance contract were made accurately reflects the contractual obligations which would arise under the law presumed to be applicable to that contract.

 (3) Subsections (2) to (5) of section 16B of the Act (declaration by the debtor as to the purposes of the agreement) apply for the purposes of paragraph (1).

8 Manner of disclosure

 (1) The pre-contract credit information must be disclosed by means of the form contained in Schedule 1.

 (2) The form must be—

  (a) in writing, and

  (b) of a nature that enables the debtor to remove it from the place where it is disclosed to him.

 (3) The form must be completed as specified in this paragraph—

  (a) the relevant pre-contract credit information is to be provided in the appropriate row,

  (b) the form is to be completed in accordance with the notes to that form,

  (c) the asterisks and notes may be deleted,

  (d) gridlines and boxes may be omitted, and

  (e) any information contained in the form must be clear and easily legible.

(4) Any additional information relating to the credit which is provided in writing by the creditor to the debtor must be provided in a separate document to the form.

(5) Where a consumer credit agreement is a multiple agreement containing more than one part for the purposes of section 18 of the Act, the pre-contract credit information in respect of each part may be provided in the same form provided that—

> (a) information that is not common to each part of the agreement is disclosed separately within the relevant section of the form, and
>
> (b) it is clear which information relates to which part.

9 Information to be disclosed: pawn agreements

(1) This Regulation applies to a pawn agreement.

(2) In good time before a pawn agreement is made (unless the debtor is a new customer), the creditor must inform the debtor of his right to receive the pre-contract credit information in the form contained in Schedule 1, free of charge, on request.

Information to be disclosed: overdraft agreements

10.—(1) This regulation applies to an agreement which is an authorised non-business overdraft agreement.

(2) In good time before an authorised non-business overdraft agreement is made, the creditor must disclose to the debtor, the information in paragraph (3) in the manner set out in regulation 11.

(3) The information referred to in paragraph (2) is as follows—

> (a) the type of credit,
>
> (b) the identity and geographical address of the creditor and, where applicable, of the credit intermediary,
>
> (c) the total amount of credit,
>
> (d) the duration of the agreement,
>
> (e) the rate of interest charged, any conditions applicable to that rate, any reference rate on which that rate is based and any information on any changes to the rate of interest (including the periods that the rate applies, and any conditions or procedure applicable to changing the rate),
>
> (f) where different rates of interest are charged in different circumstances the creditor must provide the information in paragraph (e) in respect of each rate,
>
> (g) the conditions and procedure for terminating the agreement,
>
> (h) where applicable, an indication that the debtor may be requested to repay the amount of credit in full on demand at any time,
>
> (i) the rate of interest applicable in the case of late payments and the arrangements for its adjustment, and, where applicable, any charges payable for default,
>
> (j) the requirement for a creditor to inform a debtor in accordance with section 157(A1) of the Act that a decision not to proceed with a prospective regulated consumer credit agreement has been reached on the basis of information from a credit reference agency and of the particulars of that agency,
>
> (k) the charges, other than the rates of interest, payable by the debtor under the agreement (and the conditions under which those charges may be varied),
>
> (l) if applicable, the period of time during which the creditor is bound by the information set out in this paragraph.

(4) Paragraph (2) does not apply to—

> (a) an agreement made by a voice telephone communication (whether or not it is a distance contract),
>
> (b) an agreement made at the debtor's request using a means of distance communication, other than a voice telephone communication, which does not enable the provision of the information required by paragraph (2) before the agreement is made, or
>
> (c) an agreement that does not come within sub-paragraph (a) or (b) but where the debtor requests the overdraft be made available with immediate effect.

(5) In the case of an agreement that falls within paragraph (4)(a) that is also a distance contract, where the debtor explicitly consents the creditor must disclose the following information before the agreement is made—

(a) the identity of the person in contact with the debtor and that person's link with the creditor,

(b) a description of the main characteristics of the financial service including at least the information in paragraph (3)(c), (e), (f), (h) and (k),

(c) the total price to be paid by the debtor to the creditor for the credit including all taxes paid via the creditor or, if an exact price cannot be indicated, the basis for the calculation of the price enabling the debtor to verify it,

(d) notice of the possibility that other taxes or costs may exist that are not paid via the creditor or imposed by the creditor,

(e) whether or not there is a right to cancel under regulation 9 of the Financial Services (Distance Marketing) Regulations 2004 and where there is such a right, its duration and the conditions for exercising it including information on the amount which the consumer may be required to pay in accordance with regulation 13 of those regulations, as well as the consequences of not exercising that right, and

(f) that other information is available on request and the nature of that information.

[(5A) In the case of an agreement that falls within paragraph (4)(a) that is also a distance contract, where the debtor does not explicitly consent to the disclosure of the information in paragraph (5), the creditor must disclose the information in paragraph (3) to the debtor before the agreement is made.]

(6) In the case of an agreement that falls within paragraph (4)(a) that is not a distance contract the creditor must disclose the information in paragraph (5)(b) before the agreement is made.

(7) In the case of an agreement that is a distance contract to which this regulation applies the creditor must ensure that the information he provides to the debtor pursuant to this regulation regarding the contractual obligations which would arise if the distance contract were concluded, accurately reflects the contractual obligations which would arise under the law presumed to be applicable to that contract.

(8) In the case of an agreement that falls within paragraph (4)(c), the creditor must disclose the information in paragraph (3)(c), (e), (f), (h), and (k) to the debtor before the agreement is made in the manner set out in regulation 11.

(9) Where a current account is an agreement for two or more debtors jointly the creditor may comply with paragraphs (5), [(5A),] (6) or (8) by disclosing the information to one debtor provided that each of the debtors have given the creditor their consent that the creditor may not comply in each debtor's case with the relevant paragraph.

11.—(1) Where regulation 10(2) applies, the creditor must comply with that regulation by—

(a) disclosing the information by means of the European Consumer Credit Information form set out in Schedule 3 to these Regulations and as specified in paragraph (2), or

(b) disclosing the information in writing so that all information is equally prominent.

(2) The specifications referred to in paragraph (1)(a) are that—

(a) the relevant information must be provided in the appropriate row,

(b) the form must be completed in accordance with the notes to that form,

(c) the asterisks and notes may be deleted,

(d) gridlines and boxes may be omitted, and

(e) any information contained in the form must be clear and easily legible.

(3) Where regulation 10(8) applies, the creditor may provide the information orally.

12 Modifying agreements

(1) Subject to paragraphs (2) to (4), these Regulations apply to a modifying agreement which varies or supplements an earlier agreement and which is, or is treated under section 82(3) of the Act as, a regulated agreement.

[(2) Where a modifying agreement modifies an earlier consumer credit agreement, the requirements of regulations 3, 4 and 10 will be deemed to be satisfied if—

    (a) in good time before the modifying agreement is made—

        (i) the information specified by regulations 3(4) and 10(3) is disclosed to the debtor in respect of any provision of the earlier agreement which is varied or supplemented, and

        (ii) the creditor informs the debtor in writing that the other information in the earlier agreement remains unchanged, and

    (b) where the Financial Services (Distance Marketing) Regulations 2004 apply, the creditor complies with regulations 7 and 8 of those Regulations.]

    (3) Where a modifying agreement is made in a manner that does not allow the creditor to comply with the requirement in [paragraph (2)(a)(ii)], the creditor is deemed to have complied with that requirement if—

    (a) before the agreement is made the creditor informs the debtor orally that the other information in the earlier agreement remains unchanged, and

    (b) this is confirmed to the debtor in writing immediately after the agreement is made.

    (4) This regulation does not apply to an excluded pawn agreement.

Regulation 8(1)

SCHEDULE 1

PRE-CONTRACT CREDIT INFORMATION

(Standard European Consumer Credit Information)

1. Contact details

Creditor.	[Identity.]
Address.	[Geographical address of the creditor
Telephone number(s).*	to be used by the debtor.]
E-mail address.*	
Fax number.*	
Web address.*	
If applicable	
Credit intermediary.	[Identity.]
Address.	[Geographical address of the credit
Telephone number(s).*	intermediary to be used by the debtor.]
E-mail address.*	
Fax number.*	
Web address.*	

* This information is optional for the creditor. The row may be deleted if the information is not provided.

    Wherever "if applicable" is indicated, the creditor must give the information relevant to the credit product or, if the information is not relevant for the type of credit considered, delete the respective information or the entire row, or indicate that the information is not applicable.

    Indications between square brackets provide explanations for the creditor and must be replaced with the corresponding information.

2. Key features of the credit product

[The type of credit].	
The total amount of credit. This means the amount of credit to be provided under the proposed credit agreement or the credit limit.	[The amount is to be expressed as a sum of money. In the case of running-account credit, the total amount may be expressed as a statement indicating the manner in which the credit limit will be determined where it is not practicable to express the limit as a sum of money.]
How and when credit would be provided.	[Details of how and when any credit being advanced is to be drawn down.]
The duration of the credit agreement.	[The duration or minimum duration of the agreement or a statement that the agreement has no fixed or minimum duration.]
Repayments. If applicable: Your repayments will pay off what you owe in the following order.	[The amount (expressed as a sum of money), number (if applicable) and frequency of repayments to be made by the debtor. In the case of an agreement for running-account credit, the amount may be expressed as a sum of money or a specified proportion of a specified amount or both, or in a case where the amount of any repayment cannot be expressed as a sum of money or a specified proportion, a statement indicating the manner in which the amount will be determined. [The order in which repayments will be allocated to different outstanding balances charged at different rates of interest.]
The total amount you will have to pay. This means the amount you have borrowed plus interest and other costs.	[The amount payable by the debtor under the agreement (where necessary, illustrated by means of a representative example). The total amount payable will be the sum of the total amount of credit and the total charge for credit payable under the agreement as well as any advance payment where required. In the case of running account credit, where it is not practicable to express the limit as a sum of money, a credit limit of £1200 should be assumed. In a case where credit is to be provided subject to a maximum credit limit of less than £1200, an amount equal to that maximum limit. The total charge for credit is to be calculated using the relevant APR assumptions set out in Schedule 2 to the Consumer Credit (Disclosure of Information) Regulations 2010 and the Total Charge for Credit Regulations, and where appropriate the relevant components of the debtor's preferred credit.]
If applicable The proposed credit will be granted in the form of a deferred payment for goods or service.] or [The proposed credit will be linked to the supply of specific goods or the provision of a service.] Description of goods/services/ land (as applicable). Cash price.	[A list or other description] [Cash price of goods or service.] [Total cash price.]
If applicable Security required. This is a description of the security to be provided by you in relation to the credit agreement.	[Description of any security to be provided by or on behalf of the debtor.]

| If applicable

Repayments will not immediately reduce the amount you owe. | [In the case of a credit agreement under which repayments do not give rise to an immediate reduction in the total amount of credit advanced but are used to constitute capital as provided by the agreement (or an ancillary agreement a clear and concise statement) where applicable, that the agreement does not provide for a guarantee of the repayment of the total amount of credit drawn down under the credit agreement.] |

3. Costs of the credit

The rates of interest which apply to the credit agreement	[Details of the rate of interest charged, any conditions applicable to that rate, where available, any reference rate on which that rate is based and any information on changes to the rate of interest (including the periods that the rate applies, and any conditions or procedure applicable to changing the rate). Where different rates of interest are charged in different circumstances, the creditor must provide the above information in respect of each rate.]
Annual Percentage Rate of Charge (APR). This is the total cost expressed as an annual percentage of the total amount of credit. The APR is there to help you compare different offers.	[% if known. If the APR is not known a representative example (expressed as a %) mentioning all the necessary assumptions used for calculating the rate (as set out in Schedule 2 to the Consumer Credit (Disclosure of Information) Regulations 2010, the Total Charge for Credit Regulations and, where appropriate, the relevant components of the debtor's preferred credit). Where the creditor uses the assumption set out in regulation 6(g) of the Total Charge for Credit Regulations, the creditor shall indicate that other draw down mechanisms for this type of agreement may result in a higher APR.]
If applicable In order to obtain the credit or to obtain it on the terms and conditions marketed, you must take out: — an insurance policy securing the credit, or — another ancillary service contract.	[Nature and description of any insurance or other ancillary service contract required.]
If we do not know the costs of these services they are not included in the APR.	
Related costs	
If applicable You must have a separate account for recording both payment transactions and drawdowns.	[Details of any account or accounts that the creditor requires to be set up in order to obtain the credit together with the amount of any charge for this.]
If applicable Charge for using a specific payment method.	[Specify means of payment and the amount of charge.]
If applicable Any other costs deriving from the credit agreement.	[Description and amount of any other charges not otherwise referred to in this form.]

If applicable Conditions under which the above charges can be changed.	[Details of the conditions under which any of the charges mentioned above can be changed.]
If applicable You will be required to pay notarial fees.	[Description and amount of any fee.]
Costs in the case of late payments.	Either [A statement that there are no charges for late or missed payments.] Or [Applicable rate of interest in the case of late payments and arrangements for its adjustment and, where applicable any charges payable for default.]
Consequences of missing payments.	[A statement warning about the consequences of missing payments, including: — a reference to possible legal proceedings and repossession of the debtor's home where this is a possibility, and — the possibility of missing payments making it more difficult to obtain credit in the future.]

4.   Other important legal aspects

Right of withdrawal.	Either: [A statement that the debtor has the right to withdraw from the credit agreement before the end of 14 days beginning with the day after the day on which the agreement is made, or if information is provided after the agreement is made, the day on which the debtor receives a copy of the executed agreement under sections 61A or 63 of the Consumer Credit Act 1974, the day on which the debtor receives the information required in section 61A(3) of that Act or the day on which the creditor notifies the debtor of the credit limit, the first time it is provided, whichever is the latest.] Or [There is no right to withdraw from this agreement – if there is a right to cancel the agreement this should be stated.] [If the right to cancel is under the Financial Services (Distance Marketing) Regulations 2004 refer to section 5 of the form.]
Early repayment. If applicable Compensation payable in the case of early repayment.	[A statement that the debtor has the right to repay the credit early at any time in full or partially.]. [Determination of the compensation (calculation method) in accordance with section 95A of the Consumer Credit Act 1974.]
Consultation with a Credit Reference Agency.	[A statement that if the creditor decides not to proceed with a prospective regulated consumer credit agreement on the basis of information from a credit reference agency the creditor must, when informing the debtor of the decision, inform the debtor that it has been reached on the basis of information from a credit reference agency and of the particulars of that agency.]
Right to a draft credit agreement.	[A statement that the debtor has the right, upon request, to obtain a copy of the draft credit agreement free of charge, unless the creditor is unwilling at the time of the request to proceed to the conclusion of the credit agreement.]

If applicable The period of time during which the creditor is bound by the pre-contractual information.	[This information is valid from [—] until [—].]or [Period of time during which the information on this form is valid.]

If applicable

5. Additional information in the case of distance marketing of financial services

(a) concerning the creditor	
If applicable The creditor's representative in your Member State of residence. Address. Telephone number(s). E-mail address.* Fax number.* Web address.*	[i.e. where different from section 1.] [Identity.] [Geographical address to be used by the debtor.]
If applicable Registration number.	[Consumer credit licence number and any other relevant registration number of the creditor.]
If applicable The supervisory authority.	[The Office of Fair Trading or any other relevant supervisory authority or both.]
(b) concerning the credit agreement	
If applicable Right to cancel the credit agreement.	[Practical instructions for exercising the right to cancel indicating, amongst other things, the period for exercising the right, the address to which notification of exercise of the right to cancel should be sent and the consequences of non-exercise of that right.]
If applicable The law taken by the creditor as a basis for the establishment of relations with you before the conclusion of the credit agreement.	[English/other law]
If applicable The law applicable to the credit agreement and/or the competent court.	[A statement concerning the law which governs the contract and the courts to which disputes may be referred.]
If applicable Language to be used in connection with the credit agreement.	[Details of the language that the information and contractual terms will be supplied in and used, with your consent, for communication during the duration of the credit agreement.]
(c) concerning redress	
Access to out-of-court complaint and redress mechanism.	[Whether or not there is an out-of-court complaint and redress mechanism for the debtor and, if so, the methods of access to it.]

* This information is optional for the creditor. The row may be deleted if the information is not provided.

SCHEDULE 2

PROVISIONS RELATING TO CALCULATION AND DISCLOSURE OF THE TOTAL CHARGE FOR CREDIT AND APR

1. Assumptions about running-account credit

(a) In the case of an agreement for running-account credit, the assumption in paragraph (b) shall have effect for the purpose of calculating the total charge for credit and any APR in place of any assumptions in regulation 6(o) of the Consumer Credit (Total Charge for Credit) Regulations 2010 that might otherwise apply—

(b) in a case where the credit limit applicable to the credit is not known at the time the pre-contract credit information is disclosed but it is known that it will be subject to a maximum limit of less than £1,200, the credit limit shall be assumed to be an amount equal to that maximum limit.

2. Permissible tolerances in disclosure of an APR

For the purposes of these Regulations, it shall be sufficient compliance with the requirement to show an APR if there is included in the pre-contract credit information—

(a) a rate which exceeds the APR by not more than one,

(b) a rate which falls short of the APR by not more than 0.1, or

(c) in a case to which paragraph 3 or 4 of this Schedule applies, a rate determined in accordance with those paragraphs or whichever of them applies to that case.

3. Tolerance where repayments are nearly equal

In the case of an agreement under which all repayments but one are equal and that one repayment does not differ from any other repayment by more whole pence than there are repayments of credit, there may be included in the pre-contract credit information a rate found under regulation 5 of the Consumer Credit (Total Charge for Credit) Regulations 2010 as if that one repayment were equal to the other repayments to be made under the agreement.

4. Tolerance where interval between relevant date and first repayment is greater than interval between repayments

In the case of an agreement under which—

(a) three or more repayments are to be made at equal intervals, and

(b) the interval between the relevant date and the first repayment is greater than the interval between the repayments,

there may be included in the pre-contract credit information a rate found under regulation 5 of the Consumer Credit (Total Charge for Credit) Regulations 2010 as if the interval between the relevant date and the first repayment were shortened so as to be equal to the interval between repayments.

Regulation 11(1)   **SCHEDULE 3**

EUROPEAN CONSUMER CREDIT INFORMATION

1. Contact details

Creditor.	[Identity.]
Address.	[Geographical address of the creditor to be used by the debtor.]
Telephone number(s).*	
E-mail address.*	
Fax number.*	
Web address.*	
If applicable	
Credit intermediary.	[Identity.]
Address.	[Geographical address of the credit intermediary to be used by the debtor.]
Telephone number(s).*	
E-mail address.*	
Fax number.*	
Web address.*	

* This information is optional for the creditor. The row may be deleted if the information is not provided.

Wherever "if applicable" is indicated, the creditor must give the information relevant to the credit product or, if the information is not relevant for the type of credit considered, delete the respective information or the entire row or indicate that the information is not applicable.

Indications between square brackets provide explanations for the creditor and must be replaced with the corresponding information.

2. Description of the main features of the credit product

[The type of credit].	
The total amount of credit. This means the amount of credit to be provided under the agreement or the credit limit.	[The amount is to be expressed as a sum of money. In the case of running account credit, the total amount may be expressed as a statement indicating the manner in which the credit limit will be determined where it is not practicable to express the limit as a sum of money.]
The duration of the credit agreement.	[The duration or minimum duration of the agreement or a statement that the agreement has no fixed or minimum duration.]
If applicable Repayment of the credit.	[A statement informing the debtor that the debtor may be required to repay the amount of credit in full on demand at any time.]

3. Costs of the credit

The rates of interest which apply to the credit agreement.	[Details of the rates of interest charged, any conditions applicable to that rate, where available any reference rate on which that rate is based and any information on changes to the rate of interest (including the periods that the rate applies and any conditions or procedure applicable to changing the rate). Where different rates of interest are charged in different circumstances, the creditor must provide the above information in respect of each rate.]
If applicable Costs. If applicable The conditions under which those costs may be changed.	[The costs applicable from the time the credit agreement is concluded.]
Costs in the case of late payments.	Either [A statement that there are no charges for late or missed payments.] Or [Applicable rate of interest, in the case of late payments and arrangements for its adjustment and, where applicable, any charges payable for default.]

4. Other important legal aspects

Termination of the credit agreement.	[The conditions and procedure for termination of the credit agreement.]
Consultation with a credit reference agency.	[A statement that if the creditor decides not to proceed with a prospective regulated consumer credit agreement on the basis of information from a credit reference agency the creditor must, when informing the debtor of that decision, inform the debtor that it has been reached on the basis of information from a credit reference agency and of the particulars of that agency.]
If applicable The period of time during which the creditor is bound by the pre-contractual information.	[This information is valid from [—] until [—] or [Period of time during which the information on this form is valid.]

If applicable

5. Additional information to be given in the case of distance marketing of financial services

(a) concerning the creditor	
If applicable The creditor's representative in [the UK] [your Member State of residence.] Address. Telephone number.* E-mail address.* Fax number.* Web address.*	[i.e. where different from section 1.] [Identity.] [Geographical address to be used by the debtor.]

If applicable Registration number.	[Consumer credit licence number and any other relevant registration number of the creditor.]
If applicable The supervisory authority.	[The Office of Fair Trading or any other relevant supervisory authority or both.]
(b) concerning the credit agreement	
If applicable The law taken by the creditor as a basis for the establishment of relations with you before the conclusion of the credit contract.	[English/other law.]
If applicable The law applicable to the credit agreement and/or the competent court.	[A statement concerning the law which governs the contract and the courts to which disputes may be referred.]
If applicable Language to be used in connection your agreement.	[Details of the language that the information and contractual terms will be supplied in and used, with the debtor's consent, for communication during the duration of the credit agreement.]
(c) concerning redress	
Access to out-of-court complaint and redress mechanism.	[Whether or not there is an out-of-court complaint and redress mechanism for the debtor who is party to the distance contract and, if so, the methods of access to it.]

* This information is optional for the creditor. The row may be deleted if the information is not provided.

Part III

EU Materials*

Council Regulation (EC) No. 44/2001 of 22 December 2000 on jurisdiction and the recognition and enforcement of judgments in civil and commercial matters

Chapter I Scope

Article 1

1. This Regulation shall apply in civil and commercial matters whatever the nature of the court or tribunal. It shall not extend, in particular, to revenue, customs or administrative matters.

2. The Regulation shall not apply to:
   (a) the status or legal capacity of natural persons, rights in property arising out of a matrimonial relationship, wills and succession;
   (b) bankruptcy, proceedings relating to the winding-up of insolvent companies or other legal persons, judicial arrangements, compositions and analogous proceedings;
   (c) social security;
   (d) arbitration.

3. In this Regulation, the term 'Member State' shall mean Member States with the exception of Denmark.

Chapter II Jurisdiction

Section 1 General provisions

Article 2

1. Subject to this Regulation, persons domiciled in a Member State shall, whatever their nationality, be sued in the courts of that Member State.

2. Persons who are not nationals of the Member State in which they are domiciled shall be governed by the rules of jurisdiction applicable to nationals of that State.

Article 3

1. Persons domiciled in a Member State may be sued in the courts of another Member State only by virtue of the rules set out in Sections 2 to 7 of this Chapter.

2. In particular the rules of national jurisdiction set out in Annex I shall not be applicable as against them.

Article 4

1. If the defendant is not domiciled in a Member State, the jurisdiction of the courts of each Member State shall, subject to Articles 22 and 23, be determined by the law of that Member State.

2. As against such a defendant, any person domiciled in a Member State may, whatever his nationality, avail himself in that State of the rules of jurisdiction there in force, and in particular those specified in Annex I, in the same way as the nationals of that State.

Section 2   Special jurisdiction

Article 5

A person domiciled in a Member State may, in another Member State, be sued:

1. (a) in matters relating to a contract, in the courts for the place of performance of the obligation in question;

   (b) for the purpose of this provision and unless otherwise agreed, the place of performance of the obligation in question shall be:
   - in the case of the sale of goods, the place in a Member State where, under the contract, the goods were delivered or should have been delivered,
   - in the case of the provision of services, the place in a Member State where, under the contract, the services were provided or should have been provided.

   (c) if subparagraph (b) does not apply then subparagraph (a) applies;

2. In matters relating to maintenance, in the courts for the place where the maintenance creditor is domiciled or habitually resident or, if the matter is ancillary to proceedings concerning the status of a person, in the court which, according to its own law, has jurisdiction to entertain those proceedings, unless that jurisdiction is based solely on the nationality of one of the parties;

3. In matters relating to tort, delict or quasi-delict, in the courts for the place where the harmful event occurred or may occur;

4. As regards a civil claim for damages or restitution which is based on an act giving rise to criminal proceedings, in the court seised of those proceedings, to the extent that that court has jurisdiction under its own law to entertain civil proceedings;

5. As regards a dispute arising out of the operations of a branch, agency or other establishment, in the courts for the place in which the branch, agency or other establishment is situated;

6. As settlor, trustee or beneficiary of a trust created by the operation of a statute, or by a written instrument, or created orally and evidenced in writing, in the courts of the Member State in which the trust is domiciled;

7. As regards a dispute concerning the payment of remuneration claimed in respect of the salvage of a cargo or freight, in the court under the authority of which the cargo or freight in question:

   (a) has been arrested to secure such payment, or

   (b) could have been so arrested, but bail or other security has been given;

provided that this provision shall apply only if it is claimed that the defendant has an interest in the cargo or freight or had such an interest at the time of salvage.

Article 6

A person domiciled in a Member State may also be sued:

1. Where he is one of a number of defendants, in the courts for the place where any one of them is domiciled, provided the claims are so closely connected that it is expedient to hear and determine them together to avoid the risk of irreconcilable judgments resulting from separate proceedings;

2. As a third party in an action on a warranty or guarantee or in any other third party proceedings, in the court seised of the original proceedings, unless these were instituted solely with the object of removing him from the jurisdiction of the court which would be competent in his case;

3. On a counter-claim arising from the same contract or facts on which the original claim was based, in the court in which the original claim is pending;

4. In matters relating to a contract, if the action may be combined with an action against the same defendant in matters relating to rights in rem in immovable property, in the court of the Member State in which the property is situated.

Article 7

Where by virtue of this Regulation a court of a Member State has jurisdiction in actions relating to liability from the use or operation of a ship, that court, or any other court substituted for this purpose by the internal law of that Member State, shall also have jurisdiction over claims for limitation of such liability.

Section 4 Jurisdiction over consumer contracts

Article 15

1. In matters relating to a contract concluded by a person, the consumer, for a purpose which can be regarded as being outside his trade or profession, jurisdiction shall be determined by this Section, without prejudice to Article 4 and point 5 of Article 5, if:
   (a) it is a contract for the sale of goods on instalment credit terms; or
   (b) it is a contract for a loan repayable by instalments, or for any other form of credit, made to finance the sale of goods; or
   (c) in all other cases, the contract has been concluded with a person who pursues commercial or professional activities in the Member State of the consumer's domicile or, by any means, directs such activities to that Member State or to several States including that Member State, and the contract falls within the scope of such activities.

2. Where a consumer enters into a contract with a party who is not domiciled in the Member State but has a branch, agency or other establishment in one of the Member States, that party shall, in disputes arising out of the operations of the branch, agency or establishment, be deemed to be domiciled in that State.

3. This Section shall not apply to a contract of transport other than a contract which, for an inclusive price, provides for a combination of travel and accommodation.

Article 16

1. A consumer may bring proceedings against the other party to a contract either in the courts of the Member State in which that party is domiciled or in the courts for the place where the consumer is domiciled.

2. Proceedings may be brought against a consumer by the other party to the contract only in the courts of the Member State in which the consumer is domiciled.

3. This Article shall not affect the right to bring a counter-claim in the court in which, in accordance with this Section, the original claim is pending.

Article 17

The provisions of this Section may be departed from only by an agreement:
   1. which is entered into after the dispute has arisen; or
   2. which allows the consumer to bring proceedings in courts other than those indicated in this Section; or
   3. which is entered into by the consumer and the other party to the contract, both of whom are at the time of conclusion of the contract domiciled or habitually resident in the same Member State, and which confers jurisdiction on the courts of that Member State, provided that such an agreement is not contrary to the law of that Member State.

Section 6 Exclusive jurisdiction

Article 22

The following courts shall have exclusive jurisdiction, regardless of domicile:

1. In proceedings which have as their object rights in rem in immovable property or tenancies of immovable property, the courts of the Member State in which the property is situated.

However, in proceedings which have as their object tenancies of immovable property concluded for temporary private use for a maximum period of six consecutive months, the courts of the Member State in which the defendant is domiciled shall also have jurisdiction, provided that the tenant is a natural person and that the landlord and the tenant are domiciled in the same Member State;

2. In proceedings which have as their object the validity of the constitution, the nullity or the dissolution of companies or other legal persons or associations of natural or legal persons, or of the validity of the decisions of their organs, the courts of the Member State in which the company, legal person or association has its seat. In order to determine that seat, the court shall apply its rules of private international law;

3. In proceedings which have as their object the validity of entries in public registers, the courts of the Member State in which the register is kept;

4. In proceedings concerned with the registration or validity of patents, trade marks, designs, or other similar rights required to be deposited or registered, the courts of the Member State in which the deposit or registration has been applied for, has taken place or is under the terms of a Community instrument or an international convention deemed to have taken place.

Without prejudice to the jurisdiction of the European Patent Office under the Convention on the Grant of European Patents, signed at Munich on 5 October 1973, the courts of each Member State shall have exclusive jurisdiction, regardless of domicile, in proceedings concerned with the registration or validity of any European patent granted for that State;

5. In proceedings concerned with the enforcement of judgments, the courts of the Member State in which the judgment has been or is to be enforced.

Section 7 Prorogation of jurisdiction

Article 23

1. If the parties, one or more of whom is domiciled in a Member State, have agreed that a court or the courts of a Member State are to have jurisdiction to settle any disputes which have arisen or which may arise in connection with a particular legal relationship, that court or those courts shall have jurisdiction. Such jurisdiction shall be exclusive unless the parties have agreed otherwise. Such an agreement conferring jurisdiction shall be either:

    (a) in writing or evidenced in writing; or

    (b) in a form which accords with practices which the parties have established between themselves; or

    (c) in international trade or commerce, in a form which accords with a usage of which the parties are or ought to have been aware and which in such trade or commerce is widely known to, and regularly observed by, parties to contracts of the type involved in the particular trade or commerce concerned.

2. Any communication by electronic means which provides a durable record of the agreement shall be equivalent to 'writing'.

3. Where such an agreement is concluded by parties, none of whom is domiciled in a Member State, the courts of other Member States shall have no jurisdiction over their disputes unless the court or courts chosen have declined jurisdiction.

4. The court or courts of a Member State on which a trust instrument has conferred jurisdiction shall have exclusive jurisdiction in any proceedings brought against a settlor, trustee or beneficiary, if relations between these persons or their rights or obligations under the trust are involved.

5. Agreements or provisions of a trust instrument conferring jurisdiction shall have no legal force if they are contrary to Articles 13, 17 or 21, or if the courts whose jurisdiction they purport to exclude have exclusive jurisdiction by virtue of Article 22.

Article 24

Apart from jurisdiction derived from other provisions of this Regulation, a court of a Member State before which a defendant enters an appearance shall have jurisdiction. This rule shall not apply where appearance was entered to contest the jurisdiction, or where another court has exclusive jurisdiction by virtue of Article 22.

Chapter III Recognition and enforcement

Article 32

For the purposes of this Regulation, 'judgment' means any judgment given by a court or tribunal of a Member State, whatever the judgment may be called, including a decree, order, decision or writ of execution, as well as the determination of costs or expenses by an officer of the court.

Section 1 Recognition

Article 33

1. A judgment given in a Member State shall be recognised in the other Member States without any special procedure being required.

2. Any interested party who raises the recognition of a judgment as the principal issue in a dispute may, in accordance with the procedures provided for in Sections 2 and 3 of this Chapter, apply for a decision that the judgment be recognised.

3. If the outcome of proceedings in a court of a Member State depends on the determination of an incidental question of recognition that court shall have jurisdiction over that question.

Article 34

A judgment shall not be recognised:

1. If such recognition is manifestly contrary to public policy in the Member State in which recognition is sought;

2. Where it was given in default of appearance, if the defendant was not served with the document which instituted the proceedings or with an equivalent document in sufficient time and in such a way as to enable him to arrange for his defence, unless the defendant failed to commence proceedings to challenge the judgment when it was possible for him to do so;

3. If it is irreconcilable with a judgment given in a dispute between the same parties in the Member State in which recognition is sought;

4. If it is irreconcilable with an earlier judgment given in another Member State or in a third State involving the same cause of action and between the same parties, provided that the earlier judgment fulfils the conditions necessary for its recognition in the Member State addressed.

Article 36

Under no circumstances may a foreign judgment be reviewed as to its substance.

Chapter V General provisions

Article 59

1. In order to determine whether a party is domiciled in the Member State whose courts are seised of a matter, the court shall apply its internal law.

2. If a party is not domiciled in the Member State whose courts are seised of the matter, then, in order to determine whether the party is domiciled in another Member State, the court shall apply the law of that Member State.

Article 60

1. For the purposes of this Regulation, a company or other legal person or association of natural or legal persons is domiciled at the place where it has its:

    (a) statutory seat, or

    (b) central administration, or

    (c) principal place of business.

2. For the purposes of the United Kingdom and Ireland 'statutory seat' means the registered office or, where there is no such office anywhere, the place of incorporation or, where there is no such place anywhere, the place under the law of which the formation took place.

3. In order to determine whether a trust is domiciled in the Member State whose courts are seised of the matter, the court shall apply its rules of private international law.

Article 61

Without prejudice to any more favourable provisions of national laws, persons domiciled in a Member State who are being prosecuted in the criminal courts of another Member State of which they are not nationals for an offence which was not intentionally committed may be defended by persons qualified to do so, even if they do not appear in person. However, the court seised of the matter may order appearance in person; in the case of failure to appear, a judgment given in the civil action without the person concerned having had the opportunity to arrange for his defence need not be recognised or enforced in the other Member States.

Chapter VII Relations with Other Instruments

Article 67

This Regulation shall not prejudice the application of provisions governing jurisdiction and the recognition and enforcement of judgments in specific matters which are contained in Community instruments or in national legislation harmonised pursuant to such instruments.

Article 68

2. In so far as this Regulation replaces the provisions of the Brussels Convention between Member States, any reference to the Convention shall be understood as a reference to this Regulation.

Annex 1

The rules of jurisdiction referred to in Article 3(2) and Article 4(2) are the following:

. . .

    — in the United Kingdom: rules which enable jurisdiction to be founded on:

        (a) the document instituting the proceedings having been served on the defendant during his temporary presence in the United Kingdom; or

        (b) the presence within the United Kingdom of property belonging to the defendant; or

        (c) the seizure by the plaintiff of property situated in the United Kingdom.

Regulation (EC) No 593/2008 of the European Parliament and of the Council of 17 June 2008 on the law applicable to contractual obligations (Rome I)

Article 1   Material scope

1. This Regulation shall apply, in situations involving a conflict of laws, to contractual obligations in civil and commercial matters.

It shall not apply, in particular, to revenue, customs or administrative matters.

    2. The following shall be excluded from the scope of this Regulation:

      (d) obligations arising under bills of exchange, cheques and promissory notes and other nego-tiable instruments to the extent that the obligations under such other negotiable instruments arise out of their negotiable character;

      (e) arbitration agreements and agreements on the choice of court;

      (g) the question whether an agent is able to bind a principal, or an organ to bind a company or other body corporate or unincorporated, in relation to a third party;

      (h) the constitution of trusts and the relationship between settlors, trustees and beneficiaries;

      (i) obligations arising out of dealings prior to the conclusion of a contract;

      (j) insurance contracts arising out of operations carried out by organisations other than undertakings referred to in Article 2 of Directive 2002/83/EC of the European Parliament and of the Council of 5 November 2002 concerning life assurance the object of which is to provide benefits for employed or self-employed persons belonging to an undertaking or group of undertakings, or to a trade or group of trades, in the event of death or survival or of discontinuance or curtailment of activity, or of sickness related to work or accidents at work.

Article 3   Freedom of choice

    1. A contract shall be governed by the law chosen by the parties. The choice shall be made expressly or clearly demonstrated by the terms of the contract or the circumstances of the case. By their choice the parties can select the law applicable to the whole or to part only of the contract.

    2. The parties may at any time agree to subject the contract to a law other than that which previously governed it, whether as a result of an earlier choice made under this Article or of other provisions of this Regulation. Any change in the law to be applied that is made after the conclusion of the contract shall not prejudice its formal validity under Article 11 or adversely affect the rights of third parties.

    3. Where all other elements relevant to the situation at the time of the choice are located in a country other than the country whose law has been chosen, the choice of the parties shall not prejudice the application of provisions of the law of that other country which cannot be derogated from by agreement.

    4. Where all other elements relevant to the situation at the time of the choice are located in one or more Member States, the parties' choice of applicable law other than that of a Member State shall not prejudice the application of provisions of Community law, where appropriate as implemented in the Member State of the forum, which cannot be derogated from by agreement.

    5. The existence and validity of the consent of the parties as to the choice of the applicable law shall be determined in accordance with the provisions of Articles 10, 11 and 13.

Article 4   Applicable law in the absence of choice

    1. To the extent that the law applicable to the contract has not been chosen in accordance with Article 3 and without prejudice to Articles 5 to 8, the law governing the contract shall be determined as follows:

      (a) a contract for the sale of goods shall be governed by the law of the country where the seller has his habitual residence;

      (b) a contract for the provision of services shall be governed by the law of the country where the service provider has his habitual residence; . . .

    2. Where the contract is not covered by paragraph 1 or where the elements of the contract would be covered by more than one of points (a) to (h) of paragraph 1, the contract shall be governed by the law of the country where the party required to effect the characteristic performance of the contract has his habitual residence.

    3. Where it is clear from all the circumstances of the case that the contract is manifestly more closely connected with a country other than that indicated in paragraphs 1 or 2, the law of that other country shall apply.

4. Where the law applicable cannot be determined pursuant to paragraphs 1 or 2, the contract shall be governed by the law of the country with which it is most closely connected.

Article 5   Contracts of carriage

1. To the extent that the law applicable to a contract for the carriage of goods has not been chosen in accordance with Article 3, the law applicable shall be the law of the country of habitual residence of the carrier, provided that the place of receipt or the place of delivery or the habitual residence of the consignor is also situated in that country. If those requirements are not met, the law of the country where the place of delivery as agreed by the parties is situated shall apply.

2. To the extent that the law applicable to a contract for the carriage of passengers has not been chosen by the parties in accordance with the second subparagraph, the law applicable shall be the law of the country where the passenger has his habitual residence, provided that either the place of departure or the place of destination is situated in that country. If these requirements are not met, the law of the country where the carrier has his habitual residence shall apply.

The parties may choose as the law applicable to a contract for the carriage of passengers in accordance with Article 3 only the law of the country where:

    (a) the passenger has his habitual residence; or

    (b) the carrier has his habitual residence; or

    (c) the carrier has his place of central administration; or

    (d) the place of departure is situated; or

    (e) the place of destination is situated.

3. Where it is clear from all the circumstances of the case that the contract, in the absence of a choice of law, is manifestly more closely connected with a country other than that indicated in paragraphs 1 or 2, the law of that other country shall apply.

Article 6   Consumer contracts

1. Without prejudice to Articles 5 and 7, a contract concluded by a natural person for a purpose which can be regarded as being outside his trade or profession (the consumer) with another person acting in the exercise of his trade or profession (the professional) shall be governed by the law of the country where the consumer has his habitual residence, provided that the professional:

    (a) pursues his commercial or professional activities in the country where the consumer has his habitual residence, or

    (b) by any means, directs such activities to that country or to several countries including that country,

and the contract falls within the scope of such activities.

2. Notwithstanding paragraph 1, the parties may choose the law applicable to a contract which fulfils the requirements of paragraph 1, in accordance with Article 3. Such a choice may not, however, have the result of depriving the consumer of the protection afforded to him by provisions that cannot be derogated from by agreement by virtue of the law which, in the absence of choice, would have been applicable on the basis of paragraph 1.

3. If the requirements in points (a) or (b) of paragraph 1 are not fulfilled, the law applicable to a contract between a consumer and a professional shall be determined pursuant to Articles 3 and 4.

4. Paragraphs 1 and 2 shall not apply to:

    (a) a contract for the supply of services where the services are to be supplied to the consumer exclusively in a country other than that in which he has his habitual residence;

    (b) a contract of carriage other than a contract relating to package travel within the meaning of Council Directive 90/314/EEC of 13 June 1990 on package travel, package holidays and package tours; . . .

Article 7   Insurance contracts

1. This Article shall apply to contracts referred to in paragraph 2, whether or not the risk covered is situated in a Member State, and to all other insurance contracts covering risks situated inside the territory of the Member States. It shall not apply to reinsurance contracts.

2. An insurance contract covering a large risk as defined in Article 5(d) of the First Council Directive 73/239/EEC of 24 July 1973 on the coordination of laws, regulations and administrative provisions relating to the taking-up and pursuit of the business of direct insurance other than life assurance shall be governed by the law chosen by the parties in accordance with Article 3 of this Regulation.

To the extent that the applicable law has not been chosen by the parties, the insurance contract shall be governed by the law of the country where the insurer has his habitual residence. Where it is clear from all the circumstances of the case that the contract is manifestly more closely connected with another country, the law of that other country shall apply.

3. In the case of an insurance contract other than a contract falling within paragraph 2, only the following laws may be chosen by the parties in accordance with Article 3:

(a) the law of any Member State where the risk is situated at the time of conclusion of the contract;

(b) the law of the country where the policy holder has his habitual residence;

(c) in the case of life assurance, the law of the Member State of which the policy holder is a national;

(d) for insurance contracts covering risks limited to events occurring in one Member State other than the Member State where the risk is situated, the law of that Member State;

(e) where the policy holder of a contract falling under this paragraph pursues a commercial or industrial activity or a liberal profession and the insurance contract covers two or more risks which relate to those activities and are situated in different Member States, the law of any of the Member States concerned or the law of the country of habitual residence of the policy holder.

Where, in the cases set out in points (a), (b) or (e), the Member States referred to grant greater freedom of choice of the law applicable to the insurance contract, the parties may take advantage of that freedom.

To the extent that the law applicable has not been chosen by the parties in accordance with this paragraph, such a contract shall be governed by the law of the Member State in which the risk is situated at the time of conclusion of the contract.

4. The following additional rules shall apply to insurance contracts covering risks for which a Member State imposes an obligation to take out insurance:

(a) the insurance contract shall not satisfy the obligation to take out insurance unless it complies with the specific provisions relating to that insurance laid down by the Member State that imposes the obligation. Where the law of the Member State in which the risk is situated and the law of the Member State imposing the obligation to take out insurance contradict each other, the latter shall prevail;

(b) by way of derogation from paragraphs 2 and 3, a Member State may lay down that the insurance contract shall be governed by the law of the Member State that imposes the obligation to take out insurance.

5. For the purposes of paragraph 3, third subparagraph, and paragraph 4, where the contract covers risks situated in more than one Member State, the contract shall be considered as constituting several contracts each relating to only one Member State.

6. For the purposes of this Article, the country in which the risk is situated shall be determined in accordance with Article 2(d) of the Second Council Directive 88/357/EEC of 22 June 1988 on the coordination of laws, regulations and administrative provisions relating to direct insurance other than life assurance and laying down provisions to facilitate the effective exercise of freedom to provide services and, in the case of life assurance, the country in which the risk is situated shall be the country of the commitment within the meaning of Article 1(1)(g) of Directive 2002/83/EC.

Article 9 Overriding mandatory provisions

1. Overriding mandatory provisions are provisions the respect for which is regarded as crucial by a country for safeguarding its public interests, such as its political, social or economic organisation, to such an extent that they are applicable to any situation falling within their scope, irrespective of the law otherwise applicable to the contract under this Regulation.

2. Nothing in this Regulation shall restrict the application of the overriding mandatory provisions of the law of the forum.

3. Effect may be given to the overriding mandatory provisions of the law of the country where the obligations arising out of the contract have to be or have been performed, in so far as those overriding mandatory provisions render the performance of the contract unlawful. In considering whether to give effect to those provisions, regard shall be had to their nature and purpose and to the consequences of their application or non-application.

Article 10   Consent and material validity

1. The existence and validity of a contract, or of any term of a contract, shall be determined by the law which would govern it under this Regulation if the contract or term were valid.

2. Nevertheless, a party, in order to establish that he did not consent, may rely upon the law of the country in which he has his habitual residence if it appears from the circumstances that it would not be reasonable to determine the effect of his conduct in accordance with the law specified in paragraph 1.

Article 11   Formal validity

1. A contract concluded between persons who, or whose agents, are in the same country at the time of its conclusion is formally valid if it satisfies the formal requirements of the law which governs it in substance under this Regulation or of the law of the country where it is concluded.

2. A contract concluded between persons who, or whose agents, are in different countries at the time of its conclusion is formally valid if it satisfies the formal requirements of the law which governs it in substance under this Regulation, or of the law of either of the countries where either of the parties or their agent is present at the time of conclusion, or of the law of the country where either of the parties had his habitual residence at that time.

3. A unilateral act intended to have legal effect relating to an existing or contemplated contract is formally valid if it satisfies the formal requirements of the law which governs or would govern the contract in substance under this Regulation, or of the law of the country where the act was done, or of the law of the country where the person by whom it was done had his habitual residence at that time.

4. Paragraphs 1, 2 and 3 of this Article shall not apply to contracts that fall within the scope of Article 6. The form of such contracts shall be governed by the law of the country where the consumer has his habitual residence.

Article 12   Scope of the law applicable

1. The law applicable to a contract by virtue of this Regulation shall govern in particular:
   (a) interpretation;
   (b) performance;
   (c) within the limits of the powers conferred on the court by its procedural law, the consequences of a total or partial breach of obligations, including the assessment of damages in so far as it is governed by rules of law;
   (d) the various ways of extinguishing obligations, and prescription and limitation of actions;
   (e) the consequences of nullity of the contract.

2. In relation to the manner of performance and the steps to be taken in the event of defective performance, regard shall be had to the law of the country in which performance takes place.

Article 14   Voluntary assignment and contractual subrogation

1. The relationship between assignor and assignee under a voluntary assignment or contractual subrogation of a claim against another person (the debtor) shall be governed by the law that applies to the contract between the assignor and assignee under this Regulation.

2. The law governing the assigned or subrogated claim shall determine its assignability, the relationship between the assignee and the debtor, the conditions under which the assignment or subrogation can be invoked against the debtor and whether the debtor's obligations have been discharged.

3. The concept of assignment in this Article includes outright transfers of claims, transfers of claims by way of security and pledges or other security rights over claims.

Article 15   Legal subrogation

Where a person (the creditor) has a contractual claim against another (the debtor) and a third person has a duty to satisfy the creditor, or has in fact satisfied the creditor in discharge of that duty, the law which governs the third person's duty to satisfy the creditor shall determine whether and to what extent the third person is entitled to exercise against the debtor the rights which the creditor had against the debtor under the law governing their relationship.

Article 16   Multiple liability

If a creditor has a claim against several debtors who are liable for the same claim, and one of the debtors has already satisfied the claim in whole or in part, the law governing the debtor's obligation towards the creditor also governs the debtor's right to claim recourse from the other debtors. The other debtors may rely on the defences they had against the creditor to the extent allowed by the law governing their obligations towards the creditor.

Article 17   Set-off

Where the right to set-off is not agreed by the parties, set-off shall be governed by the law applicable to the claim against which the right to set-off is asserted.

Article 18   Burden of proof

1. The law governing a contractual obligation under this Regulation shall apply to the extent that, in matters of contractual obligations, it contains rules which raise presumptions of law or determine the burden of proof.

2. A contract or an act intended to have legal effect may be proved by any mode of proof recognised by the law of the forum or by any of the laws referred to in Article 11 under which that contract or act is formally valid, provided that such mode of proof can be administered by the forum.

Article 19   Habitual residence

1. For the purposes of this Regulation, the habitual residence of companies and other bodies, corporate or unincorporated, shall be the place of central administration.

The habitual residence of a natural person acting in the course of his business activity shall be his principal place of business.

2. Where the contract is concluded in the course of the operations of a branch, agency or any other establishment, or if, under the contract, performance is the responsibility of such a branch, agency or establishment, the place where the branch, agency or any other establishment is located shall be treated as the place of habitual residence.

3. For the purposes of determining the habitual residence, the relevant point in time shall be the time of the conclusion of the contract.

Article 20   Exclusion of renvoi

The application of the law of any country specified by this Regulation means the application of the rules of law in force in that country other than its rules of private international law, unless provided otherwise in this Regulation.

Article 21   Public policy of the forum

The application of a provision of the law of any country specified by this Regulation may be refused only if such application is manifestly incompatible with the public policy (*ordre public*) of the forum.

Article 23   Relationship with other provisions of Community law

With the exception of Article 7, this Regulation shall not prejudice the application of provisions of Community law which, in relation to particular matters, lay down conflict-of-law rules relating to contractual obligations.

Article 25   Relationship with existing international conventions

1. This Regulation shall not prejudice the application of international conventions to which one or more Member States are parties at the time when this Regulation is adopted and which lay down conflict-of-law rules relating to contractual obligations.

2. However, this Regulation shall, as between Member States, take precedence over conventions concluded exclusively between two or more of them in so far as such conventions concern matters governed by this Regulation.

Directive 2011/7/EU of the European Parliament and of the Council of 16 February 2011 on combating late payment in commercial transactions (recast)

Article 1   Subject matter and scope

1. The aim of this Directive is to combat late payment in commercial transactions, in order to ensure the proper functioning of the internal market, thereby fostering the competitiveness of undertakings and in particular of SMEs.

2. This Directive shall apply to all payments made as remuneration for commercial transactions.

3. Member States may exclude debts that are subject to insolvency proceedings instituted against the debtor, including proceedings aimed at debt restructuring.

Article 2   Definitions

For the purposes of this Directive, the following definitions shall apply:

(1) 'commercial transactions' means transactions between undertakings or between undertakings and public authorities which lead to the delivery of goods or the provision of services for remuneration;

(2) 'public authority' means any contracting authority, as defined in point (a) of Article 2(1) of Directive 2004/17/EC and in Article 1(9) of Directive 2004/18/EC, regardless of the subject or value of the contract;

(3) 'undertaking' means any organisation, other than a public authority, acting in the course of its independent economic or professional activity, even where that activity is carried out by a single person;

(4) 'late payment' means payment not made within the contractual or statutory period of payment and where the conditions laid down in Article 3(1) or Article 4(1) are satisfied;

(5) 'interest for late payment' means statutory interest for late payment or interest at a rate agreed upon between undertakings, subject to Article 7;

(6) 'statutory interest for late payment' means simple interest for late payment at a rate which is equal to the sum of the reference rate and at least eight percentage points;

(7) 'reference rate' means either of the following:
   (a) for a Member State whose currency is the euro, either:
      (i)   the interest rate applied by the European Central Bank to its most recent main refinancing operations; or
      (ii) the marginal interest rate resulting from variable- rate tender procedures for the most recent main refinancing operations of the European Central Bank;
   (b) for a Member State whose currency is not the euro, the equivalent rate set by its national central bank;

(8) 'amount due' means the principal sum which should have been paid within the contractual or statutory period of payment, including the applicable taxes, duties, levies or charges specified in the invoice or the equivalent request for payment;

(9) 'retention of title' means the contractual agreement according to which the seller retains title to the goods in question until the price has been paid in full;

(10) 'enforceable title' means any decision, judgment or order for payment issued by a court or other competent authority, including those that are provisionally enforceable, whether for immediate payment or payment by instalments, which permits the creditor to have his claim against the debtor collected by means of forced execution.

Article 3   Transactions between undertakings

1. Member States shall ensure that, in commercial transactions between undertakings, the creditor is entitled to interest for late payment without the necessity of a reminder, where the following conditions are satisfied:

(a) the creditor has fulfilled its contractual and legal obligations; and

(b) the creditor has not received the amount due on time, unless the debtor is not responsible for the delay.

2. Member States shall ensure that the applicable reference rate:

(a) for the first semester of the year concerned shall be the rate in force on 1 January of that year;

(b) for the second semester of the year concerned shall be the rate in force on 1 July of that year.

3. Where the conditions set out in paragraph 1 are satisfied, Member States shall ensure the following:

(a) that the creditor is entitled to interest for late payment from the day following the date or the end of the period for payment fixed in the contract;

(b) where the date or period for payment is not fixed in the contract, that the creditor is entitled to interest for late payment upon the expiry of any of the following time limits:

(i) 30 calendar days following the date of receipt by the debtor of the invoice or an equivalent request for payment;

(ii) where the date of the receipt of the invoice or the equivalent request for payment is uncertain, 30 calendar days after the date of receipt of the goods or services;

(iii) where the debtor receives the invoice or the equivalent request for payment earlier than the goods or the services, 30 calendar days after the date of the receipt of the goods or services;

(iv) where a procedure of acceptance or verification, by which the conformity of the goods or services with the contract is to be ascertained, is provided for by statute or in the contract and if the debtor receives the invoice or the equivalent request for payment earlier or on the date on which such acceptance or verification takes place, 30 calendar days after that date.

4. Where a procedure of acceptance or verification, by which the conformity of the goods or services with the contract is to be ascertained, is provided for, Member States shall ensure that the maximum duration of that procedure does not exceed 30 calendar days from the date of receipt of the goods or services, unless otherwise expressly agreed in the contract and provided it is not grossly unfair to the creditor within the meaning of Article 7.

5. Member States shall ensure that the period for payment fixed in the contract does not exceed 60 calendar days, unless otherwise expressly agreed in the contract and provided it is not grossly unfair to the creditor within the meaning of Article 7.

Article 4   Transactions between undertakings and public authorities

1. Member States shall ensure that, in commercial transactions where the debtor is a public authority, the creditor is entitled upon expiry of the period defined in paragraphs 3, 4 or 6 to statutory interest for late payment, without the necessity of a reminder, where the following conditions are satisfied:

(a) the creditor has fulfilled its contractual and legal obligations; and

(b) the creditor has not received the amount due on time, unless the debtor is not responsible for the delay.

2. Member States shall ensure that the applicable reference rate:

(a) for the first semester of the year concerned shall be the rate in force on 1 January of that year;

(b) for the second semester of the year concerned shall be the rate in force on 1 July of that year.

3. Member States shall ensure that in commercial transactions where the debtor is a public authority:

(a) the period for payment does not exceed any of the following time limits:

(i)   30 calendar days following the date of receipt by the debtor of the invoice or an equivalent request for payment;

(ii) where the date of receipt of the invoice or the equivalent request for payment is uncertain, 30 calendar days after the date of the receipt of the goods or services;

(iii) where the debtor receives the invoice or the equivalent request for payment earlier than the goods or the services, 30 calendar days after the date of the receipt of the goods or services;

(iv) where a procedure of acceptance or verification, by which the conformity of the goods or services with the contract is to be ascertained, is provided for by statute or in the contract and if the debtor receives the invoice or the equivalent request for payment earlier or on the date on which such acceptance or verification takes place, 30 calendar days after that date;

(b) the date of receipt of the invoice is not subject to a contractual agreement between debtor and creditor.

4. Member States may extend the time limits referred to in point (a) of paragraph 3 up to a maximum of 60 calendar days for:

(a) any public authority which carries out economic activities of an industrial or commercial nature by offering goods or services on the market and which is subject, as a public undertaking, to the transparency requirements laid down in Commission Directive 2006/111/EC of 16 November 2006 on the transparency of financial relations between Member States and public undertakings as well as on financial transparency within certain undertakings);

(b) public entities providing healthcare which are duly recognised for that purpose.

If a Member State decides to extend the time limits in accordance with this paragraph, it shall send a report on such extension to the Commission by 16 March 2018.

On that basis, the Commission shall submit a report to the European Parliament and the Council indicating which Member States have extended the time limits in accordance with this paragraph and taking into account the impact on the functioning of the internal market, in particular on SMEs. That report shall be accompanied by any appropriate proposals.

5. Member States shall ensure that the maximum duration of a procedure of acceptance or verification referred to in point (iv) of point (a) of paragraph 3 does not exceed 30 calendar days from the date of receipt of the goods or services, unless otherwise expressly agreed in the contract and any tender documents and provided it is not grossly unfair to the creditor within the meaning of Article 7.

6. Member States shall ensure that the period for payment fixed in the contract does not exceed the time limits provided for in paragraph 3, unless otherwise expressly agreed in the contract and provided it is objectively justified in the light of the particular nature or features of the contract, and that it in any event does not exceed 60 calendar days.

Article 5   Payment schedules

This Directive shall be without prejudice to the ability of parties to agree, subject to the relevant provisions of applicable national law, on payment schedules providing for instalments. In such cases, where any of the instalments is not paid by the agreed date, interest and compensation provided for in this Directive shall be calculated solely on the basis of overdue amounts.

Article 6   Compensation for recovery costs

1. Member States shall ensure that, where interest for late payment becomes payable in commercial transactions in accordance with Article 3 or 4, the creditor is entitled to obtain from the debtor, as a minimum, a fixed sum of EUR 40.

2. Member States shall ensure that the fixed sum referred to in paragraph 1 is payable without the necessity of a reminder and as compensation for the creditor's own recovery costs.

3. The creditor shall, in addition to the fixed sum referred to in paragraph 1, be entitled to obtain reasonable compensation from the debtor for any recovery costs exceeding that fixed sum and incurred due to the debtor's late payment. This could include expenses incurred, inter alia, in instructing a lawyer or employing a debt collection agency.

Article 7   Unfair contractual terms and practices

1. Member States shall provide that a contractual term or a practice relating to the date or period for payment, the rate of interest for late payment or the compensation for recovery costs is either unenforceable or gives rise to a claim for damages if it is grossly unfair to the creditor.

In determining whether a contractual term or a practice is grossly unfair to the creditor, within the meaning of the first subparagraph, all circumstances of the case shall be considered, including:

    (a) any gross deviation from good commercial practice, contrary to good faith and fair dealing;

    (b) the nature of the product or the service; and

    (c) whether the debtor has any objective reason to deviate from the statutory rate of interest for late payment, from the payment period as referred to in Article 3(5), point (a) of Article 4(3), Article 4(4) and Article 4(6) or from the fixed sum as referred to in Article 6(1).

2. For the purpose of paragraph 1, a contractual term or a practice which excludes interest for late payment shall be considered as grossly unfair.

3. For the purpose of paragraph 1, a contractual term or a practice which excludes compensation for recovery costs as referred to in Article 6 shall be presumed to be grossly unfair.

4. Member States shall ensure that, in the interests of creditors and competitors, adequate and effective means exist to prevent the continued use of contractual terms and practices which are grossly unfair within the meaning of paragraph 1.

5. The means referred to in paragraph 4 shall include provisions whereby organisations officially recognised as representing undertakings, or organisations with a legitimate interest in representing undertakings may take action according to the applicable national law before the courts or before competent administrative bodies on the grounds that contractual terms or practices are grossly unfair within the meaning of paragraph 1, so that they can apply appropriate and effective means to prevent their continued use.

Article 8   Transparency and awareness raising

1. Member States shall ensure transparency regarding the rights and obligations stemming from this Directive, including by making publicly available the applicable rate of statutory interest for late payment.

2. The Commission shall make publicly available on the Internet details of the current statutory rates of interest which apply in all the Member States in the event of late payment in commercial transactions.

3. Member States shall, where appropriate, use professional publications, promotion campaigns or any other functional means to increase awareness of the remedies for late payment among undertakings.

4. Member States may encourage the establishment of prompt payment codes which set out clearly defined payment time limits and a proper process for dealing with any payments that are in dispute, or any other initiatives that tackle the crucial issue of late payment and contribute to developing a culture of prompt payment which supports the objective of this Directive.

Article 9   Retention of title

1. Member States shall provide in conformity with the applicable national provisions designated by private international law that the seller retains title to goods until they are fully paid for if a retention of title clause has been expressly agreed between the buyer and the seller before the delivery of the goods.

2. Member States may adopt or retain provisions dealing with down payments already made by the debtor.

Article 10   Recovery procedures for unchallenged claims

1. Member States shall ensure that an enforceable title can be obtained, including through an expedited procedure and irrespective of the amount of the debt, normally within 90 calendar days of the lodging of the creditor's action or application at the court or other competent authority, provided that the debt or aspects of the procedure are not disputed. Member States shall carry out this duty in accordance with their respective national laws, regulations and administrative provisions.

2. National laws, regulations and administrative provisions shall apply the same conditions for all creditors who are established in the Union.

3. When calculating the period referred to in paragraph 1, the following shall not be taken into account:

  (a) periods for service of documents;

  (b) any delays caused by the creditor, such as periods devoted to correcting applications.

4. This Article shall be without prejudice to the provisions of Regulation (EC) No 1896/2006.

Article 11   Report

By 16 March 2016, the Commission shall submit a report to the European Parliament and the Council on the implementation of this Directive. The report shall be accompanied by any appropriate proposals.

Article 12   Transposition

1. Member States shall bring into force the laws, regulations and administrative provisions necessary to comply with Articles 1 to 8 and 10 by 16 March 2013. They shall forthwith communicate to the Commission the text of those provisions.

When Member States adopt those measures, they shall contain a reference to this Directive or shall be accompanied by such reference on the occasion of their official publication. They shall also include a statement that references in existing laws, regulations and administrative provisions to the repealed Directive shall be construed as references to this Directive. The methods of making such reference and the formulation of such statement shall be laid down by Member States.

2. Member States shall communicate to the Commission the text of the main provisions of national law which they adopt in the field covered by this Directive.

3. Member States may maintain or bring into force provisions which are more favourable to the creditor than the provisions necessary to comply with this Directive.

4. In transposing the Directive, Member States shall decide whether to exclude contracts concluded before 16 March 2013.

Article 13   Repeal

Directive 2000/35/EC is repealed with effect from 16 March 2013, without prejudice to the obligations of the Member States relating to the time limit for its transposition into national law and its application. However, it shall remain applicable to contracts concluded before that date to which this Directive does not apply pursuant to Article 12(4).

References to the repealed Directive shall be construed as references to this Directive and be read in accordance with the correlation table set out in the Annex.

Proposal for a regulation of the European Parliament and of the Council on a common European sales law

(2011/0284 (COD))

THE EUROPEAN PARLIAMENT AND THE COUNCIL OF THE EUROPEAN UNION,

Having regard to the Treaty on the Functioning of the European Union, and in particular Article 114 thereof,

Having regard to the proposal from the European Commission,

After transmission of the draft legislative act to the national Parliaments,

Having regard to the opinion of the European Economic and Social Committee,

Having regard to the opinion of the Committee of the Regions,

Acting in accordance with the ordinary legislative procedure,

Whereas:

(1) There are still considerable bottlenecks to cross-border economic activity that prevent the internal market from exploiting its full potential for growth and job creation. Currently, only one in ten traders in the Union exports goods within the Union and the majority of those who do, only export to a small number of Member States. From the range of obstacles to cross-border trade including tax regulations, administrative requirements, difficulties in delivery, language and culture, traders consider the difficulty in finding out the provisions of a foreign contract law among the top barriers in business-to-consumer transactions and in business-to-business transactions. This also leads to disadvantages for consumers due to limited access to goods. Different national contract laws therefore deter the exercise of fundamental freedoms, such as the freedom to provide goods and services, and represent a barrier to the functioning and continuing establishment of the internal market. They also have the effect of limiting competition, particularly in the markets of smaller Member States.

(2) Contracts are the indispensable legal tool for every economic transaction. However, the need for traders to identify or negotiate the applicable law, to find out about the provisions of a foreign applicable law often involving translation, to obtain legal advice to make themselves familiar with its requirements and to adapt their contracts to different national laws that may apply in cross-border dealings makes cross-border trade more complex and costly compared to domestic trade. Contract-law-related barriers are thus a major contributing factor in dissuading a considerable number of export-oriented traders from entering cross-border trade or expanding their operations into more Member States. Their deterrent effect is particularly strong for small and medium-sized enterprises (SME) for which the costs of entering multiple foreign markets are often particularly high in relation to their turnover. As a consequence, traders miss out on cost savings they could achieve if it were possible to market goods and services on the basis of one uniform contract law for all their cross-border transactions and, in the online environment, one single web-site.

(3) Contract law related transaction costs which have been shown to be of considerable proportions and legal obstacles stemming from the differences between national mandatory consumer protection rules have a direct effect on the functioning of the internal market in relation to business-to-consumer transactions. Pursuant to Article 6 of Regulation 593/2008 of the European Parliament and of the Council of 17 June 2008 on the law applicable to contractual obligations (Regulation (EC) No 593/2008), whenever a trader directs its activities to consumers in another Member State the consumer protection provisions of the Member State of the consumer's habitual residence that provide a higher level of protection and cannot be derogated from by agreement by virtue of that law will apply, even where another applicable law has been chosen by the parties. Therefore, traders need to find out in advance whether the consumer's law provides higher protection and ensure that their contract is in compliance with its requirements. In addition, in e-commerce, web-site adaptations which need to reflect mandatory requirements of applicable foreign consumer contract laws entail further costs. The existing harmonisation of consumer law at Union level has led to a certain approximation in some

areas. However the differences between Member States' laws remain substantial; existing harmonisation leaves Member States a broad range of options on how to comply with the requirements of Union legislation and where to set the level of consumer protection.

(4) The contract-law-related barriers which prevent traders from fully exploiting the potential of the internal market also work to the detriment of consumers. Less cross-border trade results in fewer imports and less competition. Consumers may be disadvantaged by a limited choice of goods at higher prices both because fewer foreign traders offer their products and services directly to them and also indirectly as a result of restricted cross-border business-to-business trade at the wholesale level. While cross-border shopping could bring substantial economic advantages in terms of more and better offers, many consumers are also reluctant to engage in cross-border shopping, because of the uncertainty about their rights. Some of the main consumer concerns are related to contract law, for instance whether they would enjoy adequate protection in the event of purchasing defective products. As a consequence, a substantial number of consumers prefer to shop domestically even if this means they have less choice or pay higher prices.

(5) In addition, those consumers who want to benefit from price differences between Member States by purchasing from a trader from another Member State are often hindered due to a trader's refusal to sell. While e-commerce has greatly facilitated the search for offers as well as the comparison of prices and other conditions irrespective of where a trader is established, orders by consumers from abroad are very frequently refused by traders which refrain from entering into cross-border transactions.

(6) Differences in national contract laws therefore constitute barriers which prevent consumers and traders from reaping the benefits of the internal market. Those contract-law-related barriers would be significantly reduced if contracts could be based on a single uniform set of contract law rules irrespective of where parties are established. Such a uniform set of contract law rules should cover the full life cycle of a contract and thus comprise the areas which are the most important when concluding contracts. It should also include fully harmonised provisions to protect consumers.

(7) The differences between national contract laws and their effect on cross-border trade also serve to limit competition. With a low level of cross-border trade, there is less competition, and thus less incentive for traders to become more innovative and to improve the quality of their products or to reduce prices. Particularly in smaller Member States with a limited number of domestic competitors, the decision of foreign traders to refrain from entering these markets due to costs and complexity may limit competition, resulting in an appreciable impact on choice and price levels for available products. In addition, the barriers to cross-border trade may jeopardise competition between SME and larger companies. In view of the significant impact of the transaction costs in relation to turnover, an SME is much more likely to refrain from entering a foreign market than a larger competitor.

(8) To overcome these contract-law-related barriers, parties should have the possibility to agree that their contracts should be governed by a single uniform set of contract law rules with the same meaning and interpretation in all Member States, a Common Sales Law. The Common European Sales Law should represent an additional option increasing the choice available to parties and open to use whenever jointly considered to be helpful in order to facilitate cross-border trade and reduce transaction and opportunity costs as well as other contract-law-related obstacles to cross-border trade. It should become the basis of a contractual relationship only where parties jointly decide to use it.

(9) This Regulation establishes a Common European Sales Law. It harmonises the contract laws of the Member States not by requiring amendments to the pre-existing national contract law, but by creating within each Member State's national law a second contract law regime for contracts within its scope. This second regime should be identical throughout the Union and exist alongside the pre-existing rules of national contract law. The Common European Sales Law should apply on a voluntary basis, upon an express agreement of the parties, to a cross-border contract.

(10) The agreement to use the Common European Sales Law should be a choice exercised within the scope of the respective national law which is applicable pursuant to Regulation (EC) No 593/2008 or, in relation to pre-contractual information duties, pursuant to Regulation (EC) No 864/2007 of the European Parliament and of the Council of 11 July 2007 on the law applicable to non-contractual

obligations (Regulation (EC) No 864/2007), or any other relevant conflict of law rule. The agreement to use the Common European Sales Law should therefore not amount to, and not be confused with, a choice of the applicable law within the meaning of the conflict-of-law rules and should be without prejudice to them. This Regulation will therefore not affect any of the existing conflict of law rules.

(11) The Common European Sales Law should comprise of a complete set of fully harmonised mandatory consumer protection rules. In line with Article 114(3) of the Treaty, those rules should guarantee a high level of consumer protection with a view to enhancing consumer confidence in the Common European Sales Law and thus provide consumers with an incentive to enter into cross-border contracts on that basis. The rules should maintain or improve the level of protection that consumers enjoy under Union consumer law.

(12) Since the Common European Sales Law contains a complete set of fully harmonised mandatory consumer protection rules, there will be no disparities between the laws of the Member States in this area, where the parties have chosen to use the Common European Sales Law. Consequently, Article 6(2) Regulation (EC) No 593/2008, which is predicated on the existence of differing levels of consumer protection in the Member States, has no practical importance for the issues covered by the Common European Sales Law.

(13) The Common European Sales Law should be available for cross-border contracts, because it is in that context that the disparities between national laws lead to complexity and additional costs and dissuade parties from entering into contractual relationships. The cross-border nature of a contract should be assessed on the basis of the habitual residence of the parties in business-to-business contracts. In a business-to-consumer contract the cross-border requirement should be met where either the general address indicated by the consumer, the delivery address for the goods or the billing address indicated by the consumer are located in a Member State, but outside the State where the trader has its habitual residence.

(14) The use of the Common European Sales Law should not be limited to cross-border situations involving only Member States, but should also be available to facilitate trade between Member States and third countries. Where consumers from third countries are involved, the agreement to use the Common European Sales Law, which would imply the choice of a foreign law for them, should be subject to the applicable conflict-of-law rules.

(15) Traders engaging in purely domestic as well as in cross-border trade transactions may also find it useful to make use of a single uniform contract for all their transactions. Therefore Member States should be free to decide to make the Common European Sales Law available to parties for use in an entirely domestic setting.

(16) The Common European Sales Law should be available in particular for the sale of movable goods, including the manufacture or production of such goods, as this is the economically single most important contract type which could present a particular potential for growth in cross-border trade, especially in e-commerce.

(17) In order to reflect the increasing importance of the digital economy, the scope of the Common European Sales Law should also cover contracts for the supply of digital content. The transfer of digital content for storage, processing or access, and repeated use, such as a music download, has been growing rapidly and holds a great potential for further growth but is still surrounded by a considerable degree of legal diversity and uncertainty. The Common European Sales Law should therefore cover the supply of digital content irrespective of whether or not that content is supplied on a tangible medium.

(18) Digital content is often supplied not in exchange for a price but in combination with separate paid goods or services, involving a non-monetary consideration such as giving access to personal data or free of charge in the context of a marketing strategy based on the expectation that the consumer will purchase additional or more sophisticated digital content products at a later stage. In view of this specific market structure and of the fact that defects of the digital content provided may harm the economic interests of consumers irrespective of the conditions under which it has been provided, the availability of the Common European Sales Law should not depend on whether a price is paid for the specific digital content in question.

(19) With a view to maximising the added value of the Common European Sales Law its material scope should also include certain services provided by the seller that are directly and closely related to specific goods or digital content supplied on the basis of the Common European Sales Law, and in practice often combined in the same or a linked contract at the same time, most notably repair, maintenance or installation of the goods or the digital content.

(20) The Common European Sales Law should not cover any related contracts by which the buyer acquires goods or is supplied with a service, from a third party. This would not be appropriate because the third party is not part of the agreement between the contracting parties to use the rules of the Common European Sales Law. A related contract with a third party should be governed by the respective national law which is applicable according pursuant to Regulations (EC) No 593/2008 and (EC) No 864/2007 or any other relevant conflict of law rule.

(21) In order to tackle the existing internal market and competition problems in a targeted and proportionate fashion, the personal scope of the Common European Sales Law should focus on parties who are currently dissuaded from doing business abroad by the divergence of national contract laws with the consequence of a significant adverse impact on cross-border trade. It should therefore cover all business-to consumer transactions and contracts between traders where at least one of the parties is an SME drawing upon Commission Recommendation 2003/361 of 6 May 2003 concerning the definition of micro, small and medium-sized enterprises. This should, however, be without prejudice to the possibility for Member States to enact legislation which makes the Common European Sales Law available for contracts between traders, neither of which is an SME. In any case, in business-to-business transactions, traders enjoy full freedom of contract and are encouraged to draw inspiration from the Common European Sales Law in the drafting of their contractual terms.

(22) The agreement of the parties to a contract is indispensable for the application of the Common European Sales Law. That agreement should be subject to strict requirements in business-to-consumer transactions. Since, in practice, it will usually be the trader who proposes the use of the Common European Sales Law, consumers must be fully aware of the fact that they are agreeing to the use of rules which are different from those of their pre-existing national law. Therefore, the consumer's consent to use the Common European Sales Law should be admissible only in the form of an explicit statement separate from the statement indicating the agreement to the conclusion of the contract. It should therefore not be possible to offer the use of the Common European Sales Law as a term of the contract to be concluded, particularly as an element of the trader's standard terms and conditions. The trader should provide the consumer with a confirmation of the agreement to use the Common European Sales Law on a durable medium.

(23) In addition to being a conscious choice, the consent of a consumer to the use of the Common European Sales Law should be an informed choice. The trader should therefore not only draw the consumer's attention to the intended use of the Common European Sales Law but should also provide information on its nature and its salient features. In order to facilitate this task for traders, thereby avoiding unnecessary administrative burdens, and to ensure consistency in the level and the quality of the information communicated to consumers, traders should supply consumers with the standard information notice provided for in this Regulation and thus readily available in all official languages in the Union. Where it is not possible to supply the consumer with the information notice, for example in the context of a telephone call, or where the trader has failed to provide the information notice, the agreement to use the Common European Sales Law should not be binding on the consumer until the consumer has received the information notice together with the confirmation of the agreement and has subsequently expressed consent.

(24) In order to avoid a selective application of certain elements of the Common European Sales Law, which could disturb the balance between the rights and obligations of the parties and adversely affect the level of consumer protection, the choice should cover the Common European Sales Law as a whole and not only certain parts of it.

(25) Where the United Nations Convention on Contracts for the International Sale of Goods would otherwise apply to the contract in question, the choice of the Common European Sales Law should imply an agreement of the contractual parties to exclude that Convention.

(26) The rules of the Common European Sales Law should cover the matters of contract law that are of practical relevance during the life cycle of the types of contracts falling within the material and personal scope, particularly those entered into online. Apart from the rights and obligations of the parties and the remedies for non-performance, the Common European Sales Law should therefore govern pre-contractual information duties, the conclusion of a contract including formal require- ments, the right of withdrawal and its consequences, avoidance of the contract resulting from a mis- take, fraud, threats or unfair exploitation and the consequences of such avoidance, interpretation, the contents and effects of a contract, the assessment and consequences of unfairness of contract terms, restitution after avoidance and termination and the prescription and preclusion of rights. It should settle the sanctions available in case of the breach of all the obligations and duties arising under its application.

(27) All the matters of a contractual or non-contractual nature that are not addressed in the Common European Sales Law are governed by the pre-existing rules of the national law outside the Common European Sales Law that is applicable under Regulations (EC) No 593/2008 and (EC) No 864/2007 or any other relevant conflict of law rule. These issues include legal personality, the invalidity of a contract arising from lack of capacity, illegality or immorality, the determination of the language of the contract, matters of non-discrimination, representation, plurality of debtors and creditors, change of parties including assignment, set-off and merger, property law including the transfer of ownership, intellectual property law and the law of torts. Furthermore, the issue of whether concurrent contractual and non-contractual liability claims can be pursued together falls ' outside the scope of the Common European Sales Law.

(28) The Common European Sales Law should not govern any matters outside the remit of con- tract law. This Regulation should be without prejudice to the Union or national law in relation to any such matters. For example, information duties which are imposed for the protection of health and safety or environmental reasons should remain outside the scope of the Common European Sales Law. This Regulation should further be without prejudice to the information requirements of Directive 2006/123/EC of the European Parliament and of the Council of 12 December 2006 on serv- ices in the internal market.

(29) Once there is a valid agreement to use the Common European Sales Law, only the Common European Sales Law should govern the matters falling within its scope. The rules of the Common European Sales Law should be interpreted autonomously in accordance with the well-established principles on the interpretation of Union legislation. Questions concerning matters falling within the scope of the Common European Sales Law which are not expressly settled by it should be resolved only by interpretation of its rules without recourse to any other law. The rules of the Common European Sales Law should be interpreted on the basis of the underlying principles and objectives and all its provisions.

(30) Freedom of contract should be the guiding principle underlying the Common European Sales Law. Party autonomy should be restricted only where and to the extent that this is indispensa- ble, in particular for reasons of consumer protection. Where such a necessity exists, the mandatory nature of the rules in question should be clearly indicated.

(31) The principle of good faith and fair dealing should provide guidance on the way parties have to cooperate. As some rules constitute specific manifestations of the general principle of good faith and fair dealing, they should take precedent over the general principle. The general principle should therefore not be used as a tool to amend the specific rights and obligations of parties as set out in the specific rules. The concrete requirements resulting from the principle of good faith and fair dealing should depend, amongst others, on the relative level of expertise of the parties and should therefore be different in business-to-consumer transactions and in business-to-business transactions. In transactions between traders, good commercial practice in the specific situation concerned should be a relevant factor in this context.

(32) The Common European Sales Law should aim at the preservation of a valid contract when- ever possible and appropriate in view of the legitimate interests of the parties.

(33) The Common European Sales Law should identify well-balanced solutions taking account the legitimate interests of the parties in designating and exercising the remedies available in the case of non-performance of the contract. In business-to-consumer contracts the system of remedies should reflect the fact that the non-conformity of goods, digital content or services falls within the trader's sphere of responsibility.

(34) In order to enhance legal certainty by making the case-law of the Court of Justice of the European Union and of national courts on the interpretation of the Common European Sales Law or any other provision of this Regulation accessible to the public, the Commission should create a database comprising the final relevant decisions. With a view to making that task possible, the Member States should ensure that such national judgments are quickly communicated to the Commission.

(35) It is also appropriate to review the functioning of the Common European Sales Law or any other provision of this Regulation after five years of operation. The review should take into account, amongst other things, the need to extend further the scope in relation to business-to-business contracts, market and technological developments in respect of digital content and future developments of the Union acquis.

(36) Since the objective of this Regulation, namely to contribute to the proper functioning of the internal market by making available a uniform set of contract law rules that can be used for cross-border transactions throughout the Union, cannot be sufficiently achieved by the Member States and can therefore be better achieved at Union level, the Union may adopt measures, in accordance with the principle of subsidiarity as set out in Article 5 of the Treaty on the European Union. In accordance with the principle of proportionality, as set out in that Article, this Regulation does not go beyond what is necessary in order to achieve that objective.

(37) This Regulation respects the fundamental rights and observes the principles recognised in particular by the Charter of Fundamental Rights of the European Union and specifically Articles 16, 38 and 47 thereof,

HAVE ADOPTED THIS REGULATION:

Article 1   Objective and subject matter

1. The purpose of this Regulation is to improve the conditions for the establishment and the functioning of the internal market by making available a uniform set of contract law rules as set out in Annex I ('the Common European Sales Law'). These rules can be used for cross-border transactions for the sale of goods, for the supply of digital content and for related services where the parties to a contract agree to do so.

2. This Regulation enables traders to rely on a common set of rules and use the same contract terms for all their cross-border transactions thereby reducing unnecessary costs while providing a high degree of legal certainty.

3. In relation to contracts between traders and consumers, this Regulation comprises a comprehensive set of consumer protection rules to ensure a high level of consumer protection, to enhance consumer confidence in the internal market and encourage consumers to shop across borders.

Article 2   Definitions

For the purpose of this Regulation, the following definitions shall apply:

(a) 'contract' means an agreement intended to give rise to obligations or other legal effects;

(b) 'good faith and fair dealing' means a standard of conduct characterised by honesty, openness and consideration for the interests of the other party to the transaction or relationship in question;

(c) 'loss' means economic loss and non-economic loss in the form of pain and suffering, excluding other forms of non-economic loss such as impairment of the quality of life and loss of enjoyment;

(d) 'standard contract terms' means contract terms which have been drafted in advance for several transactions involving different parties, and which have not been individually negotiated by the parties within the meaning of Article 7 of the Common European Sales Law;

(e) 'trader' means any natural or legal person who is acting for purposes relating to that person's trade, business, craft, or profession;

(f) 'consumer' means any natural person who is acting for purposes which are outside that person's trade, business, craft, or profession;

(g) 'damages' means a sum of money to which a person may be entitled as compensation for loss, injury or damage;

(h) 'goods' means any tangible movable items; it excludes:
  (i) electricity and natural gas; and
  (ii) water and other types of gas unless they are put up for sale in a limited volume or set quantity;

(i) 'price' means money that is due in exchange for goods sold, digital content supplied or a related service provided;

(j) 'digital content' means data which are produced and supplied in digital form, whether or not according to the buyer's specifications, including video, audio, picture or written digital content, digital games, software and digital content which makes it possible to personalise existing hardware or software; it excludes:
  (i) financial services, including online banking services;
  (ii) legal or financial advice provided in electronic form;
  (iii) electronic healthcare services;
  (iv) electronic communications services and networks, and associated facilities and services;
  (v) gambling;
  (vi) the creation of new digital content and the amendment of existing digital content by consumers or any other interaction with the creations of other users;

(k) 'sales contract' means any contract under which the trader ('the seller') transfers or undertakes to transfer the ownership of the goods to another person ('the buyer'), and the buyer pays or undertakes to pay the price thereof; it includes a contract for the supply of goods to be manufactured or produced and excludes contracts for sale on execution or otherwise involving the exercise of public authority;

(l) 'consumer sales contract' means a sales contract where the seller is a trader and the buyer is a consumer;

(m) 'related service' means any service related to goods or digital content, such as installation, maintenance, repair or any other processing, provided by the seller of the goods or the supplier of the digital content under the sales contract, the contract for the supply of digital content or a separate related service contract which was concluded at the same time as the sales contract or the contract for the supply of digital content; it excludes:
  (i)   transport services,
  (ii) training services,
  (iii) telecommunications support services; and
  (iv) financial services;

(n) 'service provider' means a seller of goods or supplier of digital content who undertakes to provide a customer with a service related to those goods or that digital content;

(o) 'customer' means any person who purchases a related service;

(p) 'distance contract' means any contract between the trader and the consumer under an organised distance sales scheme concluded without the simultaneous physical presence of the trader or, in case the trader is a legal person, a natural person representing the trader and the consumer, with the exclusive use of one or more means of distance communication up to and including the time at which the contract is concluded;

(q) 'off-premises contract' means any contract between a trader and a consumer:

    (i)   concluded in the simultaneous physical presence of the trader or, where the trader is a legal person, the natural person representing the trader and the consumer in a place which is not the trader's business premises, or concluded on the basis of an offer made by the consumer in the same circumstances; or

    (ii)   concluded on the trader's business premises or through any means of distance communication immediately after the consumer was personally and individually addressed in a place which is not the trader's business premises in the simultaneous physical presence of the trader or, where the trader is a legal person, a natural person representing the trader and the consumer; or

    (iii) concluded during an excursion organised by the trader or, where the trader is a legal person, the natural person representing the trader with the aim or effect of promoting and selling goods or supplying digital content or related services to the consumer;

(r) 'business premises' means:

    (i)   any immovable retail premises where a trader carries out activity on a permanent basis, or

    (ii)   any movable retail premises where a trader carries out activity on a usual basis;

(s) 'commercial guarantee' means any undertaking by the trader or a producer to the consumer, in addition to legal obligations under Article 106 in case of lack of conformity to reimburse the price paid or to replace or repair, or service goods or digital content in any way if they do not meet the specifications or any other requirements not related to conformity set out in the guarantee statement or in the relevant advertising available at the time of, or before the conclusion of the contract;

(t) 'durable medium' means any medium which enables a party to store information addressed personally to that party in a way accessible for future reference for a period of time adequate for the purposes of the information and which allows the unchanged reproduction of the information stored;

(u) 'public auction' means a method of sale where goods or digital content are offered by the trader to the consumer who attends or is given the possibility to attend the auction in person, through a transparent, competitive bidding procedure run by an auctioneer and where the successful bidder is bound to purchase the goods or digital content;

(v) 'mandatory rule' means any provision the application of which the parties cannot exclude, or derogate from or the effect of which they cannot vary;

(w) 'creditor' means a person who has a right to performance of an obligation, whether monetary or non-monetary, by another person, the debtor;

(x) 'debtor' means a person who has an obligation, whether monetary or non-monetary, to another person, the creditor;

(y) 'obligation' means a duty to perform which one party to a legal relationship owes to another party.

Article 3   Optional nature of the Common European Sales Law

The parties may agree that the Common European Sales Law governs their cross-border contracts for the sale of goods, for the supply of digital content and for the provision of related services within the territorial, material and personal scope as set out in Articles 4 to 7.

Article 4   Cross-border contracts

1. The Common European Sales Law may be used for cross-border contracts.

2. For the purposes of this Regulation, a contract between traders is a cross-border contract if the parties have their habitual residence in different countries of which at least one is a Member State.

3. For the purposes of this Regulation, a contract between a trader and a consumer is a cross-border contract if:

    (a) either the address indicated by the consumer, the delivery address for goods or the billing address are located in a country other than the country of the trader's habitual residence; and

    (b) at least one of these countries is a Member State.

4. For the purposes of this Regulation, the habitual residence of companies and other bodies, corporate or unincorporated, shall be the place of central administration. The habitual residence of a trader who is a natural person shall be that person's principal place of business.

5. Where the contract is concluded in the course of the operations of a branch, agency or any other establishment of a trader, the place where the branch, agency or any other establishment is located shall be treated as the place of the trader's habitual residence.

6. For the purpose of determining whether a contract is a cross-border contract the relevant point in time is the time of the agreement on the use of the Common European Sales Law.

Article 5   Contracts for which the Common European Sales Law can be used

The Common European Sales Law may be used for:
- (a) sales contracts;
- (b) contracts for the supply of digital content whether or not supplied on a tangible medium which can be stored, processed or accessed, and re-used by the user, irrespective of whether the digital content is supplied in exchange for the payment of a price.
- (c) related service contracts, irrespective of whether a separate price was agreed for therelated service.

Article 6   Exclusion of mixed-purpose contracts and contracts linked to a consumer credit

1. The Common European Sales Law may not be used for mixed-purpose contracts including any elements other than the sale of goods, the supply of digital content and the provision of related services within the meaning of Article 5.

2. The Common European Sales Law may not be used for contracts between a trader and a consumer where the trader grants or promises to grant to the consumer credit in the form of a deferred payment, loan or other similar financial accommodation. The Common European Sales Law may be used for contracts between a trader and a consumer where goods, digital content or related services of the same kind are supplied on a continuing basis and the consumer pays for such goods, digital content or related services for the duration of the supply by means of instalments.

Article 7   Parties to the contract

1. The Common European Sales Law may be used only if the seller of goods or the supplier of digital content is a trader. Where all the parties to a contract are traders, the Common European Sales Law may be used if at least one of those parties is a small or medium-sized enterprise ('SME').

2. For the purposes of this Regulation, an SME is a trader which
- (a) employs fewer than 250 persons; and
- (b) has an annual turnover not exceeding EUR 50 million or an annual balance sheet total not exceeding EUR 43 million, or, for an SME which has its habitual residence in a Member State whose currency is not the euro or in a third country, the equivalent amounts in the currency of that Member State or third country.

Article 8   Agreement on the use of the Common European Sales Law

1. The use of the Common European Sales Law requires an agreement of the parties to that effect. The existence of such an agreement and its validity shall be determined on the basis of paragraphs 2 and 3 of this Article and Article 9, as well as the relevant provisions in the Common European Sales Law.

2. In relations between a trader and a consumer the agreement on the use of the Common European Sales Law shall be valid only if the consumer's consent is given by an explicit statement which is separate from the statement indicating the agreement to conclude a contract. The trader shall provide the consumer with a confirmation of that agreement on a durable medium price.

3. In relations between a trader and a consumer the Common European Sales Law may not be chosen partially, but only in its entirety.

Article 9   Standard Information Notice in contracts between a trader and a consumer

1. In addition to the pre-contractual information duties laid down in the Common European Sales Law, in relations between a trader and a consumer the trader shall draw the consumer's attention to the intended application of the Common European Sales Law before the agreement by providing the consumer with the information notice in Annex II in a prominent manner. Where the agreement to use the Common European Sales Law is concluded by telephone or by any other means that do not make it possible to provide the consumer with the information notice, or where the trader has failed to provide the information notice, the consumer shall not be bound by the agreement until the consumer has received the confirmation referred to in Article 8(2) accompanied by the information notice and has expressly consented subsequently to the use of the Common European Sales Law.

2. The information notice referred to in paragraph 1 shall, if given in electronic form, contain a hyperlink or, in all other circumstances, include the indication of a website through which the text of the Common European Sales Law can be obtained free of charge.

Article 10   Penalties for breach of specific requirements

Member States shall lay down penalties for breaches by traders in relations with consumers of the requirements set out in Articles 8 and 9 and shall take all the measures necessary to ensure that those penalties are applied. The penalties thus provided shall be effective, proportionate and dissuasive. Member States shall notify the relevant provisions to the Commission no later than [1 *year after the date of application of this Regulation*] and shall notify any subsequent changes as soon as possible.

Article 11   Consequences of the use of the Common European Sales Law

Where the parties have validly agreed to use the Common European Sales Law for a contract, only the Common European Sales Law shall govern the matters addressed in its rules. Provided that the contract was actually concluded, the Common European Sales Law shall also govern the compliance with and remedies for failure to comply with the pre-contractual information duties.

Article 12   Information requirements resulting from the Services Directive

This Regulation is without prejudice to the information requirements laid down by national laws which transpose the provisions of Directive 2006/123/EC of the European Parliament and of the Council of 12 December 2006 on services in the internal market and which complement the information requirements laid down in the Common European Sales Law.

Article 13   Member States' options

A Member State may decide to make the Common European Sales Law available for:

(a) contracts where the habitual residence of the traders or, in the case of a contract between a trader and a consumer, the habitual residence of the trader, the address indicated by the consumer, the delivery address for goods and the billing address, are located in that Member State; and/or

(b) contracts where all the parties are traders but none of them is an SME within the meaning of Article 7(2).

Article 14   Communication of judgments applying this Regulation

1. Member States shall ensure that final judgments of their courts applying the rules of this Regulation are communicated without undue delay to the Commission.

2. The Commission shall set up a system which allows the information concerning the judgments referred to in paragraph 1 and relevant judgements of the Court of Justice of the European Union to be consulted. That system shall be accessible to the public.

Article 15   Review

1. By... [4 years after the date of application of this Regulation], Member States shall provide the Commission with information relating to the application of this Regulation, in particular on the level of acceptance of the Common European Sales Law, the extent to which its provisions have given rise to litigation and on the state of play concerning differences in the level of consumer protection between the Common European Sales Law and national law. That information shall include a comprehensive

overview of the case law of the national courts interpreting the provisions of the Common European Sales Law.

2. By...[5 years after the date of application of this Regulation], the Commission shall present to the European Parliament, the Council and the Economic and Social Committee a detailed report reviewing the operation of this Regulation, and taking account of, amongst others, the need to extend the scope in relation to business-to-business contracts, market and technological developments in respect of digital content and future developments of the Union acquis.

Article 16   Entry into force and application

1. This Regulation shall enter into force on the 20th day following that of its publication in the *Official Journal of the European Union*.

2. It shall apply from [6 *months after its the entry into force*].

This Regulation shall be binding in its entirety and directly applicable in the Member States.

ANNEX I COMMON EUROPEAN SALES LAW

PART I INTRODUCTORY PROVISIONS

Chapter 1   General principles and application

Section 1   General principles

Article 1   Freedom of contract

1. Parties are free to conclude a contract and to determine its contents, subject to any applicable mandatory rules.

2. Parties may exclude the application of any of the provisions of the Common European Sales Law, or derogate from or vary their effects, unless otherwise stated in those provisions.

Article 2   Good faith and fair dealing

1. Each party has a duty to act in accordance with good faith and fair dealing.

2. Breach of this duty may preclude the party in breach from exercising or relying on a right, remedy or defence which that party would otherwise have, or may make the party liable for any loss thereby caused to the other party.

3. The parties may not exclude the application of this Article or derogate from or vary its effects.

Article 3   Co-operation

The parties are obliged to co-operate with each other to the extent that this can be expected for the performance of their contractual obligations.

Section 2   Application

Article 4   Interpretation

1. The Common European Sales Law is to be interpreted autonomously and in accordance with its objectives and the principles underlying it.

2. Issues within the scope of the Common European Sales Law but not expressly settled by it are to be settled in accordance with the objectives and the principles underlying it and all its provisions, without recourse to the national law that would be applicable in the absence of an agreement to use the Common European Sales Law or to any other law.

3. Where there is a general rule and a special rule applying to a particular situation within the scope of the general rule, the special rule prevails in any case of conflict.

Article 5   Reasonableness

1. Reasonableness is to be objectively ascertained, having regard to the nature and purpose of the contract, to the circumstances of the case and to the usages and practices of the trades or professions involved.

2. Any reference to what can be expected of or by a person, or in a particular situation, is a reference to what can reasonably be expected.

Article 6   No form required

Unless otherwise stated in the Common European Sales Law, a contract, statement or anyother act which is governed by it need not be made in or evidenced by a particular form.

Article 7   Not individually negotiated contract terms

1. A contract term is not individually negotiated if it has been supplied by one party and the other party has not been able to influence its content.

2. Where one party supplies a selection of contract terms to the other party, a term will not be regarded as individually negotiated merely because the other party chooses that term from that selection.

3. A party who claims that a contract term supplied as part of standard contract terms has since been individually negotiated bears the burden of proving that it has been.

4. In a contract between a trader and a consumer, the trader bears the burden of proving that a contract term supplied by the trader has been individually negotiated.

5. In a contract between a trader and a consumer, contract terms drafted by a third party are considered to have been supplied by the trader, unless the consumer introduced them to the contract.

Article 8   Termination of a contract

1. To 'terminate a contract' means to bring to an end the rights and obligations of the parties under the contract with the exception of those arising under any contract term providing for the settlement of disputes or any other contract term which is to operate even after termination.

2. Payments due and damages for any non-performance before the time of termination remain payable. Where the termination is for non-performance or for anticipated non-performance, the terminating party is also entitled to damages in lieu of the other party's future performance.

3. The effects of termination on the repayment of the price and the return of the goods or the digital content, and other restitutionary effects, are governed by the rules on restitution set out in Chapter 17.

Article 9   Mixed-purpose contracts

1. Where a contract provides both for the sale of goods or the supply of digital content and for the provision of a related service, the rules of Part IV apply to the obligations and remedies of the parties as seller and buyer of goods or digital content and the rules of Part V apply to the obligations and remedies of the parties as service provider and customer.

2. Where, in a contract falling under paragraph 1, the obligations of the seller and the service provider under the contract are to be performed in separate parts or are otherwise divisible, then if there is a ground for termination for non-performance of a part to which a part of the price can be apportioned, the buyer and customer may terminate only in relation to that part.

3. Paragraph 2 does not apply where the buyer and customer cannot be expected to accept performance of the other parts or the non-performance is such as to justify termination of the contract as a whole.

4. Where the obligations of the seller and the service provider under the contract are not divisible or a part of the price cannot be apportioned, the buyer and the customer may terminate only if the non-performance is such as to justify termination of the contract as a whole.

Article 10   Notice

1. This Article applies in relation to the giving of notice for any purpose under the rules of the Common European Sales Law and the contract. 'Notice' includes the communication of any statement which is intended to have legal effect or to convey information for a legal purpose.

2. A notice may be given by any means appropriate to the circumstances.

3. A notice becomes effective when it reaches the addressee, unless it provides for a delayed effect.

4. A notice reaches the addressee:

    (a) when it is delivered to the addressee;

    (b) when it is delivered to the addressee's place of business or, where there is no such place of business or the notice is addressed to a consumer, to the addressee's habitual residence;

    (c) in the case of a notice transmitted by electronic mail or other individual communication, when it can be accessed by the addressee; or

    (d) when it is otherwise made available to the addressee at such a place and in such a way that the addressee could be expected to obtain access to it without undue delay.

The notice has reached the addressee after one of the requirements in point (a), (b), (c) or (d) is fulfilled, whichever is the earliest.

5. A notice has no effect if a revocation of it reaches the addressee before or at the same time as the notice.

6. In relations between a trader and a consumer the parties may not, to the detriment of the consumer, exclude the application of paragraphs 3 and 4 or derogate from or vary its effects.

Article 11 Computation of time

1. The provisions of this Article apply in relation to the computation of time for any purpose under the Common European Sales Law.

2. Subject to paragraphs 3 to 7:

    (a) a period expressed in days starts at the beginning of the first hour of the first day and ends with the expiry of the last hour of the last day of the period;

    (b) a period expressed in weeks, months or years starts at the beginning of the first hour of the first day of the period, and ends with the expiry of the last hour of whichever day in the last week, month or year is the same day of the week, or falls on the same date, as the day from which the period runs; with the qualification that if, in a period expressed in months or in years, the day on which the period should expire does not occur in the last month, it ends with the expiry of the last hour of the last day of that month.

3. Where a period expressed in days, weeks, months or years is to be calculated from a specified event, action or time the day during which the event occurs, the action takes place or the specified time arrives does not fall within the period in question.

4. The periods concerned include Saturdays, Sundays and public holidays, save where these are expressly excepted or where the periods are expressed in working days.

5. Where the last day of a period is a Saturday, Sunday or public holiday at the place where a prescribed act is to be done, the period ends with the expiry of the last hour of the following working day. This provision does not apply to periods calculated retroactively from a given date or event.

6. Where a person sends another person a document which sets a period of time within which the addressee has to reply or take other action but does not state when the period is to begin, then, in the absence of indications to the contrary, the period is calculated from the moment the document reaches the addressee.

7. For the purposes of this Article:

    (a) "public holiday" with reference to a Member State, or part of a Member State, of the European Union means any day designated as such for that Member State or part in a list published in the Official Journal of the European Union; and

    (b) "working days" means all days other than Saturdays, Sundays and public holidays.

Article 12 Unilateral statements or conduct

1. A unilateral statement indicating intention is to be interpreted in the way in which the person to whom it is addressed could be expected to understand it.

2. Where the person making the statement intended an expression used in it to have a particular meaning and the other party was aware, or could be expected to have been aware, of that intention, the expression is to be interpreted in the way intended by the person making the statement.

3. Articles 59 to 65 apply with appropriate adaptations to the interpretation of unilateral statements indicating intention.

4. The rules on defects in consent in Chapter 5 apply with appropriate adaptations to unilateral statements indicating intention.

5. Any reference to a statement referred to in this Article includes a reference to conduct which can be regarded as the equivalent of a statement.

PART II MAKING A BINDING CONTRACT

Chapter 2 Pre-contractual information

Section 1 Pre-contractual information to be given by a trader dealing with a consumer

Article 13 Duty to provide information when concluding a distance or off-premises contract

1. A trader concluding a distance contract or off-premises contract has a duty to provide the following information to the consumer, in a clear and comprehensible manner before the contract is concluded or the consumer is bound by any offer:

(a) the main characteristics of the goods, digital content or related services to be supplied, to an extent appropriate to the medium of communication and to the goods, digital content or related services;

(b) the total price and additional charges and costs, in accordance with Article 14;

(c) the identity and address of the trader, in accordance with Article 15;

(d) the contract terms, in accordance with Article 16;

(e) the rights of withdrawal, in accordance with Article 17;

(f) where applicable, the existence and the conditions of the trader's after-sale customer assistance, after-sale services, commercial guarantees and complaints handling policy;

(g) where applicable, the possibility of having recourse to an Alternative Dispute Resolution mechanism to which the trader is subject and the methods for having access to it;

(h) where applicable, the functionality, including applicable technical protection measures, of digital content; and

(i) where applicable, any relevant interoperability of digital content with hardware and software which the trader is aware of or can be expected to have been aware of.

2. The information provided, except for the addresses required by point (c) of paragraph 1, forms an integral part of the contract and shall not be altered unless the parties expressly agree otherwise.

3. For a distance contract, the information required by this Article must:

(a) be given or made available to the consumer in a way that is appropriate to the means of distance communication used;

(b) be in plain and intelligible language; and

(c) insofar as it is provided on a durable medium, be legible.

4. For an off-premises contract, the information required by this Article must:

(a) be given on paper or, if the consumer agrees, on another durable medium; and

(b) be legible and in plain, intelligible language.

5. This Article does not apply where the contract is:

(a) for the supply of foodstuffs, beverages or other goods which are intended for current consumption in the household, and which are physically supplied by a trader on frequent and regular rounds to the consumer's home, residence or workplace;

(b) concluded by means of an automatic vending machine or automated commercial premises;

(c) an off-premises contract if the price or, where multiple contracts were concluded at the same time, the total price of the contracts does not exceed EUR 50 or the equivalent sum in the currency agreed for the contract price.

Article 14   Information about price and additional charges and costs

1. The information to be provided under point (b) of Article 13 (1) must include:

(a) the total price of the goods, digital content or related services, inclusive of taxes, or where the nature of the goods, digital content or related services is such that the price cannot reasonably be calculated in advance, the manner in which the price is to be calculated; and

(b) where applicable, any additional freight, delivery or postal charges and any other costs or, where these cannot reasonably be calculated in advance, the fact that such additional charges and costs may be payable.

2. In the case of a contract of indeterminate duration or a contract containing a subscription, the total price must include the total price per billing period. Where such contracts are charged at a fixed rate, the total price must include the total monthly price. Where the total price cannot be reasonably calculated in advance, the manner in which the price is to be calculated must be provided.

3. Where applicable, the trader must inform the consumer of the cost of using the means of distance communication for the conclusion of the contract where that cost is calculated other than at the basic rate.

Article 15   Information about the identity and address of the trader

The information to be provided under point (c) of Article 13 (1) must include:

(a) the identity of the trader, such as its trading name;

(b) the geographical address at which the trader is established;

(c) the telephone number, fax number and e-mail address of the trader, where available, to enable the consumer to contact the trader quickly and communicate with the trader efficiently;

(d) where applicable, the identity and geographical address of any other trader on whose behalf the trader is acting; and

(e) where different from the address given pursuant to points (b) and (d) of this Article, the geographical address of the trader, and where applicable that of the trader on whose behalf it is acting, where the consumer can address any complaints.

Article 16   Information about the contract terms

The information to be provided under point (d) of Article 13 (1) must include:

(a) the arrangements for payment, delivery of the goods, supply of the digital content or performance of the related services and the time by which the trader undertakes to deliver the goods, to supply the digital content or to perform the related services;

(b) where applicable, the duration of the contract, the minimum duration of the consumer's obligations or, if the contract is of indeterminate duration or is to be extended automatically, the conditions for terminating the contract; and

(c) where applicable, the existence and conditions for deposits or other financial guarantees to be paid or provided by the consumer at the request of the trader;

(d) where applicable, the existence of relevant codes of conduct and how copies of them can be obtained.

Article 17   Information about rights of withdrawal when concluding a distance or off-premises contract

1. Where the consumer has a right of withdrawal under Chapter 4, the information to be provided under point (e) of Article 13 (1) must include the conditions, time limit and procedures for exercising that right in accordance with Appendix 1, as well as the model withdrawal form set out in Appendix 2.

2. Where applicable, the information to be provided under point (e) of Article 13(1) must include the fact that the consumer will have to bear the cost of returning the goods in case of withdrawal and, for distance contracts, that the consumer will have to bear the cost of returning the goods in the event of withdrawal if the goods by their nature cannot be normally returned by post.

3. Where the consumer can exercise the right of withdrawal after having made a request for the provision of related services to begin during the withdrawal period, the information to be provided under point (e) of Article 13(1) must include the fact that the consumer would be liable to pay the trader the amount referred to in Article 45(5).

4. The duty to provide the information required by paragraphs 1, 2 and 3 may be fulfilled by supplying the Model instructions on withdrawal set out in Appendix 1 to the consumer. The trader will be deemed to have fulfilled these information requirements if he has supplied these instructions to the consumer correctly filled in.

5. Where a right of withdrawal is not provided for in accordance with points (c) to (i) of Article 40(2) and paragraph 3 of that Article, the information to be provided under point (e) of Article 13(1) must include a statement that the consumer will not benefit from a right of withdrawal or, where applicable, the circumstances under which the consumer loses the right of withdrawal.

Article 18   Off-premises contracts: additional information requirements and confirmation

1. The trader must provide the consumer with a copy of the signed contract or the confirmation of the contract, including where applicable, the confirmation of the consumer's consent and acknowledgment as provided for in point (d) of Article 40(3) on paper or, if the consumer agrees, on a different durable medium.

2. Where the consumer wants the provision of related services to begin during the withdrawal period provided for in Article 42(2), the trader must require that the consumer makes such an express request on a durable medium.

Article 19   Distance contracts: additional information and other requirements

1. When a trader makes a telephone call to a consumer, with a view to concluding a distance contract, the trader must, at the beginning of the conversation with the consumer, disclose its identity and, where applicable, the identity of the person on whose behalf it is making the call and the commercial purpose of the call.

2. If the distance contract is concluded through a means of distance communication which allows limited space or time to display the information, the trader must provide at least the information referred to in paragraph 3 of this Article on that particular means prior to the conclusion of such a contract. The other information referred to in Article 13 shall be provided by the trader to the consumer in an appropriate way in accordance with Article 13(3).

3. The information required under paragraph 2 is:
   (a) the main characteristics of the goods, digital content or related services, as required by point (a) of Article 13 (1);
   (b) the identity of the trader, as required by point (a) of Article 15;
   (c) the total price, including all items referred to in point (b) of Article 13 (1) and Article 14(1) and (2);
   (d) the right of withdrawal; and
   (e) where relevant, the duration of the contract, and if the contract is for an indefinite period, the requirements for terminating the contract, referred to in point (b) of Article 16.

4. A distance contract concluded by telephone is valid only if the consumer has signed the offer or has sent his written consent indicating the agreement to conclude a contract. The trader must provide the consumer with a confirmation of that agreement on a durable medium.

5. The trader must give the consumer a confirmation of the contract concluded, including where applicable, of the consent and acknowledgement of the consumer referred to in point (d) of Article 40(3), and all the information referred to in Article 13 on a durable medium. The trader must give that information in reasonable time after the conclusion of the distance contract, and at the latest at the time of the delivery of the goods or before the supply of digital content or the provision of the related service begins, unless the information has already been given to the consumer prior to the conclusion of the distance contract on a durable medium.

6. Where the consumer wants the provision of related services to begin during the withdrawal period provided for in Article 42(2), the trader must require that the consumer makes an express request to that effect on a durable medium.

Article 20   Duty to provide information when concluding contracts other than distance and off-premises contracts

1. In contracts other than distance and off-premises contracts, a trader has a duty to provide the following information to the consumer, in a clear and comprehensible manner before the contract is concluded or the consumer is bound by any offer, if that information is not already apparent from the context:

(a) the main characteristics of the goods, digital content or related services to be supplied, to an extent appropriate to the medium of communication and to the goods, digital content or related services;

(b) the total price and additional charges and costs, in accordance with Article 14(1);

(c) the identity of the trader, such as the trader's trading name, the geographical address at which it is established and its telephone number;

(d) the contract terms in accordance with points (a) and (b) of Article 16;

(e) where applicable, the existence and the conditions of the trader's after-sale services, commercial guarantees and complaints handling policy;

(f) where applicable, the functionality, including applicable technical protection measures of digital content; and

(g) where applicable, any relevant interoperability of digital content with hardware and software which the trader is aware of or can be expected to have been aware of.

2. This Article does not apply where the contract involves a day-to-day transaction and is performed immediately at the time of its conclusion.

Article 21   Burden of proof

The trader bears the burden of proof that it has provided the information required by this Section.

Article 22   Mandatory nature

The parties may not, to the detriment of the consumer, exclude the application of this Section or derogate from or vary its effects.

Section 2 Pre-contractual information to be given by a trader dealing with another trader

Article 23   Duty to disclose information about goods and related services

1. Before the conclusion of a contract for the sale of goods, supply of digital content or provision of related services by a trader to another trader, the supplier has a duty to disclose by any appropriate means to the other trader any information concerning the main characteristics of the goods, digital content or related services to be supplied which the supplier has or can be expected to have and which it would be contrary to good faith and fair dealing not to disclose to the other party.

2. In determining whether paragraph 1 requires the supplier to disclose any information, regard is to be had to all the circumstances, including:

(a) whether the supplier had special expertise;

(b) the cost to the supplier of acquiring the relevant information;

(c) the ease with which the other trader could have acquired the information by other means;

(d) the nature of the information;

(e) the likely importance of the information to the other trader; and

(f) good commercial practice in the situation concerned.

Section 3 Contracts concluded by electronic means

Article 24 Additional duties to provide information in distance contracts concluded by electronic means

1. This Article applies where a trader provides the means for concluding a contract and where those means are electronic and do not involve the exclusive exchange of electronic mail or other individual communication.

2. The trader must make available to the other party appropriate, effective and accessible technical means for identifying and correcting input errors before the other party makes or accepts an offer.

3. The trader must provide information about the following matters before the other party makes or accepts an offer:
    (a) the technical steps to be taken in order to conclude the contract;
    (b) whether or not a contract document will be filed by the trader and whether it will be accessible;
    (c) the technical means for identifying and correcting input errors before the other party makes or accepts an offer;
    (d) the languages offered for the conclusion of the contract;
    (e) the contract terms.

4. The trader must ensure that the contract terms referred to in point (e) of paragraph 3 are made available in alphabetical or other intelligible characters and on a durable medium by means of any support which permits reading, recording of the information contained in the text and its reproduction in tangible form.

5. The trader must acknowledge by electronic means and without undue delay the receipt of an offer or an acceptance sent by the other party.

Article 25 Additional requirements in distance contracts concluded by electronic means

1. Where a distance contract which is concluded by electronic means would oblige the consumer to make a payment, the trader must make the consumer aware in a clear and prominent manner, and immediately before the consumer places the order, of the information required by point (a) of Article 13 (1), Article 14(1) and (2), and point (b) of Article 16.

2. The trader must ensure that the consumer, when placing the order, explicitly acknowledges that the order implies an obligation to pay. Where placing an order entails activating a button or a similar function, the button or similar function must be labelled in an easily legible manner only with the words "order with obligation to pay" or similar unambiguous wording indicating that placing the order entails an obligation to make a payment to the trader. Where the trader has not complied with this paragraph, the consumer is not bound by the contract or order.

3. The trader must indicate clearly and legibly on its trading website at the latest at the beginning of the ordering process whether any delivery restrictions apply and what means of payment are accepted.

Article 26 Burden of proof

In relations between a trader and a consumer, the trader bears the burden of proof that it has provided the information required by this Section.

Article 27 Mandatory nature

In relations between a trader and a consumer, the parties may not, to the detriment of the consumer, exclude the application of this Section or derogate from or vary its effects.

Section 4 Duty to ensure that information supplied is correct

Article 28 Duty to ensure that information supplied is correct

1. A party who supplies information before or at the time a contract is concluded, whether in order to comply with the duties imposed by this Chapter or otherwise, has a duty to take reasonable care to ensure that the information supplied is correct and is not misleading.

2. A party to whom incorrect or misleading information has been supplied in breach of the duty referred to in paragraph 1, and who reasonably relies on that information in concluding a contract with the party who supplied it, has the remedies set out in Article 29.

3. In relations between a trader and a consumer the parties may not, to the detriment of the consumer, exclude the application of this Article or derogate from or vary its effects.

Section 5 Remedies for breach of information duties

Article 29 Remedies for breach of information duties

1. A party which has failed to comply with any duty imposed by this Chapter is liable for any loss caused to the other party by such failure.

2. Where the trader has not complied with the information requirements relating to additional charges or other costs as referred to in Article 14 or on the costs of returning the goods as referred to in Article 17(2) the consumer is not liable to pay the additional charges and other costs.

3. The remedies provided under this Article are without prejudice to any remedy which may be available under Article 42 (2), Article 48 or Article 49.

4. In relations between a trader and a consumer the parties may not, to the detriment of the consumer, exclude the application of this Article or derogate from or vary its effects.

Chapter 3 Conclusion of contract

Article 30 Requirements for the conclusion of a contract

1. A contract is concluded if:
    (a) the parties reach an agreement;
    (b) they intend the agreement to have legal effect; and
    (c) the agreement, supplemented if necessary by rules of the Common European Sales Law, has sufficient content and certainty to be given legal effect.

2. Agreement is reached by acceptance of an offer. Acceptance may be made explicitly or by other statements or conduct.

3. Whether the parties intend the agreement to have legal effect is to be determined from their statements and conduct.

4. Where one of the parties makes agreement on some specific matter a requirement for the conclusion of a contract, there is no contract unless agreement on that matter has been reached.

Article 31 Offer

1. A proposal is an offer if:
    (a) it is intended to result in a contract if it is accepted; and
    (b) it has sufficient content and certainty for there to be a contract.

2. An offer may be made to one or more specific persons.

3. A proposal made to the public is not an offer, unless the circumstances indicate otherwise.

Article 32 Revocation of offer

1. An offer may be revoked if the revocation reaches the offeree before the offeree has sent an acceptance or, in cases of acceptance by conduct, before the contract has been concluded.

2. Where a proposal made to the public is an offer, it can be revoked by the same means as were used to make the offer.

3. A revocation of an offer is ineffective if:
    (a) the offer indicates that it is irrevocable;

(b) the offer states a fixed time period for its acceptance; or

(c) it was otherwise reasonable for the offeree to rely on the offer as being irrevocable and the offeree has acted in reliance on the offer.

Article 33   Rejection of offer

When a rejection of an offer reaches the offeror, the offer lapses.

Article 34   Acceptance

1. Any form of statement or conduct by the offeree is an acceptance if it indicates assent to the offer.

2. Silence or inactivity does not in itself constitute acceptance.

Article 35   Time of conclusion of the contract

1. Where an acceptance is sent by the offeree the contract is concluded when the acceptance reaches the offeror.

2. Where an offer is accepted by conduct, the contract is concluded when notice of the conduct reaches the offeror.

3. Notwithstanding paragraph 2, where by virtue of the offer, of practices which the parties have established between themselves, or of a usage, the offeree may accept the offer by conduct without notice to the offeror, the contract is concluded when the offeree begins to act.

Article 36   Time limit for acceptance

1. An acceptance of an offer is effective only if it reaches the offeror within any time limit stipulated in the offer by the offeror.

2. Where no time limit has been fixed by the offeror the acceptance is effective only if it reaches the offeror within a reasonable time after the offer was made.

3. Where an offer may be accepted by doing an act without notice to the offeror, the acceptance is effective only if the act is done within the time for acceptance fixed by the offeror or, if no such time is fixed, within a reasonable time.

Article 37   Late acceptance

1. A late acceptance is effective as an acceptance if without undue delay the offeror informs the offeree that the offeror is treating it as an effective acceptance.

2. Where a letter or other communication containing a late acceptance shows that it has been sent in such circumstances that if its transmission had been normal it would have reached the offeror in due time, the late acceptance is effective as an acceptance unless, without undue delay, the offeror informs the offeree that the offer has lapsed.

Article 38   Modified acceptance

1. A reply by the offeree which states or implies additional or different contract terms which materially alter the terms of the offer is a rejection and a new offer.

2. Additional or different contract terms relating, among other things, to the price, payment, quality and quantity of the goods, place and time of delivery, extent of one party's liability to the other or the settlement of disputes are presumed to alter the terms of the offer materially.

3. A reply which gives a definite assent to an offer is an acceptance even if it states or implies additional or different contract terms, provided that these do not materially alter the terms of the offer. The additional or different terms then become part of the contract.

4. A reply which states or implies additional or different contract terms is always a rejection of the offer if:

(a) the offer expressly limits acceptance to the terms of the offer;

(b) the offeror objects to the additional or different terms without undue delay; or

(c) the offeree makes the acceptance conditional upon the offeror's assent to the additional or different terms, and the assent does not reach the offeree within a reasonable time.

Article 39   Conflicting standard contract terms

1. Where the parties have reached agreement except that the offer and acceptance refer to conflicting standard contract terms, a contract is nonetheless concluded. The standard contract terms are part of the contract to the extent that they are common in substance.

2. Notwithstanding paragraph 1, no contract is concluded if one party:

    (a) has indicated in advance, explicitly, and not by way of standard contract terms, an intention not to be bound by a contract on the basis of paragraph 1; or

    (b) without undue delay, informs the other party of such an intention.

Chapter 4 Right to withdraw in distance and off-premises contracts between traders and consumers

Article 40   Right to withdraw

1. During the period provided for in Article 42, the consumer has a right to withdraw from the contract without giving any reason, and at no cost to the consumer except as provided in Article 45, from:

    (a) a distance contract;

    (b) an off-premises contract, provided that the price or, where multiple contracts were concluded at the same time, the total price of the contracts exceeds EUR 50 or the equivalent sum in the currency agreed for the contract price at the time of the conclusion of the contract.

2. Paragraph 1 does not apply to:

    (a) a contract concluded by means of an automatic vending machine or automated commercial premises;

    (b) a contract for the supply of foodstuffs, beverages or other goods which are intended for current consumption in the household and which are physically supplied by the trader on frequent and regular rounds to the consumer's home, residence or workplace;

    (c) a contract for the supply of goods or related services for which the price depends on fluctuations in the financial market which cannot be controlled by the trader and which may occur within the withdrawal period;

    (d) a contract for the supply of goods or digital content which are made to the consumer's specifications, or are clearly personalised;

    (e) a contract for the supply of goods which are liable to deteriorate or expire rapidly;

    (f) a contract for the supply of alcoholic beverages, the price of which has been agreed upon at the time of the conclusion of the sales contract, the delivery of which can only take place after 30 days from the time of conclusion of the contract and the actual value of which is dependent on fluctuations in the market which cannot be controlled by the trader;

    (g) a contract for the sale of a newspaper, periodical or magazine with the exception of subscription contracts for the supply of such publications;

    (h) a contract concluded at a public auction; and

    (i) a contract for catering or services related to leisure activities which provides for a specific date or period of performance.

3. Paragraph 1 does not apply in the following situations:

    (a) where the goods supplied were sealed, have been unsealed by the consumer and are not then suitable for return due to health protection or hygiene reasons;

    (b) where the goods supplied have, according to their nature, been inseparably mixed with other items after delivery;

    (c) where the goods supplied were sealed audio or video recordings or computer software and have been unsealed after delivery;

    (d) where the supply of digital content which is not supplied on a tangible medium has begun with the consumer's prior express consent and with the acknowledgement by the consumer of losing the right to withdraw;

(e) the consumer has specifically requested a visit from the trader for the purpose of carrying out urgent repairs or maintenance. Where on the occasion of such a visit the trader
provides related services in addition to those specifically requested by the consumer or
goods other than replacement parts necessarily used in performing the maintenance or in
making the repairs, the right of withdrawal applies to those additional related services or
goods.

4. Where the consumer has made an offer which, if accepted, would lead to the conclusion of a
contract from which there would be a right to withdraw under this Chapter, the consumer may withdraw the offer even if it would otherwise be irrevocable.

Article 41   Exercise of right to withdraw

1. The consumer may exercise the right to withdraw at any time before the end of the period of
withdrawal provided for in Article 42.

2. The consumer exercises the right to withdraw by notice to the trader. For this purpose, the
consumer may use either the Model withdrawal form set out in Appendix 2 or any other unequivocal
statement setting out the decision to withdraw.

3. Where the trader gives the consumer the option to withdraw electronically on its trading website, and the consumer does so, the trader has a duty to communicate to the consumer an acknowledgement of receipt of such a withdrawal on a durable medium without delay. The trader is liable for
any loss caused to the other party by a breach of this duty.

4. A communication of withdrawal is timely if sent before the end of the withdrawal period.

5. The consumer bears the burden of proof that the right of withdrawal has been exercised in
accordance with this Article.

Article 42   Withdrawal period

1. The withdrawal period expires after fourteen days from:
   (a) the day on which the consumer has taken delivery of the goods in the case of a sales con-
       tract, including a sales contract under which the seller also agrees to provide related
       services;
   (b) the day on which the consumer has taken delivery of the last item in the case of a contract
       for the sale of multiple goods ordered by the consumer in one order and delivered sepa-
       rately, including a contract under which the seller also agrees to provide related services;
   (c) the day on which the consumer has taken delivery of the last lot or piece in the case of a
       contract where the goods consist of multiple lots or pieces, including a contract under
       which the seller also agrees to provide related services;
   (d) the day on which the consumer has taken delivery of the first item where the contract is
       for regular delivery of goods during a defined period of time, including a contract under
       which the seller also agrees to provide related services;
   (e) the day of the conclusion of the contract in the case of a contract for related services con-
       cluded after the goods have been delivered;
   (f) the day when the consumer has taken delivery of the tangible medium in accordance with
       point (a) in the case of a contract for the supply of digital content where the digital content
       is supplied on a tangible medium;
   (g) the day of the conclusion of the contract in the case of a contract where the digital content
       is not supplied on a tangible medium.

2. Where the trader has not provided the consumer with the information referred to in Article
17(1), the withdrawal period expires:
   (a) after one year from the end of the initial withdrawal period, as determined in accordance
       with paragraph 1; or
   (b) where the trader provides the consumer with the information required within one year
       from the end of the withdrawal period as determined in accordance with paragraph 1,
       after fourteen days from the day the consumer receives the information.

Article 43   Effects of withdrawal

Withdrawal terminates the obligations of both parties under the contract:

    (a) to perform the contract; or

    (b) to conclude the contract in cases where an offer was made by the consumer.

Article 44   Obligations of the trader in the event of withdrawal

1. The trader must reimburse all payments received from the consumer, including, where applicable, the costs of delivery without undue delay and in any event not later than fourteen days from the day on which the trader is informed of the consumer's decision to withdraw from the contract in accordance with Article 41. The trader must carry out such reimbursement using the same means of payment as the consumer used for the initial transaction, unless the consumer has expressly agreed otherwise and provided that the consumer does not incur any fees as a result of such reimbursement.

2. Notwithstanding paragraph 1, the trader is not required to reimburse the supplementary costs, if the consumer has expressly opted for a type of delivery other than the least expensive type of standard delivery offered by the trader.

3. In the case of a contract for the sale of goods, the trader may withhold the reimbursement until it has received the goods back, or the consumer has supplied evidence of having sent back the goods, whichever is earlier, unless the trader has offered to collect the goods.

4. In the case of an off-premises contract where the goods have been delivered to the consumer's home at the time of the conclusion of the contract, the trader must collect the goods at its own cost if the goods by their nature cannot be normally returned by post.

Article 45   Obligations of the consumer in the event of withdrawal

1. The consumer must send back the goods or hand them over to the trader or to a person authorised by the trader without undue delay and in any event not later than fourteen days from the day on which the consumer communicates the decision to withdraw from the contract to the trader in accordance with Article 41, unless the trader has offered to collect the goods. This deadline is met if the consumer sends back the goods before the period of fourteen days has expired.

2. The consumer must bear the direct costs of returning the goods, unless the trader has agreed to bear those costs or the trader failed to inform the consumer that the consumer has to bear them.

3. The consumer is liable for any diminished value of the goods only where that results from handling of the goods in any way other than what is necessary to establish the nature, characteristics and functioning of the goods. The consumer is not liable for diminished value where the trader has not provided all the information about the right to withdraw in accordance with Article 17 (1).

4. Without prejudice to paragraph 3, the consumer is not liable to pay any compensation for the use of the goods during the withdrawal period.

5. Where the consumer exercises the right of withdrawal after having made an express request for the provision of related services to begin during the withdrawal period, the consumer must pay to the trader an amount which is in proportion to what has been provided before the consumer exercised the right of withdrawal, in comparison with the full coverage of the contract. The proportionate amount to be paid by the consumer to the trader must be calculated on the basis of the total price agreed in the contract. Where the total price is excessive, the proportionate amount must be calculated on the basis of the market value of what has been provided.

6. The consumer is not liable for the cost for:

    (a) the provision of related services, in full or in part, during the withdrawal period, where:

        (i)   the trader has failed to provide information in accordance with Article 17(1) and (3); or

        (ii) the consumer has not expressly requested performance to begin during the withdrawal period in accordance with Article 18(2) and Article 19(6);

    (b) for the supply, in full or in part, of digital content which is not supplied on a tangible medium where:

        (i)   the consumer has not given prior express consent for the supply of digital content to begin before the end of the period of withdrawal referred to in Article 42(1);

(ii) the consumer has not acknowledged losing the right of withdrawal when giving the
consent; or

(iii) the trader has failed to provide the confirmation in accordance with Article 18(1) and
Article 19(5).

7. Except as provided for in this Article, the consumer does not incur any liability through the
exercise of the right of withdrawal.

Article 46   Ancillary contracts

1. Where a consumer exercises the right of withdrawal from a distance or an off-premises contract
in accordance with Articles 41 to 45, any ancillary contracts are automatically terminated at no cost
to the consumer except as provided in paragraphs 2 and 3. For the purpose of this Article an ancillary
contract means a contract by which a consumer acquires goods, digital content or related services
in connexion to a distance contract or an off-premises contract and these goods, digital content or
related services are provided by the trader or a third party on the basis of an arrangement between
that third party and the trader.

2. The provisions of Articles 43, 44 and 45 apply accordingly to ancillary contracts to the extent
that those contracts are governed by the Common European Sales Law.

3. For ancillary contracts which are not governed by the Common European Sales Law the applicable law governs the obligations of the parties in the event of withdrawal.

Article 47   Mandatory nature

The parties may not, to the detriment of the consumer, exclude the application of this Chapter or
derogate from or vary its effects.

Chapter 5 Defects in consent

Article 48   Mistake

1. A party may avoid a contract for mistake of fact or law existing when the contract was concluded if:

    (a) the party, but for the mistake, would not have concluded the contract or would have done
so only on fundamentally different contract terms and the other party knew or could be
expected to have known this; and

    (b) the other party:

        (i) caused the mistake;

        (ii) caused the contract to be concluded in mistake by failing to comply with any pre-
contractual information duty under Chapter 2, Sections 1 to 4;

        (iii) knew or could be expected to have known of the mistake and caused the contract to
be concluded in mistake by not pointing out the relevant information, provided that
good faith and fair dealing would have required a party aware of the mistake to point
it out; or

        (iv) made the same mistake.

2. A party may not avoid a contract for mistake if the risk of the mistake was assumed, or in the
circumstances should be borne, by that party.

3. An inaccuracy in the expression or transmission of a statement is treated as a mistake of the
person who made or sent the statement.

Article 49   Fraud

1. A party may avoid a contract if the other party has induced the conclusion of the contract by
fraudulent misrepresentation, whether by words or conduct, or fraudulent non-disclosure of any
information which good faith and fair dealing, or any pre-contractual information duty, required that
party to disclose.

2. Misrepresentation is fraudulent if it is made with knowledge or belief that the representation
is false, or recklessly as to whether it is true or false, and is intended to induce the recipient to make a

mistake. Non-disclosure is fraudulent if it is intended to induce the person from whom the information is withheld to make a mistake.

3. In determining whether good faith and fair dealing require a party to disclose particular information, regard should be had to all the circumstances, including:

(a) whether the party had special expertise;

(b) the cost to the party of acquiring the relevant information;

(c) the ease with which the other party could have acquired the information by other means;

(d) the nature of the information;

(e) the apparent importance of the information to the other party; and

(f) in contracts between traders good commercial practice in the situation concerned.

Article 50   Threats

A party may avoid a contract if the other party has induced the conclusion of the contract by the threat of wrongful, imminent and serious harm, or of a wrongful act.

Article 51   Unfair exploitation

A party may avoid a contract if, at the time of the conclusion of the contract:

(a) that party was dependent on, or had a relationship of trust with, the other party, was in economic distress or had urgent needs, was improvident, ignorant, or inexperienced; and

(b) the other party knew or could be expected to have known this and, in the light of the circumstances and purpose of the contract, exploited the first party's situation by taking an excessive benefit or unfair advantage.

Article 52   Notice of avoidance

1. Avoidance is effected by notice to the other party.

2. A notice of avoidance is effective only if it is given within the following period after the avoiding party becomes aware of the relevant circumstances or becomes capable of acting freely:

(a) six months in case of mistake; and

(b) one year in case of fraud, threats and unfair exploitation.

Article 53   Confirmation

Where the party who has the right to avoid a contract under this Chapter confirms it, expressly or impliedly, after becoming aware of the relevant circumstances, or becoming capable of acting freely, that party may no longer avoid the contract.

Article 54   Effects of avoidance

1. A contract which may be avoided is valid until avoided but, once avoided, is retrospectively invalid from the beginning.

2. Where a ground of avoidance affects only certain contract terms, the effect of avoidance is limited to those terms unless it is unreasonable to uphold the remainder of the contract.

3. The question whether either party has a right to the return of whatever has been transferred or supplied under a contract which has been avoided, or to a monetary equivalent, is regulated by the rules on restitution in Chapter 17.

Article 55   Damages for loss

A party who has the right to avoid a contract under this Chapter or who had such a right before it was lost by the effect of time limits or confirmation is entitled, whether or not the contract is avoided, to damages from the other party for loss suffered as a result of the mistake, fraud, threats or unfair exploitation, provided that the other party knew or could be expected to have known of the relevant circumstances.

Article 56   Exclusion or restriction of remedies

1. Remedies for fraud, threats and unfair exploitation cannot be directly or indirectly excluded or restricted.

2. In relations between a trader and a consumer the parties may not, to the detriment of the consumer, directly or indirectly exclude or restrict remedies for mistake.

Article 57   Choice of remedy

A party who is entitled to a remedy under this Chapter in circumstances which afford that party a remedy for non-performance may pursue either of those remedies.

PART III   ASSESSING WHAT IS IN THE CONTRACT

Chapter 6   Interpretation

Article 58   General rules on interpretation of contracts

1. A contract is to be interpreted according to the common intention of the parties even if this differs from the normal meaning of the expressions used in it.

2. Where one party intended an expression used in the contract to have a particular meaning, and at the time of the conclusion of the contract the other party was aware, or could be expected to have been aware, of that intention, the expression is to be interpreted in the way intended by the first party.

3. Unless otherwise provided in paragraphs 1 and 2, the contract is to be interpreted according to the meaning which a reasonable person would give to it.

Article 59   Relevant matters

In interpreting a contract, regard may be had, in particular, to:
- (a) the circumstances in which it was concluded, including the preliminary negotiations;
- (b) the conduct of the parties, even subsequent to the conclusion of the contract;
- (c) the interpretation which has already been given by the parties to expressions which are identical to or similar to those used in the contract;
- (d) usages which would be considered generally applicable by parties in the same situation;
- (e) practices which the parties have established between themselves;
- (f) the meaning commonly given to expressions in the branch of activity concerned;
- (g) the nature and purpose of the contract; and
- (h) good faith and fair dealing.

Article 60   Reference to contract as a whole

Expressions used in a contract are to be interpreted in the light of the contract as a whole.

Article 61   Language discrepancies

Where a contract document is in two or more language versions none of which is stated to be authoritative and where there is a discrepancy between the versions, the version in which the contract was originally drawn up is to be treated as the authoritative one.

Article 62   Preference for individually negotiated contract terms

To the extent that there is an inconsistency, contract terms which have been individually negotiated prevail over those which have not been individually negotiated within the meaning of Article 7.

Article 63   Preference for interpretation which gives contract terms effect

An interpretation which renders the contract terms effective prevails over one which does not.

Article 64   Interpretation in favour of consumers

1. Where there is doubt about the meaning of a contract term in a contract between a trader and a consumer, the interpretation most favourable to the consumer shall prevail unless the term was supplied by the consumer.

2. The parties may not, to the detriment of the consumer, exclude the application of this Article or derogate from or vary its effects.

Article 65   Interpretation against supplier of a contract term

Where, in a contract which does not fall under Article 64, there is doubt about the meaning of a contract term which has not been individually negotiated within the meaning of Article 7, an interpretation of the term against the party who supplied it shall prevail.

Chapter 7   Contents and effects

Article 66   Contract terms

The terms of the contract are derived from:

    (a) the agreement of the parties, subject to any mandatory rules of the Common European Sales Law;

    (b) any usage or practice by which parties are bound by virtue of Article 67;

    (c) any rule of the Common European Sales Law which applies in the absence of an agreement of the parties to the contrary; and

    (d) any contract term implied by virtue of Article 68.

Article 67   Usages and practices in contracts between traders

1. In a contract between traders, the parties are bound by any usage which they have agreed should be applicable and by any practice they have established between themselves.

2. The parties are bound by a usage which would be considered generally applicable by traders in the same situation as the parties.

3. Usages and practices do not bind the parties to the extent to which they conflict with contract terms which have been individually negotiated or any mandatory rules of the Common European Sales Law.

Article 68   Contract terms which may be implied

1. Where it is necessary to provide for a matter which is not explicitly regulated by the agreement of the parties, any usage or practice or any rule of the Common European Sales Law, an additional contract term may be implied, having regard in particular to:

    (a) the nature and purpose of the contract;

    (b) the circumstances in which the contract was concluded; and

    (c) good faith and fair dealing.

2. Any contract term implied under paragraph 1 is, as far as possible, to be such as to give effect to what the parties would probably have agreed, had they provided for the matter.

3. Paragraph 1 does not apply if the parties have deliberately left a matter unregulated, accepting that one or other party would bear the risk.

Article 69   Contract terms derived from certain pre-contractual statements

1. Where the trader makes a statement before the contract is concluded, either to the other party or publicly, about the characteristics of what is to be supplied by that trader under the contract, the statement is incorporated as a term of the contract unless:

    (a) the other party was aware, or could be expected to have been aware when the contract was concluded that the statement was incorrect or could not otherwise be relied on as such a term; or

    (b) the other party's decision to conclude the contract could not have been influenced by the statement.

2. For the purposes of paragraph 1, a statement made by a person engaged in advertising or marketing for the trader is regarded as being made by the trader.

3. Where the other party is a consumer then, for the purposes of paragraph 1, a public statement made by or on behalf of a producer or other person in earlier links of the chain of transactions leading to the contract is regarded as being made by the trader unless the trader, at the time of conclusion of the contract, did not know and could not be expected to have known of it.

4. In relations between a trader and a consumer the parties may not, to the detriment of the consumer, exclude the application of this Article or derogate from or vary its effects.

Article 70   Duty to raise awareness of not individually negotiated contract terms

1. Contract terms supplied by one party and not individually negotiated within the meaning of Article 7 may be invoked against the other party only if the other party was aware of them, or if the party supplying them took reasonable steps to draw the other party's attention to them, before or when the contract was concluded.

2. For the purposes of this Article, in relations between a trader and a consumer contract terms are not sufficiently brought to the consumer's attention by a mere reference to them in a contract document, even if the consumer signs the document.

3. The parties may not exclude the application of this Article or derogate from or vary its effects.

Article 71   Additional payments in contracts between a trader and a consumer

1. In a contract between a trader and a consumer, a contract term which obliges the consumer to make any payment in addition to the remuneration stated for the trader's main contractual obligation, in particular where it has been incorporated by the use of default options which the consumer is required to reject in order to avoid the additional payment, is not binding on the consumer unless, before the consumer is bound by the contract, the consumer has expressly consented to the additional payment. If the consumer has made the additional payment, the consumer may recover it.

2. The parties may not, to the detriment of the consumer, exclude the application of this Article or derogate from or vary its effects.

Article 72   Merger clauses

1. Where a contract in writing includes a term stating that the document contains all contract terms (a merger clause), any prior statements, undertakings or agreements which are not contained in the document do not form part of the contract.

2. Unless the contract otherwise provides, a merger clause does not prevent the parties' prior statements from being used to interpret the contract.

3. In a contract between a trader and a consumer, the consumer is not bound by a merger clause.

4. The parties may not, to the detriment of the consumer, exclude the application of this Article or derogate from or vary its effects.

Article 73   Determination of price

Where the amount of the price payable under a contract cannot be otherwise determined, the price payable is, in the absence of any indication to the contrary, the price normally charged in comparable circumstances at the time of the conclusion of the contract or, if no such price is available, a reasonable price.

Article 74   Unilateral determination by a party

1. Where the price or any other contract term is to be determined by one party and that party's determination is grossly unreasonable then the price normally charged or term normally used in comparable circumstances at the time of the conclusion of the contract or, if no such price or term is available, a reasonable price or a reasonable term is substituted.

2. The parties may not exclude the application of this Article or derogate from or vary its effects.

Article 75   Determination by a third party

1. Where a third party is to determine the price or any other contract term and cannot or will not do so, a court may, unless this is inconsistent with the contract terms, appoint another person to determine it.

2. Where a price or other contract term determined by a third party is grossly unreasonable, the price normally charged or term normally used in comparable circumstances at the time of the conclusion of the contract or, if no such price is available, a reasonable price, or a reasonable term is substituted.

3. For the purpose of paragraph 1 a 'court' includes an arbitral tribunal.

4. In relations between a trader and a consumer the parties may not to the detriment of the consumer exclude the application of paragraph 2 or derogate from or vary its effects.

Article 76 Language

Where the language to be used for communications relating to the contract or the rights or obligations arising from it cannot be otherwise determined, the language to be used is that used for the conclusion of the contract.

Article 77 Contracts of indeterminate duration

1. Where, in a case involving continuous or repeated performance of a contractual obligation, the contract terms do not stipulate when the contractual relationship is to end or provide for it to be terminated upon giving notice to that effect, it may be terminated by either party by giving a reasonable period of notice not exceeding two months.

2. In relations between a trader and a consumer the parties may not, to the detriment of the consumer, exclude the application of this Article or derogate from or vary its effects.

Article 78 Contract terms in favour of third parties

1. The contracting parties may, by the contract, confer a right on a third party. The third party need not be in existence or identified at the time the contract is concluded but needs to be identifiable.

2. The nature and content of the third party's right are determined by the contract. The right may take the form of an exclusion or limitation of the third party's liability to one of the contracting parties.

3. When one of the contracting parties is bound to render a performance to the third party under the contract, then:

    (a) the third party has the same rights to performance and remedies for non-performance as if the contracting party was bound to render the performance under a contract with the third party; and

    (b) the contracting party who is bound may assert against the third party all defences which the contracting party could assert against the other party to the contract.

4. The third party may reject a right conferred upon them by notice to either of the contracting parties, if that is done before it has been expressly or impliedly accepted. On such rejection, the right is treated as never having accrued to the third party.

5. The contracting parties may remove or modify the contract term conferring the right if this is done before either of them has given the third party notice that the right has been conferred.

Chapter 8 Unfair contract terms

Section 1 General provisions

Article 79 Effects of unfair contract terms

1. A contract term which is supplied by one party and which is unfair under Sections 2 and 3 of this Chapter is not binding on the other party.

2. Where the contract can be maintained without the unfair contract term, the other contract terms remain binding.

Article 80 Exclusions from unfairness test

1. Sections 2 and 3 do not apply to contract terms which reflect rules of the Common European Sales Law which would apply if the terms did not regulate the matter.

2. Section 2 does not apply to the definition of the main subject matter of the contract, or to the appropriateness of the price to be paid in so far as the trader has complied with the duty of transparency set out in Article 82.

3. Section 3 does not apply to the definition of the main subject matter of the contract or to the appropriateness of the price to be paid.

Article 81   Mandatory nature

The parties may not exclude the application of this Chapter or derogate from or vary its effects.

Section 2 Unfair contract terms in contracts between a trader and a consumer

Article 82   Duty of transparency in contract terms not individually negotiated

Where a trader supplies contract terms which have not been individually negotiated with the consumer within the meaning of Article 7, it has a duty to ensure that they are drafted and communicated in plain, intelligible language.

Article 83   Meaning of "unfair" in contracts between a trader and a consumer

1. In a contract between a trader and a consumer, a contract term supplied by the trader which has not been individually negotiated within the meaning of Article 7 is unfair for the purposes of this Section if it causes a significant imbalance in the parties' rights and obligations arising under the contract, to the detriment of the consumer, contrary to good faith and fair dealing.

2. When assessing the unfairness of a contract term for the purposes of this Section, regard is to be had to:

(a) whether the trader complied with the duty of transparency set out in Article 82;
(b) the nature of what is to be provided under the contract;
(c) the circumstances prevailing during the conclusion of the contract;
(d) to the other contract terms; and
(e) to the terms of any other contract on which the contract depends.

Article 84   Contract terms which are always unfair

A contract term is always unfair for the purposes of this Section if its object or effect is to:

(a) exclude or limit the liability of the trader for death or personal injury caused to the consumer through an act or omission of the trader or of someone acting on behalf of the trader;
(b) exclude or limit the liability of the trader for any loss or damage to the consumer caused deliberately or as a result of gross negligence;
(c) limit the trader's obligation to be bound by commitments undertaken by its authorised agents or make its commitments subject to compliance with a particular condition the fulfilment of which depends exclusively on the trader;
(d) exclude or hinder the consumer's right to take legal action or exercise any other legal remedy, particularly by requiring the consumer to take disputes exclusively to an arbitration system not foreseen generally in legal provisions that apply to contracts between a trader and a consumer;
(e) confer exclusive jurisdiction for all disputes arising under the contract to a court for the place where the trader is domiciled unless the chosen court is also the court for the place where the consumer is domiciled;
(f) give the trader the exclusive right to determine whether the goods, digital content or related services supplied are in conformity with the contract or gives the trader the exclusive right to interpret any contract term;
(g) provide that the consumer is bound by the contract when the trader is not;
(h) require the consumer to use a more formal method for terminating the contract within the meaning of Article 8 than was used for conclusion of the contract;
(i) grant the trader a shorter notice period to terminate the contract than the one required of the consumer;
(j) oblige the consumer to pay for goods, digital content or related services not actually delivered, supplied or rendered;
(k) determine that non-individually negotiated contract terms within the meaning of Article 7 prevail or have preference over contract terms which have been individually negotiated.

Article 85   Contract terms which are presumed to be unfair

A contract term is presumed to be unfair for the purposes of this Section if its object or effect is to:

(a) restrict the evidence available to the consumer or impose on the consumer a burden of proof which should legally lie with the trader;

(b) inappropriately exclude or limit the remedies available to the consumer against the trader or a third party for non-performance by the trader of obligations under the contract;

(c) inappropriately exclude or limit the right to set-off claims that the consumer may have against the trader against what the consumer may owe to the trader;

(d) permit a trader to keep money paid by the consumer if the latter decides not to conclude the contract, or perform obligations under it, without providing for the consumer to receive compensation of an equivalent amount from the trader in the reverse situation;

(e) require a consumer who fails to perform obligations under the contract to pay a disproportionately high amount by way of damages or a stipulated payment for non-performance;

(f) entitle a trader to withdraw from or terminate the contract within the meaning of Article 8 on a discretionary basis without giving the same right to the consumer, or entitle a trader to keep money paid for related services not yet supplied in the case where the trader withdraws from or terminates the contract;

(g) enable a trader to terminate a contract of indeterminate duration without reasonable notice, except where there are serious grounds for doing so;

(h) automatically extend a contract of fixed duration unless the consumer indicates otherwise, in cases where contract terms provide for an unreasonably early deadline for giving notice;

(i) enable a trader to alter contract terms unilaterally without a valid reason which is specified in the contract; this does not affect contract terms under which a trader reserves the right to alter unilaterally the terms of a contract of indeterminate duration, provided that the trader is required to inform the consumer with reasonable notice, and that the consumer is free to terminate the contract at no cost to the consumer;

(j) enable a trader to alter unilaterally without a valid reason any characteristics of the goods, digital content or related services to be provided or any other features of performance;

(k) provide that the price of goods, digital content or related services is to be determined at the time of delivery or supply, or allow a trader to increase the price without giving the consumer the right to withdraw if the increased price is too high in relation to the price agreed at the conclusion of the contract; this does not affect price-indexation clauses, where lawful, provided that the method by which prices vary is explicitly described;

(l) oblige a consumer to perform all their obligations under the contract where the trader fails to perform its own;

(m) allow a trader to transfer its rights and obligations under the contract without the consumer's consent, unless it is to a subsidiary controlled by the trader, or as a result of a merger or a similar lawful company transaction, and such transfer is not likely to negatively affect any right of the consumer;

(n) allow a trader, where what has been ordered is unavailable, to supply an equivalent without having expressly informed the consumer of this possibility and of the fact that the trader must bear the cost of returning what the consumer has received under the contract if the consumer exercises a right to reject performance;

(o) allow a trader to reserve an unreasonably long or inadequately specified period to accept or refuse an offer;

(p) allow a trader to reserve an unreasonably long or inadequately specified period to perform the obligations under the contract;

(q) inappropriately exclude or limit the remedies available to the consumer against the trader or the defences available to the consumer against claims by the trader;

(r) subject performance of obligations under the contract by the trader, or subject other ben-eficial effects of the contract for the consumer, to particular formalities that are not legally required and are unreasonable;

(s) require from the consumer excessive advance payments or excessive guarantees of per-formance of obligations;

(t) unjustifiably prevent the consumer from obtaining supplies or repairs from third party sources;

(u) unjustifiably bundle the contract with another one with the trader, a subsidiary of the trader, or a third party, in a way that cannot be expected by the consumer;

(v) impose an excessive burden on the consumer in order to terminate a contract of indeter-minate duration;

(w) make the initial contract period, or any renewal period, of a contract for the protracted provision of goods, digital content or related services longer than one year, unless the consumer may terminate the contract at any time with a termination period of no more than 30 days.

Section 3 Unfair contract terms in contracts between traders

Article 86   Meaning of "unfair" in contracts between traders

1. In a contract between traders, a contract term is unfair for the purposes of this Section only if:
   (a) it forms part of not individually negotiated terms within the meaning of Article 7; and
   (b) it is of such a nature that its use grossly deviates from good commercial practice, contrary to good faith and fair dealing.

2. When assessing the unfairness of a contract term for the purposes of this Section, regard is to be had to:
   (a) the nature of what is to be provided under the contract;
   (b) the circumstances prevailing during the conclusion of the contract;
   (c) the other contract terms; and
   (d) the terms of any other contract on which the contract depends.

PART IV OBLIGATIONS AND REMEDIES OF THE PARTIES TO A SALES CONTRACT OR A CONTRACT FOR THE SUPPLY OF DIGITAL CONTENT

Chapter 9 General provisions

Article 87   Non-performance and fundamental non-performance

1. Non-performance of an obligation is any failure to perform that obligation, whether or not the failure is excused, and includes:
   (a) non-delivery or delayed delivery of the goods;
   (b) non-supply or delayed supply of the digital content;
   (c) delivery of goods which are not in conformity with the contract;
   (d) supply of digital content which is not in conformity with the contract;
   (e) non-payment or late payment of the price; and
   (f) any other purported performance which is not in conformity with the contract.

2. Non-performance of an obligation by one party is fundamental if:
   (a) it substantially deprives the other party of what that party was entitled to expect under the contract, unless at the time of conclusion of the contract the non-performing party did not foresee and could not be expected to have foreseen that result; or
   (b) it is of such a nature as to make it clear that the non-performing party's future performance cannot be relied on.

Article 88   Excused non-performance

1. A party's non-performance of an obligation is excused if it is due to an impediment beyond that party's control and if that party could not be expected to have taken the impediment into account at the time of the conclusion of the contract, or to have avoided or overcome the impediment or its consequences.

2. Where the impediment is only temporary the non-performance is excused for the period during which the impediment exists. However, if the delay amounts to a fundamental non-performance, the other party may treat it as such.

3. The party who is unable to perform has a duty to ensure that notice of the impediment and of its effect on the ability to perform reaches the other party without undue delay after the first party becomes, or could be expected to have become, aware of these circumstances. The other party is entitled to damages for any loss resulting from the breach of this duty.

Article 89   Change of circumstances

1. A party must perform its obligations even if performance has become more onerous, whether because the cost of performance has increased or because the value of what is to be received in return has diminished. Where performance becomes excessively onerous because of an exceptional change of circumstances, the parties have a duty to enter into negotiations with a view to adapting or terminating the contract.

2. If the parties fail to reach an agreement within a reasonable time, then, upon request by either party a court may:
    (a) adapt the contract in order to bring it into accordance with what the parties would reasonably have agreed at the time of contracting if they had taken the change of circumstances into account; or
    (b) terminate the contract within the meaning of Article 8 at a date and on terms to be determined by the court.

3. Paragraphs 1 and 2 apply only if:
    (a) the change of circumstances occurred after the time when the contract was concluded;
    (b) the party relying on the change of circumstances did not at that time take into account, and could not be expected to have taken into account, the possibility or scale of that change of circumstances; and
    (c) the aggrieved party did not assume, and cannot reasonably be regarded as having assumed, the risk of that change of circumstances.

4. For the purpose of paragraphs 2 and 3 a 'court' includes an arbitral tribunal.

Article 90   Extended application of rules on payment and on goods or digital content not accepted

1. Unless otherwise provided, the rules on payment of the price by the buyer in Chapter 12 apply with appropriate adaptations to other payments.

2. Article 97 applies with appropriate adaptations to other cases where a person is left in possession of goods or digital content because of a failure by another person to take them when bound to do so.

Chapter 10   The seller's obligations

Section 1   General provisions

Article 91   Main obligations of the seller

The seller of goods or the supplier of digital content (in this part referred to as 'the seller') must:
    (a) deliver the goods or supply the digital content;
    (b) transfer the ownership of the goods, including the tangible medium on which the digital content is supplied;
    (c) ensure that the goods or the digital content are in conformity with the contract;
    (d) ensure that the buyer has the right to use the digital content in accordance with the contract; and

(e) deliver such documents representing or relating to the goods or documents relating to the digital content as may be required by the contract.

Article 92   Performance by a third party

1. A seller may entrust performance to another person, unless personal performance by the seller is required by the contract terms.

2. A seller who entrusts performance to another person remains responsible for performance.

3. In relations between a trader and a consumer the parties may not, to the detriment of the consumer, exclude the application of paragraph (2) or derogate from or vary its effects.

Section 2 Delivery

Article 93   Place of delivery

1. Where the place of delivery cannot be otherwise determined, it is:
   (a) in the case of a consumer sales contract or a contract for the supply of digital content which is a distance or off-premises contract, or in which the seller has undertaken to arrange carriage to the buyer, the consumer's place of residence at the time of the conclusion of the contract;
   (b) in any other case,
      (i)   where the contract of sale involves carriage of the goods by a carrier or series of carriers, the nearest collection point of the first carrier;
      (ii) where the contract does not involve carriage, the seller's place of business at the time of conclusion of the contract.

2. If the seller has more than one place of business, the place of business for the purposes of point (b) of paragraph 1 is that which has the closest relationship to the obligation to deliver.

Article 94   Method of delivery

1. Unless agreed otherwise, the seller fulfils the obligation to deliver:
   (a) in the case of a consumer sales contract or a contract for the supply of digital content which is a distance or off-premises contract or in which the seller has undertaken to arrange carriage to the buyer, by transferring the physical possession or control of the goods or the digital content to the consumer;
   (b) in other cases in which the contract involves carriage of the goods by a carrier, by handing over the goods to the first carrier for transmission to the buyer and by handing over to the buyer any document necessary to enable the buyer to take over the goods from the carrier holding the goods; or
   (c) in cases that do not fall within points (a) or (b), by making the goods or the digital content, or where it is agreed that the seller need only deliver documents representing the goods, the documents, available to the buyer.

2. In points (a) and (c) of paragraph 1, any reference to the consumer or the buyer includes a third party, not being the carrier, indicated by the consumer or the buyer in accordance with the contract.

Article 95   Time of delivery

1. Where the time of delivery cannot be otherwise determined, the goods or the digital content must be delivered without undue delay after the conclusion of the contract.

2. In contracts between a trader and a consumer, unless agreed otherwise by the parties, the trader must deliver the goods or the digital content not later than 30 days from the conclusion of the contract.

Article 96   Seller's obligations regarding carriage of the goods

1. Where the contract requires the seller to arrange for carriage of the goods, the seller must conclude such contracts as are necessary for carriage to the place fixed by means of transportation appropriate in the circumstances and according to the usual terms for such transportation.

2. Where the seller, in accordance with the contract, hands over the goods to a carrier and if the goods are not clearly identified as the goods to be supplied under the contract by markings on the goods, by shipping documents or otherwise, the seller must give the buyer notice of the consignment specifying the goods.

3. Where the contract does not require the seller to effect insurance in respect of the carriage of the goods, the seller must, at the buyer's request, provide the buyer with all available information necessary to enable the buyer to effect such insurance.

Article 97   Goods or digital content not accepted by the buyer

1. A seller who is left in possession of the goods or the digital content because the buyer, when bound to do so, has failed to take delivery must take reasonable steps to protect and preserve them.

2. The seller is discharged from the obligation to deliver if the seller:
- (a) deposits the goods or the digital content on reasonable terms with a third party to be held to the order of the buyer, and notifies the buyer of this; or
- (b) sells the goods or the digital content on reasonable terms after notice to the buyer, and pays the net proceeds to the buyer.

3. The seller is entitled to be reimbursed or to retain out of the proceeds of sale any costs reasonably incurred.

Article 98   Effect on passing of risk

The effect of delivery on the passing of risk is regulated by Chapter 14.

Section 3 Conformity of the goods and digital content

Article 99   Conformity with the contract

1. In order to conform with the contract, the goods or digital content must:
- (a) be of the quantity, quality and description required by the contract;
- (b) be contained or packaged in the manner required by the contract; and
- (c) be supplied along with any accessories, installation instructions or other instructions required by the contract.

2. In order to conform with the contract the goods or digital content must also meet the requirements of Articles 100, 101 and 102, save to the extent that the parties have agreed otherwise.

3. In a consumer sales contract, any agreement derogating from the requirements of Articles 100, 102 and 103 to the detriment of the consumer is valid only if, at the time of the conclusion of the contract, the consumer knew of the specific condition of the goods or the digital content and accepted the goods or the digital content as being in conformity with the contract when concluding it.

4. In a consumer sales contract, the parties may not, to the detriment of the consumer, exclude the application of paragraph 3 or derogate from or vary its effects.

Article 100   Criteria for conformity of the goods and digital content

The goods or digital content must:
- (a) be fit for any particular purpose made known to the seller at the time of the conclusion of the contract, except where the circumstances show that the buyer did not rely, or that it was unreasonable for the buyer to rely, on the seller's skill and judgement;
- (b) be fit for the purposes for which goods or digital content of the same description would ordinarily be used;
- (c) possess the qualities of goods or digital content which the seller held out to the buyer as a sample or model;
- (d) be contained or packaged in the manner usual for such goods or, where there is no such manner, in a manner adequate to preserve and protect the goods;
- (e) be supplied along with such accessories, installation instructions or other instructions as the buyer may expect to receive;
- (f) possess the qualities and performance capabilities indicated in any pre-contractual statement which forms part of the contract terms by virtue of Article 69; and

(g) possess such qualities and performance capabilities as the buyer may expect. When determining what the consumer may expect of the digital content regard is to be had to whether or not the digital content was supplied in exchange for the payment of a price.

Article 101   Incorrect installation under a consumer sales contract

1. Where goods or digital content supplied under a consumer sales contract are incorrectly installed, any lack of conformity resulting from the incorrect installation is regarded as lack of conformity of the goods or the digital content if:

(a) the goods or the digital content were installed by the seller or under the seller's responsibility; or

(b) the goods or the digital content were intended to be installed by the consumer and the incorrect installation was due to a shortcoming in the installation instructions.

2. The parties may not, to the detriment of the consumer, exclude the application of this Article or derogate from or vary its effects.

Article 102   Third party rights or claims

1. The goods must be free from and the digital content must be cleared of any right or not obviously unfounded claim of a third party.

2. As regards rights or claims based on intellectual property, subject to paragraphs 3 and 4, the goods must be free from and the digital content must be cleared of any right or not obviously unfounded claim of a third party:

(a) under the law of the state where the goods or digital content will be used according to the contract or, in the absence of such an agreement, under the law of the state of the buyer's place of business or in contracts between a trader and a consumer the consumer's place of residence indicated by the consumer at the time of the conclusion of the contract; and

(b) which the seller knew of or could be expected to have known of at the time of the conclusion of the contract.

3. In contracts between businesses, paragraph 2 does not apply where the buyer knew or could be expected to have known of the rights or claims based on intellectual property at the time of the conclusion of the contract.

4. In contracts between a trader and a consumer, paragraph 2 does not apply where the consumer knew of the rights or claims based on intellectual property at the time of the conclusion of the contract.

5. In contracts between a trader and a consumer, the parties may not, to the detriment of the consumer, exclude the application of this Article or derogate from or vary its effects.

Article 103   Limitation on conformity of digital content

Digital content is not considered as not conforming to the contract for the sole reason that updated digital content has become available after the conclusion of the contract.

Article 104   Buyer's knowledge of lack of conformity in a contract between traders

In a contract between traders, the seller is not liable for any lack of conformity of the goods if, at the time of the conclusion of the contract, the buyer knew or could not have been unaware of the lack of conformity.

Article 105   Relevant time for establishing conformity

1. The seller is liable for any lack of conformity which exists at the time when the risk passes to the buyer under Chapter 14.

2. In a consumer sales contract, any lack of conformity which becomes apparent within six months of the time when risk passes to the buyer is presumed to have existed at that time unless this is incompatible with the nature of the goods or digital content or with the nature of the lack of conformity.

3. In a case governed by point (a) of Article 101(1) any reference in paragraphs 1 or 2 of this Article to the time when risk passes to the buyer is to be read as a reference to the time when the

installation is complete. In a case governed by point (b) of Article 101(1) it is to be read as a reference to the time when the consumer had reasonable time for the installation.

4. Where the digital content must be subsequently updated by the trader, the trader must ensure that the digital content remains in conformity with the contract throughout the duration of the contract.

5. In a contract between a trader and a consumer, the parties may not, to the detriment of a consumer, exclude the application of this Article or derogate from or vary its effect.

Chapter 11 The buyer's remedies

Section 1 General provisions

Article 106   Overview of buyer's remedies

1. In the case of non-performance of an obligation by the seller, the buyer may do any of the following:
   - (a) require performance, which includes specific performance, repair or replacement of the goods or digital content, under Section 3 of this Chapter;
   - (b) withhold the buyer's own performance under Section 4 of this Chapter;
   - (c) terminate the contract under Section 5 of this Chapter and claim the return of any price already paid, under Chapter 17;
   - (d) reduce the price under Section 6 of this Chapter; and
   - (e) claim damages under Chapter 16.

2. If the buyer is a trader:
   - (a) the buyer's rights to exercise any remedy except withholding of performance are subject to cure by the seller as set out in Section 2 of this Chapter; and
   - (b) the buyer's rights to rely on lack of conformity are subject to the requirements of examination and notification set out in Section 7 of this Chapter.

3. If the buyer is a consumer:
   - (a) the buyer's rights are not subject to cure by the seller; and
   - (b) the requirements of examination and notification set out in Section 7 of this Chapter do not apply.

4. If the seller's non-performance is excused, the buyer may resort to any of the remedies referred to in paragraph 1 except requiring performance and damages.

5. The buyer may not resort to any of the remedies referred to in paragraph 1 to the extent that the buyer caused the seller's non-performance.

6. Remedies which are not incompatible may be cumulated.

Article 107   Limitation of remedies for digital content not supplied in exchange for a price

Where digital content is not supplied in exchange for the payment of a price, the buyer may not resort to the remedies referred to in points (a) to (d) of Article 106(1) . The buyer may only claim damages under point (e) of Article 106 (1) for loss or damage caused to the buyer's property, including hardware, software and data, by the lack of conformity of the supplied digital content, except for any gain of which the buyer has been deprived by that damage.

Article 108   Mandatory nature

In a contract between a trader and a consumer, the parties may not, to the detriment of the consumer, exclude the application of this Chapter, or derogate from or vary its effect before the lack of conformity is brought to the trader's attention by the consumer.

Section 2 Cure by the seller

Article 109   Cure by the seller

1. A seller who has tendered performance early and who has been notified that the performance is not in conformity with the contract may make a new and conforming tender if that can be done within the time allowed for performance.

2. In cases not covered by paragraph 1 a seller who has tendered a performance which is not in conformity with the contract may, without undue delay on being notified of the lack of conformity, offer to cure it at its own expense.

3. An offer to cure is not precluded by notice of termination.

4. The buyer may refuse an offer to cure only if:

   (a) cure cannot be effected promptly and without significant inconvenience to the buyer;
   (b) the buyer has reason to believe that the seller's future performance cannot be relied on; or
   (c) delay in performance would amount to a fundamental non-performance.

5. The seller has a reasonable period of time to effect cure.

6. The buyer may withhold performance pending cure, but the rights of the buyer which are inconsistent with allowing the seller a period of time to effect cure are suspended until that period has expired.

7. Notwithstanding cure, the buyer retains the right to claim damages for delay as well as for any harm caused or not prevented by the cure.

Section 3 Requiring performance

Article 110   Requiring performance of seller's obligations

1. The buyer is entitled to require performance of the seller's obligations.

2. The performance which may be required includes the remedying free of charge of a performance which is not in conformity with the contract.

3. Performance cannot be required where:

   (a) performance would be impossible or has become unlawful; or
   (b) the burden or expense of performance would be disproportionate to the benefit that the buyer would obtain.

Article 111   Consumer's choice between repair and replacement

1. Where, in a consumer sales contract, the trader is required to remedy a lack of conformity pursuant to Article 110(2) the consumer may choose between repair and replacement unless the option chosen would be unlawful or impossible or, compared to the other option available, would impose costs on the seller that would be disproportionate taking into account:

   (a) the value the goods would have if there were no lack of conformity;
   (b) the significance of the lack of conformity; and
   (c) whether the alternative remedy could be completed without significant inconvenience to the consumer.

2. If the consumer has required the remedying of the lack of conformity by repair or replacement pursuant to paragraph 1, the consumer may resort to other remedies only if the trader has not completed repair or replacement within a reasonable time, not exceeding 30 days. However, the consumer may withhold performance during that time.

Article 112   Return of replaced item

1. Where the seller has remedied the lack of conformity by replacement, the seller has a right and an obligation to take back the replaced item at the seller's expense.

2. The buyer is not liable to pay for any use made of the replaced item in the period prior to the replacement.

Section 4 Withholding performance of buyer's obligations

Article 113   Right to withhold performance

1. A buyer who is to perform at the same time as, or after, the seller performs has a right to withhold performance until the seller has tendered performance or has performed.

2. A buyer who is to perform before the seller performs and who reasonably believes that there will be non-performance by the seller when the seller's performance becomes due may withhold performance for as long as the reasonable belief continues.

3. The performance which may be withheld under this Article is the whole or part of the performance to the extent justified by the non-performance. Where the seller's obligations are to be performed in separate parts or are otherwise divisible, the buyer may withhold performance only in relation to that part which has not been performed, unless the seller's non-performance is such as to justify withholding the buyer's performance as a whole.

Section 5 Termination

Article 114   Termination for non-performance

1. A buyer may terminate the contract within the meaning of Article 8 if the seller's non-performance under the contract is fundamental within the meaning of Article 87 (2).

2. In a consumer sales contract and a contract for the supply of digital content between a trader and a consumer, where there is a non-performance because the goods do not conform to the contract, the consumer may terminate the contract unless the lack of conformity is insignificant.

Article 115   Termination for delay in delivery after notice fixing additional time for performance

1. A buyer may terminate the contract in a case of delay in delivery which is not in itself fundamental if the buyer gives notice fixing an additional period of time of reasonable length for performance and the seller does not perform within that period.

2. The additional period referred to in paragraph 1 is taken to be of reasonable length if the seller does not object to it without undue delay.

3. Where the notice provides for automatic termination if the seller does not perform within the period fixed by the notice, termination takes effect after that period without further notice.

Article 116   Termination for anticipated non-performance

A buyer may terminate the contract before performance is due if the seller has declared, or it is otherwise clear, that there will be a non-performance, and if the non-performance would be such as to justify termination.

Article 117   Scope of right to terminate

1. Where the seller's obligations under the contract are to be performed in separate parts or are otherwise divisible, then if there is a ground for termination under this Section of a part to which a part of the price can be apportioned, the buyer may terminate only in relation to that part.

2. Paragraph 1 does not apply if the buyer cannot be expected to accept performance of the other parts or the non-performance is such as to justify termination of the contract as a whole.

3. Where the seller's obligations under the contract are not divisible or a part of the price cannot be apportioned, the buyer may terminate only if the non-performance is such as to justify termination of the contract as a whole.

Article 118   Notice of termination

A right to terminate under this Section is exercised by notice to the seller.

Article 119   Loss of right to terminate

1. The buyer loses the right to terminate under this Section if notice of termination is not given within a reasonable time from when the right arose or the buyer became, or could be expected to have become, aware of the non-performance, whichever is later.

2. Paragraph 1 does not apply:

    (a) where the buyer is a consumer; or

    (b) where no performance at all has been tendered.

Section 6 Price reduction

Article 120   Right to reduce price

1. A buyer who accepts a performance not conforming to the contract may reduce the price. The reduction is to be proportionate to the decrease in the value of what was received in performance at the time performance was made compared to the value of what would have been received by a conforming performance.

2. A buyer who is entitled to reduce the price under paragraph 1 and who has already paid a sum exceeding the reduced price may recover the excess from the seller.

3. A buyer who reduces the price cannot also recover damages for the loss thereby compensated but remains entitled to damages for any further loss suffered.

Section 7 Requirements of examination and notification in a contract between traders

Article 121   Examination of the goods in contracts between traders

1. In a contract between traders the buyer is expected to examine the goods, or cause them to be examined, within as short a period as is reasonable not exceeding 14 days from the date of delivery of the goods, supply of digital content or provision of related services.

2. If the contract involves carriage of the goods, examination may be deferred until after the goods have arrived at their destination.

3. If the goods are redirected in transit, or redispatched by the buyer before the buyer has had a reasonable opportunity to examine them, and at the time of the conclusion of the contract the seller knew or could be expected to have known of the possibility of such redirection or redispatch, examination may be deferred until after the goods have arrived at the new destination.

Article 122   Requirement of notification of lack of conformity in sales contracts between traders

1. In a contract between traders the buyer may not rely on a lack of conformity if the buyer does not give notice to the seller within a reasonable time specifying the nature of the lack of conformity.

The time starts to run when the goods are supplied or when the buyer discovers or could be expected to discover the lack of conformity, whichever is later.

2. The buyer loses the right to rely on a lack of conformity if the buyer does not give the seller notice of the lack of conformity within two years from the time at which the goods were actually handed over to the buyer in accordance with the contract.

3. Where the parties have agreed that the goods must remain fit for a particular purpose or for their ordinary purpose during a fixed period of time, the period for giving notice under paragraph 2 does not expire before the end of the agreed period.

4. Paragraph 2 does not apply in respect of the third party claims or rights referred to in Article 102.

5. The buyer does not have to notify the seller that not all the goods have been delivered if the buyer has reason to believe that the remaining goods will be delivered.

6. The seller is not entitled to rely on this Article if the lack of conformity relates to facts of which the seller knew or could be expected to have known and which the seller did not disclose to the buyer.

Chapter 12 The buyer's obligations

Section 1 General provisions

Article 123   Main obligations of the buyer

1. The buyer must:
   (a) pay the price;
   (b) take delivery of the goods or the digital content; and
   (c) take over documents representing or relating to the goods or documents relating to digital content as may be required by the contract.

2. Point (a) of paragraph 1 does not apply to contracts for the supply of digital content where the digital content is not supplied in exchange for the payment of a price.

Section 2 Payment of the price

Article 124   Means of payment

1. Payment shall be made by the means of payment indicated by the contract terms or, if there is no such indication, by any means used in the ordinary course of business at the place of payment taking into account the nature of the transaction.

2. A seller who accepts a cheque or other order to pay or a promise to pay is presumed to do so only on condition that it will be honoured. The seller may enforce the original obligation to pay if the order or promise is not honoured.

3. The buyer's original obligation is extinguished if the seller accepts a promise to pay from a third party with whom the seller has a pre-existing arrangement to accept the third party's promise as a means of payment.

4. In a contract between a trader and a consumer, the consumer is not liable, in respect of the use of a given means of payment, for fees that exceed the cost borne by the trader for the use of such means.

Article 125   Place of payment

1. Where the place of payment cannot otherwise be determined it is the seller's place of business at the time of conclusion of the contract.

2. If the seller has more than one place of business, the place of payment is the place of business of the seller which has the closest relationship to the obligation to pay.

Article 126   Time of payment

1. Payment of the price is due at the moment of delivery.

2. The seller may reject an offer to pay before payment is due if it has a legitimate interest in so doing.

Article 127   Payment by a third party

1. A buyer may entrust payment to another person. A buyer who entrusts payment to another person remains responsible for payment.

2. The seller cannot refuse payment by a third party if:
   (a) the third party acts with the assent of the buyer; or
   (b) the third party has a legitimate interest in paying and the buyer has failed to pay or it is clear that the buyer will not pay at the time that payment is due.

3. Payment by a third party in accordance with paragraphs 1 or 2 discharges the buyer from liability to the seller.

4. Where the seller accepts payment by a third party in circumstances not covered by paragraphs 1 or 2 the buyer is discharged from liability to the seller but the seller is liable to the buyer for any loss caused by that acceptance.

Article 128   Imputation of payment

1. Where a buyer has to make several payments to the seller and the payment made does not suffice to cover all of them, the buyer may at the time of payment notify the seller of the obligation to which the payment is to be imputed.

2. If the buyer does not make a notification under paragraph 1 the seller may, by notifying the buyer within a reasonable time, impute the performance to one of the obligations.

3. An imputation under paragraph 2 is not effective if it is to an obligation which is not yet due or is disputed.

4. In the absence of an effective imputation by either party, the payment is imputed to that obligation which satisfies one of the following criteria in the sequence indicated:

    (a) the obligation which is due or is the first to fall due;

    (b) the obligation for which the seller has no or the least security;

    (c) the obligation which is the most burdensome for the buyer;

    (d) the obligation which arose first.

If none of those criteria applies, the payment is imputed proportionately to all the obligations.

5. The payment may be imputed under paragraph 2, 3 or 4 to an obligation which is unenforceable as a result of prescription only if there is no other obligation to which the payment could be imputed in accordance with those paragraphs.

6. In relation to any one obligation a payment by the buyer is to be imputed, first, to expenses, secondly, to interest, and thirdly, to principal, unless the seller makes a different imputation.

Section 3 Taking delivery

Article 129   Taking delivery

The buyer fulfils the obligation to take delivery by:

    (a) doing all the acts which could be expected in order to enable the seller to perform the obligation to deliver; and

    (b) taking over the goods, or the documents representing the goods or digital content, as required by the contract.

Article 130   Early delivery and delivery of wrong quantity

1. If the seller delivers the goods or supplies the digital content before the time fixed, the buyer must take delivery unless the buyer has a legitimate interest in refusing to do so.

2. If the seller delivers a quantity of goods or digital content less than that provided for in the contract the buyer must take delivery unless the buyer has a legitimate interest in refusing to do so.

3. If the seller delivers a quantity of goods or digital content greater than that provided for by the contract, the buyer may retain or refuse the excess quantity.

4. If the buyer retains the excess quantity it is treated as having been supplied under the contract and must be paid for at the contractual rate.

5. In a consumer sales contract paragraph 4 does not apply if the buyer reasonably believes that the seller has delivered the excess quantity intentionally and without error, knowing that it had not been ordered.

6. This Article does not apply to contracts for the supply of digital content where the digital content is not supplied in exchange for the payment of a price.

Chapter 13 The seller's remedies

Section 1 General provisions

Article 131   Overview of seller's remedies

1. In the case of a non-performance of an obligation by the buyer, the seller may do any of the following:

    (a) require performance under Section 2 of this Chapter;

    (b) withhold the seller's own performance under Section 3 of this Chapter;

(c) terminate the contract under Section 4 of this Chapter; and

(d) claim interest on the price or damages under Chapter 16.

2. If the buyer's non-performance is excused, the seller may resort to any of the remedies referred to in paragraph 1 except requiring performance and damages.

3. The seller may not resort to any of the remedies referred to in paragraph 1 to the extent that the seller caused the buyer's non-performance.

4. Remedies which are not incompatible may be cumulated.

Section 2 Requiring performance

Article 132   Requiring performance of buyer's obligations

1. The seller is entitled to recover payment of the price when it is due, and to require performance of any other obligation undertaken by the buyer.

2. Where the buyer has not yet taken over the goods or the digital content and it is clear that the buyer will be unwilling to receive performance, the seller may nonetheless require the buyer to take delivery, and may recover the price, unless the seller could have made a reasonable substitute transaction without significant effort or expense.

Section 3 Withholding performance of seller's obligations

Article 133   Right to withhold performance

1. A seller who is to perform at the same time as, or after, the buyer performs has a right to withhold performance until the buyer has tendered performance or has performed.

2. A seller who is to perform before the buyer performs and who reasonably believes that there will be non-performance by the buyer when the buyer's performance becomes due may withhold performance for as long as the reasonable belief continues. However, the right to withhold performance is lost if the buyer gives an adequate assurance of due performance or provides adequate security.

3. The performance which may be withheld under this Article is the whole or part of the performance to the extent justified by the non-performance. Where the buyer's obligations are to be performed in separate parts or are otherwise divisible, the seller may withhold performance only in relation to that part which has not been performed, unless the buyer's non-performance is such as to justify withholding the seller's performance as a whole.

Section 4 Termination

Article 134   Termination for fundamental non-performance

A seller may terminate the contract within the meaning of Article 8 if the buyer's non-performance under the contract is fundamental within the meaning of Article 87 (2).

Article 135   Termination for delay after notice fixing additional time for performance

1. A seller may terminate in a case of delay in performance which is not in itself fundamental if the seller gives a notice fixing an additional period of time of reasonable length for performance and the buyer does not perform within that period.

2. The period is taken to be of reasonable length if the buyer does not object to it without undue delay. In relations between a trader and a consumer, the additional time for performance must not end before the 30 day period referred to Article 167(2).

3. Where the notice provides for automatic termination if the buyer does not perform within the period fixed by the notice, termination takes effect after that period without further notice.

4. In a consumer sales contract, the parties may not, to the detriment of the consumer, exclude the application of this Article or derogate from or vary its effects.

Article 136   Termination for anticipated non-performance

A seller may terminate the contract before performance is due if the buyer has declared, or it is otherwise clear, that there will be a non-performance, and if the non-performance would be fundamental.

Article 137   Scope of right to terminate

1. Where the buyer's obligations under the contract are to be performed in separate parts or are otherwise divisible, then if there is a ground for termination under this Section of a part which corresponds to a divisible part of the seller's obligations, the seller may terminate only in relation to that part.

2. Paragraph 1 does not apply if the non-performance is fundamental in relation to the contract as a whole.

3. Where the buyer's obligations under the contract are not to be performed in separate parts, the seller may terminate only if the non-performance is fundamental in relation to the contract as a whole.

Article 138   Notice of termination

A right to terminate the contract under this Section is exercised by notice to the buyer.

Article 139   Loss of right to terminate

1. Where performance has been tendered late or a tendered performance otherwise does not conform to the contract the seller loses the right to terminate under this Section unless notice of termination is given within a reasonable time from when the seller has become, or could be expected to have become, aware of the tender or the lack of conformity.

2. A seller loses a right to terminate by notice under Articles 136 unless the seller gives notice of termination within a reasonable time after the right has arisen.

3. Where the buyer has not paid the price or has not performed in some other way which is fundamental, the seller retains the right to terminate.

Chapter 14 Passing of risk

Section 1 General provisions

Article 140   Effect of passing of risk

Loss of, or damage to, the goods or the digital content after the risk has passed to the buyer does not discharge the buyer from the obligation to pay the price, unless the loss or damage is due to an act or omission of the seller.

Article 141   Identification of goods or digital content to contract

The risk does not pass to the buyer until the goods or the digital content are clearly identified as the goods or digital content to be supplied under the contract, whether by the initial agreement, by notice given to the buyer or otherwise.

Section 2 Passing of risk in consumer sales contracts

Article 142   Passing of risk in a consumer sales contract

1. In a consumer sales contract, the risk passes at the time when the consumer or a third party designated by the consumer, not being the carrier, has acquired the physical possession of the goods or the tangible medium on which the digital content is supplied.

2. In a contract for the supply of digital content not supplied on a tangible medium, the risk passes at the time when the consumer or a third party designated by the consumer for this purpose has obtained the control of the digital content.

3. Except where the contract is a distance or off-premises contract, paragraphs 1 and 2 do not apply where the consumer fails to perform the obligation to take over the goods or the digital content and the non-performance is not excused under Article 88. In this case, the risk passes at the time when the consumer, or the third party designated by the consumer, would have acquired the physical possession of the goods or obtained the control of the digital content if the obligation to take them over had been performed.

4. Where the consumer arranges the carriage of the goods or the digital content supplied on a tangible medium and that choice was not offered by the trader, the risk passes when the goods or the digital content supplied on a tangible medium are handed over to the carrier, without prejudice to the rights of the consumer against the carrier.

5. The parties may not, to the detriment of the consumer, exclude the application of this Article or derogate from or vary its effects.

Section 3 Passing of risk in contracts between traders

Article 143   Time when risk passes

1. In a contract between traders the risk passes when the buyer takes delivery of the goods or digital content or the documents representing the goods.

2. Paragraph 1 is subject to Articles 144, 145 and 146.

Article 144   Goods placed at buyer's disposal

1. If the goods or the digital content are placed at the buyer's disposal and the buyer is aware of this, the risk passes to the buyer at the time when the goods or digital content should have been taken over, unless the buyer was entitled to withhold taking of delivery pursuant to Article 113.

2. If the goods or the digital content are placed at the buyer's disposal at a place other than a place of business of the seller, the risk passes when delivery is due and the buyer is aware of the fact that the goods or digital content are placed at the buyer's disposal at that place.

Article 145   Carriage of the goods

1. This Article applies to a contract of sale which involves carriage of goods.

2. If the seller is not bound to hand over the goods at a particular place, the risk passes to the buyer when the goods are handed over to the first carrier for transmission to the buyer in accordance with the contract.

3. If the seller is bound to hand over the goods to a carrier at a particular place, the risk does not pass to the buyer until the goods are handed over to the carrier at that place.

4. The fact that the seller is authorised to retain documents controlling the disposition of the goods does not affect the passing of the risk.

Article 146   Goods sold in transit

1. This Article applies to a contract of sale which involves goods sold in transit.

2. The risk passes to the buyer as from the time the goods were handed over to the first carrier. However, if the circumstances so indicate, the risk passes to the buyer when the contract is concluded.

3. If at the time of the conclusion of the contract the seller knew or could be expected to have known that the goods had been lost or damaged and did not disclose this to the buyer, the loss or damage is at the risk of the seller.

PART V OBLIGATIONS AND REMEDIES OF THE PARTIES TO A RELATED SERVICE CONTRACT

Chapter 15 Obligations and remedies of the parties

Section 1 Application of certain general rules on sales contracts

Article 147   Application of certain general rules on sales contracts

1. The rules in Chapter 9 apply for the purposes of this Part.

2. Where a sales contract or a contract for the supply of digital content is terminated any related service contract is also terminated.

Section 2 Obligations of the service provider

Article 148   Obligation to achieve result and obligation of care and skill

1. The service provider must achieve any specific result required by the contract.

2. In the absence of any express or implied contractual obligation to achieve a specific result, the service provider must perform the related service with the care and skill which a reasonable service provider would exercise and in conformity with any statutory or other binding legal rules which are applicable to the related service.

3. In determining the reasonable care and skill required of the service provider, regard is to be had, among other things, to:

(a) the nature, the magnitude, the frequency and the foreseeability of the risks involved in the performance of the related service for the customer;

(b) if damage has occurred, the costs of any precautions which would have prevented that damage or similar damage from occurring; and

(c) the time available for the performance of the related service.

4. Where in a contract between a trader and a consumer the related service includes installation of the goods, the installation must be such that the installed goods conform to the contract as required by Article 101.

5. In relations between a trader and a consumer the parties may not, to the detriment of the consumer, exclude the application of paragraph 2 or derogate from or vary its effects.

Article 149   Obligation to prevent damage

The service provider must take reasonable precautions in order to prevent any damage to the goods or the digital content, or physical injury or any other loss or damage in the course of or as a consequence of the performance of the related service.

Article 150   Performance by a third party

1. A service provider may entrust performance to another person, unless personal performance by the service provider is required.

2. A service provider who entrusts performance to another person remains responsible for performance.

3. In relations between a trader and a consumer the parties may not, to the detriment of the consumer, exclude the application of paragraph 2 or derogate from or vary its effects.

Article 151   Obligation to provide invoice

Where a separate price is payable for the related service, and the price is not a lump sum agreed at the time of conclusion of the contract, the service provider must provide the customer with an invoice which explains, in a clear and intelligible way, how the price was calculated.

Article 152   Obligation to warn of unexpected or uneconomic cost

1. The service provider must warn the customer and seek the consent of the customer to proceed if:

(a) the cost of the related service would be greater than already indicated by the service provider to the customer; or

(b) the related service would cost more than the value of the goods or the digital content after the related service has been provided, so far as this is known to the service provider.

2. A service provider who fails to obtain the consent of the customer in accordance with paragraph 1 is not entitled to a price exceeding the cost already indicated or, as the case may be, the value of the goods or digital content after the related service has been provided.

Section 3 Obligations of the customer

Article 153   Payment of the price

1. The customer must pay any price that is payable for the related service in accordance with the contract.

2. The price is payable when the related service is completed and the object of the related service is made available to the customer.

Article 154   Provision of access

Where it is necessary for the service provider to obtain access to the customer's premises in order to perform the related service the customer must provide such access at reasonable hours.

Section 4   Remedies

Article 155   Remedies of the customer

1. In the case of non-performance of an obligation by the service provider, the customer has, with the adaptations set out in this Article, the same remedies as are provided for the buyer in Chapter 11, namely:

(a) to require specific performance;
(b) to withhold the customer's own performance;
(c) to terminate the contract;
(d) to reduce the price; and
(e) to claim damages.

2. Without prejudice to paragraph 3, the customer's remedies are subject to a right of the service provider to cure whether or not the customer is a consumer.

3. In the case of incorrect installation under a consumer sales contract as referred to in Article 101 the consumer's remedies are not subject to a right of the service provider to cure.

4. The customer, if a consumer, has the right to terminate the contract for any lack of conformity in the related service provided unless the lack of conformity isinsignificant.

5. Chapter 11 applies with the necessary adaptations, in particular:

(a) in relation to the right of the service provider to cure, in contracts between a trader and a consumer, the reasonable period under Article 109 (5) must not exceed 30 days;
(b) in relation to the remedying of a non-conforming performance Articles 111 and 112 do not apply; and
(c) Article 156 applies instead of Article 122.

Article 156   Requirement of notification of lack of conformity in related service contracts between traders

1. In a related service contract between traders, the customer may rely on a lack of conformity only if the customer gives notice to the service provider within a reasonable time specifying the nature of the lack of conformity.

The time starts to run when the related service is completed or when the customer discovers or could be expected to discover the lack of conformity, whichever is later.

2. The service provider is not entitled to rely on this Article if the lack of conformity relates to facts of which the service provider knew or could be expected to have known and which the service provider did not disclose to the customer.

Article 157   Remedies of the service provider

1. In the case of a non-performance by the customer, the service provider has, with the adaptations set out in paragraph 2, the same remedies as are provided for the seller in Chapter 13, namely:

(a) to require performance;
(b) to withhold the service provider's own performance;
(c) to terminate the contract; and
(d) to claim interest on the price or damages.

2. Chapter 13 applies with the necessary adaptations. In particular Article 158 applies instead of Article 132 (2).

Article 158   Customer's right to decline performance

1. The customer may at any time give notice to the service provider that performance, or further performance of the related service is no longer required.

2. Where notice is given under paragraph 1:

(a) the service provider no longer has the right or obligation to provide the related service; and

(b) the customer, if there is no ground for termination under any other provision, remains liable to pay the price less the expenses that the service provider has saved or could be expected to have saved by not having to complete performance.

3. In relations between a trader and a consumer the parties may not, to the detriment of the consumer, exclude the application of this Article or derogate from or vary its effects.

PART VI DAMAGES AND INTEREST

Chapter 16 Damages and interest

Section 1 Damages

Article 159   Right to damages

1. A creditor is entitled to damages for loss caused by the non-performance of an obligation by the debtor, unless the non-performance is excused.

2. The loss for which damages are recoverable includes future loss which the debtor could expect to occur.

Article 160   General measure of damages

The general measure of damages for loss caused by non-performance of an obligation is such sum as will put the creditor into the position in which the creditor would have been if the obligation had been duly performed, or, where that is not possible, as nearly as possible into that position. Such damages cover loss which the creditor has suffered and gain of which the creditor has been deprived.

Article 161   Foreseeability of loss

The debtor is liable only for loss which the debtor foresaw or could be expected to have foreseen at the time when the contract was concluded as a result of the non-performance.

Article 162   Loss attributable to creditor

The debtor is not liable for loss suffered by the creditor to the extent that the creditor contributed to the non-performance or its effects.

Article 163   Reduction of loss

1. The debtor is not liable for loss suffered by the creditor to the extent that the creditor could have reduced the loss by taking reasonable steps.

2. The creditor is entitled to recover any expenses reasonably incurred in attempting to reduce the loss.

Article 164   Substitute transaction

A creditor who has terminated a contract in whole or in part and has made a substitute transaction within a reasonable time and in a reasonable manner may, in so far as it is entitled to damages, recover the difference between the value of what would have been payable under the terminated contract and the value of what is payable under the substitute transaction, as well as damages for any further loss.

Article 165   Current price

Where the creditor has terminated the contract and has not made a substitute transaction but there is a current price for the performance, the creditor may, in so far as entitled to damages, recover the difference between the contract price and the price current at the time of termination as well as damages for any further loss.

Section 2 *Interest on late payments: general provisions*

Article 166   Interest on late payments

1. Where payment of a sum of money is delayed, the creditor is entitled, without the need to give notice, to interest on that sum from the time when payment is due to the time of payment at the rate specified in paragraph 2.

2. The interest rate for delayed payment is:

(a) where the creditor's habitual residence is in a Member State whose currency is the euro or in a third country, the rate applied by the European Central Bank to its most recent main refinancing operation carried out before the first calendar day of the half-year in question, or the marginal interest rate resulting from variable-rate tender procedures for the most recent main refinancing operations of the European Central Bank, plus two percentage points;

(b) where the creditor's habitual residence is in a Member State whose currency is not the euro, the equivalent rate set by the national central bank of that Member State, plus two percentage points.

3. The creditor may recover damages for any further loss.

Article 167   Interest when the debtor is a consumer

1. When the debtor is a consumer, interest for delay in payment is due at the rate provided in Article 166 only when non-performance is not excused.

2. Interest does not start to run until 30 days after the creditor has given notice to the debtor specifying the obligation to pay interest and its rate. Notice may be given before the date when payment is due.

3. A term of the contract which fixes a rate of interest higher than that provided in Article 166, or accrual earlier than the time specified in paragraph 2 of this Article is not binding to the extent that this would be unfair according to Article 83.

4. Interest for delay in payment cannot be added to capital in order to produce interest.

5. The parties may not, to the detriment of the consumer, exclude the application of this Article or derogate from or vary its effects.

Section 3 *Late payments by traders*

Article 168   Rate of interest and accrual

1. Where a trader delays the payment of a price due under a contract for the delivery of goods, supply of digital content or provision of related services without being excused by virtue of Article 88, interest is due at the rate specified in paragraph 5 of this Article.

2. Interest at the rate specified in paragraph 5 starts to run on the day which follows the date or the end of the period for payment provided in the contract. If there is no such date or period, interest at that rate starts to run:

(a) 30 days after the date when the debtor receives the invoice or an equivalent request for payment; or

(b) 30 days after the date of receipt of the goods, digital content or related services, if the date provided for in point (a) is earlier or uncertain, or if it is uncertain whether the debtor has received an invoice or equivalent request for payment.

3. Where conformity of goods, digital content or related services to the contract is to be ascertained by way of acceptance or examination, the 30 day period provided for in point (b) of paragraph 2 begins on the date of the acceptance or the date the examination procedure is finalised. The maximum duration of the examination procedure cannot exceed 30 days from the date of delivery of the goods, supply of digital content or provision of related services, unless the parties expressly agree otherwise and that agreement is not unfair according to Article 170.

4. The period for payment determined under paragraph 2 cannot exceed 60 days, unless the parties expressly agree otherwise and that agreement is not unfair according to Article 170.

5. The interest rate for delayed payment is:

    (a) where the creditor's habitual residence is in a Member State whose currecy is the euro or in a third country, the interest rate applied by the European Central Bank to its most recent main refinancing operation carried out before the first calendar day of the half-year in question, or the marginal interest rate resulting from variable-rate tender procedures for the most recent main refinancing operations of the European Central Bank, plus eight percentage points;

    (b) where the creditor's habitual residence is in a Member State whose currency is not the euro, the equivalent rate set by the national central bank of that Member State, plus eight percentage points.

6. The creditor may recover damages for any further loss.

Article 169   Compensation for recovery costs

1. Where interest is payable in accordance with Article 168, the creditor is entitled to obtain from the debtor, as a minimum, a fixed sum of EUR 40 or the equivalent sum in the currency agreed for the contract price as compensation for the creditor's recovery costs.

2. The creditor is entitled to obtain from the debtor reasonable compensation for any recovery costs exceeding the fixed sum referred to in paragraph 1 and incurred due to the debtor's late payment.

Article 170   Unfair contract terms relating to interest for late payment

1. A contract term relating to the date or the period for payment, the rate of interest for late payment or the compensation for recovery costs is not binding to the extent that the term is unfair. A term is unfair if it grossly deviates from good commercial practice, contrary to good faith and fair dealing, taking into account all circumstances of the case, including the nature of the goods, digital content or related service.

2. For the purpose of paragraph 1, a contract term providing for a time or period for payment or a rate of interest less favourable to the creditor than the time, period or rate specified in Articles 167 or 168, or a term providing for an amount of compensation for recovery costs lower than the amount specified in Article 169 is presumed to be unfair.

3. For the purpose of paragraph 1, a contract term excluding interest for late payment or compensation for recovery costs is always unfair.

Article 171   Mandatory nature

The parties may not exclude the application of this Section or derogate from or vary its effects.

PART VII RESTITUTION

Chapter 17 Restitution

Article 172   Restitution on avoidance or termination

1. Where a contract is avoided or terminated by either party, each party is obliged to return what that party ("the recipient") has received from the other party.

2. The obligation to return what was received includes any natural and legal fruits derived from what was received.

3. On the termination of a contract for performance in instalments or parts, the return of what was received is not required in relation to any instalment or part where the obligations on both sides have been fully performed, or where the price for what has been done remains payable under Article 8 (2), unless the nature of the contract is such that part performance is of no value to one of the parties.

Article 173   Payment for monetary value

1. Where what was received, including fruits where relevant, cannot be returned, or, in a case of digital content whether or not it was supplied on a tangible medium, the recipient must pay its

monetary value. Where the return is possible but would cause unreasonable effort or expense, the recipient may choose to pay the monetary value, provided that this would not harm the other party's proprietary interests.

2. The monetary value of goods is the value that they would have had at the date when payment of the monetary value is to be made if they had been kept by the recipient without destruction or damage until that date.

3. Where a related service contract is avoided or terminated by the customer after the related service has been performed or partly performed, the monetary value of what was received is the amount the customer saved by receiving the related service.

4. In a case of digital content the monetary value of what was received is the amount the consumer saved by making use of the digital content.

5. Where the recipient has obtained a substitute in money or in kind in exchange for goods or digital content when the recipient knew or could be expected to have known of the ground for avoidance or termination, the other party may choose to claim the substitute or the monetary value of the substitute. A recipient who has obtained a substitute in money or kind in exchange for goods or digital content when the recipient did not know and could not be expected to have known of the ground for avoidance or termination may choose to return the monetary value of the substitute or the substitute.

6. In the case of digital content which is not supplied in exchange for the payment of a price, no restitution will be made.

Article 174   Payment for use and interest on money received

1. A recipient who has made use of goods must pay the other party the monetary value of that use for any period where:
   (a) the recipient caused the ground for avoidance or termination;
   (b) the recipient, prior to the start of that period, was aware of the ground for avoidance or termination; or
   (c) having regard to the nature of the goods, the nature and amount of the use and the availability of remedies other than termination, it would be inequitable to allow the recipient the free use of the goods for that period.

2. A recipient who is obliged to return money must pay interest, at the rate stipulated in Article 166, where:
   (a) the other party is obliged to pay for use; or
   (b) the recipient gave cause for the contract to be avoided because of fraud, threats and unfair exploitation.

3. For the purposes of this Chapter, a recipient is not obliged to pay for use of goods received or interest on money received in any circumstances other than those set out in paragraphs 1 and 2.

Article 175   Compensation for expenditure

1. Where a recipient has incurred expenditure on goods or digital content, the recipient is entitled to compensation to the extent that the expenditure benefited the other party provided that the expenditure was made when the recipient did not know and could not be expected to know of the ground for avoidance or termination.

2. A recipient who knew or could be expected to know of the ground for avoidance or termination is entitled to compensation only for expenditure that was necessary to protect the goods or the digital content from being lost or diminished in value, provided that the recipient had no opportunity to ask the other party for advice.

Article 176   Equitable modification

Any obligation to return or to pay under this Chapter may be modified to the extent that its performance would be grossly inequitable, taking into account in particular whether the party did not cause, or lacked knowledge of, the ground for avoidance or termination.

Article 177 Mandatory nature

In relations between a trader and a consumer the parties may not, to the detriment of the consumer, exclude the application of this Chapter or derogate from or vary its effects.

PART VIII PRESCRIPTION

Chapter 18 Prescription

[*Arts 178–186 omitted.*]

Appendix 1 Model instructions on withdrawal

Right of withdrawal

You have the right to withdraw from this contract within 14 days without giving any reason.

The withdrawal period expires after 14 days from the day 1.

To exercise the right of withdrawal, you must inform us ([2]) of your decision to withdraw from this contract by a clear statement (e.g. a letter sent by post, fax or e-mail). You may use the attached model withdrawal form, but it is not obligatory. [3]

To meet the withdrawal deadline, it is sufficient for you to send your communication concerning your exercise of the right of withdrawal before the withdrawal period has expired.

Effects of withdrawal

If you withdraw from this contract, we will reimburse all payments received from you, including the costs of delivery (with the exception of the supplementary costs resulting from your choice of a type of delivery other than the least expensive type of standard delivery offered by us), without undue delay and in any event not later than 14 days from the day on which we are informed about your decision to withdraw from this contract. We will carry out such reimbursement using the same means of payment as you used for the initial transaction, unless you have expressly agreed otherwise; in any event, you will not incur any fees as a result of such reimbursement.[4]

[5]

[6]

Instructions for completion:

[1] Insert one of the following texts between inverted commas here:

   a) in the case of a related service contract or a contract for the supply of water, gas or electricity, where they are not put up for sale in a limited volume or set quantity, of district heating or of digital content which is not supplied on a tangible medium: "of the conclusion of the contract.";

   b) in the case of a sales contract: "on which you acquire, or a third party other than the carrier and indicated by you acquires, physical possession of the goods.";

   c) in the case of a contract relating to multiple goods ordered by the consumer in one order and delivered separately: "on which you acquire, or a third party other than the carrier and indicated by you acquires, physical possession of the last good.";

   d) in the case of a contract relating to delivery of a good consisting of multiple lots or pieces: "on which you acquire, or a third party other than the carrier and indicated by you acquires, physical possession of the last lot or piece.";

   e) in the case of a contract for regular delivery of goods during a defined period of time: "on which you acquire, or a third party other than the carrier and indicated by you acquires, physical possession of the first good.".

[2] Insert your name, geographical address and, where available, your telephone number, fax number and e-mail address.

[3] If you give the option to the consumer to electronically fill in and submit information about his or her withdrawal from the contract on your website, insert the following: "You can also electronically fill in and submit the model withdrawal form or any other clear statement on our website [insert

internet address]. If you use this option, we will communicate to you an acknowledgement of receipt of such a withdrawal on a durable medium (e.g. by e-mail) without delay."

4 In the case of sales contracts in which you have not offered to collect the goods in the event of withdrawal insert the following: "We may withhold reimbursement until we have received the goods back or you have supplied evidence of having sent back the goods, whichever is the earliest".

5 If the consumer has received goods in connection with the contract, insert the following:

    a insert:
-    "We will collect the goods."; or
-    "You shall send back the goods or hand them over to us or ____ [insert the name and geographical address, where applicable, of the person authorised by you to receive the goods], without undue delay and in any event not later than 14 days from the day on which you communicate your withdrawal from this contract to us. The deadline is met if you send back the goods before the period of 14 days has expired."

    b insert either:
-    "We will bear the cost of returning the goods."; or
-    "You will have to bear the direct cost of returning the goods."; or
-    If, in a distance contract, you do not offer to bear the cost of returning the goods and the goods, by their nature, cannot normally be returned by post: "You will have to bear the direct cost of returning the goods, ___ EUR [insert the amount]."; or if the cost of returning the goods cannot reasonably be calculated in advance: "You will have to bear the direct cost of returning the goods. The cost is estimated to a maximum of approximately ___ EUR [insert the amount]"; or
-    If, in an off-premises contract, the goods, by their nature, cannot normally be returned by post and have been delivered to the consumer's home at the time of the conclusion of the contract: "We will collect the goods at our own expense."

    c "You are only liable for any diminished value of the goods resulting from the handling other than what is necessary to establish the nature, characteristics and functioning of the goods."

6 In the case of a contract for the provision of related services insert the following: "If you requested to begin the performance of related services during the withdrawal period, you shall pay us an amount which is in proportion to what has been provided until you have communicated us your withdrawal from this contract, in comparison with the full coverage of the contract.".

Appendix 2 Model withdrawal form

(complete and return this form only if you wish to withdraw from the contract)
- To [here the trader's name, geographical address and, where available, his fax number and e-mail address are to be inserted by the trader]:
- I/We* hereby give notice that I/We* withdraw from my/our* contract of sale of the following goods*/for the supply of the following digital content/for the provision of the following related service*
- Ordered on*/received on*
- Name of consumer(s)
- Address of consumer(s)
- Signature of consumer(s) (only if this form is notified on paper)
- Date
    * Delete as appropriate.

ANNEX II STANDARD INFORMATION NOTICE

The contract you are about to conclude will be governed by the Common European Sales Law, which is an alternative system of national contract law available to consumers in cross-border situations.

These common rules are identical throughout the European Union, and have been designed to provide consumers with a high level of protection.

These rules only apply if you mark your agreement that the contract is governed by the Common European Sales Law.

You may also have agreed to a contract on the telephone or in any other way (such as by SMS) that did not allow you to get this notice beforehand. In this case the contract will only become valid after you have received this notice and confirmed your consent.

Your core rights are described below.

THE COMMON EUROPEAN SALES LAW: SUMMARY OF KEY CONSUMER RIGHTS

Your rights before signing the contract

The trader has to give you the **important information on the contract**, for instance on the product and its price including all taxes and charges and his contact details. The information has to be more detailed when you buy something outside the trader's shop or if you do not meet the trader personally at all, for instance if you buy online or by telephone. You are entitled to damages if this information is incomplete or wrong.

Your rights after signing the contract

In most cases you have 14 days to **withdraw from the purchase if you bought the goods** outside the trader's shop or if you have not met the trader up to the time of the purchase (for instance if you bought online or by telephone). The trader must provide you with information and a Model withdrawal form.[1] If the trader has not done so, you can cancel the contract within one year.

What **can you do when products are faulty or not delivered as agreed**? You are entitled to choose between: 1) having the product delivered 2) replaced or 3) repaired. 4) Ask for a price reduction. 5) You can cancel the contract, return the product and get a refund, except if the defect is very small. 6) You can claim damages for your loss. You do not have to pay the price until you get the product without defects.

If the trader has not performed a related *service* as promised in the contract, you have similar rights. However, after you have complained to the trader, he normally has the right to first try to do the job correctly. Only if the trader fails again you have a choice between 1) asking the trader again to provide the related service, 2) not paying the price until you get the related service supplied correctly, 3) requesting a price reduction or 4) claiming damages. 5) You can also cancel the contract and get a refund, except if the failure in providing the related service is very small. **Period to claim your rights when products are faulty or not delivered as agreed**: You have 2 years to claim your rights after you realise or should have realised that the trader has not done something as agreed in the contract. Where such problems become apparent very late, the last possible moment for you to make such a claim is 10 years from the moment the trader had to deliver the goods, supply the digital content or provide the related service.

Unfair terms protection: Trader's standard contract terms which are unfair are not legally binding for you.

This list of rights is only a summary and therefore not exhaustive, nor does it contain all details. You can consult the full text of the Common European Sales Law here. Please read your contract carefully.

In case of dispute you may wish to ask for legal advice.

---

[1] Insert a link here.

Directive 2011/83/EU of the European Parliament and of the Council of 25 October 2011 on consumer rights, amending Council Directive 93/13/EEC and Directive 1999/44/EC of the European Parliament and of the Council and repealing Council Directive 85/577/EEC and Directive 97/7/EC of the European Parliament and of the Council

Chapter I   Subject matter, definitions and scope

Article 1   Subject matter

The purpose of this Directive is, through the achievement of a high level of consumer protection, to contribute to the proper functioning of the internal market by approximating certain aspects of the laws, regulations and administrative provisions of the Member States concerning contracts concluded between consumers and traders.

Article 2   Definitions

For the purpose of this Directive, the following definitions shall apply:

(1) 'consumer' means any natural person who, in contracts covered by this Directive, is acting for purposes which are outside his trade, business, craft or profession;

(2) 'trader' means any natural person or any legal person, irrespective of whether privately or publicly owned, who is acting, including through any other person acting in his name or on his behalf, for purposes relating to his trade, business, craft or profession in relation to contracts covered by this Directive;

(3) 'goods' means any tangible movable items, with the exception of items sold by way of execution or otherwise by authority of law; water, gas and electricity shall be considered as goods within the meaning of this Directive where they are put up for sale in a limited volume or a set quantity;

(4) 'goods made to the consumer's specifications' means non- prefabricated goods made on the basis of an individual choice of or decision by the consumer;

(5) 'sales contract' means any contract under which the trader transfers or undertakes to transfer the ownership of goods to the consumer and the consumer pays or undertakes to pay the price thereof, including any contract having as its object both goods and services;

(6) 'service contract' means any contract other than a sales contract under which the trader supplies or undertakes to supply a service to the consumer and the consumer pays or undertakes to pay the price thereof;

(7) 'distance contract' means any contract concluded between the trader and the consumer under an organised distance sales or service-provision scheme without the simultaneous physical presence of the trader and the consumer, with the exclusive use of one or more means of distance communication up to and including the time at which the contract is concluded;

(8) 'off-premises contract' means any contract between the trader and the consumer:

(a) concluded in the simultaneous physical presence of the trader and the consumer, in a place which is not the business premises of the trader;

(b) for which an offer was made by the consumer in the same circumstances as referred to in point (a);

(c) concluded on the business premises of the trader or through any means of distance communication immediately after the consumer was personally and individually addressed in a place which is not the business premises of the trader in the simultaneous physical presence of the trader and the consumer; or

(d) concluded during an excursion organised by the trader with the aim or effect of promoting and selling goods or services to the consumer;

(9) 'business premises' means:

    (a) any immovable retail premises where the trader carries out his activity on a permanent basis; or

    (b) any movable retail premises where the trader carries out his activity on a usual basis;

(10) 'durable medium' means any instrument which enables the consumer or the trader to store information addressed personally to him in a way accessible for future reference for a period of time adequate for the purposes of the information and which allows the unchanged reproduction of the information stored;

(11) 'digital content' means data which are produced and supplied in digital form;

(12) 'financial service' means any service of a banking, credit, insurance, personal pension, investment or payment nature;

(13) 'public auction' means a method of sale where goods or services are offered by the trader to consumers, who attend or are given the possibility to attend the auction in person, through a transparent, competitive bidding procedure run by an auctioneer and where the successful bidder is bound to purchase the goods or services;

(14) 'commercial guarantee' means any undertaking by the trader or a producer (the guarantor) to the consumer, in addition to his legal obligation relating to the guarantee of conformity, to reimburse the price paid or to replace, repair or service goods in any way if they do not meet the specifications or any other requirements not related to conformity set out in the guarantee statement or in the relevant advertising available at the time of, or before the conclusion of the contract;

(15) 'ancillary contract' means a contract by which the consumer acquires goods or services related to a distance contract or an off-premises contract and where those goods are supplied or those services are provided by the trader or by a third party on the basis of an arrangement between that third party and the trader.

Article 3   Scope

1. This Directive shall apply, under the conditions and to the extent set out in its provisions, to any contract concluded between a trader and a consumer. It shall also apply to contracts for the supply of water, gas, electricity or district heating, including by public providers, to the extent that these commodities are provided on a contractual basis.

2. If any provision of this Directive conflicts with a provision of another Union act governing specific sectors, the provision of that other Union act shall prevail and shall apply to those specific sectors.

3. This Directive shall not apply to contracts:

    (a) for social services, including social housing, childcare and support of families and persons permanently or temporarily in need, including long-term care;

    (b) for healthcare as defined in point (a) of Article 3 of Directive 2011/24/EU, whether or not they are provided via healthcare facilities;

    (c) for gambling, which involves wagering a stake with pecuniary value in games of chance, including lotteries, casino games and betting transactions;

    (d) for financial services;

    (e) for the creation, acquisition or transfer of immovable property or of rights in immovable property;

    (f) for the construction of new buildings, the substantial conversion of existing buildings and for rental of accommodation for residential purposes;

    (g) which fall within the scope of Council Directive 90/314/EEC of 13 June 1990 on package travel, package holidays and package tours;

    (h) which fall within the scope of Directive 2008/122/EC of the European Parliament and of the Council of 14 January 2009 on the protection of consumers in respect of certain aspects of timeshare, long-term holiday product, resale and exchange contracts;

    (i) which, in accordance with the laws of Member States, are established by a public office-holder who has a statutory obligation to be independent and impartial and who must ensure, by providing comprehensive legal information, that the consumer only concludes the contract on the basis of careful legal consideration and with knowledge of its legal scope;

(j) for the supply of foodstuffs, beverages or other goods intended for current consumption in the household, and which are physically supplied by a trader on frequent and regular rounds to the consumer's home, residence or workplace;

(k) for passenger transport services, with the exception of Article 8(2) and Articles 19 and 22;

(l) concluded by means of automatic vending machines or automated commercial premises;

(m) concluded with telecommunications operators through public payphones for their use or concluded for the use of one single connection by telephone, Internet or fax established by a consumer.

4. Member States may decide not to apply this Directive or not to maintain or introduce corresponding national provisions to off-premises contracts for which the payment to be made by the consumer does not exceed EUR 50. Member States may define a lower value in their national legislation.

5. This Directive shall not affect national general contract law such as the rules on the validity, formation or effect of a contract, in so far as general contract law aspects are not regulated in this Directive.

6. This Directive shall not prevent traders from offering consumers contractual arrangements which go beyond the protection provided for in this Directive.

Article 4   Level of harmonisation

Member States shall not maintain or introduce, in their national law, provisions diverging from those laid down in this Directive, including more or less stringent provisions to ensure a different level of consumer protection, unless otherwise provided for in this Directive.

Chapter II Consumer information for contracts other than distance or off-premises contracts

Article 5   Information requirements for contracts other than distance or off-premises contracts

1. Before the consumer is bound by a contract other than a distance or an off-premises contract, or any corresponding offer, the trader shall provide the consumer with the following information in a clear and comprehensible manner, if that information is not already apparent from the context:

(a) the main characteristics of the goods or services, to the extent appropriate to the medium and to the goods or services;

(b) the identity of the trader, such as his trading name, the geographical address at which he is established and his telephone number;

(c) the total price of the goods or services inclusive of taxes, or where the nature of the goods or services is such that the price cannot reasonably be calculated in advance, the manner in which the price is to be calculated, as well as, where applicable, all additional freight, delivery or postal charges or, where those charges cannot reasonably be calculated in advance, the fact that such additional charges may be payable;

(d) where applicable, the arrangements for payment, delivery, performance, the time by which the trader undertakes to deliver the goods or to perform the service, and the trader's complaint handling policy;

(e) in addition to a reminder of the existence of a legal guarantee of conformity for goods, the existence and the conditions of after-sales services and commercial guarantees, where applicable;

(f) the duration of the contract, where applicable, or, if the contract is of indeterminate duration or is to be extended automatically, the conditions for terminating the contract;

(g) where applicable, the functionality, including applicable technical protection measures, of digital content;

(h) where applicable, any relevant interoperability of digital content with hardware and software that the trader is aware of or can reasonably be expected to have been aware of.

2. Paragraph 1 shall also apply to contracts for the supply of water, gas or electricity, where they are not put up for sale in a limited volume or set quantity, of district heating or of digital content which is not supplied on a tangible medium.

3. Member States shall not be required to apply paragraph 1 to contracts which involve day-to-day transactions and which are performed immediately at the time of their conclusion.

4. Member States may adopt or maintain additional pre- contractual information requirements for contracts to which this Article applies.

Chapter III Consumer information and right of withdrawal for distance and off-premises contracts

Article 6   Information requirements for distance and off-premises contracts

1. Before the consumer is bound by a distance or off- premises contract, or any corresponding offer, the trader shall provide the consumer with the following information in a clear and comprehensible manner:

(a) the main characteristics of the goods or services, to the extent appropriate to the medium and to the goods or services;

(b) the identity of the trader, such as his trading name;

(c) the geographical address at which the trader is established and the trader's telephone number, fax number and e-mail address, where available, to enable the consumer to contact the trader quickly and communicate with him efficiently and, where applicable, the geographical address and identity of the trader on whose behalf he is acting;

(d) if different from the address provided in accordance with point (c), the geographical address of the place of business of the trader, and, where applicable, that of the trader on whose behalf he is acting, where the consumer can address any complaints;

(e) the total price of the goods or services inclusive of taxes, or where the nature of the goods or services is such that the price cannot reasonably be calculated in advance, the manner in which the price is to be calculated, as well as, where applicable, all additional freight, delivery or postal charges and any other costs or, where those charges cannot reasonably be calculated in advance, the fact that such additional charges may be payable. In the case of a contract of indeterminate duration or a contract containing a subscription, the total price shall include the total costs per billing period. Where such contracts are charged at a fixed rate, the total price shall also mean the total monthly costs. Where the total costs cannot be reasonably calculated in advance, the manner in which the price is to be calculated shall be provided;

(f) the cost of using the means of distance communication for the conclusion of the contract where that cost is calculated other than at the basic rate;

(g) the arrangements for payment, delivery, performance, the time by which the trader undertakes to deliver the goods or to perform the services and, where applicable, the trader's complaint handling policy;

(h) where a right of withdrawal exists, the conditions, time limit and procedures for exercising that right in accordance with Article 11(1), as well as the model withdrawal form set out in Annex I(B);

(i) where applicable, that the consumer will have to bear the cost of returning the goods in case of withdrawal and, for distance contracts, if the goods, by their nature, cannot normally be returned by post, the cost of returning the goods;

(j) that, if the consumer exercises the right of withdrawal after having made a request in accordance with Article 7(3) or Article 8(8), the consumer shall be liable to pay the trader reasonable costs in accordance with Article 14(3);

(k) where a right of withdrawal is not provided for in accordance with Article 16, the information that the consumer will not benefit from a right of withdrawal or, where applicable, the circumstances under which the consumer loses his right of withdrawal;

(l) a reminder of the existence of a legal guarantee of conformity for goods;

(m) where applicable, the existence and the conditions of after sale customer assistance, after-sales services and commercial guarantees;

(n) the existence of relevant codes of conduct, as defined in point (f) of Article 2 of Directive 2005/29/EC, and how copies of them can be obtained, where applicable;

(o) the duration of the contract, where applicable, or, if the contract is of indeterminate duration or is to be extended automatically, the conditions for terminating the contract;

(p) where applicable, the minimum duration of the consumer's obligations under the contract;

(q) where applicable, the existence and the conditions of deposits or other financial guarantees to be paid or provided by the consumer at the request of the trader;

(r) where applicable, the functionality, including applicable technical protection measures, of digital content;

(s) where applicable, any relevant interoperability of digital content with hardware and software that the trader is aware of or can reasonably be expected to have been aware of;

(t) where applicable, the possibility of having recourse to an out-of-court complaint and redress mechanism, to which the trader is subject, and the methods for having access to it.

2. Paragraph 1 shall also apply to contracts for the supply of water, gas or electricity, where they are not put up for sale in a limited volume or set quantity, of district heating or of digital content which is not supplied on a tangible medium.

3. In the case of a public auction, the information referred to in points (b), (c) and (d) of paragraph 1 may be replaced by the equivalent details for the auctioneer.

4. The information referred to in points (h), (i) and (j) of paragraph 1 may be provided by means of the model instructions on withdrawal set out in Annex I(A). The trader shall have fulfilled the information requirements laid down in points (h), (i) and (j) of paragraph 1 if he has supplied these instructions to the consumer, correctly filled in.

5. The information referred to in paragraph 1 shall form an integral part of the distance or off-premises contract and shall not be altered unless the contracting parties expressly agree otherwise.

6. If the trader has not complied with the information requirements on additional charges or other costs as referred to in point (e) of paragraph 1, or on the costs of returning the goods as referred to in point (i) of paragraph 1, the consumer shall not bear those charges or costs.

7. Member States may maintain or introduce in their national law language requirements regarding the contractual information, so as to ensure that such information is easily understood by the consumer.

8. The information requirements laid down in this Directive are in addition to information requirements contained in Directive 2006/123/EC and Directive 2000/31/EC and do not prevent Member States from imposing additional information requirements in accordance with those Directives.

Without prejudice to the first subparagraph, if a provision of Directive 2006/123/EC or Directive 2000/31/EC on the content and the manner in which the information is to be provided conflicts with a provision of this Directive, the provision of this Directive shall prevail.

9. As regards compliance with the information requirements laid down in this Chapter, the burden of proof shall be on the trader.

Article 7   Formal requirements for off-premises contracts

1. With respect to off-premises contracts, the trader shall give the information provided for in Article 6(1) to the consumer on paper or, if the consumer agrees, on another durable medium. That information shall be legible and in plain, intelligible language.

2. The trader shall provide the consumer with a copy of the signed contract or the confirmation of the contract on paper or, if the consumer agrees, on another durable medium, including, where applicable, the confirmation of the consumer's prior express consent and acknowledgement in accordance with point (m) of Article 16.

3. Where a consumer wants the performance of services or the supply of water, gas or electricity, where they are not put up for sale in a limited volume or set quantity, or of district heating to begin during the withdrawal period provided for in Article 9(2), the trader shall require that the consumer makes such an express request on a durable medium.

4. With respect to off-premises contracts where the consumer has explicitly requested the services of the trader for the purpose of carrying out repairs or maintenance for which the trader and the consumer immediately perform their contractual obligations and where the payment to be made by the consumer does not exceed EUR 200:

    (a) the trader shall provide the consumer with the information referred to in points (b) and (c) of Article 6(1) and information about the price or the manner in which the price is to be calculated together with an estimate of the total price, on paper or, if the consumer agrees, on another durable medium. The trader shall provide the information referred to in points (a), (h) and (k) of Article 6(1), but may choose not to provide it on paper or another durable medium if the consumer expressly agrees;

    (b) the confirmation of the contract provided in accordance with paragraph 2 of this Article shall contain the information provided for in Article 6(1).

Member States may decide not to apply this paragraph.

5. Member States shall not impose any further formal pre- contractual information requirements for the fulfilment of the information obligations laid down in this Directive.

Article 8   Formal requirements for distance contracts

1. With respect to distance contracts, the trader shall give the information provided for in Article 6(1) or make that information available to the consumer in a way appropriate to the means of distance communication used in plain and intelligible language. In so far as that information is provided on a durable medium, it shall be legible.

2. If a distance contract to be concluded by electronic means places the consumer under an obligation to pay, the trader shall make the consumer aware in a clear and prominent manner, and directly before the consumer places his order, of the information provided for in points (a), (e), (o) and (p) of Article 6(1).

The trader shall ensure that the consumer, when placing his order, explicitly acknowledges that the order implies an obligation to pay. If placing an order entails activating a button or a similar function, the button or similar function shall be labelled in an easily legible manner only with the words 'order with obligation to pay' or a corresponding unambiguous formulation indicating that placing the order entails an obligation to pay the trader. If the trader has not complied with this subparagraph, the consumer shall not be bound by the contract or order.

3. Trading websites shall indicate clearly and legibly at the latest at the beginning of the ordering process whether any delivery restrictions apply and which means of payment are accepted.

4. If the contract is concluded through a means of distance communication which allows limited space or time to display the information, the trader shall provide, on that particular means prior to the conclusion of such a contract, at least the pre-contractual information regarding the main characteristics of the goods or services, the identity of the trader, the total price, the right of withdrawal, the duration of the contract and, if the contract is of indeterminate duration, the conditions for terminating the contract, as referred to in points (a), (b), (e), (h) and (o) of Article 6(1). The other information

referred to in Article 6(1) shall be provided by the trader to the consumer in an appropriate way in accordance with paragraph 1 of this Article.

5. Without prejudice to paragraph 4, if the trader makes a telephone call to the consumer with a view to concluding a distance contract, he shall, at the beginning of the conversation with the consumer, disclose his identity and, where applicable, the identity of the person on whose behalf he makes that call, and the commercial purpose of the call.

6. Where a distance contract is to be concluded by telephone, Member States may provide that the trader has to confirm the offer to the consumer who is bound only once he has signed the offer or has sent his written consent. Member States may also provide that such confirmations have to be made on a durable medium.

7. The trader shall provide the consumer with the confirmation of the contract concluded, on a durable medium within a reasonable time after the conclusion of the distance contract, and at the latest at the time of the delivery of the goods or before the performance of the service begins. That confirmation shall include:

(a) all the information referred to in Article 6(1) unless the trader has already provided that information to the consumer on a durable medium prior to the conclusion of the distance contract; and

(b) where applicable, the confirmation of the consumer's prior express consent and acknowledgment in accordance with point (m) of Article 16.

8. Where a consumer wants the performance of services, or the supply of water, gas or electricity, where they are not put up for sale in a limited volume or set quantity, or of district heating, to begin during the withdrawal period provided for in Article 9(2), the trader shall require that the consumer make an express request.

9. This Article shall be without prejudice to the provisions on the conclusion of e-contracts and the placing of e-orders set out in Articles 9 and 11 of Directive 2000/31/EC.

10. Member States shall not impose any further formal pre- contractual information requirements for the fulfilment of the information obligations laid down in this Directive.

Article 9   Right of withdrawal

1. Save where the exceptions provided for in Article 16 apply, the consumer shall have a period of 14 days to withdraw from a distance or off-premises contract, without giving any reason, and without incurring any costs other than those provided for in Article 13(2) and Article 14.

2. Without prejudice to Article 10, the withdrawal period referred to in paragraph 1 of this Article shall expire after 14 days from:

(a) in the case of service contracts, the day of the conclusion of the contract;

(b) in the case of sales contracts, the day on which the consumer or a third party other than the carrier and indicated by the consumer acquires physical possession of the goods or:

   (i) in the case of multiple goods ordered by the consumer in one order and delivered separately, the day on which the consumer or a third party other than the carrier and indicated by the consumer acquires physical possession of the last good;

   (ii) in the case of delivery of a good consisting of multiple lots or pieces, the day on which the consumer or a third party other than the carrier and indicated by the consumer acquires physical possession of the last lot or piece;

   (iii) in the case of contracts for regular delivery of goods during defined period of time, the day on which the consumer or a third party other than the carrier and indicated by the consumer acquires physical possession of the first good;

(c) in the case of contracts for the supply of water, gas or electricity, where they are not put up for sale in a limited volume or set quantity, of district heating or of digital content which is not supplied on a tangible medium, the day of the conclusion of the contract.

3. The Member States shall not prohibit the contracting parties from performing their contractual obligations during the withdrawal period. Nevertheless, in the case of off- premises contracts,

Member States may maintain existing national legislation prohibiting the trader from collecting the payment from the consumer during the given period after the conclusion of the contract.

Article 10　Omission of information on the right of withdrawal

1. If the trader has not provided the consumer with the information on the right of withdrawal as required by point (h) of Article 6(1), the withdrawal period shall expire 12 months from the end of the initial withdrawal period, as determined in accordance with Article 9(2).

2. If the trader has provided the consumer with the information provided for in paragraph 1 of this Article within 12 months from the day referred to in Article 9(2), the withdrawal period shall expire 14 days after the day upon which the consumer receives that information.

Article 11　Exercise of the right of withdrawal

1. Before the expiry of the withdrawal period, the consumer shall inform the trader of his decision to withdraw from the contract. For this purpose, the consumer may either:

    (a) use the model withdrawal form as set out in Annex I(B); or

    (b) make any other unequivocal statement setting out his decision to withdraw from the contract.

Member States shall not provide for any formal requirements applicable to the model withdrawal form other than those set out in Annex I(B).

2. The consumer shall have exercised his right of withdrawal within the withdrawal period referred to in Article 9(2) and Article 10 if the communication concerning the exercise of the right of withdrawal is sent by the consumer before that period has expired.

3. The trader may, in addition to the possibilities referred to in paragraph 1, give the option to the consumer to electronically fill in and submit either the model withdrawal form set out in Annex I(B) or any other unequivocal statement on the trader's website. In those cases the trader shall communicate to the consumer an acknowledgement of receipt of such a withdrawal on a durable medium without delay.

4. The burden of proof of exercising the right of withdrawal in accordance with this Article shall be on the consumer.

Article 12　Effects of withdrawal

The exercise of the right of withdrawal shall terminate the obligations of the parties:

    (a) to perform the distance or off-premises contract; or

    (b) to conclude the distance or off-premises contract, in cases where an offer was made by the consumer.

Article 13　Obligations of the trader in the event of withdrawal

1. The trader shall reimburse all payments received from the consumer, including, if applicable, the costs of delivery without undue delay and in any event not later than 14 days from the day on which he is informed of the consumer's decision to withdraw from the contract in accordance with Article 11.

The trader shall carry out the reimbursement referred to in the first subparagraph using the same means of payment as the consumer used for the initial transaction, unless the consumer has expressly agreed otherwise and provided that the consumer does not incur any fees as a result of such reimbursement.

2. Notwithstanding paragraph 1, the trader shall not be required to reimburse the supplementary costs, if the consumer has expressly opted for a type of delivery other than the least expensive type of standard delivery offered by the trader.

3. Unless the trader has offered to collect the goods himself, with regard to sales contracts, the trader may withhold the reimbursement until he has received the goods back, or until the consumer has supplied evidence of having sent back the goods, whichever is the earliest.

Article 14   Obligations of the consumer in the event of withdrawal

1. Unless the trader has offered to collect the goods himself, the consumer shall send back the goods or hand them over to the trader or to a person authorised by the trader to receive the goods, without undue delay and in any event not later than 14 days from the day on which he has communicated his decision to withdraw from the contract to the trader in accordance with Article 11. The deadline shall be met if the consumer sends back the goods before the period of 14 days has expired.

The consumer shall only bear the direct cost of returning the goods unless the trader has agreed to bear them or the trader failed to inform the consumer that the consumer has to bear them.

In the case of off-premises contracts where the goods have been delivered to the consumer's home at the time of the conclusion of the contract, the trader shall at his own expense collect the goods if, by their nature, those goods cannot normally be returned by post.

2. The consumer shall only be liable for any diminished value of the goods resulting from the handling of the goods other than what is necessary to establish the nature, characteristics and functioning of the goods. The consumer shall in any event not be liable for diminished value of the goods where the trader has failed to provide notice of the right of withdrawal in accordance with point (h) of Article 6(1).

3. Where a consumer exercises the right of withdrawal after having made a request in accordance with Article 7(3) or Article 8(8), the consumer shall pay to the trader an amount which is in proportion to what has been provided until the time the consumer has informed the trader of the exercise of the right of withdrawal, in comparison with the full coverage of the contract. The proportionate amount to be paid by the consumer to the trader shall be calculated on the basis of the total price agreed in the contract. If the total price is excessive, the proportionate amount shall be calculated on the basis of the market value of what has been provided.

4. The consumer shall bear no cost for:

(a) the performance of services or the supply of water, gas or electricity, where they are not put up for sale in a limited volume or set quantity, or of district heating, in full or in part, during the withdrawal period, where:

(i)   the trader has failed to provide information in accordance with points (h) or (j) of Article 6(1); or

(ii) the consumer has not expressly requested performance to begin during the withdrawal period in accordance with Article 7(3) and Article 8(8); or

(b) the supply, in full or in part, of digital content which is not supplied on a tangible medium where:

(i)   the consumer has not given his prior express consent to the beginning of the performance before the end of the 14-day period referred to in Article 9;

(ii) the consumer has not acknowledged that he loses his right of withdrawal when giving his consent; or

(iii) the trader has failed to provide confirmation in accordance with Article 7(2) or Article 8(7).

5. Except as provided for in Article 13(2) and in this Article, the consumer shall not incur any liability as a consequence of the exercise of the right of withdrawal.

Article 15   Effects of the exercise of the right of withdrawal on ancillary contracts

1. Without prejudice to Article 15 of Directive 2008/48/EC of the European Parliament and of the Council of 23 April 2008 on credit agreements for consumers, if the consumer exercises his right of withdrawal from a distance or an off- premises contract in accordance with Articles 9 to 14 of this Directive, any ancillary contracts shall be automatically terminated, without any costs for the consumer, except as provided for in Article 13(2) and in Article 14 of this Directive.

2. The Member States shall lay down detailed rules on the termination of such contracts.

Article 16 Exceptions from the right of withdrawal

Member States shall not provide for the right of withdrawal set out in Articles 9 to 15 in respect of distance and off-premises contracts as regards the following:

(a) service contracts after the service has been fully performed if the performance has begun with the consumer's prior express consent, and with the acknowledgement that he will lose his right of withdrawal once the contract has been fully performed by the trader;

(b) the supply of goods or services for which the price is dependent on fluctuations in the financial market which cannot be controlled by the trader and which may occur within the withdrawal period;

(c) the supply of goods made to the consumer's specifications or clearly personalised;

(d) the supply of goods which are liable to deteriorate or expire rapidly;

(e) the supply of sealed goods which are not suitable for return due to health protection or hygiene reasons and were unsealed after delivery;

(f) the supply of goods which are, after delivery, according to their nature, inseparably mixed with other items;

(g) the supply of alcoholic beverages, the price of which has been agreed upon at the time of the conclusion of the sales contract, the delivery of which can only take place after 30 days and the actual value of which is dependent on fluctuations in the market which cannot be controlled by the trader;

(h) contracts where the consumer has specifically requested a visit from the trader for the purpose of carrying out urgent repairs or maintenance. If, on the occasion of such visit, the trader provides services in addition to those specifically requested by the consumer or goods other than replacement parts necessarily used in carrying out the maintenance or in making the repairs, the right of withdrawal shall apply to those additional services or goods;

(i) the supply of sealed audio or sealed video recordings or sealed computer software which were unsealed after delivery;

(j) the supply of a newspaper, periodical or magazine with the exception of subscription contracts for the supply of such publications;

(k) contracts concluded at a public auction;

(l) the provision of accommodation other than for residential purpose, transport of goods, car rental services, catering or services related to leisure activities if the contract provides for a specific date or period of performance;

(m) the supply of digital content which is not supplied on a tangible medium if the performance has begun with the consumer's prior express consent and his acknowledgment that he thereby loses his right of withdrawal.

Chapter IV Other consumer rights

Article 17   Scope

1. Articles 18 and 20 shall apply to sales contracts. Those Articles shall not apply to contracts for the supply of water, gas or electricity, where they are not put up for sale in a limited volume or set quantity, of district heating or the supply of digital content which is not supplied on a tangible medium.

2. Articles 19, 21 and 22 shall apply to sales and service contracts and to contracts for the supply of water, gas, electricity, district heating or digital content.

Article 18   Delivery

1. Unless the parties have agreed otherwise on the time of delivery, the trader shall deliver the goods by transferring the physical possession or control of the goods to the consumer without undue delay, but not later than 30 days from the conclusion of the contract.

2. Where the trader has failed to fulfil his obligation to deliver the goods at the time agreed upon with the consumer or within the time limit set out in paragraph 1, the consumer shall call upon him to make the delivery within an additional period of time appropriate to the circumstances. If the trader fails to deliver the goods within that additional period of time, the consumer shall be entitled to terminate the contract.

The first subparagraph shall not be applicable to sales contracts where the trader has refused to deliver the goods or where delivery within the agreed delivery period is essential taking into account all the circumstances attending the conclusion of the contract or where the consumer informs the trader, prior to the conclusion of the contract, that delivery by or on a specified date is essential. In those cases, if the trader fails to deliver the goods at the time agreed upon with the consumer or within the time limit set out in paragraph 1, the consumer shall be entitled to terminate the contract immediately.

3. Upon termination of the contract, the trader shall, without undue delay, reimburse all sums paid under the contract.

4. In addition to the termination of the contract in accordance with paragraph 2, the consumer may have recourse to other remedies provided for by national law.

Article 19   Fees for the use of means of payment

Member States shall prohibit traders from charging consumers, in respect of the use of a given means of payment, fees that exceed the cost borne by the trader for the use of such means.

Article 20   Passing of risk

In contracts where the trader dispatches the goods to the consumer, the risk of loss of or damage to the goods shall pass to the consumer when he or a third party indicated by the consumer and other than the carrier has acquired the physical possession of the goods. However, the risk shall pass to the consumer upon delivery to the carrier if the carrier was commissioned by the consumer to carry the goods and that choice was not offered by the trader, without prejudice to the rights of the consumer against the carrier.

Article 21   Communication by telephone

Member States shall ensure that where the trader operates a telephone line for the purpose of contacting him by telephone in relation to the contract concluded, the consumer, when contacting the trader is not bound to pay more than the basic rate.

The first subparagraph shall be without prejudice to the right of telecommunication services providers to charge for such calls.

Article 22   Additional payments

Before the consumer is bound by the contract or offer, the trader shall seek the express consent of the consumer to any extra payment in addition to the remuneration agreed upon for the trader's main contractual obligation. If the trader has not obtained the consumer's express consent but has inferred it by using default options which the consumer is required to reject in order to avoid the additional payment, the consumer shall be entitled to reimbursement of this payment.

Chapter V General provisions

Article 23   Enforcement

1. Member States shall ensure that adequate and effective means exist to ensure compliance with this Directive.

2. The means referred to in paragraph 1 shall include provisions whereby one or more of the following bodies, as determined by national law, may take action under national law before the courts or before the competent administrative bodies to ensure that the national provisions transposing this Directive are applied:

    (a) public bodies or their representatives;

    (b) consumer organisations having a legitimate interest in protecting consumers;

    (c) professional organisations having a legitimate interest in acting.

Article 24   Penalties

1. Member States shall lay down the rules on penalties applicable to infringements of the national provisions adopted pursuant to this Directive and shall take all measures necessary to ensure that they are implemented. The penalties provided for must be effective, proportionate and dissuasive.

2. Member States shall notify those provisions to the Commission by 13 December 2013 and shall notify it without delay of any subsequent amendment affecting them.

Article 25   Imperative nature of the Directive

If the law applicable to the contract is the law of a Member State, consumers may not waive the rights conferred on them by the national measures transposing this Directive.

Any contractual terms which directly or indirectly waive or restrict the rights resulting from this Directive shall not be binding on the consumer.

Article 26   Information

Member States shall take appropriate measures to inform consumers and traders of the national provisions transposing this Directive and shall, where appropriate, encourage traders and code owners as defined in point (g) of Article 2 of Directive 2005/29/EC, to inform consumers of their codes of conduct.

Article 27   Inertia selling

The consumer shall be exempted from the obligation to provide any consideration in cases of unsolicited supply of goods, water, gas, electricity, district heating or digital content or unsolicited provision of services, prohibited by Article 5(5) and point 29 of Annex I to Directive 2005/29/EC. In such cases, the absence of a response from the consumer following such an unsolicited supply or provision shall not constitute consent.

Article 28   Transposition

2. The provisions of this Directive shall apply to contracts concluded after 13 June 2014.

Article 29   Reporting requirements

1. Where a Member State makes use of any of the regulatory choices referred to in Article 3(4), Article 6(7), Article 6(8), Article 7(4), Article 8(6) and Article 9(3), it shall inform the Commission thereof by 13 December 2013, as well as of any subsequent changes.

2. The Commission shall ensure that the information referred to in paragraph 1 is easily accessible to consumers and traders, inter alia, on a dedicated website.

3. The Commission shall forward the information referred to in paragraph 1 to the other Member States and the European Parliament. The Commission shall consult stakeholders on that information.

Article 30   Reporting by the Commission and review

By 13 December 2016, the Commission shall submit a report on the application of this Directive to the European Parliament and the Council. That report shall include in particular an evaluation of the provisions of this Directive regarding digital content including the right of withdrawal. The report shall be accompanied, where necessary, by legislative proposals to adapt this Directive to developments in the field of consumer rights.

Chapter VI Final provisions

Article 31   Repeals

Directive 85/577/EEC and Directive 97/7/EC, as amended by Directive 2002/65/EC of the European Parliament and of the Council of 23 September 2002 concerning the distance marketing of consumer financial services and by Directives 2005/29/EC and 2007/64/EC, are repealed as of 13 June 2014.

References to the repealed Directives shall be construed as references to this Directive and shall be read in accordance with the correlation table set out in Annex II.

ANNEX I
INFORMATION CONCERNING THE EXERCISE OF THE RIGHT OF WITHDRAWAL

[Part A (Model instructions on withdrawal) and Part B (Model withdrawal form) are identical to Appendix 1 (Model instructions on withdrawal) and Appendix 2 (Model withdrawal form) of the Proposal for a regulation of the European Parliament and of the Council on a common European sales law (above, pp. 608–609).]

Part IV

International Materials

United Nations Convention on Contracts for the International Sale of Goods 1980*

THE STATES PARTIES TO THIS CONVENTION,

BEARING IN MIND the broad objectives in the resolutions adopted by the sixth special session of the General Assembly of the United Nations on the establishment of a New International Economic Order, CONSIDERING that the development of international trade on the basis of equality and mutual benefit is an important element in promoting friendly relations among States,

BEING OF THE OPINION that the adoption of uniform rules which govern contracts for the international sale of goods and take into account the different social, economic and legal systems would contribute to the removal of legal barriers in international trade and promote the development of international trade, HAVE AGREED as follows:

PART I SPHERE OF APPLICATION AND GENERAL PROVISIONS

Chapter I Sphere of application

Article 1

1. This Convention applies to contracts of sale of goods between parties whose places of business are in different States:

    (a) when the States are Contracting States; or

    (b) when the rules of private international law lead to the application of the law of a Contracting State.

2. The fact that the parties have their places of business in different States is to be disregarded whenever this fact does not appear either from the contract or from any dealings between, or from information disclosed by, the parties at any time before or at the conclusion of the contract.

3. Neither the nationality of the parties nor the civil or commercial character of the parties or of the contract is to be taken into consideration in determining the application of this Convention.

Article 2

This Convention does not apply to sales:

    (a) of goods bought for personal, family or household use unless the seller, at any time before or at the conclusion of the contract, neither knew nor ought to have known that the goods were bought for any such use;

    (b) by auction;

    (c) on execution or otherwise by authority of law;

    (d) of stocks, shares, investment securities, negotiable instruments or money;

    (e) of ships, vessels, hovercraft or aircraft;

    (f) of electricity.

* Reproduced with permission from the United Nations Commission on International Trade Law (UNCITRAL).

Article 3

1. Contracts for the supply of goods to be manufactured or produced are to be considered sales unless the party who orders the goods undertakes to supply a substantial part of the materials necessary for such manufacture or production.

2. This Convention does not apply to contracts in which the preponderant part of the obligations of the party who furnishes the goods consists in the supply of labour or other services.

Article 4

This Convention governs only the formation of the contract of sale and the rights and obligations of the seller and the buyer arising from such a contract. In particular, except as otherwise expressly provided in this Convention, it is not concerned with:

(a) the validity of the contract or of any of its provisions or of any usage;

(b) the effect which the contract may have on the property in the goods sold.

Article 5

This Convention does not apply to the liability of the seller for death or personal injury caused by the goods to any person.

Article 6

The parties may exclude the application of this Convention or, subject to article 12, derogate from or vary the effect of any of its provisions.

Chapter II General provisions

Article 7

1. In the interpretation of this Convention, regard is to be had to its international character and to the need to promote uniformity in its application and the observance of good faith in international trade.

2. Questions concerning matters governed by this Convention which are not expressly settled in it are to be settled in conformity with the general principles on which it is based or, in the absence of such principles, in conformity with the law applicable by virtue of the rules of private international law.

Article 8

1. For the purposes of this Convention statements made by and other conduct of a party are to be interpreted according to his intent where the other party knew or could not have been unaware what that intent was.

2. If the preceding paragraph is not applicable, statements made by and other conduct of a party are to be interpreted according to the understanding that a reasonable person of the same kind as the other party would have had in the same circumstances.

3. In determining the intent of a party or the understanding a reasonable person would have had, due consideration is to be given to all relevant circumstances of the case including the negotiations, any practices which the parties have established between themselves, usages and any subsequent conduct of the parties.

Article 9

1. The parties are bound by any usage to which they have agreed and by any practices which they have established between themselves.

2. The parties are considered, unless otherwise agreed, to have impliedly made applicable to their contract or its formation a usage of which the parties knew or ought to have known and which in international trade is widely known to, and regularly observed by, parties to contracts of the type involved in the particular trade concerned.

Article 10

For the purposes of this Convention:

(a) if a party has more than one place of business, the place of business is that which has the closest relationship to the contract and its performance, having regard to the circumstances known to or contemplated by the parties at any time before or at the conclusion of the contract;

(b) if a party does not have a place of business, reference is to be made to his habitual residence.

Article 11

A contract of sale need not be concluded in or evidenced by writing and is not subject to any other requirement as to form. It may be proved by any means, including witnesses.

Article 12

Any provision of article 11, article 29 or Part II of this Convention that allows a contract of sale or its modification or termination by agreement or any offer, acceptance or other indication of intention to be made in any form other than in writing does not apply where any party has his place of business in a Contracting State which has made a declaration under article 96 of this Convention. The parties may not derogate from or vary the effect of this article.

Article 13

For the purposes of this Convention 'writing' includes telegram and telex.

PART II FORMATION OF THE CONTRACT

Article 14

1. A proposal for concluding a contract addressed to one or more specific persons constitutes an offer if it is sufficiently definite and indicates the intention of the offeror to be bound in case of acceptance. A proposal is sufficiently definite if it indicates the goods and expressly or implicitly fixes or makes provision for determining the quantity and the price.

2. A proposal other than one addressed to one or more specific persons is to be considered merely as an invitation to make offers, unless the contrary is clearly indicated by the person making the proposal.

Article 15

1. An offer becomes effective when it reaches the offeree.

2. An offer, even if it is irrevocable, may be withdrawn if the withdrawal reaches the offeree before or at the same time as the offer.

Article 16

1. Until a contract is concluded an offer may be revoked if the revocation reaches the offeree before he has dispatched an acceptance.

2. However, an offer cannot be revoked:

(a) if it indicates, whether by stating a fixed time for acceptance or otherwise, that it is irrevocable; or

(b) if it was reasonable for the offeree to rely on the offer as being irrevocable and the offeree has acted in reliance on the offer.

Article 17

An offer, even if it is irrevocable, is terminated when a rejection reaches the offeror.

Article 18

1. A statement made by or other conduct of the offeree indicating assent to an offer is an acceptance. Silence or inactivity does not itself amount to acceptance.

2. An acceptance of an offer becomes effective at the moment the indication of assent reaches the offeror. An acceptance is not effective if the indication of assent does not reach the offeror within the time he has fixed or, if no time is fixed, within a reasonable time, due account being taken of the circumstances of the transaction, including the rapidity of the means of communication employed

by the offeror. An oral offer must be accepted immediately unless the circumstances indicate otherwise.

3. However, if, by virtue of the offer or as a result of practices which the parties have established between themselves or of usage, the offeree may indicate assent by performing an act, such as one relating to the dispatch of the goods or payment of the price, without notice to the offeror, the acceptance is effective at the moment the act is performed, provided that the act is performed within the period of time laid down in the preceding paragraph.

Article 19

1. A reply to an offer which purports to be an acceptance but contains additions, limitations or other modifications is a rejection of the offer and constitutes a counter-offer.

2. However, a reply to an offer which purports to be an acceptance but contains additional or different terms which do not materially alter the terms of the offer constitutes an acceptance, unless the offeror, without undue delay, objects orally to the discrepancy or dispatches a notice to the effect. If he does not so object, the terms of the contract are the terms of the offer with the modifications contained in the acceptance.

3. Additional or different terms relating, among other things, to the price, payment, quality and quantity of the goods, place and time of delivery, extent of one party's liability to the other or the settlement of disputes are considered to alter the terms of the offer materially.

Article 20

1. A period of time for acceptance fixed by the offeror in a telegram or a letter begins to run from the moment the telegram is handed in for dispatch or from the date shown on the letter or, if no such date is shown on the letter or, if no such date is shown, from the date shown on the envelope. A period of time for acceptance fixed by the offeror by telephone, telex or other means of instantaneous communication, begins to run from the moment that the offer reaches the offeree.

2. Official holidays or non-business days occurring during the period for acceptance are included in calculating the period. However, if a notice of acceptance cannot be delivered at the address of the offeror on the last day of the period because that day falls on an official holiday or a non-business day at the place of business of the offeror, the period is extended until the first business day which follows.

Article 21

1. A late acceptance is nevertheless effective as an acceptance if without delay the offeror orally so informs the offeree or dispatches a notice to that effect.

2. If a letter or other writing containing a late acceptance shows that it has been sent in such circumstances that if its transmission had been normal it would have reached the offeror in due time, the late acceptance is effective as an acceptance unless, without delay, the offeror orally informs the offeree that he considers his offer as having lapsed or dispatches a notice to that effect.

Article 22

An acceptance may be withdrawn if the withdrawal reaches the offeror before or at the same time as the acceptance would have become effective.

Article 23

A contract is concluded at the moment when an acceptance of an offer becomes effective in accordance with the provisions of this Convention.

Article 24

For the purposes of this Part of the Convention, an offer, declaration of acceptance or any other indication of intention 'reaches' the addressee when it is made orally to him or delivered by any other means to him personally, to his place of business or mailing address or, if he does not have a place of business or mailing address, to his habitual residence.

PART III SALE OF GOODS

Chapter I General provisions

Article 25
A breach of contract committed by one of the parties is fundamental if it results in such detriment to the other party as substantially to deprive him of what he is entitled to expect under the contract, unless the party in breach did not foresee and a reasonable person of the same kind in the same circumstances would not have foreseen such a result.

Article 26
A declaration of avoidance of the contract is effective only if made by notice to the other party.

Article 27
Unless otherwise expressly provided in this Part of the Convention, if any notice, request or other communication is given or made by a party in accordance with this Part and by means appropriate in the circumstances, a delay or error in the transmission of the communication or its failure to arrive does not deprive that party of the right to rely on the communication.

Article 28
If, in accordance with the provisions of this Convention, one party is entitled to require performance of any obligation by the other party, a court is not bound to enter a judgment for specific performance unless the court would do so under its own law in respect of similar contracts of sale not governed by this Convention.

Article 29
1. A contract may be modified or terminated by the mere agreement of the parties.

2. A contract in writing which contains a provision requiring any modification or termination by agreement to be in writing may not be otherwise modified or terminated by agreement. However, a party may be precluded by his conduct from asserting such a provision to the extent that the other party has relied on that conduct.

Chapter II Obligations of the seller

Article 30
The seller must deliver the goods, hand over any documents relating to them and transfer the property in the goods, as required by the contract and this Convention.

Section I Delivery of the goods and handing over of documents

Article 31
If the seller is not bound to deliver the goods at any other particular place, his obligation to deliver consists:
    (a) if the contract of sale involves carriage of the goods—in handing the goods over to the first carrier for transmission to the buyer;
    (b) if, in cases not within the preceding sub-paragraph, the contract relates to specific goods, or unidentified goods to be drawn from a specific stock or to be manufactured or produced, and at the time of the conclusion of the contract the parties knew that the goods were at, or were to be manufactured or produced at, a particular place—in placing the goods at the buyer's disposal at that place;
    (c) in other cases—in placing the goods at the buyer's disposal at the place where the seller had his place of business at the time of the conclusion of the contract.

Article 32

1. If the seller, in accordance with the contract or this Convention, hands the goods over to a carrier and if the goods are not clearly identified to the contract by markings on the goods, by shipping documents or otherwise, the seller must give the buyer notice of the consignment specifying the goods.

2. If the seller is bound to arrange for carriage of the goods, he must make such contracts as are necessary for carriage to the place fixed by means of transportation appropriate in the circumstances and according to the usual terms for such transportation.

3. If the seller is not bound to effect insurance in respect of the carriage of the goods, he must, at the buyer's request, provide him with all available information necessary to enable him to effect such insurance.

Article 33

The seller must deliver the goods:

    (a) if a date is fixed by or determinable from the contract, on that date;

    (b) if a period of time is fixed by or determinable from the contract, at any time within that period unless circumstances indicate that the buyer is to choose a date; or

    (c) in any other case, within a reasonable time after the conclusion of the contract.

Article 34

If the seller is bound to hand over documents relating to the goods, he must hand them over at the time and place and in the form required by the contract. If the seller has handed over documents before that time, he may, up to that time, cure any lack of conformity in the documents, if the exercise of this right does not cause the buyer unreasonable inconvenience or unreasonable expense. However, the buyer retains any right to claim damages as provided for in this Convention.

Section II Conformity of the goods and third party claims

Article 35

1. The seller must deliver goods which are of the quantity, quality and description required by the contract and which are contained or packaged in the manner required by the contract.

2. Except where the parties have agreed otherwise, the goods do not conform with the contract unless they:

    (a) are fit for the purposes for which goods of the same description would ordinarily be used

    (b) are fit for any particular purpose expressly or impliedly made known to the seller at the time of the conclusion of the contract, except where the circumstances show that the buyer did not rely, or that it was unreasonable for him to rely, on the seller's skill and judgment;

    (c) possess the qualities of goods which the seller has held out to the buyer as a sample or model;

    (d) are contained or packaged in the manner usual for such goods or, where there is no such manner, in a manner adequate to preserve and protect the goods.

3. The seller is not liable under subparagraphs (a) to (d) of the preceding paragraph for any lack of conformity of the goods if at the time of the conclusion of the contract the buyer knew or could not have been unaware of such lack of conformity.

Article 36

1. The seller is liable in accordance with the contract and this Convention for any lack of conformity which exists at the time when the risk passes to the buyer, even though the lack of conformity becomes apparent only after that time.

2. The seller is also liable for any lack of conformity which occurs after the time indicated in the preceding paragraph and which is due to a breach of any of his obligations, including a breach of any guarantee that for a period of time the goods will remain fit for their ordinary purpose or for some particular purpose or will retain specified qualities or characteristics.

Article 37

If the seller has delivered goods before the date for delivery, he may, up to that date, deliver any missing part or make up any deficiency in the quantity of the goods delivered, or deliver goods in replacement of any non-conforming goods delivered or remedy any lack of conformity in the goods delivered, provided that the exercise of this right does not cause the buyer unreasonable inconvenience or unreasonable expense. However, the buyer retains any right to claim damages as provided for in this Convention.

Article 38

1. The buyer must examine the goods, or cause them to be examined, within as short a period as is practicable in the circumstances.

2. If the contract involves carriage of the goods, examination may be deferred until after the goods have arrived at their destination.

3. If the goods are redirected in transit or redispatched by the buyer without a reasonable opportunity for examination by him and at the time of the conclusion of the contract the seller knew or ought to have known of the possibility of such redirection or redispatch, examination may be deferred until after the goods have arrived at the new destination.

Article 39

1. The buyer loses the right to rely on a lack of conformity of the goods if he does not give notice to the seller specifying the nature of the lack of conformity within a reasonable time after he has discovered it or ought to have discovered it.

2. In any event, the buyer loses the right to rely on a lack of conformity of the goods if he does not give the seller notice thereof at the latest within a period of two years from the date on which the goods were actually handed over to the buyer, unless this time-limit is inconsistent with a contractual period of guarantee.

Article 40

The seller is not entitled to rely on the provisions of articles 38 and 39 if the lack of conformity relates to facts of which he knew or could not have been unaware and which he did not disclose to the buyer.

Article 41

The seller must deliver goods which are free from any right or claim of a third party, unless the buyer agreed to take the goods subject to that right or claim. However, if such right or claim is based on industrial property or other intellectual property, the seller's obligation is governed by article 42.

Article 42

1. The seller must deliver goods which are free from any right or claim of a third party based on industrial property or other intellectual property, of which at the time of the conclusion of the contract the seller knew or could not have been unaware, provided that the right or claim is based on industrial property or other intellectual property:

   (a) under the law of the State where the goods will be resold or otherwise used, if it was contemplated by the parties at the time of the conclusion of the contract that the goods would be resold or otherwise used in that State; or

   (b) in any other case, under the law of the State where the buyer has his place of business.

2. The obligation of the seller under the preceding paragraph does not extend to cases where:

   (a) at the time of the conclusion of the contract the buyer knew or could not have been unaware of the right or claim; or

   (b) the right or claim results from the seller's compliance with technical drawings, designs, formulae or other such specifications furnished by the buyer.

Article 43

1. The buyer loses the right to rely on the provisions of article 41 or article 42 if he does not give notice to the seller specifying the nature of the right or claim of the third party within a reasonable time after he has become aware or ought to have become aware of the right or claim.

2. The seller is not entitled to rely on the provisions of the preceding paragraph if he knew of the right or claim of the third party and the nature of it.

Article 44

Notwithstanding the provisions of paragraph 1 of article 39 and paragraph 1 of article 43, the buyer may reduce the price in accordance with article 50 or claim damages, except for loss of profit, if he has a reasonable excuse for his failure to give the required notice.

Section III Remedies for breach of contract by the seller

Article 45

1. If the seller fails to perform any of his obligations under the contract or this Convention, the buyer may:

(a) exercise the rights provided in articles 46 to 52;

(b) claim damages as provided in articles 74 to 77.

2. The buyer is not deprived of any right he may have to claim damages by exercising his right to other remedies.

3. No period of grace may be granted to the seller by a court or arbitral tribunal when the buyer resorts to a remedy for breach of contract.

Article 46

1. The buyer may require performance by the seller of his obligations unless the buyer has resorted to a remedy which is inconsistent with this requirement.

2. If the goods do not conform with the contract, the buyer may require delivery of substitute goods only if the lack of conformity constitutes a fundamental breach of contract and a request for substitute goods is made either in conjunction with notice given under article 39 or within a reasonable time thereafter.

3. If the goods do not conform with the contract, the buyer may require the seller to remedy the lack of conformity by repair, unless this is unreasonable having regard to all the circumstances. A request for repair must be made either in conjunction with notice given under article 39 or within a reasonable time thereafter.

Article 47

1. The buyer may fix an additional period of time of reasonable length for performance by the seller of his obligations.

2. Unless the buyer has received notice from the seller that he will not perform within the period so fixed, the buyer may not, during that period, resort to any remedy for breach of contract. However, the buyer is not deprived thereby of any right he may have to claim damages for delay in performance.

Article 48

1. Subject to article 49, the seller may, even after the date for delivery, remedy at his own expense any failure to perform his obligations, if he can do so without unreasonable delay and without causing the buyer unreasonable inconvenience or uncertainty of reimbursement by the seller of expenses advanced by the buyer. However, the buyer retains any right to claim damages as provided for in this Convention.

2. If the seller requests the buyer to make known whether he will accept performance and the buyer does not comply with the request within a reasonable time, the seller may perform within the time indicated in his request. The buyer may not, during that period of time, resort to any remedy which is inconsistent with performance by the seller.

3. A notice by the seller that he will perform within a specified period of time is assumed to include a request, under the preceding paragraph, that the buyer make known his decision.

4. A request or notice by the seller under paragraph 2 or 3 of this article is not effective unless received by the buyer.

Article 49

1. The buyer may declare the contract avoided:

(a) if the failure by the seller to perform any of his obligations under the contract or this Convention amounts to a fundamental breach of contract; or

(b) in case of non-delivery, if the seller does not deliver the goods within the additional period of time fixed by the buyer in accordance with paragraph 1 of article 47 or declares that he will not deliver within the period so fixed.

2.　However, in cases where the seller has delivered the goods, the buyer loses the right to declare the contract avoided unless he does so:

(a) in respect of late delivery, within a reasonable time after he has become aware that delivery has been made;

(b) in respect of any breach other than late delivery, within a reasonable time:

(i)　after he knew or ought to have known of the breach;

(ii)　after the expiration of any additional period of time fixed by the buyer in accordance with paragraph 1 of article 47, or after the seller has declared that he will not perform his obligations within such an additional period; or

(iii)　after the expiration of any additional period of time indicated by the seller in accordance with paragraph 2 of article 48, or after the buyer has declared that he will not accept performance.

Article 50

If the goods do not conform with the contract and whether or not the price has already been paid, the buyer may reduce the price in the same proportion as the value that the goods actually delivered had at the time of the delivery bears to the value that conforming goods would have had at that time. However, if the seller remedies any failure to perform his obligations in accordance with article 37 or article 48 or if the buyer refuses to accept performance by the seller in accordance with those articles, the buyer may not reduce the price.

Article 51

1.　If the seller delivers only a part of the goods or if only a part of the goods delivered is in conformity with the contract, articles 46 to 50 apply in respect of the part which is missing or which does not conform.

2.　The buyer may declare the contract avoided in its entirety only if the failure to make delivery completely or in conformity with the contract amounts to a fundamental breach of the contract.

Article 52

1.　If the seller delivers the goods before the date fixed, the buyer may take delivery or refuse to take delivery.

2.　If the seller delivers a quantity of goods greater than that provided for in the contract, the buyer may take delivery or refuse to take delivery of the excess quantity. If the buyer takes delivery of all or part of the excess quantity, he must pay for it at the contract rate.

Chapter III　Obligations of the buyer

Article 53

The buyer must pay the price for the goods and take delivery of them as required by the contract and this Convention.

Section I　Payment of the price

Article 54

The buyer's obligation to pay the price includes taking such steps and complying with such formalities as may be required under the contract or any laws and regulations to enable payment to be made.

Article 55

Where a contract has been validly concluded but does not expressly or implicitly fix or make provision for determining the price, the parties are considered, in the absence of any indication to the contrary, to have impliedly made reference to the price generally charged at the time of the conclusion of the contract for such goods sold under comparable circumstances in the trade concerned.

Article 56
If the price is fixed according to the weight of the goods, in case of doubt it is to be determined by the net weight.

Article 57
1. If the buyer is not bound to pay the price at any other particular place, he must pay it to the seller:
  (a) at the seller's place of business; or
  (b) if the payment is to be made against the handing over of the goods or of documents, at the place where the handing over takes place.
2. The seller must bear any increase in the expenses incidental to payment which is caused by a change in his place of business subsequent to the conclusion of the contract.

Article 58
1. If the buyer is not bound to pay the price at any other specific time, he must pay it when the seller places either the goods or documents controlling their disposition at the buyer's disposal in accordance with the contract and this Convention. The seller may make such payment a condition for handing over the goods or documents.
2. If the contract involves carriage of the goods, the seller may dispatch the goods on terms whereby the goods, or documents controlling their disposition, will not be handed over to the buyer except against payment of the price.
3. The buyer is not bound to pay the price until he has had an opportunity to examine the goods, unless the procedures for delivery or payment agreed upon by the parties are inconsistent with his having such an opportunity.

Article 59
The buyer must pay the price on the date fixed by or determinable from the contract and this Convention without the need for any request or compliance with any formality on the part of the seller.

Section II Taking delivery

Article 60
The buyer's obligation to take delivery consists:
  (a) in doing all the acts which could reasonably be expected of him in order to enable the seller to make delivery, and
  (b) in taking over the goods.

Section III Remedies for breach of contract by the buyer

Article 61
1. If the buyer fails to perform any of his obligations under the contract or this Convention, the seller may:
  (a) exercise the rights provided in articles 62 to 65;
  (b) claim damages as provided in articles 74 to 77.
2. The seller is not deprived of any right he may have to claim damages by exercising his right to other remedies.
3. No period of grace may be granted to the buyer by a court or arbitral tribunal when the seller resorts to a remedy for breach of contract.

Article 62
The seller may require the buyer to pay the price, take delivery or perform his other obligations, unless the seller has resorted to a remedy which is inconsistent with this requirement.

Article 63
1. The seller may fix an additional period of time of reasonable length for performance by the buyer of his obligations.

2. Unless the seller has received notice from the buyer that he will not perform within the period so fixed, the seller may not, during that period, resort to any remedy for breach of contract. However, the seller is not deprived thereby of any right he may have to claim damages for delay in performance.

Article 64

1. The seller may declare the contract avoided:

   (a) if the failure by the buyer to perform any of his obligations under the contract or this Convention amounts to a fundamental breach of contract, or

   (b) if the buyer does not, within the additional period of time fixed by the seller in accordance with paragraph 1 of article 63, perform his obligation to pay the price or take delivery of the goods, or if he declares that he will not do so within the period so fixed.

2. However, in cases where the buyer has paid the price, the seller loses the right to declare the contract avoided unless he does so:

   (a) in respect of late performance by the buyer, before the seller has become aware that performance has been rendered; or

   (b) in respect of any breach other than late performance by the buyer, within a reasonable time:

   (i) after the seller knew or ought to have known the breach; or

   (ii) after the expiration of any additional period of time fixed by the seller in accordance with paragraph 1 of article 63, or after the buyer has declared that he will not perform his obligations within such an additional period.

Article 65

1. If under the contract the buyer is to specify the form, measurement or other features of the goods and he fails to make such specification either on the date agreed upon or within a reasonable time after receipt of a request from the seller, the seller may, without prejudice to any other rights he may have, make the specification himself in accordance with the requirements of the buyer that may be known to him.

2. If the seller makes the specification himself, he must inform the buyer of the details thereof and must fix a reasonable time within which the buyer may make a different specification. If, after receipt of such a communication, the buyer fails to do so within the time so fixed, the specification made by the seller is binding.

Chapter IV Passing of risk

Article 66

Loss of or damage to the goods after the risk has passed to the buyer does not discharge him from his obligation to pay the price, unless the loss or damage is due to an act or omission of the seller.

Article 67

1. If the contract of sale involves carriage of the goods and the seller is not bound to hand them over at a particular place, the risk passes to the buyer when the goods are handed over to the first carrier for transmission to the buyer in accordance with the contract of sale. If the seller is bound to hand the goods over to a carrier at a particular place, the risk does not pass to the buyer until the goods are handed over to the carrier at that place. The fact that the seller is authorized to retain documents controlling the disposition of the goods does not affect the passage of the risk.

2. Nevertheless, the risk does not pass to the buyer until the goods are clearly identified to the contract, whether by markings on the goods, by shipping documents, by notice given to the buyer or otherwise.

Article 68

The risk in respect of goods sold in transit passes to the buyer from the time of the conclusion of the contract. However, if the circumstances so indicate, the risk is assumed by the buyer from the time the goods were handed over to the carrier who issued the documents embodying the contract of carriage. Nevertheless, if at the time of the conclusion of the contract of sale the seller knew or ought to have known that the goods had been lost or damaged and did not disclose this to the buyer, the loss or damage is at the risk of the seller.

Article 69

1. In cases not within articles 67 and 68, the risk passes to the buyer when he takes over the goods or, if he does not do so in due time, from the time when the goods are placed at his disposal and he commits a breach of contract by failing to take delivery.

2. However, if the buyer is bound to take over the goods at a place other than a place of business of the seller, the risk passes when delivery is due and the buyer is aware of the fact that the goods are placed at his disposal at that place.

3. If the contract relates to goods not then identified, the goods are considered not to be placed at the disposal of the buyer until they are clearly identified to the contract.

Article 70

If the seller has committed a fundamental breach of contract, articles 67, 68 and 69 do not impair the remedies available to the buyer on account of the breach.

Chapter V Provisions common to the obligations of the seller and of the buyer

Section I Anticipatory breach and instalment contracts

Article 71

1. A party may suspend the performance of his obligations if, after the conclusion of the contract, it becomes apparent that the other party will not perform a substantial part of his obligations as a result of:

    (a) a serious deficiency in his ability to perform or in is creditworthiness; or

    (b) his conduct in preparing to perform or in performing the contract.

2. If the seller has already dispatched the goods before the grounds described in the preceding paragraph become evident, he may prevent the handing over of the goods to the buyer even though the buyer holds a document which entitles him to obtain them. The present paragraph relates only to the rights in the goods as between the buyer and the seller.

3. A party suspending performance, whether before or after dispatch of the goods, must immediately give notice of the suspension to the other party and must continue with performance if the other party provides adequate assurance of his performance.

Article 72

1. If prior to the date for performance of the contract it is clear that one of the parties will commit a fundamental breach of contract, the other party may declare the contract avoided.

2. If time allows, the party intending to declare the contract avoided must give reasonable notice to the other party in order to permit him to provide adequate assurance of his performance.

3. The requirements of the preceding paragraph do not apply if the other party has declared that he will not perform his obligations.

Article 73

1. In the case of a contract for delivery of goods by instalments, if the failure of one party to perform any of his obligations in respect of any instalment constitutes a fundamental breach of contract with respect to that instalment, the other party may declare the contract avoided with respect to that instalment.

2. If one party's failure to perform any of his obligations in respect of any instalment gives the other party good grounds to conclude that a fundamental breach of contract will occur with respect to future instalments, he may declare the contract avoided for the future, provided that he does so within a reasonable time.

3. A buyer who declares the contract avoided in respect of any delivery may, at the same time, declare it avoided in respect of deliveries already made or of future deliveries if, by reason of their interdependence, those deliveries could not be used for the purpose contemplated by the parties at the time of the conclusion of the contract.

Section II Damages

Article 74

Damages for breach of contract by one party consist of a sum equal to the loss, including loss of profit, suffered by the other party as a consequence of the breach. Such damages may not exceed the loss which the party in breach foresaw or ought to have foreseen at the time of the conclusion of the contract, in the light of the facts and matters of which he then knew or ought to have known, as a possible consequence of the breach of contract.

Article 75

If the contract is avoided and if, in a reasonable manner and with a reasonable time after avoidance, the buyer has bought goods in replacement or the seller has resold the goods, the party claiming damages may recover the difference between the contract price and the price in the substitute transaction as well as any further damages recoverable under article 74.

Article 76

1. If the contract is avoided and there is a current price for the goods, the party claiming damages may, if he has not made a purchase or resale under article 75, recover the difference between the price fixed by the contract and the current price at the time of avoidance as well as any further damages recoverable under article 74. If, however, the party claiming damages has avoided the contract after taking over the goods, the current price at the time of such taking over shall be applied instead of the current price at the time of avoidance.

2. For the purposes of the preceding paragraph, the current price is the price prevailing at the place where delivery of the goods should have been made or, if there is no current price at that place, the price at such other place as serves as a reasonable substitute, making due allowance for differences in the cost of transporting the goods.

Article 77

A party who relies on a breach of contract must take such measures as are reasonable in the circumstances to mitigate the loss, including loss of profit, resulting from the breach. If he fails to take such measures, the party in breach may claim a reduction in the damages in the amount by which the loss should have been mitigated.

Section III Interest

Article 78

If a party fails to pay the price or any other sum that is in arrears, the other party is entitled to interest on it, without prejudice to any claim for damages recoverable under article 74.

Section IV Exemptions

Article 79

1. A party is not liable for a failure to perform any of his obligations if he proves that the failure was due to an impediment beyond his control and he could not reasonably be expected to have taken the impediment into account at the time of the conclusion of the contract or to have avoided or overcome it or its consequences.

2. If the party's failure is due to the failure by a third person whom he has engaged to perform the whole or a part of the contract, that party is exempt from liability only if:

    (a) he is exempt under the preceding paragraph; and

    (b) the person whom he has so engaged would be so exempt if the provisions of that paragraph were applied to him.

    3. The exemption provided by this article has effect for the period during which the impediment exists.

    4. The party who fails to perform must give notice to the other party of the impediment and its effect on his ability to perform. If the notice is not received by the other party within a reasonable time after the party who fails to perform knew or ought to have known of the impediment, he is liable for damages resulting from such non-receipt.

    5. Nothing in this article prevents either party from exercising any right other than to claim damages under this Convention.

Article 80

A party may not rely on a failure of the other party to perform, to the extent the such failure was caused by the first party's act or omission.

Section V Effects of avoidance

Article 81

    1. Avoidance of the contract releases both parties from their obligations under it, subject to any damages which may be due. Avoidance does not affect any provision of the contract for the settlement of disputes or any other provision of the contract governing the rights and obligations of the parties consequent upon the avoidance of the contract.

    2. A party who has performed the contract either wholly or in part may claim restitution from the other party of whatever the first party has supplied or paid under the contract. If both parties are bound to make restitution, they must do so concurrently.

Article 82

    1. The buyer loses the right to declare the contract avoided or to require the seller to deliver substitute goods if it is impossible for him to make restitution of the goods substantially in the condition in which he received them.

    2. The preceding paragraph does not apply:
    (a) if the impossibility of making restitution of the goods or of making restitution of the goods substantially in the condition in which the buyer received them is not due to his act or omission;
    (b) if the goods or part of the goods have perished or deteriorated as a result of the examination provided for in article 38; or
    (c) if the goods or part of the goods have been sold in the normal course of business or have been consumed or transformed by the buyer in the course of normal use before he discovered or ought to have discovered the lack of conformity.

Article 83

A buyer who has lost the right to declare the contract avoided or to require the seller to deliver substitute goods in accordance with article 82 retains all other remedies under the contract and this Convention.

Article 84

    1. If the seller is bound to refund the price, he must also pay interest on it, from the date on which the price was paid.

    2. The buyer must account to the seller for all benefits which he has derived from the goods or part of them:
    (a) if he must make restitution of the goods or part of them; or
    (b) if it is impossible for him to make restitution of all or part of the goods or to make restitution of all or part of the goods substantially in the condition in which he received them, but he has nevertheless declared the contract avoided or required the seller to deliver substitute goods.

Section VI Preservation of the goods

Article 85

If the buyer is in delay in taking delivery of the goods or, where payment of the price and delivery of the goods are to be made concurrently, if he fails to pay the price, and the seller is either in possession of the goods or otherwise able to control their disposition, the seller must take such steps as are reasonable in the circumstances to preserve them. He is entitled to retain them until he has been reimbursed his reasonable expenses by the buyer.

Article 86

1. If the buyer has received the goods and intends to exercise any right under the contract or this Convention to reject them, he must take such steps to preserve them as are reasonable in the circumstances. He is entitled to retain them until he has been reimbursed his reasonable expenses by the seller.

2. If goods dispatched to the buyer have been placed at his disposal at their destination and he exercises the right to reject them, he must take possession of them on behalf of the seller, provided that this can be done without payment of the price and without unreasonable inconvenience or unreasonable expense. This provision does not apply if the seller or a person authorized to take charge of the goods on his behalf is present at the destination. If the buyer takes possession of the goods under this paragraph, his rights and obligations are governed by the preceding paragraph.

Article 87

A party who is bound to take steps to preserve the goods may deposit them in a warehouse of a third person at the expense of the other party provided that the expense incurred is not unreasonable.

Article 88

1. A party who is bound to preserve the goods in accordance with article 85 or 86 may sell them by an appropriate means if there has been an unreasonable delay by the other party in taking possession of the goods or in taking them back or in paying the price or the cost of preservation, provided that reasonable notice of the intention to sell has been given to the other party.

2. If the goods are subject to rapid deterioration or their preservation would involve unreasonable expense, a party who is bound to preserve the goods in accordance with article 85 or 86 must take reasonable measures to sell them. To the extent possible he must give notice to the other party of his intention to sell.

3. A party selling the goods has the right to retain out of the proceeds of sale an amount equal to the reasonable expenses of preserving the goods and of selling them. He must account to the other party for the balance.

PART IV FINAL PROVISIONS

Article 89

...

Article 90

This Convention does not prevail over any international agreement which has already been or may be entered into and which contains provisions concerning the matters governed by this Convention, provided that the parties have their places of business in States parties to such agreement.

Article 91

...

Article 92

1. A Contracting State may declare at the time of signature, ratification, acceptance, approval or accession that it will not be bound by Part II of this Convention or that it will not be bound by Part III of this Convention.

2. A Contracting State which makes a declaration in accordance with the preceding paragraph in respect of Part II or Part III of this Convention is not to be considered a Contracting State within paragraph 1 of article 1 of this Convention in respect of matters governed by the Part to which the declaration applies.

Article 93

1. If a Contracting State has two or more territorial units in which, according to its constitution, different systems of law are applicable in relation to the matters dealt within this Convention, it may, at the time of signature, ratification, acceptance, approval or accession, declare that this Convention is to extend to all its territorial units or only to one or more of them, and may amend its declaration by submitting another declaration at any time.

...

Article 94

1. Two or more Contracting States which have the same or closely related legal rules on matters governed by this Convention may at any time declare that the Convention is not to apply to contracts of sale or to their formation where the parties have their places of business in those States. Such declaration may be made jointly or by reciprocal unilateral declarations.

2. A Contracting State which has the same or closely related legal rules on matters governed by this Convention as one or more non-Contracting States may at any time declare that the Convention is not to apply to contracts of sale or to their formation where the parties have their places of business in those States.

3. If a State which is the object of a declaration under the preceding paragraph subsequently becomes a Contracting State, the declaration made will, as from the date on which the Convention enters into force in respect of the new Contracting State, have the effect of a declaration made under paragraph 1, provided that the new Contracting State joins in such declaration or makes a reciprocal unilateral declaration.

Article 95

Any State may declare at the time of the deposit of its instrument of ratification, acceptance, approval or accession that it will not be bound by subparagraph 1 (b) of article 1 of this Convention.

Article 96

A Contracting State whose legislation requires contracts of sale to be concluded in or evidenced by writing may at any time make a declaration in accordance with article 12 that any provision of article 11, article 29, or Part II of this Convention, that allows a contract of sale or its modification or termination by agreement or any offer, acceptance, or other indication of intention to be made in any form other than in writing, does not apply where any party has his place of business in that State.

Article 98

No reservations are permitted except those expressly authorized in this Convention.

Article 99

1. This Convention enters into force, subject to the provisions of paragraph 6 of this article, on the first day of the month following the expiration of twelve months after the date of deposit of the tenth instrument of ratification, acceptance, approval or accession, including an instrument which contains a declaration made under article 92.

Done at Vienna, this day of eleventh day of April, one thousand nine hundred and eighty, ...

...

CMI Rules for Electronic Bills of Lading [1990][*]

1   Scope of application
These rules shall apply whenever the parties so agree.

2   Definitions
  (a) 'Contract of Carriage', means any agreement to carry goods wholly or partly by sea.
  (b) 'EDI', means Electronic Data Interchange, i.e. the interchange of trade data effected by teletransmission.
  (c) 'UN/EDIFACT' means the United Nations Rules for Electronic Data Interchange for Administration, Commerce and Transport.
  (d) 'Transmission' means one or more messages electronically sent together as one unit of dispatch which includes heading and terminating data.
  (e) 'Confirmation' means a Transmission which advises that the content of a Transmission appears to be complete and correct, without prejudice to any subsequent consideration or action that the content may warrant.
  (f) 'Private Key' means any technically appropriate form, such as a combination of numbers and/or letters, which the parties may agree for securing the authenticity and integrity of a Transmission.
  (g) 'Holder' means the party who is entitled to the rights described in Article 7(a) by virtue of its possession of a valid Private Key.
  (h) 'Electronic Monitoring System' means the device by which a computer system can be examined for the transactions that it recorded, such as a Trade Data Log or an Audit Trail.
  (i) 'Electronic Storage' means any temporary, intermediate or permanent storage of electronic data including the primary and the back-up storage of such data.

3   Rules of procedure
  (a) When not in conflict with these Rules, the Uniform Rules of Conduct for Interchange of Trade Data by Teletransmission, 1987 (UNCID) shall govern the conduct between the parties.
  (b) The EDI under these Rules should conform with the relevant UN/EDIFACT standards. However, the parties may use any other method of trade data interchange acceptable to all of the users.
  (c) Unless otherwise agreed, the document format for the Contract of Carriage shall conform to the UN Layout Key or compatible national standard for bills of lading.
  (d) Unless otherwise agreed, a recipient of a Transmission is not authorised to act on a Transmission unless he has sent a Confirmation.
  (e) In the event of a dispute arising between the parties as to the data actually transmitted, an Electronic Monitoring System may be used to verify the data received. Data concerning other transactions not related to the data in dispute are to be considered as trade secrets and thus not available for examination. If such data are unavoidably revealed as part of the examination of the Electronic Monitoring System, they must be treated as confidential and not released to any outside party or used for any other purpose.
  (f) Any transfer of rights to the goods shall be considered to be private information, and shall not be released to any outside party not connected to the transport or clearance of the goods.

4   Form and content of the receipt message
  (a) The carrier, upon receiving the goods from the shipper, shall give notice of the receipt of the goods to the shipper by a message at the electronic address specified by the shipper.

[*] Reproduced with permission from the Comité Maritime International (CMI).

(b) This receipt message shall include:
  (i)   the name of the shipper;
  (ii) the description of the goods, with any representations and reservations, in the same tenor as would be required if a paper bill of lading were issued;
  (iii) the date and place of the receipt of the goods;
  (iv) a reference to the carrier's terms and conditions of carriage; and
  (v)   the Private Key to be used in subsequent Transmissions.
  The shipper must confirm this receipt message to the carrier, upon which Confirmation the shipper shall be the Holder.
(c) Upon demand of the Holder, the receipt message shall be updated with the date and place of shipment as soon as the goods have been loaded on board.
(d) The information contained in (ii), (iii) and (iv) of paragraph (b) above including the date and place of shipment if updated in accordance with paragraph (c) of this Rule, shall have the same force and effect as if the receipt message were contained in a paper bill of lading.

5   Terms and conditions of the Contract of Carriage

(a) It is agreed and understood that whenever the carrier makes a reference to its terms and conditions of carriage, these terms and conditions shall form part of the Contract of Carriage.
(b) Such terms and conditions must be readily available to the parties to the Contract of Carriage.
(c) In the event of any conflict or inconsistency between such terms and conditions and these Rules, these Rules shall prevail.

6   Applicable law

The Contract of Carriage shall be subject to any international convention or national law which would have been compulsorily applicable if a paper bill of lading had been issued.

7   Right of Control and Transfer

(a) The Holder is the only party who may, as against the carrier:
  (1) claim delivery of the goods;
  (2) nominate the consignee or substitute a nominated consignee for any other party, including itself;
  (3) transfer the Right of Control and Transfer to another party;
  (4) instruct the carrier on any other subject concerning the goods, in accordance with the terms and conditions of the Contract of Carriage, as if he were the holder of a paper bill of lading.
(b) A transfer of the Right of Control and Transfer shall be effected: (i) by notification of the current Holder to the carrier of its intention to transfer its Right of Control and Transfer to a proposed new Holder, and (ii) confirmation by the carrier of such notification message, whereupon (iii) the carrier shall transmit the information as referred to in article 4 (except for the Private Key) to the proposed new Holder, whereafter (iv) the proposed new Holder shall advise the carrier of its acceptance of the Right of Control and Transfer, whereupon (v) the carrier shall cancel the current Private Key and issue a new Private Key to the new Holder.
(c) If the proposed new Holder advises the carrier that it does not accept the Right of Control and Transfer or fails to advise the carrier of such acceptance within a reasonable time, the proposed transfer of the Right of Control and Transfer shall not take place. The carrier shall notify the current Holder accordingly and the current Private Key shall retain its validity.
(d) The transfer of the Right of Control and Transfer in the manner described above shall have the same effects as the transfer of such rights under a paper bill of lading.

8   The Private Key

(a) The Private Key is unique to each successive Holder. It is not transferable by the Holder. The carrier and the Holder shall each maintain the security of the Private Key.

(b) The carrier shall only be obliged to send a Confirmation of an electronic message to the last Holder to whom it issued a Private Key, when such Holder secures the Transmission containing such electronic message by the use of the Private Key.

(c) The Private Key must be separate and distinct from any means used to identify the Contract of Carriage, and any security password or identification used to access the computer network.

9   Delivery

(a) The carrier shall notify the Holder of the place and date of intended delivery of the goods. Upon such notification the Holder has a duty to nominate a consignee and to give adequate delivery instructions to the carrier with verification by the Private Key. In the absence of such nomination, the Holder will be deemed to be the consignee.

(b) The carrier shall deliver the goods to the consignee upon production of proper identification in accordance with the delivery instructions specified in paragraph (a) above; such delivery shall automatically cancel the Private Key.

(c) The carrier shall be under no liability for misdelivery if it can prove that it exercised reasonable care to ascertain that the party who claimed to be the consignee was in fact that party.

10   Option to receive a paper document

(a) The Holder has the option at any time prior to delivery of the goods to demand from the carrier a paper bill of lading. Such document shall be made available at a location to be determined by the Holder, provided that no carrier shall be obliged to make such document available at a place where it has no facilities and in such instance the carrier shall only be obliged to make the document available at the facility nearest to the location determined by the Holder. The carrier shall not be responsible for delays in delivering the goods resulting from the Holder exercising the above option.

(b) The carrier has the option at any time prior to delivery of the goods to issue to the Holder a paper bill of lading unless the exercise of such option could result in undue delay or disrupts the delivery of the goods.

(c) A bill of lading issued under Rules 10(a) or (b) shall include: the information set out in the receipt message referred to in Rule 4 (except for the Private Key); and (ii) a statement to the effect that the bill of lading has been issued upon termination of the procedures for EDI under the CMI Rules for Electronic Bills of Lading. The aforementioned bill of lading shall be issued at the option of the Holder either to the order of the Holder whose name for this purpose shall then be inserted in the bill of lading or 'to bearer'.

(d) The issuance of a paper bill of lading under Rule 10(a) or (b) shall cancel the Private Key and terminate the procedures for EDI under these Rules. Termination of these procedures by the Holder or the carrier will not relieve any of the parties to the Contract of Carriage of their rights, obligations or liabilities while performing under the present Rules nor of their rights, obligations or liabilities under the Contract of Carriage.

(e) The Holder may demand at any time the issuance of a print-out of the receipt message referred to in Rule 4 (except for the Private Key) marked as 'non-negotiable copy'. The issuance of such a print-out shall not cancel the Private Key nor terminate the procedures for EDI.

11   Electronic data is equivalent to writing

The carrier and the shipper and all subsequent parties utilizing these procedures agree that any national or local law, custom or practice requiring the Contract of Carriage to be evidenced in writing and signed, is satisfied by the transmitted and confirmed electronic data residing on computer data storage media displayable in human language on a video screen or as printed out by a computer. In agreeing to adopt these Rules, the parties shall be taken to have agreed not to raise the defence that this contract is not in writing.

CMI Uniform Rules for Sea Waybills [1990]*

1 Scope of application

  (i) These Rules shall be called the 'CMI Uniform Rules for Sea Waybills'.

 (ii) They shall apply when adopted by a contract of carriage which is not covered by a bill of lading or similar document of title, whether the contract be in writing or not.

2 Definitions

In these Rules:

'Contract of carriage' shall mean any contract of carriage subject to these Rules which is to be performed wholly or partly by sea.

'Goods' shall mean any goods carried or received for carriage under a contract of carriage.

'Carrier' and 'Shipper' shall mean the parties named in or identifiable as such from the contract of carriage.

'Consignee' shall mean the party named in or identifiable as such from the contract of carriage, or any person substituted as consignee in accordance with rule 6(i).

'Right of Control' shall mean the rights and obligations referred to in rule 6.

3 Agency

  (i) The shipper on entering into the contract of carriage does so not only on his own behalf but also as agent for and on behalf of the consignee, and warrants to the carrier that he has authority so to do.

 (ii) This rule shall apply if, and only if, it be necessary by the law applicable to the contract of carriage so as to enable the consignee to sue and be sued thereon. The consignee shall be under no greater liability than he would have been had the contract of carriage been covered by a bill of lading or similar document of title.

4 Rights and responsibilities

  (i) The contract of carriage shall be subject to any International Convention or National Law which is, or if the contract of carriage had been covered by a bill of lading or similar document of title would have been, compulsorily applicable thereto. Such convention or law shall apply notwithstanding anything inconsistent therewith in the contract of carriage.

 (ii) Subject always to subrule (i), the contract of carriage is governed by:

   (a) these Rules;

   (b) unless otherwise agreed by the parties, the carrier's standard terms and conditions for the trade, if any, including any terms and conditions relating to the non-sea part of the carriage;

   (c) any other terms and conditions agreed by the parties.

(iii) In the event of any inconsistency between the terms and conditions mentioned under subrule (ii)(b) or (c) and these Rules, these Rules shall prevail.

5 Description of the goods

  (i) The shipper warrants the accuracy of the particulars furnished by him relating to the goods, and shall indemnify the carrier against any loss, damage or expense resulting from any inaccuracy.

---

* Reproduced with permission from the Comité Maritime International (CMI).

(ii) In the absence of reservation by the carrier, any statement in a sea waybill or similar document as to the quantity or condition of the goods shall

(a) as between the carrier and the shipper be *prima facie* evidence of receipt of the goods as so stated;

(b) as between the carrier and the consignee be conclusive evidence of receipt of the goods as so stated, and proof to the contrary shall not be permitted, provided always that the consignee has acted in good faith.

6   Right of control

(i) Unless the shipper has exercised his option under subrule (ii) below, he shall be the only party entitled to give the carrier instructions in relation to the contract of carriage. Unless prohibited by the applicable law, he shall be entitled to change the name of the consignee at any time up to the consignee claiming delivery of the goods after their arrival at destination, provided he gives the carrier reasonable notice in writing, or by some other means acceptable to the carrier, thereby undertaking to indemnify the carrier against any additional expense caused thereby.

(ii) The shipper shall have the option, to be exercised not later than the receipt of the goods by the carrier, to transfer the right of control to the consignee. The exercise of this option must be noted on the sea waybill or similar document, if any. Where the option has been exercised the consignee shall have such rights as are referred to in subrule **(i)** above and the shipper shall cease to have such rights.

7   Delivery

(i) The carrier shall deliver the goods to the consignee upon production of proper identification.

(ii) The carrier shall be under no liability for wrong delivery if he can prove that he has exercised reasonable care to ascertain that the party claiming to be the consignee is in fact that party.

8   Validity

In the event of anything contained in these Rules or any such provisions as are incorporated into the contract of carriage by virtue of rule 4, being inconsistent with the provisions of any International Convention or National Law compulsorily applicable to the contract of carriage, such Rules and provisions shall to that extent but no further be null and void.

ICC Uniform Customs and Practice for Documentary Credits

(2007 Revision)

(ICC Publication No. 600LF—ISBN 978-92-842-0007-8)

Notes:
ICC Uniform Customs and Practice for Documentary Credits – 2007 Revision ICC Publication No. 600E – ISBN 92.842.1257.X / 978.92.842.1257.6

Copyright © 2006 – International Chamber of Commerce (ICC), Paris.

This edition is published by arrangement with ICC Services, Publications Department, 38 Cours Albert 1er, 75008 Paris, France; www.iccbooks.com.

Article 1   Application of UCP

The *Uniform Customs and Practice for Documentary Credits, 2007 Revision,* ICC Publication No. 600 ('UCP') are rules that apply to any documentary credit ('credit') (including, to the extent to which they may be applicable, any standby letter of credit) when the text of the credit expressly indicates that it is subject to these rules. They are binding on all parties thereto unless expressly modified or excluded by the credit.

Article 2   Definitions

For the purpose of these rules:

Advising bank means the bank that advises the credit at the request of the issuing bank.

Applicant means the party on whose request the credit is issued.

Banking day means a day on which a bank is regularly open at the place at which an act subject to these rules is to be performed.

Beneficiary means the party in whose favour a credit is issued.

Complying presentation means a presentation that is in accordance with the terms and conditions of the credit, the applicable provisions of these rules and international standard banking practice.

Confirmation means a definite undertaking of the confirming bank, in addition to that of the issuing bank, to honour or negotiate a complying presentation.

Confirming bank means the bank that adds its confirmation to a credit upon the issuing bank's authorization or request.

Credit means any arrangement, however named or described, that is irrevocable and thereby constitutes a definite undertaking of the issuing bank to honour a complying presentation.

Honour means:
(a) to pay at sight if the credit is available by sight payment.
(b) to incur a deferred payment undertaking and pay at maturity if the credit is available by deferred payment.
(c) to accept a bill of exchange ('draft') drawn by the beneficiary and pay at maturity if the credit is available by acceptance.

Issuing bank means the bank that issues a credit at the request of an applicant or on its own behalf.

Negotiation means the purchase by the nominated bank of drafts (drawn on a bank other than the nominated bank) and/or documents under a complying presentation, by advancing or agreeing to advance funds to the beneficiary on or before the banking day on which reimbursement is due to the nominated bank.

Nominated bank means the bank with which the credit is available or any bank in the case of a credit available with any bank.

Presentation means either the delivery of documents under a credit to the issuing bank or nominated bank or the documents so delivered.

Presenter means a beneficiary, bank or other party that makes presentation.

Article 3   Interpretations

For the purpose of these rules:

Where applicable, words in the singular include the plural and in the plural include the singular.

A credit is irrevocable even if there is no indication to that effect.

A document may be signed by handwriting, facsimile signature, perforated signature, stamp, symbol or any other mechanical or electronic method of authentication.

A requirement for a document to be legalized, visaed, certified or similar will be satisfied by any signature, mark, stamp or label on the document which appears to satisfy that requirement.

Branches of a bank in different countries are considered to be separate banks.

Terms such as 'first class', 'well known', 'qualified', 'independent', 'official', 'competent' or 'local' used to describe the issuer of a document allow any issuer except the beneficiary to issue that document.

Unless required to be used in a document, words such as 'prompt', 'immediately' or 'as soon as possible' will be disregarded.

The expression 'on or about' or similar will be interpreted as a stipulation that an event is to occur during a period of five calendar days before until five calendar days after the specified date, both start and end dates included.

The words 'to', 'until', 'till', 'form' and 'between' when used to determine a period of shipment include the date or dates mentioned, and the words 'before' and 'after' exclude the date mentioned.

The words 'from' and 'after' when used to determine a maturity date exclude the date mentioned.

The terms 'first half' and 'second half' of a month shall be construed respectively as the 1st to the 15th and the 16th to the last day of the month, all dates inclusive.

The terms 'beginning', 'middle' and 'end' of a month shall be construed respectively as the 1st to the 10th, the 11th to the 20th and the 21st to the last day of the month, all dates inclusive.

Article 4   Credits v. contracts

(a) A credit by its nature is a separate transaction from the sale or other contract on which it may be based. Banks are in no way concerned with or bound by such contract, even if any reference whatsoever to it is included in the credit. Consequently, the undertaking of a bank to honour, to negotiate or to fulfil any other obligation under the credit is not subject to claims or defences by the applicant resulting from its relationships with the issuing bank or the beneficiary.

A beneficiary can in no case avail itself of the contractual relationships existing between banks or between the applicant and the issuing bank.

(b) An issuing bank should discourage any attempt by the applicant to include, as a integral part of the credit, copies of the underlying contract, proforma invoice and the like.

Article 5   Documents v. goods, services or performance

Banks deal with documents and not with goods, services or performance to which the documents may relate.

Article 6   Availability, expiry date and place for presentation

(a) A credit must state the bank with which it is available or whether it is available with any bank. A credit available with a nominated bank is also available with the issuing bank.

(b) A credit must state whether it is available by sight payment, deferred payment, acceptance or negotiation.

(c) A credit must not be issued available by a draft drawn on the applicant.

(d) (i) A credit must state an expiry date for presentation. An expiry date for honour or negotiation will be deemed to be an expiry date for presentation.

(ii) The place of the bank with which the credit is available is the place for presentation. The place for presentation under a credit available with any bank is that of any bank. A place for presentation other than that of the issuing bank is in addition to the place of the issuing bank.

(e) Except as provided in sub-article 29(a), a presentation by or on behalf of the beneficiary must be made on or before the expiry date.

Article 7   Issuing bank undertaking

(a) Provided that the stipulated documents are presented to the nominated bank or to the issuing bank and that they constitute a complying presentation, the issuing bank must honour if the credit is available by:

(i) sight payment, deferred payment or acceptance with the issuing bank;
(ii) sight payment with a nominated bank and that nominated bank does not pay;
(iii) deferred payment with a nominated bank and that nominated bank does not incur its deferred payment undertaking or, having incurred its deferred payment undertaking, does not pay at maturity;
(iv) acceptance with a nominated bank and that nominated bank does not accept a draft drawn on it or, having accepted a draft on it, does not pay at maturity;
(v) negotiation with a nominated bank and that nominated bank does not negotiate.

(b) An issuing bank is irrevocably bound to honour as of the time it issues the credit.

(c) An issuing bank undertakes to reimburse a nominated bank that has honoured or negotiated a complying presentation and forwarded the documents to the issuing bank. Reimbursement for the amount of a complying presentation under a credit available by acceptance or deferred payment is due at maturity, whether or not the nominated bank prepaid or purchased before maturity. An issuing bank's undertaking to reimburse a nominated bank is independent of the issuing bank's undertaking to the beneficiary.

Article 8 Confirming bank undertaking

(a) Provided that the stipulated documents are presented to the confirming bank or to any other nominated bank and that they constitute a complying presentation, the confirming bank must:

    (i)   honour, if the credit is available by

        (a) sight payment, deferred payment or acceptance with the confirming bank;

        (b) sight payment with another nominated bank and that nominated bank does not pay;

        (c) deferred payment with another nominated bank and that nominated bank does not incur its deferred payment undertaking or, having incurred its deferred payment undertaking, does not pay at maturity;

        (d) acceptance with another nominated bank and that nominated bank does not accept a draft drawn on it or, having accepted a draft drawn on it, does not pay at maturity;

        (e) negotiation with another nominated bank and that nominated bank does not negotiate.

    (ii) negotiate, without recourse, if the credit is available by negotiation with the confirming bank.

(b) A confirming bank is irrevocably bound to honour or negotiate as of the time it adds its confirmation to the credit.

(c) A confirming bank undertakes to reimburse another nominated bank that has honoured or negotiated a complying presentation and forwarded the documents to the confirming bank. Reimbursement for the amount of a complying presentation under a credit available by acceptance or deferred payment is due at maturity, whether or not another nominated bank prepaid or purchased before maturity. A confirming bank's undertaking to reimburse another nominated bank is independent of the confirming bank's undertaking to the beneficiary.

(d) If a bank is authorized or requested by the issuing bank to confirm a credit but is not prepared to do so, it must inform the issuing bank without delay and may advise the credit without confirmation.

Article 9 Advising of credits and amendments

(a) A credit and any amendment may be advised to a beneficiary through an advising bank. An advising bank that is not a confirming bank advises the credit and any amendment without any undertaking to honour or negotiate.

(b) By advising the credit or amendment, the advising bank signifies that is has satisfied itself as to the apparent authenticity of the credit or amendment and that the advice accurately reflects the terms and conditions of the credit or amendment received.

(c) An advising bank may utilize the services of another bank ('second advising bank') to advise the credit and any amendment to the beneficiary. By advising the credit or amendment, the second advising bank signifies that it has satisfied itself as to the apparent authenticity of the advice it has received and that the advice accurately reflects the terms and conditions of the credit or amendment received.

(d) A bank utilizing the services of an advising bank or second advising bank to advise a credit must use the same bank to advise any amendment thereto.

(e) If a bank is requested to advise a credit or amendment but elects not to do so, it must so inform, without delay, the bank from which the credit, amendment or advice has been received.

(f) If a bank is requested to advise a credit or amendment but cannot satisfy itself as to the apparent authenticity of the credit, the amendment or the advice, it must so inform, without delay, the bank from which the instructions appear to have been received. If the advising bank or second advising bank elects nonetheless to advise the credit or amendment, it must inform the beneficiary or second advising bank that it has not been able to satisfy itself as to the apparent authenticity of the credit, the amendment or the advice.

Article 10   Amendments

(a) Except as otherwise provided by article 38, a credit can neither be amended nor cancelled without the agreement of the issuing bank, the confirming bank, if any, and the beneficiary.

(b) An issuing bank is irrevocably bound by an amendment as of the time it issues the amendment. A confirming bank may extend its confirmation to an amendment and will be irrevocably bound as of the time it advises the amendment. A confirming bank may, however, choose to advise an amendment without extending its confirmation and, if so, it must inform the issuing bank without delay and inform the beneficiary in its advice.

(c) The terms and conditions of the original credit (or a credit incorporating previously accepted amendments) will remain in force for the beneficiary until the beneficiary communicates its acceptance of the amendment to the bank that advised such amendment. The beneficiary should give notification of acceptance or rejection of an amendment. If the beneficiary fails to give such notification, a presentation that complies with the credit and to any not yet accepted amendment will be deemed to be notification of acceptance by the beneficiary of such amendment. As of that moment the credit will be amended.

(d) A bank that advises an amendment should inform the bank from which it received the amendment of any notification of acceptance or rejection.

(e) Partial acceptance of an amendment is not allowed and will be deemed to be notification of rejection of the amendment.

(f) A provision in an amendment to the effect that the amendment shall enter into force unless rejected by the beneficiary within a certain time shall be disregarded.

Article 11   Teletransmitted and pre-advised credits and amendments

(a) A authenticated teletransmission of a credit or amendment will be deemed to be the operative credit or amendment, and any subsequent mail confirmation shall be disregarded.

If a teletransmission states 'full details to follow' (or words of similar effect), or states that the mail confirmation is to be the operative credit or amendment, then the teletransmission will not be deemed to be the operative credit or amendment. The issuing bank must then issue the operative credit or amendment without delay in terms not inconsistent with the teletransmission.

(b) A preliminary advice of the issuance of a credit or amendment ('pre-advice') shall only be sent if the issuing bank is prepared to issue the operative credit or amendment. An issuing bank that sends a pre-advice is irrevocably committed to issue the credit or amendment, without delay, in terms not inconsistent with the pre-advice.

Article 12   Nomination

(a) Unless a nominated bank is the confirming bank, authorization to honour or negotiate does not impose any obligation on that nominated bank to honour or negotiate, except when expressly agreed to by that nominated bank and so communicated to the beneficiary.

(b) By nominating a bank to accept a draft or incur a deferred payment undertaking, an issuing bank authorizes that nominated bank to prepay or purchase a draft accepted or a deferred payment undertaking incurred by that nominated bank.

(c) Receipt or examination and forwarding of documents by a nominated bank that is not a confirming bank does not make that nominated bank liable to honour or negotiate, nor does it constitute honour or negotiation.

Article 13   Bank-to-bank reimbursement arrangements

(a) If a credit states that reimbursement is to be obtained by a nominated bank ('claiming bank') claiming on another party ('reimbursing bank'), the credit must state if the reimbursement is subject to the ICC rules for bank-to-bank reimbursements in effect on the date of issuance of the credit.

(b) If a credit does not state that reimbursement is subject to the ICC rules for bank-to-bank reimbursements, the following apply:

(i)   An issuing bank must provide a reimbursing bank with a reimbursement authorization that conforms with the availability stated in the credit. The reimbursement authorization should not be subject to an expiry date.

(ii) A claiming bank shall not be required to supply a reimbursing bank with a certificate of compliance with the terms and conditions of the credit.

(iii) An issuing bank will be responsible for any loss of interest, together with any expenses incurred, if reimbursement is not provided on first demand by a reimbursing bank in accordance with the terms and conditions of the credit.

(iv) A reimbursing bank's charges are for the account of the issuing bank. However, if the charges are for the account of the beneficiary, it is the responsibility of an issuing bank to so indicate in the credit and in the reimbursement authorization. If a reimbursing bank's charges are for the account of the beneficiary, they shall be deducted from the amount due to a claiming bank when reimbursement is made. If no reimbursement is made, the reimbursing bank's charges remain the obligation of the issuing bank.

(c) An issuing bank is not relieved of any of its obligations to provide reimbursement if reimbursement is not made by a reimbursing bank on first demand.

Article 14   Standard for examination of documents

(a) A nominated bank acting on its nomination, a confirming bank, if any, and the issuing bank must examine a presentation to determine, on the basis of the documents alone, whether or not the documents appear on their face to constitute a complying presentation.

(b) A nominated bank acting on its nomination, a confirming bank, if any, and the issuing bank shall each have a maximum of five banking days following the day of presentation to determine if a presentation is complying. This period is not curtailed or otherwise affected by the occurrence on or after the date of presentation of any expiry date or last day for presentation.

(c) A presentation including one or more original transport documents subject to articles 19, 20, 21, 22, 23, 24 or 25 must be made by or on behalf of the beneficiary not later than 21 calendar days after the date of shipment as described in these rules, but in any event not later than the expiry date of the credit.

(d) Data in a document, when read in context with the credit, the document itself and international standard banking practice, need not be identical to, but must not conflict with, data in that document, any other stipulated document or the credit.

(e) In documents other than the commercial invoice, the description of the goods, services or performance, if stated, may be in general terms not conflicting with their description in the credit.

(f) If a credit requires presentation of a document other than a transport document, insurance document or commercial invoice, without stipulating by whom the document is to be issued or its data content, banks will accept the document as presented if its content appears to fulfil the function of the required document and otherwise complies with sub-article 14(d).

(g) A document presented but not required by the credit will be disregarded and may be returned to the presenter.

(h) If a credit contains a condition without stipulating the document to indicate compliance with the condition, banks will deem such condition as not stated and will disregard it.

(i) A document may be dated prior to the issuance date of the credit, but must not be dated later than its date of presentation.

(j) When the addresses of the beneficiary and the applicant appear in any stipulated document, they need not be same as those stated in the credit or in any other stipulated document, but must be within the same country as the respective addresses mentioned in the credit. Contact details (telefax, telephone, email and the like) stated as part of the beneficiary's and the applicant's address will be disregarded. However, when the address and contact details of the applicant appear as part of the consignee or notify party details on a transport document subject to articles 19, 20, 21, 22, 23, 24 or 25, they must be as stated in the credit.

(k) The shipper or consignor of the goods indicated on any document need not be the beneficiary of the credit.

(l) A transport document may be issued by any party other than a carrier, owner, master or charterer provided that the transport document meets the requirements of articles 19, 20, 21, 22, 23 or 24 of these rules.

Article 15   Complying presentation

(a) When an issuing bank determines that a presentation is complying, it must honour.

(b) When a confirming bank determines that a presentation is complying, it must honour or negotiate and forward the documents to the issuing bank.

(c) When a nominated bank determines that a presentation is complying and honours or negotiates, it must forward the documents to the confirming bank or issuing bank.

Article 16   Discrepant documents, waiver and notice

(a) When a nominated bank acting on its nomination, a confirming bank, if any, or the issuing bank determines that a presentation does not comply, it may refuse to honour or negotiate.

(b) When an issuing bank determines that a presentation does not comply, it may in its sole judgement approach the applicant for a waiver of the discrepancies. This does not, however, extend the period mentioned in sub-article 14(b).

(c) When a nominated bank acting on its nomination, a confirming bank, if any, or the issuing bank decides to refuse to honour or negotiate, it must give a single notice to that effect to the presenter.

The notice must state:

    (i)   that the bank is refusing to honour or negotiate; and

    (ii) each discrepancy in respect of which the bank refuses to honour or negotiate; and

    (iii) (a) that the bank is holding the documents pending further instructions from the presenter; or

         (b) that the issuing bank is holding the documents until it receives a waiver from the applicant and agrees to accept it, or receives further instructions from the presenter prior to agreeing to accept a waiver; or

         (c) that the bank is returning the documents; or

         (d) that the bank is acting in accordance with instructions previously received from the presenter.

(d) The notice required in sub-article 16(c) must be given by telecommunication or, if that is not possible, by other expeditious means no later than the close of the fifth banking day following the day of presentation.

(e) A nominated bank acting on its nomination, a conforming bank, if any, or the issuing bank may, after providing notice required by sub-article 16(c)(iii)(a) or (b), return the documents to the presenter at any time.

(f) If an issuing bank or a confirming bank fails to act in accordance with the provisions of this article, it shall be precluded from claiming that the documents do not constitute a complying presentation.

(g) When an issuing bank refuses to honour or a confirming bank refuses to honour or negotiate and has given notice to that effect in accordance with this article, it shall then be entitled to claim a refund, with interest, of any reimbursement made.

Article 17   Original document and copies

(a) At least one original of each document stipulated in the credit must be presented.

(b) A bank shall treat as an original any document bearing an apparently original signature, mark, stamp, or label the issuer of the document, unless the document itself indicates that it is not an original.

(c) Unless a document indicates otherwise, a bank will also accept a document as original if it:

    (i)   appears to be written, typed, perforated or stamped by the document issuer's hand; or

    (ii)   appears to be on the document issuer's original stationery; or

    (iii) states that is original, unless the statement appears not to apply to the document presented.

    (d) If a credit requires presentation of copies of documents, presentation of either originals or copies is permitted.

    (e) If a credit requires presentation of multiple documents by using terms such as 'in duplicated', 'in two fold' or 'in two copies', this will be satisfied by the presentation of at least one original and the remaining number in copies, except when the document itself indicates otherwise.

Article 18   Commercial invoice

    (a) A Commercial Invoice:

      (i)   must appear to have been issued by the beneficiary (except as provided in article 38);

      (ii)   must be made out in the name of the applicant (except as provided in sub-article 38(g));

      (iii) must be made out in the same currency as the credit; and

      (iv) need not be signed.

    (b) A nominated bank acting on its nomination, a confirming bank, if any, or the issuing bank may accept a commercial invoice issued for an amount in excess of the amount permitted by the credit, and its decision will be binding upon all parties, provided the bank in question has not honoured or negotiated for an amount in excess of that permitted by the credit.

    (c) The description of the goods, services or performance in a commercial invoice must correspond with that appearing in the credit

Article 19   Transport document covering at least two different modes of transport

    (a) A transport document covering at least two different modes of transport (multimodal or combined transport document), however named, must appear to:

      (i)   indicate the name of the carrier and be signed by:

          • the carrier or a named agent for or on behalf of the carrier, or

          • the master or a named agent for or on behalf of the master.

          Any signature by the carrier, master or agent must be identified as that of the carrier, master or agent.

          Any signature by an agent must indicate whether the agent has signed for or on behalf of the carrier or for or on behalf of the master.

      (ii)   indicate that the goods have been dispatched, taken in charge or shipped on board at the place stated in the credit, by:

          • pre-printed wording, or

          • a stamp or notation indicating the date on which the goods have been dispatched, taken in charge or shipped on board.

          The date of issuance of the transport document will be deemed to be the date of dispatch, taking in charge or shipped on board, and the date of shipment. However, if the transport document indicates, by stamp or notation, a date of dispatch, taking in charge or shipped on board, this date will be deemed to be the date of shipment.

      (iii) indicate the place of dispatch, taking in charge or shipment, and the place of final destination stated in the credit, even if:

          (a) the transport document states, in addition, a different place of dispatch, taking in charge or shipment or place of final destination, or

          (b) the transport document contains the indication 'intended' or similar qualification in relation to the vessel, port of loading or port of discharge.

      (iv) be the sole original transport document or, if issued in more than one original, be the full set as indicted on the transport document.

      (v)   contain terms and conditions of carriage or make reference to another source containing the terms and conditions of carriage (short form or blank back transport document). Contents of terms and conditions of carriage will not be examined.

(vi) contain no indication that it is subject to a charter party.

(b) For the purpose of this article, transhipment means unloading from one means of conveyance and reloading to another means of conveyance (whether or not in different modes of transport) during the carriage from the place of dispatch, taking in charge or shipment to the place of final destination stated in the credit.

(c) (i) A transport document may indicate that the goods will or may be transhipped provided that the entire carriage is covered by one and the same transport document.

(ii) A transport document indicating that transhipment will or may take place is acceptable, even if the credit prohibits transhipment.

Article 20   Bill of lading

(a) A bill of lading, however named, must appear to:

(i) indicate the name of the carrier and be signed by:
  • the carrier or a named agent for or on behalf of the carrier, or
  • the master or a named agent for or on behalf of the master.

    Any signature by the carrier, master or agent must be identified as that of the carrrier, master or agent.

    Any signature by an agent must indicate whether the agent has signed for or on behalf of the carrier or for or on behalf of the master.

(ii) indicate that the goods have been shipped on board a named vessel at the port of loading stated in the credit by:
  • pre-printed wording, or
  • an on board notation indicating the date on which the goods have been shipped on board.

    The date of issuance of the bill of lading will be deemed to be the date of shipment unless the bill of lading contains an on board notation indicating the date of shipment, in which case the date stated in the on board notation will be deemed to be the date of shipment.

    If the bill of lading contains the indication 'intended vessel' or similar qualification in relation to the name of the vessel, an on board notation indicating the date of shipment and the name of the actual vessel is required.

(iii) indicate shipment from the port of loading to the port of discharge stated in the credit.

    If the bill of lading does not indicate the port of loading stated in the credit as the port of loading, or if it contains the indication 'intended' or similar qualification in relation to the port of loading, an on board notation indicating the port of loading as stated in the credit, the date of shipment and the name of the vessel is required. This provision applies even when loading on board or shipment on a named vessel is indicated by pre-printed wording on the bill of lading.

(iv) be the sole original bill of lading or, if issued in more than one original, be the full set as indicated on the bill of lading.

(v) contain terms and conditions of carriage or make reference to another source containing the terms and conditions of carriage (short form or blank back bill of lading). Contents of terms and conditions of carriage will not be examined.

(vi) contain no indication that it is subject to a charter party.

(b) For the purpose of this article, transhipment means unloading from one vessel and reloading to another vessel during the carriage from the port of loading to the port of discharge stated in the credit.

(c) (i) A bill of lading may indicate that the goods will or may be transhipped provided that the entire carriage is covered by one and the same bill of lading.

(ii) A bill of lading indicating that transhipment will or may take place is acceptable, even if the credit prohibits transhipment, if the goods have been shipped in a container, trailer or LASH barge as evidenced by the bill of lading.

(d) Clauses in a bill of lading stating that the carrier reserves the right to tranship will be disregarded.

Article 21   Non-negotiable sea waybill

(a) A non-negotiable sea waybill, however named, must appear to:

   (i)   indicate the name of the carrier and be signed by:
- the carrier or a named agent for or on behalf of the carrier, or
- the master or a named agent for or on behalf of the master.

        Any signature by the carrier, master or agent must be identified as that of the carrier, master or agent.

        Any signature by an agent must indicate whether the agent has signed for or on behalf of the master.

   (ii) indicate that the goods have been shipped on board a named vessel at the port of loading stated in the credit by:
- pre-printed wording, or
- an on board notation indicating the date on which the goods have been shipped on board.

        The date of issuance of the non-negotiable sea waybill will be deemed to be the date of shipment unless the non-negotiable sea waybill contains an on board notation indicating the date of shipment, in which case the date stated in the on board notation will be deemed to be the date of shipment. If the non-negotiable sea waybill contains the indication 'intended vessel' or similar qualification in relation to the name of the vessel, an on board notation indicating the date of shipment and the name of the actual vessel is required.

   (iii) indicate shipment from the port of loading to the port of discharge stated in the credit.

        If the non-negotiable sea waybill does not indicate the port of loading stated in the credit as the port of loading, or if it contains the indication 'intended' or similar qualification in relation to the port of loading, an on board notation indicating the port of loading as stated in the credit, the date of shipment and the name of the vessel is required. This provision applies even when loading on board or shipment on a named vessel is indicated by pre-printed wording on the non-negotiable sea waybill.

   (iv) be the sole original non-negotiable sea waybill or, if issued in more than one original, be the full set as indicated on the non-negotiable sea waybill.

   (v) contain terms and conditions of carriage or make reference to another source containing the terms and conditions of carriage (short form or blank back non-negotiable sea waybill). Contents of terms and conditions of carriage will not be examined.

   (vi) contain no indication that it is subject to a charter party.

(b) For the purpose of this article, transhipment means unloading from one vessel and reloading to another vessel during the carriage from the port of loading to the port of discharge stated in the credit.

(c) (i) A non-negotiable sea waybill may indicate that the goods will or may be transhipped provided that the entire carriage is covered by one and the same non-negotiable sea waybill.

   (ii) A non-negotiable sea waybill indicating that transhipment will or may take place is acceptable, even if the credit prohibits transhipment, if the goods have been shipped in a container, trailer or LASH barge as evidenced by the non-negotiable sea waybill.

(d) Clauses in a non-negotiable sea waybill stating that the carrier reserves the right to tranship will be disregarded.

Article 22   Charter party bill of lading

(a) A bill of lading, however named, containing an indication that it is subject to a charter party (charter party bill of lading), must appear to:

(i) be signed by:
- the master or a named agent for or on behalf of the master, or
- the owner or a named agent for or on behalf of the owner, or
- the charterer or a named agent for or on behalf of the charterer.

Any signature by the master, owner, charterer or agent must be identified as that of the master, owner, charterer or agent.

Any signature by an agent must indicate whether the agent has signed for or on behalf of the master, owner or charterer.

An agent signing for or on behalf of the owner or charterer must indicate the name of the owner or charterer.

(ii) indicate that the goods have been shipped on board a named vessel at the port of loading stated in the credit by:
- pre-printed wording, or
- an on board notation indicating the date on which the goods have been shipped on board.

The date of issuance of the charter party bill of lading will be deemed to be the date of shipment unless the charter party bill of lading an contains on board notation indicating the date of shipment, in which case the date stated in the on board notation will be deemed to be the date of shipment.

(iii) indicate shipment from the port of the loading to the port of discharge stated in the credit. The port of discharge may also be shown as a range of ports or a geographical area, as stated in the credit.

(iv) be the sole original charter party bill of lading or, if issued in more than one original, be the full set as indicated on the charter party bill of lading.

(b) A bank will not examine charter party contracts, even if they are required to be presented by the terms of the credit.

Article 23   Air transport document

(a) An air transport document, however named, must appear to:

(i) indicate the name of the carrier and be signed by:
- the carrier, or
- a named agent for or on behalf of the carrier.

Any signature by the carrier or agent must be identified as that of the carrier or agent.

Any signature by an agent must indicate that the agent has signed for or on behalf of the carrier.

(ii) indicate that the goods have been accepted for carriage.

(iii) indicate the date of issuance. This date will be deemed to be the date of shipment unless the air transport document contains a specific notation of the actual date of shipment, in which case the date stated in the notation will be deemed to be the date of shipment.

Any other information appearing on the air transport document relative to the flight number and date will not be considered in determining the date of shipment.

(iv) Indicate the airport of departure and the airport of destination stated in the credit.

(v) be the original for consignor or shipper, even if the credit stipulates a full set of originals.

(vi) contain terms and conditions of carriage or make reference to another source containing the terms and conditions of carriage. Contents of terms and conditions of carriage will not be examined.

(b) For the purpose of this article, transhipment means unloading from one aircraft and reloading to another aircraft during the carriage from the airport of departure to the airport of destination stated in the credit.

(c) (i) An air transport document may indicate that the goods will or may be transhipped, provided that the entire carriage is covered by one and the same air transport document.

(ii) An air transport document indicating that transshipment will or may take place is acceptable, even if the credit prohibits transhipment.

Article 24   Road, rail or inland waterway transport documents

(a) A road, rail or inland waterway transport document, however named, must appear to:

(i) indicate the name of the carrier and:
- be signed by the carrier or a named agent for or on behalf of the carrier, or
- indicate receipt of the goods by signature, stamp or notation by the carrier or a named agent for or on behalf of the carrier.

Any signature, stamp or notation of receipt of the goods by the carrier or agent must be identified as that of the carrier or agent.

Any signature, stamp or notation of receipt of the goods by the agent musty indicate that the agent has signed or acted for or an behalf of the carrier. If a rail transport document does not identify the carrier, any signature or stamp of the railway company will be accepted as evidence of the document being signed by the carrier.

(ii) indicate the date of shipment of the date the goods have been received for shipment, dispatch or carriage at the place stated in the credit. Unless the transport document contains a dated reception stamp, an indication of the date of receipt or a date of shipment, the date of issuance of the transport document will be deemed to be the date of shipment.

(iii) indicate the place of shipment and the place of destination stated in the credit.

(b) (i) A road transport document must appear to be the original for consignor or shipper or bear no marking indicating for whom the document has been prepared.

(ii) A rail transport document marked 'duplicate' will be accepted as an original.

(iii) A rail or inland waterway transport document will be accepted as an original whether marked as an original or not.

(c) In the absence of an indication on the transport document as to the number of originals issued, the number presented will be deemed to constitute a full set.

(d) For the purpose for this article, transhipment means unloading from one means of conveyance and reloading to another means of conveyance, within the same mode of transport, during the carriage from the place of shipment, dispatch or carriage to the place of destination stated in the credit.

(e) (i) A road, rail or inland waterway transport document may indicate that the goods will or may be transhipped provided that the entire carriage is covered by one and the same transport document.

(ii) A road, rail or inland waterway transport document indicating that transhipment will or may take place is acceptable, even if the credit prohibits transhipment.

Article 25   Courier receipt, post receipt or certificate of posting

(a) A courier receipt, however named, evidencing receipt of goods for transport, must appear to:

(i) indicate the name of the courier service and be stamped or signed by the named courier service at the place from which the credit states the goods are to be shipped; and

(ii) indicate a date of pickup or of receipt or wording to this effect. This date will be deemed to be the date of shipment.

(b) A requirement that courier charges are to be paid or prepaid may be satisfied by a transport document issued by a courier service evidencing that courier charges are for the account of a party other than the consignee.

(c) A post receipt of certificate of posting, however named, evidencing receipt of goods for transport, must appear to be stamped or signed and dated at the place from which the credit states the goods are to be shipped. This date will be deemed to be the date of shipment.

Article 26   'On deck', 'shipper's load and count', 'said by shipper to contain' and charges additional to freight

(a) A transport document must not indicate that the goods are or will be loaded on deck. A clause on a transport document stating that the goods may be loaded on deck is acceptable.

(b) A transport document bearing a clause such as 'shipper's load and count' and 'said by shipper to contain' is acceptable.

(c) A transport document may bear a reference, by stamp or otherwise, to charges additional to the freight.

Article 27   Clean transport document

A bank will only accept a clean transport document. A clean transport document is one bearing no clause or notation expressly declaring a defective condition of the goods or their packaging. The word 'clean' need not appear on a transport document, even if a credit has a requirement for the transport document to be 'clean on board'.

Article 28   Insurance document and coverage

(a) An insurance document, such as an insurance policy, an insurance certificate or a declaration under an open cover, must appear to be issued and signed by an insurance company, an underwriter or their agents or their proxies.

Any signature by an agent or proxy must indicate whether the agent or proxy has signed for or on behalf of the insurance company or underwriter.

(b) When the insurance document indicates that it has been issued in more than one original, all originals must be presented.

(c) Cover notes will not be accepted.

(d) An insurance policy is acceptable in lieu of an insurance certificate or a declaration under an open cover.

(e) The date of the insurance document must be no later than the date of shipment, unless it appears from the insurance document that the cover is effective from a date not later than the date of shipment.

(f) (i)   The insurance document must indicate the amount of insurance coverage and be in the same currency as the credit.

   (ii)   A requirement in the credit for insurance coverage to be for a percentage of the value of the goods, of the invoice value or similar is deemed to be the minimum amount of coverage required.

   If there is no indication in the credit of the insurance coverage required, the amount of insurance coverage must be at least 110% of the CIF or CIP value of the goods.

   When the CIF or CIP value cannot be determined from the documents, the amount of insurance coverage must be calculated on the basis of the amount for which honour or negotiation is requested or the gross value of the goods as shown on the invoice, whichever is greater.

   (iii)   The insurance document must indicate that risks are covered at least between the place of taking in charge or shipment and the place of discharge or final destination as stated in the credit.

(g) A credit should state the type of insurance required and, if any, the additional risks to be covered. An insurance document will be accepted without regard to any risks that are not covered if the credit uses imprecise terms such as 'usual risks' or 'customary risks'.

(h) When a credit requires insurance against 'all risks' and an insurance document is presented containing any 'all risks' notation or clause, whether or not bearing the heading 'all risks', the insurance document will be accepted without regard to any risks state to be excluded.

(i) An insurance document may contain reference to any exclusion clause.

(j) An insurance document may indicate that the cover is subject to a franchise or excess (deductible).

Article 29   Extension of expiry date or last day for presentation

(a) If the expiry date of a credit or the last day for presentation falls on a day when the bank to which presentation is to be made is closed for reasons other than those referred to in article 36, the expiry date or the last day for presentation, as the case may be, will be extended to the first following banking day.

(b) If presentation is made on the first following banking day, a nominated bank must provide the issuing bank or confirming bank with a statement on its covering schedule that the presentation was made within the time limits extended in accordance with sub-article 29(a).

(c) The latest date for shipment will not be extended as a result of sub-article 29(a).

Article 30   Tolerance in credit amount, quantity and unit prices

(a) The words 'about' or 'approximately' used in connection with the amount of the credit or the quantity or the unit price stated in the credit are to be construed as allowing a tolerance not to exceed 10% more or 10% less than the amount, the quantity or the unit price to which they refer.

(b) A tolerance not to exceed 5% more or 5% less than the quantity of the goods is allowed, provided the credit does not state the quantity in terms of a stipulated number of packing units or individual items and the total amount of the drawings does not exceed the amount of the credit.

(c) Even when partial shipments are not allowed, a tolerance not to exceed 5% less than the amount of the credit is allowed, provided that the quantity of the goods, if stated in the credit, is shipped in full and a unit price, if stated in the credit, is not reduced or that sub-article 30(b) is not applicable. This tolerance does not apply when the credit stipulates a specific tolerance or uses the expressions referred to in sub-article 30(a).

Article 31   Partial drawings or shipments

(a) Partial drawings or shipments are allowed.

(b) A presentation consisting of more than one set of transport documents evidencing shipment commencing on the same means of conveyance and for the same journey, provided they indicate the same destination, will not be regarded as covering a partial shipment, even if they indicate different dates of shipment or different ports or loading, places of taking in charge or dispatch. If the presentation consists of more than one set of transport documents, the latest date of shipment as evidenced on any of the sets of transport documents will be regarded as the date of shipment.

A presentation consisting of one or more sets of transport documents evidencing shipment on more than one means of conveyance within the same mode of transport will be regarded as covering a partial shipment, even if the means of conveyance leave on the same day for the same destination.

(c) A presentation consisting of more than one courier receipt, post receipt or certificate of posting will not be regarded as a partial shipment if the courier receipts, post receipts or certificates of posting appear to have been stamped or signed by the same courier or postal service at the same place and date and for the same destination.

Article 32   Instalment drawings or shipments

If a drawing or shipment by instalments within given periods is stipulated in the credit and any instalment is not drawn or shipped within the period allowed for that instalment, the credit ceases to be available for that and any subsequent instalment.

Article 33   Hours of presentation

A bank has no obligation to accept a presentation outside of its banking hours.

Article 34   Disclaimer on effectiveness of documents

A bank assumes no liability or responsibility for the form, sufficiency, accuracy, genuineness, falsification or legal effect of any document, or for the general or particular conditions stipulated in a document or superimposed thereon; nor does it assume any liability or responsibility for the description, quantity, weight, quality, condition, packing, delivery, value or existence of the goods, services or other performance represented by any document, or for the good faith or acts or omissions, solvency, performance or standing of the consignor, the carrier, the forwarder, the consignee or the insurer of the goods or any other person.

Article 35   Disclaimer on transmission and translation

A bank assumes no liability or responsibility for the consequences arising out of delay, loss in transit, mutilation or other errors arising in the transmission of any messages or delivery of letters or documents, when such messages, letters or documents are transmitted or sent according to the requirements stated in the credit, or when the bank may have taken the initiative in the choice of the delivery service in the absence of such instructions in the credit.

If a nominated bank determines that a presentation is complying and forwards the documents to the issuing bank or confirming bank, whether or not the nominated bank has honoured or negotiated, an issuing bank or confirming bank must honour or negotiate, or reimburse that nominated bank, even when the documents have been lost in transit between the nominated bank and the issuing bank or confirming bank, or between the confirming bank and the issuing bank.

A bank assumes no liability or responsibility for errors in translation or interpretation of technical terms and may transmit credit terms without translating them.

Article 36   Force majeure

A bank assumes no liability or responsibility for the consequences arising out of the interruption of its business by Acts or God, riots, civil commotions, insurrections, wars, acts of terrorism, or by any strikes or lockouts or any other causes beyond its control.

A bank will not, upon resumption of its business, honour or negotiate under a credit that expired during such interruption of its business.

Article 37   Disclaimer for acts of an instructed party

(a) A bank utilizing the services of another bank for the purpose of giving effect to the instruction of the applicant does so for the account and at the risk of the applicant.

(b) An issuing bank or advising bank assumes no liability or responsibility should the instructions it transmits to another bank not be carried out, even if it has taken the initiative in the choice of that other bank.

(c) A bank instructing another bank to perform services is liable for any commissions, fees, costs or expenses ('charges') incurred by that bank in connection with its instructions.

If a credit states that charges are for the account of the beneficiary and charges cannot be collected or deducted from proceeds, the issuing bank remains liable for payment of charges.

A credit or amendment should not stipulate that the advising to a beneficiary is conditional upon the receipt by the advising bank or second advising bank of its charges.

(d) The applicant shall be bound by and liable to indemnify a bank against all obligations and responsibilities imposed by foreign laws and usages.

Article 38   Transferable credits

(a) A bank is under no obligation to transfer a credit except to the extent and in the manner expressly consented to by that bank.

(b) For the purpose of this article:

Transferable credit means a credit that specifically states it is 'transferable'. A transferable credit may be made available in whole or in part to another beneficiary ('second beneficiary') at the request of the beneficiary ('first beneficiary').

Transferring bank means a nominated bank that transfers the credit or, in a credit available with any bank, a bank that is specifically authorized by the issuing bank to transfer and that transfers the credit. An issuing bank may be a transferring bank.

Transferred credit means a credit that has been made available by the transferring bank to a second beneficiary.

(c) Unless otherwise agreed at the time of transfer, all charges (such as commissions, fees, costs or expenses) incurred in respect of a transfer must be paid by the first beneficiary.

(d) A credit may be transferred in part to more than one second beneficiary provided partial drawings or shipments are allowed.

A transferred credit cannot be transferred at the request of a second beneficiary to any subsequent beneficiary. The first beneficiary is not considered to be a subsequent beneficiary.

(e) Any request for transfer must indicate if and under what conditions amendments may be advised to the second beneficiary. The transferred credit must clearly indicate those conditions.

(f) If a credit is transferred to more than one second beneficiary, rejection of an amendment by one or more second beneficiary does not invalidate the acceptance by any other second beneficiary, with respect to which the transferred credit will be amended accordingly. For any second beneficiary that rejected the amendment, the transferred credit will remain unamended.

(g) The transferred credit must accurately reflect the terms and conditions of the credit, including confirmation, if any, with the exception of:

- the amount of the credit,
- any unit price stated therein,
- the expiry date,
- the period for presentation, or
- the latest shipment date or given period for shipment,

any or all of which may be reduced or curtailed.

The percentage for which insurance cover must be effected may be increased to provide the amount of cover stipulated in the credit or these articles.

The name of the first beneficiary may be substituted for that of the applicant in the credit.

If the name of the applicant is specifically required by the credit to appear in any document other than the invoice, such requirement must be reflected in the transferred credit.

(h) The first beneficiary has the right to substitute its own invoice and draft, if any, for those of a second beneficiary for an amount not in excess of that stipulated in the credit, and upon such substitution the first beneficiary can draw under the credit for the difference, if any, between its invoice and the invoice of a second beneficiary.

(i) If the first beneficiary is to present its own invoice and draft, if any, but fails to do so on first demand, or if the invoices presented by the first beneficiary create discrepancies that did not exist in the presentation made by the second beneficiary and the first beneficiary fails to correct them on first demand, the transferring bank has the right to present the documents as received from the second beneficiary to the issuing bank, without further responsibility to the first beneficiary.

(j) The first beneficiary may, in its request for transfer, indicate that honour or negotiation is to be effected to a second beneficiary at the place to which the credit has been transferred, up to and including the expiry date of the credit. This is without prejudice to the right of the first beneficiary in accordance with sub-article 38(h).

(k) Presentation of documents by or on behalf of a second beneficiary must be made to the transferring bank.

Article 39   Assignment of proceeds
The fact that a credit is not stated to be transferable shall not affect the right of the beneficiary to assign any proceeds to which it may be or may become entitled under the credit, in accordance with the provisions of applicable law. This article relates only to the assignment of proceeds and not to the assignment of the right to perform under the credit.

SUPPLEMENT FOR ELECTRONIC PRESENTATION
eUCP VERSION 1.1

Article e1   Scope of the eUCP
(a) The Supplement to the Uniform Customs and Practice for Documentary Credits for Electronic Presentation ('eUCP') supplements the *Uniform Customs and Practice for Documentary Credits* (2007 Revision, ICC Publication No. 600) ('UCP') in order to accommodate presentation of electronic records alone or in combination with paper documents.

(b) The eUCP shall apply as a supplement to the UCP where the credit indicates that it is subject to eUCP.

(c) This version is Version 1.1. A credit must indicate the applicable version of the eUCP. If it does not do so, it is subject to the version in effect on the date the credit is issued or, if made subject to eUCP by an amendment accepted by the beneficiary, on the date of that amendment.

Article e2   Relationship of the eUCP to the UCP

(a) A credit subject to the eUCP ('eUCP credit') is also subject to the UCP without express incorporation of the UCP.

(b) Where the eUCP applies, its provisions shall prevail to the extent that they would produce a result different from the application of the UCP.

(c) If an eUCP credit allows the beneficiary to choose between presentation of paper documents or electronic records and it chooses to present only paper documents, the UCP alone shall apply to that presentation. If only paper documents are permitted under an eUCP credit, the UCP alone shall apply.

Article e3   Definitions

(a) Where the following terms are used in the UCP, for the purposes of applying the UCP to an electronic record presented under an eUCP credit, the term:

    (i)   **appear on their face** and the like shall apply to examination of the data content of an electronic record.

    (ii)   **document** shall include an electronic record.

    (iii)   **place for presentation** of electronic records means an electronic address.

    (iv)   **sign** and the like shall include an electronic signature.

    (v)   **superimposed, notation** or **stamped** means data content whose supplementary character is apparent in an electronic record.

(b) The following terms used in the eUCP shall have the following meanings:

    (i)   **electronic record** means

- data created, generated, sent, communicated, received or stored by electronic means

- that is capable of being authenticated as to the apparent identity of a sender and the apparent source of the data contained in it, and as to whether it has remained complete and unaltered, and

- is capable of being examined for compliance with the terms and conditions of the eUCP credit.

    (ii)   **electronic signature** means a data process attached to or logically associated with an electronic record and executed or adopted by a person in order to identify that person and to indicate that person's authentication of the electronic record.

    (iii)   **format** means the data organization in which the electronic record is expressed or to which it refers.

    (iv)   **paper document** means a document in a traditional paper form.

    (v)   **received** means the time when an electronic record enters the information system of the applicable recipient in a form capable of being accepted by that system. Any acknowledgement of receipt does not imply acceptance or refusal of the electronic record under an eUCP credit.

Article e4   Format

An eUCP credit must specify the formats in which electronic records are to be presented. If the format of the electronic record is not so specified, it may be presented in any format.

Article e5   Presentation

(a) An eUCP credit allowing presentation of:

    (i)   electronic records must state a place for presentation of the electronic records.

    (ii)   both electronic records and paper documents must also state a place for presentation of the paper documents.

(b) Electronic records may be presented separately and need not be presented at the same time.

(c) If an eUCP credit allows for presentation of one or more electronic records, the beneficiary is responsible for providing a notice to the bank to which presentation is made signifying when the presentation is complete. The notice of completeness may be given as an electronic record or paper document and must identify the eUCP credit to which it relates. Presentation is deemed not to have been made if the beneficiary's notice is not received.

(d) (i) Each presentation of an electronic record and the presentation of paper documents under an eUCP credit must identify the eUCP credit under which it is presented.

(ii) A presentation not so identified may be treated as not received.

(e) If the bank to which presentation is to be made is open but its system is unable to receive a transmitted electronic record on the stipulated expiry date and/or the last day of the period of time after the date of shipment for presentation, as the case may be, the bank will be deemed to be closed and the date for presentation and/or the expiry date shall be extended to the first following banking day on which such bank is able to receive an electronic record. If the only electronic record remaining to be presented is the notice of completeness, it maybe given by telecommunications or by paper document and will be deemed timely, provided that it is sent before the bank is able to receive an electronic record.

(f) An electronic record that cannot be authenticated is deemed not to have been presented.

Article e6   Examination

(a) If an electronic record contains a hyperlink to an external system or a presentation indicates that the electronic record may be examined by reference to an external system, the electronic record at the hyperlink or the referenced system shall be deemed to be the electronic record to be examined. The failure of the indicated system to provide access to the required electronic record at the time of examination shall constitute a discrepancy.

(b) The forwarding of electronic records by a nominated bank pursuant to its nomination signifies that it has satisfied itself as to the apparent authenticity of the electronic records.

(c) The inability of the issuing bank, or confirming bank, if any, to examine an electronic record in a format required by the eUCP credit or, if no format is required, to examine it in the format presented is not a basis for refusal.

Article e7   Notice of refusal

(a) (i) The time period for the examination of documents commences on the banking day following the banking day on which the beneficiary's notice of completeness is received.

(ii) If the time for presentation of documents or the notice of completeness is extended, the time for the examination of documents commences on the first following banking day on which the bank to which presentation is to be made is able to receive the notice of completeness.

(b) If an issuing bank, the confirming bank, if any, or a nominated bank acting on their behalf, provides a notice of refusal of a presentation which includes electronic records and does not receive instructions from the party to which notice of refusal is given within 30 calendar days from the date the notice of refusal is given for the disposition of the electronic records, the bank shall return any paper documents not previously returned to the presenter but may dispose of the electronic records in any manner deemed appropriate without any responsibility.

Article e8   Originals and copies

Any requirement of the UCP or an eUCP credit for presentation of one or more originals or copies of an electronic record is satisfied by the presentation of one electronic record.

Article e9   Data of issuance

Unless an electronic record contains a specific date of issuance, the date on which it appears to have been sent by the issuer is deemed to be the date of issuance. The date of receipt will be deemed to be the date it was sent if no other date is apparent.

Article e10   Transport

If an electronic record evidencing transport does not indicate a date of shipment or dispatch, the date of issuance of the electronic record will be deemed to be the date of shipment or dispatch. However, if the electronic record bears a notation that evidences the date of shipment or dispatch, the date of the notation will be deemed to be the date of shipment or dispatch. A notation showing additional data content need not be separately signed or otherwise authenticated.

Article e11   Corruption of an electronic record after presentation

(a) If an electronic record that has been received by the issuing bank, confirming bank, or another nominated bank appears to have been corrupted, the bank may inform the presenter and may request that the electronic record be re-presented.

(b) If the bank requests that an electronic record be re-presented:

    (i)   the time for examination is suspended and resumes when the presenter re-presents the electronic record; and

    (ii) if the nominated bank is not the confirming bank, it must provide the issuing bank and any confirming bank with notice of the request for re-presentation and inform it of the suspension; but

    (iii) if the same electronic record is not re-presented within thirty (30) calendar days, the bank may treat the electronic record as not presented, and

    (iv) any deadlines are not extended.

Article e12   Additional disclaimer of liability for presentation of electronic records under eUCP

By satisfying itself as to the apparent authenticity of an electronic record, banks assume no liability for the identity of the sender, source of the information or its complete and unaltered character other than that which is apparent in the electronic record received by the use of a commercially acceptable data process for the receipt, authentication and identification of electronic records.

United Nations Convention on Contracts for the International Carriage of Goods Wholly or Partly by Sea[*]

(The Rotterdam Rules)

[11 December 2008]

The States Parties to this Convention,

Reaffirming their belief that international trade on the basis of equality and mutual benefit is an important element in promoting friendly relations among States,

Convinced that the progressive harmonization and unification of international trade law, in reducing or removing legal obstacles to the flow of international trade, significantly contributes to universal economic cooperation among all States on a basis of equality, equity and common interest, and to the well-being of all peoples,

Recognizing the significant contribution of the International Convention for the Unification of Certain Rules of Law relating to Bills of Lading, signed in Brussels on 25 August 1924, and its

---

[*] Reproduced with permission from the United Nations Commission on International Trade Law (UNCITRAL).

Protocols, and of the United Nations Convention on the Carriage of Goods by Sea, signed in Hamburg on 31 March 1978, to the harmonization of the law governing the carriage of goods by sea,

Mindful of the technological and commercial developments that have taken place since the adoption of those conventions and of the need to consolidate and modernize them,

Noting that shippers and carriers do not have the benefit of a binding universal regime to support the operation of contracts of maritime carriage involving other modes of transport,

Believing that the adoption of uniform rules to govern international contracts of carriage wholly or partly by sea will promote legal certainty, improve the efficiency of international carriage of goods and facilitate new access opportunities for previously remote parties and markets, thus playing a fundamental role in promoting trade and economic development, both domestically and internationally,

Have agreed as follows:

Chapter 1 General provisions

Article 1 Definitions

For the purposes of this Convention:

1. "Contract of carriage" means a contract in which a carrier, against the payment of freight, undertakes to carry goods from one place to another. The contract shall provide for carriage by sea and may provide for carriage by other modes of transport in addition to the sea carriage.

2. "Volume contract" means a contract of carriage that provides for the carriage of a specified quantity of goods in a series of shipments during an agreed period of time. The specification of the quantity may include a minimum, a maximum or a certain range.

3. "Liner transportation" means a transportation service that is offered to the public through publication or similar means and includes transportation by ships operating on a regular schedule between specified ports in accordance with publicly available timetables of sailing dates.

4. "Non-liner transportation" means any transportation that is not liner transportation.

5. "Carrier" means a person that enters into a contract of carriage with a shipper.

6. (a) "Performing party" means a person other than the carrier that performs or undertakes to perform any of the carrier's obligations under a contract of carriage with respect to the receipt, loading, handling, stowage, carriage, care, unloading or delivery of the goods, to the extent that such person acts, either directly or indirectly, at the carrier's request or under the carrier's supervision or control.

    (b) "Performing party" does not include any person that is retained, directly or indirectly, by a shipper, by a documentary shipper, by the controlling party or by the consignee instead of by the carrier.

7. "Maritime performing party" means a performing party to the extent that it performs or undertakes to perform any of the carrier's obligations during the period between the arrival of the goods at the port of loading of a ship and their departure from the port of discharge of a ship. An inland carrier is a maritime performing party only if it performs or undertakes to perform its services exclusively within a port area.

8. "Shipper" means a person that enters into a contract of carriage with a carrier.

9. "Documentary shipper" means a person, other than the shipper, that accepts to be named as "shipper" in the transport document or electronic transport record.

10. "Holder" means:

    (a) A person that is in possession of a negotiable transport document; and
        (i) if the document is an order document, is identified in it as the shipper or the consignee, or is the person to which the document is duly endorsed; or
        (ii) if the document is a blank endorsed order document or bearer document, is the bearer thereof; or
    (b) The person to which a negotiable electronic transport record has been issued or transferred in accordance with the procedures referred to in article 9, paragraph 1.

11. "Consignee" means a person entitled to delivery of the goods under a contract of carriage or a transport document or electronic transport record.

12. "Right of control" of the goods means the right under the contract of carriage to give the carrier instructions in respect of the goods in accordance with chapter 10.

13. "Controlling party" means the person that pursuant to article 51 is entitled to exercise the right of control.

14. "Transport document" means a document issued under a contract of carriage by the carrier that:

    (a) Evidences the carrier's or a performing party's receipt of goods under a contract of carriage; and

    (b) Evidences or contains a contract of carriage.

15. "Negotiable transport document" means a transport document that indicates, by wording such as "to order" or "negotiable" or other appropriate wording recognized as having the same effect by the law applicable to the document, that the goods have been consigned to the order of the shipper, to the order of the consignee, or to bearer, and is not explicitly stated as being "non-negotiable" or "not negotiable".

16. "Non-negotiable transport document" means a transport document that is not a negotiable transport document.

17. "Electronic communication" means information generated, sent, received or stored by electronic, optical, digital or similar means with the result that the information communicated is accessible so as to be usable for subsequent reference.

18. "Electronic transport record" means information in one or more messages issued by electronic communication under a contract of carriage by a carrier, including information logically associated with the electronic transport record by attachments or otherwise linked to the electronic transport record contemporaneously with or subsequent to its issue by the carrier, so as to become part of the electronic transport record, that:

    (a) Evidences the carrier's or a performing party's receipt of goods under a contract of carriage; and

    (b) Evidences or contains a contract of carriage.

19. "Negotiable electronic transport record" means an electronic transport record:

    (a) That indicates, by wording such as "to order", or "negotiable", or other appropriate wording recognized as having the same effect by the law applicable to the record, that the goods have been consigned to the order of the shipper or to the order of the consignee, and is not explicitly stated as being "non-negotiable" or "not negotiable"; and

    (b) The use of which meets the requirements of article 9, paragraph 1.

20. "Non-negotiable electronic transport record" means an electronic transport record that is not a negotiable electronic transport record.

21. The "issuance" of a negotiable electronic transport record means the issuance of the record in accordance with procedures that ensure that the record is subject to exclusive control from its creation until it ceases to have any effect or validity.

22. The "transfer" of a negotiable electronic transport record means the transfer of exclusive control over the record.

23. "Contract particulars" means any information relating to the contract of carriage or to the goods (including terms, notations, signatures and endorsements) that is in a transport document or an electronic transport record.

24. "Goods" means the wares, merchandise, and articles of every kind whatsoever that a carrier undertakes to carry under a contract of carriage and includes the packing and any equipment and container not supplied by or on behalf of the carrier.

25. "Ship" means any vessel used to carry goods by sea.

26. "Container" means any type of container, transportable tank or flat, swapbody, or any similar unit load used to consolidate goods, and any equipment ancillary to such unit load.

27. "Vehicle" means a road or railroad cargo vehicle.

28. "Freight" means the remuneration payable to the carrier for the carriage of goods under a contract of carriage.

29. "Domicile" means (a) a place where a company or other legal person or association of natural or legal persons has its (i) statutory seat or place of incorporation or central registered office, whichever is applicable, (ii) central administration or (iii) principal place of business, and (b) the habitual residence of a natural person.

30. "Competent court" means a court in a Contracting State that, according to the rules on the internal allocation of jurisdiction among the courts of that State, may exercise jurisdiction over the dispute.

Article 2   Interpretation of this Convention

In the interpretation of this Convention, regard is to be had to its international character and to the need to promote uniformity in its application and the observance of good faith in international trade.

Article 3   Form requirements

The notices, confirmation, consent, agreement, declaration and other communications referred to in articles 19, paragraph 2; 23, paragraphs 1 to 4; 36, subparagraphs 1 (b), (c) and (d); 40, subparagraph 4 (b); 44; 48, paragraph 3; 51, subparagraph 1 (b); 59, paragraph 1; 63; 66; 67, paragraph 2; 75, paragraph 4; and 80, paragraphs 2 and 5, shall be in writing. Electronic communications may be used for these purposes, provided that the use of such means is with the consent of the person by which it is communicated and of the person to which it is communicated.

Article 4   Applicability of defences and limits of liability

1. Any provision of this Convention that may provide a defence for, or limit the liability of, the carrier applies in any judicial or arbitral proceeding, whether founded in contract, in tort, or otherwise, that is instituted in respect of loss of, damage to, or delay in delivery of goods covered by a contract of carriage or for the breach of any other obligation under this Convention against:

    (a) The carrier or a maritime performing party;

    (b) The master, crew or any other person that performs services on board the ship; or

    (c) Employees of the carrier or a maritime performing party.

2. Any provision of this Convention that may provide a defence for the shipper or the documentary shipper applies in any judicial or arbitral proceeding, whether founded in contract, in tort, or otherwise, that is instituted against the shipper, the documentary shipper, or their subcontractors, agents or employees.

Chapter 2 Scope of application

Article 5   General scope of application

1. Subject to article 6, this Convention applies to contracts of carriage in which the place of receipt and the place of delivery are in different States, and the port of loading of a sea carriage and the port of discharge of the same sea carriage are in different States, if, according to the contract of carriage, any one of the following places is located in a Contracting State:

    (a) The place of receipt;

    (b) The port of loading;

    (c) The place of delivery; or

    (d) The port of discharge.

2. This Convention applies without regard to the nationality of the vessel, the carrier, the performing parties, the shipper, the consignee, or any other interested parties.

Article 6   Specific exclusions

1. This Convention does not apply to the following contracts in liner transportation:

    (a) Charter parties; and

    (b) Other contracts for the use of a ship or of any space thereon.

2. This Convention does not apply to contracts of carriage in non-liner transportation except when:

(a) There is no charter party or other contract between the parties for the use of a ship or of any space thereon; and

(b) A transport document or an electronic transport record is issued.

Article 7   Application to certain parties

Notwithstanding article 6, this Convention applies as between the carrier and the consignee, controlling party or holder that is not an original party to the charterparty or other contract of carriage excluded from the application of this Convention. However, this Convention does not apply as between the original parties to a contract of carriage excluded pursuant to article 6.

Chapter 3 Electronic transport records

Article 8   Use and effect of electronic transport records

Subject to the requirements set out in this Convention:

(a) Anything that is to be in or on a transport document under this Convention may be recorded in an electronic transport record, provided the issuance and subsequent use of an electronic transport record is with the consent of the carrier and the shipper; and

(b) The issuance, exclusive control, or transfer of an electronic transport record has the same effect as the issuance, possession, or transfer of a transport document.

Article 9   Procedures for use of negotiable electronic transport records

1. The use of a negotiable electronic transport record shall be subject to procedures that provide for:

(a) The method for the issuance and the transfer of that record to an intended holder;

(b) An assurance that the negotiable electronic transport record retains its integrity;

(c) The manner in which the holder is able to demonstrate that it is the holder; and

(d) The manner of providing confirmation that delivery to the holder has been effected, or that, pursuant to articles 10, paragraph 2, or 47, subparagraphs 1 (a) (ii) and (c), the electronic transport record has ceased to have any effect or validity.

2. The procedures in paragraph 1 of this article shall be referred to in the contract particulars and be readily ascertainable.

Article 10   Replacement of negotiable transport document or negotiable electronic transport record

1. If a negotiable transport document has been issued and the carrier and the holder agree to replace that document by a negotiable electronic transport record:

(a) The holder shall surrender the negotiable transport document, or all of them if more than one has been issued, to the carrier;

(b) The carrier shall issue to the holder a negotiable electronic transport record that includes a statement that it replaces the negotiable transport document; and

(c) The negotiable transport document ceases thereafter to have any effect or validity.

2. If a negotiable electronic transport record has been issued and the carrier and the holder agree to replace that electronic transport record by a negotiable transport document:

(a) The carrier shall issue to the holder, in place of the electronic transport record, a negotiable transport document that includes a statement that it replaces the negotiable electronic transport record; and

(b) The electronic transport record ceases thereafter to have any effect or validity.

Chapter 4 Obligations of the carrier

Article 11   Carriage and delivery of the goods

The carrier shall, subject to this Convention and in accordance with the terms of the contract of carriage, carry the goods to the place of destination and deliver them to the consignee.

Article 12   Period of responsibility of the carrier

1. The period of responsibility of the carrier for the goods under this Convention begins when the carrier or a performing party receives the goods for carriage and ends when the goods are delivered.

2. (a) If the law or regulations of the place of receipt require the goods to be handed over to an authority or other third party from which the carrier may collect them, the period of responsibility of the carrier begins when the carrier collects the goods from the authority or other third party.

   (b) If the law or regulations of the place of delivery require the carrier to hand over the goods to an authority or other third party from which the consignee may collect them, the period of responsibility of the carrier ends when the carrier hands the goods over to the authority or other third party.

3. For the purpose of determining the carrier's period of responsibility, the parties may agree on the time and location of receipt and delivery of the goods, but a provision in a contract of carriage is void to the extent that it provides that:

   (a) The time of receipt of the goods is subsequent to the beginning of their initial loading under the contract of carriage; or

   (b) The time of delivery of the goods is prior to the completion of their final unloading under the contract of carriage.

Article 13   Specific obligations

1. The carrier shall during the period of its responsibility as defined in article 12, and subject to article 26, properly and carefully receive, load, handle, stow, carry, keep, care for, unload and deliver the goods.

2. Notwithstanding paragraph 1 of this article, and without prejudice to the other provisions in chapter 4 and to chapters 5 to 7, the carrier and the shipper may agree that the loading, handling, stowing or unloading of the goods is to be performed by the shipper, the documentary shipper or the consignee. Such an agreement shall be referred to in the contract particulars.

Article 14   Specific obligations applicable to the voyage by sea

The carrier is bound before, at the beginning of, and during the voyage by sea to exercise due diligence to:

(a) Make and keep the ship seaworthy;

(b) Properly crew, equip and supply the ship and keep the ship so crewed, equipped and supplied throughout the voyage; and

(c) Make and keep the holds and all other parts of the ship in which the goods are carried, and any containers supplied by the carrier in or upon which the goods are carried, fit and safe for their reception, carriage and preservation.

Article 15   Goods that may become a danger

Notwithstanding articles 11 and 13, the carrier or a performing party may decline to receive or to load, and may take such other measures as are reasonable, including unloading, destroying, or rendering goods harmless, if the goods are, or reasonably appear likely to become during the carrier's period of responsibility, an actual danger to persons, property or the environment.

Article 16   Sacrifice of the goods during the voyage by sea

Notwithstanding articles 11, 13, and 14, the carrier or a performing party may sacrifice goods at sea when the sacrifice is reasonably made for the common safety or for the purpose of preserving from peril human life or other property involved in the common adventure.

Chapter 5 Liability of the carrier for loss, damage or delay

Article 17   Basis of liability

1. The carrier is liable for loss of or damage to the goods, as well as for delay in delivery, if the claimant proves that the loss, damage, or delay, or the event or circumstance that caused or contributed to it took place during the period of the carrier's responsibility as defined in chapter 4.

2. The carrier is relieved of all or part of its liability pursuant to paragraph 1 of this article if it proves that the cause or one of the causes of the loss, damage, or delay is not attributable to its fault or to the fault of any person referred to in article 18.

3. The carrier is also relieved of all or part of its liability pursuant to paragraph 1 of this article if, alternatively to proving the absence of fault as provided in paragraph 2 of this article, it proves that one or more of the following events or circumstances caused or contributed to the loss, damage, or delay:

    (a) Act of God;

    (b) Perils, dangers, and accidents of the sea or other navigable waters;

    (c) War, hostilities, armed conflict, piracy, terrorism, riots, and civil commotions;

    (d) Quarantine restrictions; interference by or impediments created by governments, public authorities, rulers, or people including detention, arrest, or seizure not attributable to the carrier or any person referred to in article 18;

    (e) Strikes, lockouts, stoppages, or restraints of labour;

    (f) Fire on the ship;

    (g) Latent defects not discoverable by due diligence;

    (h) Act or omission of the shipper, the documentary shipper, the controlling party, or any other person for whose acts the shipper or the documentary shipper is liable pursuant to article 33 or 34;

    (i) Loading, handling, stowing, or unloading of the goods performed pursuant to an agreement in accordance with article 13, paragraph 2, unless the carrier or a performing party performs such activity on behalf of the shipper, the documentary shipper or the consignee;

    (j) Wastage in bulk or weight or any other loss or damage arising from inherent defect, quality, or vice of the goods;

    (k) Insufficiency or defective condition of packing or marking not performed by or on behalf of the carrier;

    (l) Saving or attempting to save life at sea;

    (m) Reasonable measures to save or attempt to save property at sea;

    (n) Reasonable measures to avoid or attempt to avoid damage to the environment; or

    (o) Acts of the carrier in pursuance of the powers conferred by articles 15 and 16.

4. Notwithstanding paragraph 3 of this article, the carrier is liable for all or part of the loss, damage, or delay:

    (a) If the claimant proves that the fault of the carrier or of a person referred to in article 18 caused or contributed to the event or circumstance on which the carrier relies; or

    (b) If the claimant proves that an event or circumstance not listed in paragraph 3 of this article contributed to the loss, damage, or delay, and the carrier cannot prove that this event or circumstance is not attributable to its fault or to the fault of any person referred to in article 18.

5. The carrier is also liable, notwithstanding paragraph 3 of this article, for all or part of the loss, damage, or delay if:

    (a) The claimant proves that the loss, damage, or delay was or was probably caused by or contributed to by

        (i)   the unseaworthiness of the ship;

        (ii) the improper crewing, equipping, and supplying of the ship; or

      (iii) the fact that the holds or other parts of the ship in which the goods are carried, or any containers supplied by the carrier in or upon which the goods are carried, were not fit and safe for reception, carriage, and preservation of the goods; and

  (b) The carrier is unable to prove either that:

      (i)   none of the events or circumstances referred to in subparagraph 5 (a) of this article caused the loss, damage, or delay; or

      (ii) that it complied with its obligation to exercise due diligence pursuant to article 14.

6. When the carrier is relieved of part of its liability pursuant to this article, the carrier is liable only for that part of the loss, damage or delay that is attributable to the event or circumstance for which it is liable pursuant to this article.

Article 18 Liability of the carrier for other persons

The carrier is liable for the breach of its obligations under this Convention caused by the acts or omissions of:

  (a) Any performing party;

  (b) The master or crew of the ship;

  (c) Employees of the carrier or a performing party; or

  (d) Any other person that performs or undertakes to perform any of the carrier's obligations under the contract of carriage, to the extent that the person acts, either directly or indirectly, at the carrier's request or under the carrier's supervision or control.

Article 19 Liability of maritime performing parties

1. A maritime performing party is subject to the obligations and liabilities imposed on the carrier under this Convention and is entitled to the carrier's defences and limits of liability as provided for in this Convention if:

  (a) The maritime performing party received the goods for carriage in a Contracting State, or delivered them in a Contracting State, or performed its activities with respect to the goods in a port in a Contracting State; and

  (b) The occurrence that caused the loss, damage or delay took place:

      (i)   during the period between the arrival of the goods at the port of loading of the ship and their departure from the port of discharge from the ship;

      (ii) while the maritime performing party had custody of the goods; or

      (iii) at any other time to the extent that it was participating in the performance of any of the activities contemplated by the contract of carriage.

2. If the carrier agrees to assume obligations other than those imposed on the carrier under this Convention, or agrees that the limits of its liability are higher than the limits specified under this Convention, a maritime performing party is not bound by this agreement unless it expressly agrees to accept such obligations or such higher limits.

3. A maritime performing party is liable for the breach of its obligations under this Convention caused by the acts or omissions of any person to which it has entrusted the performance of any of the carrier's obligations under the contract of carriage under the conditions set out in paragraph 1 of this article.

4. Nothing in this Convention imposes liability on the master or crew of the ship or on an employee of the carrier or of a maritime performing party.

Article 20 Joint and several liability

1. If the carrier and one or more maritime performing parties are liable for the loss of, damage to, or delay in delivery of the goods, their liability is joint and several but only up to the limits provided for under this Convention.

2. Without prejudice to article 61, the aggregate liability of all such persons shall not exceed the overall limits of liability under this Convention.

Article 21 Delay

Delay in delivery occurs when the goods are not delivered at the place of destination provided for in the contract of carriage within the time agreed.

Article 22   Calculation of compensation

1. Subject to article 59, the compensation payable by the carrier for loss of or damage to the goods is calculated by reference to the value of such goods at the place and time of delivery established in accordance with article 43.

2. The value of the goods is fixed according to the commodity exchange price or, if there is no such price, according to their market price or, if there is no commodity exchange price or market price, by reference to the normal value of the goods of the same kind and quality at the place of delivery.

3. In case of loss of or damage to the goods, the carrier is not liable for payment of any compensation beyond what is provided for in paragraphs 1 and 2 of this article except when the carrier and the shipper have agreed to calculate compensation in a different manner within the limits of chapter 16.

Article 23   Notice in case of loss, damage or delay

1. The carrier is presumed, in absence of proof to the contrary, to have delivered the goods according to their description in the contract particulars unless notice of loss of or damage to the goods, indicating the general nature of such loss or damage, was given to the carrier or the performing party that delivered the goods before or at the time of the delivery, or, if the loss or damage is not apparent, within seven working days at the place of delivery after the delivery of the goods.

2. Failure to provide the notice referred to in this article to the carrier or the performing party shall not affect the right to claim compensation for loss of or damage to the goods under this Convention, nor shall it affect the allocation of the burden of proof set out in article 17.

3. The notice referred to in this article is not required in respect of loss or damage that is ascertained in a joint inspection of the goods by the person to which they have been delivered and the carrier or the maritime performing party against which liability is being asserted.

4. No compensation in respect of delay is payable unless notice of loss due to delay was given to the carrier within twenty-one consecutive days of delivery of the goods.

5. When the notice referred to in this article is given to the performing party that delivered the goods, it has the same effect as if that notice was given to the carrier, and notice given to the carrier has the same effect as a notice given to a maritime performing party.

6. In the case of any actual or apprehended loss or damage, the parties to the dispute shall give all reasonable facilities to each other for inspecting and tallying the goods and shall provide access to records and documents relevant to the carriage of the goods.

Chapter 6   Additional provisions relating to particular stages of carriage

Article 24   Deviation

When pursuant to applicable law a deviation constitutes a breach of the carrier's obligations, such deviation of itself shall not deprive the carrier or a maritime performing party of any defence or limitation of this Convention, except to the extent provided in article 61.

Article 25   Deck cargo on ships

1. Goods may be carried on the deck of a ship only if:
    (a) Such carriage is required by law;
    (b) They are carried in or on containers or vehicles that are fit for deck carriage, and the decks are specially fitted to carry such containers or vehicles; or
    (c) The carriage on deck is in accordance with the contract of carriage, or the customs, usages or practices of the trade in question.

2. The provisions of this Convention relating to the liability of the carrier apply to the loss of, damage to or delay in the delivery of goods carried on deck pursuant to paragraph 1 of this article, but the carrier is not liable for loss of or damage to such goods, or delay in their delivery, caused by the special risks involved in their carriage on deck when the goods are carried in accordance with subparagraphs 1 (a) or (c) of this article.

3. If the goods have been carried on deck in cases other than those permitted pursuant to paragraph 1 of this article, the carrier is liable for loss of or damage to the goods or delay in their delivery that is exclusively caused by their carriage on deck, and is not entitled to the defences provided for in article 17.

4. The carrier is not entitled to invoke subparagraph 1 (c) of this article against a third party that has acquired a negotiable transport document or a negotiable electronic transport record in good faith, unless the contract particulars state that the goods may be carried on deck.

5. If the carrier and shipper expressly agreed that the goods would be carried under deck, the carrier is not entitled to the benefit of the limitation of liability for any loss of, damage to or delay in the delivery of the goods to the extent that such loss, damage, or delay resulted from their carriage on deck.

Article 26   Carriage preceding or subsequent to sea carriage

When loss of or damage to goods, or an event or circumstance causing a delay in their delivery, occurs during the carrier's period of responsibility but solely before their loading onto the ship or solely after their discharge from the ship, the provisions of this Convention do not prevail over those provisions of another international instrument that, at the time of such loss, damage or event or circumstance causing delay:

  (a) Pursuant to the provisions of such international instrument would have applied to all or any of the carrier's activities if the shipper had made a separate and direct contract with the carrier in respect of the particular stage of carriage where the loss of, or damage to goods, or an event or circumstance causing delay in their delivery occurred;

  (b) Specifically provide for the carrier's liability, limitation of liability, or time for suit; and

  (c) Cannot be departed from by contract either at all or to the detriment of the shipper under that instrument.

Chapter 7   Obligations of the shipper to the carrier

Article 27   Delivery for carriage

1. Unless otherwise agreed in the contract of carriage, the shipper shall deliver the goods ready for carriage. In any event, the shipper shall deliver the goods in such condition that they will withstand the intended carriage, including their loading, handling, stowing, lashing and securing, and unloading, and that they will not cause harm to persons or property.

2. The shipper shall properly and carefully perform any obligation assumed under an agreement made pursuant to article 13, paragraph 2.

3. When a container is packed or a vehicle is loaded by the shipper, the shipper shall properly and carefully stow, lash and secure the contents in or on the container or vehicle, and in such a way that they will not cause harm to persons or property.

Article 28   Cooperation of the shipper and the carrier in providing information and instructions

The carrier and the shipper shall respond to requests from each other to provide information and instructions required for the proper handling and carriage of the goods if the information is in the requested party's possession or the instructions are within the requested party's reasonable ability to provide and they are not otherwise reasonably available to the requesting party.

Article 29   Shipper's obligation to provide information, instructions and documents

1. The shipper shall provide to the carrier in a timely manner such information, instructions and documents relating to the goods that are not otherwise reasonably available to the carrier, and that are reasonably necessary:

  (a) For the proper handling and carriage of the goods, including precautions to be taken by the carrier or a performing party; and

(b) For the carrier to comply with law, regulations or other requirements of public authorities in connection with the intended carriage, provided that the carrier notifies the shipper in a timely manner of the information, instructions and documents it requires.

2. Nothing in this article affects any specific obligation to provide certain information, instructions and documents related to the goods pursuant to law, regulations or other requirements of public authorities in connection with the intended carriage.

Article 30   Basis of shipper's liability to the carrier

1. The shipper is liable for loss or damage sustained by the carrier if the carrier proves that such loss or damage was caused by a breach of the shipper's obligations under this Convention.

2. Except in respect of loss or damage caused by a breach by the shipper of its obligations pursuant to articles 31, paragraph 2, and 32, the shipper is relieved of all or part of its liability if the cause or one of the causes of the loss or damage is not attributable to its fault or to the fault of any person referred to in article 34.

3. When the shipper is relieved of part of its liability pursuant to this article, the shipper is liable only for that part of the loss or damage that is attributable to its fault or to the fault of any person referred to in article 34.

Article 31   Information for compilation of contract particulars

1. The shipper shall provide to the carrier, in a timely manner, accurate information required for the compilation of the contract particulars and the issuance of the transport documents or electronic transport records, including the particulars referred to in article 36, paragraph 1; the name of the party to be identified as the shipper in the contract particulars; the name of the consignee, if any; and the name of the person to whose order the transport document or electronic transport record is to be issued, if any.

2. The shipper is deemed to have guaranteed the accuracy at the time of receipt by the carrier of the information that is provided according to paragraph 1 of this article. The shipper shall indemnify the carrier against loss or damage resulting from the inaccuracy of such information.

Article 32   Special rules on dangerous goods

When goods by their nature or character are, or reasonably appear likely to become, a danger to persons, property or the environment:

(a) The shipper shall inform the carrier of the dangerous nature or character of the goods in a timely manner before they are delivered to the carrier or a performing party. If the shipper fails to do so and the carrier or performing party does not otherwise have knowledge of their dangerous nature or character, the shipper is liable to the carrier for loss or damage resulting from such failure to inform; and

(b) The shipper shall mark or label dangerous goods in accordance with any law, regulations or other requirements of public authorities that apply during any stage of the intended carriage of the goods. If the shipper fails to do so, it is liable to the carrier for loss or damage resulting from such failure.

Article 33   Assumption of shipper's rights and obligations by the documentary shipper

1. A documentary shipper is subject to the obligations and liabilities imposed on the shipper pursuant to this chapter and pursuant to article 55, and is entitled to the shipper's rights and defences provided by this chapter and by chapter 13.

2. Paragraph 1 of this article does not affect the obligations, liabilities, rights or defences of the shipper.

Article 34   Liability of the shipper for other persons

The shipper is liable for the breach of its obligations under this Convention caused by the acts or omissions of any person, including employees, agents and subcontractors, to which it has entrusted the performance of any of its obligations, but the shipper is not liable for acts or omissions of the carrier or a performing party acting on behalf of the carrier, to which the shipper has entrusted the performance of its obligations.

Chapter 8 Transport documents and electronic transport records

Article 35 Issuance of the transport document or the electronic transport record

Unless the shipper and the carrier have agreed not to use a transport document or an electronic transport record, or it is the custom, usage or practice of the trade not to use one, upon delivery of the goods for carriage to the carrier or performing party, the shipper or, if the shipper consents, the documentary shipper, is entitled to obtain from the carrier, at the shipper's option:

(a) A non-negotiable transport document or, subject to article 8, subparagraph (a), a non-negotiable electronic transport record; or

(b) An appropriate negotiable transport document or, subject to article 8, subparagraph (a), a negotiable electronic transport record, unless the shipper and the carrier have agreed not to use a negotiable transport document or negotiable electronic transport record, or it is the custom, usage or practice of the trade not to use one.

Article 36 Contract particulars

1. The contract particulars in the transport document or electronic transport record referred to in article 35 shall include the following information, as furnished by the shipper:

(a) A description of the goods as appropriate for the transport;

(b) The leading marks necessary for identification of the goods;

(c) The number of packages or pieces, or the quantity of goods; and

(d) The weight of the goods, if furnished by the shipper.

2. The contract particulars in the transport document or electronic transport record referred to in article 35 shall also include:

(a) A statement of the apparent order and condition of the goods at the time the carrier or a performing party receives them for carriage;

(b) The name and address of the carrier;

(c) The date on which the carrier or a performing party received the goods, or on which the goods were loaded on board the ship, or on which the transport document or electronic transport record was issued; and

(d) If the transport document is negotiable, the number of originals of the negotiable transport document, when more than one original is issued.

3. The contract particulars in the transport document or electronic transport record referred to in article 35 shall further include:

(a) The name and address of the consignee, if named by the shipper;

(b) The name of a ship, if specified in the contract of carriage;

(c) The place of receipt and, if known to the carrier, the place of delivery; and

(d) The port of loading and the port of discharge, if specified in the contract of carriage.

4. For the purposes of this article, the phrase "apparent order and condition of the goods" in subparagraph 2 (a) of this article refers to the order and condition of the goods based on:

(a) A reasonable external inspection of the goods as packaged at the time the shipper delivers them to the carrier or a performing party; and

(b) Any additional inspection that the carrier or a performing party actually performs before issuing the transport document or electronic transport record.

Article 37 Identity of the carrier

1. If a carrier is identified by name in the contract particulars, any other information in the transport document or electronic transport record relating to the identity of the carrier shall have no effect to the extent that it is inconsistent with that identification.

2. If no person is identified in the contract particulars as the carrier as required pursuant to article 36, subparagraph 2 (b), but the contract particulars indicate that the goods have been loaded on board a named ship, the registered owner of that ship is presumed to be the carrier, unless it proves that the ship was under a bareboat charter at the time of the carriage and it identifies this bareboat charterer and indicates its address, in which case this bareboat charterer is presumed to be the carrier. Alternatively, the registered owner may rebut the presumption of being the carrier by identifying the carrier and indicating its address. The bareboat charterer may rebut any presumption of being the carrier in the same manner.

3. Nothing in this article prevents the claimant from proving that any person other than a person identified in the contract particulars or pursuant to paragraph 2 of this article is the carrier.

Article 38   Signature

1. A transport document shall be signed by the carrier or a person acting on its behalf.

2. An electronic transport record shall include the electronic signature of the carrier or a person acting on its behalf. Such electronic signature shall identify the signatory in relation to the electronic transport record and indicate the carrier's authorization of the electronic transport record.

Article 39   Deficiencies in the contract particulars

1. The absence or inaccuracy of one or more of the contract particulars referred to in article 36, paragraphs 1, 2 or 3, does not of itself affect the legal character or validity of the transport document or of the electronic transport record.

2. If the contract particulars include the date but fail to indicate its significance, the date is deemed to be:

   (a) The date on which all of the goods indicated in the transport document or electronic transport record were loaded on board the ship, if the contract particulars indicate that the goods have been loaded on board a ship; or

   (b) The date on which the carrier or a performing party received the goods, if the contract particulars do not indicate that the goods have been loaded on board a ship.

3. If the contract particulars fail to state the apparent order and condition of the goods at the time the carrier or a performing party receives them, the contract particulars are deemed to have stated that the goods were in apparent good order and condition at the time the carrier or a performing party received them.

Article 40   Qualifying the information relating to the goods in the contract particulars

1. The carrier shall qualify the information referred to in article 36, paragraph 1 to indicate that the carrier does not assume responsibility for the accuracy of the information furnished by the shipper if:

   (a) The carrier has actual knowledge that any material statement in the transport document or electronic transport record is false or misleading; or

   (b) The carrier has reasonable grounds to believe that a material statement in the transport document or electronic transport record is false or misleading.

2. Without prejudice to paragraph 1 of this article, the carrier may qualify the information referred to in article 36, paragraph 1 in the circumstances and in the manner set out in paragraphs 3 and 4 of this article to indicate that the carrier does not assume responsibility for the accuracy of the information furnished by the shipper.

3. When the goods are not delivered for carriage to the carrier or a performing party in a closed container or vehicle, or when they are delivered in a closed container or vehicle and the carrier or a performing party actually inspects them, the carrier may qualify the information referred to in article 36, paragraph 1, if:

   (a) The carrier had no physically practicable or commercially reasonable means of checking the information furnished by the shipper, in which case it may indicate which information it was unable to check; or

(b) The carrier has reasonable grounds to believe the information furnished by the shipper to be inaccurate, in which case it may include a clause providing what it reasonably considers accurate information.

4. When the goods are delivered for carriage to the carrier or a performing party in a closed container or vehicle, the carrier may qualify the information referred to in:

(a) Article 36, subparagraphs 1 (a), (b), or (c), if –

    (i) The goods inside the container or vehicle have not actually been inspected by the carrier or a performing party; and

    (ii) Neither the carrier nor a performing party otherwise has actual knowledge of its contents before issuing the transport document or the electronic transport record; and

(b) Article 36, subparagraph 1 (d), if –

    (i) Neither the carrier nor a performing party weighed the container or vehicle, and the shipper and the carrier had not agreed prior to the shipment that the container or vehicle would be weighed and the weight would be included in the contract particulars; or

    (ii) There was no physically practicable or commercially reasonable means of checking the weight of the container or vehicle.

Article 41   Evidentiary effect of the contract particulars

Except to the extent that the contract particulars have been qualified in the circumstances and in the manner set out in article 40:

(a) A transport document or an electronic transport record is prima facie evidence of the carrier's receipt of the goods as stated in the contract particulars;

(b) Proof to the contrary by the carrier in respect of any contract particulars shall not be admissible, when such contract particulars are included in:

    (i) A negotiable transport document or a negotiable electronic transport record that is transferred to a third party acting in good faith; or

    (ii) A non-negotiable transport document that indicates that it must be surrendered in order to obtain delivery of the goods and is transferred to the consignee acting in good faith.

(c) Proof to the contrary by the carrier shall not be admissible against a consignee that in good faith has acted in reliance on any of the following contract particulars included in a non-negotiable transport document or a non-negotiable electronic transport record:

    (i) The contract particulars referred to in article 36, paragraph 1, when such contract particulars are furnished by the carrier;

    (ii) The number, type and identifying numbers of the containers, but not the identifying numbers of the container seals; and

    (iii) The contract particulars referred to in article 36, paragraph 2.

Article 42   "Freight prepaid"

If the contract particulars contain the statement "freight prepaid" or a statement of a similar nature, the carrier cannot assert against the holder or the consignee the fact that the freight has not been paid. This article does not apply if the holder or the consignee is also the shipper.

Chapter 9 Delivery of the goods

Article 43   Obligation to accept delivery

When the goods have arrived at their destination, the consignee that demands delivery of the goods under the contract of carriage shall accept delivery of the goods at the time or within the time period and at the location agreed in the contract of carriage or, failing such agreement, at the time and location at which, having regard to the terms of the contract, the customs, usages or practices of the trade and the circumstances of the carriage, delivery could reasonably be expected.

Article 44   Obligation to acknowledge receipt

On request of the carrier or the performing party that delivers the goods, the consignee shall acknowledge receipt of the goods from the carrier or the performing party in the manner that is customary at the place of delivery. The carrier may refuse delivery if the consignee refuses to acknowledge such receipt.

Article 45   Delivery when no negotiable transport document or negotiable electronic transport record is issued

When neither a negotiable transport document nor a negotiable electronic transport record has been issued:

(a) The carrier shall deliver the goods to the consignee at the time and location referred to in article 43. The carrier may refuse delivery if the person claiming to be the consignee does not properly identify itself as the consignee on the request of the carrier;

(b) If the name and address of the consignee are not referred to in the contract particulars, the controlling party shall prior to or upon the arrival of the goods at the place of destination advise the carrier of such name and address;

(c) Without prejudice to article 48, paragraph 1, if the goods are not deliverable because

  (i) the consignee, after having received a notice of arrival, does not, at the time or within the time period referred to in article 43, claim delivery of the goods from the carrier after their arrival at the place of destination,

  (ii) the carrier refuses delivery because the person claiming to be the consignee does not properly identify itself as the consignee, or

  (iii) the carrier is, after reasonable effort, unable to locate the consignee in order to request delivery instructions,

the carrier may so advise the controlling party and request instructions in respect of the delivery of the goods. If, after reasonable effort, the carrier is unable to locate the controlling party, the carrier may so advise the shipper and request instructions in respect of the delivery of the goods. If, after reasonable effort, the carrier is unable to locate the shipper, the carrier may so advise the documentary shipper and request instructions in respect of the delivery of the goods;

(d) The carrier that delivers the goods upon instruction of the controlling party, the shipper or the documentary shipper pursuant to subparagraph (c) of this article is discharged from its obligations to deliver the goods under the contract of carriage.

Article 46   Delivery when a non-negotiable transport document that requires surrender is issued

When a non-negotiable transport document has been issued that indicates that it shall be surrendered in order to obtain delivery of the goods:

(a) The carrier shall deliver the goods at the time and location referred to in article 43 to the consignee upon the consignee properly identifying itself on the request of the carrier and surrender of the non-negotiable document. The carrier may refuse delivery if the person claiming to be the consignee fails to properly identify itself on the request of the carrier, and shall refuse delivery if the non-negotiable document is not surrendered. If more than one original of the non negotiable document has been issued, the surrender of one original will suffice and the other originals cease to have any effect or validity;

(b) Without prejudice to article 48, paragraph 1, if the goods are not deliverable because

  (i) the consignee, after having received a notice of arrival, does not, at the time or within the time period referred to in article 43, claim delivery of the goods from the carrier after their arrival at the place of destination,

  (ii) the carrier refuses delivery because the person claiming to be the consignee does not properly identify itself as the consignee or does not surrender the document, or

  (iii) the carrier is, after reasonable effort, unable to locate the consignee in order to request delivery instructions, the carrier may so advise the shipper and request instructions in respect of the delivery of the goods. If, after reasonable effort, the carrier is unable to locate the shipper, the carrier may so advise the documentary shipper and request instructions in respect of the delivery of the goods;

(c) The carrier that delivers the goods upon instruction of the shipper or the documentary shipper pursuant to subparagraph (b) of this article is discharged from its obligation to deliver the goods under the contract of carriage, irrespective of whether the non-negotiable transport document has been surrendered to it.

Article 47   Delivery when a negotiable transport document or negotiable electronic transport record is issued

1. When a negotiable transport document or a negotiable electronic transport record has been issued:

(a) The holder of the negotiable transport document or negotiable electronic transport record is entitled to claim delivery of the goods from the carrier after they have arrived at the place of destination, in which event the carrier shall deliver the goods at the time and location referred to in article 43 to the holder:

   (i)   Upon surrender of the negotiable transport document and, if the holder is one of the persons referred to in article 1, subparagraph 10 (a)(i), upon the holder properly identifying itself; or

   (ii) Upon demonstration by the holder, in accordance with the procedures referred to in article 9, paragraph 1, that it is the holder of the negotiable electronic transport record.

(b) The carrier shall refuse delivery if the requirements of subparagraph (a)(i) or (a)(ii) of this paragraph are not met;

(c) If more than one original of the negotiable transport document has been issued, and the number of originals is stated in that document, the surrender of one original will suffice and the other originals cease to have any effect or validity. When a negotiable electronic transport record has been used, such electronic transport record ceases to have any effect or validity upon delivery to the holder in accordance with the procedures required by article 9, paragraph 1.

2. Without prejudice to article 48, paragraph 1, if the negotiable transport document or the negotiable electronic transport record expressly states that the goods may be delivered without the surrender of the transport document or the electronic transport record, the following rule applies:

(a) If the goods are not deliverable because

   (i)   the holder, after having received a notice of arrival, does not, at the time or within the time period referred to in article 43, claim delivery of the goods from the carrier after their arrival at the place of destination,

   (ii) the carrier refuses delivery because the person claiming to be a holder does not properly identify itself as one of the persons referred to in article 1, subparagraph 10 (a)(i), or

   (iii) the carrier is, after reasonable effort, unable to locate the holder in order to request delivery instructions,

   the carrier may so advise the shipper and request instructions in respect of the delivery of the goods. If, after reasonable effort, the carrier is unable to locate the shipper, the carrier may so advise the documentary shipper and request instructions in respect of the delivery of the goods;

(b) The carrier that delivers the goods upon instruction of the shipper or the documentary shipper in accordance with subparagraph 2 (a) of this article is discharged from its obligation to deliver the goods under the contract of carriage to the holder, irrespective of whether the negotiable transport document has been surrendered to it, or the person claiming delivery under a negotiable electronic transport record has demonstrated, in accordance with the procedures referred to in article 9, paragraph 1, that it is the holder;

(c) The person giving instructions under subparagraph 2 (a) of this article shall indemnify the carrier against loss arising from its being held liable to the holder under subparagraph 2 (e) of this article. The carrier may refuse to follow those instructions if the person fails to provide adequate security as the carrier may reasonably request;

(d) A person that becomes a holder of the negotiable transport document or the negotiable electronic transport record after the carrier has delivered the goods pursuant to subparagraph 2 (b) of this article, but pursuant to contractual or other arrangements made before such delivery acquires rights against the carrier under the contract of carriage, other than the right to claim delivery of the goods;

(e) Notwithstanding subparagraphs 2 (b) and 2 (d) of this article, a holder that becomes a holder after such delivery, and that did not have and could not reasonably have had knowledge of such delivery at the time it became a holder, acquires the rights incorporated in the negotiable transport document or negotiable electronic transport record. When the contract particulars state the expected time of arrival of the goods, or indicate how to obtain information as to whether the goods have been delivered, it is presumed that the holder at the time that it became a holder had or could reasonably have had knowledge of the delivery of the goods.

Article 48   Goods remaining undelivered

1. For the purposes of this article, goods shall be deemed to have remained undelivered only if, after their arrival at the place of destination:

(a) The consignee does not accept delivery of the goods pursuant to this chapter at the time and location referred to in article 43;

(b) The controlling party, the holder, the shipper or the documentary shipper cannot be found or does not give the carrier adequate instructions pursuant to articles 45, 46 and 47;

(c) The carrier is entitled or required to refuse delivery pursuant to articles 44, 45, 46 and 47;

(d) The carrier is not allowed to deliver the goods to the consignee pursuant to the law or regulations of the place at which delivery is requested; or

(e) The goods are otherwise undeliverable by the carrier.

2. Without prejudice to any other rights that the carrier may have against the shipper, controlling party or consignee, if the goods have remained undelivered, the carrier may, at the risk and expense of the person entitled to the goods, take such action in respect of the goods as circumstances may reasonably require, including:

(a) To store the goods at any suitable place;

(b) To unpack the goods if they are packed in containers or vehicles, or to act otherwise in respect of the goods, including by moving them; and

(c) To cause the goods to be sold or destroyed in accordance with the practices or pursuant to the law or regulations of the place where the goods are located at the time.

3. The carrier may exercise the rights under paragraph 2 of this article only after it has given reasonable notice of the intended action under paragraph 2 of this article to the person stated in the contract particulars as the person, if any, to be notified of the arrival of the goods at the place of destination, and to one of the following persons in the order indicated, if known to the carrier: the consignee, the controlling party or the shipper.

4. If the goods are sold pursuant to subparagraph 2 (c) of this article, the carrier shall hold the proceeds of the sale for the benefit of the person entitled to the goods, subject to the deduction of any costs incurred by the carrier and any other amounts that are due to the carrier in connection with the carriage of those goods.

5. The carrier shall not be liable for loss of or damage to goods that occurs during the time that they remain undelivered pursuant to this article unless the claimant proves that such loss or damage resulted from the failure by the carrier to take steps that would have been reasonable in the circumstances to preserve the goods and that the carrier knew or ought to have known that the loss or damage to the goods would result from its failure to take such steps.

Article 49   Retention of goods

Nothing in this Convention affects a right of the carrier or a performing party that may exist pursuant to the contract of carriage or the applicable law to retain the goods to secure the payment of sums due.

Chapter 10   Rights of the controlling party

Article 50   Exercise and extent of right of control

1. The right of control may be exercised only by the controlling party and is limited to:
   (a) The right to give or modify instructions in respect of the goods that do not constitute a variation of the contract of carriage;
   (b) The right to obtain delivery of the goods at a scheduled port of call or, in respect of inland carriage, any place en route; and
   (c) The right to replace the consignee by any other person including the controlling party.
2. The right of control exists during the entire period of responsibility of the carrier, as provided in article 12, and ceases when that period expires.

Article 51   Identity of the controlling party and transfer of the right of control

1. Except in the cases referred to in paragraphs 2, 3 and 4 of this article:
   (a) The shipper is the controlling party unless the shipper, when the contract of carriage is concluded, designates the consignee, the documentary shipper or another person as the controlling party;
   (b) The controlling party is entitled to transfer the right of control to another person. The transfer becomes effective with respect to the carrier upon its notification of the transfer by the transferor, and the transferee becomes the controlling party; and
   (c) The controlling party shall properly identify itself when it exercises the right of control.
2. When a non-negotiable transport document has been issued that indicates that it shall be surrendered in order to obtain delivery of the goods:
   (a) The shipper is the controlling party and may transfer the right of control to the consignee named in the transport document by transferring the document to that person without endorsement. If more than one original of the document was issued, all originals shall be transferred in order to effect a transfer of the right of control; and
   (b) In order to exercise its right of control, the controlling party shall produce the document and properly identify itself. If more than one original of the document was issued, all originals shall be produced, failing which the right of control cannot be exercised.
3. When a negotiable transport document is issued:
   (a) The holder or, if more than one original of the negotiable transport document is issued, the holder of all originals is the controlling party;
   (b) The holder may transfer the right of control by transferring the negotiable transport document to another person in accordance with article 57. If more than one original of that document was issued, all originals shall be transferred to that person in order to effect a transfer of the right of control; and
   (c) In order to exercise the right of control, the holder shall produce the negotiable transport document to the carrier, and if the holder is one of the persons referred to in article 1, sub-paragraph 10 (a)(i), the holder shall properly identify itself. If more than one original of the document was issued, all originals shall be produced, failing which the right of control cannot be exercised.
4. When a negotiable electronic transport record is issued:
   (a) The holder is the controlling party;
   (b) The holder may transfer the right of control to another person by transferring the negotiable electronic transport record in accordance with the procedures referred to in article 9, paragraph 1; and

(c) In order to exercise the right of control, the holder shall demonstrate, in accordance with the procedures referred to in article 9, paragraph 1, that it is the holder.

Article 52   Carrier's execution of instructions

1. Subject to paragraphs 2 and 3 of this article, the carrier shall execute the instructions referred to in article 50 if:

(a) The person giving such instructions is entitled to exercise the right of control;

(b) The instructions can reasonably be executed according to their terms at the moment that they reach the carrier; and

(c) The instructions will not interfere with the normal operations of the carrier, including its delivery practices.

2. In any event, the controlling party shall reimburse the carrier for any reasonable additional expense that the carrier may incur and shall indemnify the carrier against loss or damage that the carrier may suffer as a result of diligently executing any instruction pursuant to this article, including compensation that the carrier may become liable to pay for loss of or damage to other goods being carried.

3. The carrier is entitled to obtain security from the controlling party for the amount of additional expense, loss or damage that the carrier reasonably expects will arise in connection with the execution of an instruction pursuant to this article. The carrier may refuse to carry out the instructions if no such security is provided.

4. The carrier's liability for loss of or damage to the goods or for delay in delivery resulting from its failure to comply with the instructions of the controlling party in breach of its obligation pursuant to paragraph 1 of this article shall be subject to articles 17 to 23, and the amount of the compensation payable by the carrier shall be subject to articles 59 to 61.

Article 53   Deemed delivery

Goods that are delivered pursuant to an instruction in accordance with article 52, paragraph 1, are deemed to be delivered at the place of destination, and the provisions of chapter 9 relating to such delivery apply to such goods.

Article 54   Variations to the contract of carriage

1. The controlling party is the only person that may agree with the carrier to variations to the contract of carriage other than those referred to in article 50, subparagraphs 1 (b) and (c).

2. Variations to the contract of carriage, including those referred to in article 50, subparagraphs 1 (b) and (c), shall be stated in a negotiable transport document or in a non-negotiable transport document that requires surrender, or incorporated in a negotiable electronic transport record, or, upon the request of the controlling party, shall be stated in a non-negotiable transport document or incorporated in a non-negotiable electronic transport record. If so stated or incorporated, such variations shall be signed in accordance with article 38.

Article 55   Providing additional information, instructions or documents to carrier

1. The controlling party, on request of the carrier or a performing party, shall provide in a timely manner information, instructions or documents relating to the goods not yet provided by the shipper and not otherwise reasonably available to the carrier that the carrier may reasonably need to perform its obligations under the contract of carriage.

2. If the carrier, after reasonable effort, is unable to locate the controlling party or the controlling party is unable to provide adequate information, instructions or documents to the carrier, the shipper shall provide them. If the carrier, after reasonable effort, is unable to locate the shipper, the documentary shipper shall provide such information, instructions or documents.

Article 56   Variation by agreement

The parties to the contract of carriage may vary the effect of articles 50, subparagraphs 1 (b) and (c), 50, paragraph 2, and 52. The parties may also restrict or exclude the transferability of the right of control referred to in article 51, subparagraph 1 (b).

Chapter 11 Transfer of rights

Article 57 When a negotiable transport document or negotiable electronic transport record is issued

1. When a negotiable transport document is issued, the holder may transfer the rights incorporated in the document by transferring it to another person:

    (a) Duly endorsed either to such other person or in blank, if an order document; or

    (b) Without endorsement, if:

        (i) A bearer document or a blank endorsed document; or

        (ii) A document made out to the order of a named person and the transfer is between the first holder and the named person.

2. When a negotiable electronic transport record is issued, its holder may transfer the rights incorporated in it, whether it be made out to order or to the order of a named person, by transferring the electronic transport record in accordance with the procedures referred to in article 9, paragraph 1.

Article 58 Liability of holder

1. Without prejudice to article 55, a holder that is not the shipper and that does not exercise any right under the contract of carriage does not assume any liability under the contract of carriage solely by reason of being a holder.

2. A holder that is not the shipper and that exercises any right under the contract of carriage assumes any liabilities imposed on it under the contract of carriage to the extent that such liabilities are incorporated in or ascertainable from the negotiable transport document or the negotiable electronic transport record.

3. For the purposes of paragraphs 1 and 2 of this article, a holder that is not the shipper does not exercise any right under the contract of carriage solely because:

    (a) It agrees with the carrier, pursuant to article 10, to replace a negotiable transport document by a negotiable electronic transport record or to replace a negotiable electronic transport record by a negotiable transport document; or

    (b) It transfers its rights pursuant to article 57.

Chapter 12 Limits of liability

Article 59 Limits of liability

1. Subject to articles 60 and 61, paragraph 1, the carrier's liability for breaches of its obligations under this Convention is limited to 875 units of account per package or other shipping unit, or 3 units of account per kilogram of the gross weight of the goods that are the subject of the claim or dispute, whichever amount is the higher, except when the value of the goods has been declared by the shipper and included in the contract particulars, or when a higher amount than the amount of limitation of liability set out in this article has been agreed upon between the carrier and the shipper.

2. When goods are carried in or on a container, pallet or similar article of transport used to consolidate goods, or in or on a vehicle, the packages or shipping units enumerated in the contract particulars as packed in or on such article of transport or vehicle are deemed packages or shipping units. If not so enumerated, the goods in or on such article of transport or vehicle are deemed one shipping unit.

3. The unit of account referred to in this article is the Special Drawing Right as defined by the International Monetary Fund. The amounts referred to in this article are to be converted into the national currency of a State according to the value of such currency at the date of judgement or award or the date agreed upon by the parties. The value of a national currency, in terms of the Special Drawing Right, of a Contracting State that is a member of the International Monetary Fund is to be calculated in accordance with the method of valuation applied by the International Monetary Fund in effect at the date in question for its operations and transactions. The value of a national currency, in terms of the Special Drawing Right, of a Contracting State that is not a member of the International Monetary Fund is to be calculated in a manner to be determined by that State.

Article 60   Limits of liability for loss caused by delay

Subject to article 61, paragraph 2, compensation for loss of or damage to the goods due to delay shall be calculated in accordance with article 22 and liability for economic loss due to delay is limited to an amount equivalent to two and one-half times the freight payable on the goods delayed. The total amount payable pursuant to this article and article 59, paragraph 1 may not exceed the limit that would be established pursuant to article 59, paragraph 1 in respect of the total loss of the goods concerned.

Article 61   Loss of the benefit of limitation of liability

1. Neither the carrier nor any of the persons referred to in article 18 is entitled to the benefit of the limitation of liability as provided in article 59, or as provided in the contract of carriage, if the claimant proves that the loss resulting from the breach of the carrier's obligation under this Convention was attributable to a personal act or omission of the person claiming a right to limit done with the intent to cause such loss or recklessly and with knowledge that such loss would probably result.

2. Neither the carrier nor any of the persons mentioned in article 18 is entitled to the benefit of the limitation of liability as provided in article 60 if the claimant proves that the delay in delivery resulted from a personal act or omission of the person claiming a right to limit done with the intent to cause the loss due to delay or recklessly and with knowledge that such loss would probably result.

Chapter 13 Time for suit

Article 62   Period of time for suit

1. No judicial or arbitral proceedings in respect of claims or disputes arising from a breach of an obligation under this Convention may be instituted after the expiration of a period of two years.

2. The period referred to in paragraph 1 of this article commences on the day on which the carrier has delivered the goods or, in cases in which no goods have been delivered or only part of the goods have been delivered, on the last day on which the goods should have been delivered. The day on which the period commences is not included in the period.

3. Notwithstanding the expiration of the period set out in paragraph 1 of this article, one party may rely on its claim as a defence or for the purpose of set-off against a claim asserted by the other party.

Article 63   Extension of time for suit

The period provided in article 62 shall not be subject to suspension or interruption, but the person against which a claim is made may at any time during the running of the period extend that period by a declaration to the claimant. This period may be further extended by another declaration or declarations.

Article 64   Action for indemnity

An action for indemnity by a person held liable may be instituted after the expiration of the period provided in article 62 if the indemnity action is instituted within the later of:

(a) The time allowed by the applicable law in the jurisdiction where proceedings are instituted; or

(b) Ninety days commencing from the day when the person instituting the action for indemnity has either settled the claim or been served with process in the action against itself, whichever is earlier.

Article 65   Actions against the person identified as the carrier

An action against the bareboat charterer or the person identified as the carrier pursuant to article 37, paragraph 2, may be instituted after the expiration of the period provided in article 62 if the action is instituted within the later of:

(a) The time allowed by the applicable law in the jurisdiction where proceedings are instituted; or

(b) Ninety days commencing from the day when the carrier has been identified, or the registered owner or bareboat charterer has rebutted the presumption that it is the carrier, pursuant to article 37, paragraph 2.

Chapter 14 Jurisdiction

Article 66   Actions against the carrier

Unless the contract of carriage contains an exclusive choice of court agreement that complies with article 67 or 72, the plaintiff has the right to institute judicial proceedings under this Convention against the carrier:

(a) In a competent court within the jurisdiction of which is situated one of the following places:
   (i)   The domicile of the carrier;
   (ii) The place of receipt agreed in the contract of carriage;
   (iii) The place of delivery agreed in the contract of carriage; or
   (iv) The port where the goods are initially loaded on a ship or the port where the goods are finally discharged from a ship; or
(b) In a competent court or courts designated by an agreement between the shipper and the carrier for the purpose of deciding claims against the carrier that may arise under this Convention.

Article 67   Choice of court agreements

1. The jurisdiction of a court chosen in accordance with article 66, paragraph (b), is exclusive for disputes between the parties to the contract only if the parties so agree and the agreement conferring jurisdiction:

(a) Is contained in a volume contract that clearly states the names and addresses of the parties and either (i) is individually negotiated or (ii) contains a prominent statement that there is an exclusive choice of court agreement and specifies the sections of the volume contract containing that agreement; and
(b) Clearly designates the courts of one Contracting State or one or more specific courts of one Contracting State.

2. A person that is not a party to the volume contract is bound by an exclusive choice of court agreement concluded in accordance with paragraph 1 of this article only if:

(a) The court is in one of the places designated in article 66, paragraph (a);
(b) That agreement is contained in the transport document or electronic transport record;
(c) That person is given timely and adequate notice of the court where the action shall be brought and that the jurisdiction of that court is exclusive; and
(d) The law of the court seized recognizes that that person may be bound by the exclusive choice of court agreement.

Article 68   Actions against the maritime performing party

The plaintiff has the right to institute judicial proceedings under this Convention against the maritime performing party in a competent court within the jurisdiction of which is situated one of the following places:

(a) The domicile of the maritime performing party; or
(b) The port where the goods are received by the maritime performing party, the port where the goods are delivered by the maritime performing party or the port in which the maritime performing party performs its activities with respect to the goods.

Article 69   No additional bases of jurisdiction

Subject to articles 71 and 72, no judicial proceedings under this Convention against the carrier or a maritime performing party may be instituted in a court not designated pursuant to articles 66 or 68.

Article 70   Arrest and provisional or protective measures

Nothing in this Convention affects jurisdiction with regard to provisional or protective measures, including arrest. A court in a State in which a provisional or protective measure was taken does not have jurisdiction to determine the case upon its merits unless:

(a) The requirements of this chapter are fulfilled; or

(b) An international convention that applies in that State so provides.

Article 71   Consolidation and removal of actions

1. Except when there is an exclusive choice of court agreement that is binding pursuant to articles 67 or 72, if a single action is brought against both the carrier and the maritime performing party arising out of a single occurrence, the action may be instituted only in a court designated pursuant to both article 66 and article 68. If there is no such court, such action may be instituted in a court designated pursuant to article 68, subparagraph (b), if there is such a court.

2. Except when there is an exclusive choice of court agreement that is binding pursuant to articles 67 or 72, a carrier or a maritime performing party that institutes an action seeking a declaration of non-liability or any other action that would deprive a person of its right to select the forum pursuant to article 66 or 68 shall, at the request of the defendant, withdraw that action once the defendant has chosen a court designated pursuant to article 66 or 68, whichever is applicable, where the action may be recommenced.

Article 72   Agreement after a dispute has arisen and jurisdiction when the defendant has entered an appearance

1. After a dispute has arisen, the parties to the dispute may agree to resolve it in any competent court.

2. A competent court before which a defendant appears, without contesting jurisdiction in accordance with the rules of that court, has jurisdiction.

Article 73   Recognition and enforcement

1. A decision made in one Contracting State by a court having jurisdiction under this Convention shall be recognized and enforced in another Contracting State in accordance with the law of such latter Contracting State when both States have made a declaration in accordance with article 74.

2. A court may refuse recognition and enforcement based on the grounds for the refusal of recognition and enforcement available pursuant to its law.

3. This chapter shall not affect the application of the rules of a regional economic integration organization that is a party to this Convention, as concerns the recognition or enforcement of judgements as between member States of the regional economic integration organization, whether adopted before or after this Convention.

Article 74   Application of chapter 14

The provisions of this chapter shall bind only Contracting States that declare in accordance with article 91 that they will be bound by them.

Chapter 15 Arbitration

Article 75   Arbitration agreements

1. Subject to this chapter, parties may agree that any dispute that may arise relating to the carriage of goods under this Convention shall be referred to arbitration.

2. The arbitration proceedings shall, at the option of the person asserting a claim against the carrier, take place at:

(a) Any place designated for that purpose in the arbitration agreement; or

(b) Any other place situated in a State where any of the following places is located:

    (i)   The domicile of the carrier;

    (ii) The place of receipt agreed in the contract of carriage;

    (iii) The place of delivery agreed in the contract of carriage; or

(iv) The port where the goods are initially loaded on a ship or the port where the goods are finally discharged from a ship.

3. The designation of the place of arbitration in the agreement is binding for disputes between the parties to the agreement if the agreement is contained in a volume contract that clearly states the names and addresses of the parties and either:

(a) Is individually negotiated; or

(b) Contains a prominent statement that there is an arbitration agreement and specifies the sections of the volume contract containing the arbitration agreement.

4. When an arbitration agreement has been concluded in accordance with paragraph 3 of this article, a person that is not a party to the volume contract is bound by the designation of the place of arbitration in that agreement only if:

(a) The place of arbitration designated in the agreement is situated in one of the places referred to in subparagraph 2 (b) of this article;

(b) The agreement is contained in the transport document or electronic transport record;

(c) The person to be bound is given timely and adequate notice of the place of arbitration; and

(d) Applicable law permits that person to be bound by the arbitration agreement.

5. The provisions of paragraphs 1, 2, 3 and 4 of this article are deemed to be part of every arbitration clause or agreement, and any term of such clause or agreement to the extent that it is inconsistent therewith is void.

Article 76   Arbitration agreement in non-liner transportation

1. Nothing in this Convention affects the enforceability of an arbitration agreement in a contract of carriage in non-liner transportation to which this Convention or the provisions of this Convention apply by reason of:

(a) The application of article 7; or

(b) The parties' voluntary incorporation of this Convention in a contract of carriage that would not otherwise be subject to this Convention.

2. Notwithstanding paragraph 1 of this article, an arbitration agreement in a transport document or electronic transport record to which this Convention applies by reason of the application of article 7 is subject to this chapter unless such a transport document or electronic transport record:

(a) Identifies the parties to and the date of the charterparty or other contract excluded from the application of this Convention by reason of the application of article 6; and

(b) Incorporates by specific reference the clause in the charterparty or other contract that contains the terms of the arbitration agreement.

Article 77   Agreement to arbitrate after a dispute has arisen

Notwithstanding the provisions of this chapter and chapter 14, after a dispute has arisen the parties to the dispute may agree to resolve it by arbitration in any place.

Article 78   Application of chapter 15

The provisions of this chapter shall bind only Contracting States that declare in accordance with article 91 that they will be bound by them.

Chapter 16 Validity of contractual terms

Article 79   General provisions

1. Unless otherwise provided in this Convention, any term in a contract of carriage is void to the extent that it:

(a) Directly or indirectly excludes or limits the obligations of the carrier or a maritime performing party under this Convention;

(b) Directly or indirectly excludes or limits the liability of the carrier or a maritime performing party for breach of an obligation under this Convention; or

    (c) Assigns a benefit of insurance of the goods in favour of the carrier or a person referred to in article 18.

  2. Unless otherwise provided in this Convention, any term in a contract of carriage is void to the extent that it:

    (a) Directly or indirectly excludes, limits or increases the obligations under this Convention of the shipper, consignee, controlling party, holder or documentary shipper; or

    (b) Directly or indirectly excludes, limits or increases the liability of the shipper, consignee, controlling party, holder or documentary shipper for breach of any of its obligations under this Convention.

Article 80   Special rules for volume contracts

  1. Notwithstanding article 79, as between the carrier and the shipper, a volume contract to which this Convention applies may provide for greater or lesser rights, obligations and liabilities than those imposed by this Convention.

  2. A derogation pursuant to paragraph 1 of this article is binding only when:

    (a) The volume contract contains a prominent statement that it derogates from this Convention;

    (b) The volume contract is (i) individually negotiated or (ii) prominently specifies the sections of the volume contract containing the derogations;

    (c) The shipper is given an opportunity and notice of the opportunity to conclude a contract of carriage on terms and conditions that comply with this Convention without any derogation under this article; and

    (d) The derogation is neither (i) incorporated by reference from another document nor (ii) included in a contract of adhesion that is not subject to negotiation.

  3. A carrier's public schedule of prices and services, transport document, electronic transport record or similar document is not a volume contract pursuant to paragraph 1 of this article, but a volume contract may incorporate such documents by reference as terms of the contract.

  4. Paragraph 1 of this article does not apply to rights and obligations provided in articles 14, subparagraphs (a) and (b), 29 and 32 or to liability arising from the breach thereof, nor does it apply to any liability arising from an act or omission referred to in article 61.

  5. The terms of the volume contract that derogate from this Convention, if the volume contract satisfies the requirements of paragraph 2 of this article, apply between the carrier and any person other than the shipper provided that:

    (a) Such person received information that prominently states that the volume contract derogates from this Convention and gave its express consent to be bound by such derogations; and

    (b) Such consent is not solely set forth in a carrier's public schedule of prices and services, transport document or electronic transport record.

  6. The party claiming the benefit of the derogation bears the burden of proof that the conditions for derogation have been fulfilled.

Article 81   Special rules for live animals and certain other goods

Notwithstanding article 79 and without prejudice to article 80, the contract of carriage may exclude or limit the obligations or the liability of both the carrier and a maritime performing party if:

    (a) The goods are live animals, but any such exclusion or limitation will not be effective if the claimant proves that the loss of or damage to the goods, or delay in delivery, resulted from an act or omission of the carrier or of a person referred to in article 18, done with the intent to cause such loss of or damage to the goods or such loss due to delay or done recklessly and with knowledge that such loss or damage or such loss due to delay would probably result; or

    (b) The character or condition of the goods or the circumstances and terms and conditions under which the carriage is to be performed are such as reasonably to justify a special agreement, provided that such contract of carriage is not related to ordinary commercial shipments made in the ordinary course of trade and that no negotiable transport document or negotiable electronic transport record is issued for the carriage of the goods.

Chapter 17 Matters not governed by this Convention

Article 82   International conventions governing the carriage of goods by other modes of transport

Nothing in this Convention affects the application of any of the following international conventions in force at the time this Convention enters into force, including any future amendment to such conventions, that regulate the liability of the carrier for loss of or damage to the goods:

(a) Any convention governing the carriage of goods by air to the extent that such convention according to its provisions applies to any part of the contract of carriage;

(b) Any convention governing the carriage of goods by road to the extent that such convention according to its provisions applies to the carriage of goods that remain loaded on a road cargo vehicle carried on board a ship;

(c) Any convention governing the carriage of goods by rail to the extent that such convention according to its provisions applies to carriage of goods by sea as a supplement to the carriage by rail; or

(d) Any convention governing the carriage of goods by inland waterways to the extent that such convention according to its provisions applies to a carriage of goods without transshipment both by inland waterways and sea.

Article 83   Global limitation of liability

Nothing in this Convention affects the application of any international convention or national law regulating the global limitation of liability of vessel owners.

Article 84   General average

Nothing in this Convention affects the application of terms in the contract of carriage or provisions of national law regarding the adjustment of general average.

Article 85   Passengers and luggage

This Convention does not apply to a contract of carriage for passengers and their luggage.

Article 86   Damage caused by nuclear incident

No liability arises under this Convention for damage caused by a nuclear incident if the operator of a nuclear installation is liable for such damage:

(a) Under the Paris Convention on Third Party Liability in the Field of Nuclear Energy of 29 July 1960 as amended by the Additional Protocol of 28 January 1964 and by the Protocols of 16 November 1982 and 12 February 2004, the Vienna Convention on Civil Liability for Nuclear Damage of 21 May 1963 as amended by the Joint Protocol Relating to the Application of the Vienna Convention and the Paris Convention of 21 September 1988 and as amended by the Protocol to Amend the 1963 Vienna Convention on Civil Liability for Nuclear Damage of 12 September 1997, or the Convention on Supplementary Compensation for Nuclear Damage of 12 September 1997, including any amendment to these conventions and any future convention in respect of the liability of the operator of a nuclear installation for damage caused by a nuclear incident; or

(b) Under national law applicable to the liability for such damage, provided that such law is in all respects as favourable to persons that may suffer damage as either the Paris or Vienna Conventions or the Convention on Supplementary Compensation for Nuclear Damage.

Chapter 18 Final clauses

Article 87   Depositary

The Secretary-General of the United Nations is hereby designated as the depositary of this Convention.

Article 88   Signature, ratification, acceptance, approval or accession

1. This Convention is open for signature by all States at Rotterdam, the Netherlands, on 23 September 2009 and thereafter at the Headquarters of the United Nations in New York.

2. This Convention is subject to ratification, acceptance or approval by the signatory States.

3. This Convention is open for accession by all States that are not signatory States as from the date it is open for signature.

4. Instruments of ratification, acceptance, approval and accession are to be deposited with the Secretary-General of the United Nations.

Article 89   Denunciation of other conventions

1. A State that ratifies, accepts, approves or accedes to this Convention and is a party to the International Convention for the Unification of certain Rules relating to Bills of Lading signed at Brussels on 25 August 1924; to the Protocol signed on 23 February 1968 to amend the International Convention for the Unification of certain Rules relating to Bills of Lading signed at Brussels on 25 August 1924; or to the Protocol to amend the International Convention for the Unification of certain Rules relating to Bills of Lading as Modified by the Amending Protocol of 23 February 1968, signed at Brussels on 21 December 1979 shall at the same time denounce that Convention and the protocol or protocols thereto to which it is a party by notifying the Government of Belgium to that effect, with a declaration that the denunciation is to take effect as from the date when this Convention enters into force in respect of that State.

2. A State that ratifies, accepts, approves or accedes to this Convention and is a party to the United Nations Convention on the Carriage of Goods by Sea concluded at Hamburg on 31 March 1978 shall at the same time denounce that Convention by notifying the Secretary-General of the United Nations to that effect, with a declaration that the denunciation is to take effect as from the date when this Convention enters into force in respect of that State.

3. For the purposes of this article, ratifications, acceptances, approvals and accessions in respect of this Convention by States parties to the instruments listed in paragraphs 1 and 2 of this article that are notified to the depositary after this Convention has entered into force are not effective until such denunciations as may be required on the part of those States in respect of these instruments have become effective. The depositary of this Convention shall consult with the Government of Belgium, as the depositary of the instruments referred to in paragraph 1 of this article, so as to ensure necessary coordination in this respect.

Article 90   Reservations

No reservation is permitted to this Convention.

Article 91   Procedure and effect of declarations

1. The declarations permitted by articles 74 and 78 may be made at any time. The initial declarations permitted by article 92, paragraph 1, and article 93, paragraph 2, shall be made at the time of signature, ratification, acceptance, approval or accession. No other declaration is permitted under this Convention.

2. Declarations made at the time of signature are subject to confirmation upon ratification, acceptance or approval.

3. Declarations and their confirmations are to be in writing and to be formally notified to the depositary.

4. A declaration takes effect simultaneously with the entry into force of this Convention in respect of the State concerned. However, a declaration of which the depositary receives formal notification after such entry into force takes effect on the first day of the month following the expiration of six months after the date of its receipt by the depositary.

5. Any State that makes a declaration under this Convention may withdraw it at any time by a formal notification in writing addressed to the depositary. The withdrawal of a declaration, or its modification where permitted by this Convention, takes effect on the first day of the month following the expiration of six months after the date of the receipt of the notification by the depositary.

Article 92   Effect in domestic territorial units

1. If a Contracting State has two or more territorial units in which different systems of law are applicable in relation to the matters dealt with in this Convention, it may, at the time of signature, ratification, acceptance, approval or accession, declare that this Convention is to extend to all its territorial units or only to one or more of them, and may amend its declaration by submitting another declaration at any time.

2. These declarations are to be notified to the depositary and are to state expressly the territorial units to which the Convention extends.

3. When a Contracting State has declared pursuant to this article that this Convention extends to one or more but not all of its territorial units, a place located in a territorial unit to which this Convention does not extend is not considered to be in a Contracting State for the purposes of this Convention.

4. If a Contracting State makes no declaration pursuant to paragraph 1 of this article, the Convention is to extend to all territorial units of that State.

Article 93   Participation by regional economic integration organizations

1. A regional economic integration organization that is constituted by sovereign States and has competence over certain matters governed by this Convention may similarly sign, ratify, accept, approve or accede to this Convention. The regional economic integration organization shall in that case have the rights and obligations of a Contracting State, to the extent that that organization has competence over matters governed by this Convention. When the number of Contracting States is relevant in this Convention, the regional economic integration organization does not count as a Contracting State in addition to its member States which are Contracting States.

2. The regional economic integration organization shall, at the time of signature, ratification, acceptance, approval or accession, make a declaration to the depositary specifying the matters governed by this Convention in respect of which competence has been transferred to that organization by its member States. The regional economic integration organization shall promptly notify the depositary of any changes to the distribution of competence, including new transfers of competence, specified in the declaration pursuant to this paragraph.

3. Any reference to a "Contracting State" or "Contracting States" in this Convention applies equally to a regional economic integration organization when the context so requires.

Article 94   Entry into force

1. This Convention enters into force on the first day of the month following the expiration of one year after the date of deposit of the twentieth instrument of ratification, acceptance, approval or accession.

2. For each State that becomes a Contracting State to this Convention after the date of the deposit of the twentieth instrument of ratification, acceptance, approval or accession, this Convention enters into force on the first day of the month following the expiration of one year after the deposit of the appropriate instrument on behalf of that State.

3. Each Contracting State shall apply this Convention to contracts of carriage concluded on or after the date of the entry into force of this Convention in respect of that State.

Article 95   Revision and amendment

1. At the request of not less than one third of the Contracting States to this Convention, the depositary shall convene a conference of the Contracting States for revising or amending it.

2. Any instrument of ratification, acceptance, approval or accession deposited after the entry into force of an amendment to this Convention is deemed to apply to the Convention as amended.

Article 96   Denunciation of this Convention

1. A Contracting State may denounce this Convention at any time by means of a notification in writing addressed to the depositary.

2. The denunciation takes effect on the first day of the month following the expiration of one year after the notification is received by the depositary. If a longer period is specified in the notification, the denunciation takes effect upon the expiration of such longer period after the notification is received by the depositary.

DONE at New York, this eleventh day of December two thousand and eight, in a single original, of which the Arabic, Chinese, English, French, Russian and Spanish texts are equally authentic.

IN WITNESS WHEREOF the undersigned plenipotentiaries, being duly authorized by their respective Governments, have signed this Convention.

Codes

Banking: Conduct of Business Sourcebook (BCOBS)

[Reproduced with permission of the Financial Services Authority]   [as at **14 May 2011**]
[G = Guidance; P = principle; R = Rule.]

1. APPLICATION

1.1 General application

The general application rule

1.1.1 R   This sourcebook applies to a *firm* with respect to the activity of *accepting deposits* from *banking customers* carried on from an establishment maintained by it in the *United Kingdom* and activities connected with that activity.

Limitations on the general application rule

1.1.2 R   The general application *rule* is modified in the chapters of this sourcebook for particular purposes.

1.1.3 R   Except as provided for in BCOBS 1.1.4R, this sourcebook does not apply to:
   (1) *payment services* where Part 5 and 6 of the *Payment Services Regulations* apply; or
   (2) a *person* or *firm* which has permission for *accepting deposits* but only for the purposes of, or in the course of, an activity other than *accepting deposits*.

1.1.4 R   (1) Chapters 2, 5 and 6 of BCOBS (except for BCOBS 5.1.11 R to BCOBS 5.1.19 R) apply to payment services where Parts 5 and 6 of the Payment Services Regulations apply.
   (2) Chapter 3 of *BCOBS* applies to *payment services* where Parts 5 and 6 of the *Payment Services Regulations* apply with the modifications set out in BCOBS 3.1.2 R(2).
   (3) A *firm* will not be subject to *BCOBS* to the extent that it would be contrary to the *United Kingdom's* obligations under an *EU* instrument.

1.1.5 R   BCOBS 4.1.4AG(2)(a), BCOBS 5.1.3AG, BCOBS 5.1.3BG and BCOBS 5.1.13 R do not apply to a *credit union*.

Exclusion of liability

1.1.6 R   A firm must not seek to exclude or restrict, or rely on any exclusion or restriction of, any duty or liability it may have to a *banking customer* unless it is reasonable for it to do so and the duty or liability arises other than under the *regulatory system*.

1.1.7 G   The general law, including the *Unfair Terms Regulations*, also limits the scope for a *firm* to exclude or restrict any duty or liability to a *consumer*.

2. COMMUNICATIONS WITH BANKING CUSTOMERS AND FINANCIAL PROMOTIONS

2.1 Purpose and Application: Who and what?

2.1.1 G   *Principle* 6 requires a *firm* to pay due regard to the interests of its *customers* and treat them fairly. *Principle* 7 requires a *firm* to pay due regard to the information needs of its clients and communicate information to them in a way which is clear, fair and not misleading. This chapter reinforces these requirements by requiring a *firm* to pay regard to the information needs of *banking customers* when communicating with, or making a *financial promotion* to, them and to communicate information in a way that is clear, fair and not misleading.

2.1.2 R   In addition to the general application *rule* (BCOBS 1.1.1 R), this chapter applies to the *communication*, or *approval* for *communication*, to a *person* in the *United Kingdom* of a *financial promotion* of a *retail banking service* unless it can lawfully be *communicated* by an *unauthorised person* without *approval*.

2.1.3 R   This chapter applies to a *firm*:
   (1) communicating with a *banking customer* in relation to *accepting deposits*;
   (2) *communicating* a *financial promotion* that is not an *excluded communication*; or
   (3) *approving* a *financial promotion*.

2.2   The fair, clear and not misleading rule

2.2.1 R   A *firm* must take reasonable steps to ensure that a communication or a *financial promotion* is fair, clear and not misleading.

2.2.2 G   The fair, clear and not misleading *rule* applies in a way that is appropriate and proportionate taking into account the means of communication and the information that it is intended to convey. So a communication addressed to a *banking customer* who is not a *consumer* may not need to include the same information, or be presented in the same way, as a communication addressed to a *consumer*.

2.2.3 G   The *rules* in SYSC 3 (Systems and Controls) and SYSC 4 (General organisational requirements) require a *firm* to put in place systems and controls or policies and procedures in order to comply with the *rules* in COBS 4.6 (Past, simulated past and future performance), COBS 4.7.1 R (Direct offer financial promotions), COBS 4.10 (Systems and controls and approving and communicating financial promotions) and this chapter of *BCOBS*.

2.2.4 G   Section 397 (Misleading statements and practices) of the *Act* creates a criminal offence relating to certain misleading statements and practices.

2.2.5 G   A communication or a *financial promotion* should not describe a feature of a product or service as "guaranteed", "protected" or "secure", or use a similar term unless:
   (1) that term is capable of being a fair, clear and not misleading description of it; and
   (2) the *firm* communicates all of the information necessary, and presents that information with sufficient clarity and prominence, to make the use of that term fair, clear and not misleading.

2.3   Other general requirements for communications and financial promotions

2.3.1 R   A *firm* must ensure that each communication made to a *banking customer* and each *financial promotion communicated* or *approved* by the *firm*:
   (1) includes the name of the *firm*;
   (2) is accurate and, in particular, does not emphasise any potential benefits of a *retail banking service* without also giving a fair and prominent indication of any relevant risks;
   (3) is sufficient for, and presented in a way that is likely to be understood by, the average member of the group to whom it is directed, or by whom it is likely to be received; and
   (4) does not disguise, diminish or obscure important information, statements or warnings.

2.3.2 G   The name of the *firm* may be a trading name or shortened version of the legal name of the *firm*, provided the *banking customer* can identify the *firm* communicating the information.

2.3.3 G   In deciding whether, and how, to *communicate* information to a particular target audience, a *firm* should take into account the nature of the *retail banking service*, the *banking customer's* likely or actual commitment, the likely information needs of a reasonable recipient, and the role of the communication or *financial promotion* in the sales process.

2.3.4 G   If a communication or a *financial promotion* names the *FSA* as the regulator of a *firm* and refers to matters not regulated by the *FSA*, the *firm* should ensure that the communication or *financial promotion* makes clear that those matters are not regulated by the *FSA*.

2.3.5 G   When *communicating* information, a *firm* should consider whether omission of any relevant fact will result in information given to the *banking customer* being insufficient, unclear, unfair or misleading.

2.3.6 G   The Credit Institutions (Protection of Deposits) Regulations 1995 may apply in relation to communications with a *banking customer*.

2.3.7 R   If a communication or a *financial promotion* compares a *retail banking service* with one or more other *retail banking service* (whether or not provided by the *firm*), the *firm* must ensure that the comparison is meaningful and presented in a fair and balanced way.

2.3.8 R   If a communication or a *financial promotion* in relation to a *retail banking service* refers to a particular tax treatment or rate of interest payable, a *firm* must ensure that a prominent statement that the tax treatment or the rate of interest payable:

(1) depends on the individual circumstances of each *banking customer*; and

(2) may be subject to change in the future;

is either included in that communication or *financial promotion*, or provided to the *banking customer* on paper or in another *durable medium* in good time before the *banking customer* is bound by the contract for that *retail banking service*.

2.3.9 G   When designing a *financial promotion*, a *firm* may find it helpful to take account of the British Bankers' Association/Building Societies Association Code of Conduct for the Advertising of Interest Bearing Accounts.

2.4   Structured deposits, cash deposit ISAs and cash deposit CTFs

2.4.1 G   If a *financial promotion* relates to a *structured deposit*, *rules* in COBS 4.6 (Past, simulated past and future performance) will also apply.

2.4.2 G   If a *financial promotion* relates to a *cash deposit ISA* or *cash deposit CTF*, COBS 4.7.1 R (Direct offer financial promotions) also applies.

3.   DISTANCE COMMUNICATIONS

3.1   Distance marketing

Application

3.1.1 R   This section applies to a *firm* that carries on any distance marketing activity from an establishment in the *United Kingdom*, with or for a *consumer* in the *United Kingdom* or another *EEA State*.

The distance marketing disclosure rules

3.1.2 R   (1) Subject to (2), a *firm* must provide a *consumer* with the distance marketing information (BCOBS 3 Annex 1 R) in good time before the *consumer* is bound by a *distance contract* or offer.

(2) Where a *distance contract* is also a contract for *payment services* to which the *Payment Services Regulations* apply, a *firm* is required to provide to the consumer only the information specified in rows 7 to 12, 15, 16 and 20 of BCOBS 3 Annex 1 R.

3.1.3 R   A *firm* must ensure that the distance marketing information, the commercial purpose of which must be made clear, is provided in a clear and comprehensible manner in a way appropriate to the means of distance communication used with due regard, in particular, to the principles of good faith in commercial transactions and the legal principles governing the protection of those who are unable to give their consent, such as minors.

3.1.4 R   When a *firm* makes a voice telephony communication to a *consumer*, it must make its identity and the purposes of its call explicitly clear at the beginning of the conversation.

3.1.5 R   A *firm* must ensure that information on contractual obligations to be communicated to a *consumer* during the pre-contractual phase is in conformity with the contractual obligations which would result from the law presumed to be applicable to the *distance contract* if that contract is concluded.

Terms and conditions, and form

3.1.6 R   A *firm* must communicate to the *consumer* all the contractual terms and conditions and the information referred to in the distance marketing disclosure *rules* (BCOBS 3.1.2R to 3.1.5R) in a *durable medium* available and accessible to the *consumer* in good time before the *consumer* is bound by any *distance contract* or offer.

3.1.7 G   A *firm* will provide information, or communicate contractual terms and conditions, to a *consumer* if another *person* provides the information, or communicates the terms and conditions, to the *consumer* on its behalf.

Commencing performance of the distance contract

3.1.8 R   The performance of the *distance contract* may only begin after the *consumer* has given his approval.

Exception: successive operations

3.1.9 R   In the case of a *distance contract* comprising an initial service agreement, followed by successive operations or a series of separate operations of the same nature performed over time, the *rules* in this chapter only apply to the initial agreement.

3.1.10 R   (1)   If there is no initial service agreement but the successive operations or separate operations of the same nature performed over time are performed between the same contractual parties, the distance marketing disclosure *rules* (BCOBS 3.1.2R to 3.1.5R) will only apply:

    (a)   when the first operation is performed; and

    (b)   if no operation of the same nature is performed for more than a year, when the next operation is performed (the next operation being deemed the first in a new series of operations).

  (2)   In this section:

    (a)   "initial service agreement" includes the opening of a bank account;

    (b)   "operations" includes the deposit or withdrawal of funds to or from a bank account; and

    (c)   adding new elements to an initial service agreement, such as the ability to use an electronic payment instrument together with an existing *retail banking service*, does not constitute an "operation" but an additional contract to which the rules in this chapter apply.

Exception: voice telephony communications

3.1.11 R   In the case of voice telephony communication, and subject to the explicit consent of the *consumer*, only the abbreviated distance marketing information (BCOBS 3 Annex 2 R) needs to be provided during that communication. However, a *firm* must still provide the distance marketing information (BCOBS 3 Annex 1 R) in a *durable medium* available and accessible to the *consumer* in good time before the *consumer* is bound by any *distance contract* or offer, unless another exception applies.

Exception: means of distance communication not enabling disclosure

3.1.12 R   A *firm* may provide the distance marketing information (BCOBS 3 Annex 1 R) and the contractual terms and conditions in a *durable medium* immediately after the conclusion of a *distance contract*, if the contract has been concluded at a *consumer's* request using a means of distance communication that does not enable the provision of that information in that form in good time before the *consumer* is bound by any *distance contract* or offer.

Exception: contracts for payment services

3.1.13 G   Where a *distance contract* covers both *payment services* and non-*payment services*, the exception in BCOBS 3.1.2R (2) applies only to the *payment services* aspects of the contract.

A *firm* taking advantage of this exception will need to comply with the information requirements in Part 5 of the *Payment Services Regulations*.

Consumer's right to request paper copies and change the means of communication

3.1.14 R   At any time during the contractual relationship, the *consumer* is entitled, at his request, to receive the contractual terms and conditions on paper. The *consumer* is also entitled to change the means of distance communication used unless this is incompatible with the contract concluded or the nature of the service provided.

Unsolicited services

3.1.15 R   (1) A *firm* must not enforce, or seek to enforce, any obligations under a *distance contract* against a *consumer*, in the event of an unsolicited supply of services, the absence of a reply not constituting consent.

(2) This *rule* does not apply to the tacit renewal of a *distance contract*.

Mandatory nature of a consumer's rights

3.1.16 R   If a *consumer* purports to waive any of the *consumer's* rights created or implied by the *rules* in this section, a *firm* must not accept that waiver, nor seek to rely on or enforce it against the *consumer*.

Contracts governed by law of a third party state

3.1.17 R   If a *firm* proposes to enter into a *distance contract* with a *consumer* that will be governed by the law of a country outside the *EEA*, the *firm* must ensure that the *consumer* will not lose the protection created by the *rules* in this chapter if the *distance contract* has a close link with the territory of one or more *EEA States*.

3.2   E Commerce

Application

3.2.1 R   This section applies to a *firm* carrying on an *electronic commerce activity* from an *establishment* in the *United Kingdom* with or for a *person* in the *United Kingdom* or another *EEA State*.

Information about the firm and its products or services

3.2.2 R   A *firm* must make at least the following information easily, directly and permanently accessible to the recipients of the *information society services* it provides:

(1) its name;

(2) the geographic address at which it is established;

(3) the details of the *firm* including its e-mail address, which allow it to be contacted rapidly and communicated with in a direct and effective manner;

(4) an appropriate statutory status disclosure statement (GEN 4 Annex 1 R), together with a statement which explains that it is on the *FSA Register* and includes the *FSA* registration number;

(5) if it is a *professional firm*, or a person regulated by the equivalent of a *designated professional body* in another *EEA State*:

(a) the name of the professional body (including any *designated professional body*) or similar institution with which it is registered;

(b) the professional title and the *EEA State* where it was granted;

(c) a reference to the applicable professional rules in the *EEA State* of establishment and the means to access them; and

(d) where the *firm* undertakes an activity that is subject to VAT, its VAT number.

3.2.3 R   If a *firm* refers to price, it must do so clearly and unambiguously, indicating whether the price is inclusive of tax and delivery costs.

3.2.4 R   A *firm* must ensure that commercial communications which are part of, or constitute, an *information society service*, comply with the following conditions:

(1) the commercial communication must be clearly identifiable as such;

(2) the *person* on whose behalf the commercial communication is made must be clearly identifiable;

(3) promotional offers must be clearly identifiable as such, and the conditions that must be met to qualify for them must be easily accessible and presented clearly and unambiguously; and

(4) promotional competitions or games must be clearly identifiable as such, and the conditions for participation must be easily accessible and presented clearly and unambiguously.

3.2.5 R An unsolicited commercial communication sent by e-mail by a *firm* established in the *United Kingdom* must be identifiable clearly and unambiguously as an unsolicited commercial communication as soon as it is received by the recipient.

Requirements relating to the placing and receipt of orders

3.2.6 R A *firm* must (except when otherwise agreed by parties who are not *consumers*):

(1) give an *ECA recipient* at least the following information, clearly, comprehensibly and unambiguously, and prior to the order being placed by the recipient of the service:

(a) the different technical steps to follow to conclude the contract;

(b) whether or not the concluded contract will be filled in by the *firm* and whether it will be accessible;

(c) the technical means for identifying and correcting input errors prior to the placing of the order; and

(d) the languages offered for the conclusion of the contract;

(2) indicate any relevant codes of conduct to which it subscribes and information on how those codes can be consulted electronically;

(3) (when an *ECA recipient* places an order through technological means) acknowledge the receipt of the recipient's order without undue delay and by electronic means; and

(4) make available to the *ECA recipient* appropriate, effective and accessible technical means allowing the recipient to identify and correct input errors prior to the placing of an order.

3.2.7 R For the purposes of BCOBS 3.2.6R (3), an order and an acknowledgement of receipt are deemed to be received when the parties to whom they are addressed are able to access them.

3.2.8 R Contractual terms and conditions provided by a *firm* to an *ECA recipient* must be made available in a way that allows the recipient to store and reproduce them.

Exception: contract concluded by e mail

3.2.9 R The requirements relating to the placing and receipt of orders (BCOBS 3.2.6R (3)) do not apply to contracts concluded exclusively by exchange of e-mail or by equivalent individual communications.

3   **Annex 1 Distance marketing information**

R   This Annex belongs to BCOBS 3.1.2 R (The distance marketing disclosure rules)

Information about the firm	
(1)	The name and the main business of the *firm*, the geographical address at which it is established and any other geographical address relevant for the *consumer's* relations with the *firm*.
(2)	Where the *firm* has a representative established in the *consumer's EEA State* of residence, the name of that representative and the geographical address relevant for the *consumer's* relations with that representative.
(3)	Where the *consumer's* dealings are with any professional other than the *firm*, the identity of that professional, the capacity in which he is acting with respect to the *consumer*, and the geographical address relevant to the *consumer's* relations with that professional.

(4)   The particulars of the public register in which the *firm* is entered, its registration number in that register and the particulars of the relevant supervisory authority, including an appropriate statutory status disclosure statement (GEN 4), a statement that the *firm* is on the *FSA Register* and its *FSA* registration number.

Information about the financial service

(5)   A description of the main characteristics of the service the *firm* will provide.

(6)   The total price to be paid by the *consumer* to the *firm* for the financial service, including all related fees, charges and expenses, and all taxes paid through the *firm* or, where an exact price cannot be indicated, the basis for the calculation of the price enabling the *consumer* to verify it.

(7)   Where relevant, notice indicating that the service is related to instruments involving special risks related to their specific features or the operations to be executed, or whose price depends on fluctuations in the financial markets outside the *firm's* control and that past performance is no indicator of future performance.

(8)   Notice of the possibility that other taxes or costs may exist that are not paid via the *firm* or imposed by it.

(9)   Any limitations on the period for which the information provided is valid, including a clear explanation as to how long a *firm's* offer applies as it stands.

(10)   The arrangements for payment and performance.

(11)   Details of any specific additional cost to the *consumer* for using a means of distance communication.

Information about the contract

(12)   The existence or absence of a right to cancel under the cancellation rules (BCOBS 6) and, where there is such a right, its duration and the conditions for exercising it, including information on the amount which the *consumer* may be required to pay (or which may not be returned to the *consumer*) in accordance with those *rules*, as well as the consequences of not exercising the right to cancel.

(13)   The minimum duration of the contract, in the case of services to be performed permanently or recurrently.

(14)   Information on any rights the parties may have to terminate the contract early or unilaterally under its terms, including any penalties imposed by the contract in such cases.

(15)   Practical instructions for exercising any right to cancel, including the address to which any cancellation notice should be sent.

(16)   The *EEA State* or States whose laws are taken by the *firm* as a basis for the establishment of relations with the *consumer* prior to the conclusion of the contract.

(17)   Any contractual clause on the law applicable to the contract or on the competent court, or both.

(18)   In which language, or languages, the contractual terms and conditions and the other information in this Annex will be supplied, and in which language, or languages, the *firm*, with the agreement of the *consumer*, undertakes to communicate during the duration of the contract.

Information about redress

(19)   How to complain to the *firm*, whether complaints may subsequently be referred to the *Financial Ombudsman Service* and, if so, the methods for having access to that body, together with equivalent information about any other applicable named complaints scheme.

(20)   Whether compensation may be available from the *compensation scheme*, or any other named compensation scheme, if the *firm* is unable to meet its liabilities.

[Note: Recitals 21 and 23 to, and article 3(1) of, the *Distance Marketing Directive*]

3   Annex 2 Abbreviated distance marketing information

R   This Annex belongs to BCOBS 3.1.11 R

(1)	The identity of the *person* in contact with the *consumer* and his link with the *firm*.
(2)	A description of the main characteristics of the financial service.
(3)	The total price to be paid by the *consumer* to the *firm* for the financial service including all taxes paid via the *firm* or, when an exact price cannot be indicated, the basis for the calculation of the price enabling the *consumer* to verify it.
(4)	Notice of the possibility that other taxes and/or costs may exist that are not paid via the *firm* or imposed by him.
(5)	The existence or absence of a right to cancel in accordance with the cancellation rules (BCOBS 6) and, where the right to cancel exists, its duration and the conditions for exercising it, including information on the amount the *consumer* may be required to pay on the basis of the cancellation rules.
(6)	That other information is available on request and what the nature of that information is.

[Note: article 3(3)(b) of the *Distance Marketing Directive*]

4   INFORMATION TO BE COMMUNICATED TO BANKING CUSTOMERS

4.1   Enabling banking customers to make informed decisions

The appropriate information rule

4.1.1 R   A *firm* must provide or make available to a *banking customer* appropriate information about a *retail banking service* and any *deposit* made in relation to that *retail banking service*:

(1) in good time;

(2) in an appropriate medium; and

(3) in easily understandable language and in a clear and comprehensible form;

so that the *banking customer* can make decisions on an informed basis.

4.1.2 G   (1) In determining:

(a) what is "in good time";

(b) the appropriate medium for communicating information; and

(c) whether it is appropriate to provide information (that is, send or give it directly to the *banking customer*) or make it available (that is, make it available to obtain at the *banking customer's* option);

a *firm* should consider the importance of the information to the decision-making process of the *banking customer* and the time at which the information may be most useful. Distance communications requirements are also relevant.

(2) For example, (unless BCOBS 3 applies) a *firm* should provide the terms and conditions of the contract for a *retail banking service* on paper or in another *durable medium* in good time before a *banking customer* is bound by them.

(3) Where a *firm* proposes to exercise a power to make:

(a) a change to any term or condition of the agreement;

(b) a change to any charge; or

(c) a material change to any rate of interest;

that applies to the *retail banking service* and that will be to the disadvantage of a *banking customer*, the *firm* should provide reasonable notice to the *banking customer* on paper or in another durable medium before the change takes effect, taking into account the period of notice required by the *banking customer* to terminate the contract for the *retail banking service*. Whether a change to a rate of interest is "material" should be determined having regard to the size of the balance of the account and the size of the change in the rate.

(4) Where a *firm* notifies a *banking customer* of a material change to a rate of interest that applies to a *retail banking service* and that will be to the disadvantage of a *banking customer*, this notification should, where applicable:

(a) refer to the fact that the *firm* offers a comparable *retail banking service* for which the *banking customer* is eligible;

(b) indicate that the *banking customer* may move to that *retail banking service* or a *retail banking service* provided by another *firm*; and

(c) indicate that the *firm* will assist the *banking customer* to move to another *retail banking service* if he wishes to do so.

(5) Where, under a contract for a *retail banking service*, an introductory, promotional or preferential rate of interest applies to the *retail banking service* until a specified future date or the end of a fixed period, a *firm* should, where appropriate, provide notice of the expiry of the application of that rate of interest to the *banking customer* on paper or in another durable medium within a reasonable period before that rate of interest ceases to apply.

(6) In determining whether it is appropriate to provide the notice referred to in (5), a *firm* should consider:

(a) whether there is a material difference between the introductory or promotional rate of interest and the rate of interest that will apply to the *retail banking service* following the expiry of the introductory or promotional rate of interest;

(b) the size of the balance of the account; and

(c) the period of time that has elapsed since the *firm* last provided information to the *banking customer* in relation to the period for which the introductory or promotional rate of interest is applicable and the effect of its expiry.

(7) The general law, including the *Unfair Terms Regulations*, also limits the scope for a *firm* to use or rely on a variation clause in a contract with a *consumer*.

4.1.3 R   Where a *rule* in this chapter requires information to be provided on paper or in another *durable medium* before a *banking customer* is bound by the terms and conditions of the contract, a *firm* may instead provide that information in accordance with the distance communication timing requirements (see BCOBS 3.1.11 R and BCOBS 3.1.12 R).

4.1.4 G   The appropriate information *rule* applies before a *banking customer* is bound by the terms of the contract. It also applies after a *banking customer* has become bound by them. In order to meet the requirements of the appropriate information *rule*, information provided or made available by a *firm* to a *banking customer* should include information relating to:

(1) the *firm*;

(2) the different *retail banking services* offered by the *firm* which share the main features of the *retail banking service* the *banking customer* has enquired about, or which have the product features the *banking customer* has expressed an interest in, unless the *banking customer* has expressly indicated that he does not wish to receive that information;

(3) the terms and conditions of the contract for a *retail banking service* and any changes to them;

(4) the rate or rates of interest payable on any deposit, how and when such interest is calculated and applied and any changes to that rate or those rates;

(5) any charges at any time payable by or on behalf of a *banking customer* in relation to each *retail banking service* and any changes to those charges;

(5A) the time at which any funds placed with or transferred to the *firm* for credit to the *banking customer's* account will be made available to the *banking customer*;

(6) a *banking customer's* rights to cancel a contract for a *retail banking service*;

(7) how a *banking customer* may make a complaint (at the time and in the manner required by DISP 1.2);

(8) the terms of any compensation scheme if the *firm* cannot meet its obligations in respect of the *retail banking service*;

(9) basic bank accounts but only if the *firm* offers a basic bank account and the *banking customer* meets the *firm's* eligibility criteria for such an account; and

(10) the timescales for each stage of the cheque clearing process.

4.1.4A G   (1) This *guidance* applies to a *firm* only with respect to its *communications* and dealings with *consumers* where a *firm* has a *right of set-off*.

(2) To ensure compliance with the appropriate information *rule*, the *firm* should:

    (a) (i) provide an explanation of the nature and extent of the *firm's right of set-off*; and

        (ii) if the *firm* considers that it is entitled to exercise a right to set off or combine a debt due solely from a *consumer*, or a debit balance on an account held in the sole name of a *consumer*, against or with a credit balance on an account held in the joint names of that *consumer* and another *consumer*, also provide an explanation of that right to the *consumers* in whose names the joint account is held;

    in good time before the *consumer* is bound by the contract for the *retail banking service*. This information may be incorporated in the terms and conditions that apply to the contract for the *retail banking service*;

    (b) (i) on the first occasion that the *firm* proposes to exercise a *right of set-off* in its dealings with the *consumer*; and

        (ii) where appropriate, on any subsequent occasion that the *firm* proposes to exercise a *right of set-off* in its dealings with the *consumer*;

    provide general information in relation to the nature of the *firm's right of set-off* and the generic circumstances in which the *firm* may rely on that right within a reasonable period before the *firm* seeks to exercise its *right of set-off*. The *FSA* considers that this information should be provided at least 14 *days* before the *firm* seeks to exercise its *right of set-off*. It may be incorporated in another communication sent by the *firm* to the *consumer*; and

    (c) where it has exercised a *right of set-off*, provide prompt notification of this to the *consumer*. This notification should clearly identify the date that the *firm* exercised its *right of set-off* and the amount debited from the *consumer's* account in reliance on that right.

(3) The information referred to in (2) should be provided in plain and intelligible language on paper or in another *durable medium*.

(4) In determining whether it is appropriate to provide general information under (2)(b)(ii), the *firm* should consider the period of time that has elapsed since the *firm* last provided that information under (2)(b)(i) or (ii).

(5) Nothing in (2)(a)(ii) should be considered as expressing a view on the validity, enforceability or fairness of any *right of set-off* in relation to a joint account that a *firm* considers it is entitled to exercise.

4.1.5 G The information required by the appropriate information *rule* may vary according to matters such as:

(1) the *banking customer's* likely or actual commitment;

(2) the information needs of a reasonable recipient having regard to the type of *retail banking service* that is proposed or provided and its overall complexity, main benefits, risks, limitations, conditions and duration;

(3) distance communication information requirements (for example, under the distance communication *rules* less information can be given during certain telephone sales than in a sale made purely by written correspondence (see BCOBS 3.1)); and

(4) whether the same information has been provided to the *banking customer* previously and, if so, when that was.

4.1.6 G The existence of cancellation rights does not affect what information it is appropriate to give a *banking customer* in order to enable him to make an informed purchasing decision.

4.1.7 G If the *retail banking service* is a *cash deposit ISA* or a *cash deposit CTF*, the rules in COBS 13.1 (Preparing product information) and COBS 14.2 (Providing product information to clients) also apply.

4.2   Statements of account

4.2.1 R (1) A *firm* must provide or make available to a *banking customer* on paper or in another *durable medium* such regular statements of account as are appropriate to the type of *retail banking service* provided, but need not do so where:

(a) the *firm* has provided a *banking customer* with a pass book or other document in a *durable medium* that records transactions in relation to the *retail banking service*;

(b) the *retail banking service* is provided at a distance by means of electronic equipment where the *banking customer* can access his account balance, view transactions and give instructions in relation to the *retail banking service* at a distance by such means;

(c) a *banking customer* has elected not to receive periodic statements of account, and for so long as such election is in force; or

(d) it has reasonable grounds to believe that the *banking customer* is not resident at the address last known to it as the address of the *banking customer* and it is not practicable after reasonable inquiry to ascertain the *banking customer's* address.

(2) A *firm* must not charge for providing information which is required to be provided by (1).

(3) A *firm* must provide a *banking customer* with a true copy of any statement of account provided to him under (1) on paper or in another *durable medium* within a reasonable period of time following a request to that effect made by or on his behalf.

(4) A *firm* and a *banking customer* may agree on a charge for:

(a) providing a copy of a statement of account under (3); or

(b) providing statements of account more frequently than required by (1);

at the request of the *banking customer*. Any such charge must reasonably correspond to the *firm's* actual costs.

4.2.2 G A *firm* should indicate the rate or rates of interest that apply to a *retail banking service* in each statement of account provided or made available to a *banking customer* in respect of that *retail banking service* in accordance with BCOBS 4.2.1R.

5   POST SALE

5.1   Post sale requirements

Service

5.1.1 R A *firm* must provide a service in relation to a *retail banking service* which is prompt, efficient and fair to a *banking customer* and which has regard to any communications or *financial promotion* made by the *firm* to the *banking customer* from time to time.

5.1.2 G In determining the order in which to process payment instructions in relation to the *retail banking service*, a *firm* must have regard to its obligation to treat *banking customers* fairly.

5.1.3 G To the extent that it relates to a *retail banking service*, a *firm* may find it helpful to take account of the British Bankers' Association "A Statement of Principles: Banks and businesses-working together".

Dealings with customers in financial difficulty

5.1.4 G Principle 6 requires a *firm* to pay due regard to the interests of its customers and to treat them fairly. In particular, a *firm* should deal fairly with a *banking customer* whom it has reason to believe is in financial difficulty.

Moving a retail banking service

5.1.5 R A *firm* must provide a prompt and efficient service to enable a *banking customer* to move to a *retail banking service* (including a *payment service*) provided by another *firm*.

5.1.6 G Where a *banking customer* wishes to move a *retail banking service* and there are no arrangements between the *firm* the *banking customer* wishes to move from and the *firm* that the *banking customer* wishes to move to, the service provided by the former *firm* will extend only to providing a prompt and efficient service in respect of termination of the *retail banking service*, for example by closing an account and returning any *deposit* (with interest as appropriate) to the *banking customer*.

5.1.7 G   Where a *banking customer* wishes to move a *retail banking service* and there are arrangements between the *firm* the *banking customer* wishes to move from and the *firm* that the *banking customer* wishes to move to, the service provided by the former *firm* will include providing a prompt and efficient service in respect of termination of the *retail banking service*, for example by closing an account, transferring any account balance and making arrangements in respect of any direct debits or standing orders.

5.1.8 G   A firm may find it helpful to take account of the European Banking Industry Committee Common Principles for Bank Account Switching and the Cash ISA to Cash ISA Transfers Industry Guidelines.

Lost and dormant accounts

5.1.9 R   A *firm* must make appropriate arrangements to enable a *banking customer*, so far as is possible, to trace and, if appropriate, to have access to a *deposit* held (or formerly held) in a *retail banking service* provided by the *firm*. This applies even if:

(1) the *banking customer* may not be able to provide the *firm* with information which is sufficient to identify the *retail banking service* concerned; or

(2) the *banking customer* may not have carried out any transactions in relation to that *retail banking service* for an extended period of time.

5.1.10 R   If a *firm* participates in the scheme under the Dormant Bank and Building Society Accounts Act 2008, it must inform a *banking customer* of this fact and provide appropriate information regarding the terms of the scheme on entering into communications with a *banking customer* regarding a *dormant account*.

Firm's liability for unauthorised payments

5.1.11 R   (1) Where a *banking customer* denies having authorised a payment, it is for the *firm* to prove that the payment was authorised.

(2) Where a payment from a *banking customer's* account was not authorised by the *banking customer*, a *firm* must, within a reasonable period, refund the amount of the unauthorised payment to the *banking customer* and, where applicable, restore the *banking customer's* account to the state it would have been in had the unauthorised payment not taken place.

Banking customer's liability for unauthorised payments

5.1.12 R   (1) Subject to (2) and (3), a *firm* may, in an agreement for a *retail banking service*, provide for a *banking customer* to be liable for an amount up to a maximum of £50 for losses in respect of unauthorised payments arising:

(a) from the use of a lost or stolen *payment instrument*; or

(b) where the *banking customer* has failed to keep the personalised security features of the *payment instrument* safe, from the misappropriation of the *payment instrument*.

(2) A *firm* may, in an agreement for a *retail banking service*, provide for a *banking customer* to be liable for all losses in respect of unauthorised payments:

(a) where a *banking customer* has acted fraudulently; or

(b) (subject to (3)) where a *banking customer* has intentionally, or with gross negligence, failed to comply with his or her obligations under the agreement for the *retail banking service* in relation to the issue or use of the *payment instrument* or to take all reasonable steps to keep its personalised security features safe.

(3) Except where a *banking customer* has acted fraudulently, a *firm* must not, in an agreement for a *retail banking service*, seek to make a *banking customer* liable for any losses in respect of unauthorised payments where:

(a) the unauthorised payment arises after the *banking customer* has notified the *firm* of the loss, theft, misappropriation or unauthorised use of the *payment instrument*;

    (b) the *firm* has failed to ensure that appropriate means are available at all times to enable the *banking customer* to notify it of the loss, theft, misappropriation or unauthorised use of a *payment instrument*; or

    (c) the *payment instrument* has been used in connection with

        (i) a *distance contract*; or

        (ii) a *distance selling contract* other than an *excepted contract*.

(4) Except as provided in (1) to (3), a *firm* must not, in an agreement for a *retail banking service*, seek to make a *banking customer* liable for any consequential loss in respect of an unauthorised payment.

Value date

5.1.13 R (1) The reference date used by a *firm* for the purpose of calculating interest on funds credited to an account of a *banking customer* held with it must be no later than:

    (a) the *business day* on which the funds are credited to the account of the *firm*; or

    (b) in the case of cash placed with a *firm* for credit to a *banking customer's* account in the same currency as that account, immediately after the *firm* receives the funds.

(2) Paragraph (1) does not apply to funds credited to a *banking customer's* account by means of a paper cheque.

Set-off

5.1.3A G To ensure compliance with its obligations under BCOBS 5.1.1 R and *Principle* 6, on any occasion where it proposes to exercise a *right of set-off*, a firm (other than a *credit union*) should, with respect to its dealings with *consumers*:

(1) review the information available and accessible to the *firm* relating to the *consumer's* account, on an individual basis, and estimate the amount of any *subsistence balance*;

(2) refrain from seeking to set off or combine:

    (a) any debt due from, or a debit balance on an account held by, a *consumer* against or with that *subsistence balance*;

    (b) any debt due from, or a debit balance on an account held by, a *consumer* in a personal capacity against or with any sum of money payable by the *firm* to the *consumer* or standing to the credit of the *consumer* in an account held with the *firm*, where the *firm* knows or reasonably ought to know that:

        (i) a third party is beneficially entitled to that money or that the *consumer* is a fiduciary in respect of that money; or

        (ii) the *consumer* has received that money from a government department, local authority or NHS direct payment body for a specific purpose or is under a legal obligation to a third party to retain and deal with that money in a particular way.

5.1.3B G (1) If it becomes apparent to a *firm* after it has exercised a *right of set-off* that it has set off or combined a debt due from, or a debit balance on an account held by, a *consumer* against or with:

    (a) the *consumer's subsistence balance*; or

    (b) money payable by the *firm* to the *consumer*, or standing to the credit of the *consumer* in an account held with the *firm*, that falls within BCOBS 5.1.3AG (2)(b)(i) or (ii);

the *firm* should refund to the *consumer* the sum debited from the account of the *consumer* in exercise of the *right of set-off* unless it is fair not to do so.

(2) If, in the circumstances referred to in (1), the *firm* does not provide a refund of the sum debited from the account in exercise of the *right of set-off*, the *firm* should be able to justify that it is fair not to do so and should consider taking other remedial action having regard to its obligations under BCOBS 5.1.1 R and *Principle* 6.

Non-execution or defective execution of payments

5.1.14 R (1) Where a *banking customer* claims that a payment has not been correctly executed, it is for the *firm* to prove that the payment was authenticated, accurately recorded, entered in the *firm's* accounts and not affected by a technical breakdown or some other deficiency.

(2) In paragraph (1) "authenticated" means the use of any procedure by which a *firm* is able to verify the use of a specific *payment instrument*, including its personalised security features.

5.1.15 R (1) Where a payment from an account of a *banking customer* is executed in accordance with the *payment routing information* provided in respect of that payment, it shall be treated as correctly executed by each *firm* involved in executing the payment.

(2) Where incorrect *payment routing information* has been provided to a *firm* in respect of a payment:

(a) BCOBS 5.1.16R and BCOBS 5.1.17R do not apply in relation to that payment; and

(b) the *firm* must make reasonable efforts to recover the funds involved in the transaction.

(3) A *firm* and a *banking customer* may agree on a charge for taking the steps referred to in (2)(b). Any such charge must reasonably correspond to the *firm's* actual costs.

5.1.16 R (1) Where a *banking customer* instructs or requests a *firm* to make a payment from his or her account and the payment is not correctly executed, the *firm* must, without undue delay:

(a) refund to the *banking customer* the amount of the non-executed or defective payment; and

(b) where applicable, restore the *banking customer's* account to the state in which it would have been had the defective payment not taken place; unless:

(c) the *firm* can prove that the amount of the payment was received by another *firm* (referred to in this *rule* as "firm B") with which the relevant account of the intended recipient is held.

(2) Where (1)(c) applies, firm B must:

(a) immediately make available the amount of the payment to the intended recipient; and

(b) where applicable, credit the corresponding amount to the intended recipient's account.

5.1.17 R Where:

(1) an instruction or request for a payment to be made from a *banking customer's* account is given by the intended recipient of that payment to a *firm*;

(2) that *firm* can prove that it correctly transmitted the instruction or request to the *firm* with which the relevant account of the *banking customer* is held (in this rule referred to as "firm A"); and

(3) the payment is not correctly executed;

firm A must, as appropriate and without undue delay:

(4) refund to that *banking customer* the amount of the payment; and

(5) restore that *banking customer's* account to the state in which it would have been had the defective payment not taken place.

5.1.18 R Where a *firm* is required to give a refund or take other remedial action under BCOBS 5.1.16R or BCOBS 5.1.17R, it must also refund:

(1) any charges for which a *banking customer* is responsible; and

(2) any interest which a *banking customer* must pay;

as a consequence of the non-execution or defective execution of the payment.

5.1.19 R Where the non-execution or defective execution of a payment by a *firm* is due to abnormal and unforeseeable circumstances beyond the *firm's* control, the consequences of which would have been unavoidable despite all efforts to the contrary, BCOBS 5.1.16R to BCOBS 5.1.18R shall not apply with respect to that incorrectly executed payment.

6 CANCELLATION

6.1 The right to cancel

Introduction

6.1.1 R Except as provided for in BCOBS 6.1.2 R, a *banking customer* has a right to cancel a contract for a *retail banking service* (including a *cash deposit ISA*) without penalty and without giving any reason, within 14 calendar days.

6.1.2 R There is no right to cancel:

    (1) a contract (other than a *cash deposit ISA*) where the rate or rates of interest payable on the *deposit* are fixed for a period of time following conclusion of the contract;

    (2) a contract whose price depends on fluctuations in the financial market outside the *firm's* control that may occur during the cancellation period; or

    (3) a *cash deposit CTF* (other than a *distance contract*).

6.1.3 G A *firm* may provide longer or additional cancellation rights voluntarily but, if it does, these should be on terms at least as favourable to the *banking customer* as those in this chapter, unless the differences are clearly explained.

Beginning of cancellation period

6.1.4 R The cancellation period begins:

    (1) either from the day of the conclusion of the contract for the *retail banking service*; or

    (2) from the day on which the *banking customer* receives the contractual terms and conditions of the *retail banking service* and any other pre-contractual information required under this sourcebook, if that is later than the date referred to in (1) above.

Disclosing the right to cancel

6.1.5 R (1) The *firm* must disclose to a *banking customer* in good time or, if that is not possible, immediately after the *banking customer* is bound by a contract for a *retail banking service*, and in a *durable medium*, the existence of the right to cancel, its duration and the conditions for exercising it including information on the amount which the *banking customer* may be required to pay, the consequences of not exercising it and practical instructions for exercising it, indicating the address to which the notification of cancellation should be sent.

    (2) This *rule* applies only where a *banking customer* would not otherwise receive the information referred to in (1) under a *rule* in this sourcebook from the *firm* (such as under BCOBS 3.1.2 R to 3.1.5 R (the distance marketing disclosure rules)).

6.2 Exercising the right to cancel

6.2.1 R If a *banking customer* exercises his right to cancel he must, before the expiry of the cancellation period, notify this following the practical instructions given to him. The deadline shall be deemed to have been observed if the notification, if in a *durable medium* available and accessible to the recipient, is dispatched before the cancellation period expires.

6.2.2 G The *firm* should accept any indication that the *banking customer* wishes to cancel as long as it satisfies the conditions for notification. In the event of any dispute, unless there is clear written evidence to the contrary, the *firm* should treat the date cited by the *banking customer* as the date when the notification was dispatched.

Record keeping

6.2.3 R The *firm* must make adequate records concerning the exercise of a right to cancel and retain them for at least three years.

6.3   Effects of cancellation

6.3.1 R   By exercising a right to cancel, a *banking customer* withdraws from the contract and the contract is terminated.

Payment for the service provided before cancellation

6.3.2 R   (1) This *rule* applies in relation to a contract for a *retail banking service* that is not a *cash deposit ISA* or a *cash deposit CTF*.

(2) When a *banking customer* exercises the right to cancel he may only be required to pay, without any undue delay, for the service actually provided by the *firm* in accordance with the contract. The amount payable must not:

(a) exceed an amount which is in proportion to the extent of the service already provided in comparison with the full coverage of the contract;

(b) in any case be such that it could be construed as a penalty.

Banking: Conduct of Business Sourcebook

(3) The *firm* may not require a *banking customer* to pay any amount on the basis of this *rule* unless it can prove that the *banking customer* was duly informed about the amount payable and, in the case of a contract which is a *distance contract*, in conformity with the distance marketing disclosure rules. However, in no case may the *firm* require such payment if it has commenced the performance of the contract before expiry of the cancellation period without the *banking customer's* prior request.

6.4   Obligations on cancellation

Firm's obligation

6.4.1 R   The *firm* must, without undue delay and within 30 calendar days, return to the *banking customer* any sums it has received from him except for any amount that the *banking customer* may be required to pay under BCOBS 6.3.2 R. This period begins from the day on which the *firm* receives the notification of cancellation.

Banking customer's obligation

6.4.2 R   The *firm* is entitled to receive from the *banking customer* any sums or property he has received from the *firm* without any undue delay and no later than within 30 calendar days. This period begins from the day on which the *banking customer* dispatches the notification of cancellation.

6.4.3 R   Any sums payable under this section on cancellation of a contract are owed as simple contract debts and may be set off against each other.

6.5   Other applicable legislation

6.5.1 R   This chapter applies as modified to the extent necessary for it to be compatible with any enactment, including legislation relating to child trust funds.

TRANSITIONAL PROVISIONS AND SCHEDULES (BCOBS TRANSCHEDULE)

Sch 1   RECORD-KEEPING REQUIREMENTS

Notes:	
1	The aim of the *guidance* in the following table is to give the reader a quick overall view of the relevant record-keeping requirements.
2	It is not a complete statement of those requirements and should not be relied on as if it were.

Handbook reference	Subject of record	When record must be made	Contents of record	Retention period
BCOBS 6.2.3 R	Cancellation: exercise of right	Exercise of the right to cancel	Date of exercise	At least three years

Sch 5   RIGHTS OF ACTION FOR DAMAGES

5.1   The table below sets out the *rules* in *BCOBS* contravention of which by an *authorised person* may be actionable under section 150 of the *Act* (Actions for damages) by a *person* who suffers loss as a result of the contravention.

5.2   If a "Yes" appears in the column headed "For private person?", the *rule* may be actionable by a *private person* under section 150 (or, in certain circumstances, his fiduciary or representative; see article 6(2) and (3)(c) of the Financial Services and Markets Act 2000 (Rights of Action) Regulations 2001 (SI 2001/2256)). A "Yes" in the column headed "Removed" indicates that the *FSA* has removed the right of action under section 150(2) of the Act. If so, a reference to the *rule* in which it is removed is also given.

5.3   The column headed "For other person?" indicates whether the *rule* may be actionable by a *person* other than a *private person* (or his fiduciary or representative) under article 6(2) and (3) of those Regulations. If so, an indication of the type of *person* by whom the *rule* may be actionable is given.

Rule	Right of action under section 150		
	For private person?	Removed?	For other person?
Any rule in *BCOBS* which prohibits an authorised person from seeking to make provision excluding or restricting any duty or liability	Yes	No	Yes Any other person
All other rules in *BCOBS*	Yes	No	No

Sch 6   RULES THAT CAN BE WAIVED

6.1   As a result of regulation 10 of the Regulatory Reform (Financial Services and Markets Act 2000) Order 2007 (SI 2007/1973) the FSA has power to waive all its rules. However, if the rules incorporate requirements laid down in European directives, it will not be possible for the FSA to grant a waiver that would be incompatible with the United Kingdom's responsibilities under those directives.

The Lending Code

Setting standards for banks, building societies and credit card providers

[Reproduced with permission of the British Bankers' Association, the Building Societies Association, the UK Cards Association and the Lending Standards Board.]

[March 2011] (Revised 1 May 2012)

To discuss this Code you can contact:

British Bankers' Association	Building Societies Association	UK Cards Association
Pinners Hall	6th Floor, York House	
105–108 Old Broad Street	23 Kingsway	2 Thomas More Square
London EC2N 1EX	London WC2B 6UJ	London E1W 1YN
Email: info@bba.org.uk	Email: information@bsa.	Email / contact through the
Tel: 0207 216 8800	org.uk	website:
	Tel: 0207 520 5900	www.theukcardsassociation.
		org.uk

Introduction

1. This is a self-regulatory Lending Code setting minimum standards of good practice when dealing with the following customers in the UK:

- Consumers;
- Micro-enterprises[1]; or
- Charities with an annual income of less than £1 million. For ease of reference, in the text of the Code, references to "micro-enterprise customers" includes charities of this nature.

[[1] *A micro-enterprise is defined as a business that employs fewer than 10 persons and has a turnover or annual balance sheet that does not exceed €2 million.*]

3. The Lending Code covers good practice in relation to:

- loans;
- credit cards;
- charge cards[2]; and
- current account overdrafts.

It does not apply to merchant services, non-business borrowing secured on land, or to sales finance.

[[2] *Charge cards are subject to the Key Commitments and general provisions of this Code, where a requirement is not specific to another product.*]

4. The Code applies to lending in sterling. However, subscribers are not precluded from applying the Code's standards to lending in other currencies.

5. Compliance with the terms of this Code is independently monitored and enforced by the Lending Standards Board (LSB). A list of subscribers to the Code and contact details for the LSB can be found at www.lendingstandardsboard.org.uk.

6. This Code sets standards of good lending practice but subscribers must—at all times—ensure they are compliant with:

- the Consumer Credit Act 1974, as amended and associated Regulations made under it;
- the Consumer Credit (EU Directive) Regulations 2010;
- the Equality Act 2010; and
- other relevant legislation (such as the Payment Services Regulations (PSRs) and, for consumers, the Consumer Protection from Unfair Trading Regulations).

Subscribers should also have regard to relevant Office of Fair Trading Guidance.

7. It is important that, when considering how the Code will affect products and services, all delivery channels are catered for. The Code applies regardless of how a product or service is delivered.

8. It is the responsibility of subscribers to ensure that any third party or agent acting on their behalf complies with the Code in relation to any products or services covered by this Code.

9. Subscribers should make information available to customers to inform them that they follow the Lending Code. This should include providing a link to the Code on their website and, where appropriate, making reference to the Code within relevant literature.

10. Subscribers should make copies of the 'Guide to the Lending Code' available on request in branch. Additionally, from 1 July 2011, new customers of products covered by the Code should be provided with a copy of the 'Guide to the Lending Code' when they open their product. This can be provided in hard copy or electronically, at point of sale or in account opening material, such as a welcome pack. This requirement to provide a copy of the Guide does not apply in relation to the provision of a new overdraft facility to an existing current account customer.

11. Commitments previously provided by the BBA Statement of Principles for small businesses have been incorporated into the Lending Code and the customer-facing document has been replaced by the 'Guide to the Lending Code for micro-enterprises'.

12. Unless otherwise specified all references in this Code to 'customer' or 'customers' apply to personal and micro-enterprise customers.

13. This Code uses the terms 'provide', 'give', 'tell' and 'make available' interchangeably. These terms are not defined to specify how information is made accessible to the customer. Instead, firms should determine the most appropriate way for customers to access information at the right time in order to make informed decisions.

14. However, where this Code requires that certain information is given to customers 'personally', this means that some form of notification is given or sent to them, rather than being told by a general notice or advertisement. Such notification could be made by letter, by e-mail or by an alternative method that reflects the manner in which the product or service is normally operated.

Section 1:   Key commitments

15. Subscribers will act fairly and reasonably in all their dealings with customers by, as a minimum, meeting all the commitments and standards in this Code. The key commitments are shown below.

- Subscribers will make sure that advertising and promotional literature is fair, clear and not misleading and that customers are given clear information about products and services.
- Customers will be given clear information about products and services before, during and after the point of sale, including how they work, their terms and conditions and the interest rates and charges that apply to them.
- Regular statements will be made available to customers (if appropriate). Customers will also be informed about changes to the interest rates, charges or terms and conditions.
- Subscribers will lend money responsibly.
- Subscribers will deal quickly and sympathetically with things that go wrong and act sympathetically and positively when considering a customer's financial difficulties.
- Personal information will be treated as private and confidential, and subscribers will provide secure and reliable banking and payment systems.
- Subscribers will make sure their staff are trained to put this Code into practice.

Section 2:   Communications and financial promotions

16. This section applies to financial promotions for lending products and services and communications to customers during the lifetime of the product or service.

17. The key consideration for subscribers is to ensure communications are clear, fair and not misleading and that customers are provided with appropriate information at the right time in order to make informed decisions. Subscribers will use plain language in all communications with customers in order to help them to better understand the information being provided and wherever possible avoid the use of technical or legal language.

18. Subscribers should ensure that financial promotions are compliant with relevant advertising legislation and industry codes of practice, such as the Consumer Credit (Advertisements) Regulations 2010 and the Committee of Advertising Practice Codes.

19. For promotions to personal customers that are made at a distance subscribers should follow the requirements of the Financial Services (Distance Marketing) Regulations 2004.

20. For direct sales of credit cards, subscribers should follow the relevant best practice guidelines issued by The UK Cards Association, which can be found at http://www.theukcardsassociation.org.uk/best_practices

21. For unsecured personal loans, if a subscriber chooses to provide key product information within financial promotions and pre-sale information in the form of a summary box, it should follow the standard format set out in Annex A.

22. To ensure financial promotions and communications are clear, fair and not misleading sub-scribers should have regard to:

- presenting information in plain language and wherever possible avoiding the use of technical or legal language;
- the way the communication or financial promotion is being made e.g. direct mail, letter, email, text message, branch or web material;
- the type and complexity of information that is being presented, the actions the information might elicit from the customer, the channels by which the information is accessible and the passage of time, if any, since the information was last provided; and
- the appropriate format and content of the communication based on its intended audience. For instance, a communication to a personal customer might include different information to that for a micro-enterprise, where needs may differ.

Marketing and advertising

23. Subscribers must have the customer's specific permission to pass the customer's name and address to any company, including other companies in the subscriber's group, for marketing purposes.

24. There are various acceptable methods of obtaining the customer's consent. It may, for example, be given by way of a clear and unambiguous clause above a signature box on an application form, or a positive 'click' on an internet application, or a positive reply to a specific question on the telephone. Subscribers should also be aware of the Information Commissioner's Guidance for Direct Marketers and telecoms licensing requirements. Consent should not be required in return for the provision of standard account services.

25. Subscribers can tell customers about another company's services or products but no confidential information about the customer should be passed to the other company by the subscriber without customer consent.

26. If the customer is interested in the other company's products or services and they respond, then they are themselves releasing confidential information. For example, a subscriber may have a subsidiary which offers general insurance products. The subscriber could send their customer details of those products. The subscriber should make clear to the customer that the third party is a separate legal entity, and is not a division of the subscriber's company, since this will not always be clear to the customer from the name of the third party. It is only if the customer chooses to respond positively that the subsidiary will learn any details about the customer, or even that the customer has been sent the information in the first place.

27. Customers must be given the opportunity to opt out of receiving the subscriber's marketing information. They should be reminded of this option at least once every three years.

28. Account opening forms (whether paper, internet-based, questions over the telephone, or other 'welcome pack' information) should contain a section or question to allow customers to signify that they do not wish to receive 'marketing approaches.' Examples of marketing approaches include literature through the post, e-mails and telephone calls. The types of approaches could be listed so the customer can object to some rather than all.

29. Subscribers should ensure that unsolicited promotional emails sent to customers include an option for the customer to 'unsubscribe' from future email promotional material from the subscriber.

30. 'Marketing approaches' means information designed to sell additional products and services. This means that if there is a clear intention to sell a product or service which the customer does not already have it will be caught by these provisions, however it is sent. However, the provision of information relating to product or service improvements or the availability of new channels (e.g. that the customer's existing account(s) can be accessed via the internet) are excluded from these provisions, as are changes to administrative details, such as new branch or telephone helpline opening hours.

31. As an illustration, advising a customer that they have free annual travel insurance with their credit card is not a marketing approach, whereas promoting an enhanced credit card to a standard credit cardholder is.

32. Subscribers should consider carefully whether the purpose of a customer communication is operational or promotional. Where 'combined' messages are used, a non-promotional version may be needed for customers who have opted out of receiving marketing material.

33. Express consent is not required to send information relating to product or service improvements or the availability of new channels of delivery, but customers must be given a clear opportunity to opt out of receiving it. Subscribers should, however, be aware (in the case of direct marketing telephone calls) of the Information Commissioner's Guidance in relation to the Privacy and Electronic Communications (EU Directive) Regulations 2003.

34. It will not be sufficient to state only in terms and conditions that customers can opt out by writing to a particular address; however, provided it is clear and unambiguous, a notification can be included in, for example, an account opening pack. In addition, existing customers have to be reminded, at least once every three years, that they can opt out of receiving this information. This reminder could be by letter, e-mail, telephone or other method, such as being included in an annual mailing, provided it is sent personally to each customer and is clear. Whatever notification method is chosen, subscribers should ensure they are familiar with the various pieces of guidance issued by the Information Commissioner under the Data Protection Act 1998.

35. The three year notice can also be covered by subscribers adopting a more frequent approach, for example on all statements and/or marketing material.

Section 3: Credit reference agencies

36. When customers apply for a credit product, subscribers should tell them if checks (searches) will be made at credit reference agencies (CRAs) and if a record of the search is kept at the CRA and, if so, that this could impact the customer's ability to obtain credit elsewhere within a short period of time.

37. At the same time, subscribers should also tell customers if details of the account, if opened, will be passed to CRAs and that that information will be accessed and used by others. This will include information about the running of the account such as the limit and balances as well as payment performance. The Information Commissioner accepts that such permission may be made a condition of borrowing.

38. See also the Information Commissioner's Guidance on the Data Protection Act 1998 which sets out the conditions under which data may be collected, shared or processed. (Useful information can be found at www.ico.gov.uk).

39. The requirement to share data does not apply in specialist customer segments such as private banking where sharing CRA data is not always appropriate.

40. Subscribers can give CRAs default information about a customer's debts if:
- the customer has fallen behind with their payments;
- the amount owed is not being disputed by the customer; and
- the customer has not made a proposal that satisfies the subscriber for repaying the debt following the subscriber's formal demand.

41. But, in all cases, the customer must be given further notice of the intention to disclose the information at least 28 days before the disclosure is made (for example, when a default notice or formal demand is given). At the same time, customers must be given an explanation about how default information registered against them may affect their ability to obtain credit in the future. This notice will mean that customers have 28 days to try to repay or come to some arrangement with the subscriber before default information is passed to the CRA.

42. For the purposes of the second bullet in paragraph 40, a customer dispute is relevant if it refers to the amount of money owed by the customer and is genuine, reasonable and unresolved. Further detail is provided in the ICO guidance referenced below.

43. Subscribers should refer to the Information Commissioner's Data Protection Technical Guidance on Filing Defaults with CRAs (www.ico.gov.uk).

44. If a customer asks, subscribers should tell them which CRAs they use and how to get a copy of the information CRAs hold about them, or give the customer a copy of the Guide to the Lending Code and/or one of their leaflets that explain how credit referencing works.

45. If an application for credit is declined, subscribers should advise the customer if information from CRAs made a contribution to the decision and advise the customer to obtain a copy of the information that CRAs hold about them, preferably before making any further applications.

46. If a subscriber offers an indicative quotation facility for a risk-priced credit product, it should be transparent about the availability of this facility.

47. If asked by a customer for an indication of the likely interest rate for a risk-priced product, subscribers should either:

- as industry best practice, provide an indicative quotation, in respect of which any credit search undertaken is not registered as a full application search at CRAs i.e. it is not used by lenders in their risk assessment; or
- inform the customer that it does not offer an indicative quotation facility and ensure that the customer is aware that, if they proceed, an application search will be registered at the CRA(s).[3]

[3 *This paragraph is effective from 1 July 2011.*]

48. With the customer's permission, subscribers can share information about the day-to-day running of the customer's account, including positive data, with CRAs where the firm has agreed to follow the industry's Principles of Reciprocity. It is consistent with the legal position that any other disclosure to CRAs can be made only with the customer's consent, usually by way of a declaration on an application form. The Information Commissioner accepts that such permission may be made a condition of borrowing.

49. See also the Information Commissioner's Guidance on the Data Protection Act 1998. The 'permission' can be covered in a number of ways, for example, in terms and conditions, in an account opening pack, or it can be obtained at the time the disclosure is made. (Useful information can be found at www.ico.gov.uk)

Section 4:   Credit assessment

Personal customers

50. Before lending any money, granting or increasing an overdraft or other borrowing, subscribers should assess whether the customer will be able to repay it in a sustainable manner. They should do this by considering information from CRAs, including existing financial commitments where provided, as well as the following, as appropriate:

- The type and amount of credit being sought;
- How the customer has handled their finances in the past;
- Internal credit scoring techniques (if used by the subscriber);
- The customer's declared income;
- Why the customer wants to borrow the money and for how long; and
- Any security provided.

51. Subscribers should take a view on which of the above factors it is appropriate to consider in any particular circumstance dependent on, for example, the type and amount of credit being sought and the potential risks to the borrower.

52. Assessment may also include other checks that have not been listed above.

53. The requirement to consider information from CRAs does not apply in specialist customer segments such as private banking where use of CRA data may not be appropriate.

54. Where income is one of the factors considered when assessing ability to repay a personal loan and the loan is agreed only if the income of another person is taken into account, normally the loan should be provided on a joint and several basis. However there may be circumstances when it is appropriate to provide a loan on a sole basis.

55. Subscribers should ensure they are familiar with the requirements of the Code Sponsors' Guide to Credit Scoring and the explanations that need to be given to customers if credit scoring is used.

56. If a lending application is declined following credit assessment, the subscriber should explain the main reason why if asked by the customer. If the decline is as a result of information obtained from a CRA search, the subscriber should provide the customer with contact details for the CRA.

Micro-enterprise customers

57. Before lending any money, granting or increasing an overdraft or other borrowing, subscribers should assess whether the customer will be able to repay it by considering some or all of the following, as appropriate:

- Why the business wants to borrow the money;
- The business plan and accounts;
- The business's cash flow, profitability and existing financial commitments;
- Any personal financial commitments which may affect the business;
- How the customer has handled their finances in the past;
- Information from credit reference agencies and, with the customer's permission, others, such as other lenders and the customer's landlord (where relevant);
- Credit-assessment techniques, such as credit scoring; and
- Any security provided.

58. If the subscriber requires a micro-enterprise customer to hold a current account in order to get a loan the reasons for this should be explained to the customer before the loan application is completed.

59. Subscribers will confirm the conditions of any facility in writing. The document should include, as appropriate:

- the amount and purpose of the facility;
- whether the facility is for a particular period or whether it is repayable on demand;
- details of repayments;
- the interest rate and any other charges for the facility, and whether these are variable;
- when the facility will normally be reviewed;
- the existing or new security and guarantees, including any minimum values to be maintained;
- what sort of circumstances will lead to an earlier review or require repayment;
- the information the customer will need to give before they can use the facility; and
- what action the subscriber will take if repayments are not met.

60. Subscribers should recommend that the customer gets independent advice before accepting the facility.

61. Subscribers should allow customers to bring their professional advisers with them to support them in the discussions and should co-operate with the customer's advisers to explain the facility and to clarify anything during the relationship. Subscribers may need to ask for the customer's explicit consent to engage with the adviser, if the customer will not be present.

62. Before the customer accepts the facility, the subscriber should agree with the customer what sort of monitoring information they need about the firm's performance and how often they need it. Subscribers should write to customers setting out what information is required from them and by when. Examples of what might be included are:

- a comparison of the forecasts in the business plan, with actual results;
- progress on important aspects of the business plan, such as contract renewals;
- revised cash-flow forecasts;
- major capital spending proposals;
- annual accounts and regular management accounts;
- details of how much the customer owes creditors, and are owed by debtors, and for how long these have been due; and
- proof that the customer is meeting any special conditions agreed.

63. Subscribers should provide either in-house guides or industry-standard literature to provide guidance on the factors that determine pricing. The BBA has also published a factsheet, available at www.bba.org.uk/content/1/c6/01/79/71/Small_business_lending_bankfact.pdf

64. Subscribers should inform the customer of the time it will take for a lending decision to be made, starting from the point when a full suite of information is provided to complete an application.

65. Subscribers should ensure they have fair and effective processes in place to review decisions to decline a lending application.

66. If a lending application is declined, wherever practical the subscriber should provide pro-active and clear feedback to the customer on the main reason why the application was declined and have fair and effective processes in place to review decisions to decline a lending application. Each bank should have their individual solution to handle a request to review an application that was turned down. Examples for this include: a second bank manager reviewing the decision on request or a central telephone hotline to make the application again.

Guarantees for personal and micro-enterprise lending

67. Regular financial information about the person on whose behalf a guarantee/indemnity or other security is given should always be made available to the guarantor or granters of third party security ('granters'), so that they can assess the likelihood of being called upon to pay, as long as permission is given and confidentiality is not breached.

68. If the guarantor or granter requests confidential financial information (with the exception of the current level of liability), such as details of balances, copy statements, etc, the customer's consent should first be obtained.

69. It is important that guarantors or granters receive independent legal advice to help them understand the full nature of their commitment and the potential implications of their decision. Case law on this issue is well developed and subscribers should encourage, as far as possible, potential guarantors or granters to take independent advice. Subscribers may wish to go further than what is covered in this section and require a potential guarantor or granter who refuses to take legal advice to sign a declaration to that effect. In any case, the recommendation to take independent legal advice, and the potential consequences of their decision, should be stated clearly on all appropriate documents that the guarantor or granter is asked to sign.

70. In relation to guarantees/indemnities, subscribers must also inform guarantors or granters that, by giving the guarantee/indemnity or other third party security, they may have to pay instead of or as well as the customer. Subscribers must also tell the guarantor the extent of their liability, including the addition of interest and charges after demand has been made. When independent legal advice has been given, it may be assumed that the solicitor will have explained the nature of all monies and continuing security, if appropriate. Depending on the nature and structure of facilities, subscribers may choose to explain these features to those customers who have declined independent legal advice (and should always do so when requested by any guarantor).

71. Subscribers should not take an unlimited guarantee from an individual other than to support a customer's liabilities under a merchant agreement. However, other forms of unlimited third party security may be taken from an individual, provided that the limit of the granter's liability is explained in a side letter. This is to avoid the need to take fresh security, with the associated expense and inconvenience to customers, each time a facility changes.

72. 'Unlimited' applies to the capital amount of the loan and excludes interest, charges and arrears etc. An explanation of this should be covered in the guarantee/indemnity or other security documents that the guarantor is asked to sign.

73. In the case of limited companies, which are part of the same group structure, subscribers may continue to take unlimited guarantees from the constituent companies in support of borrowing by other companies in the group.

Security for micro-enterprise lending

74. If a subscriber asks for security to support a business's borrowing or other liabilities it should tell the business why it needs the security and confirm what is needed in writing. Documents should be easy to understand and avoid technical language whenever possible. Customers should have the opportunity to discuss with the subscriber anything about which they are unsure.

75. If asked by the customer, the subscriber should tell the customer under what circumstances they will agree to release the security. It should be made clear that the security will be released once the facility is repaid unless contrary instructions are received from the customer (i.e. security should not be retained beyond the life of the borrowing without the customer's express agreement).

Section 5:   Current account overdrafts

The following provisions relate to arranged and unarranged overdrafts unless otherwise indicated. Provisions relating to the promotion and operation of current accounts with an opt out facility will be effective from 1 July 2011 and do not apply to private banking customers, who would typically have a designated relationship manager, or micro-enterprise customers.

Pre-sale information

76. When providing customers with information, before a contract is entered into, about a current account offering an arranged overdraft facility, subscribers should include clear, fair and not misleading information outlining the availability of the overdraft, including whether there are qualifying criteria for accessing the overdraft.

77. The customer must be provided, where relevant, with details of any charges payable, the interest rate to be applied or, if reference interest rates are to be used, the method for calculating the actual interest and the relevant date and index or base for determining such reference interest rates.

78. Where a subscriber provides within its current account range one or more accounts that provide customers with the ability to opt out from unarranged overdrafts:

- Details of such accounts must be provided to customers applying for a new current account, together with a comparison of this type of account against other current accounts offered by the subscriber without such facility, in order that the customer may make an informed choice. However, such information need not be provided where the subscriber reasonably believes or is advised that the customer has already decided on another current account product in the subscriber's range of current accounts (e.g. a Basic Bank Account). The comparison only needs to include comparable current account products on which overdrafts are permitted.
- If a customer requests a current account which includes an opt out from unarranged overdrafts, the subscriber shall not offer a Basic Bank Account as an appropriate account to meet this requirement unless the limited functionality of such an account is suitable for the customer's circumstances.
- The information to be provided by the subscriber should be in plain and simple language and have sufficient detail to enable the customer to understand how the product works. As a minimum, the information to be provided should include an explanation of:
  - what an unarranged overdraft is and how it operates;
  - how the opt out will work and the benefits to the customer in terms of allowing greater control and certainty;
  - the potential detrimental impact of opting out e.g. return of items or authorisation refusal even if only a very small overdraft would result if the item had been paid;
  - why some items (such as point of sale transactions that were not subject to on-line authorisation, charges, payments against uncleared cheques which are subsequently returned unpaid) are excluded from the opt out and the consequences of this;
  - costs and charges including any account fees and unpaid item charges;
  - how the customer can select the option and whether a switch of account is required. The ability to reverse the decision subsequently and any restrictions on this;
  - how any items in transit will be treated when the facility becomes live;
  - the availability of a buffer zone, if applicable, including the amount of the buffer zone and any costs incurred if utilised; and

    – general information on how customers can avoid overdrafts e.g. through account monitoring, changing dates of direct debits, if not provided via other communications.

- The information to be provided to customers as outlined above should be provided in a leaflet or key features document or some other durable medium and should include a glossary or explanation of terms to aid customer understanding.

79. This information must be provided either in good time, before the customer is bound by the contract, or where the contract concludes at the payment service user's request, using a means of distance communication, immediately after the conclusion of the contract.

Point of sale and post-sale information

80. If a customer is offered an arranged overdraft, or an increase in their existing arranged overdraft limit, subscribers should tell the customer if the overdraft is repayable on demand. The explanation could be contained in a facility letter or the terms and conditions.

81. Where a subscriber introduces the facility for current account customers to opt out of unarranged overdrafts or launches a new product with this facility, the subscriber must provide the information set out in paragraph 78 (bullet 3) to:

- all those customers with an account of the type to which the facility is to be added, in the case of a new enhancement to the existing range of current accounts. The required changes to terms and conditions must be advised to customers within 30 days in accordance with paragraph 176; and
- within three months of the introduction of the new product, to all current account customers who have incurred unarranged overdraft charges in the previous 12 months.

82. Where a subscriber offers current accounts that enable customers to opt out of unarranged overdrafts, information about the opt out facility must be provided to:

- all customers who incur an unarranged overdraft charge, on the first occasion that such a charge is incurred, either as part of the communication regarding the charge/usage of the unarranged overdraft or by separate communication; and
- all current account customers who have incurred unarranged overdraft charges in the previous 12 months, unless a reminder of the availability of an opt out was sent when the charge was incurred.

83. If an existing current account customer wishes to opt out of unarranged overdrafts on their account, the subscriber should enable the customer to exercise this option and remind them what the effect will be on the operation of their account. Such information may be provided in a leaflet or letter or electronically, according to the normal channel of communication with the customer.

84. The information to be provided under paragraphs 81 and 82 may include a summary of the information outlined in paragraph 78 (bullet 3) and/or signposting to a leaflet or web page for detailed information.

85. If a customer requests to opt out of unarranged overdrafts, a subscriber should not, in response offer the customer a Basic Bank Account unless the limited functionality of a Basic Bank Account is appropriate for the customer's circumstances.

86. Although a customer's decision to opt out of unarranged overdrafts is capable of being revoked by the customer, a subscriber may place restrictions on the number and frequency of permitted switches that a customer may make in respect of unarranged overdrafts.

87. The decision by a current account customer to opt out of unarranged overdrafts will not of itself have any negative impact on the customer's credit record. However, whether or not a customer chooses to opt out, their credit record may be damaged as a result of returned items.

88. If a customer's overdraft application is declined, the subscriber should explain the main reason why if asked by the customer. This could be provided in writing or electronically, if requested.

89. The written explanation could be given in the form of a leaflet if this is sufficiently focused. With regard to refusals based on credit scoring, the Code Sponsors' Guide to Credit Scoring refers and can be found at: http://www.bba.org.uk/bba/jsp/polopoly.jsp?d=135&a=6612. Subscribers should have regard to the potential for financial crime in the information they provide and will want to avoid compromising their security procedures.

Interest rates and charges

90. Subscribers should make information about overdraft interest rates available to customers via:

- a telephone helpline;
- a website;
- notices in branches; or
- information from staff.

91. If an overdraft is provided subscribers should give customers information on the interest rates which apply and when interest will be collected. If a customer asks, subscribers should also give a full explanation of how interest is worked out.

91.1 In relation to personal customers, before taking interest and overdraft charges, subscribers should give at least 14 days notice of how much will be taken.

91.2 In relation to micro-enterprise customers, before taking interest and arranged overdraft charges, subscriber should give at least 14 days notice of how much will be taken.

92. In sub-paragraphs 91.1 and 91.2 'charges' do not include up-front arrangement fees which are subject to prior agreement with the customer.

93. Subscribers should inform customers about changes to the interest rates on their overdraft in compliance with the relevant regulatory requirement applying to the subscriber's overdraft terms. To help compare rates, the old rate should also be included.

94. Within three working days of a rate change, notices should be put in branches and newspapers, unless all customers affected by the rate change have already been personally notified. To help compare rates, the old rate should also be included.

95. Where an overdraft interest rate tracks changes to an index rate, the requirement to inform customers of changes does not apply.

96. Subscribers should make available to customers information about any charges for overdrafts via:

- a telephone helpline;
- a website; or
- by asking staff.

97. Subscribers should tell customers personally at least 30 days before increasing an overdraft charge or introducing a new overdraft charge.

98. Further guidance on charges information for current accounts, which are regulated under the Payment Services Regulations (PSRs), can be found at: http://www.fsa.gov.uk/pubs/other/PSD_approach.pdf

Section 6:   Credit cards

All customers
Pre-sale information

99. Information provided to customers should be clear, fair and not misleading. Subscribers should present information about the main features of a credit card in a summary box, as set out in The UK Cards Association Best Practice Guidelines http://www.theukcardsassociation.org.uk/best_practices/

100. The summary box should be provided to the customer prior to their acceptance of the credit agreement.

101. All integral features of the product, such as introductory rates, should be included in the summary box. Information on free-standing or optional product features, such as Payment Protection Insurance (PPI), credit card cheques or other free-standing product features should not be shown in the summary box. Information on such free-standing features should be provided separately and should comply with any relevant best practice guidelines.

102. Pre-contract, the summary box should appear prominently on, or within, any application form/pack, acting as a final reminder for the consumer. This will typically cover direct mail pieces, free-standing leaflets, inserts etc. but not media such as television, radio, cinema or outdoor advertising.

103. For internet applications, a click-through to a page containing the summary box should be available.

104. Credit card issuers are not precluded from using the summary box in any advertising media they choose or at any point post-contract.

105. Subscribers should only send a credit card to a customer if they request one or to replace a credit card the customer already has.

106. If an application for a credit card made by a personal customer is declined following credit assessment, the subscriber should explain the main reason why if asked by the customer. If the decline is as a result of information obtained from a CRA search, the customer should be given contact details for the CRA.

107. If a credit card application by a micro-enterprise customer is declined, wherever practical the subscriber should provide proactive and clear feedback to the customer on the main reason why the application was declined and inform the customer of their right to appeal that decision.

Point of contract information

108. Before a customer enters into the contract for a credit card (and when they accept the product for the first time) they should be given information relating to the following:

- An explanation of how interest is calculated and charged; for example, whether it is charged on the full statement balance or only on any balance remaining after the customer has made the monthly payment;
- The PSRs require that the customer must be provided, where relevant, with details of the interest and exchange rates to be applied or, if reference interest and exchange rates are to be used, the method for calculating the actual interest and the relevant date and index or base for determining such reference interest or exchange rates;
- This information must be provided either in good time before the customer is bound by the contract, or where the contract is concluded at the payment service user's request, using a means of distance communication, immediately after the conclusion of the contract;
- Details of how monthly payments are applied to any outstanding balance across transaction types including promotional offers;
- An explanation of recurring transactions;
- Details of charges for the day-to-day running of the account, including any annual fee, dormancy fee, charge for exceeding credit limit, charge for delayed monthly payment, charges for overseas transactions, cash withdrawal fees for card usage at an ATM or over the counter, fees for any cash equivalent transactions, balance transfer fees, returned payment fees due to insufficient funds, and any other applicable fees;
- The distinction between being the principal cardholder and an additional cardholder should be explained i.e., that the principal cardholder is responsible for all spending, including that by additional cardholders, and is responsible for repayments on the credit card;
- The interest rates applicable to different types of transactions (e.g., purchases, balance transfers, credit card cheque transactions and cash transactions) and the ways in which customers will be told about changes in interest rates; and
- Sufficient details to enable customers to pay on time, including via automated payments. Subscribers should also ensure that, where customers are offered the facility to pay by cheque by post, sufficient time is given to allow payments to be made in time, taking account of the postal delivery system and the length of the clearing cycle.

Chip and PIN

109. Subscribers should issue the customer's PIN separately from their card.

110. Subscribers should have systems in place to allow customers to change their PIN and should tell customers how to do so, for example in credit card welcome packs or on PIN notifications.

111. Subscribers will ensure that guidance is provided to customers on the need to protect their card and PIN.

112. Subscribers should make reference to the availability of alternatives to chip and PIN in materials accompanying card issuance and in any discussion with the customer where they express difficulty with using a PIN.

Interest rates

113. Subscribers should make current credit card interest rates available to customers via one or more of the following:

- A telephone helpline;
- A website;
- Notices in branches; or
- By asking staff.

Communication of interest rate changes

114. Subscribers should inform customers about changes to the interest rates on their credit card in compliance with the relevant regulatory requirement applying to the subscriber's credit card terms.

Credit card limits

115. Before giving a customer a credit limit, or increasing an existing limit, subscribers should assess whether they feel the customer will be able to repay it. Subscribers should follow The UK Cards Association Best Practice Guidelines for credit card limit increases http://www.theukcardsassociation.org.uk/best_practices/

116. Customers may at any time request an increase in their existing credit limit.

117. Where an emergency increase to a credit card limit is granted (i.e. when a transaction goes for authorisation and will take the customer over their pre-agreed limit) the subscriber should always assess the customer's ability to repay.

118. Subscribers should advise customers that checks are made before a limit is increased (the method and timing of advice will be at the subscriber's discretion).

119. Credit card limit increases should not be offered on accounts that are in arrears and should not be granted for accounts that fall below credit scoring thresholds.

120. Subscribers should periodically review customers' credit card limits using credit reference agency and internal data. The requirement to use CRA data does not apply in specialist customer segments, such as private banking, where use of CRA data is not always appropriate.

121. Where the subscriber feels it is appropriate, the credit card limit should be reduced and notification given to the customer. The subscriber should ensure that the notification includes, or signposts to, relevant contact details so that the customer can discuss with the lender any concerns they have about their card or their financial position[4].

[4 *This paragraph is effective from 1 July 2011.*]

Credit card promotional period

122. If a credit card has an introductory promotional rate the expiry date of the introductory promotional offer should be shown on the front of the statement or in a separate, prominent personal notification to the customer. This should be given between four and eight weeks before the offer expires.

123. It is acceptable to exceed the four or eight week period if the best way to provide information about the expiry of an introductory promotional rate is by a message in, or with, a monthly statement.

124. This requirement does not apply where the customer is in breach of the terms and conditions of the account and the subscriber is concerned that giving the customer warning that the promotional period is about to end may result in abuse of the card, or where the account is not being used and the customer is not receiving a monthly statement.

Credit card statements

125. Subscribers should provide customers with a monthly statement for their credit card unless the account has a zero balance and has not been used. The monthly statement will include information about transactions since the last statement date, any interest which applies, the minimum repayment and other useful information compliant with the Consumer Credit Act 1974, such as the allocation of payments.

126. Subscribers should follow The UK Cards Association Best Practice Guidelines for the Cardholder Statement Summary Box http://www.theukcardsassociation.org.uk/best_practices/

127. There are a number of specific pieces of information which should be included on every credit card statement (and where appropriate on a link from an electronic statement):

- Sufficient details to enable customers to pay on time, including via automated payments;
- The current interest rate should be printed on each statement. Also, if more than one interest rate applies to an outstanding balance (for example, where one rate applies to a transferred balance and different rates to new borrowing and cash transactions) this should be made clear;
- A clear statement that if the account is not fully cleared, interest will be charged on the total value of the statement, and not just on the outstanding balance;
- A clear statement that interest will be charged on a daily basis and that interest payments therefore increase the longer payment is delayed (even before the monthly payment date);
- A brief summary on the allocation of monthly payments on the front or back of the statement (or a link from an online statement);
- The front of each credit card statement should show a cash figure indicative of the amount of interest which would be payable by the customer if they paid the minimum amount and it reached the subscriber on the last day for payment; and
- A warning about the risk of only making minimum payments—this should be worded as follows, 'If you make only the minimum payment each month, it will take you longer and cost you more to clear your balance.'

128. In the event that a customer has missed a payment, subscribers should also include in any notification sent to a customer in respect of the first missed payment, reference to the option of paying by automated payment to avoid missing future payments.

Credit card repayments

129. Subscribers should ensure that the minimum monthly repayment covers more than that month's interest. This means that the minimum repayment will cover that month's interest and a proportion of the balance outstanding from the previous month.

130. The principle should be that the minimum repayment on a credit card should reduce month by month if there have been no further transactions on the card and the lower minimum payment threshold of the card has not been reached, assuming all other conditions of the product remain unchanged. The term 'transactions' includes any fees, charges or PPI premiums incurred on the card.

131. The minimum payment amount on the account should be clearly shown. This amount should normally be sufficient to avoid negative amortisation over a period of 12 months (i.e. the sum of 12 minimum payments would exceed the sum of additional interest added to the account over the same 12 month period).

132. It is acceptable for the minimum payment amount to be calculated as a percentage of the balance carried forward, so long as the percentage would normally prevent negative amortisation. Other methods for calculating the minimum payment are also acceptable, provided this principle can be demonstrated.

133. Subscribers may offer payment holidays and should clearly explain the terms and that customers can reject the holiday by continuing payment. Where a payment holiday is provided the minimum repayment afterwards should be sufficient to avoid negative amortisation over a period of 12 months from the start of the holiday.

Credit card cheques

134. Subscribers should follow The UK Cards Association Best Practice Guidelines for credit card cheques including the provision of clear information through a summary box provided with all credit card cheques: http://www.theukcardsassociation.org.uk/best_practices/

135. The following customers should not be issued credit card cheques:

- Customers who are in arrears or over-limit[5];
- Customers with limited scope to borrow more or who are at their limit;
- Customers who have opted out of receiving cheques; and
- Accounts where there are fraudulent activities or lost/stolen procedures pending.

[5 *This means customers who are in arrears with their payments or over-limit at the time of selection for receipt of credit card cheques.*]

136. Subscribers should not send out unsolicited credit card cheques with a pre-completed amount.

137. In addition to the summary box, subscribers should clearly and transparently highlight in the main body of any communication accompanying the provision of credit card cheques the following (where applicable):

- Credit card cheques do not provide the same level of consumer protection as a normal credit card purchase;
- The transaction fee per cheque;
- Whether there is an interest free period; and

An alert to the Summary Box (e.g. "see important information overleaf").

Unauthorised transactions

138. If a credit card transaction has not been authorised by the customer then any interest that may have been charged on this transaction will be refunded unless the customer has acted fraudulently or with gross negligence.

139. Unless the subscriber can show that the customer acted fraudulently or with gross negligence, their liability for their credit card being misused will be limited as follows:

- If someone else uses the card, before the customer informs the subscriber that it has been lost or stolen or that someone else knows the PIN, the most the customer will have to pay is £50;
- If someone else uses the card details without the customer's permission, and the card has not been lost or stolen, the customer will not have to pay anything;
- If someone else uses the card details without the customer's permission for a transaction where the cardholder does not need to be present (e.g buying something over the internet), the customer will not have to pay anything; and
- If the card is used before the customer has received it, the customer will not have to pay anything.

140. The second bullet in paragraph 139 refers to fraudulent situations where, for example, a customer's card has been cloned. Unless the customer has acted fraudulently or with gross negligence (which the subscriber must prove—see below), the customer is liable for a maximum of £50 in total (i.e. not for each transaction) before they give notification of loss etc., if the card is out of their possession.

141. If card details are misused while the card is still in the customer's possession (i.e. it has not been lost or stolen), the customer cannot be liable, unless they have acted fraudulently or with gross negligence. This would include misuse of card details in the case of distance transactions (this reflects the requirements of the EU Distance Selling Directive). Under the Consumer Credit Act 1974, if the card was used as a credit token, then the consideration of gross negligence is irrelevant.

142. In relation to unauthorised transactions, the burden of proof lies with the subscriber and not with the customer, so the subscriber will have to provide proof if necessary.

Unsatisfied transactions

143. Subscribers will ensure that customers are made aware of the protections available to them in the event of an unsatisfied transaction[6].

[[6] *This paragraph is effective from 1 July 2011.*]

Additional provisions for personal customers
Credit card re-pricing

144. Except where the exemptions set out below apply, subscribers should follow the Statement of Principles relating to Credit Card Re-pricing issued by The UK Cards Association that can be found at: http://www.theukcardsassociation.org.uk/best_practices/

The following definitions apply:

- Risk-based re-pricing: this affects individual customers or specific groups of customers with similar risk profiles
- General re-pricing: subject to the exemptions set out below, any type of re-pricing, other than that which is risk-based.

The exemptions, which apply to paragraphs 145–154:

- An interest rate set to directly track the movement in an external index (such as a base rate), which has been clearly stated in the product's terms and conditions
- A promotional interest rate that has come to the scheduled end of its duration, or has been revoked early by the subscriber (for example where a payment is missed)
- An interest rate decrease.

Pre-notification of interest rate increases

145. Subscribers will provide written notice (which may include individual electronic communication where the customer has indicated his willingness to receive communications in this form) to customers of any interest rate increase.

146. Such notice must be given at least 30 days before the interest rate increase takes effect. The notice will explain in clear language how the rate is changing, what it will cost and the options available to them and will include the following information:

- Current interest rate;
- The new increased interest rate;
- An indicative cost impact of the increase (by either a generic or personalised example); and
- Notification of the customer's ability to reject the increase during the period of 60 days specified in the notice and pay the outstanding balance in full at the current rate.

If the subscriber offers alternative lending products, it may also provide the customer with the option to transfer the balance to such a product at the existing (or lower) rate of interest.

147. For a risk-based rate increase, the notice of interest rate increase will be a communication sent separately from any account statement.

148. For a general interest rate increase, the notice may be sent with the customer's statement, via a separate piece of paper.

Rejection of interest rate increases

149. The 60 day rejection period (referred to in paragraph 146) may run concurrently with the 30 day notice period and if this is the case, the written notice will make this clear to the customer.

150. During the 60 day rejection period, the subscriber will remind the customer of their right to reject the interest rate increase, which will require the subscriber to close the account and the customer to repay the outstanding balance. This reminder may be included on or with the customer's account statement and does not need to repeat the detail included in the original notification.

151. The customer may tell the subscriber, at any time during the 60 day rejection period specified in the notice of increase that they wish to reject the interest rate increase. Where the customer rejects the rate increase:

- the customer's credit card account will be closed by the subscriber; and
- the customer will be permitted to pay their outstanding credit card balance at their pre-notification interest rate within a reasonable period[7].

[7 *Having due regard to the level of minimum payments and the customer's financial situation.*]

152. Subscribers will, if asked by the customer, explain why the interest rate is being increased and make available an industry standard explanation of how credit card re-pricing works.

Selection of accounts for re-pricing

153. Where a customer manages their account within the subsciber's terms and conditions, the subscriber will not increase interest rates:

- for risk-based re-pricing—within the first 12 months of a customer having the credit card; or
- for risk-based re-pricing and general re-pricing—more often than 6 monthly, other than in exceptional circumstances.[8]

[8 *The exception applies to general re-pricing only and, for example may be a rapid escalation in underlying interest rates, or a change to legislation/ regulation, that significantly increases costs, or decreases income.*]

154. Subscribers will not increase the interest rate when they are aware that:

- the customer is currently two or more payments in arrears;
- an agreed repayment plan is in place in respect of the account; or
- the customer is in serious discussion with a debt advice agency (and the subscriber has been formally notified of this by the agency).

155. Further guidance on dealing with cases of financial difficulty is included in Section 9.

Credit card limits

156. Customers may at any time:

- request a reduction in their existing credit limit;
- reject an unsolicited credit limit increase;
- inform the subscriber that they do not want to be given a credit limit increase at all in the future; and
- request an increase in their credit limit.

If a customer exercises any of these rights it does not prevent them from asking for a credit limit I increase at a later date.

In the case of the first two bullets above, subscribers will make it as easy as possible for customers to exercise these options by offering them automated methods of communication, such as online (for example, using a specified proforma) or through an automated telephone system (or another automated communication method) notwithstanding the customer's right to speak to a human operator.

Communication of unsolicited credit limit increases

157. A subscriber will provide written notice to a customer (which may include individual electronic communication where the customer has indicated his willingness to receive communications in this form) of its intention to increase the customer's credit limit and such notice will be given at least 30 days before the limit increase is due to take effect. This communication will be separate from any account statement and will include the following information:

- Current credit limit;
- The new increased credit limit;
- The customer's right to reject the credit limit increase; and
- How the customer can reject the proposed credit limit increase and reassurance that the subscriber will not treat them any differently simply because they exercise their right to reject a credit limit increase.

Such notice need not be given where a subscriber gives a customer a temporary or an emergency credit limit increase.

Allocation of payments

158. Subscribers will apply customers' repayments to the most expensive parts of the credit card balance first. This means that repayments will be applied to the various elements within the balance ranked by order of their annual interest rate (not APR) on a pure high to low basis. In allocating customer repayments, subscribers will apply them to, at least, statemented transactions.

159. In the case of hybrid credit products, where the total credit provided and accordingly the balance may be made up of both fixed and revolving credit elements, the requirement to allocate payments to the most expensive part of the balance first applies only in respect of any payment made in excess of that required to satisfy the fixed instalment(s) as specified in the agreement.

Minimum payments

160. Subscribers should ensure that for customers entering a new credit agreement on or after 31 March 2011 that the calculated minimum payment will always cover at least:
- 1% of the principal owing;
- the amount of interest that appears on the statement;
- default fees/charges; and
- annual fees that may be levied (whether as a single sum, twelve equal instalments or other method).

The 'principal owing' means the outstanding balance shown on the statement less the current month's interest and fees. 'Fees' do not include fees for services such as balance transfers or cash advances.

161. Subscribers must follow the industry agreement developed by The UK Cards Association on the sending of a separate advice communication where a customer, without good reason, has made frequent minimum repayments or low repayments.

Automated payments

162. Subscribers will provide customers with online capability to set up an automated payment, for any amount they choose between the minimum payment and full payment, which will be used to reduce their balance. 'Online' could include a customer sending an instruction to the subscriber via email if the subscriber has agreed to receive instructions using this method.

Credit card cheques

163. In the case of personal customers, subscribers may only provide credit card cheques:
- to a customer who has asked for them;
- on a single occasion in respect of each request that is made; and
- the number of cheques provided must not exceed three, or, if less, the number requested

Additional provisions for micro-enterprise customers
Credit card cheques

164. New customers should be given a first time opt out from receiving credit card cheque mailings.

165. When unsolicited credit card cheques are provided to a micro-enterprise customer, the customer should be given prominent information about how to opt out of receiving cheques and how to destroy unwanted credit card cheques and supporting material.

Section 7: Loans

Declining an application

166. If a personal customer's loan application is declined following credit assessment, the subscriber should explain the main reason why if asked by the customer. This could be provided in writing or electronically, if requested. If the decline is as a result of information obtained from a CRA search, the customer should be given contact details for the CRA.

167. If a micro-enterprise customer's loan application is declined, wherever practical the subscriber should provide proactive and clear feedback to the customer on the main reason why the application was declined and inform the customer of their right to appeal that decision

168. The written explanation for both personal and micro-enterprise customers could be given in the form of a leaflet if it is sufficiently focused. In regard to refusals based on credit scoring, the Code Sponsors' Guide to Credit Scoring (in particular, section 6 of the Guide) refers. Subscribers should have regard to the potential for financial crime in the information they provide and will want to avoid compromising their security procedures.

169. If, after declining an application for credit, subscribers wish to refer a customer to another lender, they should seek the customer's consent and make the customer aware that a referral is not an indication that a subsequent application for credit will be successful.

Section 8:   Terms and conditions

Introduction

170. Unless it is impracticable to do so, as in the case of products purchased by telephone, customers should be provided with relevant product terms and conditions—and be encouraged to read them—before they commit to purchasing the product.

171. All terms and conditions should be written in clear and intelligible language. They should be fair in substance and, when relating to personal lending, should reflect the requirements of the Unfair Terms in Consumer Contracts Regulations.

172. Terms and conditions supplied to customers in paper format should be easy to read by someone with normal or corrected eyesight.

173. Customers should be told how they will be notified of changes to terms and conditions when they become a customer.

174. Subscribers must not insist that a customer buys an insurance product from them as a condition of providing the customer with a lending product.

Changes to terms and conditions

175. If terms and conditions are changed to the customer's detriment customers should be given at least 30 days personal notice (for example, by letter, e-mail, etc) before the change takes effect. At any time during the 60 days from the date of the notification, the customer must be free to close or switch their account without having to give notice. Customers should also be free to close or switch accounts without any financial penalty.

176. Where a change to terms and conditions is not to the customer's disadvantage it can be made immediately. However, the customer should be notified of the change within 30 days. Notification can be made in a number of ways, for example: by press advertisements; branch notices; information on the website; etc. The method chosen should be appropriate for the distribution channel. So, for example, a branch notice would not be appropriate to advertise changes in the terms of an internet-only account.

177. If a firm makes a major change or a lot of minor changes to terms and conditions in any one year it should provide the customer with a summary of the changes and make available a full copy of the terms and conditions.

Section 9:   Financial difficulties

Introduction

178. Subscribers should be sympathetic and positive when considering a customer's financial difficulties. Although there is an onus on customers to try to help themselves, the first step, when a subscriber becomes aware of a customer's financial difficulties, should be to try to contact the customer to discuss the matter. This applies to both personal and micro-enterprise customers.

179. Personal customers should be considered to be in financial difficulty when income is insufficient to cover reasonable living expenses and meet financial commitments as they become due. This may result from a change in lifestyle, often accompanied by a fall in disposable income and/or increased expenditure, such as:

- loss of employment;
- disability;

- serious illness;
- relationship breakdown;
- death of a partner;
- starting a lower paid job;
- parental/carer leave;
- starting full-time education; and
- imprisonment.

180. Financial difficulties may become evident to a subscriber from one or more of the following events:

- Items repeatedly being returned unpaid due to lack of available funds;
- Failing to meet loan repayments or other commitments;
- Discontinuation of regular credits;
- Notification of some form of insolvency or court proceedings;
- Regular requests for increased borrowing or repeated rescheduling of debts;
- Making frequent cash withdrawals on a credit card at a non-promotional rate of interest;
- Repeatedly exceeding a credit card or overdraft limit without agreement; and
- The customer informing the subscriber that they are, or at risk of being in financial difficulties.

This list is illustrative and non-exhaustive.

181. Additionally, for micro-enterprise customers, financial difficulties may also become evident to subscribers because:

- the customer goes overdrawn without agreement;
- the customer goes over their agreed overdraft limit, especially more than once;
- there are large increases or decreases in the business's turnover;
- the business is trading at a loss;
- the business suddenly loses a key customer or employee;
- a large part of the business is sold;
- a facility is used for purposes other than those agreed with the subscriber;
- the customer does not keep to conditions set out in the loan agreement;
- the customer does not supply agreed monitoring information on time; and
- another creditor brings a winding-up petition or other legal action against the business.

Proactive contact

182. If a subscriber becomes aware via their existing systems or from external data feeds (e.g. CRAs) or from information provided by the customer that the customer may be at risk of being in financial difficulties, the subscriber should contact the customer in order to:

- outline their approach to financial difficulties;
- encourage the customer to contact the subscriber if the customer is worried about their position;
- offer the customer appropriate and timely options where possible to help reduce the risk of deterioration in the customer's financial well- being; and
- provide signposts to sources of free, independent money advice.

The subscriber's contact with a customer identified as being at risk of being in financial difficulties should be through the normal channel of communication with the customer concerned, such as letter, telephone, email or text.

183. Signs or indicators that a personal customer may be at risk of being in financial difficulties may include:

- regular unarranged overdrafts or excesses on agreed overdraft facilities;
- high or increasing numbers of unarranged overdraft charges being incurred by the customer, particularly where the total charges are high compared to the customer's monthly income (where known);

- regular returned items or refused authorisations in respect of Point of Sale or ATM transactions;
- frequent requests for increased overdraft limits;
- hardcore borrowing or increasing dependence on unauthorised overdrafts developing;
- change in account behaviour such as significantly reduced credit turnover;
- missed or overdue payments in respect of products held by the customer; and
- deteriorating trend in third party data e.g. CRA data.

This list is not intended to be exhaustive, nor are the above necessarily indicators that a customer may be at risk of being in financial difficulties. Subscribers should consider what other information they have available that might indicate that a customer is or is not at risk of experiencing financial difficulties.

184. Once a personal customer has been identified as being in or at risk of being in financial difficulties, the subscriber should determine the appropriate level of intervention required dependent on the individual customer's position.

185. Subscribers should consider a range of solutions to assist personal customers who are identified as being at risk of being in financial difficulties, which may include:
- Account management guidance:
  - Changing the date of regular payments so that for instance a mortgage or rent payment is made immediately after receipt of a salary;
  - Set up text/email alerts (if available).
- Changes to account functionality:
  - Promotion of availability of opt out from unarranged overdrafts (where offered—see Section 5)
  - Downgrade account and facilities, e.g. to a Basic Bank Account, if the reduced functionality of such an account is appropriate for the customer's needs.
- Intervention:
  - Cancellation of regular payments, with customer making alternative arrangements to meet essential bills;
- Restructuring:
  - Re-schedule borrowing, possibly moving hardcore borrowing to a loan account with regular payments, subject to affordability assessment;
  - Agreement to a formal arranged overdraft, subject to affordability assessment.
- Concessions/forbearance
  - Charges and interest concessions (see paragraphs 224–227).
- Referral to third party debt adviser
  - Breathing space (see paragraphs 201–203).

Any arrangements agreed and made between the subscriber and a customer or their adviser must be confirmed in writing.

186. In cases where the subscriber's internal review and/or discussions with a personal customer establish that the customer is not at risk of being in financial difficulties, the subscriber need take no further action, subject always to paragraph 182 (pro-active contact) above.

Provisions for personal customers
Communicating with personal customers and their advisers

187. Subscribers should make available to customers straightforward information in plain English on their procedures and systems for dealing with customers in financial difficulty. This might explain, for example, the main rights and responsibilities of customers and subscribers, and what is involved in legal demands or a referral to a debt recovery unit. The BBA publishes a leaflet, Dealing with Debt, which is available on the BBA and The UK Cards Association websites.

188. Where a customer requests that the subscriber deals with them in writing or email (providing that facility is available) rather than by telephone, they should do so as long as the customer remains co-operative and in regular dialogue.

189. Communications with customers and/or their advisers should, wherever possible, acknowledge and reflect any previous discussions that have taken place. Subscribers should be willing to communicate with customers and/or their advisers by phone, post, secure email or fax. Normally, the subscriber will communicate through the adviser, if an authority has been received. This does not preclude subscribers from copying correspondence to customers if they choose. In certain circumstances it may be beneficial for discussions (either face-to-face or over the telephone) between the adviser and subscriber to take place with the customer present.

190. On occasions the subscriber may need to contact the customer directly, even when an authority is in place. These occasions may be the result of the adviser not being available, failing to provide requested information within a reasonable period of time, or other similar circumstances. If a subscriber does contact a customer directly when an authority is in place, it will explain to the customer why it is doing so.

191. Subscribers should give a phone number on all communications that will put the customer in contact with a named person or a team dedicated to dealing with cases of financial difficulty.

Consolidation loans

192. Where a consolidation loan is being provided to a personal customer and the subscriber considers the customer to be in financial difficulties, the subscriber should reduce or pay off the existing in-house borrowing that it is aware is being consolidated. This applies only where the existence of such in-house borrowing is apparent to subscribers via their existing in-house systems.

193. Exceptionally there may be circumstances in which it is appropriate not to reduce or pay off existing borrowing.

194. Other than in exceptional circumstances, where a consolidation loan is being provided to a personal customer and the subscriber considers the customer to be in financial difficulties, the monthly repayments on the consolidation loan should not exceed the total monthly repayments of the debts being consolidated. Exceptional circumstances may for example include where the customer has a repayment holiday or an interest-free period under their existing arrangement, which is shortly to end.[9]

[9 *This paragraph is effective from 1 July 2011.*]

Use of the right of set-off

195. Before set-off is used, a subscriber should contact the customer to inform them in clear and simple language the generic circumstances in which set-off would be used and when e.g. if the customer does not contact the subscriber and/or address the missed payment. This contact should be made at a time when the lender is actively considering or is likely to exercise set-off and not so far in advance of the event that the customer may no longer be aware that it may be undertaken. This information should be as prominent in written communications and telephone scripts as other information.

196. Before applying set-off a subscriber should take account of information that they have available to them to identify whether the customer may be or may be heading towards financial difficulties. In all cases where set-off is to be applied and the subscriber has established that the customer is in financial difficulties, the customer must be left with sufficient money to meet their reasonable day-to-day living expenses and priority debts, where these have been identified. There are a number of ways that subscribers can make this assessment. Where more than one payment has been missed, the assessment could include reviewing income and expenditure statements (if the subscriber has these), and/or account turnover and behaviour, and/or analysis of the type and frequency of credits to the account. Particular care is required where it can be identified that a customer's balance is made up wholly or in part of state benefits.

197. If the customer does not respond to contact or is not co-operative and there is no evidence available to the subscriber that using set-off will cause or exacerbate the customer's financial difficulties, then set-off may be exercised.

198. Set-off should normally only be used to make up the most recent missed payment. However if the subscriber has contacted the customer about missed payments, told the customer that set-off

is an option, and used the information available to them to assess whether the customer will be able to meet reasonable living expenses and pay priority debts, it may be used to make up earlier missed payments. A subscriber may also take more than one missed payment where the customer is not cooperating with the subscriber, for example by not responding to repeated attempts to make contact.

199. At least on the first occasion after set-off has been used, a subscriber should contact the customer to advise them and the customer should be encouraged to take appropriate action in the future to avoid missed payments.

200. If it is evident from subsequent contact with the customer that they are in financial difficulty either as a result of the use of set-off or otherwise, appropriate action should be taken promptly to ensure that they are treated fairly, sympathetically and positively as required by the Code.

Breathing space for personal customers

201. Where a customer can demonstrate to a subscriber that they are making a genuine effort to develop a repayment plan, using either a debt advice agency or a self-help tool[10], the subscriber should suspend collections activity related to the customer's current account, credit card and/or unsecured personal loan while discussions continue, for a period of 30 days.

[10 *The extension of paragraph 201 to self-help customers is effective from 1 July 2011.*]

202. The subscriber should confirm with the customer and/or their adviser that collections calls and letters will be suspended during the 'breathing space' period (except where required under Consumer Credit legislation) and should discuss with the customer and/or their adviser how the account will continue to operate during the 30 day period.

203. Where the customer and/or their adviser provides clear evidence of demonstrable progress being made in developing a genuine repayment plan, but work has not yet concluded, subscribers should extend the breathing space for up to an additional 30 days.

Common Financial Statement

204. Money advisers may use the BBA/MAT/FLA Common Financial Statement format and principles when submitting information to subscribers[11].

[11 *More information on the BBA/MAT/FLA statement is available from the British Bankers' Association or Money Advice Trust as well as the agencies supported by MAT, e.g. the National Associations of Citizens Advice Bureau Service, Advice UK, Money Advice Association, Money Advice Scotland and National Debtline.*]

205. Subscribers should accept the CFS (and other similar statements such as that used by the Consumer Credit Counselling Service (CCCS)). The CFS—or equivalent details of the customer's income, expenditure and assets—is necessary to enable the subscriber to gather information to assess if an 'offer to pay' will enable the customer to be accepted onto a formal debt management plan (DMP), or enable the subscriber to reduce or suppress interest and fees.

206. If a customer works with a debt-counselling organisation to complete a CFS, in support of a debt management plan, the subscriber should accept the CFS as the basis for pro-rata distribution amongst creditors covered by the plan. Repayment offers based upon expenditure falling within the trigger figures of the CFS should only be challenged by the subscriber if it has reasonable cause to believe that the customer's income and expenditure figures may be incomplete or inaccurate. This provision is designed to help people in or at risk of being in financial difficulties, and subscribers should use the provision when accounts have gone into default or at an earlier stage if it benefits both them and the customer.

207. The third party money adviser should ensure that their authority to act on behalf of the customer is promptly sent to all creditors identified by the customer. It is also the responsibility of the adviser to ensure that a CFS or equivalent is sent to the creditors shortly after the authority. In these circumstances, where a money adviser has been appointed and there are debts with many creditors subscribers will not normally be able to work with the customer until a CFS or equivalent has been received.

208. In general, subscribers should then be prepared to accept an offer of repayment which is based on the principle of equitable distribution of available income (after priority payments), in line with the amount outstanding to each creditor.

Alternative means of calculating the distribution of available income by the customer or their adviser may be agreed on a case-by-case basis. A subscriber may accept an offer of payment, even though the offer is not sufficient to enable the customer to be accepted onto a formal DMP.

209. There is no reason why the content of the income and expenditure statement should not be challenged but if the figures appear to be reasonable and in line with trigger figures where a CFS is used, then these principles should apply.

210. Subscribers should follow the CFS Creditor Good Practice checklist which promotes clear communications between creditors and customers[12]. The CFS checklist is available at http://www.cfs.moneyadvicetrust.org/editorial.asp?page_id=42

[12 *This paragraph is effective from 1 July 2011.*]

211. Subscribers should also comply with the Code's standards for CFS-based negotiations when considering debt repayment proposals made using other repayment models that are endorsed by the Lending Code sponsors. Currently, the CCCS Debt Remedy service and self-help tool CASHflow developed by the MAT are recognised and others will be reviewed from time to time.[13]

[13 *This paragraph is effective from 1 July 2011.*]

212. Personal customers may choose a self-help approach to negotiating debt repayment. Subscribers should ensure that such proposals are given equal consideration as those presented through a debt adviser.

Token offers and write-offs

213. Token offers should be accepted where the customer has demonstrated they have no surplus income available for their 'non-priority' creditors and there is a realistic prospect of the customer's circumstances improving[14]. A token offer will not necessarily be regarded as an agreed repayment plan and will not prevent the debt from being registered as in default with a CRA, or sold to a third party debt recovery agent.

[14 *This paragraph is effective from 1 July 2011.*]

214. Where the subscriber considers the customer's personal and financial circumstances to be exceptional and unlikely to improve, the subscriber may, among other options, consider writing off or not pursuing part or all of the customer's debt(s). Where write-off is requested by a customer or adviser but is not considered appropriate by the subscriber, the subscriber must give their reasons in writing. If the subscriber agrees to a write-off, then the debt may be registered as a default with the credit reference agencies.

Debt recovery procedures

215. If the customer does not co-operate with the subscriber, a plan cannot be developed and the subscriber may proceed with normal debt recovery procedures. Lack of co-operation would include not responding to the subscriber's attempts at contact and unreasonable demands by the customer (for example, a request that the debt be written off or repaid over a very long period, even though the customer could afford to make reasonable repayments).

216. A subscriber should ensure that any enforcement action initiated by them or on their behalf by another party to recover debt is carried out within the appropriate legal jurisdiction.

217. If a customer has assets which could reasonably be expected to be sold to reduce outstanding debts, the subscriber may request that the customer, and if appropriate, their adviser, considers this option. Thereafter, the subscriber should acknowledge that income should only be used to repay 'non-priority' debts once provision has been made for any 'priority' debts. The subscriber should leave the customer with sufficient money for reasonable day-to-day expenses, taking into account individual circumstances.

218. A debt is considered 'priority' where the customer's failure to pay could lead directly to the loss of one or more of the following:

- The customer's home (e.g., rent, mortgage, secured loans);
- The customer's liberty (e.g., council tax, child support maintenance, income tax, court fines);
- The customer's utility supplies (e.g. water, gas, electricity); or
- The customer's essential goods or services (e.g., a cooker, a fridge, or the means to travel to work).

219. Subscribers will not subject customers to harassment or undue pressure when discussing their problems.

Provisions applicable to both personal and micro-enterprise customers
Repayment plans
220. The subscriber should explore a range of options with the customer. Usually this will require the customer to disclose to the subscriber details of their income, expenditure, assets and liabilities, including amounts (if any) owed to other creditors. This information will be used to develop a plan for dealing with the liabilities. In cases where there are liabilities to multiple creditors, subscribers should recommend a free money advice service.

221. The initial arrangements for repaying the debt should be in writing or other durable medium. This will not always be treated as a formal debt management plan, and there may be departures from this plan, if it is in the interests of subscribers and customers. There is no need for every small departure from the basic plan to be in writing (for example an agreement to accept a lower repayment for one week), but any amendments that change the fundamental nature of the plan should be in writing. If, at the subscriber's discretion, the plan includes an agreement to accept smaller repayments, the subscriber should tell the customer whether this is regarded as 'falling behind with repayments' and whether information will be passed to Credit Reference Agencies.

222. Repayment plans between subscribers and customers may be subject to regular review but a subscriber should not expect a customer to increase their repayment at the review stage unless the customer's financial position has improved. Any review period will be agreed with the customer or their adviser, and subscribers should seek to revise contributions only at the end of the review period or if a customer's personal circumstances change. (Customers and/or their advisers should inform the subscriber if the customer's personal situation changes.)

223. Where a customer is unable to make repayments that are sufficient to meet a lender's minimum requirements for a repayment plan, the customer must be given clear information on the effect this will have on his position and the options open to him. However this should never be in a way that is designed to encourage a customer to pay more than they can afford as demonstrated by an income and expenditure statement.

Interest and charges concessions
224. Subscribers should consider reducing or stopping interest and charges when a customer evidences that they are in financial difficulties. Such reduction/suspension decision should be based upon an income and expenditure statement indicating that they are unable to make repayments sufficient to meet contractual terms. Where a customer is able to make only token payments, their debt should not increase as a result of interest and charges levied. The assessment should reflect the customer's lack of ability to pay rather than the stage an account has reached in the arrears cycle or whether they are using free sources of debt advice. Where a firm declines to allow concessions, they should be prepared to explain why to the customer or their adviser if requested to do so.

225. It is inappropriate for interest and charges to continue to be taken where the result would be that the repayment period for the customer becomes excessive. In forming a judgement on what might be excessive, a subscriber should take into account the type of product and the individual circumstances of the borrower.

226. Concessions should not be arbitrarily withdrawn irrespective of a customer's ability to pay or without any evidence of a change in the customer's circumstances. Expiry of a repayment arrangement should not automatically lead to the withdrawal of concessions. This does not rule out regular reviews and if a customer's position has improved then interest and charges can be reintroduced.

227. Where possible, subscribers should have consistent policies for customers holding more than one product type in terms of charges and interest concessions.

Debt collection agencies and debt sales

228. Subscribers should follow a due diligence process when selecting third parties for debt management, which should include third party compliance with data protection legislation, consumer credit legislation, Office of Fair Trading guidance on debt collection and debt management, and the code of the Credit Services Association.

229. Subscribers should ensure that the Code standards for handling financial difficulties are applied by such agents, through due diligence and periodic audit and review. Code compliance standards should form part of all third party contracts.

230. Subscribers should ensure that all relevant available information held by the subscriber relating to the debt is passed to any DCA or any debt purchaser.

231. Subscribers should inform the third party of any relevant arrangements currently being complied with by the customer. The provisions in paragraph 222 relating to repayment plans continue to apply where a debt has been passed to a DCA or sold. Existing repayment plans which have been agreed with the customer and which are being met must be respected until the scheduled review date.

232. Customers should follow a due diligence process when selecting any third party for debt sale. Any new contract should ensure that the third party will comply with data protection legislation, consumer credit legislation, Office of Fair Trading guidance on debt collection and debt management, the code of the Credit Services Association and the Lending Code's standards for handling financial difficulties even if the debt purchaser is not a subscriber.

233. Additional care needs to be taken when dealing with certain types of debt. Where a customer or his agent has provided appropriate and relevant evidence of an ongoing mental health problem that affects the customer's ability to repay their debts, the debt should not be sold.

234. Subscribers should undertake appropriate monitoring in order to satisfy themselves that debt purchasers to whom they have sold customers' debts continue to deal with such customers in a manner that is consistent with the relevant requirements of the Code and the relevant contractual terms. Such monitoring should be conducted at least annually where subscribers continue to sell debt to a purchaser, and for a further two years after they have stopped selling debt to that purchaser.

235. The results of the monitoring referred to above should be used to satisfy the subscriber and the LSB that all of the relevant Lending Code requirements in respect of the debts sold are being adhered to. Where instances of non-compliance are identified through monitoring, subscribers must be able to evidence that appropriate action has been taken to remedy any breakdown of control or customer detriment

236. Where a subscriber agrees to a subsequent sale of the debt, they must satisfy themselves that appropriate arrangements are in place to ensure that following the sale of the debt, the subsequent debt purchaser will continue to deal with customers in a manner that is consistent with the requirements set out in the Code for the treatment of customers in financial difficulties.

237. Customers should be advised before or at the time their debt is passed or sold to a third party by a subscriber. The intended outcome of this provision is that a customer should not experience collections activity from the party to whom the debt has been passed or sold without having received prior notification from the subscriber of the transfer.

238. It is common practice for third parties taking on a debt to request a new statement of income, expenditure and assets to understand the customer's most up-to-date position. However, if a statement has only recently been completed or a repayment plan is being maintained and the review date has not yet been reached, it would be inappropriate to request an updated statement.

Specialist assistance

239. Subscribers are encouraged to have a specialist team or staff trained to provide specialist advice, to deal with customers in financial difficulty who have specialist needs. These may for example include customers with a mental health condition.

240. If it becomes clear to the subscriber that the customer needs specialist assistance, the customer should be referred promptly to a specialist team that deals with customers in financial difficulties, if one exists. In some cases, referral to a debt recovery unit may also be necessary.

Debt and mental health

241. The impacts of financial difficulty can be especially acute for customers with mental health problems. Subscribers should ensure that their processes and systems are responsive to a customer in financial difficulties, from the point at which they are made aware of a mental health problem.

242. The appropriate response will differ in each case and could involve a range of approaches, including:

- working positively with an advice agency;
- promptly carrying out agreed actions;
- being flexible in responding to offers or schedules of repayment;
- sensitively managing communications with the customer (for example preventing unnecessary and unwelcome mailings);
- asking customers how their mental health problem impacts on their ability to repay their debt;
- suggesting the customer obtain support from a family member or carer; and
- signposting to a free, independent money advice agency.

243. Where it is appropriate and with a customer's consent, subscribers should work with advice agencies and health and social care professionals in a joined-up way to exchange information and ensure an effective dialogue.

244. With a customer's explicit consent and in line with requirements of the Data Protection Act, where it is possible and appropriate subscribers should record relevant information about the customer on their account so that staff can deal appropriately with the customer. Subscribers should inform customers how their information will be used and for what purposes.

245. If a subscriber has specialist staff to deal with cases of debt and mental health problems, they should ensure that appropriate mechanisms exist to refer the customer to the appropriate support.

246. If a customer informs a subscriber that they have a mental health problem that is impacting on their ability to manage their financial difficulties, the subscriber should allow the customer a reasonable period (e.g. 28 days) of time to collect and submit relevant evidence to the subscriber. This evidence will help the subscriber to work with the customer, advice agencies and health/social professionals where appropriate to determine the most appropriate action to deal with the customer's financial difficulties.

247. The Money Advice Liaison Group (MALG) has produced a Debt and Mental Health Evidence Form (DMHEF) which provides a standardised methodology for advisors and creditors to share relevant information about the customer's condition from health and social care professionals.

248. Subscribers should consider the DMHEF if it is presented by the customer or (with the customer's consent) their adviser or medical practitioner.

249. If a subscriber has received appropriate and relevant evidence of a customer's mental health problems that affect the customer's ability to repay their debts, the debt should not be sold. In these circumstances subscribers should also consider whether it is appropriate to pass the customer's debt to a DCA.

250. Where subscribers pass a debt to a DCA, the DCA should (subject to compliance with paragraph 244) be provided with relevant and appropriate information about the customer's condition to enable them to deal sympathetically and positively with a customer with ongoing mental health problems

251. The subscriber should also only initiate court action to pursue the debt as a last resort and when it is appropriate and fair to do so.

252. Further and more detailed good practice guidelines have been produced by MALG and are available at: http://www.moneyadvicetrust.org/download.asp. The MALG guidelines will not be monitored and enforced by the Lending Standards Board.

Additional provisions for micro-enterprise customers

253. Subscibers may ask a micro-enterprise customer for more financial information to help it to work with the customer to understand any problems.

254. Subscribers may suggest that an independent review of the customer's business is undertaken in order to provide an independent view of the future prospects of the business. In these circumstances, the subscriber should explain the reasons for the review, what they think should be done and how the review will take place, including who should carry out the review and the costs the customer will have to pay.

A review will usually cover all the options, including assessing:

- opportunities for improving cash flow and profitability;
- the main business activities or new markets;
- investment needs and refinancing options; and
- recommendations for the future.

255. If a customer's business is reviewed, the subscriber should discuss with the customer (and their advisers) the information provided before reaching any conclusions or taking any action.

256. If an agreement to continue to support the business cannot be reached the subscriber should make it clear why. Subscribers should advise the customer when they will withdraw their support and will communicate these changes personally.

257. A subscriber will support a rescue plan if it believes it will succeed. If the subscriber does not believe that the rescue plan will succeed, they should explain the reasons why and help the customer and their advisers to consider other options.

258. If the customer makes the agreed changes early enough to save the main business, the subscriber will not, other than in exceptional circumstances, start action to recover the amount borrowed.

259. A subscriber will work positively with a customer to support a lasting solution for a successful running of the customer's business, provided the customer:

- acts in good faith;
- keeps the subscriber informed about developments;
- keeps to its agreement with the subscriber;
- carefully considers what their own and any independent advisers say; and
- is prepared to make the necessary changes early enough.

260. If, after reviewing all the options with the customer, appointing an administrator or an administrative receiver (receiver, in Scotland) is considered to be the most appropriate action to take, the decision to appoint the receiver will be confirmed within the subscriber at a senior level.

In most cases, the customer invites the lender to appoint an administrator or administrative receiver after accepting that it is the most appropriate insolvency process based on very careful consideration of all the options available to protect the interests of the business, including the employees and creditors.

Insolvency practitioners will decide whether to accept a formal appointment after considering guidance on ethical standards. As a result of the Enterprise Act, an administrative receiver can only be appointed under security taken before 15 September 2003.

If the customer gives good reasons why a member of the firm that has carried out an independent review should not be appointed as administrator, the subscriber should appoint a different administrator (unless there are exceptional circumstances). The same principle applies for administrative receivers and receivers in Scotland.

Section 10:   Complaints

261. In line with the FSA DISP Rules, all subscribers should have a set of internal procedures for handling complaints, and staff dealing with customers should know what these are so that customers can be informed if the need arises. Procedures should be clear and well defined.

262. On entering a contract, customers should be informed about where they can find details of the subscriber's complaints handling procedures.

263. Details of the internal complaints procedures should be given to customers who wish to make a complaint.

264. If a subscriber is unable to resolve a complaint to the customer's satisfaction by the close of business on the day following receipt of the complaint, the subscriber should provide a prompt written acknowledgement that the complaint is being considered.

265. Customers should be kept informed about the subscriber's progress in dealing with the complaint and within eight weeks should receive a final response or an explanation as to why a final response has not yet been reached. The Customer should also be informed that they can refer their complaint to the Financial Ombudsman Service (where applicable) and how to do so.

266. Enforcement of compliance with these requirements is the FSA's responsibility.

Section 11:   Monitoring

267. Subscribers should appoint a Code Compliance Officer who is likely to be the contact person for co-ordinating the annual statement of compliance, compliance visits and other contact with the Lending Standards Board.

268. Further details about the Lending Standards Board can be found at www.lendingstand-ardsboard.org.uk.

Annex A: Unsecured personal loan(s)—summary box

The Summary Box is a voluntary initiative that subscribers can choose to use in any advertising media or pre-contract information provided that it is used in compliance with relevant regulations.

The content and order of the summary box is outlined below and should be relevant to the features of the financial promotion to which it relates.

	SUMMARY BOX			
	Key Information for our xxx personal loan(s) from £x to £xx			
Representative APR	*If priced by risk:-*			
	Representative x.x % APR			
	If successful, the interest rate you will pay is based on your personal circumstances, [the time period over which the loan is repaid] and [the amount you choose to borrow].			
	Or, if not priced by risk:-			
	Representative x.x % APR			
	If successful, the interest rate you will pay is based on the amount you choose to borrow, [and the time period over which the loan is repaid].			
APR ranges	Loan size range	From %	To %	Indicative APR
	£5,000 – 7,500	17.3	19.9	18.0
	£7,501 – 10,000	14.9	18.9	16.0
	To include sufficient information for the consumer to see the interest rates / ranges for all the loan size bands /tiers used in the financial promotion. If price is affected by the repayment period the From % and To % should fully reflect this.)			

Interest charging information	To include :- Is rate fixed for life of loan? Basis of interest calculation: (daily/monthly/annual balance; in arrears/ advance)
Repayment information	To include :- Method and frequency of repayment Date when first repayment is due Are payment holidays permitted? Is deferral of payments permitted at start of loan?
Repayment period	To include the range of time periods over which a loan can be repaid
Amount of loan available	To include the range of £ amounts for which loans are available and applicable increments
Application/Arrangement fee	To include the £ amount of any set up fees, whatever they may be called
Other fees	To include any optional fees, such as "fast delivery" costs, "payment date change fees" & "fees for paying by credit card"
Default fees	To include a list of all default charges applied by the loan provider, their £ costs, and any rules about when charged. "Default" to be defined so customer knows when applicable. If none are charged then show: "none". (Examples might include: returned item charges for unpaid standing orders / direct debits.)
Early settlement	To include details of any early settlement fees
* Optional example	*Subscribers can provide one or more illustrative examples in addition to the prescribed Representative Example, if they choose, but must ensure that any example given complies with the Consumer Credit (Advertisements) Regulations 2010.*

Layout

Presentation should be clear and legible and in compliance with the Consumer Credit Advertising Regulations. The summary box can include key product information for more than one of the subscriber's unsecured loan products, but information for each product should be presented in an individual column.

Subscribers are encouraged to use the standardised wording shown above, where applicable.

Left hand column

The sequence of information presented in the left hand column should be the same for each product and in the order outlined above

Right hand column

This text provides examples of the types of information that should be presented for each key product feature, but these examples are not prescriptive or exhaustive. Subscribers should ensure that information relevant to the key product feature (left hand column) is included in the right hand column. Subscribers are not required to include information in the right hand column on features that the product does not include e.g. 'Not applicable' can be inserted. Subscribers should ensure that they are compliant with customer information requirements under relevant consumer credit legislation.

Representative APR

Subscribers need only show whichever of the two suggested examples is relevant to the way the product is priced.

Subscribers are encouraged to include whichever of the variables included in the example summary box above is relevant to the way the product is priced i.e. personal circumstances; time period over which the loan is repaid; the amount you choose to borrow.

APR ranges

The ranges should be based on the price bands used in the financial promotion. In the example above, the financial promotion is for loans of £5000 to £10,000.

If the APR will be affected by the repayment period this should be articulated.

Interest charging information

An example of the way in which this information could be presented is:

Once agreed, the APR is fixed and guaranteed for the life of your loan. The interest, at the agreed rate, will be calculated on the amount of loan outstanding each day and debited from your account monthly in arrears.

Other fees

This should include any fees that can be incurred by the customer which are not outlined in other sections of the summary box. Information should include whether fees are added to the loan; paid monthly; paid in advance/arrears; interest bearing etc.

Glossary

These definitions explain the meaning of words and terms used in the Lending Code. They are not precise legal or technical definitions.

Annual Percentage Rate (APR): APR is a way of representing the total cost of credit on a loan, or credit card on an annual basis to allow consumers to be able to compare the costs associated with borrowing across from a range of products and/or from a range of lenders.

ATM (automated teller machine): Also known as a 'cash machine', a free-standing machine in which a customer can use their card to obtain cash, information or other services

Basic bank account: A basic bank account will normally have the following features:

Employers can pay income directly into the account;

- The Government can pay pensions, tax credits and benefits directly into the account;
- Cheques and cash can be paid into the account;
- Bills can be paid by direct debit, by transferring money to another account or by a payment to a linked account;
- Cash can be withdrawn at ATMs;
- There is no overdraft facility;

Buffer zone: A small overdraft facility that a current account provider will allow a customer to use, either on an account with no formal borrowing arrangement or beyond a formal agreed limit. The customer will be informed if a buffer zone is available (except in respect of basic bank accounts).

Charge card: A card which allows a customer to make purchases and to draw cash, up to an arranged credit limit. The terms include paying the balance in full at the end of a set period. The customer will normally be charged a fee each year.

Common Financial Statement (CFS): A review of the financial position of a customer in financial difficulties that is completed with the help of a money adviser. It allows the customer to offer repayments from their available income to a group of creditors.

Consolidation loan: A loan that is used to pay off existing borrowings from one or more providers. Typically consolidation loans are used to help a customer who is seeking to repay their debts over a longer period and/or at reduced monthly payments.

Consumer: Any individual who is acting for purposes which are not linked to their trade, business or profession. (This definition is based on the one used in European legislation and by the Financial Services Authority with the title of either 'consumer' or 'retail customer'.)

In practice, consumers may act in a number of capacities. Examples of consumers acting in capacities that are included in the above definition are:

- personal representatives, including executors, unless they are acting in a professional capacity, for example, a solicitor acting as executor; and
- private individuals acting in personal or other family circumstances, for example, as trustee of a family trust.

- The term 'consumer' does not include an individual acting, for example:
- as trustee of a trust such as a housing or NHS trust; or
- as a member of the governing body of a club or other unincorporated association such as a trade body or a student union; or
- as a pension trustee

Credit card: A card that allows a customer to make purchases and to draw cash up to an arranged credit limit. The customer can pay off the credit granted in full or in part by a set date. Interest is usually charged when the balance is not paid in full. In the case of cash withdrawals, interest is normally charged from the transaction date. The customer may also have to pay an annual fee.

Credit card cheque: A cheque drawn against a credit card account that gives the cardholder another way of accessing funds up to their credit limit. Credit card cheques are often used to make transactions where credit cards are not accepted. Interest is normally charged from the transaction date.

Credit reference agencies (CRAs): Organisations, licensed under the Consumer Credit Act 1974, which hold information about people that is useful to lenders. Financial institutions may contact these agencies for information to help them make various decisions, for example, whether or not to open an account or provide loans or grant credit. Financial institutions may also give the agencies information.

Credit scoring: A system that lenders use to help them make decisions about whether to open an account or lend money. Credit scoring measures the likelihood that a customer will run an account in an acceptable way or repay a loan or other borrowing on time.

Debt collection agency (DCA): A third party (appropriately licensed under the Consumer Credit Act) appointed by a lender to seek repayment of a debt from a customer. The DCA is the agent of the lender and so must comply with all of the requirements of the Lending Code, as if it were the lender.

Debt management plan (DMP): An agreement made between a customer and their lenders, arranged and operated by a third party, facilitating payments to the customer's creditors when the customer is unable to maintain their contractual payments due to financial difficulties. (See also **Repayment plan**)

Durable medium: Any means by which a customer is able to store information addressed personally to them in such a way that it is accessible for future reference for a period of time adequate for the purposes of the information and which allows the unchanged reproduction of the information. Such means may include letters, paper bank statements, emails and other communications that can be saved and reproduced/printed at a future time.

Guarantee: A promise given by a person called 'the guarantor' to pay another person's debts if that person does not pay them.

Hardcore borrowing: Hardcore borrowing refers to the position where a customer's current account overdraft remains persistently overdrawn for more than a month without returning to credit during that period.

Indicative quotation: An indicative quotation is information provided by a lender in response to a customer who wishes to know the likely cost of borrowing a specific amount on one or more risk-priced products. An indicative quotation does not bind the customer to borrow or the lender to provide credit but it can be used to enable a customer to compare different products and costs. Any credit search undertaken to provide the indicative quotation is not registered as a full application search at CRAs.

Interest: A charge for borrowing money which is usually shown as a percentage of the amount borrowed.

Joint and several liability: When two or more people have a loan, credit card or account or guarantee, they have 'joint and several liability' which means that each is individually responsible for the full amount of any borrowing.

Micro-enterprise: A business that employs fewer than 10 persons and has a turnover, or annual balance sheet, that does not exceed €2million.

Overdraft: A facility provided as a current account service that allows the customer to spend more money from their account than they have in it. An overdraft can be either:

arranged, where a formal facility is agreed by the lender with the customer

unarranged, where borrowing is undertaken without the prior agreement of the lender

Payment service user: A person making use of a payment service in the capacity of either payer or payee, or both.

PIN (personal identification number): A confidential number which enables a customer to authorise a transaction on a bank account or credit or charge card at a point of sale terminal.

Private banking: Accounts and services made available to customers that provide them with access to relationship-based banking services and bespoke borrowing arrangements.

Recurring transaction: A regular payment (other than a direct debit or standing order) collected from a customer's card account, in line with the customer's instruction. Recurring transactions are not covered by the Direct Debit Guarantee.

Repayment plan: An agreement made between a customer and one or more of their creditors when the customer is unable to meet their full contractual payment terms. (See also **Debt management plan**)

Right of set-off (ROSO): The right of a bank or building society to recover moneys due to it by using a credit balance on a customer's account to make up all or part of a debt due to the bank or building society on another account such as a loan or a credit card, for example because of a missed payment.

Security: A word used to describe valuable items such as title deeds to houses, share certificates, life policies and so on, which represent assets used as support for a loan or other liability. Under a secured loan, the lender has the right to sell the security if the loan is not repaid.

In the case of limited companies, security may include guarantees from other group companies or from company directors or a mortgage debenture, which is a form of security that includes a charge on all the assets of the company.

Standard account services: Opening, maintaining and running accounts for transmitting money (for example, by cheque or debit card).

Summary Box: This provides the customer with a brief summary in a standard format of the key features of the credit card or loan they are considering so that they can understand and compare different products more easily.

Token offer (or payment): An offer of payment of a small amount, e.g. £1, made by a customer who has no surplus income available for their 'non-priority' creditors and whose circumstances have a realistic prospect of improving so that they will be able to resume full or increased payments

Unsatisfied transaction: A credit card transaction in which the seller fails to provide the goods or services as described, e.g. the goods are damaged or are not received by the customer, or the service is not, or not adequately, provided.

Working day: Monday to Friday, not including bank holidays.

Index

STATUTE LAW SOCIETY

The Lord Rodger Essay Prize

Sponsored by Oxford University Press

The Statute Law Society ('the Society') invites applications for the Lord Rodger Essay Prize.

The Society is a charitable body, which aims to educate the legal profession and the public about the legislative process, with a view to encouraging improvements in statute law. It was founded in 1968 and has members throughout Britain, Europe and the Commonwealth.

Lord Rodger of Earlsferry SCJ was Chair of the Society from 2002 until his death in 2011. He was involved in the legislative process at various stages of his career and retained a strong interest in the making and interpretation of statute law.

In memory of Lord Rodger, the Society has established an annual essay prize worth £1,000.

➤ Essays submitted must concern one or more of the following topics:
  ➢ the legislative process,
  ➢ the use of legislation as an instrument of public policy,
  ➢ the drafting of legislation,
  ➢ the interpretation of legislation.

➤ Essays may relate to the United Kingdom and/or any other jurisdiction or jurisdictions.

➤ Essays must be written in English and must be between 5,000 and 8,000 words long, including footnotes. They must be preceded by an abstract of no more than 200 words.

➤ Essays may be submitted by anyone who is reading for an undergraduate degree at any University and in any subject; or has held their first (or only) undergraduate degree for not more than five years.

Full information about the prize including entry instructions and deadline details can be found on **www.statutelawsociety.org** and at **www.oxfordtextbooks.co.uk/statutes**

Please refer to the website for submission instructions, and to download an entry form. The closing date for the essay prize is mid-September each year.

The winning essay will be chosen by a jury consisting of three members of the Council of the Society. The prize will be presented by the Chairman of the Law Society, at the Society's Annual Lord Renton Lecture in November.

The prize sum is £1,000. The winning essay will be considered for publication in the *Statute Law Review,* which is published by Oxford University Press, in association with the Society.

OXFORD
UNIVERSITY PRESS

www.statutelawsociety.org
www.oxfordtextbooks.co.uk/law